59.99

Handbook
of
Public Personnel
Administration

PUBLIC ADMINISTRATION AND PUBLIC POLICY

A Comprehensive Publication Program

Executive Editor

JACK RABIN
Professor of Public Administration and Public Policy
Division of Public Affairs
The Capital College
The Pennsylvania State University—Harrisburg
Middletown, Pennsylvania

Additional Volumes in Preparation

ANNALS OF PUBLIC ADMINISTRATION

Handbook
of
Public Personnel
Administration

edited by

Jack Rabin
The Pennsylvania State University–Harrisburg
Middletown, Pennsylvania

Thomas Vocino
Auburn University at Montgomery
Montgomery, Alabama

W. Bartley Hildreth
Wichita State University
Wichita, Kansas

Gerald J. Miller
Rutgers University at Newark
Newark, New Jersey

Taylor & Francis
Taylor & Francis Group

Boca Raton   London   New York   Singapore

A CRC title, part of the Taylor & Francis imprint, a member of the
Taylor & Francis Group, the academic division of T&F Informa plc.

Published in 1995 by
CRC Press
Taylor & Francis Group
6000 Broken Sound Parkway NW, Suite 300
Boca Raton, FL 33487-2742

© 1995 by Taylor & Francis Group, LLC
CRC Press is an imprint of Taylor & Francis Group

No claim to original U.S. Government works
Printed in the United States of America on acid-free paper
10 9 8 7 6 5 4 3

International Standard Book Number 0-8247-9231-9 (Hardcover)
Library of Congress Card Number 94-22534

Library of Congress Cataloging-in-Publication Data

Handbook of public personnel administration / edited by Jack Rabin...[et al.].
    p. cm.—(Public administration and public policy ; 58)
    Includes bibliographical references and index.
    ISBN 0-8247-9231-9 (alk. paper)
    1. Civil service—United States—Personnel management—Handbooks,
manuals, etc. I. Rabin, Jack. II. Series.
JK765.H34   1995
350.1'00973—dc20   94-22534

Taylor & Francis Group
is the Academic Division of T&F Informa plc.

Visit the Taylor & Francis Web site at
http://www.taylorandfrancis.com

and the CRC Press Web site at
http://www.crcpress.com

Preface

The *Handbook of Public Personnel Administration* consists of a set of bibliographic treatises dealing with each aspect of the human resources process. Each chapter provides the reader with a basic overview of a particular human resource field; for the advanced student or practitioner, each chapter also gives in-depth and current citations for continued research or practice.

This book is designed as an introductory text primarily for graduate courses in human resources administration. It should also prove a valuable reference for libraries as well as for practitioners. The book's foundation is a number of chapters produced in 1983 for the *Handbook of Public Personnel Administration and Labor Relations*. Many of those chapters, updated and expanded, are found here. However, most of this text consists of newly written material, attesting to the enormous growth of the human resources field over the last decade.

During that time period, public service has been under attack from both within and without government. Presidents have "run against" the public service for years. Moreover, the image of public service, as well as the morale of public servants, have continued their downward spirals.

Ironically, our need for well-motivated, highly professional public servants has never been greater as witnessed by the current stress on service delivery, client satisfaction, total quality management, and the efficiency and effectiveness of governmental services.

Public servants are the usual scapegoats for both officeholders and citizens, yet both turn to governmental employees to deliver critical services. It is no wonder that public sector unions have been growing at a rapid pace over the last 30 years, while their private sector counterparts have been contracting.

We welcome your comments and feedback concerning this volume as well as its companion tome, the *Handbook of Public Sector Labor Relations*.

Jack Rabin
Thomas Vocino
W. Bartley Hildreth
Gerald J. Miller

Contents

Contributors

Brad Baptiste MPA Candidate, Public Administration Institute, College of Business Administration, Louisiana State University, Baton Rouge, Louisiana

Jeffrey L. Brudney, Ph.D. Professor and Director, Doctor of Public Administration Program, Department of Political Science, University of Georgia, Athens, Georgia

David G. Carnevale, Ph.D. Director, Off-Campus Programs in Public Administration, Department of Political Science, University of Oklahoma, Norman, Oklahoma

James D. Carroll Professor, Department of Public Administration, Florida International University, North Miami, Florida

Paula Phillips Carson, Ph.D. Assistant Professor of Management and Professional Women's Endowed Professor of Business Administration, Department of Management and Quantitative Methods, University of Southwestern Louisiana, Lafayette, Louisiana

N. Joseph Cayer, M.P.A., Ph.D. Professor, School of Public Affairs, Arizona State University, Tempe, Arizona

Hon S. Chan, M.Phil., Ph.D. Lecturer, Department of Public and Social Administration, City Polytechnic of Hong Kong, Hong Kong

Dennis M. Daley, Ph.D. Associate Professor, Department of Political Science and Public Administration, North Carolina State University, Raleigh, North Carolina

Linda deLeon, Ph.D. Assistant Professor, Graduate School of Public Affairs, University of Colorado at Denver, Denver, Colorado

Robert B. Denhardt, Ph.D. Professor, Department of Public Administration, University of Central Florida, Orlando, Florida

Elliot F. Eisenberg, M.P.A. Doctoral Candidate, Department of Public Administration, Maxwell School of Citizenship and Public Affairs, Syracuse University, Syracuse, New York

Robert H. Elliott Professor and Associate Dean, Department of Political Science, Auburn University at Montgomery, Montgomery, Alabama

Arthur L. Finkle, M.G.A. Adjunct Associate Professor, Graduate School of Education and Human Services, Rider University, Lawrenceville, New Jersey

John J. Gargan, Ph.D. Professor, Department of Political Science, Kent State University, Kent, Ohio

G. David Garson, Ph.D. Associate Dean and Professor, Department of Political Science and Public Administration, North Carolina State University, Raleigh, North Carolina

Rodger W. Griffeth, Ph.D. Professor, Department of Management, and the W. T. Beebe Institute of Personal and Employment Relations, Georgia State University, Atlanta, Georgia

Arie Halachmi, Ph.D. Professor, Institute of Government, Tennessee State University, Nashville, Tennessee

Steven W. Hays, Ph.D. Professor, Department of Government and International Studies, University of South Carolina, Columbia, South Carolina

W. Bartley Hildreth Regents Distinguished Professor, Hugo Wall School of Urban and Public Affairs, and Barton School of Business, Wichita State University, Wichita, Kansas

Marc Holzer Professor, Graduate Department of Public Administration, Rutgers University at Newark, Newark, New Jersey

Peter W. Hom, Ph.D. Associate Professor, Department of Management, Arizona State University, Tempe, Arizona

Steven Housel Doctoral Candidate, Department of Political Science, University of Oklahoma, Norman, Oklahoma

A. C. Hyde, Ph.D. Visiting Associate Professor, Department of Public Administration, The American University, Washington, D.C.

Patricia W. Ingraham, Ph.D. Professor, Department of Public Administration and Political Science, Maxwell School of Citizenship and Public Affairs, Syracuse University, Syracuse, New York

Richard C. Kearney, M.P.A., Ph.D. Professor and Director, Master of Public Affairs Program, Department of Political Science, University of Connecticut, Storrs, Connecticut

Donald E. Klingner, Ph.D. Professor, Department of Public Administration, Florida International University, Miami, Florida

Tao-chiu Lam, M.Phil. Assistant Professor, Faculty of Social Science and Humanities, University of Macau, Macau

James Ledvinka Professor, Department of Management, Terry College of Business, University of Georgia, Athens, Georgia

Richard A. Loverd, M.P.A., M.B.A., Ph.D. Assistant Professor, Department of Political Science, Northeastern University, Boston, Massachusetts

Larry S. Luton, Ph.D. Professor, Graduate Program in Public Administration, Eastern Washington University, Cheney, Washington

Barbara Clark Maddox Office of the City Manager, Richmond, Virginia

Thomas J. Pavlak, Ph.D.   Professor and Director, Public Administration Institute, Fairleigh Dickinson University, Rutherford, New Jersey

Marsha L. Reilly, M.P.A.   Business Manager, Archaeological and Historical Services, Eastern Washington University, Cheney, Washington

Mitchell F. Rice, Ph.D.   Professor, Public Administration Institute, College of Business Administration, Louisiana State University, Baton Rouge, Louisiana

David H. Rosenbloom   Distinguished Professor, Department of Public Administration, American University, Washington, D.C.

Debra W. Stewart, M.A., Ph.D.   Dean and Professor of Political Science and Public Administration, Graduate School, North Carolina State University, Raleigh, North Carolina

Stephen K. Straus, M.P.A., Ph.D.   Visiting Associate Professor, Department of Political Science and Public Administration, North Carolina State University, Raleigh, North Carolina

Natalia Trogen   Doctoral Candidate, School of Public Administration and Policy, Florida State University, Tallahassee, Florida

Thomas Vocino, Ph.D.   Professor and Department Head, Department of Political Science and Public Administration, Auburn University at Montgomery, Montgomery, Alabama

Barton Wechsler, Ph.D.   Associate Professor and Director of Graduate Studies, School of Public Administration and Policy, Florida State University, Tallahassee, Florida

James D. Werbel, Ph.D.   Associate Professor, Department of Management, College of Business, Iowa State University, Ames, Iowa

Marcia Lynn Whicker, Ph.D.   Professor, Graduate Department of Public Administration, Rutgers University at Newark, Newark, New Jersey

Blue Wooldridge, D.P.A.   Associate Professor, Department of Public Administration, Virginia Commonwealth University, Richmond, Virginia

Virgil B. Zimmermann   Professor Emeritus, Department of Public Administration and Policy, Rockefeller College of Public Affairs and Policy, State University of New York at Albany, Albany, New York

About the Editors

JACK RABIN is Professor of Public Administration and Public Policy at The Pennsylvania State University—Harrisburg, Middletown, Pennsylvania. Previously, he was Associate Professor and Chair in the Graduate Program in Human Services Administration at Rider College in Lawrenceville, New Jersey. He serves as editor/coeditor of five journals: the *International Journal of Public Administration* (Marcel Dekker, Inc.), *Public Administration Quarterly*, the *Journal of Health and Human Resources Administration*, *Public Budgeting and Financial Management*, and the *Journal of Management History*. Dr. Rabin is author or editor of numerous books including the *Handbook of Public Budgeting*, the *Handbook of Public Budgeting and Financial Management* (ed., with Thomas D. Lynch), *Public Budgeting and Finance* (ed., with Robert T. Golembiewski), the *Handbook on Public Personnel Administration and Labor Relations* and the *Handbook of Public Sector Labor Relations* (ed., with Thomas Vocino, W. Bartley Hildreth, and Gerald J. Miller), *Politics and Administration* (ed., with James S. Bowman), *Managing Administration* (ed., with Samuel Humes and Brian S. Morgan), *State and Local Government Administration* (ed., with Don Dodd), the *Handbook of Information Resource Management* (ed., with Edward M. Jackowski), the *Handbook of Human Services Administration* (ed., with Marcia B. Steinhauer), the *Handbook of Public Administration* (ed., with W. Bartley Hildreth and Gerald J. Miller), and the *Handbook of Strategic Management* (ed., with Gerald J. Miller and W. Bartley Hildreth) [all titles, Marcel Dekker, Inc.]. In addition, he has published *Dilemmas of Political Participation* (ed., with Robert T. Golembiewski and J. Malcolm Moore), *Contemporary Public Administration* (ed., with Thomas Vocino), *Personnel: Managing Human Resources in the Public Sector* (coauthored with C. E. Teasley III, Arthur Finkle, and Luther F. Carter), the *Public Budgeting Laboratory* (coauthored with W. Bartley Hildreth and Gerald J. Miller), and an annotated bibliography, *Public Budgeting and Financial Management* (coauthored with Ernest C. Cerino, Maria E. Dimas, and Deborah Donahue). Dr. Rabin, moreover, was a consultant in budgeting and strategic planning in the Executive Office of the President of the United States. He also serves as executive editor of the *Public Administration and Public Policy Series* (Marcel Dekker, Inc.). Dr. Rabin received the Ph.D. degree (1972) in political science from the University of Georgia, Athens.

THOMAS VOCINO is Professor in and Head of the Department of Political Science and Public Administration at Auburn University at Montgomery, Alabama. He serves as coeditor of the *International Journal of Public Administration* and the *Public Administration Quarterly*. He is the author or coauthor of over 50 articles and technical reports and coeditor of *Public Administration Education in Transition* (with Richard Heimovics), the *Handbook on Public Personnel Administration and Labor Relations*, and the *Handbook of Public Sector Labor Relations* (with Jack Rabin, W. Bartley Hildreth, and Gerald J. Miller). His work has been published in numerous journals such as the *Administrative Science Quarterly*, the *Public Administration Review, Administration and Society*, and the *American Review of Public Administration*. Dr. Vocino chaired the Program Committee for the 1982 American Society for Public Administration (ASPA) national conference and was the 1991 recipient of the Don Stone Service to the ASPA Award of the ASPA. He has also served terms on the governing boards of the ASPA, the National Association of Schools of Public Affairs and Administration, the Policy Studies Organization, and the Southern Political Science Association.

W. BARTLEY HILDRETH is Regents Distinguished Professor of Public Finance at the Hugo Wall School of Urban and Public Affairs and the Barton School of Business, and Director of the Kansas Public Finance Center, Wichita State University, Kansas. Dr. Hildreth is the former Director of Finance for the city of Akron, Ohio. Previously, he served as Associate Professor of Finance and Public Administration in the Graduate School of Management at Kent State University, Ohio; and, Professor of Public Administration in the College of Business Administration at Louisiana State University, Baton Rouge. His work has been published in numerous journals, including the *Public Administration Review*, the *American Review of Public Administration*, the *Public Administration Quarterly*, and the *International Journal of Public Administration* (Marcel Dekker, Inc.). Dr. Hildreth is Editor-in-Chief of the *Municipal Finance Journal* and Chair of the Association for Budgeting and Financial Management, a section of the American Society for Public Administration. He is the coeditor of the *Handbook on Public Personnel Administration and Labor Relations* and the *Handbook of Public Sector Labor Relations* (with Jack Rabin, Thomas Vocino, and Gerald J. Miller) and (with Jack Rabin and Gerald J. Miller) the *Handbook of Public Administration* and the *Handbook of Strategic Management* (all titles, Marcel Dekker, Inc.). He serves on several journal editorial boards and is the book review editor for the *International Journal of Public Administration*. An active consultant, his clients have included a public employee union, a Chamber of Commerce, state and local governments, the U.S. Advisory Commission on Intergovernmental Relations, and the Government Finance Officers Association of the U.S. and Canada. His research seeks to inform public policy on the efficient and effective management of public resources, thereby enhancing economic development. He received the B.A. degree in political science from the University of Alabama, the M.P.A. degree from Auburn University at Montgomery, Alabama, and the D.P.A. from the University of Georgia, Athens.

GERALD J. MILLER is Associate Professor of Public Administration at Rutgers-The State University of New Jersey in Newark. The author of over 50 research articles, his work has been published in numerous journals in the United States and abroad, including the *Public Administration Review*, the *Policy Studies Journal, Public Productivity and Management Review*, the *International Journal of Public Administration*, and the *Public Administration Quarterly*. Having published over 20 books, he is the author of *Government Financial Management*, coeditor of the *Handbook of Strategic Management* and the *Handbook of Public Administration* (both with Jack Rabin and W. Bartley Hildreth), and coeditor of the *Handbook of Public Personnel Administration and Labor Relations* and the *Handbook of Public Sector Labor Relations* (both with Jack Rabin, Thomas Vocino, and W. Bartley Hildreth.) [all titles, Marcel Dekker, Inc.]. In addition, his is coauthor of the *Public Budgeting Laboratory* (with Jack Rabin and W. Bartley Hildreth) and coeditor of *Managerial Behavior and Organization Demands* (with Robert T. Golembiewski and

Frank K. Gibson) and *Budget Management* and *Budgeting: Formulation and Execution* (both with Jack Rabin and W. Bartley Hildreth). He is an editorial board member of the *International Journal of Public Administration* (Marcel Dekker, Inc.), the *Municipal Finance Journal, Public Productivity and Management Review,* the *Journal of Public Management,* and the *Journal of Health and Human Resources Administration.* He also serves as a book review editor for the *Public Administration Quarterly.* As a former investment banker with the firm of Rauscher, Pierce, Refsnes, Inc., Phoenix, Arizona, Dr. Miller continues an active consulting practice in the United States, Canada, and Western Europe with clients including national, state, and local government organizations in legislative, executive, and judicial branches of government, as well as private business and business and public sector associations. His research seeks understanding and asserts the dominance of resource allocation in the control of public organizations; his work has received continuous and substantial support from government and private donors in the United States, Canada, England, Wales, and the European Union. Dr. Miller received the B.S. degree in economics and the M.P.A. degree from Auburn University, Alabama, and the Ph.D. degree in political science from the University of Georgia, Athens.

Handbook
of
Public Personnel
Administration

1

Analyzing the Historical Development of the American Civil Service

RICHARD A. LOVERD   Northeastern University, Boston, Massachusetts

THOMAS J. PAVLAK   Fairleigh Dickinson University, Rutherford, New Jersey

> Personnel administration lies at the very core of administrative management. The effective conduct of the work of the government depends upon the men and women who serve it. Improved plans for governmental organization and management are of little values unless simultaneous recognition is given to the need for attracting, retaining and developing human capacity in the public service. (President's Committee on Administrative Management, 1937: 1)

> When a man assumes a public trust, he should consider himself as public property. (Thomas Jefferson, quoted in Rayner, 1834: 356)

I. INTRODUCTION: RAISING ANSWERS AND QUESTIONS

If personnel management is the answer, what are the questions? Although personnel management may not be the only answer to the problems of effective management of government organizations, its practice certainly does raise a good many questions. For example, just how can government best attract, retain, and develop "human capacity in the public service?" What can public managers do to make the most effective use of government personnel? And more broadly, what can all who serve in the public domain do to earn the "public trust" we expect of them?

In this chapter, it will be demonstrated that the history of the American civil service has been characterized by a number of competing perspectives on personnel administration that not only have been dominant at different times in the past but continue to command attention today. In this sense, analyzing the proper role of public personnel management is rather like trying to get a "fix" on a moving target; that is, there is no "one best way" but rather a series of ways in which to attempt the management of people in government.

II. THE CONCEPT OF A CIVIL SERVICE

The concept of a civil service is central to an understanding of the various perspectives on personnel management that have characterized the historical development of the public service in the United States. One way to characterize the civil service is to recognize that, at base, it "merely distinguishes civilian pursuits in government from military [ones]" (Stahl, 1976, p. 41). Further, when we speak of the civil service, we are referring to those public service positions that are nonelective, appointive posts.

1

The methods used to fill such appointive posts may, however, vary (McMurty, 1976). The two primary appointment methods receiving the most attention over the years have been broadly labeled as *political*, or patronage-oriented, and *nonpolitical*, or merit-based. As Van Riper (1958, p. 8) notes, *either* type of approach can exist within the civil service framework:

> An entire civil service may be either nonpolitical or political or some combination thereof. Public employees selected through an examination system open widely to public competition have been a novelty, except in the orient, until relatively recent times. Before the nineteenth century most civil servants were chosen upon what have been called, not always too appropriately, political grounds. That is, most public appointments were made on the basis of partisanship, influence, wealth, family, personal loyalty, blackmail or charity, rather than intelligence or competence to do the work. This is the system of patronage as opposed to the merit system.

Of course, appointing civil servants on political bases in the absence of formal competitive examinations does not necessarily confirm the existence of government incompetence and corruption. Indeed, as we shall see in the historical review that follows, many competent and honest individuals served the government long before the formal establishment of competitive merit selection processes in the late nineteenth century. Nonetheless, with the institutional establishment of merit appointments to the civil service, it was expected that competence in the administration of the government could be more readily assured.

III.   THE FOUR STAGES OF CIVIL SERVICE DEVELOPMENT: A PREVIEW

Scholars have devised a variety of analytic schemes to trace the historical development of the American civil service. For example, Leonard White (1948, 1951, 1954, 1958) chose to analyze developments by major political eras: *The Federalists, The Jeffersonians, The Jacksonians,* and *The Republican Era*. Others were more specifically concerned with the civil service per se. Mosher (1968) identified six major trends in the U.S. civil service, whereas Van Riper (1958), in writing about the U.S. Civil Service Commission, presented no less than 13 historical periods.

In our view, the work of these authors and others (e.g., Kaufman, 1965; U.S. Civil Service Commission, 1974; Shafritz, 1975; McMurty, 1976) can be encompassed by a framework comprising four major general historical periods. The first era can best be described in a phrase coined by Mosher (1968, p. 55) as one of "government by gentlemen," a relatively stable period from 1789 to 1829 when civil servants tended to be selected from the aristocratic "upper crust" of society. The second, more turbulent period, from 1829 to 1883, was in large measure a reaction to the first and emphasized "government by any man"; in so doing it stressed the need for a more egalitarian and democratic public service. The excesses of that period in turn led to an era of "merit expansion" from 1883 to 1937, when merit systems were established at all levels of government to correct the evils and inefficiencies of the "spoils system." Since 1937, the merit system itself has in turn come under increasing scrutiny, leading to a variety of (often conflicting) demands for more "positive personnel management."

As these brief previews suggest, each of these historical periods is characterized by a different domain perspective of public personnel administration which was controversial and which in turn led to demands for change. Indeed, contemporary public personnel administration is no exception to such controversy. In the sections that follow, we shall examine each of the four historical periods in greater detail, focusing on the views and practices of public personnel management that were dominant, the controversies surrounding them, and their consequences for the civil service. Then we shall conclude with a look at some of the enduring questions of public personnel administration in the United States, including some suggestions for future research.

IV. GOVERNMENT BY GENTLEMEN: 1789–1829

In this first era of the American civil service, a strong aristocratic preference permeated governmental appointments. Although the rationales offered varied, the staffing outcomes were the same: "The government of our early days was a government led by the well-educated, the well-born, the prosperous and their adherents. In short, it was a government of the upper classes" (Van Riper, 1958, pp. 17–18).

As president, George Washington was the first to demonstrate this upper class preference with this "rule of fitness," a rule in which what most concerned him was not technical competence but rather the personal integrity and community standing of his prospective prominent appointees. Through his government appointments, Washington hoped that he might "give dignity and lustre to our National Character." Additionally, according to White (1948, p. 259), Washington sought to "consolidate the position and prestige of the new government among the people in all parts of the country." One result of his appointment policy was "a group of civil servants selected more from the gentry than from other elements of the population" (Kaufman, 1965, p. 13).

Other early presidents, including John Adams and Thomas Jefferson, provided additional support for maintaining an elitist public service. For Adams, *talent* rather than upper class standing was the primary criterion for appointment, but he defined such talent largely in terms of a liberal arts college education, a luxury that few but the wealthy of his day could afford. Indeed, this view led Adams to admit that education, wealth, and family are usually found together; thus, "the gentleman will ordinarily, notwithstanding some exceptions to the rule, be the richer, and born of more noted families" (Aronson, 1964, p. 4). And given the absence of much gentlemanly talent among the common people, Adams viewed their role as one unsuited to government service: "The proposition that they [the people] are the best keepers of their own liberties is not true. They are the worst conceivable; they are no keepers at all. They can neither act, judge, think or will" (Aronson, 1964, p. 5).

Jefferson similarly regarded talent as being of paramount importance for appointment to a government post, but he offered a stronger ideological apologia. Although he advocated a "natural aristocracy" of virtue and talents over an artificial one of wealth and birth, and believed that native ability was "sown as liberally among the poor as the rich," Jefferson also recognized that ability would not survive if not "sought and cultivated" (Aronson, 1964, p. 10). Consequently, for Jefferson, schools should play a pivotal role in nurturing talent by providing equality of opportunity for students "from every condition of life" and producing a genuine aristocracy of talent to overcome the "competition of wealth and birth for public trusts." Unfortunately, as Aronson (1964, p. 10) observes, in this regard Jefferson well knew that no such educational opportunities were available to the masses, thereby precluding equality of opportunity in fact. Thus, given his insistence on higher education as a condition for appointment to public service, Jefferson was led to the same sort of upper class bias as his predecessors.

Within this "upper crust" atmosphere, there also were other considerations for appointment to prominent positions in government. For example, those chosen for government service had to be *loyal to the new government*. As Fish (1904, p. 9) notes, "Political orthodoxy was considered as one of the elements of fitness for office," and, starting with the latter part of Washington's term, as the Federalist and Republican political parties began to take shape, definitions of loyalty included *partisan considerations* as well.

Geography also played a role in upper level appointments. Wherever possible, our early presidents sought to have every region of the country represented in the national government in order that this symbolic representation might contribute to the legitimacy of the government in the eyes of the public. For example, Washington's first cabinet had members from Massachusetts, New York, and Virginia; and the first supreme court was composed of justices from New York, Massachusetts, Pennsylvania, Virginia, Maryland, and South Carolina. At the field office level, considerations of residence and representation were even more extensive: appointments were taken "from the state and locality in which the officials were to serve; local jealousy would have tolerated nothing less" (White, 1948, p. 260).

Thus far, most of the discussion concerning government appointments relates to the highly visible, upper level policymaking posts. Although, for obvious reasons, those posts command our attention and set the tone for the historical period, personnel practices relating to the many workers at the middle and lower levels, who, according to Mosher (1968, pp. 58–59), "correspond roughly to those now covered in the [merit] civil service system," also are important. Unlike their wealthy superiors, these individuals came mostly from the middle and upper middle classes, performed more mundane tasks requiring a minimum of an elementary education, and tended to retain their positions for life. Whereas senior officials came and went with shifts in political party fortunes or presidential administrations, such "rotation in office" was not expected to occur at lower levels; indeed, it was discouraged. Federalist Senator George Reed expressed the sentiments of the time well when he wrote that rotation

> has always appeared to me an insincere reason urged by those who use it . . . when a fit character has been selected for office . . . and he discovers such fitness by an able discharge of duty over time, such person hath a reasonable claim to an after-continuance in office . . . by means of the improved knowledge of the duties of office which he acquires (White, 1948, p. 257).

Much the same view was demonstrated by Thomas McKenney, Superintendent of Indian Trade, when in 1816 he noted that

> to dismiss from office, in those days, without cause, would have been deemed an outrage, not less against the public interests than the party proscribed. Hence, competency, zeal, and honesty, being the characteristics of the clerks I found in the Office of Indian Trade, when I succeeded to its management, it no more occurred to me to turn them out, than it did to cut their throats (Rosenbloom, 1971, pp. 42–43).

Therefore, given such attitudes, the number of dismissals among workers in the "lesser offices" was quite small and was largely related to fault or delinquency in employee performance. Consequently, the bulk of the public work force remained relatively stable.

The picture that emerges from this first stage of civil service development is, on balance, an encouraging one. Although White (1948, p. 258) might have leaned a bit toward hyperbole in suggesting that early "rules of selection shone in statesmanlike splendor," there was much to applaud. With few formal constraints on exercising leadership in the personnel area, our early presidents, for the most part, selected responsible subordinates, fully recognizing that, in Washington's words, "if injudicious or unpopular measures should be taken by the Executive under the New Government with regard to appointments, the Government itself would be in the utmost danger of being utterly subverted by those measures" (White, 1948, p. 258). In building popular support, they sought to appoint public servants who were of the "first character," while recognizing the need to appoint them along geographic and partisan lines as well.

If any particular criticism can be lodged against the civil service of this period, it is that it was too elitist and its definition of competence too limited. By seeking citizens of good community standing, individuals from wealthy and noted families tended to receive primary consideration; and by defining talent in terms of college education "at a time when less than two Americans out of every thousand went to college" (Aronson, 1964, p. 194), those patrician perspectives were only further accentuated.

V. GOVERNMENT BY ANY MAN: 1829–1883

Although the descriptive title for this historical period of U.S. public personnel development may seem a bit exaggerated, the fact is that ideas regarding the nature of the public service and its staffing changed somewhat dramatically. No longer was government service portrayed as the preserve of the elite; instead, the dominant theme characterizing the era was that "any applicant could aspire to any office" (Fish, 1904, p. 113). This idea was very much in keeping with the widespread enfranchisement of adult male citizens, their organization into political parties, and the accompanying surge of democratic sentiment during that time (White, 1954, p. 11).

Many authors identify Andrew Jackson as the ideological spokesman for the period, not because he originated the ideas and activities associated with government by any man [indeed, as Fish (1904) notes, they already were well established in a number of states and localities long before he came into office], but rather as a consequence of his having "*introduced* them to the national government on a wider scale than any of his predecessors, and for carrying them out *openly*—indeed proudly—rather than apologetically and quietly" (Kaufman, 1965, p. 20).

What might there be to apologize about? The ideas that Jackson introduced served to legitimize the highly abused spoils system. However, before describing the spoils system, it is useful to examine the elements of Jackson's ideology more carefully, for this ideology was itself a reaction to the elitist tendencies of the previous era.

In Jackson's view, the importance of government jobs and the abilities necessary to perform them well had been exaggerated and misguided. To him, few tasks in public service were that difficult; indeed, in his first message to Congress, he stated that "the duties of all public offices are, or at least admit of being made so plain and simple, that men of intelligence may readily qualify themselves for this performance" (Richardson, 1896, pp. 448–449).

In addition to viewing public office as being relatively undemanding, Jackson also exhibited greater confidence in the abilities of the common man than did his predecessors. He believed that competence was available throughout society rather than being found only among the wealthy, college-educated ranks. Jackson further believed that high moral qualities were equally present in the masses. To him, the "farmer, the mechanic and the laborer were the bone and sinew of the country" (Aronson, 1964, p. 16). In sum, for Jackson, representatives from any segments of society had just as much competence and moral fiber as the upper classes, and the social and political costs of their continued exclusion from public posts were too high; for "let it be known that any class or portion of citizens are or ought to be proscribed and discontent and dissatisfaction will be engendered (Aronson, 1964, p. 14).

Nonetheless, there still remained the problem of providing access for Jackson's new appointees. How could he bring in his many new officers when past practices dictated lifetime tenure for most employees whose presence would stand in the way of his own personnel? Jackson's solution was to introduce a new rationale to justify the removal of current employees: *rotation in office*. In his oft-quoted first annual message to Congress, he stressed, somewhat ironically, that rotation in office would serve to control corruption:

I cannot but believe that more is lost by the long continuance of men in office than is generally to be gained by their experience. . . . There are, perhaps, few men who can for any great length of time enjoy office and power without being more or less under the influence of feelings unfavorable to the faithful discharge of their public duties. Their integrity may be proof against improper considerations immediately addressed to themselves, but they are apt to acquire a habit of looking with indifference upon the public interests and of tolerating conduct from which an unpracticed man would revolt. Office is considered as a species of property, and government rather as a means of promoting individual interests than as an instrument created solely for the service of the people. Corruption in some and in others a perversion of correct feelings and principles divert government from its legitimate ends and make it an engine for the support of the few at the expense of the many (Richardson, pp. 448–449).

Thus, in this classic defense of rotation in office, Jackson emphasized its moral purpose. This emphasis on morality was to be expected because, according to White (1954, p. 319), Jackson was a man of rigid integrity: "Jackson made no reference to the party advantage that rotation would induce, nor to its effect upon executive power. He made no defense of the abuses that might follow . . . and he would certainly have denounced them could he have foreseen them."

However, others among Jackson's contemporaries and subsequent leaders were not so noble. They saw the practical political advantages of rotation in office and, in keeping with the oft-cited 1832 sentiment of Senator William L. Marcy of New York, "[saw] nothing wrong in the rule that to the victor belong the spoils of the enemy" (Tolchin and Tolchin, 1971, p. 1; Shafritz et al., 1992, p. 7). With job rotation came tremendous opportunities to exercise patronage by rewarding faithful party followers from all segments of society with these new-found spoils of public office. In so doing, there were equally tremendous opportunities for abuse of that patronage power, leading some observers of the time to exclaim that "the government, formerly served by the elite of the nation, is now served to a very considerable extent by its refuse" (Parton, 1887, p. 20) and that "at present, there is no organization save that of corruption; no system save that of chaos; no test of integrity save that of partisanship and no test of qualification save that of intrigue" (Bing, 1868, in Hoogenboom, 1961, p. 1).

Although these indictments of the spoils system may suffer from exaggeration, they do point up the problems inherent in its practice. The public service, previously viewed as an honorable pursuit for gentlemen, now became strongly associated with partisan politics, incompetence, inefficiency, and corruption (Mosher, 1968, p. 63). For example, with regard to political parties, although any man could indeed gain access to a public post, such access was based on partisan service rather than individual competence. Government jobs were used as rewards, prizes for a job well done in working for the party and getting candidates elected to office; actual performance on the job, being "so plain and simple," was of lesser importance. As a consequence, those selected for public employment were not always qualified for the duties they were hired to perform, and a "premium was placed on the creation of extra jobs to provide additional political currency and also lighten the workload so that loyal political partisans would have time for their assigned political tasks" (Kaufman, 1965, p. 31).

Thus, for political parties, government service was of little importance except as it contributed to party power. Jobs were forms of patronage to be used to strengthen any party and, according to Sorauf (1960), they did so in at least six different ways, by (1) maintaining an active party organization, (2) promoting intraparty cohesion, (3) attracting voters and supporters, (4) financing the party and its candidates, (5) procuring favorable governmental action, and (6) creating party discipline in policymaking.

For those party faithful holding government posts, there was a great temptation to make the most of their possible short-term employment, in light of shifting partisan electoral fortunes. Thus, contrary to Jackson's arguments, rotation contributed to corruption. As Henry Clay observed in 1829, "Incumbents, feeling the instability of their situation, and knowing their liability to periodic removals, at short terms, without any regard to the manner in which they have executed their trust, will be disposed to make the most of their uncertain offices while they have them, and hence we may expect immediate cases of fraud, predation and corruption" (Fish, 1904, p. 140).

Perhaps one party leader, New York City Tammany Ward boss George Washington Plunkett, best described the temptations of office when he said, "I seen my opportunities and I took 'em" (Riordan, 1963, p. 3). Many of his cohorts at all levels of government did just that. For example, in 1868, an Indian Peace Commission observed that "agents have pocketed funds appropriated by the government and driven the Indians to starvation . . . these officers have been selected from partisan ranks, not so much on account of honesty and qualifications as for devotion to party interests and their willingness to apply the money of the Indian to promote selfish schemes of local politicians" (Rosenbloom, 1971, p. 67). Van Riper (1958, p. 75) also cites a host of exploitive incidents that occurred during the infamous Grant administration and concludes by saying: "When one considers that corruption was just as rife in state and local government . . . it is no wonder that many were exercised over the state of the nation. Never had public morals fallen so low."

In addition to partisan corruption and abuse, there were inefficiencies inherent in the very nature of rotation in office. Periodic staff turnover did little for staff morale or career development opportunities (Lee, 1987, p. 19) and, of course, considerable amounts of energy for orientation and training of the work force were expended with every change in administrations (Kaufman, 1965, p. 31).

For chief executives, the spoils system proved to be a mixed blessing. On the one hand, patronage provided considerable opportunities for executive leadership. Parceled out judiciously, government posts could be used to win elections and subsequently to secure legislative approval of proposed policies and programs. "A mayor, for example, could win legislative votes by appointing the friends of city council members" (Lee, 1987, p. 19). In addition, patronage could encourage more responsiveness from government employees through the ever-present threat of dismissal.

On the other hand, the spoils system was not without its liabilities. Not all "political friends" were necessarily in agreement with the political views of the chief executive. For example, "executives, by appointing political friends of legislators, in many instances named people who were not in agreement with them. To win an election, a person needed the support of all factions or wings of the political party, and once elected, was obligated to appoint individuals from all wings of the party" (Lee, 1987, p. 20). As a consequence, once appointed, the allegiance of those "friends" to the chief executive and his main functionaries was by no means assured. For example, in its official history, the U.S. Civil Service Commission (1974, p. 24) noted that during the Mexican–American War, General Winfield Scott found his command seriously hindered by insubordinate volunteer officers who have been appointed for political reasons. It further observed that "the spoils system, having been extended into the Army and the Navy, impaired the effectiveness of our forces not only in 1848 but also in many Civil War campaigns." And should any of those insubordinate political friends be subsequently dismissed, the executive ran the risk of incurring the wrath of their original sponsors.

In a larger sense, the spoils system also proved to be both demeaning and annoying to the chief executive, reducing his role to that of "petty job broker and diverting his strength and attention from more important matters of state to the dispensation of hundreds of posts under the

greatest pressure" (Kaufman, 1965, pp. 31–32). For example, the sheer strain of making appointments led President James Polk to exclaim: "Will the pressure for office never cease! It is one
year today since I entered on the duties of my office, and still the pressure for office has not abated.
I most sincerely wish I had no offices to bestow" (White, 1954, p. 304). President William Henry Harrison died soon after taking office, leading the U.S. Civil Service Commission (1974, p.
22) to note that "the official certificate gave pneumonia and general weakness as the causes of death,
but the opinion of many historians is that the real cause was the spoils system." And perhaps
President William Howard Taft described the greatest danger of all when he noted that a patronage appointment creates "nine enemies and one ingrate" (Shafritz, 1975, p. 25). Indeed, it was
one such "enemy," a disappointed office seeker named Charles J. Guiteau, who assassinated
President James A. Garfield in 1881.

   In summarizing this second stage of civil service development, we can note several new trends
in personnel ideologies and practices. With the legitimation of rotation in office and the accompanying notion that any person was competent to hold public posts came increased opportunities
for the common man to gain access to employment in positions throughout the government. Although this access admittedly was secured through party service, it nonetheless indicated that the
public's work was no longer the preserve of the upper classes. Thus, one major benefit of the spoils
system was the increased representativeness of public bureaucracy.

   However, substantial costs for the public service also resulted. As patronage increased, the
intrinsic worth and prestige of public employment declined. Besides being considered as "plain
and simple," the association of public service with the worst aspects of partisan politics grew
stronger. Frequently, those chosen to fill such jobs were of questionable competence; in the
workplace, they might be expected to serve their party as much as their government; and the
incidence of corruption led many to believe that appointees were, in fact, only serving themselves.

   For chief executives, the picture is less clear. In the hands of an able leader, patronage could
be used to win elections and to secure favored policies and programs. However, the actual management of the government through the spoils system proved more problematic. Party-selected
personnel not only could be incompetent but also could be unwilling to follow the chief executive's lead. And, throughout the process of making and managing appointments, one always ran
the risk of creating more enemies than allies.

VI. MERIT EXPANSION: 1883–1937

The public's concern about the abuses of the spoils system grew more intense with the assassination of President Garfield, leading to mounting demands for civil service reform. Unlike the previous two eras, this period of civil service development was characterized by an administrative
combination of morality and competence. On the one hand, the initial impetus for this reform
movement stressed the morality of stamping out partisan political spoils. As White (1939, p. 282)
notes, reformers sought to achieve "purified elections and a more wholesome democracy." Waldo
(1948, p. 28) also suggests that "the primary issue was moral" and cites R. Fulton Cutting's comments as reflecting the dominant sentiment of the early part of this period: "The real crime committed against society by the spoils system is moral . . . it poisons our institutions at the fountain-
head, corrupting the electorate and creating a political conscience antagonistic to morals." Indeed,
for Mosher (1968, p. 65), "Few reform movements in American history could draw so clear a
distinction between right and wrong, between the 'good guys' and the 'bad guys.' It was a campaign to stamp out evils that were clear and obnoxious."

   However, there was another dimension to this personnel period that soon became evident,
one that stressed the need for competence. As Waldo (1948, p. 38) observes, "there was a con-

stant secularizing tendency through all the latter part of the century, an increasing disposition to view the reform of personnel not as a high moral endeavor but as a matter of improving the quality of administration . . . Not only must persons not be given positions as party plunder, not only must they be honest: they must be trained and capable. After all, the environment surrounding public service was growing more demanding and complex, and the age of plain and simple jobs was fast disappearing. As Rosenbloom (1971, p. 71) notes, "Civil service reform of some kind was almost inevitable as government became more positive, as public policy became more regulatory, as technology and business methods advanced, and as the size of the civil service grew in conjunction with these factors."

The way to meet these demands for both morality and competence was sought through the formal establishment and expansion of *merit systems* for civil servants. This establishment occurred at the federal level with the passage of the Pendleton Act of 1883, followed by a modest number of states including New York (1883), Massachusetts (1884), Wisconsin and Illinois (1905), Colorado (1907), New Jersey (1908), and Ohio (1912). Albany, New York (1884) was the first municipality to pass a merit law, and Cook County, Illinois (1895) was the first county (Dresang, 1978; Nigro and Nigro, 1981). Although interpretations of this and succeeding merit legislation varied in scope and emphasis (e.g., see U.S. Civil Service Commission, 1956, 1958; Van Riper, 1958; Intergovernmental Personnel Act of 1970; Macy; 1971; Rosen, 1975; Civil Service Reform Act of 1978), McMurty (1976, p. 7) notes that

> one can sift through the respective definitions and ultimately arrive at three central principles of the merit system. . . . First among the historic principles is recruitment via competitive examinations, or on the basis of job ability or individual competence. A second major principle is absence or arbitrary removals, or relative security of tenure. The third fundamental principle is that of political neutrality in the civil service.

Much the same merit ideas were expressed more precisely by Heclo (1977, p. 20) when he noted that

1. The selection of subordinate government officials should be based on merit, the ability to perform the work rather than any form of personal or political favoritism,
2. Since jobs are to be filled by weighing the merits of applicants, those hired should have tenure regardless of political changes at the top of the organization, and
3. The price of job security should be a willing responsiveness to the legitimate political leaders of the day.

Thus, able people would be selected through open, competitive examinations; the corrupting influences of partisan politics would be kept out of the selection and appointment process; and the successful applicants would in turn be protected from abuse by job tenure in public employment. Furthermore, this ability and tenure also would result in a cadre with politically neutral competence, one that "envisions a continuous, uncommitted facility at the disposal of, and for the support of, political leadership" (Heclo, 1975, p. 81).

Although the issues of ability and tenure were clear enough, the concept of neutrality caused problems for civil service reformers. As Mosher (1968, p. 67) notes, it "gave the early enthusiasts of civil service reform difficulties, even as it continues to give difficulties today. How can a public service which is neutral in political matters and which is protected by responsive to a public which expresses its wishes through the machinery of elections and political parties?"

One significant attempt to provide an answer to this neutrality dilemma was the development of a doctrine of espousing the separation of policy and political activity from administration. The legislature, the chief executive, and his political appointees would determine policy whereas the protected merit civil service would faithfully implement that policy in the most able, efficient way possible. It was assumed by reformers that "the civil service is a neutral instrument, without policy preferences of its own (taken as a body) and without any inclination to attempt to impose any policy on the country. For the civil service reformers, the civil service was like a hammer or a saw; it would do nothing at all by itself, but it would serve any purpose, wise or unwise, good or bad, to which any user put it" (Kaufman, 1965, p. 39).

Many of these ideas were well expressed by civil service reformer and future President Woodrow Wilson in his classic essay on "The Study of Administration" (1887, pp. 197–222). In it he reaffirmed the "truth already so much and so fortunately insisted upon by our civil service reforms; namely that administration lies outside the proper sphere of politics. Administrative questions are not political questions. Although politics sets the tasks for administration, it should not be suffered to manipulate its offices." Further describing this doctrine, Wilson states that "the field of administration is a field of business. It is removed from the hurry and strife of politics. . . . It is a part of political life only as the methods of the counting-house are a part of the life of society; only as machinery is a part of the manufactured product." Thus, for Wilson, as well as for other reformers and writers of this period (Goodnow, 1900; Willoughby, 1927), it was expected that those placed in the protected merit civil service under the recently enacted legislation would not develop policy preferences of their own; their policy direction would come from political levels and their function would be to execute those policies in an able, "businesslike" fashion. Nonetheless, as Mosher mentions, the political neutrality of civil servants would continue to "give difficulties" to those wary of possible overprotection of public servants and fearful of the creation of a self-directed administrative class.

The basic administrative vehicle established by the civil service legislation to serve as a guardian of the merit system was the independent civil service commission. Rather than place merit protection in an executive agency under the direct control of the chief executive, the commission form was chosen in the hope that it would "be above and outside the political arena" and thereby more readily "immunize appointments and in-service activity from political influence" (Mosher, 1968, p. 69). The civil service commissions were usually composed of three to seven members, appointed by the chief executive with the consent of the legislature, and bipartisan "so that no single leader might undermine its political neutrality" (Lee, 1979, p. 31; Mosher, 1968, p. 69). For example, at the federal level, the Pendleton Act established a bipartisan, three-member Civil Service Commission appointed by the president and confirmed by the Senate.

In the critical area of merit selection, the civil service commission did not itself make merit appointments. Rather, it served as a clearinghouse, screening applicants and providing lists of those best qualified (usually the best of three, leading to the so-called rule of three) from which the appointing officer could choose. And in all phases of merit system personnel practices, it acted as a watchdog, looking for instances of abuse and striving to keep them in check.

Further enhancing the merit system and the oversight activities of the Civil Service Commission was the development during this period of more scientific methods of personnel administration, a pursuit very much in keeping with the scientific management movement of the early twentieth century. As Mosher (1968, pp. 70–71) notes,

> The civil service merit system provided a compatible base for the development during the first third of this century of technology and specialization. Its emphasis upon objectivity, upon relating qualifications with job requirements, and upon eliminating as far as possible considerations of personality and individual belief from personnel decisions were perfectly consistent with the ethos of scientific management. Further, the organizational separation and semi-independence of civil service administration provided encouragement to the development of scientific techniques in the personnel field itself.

Thus, the stage of merit expansion witnessed the development by civil service commissions of such scientific personnel methods as job analysis, position classification, and pay systems (particularly with regard to the notion that those performing "equal work" should receive "equal pay"), more objective and systematically devised examinations, job-related training programs, and efficiency ratings (Waldo, 1948; Sayre, 1948; Mosher, 1968; Shafritz, 1973; Wilson, 1973).

For the chief executive, the establishment of merit systems proved to be of mixed value. Although a merit system obviously curtailed the chief executive's ability to use patronage for his own political belief, a more consistent, competent group of politically neutral civil servants might be available to serve him once he attained office. Such a group, with its professional experience and its knowledge of the intricacies of the public bureaucracy, could help him to get what he wanted from the government. Having worked with a number of administrations, civil servants also would have developed an appreciation of the need for continuity and a well-honed "institutional memory" on which they might draw to deal with current problems. They also could add a more impartial view to the other, more immediate, limited, short-term "sectional appeals in government" and, in general, "keep the government mechanism well-oiled and in working order" (Heclo, 1975, p. 83). Of course, the preceding description provides the best of all possible scenarios for chief executives. Those same civil servants, protected in their jobs by the merit system, might also use their abilities and merit protections to limit executive initiatives and promote inaction on the basis of their past experience.

In reviewing this third stage of civil service development, it should be noted that its initial impetus was a moral one. The primary concern of the reformers was to keep out the corruption and abuse of the "spoils" period by creating institutional protections for civil servants that would enforce a more administratively responsible system of government.

Complementing those merit system protections was an emphasis on competence, i.e., using ability rather than politics as the basis for appointment to the nonpolitical positions of the public service. As reformer George William Curtis noted at the time, choosing merit civil servants on the basis of politics made as much sense as appointing "a man surveyor of highways because he played sweetly on the French horn" (Rosenbloom, 1971, p. 76). In the view of civil service reformers, selection for public employment had to be based on ability, and the scientific management methods of the time could help foster that ability in an era when jobs were becoming less plain and simple. In so doing, it was believed that a more equitable as well as more efficient public work force would result.

It was believed that access to public jobs still would be widespread, except that competence rather than party service would be the main criterion for entry into public service. Further, judgments of competence would not rest on ascriptive attributes such as a college education; instead ability would be determined by open and competitive examinations of a practical rather than an academic nature.

For chief executives, the consequences were not so clear. Obviously, they would have less patronage to dispense and therefore less opportunity to select and dismiss those in the merit ranks. However, in return, they might benefit from the services of a more competent and a more responsive work force.

VII. THE CONTEMPORARY CIVIL SERVICE: 1937 TO PRESENT

In this last and most contemporary phase of civil service development, the merit system in turn has come under scrutiny. The nature of that scrutiny was first formally expressed in 1937, when the President's Committee on Administrative Management (1937, p. 9) noted the achievements and the inadequacies of the merit system. As an agency "set up to protect the federal executive establishment against the evils of patronage," the Committee observed that the federal Civil Service Commission had "endeavored conscientiously to observe the statutes and orders that have been laid down for its guidance . . . achieved its greatest success in the administration of open competitive examinations. . . . and pioneered in personnel research and efficiency ratings." Despite these advances, the Committee (1937, pp. 9–10) then went on to state that "the existing civil service system is poorly adapted to meet the larger responsibilities of serving as a central personnel agency for a vast and complicated governmental administration," and the agency itself reflects "a negative, protective and legalistic role, whereas the need today is for a positive, constructive and active personnel agency."

Thirty-seven years later, in its own official history, the U.S. Civil Service Commission (1974, p. 67) made a similar pronouncement when it observed that "the big test . . . was whether a system conceived for an essentially negative purpose, i.e., control of patronage and corruption in appointment to public office, could be adapted to modern needs, discoveries and requirements in personnel management." Far from running its course, this "test" continues today.

In particular, the merit system currently is being challenged in a number of important ways. A first test, one that is probably most familiar to readers, is the criticism that opportunities for the exercise of executive leadership and managerial authority are too constrained. For example, rather than helping supervisors, at times it seems that civil service merit systems and their staff specialists are rigid in their views and behavior toward management, actually stifling and circumscribing managerial initiatives. As the guardians against violations of the merit system, their concerns seem to lie more in adherence to personnel rules and procedures than in the support of management. In this regard, a report by the Committee for Economic Development (1974, pp. 44–46) noted a number of common merit system deficiencies: (1) recruitment by personnel offices is often slow, unimaginative, and unaggressive; (2) bureaucratic delays prevent the prompt filling of job vacancies, many times leading to the loss of top applicants to other job opportunities; (3) rigid classification systems impede efficient assignment of work; and (4) managers lack the authority to reward superior performers and discipline or fire nonperformers. In a similar vein, Hays and Reeves (1984, pp. 268–270) criticized (1) the overemphasis on job security, (2) the lack of incentives, and (3) the obsession with centralized rules and procedures that provide little opportunity for managerial initiative and direction. As a consequence, "the supervisor does not control the selection and removal process very directly and, as protections for employee job security develop, the employee has a degree of independence (Cayer, 1980, pp. 37). And, of course, greater employee independence serves to weaken the authority of the supervisor.

The merit system, with its attendant employee protections, also can encourage self-direction on the part of career civil servants in government agencies, a direction that may not reflect the policies desired by the public and its legitimate representatives. As the eminent sociologist Max Weber observed many years ago, "the power position of a fully developed bureaucracy is always overtowering. The 'political master' finds himself in the position of the 'dilettante' who stands opposite the 'expert,' facing the trained official who stands within the management of administration" (Gerth and Mills, 1946, p. 232). Indeed, Rourke (1976, p. 14) has observed that "no fear has been more constant in modern politics—shared by revolutionaries and reactionaries alike—than the apprehension that bureaucrats might become a power elite and dominate the governmental process in which they are meant to play a subordinate role." The fear is that government bureaucrats, shielded by the protections of the merit system, might be tempted to exceed their authority and to intimidate or ignore their political superiors on the basis of their experience and professional allegiance.

Another test for the merit system relates to instances in which its restrictions are viewed as being too strong and too debilitating for managers. In those circumstances, managers might be tempted to avoid the merit system altogether. For example, merit system restrictions can be avoided simply by the creation of new government positions outside the merit system. Presidents Roosevelt and Eisenhower were particularly adept at this approach; the former established a host of new agencies exempt from merit, whereas the latter created an exempt category of "Schedule C" jobs of a confidential or policymaking nature (Kaufman, 1965, pp. 46–49). And at the state level, Roberts (1991, p. 191) notes that "since 1970, twenty-eight states have made significant policy changes [to make top bureaucracies more responsive to their political superiors], almost all in the direction of *increasing the number of exempted top managers and policy-making careerists from civil service protection and giving governors and appointed superiors more personnel discretion.*"

More covert means of merit avoidance include the creation of informal parallel systems of "temporary" or "provisional" civil service positions that continue for years, a strategy that has been a particular favorite of the political party machines in New York City and Chicago (Tolchin and Tolchin, 1971, pp. 4–41). Indeed, as Dresang (1991, p. 31) notes somewhat ironically, in some jurisdictions, the formal adoption of merit systems was little more than a "symbolic gesture":

> Cook County in Illinois was the first county government to adopt a civil service ordinance, yet, primarily through the extensive use of "temporary" and "acting" appointments, Cook County became notorious as one of the strongest patronage-based political machines in the country. Similarly, Massachusetts, the second state to adopt the merit system, developed a reputation for patronage appointments.

Also, the attempted "bending" of civil service rules to oust neutral personnel and replace them with more tractable loyalists has been aptly described in the unofficial "Federal Political Personnel Manual" or "Malek Manual" (U.S. House, 1976) prepared during the Nixon "Watergate" years and subsequently criticized in a National Academy of Public Administration report (Mosher, 1974). One final means of avoiding merit protection that has grown popular in recent years involves the use of outside contractors or "privatization" for public service, i.e., rather than continuing to work with less compliant civil servants, many chief executives prefer to contract with private and non-profit agencies or permanently jettison activities to the private sector to do the public's work (Guttman and Willner, 1976; Hanrahan, 1977; U.S. General Accounting Office, 1981; Musolf and Seidman, 1980; Hanke, 1987; Savas, 1987; Rehfuss, 1989; Kettl, 1991; Osborne and Gaebler, 1992).

The scientific personnel methods developed along with the establishment of merit systems are also being challenged, leading observers such as Sayre (1948) to question whether they reflect a "triumph of techniques over purpose." Sayre (1948, p. 137) charges that methods such as "job classification, factor analysis, numerical efficiency ratings, formal promotion charts and all their procedural relatives" may be impressive, but they "lack the objectivity which is their sole claim to usefulness; they provide merely the appearance, not the substance, of the relevant measurement of ability and merit. The variables of personnel administration are too many and too subtle to be contained within a purely statistical frame of reference." Consequently, new ways may be necessary to measure and encourage merit and thereby "tame techniques for public purposes" (Loverd, 1981).

Public employee unions, minority groups, and women share a similar distrust of such scientific techniques. For example, public employee unions desire to have a greater voice in personnel decisions by bilaterally negotiating issues such as position classification, pay, and promotion that were previously assumed to be unilaterally, scientifically, and objectively determined with the help of civil service commissions (Nollen, 1975, p. 17). In realizing that desire, Stanley (1970, p. 109) predicts that, as union strength grows in numbers and influence, "civil service commissions may not go out of business, but more and more of their vital organs will be removed by the bargaining process."

For minorities and women, the merit system frequently is perceived as having operated to exclude them from government job opportunities. Their underrepresentation in the public service and their concentration in the lowest ranking jobs at all levels of government (Krislov, 1967; Kranz, 1976; Slack, 1988; Ban, 1991; Riccucci, 1991) lead them to question the equity and integrity of merit procedures, and in many instances their questions are justified. For example, in a report of the U.S. Commission on Civil Rights (1969, pp. 31–69), it was noted that civil service procedures could be held responsible for excluding minority groups through such actions as the use of unvalidated written tests, rigid education and experience requirements, automatic disqualification in the instance of arrest records, and the absence of efforts to recruit minorities. Canfield and Reece (1975, p. 11) further note that traditional merit procedures, by "choosing the 'best' or 'better' qualified' rather than the potentially or the minimally qualified, [have] tended historically to elevate the formally educated, credentialed, and licensed, and recently the white middle class."

Further demonstration of the need to reexamine past discriminatory merit personnel practices were stimulated by the 1971 decision of the U.S. Supreme Court in the *Griggs v. Duke Power Company* case. In that case, the Court made it clear that employment selection processes that have a disparate effect on persons of a different sex, religion, race, or national origin must be proven to be job-related. If such job-relatedness cannot be shown, unlawful discrimination is present. Since *Griggs*, numerous cases have been litigated, and won, by minorities and women on that very basis (Nigro and Nigro, 1981, pp. 16–20).

All of the preceding tests for the merit system (i.e., constraints on executive leadership; excessive bureaucratic autonomy; overt and covert merit protection avoidance mechanisms; questionable scientific management methods; and challenges by unions, minorities, and women) suggest the need for yet a new approach to public personnel management. In fact, one has emerged during this most recent period, an approach that stresses that there need to be more positive and flexible personnel forms and functions to allow greater opportunities for executive leadership and discretion. This "positive personnel management" approach has been advanced by numerous organizations, including the President's Committee on Administrative Management (1937), the first and second Hoover Commissions (1949 and 1955), the Municipal Manpower Commission (1962), the National Civil Service League (in its 1970 Model Public Personnel Administration Law), the President's 1977 Federal Personnel Management Project (which furthered the passage of the Civil Service Reform Act of 1978), and the Committee for Economic Development (1978).

Advocates of positive personnel management maintain that the concern with limiting abuses has been overemphasized. This concern must be complemented by opportunities for positive executive leadership that can, in turn, foster a more competent, responsible, and representative bureaucracy. Indeed, in a report by the U.S. Office of Personnel Management (the successor to the U.S. Civil Service Commission), it was noted that "the dominant theme in public personnel reform is to improve the responsiveness of civil service personnel to management and hence to the general public to which management is ultimately accountable" (U.S. Office of Personnel Management, 1979, p. 1).

The different means by which one might improve merit civil service responsiveness to executive direction start with a restructuring of the personnel agency itself. If it is to serve as an arm of the chief executive and to enhance his or her leadership abilities, the older independent commission form that, in Nigro and Nigro's words (1981, p. 93), "[kept] a safe distance between merit system administrators and chief executives" would have to be abandoned. In its place, what is needed is a personnel staff agency directly responsible to the chief executive and subject to his or her direction.

In addition to strengthening the management authority of the chief executive, the public would benefit as well, because chief executives and their managerial subordinates could be held more directly accountable for personnel actions initiated. Moreover, it has been argued that such an organizational reform is only fair. As the National Civil Service League (1970, p. 5) stressed in promulgating its model personnel law proposals, "Most public jurisdictions have reached the point where sound administrative practices as well as a sense of political fair play demand that the chief elected official be given greater authority over the personnel function if we are to continue to charge him with the ultimate responsibility of administering the jurisdiction."

Securing such structural reform entails a readjustment in personnel functions as well. Among the expected functional improvements are the provision of more opportunities for the delegation of personnel authority to agency heads; greater discretion in examination and selection processes; increased managerial authority to appraise, reward, and discipline employee performance; and a more flexible "rank-in-person" system of classification at the upper echelons of the merit civil service, which encourages those individuals to be more responsive to the political executives charged with running the government and allows them to be more readily reassigned to tasks where their talents are most needed (Campbell, 1978).

Of course, these positive personnel initiatives have not been received without criticism. For example, Thayer (1978) argues that such reforms may encourage a style of government management that is authoritarian and oppressive. For unions, there is suspicion that positive personnel initiatives are too management-oriented (Shafritz et al., 1992, p. 21). Minorities and women question whether improved executive leadership will lead to improved opportunities for their numbers (Howard, 1978). And, permeating all the criticism is the suspicion that a more flexible system of personnel management will only serve to reinstitute, and perhaps even legitimize, the civil service spoils and abuses of the past (Rosen, 1978).

Nonetheless, despite the criticisms, if our contemporary merit system is to meet its "tests" and move ahead, positive personnel reforms may very well provide direction. As Alan K. Campbell (1978, p. 103), first director of the U.S. Office of Personnel Management, observed in challenging the more protective postures of the past:

> One could envision a system in which every action would have a check and balance, and every decision a multi-level review. This might eradicate abuse but it would also thwart productivity. A balance must be struck between the freedom necessary to service the public's needs and the oversight required to protect the system's integrity.

Consequently, for Campbell and other modern day reformers, the way to strike such a balance is to give greater weight to executive leadership than has been accorded to it in the past.

Unfortunately, in a very real sense, many of the positive personnel reforms promulgated by Campbell and others have yet to reach fruition. As Dresang (1991, p. 337) observes, given antigovernmental popular sentiment, recessions, taxpayer revolts, the emphasis on privatization and downsizing government, "the 1980's were not kind to government in general and not conducive to achieving the vision of civil service reformers in particular. . . . These factors led to incomplete implementation." Nonetheless, Dresang goes on to suggest that, with the creation of the Volcker Commission to attempt to reinvigorate the public service and a change in attitude at the presidential level, a possible shift in sentiment in the 1990s may be in the offing.

VIII.   ONGOING RESEARCH QUESTIONS

At the outset of this chapter, it was suggested that there is more than one way to attempt the management of government personnel. As our review of the history of the American civil service has demonstrated, a number of different approaches is indeed possible. Clearly, each of the four historical periods presented reflects different emphases in the use of human resources.

However, in addition to recognition of the fact that personnel management emphases can shift from era to era, we, along with certain other authors (Kaufman, 1969; Mosher, 1968), believe that a number of enduring themes can be culled from history that can prove helpful in the analysis of any past or present civil service settings. In this regard, four such themes seem particularly useful, themes that might best be put forth in the form of questions. In the first instance, those analyzing the civil service should consider the *competence* of personnel. What kinds of more or less talented individuals are being drawn into government service? How are their abilities being determined and put to use? A second theme emphasizes the degree of access by the public to government jobs and the subsequent level of representatives of the public service in relation to the public at large. Are certain interests being favored more heavily than others in the staffing patterns of the government? Is the government too elitist or too inclined toward only certain kinds of personnel to the exclusion of others? This theme is of particular concern to those interests who sense exclusion from the government's administrative decision-making processes.

In the third instance, an investigation of the opportunities for *executive leadership* is in order. Is there the administrative flexibility present to accomplish executive branch leadership, or are civil servants provided with so many merit protections or competing loyalties as to make their activities resistant to executive direction? And the fourth and final theme suggests that personnel be examined with regard to the quality of their responsible behavior. Because public servants do, after all, hold a public trust, we need to ask whether their administrative activities reflect behavior that is moral, fair, and free of corruption and scandal.

In our view, all four of the preceding themes should be used in researching civil service settings. Each helps to highlight dimensions of personnel management that took precedence in the past and continue to vie for attention in the present. For example, during the period of "government by gentlemen," it could be argued that the key theme was competence, whereas the era of "government by any man" reflected a desire for increased representation of wide segments of the public in the government. As well, the "merit expansion" phase, in fighting corruption, might be viewed as one that expressed the need for more responsible behavior on the part of merit civil servants and their political superiors, whereas "the contemporary civil service," in emphasizing a more "positive personnel management," could be seen as stressing improved executive leadership.

In addition to shifting thematic emphases, examination of the shifting interpretation of those themes is also worthy of study. For example, history demonstrates that notions of competence can change. Whereas for some observers its presence might be proven through the successful attainment of a college education and community standing, others might assume that competence is more widespread for the plain and simple work demanded by government; still others might favor job-related, scientifically devised tests to confirm such ability. History also suggests that interpretations of representatives can vary. They can shift from a perceived need for elite public servants, to party regulars, to open representation based on a test.

Beyond shifting thematic emphases and interpretations lie questions concerning the larger contextual factors that help shape the quality of any civil service system and the management of personnel within it. For example, writ large, further study of the differences between the managerial climates of the public and private sectors could be in order (Allison, 1983; Loverd, 1982; Lynn, 1981). Then again, within the public sector, further analysis of the different types of value systems or political cultures that help shape personnel behavior and thereby limit or enhance managerial initiatives could be studied (Elazar, 1972; Shafritz, 1974). And finally, further analysis of the different sorts of sometimes contradictory environmental demands that come to bear in shaping personnel decisions could help managers in balancing their priorities (Levine and Nigro, 1975; Mushkin and Sandifer, 1978; Demarco, 1983; Loverd, 1992).

At base, the shifting thematic emphases, interpretations, and contextual factors noted above raise more questions than they answer. In so doing, they provide ample evidence that the field of civil service research is a fertile one, well worth pursuing from a variety of vantage points that suggest not one best way but many competing ways in which to make the most effective use of government personnel.

REFERENCES

Allison, G. (1983). Public and private management: are they fundamentally alike in all unimportant respects? *Public Administration: Concepts and Cases* (R. Stillman, ed.)., Houghton, Mifflin, Boston.

Aronson, S. (1964). *Status and Kinship in the Higher Civil Service: Standards of Selection in the Administration of John Adams, Thomas Jefferson and Andrew Jackson*, Harvard University Press, Cambridge, MA.

Ban, C. (1991). The realities of the merit system, *Public Personnel Management: Current Concerns—Future Challenges* (C. Ban and N. Riccucci, eds.), Longman, New York.

Bing, J. (1868). Our civil service, *Putnam's Magazine, 2*: 233–236.

Campbell, A. (1978). Civil service reform: a new commitment, *Public Admin. Rev., 38*: 99–103.

Canfield, R., and Reece, B. (1975). *What Achieves Affirmative Action in Cities?* Public Services Laboratory, Georgetown University, Washington, D.C.

Cayer, N. J. (1980). *Managing Human Resources*, St. Martin's Press, New York.

Committee for Economic Development (1978). *Improving Management in the Public Workforce*, Committee for Economic Development, New York.

Demarco, J. (1984). Productivity and personnel management in government organizations, *Public Personnel Administration: Problems and Prospects* (S. Hays and R. Kearney, eds.), Prentice-Hall, Englewood Cliffs, NJ.

Dresang, D. (1978). Public personnel reform: a summary of state government activity, *Public Personnel Manage., 7*: 287–294.

_____(1991). *Public Personnel Management and Public Policy*, 2nd Ed., Longman, New York.

Elazar, D. (1972). *American Federalism: A View from the States*, 2nd Ed., Crowell, New York.

Federal Personnel Management Project (1977a). Final Staff Report, U.S. Government Printing Office, Washington, D.C.

_____(1977b). *Option Paper Number Two: Roles, Functions and Organizations for Federal Personnel Management and Related Issues*, U.S. Government Printing Office, Washington, D.C.

Fish, C. (1904). *The Civil Service and the Patronage*, Longmans, Green, New York.

Gerth, H.H., and Mills, C. W. (1946). *From Max Weber: Essays in Sociology*, Oxford University Press, New York.

Goodnow, F. (1900). *Politics and Administration*, Macmillan, New York.

Guttman, D., and Willner, B. (1976). *The Shadow Government*, Pantheon, New York.

Hanke, S. (1987). *Prospects for Privatization*, Academy of Political Science, New York.

Hanrahan, J. (1977). *Government for Sale: Contracting-Out the New Patronage*, American Federation of State, County and Municipal Employees, Washington, D.C.

Hays, S., and Reeves, T. (1984). *Personnel Management in the Public Sector*, Allyn and Bacon, Boston.

Heclo, H. (1975). OMB and the presidency: the problem of neutral competence, *The Public Interest, 38*: 80–98.

_____(1977). *A Government of Strangers: Executive Politics in Washington*, Brookings Institution, Washington, D.C.

Hoogenboom, A. (1961). *Outlawing the Spoils*, University of Illinois Press, Urbana.

Howard, L. (1978). Civil service reform: a minority and woman's perspective, *Public Administration Review 38*: 305–309.

Kaufman, H. (1965). The growth of the federal personnel system, *The Federal Government Service*, 2nd Ed. (W. Sayre, ed.), Prentice-Hall, Englewood Cliffs, NJ.

_____(1969). Administrative decentralization and political power, *Public Admin. Rev., 29*: 3-15.

Kettl, D. (1991). Privatization: implications for the public workforce, *Public Personnel Management: Current Concerns—Future Challenges* (C. Ban and N. Riccucci, eds.), Longman, New York.

Kranz, H. (1976). *The Participatory Bureaucracy*, Lexington Books, Lexington, MA.

Krislov, S. (1967). *The Negro in Federal Employment*. University of Minnesota Press, Minneapolis.

Lee, R. (1987). *Public Personnel Systems,* 2nd Ed., University Park Press, Baltimore, MD.

Levine, C., and Nigro, L. (1975). The public personnel system: can juridicial administration and manpower management coexist? *Public Admin. Rev., 35*: 98-107.

Loverd, R. (1992). Rewarding and punishing for productive performance, *Public Productivity Handbook* (M. Holzer, ed.), Marcel Dekker, New York.

_____(1981). Taming techniques for public purposes: a personnel management challenge for the eighties. *Public Admin. Rev., 41*: 504-506.

_____(1982). Taming techniques for public purposes: some business views and an overview. *Public Admin. Rev., 42*: 484-487.

Lynn, L. (1981). *Managing the Public's Business: The Job of the Government Executive*, Basic Books, New York.

Macy, J. (1971). *Public Service: The Human Side of Government*, Harper & Row, New York.

McMurty, V. (1976). Merit principles and the federal civil service: 1789 to the present, *History of Civil Service Merit Systems of the United States and Selected Foreign Countries*, U.S. House of Representatives, Committee on Post Office and Civil Service, Washington, D.C.

Mosher, F. (1968). *Democracy and the Public Service*, Oxford University Press, New York.

_____(1974). *Watergate: Implications for Responsible Government*, Basic Books, New York.

Municipal Manpower Commission (1962). *Government Manpower for Tomorrow's Cities*, McGraw-Hill, New York.

Mushkin, S., and Sandifer, F. (1978). *Personnel Management and Productivity in City Government*, Georgetown University Public Services Laboratory, Washington, D.C.

Musolf, L., and Seidman, H. (1980). The blurred boundaries of public administration. *Public Admin. Rev., 40*: 124-130.

National Civil Service League (1970). *A Model Public Personnel Administration Law*, National Civil Service League, Chevy Chase, MD.

Nigro, F., and Nigro, L. (1981). *The New Public Personnel Administration*, 2nd Ed., Peacock, Itasca, IL.

Nollen, S. (1975). *The Effect of Collective Bargaining on Municipal Personnel Systems: A Research Review*, Public Services Laboratory, Georgetown University, Washington, D.C.

Osborne, D. and Gaebler, T. (1992). *Reinventing Government*, Addison-Wesley, Reading, MA.

Parton, J. (1887). *The Life of Andrew Jackson*, Vol. 3, Houghton, Mifflin, Boston.

President's Committee on Administrative Management (1937). *Report with Special Studies*, U.S. Government Printing Office, Washington, D.C.

Rayner, B. L. (1834). *The Life of Thomas Jefferson*, Lilly, Wait, Colman and Holden, Boston.

Rehfuss, J. (1989). *Contracting Out in Government*, Jossey-Bass, San Francisco.

Riccucci, N. (1991). Affirmative action in the twenty-first century: new approaches and developments, *Public Personnel Management: Current Concerns—Future Challenges* (C. Ban and N. Riccucci, eds.), Longman, New York.

Richardson, J. (ed.) (1896). *A Compilation of the Messages and Papers of the Presidents of the United States*, 1889-1897, Vol. 2, U.S. Government Printing Office, Washington, D.C.

Riordan, W. (1963). *Plunkett of Tammany Hall*, Dutton, New York.

Roberts, D. D. (1991). A personnel chameleon blending the political appointee and careerist traditions: exempt managers in state government, *Public Personnel Management: Current Concerns—Future Challenges* (C. Ban and N. Riccucci, eds.), Longman, New York.

Rosen, B. (1975). *The Merit Systems in the United States Civil Service*, U.S. House of Representatives, Committee on Post Office and Civil Service, Washington, D.C.

_____(1978). Merit and the president's plan for changing the civil service system, *Public Admin. Rev., 38*: 301-104.

Rosenbloom, D. (1971). *Federal Service and the Constitution*, Cornell University Press, Ithaca, N.Y.

Rourke, F. (1976). *Bureaucracy, Politics and Public Policy*, 2nd Ed., Little, Brown, Boston.

Savas, E. S. (1987). *Privatization: The Key to Better Government*, Chatham House, Chatham, NJ.

Sayre, W. (1948). The triumph of techniques over purpose, *Public Admin. Rev., 8*: 134–137.

Shafritz, J. (1973). *Position Classification: A Behavioral Analysis of the Public Service*, Praeger, New York.

_____(1974). Political culture: the determinant of merit system variability, *Public Personnel Manage.*

_____(1975). *Public Personnel Management: The Heritage of Civil Service Reform*, Praeger, New York.

Shafritz, J., Riccucci, N., Rosenbloom, D., and Hyde, A. (1992). *Personnel Management in Government*, 4th Ed., Marcel Dekker, New York.

Slack, J. (1988). Affirmative action and merit in public administration, *Am. Rev. Public Admin., 18*: 377–387.

Sorauf, F. (1960). The silent revolution in patronage, *Public Admin. Rev., 20*: 28–34.

Stahl, O. G. (1976). *Public Personnel Administration*, 7th Ed., Harper and Row, New York.

Stanley, D. (1970). What are unions doing to merit systems? *Public Personnel Rev.* 31: 108–113.

Thayer, F. (1978). The President's management "reforms": theory X triumph. *Public Admin. Rev., 38*: 309–314.

Tolchin, M. and Tolchin, S. (1971). *To the Victor: Political Patronage from the Clubhouse to the White House*, Vintage, New York.

U.S. Civil Service Commission (1956). Seventy-Third Annual Report, U.S. Government Printing Office, Washington, D.C.

_____(1958, 1974). *Biography of an Ideal: A History of the Federal Civil Service*, U.S. Government Printing Office, Washington, D.C.

U.S. Commission on Civil Rights. (1969). *For All the People . . . By All the People: A Report on Equal Opportunity in State and Local Government*, U.S. Government Printing Office, Washington, D.C.

U.S. General Accounting Office (1981). *Civil Servants and Contract Employees: Who Should Do What for the Federal Government?* U.S. Government Printing Office, Washington, D.C.

U.S. House of Representatives, Committee on Post Office and Civil Service (1976). Federal political personnel manual (1976), *Final Report on Violations and Abuses of Merit Principles in Federal Employment*, U.S. Government Printing Office, Washington, D.C.

U.S. Office of Personnel Management (1979). *Common Themes in Public Personnel Reform*, Office of Intergovernmental Personnel Programs, Washington, D.C.

Van Riper, P. (1958). *History of the United States Civil Service*, Row, Peterson, Evanston, IL.

Waldo, D. (1948). *The Administrative State*, Ronald, New York.

White, L. (1939). *Introduction to the Study of Public Administration*, Macmillan, New York.

_____(1948). *The Federalists*, Macmillan, New York.

_____(1951). *The Jeffersonians*, Macmillan, New York.

_____(1954). *The Jacksonians*, Macmillan, New York.

_____(1958). *The Republican Era*, Macmillan, New York.

Willoughby, W. (1927). *Principles of Public Administration*, Brookings Institution, Washington, D.C.

Wilson, V.S. (1973). The relationship between scientific management and personnel policy in North American administrative systems, *Public Admin., 51*: 193–205.

Wilson, W. (1887). The study of administration. *Poli. Sci. Quart., 2*: 197–222.

2
Great Thinkers in Personnel Management

ROBERT B. DENHARDT   University of Central Florida, Orlando, Florida

LINDA deLEON   University of Colorado at Denver, Denver, Colorado

From its beginnings, the formal study of public administration has given attention to the problems of managing personnel. For decades the subject matter changed relatively little, although the technical sophistication of the techniques described increased over the years. Recently, however, the field—both scholarship and practice—has been changing in several ways. There has been movement from purely practical to theory-based knowledge, from particular techniques to more strategic thinking, and from an implicit assumption that organizations are hierarchical to recognition of a broader range of alternatives.

Managing the human resources of public agencies involves, first, energizing or motivating people to exert their best efforts. Next, an organization's structures and processes must be appropriate to its mission, which may necessitate organizational change. Third, providing direction for human energies and facilitating prudent change requires skillful leadership. Finally, the requirement that public administration conform to democratic norms requires attention to issues of ethics and equity. In this chapter, we will dip into four important streams of theory—motivation and job design, organizational change, leadership, and ethics—that nourish the roots from which public personnel practice springs. Then we will return to an examination of how the field is changing, where the most progress has occurred, and where more work is most urgently needed.

I. MOTIVATION AND JOB DESIGN

Those interested in both public and private organizations have always paid keen attention to the topic of motivation and the related issue of job design. Theorists have assumed that the key ingredients in determining the outputs or productivity of the employees of an organization were the ability of the individual, the resources of support provided to the individual, and the individual's willingness to contribute. The topic of motivation largely centers on the latter concern, i.e., how people might be stimulated to contribute greater efforts.

The answers theorists have provided to this central question have varied considerably over the years. The early scientific management theorists largely assumed that people found work unpleasant and were therefore primarily motivated by money. Basically, they were bribed to contribute to the organization. The human relations theorists recognized that money is only one of several factors affecting an individual's level of performance and that social as well as economic factors affected the individual's contributions. Largely, these theorists felt that the greater the level of satisfaction individuals received from their organizational involvement, the greater their contributions would be. (There was, however, considerable debate over what constituted satisfaction.) More recent theorists, including many persons we would associate with the human resources movement, have moved past these somewhat simplistic and rationalistic explanations of human behavior to suggest that individuals in organizations are assets or resources not only available to the organization but willing and able to make a positive contribution to it. In this section, we will examine traditional approaches to the question of motivation; in the following two sections we will see how these concerns have, under the banner of human resources management, begun to blend with concerns for organizational change and especially leadership.

As we noted earlier, while early exponents of the scientific management approach saw workers as responding primarily to economic stimuli, the human relations movement of the 1930s and 1940s began to place more emphasis on social factors in motivating employees. The well-known Hawthorne experiments (Roethlisberger and Dickson, 1940), while originally designed to measure the effect of heat, lighting, and other working conditions on worker productivity, led instead to the conclusion that informal or social factors explained much of the workers' behavior. Indeed, the attention given to the workers by the experimenters themselves seemed to have affected the "values and objectives" of the workers (p. 561).

The question of how social factors affect the performance of employees took an interesting turn in public administrationist Herbert Simon's rational model of administration. In *Administrative Behavior* (1957), Simon outlined a theory of organizations on the assumption that organizations are created to achieve their objectives in the most efficient way possible. In the abstract, according to Simon, it was not difficult to design such a system; but when human beings were introduced into that system, things became more complicated. For this reason, Simon was concerned with how members of an organization might more closely approximate the rationality of the organization itself.

Assuming that human beings act with some considerable, though limited, rationality, Simon argued that people would remain in an organization as long as the satisfactions they received from their involvement outweighed the satisfactions they would receive elsewhere. Similarly, employees would contribute to the organization in a way consistent with the wishes of the "controlling group" in proportion to the inducements they received from the organization. The trick for management then became that of manipulating the available inducements—whether money, recognition, pride, or whatever—so that people in the organization would contribute to the fullest.

If one follows the logic of the rational model of administration, individuals will be motivated by the "inducements" or "satisfactions" they receive from the organization. But what incentives will be most important? Early theorists had said money was the key. Later theorists proposed a variety of alternatives. For example, many drew on the work of the psychologist Abraham Maslow (1954), who suggested a hierarchy of needs ranging from very basic needs for survival to those having to do with self-fulfillment or "self-actualization." At the bottom were physical needs related to food, water, heat, light, etc. At the next level were safety or security needs providing freedom from physical, psychological, or financial harm. They came belongingness or social needs, such as the need for love, friendship, and association with others. Ego or status needs, at the next level, included self-esteem as well as recognition by others. Finally, at the top of the hierarchy were such needs as self-fulfillment, self-realization, and what Maslow termed self-actualization.

The logic of Maslow's hierarchy of needs was intuitively compelling—that one must satisfy one's basic needs before satisfying higher needs. For example, the need for friendship and affection is less important if there isn't enough to eat. But perhaps more important was simply Maslow's identification of the range of needs that individuals seek to satisfy. If managers wished to motivate their employees, attention to basic needs—such as money to provide food and shelter—was important, but it was only the beginning. Once basic needs had been satisfied, a far different range of needs came into play. To the extent that management could provide inducements that would meet these higher order needs, perhaps through providing recognition or prestige, then presumably the motivation of the employees would be increased.

Critics questioned Maslow's hierarchy, pointing out that often people seem to express needs at several levels simultaneously. Some even forego basic needs in order to reach for higher level needs. In response, Clayton Alderfer (1972) proposed a somewhat clearer and more direct formulation, suggesting that humans have the need for existence, relatedness, and growth. Existence needs correspond to Maslow's basic needs, those related to material and physiological desires; relatedness needs involve relationships with significant other people; growth needs "impel a person to make a creative or productive effect on himself and the environment" (p. 11). In Alderfer's view, all people possess all of these categories of needs, though individuals differ with respect to which needs are strongest. Moreover, there is no presumption that "lower" order needs must be met before "higher" order needs are activated. Instead, people may move back and forth in their emphasis on the various needs.

While some studies seemed to imply that people were either satisfied or not, that satisfaction and dissatisfaction were part of a continuum, research by Frederick Herzberg and his colleagues (1959) suggested that the matter was more complicated than that. Herzberg asked a group of accountants and engineers to think of the times they were most satisfied with their work and found that issues such as recognition, achievement, growth, and advancement were most important. These were labeled "motivators" or "job content" factors. But when people were asked when they were most dissatisfied, they mentioned what Herzberg called "hygiene" or "job context" factors, items such as low pay and benefits, poor supervision, inadequate working conditions, security, etc.

Herzberg concluded that satisfaction and dissatisfaction were different phenomena. Inadequate hygiene factors might cause one to be dissatisfied, but a better job context did not assure satisfaction. It simply led to less dissatisfaction. Similarly, the absence of motivators did not necessarily lead to dissatisfaction, but rather to the absence of satisfaction. Satisfaction and dissatisfaction appeared to operate independently, two factors affecting the motivation of employees. In order to limit dissatisfaction, management needed to be attentive to hygiene factors; in order to increase satisfaction, it was necessary to attend to motivators. While managers might be able to deal with complaints by changing job context factors, promoting positive job satisfaction requires attention to job content. And, of course, as with previous theories, the assumption was that more satisfied workers were more productive.

A final approach to understanding human needs in the workplace is based on the work of psychologist David McClelland (1961). McClelland posited three primary sets of needs, those for achievement, affiliation, and power. Achievement needs relate to the desire to accomplish a goal or task; affiliation needs refer to the desire to have close relationships with others; and power needs are concerned with the desire for influence and authority. McClelland's early work suggested that the need for achievement was especially important to business people, scientists, and professionals; however, later work suggested the importance of the need for power among managers. In any case, McClelland argues that recognizing the needs one exhibits in the workplace, as well as the needs being expressed by others, aids in improving productivity.

Most of the theories just reviewed share an interest in human needs and an assumption that meeting or satisfying those needs will lead to enhanced motivation. More satisfied workers will be more productive workers. Left open is the question of how changes in employee motivation can be brought about. Other theorists, with widely differing approaches, have explored this topic.

B. F. Skinner (1971) is perhaps the name most clearly identified with the manipulation of rewards and punishments in order to change individual behavior. Skinner's work focused on what he termed "operant behavior," i.e., behavior controlled by the individual. The question that Skinner asked was how behavior can be conditioned so that desired outcomes occur (thus the phrase "operant conditioning"). There are four different approaches that can be used. "Reinforcement" refers to those consequences of a particular action that increase the likelihood of that action being repeated. For example, receiving praise for a job well done may increase the likelihood of similar work being done in the future. "Positive reinforcement" involves a positive reward being given; "negative reinforcement" refers to the removal of a negative consequence following the act. For example, being taken away from an unpleasant assignment following a given action might be called negative reinforcement.

This approach is to be distinguished from punishment, a third form of operant conditioning. Punishment, as is obvious, refers to consequences that reduce the likelihood of the same action being repeated. Receiving a stern lecture may be a form of punishment for many workers. Finally, there is the concept of extinction, which involves removal of a previously valued consequence. A manager, recognizing that new circumstances require new behaviors, may withdraw praise for certain previously valued actions, thus causing a decrease or cessation of those actions. Note that reinforcements of all types can be given frequently or infrequently, on a scheduled or unscheduled basis. Since psychologists such as Skinner worked more with rats than humans, it remains for the manager to figure out what approach will be more effective in any given situation.

Victor Vroom (1964) is credited with the development of a more managerial approach to motivation known as expectancy theory. The basic question raised in expectancy theory is under what conditions a person will put forth maximum effort. Vroom outlines three factors that are likely to affect such a decision: expectancy, instrumentality, and valence. Expectancy is defined as "a momentary belief concerning the likelihood that a particular act will be followed by a particular outcome" (p. 11). A person might believe that if he or she works hard enough a particular project can be completed. Instrumentality refers to the belief that the performance of a specific task will lead to a desired outcome, e.g., that completing the project will lead to a promotion. Finally, valence refers to the value that the individual assigns to the outcomes. For example, how important is the promotion?

Vroom suggests that these factors are related, so that in practice the appeal of a given reward or inducement in a particular situation may vary considerably, depending on whether the person feels the job can be done, whether he or she expects a specific outcome, and whether that outcome is important. A lack of any of these factors of their combination will limit the likelihood that the reward will actually make a difference in the individual's behavior. The lesson for the manager is clear: in order to increase motivation, efforts must be made to maximize expectancies, instrumentalities, and valences. In other words, the manager tries to create a climate in which individuals feel that completing organizational tasks will lead to highly desired rewards.

A final approach to motivation that has been receiving attention in recent years is goal setting theory. Proposed first by Edwin Locke (see Locke and Latham, 1984), this approach suggests that people are motivated to achieve goals that are set for them. People who have goals they are trying to meet are more likely to perform at a higher level than those who do not. Moreover, more specific goals are seen as better motivators than general goals. Also, individuals are likely to reject goals they see as unrealistic or beyond their capabilities. Obviously, acceptance of a particular goal or set of goals is critical, but the question of what makes a person more or less likely to accept a particular goal may lead back to many of the factors already discussed. In any case, the goal-setting approach views individual contributions to the organization in a considerably more positive light than previous examinations of rewards and punishments.

A final aspect of motivation theory that should be noted here relates to questions of organizational design and, more specifically, the design of specific jobs. While job design can be discussed in terms of issues such as the division of labor or the specialization of tasks, issues central to traditional discussions of organizational structure, more recent approaches to job design have centered on how the design of specific jobs might increase the quality of various individual's experience in the organization and in turn motivate them to greater productivity. Discussions of the quality of work life and job enrichment (see Hackman, 1975, 1977) have suggested several characteristics that may be manipulated so as to "enrich" the job. These include skill variety (whether there are a variety of activities involved in the job), task identity (whether the job takes in an entire operation), task significance (whether the job is felt to have an important impact on others), autonomy (whether the individual has substantial freedom), and feedback (whether the individual receives clear and correct feedback). Again, this approach suggests a considerably more positive role for the individual and suggests a great degree of freedom and autonomy in order for the individual to exercise that positive role. As we will see in our later discussion of contemporary approaches to organizational leadership, these aspects of contemporary organizational life are becoming more and more important.

II. ORGANIZATIONAL CHANGE

Those interested in managing public organizations both more effectively and more responsibly inevitably confront the challenges of organizational change. It has been argued that modern society is best described as (1) highly turbulent, subject to sudden and dramatic shifts, (2) highly interdependent, requiring cooperation across many different sectors, and (3) very much in need of creative and integrative solutions to the problems we face. Under such conditions, the capacity of public managers to understand the change process, to cope with the effects of change, and to move change in positive directions has become critically important.

Kurt Lewin (1947) provided the classic interpretation of the change process by suggesting that individuals must go through three phases in order for change to occur. First, the individual must unfreeze the existing situation through loosening the physical, structural, or intellectual boundaries that define the present. Unfreezing may occur when important conflicts arise in the organization, when declining performance indicates a problem, or when there is simply an impression of a need for improvement. Second, the individual must move to a new and hopefully more desirable pattern of behavior or performance. Note that moving too quickly into the change phase before the older situation is completely unfrozen can lead to serious resistance to change. Third, the individual must refreeze the new pattern, i.e., the new pattern of behavior must become the norm for the individual or the organization. Evaluation and feedback are critical in this stage of the change process.

Historically, the approach to change most favored by managers was one in which force or coercion was key to making people do things differently. The ability of the manager to exercise authority and to manipulate rewards and punishments was the key to getting things done differently. Such an approach to change, however, was soon revealed to breed tremendous resistance on the part of subordinates, to build resentment and even rebelliousness in the organization, and at best to achieve only temporary changes.

This matter was explored early on by Douglas McGregor (1960, p. 561), who argued that successful management depends on "the ability to predict and control human behavior" and that developments in the social sciences might provide the basis for a new approach to more effective management. McGregor then contrasted this new approach to management with more traditional forms, based on the assumptions it makes about human behavior. According to McGregor, managers in industry and writers on management have made the following assumptions about the worker:

1. The average human being has an inherent dislike of work and will avoid it if possible.
2. Because of this distaste for work, most people must be coerced, controlled, directed, or threatened with punishment to get them to put forth adequate effort toward the achievement of organizational objectives.
3. The average human being prefers to be directed, wishes to avoid responsibility, has relatively little ambition, and wants security above all (pp. 33–34).

These "theory X" assumptions lead to a management style that relies on rewards and punishments, incentives and threats, coercion and control. But McGregor holds that such an approach to management is ineffective because it neglects the social and ego needs of the individual.

McGregor suggests an alternative set of assumptions about human behavior, assumptions that in turn lead to an alternative approach to management. These new assumptions are:

1. The expenditure of physical and mental effort in work is as natural as play or rest.
2. External control and the threat of punishment are not the only means for bringing about effort toward organizational objectives. People will exercise self-direction and self-control in the service of objectives to which they are committed.
3. Commitment to objectives is a function of the rewards associated with their achievement.
4. The average human being learns, under proper conditions, not only to accept but to seek responsibility.
5. The capacity to exercise a relatively high degree of imagination, ingenuity, and creativity in the solution of organizational problems is widely, not narrowly, distributed in the population.
6. Under conditions of modern industrial life, the intellectual potentialities of the average human being are only partially utilized (McGregor, 1960, pp. 47–48).

Based on these new assumptions, a style of management more attentive to the needs and interests of the individual can be devised.

A similar perspective was developed by Blake and Mouton (1981), an approach they discussed in terms of a "managerial grid." The grid is created along two dimensions: the manager's concern for production and the manager's concern for people. This leads to several prototypical styles of management based on the various combinations of concern for productivity and people. For example, the combination of high concern for production and low concern for people is called the "authority–obedience" approach and assumes that superiors should simply give orders and expect that they will be obeyed, making unnecessary any attention to human factors. Blake and Mouton argue, however, that another combination, high concern for production and high concern for people, is the most "positively associated with success, productivity, and profitability in comparison with any other theory" (p. 128). This approach, "team administration," emphasizes interdependence, trust, and respect between managers and workers in the pursuit of the organization's objectives. Like McGregor's theory Y, team administration seeks an integration of individual and organizational objectives through a style of management that is more attentive to human factors.

One question that arises from the work of both McGregor and Blake and Mouton is whether their recommended approaches are suitable to all situations. Blake and Mouton do argue that team management has been "scientifically" proved to be the "one best way" to manage, thus rejecting contingency theory; however, they leave open the possibility of "versatility" on the part of managers. Similarly, McGregor (1960, p. 56) seeks the implementation of theory Y wherever possible but recognizes that this approach will not always work: "Authority is an appropriate means for control under certain circumstances—particularly where genuine commitment to objectives cannot be achieved." Critics argue that this approach to organizational change, while providing a recognition of the human factors in organizational life, ultimately treats these factors as inducements to be manipulated in the pursuit of managerial control.

A more sophisticated interpretation of the relationship between the individual and the organization is found in the work of Chris Argyris. Argyris gained early prominence with the publication of *Personality and Organization* (1957), a review and synthesis of previous literature on the interchange between the individual personality and the demands of the organization. Later studies examined various aspects of his theory, especially interpersonal competence and organizational effectiveness. More recently, Argyris has focused on management and organization development or, more broadly, what he terms "organizational learning."

In *Interpersonal Competence and Organizational Effectiveness* (1962), Argyris argued that formal organizational structures and traditional management practices tend to be at odds with certain basic tendencies toward individual growth and development. Reviewing studies of personality development, Argyris concluded that persons in our society tend, in their growth from infancy to adulthood, to move from passivity to activity, from dependence to independence, from a limited to a greater range of behaviors, from shallow to deeper interests, from a shorter to a longer time perspective, from a subordinate position to a position of equality or superordination, and from a lack of awareness to greater awareness (p. 50). Movement along each of these dimensions constitutes growth in the direction of a more healthy adult personality.

In contrast, traditional management practices, based on command and control, inhibit the growth of the individual. The specialization of tasks and the concentration of power and information that characterize formal organizations imply certain assumptions about the human personality, assumptions that better describe infants than adults. For example, in traditional organizations, employees have very little control over their work and are expected to be dependent, submissive, and limited in the range of their responses. Under such conditions, in which normal opportunities for growth and development are restricted, employees experience considerable frustration, which manifests itself in many ways, ranging from regression to hostility. Moreover, individuals employing these patterns of adaptation are given support by others similarly situated, and their behavior is thereby reinforced.

From the perspective of management, this behavior is highly dysfunctional and interferes with the smooth operation of the organization. A typical response on the part of management might be to "crack down," to take strong actions to control what is seen as negative behavior. If managers assume (as in theory X) that workers are basically lazy, then the apathy exhibited by a frustrated employee just confirms their view and elicits an authoritarian response. But, of course, such as response simply leads to further frustration on the part of workers, which is in turn met by further crackdowns by management, thereby continuing the cycle. As a strategy for organizational change, this approach is doomed from the beginning.

In alternative efforts at planned change, based on the work of behavioral scientists, Argyris finds an approach with promise of moving organizations and their members toward more positive and congruent relationships. This approach is commonly termed "organizational development," or OD. Most organizational development programs involve an interventionist, typically someone from outside the organization who works with those in the client system either to improve the effectiveness of existing interpersonal relationships or to facilitate the implementation of planned changes in the organization's operations. The interventionist if not called in to recommend new ways of acting but rather to guide the group to discover new approaches based on their own experiences. Argyris's particular formulation of the task of the interventionist is suggestive of the nature of this relationship. Argyris (1970, pp. 12–13) recommends that the primary tasks of the interventionist are three: "(1) to help generate valid and useful information; (2) to create conditions in which clients can make informed and free choices; and (3) to help clients develop an internal commitment to their choice." The role of the interventionist is not to impose his or her own values and approaches, but to assist the client group in personal and organizational learning.

The question of organizational learning then becomes central to understanding organizational change. Writing with Donald Schön, Argyris (1978) argues that individuals and organizations hold "espoused theories" (those theories of action we profess to follow in our behavior) and "theories in use" (those we actually do follow). For effective learning to occur—that is, for learning to affect action—our espoused theories and our theories in use should be compatible and able to change when problems in the environment require them to do so. When the members of an organization discover problems that affect the ability of the organization to carry out its theories in use, they may engage in what Argyris and Schön call "single-loop learning" (p. 24). That is, they adjust their theories to meet new conditions and they adapt their behaviors to those new theories. Beyond this, individuals and organizations may also engage in "deutero learning," which is essentially learning about learning. Here people examine previous instances of learning or failing to learn. "They discover what they did that facilitated or inhibited learning, they invent new strategies for learning, they produce these strategies, and they evaluate and generalize what they have produced" (p. 27). The conclusion seems to be that organizations and individuals facing the complexities and turbulence associated with modern life must constantly inquire into their own capacities to learn effectively.

Another proponent of organizational development as a strategy for organizational change, one more clearly situated in the field of public administration, is Robert T. Golembiewski. While Golembiewski has written extensively on this subject, his approach is perhaps stated most clearly in his book *Renewing Organizations*, published in 1972 and revised and extended in 1979 under the title *Approaches to Planned Change*. In these works, Golembiewski relies on a laboratory approach to organizational change, one particularly sensitive to the experiences of individuals in small groups. His approach deviates little, if at all, from mainstream OD practice, using standard techniques such as organization development, survey feedback, team building, and career development. However, Golembiewski seems far more oriented toward the value implications of his work than other writers.

Golembiewski (1972, pp. 60–66) sees five "metavalues" guiding the laboratory approach to personal and organizational change: (1) acceptance of inquiry based on mutual accessibility and open communication; (2) expanded consciousness and recognition of choice, especially the willingness to experiment with new behaviors and choose those that seem most effective; (3) a collaborative concept of authority, emphasizing cooperation and willingness to examine conflicts openly and with an eye toward their resolution; (4) mutual helping relationships with a sense of community and responsibility for others; and (5) authenticity in interpersonal relationships. These values not only define the structure of the laboratory situation (e.g., the T group) but also provide a model for the organization as a whole. These are the values followed by the interventionist, but also the values that the interventionist seeks to establish in the organization.

Like others we have seen, Golembiewski argues that the traditional pyramidal values are indeed often dysfunctional and in need of replacement. His alternative is a collaborative-consensual system of management emphasizing openness, confrontation, feedback, and shared responsibility. But following McGregor and others, he considers this alternative not a direct substitute for bureaucracy but rather a convenient alternative to be used where possible. In certain kinds of organizations, such as the Strategic Air Command, mechanical or functional systems may be required. "Inducing aspirations about consensus in such organizations, consequently, may be foolhardy. Or inducing such aspirations may even be cruel, if compelling considerations require a structure within which only centralized conventions for decision making are realistic (1972, p. 571).

III. RECENT STUDIES OF LEADERSHIP BEHAVIOR

Earlier studies of motivation and management style as determinants of organizational change have in recent years given way to a far greater emphasis on leadership. Unfortunately, one of the difficulties in understanding leadership is that the term is used in so many different ways. Early efforts to describe leadership focused on trying to identify the leadership traits and personal characteristics of well-known leaders. However, this effort proved difficult because history provides examples of leaders who exhibited vastly different personal qualities and yet achieved major accomplishments. Some were tall and some were short; some were magnificent speakers, others were almost shy. Similarly, leaders appear to have led by a variety of means. Some are thought to have been able to lead by virtue of their personal power or "charisma." Others seem to have led because of the moral vision they were able to elicit from their followers.

One contemporary version of the effort to identify traits or personal characteristics suited to leadership, Fred E. Fiedler's cognitive resource theory (1987), appears to have encountered similar difficulties. Intuitively, it would seem that the most effective group leaders should be the ones who are the most intelligent, the most competent, and the most experienced in the nature of the work being done. And, indeed, Fiedler concludes that "more intelligent leaders develop more plans, decisions and action strategies than do less intelligent leaders; that is, plans and decisions more likely to result in effective performance" (Fiedler and Garcia, 1987, p. 201). Other studies, however, have shown "the rather counterintuitive finding that measures of leader intelligence show only a low positive correlation with the performance of their groups or organizations" (p. 201).

Other work explores the character of the individual personality. For example, Abraham Zaleznik (1977) believes that "managers and leaders differ fundamentally in their world views. The dimensions for assessing these differences include managers' and leaders' orientation toward their goals, their work, their human relations, and their selves" (p. 70). He speculates that leaders may have a different psychological grounding than managers: "Managers and leaders have different attitudes toward their goals, careers, relations with others, and themselves . . . leaders are of a psychologically different type than managers" (p. 67). The consequences of these differences for groups are that managers and leaders may lead groups to produce entirely different outcomes. Managers help groups decide how to do something whereas leaders help groups decide what to do, if indeed they need to do anything at all. As Warren Bennis and Burt Nanus (1984) comment, "Managers do things right. Leaders do the right thing" (p. 21).

More compelling is the work of James MacGregor Burns (1978), who recognizes the interactive nature of leadership by referring to its transactional, transformational, and moral aspects (pp. 448–454). In Burns's view, the terms *transactional* and *transformational* describe two basic leadership types. The transactional leader essentially uses a bargaining process to maintain control; politicians who exchange votes for jobs illustrate this kind of "transaction." Transformational leadership implies the attempt to reach the basic needs and aspirations of its followers, moral leadership adds the dimension of social action and change.

Burns argues that the legacy of the leadership process is a changed society, of which "the most lasting tangible act of leadership is the creation of an institution—a nation, a social movement, a political party, a bureaucracy—that continues to exert moral leadership and foster needed change long after creative leaders are gone" (p. 454). He believes this ongoing change is perpetuated by morally purposeful individuals who elevate both followers and themselves in the process. Burns recognizes that the creation of an institution enhances the opportunity for continued social change, but he understands that it does not necessarily guarantee such change. He suggests that "the most lasting and pervasive leadership of all is intangible and noninstitutional. It is the leadership of influence fostered by ideas embodied in social or religious or artistic movements, in books, in great seminal documents, in the memory of lives greatly lived" (p. 455). It is the perpetuation of those great ideas, "in the hope of enabling more lives to be greatly lived" at all levels of society, that leads us to focus on the relationship between leadership and development.

More recently, a variety of authors have written about leadership; indeed, leadership studies almost constitute a contemporary "fad" in the management literature. Rather than summarize these works in detail, we will review here only a few representative works. Bennis and Nanus discuss leadership in the context of a changing environment, one in which ambiguity will increasingly be a hallmark of decision making and the involvement (rather than the control) of many individuals in group decisions will be necessary. Bennis (1983) writes: "Leadership . . . will become an increasingly intricate process of multilateral brokerage, including consistencies both within and without the organization. More and more decisions will be public decisions, that is, the people that they affect will insist on being heard" (p. 16). As for Burns, power is central to Bennis and Nanus' (1984) discussion. Power is the key to leadership, they suggest, but power must be used wisely: "Power is the basic energy needed to initiate and sustain action or, to put it another way, the *capacity to translate intentions into reality and sustain it.* Leadership is the wise use of this power" (p. 17).

Kouzes and Posner (1987) interviewed a number of managers about their experiences in leadership positions and then developed an inventory to confirm the lessons they heard expressed by the leaders. As leaders talked about their "personal best" leadership experiences, some five approaches were developed. These in turn led to the postulation of 10 "behavioral commitments" that potential leaders might follow: search for opportunities, experiment and take risks, envision the future, enlist others, foster collaboration, strengthen others, set the example, plan small wins, recognize individual contributions, and celebrate accomplishments (p. 14). Correspondingly, when people were asked about the traits they valued most in leaders, they replied that they wanted leaders who were honest, competent, forward-looking, and inspiring. In a word, they wanted leaders who had credibility (p. 21).

Similarly, John Kotter (1980) developed a lengthy research program to identify how senior and middle-level executives might further their leadership skills. Interestingly, some of the findings seem to take the study of leadership full circle, back to the trait approach of many years ago. Kotter found, for example, that among the requirements for effective leadership in senior management jobs in complex business settings were the following: broad knowledge of the industry, broad knowledge of the company, a broad set of relationships in the firm and the industry, an excellent reputation and track record, a keen mind, strong interpersonal skills, high integrity, a high energy level, and a strong drive to lead (p. 30).

While power has been central to nearly all concepts of leadership in the past, with the advent of notions of empowerment and shared leadership, there is now attention being given to new ideas about leadership, ideas more clearly associated with group development. Harlan Cleveland (1985), for example, argues that the advent of plentiful and cheap information is changing the very nature of control in hierarchical organizations—indeed, it is undermining hierarchy throughout society. Because information cannot easily be bottled up, especially in an age of microcomputers and telecommunications, it is difficult, if not impossible, to prevent its dissemination. And because those who understand the value of information are becoming more and more prevalent in our information-rich society, the structure of decision-making groups must, by necessity, change. With more universal access to an understanding of information, leadership becomes even less a function of the power associated with controlling a scarce resource. Instead, the leader will be the one who is able to elicit purposeful group action based on shared information, i.e., the one who asserts public leadership. The possibility for control is diminished, but the opportunity for leadership, as we define it, is enhanced.

More recently, Robert Denhardt (1993) defined leadership as "the character of the relationship between an individual and a group or organization that stimulates or releases some latent energy within the group so that those involved more clearly understand their own needs, desires, interests, and potentialities and begin to work toward their fulfillment" (p. xx). Leadership, in this view, is seen as less related to power than to issues of group development. Leadership refers to the actions of an individual but always in relation to the group or organization.

Such an approach can be contrasted with the view of leadership as power, a view that seems increasingly to be called into question, as leaders attempting to bring about change enforce systems of power and control. A leader pursuing his or her own interests—perhaps even exercising rigid control—may be successful for a time, for even under these circumstances the latent energy of the group or organization may be tapped and leadership may occur. If the leader's interests happen to coincide with those of the group, or if members happen to recognize an interest of their own reflected in the actions of the leader, change may come about. Typically, however, as soon as the leader's interests or purposes begin to diverge from those of the group, the leader begins to close communications and to resort to the exercise of power rather than leadership. Under such circumstances, leadership soon dissolves into control, as so often happens in large organizations. Traditional modes of hierarchical organization are paradigmatic examples of the dissolution of leadership into institutionalized mechanisms for control.

IV. ETHICS AND EQUITY IN PERSONNEL MANAGEMENT

The most fundamental normative question for public administrators surely is the one that asks on what basis do they justify their authority to make policy decisions. The Constitution of the United States created legislative, executive, and judicial branches of government, but it says almost nothing about administration. Perhaps because the political theory known to the founders did not include analysis of a "fourth branch" (i.e., administrative structures), they did not incorporate their vision of the public service into the constituting document, although their other writing contained much discussion of administration (Rohr, 1978; Nigro and Richardson, 1992). Their omission left a vacuum that has since been filled by extended debate over the basis of legitimacy for the public service.

In his seminal book, *Democracy and the Public Service*, Frederick Mosher (1968) explores this problem by dividing the history of the American civil service into several periods. "Government by gentlemen," in which public servants were drawn principally from the economic and social elite of the country, prevailed at the beginning of the republic. In those early days, when only the well-to-do could afford higher education, high social status was a surrogate for competence or merit. The second era, which Mosher styled "government by the common man," saw the spoils system take root and eventually flourish. Although later reformers painted the effects of patronage in somber colors, the spoils system did have some beneficial effects. It served the needs of the poor and ethnic minorities whose votes were sought (and often bought) by the political machines, and it brought a much wider variety of people into the public service, making it more representative of the population. On this basis, its proponents argued that it was more democratic than its predecessor (government by social elites) or its successor (meritocracy).

In Mosher's third era, "government by the good," the progressive or reform movement had among its goals the universal implementation of merit systems of employment, in which public employees would be selected on the basis of competitive examinations. The purpose of these examinations was not so much to ensure that employees were competent at particular jobs, however, as to ascertain their general intelligence and basic education. An even more important purpose was that a merit system would break the hold of political parties over the government service. Thus, initially, the idea of merit signified political neutrality even more than it meant ability.

The next era began in 1906, when scientific management ushered in "government by the efficient." During this period, merit acquired the further meaning of expertise or "scientific" knowledge. In 1937, the report of the Brownlow Commission marked a fifth era, "government by administrators," in which management skill—as opposed to narrower technical competence—was elevated in importance. These three eras, however, all pursued a merit ideal. So, in this historical sequence, the normative bases alternate: from merit (as indicated by social class) to representation (of the "common man"), and again to merit (reform, scientific management, and administration).

Another influential framework for analyzing the value basis of public administration was advanced by Herbert Kaufman (1956, 1969). In his view, the doctrines of public administration have been based successively on representativeness, neutral competence, and executive leadership. Kaufman's "representativeness" was the basic value during the period Mosher called "government by the common man." "Neutral competence" conveys much the same idea as "merit," combining the two aspects—neutrality and ability—that Mosher had identified separately. And Kaufman's "executive leadership" echoes Mosher's description of government by administrators, when the Brownlow committee's preference for centralizing power in the president won favor.

Merit enjoyed a long heyday, but in the 1960s and 1970s there was a renewal of interest in promoting the representativeness of the civil service, championed by the members of a theoretical movement known as the new public administration. Theorists in this group believed that the legitimacy of the public service derives from its capacity to promote social equity, i.e., social justice and equality. Prominent among those interested in the concept of social equity is George Frederickson. In the volume that marked the emergence of the new public administration as a self-conscious theoretical initiative (Frederickson, 1971), he proposed social equity as the "third pillar" (with economy and efficiency) of public administration. Equity or fairness, according to Frederickson (1990), requires that each person be guaranteed equal basic liberties and that "inequalities be managed so that they are of greatest benefit to the least advantaged (p. 230). In his "compound theory of social equity" (1990), he identified three types of equality: simple equality, in which every individual is equal to every other; segmented equality, in which social groups may be treated differently but individuals within each group are treated the same; and block equality, in which groups are treated the same, though individuals within them may be unequal to each other.

Theorists of the new public administration gave particular attention to two different means for achieving social equity. The first of these was the achievement of a representative bureaucracy, a term that had first been used by J. Donald Kingsley (1944) in a study of the British civil service. Kingsley's analysis showed that the dominance of social, political, and economic elites in British bureaucracy had resulted in policies and programs that failed to meet the needs of all social classes. As applied to the American public service, however, representative bureaucracy usually connotes greater inclusion of ethnic minorities and women rather than the lower socioeconomic classes. A strong case for representative bureaucracy was argued by Samuel Krislov and David Rosenbloom (1981). They believe that representativeness in the bureaucracy would effectively increase public control over policy, especially if combined with citizen participation, institutionalized accountability, and other appropriate mechanisms. A representative bureaucracy will also increase efficiency, since it will be attuned to the political culture in which it operates. And inclusion in the government will not only result in policies that serve all social groups. Those groups will also—in consequence—develop greater loyalty to the regime and to the programs they have had a hand in shaping.

The new public administration also advocated a second means by which social equity could be achieved, one that represented a radical departure from previous views of the legitimate role of administration in a democracy, even in a representative bureaucracy. Mosher (1968) had distinguished two forms that representative bureaucracy might take. In the passive form, the composition of the civil service merely echoes the ethnic and gender mix of the population from which it is drawn. In the active form, administrators work to advance the ideas of the groups from which they come. By contrast, Michael Harmon (one of the new public administration theorists) proposed that administrators take a "more affirmative and activist" stance (p. 174). Rather than merely reacting (being politically responsive) to the demands of others, they should pursue self-actualization through "greater involvement in the advocacy and support of policy" (p. 180). This position, often called "proactive" administration, portrays administrators as advocates for disadvantaged groups, even when they themselves are not members of those groups.

Harmon explicitly rejects the ethic of neutrality: "Administrators are human beings rather than machines and . . . ethical neutrality is an abstraction incapable of providing a viable basis for administrative responsibility" (p. 182). In his view, self-actualizing administrators would not be above the law. But other theorists—Mosher (1968), for example—worried about the scope of power in the hands of professionals in government. Most public administrators work in bureaucratic organizations, and bureaucracies are supposed to be the type of structure most readily amenable to control. But professional work requires a high level of expert knowledge and discretion over the means by which work is accomplished, which gives the worker an independent power base. In addition, professional workers who operate within organizations have multiple allegiances—to their clients and to their professional colleagues as well as to the organization. Both these factors make professional workers harder to manage than other employees (Raelin, 1986; Benveniste, 1987). In a dispute with management, professionals can justify resistance on the basis of their superior knowledge, and they can call on client groups and their professional association as allies. For these reasons, it becomes particularly important to ensure that professionals in public organizations will act in the public interest, ethically and responsibly.

John Rohr addresses this problem in his book, *Ethics for Bureaucrats* (1978). Rohr starts from the premise that administration needs to establish a basis for legitimacy. He reviews the struggle between the "spoils" and "merit" systems, which ended with the victory of the politics/administration dichotomy described by Woodrow Wilson (1887) and its ethic of neutral competence. Consonant with the ethos of science, professional public servants were to be technically expert but ideologically neutral. After Wilson, however, the politics/administration dichotomy was increasingly discredited as it became apparent that legislators could never write laws sufficiently explicit as to exclude all room for administrative discretion. If discretion is a fact of administrative life, then it becomes essential that administrators make their decisions in accord with the values of the electorate, just as elected officials serve the will of the people. Administrators should also be responsible and accountable, i.e., there should be a time and place where they can be called on to answer for their decisions.

Rohr suggests that in order to achieve ethical administration, bureaucrats must be taught moral reasoning, or how to think carefully and systematically about ethical questions. Using these reasoning skills, they must examine social values in an effort to learn what values their administrative decisions should serve. Specifically, the values they serve are grounded in the Constitution, since that is the basic document on which our political system is built, the statement of the social compact that first formed our society. These values (such as freedom, equality, and property, each of which is the focus of a single chapter in Rohr's book) change gradually over time, however, as society changes, which means that administrators must somehow keep up to date with these shifts. Court decisions, according to Rohr, are a reasonably good reflection of society's values, so an ethical administrator will need to keep abreast of important ones that affect his or her work.

When all is said and done, Rohr's vision of ethical administration still has the bureaucrat hewing carefully to the line set down by the values of the society in which he or she lives. But what about the cases where society's values are not entirely clear, where they are ambiguous or in conflict with each other? Terry Cooper addresses this important question in his book, *The Responsible Administrator*, first published in 1981. Like Rohr, Cooper begins by acknowledging that public professionals have extensive discretionary power, which must be used responsibly. He cites the well-known "debate" between Carl Friedrich (1940) and Herbert Finer (1941), in which Finer emphasized the importance of external controls on discretion while Friedrich argued that the "inner check" of an administrator's personal conscience was a firmer defense against maladministration. In Cooper's assessment, Friedrich has "won" the debate, at least in the contemporary moment, among ethicists in the field of administration.

The importance of Cooper's work lies in its analysis of the competing responsibilities that administrators must try to integrate in their practice. These include responsibility *to* superiors as well as responsibility *for* subordinates, in a complex calculus that must also acknowledge the values of the organization and of the administrator's profession, and the personal interests of the administrator, as well as the public interest. Cooper gives more attention to the *process* of reasoning that administrators should use than to its *substance*. Although he seems to agree with Rohr that the Constitution is an appropriate basis for administrative ethics, his other points of reference include codes of ethics and ethics legislation.

Although Cooper believes that subjective responsibility—the "inner check" of the administrator's carefully considered personal values—is the best guarantor of ethical conduct, he also suggests that other sources of control over administrative conduct should include the organization's structure and culture, as well as public oversight. In her book, *The Ethics of Public Service* (1988), Kathryn Denhardt goes beyond this essentially negative view of the organization as a constraint. She provides a thorough, explicit analysis of ways in which organizations can either support or inhibit ethical behavior by the individuals who work in them. Ethical organizations protect ethical individuals and encourage ethical discourse. They can be the nourishing matrix for the growth of ethical organizational cultures—not just a system of restraints against unethical behavior by individuals—if they pay careful attention to the effects of their structures and processes.

Like Rohr and Cooper, Denhardt gives due consideration to the necessity for training administrators in ethical reasoning and in a solid knowledge of the Constitution. She is willing to advance further, however, by suggesting that it is possible to identify specific values that should be at the center of an administrative ethic: honor, benevolence, and justice (K. Denhardt, 1991).

In all the preceding discussion of administrative values, it is clear that they can appear in a variety of combinations. Under "executive leadership," administration would be the responsive tool of an elected executive. Such a bureaucratic apparatus would be competent (the merit ideal) but *not* neutral. The spoils system was representative and responsive, but *not* competent. The new public administration proposed a representative bureaucracy that would be proactive, and *not* always responsive. Thus, there appear to be two separate factors underlying the five values identified thus far. One is a continuum with political responsiveness at one end and independent action (proactiveness) at the other, with political neutrality at the midpoint. The other dimension counterposes competence and representativeness. Upon closer examination, this latter turns out to be a familiar idea, the classic polarity of equity vs. efficiency. Merit systems, though desirable, are not an end in themselves; they are a means to select competent civil servants, which results in *efficient* administration. Similarly, representativeness is not an end in itself but a way to make administration serve all social groups more *equitably* (Nalbandian, 1989).

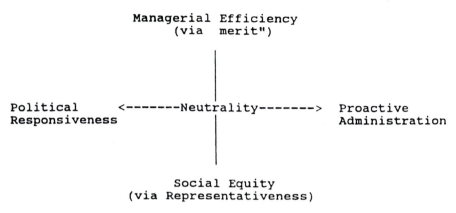

Figure 1 Two dimensions of the normative basis of public service.

The values discussed thus far and portrayed in Figure 1 are ones that have figured prominently in the scholarly debate over the normative basis for the public service. In addition, personnel management may pursue other values, such as the protection of individual employee rights. This value, while important, is not a basis for legitimacy; in other words, the *mission* of the administration is to produce efficiency or equity in the provision of public services, while protection of employee rights is a secondary aim. In fact, the attention given to employee rights is largely a recent phenomenon (Ingraham and Rosenbloom, 1990). And some authors (Klingner and Nalbandian, 1985) argue that the role of a personnel department must be to serve agency management, not employees; unions and the courts have the responsibility to protect employee interests (p. 58). Nalbandian (1989), however, cites supreme court decisions that he believes represent an emerging reemphasis on efficiency values and a reduction of the importance give to both social equity concerns and individual employee rights.

V. AN ASSESSMENT

The four streams of theory reviewed above have nourished the development of contemporary public personnel management. From them flow our understanding of how people relate to organizations and to other persons in the organization. But returning to the three vectors suggested at the beginning of this essay, how is theory currently being used?

A. From Practice to Theory

In the past decade or so, the field of public personnel management has placed greater importance on linking practice to a basis in theories of organization behavior. For many years, both scholarship and practice had for the most part been limited to the procedural details of recruitment, selection and testing, job analysis and evaluation, position classification, performance appraisal, etc. Reviewing 10 years (1980–1990) of research in two of the field's leading journals, Houston and Delevan (1991) found that public personnel management's focus had expanded to include topics such as motivation, decision making, leadership, and communication (cf. Nigro, 1990). Both the journals studied, *Public Personnel Management (PPM)* and the *Review of Public Personnel Administration (ROPPA)*, exemplified this trend over all the years studied.

The development of a more theoretical approach has primarily taken the form of positive research, which "strives to build theories that explain and predict natural and social events" (White, 1986). Houston and Delevan found that 67% of the articles published in *ROPPA* from 1980 to 1990 involve correlational studies (those that test relationships among variables) and another 5% are policy evaluation research; the remainder were largely conceptual in nature. While public personnel as a subfield can take modest pride in the fact that *ROPPA* published more theory-building work than journals in other specialized fields of public administration, most of this research was not at a very high level of methodological sophistication: only 41% went beyond bivariate analysis, and only 66% reported the results of statistical hypothesis testing. Houston and Delevan note that since public personnel research does not use statistics to control for plausible rival hypothesis (e.g., through hypothesis testing, experimental designs, or multivariate analysis), its causal conclusions must be regarded as weak. Still, the fact that public personnel research does seek to build on previous theoretical work represents the academic maturing of the subfield.

Despite the emphasis on empirical research, observers of the field of personnel management maintain that its linkages to theories in organization behavior and organization theory are still minimal (Nigro, 1990; K. Denhardt, 1991). Most currently popular textbooks in the field pay much less attention to underlying theory than to practical applications. Reviewing the recently published *Handbook of Public Administration* (Perry, 1989), R. Denhardt (1991) notes that even this 700-page compendium of state-of-the-art thinking devotes only 14 pages to topics such as motivation, decision making, and group dynamics. There is no mention of interpersonal skills, negotiation, stress management, or time management.

Even were positive research in public personnel management to be statistically sophisticated and clearly linked to theories of organizational behavior, it would not be enough to constitute "great thinking." Other sorts of theory also are needed to round out the portfolio of the human resources management (HRM) subfield (and, for that matter, the field of public administration as well, but that is another matter). Alternative modes of theorizing include the "interpretive," which attempts to discover the meanings that actors in social situations give to their own words and deeds, and "critical" theory, which seeks to uncover the unconscious roots of action or belief in order to change behavior in a beneficial direction (White, 1986). Houston and Delevan (1991) note that there is very little research self-consciously using these alternative methods, yet a case can be made that without critical theory, evaluative research is crippled, and without an understanding of the worlds of actors in public administration, science becomes alienated from practice and thus useless to it.

B. From Technique to Strategy

In 1990, Lloyd Nigro argued that public personnel management had shifted its emphasis from "personnel *for* managers" to "personnel *by* managers." The first approach,

> originally based in the policing norms of the first civil service reform movement but now anchored in the personnel system technologies that emerged from that era, sees personnel administration as something done for those in the line. The other, stressing performance and responsiveness, assigns a leading role to public managers" (p. 187).

The problem is that the transition has proceeded unevenly. Everyone agrees that the skillful and purposive deployment of human resources should be a focus of managers from the supervisory to the executive levels. But, says Nigro, the specific techniques for realizing these objectives, which have been the bread and butter of training in personnel management, are too detailed and technical to be mastered by generalist managers. Using tennis as a metaphor, Nigro views the human resource management ball as having been served into the court of the line administrator, who must then return it to the personnel specialist, who understands "the implementing technologies" (p. 195).

His solution to the problem is styled "strategic simplification," in which personnel specialists handle the nuts-and-bolts issues, but they send up the hierarchy (or back to the line manager) problems of coordination among units that cannot be resolved at lower levels. Also, they forward up or out the problems regarding critical and strategic choices, but in a form that has been simplified, clarified, and sharpened for the benefit of the higher level decision makers.

A related perspective is offered by Donald Klingner (1992), who points out that a generation ago public personnel management was merely "a collection of administrative technologies devoid of a conceptual focus or public policy implications. . . . Now, of course, academicians have come to recognize what public personnel managers have known all along. Public personnel management . . . is the policy process by which public jobs are allocated" (p. 211).

In the realm of practice, the emphasis on strategic functions was evidenced by the name change of the major professional organization of personnel managers in the private sector. Formerly called the "American Society for Personnel Management (or, to public administrators, "the other ASPA"), in 1989 it was renamed the Society for Human Resource Management. In part, the name change was a tactical move by personnelists. Long relegated to second-class citizenship as "staff," human resource managers aspired to a seat on the executive committees of their organizations. Typically, however, line management is the path to the top levels, although more recently expertise in financial management has provided an alternative route. In attempting to assert the strategic importance of their function, human resource professionals were laying claim to executive status.

Compared to its success in moving from practical procedural details to cumulative theory building, the field has been far less successful in developing its theories to the degree that strategic action is well supported. Strategic choices among alternative personnel systems require a solid understanding of the contingencies and consequences of various personnel policies, and knowledge linking conditions, practices, and consequences requires highly developed, well-tested theory. Absent knowledge of how personnel practices affect mission accomplishment, efficiency, effectiveness, diversity, personal satisfaction, and human growth and development, public managers cannot make the farsighted choices that will produce the sorts of organizations and people that our ideals envision.

There are a few examples of the sort of work that needs to be done, however. Klingner and Nalbandian's text (1985) is organized around four basic values and five core functions of personnel management. The values are managerial efficiency, political responsiveness, social equity, and individual rights; the core functions are allocation, recruitment, appraisal, training, and system creation. Each section of the book focuses on one of the functions, and each chapter contains ample discussion of how the four values are related to the function being treated. For example, recruitment and selection can serve managerial efficiency ("merit"), political responsiveness ("spoils"), or social equity (affirmative action to achieve representative bureaucracy). And any of these values must be balanced against due concern for the rights of individuals (seniority, equal opportunity). However, the utility of Klingner and Nalbandian's book is limited by the fact that it is structured around traditional personnel topics rather than around the values themselves. A manager wanting to know how to design a personnel system that maximizes, say, social equity, would have to comb through each chapter collecting ideas.

Other current work that attempts to sort out the consequences for personnel management of varying organizational structures includes an article by David Carnavale (1992) contrasting the traditional model of an organization with what he terms the learning support model. The traditional model is "intensely bureaucratic," while the learning support model "responds to the challenges of postindustrial workers by developing their problem-solving capacities" (p. 19). Carnavale explores the implications of this contrast for a variety of personnel practices, including job design, compensation, training and development, and productivity improvement (quality management). Ingraham and Ban (1986) describe four models of public management—neutral competence, responsive competence, managerial competence, and a public service model—and discuss their seffects on the relationships of political and career executives. But these initiatives are only a start on the much greater project of developing a thorough understanding of how personnel practice grows from values and theories, and how it affects structure and procedures.

C. From Hierarchy to Variety

On the final dimension of change, from an exclusive focus on hierarchical organizations to a serious consideration of alternative models, we find that the study of personnel management has progressed by mere inches. For most of its history, the field either has been unconcerned with the models of organization that underlie its precepts and practices or has implicitly assumed that the personnel function was exercised in, and in the service of, a hierarchically organized bureaucracy. Only recently has attention been paid to the ways in which administration of the personnel function takes place in a variety of organizational forms. This new development is certainly encouraged by the emphasis on strategic management because it increases managers' awareness of the pervasive impact of structures, and the values that underlie them, on personnel practices.

Klingner (1992), reviewing a collection of essays edited by Ban and Riccucci (1991), hopes that the next generation of texts in public personnel management will "more clearly define the field . . . within a comparative and contextual focus comprising competing alternatives systems and values" (p. 211). To understand how far we still must go to achieve this goal, consider the topics taken up in all of the major texts: recruitment, selection, job analysis and evaluation, classification and compensation, performance appraisal, discipline, etc. Then consider the topics that are *omitted* from this list. There is much attention to coordination and conflict management, but much less to building group cohesion and maturity. There is treatment of team building, but though the teams being constructed sometimes include supervisors or managers, they do not commonly include members of the organization's top leadership. The thrust of team building is usually not toward increasing egalitarianism or genuinely empowering all organization participants: in all the fuss over "empowerment," when managers use the word, it too often means something very like old-fashioned "delegation!"

Finally, motivating employees and channeling their energy toward the organization's purposes seems to be very important, but stimulating creativity and engendering ethical behavior are hardly mentioned at all. In most texts, job design and redesign—which would help develop work that fosters more creativity—rates less attention than the details of job analysis, description, and classification. Discussions of compensation focus almost entirely on monetary rewards; treatment of nonmonetary compensation is confined to the trivialities of suggestion boxes. All this suggests that the fundamental model of organization that underlies most contemporary texts (and articles in scholarly journals) is more bureaucratic than otherwise.

It may be that much of what is left out of human resource management texts are functions the authors consider to be prerogatives of organization leadership. This has two interesting implications. First, it suggests that despite Nigro's view that a shift has taken place from personnel *for* managers to personnel *by* them, textbook writers still consider themselves to be training personnelists (staff functionnaries), not public managers (line authorities). Second, if shaping the organization is a function reserved for top management or line management, then there is little room for genuine employee empowerment, buzz words to the contrary notwithstanding. Similarly, critical functions such as formulating the agency's mission and encouraging discourse concerning ethics are not seen as something that *every* employee should be involved in doing.

Klingner and Nalbandian address directly the question of who is served by the personnel management function: the organization's formal authorities, or the employees (or perhaps both). They give the nod to management, on the ground that unions and statutory law are the employees' protectors. Such a stance is clearly far more consonant with a view of organizations as rational hierarchies than with the vision of organizations that genuinely aspire to nurture the maturity, independence, and creativity of each employee. An interesting contrasting view is that of Shafritz et al. (1992), who suggest that the time is near when public managers will have to consider their work force a given—because shortages of skilled labor will restrict hiring and due process restrictions will restrict firing—and their task as simply to make the best of what they have (p. 90). Such an eventuality can be met, of course, with either grim determination or radiant welcome.

The problems that still bedevil the public work force represent formidable challenges. How can we find the best talent, keep morale high, build commitment to the public good, and maintain a sterling standard of conduct? Beyond that, how can we inspire creativity, build cohesion, win public respect, and still provide efficient, effective, responsible service? As a field of scholarship and of practice, our challenge is threefold. We need to develop critical theory showing how our personnel practices affect both the public welfare and the well-being of public employees. Next, we need to continue to expand our base of empirical data and positive theory concerning causes and effects. Finally, we need to translate both critical and positive knowledge into effective practice that serves the fundamental personnel function, supporting the efforts of public employees to achieve public purposes. These challenges constitute a daunting agenda, but one with so much promise!

REFERENCES

Alderfer, C. P. (1972). *Existence, Relatedness, and Growth*, Free Press, New York.

Argyris, C. (1975). *Personality and Organization*, Harper & Row, New York.

Argyris, C. (1962). *Interpersonal Competence and Organizational Effectiveness*, Brooks-Cole, Pacific Grove, CA.

Argyris, C. (1970). *Intervention Theory and Method: A Behavioral Science View*, Addison-Wesley, Reading, MA.

Argyris, C., and Schön, D. (1978). *Organizational Learning: A Theory of Action Perspective*, Addison-Wesley, Reading, MA.

Ban, C., and Riccucci, N. M. (1991). *Public Personnel Management: Current Concerns: Future Challenges*, Longman, New York.

Bennis, W. (1983). The artform of leadership, *The Executive Mind* (Suresh Srivastva, ed.), Jossey-Bass, San Francisco, pp. 15–24.

Bennis, W., and Nanus, B. (1985). *Leaders*, Harper and Row, New York.

Benveniste, G. (1987). *Professionalizing the Organization: Reducing Bureaucracy to Enhance Effectiveness*, Jossey-Bass, San Francisco.

Blake, R., and Mouton, J. (1981). *The Academic Administrator Grid*, Jossey-Bass, San Francisco.

Burns, J. M. (1978). *Leadership*, Harper and Row, New York.

Carnavale, D. (1992). The learning support model: personnel policy beyond the traditional model, *Am. Rev. Public Admin., 22*: 19–36.

Cleveland, H. (1985). The twilight of hierarchy, *Public Admin. Rev., 45*: 185–195.

Cooper, T. L. (1982). *The Responsible Administrator: An Approach to Ethics for the Administrative Role*, Kennikat Press, Port Washington, New York.

Denhardt, K. (1988). *The Ethics of Public Service*, Greenwood Press, New York.

Denhardt, K. (1991). Unearthing the moral foundations of public administration: Honor, benevolence, and justice, *Ethical Frontiers in Public Management* (J. S. Bowman, ed.), Jossey-Bass, San Francisco, pp. 91–113.

Denhardt, R. B. (1991). A statement of who we are: a summary of the discipline, *Public Admin. Rev., 51*: 80–81.

Denhardt, R. B. (1993). *The Pursuit of Significance*, Wadsworth, Belmont, CA.

Fiedler, F., and Garcia, J. (1987). *New Approaches to Effective Leadership: Cognitive Resources and Organizational Performance*, Wiley, New York.

Finer, H. (1941). Administrative responsibility in democratic government, *Am. Polit. Sci. Rev., 1*: 335–350.

Frederickson, H. G. (1971). Toward a new public administration, *Toward a New Public Administration* (F. Marini, ed.), Chandler, Scranton, PA, pp. 309–331.

Frederickson, H. G. (1990). Public administration and social equity, *Public Admin. Rev., 50*: 228–237.

Friedrich, C. (1940). Public policy and the nature of administrative responsibility, *Public Policy, 1*: 3–24.

Golembiewski, R. T. (1972). *Renewing Organizations*, Peacock, Itasca, IL.

Golembiewski, R. T. (1979). *Approaches to Planned Change*, Marcel Dekker, New York.

Hackman, R., and Oldham, G. R. (1975). Development of the job-diagnostic survey, *J. Appl. Soc. Psychol., 60*: 161–162.

Hackman, R., and Suttle, L., eds. (1977). *Improving Life at Work*, Goodyear, Santa Monica, CA.

Harmon, M. (1971). Normative theory and public administration: Some suggestions for a redefinition of administrative responsibility, *Toward a New Public Administration* (F. Marini, ed.), Chandler, Scranton, PA, pp. 172–184.

Herzberg, F., Mausner, B., and Snyderman, B. B. (1959). *The Motivation to Work*, Wiley, New York.

Houston, D. J., and Delevan, S. M. (1990). Public administration research: an assessment of journal publications, *Public Admin. Rev., 50*: 674–682.

Houston, D. J., and Delevan, S. M. (1991). The state of public personnel research, *Rev. Public Personnel Admin., 11*: 97–111.

Ingraham, P. W., and Ban, C. R. (1986). Models of public management: are they useful to federal managers in the 1980s, *Public Admin. Rev., 46*: 152–160.

Ingraham, P. W., and Rosenbloom, D. H. (1989). The new public personnel and the new public service, *Public Admin. Rev., 49*: 116–124.

Kaufman, H. (1956). Emerging conflicts in the doctrines of public administration, *Am. Polit. Sci. Rev., 50*: 1057–1073.

Kaufman, H. (1969). Administrative decentralization and political power, *Public Admin. Rev., 29*: 3–15.

Kingsley, J. D. (1944). *Representative Bureaucracy: An Interpretation of the British Civil Service*, Antioch Press, Yellow Springs, AK.

Klingner, D. E. (1992). Public personnel management (book review essay), *Public Admin. Rev., 52*: 211.

Klingner, D. E., and Nalbandian, J. (1985). *Public Personnel Management: Contexts and Strategies*, 2nd ed., Prentice-Hall, Englewood Cliffs, NJ.

Kotter, J. (1988). *The Leadership Factor*, Free Press, New York.

Kouzes, J. M., and Posner, B. (1987). *The Leadership Challenge*, Jossey-Bass, San Francisco.

Krislov, S., and Rosenbloom, D. H. (1981). *Representative Bureaucracy and the American Political System*, Praeger, New York.

Lewin, K. (1948). *Resolving Social Conflict*, Harper, New York.

Locke, E. A. and Latham, G. P. (1984). *Goal-Setting: A Motivational Technique That Works*, Prentice-Hall, Englewood Cliffs, NJ.

Maslow, A. (1954). *Motivation and Personality*, Harper and Row, New York.

McClelland, D. (1961). *The Achieving Society*, D. Van Nostrand, Princeton, NJ.

McGregor, D. (1960). *The Human Side of Enterprise*, McGraw-Hill, New York.

Mosher, F. C. (1968). *Democracy and the Public Service*, Oxford University Press, New York.

Nalbandian, J. (1989). The U.S. supreme court's "consensus" on affirmative action, *Public Admin. Rev., 49*: 38–45.

Nigro, L. G. (1990). Personnel for and personnel by public administrators: bridging the gap, *Public Administration: The State of the Discipline* (N. B. Lynn and A. Wildavsky, eds.), Chatham House, Chatham, NJ, pp. 185–202.

Nigro, L. G., and Richardson, W. D. (1992). The founders' unsentimental view of public service in the American regime, *Agenda for Excellence* (P. W. Ingraham and D. F. Kettl, eds.), Chatham House, Chatham, NJ, pp. 3–24.

Perry, J. L. (ed.) (1989). *The Handbook of Public Administration*, Jossey-Bass, San Francisco.

Raelin, J. A. (1986). *The Clash of Cultures: Managers and Professionals*, Harvard Business School Press, Boston.

Roethlisberger, F., and Dickson, W. (1940). *Management and the Worker*, Harvard University Press, Cambridge, MA.

Rohr, J. A. (1978). *Ethics for Bureaucrats: An Essay on Law and Values*, Marcel Dekker, New York.

Shafritz, J. M., Riccucci, N. M., Rosenbloom, D. H., and Hyde, A. C. (1992). *Personnel Management in Government*, 4th Ed., Marcel Dekker, New York.

Simon, H. A. (1957). *Administrative Behavior*, 2nd Ed., Free Press, New York.

Skinner, B. F. (1971). *Beyond Freedom and Dignity*, Knopf, New York.

Vroom, Victor H. (1964). *Work and Motivation*, Wiley, New York.

White, J. D. (1986). On the growth of knowledge in public administration, *Public Admin. Rev., 46*: 15–24.

Wilson, W. (1887). The study of administration, *Polit. Sci. Quart., 2*: 197–222.

Zaleznik, A. (1977). Managers and leaders: are they different?", *Harvard Business Rev.* (May–June): 67–78.

3
Assuring Equal Employment Opportunity in the Organization

STEPHEN K. STRAUS and DEBRA W. STEWART   North Carolina State University, Raleigh, North Carolina

One of the greatest challenges to the management of human resources is meaningful achievement of equal employment opportunity (EEO). Though, as a value, EEO is deeply rooted in the American political tradition, as a policy enactment it is essentially redistributive and "in-process" in nature. As such, it inevitably generates opposition and conflict in implementation. Nevertheless, a sound understanding of EEO policy is pivotal to effective executive action.

This chapter explores EEO from a variety of perspectives essential to its incorporation into effective human resources management practice. The manager must know the nature of EEO as it emerges in substantive public policy and is implemented in Washington. As well, the manager needs to bring to EEO implementation a sensitivity to the equity issues involved and to the judicial pronouncements on these issues. Finally, the effective executive implements EEO policy by understanding its principles and assimilating them into sound human resource management practices.

I.   EQUAL EMPLOYMENT OPPORTUNITY AS PUBLIC POLICY

The major laws and regulations covering EEO today include Title VII of the Civil Rights Act of 1964 (as amended by the Equal Employment Opportunity Act of 1972) and the Civil Rights Act of 1991, the Equal Pay Act of 1963, Executive Order 11246, the Age Discrimination Act of 1967 (as amended in 1986), the Rehabilitation Act of 1973, and the Americans with Disabilities Act of 1990. Also, significant implementation regulations in the form of the Equal Employment Opportunity Commission (EEOC) and the Office of Federal Contract Compliance Programs (OFCCP) guidelines have been issued and revised periodically since the 1960s. *The Uniform Guidelines for Employee Selection Procedures* issued in 1978 is one of the most significant of these documents. A brief description of the coverage, practices prohibited, specific judicial interpretations, and administrative enforcement of such enactment provides important background information for the public manager.

A.   Civil Rights Acts of 1964 and 1991

The Civil Rights Act of 1964 was the most comprehensive piece of civil rights legislation ever enacted in the United States. From the employer's perspective, Title VII of that act constitutes the critical part. Practically speaking, most employers are covered by the 1964 Civil Rights Act, as are all unions and employment agencies dealing with employers.[1] Since Title VII was amended by the Equal Employment Opportunity Act of 1972, state and local government employers as well as private and public educational institutions are also covered.[2] The 1964 Civil Rights Act prohibits an employer from using race, color, religion, sex, or national origin as a basis for (1) failing or refusing to hire any individual; (2) discriminating against any individual regarding compensation terms, conditions, or privileges of employment; and (3) limiting, segregating, or classifying employees or applicants in any way that would tend to deprive that person of employment opportunities or adversely affect his or her status. In response to several 1989 supreme court decisions that were adverse to the interest of alleged victims of employment discrimination under Title VII, the U.S. Congress passed the 1991 Civil Rights Act. In general, the new act reaffirms legal interpretations of Title VII rendered before 1989.

Because Title VII and the 1991 Civil Rights Act are so comprehensive, judicial interpretation of the discrimination they prohibit, the coverage they provide, and the legitimacy of their enforcement hold important information for the public manager. Thus, this chapter addresses these two civil rights acts in some depth, while treating the other enactments in synoptic form.

Perhaps the most basic question put to the courts from the genesis of Title VII litigation was simply, what counts as discrimination? Three stages in judicial thinking emerge clearly in court decisions. In the early days of Title VII enforcement, discrimination was assumed to be a motivational or moral problem, i.e., a human relations difficulty. Congressional oversight hearings in 1971 on the EEOC captured this phase well: "In 1964, employment discrimination tended to be viewed as a series of isolated and distinguishable events, for the most part due to ill will on the part of some identifiable individual or organization" (Senate Committee on Labor and Public Welfare, 1971).

A second stage of thinking regarding discrimination evolved in the 1960s around the notion of disparate treatment. Discrimination here occurs when an employer treats some people less favorably than others because of their race, sex, color, religion, or national origin. The courts have noted that even with disparate treatment, proof of discriminatory motive is critical, "although it can in some situations be inferred from the mere fact of differences in treatment" (Teamsters v. United States, 1977). Significant in this shift from "intent" to "treatment" is the new focus on behavior and not simply attitude.

The third stage in the evolving definition of discrimination came in terms of "effects," "consequences," or "impacts." Discrimination under this rule, often referred to by the courts as "disparate impact," involves employment practices that are neutral on their face in treatment of different groups "but that in fact fall more harshly on one group than another and cannot be justified by business necessity" (*Teamsters v. United States*, 1977). The third stage was first fully articulated by the U.S. Supreme Court in the case of *Griggs v. Duke Power Company* (1971).

Griggs, arguably the most important case ever decided under Title VII, significantly broadened the meaning of discrimination. Under disparate impact, it was no longer necessary to prove a discriminatory motive, nor was it necessary to show that employers were using different stan-

---

[1]Title VII covers employers of 15 or more workers if they are engaged in industry affecting commerce and if they have at least 15 employees for each working day in each of the 20 calendar weeks in the current or preceding years.

[2]The exemption from coverage is really quite narrow: religious corporations and associations, employers of aliens outside of the United States, Indian tribes, and bona fide tax-exempt nonmembership clubs, excepting labor unions, are exempt. Also exempt from the law are elected officials and their personal staffs, as well as their appointees on the policymaking level. (This exemption for elected officials and their staffs was removed in the 1991 Civil Rights Act.)

dards in evaluation employees. Discrimination could reside simply in the effect of an action. A full understanding of the meaning of discrimination under Title VII requires detailed discussion of the Griggs case (Blumrosen, 1972).

The Griggs case involved the legality of two of Duke Power's employment selection instruments: a standardized general intelligence test and a high school diploma requirement. According to statistical evidence, significantly more African-Americans failed the tests and thus were excluded from employment than whites. The Court found Duke Power guilty of discrimination because neither standard was shown to be significantly related to job performance, both requirements operated to disqualify African-Americans at a substantially higher rate than white applicants, and the job in question formerly had been filled by white employees as part of a longstanding practice of giving preference to whites. From one perspective *Griggs* was a test case, but its impact has been broad, reaching well beyond the narrow issue of testing.

The departure from definitions of discrimination prevalent in the 1960s emerged clearly in the Supreme Court's reasoning. Moving beyond the motivation definition, the Court said, "Congress directed the thrust of the act [Title VII of the Civil Rights Act of 1964] to the consequences of employment practices, not simply motivation." Accordingly, the justices set forth a standard higher than merely equal treatment: "The Act proscribes not only overt discrimination but also practices that are fair in form, but discriminatory in operation." Although it is true that the Civil Rights Act of 1964 describes the discriminator as one who "intentionally engaged in unlawful employment practice," intentionally means, simply, "not by accident." Thus, any employment practice is intentional because the employer presumably intends the natural consequences of his or her action (*EEO Compliance Manual*, 1979). In other words, in the post-*Griggs* era, any employment practice yielding *adverse impact* on a group protected under Title VII can be unlawful even if the employer's intentions were nondiscriminatory or even if he or she was mistaken as to what the impact of the action would be (*EEO Compliance Manual*, 1979).

The extensive applicability of the *Griggs* rule beyond the testing issue needs to be addressed. The effect of the decision was to broaden coverage to any employment practice that could be shown statistically to have an adverse impact on any group protected by Title VII. Height and weight requirements, arrest records, credit checks, and educational requirements have all been struck down under the *Griggs* interpretation of Title VII. They have fallen because they "operate to exclude" protected group members. Much of the ensuing discussion on discrimination under Title VII revolves around the basis for measuring this exclusion. The question is what statistical data would be relevant to proving discrimination.

In the Griggs case, the Supreme Court did not require that the plaintiff show that the high school diploma requirement had an exclusionary effect on the actual applicants at Duke Power. Rather it turned to the statistics of high school education for the entire state of North Carolina for evidence. In footnote 6 of the *Griggs* decision, the Supreme Court notes: "In North Carolina, 1960 census statistics show that while 34% of the white males had completed high school, only 12% of negro males had done so." In *Griggs*, the Court was persuaded by the view that the existence of the requirement in and of itself may have discouraged non–high school applicants and therefore disproportionately excluded African-Americans. Thus, to measure the real impact, one would have to look at broader census data.

When evidence does show that a practice operates to exclude members of a protected group, the only defense the employer has is business necessity. In the words of the Court in *Griggs*, the "touchstone is business necessity." Duke Power failed to show that either the high school diploma or the written test constituted a business necessity.

The *Griggs* decision marked a critical turning point in the understanding of discrimination as it was prohibited by the Civil Rights Act of 1964. In *Griggs*, the Court clearly defined discrimination in terms of impact or effect. When Congress passed the Equal Employment Opportunity Act of 1972, it unambiguously ratified the *Griggs* definition of employment discrimination.

Throughout the 1970s and much of the 1980s, the courts continued to clarify the conditions that trigger Title VII applicability. They decided that when a statistical disparity between groups was caused by discrimination occurring since Title VII took effect, and no discrimination had occurred since that time, the statistical evidence could not be used to indicate a violation of the law (*Hazelwood School District v. United States*, 1977). (Because state and local governments were not covered before 1972, statistics generated by action before that time would probably fail as evidence.) Furthermore, the Court ruled that bona fide seniority systems may be maintained even when those systems may perpetuate discrimination that occurred before the Title VII enactment (*Teamsters v. United States*, 1977), set forth the conditions required for seniority systems to be deemed "bonafide" (*Pullman Standard v. Swint*, 1982), generally ruled against establishing sex as a bona fide occupational qualification, BFOQ (*Berl v. Westchester County*, 1988; *Wilson v. Southwest Airlines*, 1981; *Weeks v. Southern Bell*, 1969), and expanded its interpretation to include subjective practices such as interviews (*Watson v. Ft. Worth Savings and Loan*, 1988). Included as well were objective hiring practices, such as written aptitude tests (*Albermarle Paper Company v. Moody*, 1975), written tests of verbal skills (*Washington v. Davis*, 1976), and written examinations (*Connecticut v. Teal*, 1982).

Moreover, although sexual harassment claims are not specifically prohibited by Title VII, the courts began in 1977 (*Barnes v. Costle*) to rule that Title VII also covered discrimination in the form of sexual harassment. The courts have accepted two types of such claims under the act: loss of tangible job benefits and hostile environment claims. In the former type of claim, an employee is rewarded or punished for his or her response to requests for sexual benefits. In the latter type of claim, a work environment is considered hostile if it alters the conditions of the victim's employment. The Court made its initial ruling on hostile environment claims in *Meritor Savings Bank v. Vinson* (1986), holding that a plaintiff need not demonstrate an economic effect of her employment (i.e., being fired or quitting). Instead, the psychological environment created in the workplace was actionable. Although the Court did not hold Meritor liable, it agreed that the employer would have been liable had it known about the situation. The Court left the lower courts with the responsibility of specifying under what conditions employers would be held liable (Neugarten, 1990). Section IV of this chapter explains employer obligations to reduce the threat of sexual harassment in the workplace.

The Supreme Court's broad interpretations of Title VII cases abruptly ended during the 1989 session. The most noteworthy case that reversed the previous trend was *Wards Cove Packing v. Atonio* (1989), which rewrote the requirements for statistical proof and made if significantly harder for protected groups to win disparate impact claims. A group of Asian and Alaskan salmon cannery employees alleged that the company filled low-skill level jobs with minorities while hiring whites for salaried and supervisory positions. The plaintiffs attempted to demonstrate disparate impact under Title VII by referring, as was done in *Griggs*, to the discrepancy between the percentage of minorities in the geographic labor market with the number of skilled jobs at the cannery. The Court, however, ruled that the proper comparison should be between the racial composition of the *qualified* persons in the labor market and those in the employer's work force. Moreover, with respect to the legal burden on plaintiffs, the Court reversed the trend established in *Griggs* and subsequent cases. In those earlier cases, when employment practices resulted in a disparate impact on a protected class, employers had to prove that the challenged practices were "job-related" and a "business necessity." Instead of holding to these standards, the Court, in *Wards Cove*, ruled that the employer merely had to produce a business justification to rebut challenges to its practices.

In other cases considered during the 1989 session, the Court further eroded the gains made by employees in Title VII discrimination cases. In *Martin v. Wilkes*, the Court allowed white firefighters to challenge an affirmative action plan as "reverse discrimination" although that plan had been approved years earlier as part of a consent decree by a lower court. The Court interpretation also reduced the statute of limitations on Title VII cases to effectively reduce the time that complainants would have to file charges. In *Lorance v. AT&T Technologies* (1989), the Court held that the period for filing a challenge to an allegedly discriminatory seniority rule begins to run on the date the rule is adopted, not on the date when the rule adversely affects an employee. Also, the Court supported employers proving "mixed motives." That is to say, employers, despite having made a discriminatory decision, would not be held liable when they could demonstrate that they would have made the same decision on nondiscriminatory grounds (*Price Waterhouse v. Hopkins*, 1989).

The U.S. Congress sought to overturn this conservative swing of the Court by passing the 1991 Civil Rights Act which, in general, reversed the Court's 1989 rulings. In its purposes section, the 1991 Act declares that it is intended to uphold the concepts of job-relatedness and business necessity established in *Griggs*. Specifically, the act reversed *Wards Cove* by stipulating that practices producing a disparate impact on a protected class are unlawful unless the employer can prove that they are job-related and a business necessity. The new act requires, when possible, that plaintiffs demonstrate how each particular challenged practice causes a disparate impact, but also holds employers responsible when a less discriminatory practice is available but they refuse to use it. However, the act did not address the stricter statistical requirement used to demonstrate adverse impact in *Wards Cove*.

The 1991 Civil Rights Act also overturns *Martin* by barring challenges to consent decrees made by individuals who had actual notice of the provision of the consent decrees unless there is a subsequent change in the law or the facts. The narrow interpretation of the statute of limitations made in *Lorance* was overruled. The act stipulates that an intentionally discriminatory seniority system may be challenged when a person is actually injured by it. Moreover, it holds that in "mixed motive" cases such as *Price Waterhouse*, employers who demonstrate that the same action would have been taken without the discriminatory motive may be prohibited from considering the discriminatory factor in the future and may be required to pay declaratory relief and attorney fees and costs.

Finally, the 1991 Civil Rights Act also revamps the damages available to victims. Before, only victims of intentional racial or ethnic bias could receive compensatory and punitive damages. The new act enables victims of discrimination based on sex, religion, or disability to obtain such damages, but the new damages will be capped at a maximum of $300,000 depending on the size of the employer. All employers may be held liable for compensatory damages in cases of intentional discrimination, and all nonpublic employers who act with "malice or with reckless indifference" may be held accountable for punitive damages.[3]

Throughout the litigation on the issues of the meaning of discrimination and the coverage of certain types of cases, the legitimacy of the EEOC's judgments has itself been an issue. It is fitting, therefore, to conclude this discussion of the civil rights acts with a brief chronology of the EEOC's role in the implementation process.

---

[3]The act limits the damages that each individual complainant can receive to $50,000 for employers with 100 or fewer employees, $100,000 for employers with up to 201 workers, $200,000 for employers with up to 501 workers, and $300,000 for employers with more than 500 workers. Back pay, and any interest accrued on back pay, are not included in these amounts.

The EEOC was established by legislation to administer Title VII. As the enforcement agency, it investigates charges of discrimination and initially attempts to reach a voluntary settlement with the employer. It is also empowered to initiate its own investigations. However, in deference to the principles of federalism, the proper complaint procedure must first be brought under any applicable state or local statute. An individual complainant may not file a charge with the EEOC for 60 days after state or local proceedings have been initiated. When the EEOC itself initiates a complaint, state or local officials must be given at least 60 days to act before the commission proceeds. When investigating a complaint against a state or local government employer, the EEOC follows the standard pattern of attempting to forge a voluntary settlement. However, when such efforts fail, the complaint with the EEOC findings is referred to the Department of Justice for litigation.

In addition to enforcement, the EEOC is also responsible for developing specific written regulations from the general standards spelled out by Congress in the 1964 and 1991 civil rights acts (as well as the Americans with Disabilities Act of 1990). Through this activity of implementation, the terms and scope of discrimination achieve definition. As with the pronouncement of any administrative agency, the courts ultimately pass on the bureaucratic refinements of public policy. The formulation of implementation policy on testing under Title VII best illustrates this history.

In 1966, in response to complaints alleging that employers discriminated on the basis of written tests, the EEOC assembled a panel of industrial psychologists to study bias in employment testing. Based on the results of this study, the EEOC issued its first guidelines on employment testing procedures. Bold for their time, these guidelines advised that a violation of Title VII had occurred whenever a test had an adverse impact on women or minorities and had not been validated as predicting job success. Courts were far from uniform in accepting this interpretation. In 1970, the EEOC issued a revised set of principles, more fully defining these same standards for validation. Throughout this period, the legitimacy of the EEOC's role in defining standards was challenged routinely. In *Griggs v. Duke Power*, the court not only shaped significantly the definition of discrimination, but also lent substantial legitimacy to EEOC interpretation of the law.

In the Griggs case, the U.S. Chamber of Commerce had filed a brief arguing that the EEOC "departed from previous notions of what discrimination is" and urged the court not to defer to the EEOC guidelines. The court, however, rejected this request, explicitly giving deference to EEOC rules. In 1972, the deference to the EEOC's standard-setting legitimacy was reinforced in the Equal Employment Opportunity Act of 1972, where the guidelines were clearly incorporated by Congress into the text of the statute. In 1976, the EEOC reissued its 1970 guidelines with a preamble indicating that they applied to the full coverage of Title VII as it had been expanded in 1972. By the late 1970s the legitimacy of the EEOC to flesh out the skeleton of Title VII law appeared well established (see subsection F for further background on the *Uniform Guidelines*).

Congressional legislation passed in 1990 and 1991 seemingly expanded the responsibilities of EEOC even further. EEOC was given new powers under the 1990 Americans with Disabilities Act to enforce fair employment for people with disabilities. Furthermore, the 1991 Civil Rights Act provided that EEOC establish a Technical Assistance Training Institute to provide educational and outreach activities to individuals who historically have been the victims of job bias. However, certain actions taken by the Bush administration at the time of the passage of the 1991 Civil Rights Act stirred doubts about the future role of EEOC. These actions and the concerns they raise about the future of EEOC will be discussed further in Section IV of this chapter.

B. Equal Pay Act

The Equal Pay Act (EPA), enacted in 1963 as an amendment to the Fair Labor Standards Act (FLSA) of 1938 (amended in 1985), requires employers to pay equal wages regardless of sex for work that is equal in skill, effort, and responsibility. More narrowly drawn than the civil rights acts of 1964 and 1991, the EPA prohibits discrimination in wages only, but its coverage is comprehensive, applying to all employers subject to the minimum wage provision of the FLSA. Although state and local government units were not subject to that provision until 1985, most court decisions upheld the applicability of the EPA to those jurisdictions. In 1985, the Supreme Court put any doubts to rest about the coverage of public agencies when it held, in *Garcia v. San Antonio Metro Transit*, that FLSA applied to state and local governments.

Although the EEOC also has enforcement responsibilities for this Act, the EPA has not required the extensive administrative interpretation given to the civil rights acts, largely because of the relative narrowness of the EPA's proscribed actions. Nevertheless, a significant amount of litigation has occurred, giving increased precision to the Act. A few of the EPA cases serve to illustrate these important refinements.

One EPA issue honed by litigation is the definition of wages. Clearly, under the Act, wages include all payments made as remuneration for employment. Counted as well as payments are commissions, bonuses, attendance payments, or any payments established to compensate for hazardous or disagreeable working conditions. The courts have also interpreted wages under the EPA to include the cost to employees for providing for room and board and other services. For example, in the case of *Laffey v. North West Airlines, Inc.* (1976), a federal court found it unlawful for North West Airlines to provide more expensive layover accommodations for male pursers than for female stewardesses, and to provide the pursers, but not the stewardesses, with a cleaning allowance.

A second area for EPA litigation concerns the basis for comparing jobs. The standard that has evolved is that jobs need not be identical but only substantially similar in all three requirements—skill, effort, and responsibility—to evoke coverage of the EPA. With regard to the skill requirement, the focus is on the position, not the employee in that position. Therefore, even if an employee's qualifications exceed those required for adequate job performance, those additional skills may not be considered in comparing the skill requirements of two jobs [29 C.F.R. 1620.15(a)]. The effort requirement is concerned with the degree, not the type, of effort (i.e., physical or mental). In *Hodgson v. Daisy Manufacturing Company* (1970), the Court found that although male employees exerted greater physical effort, the female employees performed a variety of operations requiring greater mental alertness and greater job responsibility. Paying the men more, therefore, violated the Act. The responsibility requirement concerns the degree of responsibility required for job performance [C.F.R. 1620.17 (a)].

A third area for EPA litigation concerns one of the permissible grounds for discrimination written into the Act. Explicit pay differentials are permitted under the EPA if the wage rates are based on a seniority system, a merit system, a system that measures earnings by quality or quantity of production, or any factor other than sex. The most controversial of these is the "factor other than sex." For example, in *Horner v. Mary Institute* (1980), the Eighth Circuit Court of Appeals ruled that a school was justified in paying a male gym teacher more than a female because he was the best person available and the higher salary was necessary to get him to take the job. Defining "market conditions" as a legitimate factor-other-than-sex exception, the court said, "An employer may consider the market place value of the skills of a particular individual when determining his or her salary."

Throughout the 1970s the courts stuck to these requirements despite the emergence of the comparable worth debate. Comparable worth proponents argue that in a male-dominated society, women have been steered to certain jobs that paid less than those jobs were worth to their employers. These proponents called for the courts to rely on the broader provisions of Title VII rather than the EPA in resolving legal disputes concerning pay. However, the courts countered this argument by relying on the Bennett Amendment to Title VII, which stipulates that "it shall not be an unlawful employment practice under this title for an employer to differentiate upon the basis of sex in determining the amount of wages or compensation paid . . . if such differentiation is authorized by [The Equal Pay Act]" [Sec. 703 (b)]. That is to say, illegal discrimination would exist only where there has been unequal pay for equal work.

In the early 1980s, the federal district court in the state of Washington accepted the claim that Title VII should cover sex bias in compensation beyond the equal work issue in *County of Washington v. Gunther* (1981) and, in a more publicized case, *American Federation of State, County, and Municipal Employees (AFSCME) v. The State of Washington* (1983). The plaintiffs in both cases were female public sector employees. In *Gunther*, the plaintiffs were county prison guards, and in *AFSCME* they were state employees who were union members. In both cases, the plaintiffs claimed that pay differentials were based on intentional sex discrimination because their employers had conducted but not implemented job evaluation studies to set their pay.

Gunther went all the way to the Supreme Court, which did not fully sanction the concept of comparable worth. Nevertheless, the court opened the door for future comparable worth claims by ruling that Title VII claims were not limited solely to the "equal work" standard of EPA. Although the Court did not find that the jobs of the male and female guards were substantially equivalent, it did agree that the females were victims of intentional sex discrimination.

In *AFSCME*, the federal district court in Washington State ruled that the state was liable for practices having a "disparate impact" on a protected group. The Court's ruling was overturned by the Ninth Circuit Court of Appeals in 1985, but in 1986 the federal district court approved a $482 million settlement between the union and the state (Johansen, 1990, p. 197).

The courts have not supported subsequent comparable worth claims. The six courts of appeals that ruled on comparable worth claims since *AFSCME* rejected them unanimously (Cascio, 1987). Moreover, the U.S. Civil Rights Commission also rejected the comparable worth theory and urged Congress and other federal agencies to do likewise (Williams, 1985). In sum, while the relationship between Title VII and pay discrimination claims of the EPA have been broadened, employees have not been very successful in getting legal support for comparable worth.

C. Age Discrimination in Employment Act of 1967

The Age Discrimination in Employment Act of 1967 (ADEA) aims both to promote the hiring of workers over 40 and to prohibit discrimination against older workers. The 1986 amendment to that act removed the age cap of 70 and stipulated coverage for employees over 40. The ADEA applies to all action elements covered in Title VII: hiring, firing, wages, terms, conditions, or privileges of employment. State, local, and federal government agencies are all covered under the ADEA.

In design and rationale, the ADEA was premised on an analogy between race discrimination and age discrimination. However, the analogy breaks down for certain positions because the courts have permitted exemptions, particularly for those positions concerned with public safety. For example, in *EEOC vs. City of East Providence* (1986) and *EEOC v. Missouri State Highway Patrol* (1985), the courts supported the establishment of a mandatory retirement age. Admittedly, this exemption is somewhat muddied by the courts. In *EEOC v. Pennsylvania* (1987) and *Heiar v. Crawford County, Wisconsin* (1984), the courts found that law enforcement departments had arbitrarily established mandatory retirement ages for their officers. Likewise, in *Haughton v. McDonnell Douglas Corporation* (1977), the Supreme Court held that a test pilot over 50 could not be grounded because of evidence of a general nature about the physical condition of people over 50. In addition, the Wage and Hour Division has interpreted the ADEA as not applying to bona fide apprenticeship programs because the purpose of such programs is generally to train young people for future careers.

The courts have generally applied the disparate treatment theory used in Title VII cases for ADEA cases involving hiring, discipline, and dismissal. That theory requires the plaintiff to demonstrate the following:

1. The applicant is between 40 and 70 years old.
2. The applicant was qualified for a job for which the employer was hiring, or was performing the job at a level that met the employer's legitimate expectations (discipline or dismissal).
3. The applicant was not hired, or the employee was demoted or disciplined.
4. After the applicant/employee was rejected, demoted, or dismissed, the employer continued to seek candidates with the his or her qualifications to perform the same work (Allred, 1990, pp. 73–75).

To rebut these claims, the employer must demonstrate that the action was based on some legitimate, nondiscriminatory reason. Finally, the plaintiff may attempt to rebut this employer's explanation by demonstrating that it is a pretext for age discrimination (Allred, 1990, pp. 73–75).

The courts have also upheld disparate impact claims under ADEA. Such claims may be filed when standard operating procedures of employers produce statistically significant differences in treatment that cannot be justified as a business necessity. For example, in *Geller v. Markham* (1980), the Court ruled that a policy of excluding teachers above a certain step in a salary schedule had a disparate impact on older teachers, despite the claim of the school system that such cost-cutting measures constituted a business necessity.

Since 1979 the EEOC has held enforcement responsibility for ADEA. EEOC is authorized to review and evaluate all agency programs designed to carry out the law, to obtain progress reports on covered agencies, to issue rules and regulations for enforcing the law, to consult with interested persons and groups regarding nondiscrimination on account of age, and to provide for processing complaints of age discrimination in the federal government.

A common thread weaving together the civil rights acts, the Equal Pay Act, and the Age Discrimination and Employment Act is their uniform endorsement of nondiscrimination. Under each act, the employer may be ordered by the conciliation agency or by a court to provide some remedy only after a finding of discrimination. The remedies may vary. In a Title VII case, an injunction may be granted against engaging in further discriminatory practices and affirmative action ordered. Under the Equal Pay Act or Age Discrimination in Employment Act, the payment of back wages, as well as liquidated damages or even criminal penalties, may be ordered. Whatever the remedy, the objective in each case is to correct a specific documented act or pattern of discrimination. Executive Order 11246, by way of contrast, requires affirmative action irrespective of specific judicial or administrative finding of discrimination.

D. Executive Order 11246

Presidential Executive Order 11246, as amended by Executive Order 11375 (October 1967), prohibits discrimination by federal contractors and subcontractors. "Contract" is defined very broadly to cover virtually all government contracts and, in some instances, grants are also considered as contracts under the executive order. Contractors with grants of more than a total of $10,000 are obliged under the executive order to take affirmative action to assure nondiscrimination. If a contractor has 50 or more employees and a contract of $50,000 or more, a written affirmative action plan is required. The specific affirmative action proposal developed must be based on a comprehensive analysis of the utilization of minorities and women in the work force as compared to their availability in the labor force. Numerical goals and timetables must be established for correcting any deficiencies revealed in the utilization analysis. The program must be publicized, and its implementation must be carefully monitored.

Most of the litigation surrounding the executive order has concerned the legality of quota-type programs that are established under executive order requirements but are alleged to violate Title VII's nondiscrimination provisions.

The Office of Federal Contract Compliance Programs (OFCCP) of the Department of Labor is directly responsible for enforcement of the executive order. If, in response to a complaint, a violation is found and reconciliation efforts fail, it is possible for the OFCCP to order penalties and sanctions after a formal hearing. Included among the penalties are canceling or suspending contracts in whole or in part, blacklisting the contractors, recommending to the attorney general that legal action be taken to enforce the EEO clause of a contract, and recommending to the EEOC or the Justice Department that action be taken under Title VII.

E. The Rehabilitation Act of 1973 and the Americans with Disabilities Act of 1990

The Rehabilitation Act of 1973 (Section 503) prohibits employers with federal contracts over $2500 from discriminating against handicapped people in all employment policies, including hiring, upgrading, demotion or transfer, recruiting, advertising, layoff, rate of pay, or other forms of compensation. As well, the act requires that employers take affirmative action for such handicapped employees. Under the legislation, a handicapped person is defined as anyone who (1) has a physical or mental impairment substantially limiting that person's life activities, (2) has a record of such impairment, or (3) has been regarded as having such impairment. "Life activities" are defined as those that affect employability, and "substantially limits" refers to the extent to which the handicap limits employability for a particular person.

The law requires that reasonable accommodation must be made by the employer to facilitate employment for the handicapped individual. "Reasonable accommodation" means making necessary adaptations to enable a qualified handicapped person to work. According to the legislation, this may include making facilities used by all employees accessible to handicapped people (ramps, restroom adaptations, wide isles) or making modifications in jobs, work schedules, equipment, or work areas (such as simplifying a job so that a retarded person can fill it or changing working hours so that a paraplegic person does not have to fight traffic).

Under the Rehabilitation Act, a federal contractor or subcontractor with 50 or more employees and a contract of $50,000 or more is obligated to prepare a written affirmative action program that may or may not be integrated into the affirmative action program required under Executive Order 11246. Although neither utilization analysis nor goals and timetables are required under the act, the recruitment and policy dissemination requirements are the same as those required under Executive Order 11246. The program itself must be available for inspection by government officials on demand; however, employers are not required to submit these programs to federal officials.

A unique feature of this act as compared to Executive Order 11246 is that employers are obligated to invite employees or applicants who think they are covered by the act and who want the benefits of the affirmative action program to identify themselves. However, an employer is not required to search employee files in order to discover a handicap.

Despite having passed the Rehabilitation Act, Congress by 1990 recognized that certain forms of discrimination, including segregation and isolation, continue to be a problem for individuals with disabilities. Moreover, the size of the problem in America has continued to grow. More than 43 million Americans have physical or mental disabilities and that number is increasing as the overall population gets older (Susser, 1990, p. 158). In response to this growing concern, Congress passed the 1990 Americans with Disabilities Act (ADA), which covers not only employment but also such vital areas as housing, public accommodations, access to public services, and institutionalization.

With regard to employment, the ADA expands and specifies coverage provided by the Rehabilitation Act. Rather than covering contractors with the federal government, effective July 1992, the ADA prohibits discrimination by all employers with 25 or more employees and, effective July 1994, all employers with 15 or more employees. Using the more sensitive and up-to-date term "disabled," the ADA still covers essentially the same persons referred to as "handicapped" by the Rehabilitation Act. Under the Rehabilitation Act, the courts had found a number of conditions to be handicaps including dyslexia (*Stutts v. Freeman*, 1983), missing limbs (*Coleman v. Casey*, 1980), and hypersensitivity to tobacco smoke (*Vickers v. Veterans Administration*, 1982). Perhaps most importantly, a case involving a teacher with tuberculosis (*School Board of Nassau County v. Arline*, 1987) opened the door to covering victims *regarded* as having a disability (such as HIV) but whose impairment does not substantially limit their life activities. The ADA covers any person with a physical or mental impairment that substantially limits major life activity and specifies coverage of persons with HIV and AIDS. Moreover, it protects the individual not currently using drugs but who has successfully completed or is enrolled in a rehabilitation program—even if that person is erroneously regarded as a drug user. As in the case of recovering drug users, the act also protects recovering alcohol abusers as long as they meet acceptable performance standards, and it does not expressly prohibit drug testing.[4]

Like the Rehabilitation Act, the ADA prohibits discrimination in the terms and conditions of employment for disabled persons who are otherwise qualified to perform the essential functions of a job. The new act requires accommodation unless the employer can prove "undue hardship," i.e., "action requiring significant difficulty or expense" in light of circumstances such as the size and financial resources of the employer. Specifically, "reasonable accommodation" includes making facilities accessible, job restructuring (such as modifying work schedules), reassignment to vacant jobs (without bumping other employees), acquisition or modification of existing equipment, adjusting or modifying testing or training methods, and providing qualified readers or interpreters.

Like the Rehabilitation Act, the ADA permits employees to self-identify, but the ADA prohibits preemployment inquiries about whether a candidate has a disability and permits preemployment medical examinations only if job-related and consistent with business necessity and after a job offer has been made.

The Rehabilitation Act is enforced and administered by the OFCCP. Therefore, complaints must be filed with the Department of Labor and, after the employer has reviewed the complaint through his or her internal procedures (after 60 days), the Department of Labor will investigate. As with Executive Order 11246, disputes are settled by informal means when possible, but penalties and sanction can be invoked when all else fails. In contrast, ADA has more teeth because it incorporates the powers, procedures, and remedies set forth in Title VII. As a result, complainants no longer must rely on government agencies to institute actions on their behalf, but can take private action after filing charges with EEOC and receiving a Notice of Right to Sue.[5]

---

[4]Unlike the Rehabilitation Act, the ADA specifically excludes the following conditions or disorders from coverage: homosexuality, bisexuality, transvestism, transsexualism, pedophilia, exhibitionism, voyeurism, gender identity disorders, compulsive gambling, kleptomania, pyromania, other sexual behavior disorders, and psychoactive substance abuse disorders resulting from illegal drug use.

[5]Complainants must file EEOC charges within 180 days after discrimination (300 days in states with a deferral agency) and must file private suit within 90 days after receipt of Notice of Right to Sue.

F.   Uniform Guidelines on Employee Selection Procedures

Prior to fall 1978, all of the agencies with EEO authority at the federal level were not operating under the same guidelines for employee selection. The burden fell on state and local agencies to patch together selection procedures acceptable to all federal authorities. In September 1978, the four federal agencies involved—the EEOC, the Civil Service Commission, the Department of Labor, and the Department of Justice—did come to accept and adopt *Uniform Guidelines on Employee Selection Procedures*. The critical areas affected by the *Guidelines* include hiring, promotion, and eligibility for training.

The selection rule prescribed in the *Guidelines* is as follows: if the selection procedure used for making employment decisions has an adverse impact on members of any racial, ethnic, or sex group, the procedures must be validated with the *Guidelines*. It is important to note that it is the effect of the total selection process for a job category that triggers the requirement. If a selection process does not have adverse impact, the employer is not required to look at individual procedures. However, if it does have adverse impact, the procedures must be examined to ensure that they are valid. The employer is also obliged to keep records showing the impact that selection procedures have.

The critical issue here is what counts as adverse impact. Under the *Guidelines*, adverse impact is defined as the selection rate of protected racial, ethnic, or sex group members at a rate lower than the selection rate for members of other groups. Generally, a selection rate for any racial, ethnic, or sex group that is less than four-fifths (80%) of the group with the higher selection rate will be regarded as evidence of adverse impact. The rate of selection for each group is determined by dividing the number of applicants selected from that group by the total number of applicants and by comparing the results with the result derived in the same way for the group with the highest selection rate. For example, if, over a 6-month period, there are 120 applicants (80 white, 40 African-American), of whom 60 were hired (48 white and 12 African-American), the selection rate for the white group would be 48/80 or 60%, whereas the selection rate for African-Americans would be 12/40 or 30%. Here the selection process adversely affected African-Americans. Their selection rate was only half that of whites (30 percent as compared to 60 percent). But if the selection rate for African-Americans had been within the four-fifths or 80% of the rate for the group with the highest rate, the impact would not be considered adverse.

A second example will illustrate this point. If there were 120 applicants, 80 white and 40 African-American, and 42 whites were selected whereas 18 African-Americans were selected, the selection rate for whites would be 42/80 or 52.5%, and the selection rate for African-Americans would be 18/40 or 45%. The comparative selection rate would be calculated by taking 45/52 and would produce a comparative selection rate of 86%. This would be above the 80% or four-fifths rule-of-thumb, and therefore it would be determined that the difference in impact is not substantial.

Managers should recognize that the four-fifths rule-of-thumb does not, however, mean that the *Guidelines* will tolerate up to 20% discrimination. Rather, its purpose is merely to establish a numerical basis for drawing inferences and for requiring additional information. Regardless of the amount of difference in selection rates, unlawful discrimination may be present and may be demonstrated through appropriate evidence.

Of course, part of the strength of adverse impact data depends on the magnitude of the number on which the percentage calculations are based. For example, if an employer selected three men and one woman from an applicant pool of 20 men and 10 women, the four-fifths rule would indicate adverse impact (the selection rate for women is 10%); the selection rate for men is 15%; 10/15 or 66.6% is less than 80%). Yet the numbers are so small that a difference in one person hired could show a difference the other way. In such circumstances, the enforcement agency would not require validity evidence in the absence of additional information. Section IV of this chapter describes challenges made by the Bush administration to the *Guidelines*.

II. ORGANIZATIONAL ISSUES IN EEO ENFORCEMENT

A. Legal Test for the EEO Structure

Throughout much of the 1970s, tension around implementation of the EEO policy outlined above centered on the existence of multiple and at times even conflicting rules and regulations emanating from the various agencies with enforcement responsibility. This tension culminated in court action brought by Sears, Roebuck and Company against an array of federal agencies involved in EEO enforcement. The facts of the case, as well as its ultimate outcome, are instructive for the public sector manager.

Sears was charged with employment discrimination by the EEOC in 1973. Four years later, the EEOC found reasonable cause to believe that Sears in fact had discriminated against minorities and women. In November 1978, the EEOC filed lawsuits in a number of cities charging Sears with job discrimination against both groups. Then, in 1979, Sears sued the federal government, taking the position that it was conflicting government policies that contributed to the disadvantageous position of women and minorities in the labor market and that the conflicts inherent in the law made it impossible for employers to comply with federal directives. Sears claimed that historically the social security system had assumed the man as the primary breadwinner, the extensive provisions for veterans had routinely given the edge to male workers, and the Age Discrimination in Employment Act had ensured that men placed in the past would hold onto their jobs longer by raising the retirement age to 70. In addition to conflicting with one another, some laws, Sears argued, were not even enforced.

The Federal District Court dismissed the suit in May 1979, saying that whereas providing equal opportunity for all citizens is a "formidable task . . . [it is] . . . not beyond the notable skill and competence of Sears" (*Sears, Roebuck and Company v. Attorney General*, 1979). The Court did not deny that some incompatibility or inconsistency in the law may exist, but it took the position that these difficulties should be handled by the Congress or the president, not by the courts.

B. Reorganization of 1978: Consolidation and Priority Setting

Though the court rejected the main thrust of the Sears allegation about the government working at cross-purposes, it was nonetheless true that throughout much of the late 1960s and 1970s EEO enforcement was characterized by decentralization across government agencies and significant overlapping of jurisdiction. Table 1 indicates the changes that were effected as a result of President' Carter's Reorganization Order Number 1. (Subsequent changes made by the 1990 Americans with Disabilities Act and the 1991 Civil Rights Act are also noted.)

The principal change was that responsibility for coordination of all Title VII enforcement was placed under the EEOC, as well as EEO in federal employment, the Equal Pay Act, and the Age Discrimination in Employment Act was placed under the EEOC. All contract compliance enforcement responsibility under Executive Order 11246, as well as the antidiscrimination legislation regarding handicapped participation in federal contracts, was lodged in the Department of Labor. The Justice Department maintained responsibility for enforcement in state and local government and added responsibility for investigation.

The major impact of this reorganization, viewed from the perspective of public as well as private employers, was the EEOC's emergence as the equal employment opportunity agency with

Table 1   Reorganization of Federal EEO Structure

Old structure	New structure

EEO Coordinating Council
    Coordinates all EEO enforcement
	EEOC
	    Coordinates all EEO enforcement
	    Title VII of Civil Rights Act, 1964
	    Americans with Disabilities Act
	    1991 Civil Rights Act

EEOC
    Title VII of Civil Rights Acts, 1964
	Age discrimination
	    Equal pay
	    EEO in federal employment

Department of Labor
    Age discrimination
    Equal pay
    Handicapped
    Executive Order 11246 (Labor coordinates
        cabinet department enforcement
	Department of Labor
	    Rehabilitation Act
	    Executive Order 11246 (direct enforcement)

Office of Personnel Management EEO in federal employment	

Justice Department
    State and local government enforcement
	Justice Department
	    State/local government investigation and
	        enforcement

broad responsibility for priority setting. Early on, then EEOC Chair Eleanor Holmes Norton issued a new order of priorities in the use of the EEOC's significantly enlarged resources. The thrust of the change was that the EEOC would spend more of its resources weeding out systemic discrimination and less on individual charges. To accomplish this task, two new selection programs were initiated. One program, the Early Litigation Identification Program, was designed to select and process quickly a certain set of cases where the case would be limited to the charges made. Under the second program, the Systemic Discrimination Program, cases broad in scope were selected and initiated by the EEOC in its effort to pursue model or test cases.

The initial thrust of these reforms appeared effective. From 1978 to 1979, total cases resolved increased by 96% and the time required for case resolution fell to an average of 150 days. During the 1980s, however, EEOC's effectiveness diminished substantially. Case resolution, on average, rose to 349 days in 1985, and in 1988 the *New York Times* reported that the agency had ignored over 900 age complaints thereby causing most of the complainants to miss their 2-year deadline to file in court (Perman, 1988). Furthermore, a study conducted by the Washington Council of Lawyers for the House Subcommittee on Employment and Housing found that agency staff lacked the skill, the authority, and the time to resolve complaints effectively (Perman, 1988).

Ironically, the centralization of responsibility under EEOC achieved by supporters of EEO in the 1970s provided opponents with a politically expedient mechanism to erode enforcement of EEO in the 1980s. Ideologically opposed to strong EEO enforcement, the Reagan administration did not need to resort to highly visible methods to reduce enforcement of EEO, such as challenging existing law or changing interpretive guidelines. Instead, the Reagan administration could reduce EEO enforcement by relying on more covert methods that sapped the vigor of the principal federal agency responsible for enforcement (EEOC) and that eluded detection by all but the most astute observers.

The decline on EEOC's effectiveness during the Reagan years can be attributed to appointment decisions, staff mismanagement, and the budgeting process. President Reagan's initial appointee to chair the agency, William M. Bell, "appeared to possess few qualifications for the job" (Thompson, 1984). A later appointee, Clarence Thomas, now a supreme court justice, testified in May 1982 that the federal EEO system is unworkable, yet he demonstrated little initiative to improve it (Subcommittee of the Committee on Government Affairs, 1987). Under Thomas's administration, investigative staff often lacked the specialized knowledge of the law to handle the types of cases they were assigned and received inadequate support and training to improve (Perman, 1988). Consequently, the staff demonstrated a lack of uniformity in their approach to investigations and often failed to cross-check statements of witnesses. Despite the ineffectiveness of his agency, Thomas "blamed Congress and low appropriations for much of the enforcement gap." Legislators, however, held that Thomas had agreed to budget cuts and he "steered the agency away from vigorous enforcement of antidiscrimination" (Perman, 1988).

Despite such posturing, the Reagan administration clearly was able to limit EEO through its administrative control over EEOC. Events surrounding President Bush's signing of the 1991 Civil Rights Bill suggest that more covert methods might be taken to limit the authority of EEOC. These developments will be discussed further in Section IV.

III. PREFERENTIAL TREATMENT AND THE PROVISION OF EQUITY

A. The Philosophical Debate

Serious philosophical, even moral questions have been raised in the debate over affirmative action designed to enhance employment opportunity for disadvantaged groups in society. Some argue that the underlying philosophical principles of affirmative action are at the core of the American political value system, whereas others maintain that affirmative action programs that rely on "goal"-based selection strike at the heart of that tradition. The difference resides largely in which part of that tradition is given emphasis, with the equality element of the tradition being heard strongly in the former and the liberty aspect of the tradition in the latter. Understanding this philosophical debate serves to clarify one's own thinking on these issues. Still, because such values often shape the formulation and implementation of affirmative action programs, conscious reflection on them is well worth the effort for a public executive.

In the world of the practitioner, debates on preferential treatment and reverse discrimination stem from efforts to develop numerical measures as part of affirmative action programs and from concerns about the impact of preferential treatment on organizational efficiency and effectiveness. Opponents of numerical guidelines typically call them quotas, whereas supporters see them as goals. As one author suggests, the difference in terminology betrays a difference in perspective: "Those who use the term 'quotas' pejoratively tend to assume that the numerical standards will be set so high or enforced so rigidly that strong reverse discrimination—that is, the deliberate hiring of demonstrably less well-qualified candidates—will be necessary to implement them. The term 'goal,' on the other hand, suggests that this will not be the case, and that good faith efforts to comply with these standards by means short of strong reverse discrimination will be acceptable" (Warren, 1977).

Practitioners opposing preferential treatment also argue that merit-based selection methods improve efficiency because more qualified employees produce at higher levels than less qualified workers (Black 1974; Schmitt and Noe, 1986). Advocates, on the other hand, assert that when protected individuals meet minimum qualifications, preferential hiring helps broaden the organizational talent pool and improves the quality of outputs, particularly for service-providing public agencies, such as social service or law enforcement agencies (Kennedy, 1986; Shaw, 1988).

Basically, the literature presents three philosophical arguments in favor of the practice of preferential treatment of protected group members in employment. Some advocates put forth a compensatory argument. This view is "backward looking" in the sense that it supports preferential treatment as a just means for compensating individuals or groups for past injustice (Taylor, 1973; Minas, 1977). Others, some of whom also support the first rationale, rely on a "consequentialist argument" (Bar-On, 1990). This perspective is "forward looking" in that it justifies preferential treatment as a way of bringing about some future good, such as reducing the income gap between races or providing role models for women (Nagel, 1973; Sher, 1975; Broxhill, 1985). Still others see preferential treatment as necessary merely to create conditions similar to the ones white males face in an ongoing just society. Such actions simply raise the protected group members' chances and lower white males' chances roughly to the equivalent of what they would be in a society where discrimination never existed (Warren, 1977; Bar-On, 1990).

On the negative side, there are two principal arguments against preferential treatment as it is embodied in most affirmative action programs. Both address the view of preferential treatment as compensation. One argument is directed to the question of who are the proper beneficiaries of affirmative action. Often the individuals who benefit from affirmative action programs are those who already have critical advantages (e.g., middle-class African-Americans). Moreover, preferential hiring carries with it an unintentional but adverse psychological effect; it sets up a dichotomy between "best" and "best black," which denigrates the real accomplishments of minorities (Shaw, 1988; Nacoste, 1991). As a result, some writers have suggested establishing affirmative action programs based on class distinctions (i.e., economic need) rather than racial criteria because class distinctions appear to garner greater ideological support than does preferential treatment based on race (Holmes, 1991; Stein, 1991; and Sniderman et al., 1991).

The second argument against preferential programs posits that even if compensation of some kind is due to members of disadvantaged groups, the burden of compensation should not be placed on young white men who themselves have not participated in the discrimination (Newton, 1973; Cohen, 1975). This is the conventional opposition to preferential treatment, and is heard most frequently in discussions with public officials.

Both of these objections to preferential treatment raise significant equity questions, but from the vantage point of affirmative action supporters, each carries a fatal flaw. The first argument founders on the fact that although preferential treatment may advantage the least harmed in some cases, it is still working to the advantage of the disadvantaged (e.g., African-Americans over whites) and thus can be justified on those grounds alone. Philosophically and perhaps even ideologically, it would be most appropriate to base preferential hiring on class rather than on racial distinctions. However, tests of social and economic status for employment decisions would be exceedingly complex and cumbersome, and maybe impossible. Rather than relying on class distinctions, traditional affirmative action programs can be positive organizational experiences if they are managed in ways that enhance perceptions of their fairness to all races and groups (Nacoste, 1991). Organizations can increase the perceived fairness of affirmative action through educational programs that address issues of race and gender and that explain the details of their affirmative action program (Crosby and Clayton, 1991). They can make their programs fairer by reducing the emphasis on goals and using race or gender as one factor among others when filling positions that are traditionally underrepresented (Singer and Singer, 1991). Section IV discusses how to manage affirmative action programs in greater depth.

The second argument against affirmative action is rejected by program supporters because although young white males themselves bear no guilt of past discrimination, they do benefit from a past discrimination that provided them with "conditions for both becoming and being considered better qualified" for employment. Social circumstance helps white males *become* more qualified because past discrimination has given them more resources and more role models for success. Moreover, white males have an advantage in "being considered" more qualified because the standards for performance in our society have been established by those "in charge"—white males (Bar-On, 1990). Just as feminine characteristics play a part in shaping stereotypes about what constitutes a good secretary, white male characteristics influence our expectations about features required of good professionals, such as lawyers, doctors, and managers. Because past discrimination contributed to these advantages, white males rightly bear some of the costs of redistributing the advantage (Bar-On, 1990).

While philosophical debate on these basic equity questions continues, the courts have been fashioning remedies that seem to use a temporary preferential treatment routinely to implement EEO policy.

B. Evolving Notions of Equity: Judicial Use of Quotas as Remedies

The courts have often ordered affirmative action plans under Title VII and under the Fourteenth Amendment (the equal protection clause) as a remedy for past discrimination, and the Supreme Court has generally backed such corrective measures. Perhaps the most instructive case in this area was *Communications Workers of America v. EEOC* (1978), which speaks directly to the philosophical objections raised against affirmative action. In 1973, American Telephone and Telegraph (AT&T) signed a consent decree with the EEOC agreeing to set goals and timetables to promote full utilization of all racial, sex, and ethnic groups. The decree included a seniority overrule provision. In May 1975, the unions involved sued, claiming that the consent decree violated the seniority provision of their contract, Title VII, and the U.S. Constitution. The Court of Appeals responded that, under *Franks v. Bowman* (1976), seniority override was allowed as a remedy. It went on to say that, regarding the quotas and requirements, even if they operate "to the disadvantage of members of groups which have not previously been discriminated against as compared to those groups which have been discriminated against," they are needed to counter the effects of past practice. Also, the court rejected the union's claim that the remedies should go only to identifiable victims of past discrimination and affirmed the correctness of a remedy to benefit a class of persons who had been wronged. The Supreme Court refused to review the Third Circuit Court of Appeals decision, leaving quotas in this fashion an appropriate remedy for discrimination.

Support for court-ordered affirmative action appeared to erode with a noteworthy 1984 Supreme Court decision. In *Firefighters Local Union No. 1784 v. Stotts* (1984) a lower court had ordered that certain white employees with greater seniority be laid off so that a specified number of African-American employees could be retained. Holding that Title VII protects bona fide seniority systems, the Supreme Court overturned that decision. Second, and more importantly, the Court appeared to reverse its position in *Communications Workers of America v. EEOC* by ruling that Title VII covered only those "who were actual victims of past discrimination."

In 1986, however, the Court reversed its "actual victims" position on *Stotts*. In cases that again involved unions and the question of seniority, *Local 28, Sheet Metal Workers International Association v. EEOC* (1986) and *Local 93, International Association of Firefighters v. City of Cleveland* (1986), the Court ruled that under Title VII preferential treatment may be ordered in consent decrees to remedy past discrimination even if it benefits those who are not actual victims of past discrimination.

Moreover, in *United States v. Paradise* (1987), the Court upheld a court-ordered quota under the equal protection clause. In that case, the Alabama Department of Corrections, because of its historic, pervasive, and systematic discrimination, was ordered to promote African-Americans on a one-to-one basis with whites.

In summary, during the 1980s the Court has upheld court-ordered plans that benefit individuals who prove they are actual victims of past discrimination or that are designed to remedy past discrimination by employers. In the 1980s, the Court also began upholding voluntary plans established by public employers.

C. Legal Status of Voluntary Affirmative Action

Some have argued, from a practical managerial perspective, that voluntary affirmative action creates a legal "catch-22" for the well-intentioned employer. Public employers often are urged to develop affirmative action programs or, if they are federal contractors, are obligated to do so. Yet acting aggressively in this regard simply invites reverse discrimination suits, with only those employers found guilty of discrimination in the past able to defend affirmative action measures such as numerical objectives. A review of major decisions helps clarify the legal status of voluntarily adopted affirmative action programs.

United Steel Workers of America v. Weber (1978) is the landmark case in affirmative action because it represents the first case on preferential treatment in employment decided by the Court and because Congress relied on the principles set forth in the *Weber* decision to design the 1991 Civil Rights Act. Before 1974, only 2% of the craft workers at the Kaiser Aluminum's Graymercy, Louisiana plant were African-American—a condition produced by a longstanding policy of hiring only experienced workers. As part of an affirmative action program at Kaiser, the union agreed to establish a training program in which half of the trainees assigned would be African-American. Two lists were established, and the most senior were selected from each of the lists. Brian Weber, a white employee, applied for the program and was denied admission, whereas blacks with less seniority were accepted under the two-list arrangement. Weber brought suit, claiming reverse discrimination—a violation under Title VII of the Civil Rights Act of 1964. A federal district court ruled in favor of Weber, but the Supreme Court reversed the lower court's decision and supported the voluntary affirmative action under which Weber had been denied admission to the training program. The court reasoned that the plan in question furthered the objectives of Title VII—to open job opportunities for African-Americans—and it did not "unnecessarily trammel the interest of white employees," i.e., no whites lost their jobs in the process. The Court carefully considered the section in Title VII which says that no employer is required "to grant preferential treatment to any individual or to any group because of race" but it concluded that a proper reading interprets the section to mean that employers are not required to make preferences rather than that employers are forbidden to make preferences in voluntary affirmative action.

Because Weber dealt with private sector employment, its application to the public sector remained unclear. Three cases decided in the late 1980s revealed the principles that appear to shape the legal status of affirmative action in the public sector. In *Wygant v. Jackson Board of Education* (1986), the Court devised a two-part criteria for voluntarily adopted affirmative action plans when it ruled against a voluntary plan that permitted a school board to lay off white teachers with greater seniority than minority teachers. The first criterion requires that the plan comply with the equal protection clause. The school argued that minority teachers should be retained in order to provide role models for the students. Nevertheless, the Court rejected the role model justification, ruling instead that a demonstration of prior discrimination was required to justify the plan. Second, the plan must be properly tailored to remedy the discrimination found. The Court specifically distinguished between the layoff system in the plan and hiring goals, holding that minority hiring goals impose a lesser burden on innocent third parties than layoffs.

In *Johnson v. Transportation Agency, Santa Clara County* (1987), the Court upheld a voluntary affirmative action plan under Title VII. In that decision the Court found that the plan, which did not establish quotas but did use race and gender as factors in hiring decisions, did not trammel the rights of innocent third parties. The Court found the plan justified by evidence of a manifest imbalance reflecting underrepresentation of women in traditionally segregated job categories.

The third and most recent case, *City of Richmond v. J.A. Croson Company* (1989), involved a minority set-aside program that required prime contractors with the city to subcontract at least 30% of the dollar amount of the contract to minority businesses. Croson bid on a city contract and sought a waiver of the set-aside requirement. When his waiver was denied, he sued. In its decision, the Court relied again on the two-part rule it had applied in *Wygant*. It found that general discrimination within the industry was insufficient evidence of past discrimination to justify race-based relief under the equal protection clause. Moreover, Richmond's program was not narrowly tailored because the City could not demonstrate that it had considered race-neutral means to increase minority participation and that the rigid quota in the plan was too inflexible to take into account individualized, case-by-case factors.

In sum, the rules used by the Court to review voluntarily adopted affirmative action plans appear to be the following:

1. Public employers must demonstrate substantial prior discrimination. Prior discrimination may be proven when employers show that a substantial difference exists between the percentage of minorities and females in the work force compared to the percentages in the available population. For job categories that require specialized skills, education, or experience, comparative data should be based on the percentages of minorities and women with such qualifications.
2. The plan should be based on flexible goals, not fixed quotas. Race and gender should be considered as one factor to be used in employment decisions. No unqualified candidates should be considered.
3. The plan should be temporary, lasting only long enough to correct manifest imbalances.
4. The plan should involve only hiring and promotions, not terminations (Allred, 1990, pp. 108–114; Graham, 1990).

Court-ordered or voluntary affirmative action programs as well as equal employment opportunity efforts must be appropriately implemented by public managers to ensure organizational compliance and responsiveness to evolutions in the law and its interpretation.

IV. THE MANAGER'S ROLE: IMPLEMENTATION STRATEGIES AND OPENNESS TO CHANGE

The public manager today faces a difficult and challenging task in implementing equal employment opportunity/affirmative action (EEO/AA) policy. The managerial role calls for awareness of the place of management and organization in the overall task of working toward EEO objectives. As well, it demands a sensitivity to the evolving character of EEO/AA policy. The former makes it possible to work effectively with what the law is; the latter keeps the manager open to future permutations in the definition of equal opportunity policy.

A. Implementation Strategies

Managerial action to promote conditions favorable to effective implementation of EEO/AA policy must be premised on assumptions about how change in organizations in general is produced. The structural model sees the organization itself—its systems, procedures, and controls that structure activity—as the change lever (Chapple and Sayles, 1961; Kanter, 1977). The attitudinal model sees attitudes of organization members—their feelings, values, and ideas—as the factor to be manipulated in effecting change (Roethlisberger and Dickson, 1939; McGregor, 1960; Zaleznick and Moment, 1964; Argyris, 1964).

Research indicates that both models of change should be applied in effecting a sound EEO/AA program, and, furthermore, how management chooses to implement that change is critical (Crosby and Clayton, 1990). In other words, both the structural and attitudinal interventions can founder on the shoals of inept management. Notwithstanding this research, fears of potential legal damages and public discrediting often lure managers, who would otherwise espouse collaborative methods, to impose EEO/AA policies through unilateral actions that negatively affect organizational commitment to those policies (Levine and Nigro, 1975; Nalbandian, 1981). These controlling behaviors are premised on a belief that supervisors and employees are unwilling and unable to carry out EEO/AA policies appropriately. Management manifests this belief when it imposes structural changes designed to control the behavior of supervisors and employees or when it strives to manipulate attitudes without first gaining commitment to EEO/AA policies.

Typically, the first instance occurs when the human resources department is cast in the role of the "bad guy" in the service of controlling managers, reviewing interview questions to ensure their legality (not their effectiveness), holding up personnel decisions because the "right person" was not hired or promoted, and threatening and cajoling supervisors to improve the statistical representation of protected groups in job classes.

In the second instance, by attempting to manipulate attitudes, controlling managers contribute to a decline in organizational performance and a lack of support for the EEO/AA program. Research indicates that when managers fail to involve people by providing relevant information, organizational members make negative assumptions about those persons who appear to benefit from the program—a phenomenon termed *negative expectancy effect* (Nacoste, 1991). When management withholds relevant information about EEO/AA, individuals who might be given special considerations can only infer whether they are in fact included as a member of a policy target group. As a result, those individuals will "be prone to vulnerability manifested as evaluation apprehension," i.e., they will be particularly sensitive to negative feedback about their accomplishments (Nacoste, 1991, p. 4). Nontarget group members will tend to provide that negative feedback because they discount the abilities of target group members and, accordingly, will tend to behave in ways that demonstrate a desire to be socially distant from them. This social distancing will reinforce the negative self-images of target group members and undermine their self-confidence (Nacoste, 1991). Clearly, a self-fulfilling prophesy is at work. Because public organizations require increasing cooperation and coordination among members in order to provide services, these mutually reinforcing negative images will tend to contribute to lower levels of performance throughout the organization (Carson, 1991).

Although these performance implications are grave, the controlling approach has further implications for EEO/AA policies and the managers who promulgate them. Research indicates that by focusing on statistical goals and legal liability rather than on fair processes, managers arouse further resistance to EEO/AA policies (Crosby and Clayton, 1990). Moreover, because they have taken control of the EEO/AA program and of related human resource activities, management and the human resource staff may find their support eroding as organizational members observe the decline in performance associated with EEO/AA policies and the imposition of seemingly unfair personnel decisions based on nontraditional, undisclosed, and vague criteria (Shafritz, 1975; Nalbandian, 1981; Straus, 1991).

In this context, efforts to inspire attitudinal change are doomed to failure. Management is left to plead its case for support in an environment that, at best, is unsupportive of and, at worst, is hostile to EEO/AA. When organizational members perceive that laws and policies are unfair, management efforts to recapture support by providing ethical or legal justifications will only exacerbate the sense of injustice (Singer and Singer, 1991).

To implement EEO/AA policies effectively, management should rely on an empowering approach which assumes that by providing appropriate information, involvement, and support organizational members will take responsibility for implementing EEO/AA effectively. Management becomes empowering by collaborating with supervisors and employees to design and carry out EEO/AA policies. Such an active and involving approach to structural change pays off attitudinally by spurring commitment and support for EEO/AA policies (Vogt and Murrel, 1990).

Structurally, management should concentrate primarily on proactive processes, i.e., to enable supervisors to understand, to participate in designing, and to take responsibility for carrying out effective human resource processes. For example, rather than focusing on illegal interview questions, trainers would demonstrate that the legal requirements of reliability and job relatedness are essential for hiring the best person for the job, and that a work force that is representative with regard to race, gender, age, and disability can improve citizen/client responsiveness to services. Supervisors would then learn how to design and carry out selection and promotional processes that are valid and reliable and that involve other supervisors and employees, e.g., through interview panels or assessment centers (Straus, 1988).

When supervisors employ effective selection and promotional methods, understand the importance of EEO/AA, and are held accountable for their human resource decisions, management's need to be preoccupied with outcomes diminishes. Supervisors will take more responsibility for sound human resource decisions and decision making because they will have greater ownership of those decisions (Vogt and Murrel, 1990). Certainly discrepancies will arise. However, management should only question hiring and promotional decision results when underrepresentation persists or when performance slips. Even in these circumstances, management and the human resource staff should not question hiring or promotional decisions first, but instead should begin by reviewing and even observing the validity and reliability of the processes used by supervisors to make those decisions. If those processes prove to be valid and reliable, then management and the human resource staff should work with supervisors to improve recruitment of the underrepresented groups and to enhance the attractiveness of relevant positions.

Such an empowering process should promote greater support for EEO/AA and cultivate openness to fair employment. Rather than the negative expectancy effect, non–target group members who have taken responsibility for hiring and promotional decisions will tend to give positive feedback to target group members (Fairfield-Sonn, 1984). Management can build on the enhanced organizational climate by implementing ongoing training, based on sound adult-learning principles, that fosters understanding about the nature and extent of bias and promotes the organizational benefits of diversity (Crosby and Clayton, 1991).

B. Openness to Change

The second area demanding serious managerial attention centers on the process and character of change in EEO policy. This section addresses that issue first, by looking at the 1964 and 1991 civil rights acts, to illustrate legislative, judicial, and administrative interaction in the change process. Next, we explore how that interaction may shape other critical but still evolving issues with significant implications for managers in the 1990s.

1. The 1964 and 1991 Civil Rights Act

The 1964 Civil Rights Act passed with overwhelming support in both houses of Congress. That legislation was the culmination of efforts by the civil rights movement that favorably shaped the opinions of affluent and well-educated Americans toward the rights of minorities (Dye, 1987, p. 62).

As documented earlier in this chapter, during the 1970s and 1980s, the courts played a critical role in shaping the implementation of Title VII. In general, the courts expanded the interpretation of that act, supporting affirmative action and including coverage of sexual harassment and comparable worth claims. During the 1989 session, however, the Supreme Court issued several decisions (particularly, *Wards Cove*) that reversed years of more progressive interpretations of the act.

While the judicial rulings on Title VII demonstrate the creative nature of court action, the policymaking process is a dynamic one in which the courts do not always have the final word. Events since 1989 underscore the impact that the legislature and the administration may also have on equal employment policy. Faced with the 1989 judicial reversal, proponents of progressive equal opportunity policy returned to pressure Congress in 1990. During that session Congress passed a civil rights bill only to have it vetoed by President Bush, who labeled it a "quota bill."

Gravely concerned about the divisiveness that emerged during the debates over the 1990 bill, the Business Roundtable, an organization of leading U.S. business executives, held a series of meetings with the Leadership Conference on Civil Rights to seek common ground on the bill. The two groups reached an accord on all issues except for the language addressing the issue of quotas and the limit on damages that could be assessed against employers. After further efforts, the two groups reconciled their differences on the former issue, but before they could proceed with the latter concern, the Bush administration pressured the Roundtable to withdraw from the meetings. After some delay, however, the Roundtable executives voted unanimously to continue the talks despite the objections of Bush staff members and were able to resolve their differences on damage limitations with the Leadership Conference (Mann, 1991). Congress followed with an overwhelming vote to approve the new legislation (93-5 in the Senate and 381-38 in the House).

Facing a tidal wave of opposition, the Bush administration reversed its position, and the president signed the 1991 Civil Rights Act. Nevertheless, on the day before the signing ceremony the White House staff issued a directive to federal agencies that would bar the federal government from enforcing "quotas, preferences, set-asides, or other similar devices" (Gigot, 1991). The directive was specifically designed to undercut the uniform guidelines administered by the EEOC.

Under a storm of protest including boycotts of the signing ceremony by several legislative and civil rights leaders, the Bush administration withdrew its directive. Nonetheless, the White House ordered federal agencies to interpret the 1991 Civil Rights Act on the basis of the *Wards Cove* decision—an interpretation that appears to directly contradict the act (Freiberg, 1992). Moreover, the threat of further administrative reaction remained as voiced by the soon-to-be-departed chief of the White House, John Sununu, who rationalized that the withdrawal did not reflect disagreement on the substance of the directive but rather on the timing (Gigot, 1991).

Certainly, questions persist about how the courts and EEOC will interpret the 1991 Act. The quota issue remains the most highly charged question to be decided. Opponents argue that despite the explicit language to the contrary, the Act still encourages quotas particularly for employers facing budgetary constraints. These critics hold that certain stipulations in the act, particularly those broadening permitted punitive damages and shifting the burden of proof to the employer, will prove too onerous for employers facing budgetary constraints. Rather than spending funds to validate their selection methods, those employers will opt instead for informal quotas that reduce the likelihood of a suit based on disparate impact (Ross, 1990; Noah and Karr, 1991).

Advocates of the act disagree with the concerns regarding punitive damages and burden of proof. They assert that the damage limitation established for suits based on gender, religious affiliation, and disability are well within the average amount awarded by the courts in findings of racial bias and that the burden of proof appropriately returns to the party most able to bear those economic costs—the employer (Freiberg, 1992). In sum, the bill essentially returns the legal playing field to the conditions experienced before 1989, and those conditions did not unleash a rush to quotas.

The case of the 1964 and 1991 civil rights acts suggests that managers who want to be flexible and open to the future in EEO program planning should be sensitive to the possibilities of policy change beyond the courts. To be sure, the conventional pattern will remain that administrative agencies interpret the law and the courts sit in judgment on that interpretation. Nonetheless, there are routes to be taken if any one branch disagrees with policy. Certainly, returning to the legislature is not the first choice of advocates for a particular interpretation of the EEO law. That avenue is costly and time consuming. However, that route always remains open. The effective manager will design EEO programming with alternative futures in mind.

2. Other Open Issues

EEO law has been on the books since the mid-1960s, and the courts, the administrative interpreters, legislative bodies, and time have all contributed to its expansion and comprehensibility. In three areas—employment of the disabled, sexual harassment, and women in management—a still-unfolding process raises critical concerns about the role each branch of government will play in refining EEO and holds some important insights on future policy trends for the public manager.

a. Employment of the Differently Abled. With the passage of the Americans with Disabilities Act and the issuance of administrative guidelines, the courts now shoulder the responsibility for interpreting the act. With regard to the employment provisions, two key definitions—essential job functions and reasonable accommodation—will require substantial judicial clarification.

Under ADA, employers cannot discriminate against disabled individuals who are able to perform the essential job functions, with or without reasonable accommodation. "Essential job functions" is not specifically defined by the act, but it can be inferred that the phrase refers to the primary duties intrinsic to a position, not marginal or peripheral duties that are incidental to performing the primary job duties. The act does explicate several methods for identifying the essential job functions including the employer's judgment, written job descriptions, the amount of time it takes to perform the function, the consequences of not performing that function, and the work experience of current employees in similar jobs.

The courts will frequently be asked to make judgments about this definition. For example, firefighters in a particular municipality rarely have to pull victims out of a burning house, and when they do, any one of several members of a fire-fighting unit could respond. Is that ability sufficiently critical to be termed an essential function?

The act sets forth several examples of possible reasonable accommodations, such as making existing facilities accessible and usable; the acquiring or modifying equipment or devices; providing of qualified readers or interpreters; appropriately adjusting or modifying examinations, modifying work schedules, and restructuring jobs. The act does not require employers to fundamentally alter the essential functions of a job to make reasonable accommodation or to undertake changes that would create an "undue hardship." Undue hardship is defined in terms of several factors including the nature and cost of the accommodation required, financial resources, and the size of the organization.

The courts will be asked to decide how much weight to give these factors to determine if individual employers must make reasonable accommodation. To illustrate, if writing investigative reports is an essential function for a police investigator, must a department provide secretarial support for an investigator with dyslexia?

Other types of employment issues covered by ADA will certainly receive judicial scrutiny. Perhaps the most explosive of these will be the employer's obligation to hire the disabled regardless of the effect on the cost of benefits. One could imagine the hypothetical case of a rejected job candidate who has a condition covered under the act that requires expensive medical treatment questioning the basis of an employer's decision to reject her. Moreover, scientific advances enable employer's decision to reject her. Moreover, scientific advances enable employers to use genetic testing to screen candidates. Testing for some diseases, such as sickle cell anemia in African-Americans, might be prohibited as race discrimination under the Civil Rights Act. Will the courts rule out all genetic tests under ADA because they discriminate against individuals regarded as having an impairment (Zeitz, 1991)? All of these questions remain to be answered.

b.   Sexual harassment.   While future policy initiatives concerning the disabled will likely stem from the judicial system, administrative actions will probably have the biggest impact on policy in the area of sexual harassment. The courts have set forth their interpretation of the law quite clearly. As explained in Section I of this chapter, the courts, having established that sexual harassment claims are actionable under Title VII, hold employers responsible not only for the loss of tangible job benefits of sexually harassed employees but for the psychological aspects of the workplace.

The latter source of liability particularly has placed the onus on employers to become proactive. Administrators should recognize, not tolerate, and respond appropriately to sexually harassing behavior in the workplace. A policy against sexual harassment and a grievance procedure is not sufficient. Employers should also establish special training programs, conduct relevant employee surveys, investigate claims appropriately, and administer proper disciplinary action.

Ongoing special training programs are needed to alert employees to the nature of the problem. In many cases, sexual harassment is difficult to define. Several forms of behaviors, such as attempted rape or sexual assault, may be confidently termed "sexual harassment" when they affect the conditions or the environment of employment, but other types of behavior, such as unwelcome sexual advances, joking, or suggestive looking, may or may not. Whether these latter behaviors can be termed sexual harassment depends largely on the perceptions and responses of the potential victim. Training programs should help employees understand the potential problems caused by such behavior and should also inform employees about their rights and proper courses of action. Even in the federal government, which has developed progressive sexual harassment programs, which has developed progressive sexual harassment programs, many employees still do not understand their legal rights or the remedies available to them (U.S. Merit Systems Protection Board, 1988).

Employee surveys may be helpful for designing further training and for better understanding the extent and nature of the problem. To deal with complaints, investigative procedures should be developed that fairly and impartially treat alleged victims and perpetrators. These investigations should be carried out discreetly to protect the interests of all parties. Also, counseling should be made available to the affected parties. Finally, proper disciplinary action should be taken against proven perpetrators or against alleged victims who have made false accusations (Neugarten, 1990).

d.   Women in Management.   Unlike the other issues discussed in this section, the initiative for addressing the underrepresentation of women in management does not appear to lie with any particular branch of government at this time. Rather, the problem requires simultaneous action at all levels and in all branches of government. Statistically, women are well represented on the management level in our public organizations (better represented than in private organizations), but they are concentrated in the low to middle levels (Franklin and Sweeney, 1988). Although women have made some gains since the civil rights legislation of the 1960s, they still compose less than 8% of top management positions at all levels of government (Fox, 1987; Slack, 1987). Moreover, since 1980, sex discrimination complaints with EEOC have risen over 14% annually.

The reasons for this underrepresentation are multiple and complex. Women are often socialized to view their professional careers as secondary to the family caretaker role. To move up the organization, women must demonstrate their abilities on the job to a greater extent than men. Yet, when they enter organizations, women often encounter structural and situational barriers that impede their progress, such as travel and leave requirements that conflict with their role as family caretaker. Moreover, aspiring women have less support than men. Although most high-level managers attribute their professional success to having worked closely with a mentor of the same sex, there are obviously fewer female role models in top management (Guy, 1990).

The courts' interpretations of the Civil Rights Act will certainly influence the progress that women make. However, legislative and administrative initiatives are also critical. Congress provided a mechanism for studying the problem further when it passed the 1991 Civil Rights Act. Title II of that act, called the Glass Ceiling Act of 1991, established a commission to study artificial barriers to the advancement of women and minorities in the workplace and to make recommendations for overcoming those barriers. Some public managers are also beginning to address causes of the problem by establishing on-site day care centers, by increasing the percentage of women promoted from lower levels, by closely tracking the advancement of women in the organization, by establishing mentoring programs, and by offering training designed to counter the stereotypes facing female managers (Guy, 1990).

Again, in this area, the issue remains somewhat open with legal interpretations and further research into the nature of the problem and of the effectiveness of current programs holding the key to management action.

V. CONCLUSION

This chapter was premised on the thesis that assuring equal employment opportunity in the organization turns of qualities of organizational management. EEO progress is fueled by a management knowledgeable about EEO policy and its institutional regulators, sensitive to the equity issues involved, and cognizant of the constraints and opportunities inherent in the managerial role. Today the human resource may be the most critical element in the manager's resource package. Effective management of those total resources may pivot largely on the executive's capacity to assure genuine equality of opportunity within the organization. From the perspective of EEO implementation, we can increasingly expect changes in EEO policy to occur less at the center and more at the margins of public policy as it is now defined. To the measure that this forecast is on target, the strategic factors in assuring success are management knowledge of, skill in, and commitment to equal employment opportunity as public policy.

REFERENCES

Albermarle Paper Company v. Moody (1975). 422 U.S. 405.

Allred, S. (1990). *Local Government Employment Law in North Carolina*, Institute of Government, University of North Carolina at Chapel Hill.

American Federation of State, County, and Municipal Employees v. State of Washington (1983). 770 F.2d 1401.

Argyris, C. (1964). *Integrating the Individual into the Organization*, Wiley, New York.

Bar-On, Dorit (1990). Discrimination, individual justice and preferential treatment, *Public Affairs Quart.*, *4(2)*: 111–137.

Barnes v. Costle (1977). 561 F.2d 983.

Berl v. Westchester County (1988). 849 F.2d 712.

Black, V. (1974). The erosion of legal principles in the creation of legal policies, *Ethics, 84*: 72–74.

Blumrosen, A. W. (1972). Strangers in paradise: *Griggs vs. Duke Power Company* and the concept of employment discrimination, *Michigan Law Rev., 71*: 59–110.

Broxhill, B. (1972). The morality of reparations, *Social Theory Pract., 2*: 113–122.

Carson, K. P. (November 22, 1991). New civil rights law shoots itself in the foot, *New York Times*, p. A12.

Cascio, Wayne F. (1987). *Applied Psychology in Personnel Management*, Prentice-Hall, Englewood Cliffs, NJ.

Chapple, E. D., and Sayles, L. R. (1961). *The Measure of Management: Designing Organizations for Human Effectiveness*, Macmillan, New York.

City of Richmond v. J.A. Croson Company (1989). 488 U.S. 469.

Cohen, C. (1975). Race and the Constitution. *The Nation, 2*: 8.

Coleman v. Casey (1980). 510 F. Supp. 301.

Communications Workers of America v. EEOC (1978). 556 F.2d 167, Cert. Den., 438 U.S. 915.

Connecticut v. Teal (1982). 457 U.S. 440.

County of Washington v. Gunther (1981). 452 U.S. 161.

Crosby, F., and Clayton, S. (1990). Affirmative action and the issue of expectancies, *J. Social Issues, 46(2)*: 61–79.

Dye, T. R. (1987). *Understand Public Policy*, 6th Ed. Prentice-Hall, Englewood Cliffs, NJ.

EEO Compliance Manual (1979). Prentice-Hall, Englewood Cliffs, NJ, par. 70,053.

EEOC v. City of East Providence (1986). 798 F.2d 524.

EEOC v. Missouri State State Highway Patrol (1985). 474 U.S. 828, Cert. Den., 474 U.S. 860.

EEOC v. Pennsylvania (1987). 485 U.S. 935, Cert. Den., 485 U.S. 935.

Fairfield-Sonn, J. W. (1984). Work group reactions to new members: Tool or trap in making selection decisions? *Public Personnel Manage. J., 13(4)*: 485–493.

Firefighters Local Union No. 1784 v. Stotts (1984). 467 U.S. 561.

Fox, S. F. (1987). Rights and obligations: critical feminist theory, the public bureaucracy, and policies for mother-only families. *Public Admin. Rev., 47*: 436–440.

Franklin, D. W., and Sweeney, J. L. (1988). Women and corporate power, *Women Power and Policy* (E. Boneparth and E. Stoper, eds.), Pergamon Press, New York.

Franks v. Bowman Transportation Company (1976). 424 U.S. 747.

Freiberg, P. (1992). Civil rights act is signed. *APA Monitor, 23(1)*: 12.

Garcia v. San Antonio Metropolitan Transit Authority (1985). 469 U.S. 528.

Gellar v. Markham (1980). 451 U.S. 945., Cert. Den., 451 U.S. 945, Cert. Den. 451 U.S. 945.

Gigot, P. (1991, November 22). Without beliefs, Bush stumbles into Carterism, *Wall Street Journal*, p. A12.

Graham, C. B. (1990). Equal employment opportunity and affirmative action: Policies, techniques, and controversies, *Public Personnel Administration: Problems and Prospects* (S. Hayes and R. Kearney, eds.), Prentice-Hall, Engelwood Cliffs, NJ.

Griggs v. Duke Power Company (1971). 401 U.S. 424.

Gunther v. The County of Washington (1979). 9th Cir, 8-16-79, No. 76-3448.

Guy, M. E. (1990). Women in management, *Public Personnel Administration: Problems and Prospects* (S. Hayes and R. Kearney, eds.), Prentice Hall, Engelwood Cliffs, NJ.

Haughton v. McDonnell Douglas Corporation (1977). 553 F. 2d 561, Cert. Den., 434 U.S. 966.

Hazelwood School District v. United States (1977). 433 U.S. 299.

Heiar v. Crawford County, Wisconsin (1985). 472 U.S. 1027, Cert. Den., 472 U.S. 1027.

Hodgson v. Daisy Manufacturing Company (1970). 445 F. 2d 823.

Holmes, S. (August 8, 1991). Mulling the idea of affirmative action for poor whites, *New York Times*, p. E3N, E3L.

Horner v. Mary Institute (1980). 1613 F. 2d 706.

Johansen, E. (1990). The comparable worth debate, *Public Personnel Administration: Problems and Prospects* (S. Hayes and R. Kearney, eds.), Prentice-Hall, Engelwood Cliffs, NJ.

Johnson v. Transportation Agency, Santa Clara County (1987). 480 U.S. 616.

Kanter, R. M. (1977). *Men and Women of the Corporation*, Basic Books, New York.

Kennedy, R. (1986). Persuasion and distrust: a comment in the affirmative action debate, *Harvard Law Rev., 99*: 1327–1344.

Laffey v. North West Airlines, Inc. (1976). 567F.2d 429.

Levine, C. H. and Nigro, L. (1975). The public personnel system: can juridical administration and manpower management coexist? *Public Admin. Rev., 35*: 98–107.

Local 28, Sheet Metal Workers International Association v. EEOC (1986). 478 U.S. 421.

Local 93, International Association of Firefighters v. City of Cleveland (1986). 478 U.S. 501.

Lorance v. AT&T (1989). 49 FEP Cases 1656.

Mann, J. (1991, May 24). Heartening ray of civility on civil rights, *Washington Post*, p. C3.

Martin v. Wilkes (1989). 109 S. Ct. 2180.

McDonald v. Santa Fe Trail Transportation Company (1976). 427 U.S. 273, 281.

McGregor, D. (1960). *The Human Side of Enterprise*, McGraw-Hill, New York.

Meritor Savings Bank v. Vinson (1986). 106 S.Ct. 2399.

Minas, A. C. (1977). How reverse discrimination compensates women, *Ethics, 88*: 74–79.

Nacoste, R. B. (1991). If empowerment is the goal. . . : Affirmative Action and Social Interaction. Paper presented at the Third International Conference on Social Justice Research.

Nagel, T. (1973). Equal treatment and compensatory discrimination, *Phil. Public Affairs, 2*: 348–363.

Nalbandian, J. (1981). From compliance to consultation: the changing role of the public personnel administrator, *Rev. Public Personnel Admin., 1*: 37–51.

Neugarten, D. A. (1990). Sexual harassment in public employment, *Public Personnel Administration: Problems and Prospects* (S. Hayes and R. Kearney, eds.), Prentice-Hall, Engelwood Cliffs, NJ.

Newton, L. H. (1973). Reverse discrimination is unjustified. *Ethics, 83*: 308–312.

Noah, T., and Karr, A. (November 4, 1991). What new civil rights law will mean. *Wall Street Journal*, p. B7.

Perman, F. (1988). The players and the problems in the EEO enforcement process: a status report, *Public Admin. Rev., 48*: 827–833.

Price v. Civil Service Commission (1980). 1-25-80, 80 Daily Journal, D.A.R. 273.

Price Waterhouse v. Hopkins (1989). 104 L.Ed.2d 268.

Pullman-Standard v. Swint (1982). 456 U.S. 273.

Roethlisberger, E. J., and Dickson, W. J. (1939). *Management and the Worker*, Harvard University Press, Cambridge, MA.

Ross, Patrick (1990). Are quotas making a comeback? *Personnel J., 9*: 42–44.

Schmitt, N., and Noe, R. A. (1986). Personnel selection and equal employment opportunity, *International Review of Industrial and Organizational Psychology* (M. Smith and I. Robertson, eds.), Wiley, New York.

School Board of Nassau County v. Arline (1987). 480 U.S. 273.

Sears, Roebuck, and Company v. Attorney General of the U.S. (D. D.C. 5-15-79) No. 79244.

Senate Committee on Labor and Public Welfare (1971). Senate Report 92-415, October 28, 1971.

Schultz v. Wheaton Glass Company (1970). 421 F.2d 257.

Shafritz, J. (1974). The cancer eroding the public personnel professionalism, *Public Personnel Manage., 3*: 486–492.

Shaw, B. (1988). Affirmative Action: an ethical evaluation, *J. Bus. Ethics, 7*: 763–770.

Sher, G. (1975). Justifying reverse discrimination in employment, *Phil. Public Affairs, 4*: 159–170.

Slack, J. D. (1987). Affirmative action and city managers: attitudes toward recruitment of women, *Public Admin. Rev., 47*: 199–206.

Sniderman, Paul, et al., (1991). The new politics of race. Paper presented at the Annual Meeting of the American Political Science Association Meetings.

Stein, H. (1991, September 3). On discrimination, *Wall Street Journal*, p. A18.

Straus, S. K. (1991). Multiple activities constituencies and constituencies and standards: a framework for evaluating the effectiveness of public personnel departments, *Rev. Public Personnel Admin., 11*: 55–70.

Straus, S. K. (1988). Selecting Employees Though Systematic Interviewing, *Popular Government, 53*(4): 21–26.

Stutts v. Freeman (1983). 694 F.2d 666.

Subcommittee of the Committee on Government Affairs (1987, June 25). *Processing EEO Complaints in the Federal Sector: Problems and Solutions*, p. 1.

Susser, P. A. (1990). The ADA: dramatically expanded federal rights for disabled Americans, *Employee Relations Law J., 16*: 157–176.

Taylor, P. W. (1973). Reverse discrimination and compensatory justice. *Analysis, 33*: 177–182.

Teamsters v. United States (1977). 431 U.S. 324.

Thompson, J. J. (1975). Preferential hiring. *Phil. Public Affairs, 2*: 364–384.

Thompson, F. J. (1984). Deregulation at the EEOC: Prospects and implications. *Rev. Public Personnel Admin., 4*: 41–56.

United States Merit Systems Protection Board (1981). *Sexual Harassment in the Federal Workplace: Is It a Problem?* 344 46 3. Government Printing Office, Washington, D.C.

United States v. Paradise (1987). 480 U.S. 149.

United Steel Workers of America v. Weber (1978). 443 U.S. 193.

Vickers v. Veterans Administration (1982). 549 F. Supp 85.

Vogt, J., and Murrel, K. L. (1990). *Empowerment in Organizations*, University Associates, San Diego.

Warren, M. A. (1977). Secondary sexism in quota hiring. *Phil. Public Affairs, 6*: 240–261.

Wards Cove Packing Company v. Atonio (1989). 109 S. Ct. 2115.

Washington v. Davis (1976). 426 U.S. 229.

Watson v. Ft. Worth Savings and Loan (1988). 487 U.S. 977.

Weeks v. Southern Bell Telephone and Telegraph Company (1969). 408 F. 2d 228.

Williams, W. (1985, June 9). White collar crime: booming again, *New York Times*, pp. 1F, 6F.

Wilson v. Southwest Airlines (1981). 517 F.2d 712.

Wygant v. Jackson Board of Education (1986). 476 U.S. 267.

Zalesnik, A., and Moment, D. (1964). *The Dynamics of Interpersonal Behavior*, Wiley, New York.

Zeitz, K. (1991). Employer genetic testing: a legitimate screening device or another method of discrimination? *Labor Law J., 4*: 230–238.

4

Public Personnel Administration and Law

DAVID H. ROSENBLOOM   American University, Washington, D.C.

JAMES D. CARROLL   Florida International University, North Miami, Florida

Public personnel administration in the United States has always had a substantial legal framework. In part this reflects Americans' abiding distrust of government officeholders generally. The Declaration of Independence complains that King George III "erected a Multitude of new Offices, and sent hither Swarms of Officers to harass our People, and eat out their Substance." Article II of the Constitution provides that federal offices "shall be established by law" and thereby vests a great deal of responsibility for personnel matters in Congress. However, it was not until the enactment of the Civil Service Act (Pendleton Act) of 1883 that the modern system of personnel law began to develop. Today that system is usefully conceptualized as consisting of two tiers: one of constitutional principles and the other of statutory and administrative regulations. A comprehensive detailed treatise on the law of public personnel administration in the United States would be a multivolume work. The objective of this chapter is more modest. It is to explain the development and general content of public personnel administration's legal framework. The discussion consists of two parts: Part I presents the constitutional law of public personnel administration; Part II provides an overview of the statutory framework for federal personnel management.

I   THE CONSTITUTION AND PUBLIC PERSONNEL ADMINISTRATION

A.   General Considerations

1.   The Scope of Executive Power

Personnel administration is intimately connected to executive power because executives are charged with faithful execution of the law and with the implementation of legislative policy. At the federal level, the main historical issue has been whether the Constitution allows the president to dismiss those personnel who are appointed with the advice and consent of the Senate alone, or whether the concurrence of that body is necessary. The larger the Senate's role in dismissals, of course, the greater its leverage over the operation of executive branch agencies.

The Constitution itself is unclear regarding the dismissal of federal employees. It allows removal upon impeachment, but this has been interpreted as a legislative check on the executive rather than the only means of termination. Writing in *Federalist Paper* No. 77, Hamilton indicated that

> it has been mentioned as one of the advantages to be expected from the co-operation of the Senate, in the business of appointments, that it would contribute to the stability of the ad-

ministration. The consent of that body would be necessary to displace as well as to appoint. A change of the Chief Magistrate, therefore, would not occasion so violent or so general revolution in the officers of the government as might be expected if he were the sole disposer of offices (Publius, 1961, p. 459).

But, in this instance, Hamilton was less than prescient.

In the course of establishing the Department of Foreign Affairs in 1789, Congress fully confronted the issue of the president's removal power. Members of the House and Senate set forth four constitutional interpretations:

1. That the power to remove was part of the executive power granted to the president by the Constitution and therefore his to exercise without the consent of the Senate
2. That the power to remove was connected to the power to appoint and therefore the Constitution required the Senate's concurrence
3. That the only constitutional means of removal was through impeachment
4. That since all offices must be established by law, the Constitution gave Congress the power to decide where to vest the removal power

The Decision of 1789 was that the president alone was authorized to dismiss the Secretary of Foreign Affairs. Congress reached this conclusion by a vote in the House of Representatives of 31:19 (with 9 not voting) and by virtue of Vice President John Adams's tie-breaking vote in the Senate. However, the decision was not a clear constitutional precedent because the majority in favor of it included those who subscribed to the position that the removal power was part of the executive's constitutional power as well as those who believed that Congress had the power to control removals but that, as a matter of policy, it should vest that power in the president alone (see Rohr, 1989 for a comprehensive discussion).

The Decision of 1789 was nullified by the Tenure of Office Act of 1867, which provided the legal basis for the impeachment proceedings against President Andrew Johnson. Failure to convict Johnson for firing the Secretary of War Edwin Stanton without the Senate's consent hardly resolved the constitutional issue, which arose again in *Myers v. United States* (1926).

Myers was a postmaster in Portland, Oregon, who had been appointed for a 4-year term under a statute that provided such officials "shall be appointed and may be removed by the President with the advice and consent of the Senate." After President Wilson removed Myers before the expiration of his term and without the consent of the Senate, Myers sued for back pay. The government counterargued that the power to remove such appointees was granted to the president alone as part of the executive power contained in Article II of the Constitution. Chief Justice Taft, who had been president from 1909 to 1913, spoke for the Supreme Court's majority in reasoning that the government's position was correct because "made responsible under the Constitution for the effective enforcement of the law, the President needs as an indispensable aid to meet it the disciplinary influence upon those who act under him of a reserve power of removal" (*Myers v. U.S.*, 1926, p. 132). However, the case was not an easy one. There were three dissenters and the entire text of the decision runs almost 300 pages. Moreover, the majority conceded that its interpretation of Article II did not apply to "inferior officers" whose removal could be regulated by Congress under Article II, §2, which allows the legislature to vest appointment "in the President alone, in the Courts of Law, or in the Heads of Departments."

The scope of the *Myers* decision was subsequently limited by Supreme Court rulings that the president's power under Article II to dismiss those appointed with the advice and consent of the Senate without that body's concurrence applied only to those officers whose functions were purely executive. *Humphrey's Executor v. United States* (1935) concerned the dismissal of William

Humphrey, who had been appointed to the Federal Trade Commission (FTC) by President Hoover for a 7-year term expiring in 1938. The FTC Act provides that such an appointee can be removed during his or her term "by the President for inefficiency, neglect of duty, or malfeasance in office." However, President Franklin D. Roosevelt sought to dismiss Humphrey not for any of these reasons but because he thought "that the aims and purposes of the Administration with respect to the work of the Commission can be carried out most effectively with personnel of my own selection" (*Humphrey's Executor v. U.S.*, 1935, p. 618). Humphrey declined to resign and was removed by the president. He never acquiesced in his dismissal and continued to consider himself part of the FTC.

Humphrey's suit for back pay eventually reached the Supreme Court. Justice Sutherland's opinion for the Court severely narrowed the import of the *Myers* holding: "The necessary reach of the decision goes far enough to include all purely executive officers. It goes no farther; much less does it include an officer who occupies no place in the executive department and who exercises no part of the executive power vested by the Constitution in the President" (*Humphrey's Executive v. U.S.*, 1935, pp. 627–628). Sutherland went on to explain that the FTC is "wholly disconnected from the executive department" and "was created by Congress as a means of carrying into operation legislative and judicial powers, and as an agency of the legislative and judicial departments" (p. 630). Therefore, Congress could by statute specify the grounds on which an officer like Humphrey could be dismissed by the president.

The Humphrey decision was a blow to executive power over independent commissions and agencies. By the late 1930s, it was common to refer to such units as comprising a "headless fourth branch" of government and efforts were made, unsuccessfully, to consolidate them into the executive branch departments (President's Committee on Administrative Management, 1937). In theory and practice, the independence of such units was strengthened by the next major case in this line to be decided by the Supreme Court.

In *Weiner v. United States* (1958), the Court held that the president lacked the constitutional power to dismiss a member of the War Claims Commission, even though in creating the agency Congress did not specify a removal procedure or permissible grounds for dismissals. The Court reasoned that because the Commission's functions were essentially judicial, the limited executive power of removal as articulated in *Myers* did not reach its appointees.

Morrison v. Olson (1988) is the Supreme Court's most recent major decision in the line of cases dating back to *Myers*. *Morrison* involved the constitutionality of several provisions of the Ethics in Government Act of 1978. The Act created a special court, called the Special Division, and authorized it to appoint an independent counsel, who was located in the Department of Justice and who could be removed from office by the attorney general only for good cause. The independent counsel, as the title suggests, enjoyed autonomy in exercising her prosecutorial powers. Among the issues analyzed by the Court were the Act's constitutionality under the appointments clause and whether, taken as a whole, it violated the separation of powers. The appointments clause of Article II provides that the president:

> shall nominate, and by and with the Advice and Consent of the Senate, shall appoint Ambassadors, other public Ministers and Consuls, Judges of the supreme Court, and all other Officers of the United States, whose Appointments are not herein otherwise provided for, and which shall be established by Law: but the Congress may by Law vest the Appointment of such inferior Officers, as they think proper, in the President alone, in the Courts of Law, or in the Heads of Departments (Article II, §2, clause 2).

The clause would be violated if the independent counsel were a principal (i.e., not an "inferior") officer, whose appointment must be vested in the president with the advice and consent of the

Senate. It would also be infringed if it were read to prohibit Congress from creating "interbranch" appointments, such as that involved in the appointment of the independent counsel by a court.

The Court, per Chief Justice William Rehnquist, interpreted Congress's powers very broadly. It found no constitutional infirmity with respect to the appointments clause. Rehnquist noted that "the line between 'inferior' and 'principal' officers is one that is far from clear, and the Framers provided little guidance into where it should be drawn" (*Morrison v. Olson*, 1988, p. 671). However, he concluded that the independent counsel was an inferior officer because (1) she was subject to removal by a higher executive branch official; (2) she had only certain, limited duties; (3) she had limited jurisdiction; and (4) her term was limited. Regarding interbranch appointments, the Court noted that while such appointments could violate the separation of powers and/or be unconstitutionally incongruous, it is not "impermissible for Congress to vest the power to appoint independent counsel in a specially created federal court" (*Morrison v. Olson*, 1988, p. 676).

Upon turning to the larger separation-of-powers questions, the Court addressed two issues. First, it addressed whether the limitation on dismissal of the special counsel violated the executive power in Article II as interpreted by *Myers*. Here, the Court articulated a highly flexible approach:

> . . . our present considered view is that the determination of whether the Constitution allows Congress to impose a "good cause"-type restriction on the President's power to remove an official cannot be made to turn on whether or not that official is classified as "purely executive." The analysis contained in our removal cases is designed not to define rigid categories of those officials who may or may not be removed at will by the President, but to ensure that Congress does not interfere with the President's exercise of the "executive power" and his constitutionally appointed duty to "take care that the laws be faithfully executed" under Article II (*Morrison v. Olson*, 1988, pp. 689–690).

In other words, the "real question is whether the removal restrictions are of such a nature that they impede the President's ability to perform his constitutional duty" (*Morrison v. Olson*, 1988, p. 691). The Court's answer was that the Act did not impermissibly burden presidential power in this regard.

A second separation-of-powers issue was whether the act unduly interfered with the executive branch's role in government. The Court concluded that it did not because the attorney general retained substantial controls over the independent counsel. Among these were that the appointment of a special counsel depended on a request for one by the attorney general; that, as already discussed, the attorney general could dismiss the independent counsel for good cause; and, finally, that the attorney general plays a substantial role in defining the independent counsel's jurisdiction.

The full import of the Court's decision in *Morrison* was perhaps best brought out by Justice Scalia in dissent:

> There are now no lines. If the removal of a prosecutor, the virtual embodiment of the power to "take care that the laws be faithfully executed," can be restricted, what officer's removal cannot? This is an open invitation for Congress to experiment (*Morrison v. Olson*, 1988, p. 726).

He went on to say that "today's decision on the basic issue of fragmentation of executive power is ungoverned by rule, and hence ungoverned by law" (p. 733).

The net result of the line of cases dealing with the executive removal power is twofold. First, they recognize a very broad legislative power in fixing the conditions for the appointment and dismissal of inferior executive branch officers and the dismissal of agency appointees having other than purely executive functions. Under *Morrison*, as Scalia argued, it is conceivable that even the removal of assistant secretaries, who are confirmed by the Senate, could be limited by Congress (*Morrison v. Olson*, 1988, p. 726). Had these cases developed a broader conception of the executive power of removal, much of today's civil service law dealing with dismissals might have been found an unconstitutional legislative encroachment on executive power under Article II. Congress's power to vest the appointment of inferior officers in the president, the department heads, or courts does not have to be read to include the power to limit the removal of these appointees. But as Scalia's dissent in *Morrison* emphasizes, the Court has chosen to interpret Congress's powers as very great indeed. Second, other than separation-of-powers issues, the cases did not address constitutional limits on the reasons for which a federal appointee could be dismissed from office. Impeachment would have been impractical, even if just confined to the heads of departments and other high-ranking administrative officers. However, it would have guaranteed substantial job protection to such officials. As it turned out, it was not until the 1950s that the Constitution began to be read as an important constraint on the treatment of federal employees.

2. The Doctrine of Privilege

Until the 1950s, other than in the context of the scope of executive power, the Constitution was not a significant constraint on public personnel administration. The relationship between the government and its employees was conceptualized as similar to that between private employers and their workers. In practice, this meant that the government could place almost any conditions on its employees without violating the Constitution. This is because, with the exception of the Thirteenth Amendment, the private employment relationship is not directly constrained by the Constitution, which does not regulate purely private relationships other than slavery. Eventually, this approach to public employment was called the "doctrine of privilege." It drew a strict distinction between rights on the one hand and privileges on the other. Public employment was defined as a privilege to which and in which one had no rights. The public employee accepted his or her job along with all the conditions the government placed on it—including, for instance, being a member of the political party in power or not taking an active part in partisan campaigning. Not having a right to a position in the public service, the employee, upon dismissal, lost nothing to which he or she had a right. The most concise expression of this approach was Justice Oliver Wendell Holmes's holding while on the Supreme Court of Massachusetts that "the petitioner may have a constitutional right to talk politics, but he has no constitutional right to be a policeman" (*McAuliffe v. New Bedford*, 1892, p. 220). In sum, the doctrine's

> central premise is that office is held at the pleasure of the government. Its general effect is that the government may impose upon the public employee any requirement it sees fit as conditional to employment. From the point of view of the state, public employment is maintained as an indulgence; from the position of the citizen, his job is a grant concerning which he has no independent rights (Dotson, 1955, p. 77).

Historically, in the absence of constitutional constraints on their treatment of public employees, personnel practices often interfered substantially with such employees' ordinary constitutional rights as citizens. Dismissals based on political association occurred during the presidencies of John Adams and Thomas Jefferson and then became characteristic of the federal personnel system after the inauguration of President Andrew Jackson in 1829. Adams's dismissal of Trench Coxe, Commissioner of Revenue, in 1797 is believed to be the first partisan dismissal under the constitutional regime established in 1789 (Fish, 1905, p. 19). In 1801, Jefferson issued a circular that prohibited federal employees from attempting "to influence the votes of others, or tak[ing] any part in the business of electioneering, that being inconsistent with the spirit of the Constitution and his duties to it" (Richardson, 1899, Vol. 10, pp. 98–99). The Tenure of Office Act of 1820 confirmed the absence of constitutional protection in federal employment by placing a 4-year term on most employees handling public money. Moreover, the Act did not restrict dismissals during the term.

Nevertheless, until 1829, there was a broad sense that it was wrong to dismiss federal employees without cause. As Thomas Kinney, Superintendent of Indian Trade in 1816, expressed what appears to have been the prevailing mood:

> To dismiss from office, in those days, without cause, would have been deemed an outrage, not less against the public interest than the party proscribed. Hence competency, zeal, and honesty, being the characteristics of the clerks I found in the office of Indian Trade, when I succeeded to its management, it no more occurred to me to turn them out, than it did to cut their throats (White, 1965a, p. 511).

Further, it was common throughout the government to provide notice to individuals whose character was implicated by an impeding dismissal (Rosenbloom, 1971: 43). In some respects, office was even treated as a form of property that could be handed down within families (Rosenbloom, 1971, pp. 43–44).

The introduction of the spoils system by President Andrew Jackson in 1829 immensely strengthened the view that there were no constitutional constraints on the treatment of federal employees. It also led to a long eclipse of the view that public employees have a property interest in their jobs, which eventually gained clear constitutional dominance only in the 1980s. Jackson advocated rotation in office as "a leading principle in the republican creed" that would "give healthful action to the system" and would "destroy the idea of property now so generally connected with official station" (Richardson, 1899, Vol. 2, p. 449). Political opposition to Jackson's personnel "reforms," though substantial, crumbled in 1841 when the opposition party, the Whigs, led by William Henry Harrison and John Tyler, embraced it. Any prospect of constitutional impediment to dismissals at will was eliminated by the Supreme Court's decision in *Ex Parte Hennen* (1839).

The *Hennen* case involved the removal of a clerk in a federal district court for reasons having nothing to do with his performance or conduct. The federal judge who dismissed him explained that

> unreservedly,. . . . the business of the office for the last two years had been conducted promptly, skilfully and uprightly, and that, in appointing . . . [a successor], he had been actuated purely by a sense of duty and feelings of kindness towards one whom he had long known, and between whom and himself the closest friendship had ever subsisted (*Ex Parte Hennen*, 1839, p. 256).

The dismissal was arbitrary. However, the Supreme Court was not ready to find a constitutional constraint on it. The Court held that "it cannot be admitted that it was the intention of the Constitution, that those offices which are denominated inferior offices should be held during life" (*Ex Parte Hennen*, 1839, p. 259). Therefore, in its view, Hennen had no right to the office and could be dismissed for any reason.

By today's standards, the Court's reasoning in *Hennen* was unsophisticated or even erroneous. Arbitrary dismissals can be constrained by the Constitution without declaring that offices are held for life. But one precedent before the Court was *Hoke v. Henderson* (1833), a North Carolina case holding that public office was a property right and the law at the time apparently suggested no middle ground.

The *Hennen* decision condoned a host of practices that became associated with the spoils system. Partisan removals were standard operating procedure. Employees were forced to contribute a portion of their salaries, generally between 1% and 6%, to the party in power (Rosenbloom, 1971, p. 63). They were also coerced into electioneering and other partisan activity.

The advent of civil service reform in the 1870s and 1880s (discussed below) sought to end these practices. But it too placed restrictions on the ordinary constitutional rights of public employees. The reformers generally though the best way to eliminate partisanship within the federal service, voluntary or coerced, was to prohibit employees from engaging in partisan activity itself. Section 6 of an act of August 15, 1876 provided that

> all executive officers or employees of the United States not appointed by the President, with the advice and consent of the senate, are prohibited from requesting, giving to, or receiving from, any other officer or employee of the government any money or property or other thing of value for political purposes (*Ex Parte Curtis*, 1882, p. 371).

The Supreme Court upheld the law's constitutionality on the grounds that Congress could use its legislative power to promote the efficiency of the civil service and could legitimately place restrictions on federal employees for this end. Moreover, the act was not a major interference with the political rights of the employees because it did not prohibit them from giving funds to political parties. Rather it only prohibited such giving through officers appointed by the President with the advice and consent of the Senate. It is interesting to note, however, that Justice Bradley dissented on the basis that Congress lacked the constitutional authority to prohibit voluntary political contributions by federal employees.

In a sense, the logic of the *Curtis* decision remains good law to this day. Political neutrality requirements, such as the Hatch Acts, have been repeatedly upheld by the Supreme Court (see discussion below). However, political neutrality has become a clear exception to the constitutional law of public employment generally and is best viewed as an anomaly.

The doctrine of privilege also permitted discrimination against people based on their social characteristics, including race and gender (Rosenbloom, 1977, chapter 3). An 1810 law barring blacks from conveying the mail was reenacted in 1825, though modified by departmental order in 1828 to allow African-Americans to carry mailbags from stage coaches to post offices under the supervision of whites (*Statutes at Large*, 1825, Vol. 4, p. 104). Although it was repealed in 1865—after several attempts—discrimination against blacks in the federal service was common. Racial segregation was established in the federal service in Washington, D.C. under President Woodrow Wilson, who believed it to be in the interest of African-Americans (Rosenbloom, 1977, p. 54). By the 1920s, physical separation of the races was common in the offices, cafeterias, and restrooms of several large agencies (Rosenbloom, 1977, p. 55).

Women were also barred by law from some jobs and discriminated against generally. An 1870 statute allowed the department heads to appoint women to clerkships at their discretion (Rosenbloom, 1977, p. 56). Unequal pay was legally condoned until the Classification Act of 1923 provided that the principle of equal compensation for equal work irrespective of sex would be followed. Some regulations discriminated against married women (Rosenbloom, 1977, p. 57). Even after gaining entrance to the federal service, women were very disproportionately confined to its lower levels.

The Fourteenth Amendment (1868), which prohibits the states from denying persons within their jurisdictions equal protection under the laws, could have been read to prohibit discrimination based on race or sex. However, the logic of the doctrine of privilege and prevailing social practice were strong enough to prevent such a general interpretation until the 1950s and later.

Indeed, some court decisions were remarkable in their assertions that public employment was unrestrained by the Constitution. In 1917, the Supreme Court of Illinois held that

> the [school] board has the absolute right to decline to employ or reemploy any applicant for any reason whatever or for no reason at all. . . . It is no infringement upon the constitutional rights of anyone for the board to decline to employ him . . and it is immaterial whether the reason for the refusal . . is because the applicant is married or unmarried, is of fair complexion or dark, is or is not a member of a trades union, or whether no reason is given for such refusal (*Fursman v. Chicago*, 1917, p. 318).

As late as 1939, a federal district court in Maryland found no constitutional barrier to unequal salaries for white and African-American school teachers in racially segregated systems. In *Mills v. Lowndes*, it held that "the right of the state to prescribe the qualifications for and the salary annexed to a public office . . . is ordinarily free from restriction; and it would not seem that a state employee who has accepted employment . . . could complain" (*Mills v. Lowndes*, 1939, p. 801).

3. The Demise of the Doctrine of Privilege

By the late 1940s, the Supreme Court began to show some unease with the logic of the doctrine of privilege. Greater racial equality had become an important federal policy goal. A Fair Employment Practice Committee had been created in 1941 to eliminate racial, ethnic, and religious discrimination in federal employment (see Rosenbloom, 1977, chapter 3) and civil rights had become an important political issue. In a case dealing with the constitutionality of political neutrality regulations under the Hatch Act, the Court had occasion to say:

> Appellants urge that federal employees are protected by the Bill of Rights and that Congress may not "enact a regulation providing that no Republican, Jew or Negro shall be appointed to federal office, or that no federal employee shall attend Mass or take any active part in missionary work." None would deny such limitations on Congressional power (*United Public Workers v. Mitchell*, 1947, p. 100).

The doctrine of privilege also fell under heavy attack as a result of widespread abuses under federal and other governmental loyalty/security programs that developed during the early cold war and McCarthy eras (see Rosenbloom, 1971, chapter 6). Under President Truman's "Loyalty Order" (Executive Order 9835, 1947), the loyalty of every person entering civilian federal employment was investigated and disloyal incumbent employees were to be dismissed. By contemporary standards, due process protections for applicants and employees were primitive. Originally the standard for action against an individual was that "reasonable grounds exist" for believing him or her to be disloyal to the government. In 1951, it was changed to whether there was a "reasonable doubt as to the loyalty of the person involved" (Executive Order 10241, 1951). However, loyalty was never fully defined and its meaning tended to be open-ended. The Loyalty Order was superseded by President Dwight D. Eisenhower's "Security Order" of 1953 (Executive Order 10450, 1953). It provided that the department and agency heads establish procedures to assure that the selection and retention of employees was "clearly consistent with the interests of the national security." Again, the key condition that would make one vulnerable under the order was ill defined. Theoretically, someone in a sensitive position who was careless with a briefcase or a secretary with "loose lips" could be considered a risk to national security. Several agencies treated the employment of homosexuals as *ipso facto* contrary to the interests of national security.

In practice, investigations of employees, interrogations of them, and charges leveled under these programs ranged far and wide. Subjects of loyalty/security investigations were asked about their views on racial equality and female chastity; whether they read the *New York Times* and other material; whether they attended church services and provided religious training for their children; whether they believed in marriage; whether they believed in government ownership of public utilities; and whether they were sympathetic to the underprivileged (Rosenbloom, 1971, pp. 160–165). Eventually, litigation arising out of these kind of programs reached the Supreme Court and destroyed the foundation of the doctrine of privilege.

Bailey v. Richardson (1950) arose under the Loyalty Order. Dorothy Bailey was removed from a nonsensitive federal job after the government concluded that there were reasonable grounds for belief that she was disloyal. She had a hearing before the Fourth Regional Loyalty Board and, on appeal, the Loyalty Review Board (both of which were established pursuant to the Loyalty Order). She was not afforded an opportunity to confront or cross-examine the informants against her, whose statements were apparently unsworn and who were unknown to the hearing officials (Rosenbloom, 1971, p. 171). Among the matters of concern was whether she had ever written a letter to the Red Cross protesting the segregation of blood by race.

The constitutionality of Bailey's dismissal was eventually upheld by an equally divided Supreme Court. But the case exposed the central weakness of the doctrine of privilege. The majority on the Circuit Court of Appeals for the District of Columbia had clung tightly to the doctrine of privilege in finding that neither Bailey's hearings nor the reasons for her dismissal were unconstitutional. It found that she had no right to a fair procedure because "due process of law is not applicable unless one is being deprived of something to which he has a right" (*Bailey v. Richardson*, 1950, p. 58). Moreover,

> The plain hard fact is that so far as the Constitution is concerned there is no prohibition against the dismissal of Government employees because of their political beliefs, activities or affiliations. . . . The First Amendment guarantees free speech and assembly, but it does not guarantee Government employ (*Bailey v. Richardson*, 1950, p. 59).

Although the Supreme Court justices were deadlocked 4:4 (with Justice Thomas Clark, formerly attorney general taking no part), several expressed their views in another loyalty case decided the same day. Justices William O. Douglas and Robert Jackson explicitly rejected the logic of the doctrine of privilege. Jackson found it to be a non sequitur: "The fact that one may not have a legal right to get or keep a government post does not mean that he can be adjudged ineligible illegally" (*Joint Anti-Fascist Refugee Committee v. McGrath*, 1951, p. 185). Justice Black, who went on record against the doctrine of privilege in the *United Public Workers* (1947) political neutrality case, indicated that he would have reversed in *Bailey*, as did Justice Frankfurter. The latter clearly abandoned the doctrine of privilege a few months later in *Garner v. Los Angeles* (1951), another loyalty case: "It does not at all follow that because the Constitution does not guarantee a right to public employment, a city or a state may resort to any scheme for keeping people out of such employment. . . . To describe public employment as a privilege does not meet the problem" (*Garner v. Los Angeles*, 1951, p. 725).

The doctrine of privilege was finally rejected by the Court in a 1952 Oklahoma loyalty oath case. Justice Clark, writing for the majority, reasoned that

> we need not pause to consider whether an abstract right to public employment exists. It is sufficient to say that the constitutional protection does extend to the public servant whose exclusion pursuant to a statute is patently arbitrary or discriminatory (*Weiman v. Updegraff*, 1952, p. 192).

Subsequent cases solidified this rejection to the extent that in 1972 the Court stated that it had "fully and finally rejected the wooden distinction between 'rights' and 'privileges' that once seemed to govern the applicability of procedural due process rights" (*Board of Regents v. Roth*, 1972, p. 571). In 1973, it reiterated that "this Court has now rejected the concept that constitutional rights turn upon whether a governmental benefit is characterized as a 'right' or as a 'privilege'" (*Sugarman v. Dougall*, 1973, p. 644).

4. Collateral Constitutional Development: The Rise of "New Property"

In a brilliant analysis of the impact of the rise of the administrative state on the function of private property as a shield from governmental intrusion, Charles Reich observed:

> One of the most important developments in the United States during the past decade [1950s] has been the emergence of government as a major source of wealth. Government is a gigantic syphon. It draws in revenue and power, and pours forth wealth: money, benefits, services, contracts, franchises, and licenses. Government has always had this function. But while in early times it was minor, today's distribution of largess is on a vast, imperial scale.
>
> The valuables dispensed by government take many forms, but they all share one characteristic. They are steadily taking the place of traditional forms of wealth—forms which are held as private property. Social insurance substitutes for savings; a government contract replaces a businessman's customers and goodwill, the wealth of more and more Americans depends upon a relationship to government. Increasingly, Americans live on government largess (Reich, 1964, p. 733).

He correctly noted that in the absence of constitutional protections, the citizenry's dependence on government largess could lead to an erosion of their rights: "when government—national, state, or local—hands out something of value, whether a relief check or a television license, government's power grows forthwith; it automatically gains such power as is necessary and proper to supervise its largess. It obtains new rights to investigate, to regulate, and to punish" (Reich, 1964, p. 746). Examples of arbitrary administrative action infringing on the constitutional rights of the recipients of largess were replete (Rosenbloom, 1983, chapter 3).

Reich's solution to the threat posed by the administrative state to individual rights and independence was to constitutionalize largess as a form of "new property" entitled to protection under procedural due process. The Fifth and Fourteenth Amendment clauses prohibiting deprivation of "life, liberty, or property, without due process of law" would be read to protect largess as though it were traditional property. This is the revolutionary path that the Supreme Court eventually took.

By the early 1970s, the Court was clearly treating new property similarly to traditional property in important respects. In *Goldberg v. Kelly* (1970), a dissenting Justice Hugo Black captured the scope of the change:

> The Court . . . relies upon the Fourteenth Amendment and in effect says that the failure of the government to pay a promised charitable installment to an individual deprives that individual of *his own property*, in violation of the Due Process Clause of the Fourteenth Amendment. It somewhat strains credulity to say that the government's promise of charity to an individual is property belonging to that individual when the government denies that the individual is honestly entitled to receive such a payment (*Goldberg v. Kelly*, 1970, p. 275).

The Court noted that public employment could also be a property interest in *Board of Regents v. Roth* (1972) and *Perry v. Sindermann* (1972). In 1985, a majority of the Court had no difficulty finding that an Ohio civil service statute created "property rights in continued employment" (*Cleveland Board of Education v. Loudermill*, 1985, p. 538).

The new property approach protects one's property interests in largess against arbitrary or capricious deprivation by the government. General liberty interests are given similar protection under a variety of related approaches (Van Alstyne, 1968). In essence, the Bill of Rights has been brought to bear on both the citizen's encounters with government as a client and his or her interaction with it as a public employee.

B. The Contemporary Approach: The Public Service Model

Public employment is a subset of a larger constitutional picture that applies to other recipients of government benefits as well. It is also unique in several respects. Citizens have constitutional protections against government action, but the government cannot function as an efficient and effective employer if it does not have sufficient authority over its employees. To take a simple example, the government cannot tell a private individual seeking nothing from it what to wear or where and when to arrive at work or eat lunch. At the same time, though, the contemporary constitutional law does guarantee public employees a broad set of rights. Developing a constitutional doctrine that would clearly demarcate the line of acceptable governmental authority over public employees has been difficult.

Several approaches, or perhaps only tendencies, have been used, but all have been wanting in some respects. Initially, it appeared that an individual rights model might apply to the constitutional aspects of public personnel management. Such an approach would guarantee public employees a broad range of rights and liberties. A heavy burden would be placed on the government to show why it was necessary to deprive employees of their rights as ordinary citizens. For example, one court reasoned that a "citizen's right to engage in protected expression or debate is substantially unaffected by the fact that he is also an employee of government and as a general rule he cannot be deprived of his employment merely because he exercises those rights'" (*Kiiskila v. Nichols* 1970, p. 749). However, this approach seemed to put the government at a serious disadvantage in managing its employees and did not prevail, in part because President Richard Nixon appointed a number of conservative judges and justices to the bench (Rosenbloom, 1983, pp. 121–125).

If public employees could not have the full panoply of constitutional rights afforded to private citizens, they still were entitled to protections against the kind of abuses suffered by Dorothy Bailey, African-Americans, women, and others seeking or holding jobs in the public sector. Being unable to develop a general doctrine, the courts turned to a traditional legal incrementalism. They more or less reasoned that each nonrepetitive case should be decided on the basis of the individual facts and circumstances presented. For instance, under this approach it was permissible to ban aliens from some but not all public service jobs depending on how closely related the positions were to maintaining the values of political community (*Ambach v. Norwick*, 1979; *Foley v. Connelie*, 1978). Race might be used as a basis for making specific but not general personnel assignments (*Baker v. City of St. Petersburg*, 1968). Maternity leaves, other than those commencing very late in the normal term of pregnancy, had to be based on an individual medical determination (*Cleveland Board of Education v. LaFleur*, 1974).

The case-by-case approach to defining the constitutional rights of public employees may have promoted justice, but it also had a number of undesirable consequences. It promoted litigation as well. It failed to provide clear guidelines on the scope and structure of public employees' rights. Consequently, governmental employers had little instruction from the courts regarding how to think about the limits of their own authority. Nor did the approach seem to pay much attention to normal personnel categories such as classified, excepted, sensitive, and nonsensitive positions (Rosenbloom, 1975).

In the mid- to late 1970s, it appeared that the Supreme Court wanted to reduce the federal courts' involvement in public personnel management. The work load of the courts had been growing dramatically and it appeared that cuts would have to be made somewhere. Chief Justice Warren

Burger pointed out that the number of cases docketed by the Supreme Court had gown from 1092 in 1935 to over 4000 in 1975. He warned that "we must face up to the flinty reality that there is a necessity for a choice: If we wish to maintain the Court's historic function with a quality that will command public confidence, the demands we make on it must be reduced to what they were a generation ago" (*New York Times*, 1975, p. 31).

A majority on the Court seemed to agree with Burger. In a 1976 case it declared that "we must accept the harsh fact that numerous individual mistakes are inevitable in the day-to-day administration of our affairs. The United States Constitution cannot feasibly be construed to require federal judicial review for every such error" (*Bishop v. Wood*, 1976, pp. 349–350). In *Codd v. Velger* (1977) it held that procedural due process protections did not require a hearing where there was no factual dispute involved in the dismissal of a probationary employee. In *Washington v. Davis* (1976), the Court held that the Equal Protection Clause of the Fourteenth Amendment applied to public personnel only where racial or other covered discrimination was intentional.

Despite such cases, however, the judiciary did not disengage from public personnel administration. Rather, it slowly developed what is usefully referred to as the "public service model" for considering the constitutional rights of public employees (*Harvard Law Review*, 1984). Under this approach three sets of interests are taken into account in defining public employees' constitutional rights: (1) the employee's interests in exercising protected freedoms or enjoying constitutional protections; (2) the government's interest as an employer in dealing with its work force; and (3) the public's interest in the way its affairs are run by public administrators. Importantly, the public's interest can coincide with that of either the employee or the government, depending on the circumstances. For instance, the public has an interest in public employees' First Amendment rights to whistleblow as well as in the government's effort to promote cost-effective implementation of the law. However, a major difficulty with this model is that in several areas, including free speech and procedural due process, it requires elaborate balancing of concerns—and reasonable people may disagree on where the appropriate balance lies. Among its virtues, though, is that it clearly identifies the concerns that must be weighed and the model for balancing them.

We turn now to a review of the contemporary constitutional rights of public employees. The discussion is organized according to the order in which the relevant rights are found in the Constitution. The discussion focuses on U.S. Supreme Court decisions because they are more definitive than federal district and circuit court decisions, which do not apply nationally. State court decisions may effectively afford public employees more expansive rights under state constitutions than does the Supreme Court under the federal Constitution. However, a comprehensive comparative study of such decisions would be voluminous.

C. The Scope of Public Employees' Constitutional Rights Today

1. Nonpartisan Free Speech

The leading case regarding public employees' freedom to engage in nonpartisan speech is *Rankin v. McPherson* (1987). The case applied existing constitutional doctrine under *Pickering v. Board of Education* (1968) to what appears to be its outer limits. The Supreme Court took pains to explain the construction of the right involved. Ardith McPherson was a 19-year-old probationary clerical employee in the office of a constable in Texas. She had been talking with a coworker, who according to the Court was "apparently her boyfriend" (p. 381). Upon hearing that there was an attempted assassination of President Ronald Reagan, she remarked, ". . .Shoot, if they go for him again, I hope they get him" (p. 381). She may have intended the statement to convey her disgust with the impact of Reagan's administration on African-Americans. It was overheard by another employee, who reported it to Constable Rankin. Rankin discussed the remark with

McPherson, who admitted making it but claimed that she "didn't mean anything by it" (p. 382). Rankin dismissed her. The Court, by a 5:4 margin, found the dismissal in violation of McPherson's constitutional right to freedom of expression.

The majority noted that "even though McPherson was merely a probationary employee, and even if she could have been discharged for any reason or for no reason at all, she may nonetheless be entitled to reinstatement if she was discharged for exercising her constitutional right to freedom of expression" (pp. 383–384). It went on to outline the structure of that right:

> The determination whether a public employer has properly discharged an employee for engaging in speech requires "a balance between the interests of the [employee], as a citizen, in commenting upon matters of public concern and the interest of the State, as an employer, in promoting the efficiency of the public service it performs through its employees." . . . This balancing is necessary in order to accommodate the dual role of the public employer as a provider of public services and as a government entity operating under the constraints of the First Amendment (p. 384).

The public interest is brought into this balancing by the requirement that the employee's speech be on a matter of public concern. If an employee's remarks do not reach this threshold, then there is no public interest in them. Whether a remark is of public concern depends on its content, not the forum in which it is uttered. Some comments, including those relating to office management, may not reach the threshold. However, in many cases it will be a close call. The district court and four dissenting Supreme Court justices did not think McPherson's remark was on a matter of public concern. The court of appeals thought it was, as did the majority of the Supreme Court. Once the threshold issue of public concern is reached, the manner, time, and place in which the remark is made are of relevance. Private remarks by public employees on matters of public concern "will rarely, if ever, justify discharge of a public employee" (p. 327, note 13). By contrast, government action is more likely to be justified if the remark impairs discipline or harmony in the workplace, jeopardizes close working relationships, interferes with normal operations, or detracts from the employee's ability to do his or her job.

The nature of the employee's position is also important. The remarks of employees who do not hold confidential, policymaking, or public contact positions are generally less likely to be significantly damaging to the employer's interests as an employer. But even damaging remarks, if on matters of public concern as in the case of whistleblowing, will often be protected if they help inform the public about government operations. In principle, such remarks may be protected even if they are erroneous, as long as they are not made with reckless disregard for their truth or falsity or with the knowledge that they are false (*Pickering v. Board of Education*, 1968).

It is evident that the elaborate balancing of several factors under the *Rankin* case offers public administrators more guidance on how to think about public employees' freedom of expression and what factors to consider than on how to resolve difficult issues concretely. The law may be too complex to be implemented with confidence, except by giving employees' speech wide berth.

2. Partisan Expression and Activity

Public employees' partisan speech forms a major exception to the general constitutional law regarding their First Amendment rights. As noted above, the explanation for this is historical and jurisprudential. The idea of political neutrality at the national level was apparently first introduced by President Thomas Jefferson. Presidents William H. Harrison and John Tyler also considered it desirable to limit the partisan activity of federal employees (Richardson, 1899, Vol. 4, pp. 38, 52), as did Congress in 1839 (*Congressional Globe*, 1839, Part 1, pp. 59, 189). But it was the civil service reform movement of the 1870s–1890s that successfully implanted the idea that the public service should be removed from partisan politics.

It is necessary to understand the history of political neutrality in order to understand both the contemporary constitutional law and the debate regarding specific restrictions on the partisan activities of public employees. The civil service reformers viewed depoliticization of the public service as a means to a political end. For them, "the question [of] whether the Departments at Washington are managed well or badly [was], in proportion to the whole problem, an insignificant question" (Schurz, 1913, Vol. 2, p. 123). The significant issue was changing the quality of the nation's political leadership. The reformers believed that patronage and the mobilization of public employees for partisan ends enabled unfit politicians to gain substantial control of the political system. In the words of Carl Schurz, a federal official and reformer, the purpose of reform was to

> rescue our political parties, and in great measure the management of our public affairs, from the control of men whose whole statesmanship consists in the low arts of office mongering, and many of whom would never have risen to power had not the spoils system furnished them the means and opportunity for organizing gangs of political followers as mercenary as themselves (Schurz, 1893, p. 614).

Other leading reformers complained that machine politics excluded "able and upright men from public life" (Curtis, 1884, p. 19) and that "politics have tended more and more to become a trade, or separate occupation. High character and capacity have become disassociated from public life in the popular mind" (Eaton, 1880, p. 392). Their solution to the problem included eliminating patronage through the introduction of a merit system and prohibiting certain partisan activities on the part of public employees.

The struggle for political neutrality was difficult because the public service had been so intimately connected with political parties under the spoils system. The reformers viewed it as "one of the greatest anomalies of our politics . . . that we have had no prevailing public opinion which has fixed any well-defined limits to the use of official authority for political or even for partisan ends" (Eaton, 1880, pp. 409–410). But there is little evidence that the rest of the society found the system odd. Consequently, early reform efforts at establishing political neutrality were ineffective.

The first political neutrality order based on the concepts of reform was issued by President Rutherford B. Hayes in 1877:

> No officer should be required or permitted to take part in the management of political organizations, caucuses, conventions, or election campaigns. Their right to vote and to express their views on public questions, either orally or through the press is not denied, provided it does not interfere with the discharge of their official duties (Richardson, 1899, Vol. 7, pp. 450–451).

However, the order was not enforced (White, 1965b, p. 330).

Hayes's order was followed by one issued by President Grover Cleveland in 1886. Cleveland sought to prohibit federal employees from "offending by a display of obtrusive partisanship" (Richardson, 1899, Vol. 8, p. 494), but he apparently found activity by Republicans more offending and obtrusive and made dismissals accordingly (Sageser, 1935, p. 121).

A more lasting and effective system for political neutrality was introduced by President Theodore Roosevelt, who had been a reformer and Civil Service Commissioner among other political activities. After taking a limited step in the direction of political neutrality in 1902

(Rosenbloom, 1971, pp. 98–99), Roosevelt amended Civil Service Rule I by executive order to read:

> Persons who by the provisions of these rules are in the competitive classified service, while retaining the right to vote as they please and to express privately their opinions on all political subjects, shall take no active part in political management or in political campaigns (Civil Service Commission, 1907, p. 9).

Unlike earlier efforts, Rule I was effective and strictly enforced. By 1940, the enforcement agency, the U.S. Civil Service Commission (CSC), had developed something of a case law involving over 3000 decisions.

Nevertheless, the system of political neutrality was threatened with breakdown during the New Deal. Between President Franklin D. Roosevelt's inauguration in 1933 and the end of 1934, some 60 new agencies were created, with all but five being outside the jurisdiction of the CSC (Van Riper, 1958, p. 320). The number of employees who were covered by Rule I dropped from almost 80% in 1933 to about 66% in 1939, while the overall size of the federal service was growing rapidly. This situation raised considerable concern, as the following statement by Congressman Rees (R–Kansas) in 1939 indicates:

> We have created bureaus and commissions in the name of emergency, and have given them power and authority beyond all expectations. We have added group after group of employees. The policy of this Congress is to increase these bureaus as well as the number of employees, rather than to decrease them. . . . Today we have approximately 900,000 Federal employees, 300,000 of whom secured their positions because of political patronage. . . . If this Congress continues its present practice, we are going to foster and approve the most gigantic political machine that is known in any nation anywhere (*Congressional Record*, 1939, Part 9, p. 9603).

Pressures for bringing almost all federal employees under political neutrality resulted in the Hatch Act of 1939 (also known as the First Hatch Act). Section 9(a) of the Act basically extended Rule I to all federal employees in the executive branch other than the president, vice president, department heads and assistant heads, and presidential officers engaged in formulating or implementing foreign policy or in the nationwide administration of the laws. However, its wording was not identical to Rule I because it permitted federal employees to express their views on all political subjects rather than to express them "privately" only. The change was deliberate and the Rule I was changed to match its wording in 1941. From a theoretical perspective, the Act was confusing because its Section 15 said that it should be interpreted to prohibit the same activities that the CSC had already found in violation of Rule I, which did not allow public expression on all political subjects. In practice, the contradiction did not stand in the way of the Act's constitutionality.

The Supreme Court first upheld the constitutionality of the Hatch Act and political neutrality in *United Public Workers v. Mitchell* (1947). The majority admitted that restrictions on federal employees' political activity interfered with their constitutional rights to freedom of expression. However, relying on the logic of the doctrine of privilege, it concluded that "for regulation of [federal] employees it is not necessary that the act regulated be anything more than an act reasonably deemed by Congress to interfere with the efficiency of the public service" (*United Public Workers v. Mitchell*, 1947, p. 101). The dissenters thought considerably more would be necessary to limit employees' speech constitutionally.

The Hatch Act and the kind of restrictions that it incorporates have always been controversial. On the one hand, they abridge the political rights of a significant segment of the electorate, and one that includes many who are very knowledgeable about government and public policy. On the other hand, political neutrality also protects public employees from being coerced into partisan activity. It has never been clear whether such regulations are a net gain or loss for civil servants. Not surprisingly, federal employees' opinion on such restrictions has been divided (Commission on Political Activity of Government Personnel, 1968). There is also presumed to be a public interest in the appearance of nonpartisanship in public administration, but how intensely most people feel about the matter is unknown.

In the early 1970s, it appeared that upon reconsideration the Supreme Court might find the Hatch Act unconstitutional. Both the scope of federal employment and the constitutional law of public employment had changed considerably. In *National Association of Letter Carriers v. Civil Service Commission* (1972), a federal district court held that past decisions "coupled with changes in the size and complexity of public service, place *Mitchell* among other decisions outmoded by the passage of time" (p. 585). On appeal, however, the Supreme Court upheld the Hatch Act in no uncertain terms:

> We unhesitatingly reaffirm the *Mitchell* holding that Congress had, and has, the power to prevent [federal employees] from holding a party office, working at the polls, and acting as party paymaster for other party workers. An act of Congress going no farther would in our view unquestionably be valid. So would it be if, in plain and understandable language, the statute forbade activities such as organizing a political party or club; actively participating in fund-raising activities for a partisan candidate or political party; becoming a partisan candidate for, or campaigning for, an elective public office; actively managing the campaign for a partisan candidate for public office; initiating or circulating a partisan nominating petition or soliciting votes for a partisan candidate for public office; or serving as a delegate, alternate, or proxy to a political party convention (*Civil Service Commission v. National Association of Letter Carriers*, 1973: 556).

In a companion case, *Broadrick v. Oklahoma* (1973), the Court was willing to uphold political neutrality regulations that were so ambiguously worded as to potentially inhibit speech that was clearly constitutionally protected.

In the course of issuing these opinions, the Court seemed to indicate its own policy preference for political neutrality. In more recent years, however, such regulations have increasingly fallen out of favor. By 1993, over 40 states had relaxed restrictions on the political activities of state and local public servants (Sturdivant, 1993, p. A14) and the federal government adopted a set of Hatch Act reforms that allowed federal employees to engage in a wider range of partisan activities. Among these are distributing partisan campaign literature, soliciting votes, working for partisan campaigns, and holding office in political parties. The reform did not extend to the Senior Executive Service, and some agencies were excepted. The federal reform prohibits coercion of employees to engage in partisan activities. A key to its success will be the effectiveness with which employees are protected from partisan pressures. As is discussed below in Section II, there are several ajudicatory systems intended to protect federal employees from prohibited treatment and unfair labor practices.

3.   Freedom of Association

Historically, public employees' constitutional right to freedom of association has been a significant issue in terms of membership in subversive groups and labor unions. Today the focus is on their right *not* to join groups, including political parties and unions, as well.

(a)   Subversive Groups.   Modern restrictions on federal employees' membership in subversive organizations began in 1939. Section 9A of the Hatch Act prohibited federal employees from being

members of political parties or organizations advocating the overthrow of constitutional government in the United States. (Section 9A is not to be confused with Section 9(a) which, as discussed above, involved political neutrality.) Soon thereafter, the CSC modified its rules to prevent members of Communist, Nazi, or fascist organizations from gaining federal employment. Truman's Loyalty Order included as a ground for belief that an employee was disloyal to the government

> membership in, affiliation with or sympathetic association with any foreign or domestic organization, association, movement, group or combination of persons, designated by the Attorney General as totalitarian, fascist, communist, or subversive, or as having adopted a policy of advocating or approving the commission of acts of force or violence to deny other persons their rights under the Constitution . . . or as seeking to alter the form of government . . . by unconstitutional means (Executive Order 9835, 1947).

The first public listing of such groups by the attorney general was released in March 1948 (*Federal Register*, 1948, Part 3, p. 1473).

These provisions were subsequently modified (see Rosenbloom, 1971, chapter 6), but membership in a group on the attorney general's list remained a major basis for dismissals of federal employees and disqualification of applicants for the federal service. A major shift in the constitutional law regarding public employees' membership in such groups was effectuated by the Supreme Court's decision in *Elfbrandt v. Russell* (1966). It found an Arizona loyalty oath for public employees unconstitutional because it proscribed membership in any organization having for "one of its purposes" (*Elfbrandt v. Russell*, 1966, p. 13) the overthrow of the government. The Court reasoned that the oath was too broad because "those who join an organization but do not share its unlawful purposes and . . . activities surely pose no threat, either as citizens or as public employees" (*Elfbrandt v. Russell*, 1966, p. 17). As a result, mere membership in a subversive group can no longer be the basis for an adverse public personnel action. Among other things, this means that prison guards and even police may be members of groups like the Ku Klux Klan as long as they do not share in their illegal purposes.

The *Elfbrandt* ruling shifted inquiries about public employees' loyalty away from membership alone and focused them more on their beliefs. In practice, whatever their effectiveness, loyalty oaths have been the major legal mechanism for ensuring that public employees are not subversives. Narrowly drawn loyalty oaths requiring employees to "oppose the overthrow of the government of the United States of American or of [a state] by force, violence or by any illegal or unconstitutional method" will be constitutional (*Cole v. Richardson*, 1972).

(b) Membership in Unions. Public employees' membership in labor unions was once widely prohibited in the United States. Today, it is difficult to imagine how threatening civil service unions appeared in the past. In 1943, for instance, New York State's highest court had occasion to declare that

> to tolerate or recognize any combination of Civil Service employees of the Government as a labor organization or union is not only incompatible with the spirit of democracy, but inconsistent with every principle upon which our government is founded (*Railway Mail Association v. Murphy*, 1943, p. 607).

By the 1960s, however, such opposition declined. Unions began to view the mostly unorganized public sector as fertile territory. In 1956, the Democratic Party platform endorsed union representation in the public sector. In 1962, President John F. Kennedy dispelled any lingering doubt as to the legitimacy of civil service unionism with Executive Order 10988 (1962), which proclaimed that "participation of employees in the formulation and implementation of personnel policies affecting them contributes to the executive conduct of the public business." Soon thereafter, the federal government and several states implemented comprehensive programs for labor relations with unionized employees. Nowadays the public sector has a higher rate of union representation than is found in the private sector (Shafritz et al., 1992, chapters 10 and 11). By the late 1960s, the federal judiciary had fully confirmed public employees' constitutional right to freedom of association included the right to join unions (*McLaughlin v. Tilendis*, 1968; *AFSCME v. Woodward*, 1969). However, under the federal Constitution, there is neither a right to bargain collectively with one's employer nor a right to strike (i.e., those engaging in strikes can be dismissed or otherwise penalized).

Freedom of association includes the right *not* to associate. In the context of public sector collective bargaining, this has placed strains on union security arrangements. In *Abood v. Detroit Board of Education* (1977), the Supreme Court made it clear that public employees could not constitutionally be compelled to join unions. However, it "rejected the claim that it was unconstitutional for a public employer to designate a union as the exclusive collective bargaining representative of its employees, and to require nonunion employees, as a condition of employment, to pay a fair share of the union's cost of negotiating and administering a collective bargaining agreement" (*Chicago Teachers Union v. Hudson*, 1986, pp. 301). The Court noted that "such interference as exists [with freedom of association] is constitutionally justified by the legislative assessment of the important contribution of the union shop to the system of labor relations" (*Abood v. Detroit Board of Education*, 1977, p. 222). It admonished that it would violate the Constitution if employees were forced to financially support a union's spending "for the expression of political views, on behalf of political candidates, or toward the advancement of other ideological causes not germane to its duties as collective bargaining representative" (*Abood v. Detroit Board of Education*, 1977, p. 235). The Court recognized that "there will, of course, be difficult problems in drawing lines between collective bargaining activities, for which contributions may be compelled, and ideological activities unrelated to collective bargaining, for which such compulsion is prohibited" (*Abood v. Detroit Board of Education*, 1977, p. 236).

In *Chicago Teachers Union v. Hudson* (1986), the Court set forth a procedure enabling public employees to avoid being charged for union activities other than those involving collective bargaining. It held "that the constitutional requirements for the Union's collection of agency fees include an adequate explanation of the basis for the fee, a reasonably prompt opportunity to challenge the amount of the fee before an impartial decision maker, and an escrow for the amounts reasonably in dispute while such challenges are pending" (*Chicago Teachers Union v. Hudson*, 1986, p. 310). In practice, *Chicago Teachers Union* promotes further judicialization of public sector labor relations.

(c) *Political Parties.* Historically, American public employees' constitutional right to join or refuse to join political parties was seriously impaired. Under the spoils system that dominated federal personnel administration from 1829 until the 1880s or 1890s, employees were routinely dismissed for membership in the opposition party, failure to vote for the winning party's ticket (the secret ballot was introduced in the United States in 1888), or failure to financially support the party in power (referred to as "political assessment" of public employees). These and other coercive practices were outlawed at the federal level by the Civil Service Act of 1883 (Pendleton Act) and by a host of state and local regulations drafted in the 1880s and afterward. Surprisingly, however, what was once routine and then illegal is now wholly unconstitutional.

In a series of decisions since 1976, the Supreme Court incrementally established a substantial constitutional barrier to the use of partisanship in public personnel actions. In *Elrod v. Burns* (1976), a majority of the Court found the patronage dismissals of employees in the Cook County, Illinois Sheriff's Department to be unconstitutional. The plurality opinion, written by Justice William Brennan, noted that "the cost of the practice of patronage is the restraint it places on freedoms of belief and association" (*Elrod v. Burns*, 1976, p. 355) and concluded that partisan dismissals are not the least restrictive way of promoting the legitimate governmental ends of efficiency, effectiveness, and loyalty in the public service.

Justice Potter Stewart, joined by Justice Harry Blackmun, concurred on the narrower ground that "a nonpolicymaking, nonconfidential government employee" cannot constitutionally "be discharged . . . from a job that he is satisfactorily performing upon the sole ground of his political beliefs" (*Elrod v. Burns*, 1976, p. 375). To the extent that it dominated this area of the law, Stewart's opinion would require that policymaking and confidential employees be clearly identified and distinguished from all others. Since such distinctions are inherently contestable at their margins, the opinion was an open-ended invitation to further litigation.

In *Branti v. Finkel* (1980), the Court established a much clearer standard for the constitutionality of patronage dismissals. The case involved two assistant public defenders from Rockland County, New York, who were dismissed solely on the basis of their partisan political beliefs. Writing for the majority, Justice John Paul Stevens indicated that "the ultimate inquiry is not whether the label 'policymaker' or 'confidential' fits a particular position; rather the question is whether the hiring authority can demonstrate that party affiliation is an appropriate requirement for the effective performance of the public office involved" (*Branti v. Finkel*, 1980, p. 518). This standard obviously places a heavy burden of persuasion on those who would make patronage dismissals.

Justice Lewis Powell wrote strong dissents in both these cases. In *Elrod* he was joined by Chief Justice Burger and by Justice Rehnquist; in *Branti* by Rehnquist alone. Powell argued that the majority seriously underestimated the contribution patronage could make to governance. He was also unable to accept the Court's constitutionalization of such a venerable political practice. But his logic was not compelling and subsequently, in *Rutan v. Republican Party of Illinois* (1990), the Court held that "the rule of *Elrod* and *Branti* extends to promotion, transfer, recall, and hiring decisions based on party affiliation and support" (p. 2739). Consequently, public employees now enjoy very substantial constitutional protection of the right to associate (or not associate) with political parties.

4. Privacy

The Supreme Court squarely addressed public employees' constitutional protection against unreasonable searches and seizures for the first time in 1987. Some earlier federal circuit court decisions had considered the role of Fourth Amendment protections in the federal workplace (*Powell v. Zuckert*, 1966; *Saylor v. United States*, 1967). However, in *O'Connor v. Ortega* (1987), the Supreme Court treated the question as essentially one of first impression. As is often true under such conditions, it was unable to draw any bright lines that would clearly instruct public sector personnelists, managers, and employees in this area of the constitutional law.

O'Connor v. Ortega originated when Dennis O'Connor, Executive Director of the Napa State Hospital in California, heard of alleged improprieties in Dr. Magno Ortega's management of the hospital's resident training program. Ortega had been suspected of sexual harassment of two female employees and of coercing residents to contribute to the purchase of a computer for him. He was placed on paid administrative leave and subsequently his office was searched and several items were seized. Ortega was eventually dismissed. Among the items taken was a Valentine's Day card sent to him by a former resident physician, whose credibility consequently suffered when she testified on his behalf at a hearing before the California State Personnel Board.

Justice Sandra Day O'Connor announced the Court's judgment to remand the case for trial at the district court level. Her plurality opinion started with the premise that "individuals do not lose Fourth Amendment rights merely because they work for the government instead of a private employer" (*O'Connor v. Ortega*, 1987, p. 723)—a proposition with which all the justices would agree. However, the scope of Fourth Amendment protections, as defined by O'Connor's opinion, are highly judgmental.

The threshold question is whether the employee has a reasonable expectation of privacy in the workplace. To be reasonable, such an expectation must be one that society is prepared to share. O'Connor's opinion offered no general guidance as to when this would be the case: "Given the great variety of work environments in the public sector, the question of whether an employee has a reasonable expectation of privacy must be addressed on a case-by-case basis" (*O'Connor v. Ortega*, 1987, p. 723). However, even if the employee does have a reasonable expectation of privacy, the search will be constitutional if the government can show that "both the inception and the scope of the intrusion . . . [were] reasonable" (O'Connor v. Ortega, 1987, p. 728). Of course, what is reasonable or unreasonable in this context will often be determined only by adjudication.

Justice Antonin Scalia, who concurred in the Court's judgment, contended that the plurality had created a "a standard so devoid of content that it produces rather than eliminates uncertainty in this field" (*O'Connor v. Ortega*, 1987, p. 731). He would have issued a blanket rule that "searches to retrieve work-related materials or to investigate violations of workplace rules—searches of the sort that are regarded as reasonable and normal in the private-employer context—do not violate the Fourth Amendment" (*O'Connor v. Ortega*, 1987, pp. 732–733). On the other end of the spectrum of opinions, Justice Harry Blackmun argued in dissent that the plurality and Scalia were too quick to dispense with the usual Fourth Amendment requirements that either search warrants be issued or that probable cause be present for the belief that evidence would be lost if not seized promptly.

It is evident that the framework for analyzing the Fourth Amendment rights of public employees established in *O'Connor* is imperfect. To a considerable extent, it is almost irrelevant to the major privacy issues facing the public sector today: mandatory testing for drug use and blood testing for HIV status. These procedures raise a complicated constitutional issue because unlike most Fourth Amendment matters, they often involve invasions of privacy in the absence of a suspicion that any particular employee is engaging in proscribed behavior or presents a danger to others.

The Supreme Court wrestled with the drug testing issue in *National Treasury Employees Union v. Von Raab* (1989). The case involved mandatory drug screening in the Customs Service, which required employees to produce a urine sample while being monitored by someone of the same sex. Employees who tested positively, without satisfactory explanation, were dismissed. Without disparaging the importance of the employees' privacy interests, the Court, per Justice Anthony Kennedy, held that

> the suspicionless testing of employees who apply for promotion to positions directly involving the interdiction of illegal drugs, or to positions which require the incumbent to carry a firearm, is reasonable. The Government's compelling interests in preventing promotion of drug users to positions where they might endanger the integrity of our Nation's borders or the life of the citizenry outweigh the privacy interests of those who seek promotion to these positions, who enjoy a diminished expectation of privacy by virtue of the special, and obvious, physical and ethical demands of those positions (*National Treasury Employees Union v. Von Raab*, 1989, pp. 679).

Justice Thurgood Marshall was joined by Justice William Brennan in a dissent arguing that probable cause was required for the Customs Service searches and that even if he accepted the Court's weaker balancing approach, he would find them unconstitutional. Justice Scalia also dissented in an opinion joined by Justice Stevens. Scalia found the government's procedure unreasonable because there was no evidence that employees who used illegal drugs, if any, were more likely to engage in improper law enforcement.

Mandatory HIV testing has not yet been ruled on by the Supreme Court. In *Glover v. Eastern Nebraska Community Office of Retardation* (1989), a circuit court, using the kind of balancing approach outlined in *O'Connor* and *National Treasury Employees Union*, found such testing unconstitutional for state employees who had direct contact with developmentally disabled persons. The Supreme Court declined to review the decision, but it will almost certainly address the issue in the future.

5. Procedural Due Process

Procedural due process is a constitutional right that has had a dramatic impact on public personnel management. Until the 1950s, under the doctrine of privilege, public employees had no constitutional right to a fair procedure when facing adverse actions. Dismissals could be arbitrary and one had no constitutional right to notice of the grounds on which they were based, an opportunity to respond, or a hearing. Constitutional change in this area began during the loyalty/security era. The Supreme Court held that procedural due process was applicable where the government was denying private individuals security clearances or employment (*Greene v. McElroy*, 1959; *Cafeteria Workers v. McElroy*, 1961). However, it was not until *Board of Regents v. Roth* (1972) that the Court squarely brought procedural due process into the public employment relationship.

In *Roth*, the Court indicated that public employees would have a right to a hearing in dismissals that (1) were in retaliation for the exercise of protected rights, such as freedom of speech or invoking the constitutional protection against self-incrimination (*Garrity v. New Jersey*, 1967; *Uniformed Sanitation Men's Association v. Commissioner*, 1968; *Gardner v. Broderick*, 1968); (2) could injure the employee's reputation or honor; (3) impaired his or her future employability; or (4) interfered with a property interest in the position, such as tenure or contractual rights. Although subsequent cases seemed to narrow *Roth's* application (*Arnett v. Kennedy*, 1974; *Bishop v. Wood*, 1976; *Codd v. Velger*, 1977), the Court reiterated the importance of procedural due process in *Cleveland Board of Education v. Loudermill* (1985).

The *Loudermill* decision sets forth the current structure of public employees' procedural due process rights. The case involved the dismissal of a security guard from the Cleveland school system for having falsely stated on his job application that he had never been convicted of a felony. The Court held that

> an essential principle of due process is that a deprivation of life, liberty, or property "be preceded by notice and opportunity for hearing appropriate to the nature of the case." . . . We have described "the root requirement" of the Due Process Clause as being "that an individual be given an opportunity for a hearing *before* he is deprived of any significant property interest. . . ." This principle requires "some kind of a hearing" prior to the discharge of an employee who has a constitutionally protected property interest in his employment (p. 542).

The extent of procedural protection necessary depends on a balancing of three factors: "the private interest in retaining employment, the governmental interest in the expeditious removal of unsatisfactory employees and the avoidance of administrative burdens, and the risk of an erroneous termination" (pp. 542–543). The Court emphasized that where the individual has "property rights in continued employment" (p. 532), the need for accurate decision making in dismissals is crucial. Consequently, if the action is based on disputed facts, an elaborate procedure for finding the truth may be constitutionally required. By contrast, where the procedure used is adequate or either cannot be improved at all or can be improved only at great expense, the employee's claim for more elaborate protection will not prevail.

The bottom line in *Loudermill*, which applies generally where posttermination hearings are available, is that "the tenured public employee is entitled to oral or written notice of the charges against him, an explanation of the employer's evidence, and an opportunity to present his side of the story [prior to termination]" (p. 546). If there is no right to a posttermination procedure, then the employee may be entitled to more elaborate pretermination protection, depending on the result of the threefold balancing discussed above. In practice, of course, many civil service systems already provide for a greater degree of procedural due process than is actually required by the constitutional law.

6. Equal Protection

Contemporary constitutional equal protection analysis is both highly complex and relevant to public personnel management. Historically, unequal treatment of African-Americans and women was standard personnel procedure in the federal service (Rosenbloom, 1977, chapter 3). There is no doubt that other groups, including Hispanics and Asians, faced widespread discrimination, but the historical record of it is less developed. Although the first federal equal employment opportunity (EEO) program was established in 1941, equal protection analysis had a minimal impact on personnel systems until the 1950s. It was only after the Supreme Court held that legally grounded racial segregation in public education was unconstitutional in *Brown v. Board of Education of Topeka* (1954) that barriers to the public employment of African-Americans and racial discrimination within public personnel systems could be effectively challenged. However, the Civil Rights Act of 1964 and the Equal Employment Opportunity Act of 1972 soon eclipsed equal protection as the most effective vehicles for challenging racial, ethnic, gender, and religious discrimination in the public sector. (Section II of this chapter outlines the current legislative framework for equal employment opportunity.)

Today equal protection analysis regarding public personnel administration is rooted in the Supreme Court's decision in *Washington v. Davis* (1976). The case presented a challenge to the constitutionality of a written qualifying examination for police training in the District of Columbia. It had a disparate impact on African-Americans, disqualifying four times as many of them as whites. Several lower court decisions had held that such a disparity would violate equal protection unless the governmental employer could demonstrate that the exam served a compelling state interest (Rosenbloom and Obuchowski, 1977). This generally required the government to show that exam scores were related to job performance, which was often difficult conceptually and statistically (Rosenbloom and Obuchowski, 1977). Remedies in such cases frequently discontinued the exam and require that fair substitute procedures be developed. These cases often brought the judiciary into the thick of personnel management.

In *Washington v. Davis*, the Supreme Court, which had shown growing skepticism at judicial involvement in administrative affairs (e.g., *Milliken v. Bradley*, 1974), changed the structure of such equal protection analysis. It held that those challenging public personnel practices must prove that they embody "an invidious discriminatory purpose" (p. 242):

> This is not to say that the necessary discriminatory racial purpose must be express or appear on the face of the statute, or that a law's disproportionate impact is irrelevant in cases involving Constitution-based claims of racial discrimination. . . .
>
> Necessarily, an invidious discriminatory purpose may often be inferred from the totality of the relevant facts, including the fact, if it is true, that the law bears more heavily on one race than another (pp. 241–242).

This approach was less drastic in public personnel than in other areas of public policy because, as noted alone, most claims that could be brought under equal protection could also be brought under federal civil rights law. Under then-prevailing judicial interpretation, statutorily based challenges to personnel practices required plaintiffs to show disparate impact only, not intent. Once such an impact was shown, a difficult burden of persuasion shifted to the employer to demonstrate the legality of the practices involved (*Griggs v. Duke Power Company*, 1971).

However, *Washington v. Davis* did have a major impact on litigation involving veteran preference practices in public employment, which are specifically exempted from challenge under the Equal Employment Opportunity Act of 1972. In *Personnel Administrator v. Feeney* (1979), the Supreme Court noted that a Massachusetts veteran preference law had a severe negative impact on the employment opportunities of women. Nevertheless, the Court upheld the law, reiterating that "purposeful discrimination is the condition that offends the Constitution" (*Personnel Administrator v. Feeney*, 1979, p. 274).

Washington v. Davis did not deal with affirmative action, which includes differential treatment of individuals based on race, ethnicity, and gender. Public policies that classify individuals by race or ethnicity have long been "suspect" under equal protection analysis. They are subject to strict scrutiny by the courts. Classifications by gender are not suspect by definition, but in recent years the courts have probed their rationality with greater care than in the past (*Craig v. Boren*, 1976). Suspect classifications will be constitutional only if, in the courts' view, they serve a compelling governmental interest and do so in the fashion least damaging to equal protection. In practice, very few if any classifications that purposively restrict the rights or opportunities of racial or ethnic minorities are likely to survive contemporary equal protection analysis.

However, whereas historically, racial, ethnic, and gender classifications have typically worked to the disadvantage of equality for minorities and women, modern affirmative action is intended to promote equality. Consequently, the federal judiciary has been presented with new issues of equal protection and the Supreme Court has been forging new law in this area.

Under present rulings, affirmative action at the state and federal levels is treated somewhat differently from one another. This is because the Fourteenth Amendment includes a clause providing that "the Congress shall have power to enforce, by appropriate legislation, the provisions of this article" (§5). The Supreme Court has been deferential to Congress's judgment regarding minority business set-asides to promote racial equality (*Fullilove v. Klutznick*, 1980) and to those of agencies exercising congressionally delegated authority (*Metro Broadcasting v. Federal Communications Commission*, 1990). The test for federal affirmative action is whether the policy serves important government objectives and, if so, whether the specific practices used are substantially related to the achievement of those objectives.

Nonfederal public sector affirmative action schemes involving race are subject to strict scrutiny to assure that they are "benign," i.e., they do not involve invidious or demeaning denials of equal protection (*City of Richmond v. Croson*, 1989). Further, such affirmative action must be "narrowly tailored" to survive constitutional challenge. The specifics of narrow tailoring may vary with the precise purpose and method of affirmative action. However, the following conditions, as set forth by Justice Powell in a concurring opinion in *U.S. v. Paradise* (1987), are the general criteria for narrow tailoring.

1. *The efficacy of alternative remedies.* Affirmative action is used for different purposes. It can be used to remedy the impact of past discrimination in public personnel systems, as a tool for assuring equal opportunity or to change the composition of the governmental work force. In some circumstances, racial, ethnic, and gender classifications may be only marginally better, if better at all, than other approaches. For instance, if their purpose is to assure equal opportunity, substantial fines levied on discriminatory jurisdictions or officials may prove equally or more efficacious, while avoiding the kinds of classifications abhorred by the Fourteenth Amendment. Less explicit ways of taking race, ethnicity, or gender into account in hiring and promotion decisions may work as well as affirmative action goals and timetables in changing the composition of an

agency's work force. Where alternative remedies are more efficacious and less damaging to equal protection, they clearly should be used. However, sometimes the less explicit the affirmative action categories and objectives, the less successful an equal opportunity policy may be (Rosenbloom, 1977, chapters 5 and 6; *Regents v. Bakke*, 1978).

2. *The planned duration of the remedy*. Affirmative action classifications are viewed as a means to an objective rather than a system of indefinite differential treatment. The remedy using racial, ethnic, or gender classifications should have a clear cutoff point.

3. *The relationship between the percentage of minority workers to be employed and the percentage of minority group members in the relevant population or work force*. The intended distributive effects of affirmative action policies must be balanced. For instance, in *City of Richmond v. Croson* (1989), the Supreme Court found a 30% minority business set-aside scheme that applied to a variety of minorities, including Eskimos, to be unconstitutional.

4. *The availability of waiver provisions if the hiring or promotion goals cannot be achieved*. In other words, affirmative action policies should not absolutely require that no one other than a member of a minority group or a woman be hired, promoted, retained, and so forth, regardless of availability or qualifications.

5. *The effect of the remedy on innocent third parties*. Individuals who are not in the affirmative action target groups are inevitably disadvantaged by affirmative action. They fail to obtain jobs, training, and promotions because of the public policy desire to advance the opportunities and careers of others. In *Wygant v. Jackson* (1986), the Supreme Court found an affirmative action scheme leading to the dismissal of white school teachers in favor of the retention of nonwhites unconstitutional because it placed a very heavy burden on innocent third parties. However, in *Steelworkers v. Weber* (1979), the Court suggested, though it did not squarely hold, that the denial of training opportunities as part of an affirmative action program was not so substantial a burden on innocent third parties.

The complexity of equal protection analysis presents difficulties for public personnel management. The federal Office of Personnel Management, and perhaps individual agencies as well, has more leeway than the states in fashioning affirmative action approaches. The application of strict scrutiny and the requirement of narrow tailoring require that state and local governments construct their affirmative action arrangements with great care.

7. Liberty

In *Cleveland Board of Education v. LaFleur* (1974), the Supreme Court recognized that public employees may have a constitutional right to "liberty" under the Fourteenth Amendment. The content of such liberty, often thought of as "substantive due process," is inherently unspecified by the Constitution. In *LaFleur*, the Court recognized that "freedom of personal choice in matters of marriage and family life is one of the liberties protected by the due process clause of the Fourteenth Amendment" (p. 639). It went on to hold that "by acting to penalize the pregnant teacher for deciding to bear a child, overly restrictive maternity leave regulations can constitute a heavy burden on the exercise of these protected freedoms" (p. 640) and that consequently, rules regarding such leaves must not "needlessly, arbitrarily, or capriciously impinge upon this vital area of a teacher's constitutional liberty" (p. 649). The Court then found several features of the maternity leave policies at issue to be defective.

Despite the sweeping construction of public employees' liberty outlined in *LaFleur*, the Court has declined to expand the range of protected liberties significantly. In *Kelley v. Johnson* (1976), the Court declined to find grooming regulations for male police officers an unconstitutional infringement on protected liberty. The Suffolk County, New York regulations provided that "hair will not touch the ears or the collar"; "sideburns will not extend below the lowest part of the exterior ear opening, will be even width (not flared), and will end with a clean-shaven horizontal line"; "mustaches . . . shall not extend over the top of the upper lip or beyond the corners of the mouth"; "beards and goatees are prohibited, except that a Police Surgeon may grant a waiver . . . for medical reasons. . . . When a Surgeon prescribes that a member not shave . . . all beard hairs will be kept trimmed so that they do not protrude more than one-half inch from the skin surface of the face" (*Kelley v. Johnson*, 1976, note 1). The government defended these regulations on the flimsy grounds that they enhanced the public's ability to identify police officers (who were already uniformed) and that they promoted an *esprit de corps* among the police (who brought suit against them). Justice Marshall, joined by Justice Brennan in dissent noted that

> an individual's personal appearance may reflect, sustain, and nourish his personality and may well be used as a means of expressing his attitude and lifestyle. In taking control over a citizen's personal appearance, the Government forces him to sacrifice substantial elements of his integrity and identity (pp. 250–251).

However, the majority of the Court placed the burden of persuasion on the police officers to "demonstrate that there was no rational connection between the regulation . . . and the promotion of safety of persons and property" (p. 247) and found the officers unable to meet this challenge.

Similarly, in *McCarthy v. Philadelphia Civil Service Commission* (1976) the Court declined to include the right to reside in a place of one's choosing within the range of public employees' constitutionally protected liberties. The facts of the case were particularly appealing. McCarthy, a firefighter, moved from Philadelphia for the safety of his wife and children who felt insecure in their Philadelphia domicile which had been vandalized. He resided in Philadelphia when on duty and continued to go to church there. However, in a very short opinion, the Supreme Court found that the "bona fide continuing residence requirement" involved was constitutionally permissible.

It is evident from these decisions that the scope of liberties conveyed by a substantive due process reading of the Fourteenth Amendment is quite limited. Consequently, public employees seeking to expand their constitutional liberty within the public employment relationship are likely to be more successful when they can point to rights that are specifically enumerated in the First, Fourth, and Fifth Amendments.

B. Enforcement of Public Employees' Constitutional Rights

It is axiomatic that there is sometimes a gap between the Supreme Court's articulation of constitutional rights for individuals and the respect accorded these rights by government agencies. For example, overly zealous or excessively forceful police activity that violates individuals' Fourth Amendment rights is a staple of media attention and the subject of considerable litigation. Public personnelists may have a better record in this regard, but there have been enough suits to indicate that it is far from perfect. Indeed, apparently about a quarter of all liability suits brought against public officials, agencies, and administrators for violations of constitutional rights are filed by public employees (Lee, 1987). The Supreme Court has established two mechanisms of importance to public employees' ability to vindicate their constitutional rights.

1. The Mt. Healthy Rule

Adverse actions against public employees may involve a mixture of constitutionally protected and unprotected behavior. For instance, an employee may be insubordinate, rude, and uncooperative, and also be publicly critical of the agency for which he or she works. Although the public criticism may be protected under the *Rankin v. McPherson* (1987) formula discussed above, the employee's rudeness may present legitimate grounds for dismissal, suspension, or demotion. In *Mt. Healthy City School District Board of Education v. Doyle* (1977), the Supreme Court provided a formula for dealing with such cases. First, the employee has the burden of showing that an impermissible factor, such as the exercise of free speech, motivated the public employer to take action against him or her. If the employee successfully carries this burden of persuasion, the employer then has to show "by a preponderance of the evidence that it would have reached the same decision . . . even in the absence of the protected conduct" (p. 287). In other words, a public employer's action implicating the constitutionally protected rights of an employee substantially raises the legal burden faced by the employer when disciplining the employee. This should deter public employers from allowing protected behavior to motivate their decisions.

2. Liability for Constitutional Torts

A second enforcement mechanism makes public employees and employers who violate the constitutional rights of others potentially liable for money damages in civil suits. The chief vehicle for the liability of nonfederal public administrators and agencies is derived from the Civil Rights Act of 1871, now codified as 42 U.S. Code §1983. In relevant part, it reads:

> Every person who, under color of any statute, ordinance, regulation, custom, or usage, of any State or Territory or the District of Columbia, subjects, or causes to be subjected, any citizen of the United States or other person within the jurisdiction thereof to the deprivation of any rights, privileges, or immunities secured by the Constitution and laws, shall be liable to the party injured in an action at law, suit in equity, or other proper proceeding for redress. For the purposes of this section, any Act of Congress applicable exclusively to the District of Columbia shall be considered to be a statute of the District of Columbia.

Federal officials and employees face identical or very similar liabilities directly under the First, Fourth, Fifth, and Eighth Amendments (e.g., *Bivens v. Six Unknown Named Federal Narcotics Agents*, 1971; *Davis v. Passman*, 1979; *Carlson v. Green*, 1980; see also, *Bush v. Lucas*, 1983).

Under contemporary standards, the public personnel manager may be personally liable for compensatory and punitive damages for violation of an individual's "clearly established statutory or constitutional rights of which a reasonable person would have known" (*Harlow v. Fitzgerald*, 1982, p. 818; *Smith v. Wade*, 1983). Municipalities may be liable for compensatory damages only when their personnel policies violate employees' constitutional rights (*Owen v. City of Independence*, 1980; *Pembaur v. City of Cincinnati*, 1986). States and their agencies cannot be found liable for money damages for constitutional torts under federal law, but they can be sued for injunctive relief (*Will v. Michigan Department of State Police*, 1989). State officials and employees can be sued in their personal capacities for such torts arising out of the performance of their duties (*Hafer v. Melo*, 1991), though they cannot be sued as surrogates of the state. Federal agencies cannot be sued for money damages as redress for their constitutional torts (*Federal Deposit Insurance Corporation v. Meyer*, 1994).

Exceptions to the general rule of liability for constitutional torts are as follows. At the federal level, a civil suit for damages will not be an available remedy if Congress has specified an alternative, such as appeal to the Merit Systems Protection Board (*Bush v. Lucas*, 1983). Public employees and officials are absolutely immune from civil suits for money damages arising out of the performance of adjudicatory functions, such as serving as hearing examiners, administrative law judges, or agency "prosecutors" (*Butz v. Economou*, 1978; *Forrester v. White*, 1987; *Burns v. Reed*, 1991). It is important to emphasize that such immunity depends on the function the employee is performing, not on his or her job title. Thus, an adjudicatory official may be liable for violating an individual's constitutional rights in the context of a personnel action.

The Supreme Court has explicitly stated that these liabilities are formulated to "create an incentive for officials who may harbor doubts about the lawfulness of their intended actions to err on the side of protecting . . . constitutional rights" (*Owen v. City of Independence*, 1980, p. 652). Moreover, a plaintiff in such cases does not have to show that the personnelists or other public employee acted in bad faith, with malice, or ill will, etc., but only that he or she violated constitutional rights of which a reasonable person should have been aware. At the federal level, training in constitutional rights has been offered by the U.S. Office of Personnel Management and its subordinate Federal Executive Institute (1992). It is noteworthy in this context that public employees have a constitutional right to disobey unconstitutional directives insofar as 1) they sincerely believe obedience would violate another's constitutional rights and 2) they are correct in so believing (*Harley v. Schuylkill County*, 1979; Vaughn, 1984).

C. Conclusion

It is evident that constitutional law has become central to contemporary public personnel management. Public employees have far-reaching rights under the First, Fourth, Fifth, and Fourteenth Amendments. Many personnel matters that were once unregulated by the Constitution are now controlled by it. Perhaps the Supreme Court's decisions finding patronage practices unconstitutional are the most striking example. But even where public personnel administration may undertake measures that impinge on employees' ordinary constitutional rights, as in drug testing, these must be constructed carefully and narrowly to avoid violating the Constitution. In particular, contemporary public personnel management has been infused with procedural due process. Moreover, the Supreme Court's decisions regarding the liability of public administrators for constitutional torts make it crystal clear that that the Court considers knowledge of constitutional rights a matter of basic job competence. In the Court's words: "A reasonably competent public official should know the law governing his conduct" (*Harlow v. Fitzgerald*, 1982, p. 818). Law is now more than an "add-on" to good management; it is a defining element of public personnel administration. Personnelists who ignore it or subordinate constitutional values like due process to managerial values such as efficiency risk costly, time-consuming suits, and even having money damages assessed against them personally. But the challenge public personnelists face in mastering the relevant constitutional law pales in comparison to the larger challenge of which it is a substantial part, i.e., fully integrating the modern American administrative state into the constitutional framework. This will be accomplished only when public administrators fully embrace constitutional values and apply them in the thousands of administrative actions taken on a daily basis.

II. THE STATUTORY FRAMEWORK OF FEDERAL PERSONNEL ADMINISTRATION

The rights and responsibilities of public employees are defined not only in constitutional provisions and court decisions, but also in statutes and regulations, administrative rulings, and to an indeterminate extent in the customs and practices of the federal government, the 50 state governments, and local governments acting under the authorization of state law. This section reviews the main elements of the statutory, regulatory, and organizational framework of federal executive branch public employment law and selected statutory issues.

A. The Framework of Federal Public Employment Law

1. The Civil Service

The framework of federal public employment law is based on the concept of the civil service, initially established by the Pendleton Act in 1883. The civil service by statute includes appointive positions in the executive, judicial, and legislative branches (5 U.S.C. 2101). It does not include positions in the uniformed services—the armed forces, the commissioned corps of the Public Health Service, and the commissioned corps of the National Oceanic and Atmospheric Administration. Six categories of officials or their designees can make appointments to the civil service (5 U.S.C. 2105 [a][1]). These include the president, the Congress, or a member of Congress, and the head of a government-controlled corporation. An appointment is effective when an authorized official signs a Standard Form 50, administered by the Office of Personnel Management, which specifies the terms and conditions of the appointment. Standard Form 50 designates the legal status of the employee and substantially determines his or her statutory rights. Designation in a particular category triggers application of a set of rights. The appointment determines such matters as whether the employee is a member of the competitive or excepted service (see discussion below), whether the employee is entitled to certain preferences based on service in the armed services, and whether the employee is assigned to an agency with special statutory provisions that define the rights and duties of its employees. The agencies with special provisions include government corporations, the General Accounting Office, the Federal Bureau of Investigation, the Central Intelligence Agency, the Defense Intelligence Agency, the National Security Agency, and any other entity the president may designate because of its foreign intelligence or counterintelligence activities (5 U.S.C. 2302 [a][2][c]). The statutory rights of employees in these agencies depend on the particular statutes and regulations that apply to the particular agency.

The general principles of federal employment law apply to positions in the competitive service as distinguished from the excepted service, although there is overlap between the two. The distinctions between the competitive service and the excepted service reflect judgments that certain positions, such as positions involving confidential matters, cannot effectively be administered through standard competitive appointment and tenure procedures. Positions in the *executive* branch are in the competitive service except positions in the Senior Executive Service, to which particular provisions apply (5 U.S.C. 2101 [a]). Most appointments requiring confirmation by the Senate are excepted, as are positions for which examinations are inappropriate. These include attorney positions (5 C.F.R. 213.3101), policymaking and confidential positions (5 C.F.R. 213.3301), or "Schedule C" positions; and certain positions when filled by handicapped or mentally retarded individuals (5 C.F.R. 213.3101).

Generally, the competitive service does not include positions in the legislative and judicial branches. However, the merit system principles and prohibited personnel practices discussed immediately below do apply generally to appointments to the judicial branch made through the Administrative Office of the United States and appointments to the Government Printing Office, which is under the jurisdiction of Congress, and to certain other positions by special statutory provisions. (Special statutory provisions that apply to employees of the legislative and judicial branches, and in some instances to the executive branch, are not reviewed in this chapter.)

For 1990, the Office of Personnel Management reported federal civilian employment at 2.94 million. It reported 1.694 million employees in the competitive service and 1.246 million in the excepted and Senior Executive Services (*Statistical Abstract of the United States*, 1992). While some differences between the competitive service and the expected service remain, e.g., appointment processes, the Civil Service Due Process Amendments (PL 101-376), enacted August 17, 1990, narrowed the differences. This law granted most members of the excepted service who have served at least one year a right to appeal an adverse personnel action (discussed below) to the Merit System Protection Board. As the title of the law indicates, Congress believed that the due process rights of members of the excepted service to appeal personnel actions taken against them were inadequately protected under existing statutes and case law.

2. Merit Principles

The merit system principles codified in the Civil Service Reform Act of 1978 (5 U.S.C. 230 [b]) provide the statutory framework for the competitive service. The principles have been held to provide direction and guidance to interpretation of rights otherwise expressed in statutory and regulatory form (*Wells v. Harris*, 1979). The principles (see Table 1) state that recruitment and advancement should be based on ability; that employees should be treated fairly, without discrimination, and with due regard for their privacy and other constitutional rights; and that employees should receive equal pay for equal work. Employees should be retained and promoted on the basis of performance. They should be disciplined or discharged if they fail to meet standards of satisfactory performance. They should be free from coercion for partisan political purposes, and from reprisal for disclosing information about violations of law or mismanagement.

Table 1   Merit System Principles

Federal personnel management should be implemented consistent with the following merit system principles:

(1) Recruitment should be from qualified individuals from appropriate sources in an endeavor to achieve a work force from all segments of society, and selection and advancement should be determined solely on the basis of relative ability, knowledge, and skills, after fair and open competition which assures that all receive equal opportunity.

(2) All employees and applicants for employment should receive fair and equitable treatment in all aspects of personnel management without regard to political affiliation, race, color, religion, national origin, sex, marital status, age, or handicapping condition, and with proper regard for their privacy and constitutional rights.

(3) Equal pay should be provided for work of equal value, with appropriate consideration of both national and local rates paid by employers in the private sector, and appropriate incentives and recognition should be provided for excellence in performance.

(4) All employees should maintain high standards of integrity, conduct, and concern for the public interest.

(5) The federal work force should be used efficiently and effectively.

(6) Employees should be retained on the basis of the adequacy of their performance, inadequate performance should be corrected, and employees should be separated who cannot or will not improve their performance to meet required standards.

(7) Employees should be provided effective education and training in cases in which such education and training would result in better organizational and individual performance.

(8) Employees should be:

    (A) protected against arbitrary action, personal favoritism, or coercion for partisan political purposes, and

    (B) prohibited from using their official authority or influence for the purpose of interfering with or affecting the result of an election or a nomination for election.

(9) Employees should be protected against reprisal for the lawful disclosure of information which the employees reasonably believe evidences:

    (A) a violation of any law, rule, or regulation, or

    (B) mismanagement, a gross waste of funds, an abuse of authority, or a substantial and specific danger to public health or safety.

Source: 5 U.S. Code, Sec. 2301.

3. Prohibited Personnel Practices

The Civil Service Reform Act specifies 11 prohibited personnel practices (5 U.S.C. 2302). These practices are violations of the merit system. These prohibitions create a legal cause of action for redress by an employee injured by a violation. The prohibitions apply to personnel action. "Personnel action" means an appointment or promotion, or disciplinary or corrective action, detail, transfer, or reassignment; reinstatement, restoration, or reemployment; performance evaluation; a pay, benefit, or award or education or training decision; or any other change in duties or responsibilities inconsistent with an employee's salary or grade level. The prohibitions apply to specified positions—any position in the competitive service, career appointee positions in the Senior Executive Service, and some positions in the excepted service. They do not apply to excepted positions involving confidential, policymaking responsibilities. The prohibitions can be interpreted as declarations of positive rights of covered employees—the right to be free from various forms of interference in employment.

The prohibited practices are:

Discrimination on the basis of race, color, religion, sex, national origin, age, handicapping condition, marital status, or political affiliation.

Use of information in a personnel action other than information based on the personal knowledge or records of the person providing the information concerned with the work experience and suitability of the employee or applicant (essentially a prohibition against political recommendations)

Coercion to engage in political activity

Obstruction of the right to compete for employment

Exercise of influence to secure advantage of one candidate over another

Nepotism

Reprisal for lawful disclosure of information about violations of law or mismanagement (whistleblowing)

Reprisal for exercising appeal rights

Adverse judgments on the basis of conduct that does not adversely affect the work performance of the employee or others (private conduct)

Actions that otherwise violate laws or regulations implementing merit principles

Current assessments of the merit system in operation indicate persistent tensions between the principles summarized above, political pressures, informal "old boy" networks, and the needs of managers for greater flexibility (Ban, 1991).

4. Unfair Labor Practices and Other Matters

In addition to the merit principles and prohibited personnel actions, the federal framework defines the rights and duties of management and labor in the conduct of labor relations (5 U.S.C. Chapter 71). The core rights and duties of management and labor are defined as 16 unfair labor practices, 8 of which apply to management and 8 of which apply to unions (see Table 2).

Management generally is required to allow employees to organize, to refrain from sponsoring or discouraging membership in a union, and to negotiate in good faith with a union on matters authorized by law. Unions are required to bargain in good faith with an agency and to refrain from hindering an employee's work performance.

Several other statutes and regulations establish other rights of employees in various circumstances, such as the right of an employee to challenge a position classification, rights to life and health insurance, and rights to compensation for overtime and for back pay in certain circumstances (see Bussey, 1990).

Table 2 Unfair Labor Practices

(a) It shall be an unfair labor practice for an agency:

(1) To interfere with, restrain, or coerce any employee in the exercise by the employee of any right under this chapter;

(2) To encourage or discourage membership in any labor organization by discrimination in connection with hiring, tenure, promotion, or other conditions of employment;

(3) To sponsor, control, or otherwise assist any labor organization, other than to furnish, upon request, customary and routine services and facilities if the services and facilities are also furnished on an impartial basis to other organizations having equivalent status;

(4) To discipline or otherwise discriminate against an employee because the employee has filed a complaint, affidavit, or petition, or has given any information or testimony under this chapter;

(5) To refuse to consult or negotiate in good faith with a labor organization as required by this chapter;

(6) To fail or refuse to cooperate in impasse procedures and impasse decisions as required by this chapter;

(7) To enforce any rule or regulation (other than a rule or regulation implementing Section 2302 of this title) which is in any conflict with any applicable collective bargaining agreement if the agreement was in effect before the date the rule or regulation was prescribed; or

(8) To otherwise fail or refuse to comply with any provision of this chapter.

(b) It shall be an unfair labor practice for a labor organization:

(1) To interfere with, restrain, or coerce any employee in the exercise by the employee of any right under this chapter;

(2) To cause or attempt to cause an agency to discriminate against any employee in the exercise by the employee of any right under this chapter;

(3) To coerce, discipline, fine, or attempt to coerce a member of the labor organization as punishment, reprisal, or for the purpose of hindering or impeding the member's work performance or productivity as an employee or the discharge of the member's duties as an employee;

(4) To discriminate against an employee with regard to the terms or conditions or membership in the labor organization on the basis of race, color, creed, national origin, sex, age, preferential or nonpreferential civil service status, political affiliation, marital status, or handicapping condition;

(5) To refuse to consult or negotiate in good faith with an agency as required by this chapter;

(6) To fail or refuse to cooperate in impasse procedures and impasse decisions as required by this chapter;

(7) (A) To call, or participate in, a strike, work stoppage, or slowdown, or picketing of an agency in a labor–management dispute if such picketing interferes with an agency's operations, or

   (B) To condone any activity described in subparagraph (A) of this paragraph by failing to take action to prevent or stop such activity; or

(8) To otherwise fail or refuse to comply with any provision of this chapter.

Source: 5 U.S. Code, Section 7116.

5. Ethics Law

A complex body of federal ethics laws and regulations has evolved over almost 200 years (Roberts, 1991). On August 7, 1992, the Office of Government Ethics, the organization legally authorized to interpret the laws, issued an official text of regulations organizing and implementing the laws, *Standards of Ethical Conduct for Employees of the Executive Branch* (5 C.F.R. 2635).

The regulations define the basic obligations of public service, and specify forms of disciplinary and corrective action. They define standards for seven forms of conduct:

1. Gifts from outside sources
2. Gifts between employees
3. Conflicting financial interests
4. Impartiality in performing official duties
5. Seeking other employment
6. Misuse of position
7. Outside activities

In the 1980s and 1990s, extensive controversy developed over lobbying by former government officials and postemployment revolving door restrictions. In the Ethics Reform Act of 1989 (PL 101-194), the Congress strengthened existing prohibitions and refused to rescind extensive limitations enacted in 1988 on the postemployment activities of executive branch employees who perform procurement functions. While some parties criticize ethics laws as deterrents to recruitment of people to public service (see Roberts, 1991), others call for further restrictions in such areas as lobbying by former government officials for foreign governments (Choate, 1991).

6. Enforcement: Agency Jurisdiction

As Table 3 indicates, jurisdiction over disputes and appeals arising under employee rights legislation is vested in several agencies and in a few instances directly in federal district courts. In addition, disputes in the form of grievances can often be pursued under negotiated grievance procedures if the applicable collective bargaining agreement covers the matter in dispute. There is some overlap in the jurisdictions of appellate bodies. In cases involving two or more issues, employees seeking review of an agency action must choose between different procedures and appellate bodies.

B. Disputes and Appeals

Employment rights cases arise when an agency takes a personnel action to which an employee objects. After following prescribed agency procedures, the employee can initiate an appeal to the agency with the relevant jurisdiction or initiate a grievance procedure under collective bargaining. These appeals fall into several categories.

1. Adverse Actions

Adverse actions are disciplinary steps taken by an agency for misconduct by an employee. An adverse action can be taken for "such cause as will promote the efficiency of the service" (5 U.S.C. 7313 [a]). An agency action based on misconduct is an adverse action if the penalty is removal, suspension for more than 14 days, reduction in pay or grade, or a furlough of 30 days or less. The employee must be given a 30-day advance, written notice of the charge, and an opportunity to respond. The employee is entitled to representation by counsel and to review all information on which the charge is based. The agency has the burden of proving that the conduct in question adversely affected the performance of the employee or of others, and that the adverse action is being taken "to promote the efficiency of the service."

Adverse action directed to on-the-job behavior is somewhat easier to uphold than adverse action directed to off-duty behavior. Such on-the-job behavior as intentionally falsifying a travel voucher (*Allen v. Department of the Air Force*, 1987) or misappropriating government property (*Major v. Department of the Navy*, 1986), if proven, on its face affects the efficiency of the service. Off-

Table 3 Agency Jurisdiction over Federal Personnel

Agency	Jurisdiction
Merit Systems Protection Board	(1) Disciplinary action for misconduct, such as removal, suspension for more than 14 days, and reduction in grade or pay
	(2) Disciplinary action for unacceptable performance, based on a performance appraisal
	(3) Corrective action to remedy violations of prohibited personnel practices
Office of Special Counsel	(1) Investigations and recommendations concerning prohibited personnel practices
	(2) Whistle blowing—protection of lawful disclosure of information on violations of law and official wrongdoing
Federal Labor Relations Authority	(1) Unfair labor practices
	(2) Grievances under collective bargaining
Equal Employment Opportunity Commission	Complaints of unlawful discrimination
Office of Personnel Management	(1) Position classification appeals
	(2) Claims under health and life insurance, and retirement systems
	(3) Examination ratings question
	(4) Fair Labor Standards Act issues
Federal District Courts and the Court of Appeals for the Federal Circuit	(1) Age discrimination complaints (concurrent with the federal Equal Employment Opportunity Commission)
	(2) Appeals of final decisions under negotiated grievance procedures[a]
	(3) General appellate jurisdiction based on statutory and constitutional grounds
Office of Government Ethics	(1) Interpretation of federal ethics laws and regulations for the executive branch
	(2) Issuance of ethical conduct standards rules

[a]Negotiated grievance procedures apply in some matters for employees who are members of collective bargaining units.

duty behavior, such as sexual conduct, may not be sufficiently related to the efficiency of the service to justify an adverse action. The agency must prove a close connection or nexus between the behavior and the efficiency of the service to justify an adverse action. This question is discussed below under "Selected Statutory and Regulatory Issues."

2. Performance-Based Actions

Performance-based actions are cases in which a disciplinary action is taken against an employee for failure to meet established standards in a critical element of the employee's position. These actions arise out of the performance appraisal process required by the Civil Service Reform Act of 1978 (5 U.S.C. 4301–4305). In this process, a negative appraisal can result in a disciplinary action such as reduction in grade or removal. An employee must be given 30 days advance notice of a finding of unacceptable performance and can contest the finding, with the assistance of counsel, to the supervisor of the individual making the original determination of unacceptable performance. The employee must also be given an opportunity to correct the deficiency in performance before disciplinary action takes effect. If the agency's finding is sustained after the opportunity to correct the deficiency has been given, the employee can appeal the agency's decision to the Merit Systems Protection Board. The agency must support its decision with substantial evidence, and demonstrate that the employee was properly notified and given a fair opportunity to correct the deficiency (*Archuleta v. Department of Agriculture*, 1987). The Merit Systems Protection Board can uphold or reverse the agency's finding, but cannot change the penalty imposed by the agency (*Lisiecki v. MSPB*, 1985). The employee can appeal the Board's decision to the Federal Circuit Court of Appeals.

3. Other Actions

In addition to adverse actions and performance-based actions, various other actions can give rise to appeals, such as reductions in force, restoration of rights after a compensable injury, and actions affecting the Senior Executive Service.

4. Prohibited Practice Actions

The Whistleblower Protection Act of 1989 established the Office of Special Counsel (OSC) as an independent federal agency. The position of special counsel had been attached to the Merit Systems Protection Board. Its mission is to protect employees from the prohibited personnel practices discussed above through investigation and remedial actions, particularly through proceedings before the Merit Systems Protection Board. The Office was established as a result of a finding by Congress that federal employees in general and whistleblowers in particular need more extensive and effective protection from prohibited practices. The basic concern was reprisal for whistleblowing. Under the 1989 Act, a violation of the prohibited practice of reprisal for lawfully disclosing information exists if the disclosure is found to be a "contributing factor" to a personnel action (5 U.S.C. 1214[b][4][B][i] and 1221[e][1]). Under prior law, the complainant had to prove a direct causal connection between the disclosure and retaliatory action.

The OSC has extensive powers to investigate; to request stays of personnel actions; to report and recommend corrective action to the agency, the Merit Systems Protection Board, and the Office of Personnel Management, as well as to the president, the attorney general, congressional committees, and the comptroller general, in appropriate cases; to intervene in Merit Systems Protection Board proceedings; and to take other actions. OSC is required to transmit to appropriate authorities information on violations of law, mismanagement, waste, or danger to public health and safety disclosed to it by an employee, former employee, or applicant for employment.

5. Equal Employment Opportunity Actions

Equal employment opportunity actions are based on an employee's claim that he or she has been discriminated against under the provisions of the following statutes of Title VII of the Civil Rights Act of 1964, as amended in 1972 to apply to federal government: the Civil Rights Act of 1991; the Age Discrimination in Employment Act of 1967, as amended in 1974 and 1978; the Rehabilitation Act of 1973, as amended in 1978 and 1990, to prevent discrimination based on handicapping conditions; and the Equal Pay Act of 1963, as amended in 1974, to prohibit paying men and women different wages for work requiring equal skill, effort, and responsibility. These statutes and appeals under them generally express the policy adopted in the Civil Service Reform Act of 1978 to establish a "work force reflective of the Nation's diversity." The central objective of equal employment opportunity (EEO) was to remove obstacles to employment of members of groups that have been discriminated against, in all phases and levels of work, consistent with merit principles. Today, the emphasis has shifted to positive action to recruit and develop a work force from diverse cultural backgrounds.

Under the reforms initiated by the Civil Service Reform Act of 1978, primary responsibilities for enforcing equal employment opportunities were vested in the Equal Employment Opportunity Commission (EEOC). At the same time, other organizations have retained important responsibilities for equal employment, such as federal recruitment policy by the Office of Personnel Management. Responsibilities for developing plans and procedures have been decentralized to operating agencies. Each agency has adopted complaint procedures under regulations administered by the EEOC. These procedures provide for both individual and class complaints. The procedures require consultation with an EEO counselor, investigation of the complaint, agency response, and a decision based on a hearing, if requested. If discrimination is found, the agency must take corrective action, including determining whether disciplinary action against officials responsible for the discrimination is warranted, and determining an award of costs and attorney fees.

A complainant can appeal an agency decision to the EEOC by filing notice of appeal within 20 days of the decision. The Office of Review and Appeals of the EEOC can grant or deny the appeal, remand the case to the agency for a rehearing or further investigation, or order further investigation by EEOC. The decision of the Office of Review and Appeals can be appealed to the EEOC commissioners, whose decision is the final administrative action. The complainant can then initiate suit in a federal district court, in which the case is tried as an original action.

6. Unfair Labor Practice Actions

Unfair labor practice actions can be filed by any employee against either an agency or a union. The person initiating the action is designated the "charging party." Charges are filed with a regional office of the Federal Labor Relations Authority (FLRA), which investigates the charge. If the investigation warrants, the regional director can issue a complaint, stating the basis of the charge and specifying the time and place for a hearing. The hearing is conducted by an administrative law judge, who then decides the issues and appropriate remedy. An appeal may be taken to the FLRA, and the FLRA's decision may be appealed to the U.S. Court of Appeals.

While there are many significant forms of unfair labor practice, the prohibition against a strike, work stoppage, or slowdown (5 U.S.C. 7116[b][7]) distinguishes labor relations in the public sector from those in the private sector. This was dramatically demonstrated in 1981, when the FLRA found the Professional Air Traffic Controllers Organization (PATCO) guilty of prohibited strike activity and revoked PATCO's status as a recognized labor organization, a decision that was upheld on appeal (PATCO v. FLRA, 1982).

C. Selected Statutory and Regulatory Issues

The rights of federal employees have been in dispute in a number of statutory and regulatory issues in the late 1980s and 1990s. These issues include civil rights in employment; sexual harassment; off-duty behavior and the status of homosexuals; and statutory liabilities of federal employees for common law torts. Some of these issues raise question of constitutional as well as statutory interpretation. Others affect public employment through changes in doctrines that affect interpretations of both public and private employment law.

1. The Civil Rights and Women's Equity in Employment Act of 1991 (PL 102-166)

On November 21, 1991, President Bush signed into law civil rights legislation with broad implications for both public and private employment, the Civil Rights and Women's Equity in Employment Act. The legislation has three purposes. The first is to address "glass ceiling" concerns, defined as underrepresentation of women and minorities in executive, management, and senior decision-making positions. The second is to respond to Supreme Court decisions limiting civil rights protections in employment. The third is to strengthen remedies for employment discrimination, deter further discrimination, and ensure compensation for intentional discrimination (U.S. House of Representatives Reports, 1991).

The glass ceiling provisions of the Act reinforced the commitment of the federal government to eliminating artificial barriers to the advancement of women and minorities in employment. In addressing glass ceiling barriers in private employment, the Act also reinforced mechanisms for reducing discrimination in federal employment. The provisions of the 1978 Civil Service Reform Act establishing recruitment of a representative work force have been generally interpreted to require removal of barriers in federal employment. The 1991 Act established a Pay Equity Technical Assistance Program in the Department of Labor to promote research and disseminate information on methods of eliminating wage disparities and to provide technical assistance to employers to correct wage-setting practices. The Act also authorized the EEOC to make grants to state and local governments and private organizations to conduct educational programs on glass ceiling legal and administrative requirements. Finally, the Act requires the Office of Federal Contract Compliance Programs in the Department of Labor to submit an annual report on wage differentials among and within industries, occupations, job groups, and job titles.

The Act reversed several Supreme Court statutory decisions limiting civil rights protections in employment. In two of its most important provisions, Sections 201 and 202, the Act reversed the Supreme Court's decision in *Wards Cove Packing Co. v. Atonio* (1989). In *Griggs v. Duke Power Co* (1971), the Supreme Court held that Title VII of the Civil Rights Act of 1964 forbids employment practices that have discriminatory effects. Title VII was held to forbid both practices with a discriminatory motive and practices with discriminatory effects. Under *Griggs*, the complaining party was required to prove that an employer's practices had a disparate impact on qualified applicants. The employer then was required to prove that the practices were justified by "business necessity." If the employer established business necessity, the employer won the suit unless the complaining party could show that alternative practices could satisfy the employer's needs without discriminatory effect.

In *Wards Cove*, the Supreme Court held that the test was not business necessity but whether a challenged practice served "legitimate employment goals" of the employer. Exclusionary employment practices not essential to successful performance were permissible if the practices significantly advanced the business objectives of the employer. The decisions also shifted the burden of proof from the employer to the plaintiff to establish whether a practice was justified. Since the employer often possessed information about its practices not available to the plaintiff, it was argued that this decision made it difficult for the plaintiff to establish how the employer's practice produced a discriminatory effect.

The Civil Rights Act of 1991 reestablished business necessity as the test of whether an employment practice with discriminatory effect can be justified. "Business necessity" is defined to mean that a hiring practice has a significant relationship to successful performance on the job. The employer must prove this relationship through statistical studies, validation studies, documented experience, or other evidence. Once a plaintiff proves that an employment practice has a disparate impact, the employer must prove that the practice is justified by business necessity.

The Act also reversed the holding in *Price Waterhouse v. Hopkins* (1989). In that case, the Supreme Court held that "when a plaintiff . . . proves that her gender played a motivating part in an employment decision, the defendant may avoid a finding of liability . . . by proving by preponderance of the evidence that it would have made the same decision, even if it had not taken the plaintiff's gender into account" (*Price Waterhouse v. Hopkins*, 1989, p. 1795).

Under the 1991 Act, the plaintiff must only demonstrate that discrimination was a *contributing factor* to establish the employer's liability. Proof that the employer would have made the same decision is relevant only to determine the remedy for discrimination.

The 1991 Act also reversed *Martin v. Wilks* (1989). This case held that a new employment discrimination suit could be filed when an employer hired or promoted an individual under an approved court decree. Each employee was entitled to litigate the validity and effect of the decree as it applied to the employee. The 1991 Act precludes challenges when a potential claimant had actual notice of the decree and an opportunity to object; when a court determines that the interests of the claimant were actually represented by another person who challenged the decree; and when the court determines that reasonable efforts were made to provide notice to potential claimants.

The Act also clarified when the statute of limitations begins to run in employment discrimination cases, in part reversing a Supreme Court decision in *Lorance v. AT&T* (1990). The statute begins to run when an unlawful employment practice occurs or when the practice is applied adversely to the claimant, whichever is later. The Act also provides comparable statutes of limitations for all discrimination claims.

In the third major category of concern, intentional discrimination, the Act authorizes jury trials and compensatory and punitive damages with specified limits for all types of discrimination. It also authorizes recovery of interest on awards in actions against the federal government and requires payment of the cost of expert witnesses for prevailing plaintiffs.

The Civil Rights and Women's Equity in Employment Act of 1991 reaffirmed and extended a broad commitment to removing gender, racial, and other barriers to access to both public and private employment and treatment in employment.

2. Sexual Harassment

In 1980, the *Harvard Business Review* published a survey of working women reporting that a majority of the respondents regarded sexual harassment in employment as an important problem (Collins and Blodgett, 1981). In 1981, the Merit Systems Protection Board reported that 42% of 23,000 female federal employees surveyed said they had experienced a form of sexual harassment in a 2-year period (1981). The Merit Systems Protection Board reported similar findings in 1988 (1988).

The law on sexual harassment continues to develop. Much of it is based on interpretations of Section 703(a)(1) of Title VII of the Civil Rights Act of 1964 and amendments under the Equal Employment Opportunity Act of 1972. These laws declare discrimination in employment based on sex to be an unlawful employment practice. In 1980 the EEOC defined sexual harassment in *The Final Guidelines on Sexual Harassment in the Work Place* as "unwelcome sexual advances, requests for sexual favors and other verbal or physical conduct of a sexual nature . . . when (1) submission to such conduct is made either explicitly or implicitly a term or condition of an individual's employment, or (2) submission to or rejection of such conduct by an individual is used as a basis for employment conditions affecting such individual, or (3) such conduct has the purpose or effect of unreasonably interfering with an individual's work performance or creating an intimidating, hostile or offensive work environment" (29 C.F.R. 1604.11, 1980).

The Supreme Court held in 1986 that most forms of sexual harassment have been prohibited by civil rights laws as a form of sex discrimination (*Meritor Savings Bank v. Vinson*, 1986). The Court indicated that the precise liabilities of employers, supervisory employees, and coworkers should be defined on a case-by-case basis. Any federal employee, male or female, except a member of the military service, can bring a sexual harassment action under Title VII (as can any employee of a private employer in interstate commerce with 15 or more employees or of a city or state government). Supervisory employees can be named as defendants along with the employer.

While the law is evolving, it seems clear that both the employer and the supervisor are liable if the supervisor harasses an employee. It is highly probable that the employer is liable for acts of supervisors outside of their line of authority, and of coworkers, if the employer knew or should have known of the harassment and failed to stop it (Davis and Wetherfield, 1992). For example, in *Reynolds v. Avalon* (1992), the Court held that a municipal employer unaware of incidents of sexual harassment of an employee until after the incidents can be held liable if the municipality failed to take steps to prevent the incidents. The Court held that failure to act can constitute a policy of deliberate indifference. In a somewhat similar case the Second Circuit Court of Appeals upheld a $264,000 jury verdict against the New York City Police Department for sex discrimination against women employees. The court held that the municipality's liability could be established by proving that the actions of officers were sufficiently widespread to constitute acquiescence of senior policymakers (*Sorlucco v. New York City Police Department*, 1992).

3.   Off-Duty Conduct and Homosexual and Lesbian Rights

As noted above, adverse actions for misconduct in most federal employment can only be taken for "such cause as will promote the efficiency of the service." It is a prohibited personnel practice to discipline an employee for conduct "which does not adversely affect the performance of the employee or applicant or the performance of others." Several cases pose the question of whether particular off-duty conduct detracts from the efficiency of the service and adversely affects the performance of the employee or others. The cases include such matters as failure to pay debts (*Cornish v. Department of Commerce*, 1982), homosexual solicitation (*George v. Department of the Air Force*, 1985), failure to pay taxes (*Eilertson v. Department of the Navy*, 1984), child sexual molestation (*Hayes v. Department of the Navy*, 1984), and possession of a controlled substance (*Parker v. Postal Service*, 1987).

The Merit Systems Protection Board has held that an agency taking an adverse action must clearly demonstrate a connection between the conduct and the efficiency of the service, or a "nexus": "A nexus determination must be based on evidence linking the employee's off-duty misconduct with the efficiency of the service or, in 'certain egregious circumstances,' on a presumption of nexus which may arise from the nature and gravity of the misconduct" (*Merritt v. Department of Justice*, 1981). The Federal Circuit Court of Appeals upheld the Board's test (*Alfred v. HHS*, 1986). In an era of heightened concern for privacy, the off-duty conduct cases challenge agencies to demonstrate clearly that off-duty behavior has a sufficiently strong adverse affect on performance to warrant disciplinary action.

Courts have held that homosexuals are not a suspect class entitled to particular protection under the equal protection clause of the Constitution, and there is no fundamental due process privacy right to pursue homosexual activity (*Bowers v. Hardwick*, 1986). If there is a rational basis for an agency regulation directed to homosexual behavior, the regulation will be upheld. In *High Tech Gays v. Defense Industrial Security Clearance Office* (1990), the Ninth Circuit Court of Appeals upheld regulations denying security clearances to homosexual civilians, based on susceptibility to blackmail, violations of criminal law, and untrustworthiness.

In the case of civilian employment unrelated to the military and national security, the question of what constitutes a rational basis for regulating homosexual behavior has not been clearly established. Under the nexus doctrine, if an employee's conduct has a demonstrably negative effect on his or her work or the work of others, regulation directed to the employee's behavior might be upheld. This remains to be determined.

4.   Liability of Managers for Libel and Slander and Assault and Battery

The Federal Employees Liability Reform and Tort Compensation Act of 1988 (28 U.S.C. 13461[6] 2671, et seq.) makes the United States the sole defendant in suits for money damage arising from activity performed by an employee within the scope of employment. This Act reversed the Supreme Court's decision in *Westfall v. Erwin* (1988), which held that managers were not immune from tort liability to their employees in some circumstances. The 1988 Act restored immunity for actions taken by a manager within the scope of employment, leaving the aggrieved employee to sue the United States under the Federal Torts Claims Act. However, under that Act the United States is not liable for claims of assault and battery or libel and slander. This may leave the aggrieved employee without recourse, unless the manager's conduct is held to be beyond the scope of his or her employment. The courts have interpreted the "scope of employment" requirement in different ways (*McKinney v. Whitfield*, 1984, holding a supervisor's act outside the scope of employment when he pushed an office chair into a subordinate's leg; *Detar v. Smith*, 1985, holding that slamming an office door, injuring the plaintiff, was within the scope of employment; *Kimbro v. U.S.*, 1992, holding that the striking of one employee by another was not within the scope of employment).

III. CONCLUSION: ENDURING ISSUES

Public personnel administration in the United States is law-bound. It is extensively regulated by a complex, multilayered legal regime. Many believe that personnel law is too restrictive to promote high levels of administrative efficiency and responsiveness. For instance, today's civil service reformers increasingly call for "deregulation" of the public service (Wilson, 1989; Osborne and Gaebler, 1992; DiIulio et al., 1993; Gore, 1993). Such reform would entail decentralization of personnel decision making away from central personnel agencies and to operating line managers; the creation of greater flexibility by a substantial reduction of government-wide personnel rules and required practices; and greater privatization to jettison much of the law altogether. Whatever the merit reformers' proposals, the discussion in this chapter strongly suggests that public personnel law will continue to be guided by three central issues.

First, what is the proper relationship between partisan politics and personnel administration? Public personnel's legal framework rests on a belief that the public service should be shielded from partisan politics. The merit system was created for this purpose in 1883, as were later restrictions on public employees' partisan political activity, and as are contemporary restrictions on partisan coercion. A great deal of federal personnel law, including the establishment and operation of the Merit Systems Protection Board, reflects a strong desire to keep partisanship out of the civil service. In fact, the belief that a nonpartisan civil service is strongly in the public interest has even been incorporated into contemporary constitutional law. Patronage practices as old as the Republic are now unconstitutional (*Rutan v. Republican Party of Illinois*, 1990). Public employees may have greater freedom to express publicly their hope that a president be assassinated than that he be reelected (compare *Rankin v. McPherson*, 1987 with *Civil Service Commission v. National Association of Letter Carriers*, 1973). Even staunch supporters of the Hatch Act reform strongly advocated protections against partisan coercion.

Second, what are the limits of government authority over public employees and how will they be exercised? A great deal of law regarding public personnel management is addressed to these questions. The civil service reformers of the 1870s–1890s thought it was an anomaly that the political system had not developed strict limits on the use of the public service for purely partisan ends. Today, we may wonder why we have failed for so long to prevent sexual harassment in the public sector workplace. Constitutional legal development since the 1950s has considerably strengthened public employees' substantive, procedural due process, and equal protection rights in the workplace. A great deal of statutory law, including the Civil Rights Act of 1964 (as amended), has also afforded public employees new rights and protections against abuse. In addition, many federal and other public employees now have extensive rights under labor law. The issue of authority also extends to the constitutional separation of powers as is fully evident in *Morrison v. Olson* (1988).

Third, what is the overarching public interest in public personnel administration? As the public service model emphasizes, the public interest goes well beyond mere administrative efficiency. The constitutional and statutory protection of whistleblowing is strongly regarded as in the public interest even when it interferes with administrative operations. Ethics law is premised on the belief that there is a strong public interest in accountability and disclosure even though they may be cumbersome. Ultimately, this question asks us to consider what the public service should be. What is the best model for now of the American public service? Or are there many models?

It is in the nature of public personnel administration that these questions are complex and political. They do not yield simple, timeless answers. Public personnel law has been a tool for enhancing thinking about them and for providing boundaries. There is no doubt that over the years public personnel administration has and will continue to change—often dramatically. But the central issues of political partisanship, authority, and the public interest will endure.

REFERENCES

Articles and Books

Ban, Carolyn (1991). The realities of the merit system, *Public Personnel Management* (Carolyn Ban and Norma Riccucci, eds.), Longman, White Plains, NY.

Bussey, Ellen, ed. (1990). *Federal Civil Service Law and Procedures*, Bureau of National Affairs, Washington, DC.

Choate, Pat (1990). *Agents of Influence*, Knopf, New York.

Collins, E. G., and Blodgett, T. B. (1981). Sexual harassment. *Harvard Business Review*, 76 (March).

Curtis, George (1884). *The Year's Work in Civil Service Reform*, National Civil Service Reform League, New York.

Davis, Martha, and Wetherfield, Alison (1992). A primer on sexual harassment law. *Clearinghouse Rev.*, 76 (March).

DiIulio, John, Garvey, Gerald, and Kettl, Donald (1993). *Improving Government Performance*, Brookings Institution, Washington, DC.

Dotson, Arch (1955). The emerging doctrine of privilege in public employment, *Public Admin. Rev.*, 15 (Spring): 77–87.

Eaton, Dorman (1880). *The Civil Service in Great Britain*, Harper and Bros., New York.

Fish, Carl (1905). *The Civil Service and the Patronage*, Longmans, Green, and Co., New York.

Gore, Al (1993). *From Red Tape to Results: Creating a Government that Works Better and Costs Less*, Government Printing Office, Washington, DC.

Harvard Law Review (1984). Developments in the law—public employment, *97*: 1611–1800 (authors not identified).

Lee, Yong S. (1987). Civil liability of state and local governments. *Public Admin. Rev.*, *47* (March/April): 160–170.

New York Times (1975). August 14.

Osborne, David, and Gaebler, Ted (1992). *Reinventing Government*, Addison-Wesley, Reading, MA.

Publius (1961). *The Federalist* (Clinton Rossiter, ed.), Mentor, New York.

Reich, Charles (1964). The new property. *Yale Law J.*, *73*: 733–787.

Richardson, James (1899). *A Compilation of the Messages and Papers of the Presidents of the United States, 1789–1897*, Government Printing Office, Washington, DC.

Roberts, Robert (1991). The public integrity quagmire. *Public Personnel Management*, (Carolyn Ban and Norma Riccucci, eds.), Longman, White Plains, NY.

Rohr, John (1989). *The President and Public Administration*, American Historical Association, Washington, DC.

Rosenbloom, David (1971). *Federal Service and the Constitution*, Cornell University Press, Ithaca, NY.

Rosenbloom, David (1975). Public personnel administration and the Constitution, *Public Admin. Rev., 35* (Jan./Feb.): 52–59.

Rosenbloom, David (1977). *Federal Equal Employment Opportunity*, Praeger, New York.

Rosenbloom, David (1983). *Public Administration and Law*, Marcel Dekker, New York.

Rosenbloom, David and Obuchowski, Carole (1977). Public personnel examinations and the Constitution. *Public Admin. Rev., 37* (Jan./Feb.): 9–18.

Sageser, A. B. (1935). *The First Two Decades of the Pendleton Act*, University of Nebraska, Lincoln.

Schurz, Carl (1913). *The Speeches, Correspondence, and Political Papers of Carl Schurz*, 6 vols. (Frederick Bancroft, ed.), G. P. Putnam's Sons, New York.

Shafritz, Jay, Riccucci, Norma, Rosenbloom, David, and Hyde, Albert (1992). *Personnel Management in Government*, Fourth ed., Marcel Dekker, New York.

Stiehm, Judith (1992). Managing the military's homosexual exclusion policy, *Univ. Miami Law Rev.*, 685.

Sturdivant, John (1993). Federal employees can handle politics, *Washington Post*, August 10, 1993, p. A14.

Sullivan, George (1992). Employer liability for sexual harassment extends to schools and universities, *Labor Law J.*, 456.

U.S. Office of Personnel Management, Federal Executive Institute (1992). *Constitutional Literacy Reader*, Federal Executive Institute, Charlottesville, VA.

Van Alstyne, William (1968). The demise of the right-privilege distinction in constitutional law. *Harvard Law Rev., 81*: 1439–1464.

Van Riper, Paul (1958). *History of the United States Civil Service*. Row, Peterson, Evanston, IL.

Vaughn, Robert (1984). *Merit Systems Protection Board*. Law Journal Seminars Press. New York.

White, Leonard (1965a). *The Jeffersonians*, Free Press, New York.

_____(1965b). *The Republican Era*, Free Press, New York.

Wilson, James Q. (1989). *Bureaucracy*, Basic Books, New York.

Cases

Abood v. Detroit Board of Education (1977). 430 U.S. 209.

AFSCME [American Federation of State, County, and Municipal Employees] v. Woodward (1969). 406 F.2d 137.

Alfred v. Department of Health and Human Services (1986). 786 F.2d 1128.

Allen v. Department of the Air Force (1987). 34 MSPB 314.

Ambach v. Norwick (1979). 41 U.S. 68.

Archuleta v. Department of Agriculture (1987). 34 MSPB 22.

Arnett v. Kennedy (1974). 416 U.S. 134.

Bailey v. Richardson (1950). 182 F.2d 46.

Baker v. City of St. Petersburg (1968). 400 F.2d 294.

Ben-Shalom v. Department of the Navy (1989). 881 F.2d 454.

Bishop v. Wood (1976), 426 U.S. 341.

Bivens v. Six Unknown Named Federal Narcotics Agents (1971). 403 U.S. 388.

Board of Regents v. Roth (1972). 408 U.S. 564.

Bowers v. Hardwick (1986). 478 U.S. 186.

Branti v. Finkel (1980). 445 U.S. 506.

Broadrick v. Oklahoma (1973). 413 U.S. 601.

Brown v. Board of Education of Topeka (1954). 347 U.S. 483.

Burns v. Reed (1991). 114 L.Ed.2d 547.

Bush v. Lucas (1983). 462 U.S. 367.

Butz v. Economou (1978). 438 U.S. 478.

Cafeteria Workers v. McElroy (1961). 367 U.S. 886.

Carlson v. Green (1980). 446 U.S. 14.

Chicago Teachers Union v. Hudson (1986). 475 U.S. 292.

City of Richmond v. Croson (1989). 478 U.S. 1016.

Civil Service Commission v. National Association of Letter Carriers (1973). 413 U.S. 548.

Cleveland Board of Education v. LaFleur (1974). 414 U.S. 632.

Cleveland Board of Education v. Loudermill (1985). 470 U.S. 532.

Codd v. Velger (1977). 429 U.S. 624.

Cole v. Richardson (1972). 405 U.S. 676.

Cornish v. Department of Commerce (1982). 10 MSPB 382.

Craig v. Boren (1976). 429 U.S. 190.

Davis v. Passman (1979). 442 U.S. 228.

Detar v. Smith (1992). 752 F.2d 1015.

Dronenburg v. Zech (1984). 741 F.2d 1388.

Eilertson v. Department of the Navy (1984). 23 MSPB 152.

Elfbrandt v. Russell (1966). 384 U.S. 11.

Elrod v. Burns (1976). 427 U.S. 347.

Ex Parte Curtis (1882). 106 U.S. 371.

Ex Parte Hennen (1839). 13 Peters 230.

Federal Deposit Insurance Corporation v. Meyer (1994). 62 Law Week 4138.

Foley v. Connelie (1978). 435 U.S. 291.

Forrester v. White (1987). 108 S.Ct. 538.

Fullilove v. Klutznick (1980). 448 U.S. 448.

Fursman v. Chicago (1917). 278 Ill. 318.

Gardner v. Broderick (1968). 392 U.S. 273.

Garner v. Los Angeles (1951). 341 U.S. 716.

Garrity v. New Jersey (1967). 385 U.S. 493.

George v. Department of the Air Force (1985). 29 MSPB 95.

Glover v. Eastern Nebraska Community Office of Retardation (1989). 867 F.2d 461.

Goldberg v. Kelly (1970). 397 U.S. 254.

Greene v. McElroy (1959). 360 U.S. 474.

Griggs v. Duke Power Co. (1971). 401 U.S. 424.

Hafer v. Melo (1991). 116 L. Ed.2d 301.

Harley v. Schuylkill County (1979). 476 F. Supp. 191.

Harlow v. Fitzgerald (1982). 457 U.S. 800.

Hayes v. Department of the Navy (1984). 727 F.2d 1535.

High Tech Gays v. Defense Industrial Security Clearance Office (1990). 895 F.2d 563.

Hoke v. Henderson (1833). 15 N.C. 1.

Humphrey's Executor v. U.S. (1935). 295 U.S. 602.

Joint Anti-Fascist Refugee Committee v. McGrath (1951). 341 U.S. 123.

Kelley v. Johnson (1976). 425 U.S. 238.

Kiiskila v. Nichols (1970). 433 F.2d 745.

Kimbro v. U.S. (1992). D.C. DC No. 90-0873.

Lisiecki v. Merit Systems Protection Board (1985). 769 F.2d 1588.

Lorance v. AT&T (1990). 490 U.S. 900.

Major v. Department of the Navy (1986). 31 MSPB 22.

Martin v. Wilks (1989). 109 S.Ct. 2180.

McAuliffe v. New Bedford (1892). 155 Mass. 216.

McCarthy v. Philadelphia Civil Service Commission (1976). 424 U.S. 645.

McKinney v. Whitfield (1984).

McLaughlin v. Tilendis (1968). 398 F.2d 287.

Meritor Savings Bank v. Vinson (1986). 477 U.S. 57.

Merritt v. Department of Justice (1981). 6 MSPB 493.

Metro Broadcasting v. Federal Communications Commission (1990). 110 S.Ct. 2997.

Milliken v. Bradley (1974). 418 U.S. 717.

Mills v. Lowndes (1939). 26 F. Supp. 792.

Morrison v. Olson (1988). 487 U.S. 654.

Mt. Healthy City School District Board of Education v. Doyle (1977). 429 U.S. 274.

Myers v. U.S. (1926). 272 U.S. 52.

National Association of Letter Carriers v. Civil Service Commission (1972). 346 F. Supp. 578.

National Treasury Employees Union v. Von Raab (1989). 489 U.S. 656.

O'Connor v. Ortega (1987). 480 U.S. 709.

Owen v. City of Independence (1980). 445 U.S. 622.

Parker v. Postal Service (1987). 819 F.2d 113.

Patco v. FLRA (1982). 672 F.2d 109.

Pembaur v. City of Cincinnati (1986). 475 U.S. 469.

Perry v. Sindermann (1972). 408 U.S. 593.

Personnel Administrator v. Feeney (1979). 442 U.S. 256.

Pickering v. Board of Education (1968). 391 U.S. 563.

Powell v. Zuckert (1966). 366 F.2d 634.

Price Waterhouse v. Hopkins (1989). 109 S.Ct. 1775.

Railway Mail Association v. Murphy (1943). 44 N.Y.2d 601.

Rankin v. McPherson (1987). 483 U.S. 378.

Regents v. Bakke (1978). 438 U.S. 265.

Reynolds v. Avalon (1992). D.C. NJ No. 90-4250.

Rutan v. Republican Party of Illinois (1990). 110 S.Ct. 2729.

Saylor v. U.S. (1967). 374 F.2d 894.

Smith v. Wade (1983). 461 U.S. 30.

Sorlucco v. New York City Police Department (1992). C.A. 2d, No. 92-7165.

Steelworkers v. Weber (1979). 443 U.S. 193.

Sugarman v. Dougall (1973). 413 U.S. 634.

Uniformed Sanitation Men's Association v. Commissioner (1968). 392 U.S. 280.

United Public Workers v. Mitchell (1947). 330 U.S. 75.

U.S. v. Paradise (1987). 480 U.S. 149.

Wards Cove Packing Co. v. Atonio (1989). 109 S.Ct. 2115.

Washington v. Davis (1976). 426 U.S. 229.

Weiman v. Updegraff (1952). 344 U.S. 183.

Weiner v. U.S. (1958). 357 U.S. 349.

Wells v. Harris (1979). 1 MSPB 199.

Westfall v. Erwin (1988). 484 U.S. 292.

Will v. Michigan Department of State Police (1989). 109 S.Ct. 2304.

Wygant v. Jackson (1986). 478 U.S. 267.

Public Documents

Civil Service Commission (1907). *Annual Report*, 24. Government Printing Office, Washington, DC.

Commission on Political Activity of Government Personnel (1968). *Report*, 3 vols. Government Printing Office, Washington, DC.

Congress, House of Representatives (1991). *House Report* No. 102-40 (I and II) (April 24 and May 17). Government Printing Office, Washington, DC.

Congressional Globe (1839). Vol. IV, 25th Congress, 3rd session.

Congressional Record (1939). Vol. 84, 76th Congress, 1st session.

Executive Order 9835 (1947). *Fed. Reg., 12*: 1935 (March 21).

Executive Order 10241 (1951). *Fed. Reg., 16*: 3690 (April 28).

Executive Order 10450 (1953). *Fed. Reg., 18*: 2489 (April 27).

Executive Order 10988 (1962). *Fed. Reg., 27*: 551 (January 17).

Federal Register (1948). Vol. 13: 1473 (March 20).

President's Committee on Administrative Management (1937). *Report of the Committee*. Government Printing Office, Washington, DC.

Statistical Abstract of the United States (1992). Government Printing Office, Washington, DC.

Statutes at Large (1825). *4*: 104 (March 3).

U.S. Merit Systems Protection Board (1981). *Sexual Harassment in the Federal Workplace,* Merit Systems Protection Board, Washington, DC.

U.S. Merit Systems Protection Board (1988). *Sexual Harassment in the Federal Workplace: An Update*, Merit Systems Protection Board, Washington, DC.

5
Public Personnel Administration Outside the United States

VIRGIL B. ZIMMERMANN   Rockefeller College of Public Affairs and Policy, State University of New York at Albany, Albany, New York

I. INTRODUCTION

Public personnel administration has long been one of the more narrowly parochial of the many subfields of public administration. A reader of much of the professional literature on public personnel matters might gain the impression that only in the United States do systematic and merit-based procedures govern the orderly and objective recruitment, selection, and compensation of public employees. Such a notion may be forgiven for reliable and detailed sources of information on foreign systems are not readily available. After Sharp's (1931) study of the French civil service and that of Friedrich and Cole on Switzerland there was not a book length exposition of civil service law and practice in a European country until the appearance of the volumes on the civil services of France (Gregoire, 1964), Great Britain (Campbell, 1965; Gladden, 1967), and Ireland (Dooney, 1976).

From the 1950s through the 1970s, however, there was a great flowering of interest in comparative public administration and foreign civil service systems attracted a good deal of interest. Stimulated by the wartime experiences of present and future scholars and by employment overseas in foreign aid activities, this period saw the publication of books, papers, and articles that described administrative arrangements and practices including those having to do with personnel administration in many parts of the world. Many foreign students and government workers brought to the United States to study also wrote about public service practices in their homelands.

For many reasons that enthusiasm dwindled during the late 1970s and 1980 despite the existence of such journals as *International Journal of Public Administration, Journal of Comparative Administration, Administration and Society,* and the British *Journal of Administration Overseas.* Like their venerable counterpart the *International Review of Administrative Sciences,* all of these contain occasional articles on personnel practices in countries other than the United States.

With the globalization of the world's economy, however, there has been a renewed interest in comparative administration. Heady's text has come out in a fourth edition (1992) and Dwivedi and Henderson edited *Public Administration in a World Perspective* (1990) with many non-American contributors. This has excellent chapters, with considerable information on civil services and on administrative developments in the Arab world, Africa, Australia, Canada, France, India, Japan, Latin America, Southeast Asia, and the United Kingdom. The present fragmentary and incomplete survey will, it is hoped, stimulate interest in foreign civil service systems and, perhaps, an awareness that we in the United States could, if we took the effort, learn from the experiences and experiments of others.

However, the difficulties of doing research on foreign administrators and civil service systems are substantial. Unless subsidized by increasingly tight-fisted foreign aid donors, the costs of serious multinational research are enormous. The lack of a suitable theoretical foundation for comparative studies has been an impediment (Peters, 1988). Even more daunting than the scarcity of available and reliable published sources has been the problem of relevance and interpretation. Because personnel administration, at least outwardly, depends on statutes and decrees, we look to such documents but find that their terms do not adequately define themselves.[1] Even if we learn what the law commands, we may not get much insight into ongoing administrative reality. Articles and reports on non-American personnel systems are often in unfamiliar languages. Even if responsibly translated, the works of non-American authors are easily misinterpreted or leave out details essential to our understanding. Some personnel terms are quite literally untranslatable. Still more problematic is the possibility of penetrating linguistic and conceptual barriers to grasp those deep-seated, persistent, and culturally transmitted ways of thought that shape and guide administrative behavior and decisions. A thoroughly comparative study of any element of public personnel administration in a number of countries would require a suitable institutional base and mobilize a collaborative effort involving scholars located in and thoroughly familiar with the systems of each of the countries being compared.

II. SOURCES OF INFORMATION

The most useful sources of information on personnel practices, the values that inspired and sustain them, and their impact on administration are listed in the references.[2] A student might well begin with Chapman's (1959) *The Profession of Government*. Although many details are now outdated, this comprehensive account provides much insight into the forces that shaped the evolution of contemporary civil services in Europe. He attributes many features of these personnel systems to demands for a public bureaucracy that would be politically neutral, devoted to the state and to the public interest, and acting fairly and "judiciously" in the application of the "law" to specific matters. He explains, for example, that in the emerging German nation-state where education beyond an elementary level was not readily available to many and employment opportunities were scanty for those who did get more than a minimum education, the personnel arrangements that supported the *Rechstaat* were highly compatible with the self-interests of those fortunate enough to secure places in the public service. He notes also that in such states educational institutions within governmental departments, e.g., the famous French *Ecole des Ponts et Chaussées*, provided trained technical and managerial manpower not only for the government but for the private sector as well.

Five pioneer survey volumes provide useful historical perspectives. A United Nations compendium (1966) of civil service law in 38 countries provided information on each but hardly enough

---

[1]Gregoire (1964, pp. 133–138) explains the difficulty of discovering in French law or common use a single, clear, and consistent meaning for such essential terms as *corps, cadre,* and *emploi.*

[2]In addition to the listed references and other journal articles, this chapter has drawn on the unpublished "country papers" submitted to conferences of officials of European civil service academies and governmental in-service training officers held in Rome in 1968, Madrid in 1970, and Brussels in 1972; extensive interviews with civil servants responsible for personnel administration and training in Belgium, Ireland, Italy, the Netherlands, Spain, Sweden, Switzerland, and Yugoslavia in 1971–1972; and comments of students from many lands in my graduate courses in public personnel administration.

to engender confidence that one does in fact understand both the spirit and intricacies of practice. A volume edited by Hsueh (1962) contained brief descriptions of the civil services in 11 countries lying in an arc from Nepal to Japan. Braibanti (1966a) covered the former British areas of Asia in depth with special emphasis on the historical, economic, and cultural factors that have shaped their public services. Pimental (1966) provided a cursory legal-institutional description of personnel administration in Latin America and Adu (1965) depicted the evolving personnel problems of the African states as they emerged from colonial status with a concomitant loss of the numerous European expatriots who had manned the upper levels of their bureaucracies. There has been, so far as I can discover, no updating successor to any of these volumes. However, given the glacial pace at which changes in personnel systems typically occur, much contained in these volumes of three decades past may still be pertinent.

In 1984 Bruce Smith edited a volume *The Higher Civil Service in Europe and Canada: Lessons for the United States* for the Brookings Institution and it, like *The Civil Service in Liberal Democracies* (J.C. Kingdom, editor, 1990), contains much valuable information. In 1990–1991 Gordon Klang of the Office of International Affairs of the U.S. Office of Personnel Management conducted a survey of position classification and compensation in Australia, Canada, Federal Republic of Germany, France, Japan, Northern Ireland, Sweden, and the United Kingdom. The results, which are broader in scope than the title indicates, are contained in three large looseleaf notebooks available only in the Office of Personnel Management library in Washington, D.C.

One of the best of the single-country analyses based on first-hand observation by an American engaged in "technical assistance" was Siffin's first report (1962) on the Thai bureaucracy, which he described as a "wonderously complex amalgam of Oriental and Western forms" characterized by (1) strict "careerism" with only two important points of entry, related to educational achievement, (2) advancement dependent almost wholly on supervisory judgment, and (3) extreme competition for entry determined in "elaborate and exhaustive" examinations. Despite recent political turmoil in Thailand, those circumstances probably still persist. Partially as a result of such overseas service a number of book length treatments of civil services in non-European countries were published in the 1960s and 1970s. (Australia—Caiden, 1967; Algeria—Sibh, 1968; Brazil—Graham, 1968; India—Misra, 1977; New Zealand—Smith, 1974; Pakistan—Braibanti, 1966b; Goodnow, 1964; Peru—Hopkins, 1967; Thailand—Siffin, 1966).

Many of the public administration journals published outside the United States in one of the common international languages include articles on topics relating to public personnel administration. Especially pertinent are the journals of Australia, Canada, India, Ireland, New Zealand, and the Philippines. But few of these are widely available in U.S. libraries. Moreover, many of those initiated by foreign aid–supported "institutes" of public administration in developing countries have ceased publication. It may be ironic that from 1989 to mid-1993 only one article on a foreign civil service appeared in *Public Personnel Management*, the official publication of the International Personnel Management Association.

Beginning in the middle 1950s with Kelsall's study of the British bureaucracy (1955) and Berger's (1957) on Egypt there have been numerous sociopolitical studies of civil services. Crozier's analysis of *The Bureaucratic Phenomenon* (1964) and Armstrong's account of the historical origins of the *European Administrative Elite* (1973) have been acclaimed as scholarly contributions to our understanding of the relationships among environmental conditions, personnel systems, and administrative behavior. In the same vein but with greater emphasis on the political role of civil servants are Suleiman's study (1974) of the French administrative elite, the volume edited by Dogan (1975), entitled *The Mandarins of Western Europe* and Suleiman's (1985) *Bureaucrats and Policy-making*. Comparable studies have been undertaken by non-Americans working for advanced degrees in American universities, e.g., Cappelletti (1966) and Kubota (1969). There are also the essays in *Sociologia de la Administración Pública Española* (1968), in the volumes published by the Instituto per la Scienza del 'Amministrazione Pubblica (1965) on the central bureaucracy of Italy, and the studies by Scarrow (1957) and R. A. Chapman (1970) on Australia and Great Britain and by Palmer et al. (1988) on the Egyptian bureaucracy. The objective in such works has been to demonstrate the effect that characteristics of higher civil service may have on governmental policy and economic and political modernization, and to relate the values of civil servants to the cultural, religious, and socioeconomic conditions of the environment that nurtures them.

Because of the number and variety of national[3] civil service systems and the degree of change taking place in some of them, multinational generalizations are hazardous. To any broad statement there will inevitably be exceptions. Nevertheless only by attempting such generalizations can one make sense of the incredible diversity that exists. With this caveat, the comments that follow are grouped under the headings customary in treatments of public personnel administration.

III. CAREER CORPS SYSTEMS

European civil services, which long served as a pattern for most of the rest of the world, evolved well before the flowering of political democracy. Wise rulers wanted an efficient and responsible administrative apparatus, one that would collect taxes, supply and pay the bills of the military, and administer justice in a manner resistant to the particularistic local and feudal interests that impeded the centralizing efforts of the regime (Armstrong, 1973). They had readily at hand an appropriate model in the bureaucracy of the established church, whose literate clerics had provided the financial and record-keeping staffs of feudal lords. Thus, there came into being public bureaucracies based on the twin principles of initial appointment at an early age, before ties to other interests had been fixed and assurance of a lifetime career characterized by reciprocal obligations of compensation, trust and loyal obedience.

In an age when education was not widespread, it became common for departments of government to establish their own schools so that youngsters might be recruited, trained, and then deployed as needed into the bureaucracy. Even elementary education by the British in Somalia and the Dutch in Indonesia was in departmental schools that enabled the colonial power to educate the selected few who were destined to provide the public service work force.

As national bureaucracies took shape, the several ministries or departments of administration operated quite independently of one another and were given a great deal of autonomy by the head of state, at least on all matters not directly affecting its interests. This allowed the formation of departmental or ministerial "services" in which employees were grouped into *corps* (France), *classes* (United Kingdom), *ruoli* (Italy), *services* (India), or *cuerpos* (Spain). In other languages other terms identify what is essentially the same institution.

The essence of a corps is that its members are recognized, by themselves and others, as belonging to a group that has been recruited, chosen, and trained in accordance with specific criteria and appointed or promoted to a rank that identifies their status in that group. As members of a corps they are assured of lifetime employment except in case of proven and serious misconduct. Salaries and other rewards, including advancement in rank, as well as indications as to the kinds and levels of responsibilities members of a corps may discharge, are determined customar-

---

[3]Personnel systems in the international agencies pose so many unique problems that they deserve separate treatment and are not covered in this chapter.

ily by statutes or edicts applicable only to that corps. "Like a tightly organized elite profession, the corps as an institution advances the careers of its members and the members reflect credit on the corps. As a result socialization to the values and styles of individual corps is intense and highly specific" (Armstrong, 1973, p. 214). This could be said of virtually all corps, especially those at higher levels in Britian, Ireland, and Japan, and, to a lesser degree, of departmental corps in Spain, Italy, and elsewhere.

Even where separations for reasons other than "cause" on retirement are permitted, such terminations are so foreign to tradition and hedged by so many constraints as to be virtually unthinkable. The Italian civil service code of 1956, for example, permits separation of a civil servant "whose services are no longer needed," but only after 2 years notice and a severance payment of a month's pay for each prior year of service. Veteran Italian civil servants told me in 1972 that they did not recall any such terminations. Instead, if a corp's work load diminishes, the number of vacancies filled annually at the entry level may be held below the number of places specified in the applicable statute, or, in the event that an entire corps becomes superfluous, all recruitment is stopped and its members are distributed to other ministries until all members have died or retired.

Each corps is composed of a number of levels or ranks, typically from four to eight, though Gregoire (1964) notes the existence in France and elsewhere of one-rank corps. The number of posts at each rank is usually established in relatively permanent legislation. Members of a corps are considered interchangeable and rank is determined only indirectly by a member's assigned responsibilities or organizational location.

With some exceptions, initial appointment to each corps is to the lowest grade in that corps and is limited to persons below a specified maximum age, generally 28–35 for corps requiring a university degree. Lower maximums are set for corps for which educational requirements are lower, but most countries make some allowance in maximum age for military veterans. The antiquity of this tradition is evidenced by the fact that the India Act of 1784 set a minimum age of 15 and a maximum of 18 for initial appointment of "writers" by the East India Company (Blunt, 1937). This group became the British Colonial Service.

Most corps are associated with a specific governmental department, although "interministerial" corps were created in Britain in 1921 (Balogh, 1968) and in Spain in 1964 (de la Oliva de Castro and Gutiérrez Reñón, 1968). The "Senior Executive Services" created in Australia and Canada, though modeled on that of the United States, have many of the attributes of an interministerial corps. Typically the salaries of all members of a corps are budgeted as a single item irrespective of the function or organization to which they may be either temporarily or permanently assigned. This greatly simplifies both budgeting and accounting but is, of course, incompatible with anything like "program budgeting" or cost determination by activity.

Members of departmental corps may be temporarily or permanently assigned to other branches of the administration; this is indeed characteristic of such prestigious corps as those of the council of state and court of accounts in France and Italy. Small or new offices, including even the office of the prime minister, are not apt to have corps of their own but are staffed by personnel drawn from the corps of larger entities. The private secretaries and personnel staffs of ministers and their deputies often include persons enrolled in corps other than those associated with that ministry. If a department of public education, for example, needs doctors or nurses for a program, but has no such corps of its own, it will obtain them from the corps of the ministry of public health. The difficulties in negotiating and even adjudicating such interbranch assignments are sometimes troublesome especially as governmental tasks become more technical and the demands for high-quality talent more competitive. Nevertheless, the point must be made that an employee stays in his or her own corps regardless of where he or she works and advancement and future career are determined by the rules and customs applicable to that corps. Transfers between corps are typically either impossible or extremely rare.

The corporate character of the corps is frequently reinforced by the publication for each of a "staff list" that enumerates the posts at each rank as well as the name of each incumbent with the date of appointment and, sometimes, date of birth and/or of initial appointment to the corps. Where promotion is highly dependent on the existence of vacancies at higher levels and governed by seniority, as is usually the case, one may calculate from such a list the approximate time at which advancement is likely to occur.

Because governmental activities have obviously required different levels of educational preparation, most countries using the corps system have divided their public services into three or four categories, depending on whether the qualification required was a primary, secondary, vocational or technical, or university education.[4] Some statutes and rules apply at all levels, whereas others do not. Until recently passage from a corps at one level to a higher level has been rare except for those who acquire the necessary higher education and are still below the maximum age. Efforts to democratize the civil service—as well perhaps as difficulties in recruitment—have led to measures providing limited arrangements for upward movement. In France, for example, although most admissions to the Ecole des Ponts et Chaussées and the Ecole Nationale d'Administration, which lead to entry into highest level corps, are made to recent university graduates, larger numbers are now being admitted from those with experience in the inferior corps.[5] A similar possibility now also exists in Britain, Ireland, and Italy.

Departmental personnel systems coupled with the expansion of governmental functions requiring specialized training have resulted in the proliferation of corps. In mid-1960s Britain there were 47 interdepartmental classes and more than 1400 departmental classes. In Spain there were more than 220 specialized *cuerpos*, of which 61 contained fewer than 50 places. Each complemented the four general interministerial corps. There are eight corps of doctors, six of interpreters, three of architects. There are more than 200 Italian *ruoli*, not including jurists and university professors, and 450 in Greece.

Some corps carry higher status than others requiring equivalent educational qualifications. Such prestige is due partly to the power and influence that its members wield, partly to opportunities for interdepartmental mobility, partly to the reputations built by illustrious past corps members, and partly also to opportunities for access to posts making available such extra salary emoluments as fees to be obtained from membership on the governing boards of private and quasi-public organizations. In much of the world, literary culture and legal learning are much more highly prized than technical or scientific attainments, and that social esteem is reflected in the prestige of certain corps.

Although within corps occupational differences are not usually made explicit, a good deal of specialization does occur. A generalist administrator who had worked for some years in a "personnel branch" would not be likely to be assigned to do economic analysis or put in charge of a public relations unit. One hears contradictory complaints—often from persons within the same

---

[4]In France categories A, B, C, and D; in Italy *direttivo, executivo, di concento, auxiliary*; in Germany the services (*Dienst*) are *Hoherer, Gehohener, Mittleer, Einfacher*; In Australia, divisions I, II, III, IV; in Greece, AT, AR, ME, and SE. In each case the ranking is from the highest level of education required, e.g., a university degree, to the lowest. In Italy the separation of the service into "careers" and the names of the ranks were replaced by a numbered list of grades in the 1970s but the old terms persist in common use. In 1990 France dropped the D category.

[5]In the 1990 revision of its pay scales France dropped the maximum age limit for upward movement from one corps to a higher category.

ministry—that officials stagnate working in the same office on the same materials for many years or, conversely, they are moved around so often that they never get to master the rules and procedures of any branch before they are moved to another. Where all members of a corps are considered interchangeable, the level of personal competence and the presence or lack of good interpersonal relationships skills obviously have a great deal to do with task and organizational unit assignments.

Many countries using the corps principle, and some others as well, make a legal distinction between those who are "civil servants" (in German *Beamten*) whose selection, grading, pay, rights, and obligations are governed by special legislation, and other employees, whether salaried or paid hourly wages, whose conditions of employment are fixed by contract, union negotiations, or administrative determination within the constraints set by the labor law which applies to private sector employers and employees. Manual workers, both skilled and unskilled, have usually been excluded from the ranks of civil service corps as have also those employed at all salary levels in industrial or proprietary enterprises owned and managed by the government, whether or not these are located within ministries or have corporate status. Wherever this distinction is made, only those who are civil servants may take official action or "express the will of the State." This means that supervisory and managerial posts must be filled by "officials," generally with a legal preparation, even if the bulk of their staffs are technical specialists who are not civil servants. The corresponding distinction in Great Britain and in other countries using its terminology is between "established" and "nonestablished" posts, the latter normally not assuring permanency of tenure and, until 1971, not carrying entitlement to a pension.

All bottom entry corps systems have found it difficult to cope with the demands of rapidly evolving technologies and with new programs that require scientific or technical specializations. As a result, the numbers of "nonestablished", "temporary," "*non titularie,*" and contractual personnel has grown dramatically since the end of World War II. In the 1950s only about 40% of public employees in the Federal Republic of Germany were civil servants whose posts were listed in the budget and who enjoyed life tenure and opportunity for advancement (Wacke, 1959). According to Helin (1977), there were in the French public service some 380,000 temporaries including 235,000 "auxiliaries" and 106,000 *contractuels.* The British Fulton Commission strongly criticized both the number of nonestablished employees (124,000 in 1967) and the inequity of the treatment accorded them (Chowdharay-Best, 1976). Use of temporary and contractual personnel as well as "contracting out" operations to private sector enterprises has become a very common strategy for getting technically skilled personnel for laboratories, computer installations, economic planning units, and the like. Turkey found it expedient to hire such technicians on contract at higher salaries than those paid regular civil servants (Aktan, 1967). Some years ago fewer then 10% of the staff of Italy's central statistical office were members of corps, drawn from other ministries. The hundreds of others employees were all engaged on 5-year renewable contracts. In most countries where rank-in-person prevails, titles and compensation for those who are not members of a corps are increasingly controlled by some variant of position classification.

Wacke (1959) explains that in Germany, employees who are not civil servants can be dismissed by serving them with notice to that effect. There are no formal disciplinary procedures, disputes are handled by labor counts rather than by the judiciary, and there is no right to a pension but only to "social insurance." The same tends to be true in other countries as well. It should not be assumed, however, that in practice the tenure of contract, nonestablished, or private law employees is insecure, at least in Western Europe. The force of tradition plus the real need for their services has been such that all except purely seasonal workers have at least as much security as most merit system employees in the United States. A Finnish report that classifies public employees as permanent, extraordinary, and temporary points out that the latter two groups may be terminated at any time, e.g., because of insufficient funds, but that in reality they are as permanent as those so designated.

IV. POSITION CLASSIFICATION

The alternate means by which personnel management can be given an orderly structure is position classification. Its essence is an explicit identification of sets of tasks and responsibilities to be assigned, with all such similar positions grouped into "classes" identified by a title and allocated to a salary grade. Influenced by the favorable reputation of position-based merit systems in the United States and by the requirements of contracts negotiated with unions in both private and public sectors, many countries have adopted something resembling position classification for those employees who are not members of a career corps. The civil services of Australia and Canada are for the most part governed by position classification rules. In 1972 I found personnel managers in Netherlands and Sweden quite knowledgeable about position classification, and they argued that their methods are more like those in the United States than might be supposed.

Many aspects of personnel administration in Switzerland are also like those in the United States. Most federal employees are recruited as specialists to fill posts with well-defined duties—often indeed for fixed terms. Prior to appointment, positions must be described and allocated by the federal personnel office to one of 25 salary grades that are uniform across the administration on the basis of educational level required, duties, needs of the service, and the responsibilities and dangers involved in the work (Gregoire, 1964, p. 119). There are, however, no explicit standards for such allocations and similar positions do not necessarily carry the same title.

Innovations in the Spanish civil service made in 1964 involve a unique blend of corps and position-based methods. Individuals compete for admission and advance through the ranks of a corps. However, each department must now prepare descriptions for each position or group of positions with similar duties. Furthermore, the department must prepare a "staffing pattern" (*plantillas orgánicas*) based on its position descriptions. This, in turn, governs the assignment to each post of a person from the appropriate corps and at the appropriate rank. The end result is not only a better match of corps members to tasks but a more rational correspondence between organizational structure and tasks and the number of places of each rank in each corps (Gorrochategui, 1964).

Procedures akin to position classification are typically used wherever blocks of employees receive ad hoc, contractual, or temporary appointments. In most countries, position classes appear to be purely departmental; seldom are there mechanisms to assure that positions with similar duties but in different ministries or departments carry the same job title or salary. Competitive forces and informal communication do tend to bring about much uniformity and consistency.

A 1967 move to structured collective bargaining in Canada led to a drastic simplification of the occupational and class structure. Authority to classify was delegated to the several departments and pay set in union contracts. Foreign service personnel, however, were kept in a ranked corps, and a three-rank corps of senior officers was established (Kuruvilla, 1973b).

In 1977 Stahl argued that the "job" concept was spreading. After noting the efforts of both the United Nations and U.S. foreign aid efforts to facilitate adoption of position classification plans, he concluded that "some years will have to pass before the durability and practicality of classification plans in the less developed nations can be reasonably assessed" (p. 501). A decade and a half has now has elapsed and to the best of my knowledge most of the position classification systems that were so enthusiastically welcomed around the world have collapsed entirely or been honored more in the breach than the observance. For example, in Ecuador reclassification abuse is reported to be endemic with over 100,000 reclassifications from 1979 to 1985 (Mangelsdorf and Reeves, 1989). Even in Australia, Canada, and New Zealand, where position classification seemed well entrenched, recent reforms perhaps best described as "broad banding" are producing structures quite different from those that exist in most U.S. jurisdictions.

Position classification is technically complex, requires a skilled staff, and is relatively costly. Unless the class structure is kept up to date as programs and agencies are restructured and new technologies become available, the system deteriorates. In poor countries the expense of administering such a system has often become unbearable. Moreover, because of the attachment of individuals to specific sets of tasks, position-based systems have tended to be more rigid and less responsive to new and transient circumstances than corps systems.

On balance, corps systems with a limited lateral entry as well as advancement and compensation controlled by criteria not easily manipulated seem more isolated from pernicious political influence and personal favoritism. Though standards of merit may not be very exacting, corps systems seem to exhibit a commendable measure of judicious impartiality. Other things being equal, position classification seems to work only in a stable but competitive political system within which personnel administration is carried out by persons who are members of a de facto corps that has been socialized to maintain high standards of probity.

V.   SELECTION AND COMPENSATION

A.   Recruitment

Few countries resort to what we would call positive recruitment. In most parts of the world the demand for posts in the public service far exceeds governmental needs and resources—except for highly skilled, technical, and professional talents which are nearly everywhere in short supply. A recent examination for university graduates in Japan drew over 50,000 applicants for fewer than 1000 posts.

Several countries employ unusual methods. Sweden and Israel, for example, recruit and select by calling on the "labor exchanges" maintained by the trade unions. Public advertisement of vacancies is also required in many countries whenever specific posts are to be filled.

In the planned economies of China and the former Soviet Union, entry into public service appears to have been handled in the same manner as other work placements, i.e., mainly through the party apparatus. Branches of the public service requisitioned recruits from the appropriate educational institution. School officials, overseen by party functionaries, govern the transit from the school system to occupational assignments.

A number of countries have devised methods of filling specialized posts or occupations for which there are insufficient numbers of willing and qualified applicants. These include (1) employing foreigners under contract, especially common in the Middle East; (2) employing "temporaries" under contract at higher salaries than are paid to regular civil servants; (3) expanding in-service training and making such training more highly specialized; and (4) competitively selecting youths who then are provided with educational stipends with assurance that upon completion of the requisite education they will be appointed. France has long used this "cadet" system for its technicorps. Australia has offered cadetships in some 20 different professional specializations.

B.   Selection

Some form of competitive evaluation of candidates is employed wherever law and tradition operate to minimize favoritism and political influences on employment decisions. Nearly all entries into corps, or the pertinent preparatory schools, are chosen through formal examinations, customarily written. Senior officials typically dominate the selection process although academics and jurists may also participate. In France and Spain the national civil service academies have become the primary point of entry into the higher civil service and the examination for admission to the academy is highly competitive. In France and elsewhere, this selection process appears to have a strong social class bias limiting access to the higher civil service corps only to a social elite. In Italy the civil service academy was intended to be an alternative route to Italy's highest career, but it has apparently not lived up to those expectations (Caporossi, 1991).

In corps systems, the number of posts to be filled is usually specified when the competition is announced. When results are determined, appointments are offered in rank order until the fixed number have accepted. All are then appointed simultaneously so they are equal in seniority and so that successful candidates are not lost to other employers while awaiting vacancies.

Dissatisfaction with current examining practices seems to be widespread. Examinations are said to take too long to prepare and score. Candidates often question the objectivity of the scoring or the impartiality of examining boards. Corps dominated examinations are frequently perceived as rewarding conformity to the values and traditions of an entrenched body of officials. Critics also view some examination practices as giving undue advantages to candidates from certain social classes, educational institutions, or geographic areas.[6] Many doubt whether current examining practices actually identify candidates whose performance will be superior.[7] Only in the Netherlands did I encounter personnel technicians who had attempted to measure the reliability and predictive validity of the tests they had administered.[8] Judging from both documentary and oral reports, there is greater satisfaction with selection processes on the part of both managers and employees in those jurisdictions in which the process is less formal and where appointing officials choose the first acceptable candidate who applies or is referred to them.

C. Promotions

In position-based systems promotion to a higher graded post requires a vacancy at that level, possession of appropriate qualifications, and, typically, the favorable discretionary judgment of superior officials. Examinations are rarely used to select individuals for promotion. In Australia a persons who does not get appointed to a higher vacancy may appeal that decision unless the selection had been made or overseen by a committee consisting of representatives of the agency, of the Merit System Protection Board, and the relevant union. A similar committee adjudicates appeals and about a fifth are successful.

Within corps, however, advancement is typically governed by criteria laid down in statutes or rules. Seniority is generally the most important of these. Often only a limited percentage of advancements may be made on the basis of competitive examination scores or judgment of "merit" by a committee of superior officials. Promotion primarily on the basis of seniority obviously results in serious age problem among higher level officials.[9] I have found no nonmilitary corps system in which the principle of "up-or-out" is followed.

---

[6]For examples, the dominance of Oxford and Cambridge in Britain, of Tokyo Imperial University in Japan, and of residents of the metropolitan areas of Paris and Dublin in the higher civil services of these countries.

[7]In all the literature examined, I found only one discussion of statistical tests of the validity of any selection process.

[8]An Italian functionary explained that competitive promotional examinations were counterproductive because the highest scores often went to the least diligent employees who had spent time when they should be working in studying for the examination.

[9]I once found more than 70% of the "director-generals" (the highest career post) in a half-dozen Italian ministries to be 60 years of age or older.

D.   Lateral Entry

Almost without exception, lateral entry is allowed wherever personnel administration is based on the grading or classification of positions but is very limited in career corps. Even where such appointments are permitted they tend to be rare except in Britain. The impermanence of ministers in most parliamentary governments and the implicit hostility of career staff seem sufficient to discourage the appointment of outsiders except in clearly justifiable circumstances. Lateral entries tend to be made into technical and consultative posts and rarely into line management. Some foreign observers admire the U.S. practice of filling top level executive and policy posts with freely chosen, often politically sponsored "in-and-outers" but deem our practice too unsettling and too politically dangerous for them to copy.

E.   Compensation

Schemes of compensation are so varied that it is almost impossible to say much that is meaningful about them in the space allowed this chapter. Where personnel administration is decentralized, different salary scales may exist for each corps or department.[10] Much recent civil service reform has had as its primary objective the simplification of salary scales and their unification across departmental lines.

Where a high value is ascribed to age, civil servants may receive an annual or biennial increment (Italy, Spain) throughout their careers that often results in subordinates receiving much higher compensation than younger officials who have been promoted to be their superiors.

In much of the world the sad state of public finances has left compensation for governmental employees far below any decent standard. In Greece, as elsewhere, low salaries led to a complicated system of allowances, multiple job holding, and excessive payment of overtime. Pay comparability with the private sector has frequently been posed as a desirable criterion—though rejected by the recent British government—but has rarely been achieved in practice. There is an observable trend to do away with predetermined salary scales and to substitute individual or group compensation levels determined through negotiations with employee unions.

Finally, we may note that a spirit of eqalitarianism prevails in some nations, which limits the spread between the compensation of lowest and highest ranking employees. While the normal "spread" trends to run between 1–14 to 1–20, that in Japan and China is closer to 1–5, or even less. Several decades ago in Switzerland it was a mere 1–3. In all countries the spread may grow as governments face increasing competition from a more technical, more differentiated private sector with higher rewards for scarce talents.

VI.   ORGANIZATION FOR PERSONNEL MANAGEMENT

Prior to 1950 personnel management was almost everywhere a departmental responsibility and limited to record keeping and the selection of candidates for appointment or promotion in accordance with whatever criteria prevailed. Finance agencies maintained centralized control over the numbers of posts and levels of compensation. Following World War II the example set by France in establishing a central personnel agency and reinforced by numerous technical assistance programs led to the establishment of central personnel almost everywhere. Ayubi (1990) lists 19 central agen-

---

[10]Turkey may be the world's leader in complexity of compensation for a rather elaborate set of grade and class bases salaries is supplemented by over a half dozen special benefits or allowances. In the Netherlands in 1971 there were 140 different salary scales. In Japan there are currently 17.

cies for civil service established in the Arab countries between 1958 and 1985. (One, in Iraq, was abolished in 1979.) There were similar developments in Asia, Africa, and Latin America. Some were independent multimember commissions—like the former U.S. Civil Service Commissions; more often the central agency has been an office or bureau under the chief executive.

For the most part the efforts by these agencies to rationalize the civil service, to relate titles and compensation to the tasks performed, to limit political use of appointments, and generally to significantly improve the capacity of the state's administrative apparatus have been relatively unsuccessful. Recently, the effort of international and bilateral technical assistance entities to support such steps toward civil service rationalization seem to have dwindled.

Also stimulated by the French ENA model and supported by aid donors, most countries have established institutes for enhancing the educational and skill levels of public servants. In some the primary concern has been "formation" with instruction designed to overcome deficiencies in general education, which has often been excessively legalistic (Plantey, 1954). The practice of giving "short courses" with a technological or managerial focus is now exceedingly widespread though the efficacy of this technology is sometimes questionable. Perhaps the proponents of in-service training and education expected too much too soon. Undoubtedly the long-run consequences of continuing training will be clearly positive.

VII. BICULTURALISM AND "AFFIRMATIVE ACTION"

With our current concern for the rival claim of group representation and "merit" in personnel matters, we should be aware that other countries have similar problems and are coping with them with varying degree of success.

In Switzerland, Belgium, and the Netherlands distinct linguistic and religious communities are rivals for power and position. In all three a strict merit system based on competitive examinations would be unthinkable. In the Netherlands an unwritten but widely respected code dictates that appointing officers and selection committees will endeavor to maintain a "fair" representation of each group at each rank for each subunit of the bureaucracy. Ethnic and religious rivalry in Belgium has made that the most highly politicized public bureaucracy in Europe (Moulin, 1975).

Canadian officials have long recognized that the underrepresentation of the French-speaking population in the federal administration constituted a serious threat to the integrity of the nation. A series of commissions studied the situation and recommended remedial action. Quotas were rejected. Instead Canada has employed a variety of techniques including working with educational institutions, setting specific language requirements wherever possible (in particular to require that persons dealing with the public should speak the language of the majority of their clients), and implementing extensive in-service language training programs for employees (Rehfuss, 1986). Current efforts to achieve greater diversity are being directed to the indigenous population.

Both India and Pakistan are multiethnic nations with intensive regional and cultural rivalries. Kumar (1992) concludes his discussion of the affirmative action debate in India with the conclusion that "reservations [a quota system] for "backward" castes and other groups . . . will undoubtedly spread." Such quota systems have long been employed in some of the states and recommended for the central government by the Mandal Commission in 1980. As a result, "India may well have the largest affirmative action program in the world" (Kumar, p. 290). Throughout its history Pakistan has utilized a quota system of ethnic preference to meet the demands of disaffected regional, religious, and ethnic groups. The "lessons" that Kennedy (1984) drew from this experience were that (1) preferences tend to spread, (2) preferences are hard to terminate, and (3) preferences have significant "fixed costs" that should not be overlooked.

Women almost everywhere constitute a disadvantaged class in the public service. Improvement in their status is occurring, but slowly and sporadically. In only a few countries is the enhancement of opportunity for women a matter of public policy, but gradually as women's educational levels rise they are making their way into professional and technical cadres. However, it will be a long time before women as civil servants acquire even the level of equal opportunity that they enjoy in the United States.

VIII. RECENT TRENDS

In many places revolution, civil strife, and the radical replacement of former regimes has brought about drastic change in previously existing public services. Many areas such as Iran, Yugoslavia, Somalia, Sudan, Mozambique, and Iraq now have little or no civil service system worthy of the name. Ongoing political change and transformation of governmental institutions in the former nations of the Soviet bloc and in such countries as South Africa and Nicaragua are such that their civil service systems are obviously also in a transient state. To the extent that civil government exists in such troubled countries some elements of former systems must linger on, but changes now in progress are likely to be only temporary expedients until more pressing problems of the structure of the regime, borders, status of minority peoples, and political institutions are resolved.

It has been reported that in mid-1993 the Russian Parliament passed a civil service statute based on merit system principles and that after seven decades of party rule an open civil service examination was given.

In most of Africa the progress toward a more rational indigenous civil service that began with independence seems to have been reversed. Not only has there been political turmoil and armed strife in many countries, but economic growth rates almost everywhere have been negative or below the growth in population. Up to half of export earnings are consumed in debt service. Since 1980 real wages have declined by one-fourth (Mukandala, 1992). The major objective of pressure from officials of the World Bank and the International Monetary Fund seems to be directed to reducing the size and cost of the public work force rather than of changing systems in a manner consistent both with local cultural imperatives and with the construction of more efficient and effective personnel systems. A 1984 report on the civil service of Somalia produced by a team recruited by the U.S. Agency for International Development, partially in response to World Bank concerns, found that the major problem with that civil service was the fact that pay scales were so low that most public employees spent the major portion of their time away from their posts in efforts to earn enough to support themselves and their families, a situation that both Nti (1987) and Mukandala report as true throughout Africa.

In Sweden there is a strong movement away from a rational, controlled system of compensation based on classes of positions to one in which all wages are subject to negotiation. A good deal of leeway is left to employing agencies so that public wages will more nearly reflect the private sector market place.

In France there has been an effort to bring a half-million nonestablished employees within the regular structure; a general reduction in gender discrimination in initial recruitment; a great increase in the number of applications, many with higher educational qualifications than are needed; and, finally, a civil service that is becoming ever more elitist (Bodiguel and Rouban, 1988).

Perhaps nowhere is the rate of change more rapid and far-reaching than in the People's Republic of China. A tradition of a merit-based, if highly formalistic, career bureaucracy based on competitive examination had lasted for centuries until largely replaced in the 1950s by a Communist regime that made party loyalty and personal favoritism its defining characteristics. For four decades there have been two sets of personnel offices—a formal one in governmental agencies, and a parallel and dominant one in the party organization. The latter are now withering away, but it is expected that for some time to come high officials will come only from those trained in the party's central school (Li, 1990; Maharay, 1991). A national ministry of personnel and a national academy of public administration were established in 1988. A draft order creating a "modern" civil service system, owing a good deal to the U.S. prototype, has gone through 15 revisions and in 1989 was put into operation in five central departments, two provinces, and eight municipalities (Cabestan, 1992). Its basic principles involve a return to the primacy of the examination system, a system of grades and steps, emphasis on employee training, and protection of civil servants from removal or punishment except in accordance with law and legal procedure. Equality in compensation has been a premise in Communist China but, as a recent newspaper report indicates, in some provinces competition from the burgeoning free enterprise sector has led to a significant "brain drain" away from the public service. Further changes in Chinese personnel management will undoubtedly occur.

Major changes are also taking place in Great Britain, Australia, Canada, and New Zealand that merit more attention than present space limits will permit. In most of these countries the movement is toward decentralization and nonuniformity of personnel matters. By the 1970's the British "home civil service" was made more open and the structure reduced to seven grades, but without "classes." Subsequently a study by Thatcher's efficiency unit, known by its title "The Next Steps," delivered the message that uniform national personnel rules had become so dominant that individual managers had little freedom to deal with their own real-world situation. By 1990 the Parliament had passed "framework laws" under which each of 33 agencies—employing more than 80,000 persons—was excluded from the basic national personnel system and given a system adapted to its own needs. This process of devolution is continuing (Sherwood, 1991). Changes in Australia are making the system more "fluid" and tending to what some call managerialism (Halligan, 1991). In New Zealand, too, there has been a major decentralization of the personnel function. Each agency has been authorized to develop its own personnel system. Some retain the old system; in others there is no longer a career service but all employees work on term contracts (Sherwood, 1992).

In Canada over 100 senior civil servants grouped in 10 task forces produced a report, called *Public Service 2000 Report: The Renewal of the Public Service of Canada*, which was adopted by the government in 1990. It recommended an enhancement of the career service; a "cultural change" from command and control management to one of empowerment; an emphasis on "career planning" and continual retraining; promotions from within the service. A resulting Public Service Reform Act of 1991 created the Public Service Commission (Kernaghan, 1991). Other changes involved redrawing the classification structure to reduce the number of occupational groups from 72 to 23 and of "subgroups" from 106 to 8. Pay is to be set by collective bargaining for all but the "executive group." Appointment are made to a classification level only rather than to a specific position. The number of grade levels has also been reduced. These two steps will reduce classification activity and promotions and facilitate horizontal movement and structural realignment of agencies (Klang, 1991).

IX. CONCLUSIONS

What do all the differences in public personnel systems mean? Are they but chips in a kaleidoscope, crafted by the vagaries of geography, history, and economics? Are there lessons that American policymakers should learn from personnel management in other countries?

At the outset we should admit that our personnel technology is neither wholly unique nor inherently superior to other methodologies. In the beginning we drew to some extent on European experience in the fashioning of career-based, meritorious civil services. Should we not now consider whether the innovations being introduced into those systems that have been most like our own provide models that we should adapt and adopt?

One conclusion we are clearly entitled to draw is that "merit" in personnel does not require a specific, single, universally applicable set of procedures and devises. What governments do these days is so diverse that forcing all, or nearly all, employees into a single personnel system may well be obsolete. In the United States we have long accepted the necessity of having separate systems for diplomatic and military personnel, public health professionals, and postal workers. The new highly decentralized personnel systems being devised in the other English-speaking countries may well point the way toward superior methods of handling personnel matters in a time of worldwide economic competition and well-organized public employee unions.

Some other specific lessons might be drawn from personnel administration abroad. The first is to note the benefits to be gained by a conscious and systematic socialization of young recruits into the ethics and performance standards of a professional body of public employees. The pride engendered by a vital *esprit de corps* can be a powerful force conducive to the development of a work force that is honest, impartial, efficient, and responsive to legitimate authority.

Second, we should recognize the advantage to be gained by having a civil service system that provides flexibility in organizational design, and program and technological change. Rank-in-man does provide for such a desirable degree of interorganizational mobility and changes in work assignment without imposing unreasonable costs on either the government or employees or exposing the system to excessive favoritism or manipulation. The same goal might also be achieved by greatly simplifying grade and occupational structures as is now occurring in a number of countries. We probably ought to redefine appointments so that they are not made to a specific, identified "position."

Third, the lack of success so far experienced in introducing rational merit-based personnel systems in the so-called underdeveloped nations of the world should raise the question as to whether these efforts have been pointed in the right direction. In some cases they appear to have fostered political destabilization and thus hindered rather than promoted economic development. But this is a larger question than can be examined here.

Finally, I think both personnel professionals and public administrators could profit by further study of how foreign corps systems actually operate in a context of collective negotiations and changing governmental responsibilities and technology. We might thereby pick up some ideas on how a reinvention of the merit system can reduce costs and make governmental administration more satisfying both to employees and to the general public.

REFERENCES

Abbas, M.B.A. (1970). Public administration training in Pakistan: a critical appraisal, *Int. Rev. Admin. Sci.*, *36*: 256–270.

Adu, A.I. (1965). *The Civil Service in New African States*, Praeger, New York.

Aktan, T. (1967). The new state personnel department in Turkey, *Int. Rev. Admin. Sci.*, *33*: 151–154.

Argyriades, D. C. (1965). Some aspects of civil service reorganization in Greece, *Int. Rev. Admin. Sci.*, *31*: 296–309.

Armstrong, J. A. (1973). *The European Administrative Elite*, Princeton University Press, Princeton, N.J.

Attir, A. (1973). The Israel civil service since 1948, *Public Administration in Israel and Abroad*, Israel Institute of Public Administration, Tel Aviv.

Ayubi, N. N. (1990). Policy developments and administrative change in the Arab World, *Public Administration in a World Perspective* O. P. Dwivedi and K. M. Henderson, pp. 23–53.

Balogh, T. (1968). XXXXX, *Crisis in the Civil Service* (H. Thomas, ed.), Anthony Blood, London.

Berger, M. (1957). *Bureaucracy and Society in Modern Egypt: A Study of the Higher Civil Service,* Princeton University Press, Princeton, NJ.

Blunt, E. (1937). *The I.C.S.: The Indian Civil Service*, Faber and Faber, London.

Bodiguel, J. L. (1990). Political and administrative traditions of the French civil service, *Int. J. Public Admin., 13*: 707–740.

Bodiguel, J. L., and Rouban, L. (1988). Civil service policies since 1981: crisis in the administrative model or inertia in policies, *Int. Rev. Admin. Sci., 54*: 179–199.

Braibanti, R. (ed) (1966a). *Asian Bureaucratic Systems Emergent from the British Imperial Tradition*, Duke University Press, Durham, NC.

_____(1966b). *Research on the Bureaucracy of Pakistan*, Duke University Press, Durham, NC.

Cabestan, J. P. (1992). Civil service reform in China, the draft "Provisional Order Concerning Civil Servants," *Int. Rev. Admin. Sci., 58*: 421–436.

Caiden, G. E. (1967). *The Commonwealth Bureaucracy*, Melbourne University Press, Melbourne.

_____(1991). Recent administrative changes in Australia, *Int. Rev. Admin. Sci., 57*: 9–23.

Campbell, G. A. (1965). *The Civil Service in Britain*, rev. ed., Duckworth, London.

Caporossi, P. (1991). La selezione dei migliori per la pubblica amministrazione. La Scuola superiore di pubblica ammministrazione ed il reclutamento del personale direttivo dello Stato in Italia, *Rivista Trimestrale di Scienza dell'Amministrazione, 38*: 111–154.

Cappelletti, L. (1966). Interest groups and bureaucracy in Italy. Unpublished Ph.D. dissertation, University of California, Berkeley.

Chapman, B. (1959). *The Profession of Government*, Allen and Unwin, London.

Chew, D.G.E. (1990). Civil service pay in China—1955–1989, *Int. Rev. Admin. Sci., 56*: 345–364.

Chow, K. W. (1991), Reform of the Chinese cadre system: pitfalls, issues and implications of the proposed civil service system, *Int. Rev. Admin. Sci., 57*: 25–44.

Chowdharay-Best, G. (1976). A note on the temporary civil servant, *Public Admin.* (London), *54*: 333–340.

Cloutier, S. (1968). Bilingualism, biculturalism and senior public servants. *Can. Public Admin., 11*: 395–406.

Crozier, M. (1964). *The Bureaucratic Phenomenon*, University of Chicago Press, Chicago.

Curnow, G. R. (1989). The career service debate, *Politicization and the Career Service* (G. R. Curnow and B. Page, eds.), University of Canberra and the Royal Australian Institute of Public Administration, Canberra.

de la Oliva de Castro, A. (1965). La articulación en cuerpos de la función pública, *Classifición de puestos de trabajo*, Secretaria General Técnica, Presidencia del Gobierno, Madrid. Also in *Documentacion Administrativa*, no. 96.

de la Oliva de Castro, A., and A. Gutiérrez Reñón (1968). Los cuerpos de functionarios, *Documentación Administrativa*, no. 124.

Derlien, H. U. (1991). Historical legacy and recent developments in the German higher civil service, *Int. Rev. Admin. Sci., 57*: 385–401.

Direction Générale de la Sélection et de la Formation (1977). *La fonction publiue en Belgique*, Bruxelles.

Dlakwa, H. D. (1992). Salient features of the 1988 civil service reforms in Nigeria, *Public Admin. Dev., 12*: 297–311.

Dodd, C. H. (1969). *Politics and Government in Turkey*, University Press, Manchester, England.

Dogan, M., ed. (1975). *The Mandarins of Western Europe: The Political Role of Top Civil Servants*, Sage, Wiley, New York.

Dooney, S. (1976). *The Irish Civil Service*, Institute of Public Administration, Dublin.

Dussault, M. R. (1990). Public service reform in Canada, *The Bureaucrat, 19*: 23–26.

Dwivedi, O. P., and Henderson, K. M. eds. (1990). *Public Administration in a World Perspective*, Iowa State University Press, Ames, IA.

Friedrich, C., and Cole, T. (1932). *Responsible Bureaucracy: A Study of the Swiss Civil Service*, Harvard University Press, Cambridge, MA. Reprinted 1967, Russell and Russell, New York.

Gazier, F. (1965). L'Ecole National d'Administration: apparences et realites, *Int. Rev. Admin. Sci., 31*: 31–34.

Gladden, E. N., (1967). *Civil Services of the United Kingdom 1855-1970*, Kelley, Bookseller, New York.

Goodnow, H. F. (1964). *The Civil Service of Pakistan*, Yale University Press, New Haven, CT.

Gorrochategui, E. (1964). La descripción y clasificación de puestos de trabajo en la administración pública espanola, *Int. Rev. Admin. Sci., 30*: 345–353.

Graham, L. S. (1968). *Civil Service Reform in Brazil*, University of Texas Press, Austin.

Gregoire, R. (1964). *The French Civil Service*, International Institute of Administrative Sciences, Brussels.

Gutiérrez Renón, A. (1969). The Spanish civil service, *Int. Rev. Admin. Sci., 35*: 133–140.

Halligan, J. (1991). Career public service and administrative reform in Australia, *Int. Rev. Admin. Sci., 57*: 345–360.

Heady, F. (1992). *Public Administration: A Comparative Perspective*, 4th Ed., Marcel Dekker, New York.

Helin, J. C. (1977). Les agents temporaires dans la fonction publique tunisienne, *Int. Rev. Admin. Sci., 43*: 205–220.

Hopkins, J. A., (1967). *The Government Executive of Modern Peru*, University of Florida Press, Gainesville.

Hsueh, S. S. (1962). *Public Administration in South and Southeast Asia*, International Institute of Administrative Sciences, Brussels.

Kelsall, R. K. (1955). *Higher Civil Servants in Britain*, Routledge and Kegan Paul, London.

Kennedy, C. H. (1984). Policies of ethnic preference in Pakistan, *Asian Survey, 24*: 688–703.

Kernaghan, K. (1991). Career public service 2000: road to renewal or impractical vision, *Can. Public Admin., 34*: 551–572.

Kim, P. S. (1988). *Japan's Civil Service System: Its Structure, Personnel and Politics*, Greenwood Press, Westport, CT.

_____(1970). Japan's National Civil Service Commission: its origin and structure. *Public Admin. 48*: 405–422.

Kingdom, J.C, ed (1990) *The Civil Service in the Liberal Democracies,* Routledge Paul, London.

Klang, G. (ed.) (1991), *Position Classification and Compensation: Australia, Canada, Federal Republic of Germany, France, Japan, Northern Ireland, Sweden and the United Kingdom*, United States Office of Personnel Management, unpublished manuscript in OPM library.

Kubota, A. (1969), *Higher Civil Servants in Postwar Japan: Their Social Origins, Educational Backgrounds and Career Patterns*, Princeton University Press, Princeton, NJ.

Kumar, D. (1992), The affirmative action debate in India, *Asian Survey 32*: 290–302.

Kuruvilla, P.K. (1973), The career concept in the Canadian public service, *Int. Rev. of Admin. Sci. 39*: 49–55.

_____(1977), The issue of bilingualism in the public service of Canada. in *Bureaucracy in Canadian Government*, 2nd ed. W.D.K. Kernaghan (Ed.), Methuen, Toronto.

Lachaume, J. F. (1991) *La fonction publique*, Dalloz, Paris.

Leemans, A. (1987), Recent trends in the career services of European countries, *Int. Rev. of Admin. Sci. 53*: 84–92.

Li, W. (1990), Reform in the Chinese public personnel system, *Pub. Pers. Man., 19*: 163–174.

Lee, R. D. (1991), Merit protection in the Australian public service: a comparative perspective, *Rev. of Pub. Pers. Admin. 11*: 84–94.

Lovenduski, J., (1989), Implementing equal opportunities in the 1980's: An overview, *Public Administration, 67*: 7–18.

Maharay, G. (1991), Civil service reform in the People's Republic of China, *The Bureaucrat 20*: 26–31.

Mangelsdorf, K. R. and T. Z. Reeves, (1989), Implementing in the merit system in Ecuador, *Pub. Pers. Man., 18*: 193–208.

Misra, B. B., (1977), *The Bureaucracy in India*, Oxford University Press, Delhi.

Moulin, L. (1975), The politicization of the Administration in Belgium, in *The Mandarins of Western Europe*, M. Dogan (Ed.)

Mukandala, R. S. (1992), To be or not to be: the paradoxes of African Bureaucracies in the 1990's, *Int. Rev. of Admin. Sci., 58*: 555–576.

Nti, J. (1987), Public sector personnel, in *Economic Restructuring and African Public Administration*, M. J. Balogun and G. Mutahaba, (eds), Kumarion Press, West Hartford CT.

Palmer, M. L. Ali and E. S. Yassin, (1988), *The Egyptian Bureaucracy*, Syracuse University Press, New York.

Paltiel, J. (1990), Administrative reform and the politics of management training in the Peoples Republic of China, *Can. Pub. Admin., 33*: 584–604.

Perlman, B. J. (1989), Modernizing the public service in Latin America: Paradoxes of Latin American public administration, *Int. J. Pub. Admin., 12*: 671–704.

Peters, B. G. (1988), *Comparing Public Bureaucracies; Problems of Theory and Method*, University of Alabama Press, Tuscaloosa AL.

Pimental, A. F. (1966), La administracion de personal en America Latina, Int. Rev. of Admin. Sci. 21: 197–210.

Plantey, A. (1954). *La Formation et le Perfectionnement des fonctionnaires nationaux et internationaux*, International Institute of Administrative Sciences, Brussels.

Rehfuss, J.A. (1986). A representative bureaucracy? Women and minority executives in the Canadian career service. *Public Admin. Rev., 46*: 454–460.

Scarrow, H. A. (1957). *The Higher Public Service of the Commonwealth of Australia*, Duke University Press, Durham, NC.

Sharp, W. R. (1931). *The French Civil Service: Bureaucracy in Transition*, Macmillan, New York.

Sherwood, F. P. (1991). Maggie the manager: administrative reform in Britain, *The Bureaucrat, 20*: 39–44.

———(1992). Comprehensive government reform in New Zealand, *The Public Manager, 21*: 20–24.

Sibh, M, (1968). *La Fonction Publique*, Hachette, Algeria.

Siegel, G. B., and Nascimento, K. (1965). Formalism in Brazilian administrative reform: the example of position classification, *Int. Rev. Admin. Sci., 31*: 175–184.

Siffin, W. J. (1962). Personnel processes of the Thai bureaucracy, *Papers in Comparative Public Administration* (F. Heady and S. L. Stokes, eds.), Institute of Public Administration, University of Michigan, Ann Arbor, pp. 207–228.

———(1966). *The Thai Bureaucracy: Institutional Change and Development*, East-West Center Press, Honolulu.

Smith, B. L.R., ed. (1984). *The Higher Civil Service in Europe and Canada: Lessons for the United States*, Brookings Institution, Washington, DC.

Smith, T. B. (1974). *The New Zealand Bureaucrat*, Cheshire, Wellington.

Stahl, O. G. (1977). The job concept outside of North America, *Job Evaluation and Pay Administration in the Public Sector* (H. Suskin, ed.), International Personnel Management Association, Chicago, pp. 491–505.

Suleiman, E.N. (1974). *Politics, Power and Bureaucracy in France*, Princeton University Press, Princeton, NJ.

———, ed. (1985). *Bureaucrats and Policy-Making*, Holmes and Meier, New York.

Tawati, A. M. (1976). The civil service of Saudi Arabia: problems and prospects. Unpublished PhD dissertation, West Virginia University.

United Nations, Public Administration Branch (1966). *Handbook of Civil Service Laws and Practices*, United Nations, New York.

United States Merit Systems Protection Board (1992). *To Meet the Needs of the Nations: Staffing the U.S. Civil Service and the Public Service of Canada*, Washington, D. C.

Vernardis, G., and Papastathopoulos, C.D. (1989). The higher civil service in Greece, *Int. Rev. Admin. Sci., 55*: 603–629.

Wacke, G. (1959). Legal forms of state employment, *Int. Rev. Admin. Sci., 25*: 155–159.

Westrich, E. (1992). Restructuring government New Zealand style, *Public Admin., 70*: 119–135.

Wilson, V. S., and Mullins, W. A. (1978). Representative bureaucracy: linguistic/ethnic aspects in Canadian public policy, *Can. Public Admin., 21*: 513–538.

6

Comparative Examination of National Civil Service and Personnel Reforms

PATRICIA W. INGRAHAM and ELLIOT F. EISENBERG   Maxwell School of Citizenship and Public Affairs, Syracuse University, Syracuse, New York

INTRODUCTION

Efforts to reform the civil service in Western industrial nations are frequently as old as the governments themselves. As early as 1800 in the United States, for example, President Jefferson had to deal with how to reward his political supporters while not dismembering the existing public service (White, 1951). Seventy years later, the Civil Service Reform Act of 1871 was signed, and in 1883 the Pendleton Act created the merit system. Nearly 100 years later, in 1978, the Civil Service Reform Act was described as a major comprehensive reform, but in 1983 the President's Private Sector Survey on Cost Controls (the Grace Commission) examined the role of the permanent bureaucracy again. In Europe, Australia, Canada, and elsewhere, the number of governmental reform efforts have been at least as numerous.

While these reforms have been different in substance, structure, and scope, all have had the goal of reform of government in general and the civil service in particular. It is reasonable to assume that governmental reform efforts will continue well into the future. After all, times change, and so must government. Thus, it is important to keep in mind that the reforms and changes being instituted and contemplated today are necessarily the base from which new reorganizations and governmental changes will be implemented sometime in the next century. That is, each set of governmental transformations, innovations and modifications are not a final step, but rather one in a series of steps in a process that is eternal. Nevertheless, it is important to understand the intent and impact of these various current reform efforts; it is equally important to ask why they are so common.

II. A BRIEF HISTORY OF REFORM EFFORTS BETWEEN 1840 AND 1960

The first nation to make a sustained effort at governmental reform was the United Kingdom. In the 1850s, in an attempt to make government and the civil service more responsible and professional, the Trevelyan–Northcote reforms were passed. Although these reforms were not fully implemented until 1920, they had a profound impact on the British civil service. For example, the reforms recommended the adoption of a politically neutral "closed shop" approach to staffing the higher civil service. Trevelyan felt it essential that the higher civil service become a professional and permanent part of the government that did not undergo major changes after each election. The report argued that the best way to institutionalize this idea was to create a tightly knit, well-educated, and elite cadre who would commit to a lifetime of neutral public service.

Following the American Civil War, reformers in the United States also began to push for the creation of a professional and protected civil service. In particular, the reformers wanted a system that protected government employees from politics and patronage and from the postelection purges that repeatedly rocked the bureaucracy. The first attempt by Congress to limit the patronage appointments of the chief executive was the Tenure of Office Act in 1867. This reform was followed 4 years later by the Civil Service Reform Act of 1871, which was signed into law by scandal-plagued President Grant (Cayer, 1989).

However, it was not until 1883, with the passage of the Pendleton Act, that reformers were able to make serious progress towards the goal of a permanent and professional civil service. The act created competitive exams for applicants and an open entry system for ten percent of the existing federal bureaucracy (Van Riper, 1958). The remainder of the bureaucracy was to be gradually incorporated into the merit system by presidential order (Ingraham and Rosenbloom, 1992).

Spurred by these modest successes, reformers continued to push for more changes in the patronage system (Hogenboom, 1961). During the term of President Theodore Roosevelt, the distinction between classified and nonclassified employees emerged; again the concept of a politically neutral civil service was emphasized. In 1923, the Classification Act was passed. This act established the concept of job classification in the federal government.

During the 1930s and 1940s the combination of the Great Depression, the New Deal, and the outbreak of World War II led to a dramatic increase in the size and role of government (Meier, 1987). During this period the number of civilian employees more than tripled, and citizens began to depend on government for the provision of services that previously had been provided by the private sector or else not at all. As the government increased in size and stature, another set of reforms emerged. There was renewed concern for the concept of merit, as well as a new concern for managing the now unwieldy federal government (Van Riper, 1958).

One of the most significant attempts at reform during this period was the President's Committee on Administrative Management, better known as the Brownlow report. That group, named by President Franklin Roosevelt, issued its report in 1937. Most of the recommendations of the Brownlow Committee were not acted on; President Roosevelt and Congress were engaged in serious struggles for power at the time the report was released and Congress was not enthusiastic about enhancing presidential power further, as the report recommended (Arnold, 1986).

Nonetheless, the Brownlow Committee report had a long-term influence on the civil service and on the emphasis of future debate about the public service. There was a growing realization that the form and structure of government mattered and that managing government was important. The Brownlow report also came down firmly on the side of the president in the debate over who controlled the federal bureaucracy. In the view of the committee members, Congress was the overseer, but the primary responsibility for management and control was with the chief executive (Arnold, 1986; Ingraham, 1992). This debate is one of the enduring issues in U.S. civil service reform.

More recent efforts at reform have been somewhat different in both substance and intent. A number of independent factors in the late 1970s and throughout the 1980s created both different demands and different expectations for reform.

III.   RECENT REFORMS AND WHY THEY ARE DIFFERENT

Unlike the reform efforts discussed above, which most often proceeded from the assumption that a neutral and efficient civil service served a positive role in government, recent reforms have a different philosophy. Today many reforms are designed to dramatically alter the face of the civil service. The civil service is no longer perceived to be the solution to a problem; rather, it has *become* the problem in many nations.

After a period of relative calm in the 1950s, in the 1960s many industrialized nations again turned to the problem of civil service reform. In Canada, the Royal Commission on Government Organization (the Glassco Commission) was created; in the United Kingdom, the Committee on Civil Service (the Fulton Committee) reported. Both recommended major reorganization and change (Dillman, 1986; Aucoin, 1990). More recently, in Australia the Royal Commission on Australian Government Administration (the Coombs Commission) recommended sweeping changes and created the foundation for fundamental reforms (Mascarenhas, 1990).

During this same period, however, economic growth was robust, living standards in most industrial nations were rapidly rising, productivity was high, and, generally speaking, governmental performance was not perceived to be a problem. As a result, reform commissions stimulated some structural changes and often informed future debates but overall did not generate widespread enthusiasm (Wilenski, 1986).

Both economic conditions and the satisfaction with government performance changed quickly in the mid-to-late 1970s (Pollitt, 1990). During this time economic growth slowed dramatically, Keynesian economic policies of the past became discredited, unemployment and inflation began to simultaneously drift upward, and politicians advocating a sharp break with the status quo were elected around the globe (Fry, 1984). Given these radically different conditions, in many nations governmental reform took on a new urgency. A feeling that something "had to be done" suddenly began to take hold.

The elections of Margaret Thatcher in the United Kingdom in 1979, Ronald Reagan in the United States in 1980, and Brian Mulroney in Canada a few years later created opportunities for a new conservative idealogy to shape government and the efforts to change it (Savoie, 1993). Reducing the size and scope of government and increasing the political accountability of the civil service became new reform objectives. The newly elected leaders were willing and anxious to use their political capital to effect significant change (Light, 1982). In all three cases, public bureaucracies and bureaucrats were defined as the problem. Ronald Reagan summarized both the philosophy and the proposed solutions in his inaugural address: "Government," he said, "is not the solution to the problem. It *is* the problem" (Ingraham, 1992).

IV. INTELLECTUAL FOUNDATIONS OF THE RECENT REFORMS

The problems confronting national governments in the 1980s were complex and multifaceted. To some extent, the solutions proposed were simplistic by comparison. One common source of solutions emerged from an amalgam of theories and concepts such as rational choice, property rights, principle/agent theory, and transaction cost economies. This set of theories and solutions is most frequently referred to as public choice (Atkinson and Stiglitz, 1980). Public choice theory applies microeconomic theory and analysis to governmental institutions and services. The most frequently cited public choice theorist is Niskanen (1971). Niskanen argues that bureaucrats and elected officials often pursue divergent objectives. Well-informed bureaucrats, he argues, are systematically able to convince elected officials to overspend on government programs. While this allows bureaucrats to increase their budgets and power, politicians, the electorate, and the economy are not well served.

Similar analyses were used to demonstrate that bureaucrats and special interest groups often work together to provide special interests with unnecessary subsidies, grants, and other governmental services. In short, Niskanen and other public choice theorists argue, it is bureaucratic control of government that has been the engine behind rapid governmental growth. This growth is not only a threat to individual liberty but it also slowly undermining the spirit of capitalism and long-term economic vitality (Hayek, 1972; Friedman and Friedman, 1980).

The second body of work that has received considerable attention by recent civil service reformers is frequently referred to as managerialism. Reduced to its core, managerialist theory argues that the private sector model must be applied to public sector management (Hood, 1989). Only by allowing managers that freedom and opportunity to manage and maneuver as they see fit will it be possible to increase worker efficiency and productivity. Both the constraints of civil service systems and the limitations of public managers are seen as serious obstacles to effective governmental performance (Hede, 1991b).

Even on the surface, it is clear that the solutions offered by these two schools of thought will be different and probably in conflict (Aucoin, 1990). Having concluded that bureaucrats, and not elected officials, have effective control over government spending, it is a short step for public choice theorists to conclude that less government is better and that tighter control over the smaller bureaucracy is essential if control is to revert to elected officials. By contrast, managerialists recommend providing top level bureaucrats with more freedom and leeway, and fewer written rules and procedures. This would necessarily decrease political controls on their behavior and actions.

Despite these fundamentally contradictory perspectives, actual solutions to the bureaucratic problem are often remarkably similar. For example, pay for performance is a solution propounded by both schools. Managerialists argue that pay for performance gives managers more latitude to operate and to reward productivity. Public choice advocates argue that pay for performance is beneficial because it permits elected officials and appointees to set bureaucratic goals and to reward those who meet those goals (Hood, forthcoming).

It is also true that at times the reforms advocated by the two schools of thought are quite different. Some advocates recommend increased controls on spending, while others suggest privatizing entire activities that are now under the control of government. Some deal quite specifically with reforming the bureaucracy, while others push for the implementation of better information systems so that elected officials and citizens can have improved access to information necessary for better decision making.

While many different reforms have been proposed, however, it is generally possible to group them under one of three headings: structural reforms, procedural and technical reforms, and relational reforms (Ingraham and Peters, 1988). These groupings are not exhaustive, nor are they mutually exclusive. Rather, they are tools to help analyze the many governmental and bureaucratic reforms currently being debated and/or implemented worldwide. Structural reforms emphasize structure, organization, and size of government. For example, privatizing a governmental activity is a structural reform, as are reforms that decentralize governmental responsibilities from the center to the periphery (Glascott and Bowden, 1992).

Technical reforms are directed at the operations of government and at the civil service system itself. These reforms include budgetary and financial management changes, reductions in paperwork and "red tape," and simplifications in civil service rules and procedures.

The final category of reforms, relational reforms, covers reforms that are designed to reduce or eliminate the influence of the permanent bureaucracy on the policymaking process. One example of this is the emergence of the Senior Executive Service in the United States and elsewhere, and another is the emergence of political management strategies in many nations (Savoie, 1993).

Before looking at the reform efforts currently underway in a number of Western democracies, through the triad of relational, structural, and procedural and technical reforms, it may be worth placing the nations involved on a change continuum. By realizing that governmental change and reorganization is not simply binary but rather an issue of magnitude, a continuum can help us understand yet another dimension, or variant, of governmental change that is currently taking place, i.e., intensity:

Germany	France		Denmark	Canada	UK	New Zealand
	Ireland	USA	Netherlands		Sweden	Australia
Low Amounts			Moderate Amounts			High Amounts
of Change			of Change			of Change

Which horizontal level a country occupies is irrelevant. Only the vertical location of the country on the continuum is of interest. By looking at the continuum it is clear that Australia and New Zealand are currently involved in the most ambitious governmental reform efforts, while France and Germany are making relatively small changes to their systems. The remaining countries, including the United States, Canada, and the United Kingdom, lie somewhere between those two extremes.

V. RELATIONAL REFORMS

Of the three different types of reforms listed above, relational reforms are among the most popular and their impact on the civil service among the most direct. The creation of an elite cadre of senior civil servants who exchange many of the traditional protections of the civil service for increased pay, responsibility, and influence, but also for more a direct relationship to elected officials and political appointees, is the most common reform in this group (Ingraham, 1990).

Recently, Australia, New Zealand, and Canada all adopted a Senior Executive Service (SES) modeled on the system created in the United States by the Civil Service Reform Act of 1978. The American reform was modeled on the British higher service. In all cases, members of the new cadre operate under the terms of a contract, rather than the traditional civil service procedures, and compete for financial bonuses based on performance.

A. Relational Reforms: National Examples

1. Australia

The SES was introduced at the federal level in Australia in 1984. The idea itself was copied from the United States but, unlike in America, the Australians first experimented with the idea of an SES-type system at the state level, in particular the state of Victoria (Hede, 1991a). At present, the federal SES comprises approximately 1600 employees or roughly 1.1% of all federal employees. During 1990 a new professional level SES grade was also established to allow nonpolitical specialists to enter ranks of the SES. In the same year, a new "sub-SES" category was created to provide a training ground for future members of the SES.

While appointment to the SES is open to all qualified Australian citizens, there is generally a strong reluctance to hire nongovernment employees for the job. This reluctance has manifested itself in limited external advertising for open positions. Thus, the vast majority of all new SES employees, over 84%, come from either within the same department or from another governmental agency (Hede, 1991b).

The Australian Public Service Commission recently decided to introduce a pay-for-performance plan for all members of the SES. Under the plan, now in the early stages of implementation, SES managers who are poor performers see their pay actually reduced whereas top performers receive bonuses. Again, the model is provided by the pay-for-performance plan that was implemented for the State of Victoria's SES in the 1980s. A similar plan has now been implemented in the State of New South Wales.

According to the Public Service Commission of Australia, selection to the SES is based on five core criteria: (1) corporate management skills, (2) representation and interpersonal skills, (3) judgment, (4) leadership ability, and (5) analytical skills. The Australian plan, like others, aims to increase the flexibility and mobility of top executive talent so that it can be placed where it is most needed.

2. Canada

The Canadian equivalent to the SES is the management category, which was introduced in 1981 and currently has roughly 4500 members, which constitutes about 2% of the Canadian bureaucracy. The management category is currently undergoing significant changes, including the reduction of the current six managerial layers to a flatter system of only three. Additionally, the reduction of the total number of senior managers by 10% across the board is being considered (Government of Canada Report, 1990; OECD, 1991).

The Canadian Public Service Commission is the sole arbiter of all promotions to the management category, and at present all vacancies at this level are filled from within. If, however, no currently employed federal government employees are interested in or suitable for a particular job, the opening can be filled by those employed in the private sector (Hede, 1991b).

As in the United States, pay for performance for top executives is the rule. And, as was the case in the Australian State of Victoria, the Canadian system was recently reformed. The reforms undertaken have been designed so that employees rated as "fully satisfactory," the bulk of the work force, will receive a small pay raise instead of none at all (OECD, 1991).

Also as in Australia, selection to the management category is based on a set of skills including but not limited to independence, initiative, perseverance, judgment, flexibility, interpersonal relations, and leadership ability. Unlike the American SES, which is a modified rank-in-person system, the Canadian management category employs a rank-in-position system. However, in an attempt to increase executive mobility and flexibility within government, a proposal to create a rank-in-level system is being seriously considered (Public Service 2000, 1990).

3. United States

The SES was introduced into the American federal government by the Civil Service Reform Act of 1978. In 1990 the SES numbered about 8000, slightly less than half of 1% of the total civilian federal labor force (Harper, 1992). The SES was designed to provide flexibility and mobility, as well as to give greater consideration to an executive's qualifications and performance when determining salary (U.S. MSPB, 1990).

Perhaps the largest difference between the American system and the others discussed here, including the Canadian system, is that in the United States up to 10% of SES ranks can be filled by political appointees. While political SESers are supposed to be appointed to policy positions, key provisions in the law permit placement of political executives throughout the organization, thus dramatically increasing political leverage inside the organization (National Commission on the Public Service, 1989).

Entry into the SES is determined on an agency-by-agency basis. Existing rules and regulations currently require all SES vacancies to be advertised government-wide. Each agency is free to decide, however, whether to simultaneously advertise in the public and private sectors, whether to advertise in the private sector only after all eligible governmental candidates have been interviewed, or whether to advertise in the private sector at all.

The pay-for-performance provisions of the American SES contain three levels of financial incentives: performance awards, and distinguished and meritorious service awards (the latter two are presidential rank awards). The meritorious service award brings with it a one-time $10,000 bonus, while the distinguished service award brings an even larger one-time bonus of $20,000 (Ingraham, 1987). These rewards are government-wide. Performance awards are determined on an agency-by-agency basis. The awards are based on executive performance appraisal processes and proceed through the review of quality review boards and executive review boards in each agency. In 1989, 40% of the total SES membership received an average bonus of $5478; 5.4% received a presidential rank award of which 63 were distinguished service awards (Harper, 1992, p. 278).

4. United Kingdom

In the United Kingdom the highest level attainable in the civil service is known as the senior open structure. What distinguishes the British system from the other three systems briefly outlined here is its size. The senior open structure is a very exclusive and elite upper management group. At present, it has less than 1000 members, about 0.2% of the entire British civil service.

Selection into the senior open structure is virtually closed to noncareerists and for many years the career ranks have been strongly influenced by the "Oxbridge" connection, which limits access even further. However, the "Next Steps" initiative is changing the status quo quite substantially. Open recruitment has become a goal and has actually become a reality in some government agencies (Hede, 1991b).

Like the other nations in this survey, pay for performance is also a reality for top managers in the UK. In 1987 a merit pay plan was officially implemented to cover top managers. One of the major reasons for its adoption was the perceived need for greater flexibility in pay. This need had initially been identified in 1968 by the Fulton Committee report. In 1991 the pay plan was finally revised and generally led to salary increases of upward of 15%. It was also intended to reduce the disparity in executive pay between the public and private sectors.

5. Conclusion

It is worth noting that the SES programs outlined above all combine ideas from both the managerialist and the public choice perspectives. For example, most schemes actively encourage increased executive freedom and responsibility, and reduced reliance on written rules and procedures. However, they also attempt to control the behavior of executives by offering the promise of financial bonuses, which in some cases can be quite large. The tension in these objectives has been clearly reflected in the implementation experience of the SES in virtually every national setting. Particularly in the punitive political climate of the 1980s, rewarding career bureaucrats for exercising discretion was not popular with elected officials. Failure to do so was not popular with senior government executives, who were central to implementation of many of the initiatives that elected officials wished to pursue. In an important sense, a long-term conundrum had been institutionalized.

B. Relational Reforms: Budgetary

1. United Kingdom

Following her election victory of 1979, Prime Minister Margaret Thatcher wasted little time signaling her reform objectives. In an action that she described as procedural, but which had clear relational implications, Thatcher refused to implement the pay proposals of the Civil Service Pay Research Unit. This led to a long and bitter 21-week civil service strike that ended in July 1981 in total defeat for all unions concerned.

During the strike Prime Minister Thatcher appointed a new committee, headed by Sir John Megaw, to devise a more simple and less expensive civil service pay system. While the Megaw report proposed several changes in the pay structure for civil servants, the most significant change advocated was a relational reform: that the Civil Service Pay Information Board was to be composed of five persons appointed by the prime minister.

This was a sharp break with past tradition. Under the old Priestly pay system, the Pay Research Unit (the only unit empowered to make pay recommendations to the government) was an independent body not under the control of the elected government (Fry, 1988). The decision to appoint members to the Pay Board as opposed to having them be independent of the government reduced the power and autonomy of the bureaucracy and clearly increased the political aspects of pay setting.

Another technical reform that Prime Minister Thatcher used to improve the productivity of the public sector was the "Rayner scrutinies." Lord Derek Rayner, the former managing director of a large department store chain (Marks and Spencer), was hired to assist the government in identifying areas where productivity could be enhanced, waste eliminated, and cost reductions made without, of course, reducing the quality of government service.

Between 1979 and 1983, when Lord Rayner returned to the private sector, 155 "scrutinies" were performed. Rayner estimated that if all were implemented the government could save approximately 421 million pounds sterling per annum. These savings were to be achieved through eliminating duplication, reducing rules and regulations, and using better information management systems. By 1985, recommendations totally 271 million pounds sterling had been approved by the government (Fry, 1988).

Despite the importance placed on the scrutinies by the prime minister, however, Lord Rayner was given only a small staff and was not permitted to investigate or scrutinize a department unless invited. Not surprisingly, implementation of the recommendations has proved to be far more difficult than conducting them and progress in achieving their objectives has been slow (Pollitt, 1990a).

2. United States

Much like Margaret Thatcher, Ronald Reagan also wanted to increase the efficiency and reduce the size of the public sector. Like Thatcher, he too turned to the private sector for advice and solutions. The President's Private Sector Survey on Cost Control (PPSSCC), also known as the Grace Commission, issued its report in January 1983. The Commission recommended the adoption of a set of proposals that it estimated would save the government more than $400 billion over 3 years. The proposals included the elimination of some programs, the privatization of others, and the reform of both the pay and pension systems in place for federal employees (PPSSCC, 1983).

The president also established the National Productivity Advisory Committee and the President's Council on Integrity and Efficiency. While these groups were slightly different in their orientation, they both had as their main task the identification of fraud, waste, and abuse in government programs, and the enhancement of productivity in both the public and private sectors (Dillman, 1986).

The outcomes of these activities were much more limited than the reports promised. The General Accounting Office reported that the Grace Commission greatly overestimated the potential savings. The other groups focused on paperwork and regulatory reduction, but specific recommendations and solutions were limited (Ingraham, 1992).

VI. TECHNICAL REFORMS

A. Technical Reforms: Pay for Performance

Among all technical reforms, pay for performance is without doubt the most popular. Over a dozen OECD nations have already introduced pay-for-performance plans, and other nations are investigating the concept. While there are many pay-for-performance systems currently in operation, they are not identical.

Some nations, such as the United States, offer sizable bonuses; bonuses in some others, such as the Netherlands, are quite small. In some countries the bonuses are pensionable, whereas in others they are not. In addition, some plans are designed to operate at only the highest levels of management, while elsewhere midlevel managers and sometimes blue collar employees are included. Finally, in some cases the schemes are very centralized so that all civil servants operating under a pay-for-performance plan receive standardized treatment, whereas some nations, such as New Zealand, decentralize the systems and processes. What follows is a discussion of the history and development of some of the pay plans now in operation in several OECD nations.

1. Ireland

Merit pay was introduced in 1990 and at present there are different pay plans in operation for different types of employees including assistant secretaries, top managers, and chief executives of a few government trading corporations. The plan described here is designed exclusively for the 95 assistant secretaries currently employed.

This system is based on a four-point rating, with all merit increments being added to base salary on an annual basis. For "outstanding" employees the pay increase is 2830 pounds, falling to 1415 pounds for employees rated "more than satisfactory" and 943 pounds for all employees rates "satisfactory." For employees rated unsatisfactory no merit increase is provided. An employee who is consistently rated outstanding can quickly reach the top of the pay range for assistant secretaries, which ranges from 35,212 to 43,701 pounds.

As a result of this dilemma, the Irish are considering revising the pay range upward so that most employees can continue to earn merit increases (OECD, 1991). Unlike other systems, the Irish plan uses no quotas and does not separately budget for performance awards. Rather, it considers the costs of the several plans to be a normal part of the wage bill. At present the plan seems to be working well with the only major criticism being that the increases for "satisfactory" and "more than satisfactory" are too low (OECD, 1991).

2. Denmark

The first steps toward pay for performance were made in 1985–1986. Not until 1989, however, did pay for performance begin in earnest. In that year two virtually identical plans were adopted: one for lower level civil servants and one for senior managers.

At present, the system has three methods of payment including one-time lump sum bonuses, temporary salary increases, and permanent salary increases. While the national government has issued few guidelines regarding pay bonuses, it recommends offering lump sum bonuses as they are not long-term commitments and allow for greater future financial flexibility.

It is important to note, however, that the budget for pay bonuses is a scant 0.3% of the entire wage bill. And while the system is quite new, one criticism of the plan is that the amount of money budgeted for bonuses is simply too small for effective performance–related pay allocations. As a result of this the government is planning to increase the size of the bonus pool to 0.8% of the wage bill in the near future. However, even if the bonus pool is in fact nearly tripled in size, it would still be quite small compared to other countries with pay-for-performance systems in place. As a result, it would not be surprising if the criticism that the plan allocates insufficient funds for bonuses remains.

An additional problem has been that departments have been mixed in their opinions regarding the effectiveness of the scheme. However, despite these reservations there has been virtually unanimous agreement among bureaucrats that the program should be continued. As a result of this enthusiasm, the government is planning to expand the scope of this program to cover more than 95% of all civil servants.

One unusual aspect of the Danish pay plan is that awards do not have to be based on formal appraisals. Instead, the government recommends that awards be based on efficiency, willingness to change, and creativity. As a result there have been wide variations in the criteria used to determine pay bonuses. Some departments have used the flexibility to be somewhat innovative in attempting to solve local pay problems, while other departments have simply allocated awards based on seniority. Because of these large differences there is currently a willingness on the part of managers to develop some sort of standardized appraisal system (OECD, 1991).

3. Netherlands

The Dutch plan is in many ways very similar to the Danish plan. Both plans are new, both are very decentralized, neither requires performance appraisals, and both believe it important to have all state employees involved in some sort of pay-for-performance plan. Both governments also permit performance payouts to be made in any one of three ways. In particular, the Dutch permit permanent pay raises, one-time bonuses paid over the course of a year (quite similar to the Danish temporary pay raises), and bonuses for special achievement that can be awarded at any time and are usually worth less than $100.

The Dutch, like the Danes, have also chosen to provide only modest funding for their merit pay plan. While other nations, such as Canada, set aside 5% of the wage bill for performance incentives, and the State of Victoria 10%, the Dutch have made a mere 0.25% of the pay bill available for merit raises of any kind. As a result, the Dutch permit departments to supplement their bonus budgets with additional funds from other sources. However, at present there appears to be little indication that much of this activity is taking place (OECD, 1991).

Interviews conducted with managers operating in this decentralized environment found substantial uncertainty about the objectives of the plan and as a result there is an unwillingness to commit financial resources or time to it. The managers interviewed also indicated a lack of clarity about the objectives of the pay-for-performance plan due to the vague guidelines and lack of information provided by the ministry. Finally, managers were frustrated by the meager amounts of money available for bonuses (Ingraham, 1993).

4. New Zealand

Like many other nations, New Zealand only recently adopted a pay-for-performance plan. Created in 1989, the New Zealand plan is limited to chief executives and a small minority of senior managers, and is based on a common five-point appraisal system. The rating earned by an executive is based on his or her contribution to department-wide goals, and his or her personal accomplishments and successes compared to an agreed on set of objectives.

A somewhat unusual aspect of this plan is that supplementary criteria over which an employee has no control can also be used to determine an employee's salary increases. The ease or difficulty of recruiting and/or retaining people at certain positions, for example, can also be factored into an employee's merit pay increase (OECD, 1991).

Another difference between this plan and many others is that it requires unequal awards to be made to employees earning the same performance ratings while doing the same job but who happen to be at different levels in the salary range. For example, employees closer to the top of the salary range receive smaller bonuses than employees doing the same job who receive the same rating but whose base salary is less (OECD, 1991).

Because the scheme is quite recent, no formal evaluations of this pay plan have been undertaken. However, there are indications that wage drift, which was supposed to be reduced with the use of pay for performance, has not improved. Furthermore, because merit pay was introduced in combination with more fundamental governmental reforms, it is very difficult to disentangle the effects of pay for performance on government employees from the other reforms.

5. Germany

While opposed to the idea of pay for performance in general, Germany recently introduced it at the Deutsche Bundespost (Federal Postal and Telecommunication Services). However, this step was taken only because the entire postal service was reorganized to expose it to market forces whenever and wherever possible. As a result of this reorganization, it was determined that unless the employees in the organization were also exposed to market forces and pay incentives, the reorganization would not result in any significant productivity increases.

The aim of the bonus plan is to reward outstanding employee achievements that are considered to be above and beyond their job description. In particular, close attention is placed on quality of work, economic efficiency, and the amount of work done. If it is determined that an employee's quality of work is considerably above average and better than the achievements of comparable civil servants, then that employee can be rewarded with a merit increase (OECD, 1991).

If an employee displays remarkable managerial expertise such that his or her department or branch is able to accomplish more work with no additional resources, then that employee can also be rewarded with a bonus. Bonuses can also be awarded to those who achieved outstanding results in contract negotiations and to any employees who consistently produce top quality work that is substantially above average and that is quantifiable.

Given that these rewards are highly selective and infrequent, which is quite different from the pattern in other countries, it is not surprising that bonus payments made to Bundespost employees may not exceed 2% of the entire Bundespost wage bill. The bonuses themselves are to be granted for a period of a year, 3 years for superior employees, and up to 5 years for exceptional employees. Employees may continue to earn merit pay increases until their salary is equal to the lower end of the next pay band.

One problem with this plan is that there have been serious problems in determining when an employee has earned a bonus. As a result few bonuses have been granted, and there is concern that employees, thinking that bonuses are simply unattainable, may stop trying to earn them. To this end, the federal minister in charge of the Bundespost is planning an evaluation of this program to determine its strengths and weaknesses.

While the plan is different from many others in that it encourages awards to be made in relatively few cases, it is also not a true pay-for-performance plan. This is so because it eschews the use of lump sum bonuses, preferring instead to award pay increases over a period of a year or more, which greatly reduces the impact of the bonus (OECD, 1991). Further, by specifying that only quantifiable top quality work is eligible for a bonus, the system effectively discriminates against certain work activities that may be of equal or greater importance but do not lend themselves to quantification.

6. Canada

Unlike most other nations discussed here, Canada, along with the United States and the United Kingdom, was one of the first countries to implement a pay-for-performance system. The Canadian system, like the British and American systems, is centralized. Local agencies and departments have relatively little freedom in setting rules and regulations and in deciding what behavior should be rewarded.

At present, the Salary Administration Act covers most staff from the senior manager level up to, but not including, the deputy ministerial level. This represents about 2.2% of the Canadian civil service (OECD, 1991). As is the case in most centralized systems, at the start of the year a manager and his or her superior agree on a set of goals on which the manager will be evaluated.

While progression through the pay range is based exclusively on merit, with merit increases being the only way to advance up to the job rate, defined as the highest base salary for a given job, a treasury board directive prohibits awarding more than 30% of all employees one of the top two awards ("outstanding" or "superior"). In addition, there is a second stipulation that permits no more than two-thirds of those in the top two categories from being from the "outstanding" category. This rule may be in effect to prevent performance bonuses from exceeding 5% of payroll, the amount set aside by the government for performance awards.

To combat the problem of rotating rewards, the Canadian pay plan was altered in 1990. Prior to that time, a rating of "satisfactory" brought no raise, and employees at the job rate never received bonuses regardless of their performance appraisal. Under the revised plan, employees at the job rate may receive a pensionable lump sum bonus of up to 10% of their pay instead of a "merit increase" and a rating of "fully satisfactory" now adds 3–5% to base salary. The lowest two rankings, "satisfactory" and "unsatisfactory," still bring with them no pay increase, while the designation of "outstanding" still brings with it the same 7–10% increase, and the rating of "superior" also remains unchanged, bringing with it a 5–7% pay raise (OECD, 1991).

Despite the above-mentioned changes, with the release of *Public Sector 2000*, the latest effort to reform the public service in Canada, the federal government has begun discussing the possibility of phasing out the current performance pay system and replacing it with a more private sector oriented approach. In particular, the government hopes to introduce performance rewards which will be given at the discretion of departmental deputies, and which will not always be added to base pay. The government also argues that the cash value of the performance awards must be significant if they are to be effective motivators. It is hoped that if the bonus is not permanent, a higher premium will be placed on annual performance by both the manager and his/her superior (Government of Canada Report, 1990).

In *Public Sector 2000* the government also outlines the possibility of granting greater discretion to deputy ministers to create incentive awards, so that specific departmental goals can be addressed and, as a result, unusual employee contributions can be more easily recognized. In particular, the government discusses the possibility of establishing gain-sharing rewards and other types of bonus plans that showcase entrepreneurial spirit or productivity increases (p. 87).

7. United States

The Civil Service Reform Act of 1978 (CSRA) created two separate pay-for-performance systems for federal civil servants. One system was designed exclusively for the SES, while the second was designed for all midlevel managers (GS/GM13-15). While the SES pay plan went into effect immediately after passage of the CSRA, the midlevel manager plan went into effect 3 years later. It was reasoned that the members of the SES would be comfortable with their own system after a few years and as a result would better understand how to implement the new pay plan for their subordinates. The SES plan offered recipients the possibility of winning one of three lump sum bonus awards. The midlevel plan provided that the total bonus pool for this plan would be created by pooling funds from within-grade promotions for a particular unit. The plan was intended to be revenue-neutral (Perry, 1992).

One thing both plans did share, however, was early redesign. As originally written, the SES bonus plan made half of all top managers eligible for an award. However, following the first agency-wide awards, Congress reduced the percentage from 50% to 25%, and soon after that the Office of Personnel Management, using its discretionary authority, reduced the percentage even further to 20% (Ingraham, 1987). This dramatic reduction had very detrimental effects on the SES, which persisted for much of the first decade of its existence.

The midlevel manager plan was also redesigned. Following numerous complaints about both the size and inequity of the awards, the entire pay plan was terminated in 1984. Congress replaced it with the current plan, Performance Management and Recognition System (PMRS). The largest change between the two plans was the removal of the unit pay pools and their replacement with a single government-wide formula linking pay and performance. Currently pay for midlevel managers can consist of up to three components including a permanent annual comparability adjustment, a permanent merit increase, and a lump sum performance award. At present, about 8% of the total white collar work force is now covered by the PMRS (Eisenberg and Ingraham,1993). In 1993, Congress abolished PMRS and did not replace it with a new system.

While the reform redesigns may have reduced the number of problems, they did not eliminate them. Serious problems continue. Those problems include rating inflation, awards that are too small to elicit higher levels of performance, and an inability to determine whether or not the plans have actually improved organizational productivity and performance (Eisenberg and Ingraham, 1993; Perry 1992).

B. Technical Reforms: Personnel Simplification and Flexibility

1. Canada

Over the past few years the Treasury Board Secretariat has been reorienting its own management approach. While it will continue to make decisions regarding the allocation of scarce resources, it has been delegating increased amounts of authority to departmental management and has been encouraging flexibility in the use of financial and physical resources. In essence, its mandate has changed from directing to one of providing guidance and assistance where needed (Government of Canada Reports, 1990).

In the same vein, the Public Service Commission has introduced a number of measures designed to simplify the staffing process, and to decrease the number of guidelines and directives that must be followed when hiring. For example, a review of staffing policies and directives resulted in a reduction of three books of directives down to a more manageable 75 pages. A similar examination of 6000 pages of selection standards resulted in an equally dramatic reduction to 100 pages. Finally, the Treasury Board's Personnel Policy Manual has been reduced by half, from 29 volumes to 14 (Government of Canada Reports, 1990).

C. Technical Reforms: Management Information Systems

1. United Kingdom

In another effect to control the rising costs of government, Prime Minister Thatcher created a simplified and streamlined management information system so that each ministry could "put its house in order" (Heseltine, 1987). The hope was that with better information, better decisions could be made, less money spent, and —eventually—tax rates reduced. In 1981 MINIS (Management Information System for Ministers) was adopted.

While new management information systems are rarely met with enthusiasm, with repeated prodding from the prime minister, most departments had adopted some sort of system that incorporated some or even most of the features of MINIS by 1984 (Fry, 1988). In almost all cases, the new management information system was being used to improve financial management and control in general, and costs in particular. The Rayner scrutinies described earlier in combination with MINIS were considered by many to be the cornerstones of the Thatcher effort to reform the civil service (Heseltine, 1987).

More recently other nations have also adopted management information systems to improve the budget process. For example, Australia recently created the forward estimate system, the running cost system, and portfolio budgeting which are all part of the financial management improvement program. In addition, a recent OECD publication has reported that two-thirds of the nations reporting were currently involved with some sort of budgetary or financial reform (Ingraham, 1991).

VII. STRUCTURAL REFORMS

A. Structural Reforms: Privatization

One of the major explanations for the recent popularity of privatization is the ability of the conservative movement to successfully argue that while government ought to make sure certain services are provided, there is no need for the government to actually provide the service. This elaborate argument is based on three ideas (Henig et al., 1988).

First, government is a monopoly provider of goods and services, and like all monopolists it overcharges for its services and underproduces. Second, government regulation is designed to benefit the regulated and as such hurts consumers (Posner, 1974). Third, while it is understood that "public goods" are difficult to provide in an optimal way because of "free rider" problems, it is essential for government, through its taxing power, to become involved in the financing of these public goods. Their delivery, however, should be left to the more efficient private sector (Henig et al., 1988).

One additional reason why privatization has become so popular is the emergence of large budget deficits. Selling government assets reduces the size of the deficit and, conservatives argue, increases government efficiency at the same time. In this light, privatization can be seen as a solution to two problems. However, because Western industrial nations differ dramatically in the extent to which government ownership of key services is prevalent, privatization reforms, while widespread, are very different from country to country.

1. United Kingdom

The first attempts at privatization began in 1974, under the leadership of Prime Minister Heath. The election of Prime Minister Thatcher in 1979 greatly accelerated the privatization of nationalized industries. Following the second Conservative election victory in 1983, privatization took on increased importance. Between 1980 and 1983 the sale of publicly owned enterprises averaged a little less than $1 billion annually. By contrast, between 1984 and 1987 revenue to the treasury from the sale of public assets was about $4 billion annually and hit a peak of about $7 billion in 1987.

2. France

In France, efforts at privatization began in 1986 and were designed to include the industrial groups and banks nationalized by the Socialists, as well as insurance companies, advertising agencies, oil companies, glass factories, television networks, and steel mills. The entire process was to be completed by 1991, which was to coincide with the end of that session of Parliament. However, total revenues to the French treasury were much less substantial than those in Great Britain (Henig et al., 1988).

B. Structural Reforms: Decentralization

1. Sweden

One of the most innovative attempts at structural reform has been occurring in Sweden. While the size and scope of the public sector in Sweden is not under as serious attack as in the United Kingdom or New Zealand, there is a concern that the performance of the public sector be improved. A new federal ministry—the Ministry of Public Administration—was created to develop and coordinate a program for the renewal of the public sector at both the national and local levels (Gustafsson, 1987).

In general, the solutions being adopted are based primarily on arguments forwarded by managerialist advocates but are leavened by strong influences for direct citizen participation. Citizens are to be involved in service delivery and managers and civil servants who deal directly with citizens are to be given greater authority and discretion. One reform under consideration would permit the users of government services to provide specific services. For example, under this scheme parents could be given the right to run day care centers on a cooperative basis. It is hoped that by reviewing the existing system of state grants and regulations, artificial obstacles to participation will be removed and the number of voluntary organizations will increase (Gustafsson, 1987).

Efforts to improve the efficiency of the public sector through the delegation of responsibilities from federal government ministries to lower levels of government have also been undertaken. Elected officials have become a part of the reform effort by increasing reliance on management by policy objectives rather than on detailed control of financial resources.

One important aspect of the Swedish reforms was the recognition that implementation would require the enthusiastic participation of existing public sector employees. As a result, a job security agreement was developed with those employees to ease the transition to the new structures and processes (Gustafsson, 1987).

2. New Zealand

Recent reforms of the public service in New Zealand also seek to enhance and/or improve its performance through restructuring, and more than other nations New Zealand has looked primarily to the private sector for ideas and concepts. One of the most significant reforms was the reorganization of government-owned corporations into profit-making enterprises whenever possible. Rather than being protected from market forces, many government corporations are now placed on an equal footing with private sector firms and are expected to earn a return on equity that is similar to that earned by firms in the private sector.

One of the central ways this has been done is through the delegation of responsibility from the minister to the head of the government-owned enterprise, who is now known as a chief executive. Unlike past practices, when the aptly named "permanent head" had little if any discretion as an employer and most personnel decisions had to be cleared by another office, and authority to spend money was strictly controlled, the new system provides managers and executives with extensive authority and discretion (Scott and Gorringe, 1989). Also, unlike the past when responsibility for the performance of a government corporation rested with a minister who had no say in the appointment of his or her permanent head, performance is now the responsibility of the chief executive.

Under the new system, ministers are free to delegate virtually all of their powers. Thus, chief executives now exert a great deal of control over most activities in their agencies. They hire and fire, conduct industrial relations, set policy initiatives, and determine appropriate rewards for the employees.

However, in exchange for this freedom, chief executives no longer enjoy the traditional safety and security of a government job. Chief executives are hired on a contract basis; their pay and benefits are directly related to the performance of the corporations they manage. Simply put, "chief executives are being given responsibility for key managerial functions and will be judged on their results" (Mascarenhas, 1990).

This sudden change in policy and the increased emphasis on outputs has not met with uniform enthusiasm from many civil servants. Unlike the Australian model, in which reforms were adopted incrementally and first tested at the state level, New Zealand adopted all of its reforms at once. One outcome was that the "accumulated resentment against a government which had adopted the market-driven philosophy to the point of ignoring fundamental human values led to confrontation between the government and its public employees over a period of several months" (Mascarenhas, 1990). Support for the reforms came from the ministers and the potential chief executives, as well as younger government employees. Older "tenured" civil servants were generally not so supportive.

To date, the effect of these reforms on the bureaucracy has been substantial. For example, the number of public service personnel fell from 72,417 in 1986–1987 to 60,940 by 1987–1988. Some of this reduction was due to the above-mentioned creation of state-owned private corporations, but it is important to remember that those employees no longer have the same employment privileges as regular civil servants. This twin dose of reforms based on private sector practice and public management techniques is still quite new and as of yet inconclusive, but continues to be supported by the government and by many key ministers (OECD, 1993).

3. Australia

In an effort to give departmental managers authority to match their increased responsibilities, a number of initiatives aimed at reducing central controls and devolving as much responsibility as possible down to the managerial level were created. For example, cost systems have been developed under which a department receives one governmental appropriation for the entire year. This single appropriation is to cover all salaries, as well as administrative and operating expenses. If at the end of the year monies remain, they may be rolled into the next fiscal year's budget (Australia Public Service Commission, 1989).

The federal government is now trying to devolve responsibilities even further down the chain of command. For example, the state is trying to find ways to give regional offices of departments the autonomy departmental managers now have because "further devolution is needed if the real benefits of the reduction in central controls is to be achieved" (Australian Public Service Commission, 1989). The only reason the devolution of power has not proceeded more rapidly is the absence of a good management information system; that reform is now under consideration.

4. United Kingdom

In April 1991 the National Health Service (NHS) radically reformed the way it operated. Ever since it was established in 1948, all or most pay raise decisions, work rules, and issues of public health delivery were centralized. However, during the 1970s and 1980s the drive for greater efficiency and productivity caused many to reconsider the rigid centralized decision-making process.

Critics of the system complained that centralization stifled experimentation and creativity at the local level. In addition, both management and trade unions argued that local managers were effectively powerless. For this reason evading responsibility and deferring to higher levels of authority were such standard practice that local health authorities had little if any influence in the formulation of health care policy and in the quality of health care (Glascott and Bowden, 1992).

As a result, in 1985 consensus management in which doctors, nurses, treasurers, and administrators all voted on policy decisions was abandoned. A general manager was appointed who was personally accountable for decisions made and who was personally accountable for decisions made and who was hired on a contract basis. In addition, customer service began to be emphasized, and general managers began requesting more freedom in the organizing and deploying of resources under their control. However, radical changes have come to the NHS only recently with the passage of the Community Care Act (CCA) of 1990.

The biggest change in health care delivery brought on by the CCA of 1990 is the creation of internal health care "markets." Funding is no longer automatic for all hospitals, community health service organizations, and health care professionals. Rather, there are now "purchasers" and "providers" of health services, and those providers (such as doctors) are now free to purchase care for their patients from the best providers.

General manager providers are now being forced to compete for the loyalty of doctors by providing quality service. The need to compete for contract business has had a significant impact on the behavior of most health care establishments. To give the health care providers more freedom to operate in this new environment they are now being turned into autonomous NHS trusts with corporate status and a board of directors. These trusts are free to treat all patients, public or private, buy and sell land, retain operating surpluses, build cash reserves, borrow money, run their staff as they see fit, set their own rates of pay other than for junior staff, and generally depart from centralized rules that governed the old system (Glascott and Bowden, 1992).

VIII. CONCLUSION

It is clear that a great many different reform efforts are currently in place or under consideration in most of the Western industrialized nations. From the Netherlands to the United Kingdom and from the United States to Australia, bureaucracies are being radically altered. Pay for performance is slowly displacing automatic step increases, fixed term contracts are becoming increasingly common at the top managerial levels, and governmental decentralization is making its way into areas where it was until recently thought not possible.

In New Zealand, the current Labor government has undertaken an almost total restructuring of government institutions and terms of employment in what is undoubtedly the most radical governmental reform of today. In the United Kingdom, the NHS is being radically reformed to create a market for health care services, while in North America a whole host of smaller yet substantial reforms are being continually implemented.

Are these efforts successful, or will they be? At present, the answers are not clear. Evaluations are at best limited, and in many countries, the reforms have been accompanied—and buffeted—by declining economies and major governmental reductions, shifts, and upheavals. In addition, in some countries several reforms have been implemented simultaneously and as a result determining which reforms are successful and which are not may never be possible.

However, where tentative conclusions on recent reforms are available the results are not particularly promising. It seems that in countries that have instituted pay for performance the results have consistently been below expectations (Kellough and Lu, 1992; Eisenberg and Ingraham, 1993) and pay for performance is one of the most popular reforms being undertaken. Clearly, more dramatic reforms, such as those in New Zealand, require more time to take effect; it will be several years before their full impact can begin to be satisfactorily interpreted.

Nonetheless, modest conclusions can be reached. There is virtually no place in the OECD world in which it is "business as usual" for civil service systems, government employees, and traditional government organizations. Both the political and the economic climates have mandated sweeping change directed to more efficiency, more flexibility, and more accountability in both government institutions and the public service. The standardization and central control that have long marked traditional civil service and public personnel policies cannot respond adequately to demands for rapid change and renewal. Hopefully, what is replacing them will be more successful.

There are also strong commonalities among the reforms: managerialism and private sector models are found in many nations. At the same time, national governments will adopt reforms that best fit their culture and view of government. Sweden will focus on citizen participation; the United States will continue to emphasize efficiency; the English and Canadians will emphasize the quality of the higher civil service. From these many efforts emerge a number of natural experiments, both in democracy and in effective human resource management in the public sector. Closely monitoring those experiments, and learning from them, should be a key focus for academics and practitioners alike in the next decade. Otherwise, a golden opportunity—one that may not come again for some time—will be lost.

REFERENCES

Arnold, Peri (1986). *Making the Managerial Presidency*, Princeton University Press, Princeton, NJ.

Atkinson, A. B., and Stiglitz, J. E. (1980). *Lectures on Public Economics*, McGraw-Hill, New York.

Aucoin, P. (1988). Contraction, Managerialism and Decentralization in Canadian Government, *Governance, 1*: 144–161.

Aucoin, P. (1990). Administrative reform in public management: paradigms, principles, paradoxes and pendulums, *Governance, 3*: 115–137.

Australian Public Service Commission (1989). *APS 2000: The Australian Public Service Workforce of the Future*, Australian Government Publishing Service.

Barzelay, M. (1992). *Breaking Through Bureaucracy*, University of California Press, Berkeley.

Boston, J. (1987). Transforming New Zealand's public sector: labour's quest for improved efficiency and accountability, *Public Admin., 65*: 423–442.

Caiden, G. E. (1988). Public Personnel and labor relations, *Handbook of Public Administration* (J. Rabin, W. B. Hildreth, and G. J. Miller, eds.), Marcel Dekker, New York.

Dawkins, S. J. (1985). Reforms in the Canberra system of public administration, *Aust. J. Public Admin., 44*: 59–72.

Dillman, D. L. (1986). Personnel management and productivity reform: taming the civil service in Great Britain and the United States, *Int. J. Public Admin., 8*: 345–367.

Drucker, P. F. (1984). *Management: Tasks, Responsibilities, Practices*, Heineman, London.

Eisenberg, E. F., and Ingraham, P. W. (1993). Analyzing the comparative pay for performance experience: are there common lessons? *Public Product. Rev.*

Friedman, Milton, and Friedman, Rose (1980). *Free to Choose: A Personal Statement*, Penguin, New York.

Fry, G. K. (1983). Compromise with the market: the Megaw report on civil service pay 1982, *Public Admin., 61*: 90–96.

Fry, G. K. (1984). The development of the Thatcher government's "grand strategy" for the civil service: a public policy perspective, *Public Admin., 62*: 322–335.

Fry, G. K. (1988). The Thatcher government, the financial management initiative, and the new civil service, *Public Admin., 66*: 1–20.

Glascott, F., and Bowden N. (1992). The development of pay flexibility in the English national health service, *Proceedings of the OECD Symposium on Pay Flexibility in the Public Sector*, Paris.

Government of Canada Report (1990). *Public Service 2000: The Renewal of the Public Service of Canada*, Supply and Services Canada, Ottawa.

Gustafsson, L. (1987). Renewal of the public service in Sweden, *Public Admin., 65*: 179–191.

Harper, Kirke (1992). The SES after one decade, *The Promise and Paradox of Civil Service Reform* (P. W. Ingraham and D. H. Rosenbloom, eds.), University of Pittsburgh Press.

Hayek, F. A. (1972). *The Road to Serfdom*, University of Chicago Press.

Hede, A. (1991a). Managerial reform and performance: the case of the Victorian SES, *Aust. J. Public Admin., 50*: 490–504.

Hede, A. (1991b). Trends in the higher services of Anglo-American systems, *Governance, 4*: 489–510.

Henig, J. R., Hamnett, C., and Feigenbaum, H.B. (1988). The politics of privatization: a comparative perspective, *Governance, 1*: 442–468.

Heseltine, M. (1987). *Where There's a Will*, Hutchinson, London.

Hogenboom, A. (1961). *Outlawing the Spoils: A History of the Civil Service Reform Movement: 1865–1883*, University of Illinois Press, Urbana.

Hood, C. (1989). Public administration and public policy: intellectual challenges for the 1990s, *Aust. J. Public Admin., 48*: 347–358.

Hood, Christopher (forthcoming). Exploring variations in 1980s public management reform, *Civil Service Systems in Comparative Perspective* (H. Bekke, J. Perry, and T. Toonen, eds.), University of Indiana Press, Bloomington.

Ingraham, P. W. (1987). Building bridges or burning them? The president, the appointees, and the bureaucracy, *Public Admin. Rev., 47*: 425–435.

Ingraham, P. W. (1992). Commissions, cycles and change: the role of blue ribbon commissions in executive branch change, *Agenda for Excellence: Public Service in America* (P. W. Ingraham and D. Kettl, eds.), Chatham House, Chatham, NJ.

Ingraham, P. W. (1993). Of pigs in pokes and policy diffusion: another look at pay for performance, *Public Admin. Rev., 53*: 348–356.

Ingraham, P. W. (forthcoming). External stress and internal strains: the reform agenda for national civil service systems, *Civil Service Systems in Comparative Perspective* (H. Bekke, J. Perry, and T. Toonen, eds.), University of Indiana Press, Bloomington.

Ingraham, P. W., and Peters, B. G. (1988). The conundrum of reform: a comparative analysis, *Rev. Public Personnel Admin., 8*: 3–16.

Keating, M. (1990). Managing for results in the public interest, *Aust. J. Public Admin., 9*: 387–398.

Kellough, E. J., and Lu, H. (1992). The paradox of merit pay in the public sector: persistence of a problematic procedure, Unpublished manuscript.

Kernaghan, K. (1991). Career public service 2000: road to renewal or impractical vision, *Can. Public Admin., 34*: 551–572.

Light, Paul C. (1982). *The President's Agenda*, Johns Hopkins University Press, Baltimore.

Linder, S. H., and Peters, B. G. (1987). A design perspective on policy implementation: the fallacies of misplaced prescription, *Policy Stud. Rev., 6*: 459–475.

Lovrich, N. P. (1985). Contending paradigms in public administration: a sign of crisis or intellectual vitality?, *Admin. Soc., 17*: 307–330.

Mascarenhas, C. R. (1990). Reforms of the public service in Australia and New Zealand. *Governance, 3*: 75–95.

McIntosh, R. J. (1991). Public service 2000: the employee perspective, *Can. Public Admin., 34*: 503–511.

Meier, K. J. (1987). *Politics and the Bureaucracy: Policymaking in the Fourth Branch of Government*, Brooks/Cole, Monterey, CA.

Moe, R. C. (1990). Traditional organizational principles and the managerial presidency: from Phoenix to Ash, *Public Admin. Rev., 50*: 126–139.

Moore, Barry (1989). Developments in New South Wales public administration, *Aust. J. Public Admin., 48*: 109–122.

Niskanen, W. (1971). *Bureaucracy and Representative Government*, Aldine-Atherton Press, Chicago.

Organization for Economic Cooperation and Development (1991). *Proceedings from the Symposium on Pay for Performance*, Paris.

Organization for Economic Cooperation and Development (1993). *Proceedings of the Symposium on Pay Flexibilities*, Paris.

Pollitt, C. (1990a). *Managerialism and the Public Services*, Basil Blackwell, Cambridge, UK.

Pollitt, C. (1990b). Doing business in the temple? Managers and quality assurance in the public services, *Public Admin.*, *68*: 435–452.

Posner, R. (1974). Theories of economic regulation, *Bell J. Econ. Manage. Sci.*, *5*: 24–40.

Rawson, B. (1991). Public service 2000 service to the public task force: findings and implications, *Can. Public Admin.*, *34*: 490–500.

Rose, R. (1990). Charging for public services, *Public Admin.*, *68*: 297–313.

Savoie, D. (1993). *Reagan, Thatcher and Mulroney: The Politics of Reform,* University of Pittsburgh Press, Pittsburgh, PA.

Scott, G., and Gorringe, P. (1989). Reform of the core public sector: the New Zealand experience, *Aust. J. Public Admin.*, *48*: 81–91.

Tellier, P. M. (1990). Public service 2000: the renewal of the public service, *Can. Public Admin.*, *33*: 123–132.

U.S. Merit Systems Protection Board (1990). *Senior Executive Service Pay Setting and Reassignments: Expectations vs. Reality*, Washington, DC.

U.S. Office of Personnel Management (1991). *Continuous Improvement: The Quality Challenge*, Government Printing Office, Washington, DC.

Van Riper, Paul, P, (1958). *History of the United States Civil Service*, Row, Peterson, Evanston, IL.

Wilenski, P. (1986). Administrative reform: general principles and the Australian experience, *Public Admin.*, *64*: 257–276.

Wistrich, E. (1992). Restructuring government New Zealand style, *Public Admin.*, *70*: 119–135.

Young, P., and Goodman, J. C. (1986). U.S. lags behind in going private, *Wall Street Journal*, February 20.

7

Politics and Development of China's Civil Service System

HON S. CHAN   City Polytechnic of Hong Kong, Hong Kong

TAO-CHIU LAM   University of Macau, Macau

I. INTRODUCTION

Civil service, as commonly understood in public administration, has been a strange concept in China. Because of the total absorption of society and the economy by the state (Tsou, 1986), there has scarcely been any real attempt to distinguish the different types of state organizations and kinds of employment relations in China.[1] Although categories including state and collective sectors, state administrative organs (or simply administration), service units, and economic enterprises existed since the 1950s, the unifying nature of China's state administration and management remained a dominant feature.

In China, *cadre* is an all encompassing concept, referring to a wide range of employees serving within different types of state organizations (Barnett, 1967; Gong, 1985). Currently, there are more than 40 million cadres in China, of which less than 10% serves within state administrative organs. Most work in service units and economic enterprises. The management of cadres has consistently been centralized in the party committees (or party core groups) and their organization departments at various levels of government and functional areas (Chen, 1987:3; Burns, 1987:36–51). The powers of cadre management are divided vertically within the party. Changes in the vertical distribution of powers within the party were introduced from time to time in the last few decades (Burns, 1987). However, in terms of personnel administration, these changes did not attempt to horizontally differentiate between categories of cadres. Cadres in economic enterprises, for example, were managed in the same way as government officials in state administrative organs.

This unifying management system has caused many problems. First, it has failed to develop measures to cater to the needs of different types of administration and employment relationships. Second, overcentralization of power by the party led to a disjuncture between personnel management and other functional responsibilities, i.e., officials with direct administrative responsibilities sometimes lack powers' over personnel management. Third, the unifying system has also contributed to the slow development of a professionalized personnel management system. Techniques of personnel administration are widely considered to be obsolete (Chen, 1987; Zhao, 1987:xviii–xix).

The defects inherent in this unified and centralized cadre management system have plagued generations of Chinese political leaders, prompting them to develop various remedial measures in the last seven decades (Harding, 1981). Yet until recently, the need for a fundamental change in the basic framework of state personnel administration has not gained a place in the policy agenda. Chinese leaders began to look for an alternative framework for cadre and personnel management in 1984. Yet the concept of a civil service system did not emerge until late 1986 when a high-level task force, led by Zhao Ziyang, recommended that the Party Central establish a state civil service in China (Dai, 1990–1991:61–73).[2] At the Thirteenth Congress of the Communist Party of China, held in October, 1987, the decision to establish a state civil service was formally approved. From a historical perspective, the decisions to separate personnel administration in state administrative organs (1984) and to develop a civil service system (1986) are major steps in China's reform of cadre and personnel management and state building. On reflection, these changes could fundamentally alter the basic edifice of cadre and personnel management that evolved since the founding of the People's Republic of China. Since the mid-1980s, a new system has been in the making.

This chapter focuses on policy design by examining the drafting of the civil service regulations. In drafting this set of regulations, a wide range of important issues has surfaced. Different values and interests were advanced in an attempt to foreshadow what China's civil service system should look like. In fact, the concept of a civil service has created considerable controversies and tensions within Chinese leadership (Dai, 1990–1991). Policy design as an analytic concept is important for understanding Chinese politics and China's emerging civil service system. As argued by Ingraham, problems rooted in policy design could have far-reaching implications for policy implementation and policy outcomes (Ingraham, 1992: 19–36).

In examining how Chinese policy makers and drafters of the law defined problems and formulated solutions, we discuss the unique nature of the problems that characterized China's reform of the state personnel administration. We consider the extent to which the drafters of the law adopted Western principles of civil service in developing China's own system. We analyze the recently promulgated civil service regulations in order to reflect on the main features of China's civil service system and to comment on the possible obstacles lying ahead. Particular emphasis is placed on the effect of politics on designing the civil service system in China. China's political environment changed significantly following the suppression of the prodemocracy movement in June, 1989. The impact of this change on China's civil service was decisive.

The tensions created by the need to satisfy the numerous political requirements on the one hand, and the desperate need to find viable solutions to the defects of the personnel and cadre management system on the other, were evident throughout the entire drafting process. The former can be called the *political approach* and the latter the *rational approach*. Evidently, both political considerations and rational arguments were present in the drafting process. At that level, the Chinese experience is no different from that of other countries (March and Olsen, 1983). The focus of this chapter is on the question of politics. This should not be taken to suggest that rational considerations had no role. We argue, however, that the primary of politics in China in general and in this case (the drafting of the civil servant regulations) in particular, severely limits a rational policy design. This chapter concludes by discussing the dilemmas and problems faced by Chinese officials in instituting China's civil service system, given that it has been shaped by these incoherent and conflicting imperatives.

II. DRAFTING PROCESS AND INSTITUTIONAL FRAMEWORK

As our focus is on policy design, it is necessary to consider the drafting process and the changing institutional contexts within which the regulations were drafted. The effort to develop a set of regulations to govern the management of employees in state administrative organs began in 1984 and ended with the promulgation of the Provisional Regulations of State Civil Servants in August, 1993 (*Wen Hui Bao*, August 19, 1993). Overall, policy design in this case was highly centralized, and thus, a closely monitored process. Participation was limited to a small group of people holding formal government positions. As is the case of civil service reform in the United States, the political factor is of crucial importance. The somewhat checkered course of China's civil service system reflects the turbulence of China's political environment in the past decades. More importantly, because of the importance of cadre control in Chinese polity, the tie between the overall political background and the development of a civil service system is conceivably much closer. The drafting process falls mainly into four stages (Lam and Chan, 1993).

A.   The First Stage: 1984–1986

Not surprisingly, the term "civil service" was not used in this stage. Rather, *personnel of state administrative organs* continued to be used. Two main concerns initiated the change and the need for developing a more elaborate and sophisticated cadre management system. First, there was a growing realization that the personnel of state administrative organs—as contrasted to cadres and workers in service units and economic enterprises—was a separate category requiring a unique management mechanism. Second, the need for institutionalizing the management of the personnel of state administrative organs and for stabilizing it by a legal framework had received increased attention. Subsequently, the Central Secretariat of the Communist Party ordered that a law be drafted (Dai, 1990–1991; Xu, 1992:56). Ten different drafts were produced. The first stage laid the groundwork upon which future development took place. Nonetheless, the core theme—that cadres in state administrative organs should belong to a separate category and be managed by a separate system—began to take shape. This idea was later conceptualized and labeled as "management by categories" by the drafters.

B.   The Second Stage: 1986–June, 1989

Development took a decisive turn when Deng Xiaoping, China's paramount leader, sounded out the urgency of political system reform in the second half of 1986 (Deng, 1987). A high-level task force led by Zhao Ziyang, then premier and later general secretary of CPC, was quickly formed and put in charge of making overall recommendations for political system reform to the Party Central. The purview of the task force was wide-ranging and covered practically every area of importance, including the state personnel system. Seven research teams were formed in order to develop specific ideas and formulate recommendations to be considered by the task force (Chen, 1990:101–122). As part of the task force's overall recommendations for political system reform to the Party Central, the concept of a civil service was proposed and endorsed. The decision to establish a civil service system with two different types of civil servants (one an administrative affairs civil servant with permanent tenure and the other a political affairs civil servant who comes and goes with political changes) was one of the most noteworthy features of Zhao Ziyang's historic report to the party's Thirteenth Congress in October, 1987 (Burns, 1989:739–770).

This stage was characterized by strong support and commitment to the political system reform at the highest level of leadership. Deng Xiaoping's determination and support seemed to be the primary driving force. Based on the draft produced in the first stage, six further drafts were completed. The fifteenth draft was released in an international conference held in Beijing in October, 1988. In May, 1989, the sixteenth draft was issued to the personnel departments of the central ministries and the provincial-level governments for comments. It was expected that the civil service system would be implemented very soon.

One important development during this stage was the establishment of the Ministry of Personnel (making it a full-fledged ministry) in the 1988 State Council reorganization. The new ministry was explicitly charged with the task of designing and implementing a civil service system. Though power remained highly centralized, the day-to-day drafting was taken up by the new ministry. A Beijing-based academic described the drafters in the new ministry as technocrats with a strong desire to establish a scientific system of personnel management in China. This institutional development was a crucial factor for the continued support of the civil service concept even after the Party Central failed to provide the same kind and level of support in later stages.[3]

C. The Third Stage: July, 1989–January, 1991

The Tiananmen Square incident, the demise of Zhao Ziyang, and the accompanying rejection of his program of political system reform threw the development of the civil service system into heightened dispute and forced the slowdown of its development. The optimistic hope for a quick implementation of the civil service system did not materialize. A new understanding on many crucial issues (especially the party–state relationship) in the wake of the widespread spontaneous mobilization against the regime in 1989 led to the questioning of the real and potential implications of the civil service system on the party's monopoly on political power.

On the surface, Zhao Ziyang's downfall did not spell the end of China's civil service system. Tasks arranged before the political turmoil proceeded as planned. A case in point was the pilot scheme. Just before the Tiananmen Square incident, six state bureaus were chosen as an experiment.[4] In 1990, the experiment was extended to two localities, the Shenzhen Special Economic Zone in the southern province of Guangdong, and Harbin, capital of the Heilongjiang province in northeast China (Dai, 1991:22–40). In 1990, both Zhao Dongwan, personnel minister, and Cheng Lianchang, deputy personnel minister in charge of developing the civil service regulations, came out to defend the civil service system (Zhao, 1990; Cheng, 1990).

Undoubtedly, there was much uncertainty, hesitation, and conflict. On the one hand, the development of a civil service system continued to have the support from some Central Party leaders.[5] This was so partly because the reform of the cadre and personnel management system was the core spirit underlying Deng Xiaoping's thought on reforming the party and state leadership (Deng, 1983; Deng, 1987). Also, the civil service system was presented as a move to resolve the well-known and notorious defects in cadre and personnel management. Many of the problems in cadre and personnel management identified in Zhao Ziyang's Work Report still remain the most pernicious obstacles to China's attempt to develop an efficient and competent bureaucracy. While there are opposing views regarding solutions, a consensus of the seriousness of such defects and the urgency of taking immediate actions still exist.

On the other hand, when the Communist Party of China decided to intensify its control over state organizations and cadres after the Tiananmen Square incident, the civil service system became the target of criticism.[6] Conservative leaders believed that if the civil service system was to go ahead, the overall guiding principle should definitely be modified, in particular, its original intent to separate the party from the state. Organizational interests were also at stake. The proposed civil service system would benefit some organizations and harm others. Not surprisingly, therefore, the Central Party's Organization Department, whose interest had already been adversely curtailed by the proposed civil service system and, in particular, by the parallel attempt to impart a limited separation of the functions of the party from state, quickly grasped the opportunity to regain its lost jurisdictions (*Yearbook of Chinese Personnel*, 1991:492–495; Burns, 1994).

This stage, therefore, was marked by intense political and organizational struggles. The drafting did not seem to make much progress, although the drafters often justified the civil service system in terms of the new political lines (Zhao, 1989; Zhao, 1990). While the policy of establishing a civil service system was not entirely reversed, the Party Central deemed it necessary to deploy new principles to realign its development.

D. The Fourth Stage: Early 1991–August, 1993

It was in the first half of 1991 that the top leaders seemed to reach an understanding that the drafting of the regulations should continue. An important instruction regarding the civil service system was handed down by Premier Li Peng in a national meeting prepared for cadres from the personnel system in early 1991. Li Peng pointed out that China's civil service system should be in line with its national situation. National situation, or *guoqing* in Chinese, here carried a special meaning. It was a shorthand term used to contrast the earlier tendency to adopt general principles common to civil service systems in Western countries. As a matter of fact, the drafters deliberately attempted to distinguish China's civil service system from its Western counterparts.[7] According to the interpretation of a senior official of the Ministry of Personnel, national situation referred to a number of important matters, ranging from the inevitable domination of the Communist Party and the impossibility of separating the party from the state, to the long standing practice of carrying out mass line in cadre management (Xu, 1991:15–21).

Despite Li Peng's critical remarks on the proposed civil service system and the works of the Ministry of Personnel, it seemed that clear conditions and constraints for instituting China's civil service system were defined by the Party Central. Therefore, Cheng Lianchang, after attending the meeting presided by Li, said that the purposes and requirements of the Party Central became clear and exact. Drafting activity quickly resumed within the Ministry of Personnel. Deng Xiaoping's historic tour to South China in the beginning of 1992, to push China's reform policy forward, also boosted the drafting work (Cheng, 1992). More than ten further drafts were produced before the regulations were officially promulgated in August, 1993. In this stage, the content of the regulations was substantially altered and the basic spirit of the civil service system was recast.

III. THE PRIMACY OF POLITICS AND THE UNIQUE PROBLEMS FOR DEVELOPING A CIVIL SERVICE SYSTEM IN CHINA

In China, the adoption of a common term, *civil service system*, invites comparison. The starting point concerns the problems to be tackled by the civil service system. Needless to say, the final shape of China's civil service system depends not only on considerations of different alternatives to the same set of problems that are common to other countries, but also on the nature of the problems emerged at a particular historical moment. Comparative studies have indicated that the problems of one country may not be problems in another country. Since the Second World War, the closed structure of the British higher civil service was persistently considered problematic. This concern was never on the policy agenda in the United States. Similarly, American concerns for representative bureaucracy, particularly ethnic representation, are rarely mentioned in other countries. As aptly described by Mosher (1982), the perception of a problem might well be shaped by the experience of developing one's own civil service system.

In a sense, China's attempt to establish a civil service system sought to address the same problems that are behind the emergence of civil service systems in countries such as Britain and the United States in the last century. One of the basic flaws of China's personnel system was that personnel matters in state bureaucracy were not governed by adequate rules and procedures, thus opening the door to rampant nepotism and favoritism in personnel administration. In the first stage of the drafting process, there was serious concern for a limited separation of politics and administration to provide the necessary stability and continuity in state administration. There are interesting comparisons between China's civil service system to its Western counterparts. Needless to say, many generic issues arising in the West about civil service reform were raised and debated among the law drafters and the party leaders (Xu, 1989:3–4). It cannot be denied that the Western experience in developing a civil service system has been of great value to the Chinese drafters.

There are, however, limits to such comparisons. Despite the apparent similarities, the nature of the problems in China is different. Scholars studying civil service reform in the United States observed that civil service reform there "is not a spellbinding issue. It deals with the nuts and bolts of personnel administration, merit systems, labour relations, and improved efficiency and productivity of government agencies" (Ingraham, 1992:3). While reform in these areas affects the interests of different organizations and participants and also sets forth a new set of political relationships, it basically works within the established political framework (Ingraham, 1992; Rosenbloom, 1989:188–190). This is not the case in China. Here, the establishment of a civil service system is, at least potentially, a great challenge to the existing political order and the position of the Communist Party. It would be misleading to call it just an administrative reform. Similarly, a study focusing exclusively on standard personnel issues such as recruitment, performance appraisal, promotion, etc., might not enable us to fully understand the unique problems and difficulties faced by the law drafters and the nature of China's proposed civil service system (Chow, 1991:25–44).

The most unique problem facing the reformers of personnel administration in China is that it touches on sensitive political issues. One of the key questions facing the drafters of the civil service regulations is how to create a stable state administration competent to serve its critical purpose in a communist regime. This scenario ensures that the designing procedure is bound to be affected by political concerns. Politics is a relevant factor here in several senses. First, the civil service system seeks to achieve a significant political change. As discussed later, the concept of the civil service system as manifested in the earlier stage of drafting the civil servant regulations has significant implications on the scope of the party's nomenclature and the party–state relationship. Second, many issues carry important political implications. The merit principle is a case in point. While meritocracy was officially adopted in principle by all, its specific content remains controversial.

Another way to appreciate the unique nature of the problems faced by the law drafters in China is to focus on the point of departure, i.e., the existing system of personnel administration. Two main features are worth noting. First, as suggested above, China's civil service system seeks to set apart a portion of the work force from a huge pool of cadres. Such an effort is both political and technical. It is technical because the boundary between administrative units and service units is blurred in China. This will make "management by categories" difficult (that is, to distinguish personnel working in state administrative organs from cadres working in service units and economic enterprises, and to develop different systems of personnel management). The situation in recent years was further aggravated because of repeated efforts by the central government to compress the number of administrative organs. Differentiating one group of cadres from another is political because the benefits of a great number of cadres are at stake. The implementation of a civil service system is generally perceived by cadres in China as tantamount to substantially raising the compensation of those cadres to be categorized as state civil servants. Indeed, it is widely observed that to the majority of the rank-and-file members within state bureaucracy, the civil service system is only a matter of material improvement and compensation or, to use the Chinese term, wage reform. Up to now, "management by categories" is held as a principle. The drafters seemed to be fully aware of the difficulties in overcoming these technical and political problems, but chose to ignore them for the time being (Xu, 1989; 1992).

Second, the existing personnel administrative system is highly centralized and unified. A unitary structure tied closely to state administrative structure existed since the 1950s. Many issues concerning centralization and developing a unitary structure that characterize civil service reforms elsewhere were perceived to be diametrically differently in China. While some countries sought in the beginning to develop their civil service with a view to centralize power, China sought to do the opposite, i.e., to "decentralize." Yet, it is important to note that "decentralization" means in China's context striking a delicate balance between maintaining the party's overall control and improving cadre and personnel management by granting a limited extension of power on personnel management matters to state administrative organs.

IV. SEPARATION OF POLITICS AND ADMINISTRATION AND MERITOCRACY

A core academic interest in China's emerging civil service system centers upon the reception of the cluster of ideas, values, techniques, and practices generally accepted in other civil service systems. The quest for scientific management, as it first appeared at the turn of the century in the United States, emerged again 80 years or so later in a communist country, which repeatedly denounced and persistently attacked the Western model of bureaucracy (Whyte, 1973:149–163; Harding, 1981). However, as we have indicated earlier and shall discuss again later, the pursuit of scientific management, epitomized by the rational approach, is often hindered by political constraints. In this section, we discuss China's emerging civil service system in terms of two central issues: (1) separation of politics and administration, (2) meritocracy and neutral competence. It is in these issues that the tensions between the political imperatives and the quest for a scientific personnel management are manifested most clearly.

A. Separation of Politics and Administration

The reason for putting forth a civil service system is to provide a mechanism for a stable transfer of political power. One of the key problems of state building in China over the past few decades was rooted in the fact that the established governmental order failed to provide the necessary institutional stability, the obvious effect of which was that political changes at the apex of the power structure and political struggles among the top elites have produced extensive vibrations over all walks of life, disrupted the policy agenda, and hindered the party's ability to achieve governance. The extensive party control mechanism made it inevitable for all cadres (the majority of which are party members) to get involved in political struggles (Vogel, 1971:556–568; Harding, 1981). It is not surprising to see that the advocates of political system reform in China envisaged separable working rules and procedures, which could enable the state administration to function generically, and to insulate itself from, to quote Woodrow Wilson, "the hurry and strife of politics."

In Zhao Ziyang's proposal to the Thirteenth Party Congress and the sixteenth draft of the regulations, stability of state administration was the main theme. In his Work Report, stability of state administration was mentioned as one of the major objectives for implementing the civil service system. Other objectives included facilitating the growth of outstanding cadres, helping to improve the efficiency of government work, and reinforcing and improving party leadership over personnel work (Zhao, 1987). Article One of the sixteenth draft placed stability of state administration, together with achieving a government of superior quality—able, efficient, and a "clean"—as the main goals of establishing China's civil service system (Xu, 1989). Because stability of state administration was a sensitive political issue in China, it understandably did not occupy a conspicuous position in an official report such as Zhao Ziyang's Report to the Party's Thirteenth Congress. This concern for stability of state administration represents an overdue concern for providing measures against instability and fluidity brought forth by politics, which has been a constant feature in the four-decade history of communist China. In terms of personnel management, this orientation calls for a permanent civil service, which has been universally regarded as a necessary, though by no means sufficient, prerequisite for ensuring stability and continuity of state administration.

The first move to build stability and continuity in state administration was the creation of two different categories of state civil servants—political affairs and administrative affairs civil servants. Political affairs civil servants, though labeled as state civil servants, would not be managed and regulated under the civil service regulations. They would, instead, be managed in accordance with "political requirements." Viewed this way, the arrangement is similar to the way politicians are "managed" in the West. Administrative affairs civil servants would be governed by civil service regulations. The crucial distinction between these two categories, from the personnel management's viewpoint, is in the variations in term of their tenure and the degree of career protection (Zhao, 1987; Xu, 1989). The purpose of instituting a civil service with tenure and a greater degree of protection is obviously to insulate it from political interference.

The establishment of a civil service system is part of an attempt to impart a limited separation of the functions of the party and the state. As clearly spelled out by Deng Xiaoping on several occasions in the second half of 1986, China's political system reform should center on the party-state relationship. The party-state relationship in China is comparable to the analytic relationship between politics and administration in public administration literature in the West. The attempt to grant more autonomy to state administration can be understood as an effort to separate politics from administration. Though not explicitly stated, the civil service system was in fact intended to be a major instrument to achieve this objective.

Along this line of thinking, some drafters envisaged a radical change. Dai Duangqian, director of the Department of Examination and Recruitment, Ministry of Personnel, for example, projected the following picture:

> After separation of party and state has been effected, there should be a relatively major shift concerning the functions of the Organization Department of the Party committees at all levels, with exception of the cadres that are in charge of handling and managing Party affairs . . . The emphasis and focus [of the Organization Department's activities] should be placed on comprehensive researching of cadre and personnel system, on cadre and personnel policy, and on the forecasting of [personnel] conditions and the needs of cadres. (Dai, 1990–1991:66)

The immediate task, according to Dai, was to make adjustments to the existing cadre managing structure. Dai further added:

> There will have to be appropriate and corresponding adjustments to the scope and boundaries of the authority of the Party committees to manage cadres. Some of the powers will have to be delegated, while others can be handed over to related departments. Party committees shall manage only the most important cadres, while other cadres shall be managed by the relevant systems. Naturally, we have yet to decide which cadres belong to the category of the "most important" and which cadres shall be managed by localities or by the respective departments. Under this system, there will be corresponding changes in the functions and responsibilities of the Party's Organization Departments at all levels. (Dai, 1990–1991:67)

Officials within the Ministry of Personnel were particularly eager to see the separation of party and state (*Yearbook of Chinese Personnel*, 1991:428). Zhang Zhijian, one of the deputy personnel ministers, skillfully linked the civil service system to the issue of enhancing the power and autonomy of the Ministry of Personnel. He said:

On the question of how to establish a management organ for state civil servants, I think there are two points of departure. First, it should be in line with our country's requirements. That is to say, we should create the corresponding civil service management organ in accordance with the nature, principles and characteristics of our country. Second, we should implement the civil service system within the broad background of political system reform. (*Yearbook of Chinese Personnel*, 1991:428)

Specifically, Zhang Zhijian advanced two arguments demanding that more independent and autonomous power be given to the civil service management organ, i.e., the Ministry of Personnel.

1. [It should] realize the principle of separating the functions of the Party and state, overcome the defects of inseparation of the Party and state in the personnel management in the past, and give the civil service management organ more elaborate and well defined functions, and clarify clearly its jurisdictions.
2. [It should] realize the principle of management by categories. The civil service management organ should centre specifically on the management of administrative affairs civil servants. (*Yearbook of Chinese Personnel*, 1991:428)

The Ministry of Personnel was established in March, 1988. Management powers over cadres began to be delegated to the State Council and the new ministry (Burns, 1994). In August and October, 1988, two groups of cadres, originally under the control of the Party Central, were transferred to and supervised by the State Council. These cadres belonged to two categories, one from government organs at the central level and the other from service units and economic enterprises. The former category included some organizations directly subordinate to the State Council, and all state bureaus managed and coordinated by the full-fledged ministries and commissions. The second category encompassed many of the most important service units and economic enterprises in China. It included service units such as Peking University, Tsinghua University, and the Chinese Academy of Agricultural Science; and enterprises such as Anshan Steel Mill, the Capital Steel Mill, and the First Automobile Manufacturing Plant (*Selection of Documents* [1989:11]:3–5; *Yearbook of Chinese Personnel*, 1991:137–140). Although the actual scope of transferring cadre management powers from the party to the state was not detailed in the sixteenth draft of the civil service regulations, the subsequent development moved to reduce the party's involvement and expanded the Ministry of Personnel's control over cadre and personnel management. In the sixteenth draft, it was implied that all administrative affairs civil servants—the most senior being deputy ministers—should fall under the jurisdiction of the civil service management organ (Xu, 1989; Burns, 1989).

Advocates of the civil service system endeavored to develop a framework to guarantee a relatively stable state administration and to ensure policy continuity. These reformers tended to view civil service as an administrative arm of the government, performing nonlegislative and nonjudiciary tasks, and taking up the functions of implementing and coordinating policies. Simply put, this is the traditional understanding of the role of the public service state in the West. At the turn of the century, under the influence of the scientific movement, the role of the public service state was seen as a "transmission belt," merely carrying out the orders and decisions of the political leaders. This view "perceptually" coincided with Woodrow Wilson's idea that administration is government in action. In Wilson's own words:

Administration lies outside the proper sphere of politics. Administrative questions are not political questions . . . the field of administration is the field of business. It is removed from the hurry and strife of politics; . . . It is a part of political life only as the methods of the counting-house are a part of the life of society; only as machinery is part of the manufactured product. (Wilson, 1978:18)

The political developments in 1989 fundamentally altered the nature of China's civil service system. Politics began to exert a heavy toll on the effort to develop a civil service system on the basis of Western experience. Yet, emphasis was placed on Chinese characteristics. The drafters unwillingly began to adapt to the new political conditions. The objective of separating the functions of the party from the state was explicitly renounced (*Selection of Documents* [1990:12]:12–23). Subsequently, the objective of achieving a stable state administration came under question.

Compared to the sixteenth draft, the most radical change introduced after the Tiananmen Square incident was the elimination of the distinction between political affairs and administrative affairs civil servants. Under the new political circumstances, the earlier decision to create a division of labor, and hence power between the Central Party's Organization Department and the Ministry of Personnel in cadre management, was unlikely to be carried out. A newly appointed deputy personnel minister, Zhao Zhongnai, criticized the decision in the earlier draft of the regulations for reducing party control and explicitly said that the old framework of cadre management should be preserved (*Yearbook of Chinese Personnel*, 1991:492–495). In 1990, the Central Organization Department nullified the earlier decision to hand over the management of certain cadres to the State Council and the Ministry of Personnel by introducing a number of additional procedural steps that the State Council and the Ministry of Personnel must follow when making personnel decisions (*Selection of Documents* [1990:13]:35–53). The State Council and the Ministry of Personnel did not have a final say in various aspects of cadre and personnel management since, and this remains so to date.

The evolution of China's civil service system provides a vivid example of how politics affects problems of definition and the search for alternatives and solutions in the reform of a personnel management system (Ingraham, 1992:19–36). The overriding concern of Chinese leaders in the aftermath of the Tiananmen Square incident was the long-term security of the political regime. The new emphasis was on vitality and competition in state administration. Stability and vitality and competition seemed to be seen as mutually exclusive. Xu Songato, director of the Department of Policy and Regulation, Ministry of Personnel, justified this change by arguing that

> The background of establishing China's civil service system differs from the one we find in the West. Western countries practice multiparty competition. If a particular party controls the government, it usually carries out large scale reshuffling of government officials. As a result, government lacks continuity. Under this circumstance, it is necessary to stress stability of state administration. Our civil service system is developed in an environment where the career stability of cadre corp is relatively ensured. If we still stress stability of state administration and professionalization, the cadre corp will become more like a pond of dead water. Hence, we should, therefore, establish motivation and competition mechanisms to enliven the cadre corp. Seen as such, when revising the regulations, the central idea is to tighten control at the point of entry (i.e. recruitment), to exercise stringent management, and to ensure that the exit from civil service system is unimpeded. (Xu, 1992:62–63)

Deputy Personnel Minister Cheng Lianchang echoed the same view, and said in 1992 that

> The reforms of the personnel system should develop a motivational mechanism which should aim at enhancing the vitality of administrative organs . . . In the past we talked about the relative stability of cadres in state administrative organs. I think this should be understood in the following way: our entire [cadre] corp is one that is revolutionized, young, professional and well educated. At the same time, it is necessary to enable the cadre corp of our state

administrative organs to carry out some necessary mobility, transfer and adjustments. (Cheng, 1992:9)

It is not immediately clear whether stability on the one hand, and vitality and competition on the other, are really at odds with each other.

The need for providing stability in state administration and, hence, separating politics from administration, was no longer stressed. Stability of state administration was not even mentioned in the final version of the regulations. The total recast of the drafters' and the leaders' mind about the importance of stability of state administration is primarily a function of the changing political context. However, the attempt to present stability as contradictory to the objective of increasing vitality and competition is interesting. The arguments of Xu Songtao and Cheng Lianchang quoted in regard to the needs for stressing vitality and competition obviously have a point, considering the rigidity and incompetence of Chinese bureaucracy. In the meantime, the decision to stress more cadre mobility and less career security for state civil servants tends to prepare the ground for developing a "politicized bureaucracy." Measures designed to enhance vitality and competition within the state administration could have far-reaching negative effects and could also create other problems in personnel management. These measures could be abused to advance personal and political interests. Yet, it is clear that the new approach provides good opportunities to the party to elicit obedience and loyalty from state civil servants.

B. Meritocracy

Here the analysis does not provide a specific discussion to examine how merit pay is, or ought to be, integrated with salary structure as reflected in, say, the 1978 Civil Service Reform Act in the United States. The question of meritocracy in China's context is a preliminary yet fundamental one. The analysis points to the development of a general organizational principle that personnel decisions are based on relatively rational and objective criteria. As implied in Weber's concept of bureaucracy, meritocracy has been widely seen as crucial for achieving organizational efficiency and effectiveness in the modern world. Moreover, in a modern public service state, the use of a merit system had come to rely on sophisticated techniques, such as uniform classification systems, examinations, and performance appraisal systems (Rosenbloom, 1989:201–218).

Acceptance of the merit principle has been a hallmark of post-Mao China (Li and Bachman, 1989:64–94). As a matter of fact, it can be argued that this principle was never officially rejected in the history of communist China. Even under Mao, when the orthodoxies stress both "red" (desirable political qualities) and "expert" (technical know-how) criteria, the merit principle was upheld, although in reality red is preferable to expert (Whyte, 1973). Recent years have witnessed a heightened emphasis on the merit principle and a reformulation of what constitutes merit. For example, since the 1980s, the party always insisted that cadres should be revolutionized, well-educated, professionalized, and young. The first, to be revolutionized, is a political criterion and the other three all refer to different facets of technical ability. This formulation has remained one of the key ideas guiding China's cadre and personnel policy in recent years.

The merit principle has been the core spirit underlying the entire process of designing the Chinese civil service system. Two issues shaped the development of China's merit system. The first concerns the changing substance of merit. The second is related to the difficulties and the primitive nature of job analysis and position classification in China.

1. Merit: Virtue or Ability

Because cadre management is a crucial issue to the Chinese political regime, deciding on what criteria can best reflect the cadres' merit has remained a highly political matter (Harding, 1981).

In most cases, the discussion of the merit principle during the drafting process revolved around a dominant theme: combining virtue (*de*) and ability (*cai*). Yet, the meaning of this theme and the relative weight attributed to the two components varied over time.

The notions of virtue and ability can be traced back to traditional Confucian ideology. In communist China, these notions seem to have become the accepted standards in cadre management and carried a specific meaning. According to Vogel

> Virtue refers to the fervour with which a cadre carries out the wishes of the Party. It can be interpreted to mean the ability to capture what the Party or the political situation requires, but the general emphasis is placed on the responsiveness to Party directives, i.e., on the degree to which a cadre is an "obedient tool of the Party." "Ability" is generally interpreted as actual performance in one's job assignment. It includes not only knowledge, but judgement, skill, willingness to work and all other qualities necessary for carrying out the work responsibilities. (Vogel, 1967:40–41)

Before the Tiananmen Square incident, the main thrust of the merit concept emphasized ability, not virtue. Yet, out of political and ideological necessity, virtue was incorporated into the merit principle. Reformers in China repeatedly stressed that political factors should not be neglected in developing the civil service system. They adopted this strategy in order to preempt conservative opposition. It perhaps reflected a genuine intention to demand civil servants be equipped with "political qualities." Civil servants were required to "consciously be in the same political step with the line of the Chinese Communist Party" (Dai, 1990–1991:69). It was also maintained that political qualities should be taken seriously in such areas as recruitment, performance appraisal, and promotion.

After the Tiananmen Square incident, the merit principle was attacked, leading to a new emphasis in the relationship between virtue and ability in favor of the former (Zhao, 1989; 1990). In an article written in December, 1989, the personnel minister, Zhao Dongwan, admitted that there were mistakes in understanding and handling the relationships among the four criteria (i.e., to be revolutionary, educated, professional, and young). The relationship between virtue and ability was also wrongly perceived, thus weakening the value of being revolutionary and achieving virtue in cadre management. The personnel minister reformulated the principle in the following way: combining virtue and ability, but the former should be given priority (Zhao, 1989; 1990). Central Document No. 9, issued in August, 1989 provides four guidelines in recruiting and evaluating cadres. They are (1) political position, (2) moral quality, (3) leadership ability, and (4) actual working evaluation (*Selection of Documents* [1990:12]:12–23). On paper, this concept is reminiscent of the practice of placing "red" before "expert" in Maoist China.

The reformulation of the relationship between virtue and ability inevitably led to an extensive revision of the relevant articles contained in the sixteenth draft produced in May, 1989. In the twenty-second draft, produced in November, 1992, explicit political requirements were added in a number of places (Lam and Chan, 1993). Regarding the previous emphasis on actual work performance, it was conspicuously added that performance in implementing the party line should become a criterion. However, it is surprising to find that practically all these revisions were removed from the final version released in August, 1993. This perhaps suggests that notwithstanding the party's strong reaction immediately after the Tiananmen Square incident, there were important disagreements over how merit should be defined. The merit principle continues to be a hotly contested issue.

The insistence on virtue has never gained much support. Deputy Personnel Minister Cheng Lianchang suggested in early 1992 that although it was important to emphasize the necessary political qualities [of state civil servants], recruitment decisions should be based on work-related qualities (Cheng, 1992:11). On another occasion, Zhang Chun, deputy director of the Department of Performance Appraisal, Rewards and Punishments, Ministry of Personnel, did not put political attitude before professional ability when he talked about the criteria for promotion. Although he quoted Chen Yun's instruction on giving more weight to virtue, he simply paid lip service to Chen's instruction (Zhang, 1992:147–148).

Another important change in the concept of merit after the Tiananmen Square incident is the emphasis on practical experience at the grass roots level, in contrast to the emphasis on educational achievement proposed in the earlier drafts. The new civil service regulations require state civil servants to have actual working experience before they can be recruited and promoted to important positions. Two different political considerations account for this change. In light of antigovernment sentiment in the 1989 prodemocracy movement, party leaders were highly skeptical of the trustworthiness of new university graduates. It was hoped that accumulating practical experience at the grass roots level might help scale down the political passion and the antigovernment feelings of university graduates. This was driven by a genuine concern that a state civil service populated mainly by technocrats might set it further apart from the masses.

From the previous analysis, it is not difficult to see that although political criteria were accorded a higher priority in personnel management decisions after June, 1989, the actual impact was severely limited. After more than a decade of reforms, Chinese leaders (especially Deng Xiaoping) are more convinced than ever that China's economic development and modernization require a cadre corp with specialized knowledge, adequate skill, and professional competence.

2. Job Analysis and the Merit System

Despite the laudable tendency to see merit in terms of work-related qualities, the development of the merit principle and merit system in China was, and probably will be, inhibited by the slow and frustrating development of job analysis and position classification exercises. Although the merit system is accepted in general, the merit system cannot be made operational unless clear and objective criteria are established through sophisticated job analysis and the development of position classification. Developing clear and objective criteria through job analysis and position classification is fundamental because these criteria provide the bases to develop testing and other screening devices, such as preestablished criteria to determine an employee's relative qualification and performance. Clearly stating the nature and requirements of different positions, furthermore, is particularly crucial in China because Chinese bureaucracy is notorious for favoritism and nepotism.

The emphasis on position as the unit of evaluation in China is a significant advancement. Position classification focuses attention on what is done rather than who performs it. This method avoids subjective judgments when evaluating cadres. This concept, if successfully put into practice, also underscores another fundamental of position classification—that management ultimately controls the classification of position by approving the assignment of specific duties and responsibilities to be performed.

The Chinese drafters were aware of the importance of job analysis and position classification. As a principle, position classification was laid down in the sixteenth draft. Broadly speaking, Chinese drafters might have adopted a Western position classification principle in developing their own personnel management system. These principles include

1. That positions and not individuals should be classified.
2. That the duties and responsibilities pertaining to a position constitute the outstanding characteristics that distinguish it from, or mark its similarity to, other positions.
3. That qualifications in respect to education, experience, knowledge, and skill necessary for the performance of certain duties are determined by the nature of those duties. Therefore, the

qualifications of a position are important factors in the determination of the classification of the position.

4. That the individual characteristics of an employee occupying a position should have no bearing on the classification of the position.

5. That persons holding positions in the same class should be considered equally qualified for any other position in that class (Rosenbloom, 1989:201–202).

Needless to say, position classification in Chinese bureaucracy is a formidable task. While it is difficult to make a comprehensive assessment of the present development of position classification in China, we can undertake a preliminary discussion on the basis of the information we obtained from the drafting process and pilot schemes.

Despite the importance of position classification, the task was too sophisticated and technical. This explains why limited progress had been made in the pilot schemes. The unsatisfactory results obtained from implementing the pilot scheme led some drafters to reconsider whether position classification should be adopted in China. There was a brief period of time when position classification was temporarily abandoned in favor of a less sophisticated system labeled grade classification (*fenji*). A senior official specializing in this area of research pointed out that this system, in line with Chinese tradition, based its analysis mainly on a rank classification method (Wang, 1992:77). There was widespread feeling that position classification was not suitable for China because administrative duties in Chinese bureaucracy were not susceptible to a clear and exact definition. Yet, the principle of position classification was reinstated later. Position classification was recognized as a principle as well as a long-term objective.

In view of the tremendous difficulties involved, it is not entirely correct to say that slow progress in performing position classification is due to a lack of rational comprehensiveness in vision (Chow, 1991). Working out a comprehensive position classification system in such a giant bureaucracy is an impossible task. Nonetheless, during the transitional period, the lack of operationalized criteria ensures that the merit principle, as understood in the West, will not be strictly observed and enthusiastically implemented.

V. THE DILEMMAS IN DEVELOPING CHINA'S CIVIL SERVICE SYSTEM

Developing a civil service system in China is a complex endeavor. It embodies at least the two approaches discussed. Each of these approaches emphasizes values, organizational arrangements, view of the individual civil servant, and decision-making core referents that are at odds with those of the other approach. Cadres and potential civil servants in China are stuck between the proverbial rock and a hard place when called upon to act in a fashion that will integrate two approaches that may defy successful integration.

The essence of civil service is dealing with relationships among political, social, economic, organizational, managerial, legal, scientific, and technological values and systems at both micro and macro levels. By attempting to coordinate and direct these diverse and conflicting relationships, dilemmas are bound to arise. The first dilemma concerns the transfer of a huge number of cadres into the civil service system in China. There is no concretized policy so far. In our interview with officials in the National School of Administration of China in early July, 1993, it was said that the policy sought to convert them into the civil service system by providing them "training." This policy is not a viable way as far as our analysis is concerned. The key problem remains who and how to train. China has not developed a proper classification scheme to reflect the various aspects of jobs in state administration. Considering the diverse backgrounds of cadres, their ages, educational backgrounds, working experience, etc., it is difficult to provide them with some standardized training courses. It is equally difficult to provide them with tailor-made courses. Without a viable way to transfer cadres into the civil service system, the concern for enhancing stability and/or functional vitality of state administration cannot easily materialize.

A separate and higher pay scale for state civil servants was proposed and then abandoned. It is not difficult to understand that revising the pay structure for state civil servants will definitely raise a larger concern for equity and equality in society. Cadres employed in state administrative organs, enterprises, and service units actually perform the same functions. The concerns about equity and equality demand that the same treatment must be given to those employed in economic enterprises and service units, which the Party Central is unlikely to accept. The financial burden is too tremendous to bear.

Another way to encourage people to join a civil service system is to provide greater operative discretionary power. China is notorious for nepotism in political appointments. The development of a merit-based performance appraisal scheme obviously seeks to resolve favoritism, corruption and bribery, official graft, and transaction of power for money, etc. The twin purpose of setting up a merit-based position classification scheme—that management ultimately controls the classification of position by approving the assignment of specific duties and responsibilities to be performed, and that individual characteristics, like political (organizational) loyalty and belief, political performance, and moral qualities, should have no bearing on the way that he or she is evaluated—are unlikely to be adopted in the near future. The cadres' dependence on their organization and their superior for "looking after" their interests, which is the root cause for nepotism in China, has not been reduced. In instituting a civil service system, China's officials face a hard choice of whether greater discretion should be given to state civil servants in order to motivate them to work properly and responsively, or operative discretionary authority should be cut down to avoid the misuse of power.

In terms of objective assessment criteria, the concern for making use of seniority as the main criterion is one of the key issues considered throughout the entire drafting process. While seniority appears to provide an objective basis for assessment, there is no evidence to support the correlation between seniority and better performance. Given the employment arrangement in China (such as the lack of job alternatives and the absence of social security outside the state sector), there is virtually little job mobility. The analysis hinges on that seniority in this context might even be considered an additional burden. The consideration for enhancing functional vitality and placing greater emphasis on rotation in state civil service is proof that discredits the use of seniority as the reliable basis for assessment.

The Chinese government has paid great attention to civil service reform. Chinese officials are relatively well-informed on the West's civil service system's operating methods and capacities, as well as current skills and knowledge. The Chinese experience in implementing the principles developing in the Western civil service system is poor as reflected in the drafting process, which proceeded within an incoherent framework oscillating between adopting Western principles and emphasizing China's national situation.

In summary, the tensions in the design of the civil service system were evident throughout the entire drafting process. These tensions resulted in some competing solutions. The process of reform design and the assumptions that guided it created a reform package that was, at best, loosely coupled and at worst, replete with internal contradictions. Chinese officials have yet to develop comprehensive strategies for reorienting, retrenching, retraining, and redeploying their staff, let alone building an organized and nonideological civil service system. The conclusion of this analysis has perhaps raised more questions than it has answered. Reforming a public bureaucracy means shaping political values, politics, and priorities. In China's context, it means removing the Party Central's political limits so creative measures can be devised to integrate a Western civil service system into China's developing system.

NOTES

1. This, of course, is an exaggeration. In China, there has been a sharp distinction between the collective sector, which includes the rural area and certain sectors of the urban area, and the state sector. For a brief discussion, see Walder (1986), pp. 28–80.

2. The task force was called the Central Study Group on Political System Reform. Zhao Ziyang headed the team. Other members included Tian Ziyuan (deputy prime minister), Hu Qili (member of the Central Secretariat), Peng Chong (deputy director, Standing Committee of National People's Congress), and Bo Yibo (deputy director, Central Advisory Committee of the CPC). The task force was to make recommendations on a wide range of issues relating to political system reform including reform on cadres and the personnel system. Many of the recommendations were adopted in the party's Thirteenth Congress in October, 1987, although it remained doubtful whether these recommendations were fully implemented. For a brief account, see Chen (1990).

3. This line of analysis is consistent with the institutional view of politics. See Ikenberry (1988); March and Olsen (1984).

4. These six state bureaus are the State Bureau of Statistics, Construction Materials, Environmental Protection, Auditing, Tax, and Customs and Excise.

5. The overall post-Tiananmen Square incident development in China can be described as one of balancing conservative and reformist interests. Yet, there is not a strict division of opinion within the Party Central regarding the development of the civil service system and nomenclature. A Beijing-based academic told us that, for example, Li Peng, though widely depicted as the archetype of the conservatives, did not oppose the development of a civil service system. She suggested that organizational or institutional interests seemed to be able to counteract the ideological or political interests (shared among those conservatives in the Party Central), which might incline to abandon further development of a civil service system. Li Peng, representing the institutional interests of the State Council, could have benefited from the implementation of the civil service system.

6. See Central Document No. 9 issued by the Party Central in August, 1989. The full test was reprinted in the *Selection of Documents Concerning Personnel Work*, (1990:12):12–23.

7. Even a terminological distinction was stressed. In Chinese, the term "civil service" can be translated either as *gongwuyuan zhidu* or *wengguan zhidu*. As noted by a senior official in the Ministry of Personnel, while both are correct, the first translation is preferable because the second might carry a negative meaning (for instance, it might imply political neutrality). This line of thought has continued particularly after the Tiananmen Square incident. For discussion, see Zhao (1990).

REFERENCES

Barnett, D. (1967). *Cadre, Bureaucracy and Political Power in Communist China*, Columbia Univ. Press, New York.

Burns, J. (1987). China's nomenclature system, *Prob. Communism 36*(5):36–51.

Burns, J. (1989). Chinese civil service reform: The 13th Party Congress proposals, *China Q. 120*:739–770.

Burns, J. (1994). Strengthening central CCP control of leadership selection: The 1990 nomenclature, *China Q. 138*: 125–158.

Chen, Y. (1987). Political system reform is the guarantee of economic system reform, *World Economic Herald 348* (July 13).

Chen, Y. (1990). *China: Ten Year's of Reforms and the '89 Democratic Movement*, Lianjing Press, Taiwan.

Cheng, L. (1990). Interview of Cheng Lianchang, *Seeking Trust* 8:14-15.

Cheng, L. (1992). The conceptualization of state civil service system, in *Training Materials of State Civil Service System*, China Senior Civil Servants Training Centre, Ministry of Personnel, Beijing.

Chow, K. (1991). Reform of the Chinese cadre system: Pitfalls, issues and implications of the proposed civil service reform, *Int. Rev. Admin. Sci.* 57:25-44.

Dai, G. (1990-1991). Proposing a reform of the cadre and personnel system and the state, *Chinese Law Govern.* (Winter, 1990-1991):61-73.

Dai, G. (1991). A summary description of the progress of the pilot schemes of state civil service system, in *Seminar Papers on the Pilot Schemes of State Civil Service System*, China Senior Civil Servants Training Centre, Ministry of Personnel, Beijing.

Deng, X. (1983). *Selected Works of Deng Xiaoping 1975-1982*, People's Publishing, Beijing.

Deng, X. (1987). *Building Socialism with Chinese Characteristics*, Joint Publishing, Beijing.

Gong, X. (1985). *Civil Service System*, People's Publishing, Beijing.

Harding, H. (1981). *Organizing China*, Stanford Univ. Press, Stanford, CA.

Ikenberry, G. J. (1988). *Reason of State*, Cornell Univ. Press, New York.

Ingraham, P. (1992). The design of civil service reform: Good politics or good management, in *The Promise and Paradox of Civil Service*, (P. Ingraham and D. Rosenbloom, eds.), Univ. Pittsburgh Press, Pittsburgh.

Lam, T. C. and Hon S. Chan. (1993). The changing civil service concepts in China: Balancing party control with better cadre management, unpublished manuscript.

Li, C. and Bachman, D. (1989). Localism, elitism, and immobilism: Elite formation and social change in post-Mao China, *World Polit.* 42:64-94.

March, J. and Olsen, J. (1983). Organizing political life: What administrative reorganization tells us about governing, *Am. Polit. Sci. Rev.* 77:281-296.

March, J. and Olsen, J. (1984). The new institutionalism: Organizational factors in political life, *Am. Polit. Sci. Rev.* 78:734-749.

Mosher, F. (1982). *Democracy and the Public Service*, Oxford Univ. Press, London.

Rosenbloom, D. (1989). *Public Administration; Understanding Management, Politics, and Law in the Public Sector*, Random House, New York.

Selection of Documents Concerning Personnel Work. (1989:11) (1990:12, 13), Chinese Personnel Press, Beijing.

Tsou, T. (1986). *Cultural Revolution and Post-Mao Reforms*, Univ. Chicago Press, Chicago.

Vogel, E. (1967). From revolutionary to semi-bureaucrat: The regularization of cadres, *China Q.* 29:36-60.

Vogel, E. (1971). Politicized bureaucracy: Communist China, in *Frontiers of Development Administration*, D. Barnett, and F. Riggs, eds., Duke Univ. Press, Durham.

Walder, A. (1986). *Communist Neo-Traditionalism: Work and Authority in China*, Univ. California Press, CA.

Wang, L. (1992). Personnel classification of state civil servants, in *Training Materials of State Civil Service System*, China Senior Civil Servants Training Centre, Ministry of Personnel, Beijing.

Wen Hui Bao. (Hong Kong). (August 19, 1993).

Whyte, M. K. (1973). Bureaucracy and modernization in China: The Maoist critique, *Am. Soc. Rev.* 38(2):149-163.

Wilson, W. (1978). The study of administration (1887), in *Classics of Public Administration*, J. Shafritz, and A. Hyde, eds., Moore Publishing, Oak Park, IL.

Xu, S., ed. (1989). *An Explanation of Provisional Regulations of the State Civil Servant* (draft), Chinese Personnel Press, Beijing.

Xu, S. (1991). Actively and safely establishing a civil service system suitable for China's national situation, in *Seminar Papers on the Pilot Schemes of State Civil Service System*, China Senior Civil Servants Training Centre, Ministry of Personnel, Beijing.

Xu, S. (1992). The formation and development of state civil service system, in *Training Materials of State Civil Service System*, China Senior Civil Servants Training Centre, Ministry of Personnel, Beijing.

Yearbook of Chinese Personnel 1988-1989. (1991). Chinese Personnel Press, Beijing.

Zhang, C. (1992). Promotion and demotion of state civil servants, in *Training Materials of State Civil Service System*, China Senior Civil Servants Training Centre, Ministry of Personnel, Beijing.

Zhao, D. (1989). We should uphold the principle of combining virtue and ability in selection and use of cadres, *Seeking Trust 22*:15–18.

Zhao, D. (1990). Actively implement a civil service system with Chinese characteristics, *Seeking Truth 8*:38–42.

Zhao, Z. (1987). Advance along the road of socialism with Chinese characteristics, *Beijing Rev. 30*(45):i–xxvii.

8

The Economy and Public Personnel Management

MARCIA LYNN WHICKER   Rutgers University at Newark, Newark, New Jersey

Trends in the economy have important implications for the public sector for two reasons. First, the public sector in the United States is a large share of the total economy, so that some economic trends spill over into the public sector as well as impact the private sector. By the early 1990s, federal outlays constituted between one-fifth and one-fourth of the gross national product (GNP). When state and local government outlays are added, the public sector approaches one-third of the economy. Trends in labor markets, technology, and wage growth affect government employees as well as their private sector counterparts. Second, the state of the economy greatly affects the revenues available to the public sector. Government revenues in turn impact on the size of the public sector, its employment growth, and employee compensation. The chapter will examine several important economic trends that have changed the American economy in recent years. It will also examine the implications of these trends for public personnel management.

I. ECONOMIC TRENDS

A. Economic Globalization

The seeds of postwar economic globalization were sown with the establishment of the General Agreement on Trade and Tariffs (GATT) at the end of World War II (Thurow, 1992; Walters and Blake, 1992; Whicker, 1993). Subsequently, the world economy enjoyed the greatest period of free trade and flow of economic goods and services across political boundaries ever and an accompanying spurt in world productivity. Although the system began to break down with signs of protectionism, splintering into regional trading blocks, and difficulties in negotiating the Uruguay Round of GATT by the end of the 1980s, economic globalization had prospered.

Between 1950 and the early 1990s, international merchandise trade had grown on average over 5% a year. Global trade regularly grew faster than global output as a whole. Trade in services and direct investment also grew rapidly (French, 1993). The share of exports of the U.S. economy also increased, from 5% in the 1950s to over 17% by the late 1980s. Unfortunately, the U.S. trade deficit also grew as imports exceeded exports. By the 1990s, this deficit approached $100 billion.

During this period the role of transnational corporations (TNCs), megacompanies that sprawled across national boundaries, increased both in power and in share of world output (Whicker, 1993).

Satellite communications linked distant portions of the world with on-the-spot coverage, such as that provided to U.S. citizens during the 1991 Persian Gulf War. The world was truly becoming a "global village" and the United States was one of the major economic players.

B. Shift to an Information and High-Technology Economy

In 1980, Toffler predicted that a fundamental shift was occurring in the economy: a shift from second-wave mass production of similar products to third-wave production of small runs and individually tailored goods and services. Mass production was passé; unique or at least limited production was chic. The shift would require that more workers analyze, massage, interpret, and manipulate information. Computerization, robotics, and high technology were all a part of this third-wave transformation. Efficiency benefits of robots and other new technologies would be considerable. The workplace would change to one requiring more independent decision making by all employees and participatory management (Ouchi, 1981; Pascale and Athos, 1981; Naisbitt and Aburdene, 1985). Others referred to a "superindustrial" economy (Ratner et al., 1979).

By the late 1980s, many of these trends were apparent. Several hundred thousand robots toiled worldwide to augment human labor (Kennedy, 1993, p. 88). These could be divided into three classes: fixed machines with manipulators to do various tasks automatically, field robots designed to operate in an unstructured environment through sensors that allowed them to move around and respond to objects, and third-generation knowledge-based intelligent robots, designed to use artificial intelligence to solve problems as humans do. Unfortunately for the United States, unions resisted robotics, fearing their capacity to displace workers from their current jobs. While Japan employed over 60% of robots used worldwide and Western Europe employed about 17%, the United States employed only 11%, trailed only by Eastern Europe, Southeast Asia, and the rest of the world.

C. Shift in the Character of the Labor Force

With economic globalization, the character of the U.S. labor force has changed (Reich, 1989, 1991). Describing workers as "white collar" or "blue collar" to denote their positions within hierarchically structured organizations makes less sense, as organizations flatten and reorganize, and as the character of work shifts to dealing with information. Reich divides the labor force into three categories that are derived from these shifts: symbolic-analytic workers, who account for almost 20% of the jobs but over 40% of the GNP; routine production workers, who constitute over half of all jobs but only 30% of GNP; and routine service workers, who make up 30% of jobs and 20% of GNP.

Symbolic-analytic workers have good prospects economically because they produce goods and services in demand worldwide and are able to compete in the global marketplace. Symbolic-analytic workers consist of three groups: people who deploy or manipulate resources to save time and money; people who grab money from others who are too slow or naive to protect themselves; and people who entertain others. The first type enhances efficiency; the second type lives off glitches in the system; and the third type provides a real service in a world with increasing amounts of leisure time.

In contrast to symbolic-analytic workers, routine production workers and routine service workers are not globally competitive, and their economic prospects are dim. Routine production workers may work in manufacturing but increasingly may also work in information-oriented industries, processing routine forms and claims. These workers confront the possibility of their jobs being exported to cheaper labor markets. Routine service workers are poorly paid and poorly educated, and often must compete with illegal immigrants to retain the jobs they have.

D.   Growing Gap Between the Rich and Poor

The gap between the "haves" and "have-nots" grew greater (Phillips, 1990). By the mid-1980s, U.S. Census Bureau economists reported that the United States had the largest difference between the rich and poor of any major Western nation. Ironically, America, the land of opportunity, had become more economically polarized than formerly class-conscious Europe (Phillips, 1993, pp. 17–18). State level data from New York, Massachusetts, California, Illinois, and other states supported these findings by reporting that in the 1980s the share of income going to the top 1%, 5%, and 10% ballooned, while the share going to the middle 40% or 60% percent shrank substantially. In terms of additional wealth accruing to the already rich, the 1980s in the United States were likened to two earlier periods: the "roaring twenties" in the early 1900s and the "gilded age" of the late 1800s.

E.   Shrinking of the Middle Class

By the 1990s, the middle class was plainly feeling squeezed (Phillips, 1993). Not only were its numbers shrinking, but the middle-class standard of living was declining as well. By the end of the 1980s, the top 1% was approaching in income share the same proportion of pretax income as the entire middle 20%. According to the Congressional Budget Office, in 1977 the top 1% had 8.3% of pretax national income while the middle quintile had 16.3%. By 1989, those income returns were 13.0% for the top 1% and 14% for the middle 20% (Phillips, 1993, p. 25). In just the 10 years between 1977 and 1987, median family after-tax income, controlled for inflation, fell over $2000, from $25,518 to $23,508 in 1987 dollars.

F.   Growth in Two-Income Earner and Single-Parent Families

By the beginning of the 1990s, the "traditional" family structure had changed radically. Families with a male breadwinner, a stay-at-home wife, and several kids at home constituted less than a quarter of all families. Single-parent households, headed mostly by women, had increased from 13% of all families in 1970 to 27% in 1987 (Phillips, 1990, p. 203), with women holding almost half of all jobs (Lane and Wolf, 1990).

The change in family structure contributed to the growing income disparity. While the inflation-adjusted income of married couples, for example, grew by 9% from 1980 to 1986, the income of female-headed households grew by only 2%. Many two-parent households, however, maintained household income only by sending wives into the labor force and/or by taking second and third jobs. One estimate holds that husbands' inflation-adjusted salaries declined in 80% of all married couple households between 1979 and 1986. This decline was offset only by a dramatic increase (18%) in the number of hours worked by wives. And some did not manage to offset the loss.

G.   Growing Federal Deficit

One of the most disturbing economic trends is the growth in annual deficits for the United States, especially during the past two decades. Few argue that massive federal deficits are good. Rather controversy surrounds exactly how bad federal deficits are and what to do about it. Observers agree, however, that federal deficits have been rising, despite all efforts to abate or even just ameliorate their growth. By FY 1991, projected deficits were $360 billion excluding the post office service and reserves of the social security trust fund (Dentzler, 1991).

Why have deficits grown and persisted? Policymakers agree that something should be done but disagree as to what solutions should be embraced. Plausible methods of reducing the deficit all create political pain and thus are controversial. Several factors are at work in the growth of government red ink. Budgets have dual stabilization and allocation functions that may conflict. The budget process is decentralized, with no single person or authority assuming responsibility for deficits, and lacking structures in the past to coordinate fiscal policy and allocation goals. The budget process is lengthy, providing many points at which interest groups may block cuts. Redistribution drives federal budgeting, yet the budget does not include direct explicit information on who gets what. Budgeting has historically been incremental and "bottom-up." Major budget actors all have incentives for increasing federal spending.

Economic policymakers have tried several things to address deficits, some substantive, but many cosmetic. Among the approaches employed have been the adoption of a statutory national debt limit, moving expenditures off budget, and moving trust funds carrying surpluses on budget. Other strategies have been to give authority for budget reduction recommendations to a nonpartisan commission (National Economic Commission), to introduce a structure for top-down budgeting in the 1974 Congressional Budget Act, and to episodically embrace budget reforms to enhance efficiency. Some politicians have advocated constitutional amendments to deal with deficits, including a balanced budget amendment and the presidential item veto. Congress enacted the Gramm–Rudman–Hollings deficit reduction legislation in 1985 and the Budget Enforcement Act of 1990. Despite all these actions and measures, federal deficits continue relatively uncurbed. By the early 1990s, the national debt approached $4 trillion and interest payments on it approached 20% of federal spending. Critics contended that growing deficits inflicted reduced opportunities for government programs on future generations as well as higher taxes and reduced economic growth.

H. Difficulty in Implementing Macroeconomic Policy

For much of the post–World War II period, the U.S. economy was a huge productivity machine, cranking out for several decades every rising increase in the standard of living, a sense of optimism and boundless unlimitedness, and an expansion in government programs. In the 1970s, however, the productivity machine began to sputter, jerk forward more in spasms, and perform less consistently. OPEC oil shortages provided external inflationary jolts that rippled throughout the economy. Stagflation with double-digit inflation and unemployment appeared. The 1980s saw a return to prosperity, but mostly for the rich.

As before, calls for government intervention, and particularly for masterful management of the economy by the president, increased. For the first time since Keynesian fiscal policy was embraced by Franklin Roosevelt as a means to leverage the economy of the 1930s out of the Great Depression, this philosophy of macroeconomic management was seriously challenged by a competing philosophy: the supply side economics embraced by Ronald Reagan and his adherents. The nation temporarily played with supply side notions, using supply side theory to justify large cuts in government's social spending and tax cuts. Ballooning deficits and national debt forced the country to return to Keynesian economics, criticizing supply side theory as flawed.

Yet others criticize our whole notion that the economy is controllable at all. These critics of notions of the economy as an efficient machine responsive to attempts to pull financial and policy "levers" to control it contend that it is really just a metaphor for a very complex aggregation of the daily personal and commercial transactions of over 250 million Americans (Morris, 1993). Controlling it is difficult for two reasons. First, in many instances, what should be done is not clear. Economists often fiercely disagree over whether to provide more or less stimulus, whether to tighten or loosen monetary policy, whether to worry about inflation or unemployment.

Second, even if something is done, it is not always clear as to what works. For example, did the stimulus package succeed, or was recovery underway anyway? Why did it provoke a response, if it did: because of the actual economic effects, or the psychological effects of people thinking it should matter? Forecasting economic growth and performance is far more uncertain than forecasting the planetary orbits or distant celestial bodies. While using scientific language and techniques, macroeconomic policymaking remains much less than a precise science.

I. Increased Mandates and Financial Stress for States and Localities

With the growth of "fiscal federalism," states began to depend on intergovernmental transfers, in the form of categorical and block grants, and, during part of the 1980s, revenue sharing. As the federal government began to encounter its own fiscal difficulties, it reorganized and reduced intergovernmental funding efforts and increased unfunded mandates. Federal assistance to state and local governments reached a peak during the Carter administration and began a dramatic decline during Reagan's terms (Beam, 1985). The landmark Omnibus Budget Reconciliation Act of 1981 early in the Reagan administration continued a trend begun late in Carter's term of reducing the growth in intergovernmental aid. This act also achieved the first absolute reduction of federal aid in decades, including a $2 billion cut in employment and training assistance. As a proportion of total federal outlays, intergovernmental aid peaked in 1978 at 17% percent, and by 1987 had fallen to 10.8%. The result has been increased fiscal stress on states and localities.

In recent years, federal assistance has been coupled with regulatory mandates (ACIR, 1984). Four new categories of regulatory techniques, different from the specific requirements of categorical grants, were developed and applied to intergovernmental aid programs with increasing regularity. Direct orders, often used in the areas of public employment and environmental protection, are federal laws and regulations that must be fulfilled to avoid the threat of civil or criminal penalties. Cross-cutting requirements are regulations imposed on all federal aid programs to promote desirable national social and economic policies. Crossover sanctions attached to federal assistance programs impose fiscal sanctions on one program area in order to influence policy or activity in another areas. Partial exemptions establish federal standards and delegate their enforcement to states, if the states adopt standards equivalent to or more stringent than the national standards. The impact of each of these mandates has been to force spending increases by states and localities with no offsetting revenues.

J. Growing Education Deficit

American elementary and secondary education, largely funded and produced at the state and local levels of government, is not as good as the education provided throughout most of the rest of the world, including that provided in many third world countries. Estimates of the percentage of the U.S. population that is functionally illiterate approach 20%. Industry has begun a multibillion dollar education effort to try to overcome lack of worker skills in high school graduates. Despite former President George Bush's claims in his 1990 State of the Union speech that U.S. workers were the most productive in the world, the inflation-corrected wages of nonsupervisory U.S. workers had fallen 16% since 1972 and continue to fall by 1% a year (Thurow, 1990).

Underlying this fall in productivity was a growing gap in educational attainment between the United States and nations with which it competes globally. U.S. student skills in math and science are now among the lowest in the industrialized world. The language competencies of U.S. students lag far behind those of students abroad. The National Commission on Excellence in Education reported that the nation was "at risk" from an inferior and deteriorated education system. Secondary school curricula had become "homogenized, diluted, and diffused," and had lost their purpose. In comparison with other nations, state standards were very lax. Between the mid-1960s and the beginning of the 1980s, the proportion of students taking "general" courses increased from about 10% to 40% with one-fourth of those courses concentrated in physical and health education. Only one-third of recent graduates completed intermediate algebra and about 5% finished calculus. Only one-sixth took French I and geography (Whicker and Moore, 1988).

Despite growing distress in the educational system, the highly decentralized structure of U.S. education does not seem well adapted to meet these pressing needs. By the early 1990s, the high school dropout rate in America (29%) far exceeded that of Japan (6%) or Germany (9%). The United States was also outspent on elementary and secondary education. While the United States spent 4.1% of its GNP on K–12 education, Germany spent 4.6% and Japan 4.8% (Thurow, 1992, pp. 276–277). As states and localities confronted the recession of 1991, education was cut more than any other type of public spending. Yet many of the suggested improvements of education require more funds—expanding the school year from 180 days a year to 220 or 250 days, increasing requirements and pay for teachers, and imposing national standards to be met by the educational system.

K. Growing Diversity in the Labor Force

Immigration to the United States began to increase in the 1960s, especially from Puerto Rico and Cuba, and, later, from Mexico and Central America. After the Vietnam War, many Indo-Chinese refugees also entered the United States. Concentrations of minorities have varied by location. Puerto Ricans often went to New York City, Cubans to Miami, and immigrants from mainland China and Vietnam to San Francisco. Immigrants from Mexico and Central America often chose Los Angeles and various parts of the Southwest. More recently, immigrants from other parts of Asia and the Middle East have dispersed throughout the United States.

Diversity is projected to increase even further in the future. Minorities, women, and immigrants have been projected to make up 85% of growth in the labor force between 1985 and 2000 (Thomas, 1991). The highest rate of growth will occur for Asian-Americans and Hispanics, but because Hispanics are growing from a much larger base, their absolute numbers will be much larger. The share of the labor force that is white males is projected to shrink slightly. While in 1985 white males constituted 49% of the labor force, that figure is projected to be 45% in 2000 (Thomas, 1991). In 1987, blacks constituted 11% of the national labor force but were projected to provide 17% of the new entrants in the following decade. Hispanics represented 6.6% of the national work force but were projected to provide 29% of new entrants. Twenty-two percent of new entrants were projected to be immigrants from various countries, especially Asia and Latin America (Lane and Wolf, 1990, pp. 36–38).

L. Downsizing of Organizations

The 1990–1991 recession differed from previous recessions in a crucial way: when it ended on paper, the jobs that were lost did not come back (Hage et al., 1993). Also unlike other recessions, the jobs that permanently disappeared as organizations restructured and downsized were white collar middle-management jobs. In the 1981–1982 recession, employers actually increased white collar positions by 838,000 jobs before the recession began. In the 1990–1991 recession, by contrast, the number of white collar jobs shrank by 354,000. After the recession was formally over, the economy generated white collar jobs at only half the rate of the former recessions. Permanent separations accounted for 85% of the job losses in the 1990–1991 recession, but only 56% of the jobs in the four previous recessions. This permanent job loss occurred in the largest sector, since white collar jobs accounted for 6 of 10 workers.

When new jobs were generated, they were rarely of the same quality as those that were lost, often lacking pension and health benefits, and offering lower salaries. By 1993, the number of new jobs relative to the size of the labor force offered by employers had dropped 40% since the mid-1980s, and the share of new jobs offering pensions and health insurance dropped by 35% since the late 1970s. Downsizing then contributed to higher unemployment and a loss of confidence on the part of those that retained jobs. By 1993, 62% of white collar workers feared that a family member might lose his or her job, and 38% said they had fallen behind the cost of living since 1992.

M. High Resistance to Tax Increases

By the 1980s, pledges of "no new taxes" from politicians was almost a political litmus test for voter approval. Politicians who acknowledged in the heat of a campaign that they would support raising taxes, such as Democratic nominee Walter Mondale, or those who reneged on their promises of no new taxes, such as George Bush, went down to resounding defeat. Politicians who railed against new taxes, such as incumbent President Ronald Reagan, won by large margins. A key question for policymakers became how to raise adequate tax revenues to fund government in a democracy in the face of widespread resistance. An age old question, how to fund government personnel and services took on new urgency in the 1980s and beyond.

Several constraints operate on the ability of policymakers to raise taxes as demands on government grow. Low taxes relative to other nations create expectations of continued low taxes (Pechman, 1987). Taxes already constitute a large dollar volume, which makes it difficult for the average citizen to understand the need for more. Heavy reliance on highly visible and despised income taxes further generates tax resistance. The growing reliance on payroll taxes also increases resistance. Tax overlap across levels of government contributes to resentment of "overtaxation." Tax policy has been used as an instrument for stabilization and redistribution, which sometimes undercuts the goal of raising revenues to fund government. Very little progressive redistribution occurs through the tax system, so no one supports taxes because they are substantially relatively better off. Citizens get little formal education about taxes and the role of government in the economy. These factors and others have meant that the effort to raise adequate revenues to fund government personnel and services is always a political struggle, one in which sometimes the policymakers as well as the funds raised fall short.

II. IMPLICATIONS FOR PUBLIC PERSONNEL MANAGEMENT

The above economic trends will likely have several impacts on public personnel management in the future. Their effect is to increase the need for managers to be sensitive to employee needs, to facilitate employee development, and to cope with employee concerns about the labor market in an era of economic turmoil and transition.

A. Increased Emphasis on Managing Diversity

As the labor force grows more ethnically, racially, and gender diverse, so does the pool of workers from which governments draw to meet their personnel needs. During the 1980s, women and minorities began entering the federal work force at increasing rates. By 1988, women were 27% of government professionals and 35% of administrators, compared to 19% of both categories 10 years previously. In some fields, the growth in numbers of women was even more rapid. For example, by 1988, women were one-third of all IRS accountants (Lane and Wolf, 1990). Similar rates of increase occurred for blacks and other minorities. While the diversity of other levels of government has varied across the country, state and local jurisdictions have similarly been impacted by the increasing diversity of the work force.

What does managing diversity imply? Obviously, it involves attention to questions of equity in salary and promotion opportunities. Nationwide, men and women in state and local government in the United States experienced a growth, not a decline, in the gender-based salary gap across the 1980s (Guy, 1992, pp. 5–7). In 1980, men earned on average $3745 more than women; by 1990, the gender gap had grown to $5439. Guy concluded that upon closer examination the wage gap is "nowhere close to disappearing." At the federal level, women still lag behind men in achieving managerial positions above GS-9 (Lane and Wolf, 1990).

Managing diversity also implies sensitivity to workplace environment and difficulties women and minorities are likely to confront. This may include developing a sexual harassment policy and encouraging participation in racial sensitivity training. Managers can attempt to make their organizations color- and gender-blind by adopting and communicating firm philosophies that the agency is committed to any individual who demonstrates needed abilities. Promoting managers who are positive toward others and have little proclivity to discriminate is a good strategy. Agencies may also provide thorough and regular training of supervisors and managers on human relations, legal issues associated with employment discrimination, organizational policies, and how to handle discrimination problems. The human resource department may be used as an internal consulting service to provide support. Managing diversity also implies not using race, color, national origin, or any other protected characteristic of employees as a determining factor in layoffs, since doing so may result in liability in a reverse discrimination suit (Levesque, 1992).

B.   Increased Emphasis on Employee Development and Training

Reduced education levels, increased emphasis on high technology and associated skills, and an increasingly diverse work force all point to greater need in the future for employee development and training. Development and training goals themselves may be diverse, ranging from equipping employees to operate in their new environment, enabling them to understand and use new or different procedures and practices, focusing their attention on specific skills or requirements, to more broad goals of preparing them to be managers, learning conflict management and negotiation skills, and broadening individuals with potential such as through a 4-week senior management course (Moorby, 1991, p. 13). Other types of training may include preparing people for job transitions, and on occasion, for redundancy and retirement. Some training may be focused on a specific job or set of professional skills.

Other approaches to employee development may emphasize generic skills likely to be needed by general managers and employees (Tracey, 1988). Among them are listening, speaking, writing, problem sensing, inquiring or fact finding, and decision making. Others include hiring, motivating, delegating, appraising, coaching, counseling, negotiating, and team building.

C.   Greater Need for Supports for Families

The growth of dual-career couples along with that of single-parent households in the labor force has increased the need of governments to be sensitive to the needs of these groups. By one projection, by 1995, 9 of 10 married couples will be dual-income families (Bruce and Reed, 1991). One survey of the American Society for Public Administration indicated that 66% of respondents classified themselves as members of a dual-career couple, much higher than the 20% in the general labor force.

Dual-career and single-parent families imply a greater need for childcare. In 1987, while 33% of two-paycheck families had no children at home, 15% had children under 6 years of age, 34% had school age children between 6 and 17, and 18% had children between 18 and 24 living at home. With dual-career couples, while each may devote 40–50 hours each week to work, an additional 48–78 hours of work at home and for the family must be completed by each. The single parent spends 40–50 hours at work and an additional 128-plus hours on home and family responsibilities.

Sensitivity to the concerns of these groups includes attention to childcare, liberal use of flextime and sick leave for children as well as for personal use, and, in some instances, greater flexibility in setting travel and schedules. For couples wanting or anticipating having children, issues surrounding pregnancy leave and family leave are important.

D. Heightened Competition with the Private Sector for "Symbolic-Analytic" Workers

As the character of the labor force shifts to where "symbolic-analytic" workers with high-tech skills produce the largest share of national output and are highly sought after, the public sector must increasingly compete with the private sector for these workers. Professionals whom governments may wish to attract are often credentialed with higher education degrees and able to use a "critical discourse" approach to problem solving (Derber et al., 1990). Critics contend that the public sector has not succeeded in this mission and has not been unable to attract and hold competent senior officials (Huddleston, 1987). Such criticisms are often used to advance reforms in compensation and work schedules, but have the disadvantages of reinforcing negative public images of public "bureaucrats" as functionaries.

Among the objectives in designing a pay and compensation system to allow the public sector to attract its share of symbolic analysts in the future are encouraging long-term service, reducing or controlling turnover, achieving comparable worth, maintaining competitiveness in labor markets, increasing organizational performance, attracting and retaining key occupational specialists, and reducing work force costs (von Glinow, 1988; Siegel, 1992). Yet politics, the public, and partisanship complexify if not confound construction of a well-designed compensation system for the public sector.

Several trends can be identified that must be considered in establishing employee compensation and work conditions. Elected officials on occasion exploit a widely held negative image of public sector workers. Across time, the time orientation for the civil service has shifted from a long-term to a short-term perspective, including a shift away from long-term service and systems that support them. Increasingly performance is considered for compensation. These shifts have resulted in retrenchment in the level and types of benefits with reductions in each. There has been a growing fixation on political accountability, especially at the national level among political appointees. Demand for a more adaptable work force has emerged, especially in contracts management in contrast to management of service delivery and regulatory functions.

E. Occasional RIFs and Growing Uncertainty in Job Stability

With economic distress, the job security of government employment has atrophied, so that in many settings government service is no longer regarded as safe as it once was. During the 1990–1991 turndown, various governments, ranging from New Jersey to California and in between, were forced to make layoffs and reductions in force, in some instances creating widespread exercise of bumping rights. As higher, more protected employees "bumped" lower ranking employees out their jobs, some of whom had bumping rights themselves, the ripple effect was profound. Cynicism, reduced employee morale, possibly reduced productivity, and the training of the numerous people for new jobs with reduced salaries occurred. During the same time frame, civilian military employees and military personnel faced layoffs and discharges, and federal employees overall confronted limits on pay increases to below the rate of inflation. Public managers must deal with a less secure and at times disgruntled work force as creatively as possible within the bounds of public sector constraints. Public employees who feel they are learning useful job skills and advancing in their own personal and professional development will be better able to cope with economic and environmental turmoil than those who feel stymied on all fronts.

III. CONCLUSION

Plainly the challenges posed by the economy for public personnel management are great. Vision, creativity, and leadership in scanning the changing economy and environment, and incorporating the changes into personnel practices, are what is needed for the future. Business as usual will not adequately address the economic trends outlined here. Ideas, talent, and a commitment to public sector service are the order for the future if we are to build partnerships between employees and their managers as well as public officials and their clients to make the next decade a bridge to a salutary, not oppressive, brave new world.

REFERENCES

Beam, David R. (1985). New federalism, old realities: the Reagan administration and intergovernmental reform, *The Reagan Presidency and the Governing of America*, The Urban Institute, Washington, DC.

Bruce, Willa M., and Reed, Christine M. (1991). *Dual-Career Couples in the Public Sector*, Quorum Books, New York.

Dentzler, Susan (1991). $300 billion whopper: why Washington's new deficit diet may work better than the last one," *U.S. News and World Report*, Feb. 11, pp. 51–54.

Derber, Charles, Schwartz, William A., and Magrass, Yale (1990). *Power in the Highest Degree: Professionals and the Rise of a New Mandarin Order*. Oxford University Press, New York.

French, Hilary F. (1993). Reconciling trade and the environment, *State of the World*. (Lester R. Brown, ed.), Worldwatch Institute, New York, pp. 158–179.

Guy, Mary E., ed. (1992). *Women and Men of the States: Public Administrators at the State Level*. M. E. Sharpe, Armonk, NY.

Hage, David, Grant, Linda, and Impoco, Jim (1993). White collar wasteland, *U.S. News and World Report, June 28*, pp. 42–52.

Huddleston, Mark W. (1987). *The Government's Managers: Report of the Twentieth Century Fund Task Force on the Senior Executive Service*, Priority Press, New York.

Kennedy, Paul (1993). *Preparing for the Twenty-First Century*, Random House, New York.

Lane, Larry M., and Wolf, James F. (1990). *The Human Resource Crisis in the Public Sector*, Quorum Books, New York.

Levesque, Joseph D. (1992). *The Human Resource Problem-Solver's Handbook*, McGraw-Hill, New York.

Moorby, Ed (1991). *How to Succeed in Employee Development*, McGraw-Hill, New York.

Morris, Charles R. (1993). It's not the economy, stupid, *The Atlantic Monthly, July*: 49–62.

Naisbitt, John, and Aburdene, Patricia (1985). *Re-inventing the Corporation*, Warner Books, New York.

Ouchi, William G. (1981). *Theory Z*, Avon Books, New York.

Pascale, Richard Tanner, and Athos, Anthony G. (1981). *The Art of Japanese Management*, Warner Books, New York.

Pechman, Joseph A. (1987). *Federal Tax Policy*, 5th Ed., Brookings Institution, Washington, DC.

Phillips, Kevin (1990). *The Politics of Rich and Poor*, Random House, New York.

Phillips, Kevin (1993). *Boiling Point*, Random House, New York.

Ratner, Sidney, Soltow, James H., and Sylla, Richard (1979). *The Evolution of the American Economy*, Basic Books, New York.

Reich, Robert B. (1989). As the world turns: U.S. income inequality keeps on rising, *The New Republic, May 1*: 23–28.

Reich, Robert B. (1991). *The Work of Nations*, Knopf, New York.

Siegel, Gilbert B. (1992). *Public Employee Compensation and Its Role in Public Sector Strategic Management*, Quorum Books, New York.

Thomas, R. Roosevelt, Jr. (1991). *Beyond Race and Gender*, AMACON, New York

Thurow, Lester C. (1990). America adrift: today we're not facing up to our national problems, *The Washington Post*, February 11: C1.

Thurow, Lester (1992). *Head to Head*, Morrow, New York.

Toffler, Alvin (1980). *The Third Wave*, Morrow, New York.

Tracey, William R. (1988). *Critical Skills: The Guide to Top Performance for Human Resource Managers*, AMACON, New York.

U.S. Advisory Commission on Intergovernmental Relations (1984). *Regulatory Federalism: Policy, Process, Impact and Reform*, U.S. Government Printing Office, Washington, DC.

Von Glinow, Mary Ann (1988). *The New Professionals: Managing Today's High-Tech Employees*, Ballinger, Cambridge, MA.

Walters, Robert S., and Blake, David H. (1992). *The Politics of Global Economic Relations*, 4th Ed. Prentice-Hall, Englewood Cliffs, NJ.

Whicker, Marcia Lynn (1993). *Controversial Issues in Economic Regulatory Policy*, Sage, Newberry Park, CA.

Whicker, Marcia Lynn, and Moore, Raymond A. (1988). *Making America Competitive*, Praeger, Westport, CT.

9

Demographic Changes and Diversity in Personnel: Implications for Public Administrators

BLUE WOOLDRIDGE   Virginia Commonwealth University, Richmond, Virginia

BARBARA CLARK MADDOX   Office of the City Manager, Richmond, Virginia

I. INTRODUCTION

By now, practically everyone knows the statistics forecasting the characteristics of the work force in the early 21st century. The discussion of this topic started in earnest when in 1987 William Johnston published *Workforce 2000*, a report that has become an essential reference book for the personnel management community. Among the demographic "facts" that the report said would shape the economy and the work force of the future were (1) tighter labor markets due to slower work force growth and a small reservoir of well-qualified talent; (2) a continued "feminization" of the work force (i.e., a growing percentage of the work force that is female); (3) the increasing representation of blacks, Hispanics, Asians, and other minorities in the work force; and (4) the aging of the work force.

While the original forecasts have been slightly adjusted and trends on other groups added to the list, the prognostication is clear: the work force of the early 21st century will be strikingly more diverse than it was when many of us started our careers as public administrators.

In Part One of this chapter we will describe many of these trends in more detail, providing in-depth statistics for each of these demographic groups. Part Two of this chapter will discuss the implications of these demographic changes for public administrators, both those who are primarily researchers and those who are primarily leaders and managers in public organizations.

II. PART ONE: DEMOGRAPHIC TRENDS

A. Slowing Growth of the Labor Force

One of the more controversial predictions in *Workforce 2000* was that slow labor force growth, caused by declining birth rates in the post–baby boom generation, would result in tighter labor markets by the early 21st century. For example, the Bureau of Labor Statistics (BLS) projects that by the year 2005, those working or looking for work will only increase by 21% from 1990 as compared to a 33% increase over the previous 15-year period (Fullerton, 1991). The 26 million workers added to the labor force between 1990 and 2005 represent an annual increase of only 1.3%, a figure that is down sharply from the 1.9% annual change for the 1975–1990 period. This slowing of the increase in the labor force is attributed to a combination of factors including a population growth over the period of less than 1%. This slow growth is combined with a labor force participation rate that is still increasing, but only at a rate of approximately 0.3% annually in contrast to the 0.5% increased annual growth in participation over the previous 15 years. However, more recent assessments by officials of the BLS downplay this potential labor shortage. They point out that while the supply of labor has been slowing down, the demand for labor has decreased as well. With both supply and demand decreasing, widespread labor shortages are, they believe, unlikely to occur (GAO, 1992).

An important aspect of the changing composition of the labor force is in the number of 16- to 19-year-olds. In the late 1980s, a low unemployment rate in the U.S. economy and declining numbers in this age group led to discussions about a shortage of entry level workers. However, according to the latest BLS report, that problem, to the extent that it existed, is expected to diminish and should very soon begin to improve. Further, by 2005 the number of 16- to 19-year-olds should have returned to a level nearer that of the early 1980s (Kutscher, 1991).

B.   Entrants and Leavers

The labor force is projected to increase from 124.8 million in 1990 to 150.7 million in 2005, a net increase of slightly less than 26.0 million. However, that net growth results from an expected 55.8 million new entrants and nearly 30.0 million who are projected to leave the labor force some time over the 1990–2005 period. Another dimension of this dynamic change in the labor force is that the composition of the entrants and leavers is expected to be very different from that in past years. Entrants will more likely be women, blacks, Hispanics, and Asians. Thus, Hispanics, while currently only 7.7% of the labor force, are projected to represent 15.7% of labor force entrants over the 1990–2005 period. Leavers from the work force, on the other hand, are more likely to be male, and almost one-half of the leavers are projected to be White, Non-Hispanic males. The mixture of entrants and leavers explains the changes expected in the composition of the labor force between 1990 and 2005 (Kutscher, 1991).

1.   Women in the Work Force

During the 1980s, women accounted for more than 70% of growth in the labor market (Friedman, 1987). By the year 2005 women will make up approximately 47.5% of the total work force (Fullerton, 1991).

Between 1973 and 1987, the number of women employed full time in state and local government jobs increased nearly 50%, from 1.3 million to 1.9 million, so that by 1989 women were 42% of the public work force at those levels of government. Between 1970 and 1988, women's share of paid, civilian jobs in the federal sector also grew, rising from 27% to 42%. Yet while accounting for nearly half of the civilian white collar work force in the federal executive branch in 1988, women composed only about 1 in 10 of the executives. In state and local government, women were less than a third of "officials and administrators" (American Society for Public Administration, 1992).

(a)   *Women with Children.*   What effect has the increased number of working women had on the American family? While women's participation rate in the work force has changed, the most dramatic change in women's labor force participation rates in recent decades has been among married women with children. Women now constitute 44% of the work force; most of them will get pregnant at some point during their careers, work until their ninth month, and return to work soon after their babies are born. Census figures from 1984 show that 65% of American women in their childbearing years are working. Yet, according to Edward Zigler, Director of the Yale Bush Center in Child Development and Social Policy at Yale University, only 40% of working women can take paid maternity leave with reasonable certainty they will have a job to return to (O'Carolan, 1987). In 1986, 54% of women with a child under 6 were working. More than half of all married mothers were back at work by the time their child was 1 year old and usually working full time (Friedman, 1987). In 1986, some 63% of mothers with children under 18 were in the labor force, according to "Investing in Quality Child Care: A Report for AT&T" prepared by Ellen Galinsky, Director of Work and Family Life Studies at Bank Street College in New York. This is in sharp contrast to 1940, when only 8.6% were in the labor force. In 1986, some 60% of mothers worked while their youngest child was 3–5 years old, compared with 45% a decade earlier. The most dramatic increase was in the percentage of working mothers with children under 3 years of age. This group grew from 35% in 1976 to 51% in 1986 (*Richmond News Leader*, 1989). By 1995, two of three preschoolers and four of five school-aged children will have mothers in the labor force (Wider Opportunities, 1989). It has been estimated, however, that only 13% of working women with children want to work full-time regular hours (Johnston, 1987). In all, 21.5 million mothers were in the labor force in 1986, 73% of them full time; however, of approximately 6 million companies in the United States, only 4150 provided child care assistance to employees in 1986.

Given these facts, it is obvious that there has also been a dramatic increase in the proportion of families in which both husbands and wives are in the labor force. In 1960, less than 32% of working husbands' wives were in the labor force. By 1990, that percentage had more than doubled to nearly 70%. In 1980, both the husband and the wife worked in 52% of families; by 1988, that proportion had risen to 63%. Additionally, the number of single-parent households has risen 23% since 1980. Forty percent of the work force is now made up of families in which both spouses are working, with another 6% being single parents. The Bureau of National Affairs reported in 1989 that only about 4% of American families fit the stereotypical image of the father who works outside the home and the mother who stays home and cares for the children.

Approximately 24 million of the 85 million families in the United States now have dual incomes; a large percentage of these are full-time, two-income professional career families. Today the woman is the dominant earner in some 12% of husband/wife households, and this trend is expected to continue. Women now head up 93% of all single-parent households; however, they are generally underpaid in all areas (Goddard, 1989).

Numerous studies have shown that society's negative stereotypes about women are carried into the corporate structure, where they adversely affect women's careers. Between 1976–1978 and 1988, negative stereotypes about women have increased. For example, a 1976–1978 survey conducted by Fernandez (1991) found that 16% of men and 7% of women agreed that women are not serious about their professional careers; in 1988, 25% of men and 20% of women agreed. This flies in the face of the increasing numbers of women entering the permanent full-time work force.

A national study of 1500 women in management was conducted by Stoner and Hartman in 1992 and found that more than 30% of women managers felt their careers had been helped by raising a family. They related this to spouse input or ideas that aided their careers, and to family support and encouragement from spouse and children. Another 30% of those surveyed felt their careers had been hurt. They attributed this to lack of mobility, inability to follow job opportunities because of spouse's job, mobility for the furtherance of spouse's job opportunities, and inability to relocate based on perceived impact on children. The remaining 40% of those surveyed expressed no significant impact between family and career opportunities (Stoner and Hartman, 1992).

In a study that John P. Fernandez, AT&T Division Manager of Personnel Services, conducted of 5000 companies and their employees, 76% of the women and 58% of the men said that greater corporate involvement in child care would increase productivity. An unrelated study of 8000 employees in Portland, Oregon reported that they lost an average of 9 days a year, 4% of the number of days that could have been worked, dealing with child problems, while women with children under 18 missed work an average of only 11.9 days (O'Carolan, 1987).

As more women enter the labor force and the demand for child care increases, employer-assisted child care may become an increasingly powerful incentive for job seekers to choose one firm over another. In 1985, only 1% of full-time employees in medium and large establishments offered child care assistance. By 1988, that number had risen to 4%, and in 1989 to 5% (Hyland, 1990).

(b)   *Women's Participation in Management.*   Since the beginning of the century, women's participation in the work force has been steadily increasing, although women's movement into positions of organizational power has lagged greatly behind. Working women currently occupy the majority of low-status jobs (Fagenson, 1986).

Futurist Joseph Coates cites a survey of 1200 executives indicating that 68% were eager to promote women to top executive levels and 85% were eager to promote them to middle management. In addition, only 29% said women are not likely to be promoted as quickly as men (Fernandez, 1991).

Women hold 35% of the executive, administrative, and management jobs in the United States, almost double the 1972 level. However, only slightly more than 2% of general manager jobs are held by women. *Fortune* magazine found that in 800 public companies, only 19 of 4012 people serving as the highest paid officers and directors were women. Of 599 managing directors at five prominent investment banks, only 15 were women. In addition, only one woman is a chief financial officer at any of the top 250 industrial corporations. These statistics are true despite the fact that women represent more than one of three business school graduates (Fernandez, 1991).

At the federal level of government, between 1972 and 1980 the number of female managers and administrators more than doubled, while the number of male managers and administrators increased by only 22% (Guy, 1992). Between 1976 and 1986 the increase in general schedule–type jobs held by women increased by 6.5% while the white male share of these jobs decreased from 50.2% to 41.8%.

Even though women have been able to achieve positions in government, the wage gap between women's and men's earnings has widened. In 1987 the annual female–male earnings ratio for full-time workers, known as the wage gap, was 65%. This means that for every $1.00 in wages that the average man earns, a women earns $0.65 (Guy, 1992).

Well over 80% of the companies have formal policies against harassment, and about 60% offer supervisory training in harassment issues. However, efforts to help women move ahead professionally seem to lag behind. Mentor programs, support groups, and specific hiring programs remain the exception rather than the rule (Beilinson, 1990).

The white female has advanced much faster in the world of executive administration than her African-American counterpart. Whereas the African-American female represents only 0.9% of the executive ranks, the white female represents 36% (Baskerville, 1991).

The results of a survey conducted about differences between women and men in management level positions may be surprising. Women filled only 14% of middle manager jobs as compared to 46% for men. Their salaries represented only 93% of salary paid to men in the same comparable jobs and classes. Women became immobilized at lower levels of management than did men (62% vs. 52%) (Lewis, 1992).

Although U.S. law is progressive in its treatment of women, the U.S. workplace is by no means free of gender discrimination. Considering the growing number of women in the labor force, it makes good business sense to create work environments that fully encourage and utilize the talents of all employees (Fernandez, 1991).

2. Minorities

The United States is ethnically a very diverse nation. The population includes 14% of Anglo-Saxon ancestry, 13% of Germanic ancestry, 10% of Hispanic ancestry, and 2% of Asian ancestry. By the year 2050, one-half of the U.S. population will be African-American, Hispanic-American, Native American, and Asian-American.

The growing share of minorities in the labor force has been an important development of the past several decades, and BLS projects a continuation of this trend. White non-Hispanics, who accounted for 78.6% of the labor force in 1990, are still projected to be the largest group in 2005, but their share in expected to decline to 73%.

Nevertheless, the white non-Hispanic population will increase by nearly 12 million over the 1990–2005 period. The proportion of white non-Hispanics in the labor force declines because all of the other labor force groups—Blacks, Hispanics, Asian, and other—are projected to increase at a faster rate and to represent a larger share of the labor force in 2005. For blacks, this is an expansion from a 10.7% share of the labor force in 1990 to 11.8% by 2005. For Hispanics, an even faster rise is projected, from a 7.7% share in 1990 to 11.1% by 2005. The number of Hispanics in the 2005 labor force is projected to be approaching that of blacks. An important factor in their rapid increase is that a very significant share of immigrants to the United States are projected to be of Hispanic origin. The Asian/other group is projected to increase its share of the labor force from 3.1% to 4.3%.

BLS reported that while the number of whites in the labor force is expected to increase by about 17% between 1990 and 2005, the number of blacks is expected to increase by over 30%, and the number of Hispanics and Asian/other minorities is expected to increase by about 75% during this period (Fullerton, 1991).

This change in the work force is reflective of population changes in the U.S. society. The overall U.S. population became significantly less white and Anglo-Saxon during the 1980s, largely because of growth in the number of Hispanics and Asians living in this country, according to the 1990 census. The proportion of U.S. residents identifying themselves as white declined to 80.3% in 1990 from 83.1% in 1980. At the same time, the proportion of Hispanics increased to 9% in 1990 from 6.4% in 1980. In addition, blacks became a slightly larger segment of the U.S. population, increasing to 12.1% in 1990 from 11.7% in 1980, and Native Americans grew of 0.8% from 0.6%. Although still an overwhelming majority in the United States, whites have shrunk as a proportion of the population from 90% in 1960. People of Chinese descent remain the largest element in the growing U.S. population of Asians and Pacific Islanders, followed by those of Philippine and Japanese origin. In addition, the census found significant growth among certain groups from Asia—especially the Hmong, who are from mountainous regions of Laos, and people from Bangladesh, Pakistan, and Sri Lanka (Noah, 1991).

(a) *African-Americans.* The black labor force is projected to grow more rapidly than the overall labor force. However, its growth is expected to be slower than that of either the Hispanic or the Asian/other group. These groups' projected number in the labor force in 2005, 18 million, make this group still the largest minority group therein. At 11.8%, their share would be up one percentage point from 1990. The relatively faster growth of blacks in the labor force is attributable to population growth from higher birth rates and immigration, and to higher participation by black women (Fullerton, 1991).

In the year 2000, African-Americans will represent at least 14.2% of the U.S. population and 18% of the labor force growth between now and then.

Fernandez (1991) states that over the years he has found that African-American employees are by far the most critical of corporate treatment of minorities. For example, 87% of African-

Table 1 U.S. Population by Race and Ethnicity: 1990 and 1980

	1990		1980		
	Population (thousands)	Percentage of total	Population (thousands)	Percentage of total	Population growth rate: 1980–1990
White	199,686	80.3	188,372	83.1	6.0
Black	29,986	12.1	26,495	11.7	13.2
Hispanic	22,354	9.0	14,609	6.4	53.0
Asian and Pacific Islander	7,274	2.9	3,500	1.5	107.8
Native American	1,959	0.8	1,420	0.6	37.9

Source: U.S. Bureau of the Census, Racial Statistics Division.

Americans, 57% of Asians, 54% of Hispanics, 44% of Native Americans, and 35% of whites believe that minorities have a more difficult time finding a sponsor or mentor than white employees do.

The majority may feel more threatened by African-Americans than by other minority groups because African-Americans are (currently) the largest minority in the United States and compete more intensely in all areas with the majority. Thus, nonambivalent attitudes and the size of the African-American population have made African-Americans the biggest threat to the whites' dominant position in this society.

(b) *Asians.*   With a population of roughly 7.3 million, Asian-Americans today make up slightly less than 3% of the U.S. population. Table 1 shows that over the past decade, the Asian-American population share rose dramatically, from 1.5% to 2.9% of the total population. The Asian-American population more than doubled, growing by 108%, twice as fast as the Hispanic population, which grew by 53%. This figure is almost eight times as fast as the black population, which grew by 13%, and 15 times as fast as the white population, which grew by 6%. The Asian-American population is expected to continue to grow rapidly. The principle reason for the growth in the Asian-American population is the post-1965 influx of immigrants and refugees from Asia and the Pacific Islands. After 40 years of being virtually banned from the United States by immigration laws, people from Asia began to come to the United States in greater numbers starting in 1965, when the United States abandoned the "national origins" system of immigration (U.S. Commission on Civil Rights, 1992). See Table 2 for characteristics of Asian-Americans by country of origin.

A survey of highly successful executives in Fortune 500 companies revealed that only 0.3% of senior executives in the United States are of Asian descent. Thus, the representation of Asian-Americans among senior executives is just one-tenth their representation in the population as a whole (U.S. Commission on Civil Rights, 1992).

A recent study conducted by the U.S. Commission on Civil Rights showed that U.S.-born Asian-American men are between 7% and 11% more likely to be in managerial occupations than non-Hispanic white men with the same measured characteristics. Because the study only included U.S.-born Asian-Americans, it is unlikely that English language deficiencies or cultural barriers could be responsible for the finding of Asian underrepresentation among managers (U.S. Commission on Civil Rights, 1992).

Over the years, both positive and negative attitudes have been directed by Americans toward Asians. This minority group has sometimes been seen as a "model minority." However, as their

Table 2 Characteristics of Asian-Americans by Nationality of Origin

	Percentage of Asian-American population	Percentage foreign-born	Percentage who do not speak English well	Percentage who live in the West
Chinese	22.6	63.3	23	52.7
Filipino	19.3	64.7	67	68.8
Japanese	11.6	28.4	9	80.3
Asian Indian	11.2	70.4	5	19.2
Korean	11.0	81.9	24	42.9
Vietnamese	8.4	90.5	38	46.2
Laotian	2.0	93.7	69	45.7
Thai	1.3	82.1	12	43.0
Cambodian	2.0	93.9	59	55.6
Hmong	1.2	90.5	63	37.4
Pakistani	—	85.1	10	23.5
Indonesian	—	83.4	6	56.2
All Asian-Americans	100.00	62.1	15	56.4

Sources: Barbara Vobejda, Asians, Hispanics giving nation more diversity, *Washington Post,* June 12, 1991; U.S. Bureau of the Census, *We, the Asian and Pacific Islander Americans,* p. 11, table 7; and U.S. General Accounting Office, *Asian Americans: A Status Report,* p. 44, table 6.1.

numbers and their economic success increase, it is predictable that anti-Asian discrimination will increase (Fernandez, 1991).

It is important for the United States to recognize that as Asian countries increase their economic power, Asian-Americans will be a valuable resource in assisting U.S. companies to form positive economic ties with Asian nations (Fernandez, 1991).

(c) *Hispanics.* The Hispanic American population, which is very diverse in social, racial, and ethnic characteristics, will become the largest minority in the United States early in the 21st century. The major Hispanic ethnic groups in the United States are Mexicans (63%), Puerto Ricans (12%), Central and South Americans (11%), Cubans (5%), and others (9%) (Fernandez, 1991).

As well as being the fastest growing minority group in the United States, Hispanics are one of the nation's youngest groups (47% of Hispanics are below 21 years of age, compared to 35% of the total population). In 1980, Hispanics numbered about 14.6 million, or 6.4% of the population of the mainland United States. By the year 2000, this number is expected to increase to between 8.6% and 9.9% (Arbona, 1990).

There will be an increase of 589,000 jobs in the public service by the year 2000, with 29% of these jobs in the executive, administrative, managerial, and professional ranks. Government ranks third among industries where most job growth will occur between 1989 and 2000. Hispanic growth in the public administration industry only increased from 4.7% to 5.1% between 1983 and 1989; and an average of 22,733 Hispanics entered the ranks of public administration industry each year during this time period (Sisneros, 1991).

Very little research on Hispanic women who work outside of the home has been conducted (most previous research regarded their role at home), and even less is known about the over 1 in 10 (13%) Hispanic women in managerial or professional jobs. Due to their positions, these women may serve as community leaders and important role models for young Hispanic women. Because of the visible and demanding nature of their jobs, the challenges they face in majority work settings, and their break from traditional female roles, Hispanic women professionals are subjected to multiple sources of stress at home and in the workplace (Amaro et al., 1987).

With regard to family factors, having a supportive spouse has been found to be positively related to employed women's mental health, while having young children (under 6 years of age) has been associated with increased stress and mental distress among employed women. Other family-related influences, such as rigid and traditional sex role norms and expectations in Hispanic households, may also be a source of conflict and stress. The experience of ethnic discrimination is also a potential source of stress for Hispanic women's personal development and creates stress in multiple ways at work and at home (Amaro et al., 1987).

Compared to the majority population, Hispanics are disadvantaged in terms of educational and occupational attainment, which represents a serious problem considering that their presence in the labor force is expected to grow steadily in the years to come (Arbona, 1990). In 1988, 27%, or 5.8 million Hispanics, lived in poverty, and 40% of this community's children are believed to live in poverty. Hispanics are three times more likely than whites to live in physically inadequate or overcrowded housing. Unemployment is 50% higher among Hispanics than non-Hispanics. In 1988, 35% of Hispanics earned less than $10,000 (Arbona, 1990).

Hispanics were more likely to occupy lower and intermediate skill jobs during the 1980s; only 18% held managerial and professional jobs. Hispanics averaged $284 per week in 1987, which was 75% of the weekly earnings of all full-time workers in the United States (Arbona, 1990).

U.S. society must improve its tolerance of bilingual Americans, including people whose native language is Spanish. Bilingual Hispanic-Americans will be a tremendous asset to U.S. society as we deal with Spanish-speaking countries (Fernandez, 1991).

As is the case for other minorities, affirmative action and improved acceptance of people who are different are important requirements if the United States is to utilize the resource of a diverse population in the global marketplace (Fernandez, 1991).

3. Sexual Orientation

Many Americans are hesitant to acknowledge the multiple cultures in the United States. They are often even more hesitant to accept many of the different lifestyles that exist, particularly alternative sexual lifestyles. In a 1988 study conducted by John Fernandez, 10–12% of employees indicted that they were homosexual. Some believe that this figure is low, since homosexuals are still hesitant to reveal their sexual orientation. Their hesitancy is understandable, given the often violent, homophobic reaction some people, including employees and employers, have when they encounter a gay person. For example, the New York City Police Department reported an increase in attacks on gays (64 for the period January 1–July 1990 compared to 36 the entire year of 1989) (Fernandez, 1991).

Eight states have created laws protecting the rights of gays in the community. For example, in Massachusetts, a law that grew out of legislation first introduced in 1972 added to the state's civil rights protections by declaring sexual orientation an illegal reason for discriminating in credit, housing, public accommodation, and jobs. Although only eight states have created such laws, over 100 municipalities have similar statutes intended to protect homosexuals from discrimination. And in May, the State of Hawaii's Supreme Court ruled that gay marriages there may be legal.

Even as these signs of tolerance abound, organized opposition has also grown. In the fall of 1992, voters in Oregon defeated a ballot initiative declaring homosexuality to be "abnormal, wrong, unnatural and perverse," but a more subtly phrased measure passed decisively in Colorado.

According to a recent poll conducted by *U.S. News*, 53% of American voters say they personally know someone who is gay and this familiarity tends to make them think more favorably about ensuring gay rights. Forty-six percent say they do not know anyone gay and that they largely oppose ensuring gay rights. Yet at the same time, fully half of those surveyed oppose extending current civil rights laws to cover gays. Most voters still view homosexuality as a "lifestyle" choice rather than a matter of civil rights. Forty-four percent of respondents say that such laws (civil rights laws to cover gays) would end discrimination. Forty-three percent worry that it would amount to endorsing the gay lifestyle. Previous surveys have shown that most Americans mistakenly believe gays are covered by existing federal rights law (Shapiro et al., 1993).

4. Substance Abuse

Alcohol and drug use in the workplace is considered one of the most critical problems facing business and industry today. Although the precise annual loss of productivity due to drug and alcohol use is probably impossible to determine, the estimates are staggering. Among the most commonly cited figures are $30 billion of lost productivity due to illegal drug use and $60 billion in lost productivity due to alcohol abuse (Harris and Heft, 1992). In a recent Gallup survey for the Institute for a Drug-Free Workplace, one-half of those polled said that illegal drug use occurs in their workplaces, and about one-third said they had personally witnessed it (Beilinson, 1991).

In survey after survey, CEOs cite alcohol and drug dependency as a major factor in absenteeism, soaring medical claims, and plummeting productivity. Use of cocaine in particular has grown tremendously; David Britt, author of "The All-American Cocaine Story," estimates that 70% of the stimulant's users are jobholders, and 35% of these people are in managerial positions. But liquor remains the nation's most misused substance (Pope, 1990).

According to the Employee Assistants Professionals Association, an Arlington, Virginia–based organization representing 6000 of the nation's EAP (Employee Assistance Programs) professionals, 12% of America's 114 million workers are addicted to alcohol, while 7% are addicted to drugs like marijuana, cocaine, amphetamines, and barbiturates, and cross-addiction is not uncommon (Pope, 1990).

Mangione and Quinn (1975) analyzed data from a national survey of over 1000 working people regarding drug use and job satisfaction. Breaking down the sample into four subgroups on the basis of sex and age, they found that job satisfaction was significantly related to self-reported drug use within only one subgroup: men over 30 years old. Moreover, the correlation was very small. There is insufficient evidence to firmly conclude whether work conditions were actually related to alcohol consumption (Harris and Heft, 1992).

5. The Disabled Worker

Section 503 of the Rehabilitation Act of 1973 defines a handicapped person as anyone who has or is regarded as having a visible or invisible physical or mental impairment that substantially limits one or more major life activities, including employment (Buhler, 1991).

The Americans with Disabilities Act (ADA) of 1990 makes discrimination against disabled workers illegal. The passage of Title I prohibits private employers, state and local governments, employment agencies, and labor unions from discriminating against qualified individuals with disabilities in job application procedures, hiring, firing, advancement, compensation, job training, and other terms, conditions, and privileges of employment. An estimated 40 million Americans are covered by the historic Americans with Disabilities Act (Stein, 1991). By July 1992, businesses with 25 or more employees had to comply with this law, and in 1994 businesses with as few as 15 employees must comply with this law (Waldrop, March, 1991).

Under ADA, a company cannot discriminate against anyone who can perform the "essential functions" of the job; the employer must make a "reasonable accommodation" for a disability as long as it doesn't cause the firm "undue hardship" (Laplante, 1992).

More than a third (37%) of companies with fewer than 100 employees have done nothing to prepare for the effects of the ADA, according to a recent survey conducted by the law firm of Jackson, Lewis, Schnitzler, and Krupman. Though Title III of the ADA took affect only two years ago, already 70% of the companies surveyed by the firm had charges or complaints filed against them (Spargins, 1992).

In the United States there are over 43.6 million Americans who have one or more physical or mental disabilities, and this number is increasing as the population as a whole is growing older. According to a 1988 study by the Census Bureau, 13 million noninstitutionalized Americans aged 16–64 have a disability that limits the kind or amount of work they can do. Fewer than 5 million of these people are currently employed (Spargins, 1992).

Two-thirds of all disabled Americans between the age of 16 and 64 are not working at all; yet a large majority of those not working say that they want to work. Of working-age disabled persons who are not working 66% say that they would like to have a job. This means that about 8.2 million people with disabilities want to work but cannot find a job (Tysee, 1991). The following data are from Lentan and Taggart (1977):

Severely disabled:	14% employed
	6% held full-time jobs
	averaged 26 hours per week
Occupationally disabled:	71% employed
	45% held full-time jobs
	averaged 36 hours per week
Secondary work limitations:	72% employed
	59% held full-time jobs
Totally disabled:	43% employed
	29% held full-time jobs
Nondisabled:	74% employed
	61% held full-time jobs
	averaged 41 hour per week

Almost half of unemployed people with disabilities said they were not working because employers didn't recognize their ability. Forty percent said they were unable to find work, and nearly that many said they lacked job skills. Almost 30% lacked the means of transportation to get to work, and 23% said they needed special equipment to perform their job (Tysee, 1991).

In addition to people with physical and mental disabilities, there are large numbers of people at work with disabling illnesses and addictions. Illnesses include heart disease, cancer, AIDS, high blood pressure, arthritis, rheumatism, musculoskeletal diseases, depression, and chronic stress. Many disabled persons have multiple conditions that compound their problems. Severe and multiple conditions reduce the capacity to function physically and emotionally, while the discomforting symptoms may lessen work motivation. About four-fifths of the disabled in 1972 suffered from some physical limitation: two-fifths had trouble walking, three-fifths trouble lifting more than 10 pounds, and half could not stand for long periods (Levitan and Taggart, 1977).

A third of all persons aged 60–64 and a fourth of those aged 55–59 are disabled, compared with 1 in 10 among 35- to 44-year-olds. The disabled adult is more often a racial minority. Blacks represented 9% of the nondisabled adults in 1972 but accounted for 14% of the disabled. Furthermore, 58% of the blacks with disabilities could not work regularly or at all, compared with 48% among whites with a disability. The unemployed disabled adult is more often a woman. Of the disabled females, 56% are unable to work regularly or at all, as compared to 42% of the disabled males (Levitan and Taggart, 1977).

The disabled adult is more often undereducated. Of all adults with disabilities, 40% did not finish high school—three times more than nondisabled persons. The disabled adult more often lives in poverty. Of the disabled 50% had household incomes of $15,000 or less, compared with only 25% of nondisabled adults (Tysee, 1991).

One in six Americans is disabled—too many to ignore. But that's what employers have pretty much done for decades. The ADA is meant to help this group take its rightful place in the work force. But the cost and level of effort required to accommodate workers with disabilities may be surprising. According to the Job Accommodation Network, a service of the President's Committee on Employment of People with Disabilities, 50% of all workplace accommodations cost less than $50, and 31% cost nothing ("Hands On," 1992).

6. The Aging of the Work Force

The median age of the U.S. population is projected to rise from the current 32 years to 36 years by the year 2000, and to 39 years by the year 2010 (Fernandez, 1991).

The number of elderly people in the United States is increasing at a faster rate than at any other time in U.S. history. In 1987, "young old" groups—those aged 65–74 and those aged 75–84—were 8 and 12 times larger, respectively, than they had been in 1900. The "old old" group—those aged 85 years and older—was 23 times larger (Fernandez, 1991).

In 1900, only 4% of the U.S. population was 65 years or older; by the year 2000, 17% will be in this category. By the year 2030, one-third of the population will be 55 years or older, compared to one-fifth in this category now.

The 55 and older population is expected to expand as those born in the 1940s reach this age. The number of men in the labor force aged 55 and over, therefore, even with no significant change in their labor force participation rate, is projected to grow by 3.5 million or 31% of the total labor force growth. It is important to note that much of this increase will take place in the latter part of the projection period (Fullerton, 1991).

Women aged 55 and older are expected to increase by 3.8 million, or 47% of the total labor force growth between 1990 and 2005, because of population growth and projected higher labor force participation rates. Women who are moving into the 55 and older age groups have higher labor force participation than earlier cohorts. These women aged 55–64 are projected to increase their labor force participation rate from 45.3% in 1990 to 54.3% in 2005. Even at this much higher level of labor force participation, in 2005 women in this age group still are expected to have a participation rate nearly 14 percentage points lower than that for their male counterparts (Fullerton, 1991).

By the end of this century only 39% of the work force will be under age 35, vs. 49% now. Moreover, the number of people aged 50–65 will increase at more than twice the rate of the overall population (Ramirez, 1989).

In 20 years the oldest baby boomers will be senior citizens. According to Rosen and Jerdee (1988), the ratio of workers to retirees will drop from the current 4:1 level to 2:1 by the year 2050 (Rosen and Jerdee, 1988).

The 39 million workers aged 35–44 will dominate the labor force at the turn of the century. But the share of workers aged 45–54 will also rise. Of the work force, 51% will be between the ages of 35 and 54, and 11–13% will be over 55. In 1970, the median age of employees was 28; by the year 2000, it will be nearly 40 (Kelly, 1992).

In a recent survey by Towers Perrin and the Hudson Institute, 26% of companies reported that between 30% and 40% of their work force was over 40; another 20% reported their over-40 population constituted 40–50% of the work force, and 15% already had over 50% of their working population over 40 years of age (Perrin and the Hudson Institute, 1990).

7. Job Skills and Illiteracy

Workplace literacy relates to the required or needed skills of the specific or various employment sectors, types of industry, or jobs and employment. Work force or workplace illiteracy refers essentially to the absence of those skills, abilities, and attitudes (Ford, 1992). Workplace literacy means interpreting work schedules, following written instructions, and giving clear and succinct directions to others. It is explaining a complex operation to a new employee. It is taking ideas apart and putting them together again. This is the form of literacy that employers are most concerned about because of its direct connection to work, to quality, and to job performance (Ford, 1992).

Poor literacy costs the nation an estimated $25–30 billion in lost productivity, errors, and accidents attributable to poor literacy. A recent study found that nearly half of the nation's 191 million adult citizens are not proficient enough in English to write a letter about a billing error or to calculate the length of a bus trip from a published schedule, according to a 4-year federal study of literacy in America (Celis, 1993). Despite these facts, most of the 26,000 randomly selected participants in the literacy study said they were able to read and write English "well" or "very well" (*Newsweek*, 1993).

Literacy among 21- to 25-year-olds is dropping in comparison to a similar study from 1985. The likely cause is the dramatic increase in young Hispanics in the population, many of whom were born in other countries and are learning English as a second language (*Newsweek*, 1993). White Americans outscored other ethnic groups, who, with the exception of Asians/Pacific Islanders, had less education or, with the exception of African-Americans, were more likely to speak English as a second language. Blacks scored worse, according to the study, because schools they attend are poorer than ones whites attend (*Newsweek*, 1993).

Among the worst performers were immigrants, the elderly, and inmates. The elderly in particular constituted a disproportionate percentage of those in the lowest literacy level.

The survey results are especially worrisome because many employers now need workers with higher math and reading skills.

The U.S. Department of Education estimates that the functionally illiterate now account for 30% of the unskilled, 29% of the semiskilled, and 11% of the managerial, professional, and technical work force. Illiteracy is increasing by 2.3 million people per year (Lee, 1992).

The Educational Testing Service runs the National Assessment of Educational Progress, referred to as NAEP. NAEP surveyed 3600 individuals in the 21- to 25-year-old age group and found, for example, that only 60% of whites, 40% of Hispanics, and 25% of blacks could find information in a news article, and 25% of whites, 7% of Hispanics, and 3% of blacks could follow directions to travel from one location to another using a bus schedule. Between 1986 and the year 2000, 55% of the net addition to the labor force—new hires minus retirees—will be blacks, Hispanics, Asians, and other minorities (Petrini, 1989). Research suggests that the literacy profile of a typical midsized U.S. company is one in which 10% of the workers are marginally literate, 65% function at a level somewhere between fourth and ninth grades, and only 25% function at above a tenth grade literacy level (Bell, 1991).

Illiteracy among employees has profound implications for product quality, for customer service, for internal efficiency, and for workplace and environmental safety.

Illiteracy is not a new problem, but it is receiving widespread attention due in part to the growth of illiteracy in the past two decades. According to Donald Ford, perhaps half of the adult work force do not read, write, or compute well enough to perform their jobs satisfactorily (Ford, 1992).

Another reason for the growing interest in workplace illiteracy is the changing nature of work and the workplace. According to the 1990 workplace literacy survey conducted by the Society for Human Resource Management (SHRM) and Commerce Clearing House (CCH), workers hired several years ago would not be eligible for employment today due to changes in job requirements.

Of survey respondents 55% voiced the opinion that job applicants with a high school diploma are not sufficiently literate for employment. Some even said that recent college graduates could not perform at an acceptable level (Pilenzo, 1990).

By some estimates, employers are spending as much as $50 billion to try to eliminate the kind of practical illiteracy that the new study describes (*Newsweek*, 1993). However, according to a fax poll conducted by *Business Month* in May of 1990, only 26% of the respondents said that their companies conduct classes in basic skills or pay employees to finish high school (Smith, 1990).

8. HIV and AIDS

Acquired immunodeficiency syndrome (AIDS) is an epidemic that will test the strength of our society from a multitude of dimensions. Since the first official documentation of an AIDS case in the United States in 1981, the world in which we grew up, dated, and worked exists no longer. While less than half of the U.S. population believes AIDS is the most urgent medical problem that we face, we know that the 1990s will see more deaths attributed to AIDS each year in this country than were lost annually to the Vietnam War (Slack, 1991).

The federal Centers for Disease Control estimate that 1 in every 250 Americans has been infected by HIV. Most are 25–44—the core age group of the U.S. work force (Stodghill, 1993).

Even the vocabulary has adapted to reflect a workplace filled with AIDS-related situations and conditions. Most of the terms are used interchangeably. People with the virus are sometimes referred to as being HIV-infected, HIV-positive, or seropositive. Individuals with serious but less severe symptoms and illnesses may be classified as having AIDS-related complex, or ARC. Still others who have actually contracted the disease may be referred to as persons with AIDS. Regardless of whether one is at the asymptomatic seropositive stage of the disease or has actually developed a full-blown case of AIDS, all persons infected with AIDS-related conditions or impairments are normally referred to as being within the "HIV spectrum" (Slack, 1991).

Given the harsh realities of this epidemic—mainstream estimates of the number of people in the United States within the HIV spectrum range from 1.5 million to 2.5 million—as much as 1% of the total population and work force may develop the disease (Slack, 1991).

In 1989 Harold Dennison, Jr. become the first documented death resulting from occupational exposure to AIDS. A physician, Dr. Dennison contracted the disease while performing surgery on a patient who was unknowingly in the HIV spectrum. Unaware that he, too, had become HIV-infected, Dennison was diagnosed with AIDS a mere 3 weeks prior to his death. While the circumstances surrounding this case are unusual, they reinforce and exacerbate a fear in the minds of many of unwittingly contracting AIDS or becoming HIV-infected via the workplace (Slack, 1991).

Why is AIDS an issue in the workplace? It is an issue primarily because of the fears that this disease generates in employees and employers. Fears of employees generally center around the issue of contagion. Certainly most workers understand that unsafe sex and intravenous drug use are the primary conduits for the HIV virus. But medicine is an imprecise science, and the remote possibility of a worker with cuts or open sores on his or her hands transmitting the disease is worrisome to many people. It is the anxiety of uncertainty that engenders suspicion about AIDS in the workplace, as elsewhere, (Slack, 1991).

And, of course, there are many questions surrounding the legality of screening public employees for the HIV spectrum: Should tests be mandatory for all workers, new workers, those with direct contact with citizenry, or suspected homosexuals? How accurate are the tests? And what is the balance between employees' right to confidentiality in health-related matters with the citizen's right to be informed about issues that may affect the government's ability to deliver services (Slack, 1991)?

At the time that they need it most, individuals in the HIV spectrum cannot count with absolute certainty on practitioners nurturing a supportive environment. Therefore, in addition to fighting the virus inside their bodies, they may also have to fight the mixed viewpoints and opinions about AIDS that are held in the workplace. Like all other employers in the United States, local government practitioners are faced with a disease that takes more than 40 lives each day. More than 108,000 local government workers, 1% of each municipality's work force, are likely to be in the HIV spectrum.

II. PART TWO: IMPLICATIONS FOR PUBLIC ADMINISTRATORS

The preceding pages describe a work force that is strikingly diverse. This increased diversity presents both challenges and opportunities for public administration. Implications of this increased diversity, both for the public administration researcher and for leaders and managers in public organizations, will be suggested in the following sections.

A. Implications for the Research in Public Organizations

As long ago as 1976, Dunnette (1976) pointed out that one of the major gaps in the field of organizational psychology was that no extensive coverage was given to groups such as women, minorities, or the disadvantaged. In spite of the recognition of the growing diversity of the work force, this gap still exists. For example, in the matter of racial diversity, Cox and Nkomo (1990) surveyed 20 major management journals that published organization behavior research between 1964 and 1989 and found that the amount of total published research is small relative to the importance of the topic. They also found that the topics covered are not representative of the domain of organizational behavior. Amazingly, they concluded that the trend is for less rather than more research on these topics. Frideger (1992) agrees and argues that, with very few exceptions, research in organizational behavior has generally disregarded the domestic cross-cultural and interracial implications of its theories.

> Not surprisingly, some demography researchers have emphasized the following: (1) the need for developing an understanding of the effects of racial and gender diversity in the organizational content, particularly as this increasing diversity impacts individuals who are members of what have traditionally been the dominant majority group in organizations; and (2) the need for understanding the relationship between demographic attributes and process variables such as communication, conflict, influence, and decision-making (Tsui and Egan, 1992).

It is conventional wisdom that all individuals are different. However, "life attitudes are not randomly distributed through the population. Members of the same 'identity groups,' say the same age, gender, race and such, have had overlapping life experiences which may, in turn, predispose them toward more or less favorable attitudes about particular company practices and cultures" (Marvis and Kanter, 1991). Differentiation is very important in this type of research for it must be recognized that even within the same large demographic group differences exist. Married workers put different values on the flexibility of their work schedule than do single workers, for example (Marvis and Kanter, 1991).

Wooldridge et al. (1993), in their paper entitled "Changing Demographics of the Work Force: Implications for Research in Human Resource Management," identify at least 20 areas of organizational behavior whereby further research to detect significant identity group differences is required. These areas include organizational design (do any of the identity groups react significantly differently to degrees of centralization/decentralization, specialization, formalization, span of control, organization size, and/or work unit size?) (Steers, 1978); learning styles; basic personnel human resource management (P/HRM) functions (including elements such as effectiveness of recruitment strategies and performance appraisal methods); barriers to effective organizational performance; strategies for effective organizational development and growth; determinants of upward mobility; effectiveness of various incentives in motivating desired behavior; training needs and the selection of training strategies; occupational safety and health issues; organizational communication; causes of organizational conflict and effective conflict resolution strategies; magnitude of organizational influence; modes of exerting organizational influence; relationship to types of organizational culture; types and manifestation of organizational creativity; causes of and reaction to organizational stress; determinants of job satisfaction and job commitment and the relationship between these organizational elements; effects of organizational stress on job satisfaction and job performance; employees values; work-related attitudes such as involvement, loyalty, intentions to leave, cynicism; and compatibility with technology.

Cox and Nkomo (1990) conclude, at least in the area of racial diversity, that "in addition to a general lack of researcher attention, the development of research in this area has been hindered by research questions that are too simplistic, by an absence of theories of race effects and by the types of research designs employed." They observed that less than 35% of the 140 empirical studies reviewed addressed racial groups other than blacks and whites, and only 33% of the 132 organizations studied were public.

The need for this type of research is manifested by the differences based on gender and race shown by the research that has been completed. Blazini and Greenhaus (1988, as reported by Dance, 1993) asked the question: do the work values of the black woman manager differ from those of the white woman or the black or white male manager? With $N = 322$, each manager was asked to respond to the importance he or she placed on 25 job characteristics. According to the weighted score, the value was assigned to one of four principle factors: factor I–extrinsic (respect for others, job security, income, and working conditions); factor II–managerial activities (opportunity to take risks, work on important problems, supervise others, and develop personal contacts); factor III–independence (working independently and determining one's own work method); and factor IV–Intrinsic (importance of task variety, feelings of accomplishment, and recognition for a job well done). The results were enlightening. The black females and males placed a greater emphasis on extrinsic work values than did the white females or males. Under factor II there was little difference between the responses of the black females and other groups and the factors associated with managerial activities. Both black females and males placed a higher emphasis on the values of independence than did the white males or females, and finally, under factor IV, both the black females and white females placed a higher emphasis on intrinsic work values than did the white and black males.

From the research on gender differences, Segal (1991) found that men and women apparently had different styles of management. The operating style model of men was competitive and that of female managers cooperative. The organizational structure for men was vertical and hierarchical while that of women was horizontal and egalitarian. The basic objective for the male managers was found to be winning, whereas that of the females was quality output. The problem-solving approach of men was rational and objective and that of the female managers intuitive and subjective.

It is true that most managers possess the characteristics of both male and female; however, in a study that compared perceptions about male/female managers who used either an authoritarian or participative leadership style, managers were viewed more positively when they used a leadership style that was typical of and consistent with their gender (Griffin, 1992). In this study, more participants said that they would not like to work for the authoritarian women than for any of the other managers. Women managers, however, have shown that using the "command-and-control" style of managing others is not the only way to be effective and successful. They are drawing on the skills and attitudes they have developed from their shared experiences as women, not by adopting the style and habits that men have found successful (Rosener, 1990).

Research has been conducted on other than black–white racial or gender differences. Yuker (1988) reports a study in which adults worked at tasks given them by a research assistant who was either disabled or nondisabled, and either likable or obnoxious. It is expected that people would be more willing to help the disabled person than the nondisabled one when both were likable, but less willing to help the disabled person as compared with the latter when they were equally obnoxious. Contrary to the theoretical expectations, subjects in the positive/pleasant conditions were three times as willing to help the nondisabled tester as they were to help the tester who was disabled. In the negative/obnoxious condition they were just as strongly biased in the opposite direction, i.e., in the direction of giving more help to the tester with the disability. Yuker concluded that nondisabled persons tend to (1) insist that the disabled person is suffering even when there is no evidence of suffering, or (2) devalue the unfortunate person's behavior because she ought to suffer and does not. The implication of the experiment is that people become angry and annoyed with the disabled when they violate their beliefs about how people with disabilities are supposed to behave.

Differences between Hispanic (predominately Mexican-American) and Anglo employees of a general purpose local government, in terms of their attitude toward the work environment and their levels of job satisfaction with various aspects of the job, were investigated by Rubaii-Barrett et al. (1991). The chart that follows summarizes the differences and similarities in work climate attitudes and job satisfaction.

EMPLOYEES:

Differences:

Satisfaction with Personnel Policies	(Hispanics more satisfied)
Satisfaction with Supervision	(Hispanics less satisfied)
Satisfaction with Job Tasks	(Hispanics less satisfied)
Satisfaction with Rewards	(Hispanics less satisfied)
Satisfaction with Coworkers	(Hispanics less satisfied)
Satisfaction with Employee Competence	(Hispanics less satisfied)

No Difference by Ethnicity:

Satisfaction with Promotion, with Pay, with Employee Motivation, with Participatory Management, with Stress Levels, and with Overall Satisfaction with the Job.

SUPERVISORS:

Differences:

Satisfaction with Personnel Policies	(Hispanics more satisfied)
Satisfaction with Employee Competence	(Hispanics less satisfied)
Satisfaction with Participatory Mgmt.	(Hispanics less satisfied)

No Difference by Ethnicity:

Satisfaction with Supervision, with Job Tasks, with Rewards, with Coworkers, with Promotion, with Pay, with Employee Motivation, with Stress Levels, with Overall Satisfaction with the Job.

MANAGERS:

Differences:

Satisfaction with Personnel Policies	(Hispanics more satisfied)
Satisfaction with Employee Competence	(Hispanics less satisfied)

No Difference by Ethnicity:
Satisfaction with Supervision, with Job Tasks, with Participatory Management, with Rewards, with Coworkers, with Promotion, with Pay, with Employee Motivation, with Stress Levels, with Overall Satisfaction with the Job.

In their summary of organization-related research on Asian-Americans, Sue and Wagner (1973) reported that, in general, Asian-American males exhibited less need for dominance, aggressiveness, exhibitionism, autonomy, and heterosexuality, whereas Asian-American females were more deferent, nurturing, and achievement-oriented than their Caucasian counterparts.

This type of research on organizational related attributes of the members of a diverse work force can be thought of as the first step toward managing/valuing diversity (Thomas, 1991). The crime is that so little such research on these elements of a diverse work force has been conducted, and that common data on all of the organizational attributes listed in Wooldridge et al. (1993) have not been collected and analyzed for each of the identity group comprising the work force of the 21st century.

B. Implications for Public Managers

This chapter has identified several demographic trends that the authors suggest have major implications for the management of public organizations. Space does not permit the identification of appropriate public management response to all of the important issues presented here. However, the implications of some of these trends for public managers will next be outlined. The trends selected include (1) changing family structure, (2) increasing workplace illiteracy, (3) aging of the work force, (4) increased visibility of different sexual orientations, (5) the increase in the number of workers with disabilities, and finally, (6) the challenges produced by the overall increased diversity of the work force.

1. Responding to the Changing Family Structure

Many of the trends that characterize the changing of the family structure have already been presented in this paper. By the year 2005, women will make up more than 47% of the total work force (Fullerton, 1991). In 1986, some 63% of mothers with children under 18 were in the labor force with some 60% of mothers working while their youngest child was 3–5 years old. And in 1988 the proportion of families in which both the husband and wife worked had risen to 63%. Women now head up 93% of all single-parent households. There have been other changes in the family structure that have implications for public managers:

> Other changes to the American family include the facts that marriages occur later, as do births, which also occur less often; there are more single-parent families; and more elderly persons live alone, often depending upon their children for some type of assistance (GAO, 1992).

In light of these changes, there has been evidence that employees may be willing to leave traditional employers for those more willing to help them achieve their goal of a more balanced work/family lifestyle. "A growing body of research indicates that family problems affect employee productivity, recruitment, retention, and absenteeism" (GAO, 1992). In view of the trends and the research findings outlined above, many organizations, both public and private, have adopted family-friendly policies to respond to the needs and desires of their employees. The following descriptions of typical family-friendly policies is taken from the General Accounting Office's report entitled, "The Changing Workforce: Comparison of Federal and Nonfederal Work/Family Programs and Approaches." This report presents an excellent summary of such policies.

Part-Time Work: Part-time employment is defined by the Bureau of Labor Statistics as working less than 35 hours a week, and it may involve working fewer than 8 hours each work day or fewer than 5 days per week. It is considered a "family-friendly" mode of employment since employees on such schedules have more time to devote to their families or personal lives. Part-time workers have often received fewer employee benefits than workers in full-time jobs, although employees at Aetna Life and Casualty who work at least 15 hours a week receive full medical and dental benefits.

Job Sharing: Job sharing is a variation of part-time work in which two (or more) workers share the duties of one full-time job by splitting work days or weeks. As a rule, job sharers also split a job's salary and benefits.

Flexible Work Schedules: Flexible work schedule programs usually involve working a pre-scribed number of hours each payroll period, but under a non-traditional schedule. Under one variant commonly known as "flextime," employees work a full day, but can choose their starting and quitting times. Another option is the "compressed work week," which allows employees to work the equivalent of a full week in less than 5 days, or, for employees on biweekly work schedules, to complete their schedule in less than 10 full workdays. A third option is the use of both flextime and a compressed work week, sometimes known as "maxiflex."

Flexible Benefits: In flexible benefit programs, employees are allowed, within overall cost limits, to customize a benefit package to their personal and family needs by selecting benefits from a menu of available options. Flexible benefits are not synonymous with "cafeteria" benefits as defined by the Internal Revenue Service. Cafeteria benefits require a choice between taxable and nontaxable compensation.

Flexible Work Place Programs: A flexible work place, or "flexiplace" program, allows employees to work at home or closer to home at a "satellite office" for at least part of the work week. Employees are said to "telecommute" when they are in close contact with the office through telephone and computer hook-ups. Organizations that allow employees to work at home often require them to spend a certain number of days at the main office during each work week.

Parental and Family/Personal Leave: Parental leave includes both maternity leave and paternity leave. It may be granted to employees for the birth, adoption, and/or subsequent care of children. Parental leave periods usually do not exceed 6 months and commonly involve certain job guarantees of reinstatement rights upon return. In 1991, 20 states plus the District of Columbia required maternity and/or paternal leave be provided with employees guaranteed a return to the same or comparable positions.

Use of Sick or Other Leave for Family Illness: In a number of organizations, employees are permitted to use all or a portion of their paid sick leave or other leave to care for immediate family members who were ill. In some organizations, no distinction was made between time off for employee's illness and leave for family illnesses or emergencies. In some instances the definition of "family" is extended to include "partners."

On-Site/Near-Site Child Care Center: An employer may sponsor a child care center in a facility at the worksite or at a location near the worksite. The child care center may be operated by the employer or by an independent child care provider. Many employers providing on- or near-site care subsidize the cost of the center either directly or indirectly.

Facilitating Access to Family or In-Home Care: Some employers assisted employees in securing family day care and in-home care. For example, Ventura County, California participates in a "family care provider network." The child care providers, who work out of their homes, make caregiving more convenient to employees' homes.

Child Care Resources and Referral Programs: Child care resource and referral programs help parents locate child care providers. These services may be provided in-house through an organization's Employee Assistance Program or contracted to another organization. They can include limited support, such as giving employees lists of child care providers or more extensive services, such as helping parents locate providers with particular characteristics.

Developing Child Care Resources in the Community: Some organizations have attempted to increase the supply or quality of child care in their communities by providing funds to local care providers. Commonly, a condition for receiving the funds was that the organization's employees be given preferential access to the providers' service.

Sick-Child Care: Some employers have assisted their employees faced with finding care for a sick child, by providing or supporting what is known as "sick-child care." The care can be provided on-site at the organization; off-site by providers such as hospital day care centers; or by in-home services, such as visiting nurses.

Emergency Child Care: Emergency child care programs help employees secure care when regular arrangements fall through or when unexpected events occur, such as when schools are closed due to weather or when employees are required to work holidays or weekends.

School-Age Child Care: School-age child care can address the care needs of children before and after school, or during the summer or holidays when school is not in session. Employers either develop their own programs on-site or support programs in public schools, community centers, or other agencies.

Child Care Consortium with Other Employers: Child care consortiums are collaborative efforts by several employers to provide child care services to their employees with each employer sharing the costs.

Employer Contributions Toward Child Care Costs: Some employers pay a portion of their employees' child care expenses, either directly to the employee or to the child care provider. The payment may be a percentage of the employee's child care expenses or a flat rate.

Child Care Discounts: Some employers arrange a child care fee "discount" for their employees from a child care provider or several providers in exchange for publicizing the providers' programs.

Elder Care: As the American population ages, an increasing number of workers are faced with the need to provide care for their parents, grandparents, or elderly spouses. Between one quarter and one third of a typical company's workers are providing care to an aging relative, according to a recent study. For many elderly people, expensive, round-the-clock care in a nursing home is not necessary. Instead, they need assistance during the day with routine tasks such as shopping, preparing meals, and doing household chores. It is often a care-giving relative who must take time away from work to help with these tasks, resulting in increased absenteeism. Additionally, a care-giving worker must often spend time at work resolving problems of the elderly relative.

Elder care is defined as time off, paid or unpaid, to care for an elderly dependent. It also includes employer-paid or subsidized adult day care. In 1989, 3% of workers in medium and large firms were offered elder care assistance. Flexible work schedules can also be beneficial to care givers. Employers can also establish dependent care reimbursement accounts to help with elder care expenses (Hyland, 1990).

On-Site/Near-Site Day Care: Employers should support day care for the elderly at or near the employee's worksite, either as a separate facility or combined with child care (known as "intergenerational day care").

Elder Care Resource/Referral Services: Resources and referral programs for elder care operate in much the same way as the child care referral programs, providing information to employees about the types of care that can be provided to the elderly and assistance in locating the care they need. A wide range of approaches can be employed. Some organizations develop in-house programs using existing resources in the local community, while others work through outside elder care information providers or consultants.

Long-Term Care Insurance for Employees and Dependents: With the growing number of elderly in the population, the proportion of the elderly needing long-term care is also expected to grow. Long-term care insurance may be offered by an organization to help its employees manage the costs of extended in-house or institutional care for themselves or family members.

Adoption Assistance: Several organizations help employees pay for the costs of adopting a child.

School Match Programs: Organizations can support school match programs that help employees locate educational programs for their children or provide counselors who could help parents find ways to improve their child's school performance.

Dual Career Couple Programs: Some organizations have adopted other programs designed specifically to accommodate the needs of two-career families. For example, "relocation programs provide counseling, reemployment, and other assistance to the "trailing spouse" when an employee is relocated.

Counseling, Training, and Publications Work/Family Issues: Many organizations sponsor counseling to help their employees deal with work/family challenges, such as providing child care and elder care. These support services are usually provided through the organizations' Employees Assistance Programs. Additional ways the organizations educate their employees about work/family issues and available programs include newsletters and booklets, training classes, lunchtime seminars, and video cassettes employees can borrow and view at their homes.

Wooldridge and Wester (1991) found that many local public managers realize the need to adopt family-friendly policies. After surveying all local governments in the Commonwealth of Virginia with a population greater than 25,000, the following responses were recorded:

Strategy	% of respondents who will increase use of this strategy
Flexible work week	79.2
Job sharing	70.8
Sick leave for maternity	58.4
Sick leave for paternity	50.0
Flexible benefits packages	85.4
On-site day care or voucher system	70.9
Unpaid leave for extended care of an ill family member	64.6
Special employees accounts to set aside funds for catastrophic illness	50.2
Elder care leave or voucher	60.4

Job sharing and flexible benefits packages were the two strategies of this group that were ranked of greatest importance. Perhaps these local public managers are in agreement with the writer who said, "Benefits designed for a predominantly male worker in a stable economy are out of sync with the needs of today's worker" (Friedman, 1987).

The mere existence of family-friendly policies is not enough in light of a strange new phenomenon that appears to exist in some organizations. Beauvais and Kowalski (1993) reviewed literature that suggests that most U.S. organizations do very little to help men and women deal effectively with competing work and family demands. Moreover, corporate culture appears to be particularly harsh on men who desire to become actively involved in their family lives" (Beauvais and Kowalski, 1993).

> Demanding work roles, role modeling after one's own father, social attitudes regarding male and female roles, lack of support from wives or peers, lack of skills in the family domain, and *most importantly, cultural and structural barriers in the organization* are cited as major reasons why men do not participate in company programs that are family-oriented (Beauvais and Kowalski, 1993).

If the organization's culture does not support employees' involvement in their family lives, it cannot be expected that people will participate in family-oriented activities despite the promulgation of formal policies and programs on such issues. Public organizations must go beyond the mere establishment of such policies, as desirable as they may be. These organizations must demonstrate a supportive culture that will encourage workers to take advantage of such programs and thus reduce their levels of perceived work/family conflict. As Orr (1991) concludes, "In the long run, employers seem to be recognizing that satisfied employees are more productive ones, and represent a much better bargain than can be purchased through increased recruiting budgets." More public managers need to carry out this type of cost–benefit analysis.

2. Responding to Workplace Illiteracy

"In an increasingly competitive and technology-oriented world, the pool of employees who are qualified—even by historical standards, much less by those of the future—will be shrinking instead of growing" (The Changing Nature of Work, 1992, p. 66). It is well recognized that to meet the needs of the changing workplace employers must make significant investments in human capital—in the training of their employees. They will have to invest heavily in expanded, continuous educational and training programs for all employees.

The following section is summarized from Ayoub (1993). People with reading and writing deficiencies are often too smart for their own good. In fact, "These people develop strong verbal skills and remarkable memories as a means of hiding their inability to read. Many can use words in conversation that they wouldn't recognize on the printed page" (Somers as quoted in Militie, 1991). As illiterate workers become more afraid of being caught, they can develop strong reactions to commonplace office procedures. Many, for example, are extremely distrustful of memos. Illiterate people speak of feeling "scared," "inadequate," and "crippled." They withdraw and remain silent. Many who find themselves in these circumstances cling tightly to the jobs they have in order to avoid completing forms and applying for more challenging positions. Many illiterate employees become skillful at hiding their problems by becoming keen observers and mimicking the behavior they see around them. Fearful of the consequences they are loath to admit they cannot read, write, or compute. Therefore many managers are unaware of illiteracy among their employees (Ford, 1992). "The first thing a manager can do is to seriously consider whether there may be an incidence of the problem in the department or firm. A manager should never assume that everyone under his or her supervision can read and write even minimally (Jurmo, as quoted in Jakubovics, 1986).

Studies conducted by the Society for Human Resource Management have found that successful workplace literacy programs share the following characteristics:

Basic skills training is packaged as part of a broad training agenda that encourages participation.
Employees' personal goals are solicited and included in program planning.
Instructors are aware of the basic skills needed to perform the specific job tasks for which they are providing training.
Program goals and standards for measuring progress are clearly specified; pretests and posttests simulate job situations and tasks.
Learning materials are directly related to the goals.
Feedback is frequent and progress is documented.
Where possible, incentives such as the opportunity to learn new technology are provided to qualify employees for new jobs openings or to meet personal goals.
Training is scheduled wholly or partially on company time to encourage attendance (Pilenzo, 1990).

A survey of the larger local governments in the Commonwealth of Virginia indicates that many public managers are already giving consideration to the strategies they must use to accommodate the work force of the future. Nearly 40% said they plan to increase their use of "incentives for additional study"; 42% anticipated an increase in "redesigning jobs to accommodate low-skilled workers"; and 61% said that they would increase their use of the strategy "restructuring job responsibilities for individual employee skills" (Wooldridge and Wester, 1991).

Pilzeno goes on to say that it is extremely important for the organization to show commitment to the educational program and respect for the employee.

C. Responding to the Aging of the Work Force

The literature records many myths concerning older workers that when analyzed appear unfounded. Below are listed some of the myths relating to the older worker's relationship to technological innovation:

Myth: Older workers are more prone to accidents. Older workers make up about 13.6% of the labor force and account for only 9.7% of the injuries. It does take longer for them to recover than their younger counterparts (Hale, 1990).

Myth: Older workers cannot or do not want to learn new skills. Research on the older workers' desire and ability to learn new skills as summarized by Sawyer (1993) indicates that persons who are capable of learning when they are young and who continue to use their intellectual abilities maintain these abilities in later life (Humple and Lyons, 1983). Furthermore, there is considerable evidence that older people are interested in lifetime learning at quite advanced ages and make excellent students (Shea, 1991). They are trainable and retrainable and continue to develop their vocabularies, powers of judgment, and store of knowledge throughout their lives. Most suffer no marked creative or intellectual decline (Gilsdorf, 1992). There is evidence that they do learn differently from when they where younger. The brain can take longer to store and retrieve data and this can slow down the learning process, but when older workers learn new tasks, they tend to perform them with fewer mistakes than their younger counterparts (Fyock, 1991). "The ability of older adults to learn and benefit from training and education at all points in the life span is increasingly emphasized in the current adult-learning literature" (Sterns, 1987–1988).

"In contrast to the myth about older workers being reluctant to engage in training, the Travelers found in a survey in the late 1980s that 65 percent of retirees queried who had at least typing skills had also expressed an interest in learning to use a computer" (Hale, 1990). According to Karen Quitt, program coordinator for New Directions, funded by the Private Industry Council in Portland, Oregon, one reason for this program's computer training success is that it starts with the very basics. "She says many programs fail in teaching older adults . . . because the instructors assume a skill and knowledge level that just doesn't exist with many adults" (Fyock, 1990).

It does appear true that sometimes the older worker is reluctant to volunteer for or to pursue training opportunities. "This reluctance may be due to feeling of inadequacy about being able to do well in a training program, fear of failure, fear of competition with younger individuals, or the expectation that supervisors would encourage them if they felt it was appropriate" (Sterns, 1987–1988). Also, according to Knowles (1973), older workers may lack confidence in their ability to master a new technology. Therefore "it seems likely that training approaches that integrate mechanisms for building confidence with training content may be superior to training approaches that only focus on training content" (Gist et al., 1988).

Myth: Older workers are inflexible and less creative. A person's ability to handle change is related to how well that person handles stress and this is not age-related. The older worker may tend to be more of a traditionalist and not grab at the new, but this can be a balance in the organization (Sawyer, 1993).

The American Association for Retired Persons (1988) offers several suggestions, or principles, for managing older workers:

1. *Identify the needs of older workers.* To manage workers, managers must first start by understanding their needs. For older employees these often include financial security, social interaction, and making a contribution to others.
2. *Link needs to behavior.* By showing the older worker that job performance is directly related to a satisfaction of a need, the manager is more likely to influence behavior.
3. *Set goals for the older employee.* Counsel the older employee to set measurable, realistic, and attainable goals. Specify how performance will be measured and what performance level is acceptable. Work with the employee in setting time frames for completion and in prioritizing goals.
4. *Ensure that older employees have the means to achieve goals.* If additional training or retraining is needed by the older worker, follow through to ensure that this training is made available.
5. *Reward performance when employees meet their goals.* Provide recognition and rewards that are appropriate given the level of achievement.
6. *Change the nature of work.* Work can become boring and dull over time. Provide the older employee with a change of pace, additional autonomy, or new responsibilities.

Paul and Townsend (1993) suggest some useful consideration for those hiring older workers:

1. *Talk with general counsel.* Relevant portions of legislation should be discussed. Topics should include the ADEA (Age Discrimination in Employment Act) and its subsequent amendments, the Senior Community Service Employment Program of 1973, the Employee Retirement Income Security Act (ERISA), the Job Training Partnership Act of 1982, the Social Security Act and its 1983 amendments, and the Tax Reform and Budget Reconciliation Acts of 1986.
2. *Review the strategic plan.* In particular, the human resource section should be examined.
3. *Reconsider human resource policies.* Accommodating older workers by using flexible benefits, part-time work, flexible work schedules, and incentives for continued employment is desirable.

4. *Give thought to job redesign.* Jobs that require certainty, accuracy, judgment, and reason are more appropriate than those requiring speed, innovation, and creativity.

5. *Provide for career-long training.* Training for older workers involves a program that builds confidence for learning new skills and is adapted to their needs. A nonthreatening environment that does not emphasize speed or compare older workers to younger is best.

6. *Examine benefits plans.* Having a choice is important so that employees may match their specific needs. Insurance, pension credits, vacation days, extended leaves, voluntary demotions, and flexible benefits are alternatives.

7. *Reconsider incentives.* Incentives that appeal to younger workers may not motivate older workers. Recognition of accomplishments, financial rewards, recognitions by peers, and being consulted by management are more appropriate.

8. *Ensure that performance appraisal programs are current.* This step is often forgotten. Performance appraisal data does form the basis for many personnel decisions.

With careful consideration by management of these principles, and with effective training support, a successful integration can be achieved between the older worker and the technology required to improve public sector productivity.

4. Responding to the Needs of Gay, Lesbian, and Bisexual Workers

Sexual orientation—lesbian, gay, bisexual, or straight—is an extremely basic, fundamental, and highly emotional component of every employee's being. It is one of the defining characteristics of personhood (Edgerly, 1992).

Of the many issues facing employers in the 1990s, few will prove as difficult and controversial as the question of homosexual rights. Homosexuality is "far and away the scariest" diversity issue, provoking the most intense discussions because it is about sex and touches on religious beliefs (Simon and Daly, 1992).

In employment, as well as other aspects of life, gay and lesbian persons are in a classic double bind. It is very stressful and demeaning to remain "closeted" i.e., to hide an essential aspect of one's identity. However, it can also be stressful and dangerous to "come out," particularly if there are no civil rights protections of employment rights (Hixson, 1992).

In 1980, the National Gay Task Force distributed a questionnaire that focused exclusively on the experience of lesbians and gay men at work. Sixty-one percent thought that their homosexuality would be a problem at work, if it was known, whereas 32% said they would not have the same job security as heterosexuals. Twenty-six percent said that it was unlikely they would be treated as an equal by heterosexuals, and 23% of the respondents said they might lose customers or clients. Twenty-one percent indicated that they had actually experienced discrimination because of their sexual orientation (National Gay Task Force, 1981).

Levine and Leonard (1984) surveyed 203 women to explore in depth the factors affecting employment discrimination against lesbians. To shield themselves from possible discrimination, most women in the study reported that they stayed closeted; only 23% informed most or all work associates. Seventy-seven percent were partially or totally closeted on the job; 29% told some friends, 21% told only close friends, and 27% told no one at all.

Such caution appears justified. In the same article, the authors sample and average the findings of studies that surveyed the extent of anticipated employment discrimination and the extent of actual employment discrimination experienced by lesbians. "Thirty-one percent of the lesbians surveyed anticipated employment discrimination because of sexual orientation, and 13 percent had actually experienced it; 8 percent of the women had lost or had almost lost their jobs because they were lesbians. The only comparable estimates for gay men reveal that 29 percent of all gay male workers have had their careers negatively influenced by their sexual orientation" (Levine and Leonard, 1984).

Such anxiety makes gay and lesbian employees less productive. Brian McNaught (as quoted in Stewart, 1991) says, "My basic premise is that homophobia takes a toll on the ability of 10% of the workforce to produce."

The following implications for public managers are summarized from Sawyer (1993). The overwhelming research on sexual orientation issues in the workplace indicates that the biggest area of concern is discrimination. The manager is responsible for assuring a climate that is accepting of all workers. Research indicates that gay men and lesbians experience higher job satisfaction when they are able to come out of the closet. They are more likely to do this when they do not fear discrimination or negative social consequences. Public managers must be sensitive to diverse lifestyles, allow friends or partners to replace spouses at business and social functions, and let it be known that jokes and negative remarks about any lifestyle are not acceptable in the workplace. Gay men and lesbian women highly value their careers and management needs to respond by providing opportunities for advancement and career planning. Every effort should be made to break the "glass ceiling" that is experienced by gays and lesbians, as well as other social minorities. Training of all employees in issues of sexual preference must become a major element of all organizational human development efforts. For example, in West Hollywood, California's new employee orientation classes, nondiscrimination is one of the topics for discussion. Included in these classes is treatment of the subject of sexual orientation (Edgerly, 1992). Findings from research suggest that exposure to and interaction with homosexuals results in self-reported reduction in discomfort with homosexuals (Lance, 1987).

Managers must be sensitive to the possibility that gay men may have partners who are suffering or dying from AIDS. They may bring the suffering they are experiencing to the workplace and must receive the same degree of compassion that other workers would receive in similar circumstances. AIDS education should be available to all employees so that unfounded fears do not emerge if an employee is diagnosed as having AIDS.

The assistant city manager of West Hollywood, California describes the prerequisites of an effective gay/lesbian/bisexual integration program as follows:

> It appears that to be successful, a workforce integration plan must enjoy strong leadership, and consists of multiple elements, including a non-ambiguous non-discrimination policy, recognition and support of domestic partnership, and on-going identification and solving of the problems which most impact employees with differing sexual orientations (Edgerly, 1992).

5. Responding to the Increase Number of Workers with Disabilities

There are disabled people successfully employed at almost all professional levels in nearly every field. However, for people with disabilities to be integrated effectively into the work force, managers must overcome their belief in many myths associated with their hiring (McDonough, 1992). Below are some myths and misconceptions managers sometimes have regarding the hiring or retraining of otherwise "qualified" people with disabilities (Lester and Caudill, 1987).

Myth One: People with disabilities have a high turnover rate. The disabled have been shown statistically to be extremely dependable workers. As a group, research shows that the handicapped have an absenteeism rate well below that of the average worker. They have nearly five times lower turnover rates than nondisabled workers.

Myth Two: They are less productive. Again, current research does not support this assertion. Nearly one-fourth of workers with disabilities have better performance records than their nondisabled coworkers, while nearly two-thirds have at least the same.

Myth Three: They are a greater safety risk. Research indicates that 98% of workers with disabilities have better or similar accident records as nondisabled workers. Only 2% have worse.

Myth Four: Accommodating the disabled worker will be too costly. According to the Job Accommodation Network, a service of the President's Committee on Employment of People with Disabilities, 50% of all workplace accommodations cost less than $50 and 30% cost nothing.

Myth Five: They are too demanding. Studies reveal that the problem may not be demanding employees but an intolerance on the part of a few employees. Research suggests that the greatest majority of negative attitudes in this category stems not from aggressive workers with disabilities but from highly authoritarian supervisors. In reality, workers with disabilities make no more demands than their nondisabled counterparts. The worker with a disability is likely to be more satisfied, more customer-oriented, and more perceptive.

Myth Six: They would be an embarrassment to the organization. Systematic examinations in the last several years have clearly indicated that most individuals having direct contact with people with disabilities have relatively favorable perceptions. Moreover, studies show that when evaluated in peer groups, workers with disabilities are not evaluated differently from their nondisabled coworkers.

Myth Seven: Insurance rates will skyrocket. Studies tend not to support this belief. A U.S. Chamber of Commerce survey of 279 companies revealed that 90% of the respondents did not incur additional insurance costs.

Increasingly, organizations are recognizing that in order to have the skills and talents they need, they must pay more attention to individual needs (Povall, 1988). Gluskinos and Popper (1991) point out that the extent of disability may be quite independent of the individual's contribution to the organization. As with all employees, supervisors must obtain accurate information about what workers with disabilities can and cannot do, discover what special adaptive equipment would increase their capabilities, reshape job structures to allow them to make a greater contribution, and look beyond the first impression of being disabled or impaired (Navran and Sibula, 1991).

In identifying appropriate jobs for workers with disabilities, the supervisor's responsibility is to learn how the worker may be matched with appropriate job responsibilities. The key here is to evaluate each specific disability rather than making a blanket evaluation of all workers with disabilities across the board. Every worker has a unique array of qualities; managers should think of a worker's disabilities in the same way. Some workers may have a disability, but generally it is the environment that turns the disability into a handicap (Pati and Stubblefield, 1990).

Supervisors are responsible for setting performance standards, which sometimes means frank, candid, and difficult conversations with all employees regardless of their level of disability (Navran and Sibula, 1991).

Many organizations fear that new technology will be a barrier to employment of the disabled. However, the use of appropriate technology can also be a major strategy for the successful integration of people with disabilities into the work force. Much of the hope for the integration of people with disabilities into the general work force is riding on personal computers, which can be equipped with hundreds of adaptive devices and specialized software (Betts and Bozman, 1991). Less than $100 can buy a specialized keyboard or input pen for a disabled person. For just $50 more, organizations can purchase text-to-speech software for IBM-compatible PCs. Several studies conclude that 80% of all accommodations for people with disabilities cost less than $500 each. In addition, to help ease the costs to private businesses, the U.S. government is offering tax incentives to companies that are willing to make physical and technological accommodations (Marenghi, 1991). Excellent work on the use of technology to integrate workers with disabilities is being done by the Clearinghouse on Computer Accommodation (COCA) at the U.S. General Services Administration.

Obviously all public managers must become intimately familiar with the provisions of the Americans with Disabilities Act (ADA). The ADA is the most comprehensive piece of legislation affecting the workplace and the employer in 30 years (an excellent discussion of the ADA and especially its requirements for "reasonable accommodation" can be found in McDevitt, 1993). Under the ADA an organization cannot discriminate against anyone who can perform the essential functions of a job. The employer must make a reasonable accommodation for a disability as long as such acting does not cause the organization undue hardship. The antidiscrimination focus of the ADA extends beyond the hiring process to promotions, firings, job training, compensation, and all other conditions of employment (Laplante, 1992). Finally, however, the key to supervising nondisabled and disabled workers is to treat them with dignity (Navran and Sibula, 1991).

6. Responding to the Challenge of Work Force Diversity

This chapter has identified and discussed several of the major demographic trends that could have implications for the public manager. These trends include the increasing number of women, blacks, Hispanics, and Asian-Americans in the work force; the aging of the work force; increasing importance of workplace illiteracy; HIV and AIDS; substance abuse; and the increased number of workers with disabilities and with different sexual orientations. However, these are not the only elements that compose the diverse work force of the future. The increase of the "knowledge" workers, ideological diversity, ethnic diversity other than Hispanic and Asian-American, the diversity of employees from different regions, religious diversity, and employees with different work-related values are some other factors that the astute public manager must consider. Such diversity brings mixed blessings to an organization. Hernandez (1992) compared the organizational communication literature that suggests that heterogeneous (diverse) work groups have dysfunctional impact on communication which negatively effects creativity with the research that identifies higher organizational creativity associated with greater work group diversity. Tsui et al. (1992) do an excellent job of reviewing the available literature on this issue. They point out that there is evidence the diverse work groups are beneficial for tasks requiring creativity and judgment (Jackson, 1991) but also evidence that homogeneous groups are more likely to be socially integrated and experience higher satisfaction and lower turnover (O'Reilly et al., 1989). In a recent study of the interaction process and performance of culturally homogeneous and culturally diverse groups, researchers found that the homogeneous groups scored higher on both process and performance effectiveness initially.

While this chapter has focused on the impact of diversity on the "social minorities" identified, the Tsui et al. (1992) article reviews relevant literature discussing the possible impact of increased diversity on the previously dominant majority (in most instances white males). "There is evidence to suggest that the reactions of the numerical majority may not be equivalent to that of the minority, however, when members traditionally in the majority are in the minority position" (p. 558). Tsui et al. (1992) report research suggesting that women in predominantly male jobs were treated with hostility by male coworkers whereas men in predominantly female jobs experienced almost no hostility from female coworkers. Furthermore, token women were isolated whereas token men appeared to be socially well integrated into the female work group. "All else being equal, men in balanced settings and in settings containing a small proportion of women are significantly less satisfied than women in these settings" (Wharton and Baron, 1989). Research has also indicated that being in heterogeneous work groups leads to a slower level of organizational attachment for men as compared to women, and for whites as compared with minorities. While some authors indicate that race relations will improve as the proportion of minorities increases (Blau, 1977;

Kanter, 1977), others argue that discrimination by the majority will increase as the proportion of the minority increases (Blalock, 1957).

Moreover, not all demographic characteristics are equal. Research (Cummings, et al., 1993) suggests that those demographic characteristics that are more visible (e.g., gender, race) produce more negative relationships than those that are less visible (tenure on the job, age within some limits, religion).

How does an organization create a situation where the functional consequences of work force diversity are manifested instead of the dysfunctional? One suggestion is to look at the organizational culture. Chatman et al. (1993) concluded that in organizations that were characterized by the collective dimension of Hofstede's individualistic-collective dimension of culture (Hofstede, 1982) heterogeneous work groups performed better in terms of creativity, having beneficial conflict, degree of interaction and participation, and timeliness of task completion. Whereas in individualistic organizations such groups did not perform as well as homogeneous work groups. Hernandez (1992) reports that one characteristic of organizations that maximize the potential of their diverse work force is the presence of effective "valuing-diversity" programs. Such programs in the private sector are described in Jackson (1992) and Thomas (1991) and in the federal government in the papers presented at the recent Merit System Protection Board's Symposium on Diversity in the Federal Government (1992). An excellent description of a methodology for establishing Valuing-Diversity efforts can be found in Thomas's *Beyond Race and Gender*, a must reading for today's public managers.

A diverse work force is part of each public manager's present and future, and it will not go away. Public managers must make it a priority to create the kind of environment that will attract the best talent and make it possible for each employee to make his or her fullest contribution (Thomas, 1991). Whether the increased diversity of the work force leads to lower organizational performance, stress, lower commitment, and job satisfaction or to creative, effective, organizations with high performance and morale will depend largely on the skills of the public manager.

ACKNOWLEDGMENT

The authors thank their five colleagues in the Master of Public Administration program at Virginia Commonwealth University—Suha Ayoub, Bolman Bowles, Rosalyn Dance, Mary Sawyer, and Julia Walker—who participated during the Spring Semester, 1993 in PAD 691, "Special Topics: Work Force 2000: Creating Effective Organizations for the 21st Century." Many of the statistics and much of the research presented here were first identified by these participants.

REFERENCES

Amaro, Hortensia, Russo, Nancy, and Johnson, Julie (December 1987): Family and work predictors of psychological well-being among Hispanic women, professional," *Psychol. Women Q., 11*: 505–521.

American Society for Public Administration, National Capital Area Chapter (1992): *Breaking Through the Glass Ceiling: A Career Guide for Women in Government*, Washington, DC.

Arbona, Consuelo (March 1989): Hispanic employment and the Holland typology of work, *Career Dev. Q., 37*: 257–268.

Arbona, Consuelo (April 1990). Special populations forum: career counseling research and hispanics, *The Counseling Psychologist*, 18: 300–323.

Ayoub, Suha (1993): Managing illiteracy in the workplace, paper presented as partial fulfillment of requirements for PAD 691 special topics: Workforce 2000—creating effective organizations in the 21st century, Department of Public Administration, Virginia Commonwealth University, Richmond, Spring Semester.

Baskerville, Dawn, Hilliard, Sheryl, and Whittingham-Barnes, Donna, (August 1991): Women of power and influence in corporate America: black enterprise reveals the hottest African American female corporate executives, *Black Enterprise, 22*: 39.

Beauvas, Laura L., and Kowalski, Kellyann Berube (1993): Predicting work/family conflicts and participation in family-supportive work behaviors: a competing test of two theories, paper presented at the annual conference of the Academy of Management, Atlanta, GA, August.

Beilinson, Jerry (October 1990): Workforce 2000: already here? *Personnel, 67*:3–4.

Beilinson, Jerry (January 1991): Are EAP's the answer? *Personnel, 68*: 3–4.

Bell, Brenda (September 1991): Illiteracy: it's cheaper to train them, *Supervis. Manage., 36*: 4–5.

Betts, Mitch, and Bozman, Jean S (November 1991): Ready, willing and able? *Computerworld, 25*: 63–64.

Blalock, Hubert, M., Jr. (1957): Percent non-white and discrimination in the south, *Am. Sociol. Rev., 22*: 677–682.

Blau, Peter M. (1977): *Inequality and Heterogeneity*, Free Press, New York.

Bruening, John (October 1989): Workplace illiteracy: the threat to worker safety, *Occ. Hazards, 51*: 118–122.

Buhler, Patricia (June 1991): Hiring the disabled: the solution to our problem, *Supervision, 52*: 17–19.

Celis, William (1993): Study says half of adults in U.S. can't read or handle arithmetic, *New York Times*, Sept. 9.

Chatman, Jennifer A., Barsade, Sigal M., Potzer, Jeffrey T., and Neale, Margaret A. (1993): The influence of team diversity and organizational culture on decision making processes and outcomes, paper presented at the annual meeting of the Academy of Management, Atlanta, GA.

Cummings, Anne, Zhou, Jing and Oldham, Greg R. (1993): Demographic differences and employee work outcomes: effects of multiple comparative groups, paper presented at the annual meeting of the Academy of Management, Atlanta, GA.

Cox, Taylor, and Nkomo, Sheila (Nov. 1990): Invisible men and women: a status report on race as a variable in organizational behavior research, *J. Organiz. Behav., 11* (6): 419–431.

Dance, Rosalyn, A. (April 1993): African American women: how do they rate as managers, paper presented as partial fulfillment of requirements for PAD 691 Special Topics: Workforce 2000: creating effective organizations in the 21st century, Department of Public Administration, Virginia Commonwealth University, Richmond, Spring.

Doherty, Kathleen (January 1990): Parental leave: strategies for the 1990's, *Business and Health, 8*: 21–23.

Dunnett, Marvin, D., ed. (1976): *Handbook of Industrial and Organizational Psychology*, Rand McNally, Chicago.

Edgerly, Robert (April 1992): Diversity in the public workplace: integrating employee sexual orientation into a city's multi-cultural mix, paper presented at the Annual Conference of the American Society for Public Administration, Chicago.

Fagenson, Ellen (March–June, 1986): Women's work orientations: something old, something new, *Group Organiz. Studies, 24*: 76–77.

Feldman, Stuart (October 1991): Corporate America makes education its business, *Manage. Rev., 80*: 10–16.

Fernandez, John (1991): *Managing a Diverse Work Force*, Lexington Books, Lexington, MA.

Ford, Donald (November 1992): Toward a more literate workforce, *Train. Dev., 46*: 52–55.

Frideger Marcia A. (August 1992): The effect of accent on hiring decisions: human resource implications, paper presented at the Academy of Management Meeting, Las Vegas.

Friedman, Dana (August 1987): Work vs. family: war of the worlds, *Personnel Admin., 32*: 36–38.

Fullerton, Howard N., Jr. (November 1991): Labor force projections: the baby boom moves on, *Monthly Labor Rev., 114*: 31–44.

Fyock, Catherine, B. (1991): *American Workforce Is Coming of Age*, Lexington Books, Lexington, MA.

General Accounting Office. (March 1992): The changing workforce: demographic issues facing the federal government, a report to the congressional committees, U.S. Government Printing Office, Washington, DC.

Gilsdorf, J. W. (March 1992): The new generation: older workers, *Train. Dev.*

Gist, Brocades, et. al, (1988): Anglo-Scandinavian Conference on Sexually Transmitted Diseases, Royal Society of Medicine Services, vii, 120.

Gluskinos, Uri M., and Popper, Micha (1991): Towards reconceptionalization: the contribution of disabled at the workplace, *Personnel Rev.*, Vol. 27. 11–15.

Goddard, Robert (February 1989): "Workforce 2000, *Personnel J., 68*: 64–71.

Griffin, Betsy Q. (March 1992): Perceptions of managers: effects of leadership style and gender, paper presented at the Annual Meeting of the Southeastern Psychological Association.

Guy, Mary E. (April 1992): Three steps forward, two steps backward: the status of women's integration into public management, paper presented at the American Society for Public Administration Annual Conference, Chicago.

Hale, Noreen (1990): The Older Worker: Effective Strategies for Management and Human Resource Development, Jossey-Bass, San Francisco.

"Hands On" (November 1992): *Inc., 14*: 33.

Harris, Michael and Heft, Laura (1992): Alcohol and drug use in the workplace: issues, controversies, and directions for future research, *J. Manage., 18*(2): 239–266.

Hernandez, Edward (August 1992): The unclear role of workplace diversity on group level creativity, paper presented at the Academy of Management Meeting, Las Vegas.

Hixson, Emma (April 1992): Employee sexual preference: a lesson in managing diversity, paper presented at the annual conference of the American Society for Public Administration, Chicago.

Hofstede, Geert (1980): *Culture's consequences: international differences in work related values*, Sage, Beverly Hills.

Humple, Carol S., and Lyons, Morgan (1983): *Management and the Older Workforce: Policies and Programs*. American Management Association, New York.

Hyland, Stephanie (September 1990): Helping employees with family care, *Monthly Labor Rev., 113*: 22–26.

Jackson, Susan E. (1991): Team composition in organizational settings: issues in managing an increasingly diverse workforce, *Group Process and Productivity*, (S. Worchel, W. Wood, and J. Simpson, eds.), Beverly Hills, pp. 138–173.

Jackson, Susan E., and Associates (1992): *Diversity in the Workplace: Human Resources Initiatives*, Guilford Press, New York.

Jakubovics, Jerry (1986): Coping with illiteracy in the workplace, *Mgmt Solutions, 31*: 4–11.

Johnston, William (1987): *Workforce 2000: Work and Workers for the 21st Century*, Hudson Institute, Indianapolis, IN.

Johnston, William, and Hopkins, Kevin (1988): *Civil Service 2000*, a report prepared for the U.S. Office of Personnel Management, Career Entry Group, U.S. Government Printing Office, Washington, DC.

Kanter, Rosabeth M. (1977): *Men and Women of the Corporation*, Basic Books, New York.

Kelly, Joan (September 1992): The rising tide of older workers, *Nation's Business, 80*: 33–36.

Kutscher, Ronald E. (November 1991): New BLS projections: findings and implications, *Monthly Labor Rev., 114*: 3–12.

Lance, Larry, M. (1987): The effects of interaction with gay persons on attitudes towards homosexuality, *Human Relations, 40* (6): 329–336.

Laplante, Alice (1992): Attitudes still a barrier for the disabled, *Computerworld, 16*: 24–28.

Lee, Chris (April 1992): Miracle cures, *Training, 29*: 8.

Leong, Frederick (November 1985): Career development of Asian Americans, *J. College Student Personnel, 22*: 540–548.

Leong, Frederick (March 1991): Culture-specific and culture-comparative approaches: career development attributes and occupational values of Asian American and white American college students, *Career Dev. Q., 19*: 200–16.

Lester, Rick, A., and Caudill, Donald (August 1987): The handicapped workers: seven myths, *Training Dev. J.*

Levitan, Sam, and Taggart, Robert (1977): *Jobs for the Disabled*, Johns Hopkins University Press, Baltimore.

Lewis, Gregory (Winter 1992): Men and women toward the top: backgrounds, careers, and potential of federal middle managers, *Public Personnel Manage., 21*: 473–491.

Loden, Marilyn, and Loeser, Ronnie Hoffman (Spring 1991): Working diversity: managing the differences, *The Bureaucrat, 20*: 21–25.

Loveman, Gary W., and Gabarro, John (Spring 1991): The managerial implications of changing work force demographics: a scoping study, *Human Resource Manage., 30*: 7–29.

Marenghi, Catherine (November 1991): Dispelling cost myths about technologies for the disabled, *Computerworld, 25*: 66–67.

Marvis, Phillip H., and Kanter, Donald L. (Spring 1992): Beyond demography: a psychographic profile of the workforce, *Human Resource Manage., 30* (1): 45–68.

McDevitt, William J. (July 1993): Accommodating individuals with disabilities in the workplace: the challenge for public administrators, paper presented at the Annual Conference of the American Society for Public Administration, San Francisco. Available from ASPA, Washington, DC.

McDonough, Hugh H. (February 1992): Hiring people with disabilities, *Superv. Manage., 37*: 11–12.

National Gay Task Force (1981): *Employment Discrimination in New York City: A Survey of Gay Men and Women*, New York.

Navran, Frank J., and Sibula, Penny (November 1991): Managing the disabled employee, *Transport. Distr., 32*: 47–48.

Newsweek (1993): Dumber than we though, Sept. 20, 1993, 44–45.

Noah, Timothy (1991): U.S. population grew less white in the 1980's as Hispanics, Asians boosted presence, *The Wall Street Journal*, June 12, A6.

O'Carolan, Tarl (August 1987): Parenting time: whose problem is it?" *Personnel Admin., 32*: 58–63.

O'Reilly, Charles A. III, Caldwell, David F., and Barnett, William P. (1989): Work groups demography, social integration, and turnover, *Admin. Sci. Q., 34*: 21–37.

Orr, Elaine L. (Fall 1991): Policies for the family-friendly workplace, *The Bureaucrat*, 5–8.

Pati, Gopal C., and Stubblefield, Guy (December 1990): The disabled are able to work, *Personnel J.*

Paul, Robert J., and Townsend, James B. (August 1993): Managing the older worker—don't just rinse away the gray, *Academy of Management Executive, 7*(3): 67–74.

Perrin, Towers and the Hudson Institute (1990): *Workforce 2000: Competing in a Seller's Market*, Towers Perrin, New York.

Petrini, Cathy (February 1989): How do you manage a diverse workforce, *Train. Dev.* 43: 13–21.

Pilenzo, Ronald (November 1990): Why literacy is everybody's business, *Modern Office Technol., 35*: 82.

Pope, Tom (August 1990): EAP's: good idea, but what's the cost, *Manage. Rev., 79*: 50–53.

Povall, Margery, et al. (December 1988): Personnel's role in managing disability, *Personnel Manage., 20*: 42–47.

Pressley, Sue Anne (August 1991): Re-entering the world of work, *Washington Post*, WF 13.

Price, Joan (May 1989): With action and compassion, managers fight illiteracy, *Savings Inst., 110*: 52–54.

Ramirez, Anthony (January 30, 1989): Making better use of older workers, *Fortune, 119*: 179–180.

Richmond News Leader (1989): Solving the child care dilemma, May 29, A13.

Rosen, R., and T. H. Jerdee (1988): *Managing Older Workers' Careers*, JAI Press, Greenwich, CT.

Rosener, Judy B. (Nov./Dec. 1990): Ways women lead, *Harvard Business Rev., 68*(6): 119–125.

Rubaii-Barrett, Nadia, Beck, Ann and Lillibridge (1991): Minorities in the majority: implications for managing cultural diversity, *Public Personnel Mgmt, 22*: 503–21.

Sawyer, Mary F. (1993): Workforce 2000: sexual orientation, paper presented in partial fulfillment of course requirements for PAD 691, Special Topics: Workforce 2000: Creating Effective Organizations for the 21st Century, Department of Public Administration, Virginia Commonwealth University, Spring.

Schmidt, Veronica, and Scott, Norman (August 1987): Work and family life: a delicate balance, *Personnel Admin., 32*: 40–46.

Segal, Jonathan A. (June 1991): Women on the verge of . . . Equality, *HR Magazine, 36*(6): 117–123.

Shapiro, Joseph, Cook, Gareth G., and Krackov, Andrew (1993): Straight talk about gays, *U.S. News and World Report*, July 5.

Shea, Gordon F. (1991): *Managing Older Employees*, Jossey-Bass, San Francisco.

Simon, Howard A., and Daly, Erin (Summer 1992): Sexual orientation and workplace rights: a potential land mine for employers? *Employee Relations Law J., 1*(1).

Sisneros, Antonio (February 1991): Hispanics in the public service in the late 20th century, Annual Conference of Minority Public Administrators, Baton Rouge, LA.

Slack, James D. (1991): *AIDS and the Public Work Force: Local Government Preparedness in Managing the Epidemic*, University of Alabama Press.

Smith, Donald (August 1990): "Executives and illiteracy: a bias for action?" *Training, 27*: 13–14.

Solomon, Charlene Marmer (August 1989): The corporate response to work force diversity, *Personnel J., 68*: 42–53.

Spargins, Ellyn (November 1992): Tapping workers with disabilities, *Inc., 14*: 22.

Special report: new incentives for a changing work force (January 1990): *Business and Health.*

Staffing Digest (1991): MSPB calls for more action on the work and family front, Office of Personnel Management, Washington, DC.

Steers, Richard M. (1978): *Organizational Effectiveness: A Behavioral View*, Goodyear, Santa Monica.

Stein, Robert (June 1991): A new "bill of rights" for millions: the Americans with Disabilities Act of 1990, *Arbitration J., 46*: 6–9.

Stewart, Thomas (1991): Gay in corporate America, *Fortune, 124*: 42–46.

Stodghill, Ron, II. (1993): Managing AIDS, *Business Week*, Feb. 1, 48–54.

Stoner, Charles and Hartman, Richard (May–June 1990): Family responsibilities and career progress: the good, the bad, and the ugly, *Business Horizons, 33*: 7–14.

Sue, Stanley, and Wagner (1973): Asian Americans: Psychological perspectives, Science and Behavior Books.

Swerdlin, Marcy (January 1990): Child care: why bosses are becoming babysitters, *Business and Health, 8*: 26.

Thomas, R. Roosevelt Jr. (1991): *Beyond Race and Gender: Unleashing the Power of Your Total Workforce by Managing Diversity*, AMACOM, New York.

Tsui, Anne S., and Egan, Terri D. (August, 1992). Communication and conflict: the impact of ethnic and gender diversity in management teams, paper presented at the Academy of Management Meeting, Las Vegas.

Tsui, Anne S., Egan, Terri D., and O'Reilly, Charles A. III (1992): Being different: relational demography and organizational attachment, *Admin. Sci. Q., 37*: 549–579.

Tysee, G. John (1991): *The Legislative History of the Americans with Disabilities Act*, LRD, Pennsylvania.

U.S. Commission on Civil Rights (1992): *Civil Rights Issues Facing Asian Americans in the 1990's*, U.S. Government Printing Office, Washington, DC.

Waldrop, Judith (January 1991): You'll know it's the 21st century when... *Public Manage., 73*: 2–6.

Waldrop, Judith (March 1991): The cost of hiring the disabled, *Am. Demographics, 13*: 12.

Watson, Warren E., Kuman, Kamalesh, and Michaelsen, Larry K. (June 1993): Cultural diversity's impace on interaction process and performance: comparing homogeneous and diverse task groups, *Acad. Manage. J., 36*(3): 590–602.

Wharton, Amy S., and Baron, James N. (1989): Satisfaction? The psychological impact of gender segregation on women at work, paper presented at the annual meeting of the American Sociological Association.

White, Michael (Nov.–Dec. 1991): Linking compensation to knowledge will pay off in the 1990's, *Plann. Rev., 19*: 15–17.

Wider Opportunities for Women (May 1989): *Work and Child Care*. Washington, DC.

Wooldridge, Blue, Smith-Mason, Jackie, and Clark-Maddox, Barbara (July 1993): Changing demographics of the workforce: implications for research in human resource management, paper presented at the Annual National Conference of the American Society for Public Administration, San Francisco.

Wooldridge, Blue, and Wester, Jennifer (Summer 1991): The turbulent environment of public personnel administration: responding to the challenge of the changing workplace of the twenty-first century, *Public Personnel Manage., 20*(2): 207–224.

Yaffe, Jerry (Summer 1992): Workforce literacy in the local public sector, *Public Personnel Manage.*, *21*: 227–260.

Yuker, Harold E. (1988): *Attitudes Towards Persons with Disabilities*, Springer, New York.

SUGGESTED READING

Barth, Michael, and McNaught, William (Spring 1991): The impact of future demographic shifts on the employment of older workers, *Human Resource Manage.*, *30*: 31–44.

Carlson, Bradley R. (April 1992): The economics of Massachusetts' sexual orientation anti-discrimination statute: an analytic framework for estimating costs to employers, paper presented at the American Society for Public Administration Conference.

Coates, Joseph, Jarratt, Jennifer, and Mahaffie, John (May–June 1991): Future work: seven critical forces reshaping work and the work force in North America. *The Futurist, 25*: 9–19.

Cohen, Julie A. (January 1991): Managing tomorrow's workforce today, *Manage. Rev.*, *80*: 17–21.

Copeland, Lennie (May 1988): Learning to manage a multicultural workforce, *Training, 25*: 48–49.

Crispell, Diane (March 1990): Worker's in 2000, *Am. Demographics, 12*: 36–40.

Miller, William (1991): A new perspective for tomorrow's workforce, *Industry Week, 240*: May 6, 6–11.

Nelton, Sharon (July 1988): Meet your new work force, *Nation's Business, 76*: 16.

10

Human Resource Planning

JAMES LEDVINKA   University of Georgia, Athens, Georgia

This chapter presents a simple definition of human resource planning and presents a basic two-step model that follows from that definition, using as an example the federal government's planning for enforcement of the Occupational Safety and Health Act. The discussion explains how the first of the basic model's two steps involves strategic human resource planning; the second involves operational human resource planning. Also, the first step includes forecasting the organization's demand for labor, whereas the second includes forecasting the organization's labor supply. However, the basic model oversimplifies the task of human resource planning. The chapter, therefore, expands the basic model to incorporate three planning steps that organizations take to manage complications. Finally, the chapter discusses some basic considerations in establishing a human resource forecasting system to support the organization's planning activities.

I. DEFINITION AND MODEL

Human resource planning is *the process of devising methods for managing people*. Those methods include job design, performance appraisal, recruitment and selection of new employees, promotion and transfer of existing employees, training, compensation, and supervision. A synonym for "method" is *means*, and "managing" is the use of resources to accomplish some *end*. In other words, human resource management is the process by which an organization attempts to match means (methods for managing people) with ends.

As an example of human resource planning, this chapter considers the Occupational Safety and Health Act of 1970 (OSHA), a federal statute regulating worker safety and health in the private sector. This statute provided an occasion for human resource planning by creating the Occupational Safety and Health Administration (OSHA) and giving it a legislative purpose. That legislative purpose required human resources. That suggests that human resource planning involves the answers to the following questions:

1. *What are the organization's purposes?* For example, one purpose of OSHA is stated in Section 6(b)(5) of the Act, which concerns toxic materials in the workplace: "no employee will suffer material impairment of health or functional capacity even if such employee has regular exposure to the hazard . . . for the period of his working life." This congressional statement provides a criterion for evaluating the organization. Since OSHA applies to virtually all

organization's purposes	1 →	human resource objectives	2 →	management actions
no material impairment even with regular exposure to the hazard for entire working life		1000 health standard compliance officers		external recruiting

Figure 1   Basic model of human resource planning.

private employment, OSHA's mission is to ensure that no private sector worker will be significantly harmed by toxic materials on the job.

2. *What human resources would accomplish those purposes?* To provide the human resources sufficient to accomplish that mission, OSHA put together an initial staffing plan that called for the agency to hire 1000 health standard compliance officers.

3. *What management actions would produce those human resources?* The agency's initial plan was to acquire its health standard compliance officers through recruitment in the external labor force of industrial hygienists.

Those questions suggest a very basic model of human resource planning, shown in Fig. 1. The following discussion explains the two steps shown by the arrows connecting the three components of the model. The first step links purposes with human resources; the second links human resources with management actions. Briefly, step 1 is the process of *determining a configuration of human resources that would enable the organization to achieve its purposes*, and step 2 is the process of *devising a set of management actions to bring about that configuration*.

II.   IMPLICATIONS OF THE BASIC MODEL

A.   Strategic and Operational Management

The two steps divide the basic model into *strategic* human resource management and *operational* human resource management. Step 1 concerns the organization's *strategy*, which is its *methods for meeting its long-range goals*. Here, long-range goals means purposes. Step 2 concerns the organization's *operations*, which are its *processes for implementing its strategy on a day-to-day basis*.

More precisely, strategic and operational management form a means–ends continuum: at one end of the continuum are the goals that represent the organization's highest ends; next are the strategies used to achieve those goals; next are the major policies that provide general guidelines on how the organization expects its management to behave when implementing strategy; next are the procedures designed to implement those policies; and so on. Strategic management is about the ends side of that continuum—goals, strategies, and major policies—while operational management is about the opposite end of the continuum, the means side. Clearly, attainment of the ends is deeper into the future than development of the means; thus, strategic management is more long range in its orientation than is operational management.

Step 1: Strategic Human Resource Management

In a profit-making organization, strategy involves such issues as what lines of business the organization should enter, how to compete in those businesses, and how to manage its functional departments productively (Andrews, 1971; Mintzberg, 1976; Milkovich et al., 1983). For a government agency, strategy involves such issues as how to accomplish the agency's legislative missions. Strategy can emerge either from legislative oversight or from executive action. OSHA's decision to add 1000 health standard compliance officers to its staff was a strategic decision; it represented the agency's means for achieving the purpose established by Congress.

Step 1, then, constitutes strategic human resource planning. Here the main task is to ensure consistency between the organization's strategy and its human resource management, so that the objectives of the strategic plan are feasible and management ensures adequate human resources to attain those objectives. In other words, step 1 establishes the human resource means by which the organization meets its long-range goals. As the OSHA example suggests, step 1 includes establishing the staffing levels and competencies necessary to attain the organization's purposes. Through step 1, the human resource planner attempts to ensure that strategy implementation is not frustrated by failure to identify the human resources necessary for that strategy.

Human resource management often neglects strategy. Instead of designing human resource policies and programs to further the organization's overall mission, organizations often manage human resources reactively in response to demands and forces that seem beyond control. Strategic human resource management is more proactive; it regards human resource policy as a means to further the organization's purposes. The basic model above gives human resource planning a strategic dimension by explicitly connecting human resource management and organizational purpose. In that respect, the basic model resembles Walker's (1992) model of strategic realignment and Napier's (1988) model of human resource management linkages.

The basic model, then, is normative. It is a model of what human resource management ought to be, not necessarily what human resource management is. The basic model warns us that when human resource management neglects mission, it becomes a purposeless accumulation of meetings, documents, programs, and policies. When that happens, the three components of the model turn into pitfalls, points at which human resource management becomes separated from organizational purpose. For example, beginning at the right side of the model, the organization may take "management actions" (e.g., hiring, promotion, training) not because those actions will give it certain human resources but because they seem to be dictated by power, custom, perceived legal constraints, or various forms of bureaucratic inertia. Further, the organization may set certain human resource objectives not because they would facilitate stated organizational purposes but because there is room for them in the budget or because an important constituency calls for their employment. Finally, the organization may fail to clarify its purposes, leaving human resource management with no aim to guide it. In short, one or more of the three components of the model can be missing, even though each is critical to effective human resource planning.

Step 2: Operational Human Resource Management

Operations involve the details of translating strategy into action, including decisions about how to attain the staffing levels established as part of strategic planning. OSHA's decision to use external recruiting to attain the staffing level of 1000 health standard compliance officers was an operational human resource management decision. In some cases that kind of decision may be a strategic one, as when an organization decides to use external staffing as part of a broad strategy for infusing the organization with new ideas. In OSHA's case, however, the decision to staff externally was not a point of strategy in and of itself; it was simply the means chosen to implement a strategy that called for a certain staffing level.

Step 2 of the basic model constitutes operational human resource management. Here the main task is to ensure that human resource programs will allow the organization to have adequate human resources. A definition of operational human resource planning to parallel the definition of strategic human resource planning above might be *determining how to provide sufficient human resources*. Through step 2, the human resource planner attempts to ensure that the human resource programs are in place to give the organization the human resources it needs to implement its strategy.

Just as human resource management often neglects strategic considerations by failing to anticipate the human resources necessary to fulfill the organization's mission, it often neglects operational considerations by failing to anticipate whether the organization's human resource programs are to be determined by tradition, convenience, or some other motive unconnected with organizational strategy. The basic model, then, is normative in an operational sense as well as in a strategic sense.

B.   Supply and Demand

The two steps divide the basic model into labor demand and labor supply components just as they divide it into strategic and operational components. Labor *demand* refers to the human resources sought by the organization (its human resource objectives, to use the terms of the basic model). Human resource planning is mostly a matter of reconciling human resource demand with human resource *supply*, the human resources that are available to the organization through its human resource management actions.

Step 1: Determining Demand

Step 1 includes assessing demand by determining how many people need to be working at which jobs for the organization to attain its objectives. In the case of OSHA, the strategy set by Congress included the hazard abatement purpose stated in Section 6(b)(5) and repeated in Fig. 1. That purpose led OSHA to specify the human resources noted in the exhibit. This amounts to establishing human resource demand. Demand might be expressed as a certain number of employees with certain attributes in each job classification.

Determining demand is largely a matter of forecasting because it involves predicting the organization's human resource needs based on its strategic objectives. Human resource demand forecasting methods are discussed later in this chapter. But the step involves more than just forecasting. Management needs to consider alternative methods of organizing jobs that would allow the organization to meet its objectives. In OSHA's case, that would involve searching for alternative approaches to enforcement that would be consistent with legislative mandates, particularly alternatives that might be less skill-intensive or otherwise place less demand on the budget of OSHA.

Step 2: Determining Supply

Step 2 includes assessing human resource supplies by figuring out how many people would normally be available to meet human resource demand. If there is a shortage, this step would also include devising human resource programs to make up the shortage. In a larger sense, then, step 2 actually includes the entire process of determining which human resource methods will be used to meet human resource demand. Its purpose is to ensure that the right number of people with the right abilities will be in the right jobs at the right times.

Determining supply involves forecasting just as determining demand does. Supply forecasting methods predict the effects of various human resource programs (recruitment, training, career management, etc.) on the number of people flowing into, through, and out of the various job classifications in the organization, as well as the effects of those programs on employee productivity, employee skill levels, and so forth. Supply forecasting typically begins by projecting what the human resource supply would be if the organization made no changes in human resource management. Management then attempts to forecast how that projection would differ if various new programs were put into effect. The purpose of this process is to find the best combination of programs.

This chapter discusses human resource supply forecasting methods below, after the discussion of human resource demand forecasting. Before actually using any of the supply forecasting methods discussed below, the human resource planner should know enough about the range of available programs to begin making some educated guesses in advance about the impact of alternative program combinations (see Dyer, 1982). The forecasting methods, then, can compare these alternatives in a more precise way.

C. Reconciling Supply and Demand

To reconcile supply and demand, the human resource planner must arrive at a combination of human resource programs that will provide sufficient human resources. Figure 2 presents an approach for accomplishing that. The exhibit shows demand as affected by organizational objectives because demand refers to the human resources needed to attain those objectives. It shows supply as affected by the human resource programs because supply refers to the human resources provided by those programs.

As implied above, the demand forecasting component on the left side of Fig. 2 corresponds to step 1 of the basic human resource planning model. The human resource planner first arrives at a demand forecast for each organizational objective (1000 health standard compliance officers, for example). Next, the planner aggregates those forecasts for all objectives to arrive at an overall human resource demand forecast.

Likewise, the supply forecasting component on the right corresponds to step 2. Supply forecasting involves forecasting the impact of the human resource programs chosen on human resource supplies. In supply forecasting, the planner typically makes separate forecasts for internal and external human resource supplies. To arrive at an internal supply forecast, the planner estimates the supply impact of internal human resource programs (programs that affect existing employees, such as promotion and training). The internal supply forecast step involves forecasting the number of people from within the organization who will be in the job classification in question at some later time, i.e., those who will be transferred into that classification plus holdovers who are currently there.

To arrive at an external supply forecast, the planner estimates the supply impact of programs that affect those outside the organization, such as recruiting and external selection. The external supply forecast step involves forecasting the number of people from outside the organization who will be recruited into that classification.

Once the planner aggregates the internal and external supply forecasts, the next step is to determine whether the forecasted aggregate supply meets the forecasted aggregate demand. If supply does not meet demand, then the planner considers other human resource programs that might reconcile supply with demand—as shown by the arrow leading up to "choose human resource programs" on the right-hand side of the illustration.

Figure 3 elaborates on Fig. 2 by indicating some of the information that goes into forecasts of internal supply, external supply, and demand. The box labeled "net human resource requirements" is in Fig. 3 because a given combination of programs may not provide enough human resource supply to meet demand. The unmet demand is called *net human resource requirements*. When unmet demand exists, additional programs are considered and forecasts are made to see whether these programs can meet the net human resource requirements.

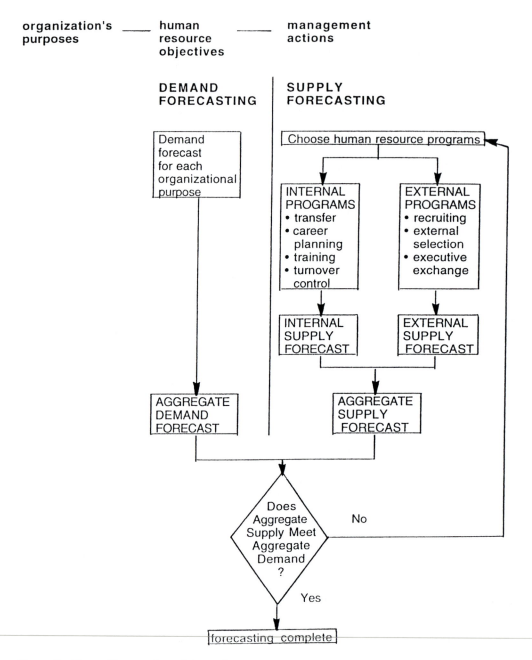

Figure 2   Reconciling supply and demand.

III.   EXPANDING THE BASIC MODEL

A.   Need for Expansion

The arrow on the right-hand side of Fig. 2 indicates that the basic model (Fig. 1) is too simple. The basic model implies that organizational purpose straightforwardly translates into a determination of sufficient human resources and from there into a determination of human resource programs.

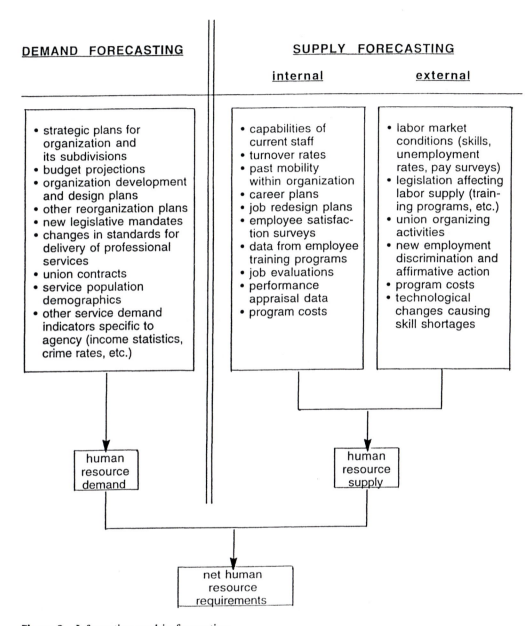

Figure 3   Information used in forecasting.

But the arrow upward on the right side of Fig. 2 implies that human resource programs may not be able to meet that demand. OSHA's initial plan to recruit 1000 industrial hygienists was unrealistic—only 2000 industrial hygienists existed in the entire U.S. labor market at the time (Northrup, 1978). Other human resource programs might be oblivious to other realities, such as budget constraints and employee skills. It seems that a sound normative model of human resource planning needs an added step to avoid management actions that fail to provide sufficient human resources.

Moreover, human resource planning should avoid a situation where the human resources specified in step 1 are unattainable by any means. OSHA's desired staffing level of 1000 industrial hygienists may have been unattainable by any means. A normative model should allow the agency to ensure that its human resource objectives are feasible.

Finally, the organization's entire mission may be unreasonable. OSHA's goal in Section 6(b)(5) was probably unreasonable, considering that the agency was charged from its outset with responsibility for virtually the entire private sector of the U.S. labor market. A complete model of human resource planning would include a process for reconsideration of organizational purpose when it conflicts with human resource reality.

B. Moving Beyond the Basic Model

Figure 4 presents an expanded model of human resource planning, one that resembles a number of models that have appeared elsewhere in the human resource planning literature (e.g., Dyer, 1982; Vetter, 1967; Walker, 1980; Milkovich and Mahoney, 1979; Groe, 1980; Coleman, 1970; Smith, 1982b). This expanded model begins with the simpler model above and continues by considering the constraints noted in the above paragraphs.

Step 3: Assessing the Effectiveness of Planned Human Resource Actions

The first step beyond the simple model is step 3, to evaluate whether the planned human resource management actions would actually provide sufficient human resources, as contemplated in step 2. If so, then planning is complete; but if not, the organization must attempt to devise a new set of actions and repeat the assessment of effectiveness for the new approach.

The key to knowing whether a program will be effective is having a knowledge of how programs operate, particularly how different programs fit together and how constraints can make a program impossible to undertake. Most of the important constraints are part of the external environment. For example:

Labor force. Skill shortages in the external labor market can make recruitment plans infeasible.

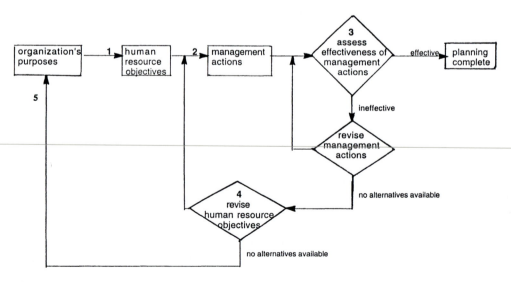

Figure 4 Expanded model of human resource planning.

Government. Equal employment opportunity regulation can make various staffing programs legally
    risky.

Labor unions. The risk of labor–management conflict may make it infeasible for the organization
    to initiate work sharing (where two employees fill one position) or to give management re-
    sponsibility to nonmanagerial workers.

Technology. Technological change can create skill shortages, the current shortage of people with
    computer skills is a good example.

Other constraints are internal to the organization. For example, skill shortages within the
organization can make promotion and training plans infeasible. Other internal constraints can be
traced to functions other than human resource: lack of the necessary finances to underwrite a human
resource program, organizational politics that make managers reluctant to give up power to those
in charge of the program, bureaucratic red tape that limits the freedom of those in charge of the
program and makes it difficult for them to innovate and be flexible, and organizational strategies
that are inconsistent with the program.

Even when human resource managers understand the factors affecting program success, they
have always had a hard time estimating the costs and benefits of human resource programs. There
are two problems. First, the costs and benefits of human resource management programs are often
difficult to anticipate. Second, even if they can be anticipated, they are usually difficult to quantify in precise dollars-and-cents terms (Dyer, 1982; Boudreau, 1990). Benefits are harder to anticipate and quantify than are costs. For example, while the human resource planner may be able
to project the costs of a training program reasonably accurately, it may be harder to come up with
firm evidence that could serve as a basis for projecting the benefits. Even when the planner can
foresee specific benefits, those benefits may not be ones that can be easily quantified in monetary
terms. The planner simply may have to say that without the program productivity declines are likely,
or that the program will make it easier to staff positions in the future or lead to a better attitude
on the part of those who receive the training.

For OSHA, step 3 would involve assessing the effectiveness of external recruitment as a means
for acquiring the 1000 health standard compliance officers. Once it became clear that external
recruitment would not suffice, management would attempt to devise internal methods for meeting human resource objectives. Such methods typically include career development and training
for existing employees. Step 3 would include an assessment of the effectiveness of those alternatives.

This process of assessing effectiveness continues either until management completes the planning process by arriving at a satisfactory array of human resource actions or until the planner
exhausts all the available management actions for attaining the human resource objectives. If no
management action will suffice, planning moves on to step 4.

Step 4: Revising Human Resource Objectives

If management exhausts all available means of meeting the human resource objectives established
in step 1, then the human resource objectives are infeasible. Step 4 is the planning step in which
management attempts to revise its human resource objectives by devising an alternative human
resource configuration that would allow the organization to fulfill its purposes. Once management
arrives at a new set of human resource objectives, planning returns to steps 2 and 3 to determine
what management actions would allow the organization to meet those objectives.

OSHA's case appears to call for step 4. The human resource objective of 1000 health standard compliance officers seems unattainable by any means. It seems that training would have taken
too long and that other forms of career management for existing employees would have failed due
to a shortage of people on OSHA's staff with the necessary qualifications to move into industrial

hygiene positions. Outside recruitment was the only option. Yet the shortage of qualified people in the external labor market made that option ineffective as well. Logic dictates, then, that the agency reconsider the advisability of attempting to effect organizational purpose by employing a staff of 1000 health compliance officers.

However, in devising an alternative human resource configuration, OSHA is limited, primarily by restrictions set forth in the Occupational Safety and Health Act itself. The Act appears to rule out any approach that shifts compliance monitoring to industry, even though such a step would have relieved OSHA's enforcement burden considerably. The Act thus rules out approaches such as self-enforcement of health standards by employers, OSHA consultation to employers, or industry associations' participation in the enforcement effort. But the statute does allow delegation to state agencies, and OSHA does use that approach. In pursuing legislative mission through state programs, OSHA provides assistance to those agencies in an attempt to ensure adequate human resources. Implicitly, this course of action involves steps 2 and 3 in that it includes specifying management actions to meet human resource objectives and assessing the feasibility of those management actions.

This sort of feasibility assessment continues either until management completes the planning process by finding a feasible set of objectives or until it becomes clear that no feasible set of objectives exists that would allow the organization to fulfill its purposes. In the latter case, the final recourse is step 5.

Step 5: Revising Organizational Purposes

If no feasible human resource configuration exists that would allow the organization to accomplish its mission, then the expanded model calls for the organization to revise that mission. Essentially, revising the mission means beginning the entire strategic management process over again. For OSHA, this step would have involved a reconsideration of OSHA's mission by Congress. For other organizations, including private sector firms, this step could involve an equally fundamental change of direction.

Although organizations do, reluctantly, change their mission, they seldom do so in response to human resource concerns. But when an organization ignores human resource inadequacies, it places its mission at risk, as management commits resources in pursuit of unattainable goals. This could explain in part why OSHA has not had the impact on safety and health envisioned by the framers of the Occupational Safety and Health Act.

IV. RECONSIDERATION: HUMAN RESOURCE PLANNING BENEFITS

In sum, management ignores human resource constraints at the risk of organizational failure. In realization of that fact, organizations have increasingly come to include human resource executives in the process of formulating strategy. Strategy is, after all, a response to strengths and weaknesses in the organization as well as to opportunities and threats in the environment (Chandler, 1971). In public administration especially, the organization's strengths and weaknesses are primarily a matter of human resources.

Nevertheless, most organizations, public sector as well as private sector, operate as though there were no connection between human resource planning and organizational effectiveness. Further, those organizations that do incorporate human resource planning experience a reality considerably more complex than even the expanded model suggests. In other words, this chapter's depiction of human resource planning is unrealistic in certain respects. Before examining the technical details of human resource forecasting, it is useful to consider the respects in which the model of human resource planning discussed above departs from reality.

A. The Model as an Oversimplification

The expanded model of human resource planning in Fig. 4 is less simplistic than the basic model, but it is still an oversimplification in several respects. For one, it portrays human resource planning as a process in which planning proceeds until some acceptable plan is found, at which point planning stops. This portrayal is simplistic in that the planner looks for more than just a barely acceptable plan. There is usually more than one possible set of human resource goals to satisfy step 1, and there is usually more than one possible set of feasible human resource programs to satisfy step 2. The planner considers as many sets of human resource goals and human resource programs as are reasonable, then chooses the set of human resource goals that best furthers the strategic plan and the set of human resource programs that best furthers the human resource goals. In short, human resource planners do not necessarily stop evaluating alternatives when they find one that satisfies their minimum criteria (see Dyer, 1982). Instead, they usually entertain several alternatives and choose the one with the greatest expected net benefits for the organization.

Another oversimplification is the implication that the main benefit of planning is the specific plans that result. If this were so, there would be little sense in planning because plans become obsolete. The organization's environment takes unexpected turns, and that makes supply and demand forecasts inaccurate. But such environmental turbulence makes planning more important because the main benefit of planning is the process of thinking and discussion that management goes through in doing it—the conscious choosing from among objectives and goals, the conscious evaluation of various programs to attain those objectives and goals, and the conscious consideration of alternative scenarios under which the likely results of program performance can be projected. This process of deliberation allows beliefs and assumptions to surface and forces management to be aware of the choices it faces (Mills and Balkaby, 1984). The result is that management is better prepared to make decisions, regardless of whether circumstances allow its plans to unfold as intended.

Consider what happens to an organization when it anticipates expansion but instead encounters cutbacks because of unexpected budget limitations or, in the private sector, because of unexpected competitive pressures. Even though the organization cannot realize its human resource plans, its approach to planning has led it to make deliberate policy choices about managing people. In making these deliberate choices, management has consciously considered the human resource philosophy underlying those choices, and this philosophy can help guide the organization through the retrenchment it faces as well as through the growth that it had anticipated. For example, management may have chosen to meet its anticipated expansion needs through the development and promotion of existing employees rather than through external hiring. This policy choice entails a philosophy of commitment to employee careers. In times of retrenchment, this philosophy would mean avoiding termination of employees. Instead of layoffs, the firm might impose involuntary part-time status on certain employees or adopt a job-sharing program. That is not to say that such a course would be more desirable than layoffs; it is only to point out that management is better off having thought through its philosophy and that planning makes management do so.

B. The Model as an Idealization

The model is also an idealization in that human resource planning is usually less rational than the model implies. Many organizations omit step 5; some dispense with other steps and instead act on the basis of common sense assumptions rather than objective evidence. An organization may fail to follow all the human resource planning steps because the planners do not have the knowledge required to undertake them. The requisite knowledge is difficult and technical; it includes human resource forecasting methods and program evaluation methods. To use those methods, the planner must seek out specialized instructions in planning methods. The last part of this chapter discusses the basic features of some of those methods, but the detailed information necessary for using them is beyond the scope of this chapter. Unless an organization makes a special effort to see that its human resource management people have this knowledge, human resource planning is likely to be inadequate.

Even if the planners have the necessary knowledge, they may still omit some of the steps. The steps involving strategy (steps 1 and 5) are the most likely to be neglected. When this happens, any resemblance between human resource programs and strategic objectives is purely coincidental. Sometimes the operations links are omitted because the organization is so attached to its existing human resource programs that it resists any effort to evaluate the feasibility and effectiveness of those programs.

In sum, human resource planning is often so poorly conducted that formal forecasting methods are pointless. Management must confront those basic problems before considering the use of approaches such as those discussed below.

V. HUMAN RESOURCE FORECASTING

Human resource forecasting is the process of projecting the organization's future human resource needs (demand) and how it will meet those needs (supply) under a given set of assumptions about the organization's policies and about the environmental conditions under which it operates. Human resource planning and decision making requires some form of forecasting; otherwise there is no way to anticipate whether a disparity between supply and demand will arise, or to tell how effective a human resource program might be in reducing that disparity.

A. Basic Considerations in Establishing a Forecasting System

Several questions face the organization that is deciding what kind of human resource forecasting system to put into effect. Among the more important ones are the following: (1) How sophisticated should the forecasting system be? (2) What is the appropriate *time frame*, i.e., how far into the future should the system forecast? (3) What use should the system make of subjective and objective forecasting methods?

1. The System's Sophistication

Not all organizations need to invest in an advanced, complex forecasting system. Scarborough and Zimmerer (1982) mention several factors that affect the complexity of the human resource forecasting system needed by an organization:

Organizational size. Planning and forecasting is not just for large organizations (Burack and Mathys, 1980). However, larger companies have more employees, more job categories, and a larger geographic area of activity. This complexity necessitates a more complex forecasting system. Larger organizations also are more likely to have the advanced computer facilities and skilled staff necessary to make a sophisticated system workable.

Organizational complexity. Complex organizations tend to have complex career pathways and diverse skill mixtures in their work forces, which requires a more complex forecasting system.

Organizational goals. The larger the gap is between the organization's current human resource situation and the desired future human resource situation, the more sophisticated is the forecasting system required to bridge that gap.

Organizational plans and strategies. The more complex the organization's plans for the future are, the more complex is the forecasting approach needed to implement those plans.

Organizational information. The more sophisticated and accurate the relevant information is, the more the organization can profit from a complex forecasting system.

2. Forecasting Time Frame

One important factor in the choice forecasting time frame (or planning horizon) is uncertainty in the organization's environment. Uncertainty reduces the accuracy of forecasts, and the problem worsens as the forecasting time frame lengthens. Among the factors that increase uncertainty are (Burack and Mathys, 1980):

Rapidly developing technology
Poor training
Rapid changes in the social, political, and economic climate
Poor information system
New legislation that may affect the organization

3. Subjective vs. Objective Forecasting

Subjective methods forecast the future by asking people what the future will be like; objective methods forecast it by using a formula based on facts about present or past trends. Common sense alone seems to argue for using objective approaches, and the technical literature offers many objective, computerized methods to improve the accuracy of human resource forecasting. Nevertheless, subjective approaches seem more common in practice, and often for good reason. Objective forecasting is generally inappropriate when

The organization lacks the expertise to use the more sophisticated objective methods properly.
The organization's computer system is inadequate.
The organization lacks the historical data on which to base an objective forecast, or the human resource database is otherwise inadequate.
There is no established method for forecasting objectively.
The forecasting horizon is too long for the available objective forecasting methods.

As a result, forecasting is often based on subjective judgment of knowledgeable observers (Gatewood and Gatewood, 1983). Human judges are asked to forecast variables such as:

Number of employees that will be needed in a job classification
Average employee productivity
Individual differences in employee productivity
Labor market trends, such as population movement into and out of commuting areas.
Expected number of applicants for a job classification
Future strategic directions of the organization
Future career pathways for employees
Vacancies in managerial positions
The extent to which the organization will hire outside applicants instead of using promotions and transfers from within the organization
The organization's anticipated plan to reduce the work force if a slowdown occurs
The percentages of people in each job who will be promoted or transferred to other jobs

One problem with subjective forecasting is that the organization often uses it carelessly. Subjective forecasting takes a lot of time, and managers may consider the procedures required to arrive at useful forecasts somewhat unnecessary. Consider the following three issues.

1. Point Estimates vs. Probability Estimates

Typically, we tend to think of forecasting as a process of producing the *one best estimate* of what will happen in the future. For example, an aerospace corporation with substantial government contract work might estimate that its demand for engineers will increase by 20%. That single-number forecast of 20% is called a *point estimate*. The problem with point estimates is that they do not give any information about the degree of *uncertainty* in the forecast. For example, the company might be more certain about the future demand for clerical staff than about the future demand for engineers because the demand for clerical staff does not depend as heavily on the unpredictable matter of whether the company will be getting new contracts.

To provide forecasts that do give information on the degree of uncertainty, the organization could express the forecast as a *confidence interval* as well as a single value. A confidence interval is a range of values, along with an estimate of the probability, or likelihood, that the actual figure will fall within the range. Instead of stating a 20% engineering growth figure, the forecast might state a 95% confidence interval of 0–30%, which would mean that there is a 95% probability that the company will need between 0% and 30% more engineers. This estimate might compare with a 95% confidence interval of 15–25% for clerical staff. Several techniques are available for soliciting point estimates and confidence intervals from forecasters in different situations (Spetzler and Stael von Holstein, 1975; Wallsten and Budescu, 1980).

2. Simple Forecasts vs. Complex Forecasts

Suppose that future demand for engineers in the aerospace firm is determined by a complex combination of factors such as the amounts of various kinds of contract work at various times in the future. In such a case, demand forecasting has two components, one simple and the other complex. The simple component is to estimate the values of the factors; the complex component is to combine the factors to arrive at an engineering demand forecast. If subjective forecasting is to have a role, what should it be—simple or complex forecasting?

The consensus among forecasting experts is that the complex forecasting should be done by objective, computerized methods as much as possible. Computers are better at complex forecasting such as uncovering the exact mathematical relationship between engineering demand and the amounts of various kinds of contract work. Human forecasting, on the other hand, is often the best way to estimate the individual factors that enter into these complex relationships. However, people find it hard to believe that a machine such as the computer could be better than a human at making complex assessments. Complex assessments seem to require judgment, not just mechanical processing of information. Machines seem better suited to simpler forecasting tasks. Thus, organizations unfortunately may be inclined to use subjective methods for the kind of forecasting work that objective methods do best and objective methods for the kind of forecasting work that subjective methods do best.

3. Individual Estimates vs. Group Estimates

If subjective forecasts are to be made, is it better to use one forecaster or several? The research findings are clear: accuracy is higher when several forecasters are employed. This is particularly true for probability estimates or confidence interval forecasts (Lichenstein et al., 1976; Fischer, 1981). Individual forecasts tend to underestimate the true confidence intervals. If objective historical data show that the true 95% confidence interval for engineering demand growth is 0–30%, an individual forecaster is more likely than a group to give an estimate that is too narrow, such as 10–25%.

Most experts think that the group should not be a face-to-face one. The problem with face-to-face interaction is that social factors can distort the group forecast. For example, conformity pressures may lead group participants to go along with others against their better judgment, or a desire to save face may lead them to persist in their publicly stated positions despite evidence to the contrary (Helmer and Rascher, 1959).

B. Forecasting Methods

Human resource planners use a variety of forecasting techniques. Some involve subjective estimation; others make use of objective data. The techniques also differ according to whether they are used more for human resource demand forecasting or for human resource supply forecasting (although some can be used for both). The remainder of this chapter discusses the basic steps in using objective forecasting models and briefly reviews some of the more widely known subjective and objective forecasting methods.

VI. STEPS IN USING OBJECTIVE HUMAN RESOURCE FORECASTING METHODS

Objective forecasting methods, also called forecasting models, are specific techniques for making forecasts. They estimate the future from information about the present and the past. More precisely, they forecast the value of some variable in the future from information about the present or past value of some variable or variables. In this discussion the present or past variables are called X variables and the forecasted future variable is called the Y variable. Objective forecasting models use a three-step forecasting process:

1. *Model building.* Determine the X variables that affect the Y variable, and specify the relationship between Y and the X variables as an equation, with Y as the unknown quantity and the X variables as known quantities. The forecasting model is this equation.
2. *Data gathering.* Collect information on the values of the X variables.
3. *Forecasting.* Enter those values into the equation from step 1 to arrive at a value for Y.

In human resource forecasting, Y is human resource supply or demand and the X variables are the factors thought to affect human resource supply or demand.

The model building step involves examining data about the past for relationships between Y and X and stating that relationship in the form of a mathematical equation. The data gathering step involves collecting either objective data on the values of the X variables or subjective human estimates of those X values. The first and third steps are usually computerized, and if the information in the second step is objective, it is often kept in a computerized database as well.

In order to take the first step, the human resource planner must specify the X variables that are to be examined for their effect on Y. This means being able to give a reasonable conjecture about the factors that might affect Y. Figure 3 lists some of the factors or variables that have been found to affect human resource supply and demand.

A. Demand Forecasting Methods

Many methods have been used to forecast human resource demand. Some are highly technical operations-research methods; others are straightforward and nontechnical. The Delphi method, a subjective approach, is one of the better known human resource demand forecasting methods. The other approaches are more objective but less frequently used than Delphi.

1. Delphi Method

Delphi is a noninteractive group forecasting procedure. In the Delphi method, the only communication received by group members is written reports from the person in charge of the forecasting procedure indicating the average group opinion (see Woudenberg, 1991). Delphi follows these steps:

Solicit estimates of forecasts from individual group members by means of a questionnaire.

Compute statistical averages of the estimates. If there is sufficient agreement among the group members about all estimates, the procedure ends.

If there is insufficient agreement (as is quite often the case), present the group's averages to the individual group members and solicit new estimates or forecasts.

Repeat steps 2 and 3 until agreement is reached.

Although the Delphi process seems simple, it is actually quite complex in practice. Anyone who considers undertaking a Delphi study should consult other sources of information (for example, Linstone and Turoff, 1975). Burack and Mathys (1980) give further information on how to use the method in human resource planning.

The Delphi method has been applied with some success in human resource demand forecasting (Milkovich et al., 1972). However, some forecasting specialists have criticized its accuracy (Armstrong, 1978; Makridakis and Wheelwright, 1978). Gatewood and Gatewood (1983) concluded that the Delphi technique may be useful for human resource forecasting in certain cases, specifically in situations in which the forecasting task is specific and there is a lack of historical information on which to base a more objective forecast.

2. Staffing Table Approach

Staffing tables are one of the simplest objective demand forecasting methods. This approach uses future sales or production estimates as X variables to predict the required number of employees for a specific job as the Y variable. The relationship between Y and the X variables is not specified as an explicit mathematical equation, as in the model building step (step 1) described above, but as a set of tables showing how many employees would be needed in each job classification at different levels of sales or production. The figures in the table are usually based on casual observation or conjectures about how many people are needed at various levels of sales, production, or service delivery. Once the tables are constructed, only sales or production forecasts are needed (step 2), and these are then entered into the staffing table to determine the demand forecast for the job classification in question (step 3).

3. Regression Analysis

A more formal version of the same basic approach is *regression analysis* (Gascoigne, 1968; Bright, 1976). Regression analysis is a form of statistical analysis applied to many problems besides human resource planning. Regression analysis differs from staffing tables in that it determines the relationship between Y variables such as the number of employees and X variables such as service delivery by actually measuring the relationship that existed in the past. Use of the method begins with a series of observations, each consisting of a value for the Y variable plus a value for each X variable. For example, the X variable for an observation could be the service delivery figures for a given month and the Y variable could be the average number of employees during that month. The observations are analyzed by computer, and the relationship between Y and the X variables is expressed as a mathematical equation rather than as a set of tables. The equation expresses the Y variable to be forecasted as a simple mathematical function of the X variable or variables.

Other X variables besides service, sales, or production can be used in regression analysis. If the organization knows the future staffing levels for some job categories but not for others, regression analysis can be used to develop an equation expressing the unknown staffing levels as a function of the known staffing levels (Schaeffer, 1974). Similarly, regression equations can express future demand for one skill as a function of the present staffing levels of another skill (Rudelius, 1976).

4. Time Series Analysis

A related regression approach is *time series analysis*, which involves forecasting future staffing levels of a job (Y) by projecting from past staffing levels of that job (X). Time series analysis is more than simple extrapolation from the past. Cyclical trends and random variation must be considered and a number of other statistical technicalities must be assessed (Bartholomew and Forbes, 1979).

B. Supply Forecasting Methods

Human resource supply forecasting typically presents different problems for public sector managers than for private sector managers. Human resource supply amounts to the flow of employees into, through, and out of the organization. But public sector managers tend to have less control over that flow than do private sector managers. Civil service laws govern external hiring as well as internal mobility, and union contracts further limit managerial discretion in staffing public sector organizations.

Among the following three methods, skill inventories and replacement and succession planning are more subjective than flow modeling. Flow modeling is the most precise and accurate demand forecasting procedure, but it is seldom used because it demands solid technical knowledge and an accurate and accessible employee information database.

1. Skills Inventory

One of oldest supply forecasting methods is the skills inventory, which is a file of information containing each employee's skills, abilities, knowledge, and experience (Bailes, 1961; Murphy, 1972; Graver, 1976; Thomsen, 1976; Niehaus et al., 1978). Although not a technically sophisticated approach, this method can be useful in revealing situations where there is an inadequate supply of skilled candidates inside the organization to fill the forecasted future demand. This ability allows management to make plans to fill the openings through outside recruiting. All in all, however, the skills inventory is an incomplete approach to supply forecasting because it focuses on the individual's *existing* skills. It should be supplemented with a method that identifies employees who have the *potential* for developing the skills needed on the job (Seaman, 1973; Shelbar, 1979).

2. Replacement and Succession Planning

Another useful approach that requires little technical knowledge is *replacement planning* and *succession planning*. Replacement planning is the process of systematically anticipating when each position will be vacated and who might fill it; succession planning is the process of making long-range plans to ensure that the candidates to fill those vacancies will be given adequate training and career development.

The principal device used in replacement planning is the *replacement chart*. Figure 5 shows a sample replacement chart that could be used for management positions. Replacement planning begins by assigning one box to a key manager who is expected to leave within the foreseeable future. The next box then is assigned to the employee who is most likely to replace the key manager, the succeeding box is assigned to the employee who is expected to fill that employee's position, and so on. The process continues until the replacement planner is satisfied that all the significant vacancies are covered.

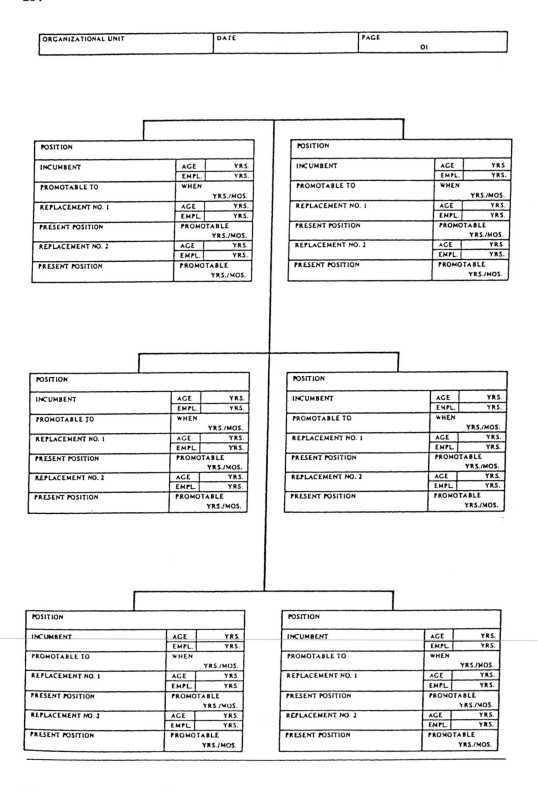

Figure 5   Replacement chart. (From Milkovich and Mahoney, 1979.)

3. Flow Modeling

A more sophisticated approach to supply forecasting is *flow modeling*, which is used in applications such as forecasting recruiting needs and setting affirmative action goals. The word *flow* refers to the flow of employees into, through, and out of the organization, including promotions, demotions, and transfers within the organization as well as terminations and new hires from outside the organization (see Jarrell, 1993; Noe et al., 1994, chapter 9; Cascio, 1993).

Most flow models forecast the size of future flows (the Y variables) from information on the size of past flows (the X variables). The information on past flows consists of either objective historical data or subjective estimates by managers who are familiar with the staffing patterns in the organization. Some flow models are built on the assumption that, for each job class, the proportion of employees leaving the class for any other given job class remains constant from year to year. Other flow models make different assumptions.

Table 1 is a simplified example of how flow models operate. The first column of numbers shows the present number of employees in each of five job categories. The matrix to the right of the first column of numbers contains the flow estimates, expressed as the average percentage of employees in each job category that moves to each of the other job categories over the course of a year, and the average percentage of employees that terminate each year. The rows represent the source job classes—where people are at the beginning of the year—and the columns represent the destinations for each flow—where people are at the end of the year. Thus, for example, from reading the second row we know that, on the average, 5% of the professional workforce is promoted to a managerial position each year, 85% remains in the professional category, 5% moves to technical positions, and 5% terminates.

It is a simple matter to use Table 1 to forecast the internal supply for each job category next year: begin with the first number in the first column, multiply it by each number in its row to forecast the flow out of the managerial category, and then continue this process with each of the remaining numbers in the first column. For example, consider the flows out of the professional category. The second number in the first column shows that there are 20 employees in the professional category. The corresponding row of the matrix indicates the percentage of those 20 employees expected to be in each column category next year. Table 2 shows these percentages converted to numbers of employees.

Once all the flows out of each job category are forecasted, the columns can be added to produce an internal supply forecast for each category. For the managerial category, the first column of Table 2 shows a forecasted internal supply of 10; of these, 9 are managers this year and one will be promoted from the professional category. The internal supply totals are shown in the row immediately below the matrix of flows in Table 2.

If human resource demand forecasts are available, it is a simple matter to use the flow model to forecast recruiting needs. The next-to-the-last row in Table 2 is a set of hypothetical demand forecasts. Recruiting needs are by definition the same as external supplies. Since the sum of the internal and external supplies must equal total staffing needs, or demand, the external supply for each job category is simply the difference between the internal supply and the demand forecast. External supplies, or recruiting needs, are shown in the last row.

Flow modeling can be applied to affirmative action by constructing separate flow matrices for each race, sex, and ethnic group. Each matrix then becomes the basis for a separate flow model to forecast the internal supplies of employees from each group (Churchill and Shank, 1976; Ledvinka et al., 1976; Chew and Justice, 1979; Milkovich and Krzystofiak, 1979).

Although flow modeling is one of the most powerful approaches available for human resource supply forecasting, such models require computer capabilities that many organizations lack. For

Table 1 Simplified Flow Model: Present Employees and Movement Percentages

Job category	Present number of employees in category	Percentage of the row category that will be in each of the following column categories next year					
		Managerial	Professional	Technical	Clerical	Service	Termination
Managerial	10	90	0	0	0	0	10
Professional	20	5	85	5	0	0	5
Technical	40	0	5	85	5	0	5
Clerical	80	0	0	5	85	0	10
Service	80	0	0	0	0	80	20

Table 2 Simplified Flow Model: Forecasts for Next Year

Job category	Present number of employees in category	Number of the row category that will be in each of the following column categories next year					
		Managerial	Professional	Technical	Clerical	Service	Termination
Managerial	10	90	0	0	0	0	1
Professional	20	1	17	1	0	0	1
Technical	40	0	2	34	2	0	2
Clerical	80	0	0	4	68	0	8
Service	80	0	0	0	0	64	16
Total internal supply		10	19	39	70	64	
Forecasted demand		10	20	42	84	84	
Difference = external supply (recruiting needs)		0	1	3	14	20	

that reason, coupled with the technical knowledge and information access requirements mentioned above, flow modeling is generally used only in the largest organizations.

C. How Widely Used Are These Methods?

Human resource planning specialists often advocate the more sophisticated and objective approaches to forecasting. However, managers apparently do not follow the experts' recommendations (Greer and Armstrong, 1980). The most popular forecasting methods are the least sophisticated ones, such as skills inventories, replacement charts, and supervisor estimates. In part, this seems due to the fact that many human resource management information systems lack the interactive capability that would allow the planner to capitalize on more sophisticated approaches such as flow modeling. Regardless of the reasons, however, these findings suggest that management may encounter resistance when it attempts to introduce advanced human resource forecasting techniques into an organization.

VII. CONCLUSION

Those observations underscore the fact that this chapter's discussion of the human resource planning process has been normative, i.e., a discussion of what human resource planning should be like rather than what it typically is like. For example:

Human resource planning should be *planning*—something done in advance rather than just as a spur-of-the-moment reaction to immediate pressures.

Human resource planning should *guide and coordinate all human resource activities* (the implementation components of the human resource management model) so that they work together to support the overall strategy rather than operate independently of one another.

Human resource planning should be *responsive to both the external environment and the organizational environment*.

Human resource planning should be *strategic*—linked with high-level planning rather than performed in isolation from the deliberations of those who are charting the overall direction for the organization, division, or functional department.

Although many organizations fall short of the ideal, it represents the direction in which the practice of human resource management seems to be evolving, particularly in those organizations that place a high value on the human resource function.

To respond to the challenge of public sector strategic management, public sector human resource managers who used to view themselves as the executors or administrators of designs imposed by others now find themselves in a more proactive role as participants in the creation of those plans. This necessitates a familiarity with forecasting methods and other management competencies that this chapter has only touched on. In short, the skill requirements for top human resource managers is expanding rapidly. Ironically, these skill demands constitute a human resource planning problem in themselves. We may hope that the profession is up to the task of solving that problem.

REFERENCES

Andrews, K. R. (1971). *The Concept of Corporate Strategy*, Irwin, Homewood, IL.

Armstrong, J. S. (1978). *Long Range Forecasting*, Wiley, New York.

Bailes S. M. (1961). Fundamental aspects of establishing a skills inventory, *Personnel J.*, 41.

Bartholomew, D.J., and Forbes, A. F. (1979). *Statistical Techniques for Manpower Planning*, Wiley, Chichester.

Boudreau, J. W. (1991). Utility analysis for decisions in human resource management, *Handbook of Industrial and Organizational Psychology*, 2nd Ed., Vol. 2 (M.D. Dunnette and L. M. Hough, eds.), Consulting Psychologists Press, Palo Alto, CA.

Bright, W. E. (1976). How one company manages its human resources, *Harvard Business Rev.* (Jan.-Feb.): 81–93.

Burack, E. H., and Mathys, J. N. (1980). *Human Resource Planning: A Pragmatic Approach to Manpower Staffing and Development*, Brace-Park, Lake Forest, IL.

Cascio, W. F. (1992). *Managing Human Resources: Productivity, Quality of Work Life, Profits*, McGraw-Hill, New York.

Chew, W. B., and Justice, R. L. (1979). EEO modeling for large, complex organizations, *Human Resource Plann.*, 2: 57–70.

Churchill, N., and Shank, J. (1976). Affirmative action and guilt-edge goals, *Harvard Business Rev. (March–April)*: 111–116.

Dyer, Lee (1982). Human resource planning. *Personnel Management* (K. M. Rowland and G. R. Ferris, eds.), Allyn and Bacon, Boston, pp. 12–78.

Fischer, G. W. (1981). When oracles fail: a comparison of four procedures for aggregating subjective probability forecasts, *Organiz. Behav. Human Perf.*, 28: 96–109.

Gascoigne, J. M. (1968). Manpower planning at the enterprise level, *Br. J. Ind. Rel.*, 6: 94–106.

Gatewood, R. D., and Gatewood, E. J. (1983). The use of expert data in human resource planning: guidelines from strategic planning, *Human Resource Plann.*, 2: 83–93.

Graver, R. T. (1976). An automated approach to affirmative action. *Personnel*, 53(5): 37–44.

Greer, C. R., and Armstrong, D. (1980). Human resource forecasting and planning: a state-of-the-art investigation. *Human Resource Plann.*, 3(2): 67–78.

Helmer, O., and Rascher, N. (1959). On the epistemology of the inexact sciences, *Manage. Sci.*

Jarrell, D. W. (1993). *Human Resource Planning: A Business Planning Approach*, Prentice-Hall, Englewood Cliffs, NJ.

Ledvinka, J., LaForge, R. L., and Corbett, T. C. (1976). Test of an affirmative action goal-setting model, *Personnel Admin.* 21 (April).

Lichtenstein, S., Fischoff, B., and Phillips, L. D. (1976). Calibration of probabilities: the state of the art, *Decision Making and Change in Human Affairs* (H. Jungerman and G. de Zeun, eds.), D. Reidel, Dordrecht.

Linstone, H. A., and Turoff, M. (1975). *The Delphi Method: Technical Techniques and Applications*, Addison-Wesley, Reading, MA.

Makridakis, S., and Wheelwright, S. C. (1978). *Forecasting: Methods and Applications*, Wiley, New York.

Milkovich, G., and Krzystofiak, F. (1979). Simulation and affirmative action planning, *Human Resource Plann.*, 2: 71–80.

Milkovich, G. T., and Mahoney, T. A. (1979). Human resources planning and PAIR policy, *Handbook of Personnel and Industrial Relations* (D. Yoder and H. G. Heneman, Jr., eds.), Bureau of National Affairs, Washington, DC, pp. 2-1-2-29.

Milkovich, G. T., Annoni, A. J., and Mahoney, T. A. (1972). The use of the Delphi procedures in manpower forecasting, *Manage. Sci.*, 19(4): 381–388.

Milkovich, G., Dyer, L., and Mahoney, T. (1983). HRM planning. *Human Resource Planning in the 1980s* (Carroll and Schuler), Bureau of National Affairs, Washington, DC, pp. 2-9-2-29.

Mills, D. Q., and Balkaby, M. L. (1984). People make the difference for human resource future, unpublished paper.

Mintzberg, H. (1976). *Patterns in Strategy Formation*, McGill University, Montreal.

Murphy, R. H. (1972). A personalized skills inventory: the North American Rockwell story. *Manpower Planning and Programming* (E. H. Burack and J. W. Walker, eds.), Allyn and Bacon, Boston.

Niehaus, R. J., Scholtz, D., and Thompson, G. (1978). Managerial tests of conversational manpower planning models, *TIMS Stud. Manage. Sci.*, 8: 153–172.

Noe, R. A., Hollenbeck, J. R., Gerhart, B., and Wright, P. M. (1994). *Human Resource Management: Gaining a Competitive Advantage*, Irwin, Homewood, IL.

Northrup, H. R. (1978). *The impact of OSHA*, University of Pennsylvania Press, Philadelphia.

Rothwell, W. J., and Kazanas, H. C. (1988). *Strategic Human Resources Planning and Management*, Prentice-Hall, Englewood Cliffs, NJ.

Rudelius, W. (1976). Lagged manpower relationships in development projects, *IEEE Trans. Eng. Manage. (Dec.)*: 88–195.

Scarborough, N., and Zimmerer, T. W. (1982). Human resource forecasting: why and where to begin, *Personnel Admin., 27*(May):55–61.

Schaeffer, R. H. (1974). Demand better results and get them, *Harvard Business Rev. (Nov.–Dec.)*: 91–98.

Seamans, L. H., Jr. (1973). What's lacking in most skills inventories, *Personnel J., 53*: 101–105.

Shelbar, P. (1979). Personnel practices review: a personnel and audit activity, *Personnel J., 58*: 211–216.

Spetzler, C. S., and Stael von Holstein, C. (1975). Probability encoding in decision analysis, *Manage. Sci., 22*:340–358.

Thomsen, D. J. (1976). Keeping track of managers in a large corporation, *Personnel, 53*:23–30.

Vetter, E. W. (1967). *Manpower Planning for High Talent Personnel*, Bureau of Industrial Relations, University of Michigan, Ann Arbor.

Walker, J. W. (1980). *Human Resource Planning*, McGraw-Hill, New York.

Walker, J. W. (1992). *Human Resource Strategy*, McGraw-Hill, New York.

Wallsten, T. S., and Budescu, D. V. (1980). *Encoding Subjective Probabilities: A Psychological and Psychometric Review*, University of North Carolina, Department of Psychology, Chapel Hill, NC.

Woudenberg, F. (1991). An evaluation of Delphi, *Technol. Forecast. Social Change (Sept.)*: 131–151.

11
Recruitment of Personnel

DAVID G. CARNEVALE and STEVEN HOUSEL University of Oklahoma,
Norman, Oklahoma

> Let the public service be a proud and lively career. And let every man and woman
> who works in any area of our national government, in any branch, at any level, be
> able to say with pride and with honor in future years: "I served the United States
> government in that hour of our nation's need."
>
> President John F. Kennedy, 1963
> (Volcker, 1989a p. 9)

I. INTRODUCTION

Government plays a tripartite economic role as a producer of goods and services, a regulator of
private enterprise, and a complementary asset to private production. Society cannot be strong
without able public servants. This is the cornerstone of a free economy and essential to the maintenance of democratic institutions (Staats, 1988; Carnevale and Carnevale, 1993).

By the late 1980s, public employment accounted for more than 17 million persons. Three
million of these were federal employees, 4 million state government workers, and over 10 million local government staff (Shafritz et al., 1992, p. 177). Government's ability to employ capable persons is vital.

The process of personnel acquisition comprises three highly interrelated activities: recruitment,
selection, and placement. These procedures can be broadly understood as "staffing" or the means
of situating individuals in organizations. The ways in which staffing is accomplished have implications for many other personnel practices, such as work force planning, training, performance
evaluation, job design, and career development (Hyde, 1983; Mosher et al., 1950). None of these
aspects of employment can be understood in isolation from the others. Each is a part of the broad
mosaic of personnel policy and the context within which it operates.

Recruitment is no exception to this point of view. Over 50 years ago a Civil Service Assembly report (Kingsley, 1942, p. 15) stated that recruitment must be understood within the context
of "a personnel *system*, rather than a collection of imperfectly related practices" (emphasis added).
In a similar vein, advocacy for a contextualistic view of human resources appears in a more recent government report. A federal committee charged with recommending how to judge the quality
of the government's work force proposed that its assessment model (Fig. 1) reflect the interactive
nature of work life. In the language of the committee, that means accounting for the interrelationships among the organizational components of inputs, processes, and outputs (Advisory Committee on Federal Workforce Quality Assessment, 1992).

Recruitment is defined as "that process through which suitable candidates are induced to
compete for appointments to the public service" (Kingsley, 1942, p. 13). It is the "cornerstone

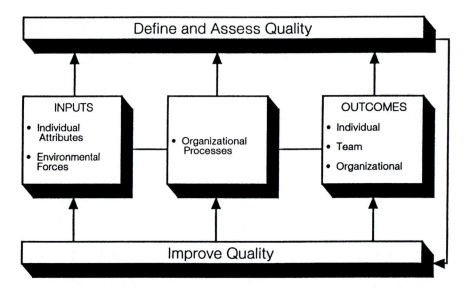

Figure 1   Workforce quality: assessment and improvement. (From Advisory Committee on Federal Workforce Quality, 1992, p. 32.)

of the whole personnel structure" (Mosher et al., 1950). Recruitment is the key facet of all comprehensive government employment systems because it functions to ensure the acquisition of the necessary knowledge, skills, and abilities (KSAs) for mission accomplishment (Nalbandian and Klingner, 1993).

Effective recruitment ensures an ample flow of human assets or capital into public organizations (Lane and Wolf, 1990). Obtaining human capital, however, is not limited to simply procuring an adequate number of available workers, but assuring the right mix of knowledge and capabilities in people (McGregor, 1988). According to the Advisory Committee on Federal Workforce Quality Assessment (1992, pp. 1–17), this means selecting persons who demonstrate the ability to use:

Resources—handling money, time, material, space, and staff
Interpersonal skills—working effectively on diverse teams, leading, serving customers, negotiating, and helping others to learn
Information—acquiring, evaluating, organizing, and communicating information
Systems—understanding systems, monitoring their operation, and adjusting their performance when required
Technology—selecting equipment and tools, applying them to specific tasks, and maintaining them

These competencies are founded on having good basic reading, writing, thinking, and personal skills (cf. U.S. Department of Labor, 1991).

In this chapter, the role of recruitment in public personnel systems will be examined. It is divided into three major parts: (1) the history of the public service and its influence on the character of modern recruitment objectives, (2) the impact of external and internal labor markets on workforce quality and recruitment strategy, and (3) the intimate relationship between recruitment and retention policies in human resource administration. Substantial attention will be paid to recruitment problems in the federal service because there is a widespread perception that the national government is unable to attract and retain a competent work force. Moreover, it is believed that there is a serious erosion of the human capital base in the U.S. civil service (Levine, 1986; Levine and Kleeman, 1986; National Commission on the Public Service, 1989). Considerable effort has been made to address this "crisis" and lessons learned have important implications for recruitment methods at all levels of public administration.

II. RECRUITMENT: THE LEGACY OF THE PAST

> The time has come in the history of America to adopt an entirely new public policy
> in the selection and appointment of men and women to carry on the day-to-day work
> of government.
>
> Commission of Inquiry on Public Service Personnel, 1935

Issues surrounding the development of effective personnel acquisition methods are enduring and closely related to the events and values that have attended the evolution of the merit system. The formation of the public service has been guided by operational tendencies that have not been helpful to the creation of impressive methods of recruitment. First, for much of its history, the primary orientation of employment systems was negative, passive, and exclusionary (Dresang, 1991). It was obsessed with keeping out the unfit rather than encouraging the best to enter government service (Mosher et al., 1950). Second, public organizations assumed they could count on a plentiful supply of qualified applicants. Each of these affinities has arrested the development of effective recruitment methods in contemporary government.

A. Keeping the Rascals Out

Historically, the essence of staffing has been for the most part reactive. It has been consumed by the idea of keeping undesirables and improper political influence out of the public service rather than concentrating on positive practices to seek the best qualified persons for appointment. Its primary purpose had been to prevent favoritism, not to actively increase the levels of professional competence of the public service (Kingsley, 1942). These goals need not be incompatible. However, until very recently, a regulatory, policing approach to recruitment was emphasized. The principal philosophical underpinning for this condition is premised on the negative reaction against the graver abuses of spoils and patronage in the late 1880s.

Prior to the passage of the Pendleton Act of 1883, the first major civil service reform effort in the United States, the bases of obtaining a government job could be divided into two periods: the pre-Jackson and post-Jackson periods (Cayer, 1975). In the pre-Jackson period, assignments were made founded on "fitness of character," which meant a good family background, educational achievement, loyalty to the new government, and military service in the revolutionary war. This period has come to be known as "government by gentlemen." The elite of society dominated the public service (Mosher, 1968). Recruitment of such individuals, while they were a distinct minority of the population, was not much of a problem and most historians agree that these selection criteria produced a highly effective and ethical public service (Moore, 1985).

During the post-Jackson period, measures for appointment shifted from those favoring the gentry of society to features which advantaged "common men." The chief rationale for securing a position was patronage and spoils—or the idea that a government job was appropriate reward for faithful service to party organizations. Moreover, Jackson believed that government work was sufficiently uncomplicated that any person could perform it. He said:

> The duties of public officers are, or at least admit of being made, so plain and simple that
> men of intelligence may readily qualify themselves for their performance; and I can not but

believe that more is lost by the long continuance of men in office than is generally to be gained by their experience (Van Riper, 1958, p. 36).

There was no shortage of applicants and recruitment was not a problem during this era. The virtues and vices of patronage systems are well known and continue to be debated even today. However, for presidents and other state officials, patronage produced endless streams of job seekers. The quadrennial job rush made life so miserable for presidents and congressmen alike that Lincoln remarked that "the spoils system might in course of time become far more dangerous to the Republic than the rebellion itself (Van Riper, 1958, p. 44). In the early days of the Garfield administration, office seekers were compared to "beasts at feeding time" (Caldwell, 1965, p. 339). Garfield himself wrote in his diary that "the core of these crowds is the . . . officeseeker who pursues his prey with the grip of death (Caldwell, 1965, p. 339).

A good many of these job hunters were not qualified to perform government work. Moreover, fraud, corruption, and other abuses of office were evident in a civil service built on political loyalty rather than any objective standards of competence. There was also a growing concern about the inefficiency of bureaucracy bred by the spoils system. Finally, the assassination of President Garfield underscored the moral failure of patronage. This catalytic event combined with the other sources of distress and precipitated passage of the Pendleton Act of 1883. This reform was the first watershed event in the history of the American public service and spearheaded the attack on the worst abuses of the spoils system (Cohen, 1984). Its primary purpose was to change how people were qualified for government jobs and established the foundation for their recruitment.

1. The Pendleton Act: The Beginning of "Merit"

The provisions of the Pendleton Act emphasized nonpolitical standards based on competitive examinations that were "practical in character." These tests were the most important element in what was then regarded as an open, egalitarian personnel system (Van Riper, 1958). The principal value embodied in the Act was the achievement of efficiency in government operations through the recruitment of employees based on merit. The new law established the initial framework of modern personnel administration and its principles expanded to include much of the federal service and influenced the design of state and local government systems. There was no real notion of recruitment in the sense of actively seeking out competent persons to apply for public work. Sufficient numbers of eligible applicants showed up to take examinations for position vacancies at all levels of government and there was no shortage of candidates for unclassified political appointment slots. Government could be passive in its recruitment approach and concentrate on refining its examination and selection techniques. The thinking was that suitable applicants would present themselves for competitive examination. Recruitment equated with testing people in this traditional model (Carnevale, 1992).

2. Criticism Emerges

The traditional model of personnel was not without its critics. In 1935 (p. v), for example, the Commission of Inquiry on Public Service Personnel identified both major and minor problems in "securing competent men and women to fill the non-elective positions and perform the day-to-day work of government." Improving recruitment methods was the major subject in their report.

The Committee on Recruiting Applicants of the Civil Service Assembly of the United States and Canada (Kingsley, 1942, p. 5) echoed a similar theme and also criticized recruitment methods of the time. It asserted:

> We do not wish to belittle in any way the contributions made by the movement for civil service reform. They were substantial, and no one familiar with American political history would

care to deny that the elimination of spoils politics was an essential step on the highroad to a career service. But because the civil service commission was first conceived as a sort of politics eliminator, and because the early reformers, typically thought in terms of a moral crusade, the concept of recruitment which developed was, to say the least, a limited one.

The Committee (1942, pp. 1, 13) went on to note that relatively few public personnel agencies in the United States had given adequate consideration to recruitment and questioned whether the no-career-service system could ever be developed without "the general acceptance of a positive concept of recruitment in contrast to the traditional negative one."

Other voices were also derogatory of personnel practices. Wallace Sayre's classic evaluation (1948) that public personnel systems had achieved the "triumph of technique over purpose" applied to the activity of recruitment. Mosher et al. (1950, p. 65) noted that:

under the historic emphasis, there was a tendency to conceive of recruitment in negative terms. The task was to keep out the unfit, rather than encourage the best to enter. It was naively assumed that, if political favoritism could be excluded from the selection process, men of ability would somehow find their way into the public service. Such an assumption long ago proved erroneous, yet only slowly did the negative emphasis give way to positive recruitment policies. How true this is must be evident to everyone who has had occasion to examine the literature and publicity issued by the average civil service commission in carrying out recruitment activities. Much of it seems designed to discourage applicants rather than to stimulate them.

Criticism mounted over time. Recruitment methods were viewed as arbitrary (Savas and Ginsburg, 1973) and "slow, unimaginative, and unaggressive" (Committee on Economic Development, 1978, p. 45). These complaints were typical. Recruitment was simply not effective and responsive enough. Significantly, new voices were also beginning to be heard.

Recruitment practices continued to exclude major segments of the population from useful involvement in the public service. However, changes in the legal environment of human resources administration caused the ascension of the value of promoting social equity in the workplace. These events added to the already considerable concerns about the quality of recruitment activities and significantly transformed interest in acquisition subsystems and the development of more aggressive induction strategies.

B. Opening Doors to the Underrepresented

The issues of social equity, representative bureaucracy, equal employment opportunity (EEO), and affirmative action are addressed in great detail elsewhere in this volume. However, it is important to note here the significance of these matters on the development of recruitment. It is obvious that personnel systems reflect the social norms of their times. In earlier periods, societal values led to personnel practices that were plainly sexist and racist (Elliott, 1985). All that is changing in the modern era. As one author notes, "the impact of EEO on merit systems, at least in terms of legal and judicial requirements, has been so great that the history of public personnel in the U.S. could be divided into two chapters: before and after EEO" (Nigro, 1984, p. 21).

The most important effect of the emergence of social equity as an operational value in public personnel systems is that government can no longer sit back and wait passively for qualified applicants to show up at its doors. It now has an obligation to measure the representativeness of its work force, evaluate whether there is evidence that its employment practices are having an adverse impact on protected classes, and take action to overcome artificial barriers that operate to exclude people.

In terms of recruitment, equalizing access demands a more thoughtful and proactive effort to ensure that notices of vacancies are widespread, all segments of society are actively encouraged to apply for positions, individual rights are respected, and the benefits of public service careers are made known to the entire population. Paying attention to applicant pools and developing tactics to become more inclusionary are mandatory. Actively improving admission to public service careers is now an important goal of human resource administration, and of recruitment in particular. Definitive expression of these beliefs is contained in one of the merit principles of the Civil Service Reform Act of 1978, which requires that "recruitment should be from qualified individuals from appropriate sources in an endeavor to achieve a work force from all segments of society, and selection . . . should be determined solely on the basis of relative ability, knowledge, and skills after fair and open competition, which assures that all receive equal opportunity" (U.S. General Accounting Office, August 1990, p. 13).

C. The Heritage of the Past and Objectives of Modern Recruitment

Public recruitment has several major objectives that arise from historical values that have shaped the field of personnel administration. The value of political responsiveness is sustained as a certain number of public jobs are set aside for political appointees. Administrative efficiency is addressed when recruitment authority is delegated and decentralized in public organizations to produce more timely hires. Social equity is met when protected groups are actively sought for employment. Individual rights are protected when every applicant is assured that hiring systems are what they appear to be. Distributive justice is served where all Americans can get their fair share of the economic pie that public employment represents (cf. Shafritz, 1975; Elliott, 1985; Klingner and Nalbandian, 1993).

In contemporary times, the first set of assumptions that have historically restrained recruitment is finally being overcome. Recruitment is less passive and more proactive. It is less negative and more positive. It is more inclusionary and less exclusionary. It responds to a wider range of values than it did, for instance, at the turn of the century. The second limiting set of assumptions, i.e., that an abundant number of able applicants could be counted on to present themselves for employment, is also being faced.

The issue of building a quality public service, particularly at the federal level, is currently an important public personnel policy issue. Defining quality and assessing the capabilities of the present work force are receiving considerable attention in both the public and private sectors. Much research has been undertaken to explore these matters as well as how labor market trends will affect recruitment. There is some debate as to what demographic trends suggest about the future supply of labor. Where the federal government and other public employers are positioned with respect to such questions is not entirely clear. However, two things are accepted: (1) the labor force is transforming its composition and (2) it is no longer assumed that a plentiful supply of qualified people exists to fill all the human capital demands of public organizations.

III. WORK FORCE QUALITY, ENVIRONMENTAL CONTINGENCIES, AND RECRUITMENT STRATEGY

Major modern recruitment issues have found expression in the federal government and have centered around questions related to assessing the overall quality of the work force, the effect of external and internal labor markets on acquisition procedures, and the development of a policy framework that supports effective human capital procurement and retention. Considerably more regard has been paid to recruitment and retention issues than perhaps any other time and much has been learned about assuring an adequate flow of human assets.

A. Analyzing Work Force Quality: The Not-So-Quiet Crisis

There is widespread agreement that America is facing a revolution in the world of work. At the heart of this upheaval is the recognition that competitive advantage depends a great deal on having able employees who know how to utilize new technologies, adapt to changing environmental contingencies, and operate new forms of work organizations (Piore and Sabel, 1982; Reich, 1984; Choate, 1986; Osborne, 1988; Carnevale, 1991). A flood of reports appeared during the latter half of the past decade scrutinizing and criticizing America's readiness to address the human capital standards represented by the "new economy" (Johnston and Packer, 1987; U.S. Congress, Office of Technology Assessment, 1988; U.S. Department of Labor, Employment and Training Administration, and the Bureau of Apprenticeship and Training, 1988; Commission on Workforce Quality and Labor Market Efficiency, 1989; Commission on the Skills of the American Workforce, 1990; Carnevale et al., 1990).

At about the same time the torrent of reports took aim at private sector organizations, a number of studies were assessing the outlook for the public sector. They specifically focused on the federal government and its future labor requirements. The conclusions of some of these investigations were alarming.

1. Civil Service 2000

One of the reports is *Civil Service 2000* (Johnston et al., 1988). This independent study was prepared by the Hudson Institute at the request of the Office of Personnel Management (OPM). A year earlier the institute had published *Workforce 2000* (Johnston and Packer, 1987), which was funded in large part by the Department of Labor. Both studies were issued against a backdrop of changing economic conditions, such as the growing importance of world trade and international competition, a decreased reliance on manufacturing, and rapid technological innovation.

The reports also echoed many of the same themes about workers and jobs. They predicted labor shortages, skill mismatches, and demographic changes. Their findings amounted to an admonition. *Civil Service 2000* warned the government of a "slowly emerging crisis of competence":

> For years, many Federal agencies have been able to hire and retain highly-educated, high-skilled workforces. . . . But as labor markets become tighter during the early 1990s, hiring qualified workers will become much more difficult. Unless steps are taken now to address the problem, the average qualifications and competence of many segments of the Federal workforce will deteriorate, perhaps so much as to impair the ability of some agencies to function (Johnston et al., 1988, p. 29).

The same report forecast that (1) competition for well-qualified employees would become intense during the coming decade, (2) the federal government would continue to need even higher skilled persons to fill its ranks, and (3) changes in the federal retirement system were likely to increase turnover. Each of these assertions has direct implications for recruitment. Accordingly, the report recommended that

Authority for personnel operations be decentralized so that agencies will have the flexibility to respond to their individual human resource needs

Continued emphasis be placed on hiring women and minorities because they will make up a larger share of new entrants in the future labor force

Agencies be encouraged to systematically invest more in the training and development of their staffs since most of the employees who will manage governmental operations in the year 2000 are already on the job

The extrinsic rewards package (mainly pay) be improved

2. Volcker Commission Report

A year after the publication of *Civil Service 2000* a report issued forth that looked at another dimension of people working in government: the integrity and dignity of public service. It called for a "renewed sense of commitment by all Americans to the highest traditions of the public service" (Volcker, 1989a, p. 1). The report is known as the Volcker Commission, but its official title is *Leadership for America: Rebuilding the Public Service* (Volcker, 1989a, 1989b). It was produced by the National Commission on the Public Service, a private, nonprofit group of noted Americans and headed by former Federal Reserve Board Chairman Paul Volcker.

The Commission claimed that the twin areas of recruitment and retention are at the heart of a "crisis" in the federal government. Before he joined the Commission, Volcker (1988, p. 12) stated that "unmistakable evidence . . . is accumulating that government in general, and the federal government in particular, is increasingly unable to attract, retain, and motivate the kinds of people it will need to do the essential work of the republic in the years and decades ahead."

The Commission's recommendations for "rebuilding the public service" are (Volcker, 1989b, pp. 75–102) as follows:

Make an exemplary public service a national priority.
Decentralize activity and delegate authority throughout government, with central personnel authority providing standards and retaining oversight responsibility.
Improve and expand recruitment efforts (especially on college campuses); simplify and clarify the federal hiring process.
Create a federal executive development strategy; support and reward executive excellence.

These reports, however, have not gone without challenge (Crispell, 1990; Mangum, 1990; Mishel and Teixeira, 1991). Some of the views they express about the qualities of the future labor market are disputed. The U.S. General Accounting Office (March 1992) summarized the detractions:

> Two of the central themes in *Workforce 2000* and *Civil Service 2000*—predictions of a tight labor market and skills mismatches between jobs and the available labor supply by the turn of the century—have been questioned by labor economists and other experts. . . . Predictions of labor market shortages require much more information than is currently available (p. 34).

The Economic Policy Institute (Mishel and Teixeira, 1991) extended the criticism even further. Its report, *The Myth of the Coming Labor Shortage*, described *Workforce 2000's* labor shortage scenario as "wrong or misleading . . . (which) leads policymakers to focus *only* on the problems with education and training and not on the types of jobs being created by the economy or on how employers structure work" (emphasis added) (pp. 4–5).

The Volcker Commission must also be included in these criticisms because it too relies on the questioned assertions contained within the year 2000 reports. Another reproach concerning the Commission's report is related to its focusing primarily on the senior administrative and professional levels of the government, which means that recruitment of college graduates received the lion's share of its attention (Volcker, 1989a, p. x). Unfortunately, this underestimates the full import of the federal government's recruitment challenge. Trends in the requirements for a future work force indicate significant growth in many occupations that do not necessarily require college degrees (Silvestri and Lukasiewicz, 1989). For example, a variety of technical jobs need only 6 months to 2 years of postsecondary training (Kutscher, 1989). In addition, the government employs over 800,000 clerical and blue collar employees (Johnston et al., 1988). These data suggest that recruitment concerns apply to workers with and without college backgrounds, and that a complete and effective human resource program must be responsive to the needs of all present and future employees regardless of educational background (Carnevale, 1990–1991).

The Volcker Commission was founded on the assumption that the quality of the federal work force was in danger of diminishing. In the preface of its report to the public the Commission (Volcker, 1989a, p. ix) said, "Simply put, too many of the best of the nation's senior executives are ready to leave government, and not enough of its most talented young people are willing to join." The Commission (Volcker, 1989a, pp. 3–4) cited a number of reports that evidently did not bode well for the future of the federal work force. One of them found that fewer than 15% of recently interviewed senior executives would recommend public employment to their children. Another reported that half of the federal personnel officers responding to a survey felt it was becoming more difficult to recruit quality workers. Two years earlier the National Academy of Public Administration (Levine and Kleeman, 1986, p. 5) characterized the recruitment and retention of public employees as being in a "process of erosion." Clearly, much conventional wisdom supported the notion that the quality of the federal work force was in decline.

Yet there was still no consensus about what was meant by "quality" or how it could be measured (Ban and Ingraham, 1988; U.S. General Accounting Office, August 1988). Even the Volcker Commission (1989, p. ix) allowed as how the impetus for the group's formation was its "perception" of a waning public service. The U.S. General Accounting Office (August 1988, p. 10) reported:

> Despite the frequency of discussion of the subject, no statutory guidelines exist that direct comprehensive or regular assessment of the quality of the federal workforce. Rather, it is analyzed using individual anecdotes, unsystematic sampling of employee or supervisor opinions, or by inferences from other data.

In 1986 the GAO was asked by a House subcommittee chairman whether a methodology could be developed that would measure and evaluate the quality of government workers. In his letter to the GAO's comptroller general the chairman wrote:

> In spite of the difficulties inherent in measuring workforce quality, there is a strong need to do so. . . . There is no good method to capture changes in quality in the past. We can, however, establish a baseline now from which future changes can be measured (U.S. General Accounting Office, August 1988, pp. 74–75).

In its response, the General Accounting Office made it clear that it perceived the quality of the work force as a "consequence of several environmental influences" (U.S. General Accounting Office, August 1988, p. 16). Figure 2 is a graphic depiction of the agency's view. Although the GAO chose to limit the focus of its measurement effort to the individual employee (the element in Fig. 2 labeled "Workforce Quality"), their use of a systems perspective is important. The model reveals both the internal and external environmental contexts of the issue of work force quality. Furthermore, it invites and accommodates several plans that may be used to fortify recruitment in government.

For example, an inferential examination of the element in Fig. 2 labeled "External Context" discloses that outside factors are associated with the recruitment challenge. Its four integral parts can be seen to show that

How the public feels about the work of the government and its employees influences acquisition activities

What people want from their career changes over time and sways the extent to which the public service is perceived as a viable vocational choice

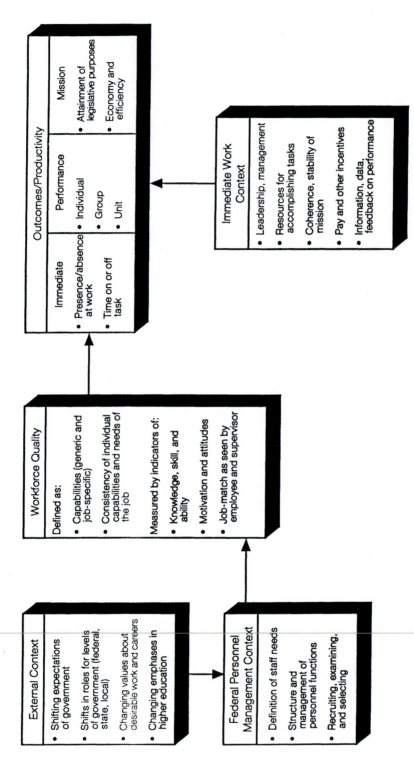

Figure 2 Workforce quality and its larger context. (From U.S. General Accounting Office, August 1988, p. 17.)

The skills preparedness workers bring to their jobs affects human resources planning, which in
    turn informs recruitment strategies

The nature and availability of labor is a central consideration in directing efforts geared to attract-
    ing applicants to government

But external factors alone cannot guarantee recruitment success or the achievement of a quality
labor force. The element in Fig. 2 depicting constituents of personnel management shows that government also needs to develop some sense of its future human capital needs. In terms of staffing
this means "anticipating loss of personnel through death, retirement, resignations, and dismissals. When these losses are compared to the anticipated expansion, reduction, or maintenance of
an organization, one can compute the human-resource needs for those who must hire new people
or lay off current employees" (Dresang, 1991, p. 85).

A general outline of human resource planning is portrayed in Fig. 3. The actual steps of the
process are not as neatly differentiated as those presented in the model; still, it is useful because
it depicts the multiple functions related to planning. Its features are also related to the surroundings within which many public activities function. That is, consideration of future staffing levels
is driven by legislative goals that are difficult to define and measure; by policies that emerge from
political values and conflicts; and by budgets that are formed in oftentimes hostile environments
(McGregor, 1991, pp. 225–226). On a positive note, the importance and feasibility of planning
is being given greater consideration, which is evidenced by the recent deluge of research on staffing
in government. The employment process is driven by more objective data analysis than ever.

Work force quality (Fig. 2) is also related to organizational outcomes. It is not enough to
recruit people with high academic credentials or other measures of achievement and to then presume that quality exists. "Quality" must be appreciated as an aspect of what government actually
produces, not just the traits of doing the work. The element labeled "Outcomes/Productivity" indicates that the work force is judged by a performance standard. This means that products and
services must address a particular need, have integrity, comply with acknowledged criteria, and
be based on the experience of knowing about the good or service being consumed (Hummel, 1987;
Garvin, 1988; Segalla, 1989). For example, it does little good to claim that a public hospital has
an effective recruitment program and a high-quality staff just because its employees have stunning
credentials from prestigious universities. What ultimately determines quality is how various stakeholders feel about the distinction of the institution's health care. Moreover, while quality and outcomes are related, they are also dependent on the caliber of mediating factors in the specific work
setting.

Recognizing the influence of the work environment completes the representation of the larger
context of work force quality (Fig. 2). "Immediate Work Context," the model's last element, illustrates that there are several components influencing the worth of outcomes. Among them are
the excellence of an organization's leadership and management competence; technological capacity; clarity of mission; reward and incentive structure; and openness to communication.

No recruitment strategy can overcome internal system deficiencies and produce quality by
itself. The same can be said for every administrative mechanism of human resource management.
This is why the authors of both of the models on work force quality (Figs. 1 and 2) portray their
views using interactive and interrelated terms. The principal lesson to be drawn from this section
of the chapter is that while one approach to quality assessment is to measure the work force in
terms of personnel.

a highly qualified workforce will not *alone* be sufficient to guarantee quality outcomes; work
environment, work systems and processes, leadership, customer expectations, and other elements are critical, too. . . . Workforce quality [is] the result of how an organization man-

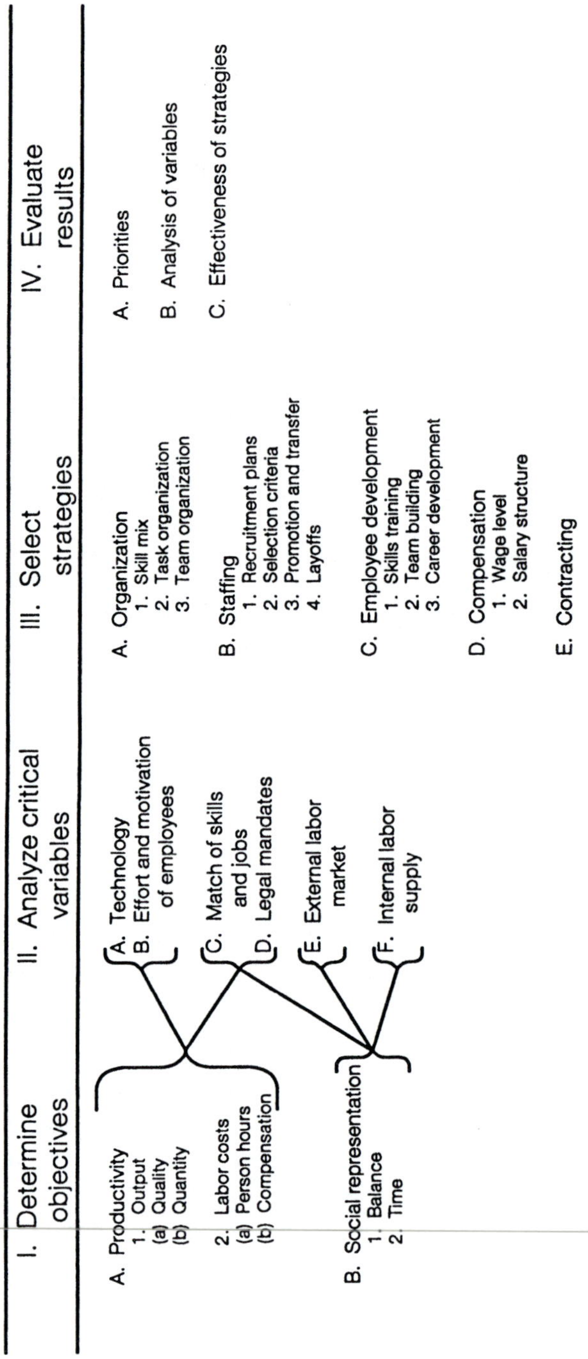

I. Determine
   objectives

II. Analyze critical
    variables

III. Select
     strategies

IV. Evaluate
    results

A. Productivity
   1. Output
      (a) Quality
      (b) Quantity

   2. Labor costs
      (a) Person hours
      (b) Compensation

B. Social representation
   1. Balance
   2. Time

A. Technology
B. Effort and motivation
   of employees

C. Match of skills
   and jobs
D. Legal mandates

E. External labor
   market

F. Internal labor
   supply

A. Organization
   1. Skill mix
   2. Task organization
   3. Team organization

B. Staffing
   1. Recruitment plans
   2. Selection criteria
   3. Promotion and transfer
   4. Layoffs

C. Employee development
   1. Skills training
   2. Team building
   3. Career development

D. Compensation
   1. Wage level
   2. Salary structure

E. Contracting

A. Priorities

B. Analysis of variables

C. Effectiveness of strategies

Figure 3   Human resource planning process. (From Dresang, 1991, p. 91.)

ages its inputs and outcomes through its various organizational processes (emphasis in original) (Advisory Committee on Federal Workforce Quality Assessment, 1992, pp. 4, 17).

IV. PRESCRIPTIONS FOR RECRUITING AND RETAINING QUALITY EMPLOYEES

There is a remarkable similarity in the ideas on how to better the employment process in government. First, there is widespread agreement that a precondition to successful recruitment depends on achieving a positive image of the public service. Second, consensus exists that improvements in the quality of working life of employees need to be realized to reduce costly turnover, which greatly leverages the extent of the recruitment problem. Third, there is accord that family-friendly policies require more attention to attract, retain, motivate, and build commitment in the emerging labor force. Fourth, continued development of career opportunities for women and minorities is considered decisive. Fifth, unanimity exists that advancements in the actual techniques or technology of recruitment are dictated.

A. The Negative Image of Public Service

Governmental employees and the American public service have suffered a serious image problem throughout modern history that has had major deleterious effects on recruitment. Trust and confidence in government is a persistent difficulty. For example, a past president of the U.S. Chamber of Commerce once observed that "the best public servant is the worst one . . . [a] thoroughly first-rate man in public service is corrosive. He eats holes in our liberties. The better he is and the longer he stays, the greater is the danger (*The Nation's Business*, November 1928). At about the same time, Leonard D. White (1979, pp. 23–24) reported that "two ideas are widely held by the American taxpayer. He believes that there is an extraordinary number of useless or overpaid public officials and he is convinced that most government employees are lazy and incompetent, and secured their positions only by 'pull.'" The Commission of Inquiry on Public Service Personnel observed (1935, p. 19) that "indiscriminate vilification lessens the morale of all public officials, dissuades capable persons from entering the public service, and discredits the authority of government." The Committee on Recruiting Applications for the Public Service of the Civil Service (Kingsley, 1942, p. 26) decried the "low prestige value for public employment" and went on to note that the "effects of such attitudes are destructive and of wide scope. They act everywhere as deterrents to the best qualified in respect to public employment [and] severely handicap recruiting activities." In short, there are problems with feelings about both bureaucracy and bureaucrats. When contemporary groups focus on how the contrary image of the public service influences staffing, they are not entertaining a fresh problem.

Bureaucrat bashing by the nation's political leadership in recent years has resulted in a widespread public perception of government as an undesirable place to work (Lane and Wolf, 1990). The Volcker Commission (1989b, p. 12) determined that "unjust negative public perceptions of the public service drive highly qualified, experienced people out of government and discourage the most qualified from joining it." Holzer and Rabin (1987, p. 4) noted the negative consequences for recruitment brought about by "attacks on government ranging from the malicious to the naive [which] demean the value of public service and minimize support for the public sector." According to one study (U.S. Merit Systems Protection Board, June 1988, p. 25), even a majority of public administration majors they interviewed cited the poor public image of "bureaucracy" and "federal employees" as reasons students may not be interested in federal employment. But it is not only the national government that is affected. Public employees everywhere are painted with the same broad brush. Negative stereotypes about public employees are widespread and make the recruitment process difficult at every level.

Changing the image and reputation of government service is a daunting task. The Volcker Commission (1989b, p. 40) suggested four general approaches for improving the reputation of government:

Emphasize public education as the principal means of counteracting the ignorance and insensitivity that underlies all stereotypes.

Improve the public image of government and government workers by increased compensation and increased recognition.

Play on the public's attraction to big business as an idealized model of managerial excellence by making the government operations seem more businesslike and government workers more entrepreneurial.

Play on the public's preference for decentralized government by decentralizing more of government's functions, thereby presumably enhancing the image of the federal government by diminishing its role.

The problem with these strategies, as with numerous others that have been suggested over time, is that people who express unfavorable attitudes about government agencies and employees also report that they have received good treatment in actual encounters with public employees. But they do not generalize from these episodes (Katz et al., 1975). Americans have a fundamental ambivalence about government that fosters a kind of political cynicism that is extremely difficult to overcome. We do not suffer from a lack of sound recommendations to improve both opinions about government and its staff. The problem is overcoming something fundamental in the American psyche (Ventriss, 1991). The likely reality is that public recruiters will always have to combat negative impressions of public service. Their job is made considerably easier, however, if elected officials can resist the temptation to engage in government bashing for short-term political gain.

B. Improving the Work Life of Government Employees

1. Compensation

In a study comparing why applicants accepted or declined federal job offers (U.S. General Accounting Office, March 1992, p. 2), "financial considerations dominated the decliner's reasons for their decisions." These results mirror the findings of other investigations. For instance, the U.S. Merit Systems Protection Board (MSPB) conducted a study (May 1990) on why employees left the federal service. Compensation and advancement were identified as the principal reasons. Another MSPB (August 1989) inquiry found that inadequate compensation was the most frequently cited reason for why senior executives left the federal service. Low salaries and noncompetitive fringe benefits were specified as being among the main explanations why federal laboratories have had difficulty recruiting high-caliber scientists and engineers (Packard, 1986). Finally, three General Accounting Office studies (May 1990, August 1990, September 1990) found starting pay for most government jobs to be a "major barrier to recruiting" throughout the public service, the primary problem in recruiting and retaining persons in specific occupations, and noncompetitive when compared to pay for comparable work in the private sector.

The Federal Pay Reform Act of 1990 goes a long way toward achieving pay equity. It mandates a series of incremental pay increases that are designed to bring government salaries into line with comparable private sector earnings. The law is also supposed to make pay adjustments in areas where the cost of living is disproportionately high (Shafritz et al., 1992, pp. 154–156). It is doubtful, however, that government compensation packages will ever be fully elevated to a level where potential hires will perceive the public service as the employer of first resort. It would be a major step forward if public compensation systems are perceived as simply being more competitive. In addition to pay, government can be more ambitious in providing other extrinsic rewards that are increasingly treasured by recruits. One such benefit relates to "work/family" programs.

2. Work/Family Programs

Despite differences on the precise nature of demographic trends, there is widespread agreement that the nature of work and families are both changing. The increased participation of women in the labor force, the number of single-parent households, and the amount of situations in which both husbands and wives work are on the increase and demand that government develop flexible policies that aid staff to balance work and family responsibilities. Doing so should confer a competitive advantage in recruitment because there is evidence that employees value these benefits (U.S. General Accounting Office, June 1992) and may be more apt to opt for employers willing to help them realize their "work/family" objectives (U.S. General Accounting Office, April 1992). In the arising seller's labor market, traditional assumptions concerning employer responsibilities in accommodating work and nonwork obligations need to be reevaluated (Romzek, 1990).

There are a number of policy options available to address these goals: (1) child care, (2) elder care, (3) parental leave, (4) diversity training, (5) alternative work scheduling arrangements, (6) job sharing, (7) flexible benefits and spending accounts, and (8) employee assistance programs (U.S. Merit Systems Protection Board, November 1991; U.S. General Accounting Office, March 1992, April 1992). And these alternatives do not exhaust the full range of possibilities. Although the Office of Personnel Management (OPM) has made federal support of these nontraditional arrangements a "high priority," the General Accounting Office (April 1992) reports that no single office in OPM is responsible for such endeavors and agency officials would like to see more leadership in this critical area. There are, however, barriers confronting OPM, and anyone else, who would care to steer such programs. Costs, of course, are a major concern. But as the U.S. Merit Systems Protection Board (November, 1991, p. 77) recently pointed out,

> many of the costs and benefits of these issues are indirect, or not immediately apparent to the casual observer, and (are) thus difficult to measure. The expenses of recruiting and training replacements, for example, or the lost productivity while positions are vacant, are real but often hidden. Similarly, an inability to attract top candidates because the Government is not viewed as a progressive employer can also be a major cost.

It is clear that the federal government must excel in the area of family-friendly policy, which should improve its competitive position in recruiting.

3. Women and Minorities

The federal government demonstrated a serious commitment to equal employment opportunity well before such practices were widely accepted in the private sector (Johnston, 1988). Similar dedication needs to be emphasized in the future. Government, like a private employer, develops a reputation based on its pledge to promote social equity and deal constructively with diversity in the workplace. Citizen evaluation of its progress in this area affects recruitment. However, it is not sufficient simply to improve the overall representativeness of the work force. Much of that has already been achieved. What is especially important in the near future is to manage major institutional changes aimed not only at recruiting women and minorities, but training and increasing their upward mobility as well (Riccucci, 1991).

While the overall numbers of protected classes are on the rise in government, their representation at top policymaking levels is still a problem (Newman, 1991). In a recent report released by the U.S. Merit Systems Protection Board (October, 1992), it was found that a "glass ceiling" existed in the federal government that serves to obstruct the upward mobility of women. Because of data developed in the MSPB report, a separate study is being performed on the opportunities for advancement for minorities in the national government. Given the changing nature of the labor pool from which applicants are drawn, the issue of advancement following appointment is a crucial issue to women and minorities and to the employers interested in recruiting them. The glass ceiling problem is also widespread in the private sector (U.S. Department of Labor, 1991). If government is to sustain its competitive advantage in attracting female and minority applicants, it must overcome the stereotypes and other institutional practices that conspire to frustrate career progression of persons underrepresented at higher levels of public administration.

4. Intrinsic Factors

Pay, work and family issues, promotional practices, and the like are certainly important. These are extrinsic motivators that help attract and retain workers. But extrinsic rewards are not the only inducements for selecting or remaining with an employer. The chance to experience meaningful and challenging work, i.e., intrinsic factors related to the work itself, is also consequential. As a matter of fact, recent personnel demonstration projects suggest that intrinsic factors are more important to young professionals than extrinsic factors (Ross, 1990). Other evidence exists that supports the idea that the nature of work is a powerful motivator for public employees (Lane and Wolf, 1990, p. 58). A major encouraging sign is the increase in innovations in workplace practices based on quality improvement schemes throughout the public sector (Hyde, 1992). Reports of successful cases are increasingly prevalent (Bowman and French, 1992; Gilbert, 1992). These ventures involve enriching the work life of employees through greater participation. As more and more governmental jurisdictions commit to such programs, the standing of public employment is enhanced making recruitment and retention easier.

In summary, recruitment is profoundly influenced by the reputation of an organization and the quality of its human resource management processes. These include not only recruitment and selection procedures, but job design, authority relations, opportunities for participation, commitment to training and development, compensation programs, and encouragement of diversity. Recruitment and retention are not enabled in impoverished work cultures. Healthy work *systems* attract and hold capable individuals.

C. Improving Methods and Techniques

> Recruitment involves more than mere announcement and passive acceptance; to meet the requirements of our present public service, it must be active, searching, selective, persistent and continuous (White, 1939, p. 316).
>
> Leonard White, 1939

> No longer will the government be able to sit back and wait for candidates for employment to present themselves and endure long delays before obtaining jobs (U.S. Senate Subcommittee hearing, 1989, p. 6).
>
> Constance Newman, 1989

As mentioned in the introduction, recruitment is a word that accommodates a variety of meanings. One of them refers to overall personnel acquisition, which is a process that includes fairly distinct personnel activities such as position classification, testing and evaluation, and human resources planning. Another meaning of recruitment pertains to efforts to advance the image of the federal service. For example, in 1942 (Kingsley, p. 25) the Civil Service Assembly asserted that "enhanc[ing] the general attractiveness and prestige of the public service" is a necessary function of any recruitment strategy. The Volcker Commission (1989a) and its Task Force on Recruitment and Retention (Volcker, 1989b) concurred, saying that the projection of a positive image of public service is essential to building a quality work force.

Another concept of recruitment limits its meaning to the utilization of specific methods for attracting potential employees. These involve techniques that can be employed without waiting for the resolution of large, complex human resource issues like safeguarding merit principles or simplifying the government's hiring process. While these types of concerns are inseparable from the general well-being and effectiveness of public sector personnel, they are not the sole determinants of successful recruitment. A case in point is the General Services Administration (GSA).

(a) *Agencies: Taking the Initiative.* During the 1980s, GSA dramatically restructured its organization. In the process the agency reduced its staff by over 44%; furthermore, it changed from employing large numbers of blue collar workers to relying more heavily on procurement and technical experts (U.S. Senate subcommittee hearing, 1989, pp. 133–134; hereafter USS). GSA believes that its revitalization was due in large measure to their college recruitment program. In testimony before a Senate subcommittee a GSA official described some of the techniques the agency employed:

A team approach to campus visits, with a program manager and a personnel specialist on every team

A high-quality brochure (with an employment application enclosed) that describes the agency's mission, goals, and accomplishments

A marketing plan that includes a college relations program and advertising—both of which are designed to communicate GSA's recruitment interests and the career opportunities within the agency (USS, 1989, pp. 24, 135–136)

Supporting these efforts is the presence of important internal factors, the most significant of which is top management's commitment to recruiting. Also salient is GSA's recognition that recruitment without retention is a hallow achievement, not to mention a costly one. Accordingly, the agency provides career development opportunities that link explicit training with the requirements of different levels of performance. In this way, employees are provided guidance along their career paths (USS, 1989, p. 137). The GSA administrator concluded his testimony by affirming his agency's belief that the government can indeed recruit quality personnel:

However, this belief is contingent on a number of factors. We must have a commitment from agency leadership, must train our recruiters, screen our representatives . . . and be prepared to receive, challenge, and make welcome our new hires (USS, 1989, p. 24).

Appearing before the same Senate subcommittee was the civilian personnel director of the U.S. Air Force. He described additional methods and practices that aid recruitment: (1) direct mailing targeted to specific classes of recipients, (2) subsidized academic education for employees, (3) training for recruiters, (4) internships for vocational and college students, and (5) greater use of television advertising. He pointed out that when the uniformed branches of the armed forces were facing recruitment problems in the 1970s, they "turned their image around through more sophisticated marketing techniques, including television and direct mailing to recruits" (USS, 1989, p. 26).

Both the GSA and Air Force representatives were asked by the subcommittee chairman about their relationship with OPM. The reason for the inquiry was no doubt similar to a concern expressed by a U.S. Merit Systems Protection Board (June 1988) study which noted that although much of the responsibility for effective on-campus recruitment necessarily and properly falls on the individual Federal agencies with the positions to be filled, there is still a need for Governmentwide coordination and centralized recruitment-related initiatives as one component of the larger picture (p. 28).

Thus the chairman's question and the MSPB report put their fingers on a fundamental personnel issue for the 1990s: What is the quality of the relationship between the central personnel authority (OPM) and the hundreds of agencies with which it is associated? The GSA representative's response provides hopeful evidence: "Mr. Chairman, we feel supported and guided by OPM . . . their very positive attitude and their willingness to listen to the agency's suggestions . . . [has] made them a true partner in recruitment" (USS, 1989, p. 28). The response by the Air Force spokesperson was equally positive.

Actually, we have come a long way from the old days of OPM. We have an excellent relationship with them now. . . . They come to us and discuss the policy changes to get the reaction of the agency users, and it has been very, very good. I think we are on the threshold . . . [of] doing some of the things that need to be done in recruiting (USS, 1989, p. 28).

(b) *Working with a Partner.*   The Presidential Management Internship (PMI) program is an encouraging example of OPM and government agencies working together in successful, ongoing recruitment efforts. PMI was established by executive order in 1977. Its purpose is to attract well-educated people who have management potential and an ethic of public service. The program is overwhelmingly supported by its participants, with over 92% endorsing its continuation and more than half reporting that their goals were either met or exceeded by their PMI experience (Johnson, 1991, pp. 147–148). Approximately one-third of the alumni said they would not have gone to work for the federal government had it not been for PMI (Goldenkoff, 1988, p. 15).

The PMI program supplements graduate level education with on-the-job training, which is accomplished during a two-year internship with a government agency. The Office of Personnel Management administers the program, recruits and screens candidates, and sponsors some of the training and development activities. It is marketed as a fast-track method of gaining substantive experience in government work (Johnson, 1991; Newcomer et al., 1990). However, the ability of OPM to make the internships meaningful and challenging is limited. Johnson (1991, pp. 19–20) says that PMI studies have consistently found that the success of most aspects of the program varies with the agencies' degree of commitment. OPM's first director of the intern program said:

Perhaps the most important lesson we have learned is that the "power" of the Office of Personnel Management, and certainly this office, is very limited. We simply can't sit back and push and pull leavers and buttons to make things happen. Instead we can talk, negotiate, plead and beg to get our position known (Blakeslee, 1980, p. 49).

Because the PMI program is decentralized, OPM can only provide direction and support from a distance. This is the general arrangement the Volcker Commission had in mind when it recommended that agencies be given greater flexibility to manage programs and human resources while at the same time relying on a central personnel authority to provide goals, guidance, and oversight (Volcker, 1989a, 1989b).

For most of the 1980s, OPM was not in the business of recruiting entry level professional positions. Agency staff reductions, decreased funding for recruitment, demoralized employees, and leadership alleged to have been both partisan and hostile all combined to deemphasize efforts to attract applicants (Rosen, 1986; U.S. Merit Systems Protection Board, April 1990, p. 5). One of the biggest deterrents to OPM-based targeted recruiting was the abolishment in 1982 of its primary competitive examination. This was the hiring mechanism through which seekers of professional and administrative jobs were tested, ranked, and presented to agencies for possible employment. The exam was eliminated after it was discovered that it was likely to have been unfair in its evaluation of minorities.

In 1990 OPM replaced the exam, but during the intervening 8 years much more recruitment was left to agencies. The trend toward decentralizing the hiring procedures had been heading in this direction since at least 1980, but the process was given a boost when OPM increased agency involvement. A comparison of the hiring rates between OPM and the agencies shows how dramatic the shift has been. In 1979 only 7% of the competitive selections came from agency-based examining, whereas 93% were via OPM. By 1992, the ratio was 70% hired by agencies and 30% by OPM (U.S. Merit Systems Protection Board, October 1989, p. 8; Klein, 1993).

The agencies that hired the bulk of the professional and administrative workers favored their new authority (U.S. Merit Systems Protection Board, September 1987, pp. 9–10; Ban and Ingraham, 1988, p. 712). They said doing their own hiring shortened the process and gave them more flexibility, particularly in the targeting of minorities and women (U.S. Merit Systems Protection Board, October 1989, p. 12). Others, however, expressed concern that turning responsibility over to the agencies puts the careful application of merit principles at risk. The American civil service is pledged by law and policy to assure that its workers are selected on the basis of fair and open competition. Upholding merit principles protects against favoritism, nepotism, and patronage.

Can the merit system be decentralized and be fair? This is one of the large, complex issues of personnel administration in the 1990s. Similar concerns are expressed about exceptions to the government's primary pay system, which permits agencies to pay different salaries to employees holding identical positions (U.S. General Accounting Office, September 1990). Agencies agree that such discretion is a very helpful recruiting aid, but the question remains as to whether, like decentralized hiring, it is a practice that violates the principles of fairness and equality.

For many observers the answer lies somewhere between the extremes. As Charles Bowsher, Comptroller General of the United States, said:

> [The severe limitation of government resources will continue for years to come. As a consequence, attention to management issues is being seen with increasing interest in the public sector.] This is reflected in efforts by state and local governments to improve services, experimentation at various levels with privatization, and other management initiatives that seek to improve services or cut costs. . . . That federal agencies must deal with change is not seriously a matter of debate (Bowsher, 1992, p. 3).

Bowsher's "serving-the-customer" approach does not exclude regard for merit principles. As his own agency, the General Accounting Office, has said many times, the central personnel authority must reinforce its oversight and evaluation efforts regarding the increased discretion exercised by government agencies (U.S. General Accounting Office, June 1989, p. 57; August 1990, p. 48; September 1991, p. 16). OPM agrees that they need to make sure agencies maintain documentation related to discretionary hiring and payment practices (U.S. General Accounting Office, April 1991, p. 17; August 1990, p. 48).

(c) *OPM: Trying to be "User-Friendly."* An on-site study by OPM of almost three dozen agency installations found that the attributes of successful agency recruitment were the very same as those described above by the GSA and the Air Force (U.S. General Accounting Office, August 1990, p. 61). However, the recruiting methods OPM has developed for its own use are somewhat different, primarily because their evolving role as a provider of support and guidance requires an alternative approach.

Besides image and pay, the most often cited barrier to effective recruitment is a hiring process that is perceived as being untimely, overly complex, and inefficient (U.S. General Accounting Office, August, 1990, p. 55; USS, 1989, p. 7) OPM has taken a twofold approach to dealing with this vexing problem. First, they have automated their system of receiving and testing applicants. Approximately 80% of the people hired by the government now apply by using optically scanned forms. OPM is thus able to process over 2000 applications an hour rather than the one or two an hour that used to be done manually. Second, OPM has also automated the process of supplying agencies with the names of interested and qualified workers (Klein, 1993).

The way in which the hiring process works today might startle some who have attempted in the past to make application to the federal government. For example, the chairman of a Senate subcommittee on the civil service once had his staff test how the government was doing in providing job seekers with employment information and assistance. Four interns from the senator's office went to various agencies in the nation's capital. They returned to report that their experiences were uniformly unfavorable (USS, 1989, pp. 2–6). In late 1990, a year and a half after the interns' experiences, a Washington-based journalist made a similar job-seeking trek. The result of his venture was like that of the interns'. He wrote:

> The job application process is so confusing that even college career counselors don't understand it. Just laying your hands on information about what positions are out there requires the investigative savvy of Bob Woodward and the patience of Job (Heileman, 1990, p. 40).

As explained by a top OPM official (Klein, 1993), government job seeking should now be a much improved experience. Today an application can be requested by calling a nationwide number. When OPM receives the completed form the pertinent information is incorporated in a central computer system. Agencies that are hiring can communicate with the master database by using touch-tone phone communication and codes that represent the specifics of their employment needs. Within half an hour, the inquiring agency receives by telefax a list of candidate referrals, which can then be used to set up interviews with prospective employees.

Most federal jobs require that applicants be tested in their area of interest and expertise. Arranging to take an examination is similar to the application process. A test sign-up form is completed, mailed to OPM, and the job seeker is scheduled to take an exam at a time and place convenient for the applicant. Testing is conducted throughout the year, regardless whether there are immediate openings.

While the "paperless" application and referral system may be the most visible improvement among OPM's attempts to improve its recruitment techniques, the agency is involved with other initiatives. Among them are:

A nationwide electronic college bulletin board system that will contain specific job information and be linked to colleges and universities

A recruiter clearinghouse that contains "models" to assist agencies with designing and implementing recruitment strategies

A work force quality database (as discussed above) to measure and compare over time the quality of government applicants and new hires

A first-class set of recruitment materials known as *Career America*, which represents a major improvement in the way the government presents itself as a place to work (USS, 1989, p. 7; U.S. General Accounting Office, August 1990, pp. 29, 72).

The methods discussed above—both the specific techniques as well as those that are broader in scope and impact—represent the direction being taken by the country's central personnel organization. Which is not to say that criticism of OPM has come to an end, even from the agency itself (U.S. General Accounting Office, January 1992, July 1992; U.S. Office of Personnel Management, October 1992). Yet Charles Bowsher's challenge to all agencies seems to be taking root at OPM. The Comptroller General said, "[Agencies] must learn not only to accept change but to embrace it" (Bowsher, 1992, p. 4). As if in response, a high OPM official described the agency's evolving view of itself:

> We are starting to see our role at OPM as providing more of a service to agencies rather than being an agent of control. I think the agencies are beginning to see us as being more customer oriented than we once were . . . as being interested in helping them get their jobs done rather than just being the cops in the system (Klein, 1993).

V. CONCLUSION

Recruitment is part of the personnel acquisition process and involves encouraging citizens to enter the public service. It is one of the most crucial activities in human resource administration. This is because recruitment serves to supply the vital human assets—people with the requisite knowledge, skills, and abilities—needed for government to competently perform its role in a democratic society.

Recruitment is a process that occurs within the context of a personnel system and is profoundly influenced by a variety of contingencies created in the external and internal operating domains of government agencies. It cannot be understood as an isolated set of techniques. Technological, demographic, and sociopolitical changes, the reputation of government as an employer, the prestige of public service, the quality of its leadership, the caliber of work life it offers employees, and its commitment to career development all bear on the magnitude and nature of the public sector's recruitment challenge.

Historically, government recruitment activities have been more negative than positive, i.e., preoccupied with keeping out the undesirable rather than aggressively seeking the best to serve. Moreover, government could always count on a plentiful supply of applicants in most occupations. There was no compelling need to improve acquisition technology as long as a sufficient supply of suitable candidates presented themselves for employment.

Elevated attention is now being paid to recruitment methods in the face of growing concern about a "crisis" of quality in government's human capital base, demographic transformations in the work force, and a "seller's" labor market in the high-skill technical and professional occupations increasingly characteristic of public work.

It is encouraging that a torrent of empirical research is being undertaken to evaluate government recruitment and the related issue of work force quality. Much of that research has focused on the federal problem. However, new research on recruitment in state and local government is appearing (Ammons and Glass, 1989; Conant and Dresang, 1992). It is also hopeful that the U.S. Office of Personnel Management, for example, is providing leadership to strengthen recruitment methods. However, evaluations of the impact of fresh approaches demonstrate that much more has to be done if the national government is to successfully compete for qualified human resources.

There are some who contend that government employees need not be the best but merely adequate. This view underestimates the importance of government in society and denigrates the notion of a public service career as a worthwhile calling. A less than capable public work force not only is unable to deliver quality goods and services but serves as a drag on the private economy. Government is nested in all of the nation's productive networks, and it matters that its staff be able, respected, and motivated to perform.

REFERENCES

Advisory Committee on Federal Workforce Quality Assessment (1992). *Federal Workforce Quality: Measurement and Improvement*, a report to the U.S. Merit Systems Protection Board and the U.S. Office of Personnel Management, Washington, DC.

Ammons, D.N., and Glass, J.J. (1989). *Recruiting Local Government Executives*, Jossey-Bass, San Francisco.

Apprenticeship 2000: Report of Public Comments, U.S. Government Printing Office, Washington, DC.

Ban, C., and Ingraham, P. (1988). Retaining quality federal employees: life after PACE, *Public Admin. Rev., 48*: 708–718.

Blakeslee, L. B. (1990). "An Interim Evaluation of the Presidential Management Intern Program." Unpublished report prepared for the U.S. Office of Personnel Management, (November).

Bowman, J., and French, B. (1992). Quality improvements in a state agency revisited, *Public Productivity & Management Review, 16*: 53–65.

Bowsher, C.A. (1992). Meeting the new American management challenge in a federal agency: lessons from the General Accounting Office, *Public Admin. Rev., 52*: 3–7.

Caldwell, R. (1965). *James A. Garfield, Party Chieftan*. Anchor Books, Hamden, CT.

Carnevale, A.P. (1991). *America and the New Economy*, Jossey-Bass, San Francisco.

Carnevale, A., and Carnevale, D. (1993). Public administration and the new economy, working paper, University of Oklahoma, Norman.

Carnevale, A.P., Gainer, L.J., and Villet, J. (1990). *Training in America*, Jossey-Bass, San Francisco.

Carnevale, D. (1990–1991). Recruitment strategies in the federal government: missing links and representative bureaucracy, *Rev. Public Personnel Admin., 11* (fall/spring): 112–120.

Carnevale, D. (1992). The learning support model: personnel policy beyond the tradional model, *Am. Rev. Public Admin., 22*: 19–36.

Cayer, J. (1975). *Public Personnel Administration in the United States*, St. Martin's Press, New York.

Choate, P., with J. Klinger (1986). *The High-Flex Society: Shaping America's Economic Future*, Knopf, New York.

Cohen, M. (1984). Two fundamental civil service reforms, *Public Personnel Update* (M. Chohen and R. Golembiewski, eds.), Marcel Dekker, New York, pp. 9–29.

Commission of Inquiry on Public Service Personnel (1935). *Better Government Personnel*, McGraw-Hill, New York.

Commission on Workforce Quality and Labor Market Efficiency (1989). *Investing in People: A Strategy to Address America's Workforce Crisis*, U.S. Department of Labor, Washington, DC.

Committee on Economic Development (1978). *Improving Management of the Public Work Force*, New York.

Conant, J.K., and Dresang, D.L. (1992). Career professional retention, morale, and recruitment in state governments, paper presented to the Commission on American State and Local Public Service.

Crispell, D. (1990). Workers in 2000, *Am. Demographics, 12*: 36, 38–40.

Dresang, D. (1991). *Public Personnel Management and Public Policy*, 2nd Ed. Longman, New York.

Elliott, R.H. (1985). *Public Personnel Administration: A Values Perspective*, Reston, Reston, VA.

Garvin, D. (1988). *Managing Quality*, Free Press, New York.

Gilbert, G.R. (1992). Quality improvement in a federal defense organization, *Public Productivity & Management Review, 16*: 53–65.

Goldenkoff, Robert (1988). That the best may serve: methods of recruiting and retaining federal entry-level personnel, unpublished study submitted to the National Commission on the Public Service.

Gullick, L. (1937). Science, values, and public administration, *Papers on the Science of Administration* (L. Gullick and L. Urwick, eds.), Institute of Public Administration, New York.

Heilemann, J. (1990). Government agencies are a haven for the mediocre because they don't try to get anybody better, *Washington Monthly, December*, 39–46.

Holzer, M., and Rabin, J. (1987). Public service: problems, professionalism, and policy recommendations, *Public Prod. Rev., 43*: 3–13.

Hummel, R. (1987). Behind quality management: what workers and a few philosophers have always known and how it adds up to quality, *Organiz. Dynamics, 16*: 71–78.

Hyde, Albert C. (1992). The proverbs of total quality management: recharting the path to quality improvement in the public sector. *Public Productivity & Management Review, 16*: 25–37.

Hyde, A. (1983). Placing the individual in the organization, *Handbook on Public Personnel Administration and Labor Relations* (J. Rabin, T. Vocino, W.B. Hildreth, and G. Miller, eds.), Marcel Dekker, New York, pp. 99–121.

Johnson, Gail (1991). *Recruiting, Retaining, and Motivating the Federal Workforces*, Quorum Books, New York.

Johnston, W.B., with contributions by S. Faul, B. Huang, and A.H. Packer (1988). *Civil Service 2000*, Office of Personnel Management, Washington, DC.

Johnston, W.B., and Packer, A.H. (1987). *Workforce 2000: Work and Workers for the 21st Century*, Hudson Institute, Indianapolis, IN.

Katz, D., Gutek, B., Kahn, R., and Barton, E. (1975). *Bureaucratic Encounters: In the Evaluation of Government Services*, Survey Research Center, Institute for Social Research, University of Michigan, Ann Arbor.

Kingsley, J.D. (1942). Recruiting applicants for the public service, a report submitted to the Civil Service Assembly by the Committee on Recruiting Applicants for the Public Service, Civil Service Assembly of the United States and Canada, Chicago.

Klein, L.R., Associate Director for Career Entry, U.S. Office of Personnel Management, personal conversation with the authors, January 1993.

Kutscher, R. (1989). Projections, summary, and emerging issues, *Monthly Labor Rev., November*: 66–74.

Lane, L., and Wolf, J. (1990). *The Human Resource Crisis in the Public Sector: Rebuilding the Capacity to Govern*, Quorum Books, New York.

Levine, C. (1986). The federal government in the year 2000: administrative legacies of the Reagan years, *Public Admin. Rev., 46*: 195–207.

Levine, C., and Kleeman, R. (1986). *The Quiet Crisis: The Federal Personnel System at the Crossroads*, National Academy of Public Administration, Washington, DC.

Mangum, S. (1990). Impending skill shortages: where is the crisis? *Challenge, Sept.–Oct.*): 46–52.

McGregor, E.B., Jr. (1988). The public sector human resource puzzle: strategic management of a strategic resource, *Public Admin. Rev., 48*: 941–950.

McGregor, E.B., Jr. (1991). *Strategic Management of Human Knowledge, Skills, and Abilities*. Jossey-Bass, San Francisco.

Mishel, L., and Teixeira, R. (1991). *The Myth of the Coming Labor Shortage: Jobs, Skills, and Incomes of America's Workforce 2000*, American Enterprise Institute, Washington, DC.

Moore, Perry (1985). *Public Personnel Management: A Contingency Approach*, Lexington Books, Lexington, Massachusetts.

Mosher, Frederick C. (1968). *Democracy and the Public Service*, Oxford University Press, New York.

Mosher, W.E., Kingsley, J.D., and Stahl, O.G. (1950). *Public Personnel Administration*, Harper & Brothers, New York.

Nalbandian, J., and Klingner, D. (1993). *Public Personnel Management: Context and Strategies*, 3rd Ed., Prentice-Hall, Englewood Cliffs, NJ.

National Commission on the Public Service (1989). *Leadership for America: Rebuilding the Public Service*, Washington, DC.

The Nations Business (November 1928). Cited in *Better Government Personnel* (1935), p. 18. Commission on Inquiry on Public Service Personnel, McGraw Hill, New York.

Newcomer, K., Johnson, G., Naccarato, T., and Collie, S. (1990). Successful recrutitment and retention: the PMIP," *The Bureaucrat, 19*: 35–42.

Newman, C. (1991). "Good Government Needs Good People." The Bureaucrat (Summer) 20: 6–10.

Nigro, F.A. (1984). Public personnel administration: from Theodore Roosevelt to Ronald Reagan, *Int. J. Public Admin., 6*: 1–54.

Osborne, D. (1988). *Laboratories of Democracy: A New Breed of Governor Creates Models for National Growth*, Harvard Business School Press, Boston.

Packard, D. (1986). The loss of government scientific and engineering talent, *Issues Sci. Technol. spring*.

Piore, M., and Sabel, C. (1982). *The Second Industrial Divide*, Basic Books, New York.

Reich, R. (1984). *The Next American Frontier*, Penguin Books, New York.

Riccucci, N. (1991). Affirmative action in the twenty-first century: new approaches and developments, *Public Personnel Management: Current and Future Challenges*. (C. Ban and N. Riccucci, eds.), Longman, New York, pp. 89–100.

Romzek, B. (1990). Employee investment and commitment: the ties that bind, *Public Admin. Rev., 50*: 374–382.

Rosen, B. (1986). Crises in the U.S. civil service, *Public Admin. Rev., 46*: 207–214.

Ross, Lynn (1990). Effective recruiting: lessons from personnel demonstration projects. *The Bureaucrat* (Fall) 19: 19–24.

Savas, E.S., and Ginsburg, S.G. (1973). The civil service: a meritless system? *The Public Interest, 32*: 70–85.

Sayre, W.S. (1948). The triumph of technique over purpose, *Public Admin. Rev., 8*: 134–137.

Segalla, E. (1989). All for quality and quality for all, *Train. Dev. J., 43*: 46–45.

Shafritz, J. (1975). *Public Personnel Management: The Heritage of Civil Service Reform*, Praeger, New York.

Shafritz, J., Riccucci, M., Rosenbloom, D., and Hyde, A. (1992). *Personnel Management in Government: Politics and Process*, 4th Ed., Marcel Dekker, New York.

Silvestri, G., and Lukasiewicz, J. (1989). Projections of occupational employment, 1988–2000, *Monthly Labor Rev., November"* 42–65.

Staats, E. (1988). Public service in the public interest, *Public Admin. Rev., 48*: 601–605.

Taylor, F. (1923). *Scientific Management*, Harper and Row, New York.

U.S. Department of Labor, Employment and Training Administration, The Bureau of Apprenticeship and Training (1988). Washington, DC.

U.S. Congress, Office of Technology Assessment (1988). *Technology and the American Economic Transition: Choices for the Future*, Washington, DC.

U.S. Department of Labor (June 1991). *What Work Requires of Schools*, Secretaries Commission on Achieving Necessary Skills, xvii–xviii.

U.S. General Accounting Office (April 1992). *Federal Pay: Private Sector Salary Differences by Locality*, Washington, DC.

U.S. General Accounting Office (June 1989). *The Public Service: Issues Affecting Its Quality, Effectiveness, Integrity, and Stewardship*, Washington, DC.

U.S. General Accounting Office (June 1992). *Federal Employment: How Federal Employees View the Government as a Place to Work*, Washington, DC.

U.S. General Accounting Office (July 1992). *Federal Employment: Poor Service Found at Federal Job Information Centers*, Washington, DC.

U.S. General Accounting Office (May 1990). *Federal Pay: Comparisons with the Private Sector by Job and Locality*, Washington, DC.

U.S. General Accounting Office (January 1992). *Federal Recruiting: College Placement Officials' Views of the Government's Campus Outreach Efforts*, Washington, DC.

U.S. General Accounting Office (March 1992). *Federal Recruiting: Comparison of Applicants Who Accepted or Declined Federal Job Offers*, Washington, DC.

U.S. General Accounting Office (August 1990). *Federal Recruiting and Hiring: Making Government Jobs Attractive to Prospective Employees*, Washington, DC.

U.S. General Accounting Office (August 1988). *Federal Workforce: A Framework for Studying Its Framework Over Time*, Washington, DC.

U.S. General Accounting Office (April 1992). *The Changing Workforce: Comparison of Federal and Nonfederal Work/Family Programs and Approaches*, Washington, DC.

U.S. General Accounting Office (March 1992). *The Changing Workforce: Demographic Issues Facing the Federal Government*, Washington, DC.

U.S. General Accounting Office (September 1990). *Recruitment and Retention: Inadequate Federal Pay Cited as Primary Problem by Agency Officials*, Washington, DC.

U.S. Merit Systems Protection Board (June 1988). *Attracting Quality Graduates to the Federal Government: A View of College Recruiting*, Washington, DC.

U.S. Merit Systems Protection Board (October 1989). *Delegation and Decentralization: Personnel Management Simplification Efforts in the Federal Government*, Washington, DC.

U.S. Merit Systems Protection Board (1987). *In Search of Merit: Hiring Entry-Level Federal Employees*, Washington, DC.

U.S. Merit Systems Protection Board (October 1992). *A Question of Equity: Women and the Glass Ceiling in the Federal Government*, Washington, DC.

U.S. Merit Systems Protection Board (November 1991). *Balancing Work Responsibilities and Family Needs: The Federal Civil Service Response*, Washington, DC.

U.S. Merit Systems Protection Board (August 1989). *Who Is Leaving the Federal Government? An Analysis of Employee Turnover*, Washington, DC.

U.S. Merit Systems Protection Board (May 1990). *Why Are Employees Leaving the Federal Government: Results of an Exit Survey*, Washington, DC.

U.S. Office of Personnel Management (October 1992). *Federal Staffing Timeliness: OPM Governmentwide Review*, Washington, DC.

U.S. Senate Subcommittee hearing (1989). *Are Federal Job Recruiting Techniques Adequate?* Hearing before the Subcommittee on Federal Services, Post Office, and Civil Service (Committee on Governmental Affairs), 101st Congress., 1st session.

Van Riper, P. (1958). *History of the United States Civil Service*, Harper and Row, New York.

Ventriss, C. (1991). The challenge of public service: dilemmas, prospects, and options, *Public Admin. Rev., 51*: 275–279.

Volcker, P.A. (1988). *Public Service: The Quit Crisis*, American Enterprise Institute for Public Policy Research, Washington, DC.

Volcker, P. (Chairman) (1989a). *Leadership for America: Rebuilding the Public Service*, report of the National Commission on the Public Service, Washington, DC.

Volcker, P. (Chairman) (1989b). *Leadership for America: Rebuilding the Public Service*, task force report of the National Commission on the Public Service, Washington, DC.

White, L.D. (1979). The personnel problem, *Classics of Public Personnel Policy* (F.J. Thompson, ed.), Moore, Oak Park, IL.

Willoughby, W. (1927). *Principles of Public Administration*, Johns Hopkins University Press, Baltimore.

12

A Review of Research Regarding Criteria Used to Select Job Applicants

JAMES D. WERBEL   Iowa State University, Ames, Iowa

Selection research can be categorized as either prescriptive or descriptive. The prescriptive approach identifies tools and techniques that recruiters should use to evaluate job applicants. It focuses on the development of valid and reliable selection processes. Some examples of this type of research include the establishment of validity for assessment centers (Gaugler et al., 1987), the use of validity generalization for testing applicants across organizations (Schmidt and Hunter, 1977), the use of situational interviews to improve the validity of interviews (Latham et al., 1980; Gabris and Rock, 1991), and the use of frame of reference training to improve interrater reliability in evaluating applicants (Maurer and Fay, 1988).

A descriptive approach to selection reflects recruiters' choice processes. It involves a cognitive assessment of an applicant's qualifications and the evaluation of a pool of applicants to select the best applicant for the vacant position. It has traditionally focused on information processing issues such as attribution theory or cognitive biases in the selection process such as stereotyping (Eder and Buckle, 1988). It could also include other issues reflecting the evaluation of applicants such as the standard deviation of criteria (Cleveland et al., 1988) or the use of evaluative criteria in the selection process (Gardner et al., 1991).

Of these two approaches, most recent literature reviews focus on the prescriptive selection perspective and have ignored or minimized the descriptive selection perspective (cf. Monohan & Muchinsky, 1983; Binning & Barret, 1989; Griffin, 1989; Harris, 1989; Guion, 1991). Furthermore, there has been a need to increase descriptive research reflecting decision processes (Arvey and Campion, 1982).

The limited number of research studies and reviews on this topic is unfortunate because there is a need to synthesize literature from both descriptive and prescriptive perspectives. This could improve selection processes in several ways. Knowing how applicants are evaluated and understanding the decision processes in comparing applicants provides a foundation for determining the strengths of existing selection processes and identifying areas that need improvement. In turn, this information could be used to prescribe selection practices that would be most readily acceptable to recruiters.

To facilitate the above objective, this chapter is divided into three parts. First, it provides an overview of the cognitive processes associated with applicant selection and provides the framework for the remainder of the chapter. The next section identifies criteria that recruiters appear to use to develop cognitive assessments of applicants. The third section identifies the relative importance of different selection criteria in selecting one applicant from a pool of applicants. In comparing the strengths and weaknesses of different applicants, we need to understand the relative importance of different attributes that could be used to either accept or reject applicants. Efforts should be made to identify those criteria that are considered to be most heavily weighted in the selection process. The final section offers recommendations to practitioners for using criteria to evaluate the competencies of job applicants.

I. SELECTION AS A CHOICE PROCESS

In the following review, I assume that selection follows a series of steps representing a rational choice process (Stumpf and London, 1981). This process assumes there are clearly defined alternatives. Criteria to assess the strengths and weaknesses of different alternatives need to be developed, and the different alternatives need to be assessed in relation to those criteria. Finally, after each alternative is evaluated individually, a choice must be made by comparing different alternatives concurrently. This describes the perfect choice process and reflects a multiattribute choice process (Fishbein and Ajzen, 1974). However, man, being subject to time pressures and stresses, may skip steps or do these steps with multiple iterations (Mintzberg et al., 1976; Janis and Mann, 1977). Nonetheless, they appear to be widely used in making decisions.

These steps appear to be relevant in applicant selection (Huber et al., 1987). The alternatives are job applicants. Criteria for selection would be commonly based on a job analysis. They include skills, knowledge, and the ability to do the job as well as personality characteristics or individual differences. These criteria are then used to guide the information gathering process to determine the extent to which an applicant has or fails to have certain aspects that could be useful in performing a job for an employer. This aspect of the selection process is most closely tied to issues associated with information processing and person perception.

The last aspect of the selection process is the comparison of different job applicants. This would probably be more closely tied to the conventional image of decision making as the process of determining the most qualified or appropriate applicant. All applicants have their strengths and weaknesses. There is seldom an ideal applicant. This aspect of the selection process determines which aspects are most associated with job performance. Thus, applicants with the best qualities in terms of the most important job criteria will probably be selected for the job.

The above information provides some assumptions about the selection process for this literature review. To understand the descriptive process to selection, it is important to understand the type of information used to form impressions of job applicants and the criteria with greatest influence in evaluating a pool of job applicants. The following seeks to clarify these two issues.

II. USE OF CRITERIA IN SELECTION

One of the central topics concerning descriptive research is the identification of commonly used information to evaluate job applicants from job applications, interviews, tests, and references. This research typically uses "paper" applicants for a hypothetical job vacancy. A standardized packet of resumes or interview videos that vary a small number of criteria are developed. Students and/or managers are then asked to evaluate the applicants for a job position and make an overall assessment about the employability of an applicant. While there may be some comparative evaluations among applicants, the evaluators usually make some overall applicant assessment against a normative standard of employability. They fail to go through the comparative process of selecting the most appropriate applicant for a job position as there is seldom an actual vacancy to fill.

The criteria used to evaluate applicants could be described as either job competency or applicant attractiveness (Graves and Powell, 1988). Job competency criteria are directly related to the skills, knowledge, and abilities that are required to do the job. Criteria representing this type of information would most commonly come from past educational experience, work experience, and nonwork activities. The prescriptive approach to selection typically recommends the exclusive use of these criteria for selection (Bowen et al., 1991).

Applicant attractiveness is a second category of criteria that could be used to select applicants. It describes the degree to which the recruiter and existing work unit members would like to work with an applicant. Van Maanen (1974) suggests that the selection process is an important element for screening potential work unit members who would disrupt the unity of the work unit due to characteristics that create interpersonal antagonisms. Criteria associated with this category could be closely related to the concept of organizational or work unit fit in the selection process (Scarpello and Campbell, 1983). Specific criteria associated with attractiveness could be personality characteristics, values, mannerisms, and physical attractiveness.

Use of Competency Criteria

Competency criteria tend to be job-specific. The types of information gathered should be appropriate to the performance of specific duties. A job analysis is helpful to identify criteria that could readily assess competency.

Tests are one of the less subjective ways to form applicant assessments. It is clear that a wide variety of tests can be used to gather information about job applicants. For some recent examples, Schmidt and his associates developed a series of tests for a specific job such as computer programmer (Schmidt et al., 1980), repairperson (Schmidt, et al., 1979), operator in the petroleum industry (Schmidt et al., 1981), and police detective (Hirsh et al., 1986). Cascio and Phillips (1979) reported firms used 19 different types of work sample tests to screen job applicants. Scarpello and Ledvinka (1988) offered different types of performances tests that have been developed for job positions ranging from sewing machine operator to engineer and magazine editor.

A complete literature review of testing is beyond the scope of this chapter. In terms of the actual use, tests do not appear to be widely used to select job applicants. While nearly 84% of 167 personnel directors responding to an American Society for Personnel Management survey reported using tests for at least one job position in the organization (Resource, 1988), most tested applicants only for clerical positions. Less than 30% of all firms reported testing management or industrial skills. Eleven percent used assessment centers and 10% gave honesty tests. While this survey reflects that competency tests are used by a significant number of firms in the selection process, the majority of firms use them to assess clerical skills only.

In spite of modest use, evaluators appear to use test scores when those scores are readily available. Two studies specifically evaluated the use of test scores in the selection process. Henneman (1977) asked undergraduate students to evaluate hypothetical applicants for insurance agent positions. They varied the test scores of applicants holding other criteria constant and noted that test scores lead to favorable impressions of job applicants.

Carlson (1971) gave insurance agents folders of hypothetical applicants with varied test scores as well as the amount of favorable information from work history. Test scores were extremely important in assessing applicant competency, accounting for 30% of the explained variance, even when tests had low validity.

Besides job-specific criteria, there have been some attempts to identify competency criteria that are generic to different types of job positions. Most of this research uses paper applicants for hypothetical entry level job positions for college graduates.

Perhaps the most commonly studied generic criteria is educational criteria such as grade point average, degree, and major. In studying grade point average, Oliphant and Alexander (1982) asked 12 human resources management professionals from a cross-section of industries to evaluate hypothetical applicants for a managerial training position. Grades varied from 2.5 to 2.8 in the low condition and 3.5 and 3.8 in the high condition. Additionally, another group had no reported grade point average. The group with no grade point average was evaluated similarly to the group with low grade point average. However, the high grade point average group was evaluated more favorably than the other two groups. The investigators also found several other complex interactions associated with grade point average. For example, married females with high grades were evaluated more favorably than single females with high grades. There was little difference with married men.

Three other studies have also examined the relationship of grades to recommendations for selection of entry level positions with hypothetical college graduates. These studies typically included both college students and recruiters as evaluators of applicants for entry level positions. Hakel et al. (1970) experimentally varied grade point averages on resumes and asked students and certified public accountants (CPAs) to evaluate the appropriateness of applicants for an accounting position. Grades were associated with more favorable applicant evaluations. Similar results using similar methodology were reported by Dipboye et al. (1975) and Wingrove et al. (1984).

Other important educational experience criteria relate to major and degree. Applicants with advanced degrees should have greater competencies than applicants with less advanced degrees. Furthermore, some majors should be more appropriate for different types of jobs than other majors.

Renwick and Tosi (1978) varied undergraduate majors (English, business, industrial sociology, history, and industrial engineering) and degree (MS in management or MBA). They asked graduate students with an MS in administration to evaluate the suitability of graduating graduate students recommended by the dean of the college for positions associated with training and development. The MBA degree was viewed as more suitable than the MS degree by MS students. Industrial sociologists and business undergraduates majors had more positive evaluations than English and history undergraduates.

Singer and Bruhns (1991) using dummy resumes varied degree for a managerial position using a New Zealand sample of personnel officers. They found that degree influenced evaluations of job applicants.

Barr and Hitt (1986) examined undergraduate degree vs. graduate degree with a sample of students and managers for a regional sales manager and a vice president of sales. They used videotapes to present materials for hypothetical applicants and asked subjects to evaluate applicant favorability. They found that students evaluated applicants with higher degrees more favorably than those with lower degrees. However, managers felt that degree was associated with applicant evaluations only for the regional sales manager job. However, in a study replicating this design (Hitt and Barr, 1989), degree was considered to be unimportant for either position with a manager-only sample.

Previous work experience is also a competency variable. Several studies examine years of work experience as well as the relevancy of the work experience for a job vacancy.

Barr and Hitt (1986), described above, varied years of work experience (10 or 15 years) for the positions of regional sales manager and vice president of sales. For managers, experience was important for vice president of sales only. For students, experience was important for both job positions. A study replicating this design (Hitt and Barr, 1989) reported similar results with a sample of managers.

Hakel et al. (1970) had CPAs evaluate resumes of hypothetical graduating accounting students. The resumes had either part-time work experience in an accounting position such as a bookkeeper or auditor or had part-time unskilled work experience such as yard worker or bus boy. Work experience was an important predictor for positive evaluations. Also, similar results were reported by Wingrove et al. (1984) in a study with recruiters evaluating resumes from college graduates in Great Britain and by Singer and Bruhns (1991) with an American sample of college graduates.

Dipboye et al. (1977) asked students to make some recommendations to hire hypothetical college graduates for a sales management position. Using resumes, they varied work experience (prior sales experience and no prior sales experience) as well as grade point average. While they failed to experimentally separate these two aspects of competency, both in combination accounted for nearly half of the explained variance in applicant evaluations.

Use of Criteria Associated with Likability

The concept of applicant likability concerns the degree to which the recruiter and/or current members in a work unit would like to work with an applicant. While one would suspect that job competency would be associated with likability, the applicant's personal qualities are also an important determinant of likability.

Research with applicant likability is more varied and more prevalent than research with job competency. This research includes a variety of research topics such as physical attractiveness, verbal and nonverbal communication, personality characteristics, demographic characteristics, and self-presentation skills. Because these criteria appear to be unrelated to job requirements and lacking content validity, they could be associated with selection biases or defective selection processes.

Physical attractiveness of applicants appears to be one of the most widely researched issues influencing applicant likability. The most common way to measure attractiveness is with facial photographs. These studies typically present photographs of applicants with biographical job information. Cash et al. (1977) using a sample of personnel directors from both private and public sectors were asked to rate paper applicants for laborer and clerical positions. They reported facial attractiveness as important in applicant evaluations. Other studies using similar methods found significant main effects for facial attractiveness (Dipboye et al., 1977; Bardach and McAndrew, 1985; Gilmore et al., 1986).

Cann et al. (1981) had students evaluate resumes with mixed qualifications. A photograph was provided. They asked students to evaluate applicants sequentially or concurrently. Facial attractiveness was only important with sequential applicant evaluation. This suggests that facial attractiveness is more important for forming assessments of applicants' qualities than actually selecting applicants for a job position.

It could be believed that physical attractiveness may have some content validity. However, Gilmore et al. (1986) failed to achieve a facial attractiveness by job type interaction for employees who engage in public contact (such as a personnel interviewer) as opposed to those who did not engage in public contact (such as a personnel records manager). This would indicate that facial attractiveness is more related to likability than to job competency.

Physical appearance in the form of attire could also be considered a part of likability. Three studies addressed this topic. Forsythe et al. (1985), using videotapes of interviews presented to personnel managers, reported that hypothetical female applicants' for manuracturing management positions dressed in feminine-style clothes were less favorably evaluated than female applicants dressed in masculine-style clothes.

Parsons and Liden (1984) using 10-min semistructured interviews for amusement park job positions had interviewers rate applicants on several criteria as well as make recommendations for hiring immediately after an actual interview. Two criteria associated with favorable applicant evaluations were cleanliness and dress. Both were highly correlated with overall recommendations but were less important than other aspects of verbal and nonverbal communication.

Gifford et al. (1985) in videotaped live interviews for a temporary public sector job found that independent assessments of dress were associated with judges' assessments of social skills and applicant interest in the job. Both of these should, in turn, be associated with overall applicant evaluations.

In a related topic, Baron (1983), using undergraduate student evaluators in mock interviews with preplanned questions and confederate responses, reported a sex and artificial scent interaction. Scented women and unscented men were evaluated more favorably the unscented women or scented men. This suggests that scent could be associated with applicant likability.

Applicant likability could also be associated with nonverbal characteristics associated with voice patterns and body language. This literature suggests that self-presentation skills are influential in relation to interpersonal attraction. For example, Gifford et al. (1984) tried to determine the mediating variables between nonverbal cues and applicant assessment. Using live videotaped interviews with 38 applicants for a part-time research assistant position, judges assessed applicants for their nonverbal behavior. Then independent judges evaluated applicants on two criteria: motivation to work and social skills. Results suggested that the average time of smiling, gesture rates, and time the applicant spent talking were positively associated with motivation to work. Gesture rates, time spent talking, and appropriate dress were associated with social skills.

Young and Beier (1977) using videotaped interviews noted that eye contact, head position, and smiling were important in applicant evaluations using mock 2-min interviews with college students.

Anderson and Shakleton (1990) examined the mediating evaluations of nonverbal communication with live campus interviews in Great Britain. They found that eye contact, postural changes, and facial expression were important forms of nonverbal communication leading to applicant acceptance. These appeared to be mediated by perceptions that the applicant was strong, successful, mature, enthusiastic, and pleasant.

Some research has demonstrated that highly intense nonverbal behavior may be perceived to be negative by recruiters. For example, Sterrett (1978) had life insurance managers evaluate videotapes of applicants who used high-, moderate-, and low-intensity nonverbal communication in the form of eye contact, gestures, pauses, and dress. The high-intensity and low-intensity groups received lower evaluations than the moderate-intensity group.

More effectively, Baron (1986) reported that high levels of eye contact and smiling were viewed negatively in mock structured interviews. Also, Tessler and Sushelsky (1978) noted that for lower level positions, medium eye contact led to more favorable evaluations than high eye contact.

Another important aspect of likability in the evaluation of applicants for job positions would be personality type or interpersonal style. One would suspect that certain personality types or interpersonal styles would fare better in job interviews than others. Tullar (1989), in studying college placement interviews, found that successful applicants in general dominated the conversation more than unsuccessful applicants. However, if the interviewer dominated the conversation, submissive applicants were evaluated more positively than dominating applicants.

Other studies involving personality assessments appear to be related to prototypes of personality. It may be viewed that certain personality characteristics are more effective for some job types than others (Holland, 1985). Two studies have been conducted of this nature. One by Rothstein and Jackson (1980) had students observe videotaped interviews that were designed to bring out certain personality characteristics considered to be either appropriate or inappropriate for engineering and accounting positions. Students evaluated applicants with congruent characteristics more favorably than incongruent characteristics. Furthermore, some students were told the congruent personality characteristics for both jobs and others were not. Still those applicants who were congruent were evaluated more favorably than incongruent applicants in both conditions.

Paunonen et al. (1987) found that personality traits based on the Strong Vocational Interest Blank for a newspaper reporter and a payroll clerk had some impact on paper applicant evaluations. However, it had a secondary impact after controlling for information about job knowledge and motivation.

Finally, there has been extensive research regarding applicant likability based on sex and race. For some reason, people may prefer to have a coworker who is male or white.

Most research on this topic appears to focus on gender. Perhaps the best summary of this research is found with meta-analysis of 19 studies (Olian et al., 1988). The results indicated that there was a small bias against women amounting to 4% of the explained variance. Curiously, they reported that one of the more important moderators was study design. Within-subject designs had more explained variance than between-subject designs. They argued that within-subject designs reflect actual selection decisions more than between-subject designs.

Studies examining race also suggest that there has been racial discrimination and that recruiters tend to evaluate minorities unfavorably (Parsons and Liden, 1984; Barr and Hitt, 1986). On the other hand, Abrahams et al. (1977) failed to note racial bias using unobtrusive measurements of applicants for naval recruits. Haefner (1977) noted similar results in selecting state employees, although whites generally received more favorable assignments than blacks. It is unclear if the effect was caused by differential application rates or subtle forms of discrimination.

Rather than observing main effects of racial discrimination, Lin et al. (1992) evaluated the effects of race similarity on applicant evaluations in situational and structured interviews. The study used archival evidence collected from 1645 interviews for a custodian job in a large public school district. Nearly all applicants were Blacks or Hispanic-Americans. Race similarity between applicant and interviewer was associated with positive evaluations for Hispanic and black applicants. No effects were found for whites but only a small number of whites applied for these job positions. This would suggest that the basis for discrimination may be more subtle than a simple refusal to hire employees from one race only.

Sex and job type also appear to be an important issue for likability. Rosen and Jerdee (1974) found strong interaction effects for sex by gender-based job types in relation to recommendations for hires in a student sample.

Based on prototype theory (Rowe, 1984) evaluators are assumed to have an image of an ideal applicant. This may include issues associated with competencies as well as personal qualities. Thus, some jobs such as managerial or engineering positions are associated with masculine qualities such as decisiveness and aggressiveness whereas other jobs are associated with feminine qualities such as nurturence and emotionality.

Based on this approach, Van Vianen and Willemsen (1992) evaluated the mediating processes of prototypes in the selection of applicants for scientific positions in the Netherlands. The study had applicants complete a personality assessment. They also asked evaluators for these jobs to define the personality attributes needed to perform scientific work. They found that female applicants were evaluated less positively than male applicants. Recruiters in this study correspondingly valued masculine qualities held by male applicants more than masculine qualities held by females or feminine qualities held by females.

These findings were supported by research using dummy resumes with photographs (Dipboye et al., 1977). Female applicants for a sales manager position were perceived to be less experienced, decisive, informed, competitive, motivated, logical, and assertive than male applicants for the same position. On the other hand, female applicants were perceived to be friendlier, warmer, and more emotional than male applicants. This may have been an important mediating variable in determining why male applicants were evaluated more positively than female applicants for this traditionally male occupation.

James et al. (1984) studying Australian police officers reported significant sex differences for personality attributes influencing subjective evaluations. They found that nine dimensions of the California Personality Inventory (CPI) had modest relationships with subjective evaluations for men, but only two were weakly associated with evaluations of women. These results suggest that evaluators may have had a clearer prototype of the personality characteristics of police officers for men than women and that the women applicants were evaluated differently than men applicants. While these results failed to show discrimination, they demonstrated that sex-based prototypes exist.

In the dress study previously mentioned (Forsythe et al., 1985), women's attire was evaluated for a managerial position. While the study failed to manipulate job type, the fact that masculine dress was evaluated more favorably for a managerial position suggests that prototypes of masculine qualities could be important in evaluating applicants for male positions.

One study (Heilman and Sarwatari, 1979) examined mediating variables for attractiveness by sex in the evaluation of résumés with photos. It varied the job type as managerial or clerical positions. In general, there was a strong interaction effect with female applicants. Attractive female applicants were valued for the clerical position and unattractive female applicants were valued for the managerial position. It was felt that attractive women were more feminine, less motivated, less decisive, and more emotional than unattractive women. These characteristics fit a shared prototype of a clerical worker more than the prototype of a manager.

In summarizing this research, there are several important issues that need to be raised from a theoretical and methodological perspective. Theoretically, there appears to be some concern with the validity of selection criteria. Based on the prescriptive literature, recruiters should be exclusively using competency-based criteria that directly assess the skills, knowledge, and abilities to perform a job. Yet likability criteria appear to be widely used to evaluate applicants in spite of their being unrelated to job performance for most job positions. This raises the question, "Why do recruiters use criteria that appear to have questionable validity?" Arvey and Campion (1982) suggest that these criteria may be used because recruiters feel that attractiveness criteria may be considered to be important for job success or that there may be a bona fide illusion of validity about these criteria. People perceive these to be important when they are in essence unrelated to job performance.

The current review takes a significantly different perspective. The question becomes neutral by asking, "Why do recruiters use selection criteria associated with likability?" Rather than focusing on validity, the emphasis is on the need to use attractiveness for selection.

There are two possible explanations as to why recruiters use these criteria. Perhaps the most positive is that likability criteria are related to job performance, especially if job performance is a function of ability, motivation, and situational constraints. Each is important if the employee is to perform the job successfully. Furthermore these could be noncompensatory. Weakness in any one area leads to poor performance.

Likability could be an important situational constraint. Situational constraints influencing job performance could be excessive if current employees are not attracted to the new employee and reject the new employee. It could lead to social isolation or perhaps situations where current employees conspire to make the new employee's job more difficult (Rothlisberger and Dickson, 1939). To avoid these problems, recruiters would be looking for applicants with certain desirable features that would lead to higher levels of interpersonal attraction with current employees.

A second explanation is that recruiters may develop prototypes of successful candidates. A prototype entails an image of an ideal applicant (Rowe, 1984). However, rather than relying exclusively on Knowledge, Skills, and Abilities (KSAs) to perform the job, prototypes entail global personal attributes or characteristics. As such, prototypes may be thought to have an intuitive construct validity. Rather than address the KSAs needed to perform the job, recruiters may be assessing broader characteristics that are believed to covary with KSAs. The research with gender attributes (Van Vianen & Willemsen, 1992; Dipboye et al., 1977) suggests that personality attributes associated with gender stereotypes are thought to covary with job performance.

Prototypes may exist not only for gender but for race, dress, facial features, or nonverbal communication. People can infer personality characteristics from these attributes. However, additional research is needed to determine the extent to which these prototypes are used to form impressions of job applicants and the types of verbal or nonverbal communication that are used to confirm or disconfirm the prototypes. Most importantly, these prototypes are associated with stereotypes or naive personality theory. As such, they would represent deficient cognitive processing in evaluating job applicants.

There also appears to be some methodological problems with this research. Perhaps the most significant problem is the use of experimental research with paper applicants. This type of design poses several problems. First, this design has some demand characteristics. For example, results appear to differ pending the use of a between- or within-subjects design (Olian et al., 1988). This seems compatible with other research indicating that framing the evaluation process guides the use of selection criteria (Huber et al., 1987). The important point to consider is that results need to be cautioned pending the design. To be truly effective, studies should include both within- and between-subject designs.

A second methodological problem concerns the use of experimental studies that vary only a small number of selection criteria. Cleveland et al. (1987) indicate that the recruiters tend to use criteria with the greatest variance. In these experimental studies that manipulate only a few dimensions, these dimensions are then used to distinguish candidates. The saliency of the manipulation may create demand characteristics that force recruiters to use these more than they would in actual decisions. They could be used or not be used, but regardless the design creates exaggerated perceptions about their use in the selection process. To avoid this problem, studies using actual selection decisions could be more useful than those experimental studies to verify if these criteria are used to form impressions of job applicants.

One final point is that more criteria should be examined. There is an absence of research about an array of criteria that could be used to select applicants. Issues such as personality characteristics, religious background, stature, posture, vocabulary, syntax, technical knowledge including computer or foreign language skills, job stability, demonstrated job knowledge, or facts about the company could be related to selection. It seems that research repeatedly examines the same criteria in different ways.

III. RELATIVE IMPORTANCE OF DIFFERENT CRITERIA

The above literature review suggests that certain criteria are used to form general impressions of job applicants. Perhaps of larger importance, particularly in relation to interview effectiveness, is the concern with the relative importance of different criteria. Engaging in a policy-capturing paradigm with actual applicant selection, the prevalence of certain criteria over others determines the most important criteria. Of central importance in this review is the relative importance of competency criteria and attractiveness criteria. While no two recruiters are likely to use these criteria identically, a general pattern could be extrapolated.

Two types of studies evaluate criteria used by recruiters. One type gives recruiters different criteria and asks them to rate the importance of those criteria. It is based on self-reports. The second type uses live recruitment situations. Some examine competency biodata from job applications and résumés, some examine nonverbal and verbal communication from the job interview, and some examine both biodata information and interview information.

Two studies asked recruiters what criteria they used to select recent college graduates. Atkins and Kent (1988) asked 100 campus recruiters what they used to select applicants. They reported that some criteria were used to reject applications and other criteria were used to accept applicants. Campus recruiters reported that they would reject applicants who had poor grammar, were dirty, had little eye contact, dressed poorly, or had poor articulation. In the order of reported importance, campus recruiters would accept applicants who had good oral communication, appeared enthusiastic, appeared motivated, had good credentials, had appropriate degree, demonstrated maturity, showed initiative, were punctual, showed good listening skills, had appropriate manners and a good appearance, and had good grades.

A second study by Gardner et al. (1991) asked campus recruiters to rank the following seven items in importance: communication skills, major grade point average (GPA), nonmajor GPA, extracurricular activities, work experience, amount of education self-financed, and course work. Campus recruiters indicated that all had some impact but communication skills and major GPA were most important for selecting college graduates.

Focusing on research with résumés and job applications that influence postinterview evaluations for campus interviews, Campion (1978) reported that belonging to a fraternity or sorority was most important, explaining 8% of the variance. GPA explained almost another 5% of the variance.

Wingrove et al. (1984) engaged in a complex study evaluating over 300 criteria from job applications by campus recruiters in the UK. They used invitations for campus interviews by three firms as the dependent variable. There was only modest consistency in evaluations across the three firms. Furthermore they reported some variation by evaluator within the firm. This suggests that each individual recruiter develops unique selection criteria to screen applicants. Nonetheless, common elements shared by at least two firms included appropriate course work (including major or a specific course), academic performance (grades or class standing), work experience, and having had positions of responsibility.

Werbel (1989) in a double-blind study evaluated the criteria used to select applicants for campus interviews based on biographic information. Of 11 criteria that focused on educational information, work experience, extracurricular activities, and demographics, only having an appropriate major and overall grade point average were widely used among 19 recruiters. However, at least one recruiter used the other criteria such as number of previous jobs, sex, and elected position in campus organizations to select applicants for campus interviews.

Gardner et al. (1991) experimentally manipulated seven criteria mentioned previously. Recruiters then evaluated 40 résumés and indicated the probability of the applicant being asked for campus interviews, a preliminary selection decision. Major GPA and communication skills (from a reference) were most widely used to select applicants. The other five criteria explained little of the selection decision. Thus, there appears to be a difference between recruiters' beliefs and recruiters' actions.

In summary, biodata criteria that appeared to be consistently most important were academic performance and appropriate course work. However, it should be noted that all of these studies focused on recent college graduates. The extent that these are used by recruiters for higher level positions would be suspect (Barr and Hitt, 1986). Perhaps most importantly, two studies reported significant variation across recruiters. While general statements can be made, it may actually be more important to study variations across recruiters. Is the variation due to different job requirements, organizational requirements, or simply some personal bias? Werbel (1989) suggested that grades were more important for professional positions than managerial positions but noted no other differences by job type. Thus, job requirements may play some role in the variation.

Five studies examined the relations between verbal and/or nonverbal communication from interviews and recruiters' choice processes. Parsons and Liden (1984) used live interviews for amusement park positions. They had interviewers evaluate aspects of nonverbal communication as well as the applicants themselves. Evaluations of facial expression and eye contact were most highly associated with applicant evaluations.

Raza and Carpenter (1987) had interviewers evaluate applicant qualities and applicant hirability using live initial interviews from the private and public sector. Using a path model, perceived intelligence had the greatest impact on hirability although it was mediated by employability and perceived skills. This was followed by perceived skill and perceived likability.

Riggio and Throckmorton (1988) had college students conduct practice interviews. Different sets of judges evaluated these for effectiveness and nonverbal/verbal communication. The researchers reported that interview errors were the most important aspect associated with interview effectiveness. This was a combined measurement that reflected poor oral communication skills such as long delays in response to questions, run-on answers, and self-deprecation. These were then followed in order of importance by dress, physical attractiveness, and fluency.

Anderson and Shakleton (1990) using videotaped campus interviews reported that facial expression and eye contact were the most important nonverbal qualities influencing selection of applicants for job interviews.

Rynes and Gerhart (1990) had recruiters conduct postcampus interview assessments of MBAs. They reported that with a sample of four recruiters, subjective interpersonal qualities were most important in applicant selection followed by applicant goal orientation and accomplishments. Assessments of applicant knowledge had little impact on applicant assessments.

While this research is limited in terms of the number of criteria considered, facial expression and eye contact appear to be the most important nonverbal qualities. This limitation as well as the use of different independent variables across studies makes it difficult to draw conclusions from these results. However, these results seem to support the notion that interpersonal attraction and likability play an important role in the interview process.

Also oral communication skill appears to be important for these job positions. Given that many jobs require good communication skills, the interview is one method to evaluate these skills. However, cross-situation specificity of interviews and a possible recruiter–applicant interaction effect would require more careful evaluation of communication skills.

Finally, some research conducts recruiters' postinterview evaluations examining information derived from a combination of interviews and biographical information. These studies compare the relative importance of interview information and biodata information.

Kinnicki and Lockwood (1985) in a study using actual campus interviews had recruiters complete postinterview applicant assessments as well as an evaluation of suitability for hiring. They reported that the ability to express ideas was most important in the selection process. This was an aggregate of recruiter-subjective assessments of appearance, communication skills, attitudes, and job interest. The second most important aspect was the attractiveness of the applicant. Gender similarity, sex, academic achievement, and relevant work experience assessed from application information were unrelated to suitability for hire.

Rasmussen (1984) in an experimental study varied résumé credentials, verbal responses, and nonverbal communication with undergraduate students. Résumé credentials varied as either high academic achievement and highly relevant work experience or low academic achievement and little previous employment. Verbal responses were concerned with the relevancy of the response. Nonverbal qualities focused on eye contact, head nodding, smiling, and hand gestures. Work experience was most important explaining 19% of the variance. This was followed by verbal responses and then nonverbal communication. Main effects were significant for all three variables.

Dougherty et al. (1986) used policy-capturing methodology with three recruiters in the energy industry. Criteria were assessed both prior to and after a recruiter interview training program that emphasized the importance of interviewing. While there was individual variation across recruiters, in general, test scores were most important followed by worker qualities and applicant work history prior to interview training. After interview training that emphasized how to use interviews to select applicants, the importance of test scores dropped significantly.

Graves and Powell (1988) asked corporate recruiters who came to campus to complete a short survey evaluating applicant qualities as well as interview ratings. They reported by path analysis that subjective applicant qualities were most important in the postinterview evaluations. They reported that subjective qualifications explained most of the interview outcomes. This included items addressing ability to express ideas, interest in company, initiative, and intelligence. Interpersonal attraction as measured by willingness to work with this person was also important. Undergraduate major had little impact on interview outcome.

Kinnicki et al. (1990) studied the impact of résumés and interviews with nursing applicants. Three recruiters evaluated the applicants. Résumés explained 1% of the selection variance. Interviews explained 42% of the selection variance. While there was variation across recruiters, perceived skills from the interview were more important than perceived worker traits and attitudes.

Graves and Karren (1992) asked trained recruiters in the financial services industry to evaluate hypothetical applicants for a customer service position. Recruiters were given a narrative statement that assessed applicant qualities for work experience, education, oral communication skills, motivation, interpersonal skills, and sex. They were asked to indicate if this was an acceptable applicant. Oral communication skills, interpersonal skills, and work experience were most important in that order. The other factors had little impact on applicant evaluation.

In summary, two of the five studies reported that biographical or test information was more important than interview information. However, one of these was an experimental study with a very strong manipulation. Three studies reported that interview information was more important. More specifically, oral communication skill was important for all studies that directly addressed that variable and from recruiters' self-reports. Worker qualities including attractiveness were also viewed as being important.

IV. DISCUSSION

In summarizing this information, it would appear that this review supports the idea of selection as a process of multiple hurdles. The first hurdle is competency. Competency is assessed through objective criteria on the résumé, job application, or tests. This information is used largely to determine if the applicant who has a requisite background can perform a job without extensive job training. Research that focuses exclusively on résumé information tends to demonstrate that work experience, tests, and educational background are important in forming positive evaluations of job applicants. While the above research focuses on competency with recent college graduates, one could infer that competency issues would also be relevant for skilled workers of various types. As jobs require fewer skills, competency issues become harder to address from résumés and job applications alone.

Once an applicant has achieved a certain degree of competency, then other issues associated with a second hurdle may become more important in the selection process such as motivation to perform the job, degree to which the individual would work well with others in the work unit, or organizational fit. It would be difficult to assess these with objective data. Thus, the interview becomes important to the subjective assessment of these qualities.

The above research indicates that recruiters use the interview to screen applicants based on significantly different criteria in comparison to résumés or job applications. They are concerned with personal appearance, oral communication skills, and subjective assessments of fit. All of these are more closely associated with interpersonal qualities than with job competency criteria. With the exception of some jobs with valid indicators of performance such as tests or biodata, it would appear that recruiters are not very concerned about competency in making postinterview evaluations. In this step of the process, recruiters are apparently mostly concerned about applicant motivation to perform a task and interpersonal attraction/skills. People would prefer to work with an applicant who is likable and has good interpersonal skills. A person who fails to fit into the existing work unit can disrupt the job performance of all members of the unit. Furthermore, an applicant with ability to sustain a high level of motivation and modest skills may perform more effectively than someone with high skills and low motivation.

Unfortunately, it is unclear as to how well the interview can be used to assess interpersonal qualities, motivation, and perceived competencies. One study reported an inverse relationship with recruiters' assessments of these qualities and job satisfaction and organizational commitment (Kinnicki et al., 1990).

One of the central issues in the interview is the importance of self-presentation skills. This would include effective oral communication skills as well as the ability to engage in political or ingratiating behaviors. For example, specificity appears to be an important aspect of the credibility of references (Knouse, 1983). Specificity of experience in the interview could also be important. Thus, individuals who are specific and provide very direct responses to questions regardless of their actual abilities or motivation levels could be evaluated more positively than those who provide less specific and direct responses. Ferris and Judge (1991) suggest that these qualities could be critical in the selection process. While some jobs may require effective self-presentation skills, particularly direct sales, many jobs do not requires these skills. Thus, it becomes difficult to estimate interpersonal qualities, motivation, and perceived competencies.

V. RECOMMENDATIONS

It would seem that personnel offices in the public sector could do a more effective job in selecting applicants in relation to competencies and the subjective qualities related to motivation and attraction. The following proposals are attempts to clarify these issues.

1. *Competency assessment.* Recruiters need to rely on the traditional methods of competency assessment and the establishment of job fit. Biodata and testing have the highest validities associated with work productivity (Asher, 1972). They should be the methods for assessing job competencies. This is important because skill testing except for clerical testing is not used that widely. While civil service exams are a step in that direction, additional testing or work samples measuring competencies for certain types of tasks could be readily achieved. Also biodata could be readily collected for many jobs in the public sector, particularly if smaller units such as cities and counties collaborated in some manner to share predictors of job productivity.

2. *Job competencies and the interview.* Avoid using job interviews to assess job competencies. The unstructured interview is not an effective tool to assess competencies. At best, it assesses some aspects of oral communication skills and an ability to create favorable initial impressions. There are more effective ways to assess oral communication skills. It is unclear as to why the ability to create favorable initial impressions would be important in most jobs. While some people may

call for structured interviews to address these problems and such interviews could be used to assess competencies, there are probably more effective ways to assess job competencies. Furthermore, recruiters will still want to assess the more intangible qualities associated with job performance.

3. *Use interviews to assess applicant attractiveness.* It is important that workers be able to function with other workers. Efforts need to be made to have work unit members participate in the interviews and at least share their impressions of applicants with the individual who is responsible for selection. If only one person conducts interviews, there may be personal biases for or against certain types of applicants. This may or may not be attractive to other group members. It can only be verified if potential coworkers interview the applicant.

There is one significant problem with this approach to selection. It may lead to discrimination against protected categories of employees. If attractiveness is overemphasized, groups may have a preference for white males under 40. The equal employment opportunity officer needs to monitor this process and be certain that group members are aware of the department's affirmative action goals to avoid potential conflicts of interest.

4. *Assess values-based motivation.* Recruiters need to be sensitive to motivational issues in organizations. Motivation is an important component of productivity. There is a need to match an organization's motivational or reward system with individual preferences. For example, public sector organizations typically accentuate job security at the expense of income potential. Thus, using money as motivator may not be readily suitable in the public sector. Those who truly value money will try to move into private sector organizations. However, public sector employees can be motivated to work through intrinsic motivation or perhaps from a sense of social responsibility. Thus employees who value intrinsic motivation, those with a high need for growth (Hackman and Oldham, 1980), or perhaps those concerned with social responsibility could be more effective in public sector organizations than those with a low need for growth or those who are unconcerned about social responsibility. To some extent these values can be assessed in interviews and could lead to the hiring of an employee with more job satisfaction than if these values were unaddressed in interviews.

VI. CONCLUSIONS

The paper indicated that there was a need to study both prescriptive and descriptive approaches to selection. This chapter looked at the descriptive process and identified the extent that selection criteria were used to select applicants for jobs.

This chapter showed that criteria used in interview are at best related to oral communication skills and an ability to create positive initial impressions. It would appear that the interview is perhaps the weakest link in the selection process. Arvey and Campion (1982) discussed this issue in length in their review of the interview literature. They came to the conclusion that the interview was used because people *believed* that it had validity based on competency.

This chapter seems to indicate that people use criteria other than competency in the interview. These criteria could be readily grouped as either personality traits and assessments or related to attractiveness of the applicant to work unit members. Personality traits seem to be related to the concept of prototypic worker. Unfortunately, this commonly has a gender bias. Attractiveness/ applicant acceptability is also important. The work unit needs to feel that the introduction of a new member will maintain work unit harmony. Thus, the prescriptive process may be out of touch with user needs. Assessments of low interview validity could be expected if interviewers and researchers are concerned with two different aspects of prediction. Perhaps researchers should heed recruiters' needs and establish validity studies with criteria other than job performance. Subjective assessments of group acceptance, perceived motivation, organizational citizenship, or organizational commitment could be important aspects for validity studies.

REFERENCES

Abrahams, N. M., Atwater, D. C., and Alf, E. F. (1977). Unobtrusive measurement of racial bias in job placement decisions, *J. Appl. Psychol., 62*: 116–119.

Anderson, N., and Shakleton, V. J. (1990). Decision making in the graduate selection interview: a field study, *J. Occup. Psychol., 63*: 63–76.

Arvey, R. D., and Campion, J. E. (1982). The employment interview: a summary and review of recent research, *Personnel Psychology, 35*: 281–322.

Asher, J. J. (1972). The biographical item: can it be improved? *Personnel Psychol., 25*: 251–269.

Atkins, C. and Kent, R. L. (1988). What do recruiters consider important during the employment interview? *J. Employ. Couns., 25*: 98–103.

Bardach, N. R., and McAndrew, F. T. (1985). The influence of physical attractiveness and manner of dress on success in a simulated personnel decision, *J. Social Psychol., 125*: 777–778.

Baron, R. A. (1983). The sweet smell of success? The impact of artificial scents on evaluation of job applicants, *J. Appl. Psychol., 68*: 709–713.

Baron, R. A. (1986). Self-presentation in job interviews: when there can be "too much of a good thing," *J. Appl. Social Psychol., 68*: 709–713.

Barr, S. H., and Hitt, M. A. (1986). A comparison of selection decision models in manager vs student samples, *Personnel Psychol., 39*: 599–617.

Binning, J. F., and Barret, G. V. (1989). Validity of personnel decisions: a conceptual analysis of the inferential and evidential biases, *J. Appl. Psychol., 74*: 478–494.

Bowen, D. E., Ledford, G. E., and Nathan, B. R. (1991). Hiring for the organization: not the job, *The Executive, 5*: 35–51.

Campion, M. A. (1978). Identification of variables most influential in determining interviewers' evaluation of applicants in a college placement center, *Psychol. Rep., 42*: 9479–952.

Cann, E., Seigfried, W.D., and Pearce, L. (1981). Forced attention to specific applicant qualification: impact of physical attractiveness and sex on applicant biases, *Personnel Psychol., 34*: 66–72.

Carlson, R. E. (1971). Effect of interview information in altering valid impressions, *J. Appl. Psychol., 55*: 66–72.

Cash, T. F. Gillen, B., and Burns, D.S. (1977). Sexism and "beautyism" in personnel consultant decision making, *J. Appl. Psychol., 62*: 301–307.

Cleveland, J. N., Festa, R.M., and Montgomery, L. (1988). Applicant pool compositions and job perceptions: Impact on decisions regarding older applicants, *J. Voc, Behav., 32*: 112–125.

Dipboye, R. L., Arvey, R. D. and Terpstra, D. (1977). Sex and physical attractiveness of raters and applicants as determinants of resume evaluation, *J. Appl. Psychol., 69*: 288–294.

Dipboye, R. L., Fromkin, H.L., and Wiback, K. (1975). Relative importance of applicant sex, attractiveness, and scholastic standing in evaluation of job applicant resume, *J. Appl. Psychol., 60*: 39–43.

Dougherty, T. W., Ebert, R. J., and Callender, J. C. (1986). Policy capturing in the employment interview, *J. Appl. Psychol., 71*: 9–15.

Eder, R. W., and Buckle, R. (1988). The employment interview: an interactionist perspective, *Research in Personnel and Human Resources Management* (K. M. Ferris and G. R. Ferris, eds.), JAI Press, Greenwich, CT.

Ferris, G. R., and Judge, T. A. (1991). Personnel/human resources management: a political perspective, *J. Manage., 17*: 447–488.

Fishbein, M., and Ajzen, I. (1974). Attitudes towards objects as predictors of single and multiple behavioral criteria, *Psychol. Rev., 81*: 59–74.

Forsythe, S., Drake, M. F., and Cox, C. E. (1985). Influence of applicant's dress on interviewer's selection decisions, *J. Appl. Psychol., 70*: 374–378.

Gabris, G. T., and Rock, S. M. (1991). Situational interviews and job performance: the results in one public agency, *Public Personnel Manage., 20*: 469–481.

Gardner, P. D., Kozlowski, S. W. J., and Hults, B. M. (1991). Wile the *real* prescreening please stand up, *J. Career Plann., Employ., 51*: 57–62.

Gaugler, B. B., Rosenthal, D. B., Thornton, G. C., and Benston, C. (1987). Meta-analysis of assessment center validity, *J. Appl. Psychol., 72*: 493–511.

Gifford, R., Ng, C. F., and Wilkinson, M. (1985). Nonverbal cues in the employment interview: links between applicant qualities and interviewer judgments, *J. Appl. Psychol., 70*: 729–736.

Gilmore, D. C., Beehr, T. A., and Love, K. G. (1986). Effects of applicant sex, applicant physical attractiveness, type of rater, and type of job on interview decisions, *J. Occup. Psychol., 59*: 103–109.

Graves, L. M., and Karren, R. J. (1992). Interviewer decision processes and effectiveness: an experimental policy capturing investigation, *Personnel Psychol., 45*: 313–340.

Graves, L. M., and Powell, G. N. (1988). An investigation of sex discrimination in recruiters' evaluations of actual applicants, *J. Appl. Psychol., 73*: 20–29.

Griffin, M. E. (1989). Personnel research on testing, selection and performance appraisal, *Public Personnel Manage., 18*: 127–137.

Guion, R. M. (1991). Personnel assessment, selection, and placement, *Handbook of Industrial and Organizational Psychology* (M. D. Dunette and L. M. Hough, eds.), Consulting Psychologists Press, Palo Alto, CA.

Hackman, J. R., and Oldham, G. R. (1980). *Work Redesign*, Addison-Wesley, Reading, MA.

Haefner, J. E. (1977). Sources of discrimination among employees: a survey investigation, *J. Appl. Psychol., 62*: 265–270.

Hakel, M. D., Dobmeyer, T. W., and Dunette, M. D. (1970). Relative importance of three content dimensions in overall suitability rating of job applicants' resumes, *J. Appl. Psychol., 54*: 65–71.

Harris, M. M. (1989). Reconsidering the employment interview: a review of recent literature and suggestions for future research, *Personnel Psychol., 42*: 691–726.

Heilman, M. E., and Sarwatari, L. R. (1979). When beauty is beastly: the effects of appearance and sex on evaluation of job applicant for managerial and nonmanagerial jobs, *Organiz. Behav. Human Perf., 23*: 360–372.

Henneman, H. G. (1977). Impact of test information and applicant sex on applicant evaluations in a selection simulation, *J. Appl. Psychol., 62*: 524–526.

Hirsh, H. R., Northrup, L. C., and Schmidt, F. L. (1986). Validity generalization results for law enforcement occupation, *Personnel Psychol., 39*: 399–420.

Hitt, M. A., and Barr, S. H. (1989). Managerial selection decision models: examination of configural cue processing, *J. Appl. Psychol., 74*: 53–61.

Holland, J.L. (1985). *Making Vocational Choices: A Theory of Careers*, Prentice Hall, Englewood Cliffs, NJ.

Huber, V. L., Neale, M. A., and Northcraft, G. B. (1987). Decision Bias in personnel selection strategies, *Organiz. Behav. Human Decision Process., 40*: 136–147.

James, S. P., Campbell, I.M., and Lovegrove, S. A. (1984). Personality in a police-selection interview, *J. Appl. Psychol., 69*: 129–134.

Janis, I. L. and Mann, L. (1977). *Decision Making: A Psychological Analysis of Conflict, Choice, and Commitment,* Free Press, NY, NY.

Kinnicki, A.J., and Lockwood, C. A. (1985). The interview process: an examination of factors recruiters use in evaluating job applicants. *J. Voc. Behav., 26*: 117–125.

Kinnicki, A. J., Lockwood, C. A. Hom, P. W., and Griffeth, R. W. (1990). Interviewer predictions of applicant qualifications and interviewer validity: aggregate and individual analyses, *J. Appl. Psychol., 75*: 477–486.

Knouse, S. B. (1983). The letter of recommendations: specificity and favorability of information, *Personnel Psychol., 36*: 331–341.

Latham, G. P., Saari, L. M., Pursell, E. D., and Campion, M. D. (1980). The situational interview, *J. Appl. Psychol., 65*: 422–427.

Lin, T. R., Dobins, G. H., and Farh, J. L. (1992). A field study of race and age similarity effect in interview ratings in conventional and situational interviews, *J. Appl. Psychol., 77*: 363–371.

Maurer, S. D., and Fay, C. (1988). Effect of situational interviews, conventional structured interviews, and training on interview rating agreement: an experimental analysis, *Personnel Psychol., 41*: 329–344.

Mintzberg, H., Raisinghani, D., and Theoret, A. (1976). The structure of unstructured decision processes, *Admin. Sci. Q., 21*: 246–275.

Monohan, C. J., and Muchinsky, P. M. (1989). Three decades of personnel selection and research: a state of the art analysis and evaluation. *J. Occup. Psychol., 56*: 215–225.

Olian, J.D., Schwab, D. P., and Haberfield, Y. (1988). The impact of applicant gender compared to qualifications on hiring recommendations: a meta-analysis of experimental studies. *Organiz. Behav. Human Decision Process., 41*: 180–195.

Oliphant, V. N., and Alexander, E. R. (1982). Reactions to resumes as a function of resume determinateness, applicant characteristics, and sex of raters, *Personnel Psychol., 35*: 829–842.

Parsons, C. K. and Liden, R. C. (1984). Interviewer perception of applicant qualifications: a multivariate field study of demographic characteristics and nonverbal cues, *J. Appl. Psychol., 69*: 557–568.

Paunonen, S. V., Jackson, D. N., and Oberman, S. M. (1987). Personnel selection decisions: Effects of applicant personality and the letter of reference, *Organiz. Behav. Human Perf., 41*: 96–114.

Rasmussen, K. G. (1984). Nonverbal behavior, verbal behavior, resume credential and selection interview outcomes, *J. Appl. Psychol., 69*: 551–556.

Raza, S. M., and Carpenter, B. N. (1987). A model of hiring decision in real employment interviews, *J. Appl. Psychol., 72*: 596–603.

Renwick, P. A., and Tosi, H. (1978). The effects of sex, marital status, and educational background on selection decisions, *Acad. Manage. J., 21*: 93–103.

Resource (June 1988). 7: 2.

Riggio, R. E., and Throckmorton, B. (1988). Effects of prior training and verbal errors on students' performance in job interviews. *J. Employ. Couns., 24*: 10–16.

Rosen, B., and Jerdee, T. H. (1974). Effects of applicant's sex and difficulty of job on evaluations of candidates for managerial positions. *J. Appl. Psychol., 59*: 9–14.

Rothlisberger, F. J., and Dickson, W. J. (1939). *Management and the Workers*, Harvard University Press, Cambridge, MA.

Rothstein, M., and Jackson, D. M. (1980). Decision making in the employment interview: an experimental approach. *J. Appl. Psychol., 65*: 271–283.

Rowe, P.M. (1984). Decision processes in personnel selection, *Can. J. Behav. Sci., 16*: 326–337.

Rynes, S., and Gerhart, B. (1990). Interviewer assessments of applicant "fit": an exploratory investigation, *Personnel Psychol., 43*: 13–35.

Scarpello, V., and Campbell, J. P. (1983). Job satisfaction and the fit between individual needs and rewards, *J. Occup. Psychol., 56*: 315–328.

Scarpello, V. G., and Ledvinka, J. (1988). *Personnel/Human Resource Management*, Kent, Boston.

Schmidt F. L., and Hunter, J. E. (1977). Development of a general solution to the problem of validity generalization, *J. Appl. Psychol., 62*: 529–540.

Schmidt, F. L., Gast-Rosenberg, I., and Hunter, J. E. (1980). Validity generalization results for computer programmers, *J. Appl. Psychol., 65*: 643–661.

Schmidt, F. L., Hunter, J. E., and Caplan, J. R. (1981). Validity generalization for two jobs in the petroleum industry, *J. Appl. Psychol., 66*: 261–273.

Schmidt, F.L., Hunter, J. E., Pearlman, K., and Shane, J. S., (1979). Further tests of the Schmidt–Hunter Bayesian validity generalization procedure, *Personnel Psychol., 32*: 257–281.

Singer, M. S., and Bruhns, C. (1991). Relative effect of applicant work experience and academic qualification on selection interview decisions: a study of between-sample generalizability, *J. Appl. Psychol., 76*: 550–568.

Sterrett, J. H. (1978). The job interview: body language and perceptions of potential effectiveness, *J. Appl. Psychol., 63*: 388–390.

Stumpf, S. A., and London, M. (1981). Management promotion: individual and organizational factor influencing the decision process, *Acad. Manage. Rev., 6*: 539–550.

Tessler, R., and Sushelsky, L. (1978). Effects of eye contact and social status on the perception of a job applicant in an employment interview situation. *J. Voc. Behav., 13*: 338–347.

Tullar, W. L. (1989). Relational control in the employment interview, *J. Appl. Psychol., 74*: 971–978.

Van Maanen, J. (1975). Police socialization: a longitudinal examination of job attitudes in an urban police department, *Admin. Sci. Q., 20*: 207–228.

Van Vianen, A. E. M., and Willemsen, T. M. (1992). The employment interview: the role of sex stereotypes in the evaluation of male and female job applicants in the Netherlands, *J. Appl. Social Psychol., 22*: 471–491.

Werbel, J. D. (1989). Selection criteria used by corporate recruiters for campus interviews. National Meeting Academy of Management, Washington, DC.

Wingrove, J., Glendinning, R., and Herriot, P. (1984). Graduate pre-selection. A research note. *J. Occup. Psychol., 57*: 169–171.

Young, I.P., and Beier, E.G. (1977). The role of applicant nonverbal communication in the employment interview. *J. Employ. Couns., 14*: 154–165.

13

Placing the Individual into the Organization: Staffing and Classification in Human Resources Management

A. C. HYDE The American University, Washington, D.C.

I. INTRODUCTION: THE TRANSFORMATION OF HUMAN RESOURCES MANAGEMENT

The process of placing individuals into organizations has extensive ramifications that deeply affect all of the general functions of human resources management. It encompasses work force planning, selection, placement, training, and evaluation, and emerging new functions such as job redesign, participative management, employee career development, and the creation of entirely new organizational management formats that are designed to function either without supervision (semiautonomous work groups) or across traditional organizational boundaries (cross-functional work teams). Clearly, as human resource management prepares for transition to the 21st century (variously referred to as workforce or workplace 2000), much about work, the work force, the workplace, and the nature of organizations has changed and is changing still.

This chapter provides a historical analysis and current assessment of the universal organizational process responsible for combining individuals with organizational structures. The process is referred to using a variety of terms and includes staffing, placement or assignment, position management, position classification, job evaluation, organizational socialization, and others. Most of these terms involve some type of focus on the inherent problems involved in integrating individuals into organizational arrangements and vice versa. As Figure 1 illustrates, each addresses in some respect how and why work is organized through the concept of the position in order to maintain both the organization's effectiveness and the individual's productivity and continued participation.

Before beginning several problems must be faced. The first involves coming up with a name that fits the topics to be addressed. This chapter's title, "Placing the Individual into the Organization," though accurate, is much too long. Simply shortening the title to "Placement," however, results in confusion with the placement process (or assignment), which is only part of what is involved here. For lack of a better term, the best choice is probably "staffing," which is defined broadly as the various organizational and management processes used to identify, structure, and evaluate work assignments for individuals and work groups within organizations and to integrate as effectively as possible individual, work group, and organizational needs.

A second problem involves recognizing the historical difficulties with staffing. Three sets of variables must be considered. First, the various ideal models for organizational structure have been

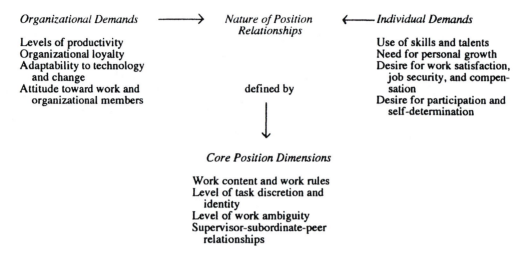

Figure 1   Matching the individual to the work.

continually changing. In the 1960s and 1970s organizational structures often seemed more like the latest fashions from Paris than more organizational theorists cared to admit. In the 1980s, a new era of downsizing marked by major reductions in work force size and reduction of managerial layers has caused organizations to drastically alter their design strategies. In the 1990s the contours of the transformation that began to take place in the private sector are reaching the public sector. The private sector is in a downsizing environment that is both a managerial restructuring and a technological/geographic relocation. The great majority of large private sector firms have reduced their demands for labor significantly (in many cases up to 30–40%). Downsizing will persist. In a recent 1991 Conference Board survey, over two thirds of 400 top U.S. firms surveyed indicated that these downsizing efforts will continue to some degree for another 5 years. Consequently, most private sector firms are not concerned about the adequacy of supply of labor; instead the issue of quality is paramount.

The quality issue has become even more acute because of the impending collapse of the "bureaucratic paradigm." When critics like Osborne and Gaebler (*Reinventing Government*, 1991) and Barzelay (*Breaking Through Bureaucracy*, 1992) call for government to be "customer driven and service-oriented," this requires public (and private sector organizations) to restructure. This entails a lot more than simply promoting entrepreneurialism. At a minimum, restructuring means regrouping the work force into teams, removing layers of hierarchy, and refocusing human resources policies to support work group cooperation and innovation at the expense of traditional command-and-control, supervisory review, and individual competition practices.

The new transformation is most critically felt in the recasting of managerial ranks in the current organizations. At its most basic level, American corporations are taking major cuts out of the midlevel, lower executive, and administrative managerial ranks. Current estimates are that the ratio of U.S. workers to managers/administrators is 8:1 compared to a 27:1 ratio in Japan. Perhaps this is why the executive order emanating out of the Clinton administration requiring a reduction in the work force by 100,000 workers by attrition included the proviso that 10% of that reduction must come from the top grade levels.

The consequences of these downsizings can be devastating. How does one develop effective staffing processes when the organizational structure in question is continually undergoing change, especially in a negative direction? This problem is made more acute by the second variable, "the amount of changes through which individuals go." There is increasing recognition that public sector employees have increasingly different skills, attitudes, preferences, job values, and needs than their predecessors.

But the greatest amount of change has been in work itself, the third variable. Actual work content and methods, because of new technology and informational processes, are becoming very different in many organizations. Further, our understanding of why work is important and what work means to individuals and organizations has changed. Changing organizations, employees, and work has meant that staffing, as a human resources management process, has experienced episodic and usually reactive development in the public sector.

The pressures on staffing and the resulting deterioration of accepted staffing methods show the final result. The history of staffing, as theory, process, and politics, is as difficult to interpret as the course of different currents running in high water. The state of the art today is much the same, reflecting the scope and significance of the problems that staffing processes have addressed in less than a century of practice in American public personnel management.

This chapter starts with the initial development of position classification at the turn of the century. Position classification theories and practices are examined up to the current controversy between "modernization" advocates and "broad-banding" reformers. From the techniques of position classification management the focus moves to the challenges presented by work redesign, quality circles, and, now, quality management teams. This in turn leads to a discussion of placement and assignment as human resources management processes. Finally, some general conclusions about all of these processes and their interrelationships within staffing are presented.

Some final caveats are in order. This chapter does not address three very significant themes that have immense interactive impacts on staffing: (1) span of control and changing supervisory–worker relationships in work, (2) computers, information, and communication technology and work functions, and (3) bias and discrimination with specific reference to gender differences in organizing work. There simply isn't space to address these themes in sufficient depth to assess their evolution and impacts. The purpose of this chapter is to provide a foundation for staffing theory and practice in the public sector. The primacy of that objective and space limitations are unfortunately a poor but necessary excuse for omitting these pivotal themes.

Lastly, it should be stated up front that this chapter is largely based on the U.S. federal government's staffing policies and experience. Given that classification got its start in the public sector in Chicago at the turn of the century, this is both ironic and unfortunate. Most of the developments in staffing and for that matter human resources management were pioneered by progressive state and local governments long before the federal government got around to implementing them. But when it comes to writing about human resources management, the personnel profession all too quickly reverts to discussing this federal law or that federal problem. Let it only be said in (admittedly weak) defense of this chapter's primary focus on the federal government's personnel system that sometimes the biggest example can be the best one to study because it still has the most to learn.

II. STAFFING AND THE NATURE OF WORK

Because work is central to the lives of so many Americans, either the absence of work or employment in meaningless work is creating an increasingly intolerable situation. The human costs of this state of affairs are manifested in worker alienation, alcoholism, drug addiction, and other symptoms of poor mental health. Moreover, much of our tax money is expended in an effort to compensate for problems with at least a part of their genesis in the world of work. A great part of the staggering national bill in the areas of crime and delinquency, mental and physical health, manpower and welfare is generated in our national policies and attitudes toward work. Likewise, industry is paying for its continued attachment to Tayloristic practices through low worker productivity and high rates of sabotage, absenteeism, and turnover.

Special Task Force to the Secretary of Health, Education, and Welfare
Work in America (1973, p. 186)

We know that much is wrong with the way people work and how they feel about the work they do. Sociologists, psychologists, economists, and others have been writing about the problems of work in society since the advent of the industrial revolution. Perhaps the classic study of this was the U.S. Department of Health, Education and Welfare (HEW) task force report, *Work in America*, written in 1971. The lone excerpt from the conclusion is sufficient to illustrate the seriousness of the problems involving work.

The large number of strikes, work stoppages, and other job actions by public employee groups are often cited as indications of a change in work attitudes. Attitudinal surveys of government employees consistently show major problems in individual attitudes about the way people work. The U.S. Merit Systems Protection Board now conducts regular surveys of the federal work force at 3-year intervals that reveal how employees feel about job satisfaction, pay levels, career prospects, and other facets of federal personnel systems. The U.S. General Accounting Office and the U.S. Office of Personnel Management also conduct special surveys of federal employees. But even given all the new information via surveys about work attitudes, this constitutes only one part of the staffing problem.

Any comprehensive assessment regarding the nature of work must examine three factors:

1. Have the methods used to accomplish work changed? (That is, how is work performed?)
2. Have the relationships of workers toward their work and their supervisors/subordinates changed? (That is, how do employees work within the organization?)
3. Have the attitudes or preferences of workers toward organizations, coworkers, and themselves changed? (That is, how do employees feel about their work?)

The *Work in America* report struck a nerve because it so graphically attested to the problems of the third factor, manifested in worker discontent and stress. Factor 1, "how work methods have changed," is less certain. Few would argue that the advances of technological changes have altered greatly the way work is performed.

Consider the computer. It is difficult to believe that the first operational computer systems were set up less than 25 years ago; that the personal computers that are now on the desks of one out of every three white collar workers in the public sector were first introduced a decade ago; that the local area networks that now connect two-thirds of all the computers in organizations, making the computer a communication processing unit as well as personal workstation, were introduced less than 5 years ago. Today, computers and communication information technology have changed nearly every facet of public sector work activity, from the processing of paychecks and entitlement payments to the issuing of library books and equipment; from collecting taxes and traffic fines to inventorying supplies and equipment.

In the last quarter century, work has been transformed into a second stage of the industrial revolution, what Cummings and Srivastva (1977) originally termed the automated technology era. This development has meant marked change in work content, especially in the public sector. They described it at the beginning as entailing the following:

The movement into the second stage of the Industrial Revolution is progressing at an astonishing rate. Principles of work design that were developed for mechanized technologies—

decomposition of the process into its simplest elementary components sequences—do not readily apply to the task requirements of newer, automated technologies. Information handling, complex decisionmaking, planning, and process control demand a new set of work design principles that account for the interdependencies and human capabilities needed to gather, combine, and evaluate diverse forms of information and to make expedient responses (p. 16).

The second factor (work relationships) is tied more to how work responsibilities are carried out than to interpersonal dimensions. Admittedly, superior–subordinate relationships are important, but only in a context of how employees view their discretion and authority to perform work. Although many industrial psychologists have examined these problems, Cummings and Srivastva provided an extremely insightful analysis that focuses directly on the work itself rather than the more commonly discussed problems of worker motivation and interpersonal relations. They used the work agreement as the major component for determining how work is to be accomplished. They developed a typology of work agreements that illustrates the scope and boundaries of work assignments along two dimensions: what is determined by the individual and what is determined by the organization. Four categories are presented, as illustrated in Table 1. Such a typology of work relationships provides an indication of how responsive or obstructive work situations can be to individual and organizational demands.

When work is accomplished in organizations using various agreement categories, the complexity of the staffing problem intensifies. Managers may seek to control work assignments by prespecifying boundaries, whereas workers may be constantly pushing to extend the bounds of their own self-determination of work. In some cases, joint determination may result; in others,

Table 1 A Typology of Work Agreements

Category of work agreement	Source of work determination	Level of worker discretion	Source of authority review
Prescribed	Not determined by self, determined by orginazation	Fixed; judgment exercised within prespecified bounds	Authority in supervisors
Contractual	Jointly determined by self and others in orgainzation	Flexible; discretion determined by bargaining and dual commitment to results	Authority in work contracts
Discretionary	Determined by self but not by others	Individual has almost total task discretion	Authority in organizational sanctions
Emergent	Work determined by environment, neither individual nor others have control	Variable and uncontrolled; individual must cope with each situation on a separate basis	Authority in environment—individuals must respond to situations and general societal/environmental laws

Source: Adapted from T.G. Cummings and S. Srivastva, *Management of Work*, Kent State University Press, Kent, OH, 1977, pp. 27–28.

individuals may outmaneuver superiors and establish almost absolute discretion. Further, the work assignments of an individual may vary considerably over time, from prescribed to contractual to discretionary or emerging, or vice versa. The point is that staffing processes must be prepared to deal with very different and dynamic formats for work relationships within organizations. This is what makes the staffing dimension so difficult to understand. Not only are individual and organizational demands changing, but work processes, work content, and work relationships are changing as well.

The above descriptions may all seem obvious, maybe even already outdated. But they provide a useful context to see where staffing is going as the pace of technology accelerates and as organizations restructure work assignments, work groups, and work processes in very dynamic environments. It was not always this way. In fact, just 80 years ago, before World War I, there was another revolution going on in American organizations. It represented the application of a set of design principles to structure work called "scientific management."

III. THE EVOLUTION OF POSITION CLASSIFICATION

> Perhaps the most prominent single element in modern scientific management is the task idea. The work of every workperson is fully planned out by the management at least one day in advance, and every worker receives in most cases complete written instructions, describing in detail the task which is to be accomplished as well as the means to be used in doing the work.
>
> Frederick Winslow Taylor
> *The Principles of Scientific Management* (1911, p. 39)

A. Origins: The Ascendancy of Scientific Management

In the beginning, salaries of public employees were individually determined by legislative statute or by departmental administrators. Consequently, the first modern position classification plans were intended to remedy conditions of excessive political and personal favoritism in determining the duties and pay of public employees. It wasn't until 1902 that the federal government began to give serious consideration to the establishment of a classification program. In its annual report, the U.S. Civil Service Commission first urged that positions be classified "on the basis of duties performed and to make compensation uniform for work of the same kind." Although Presidents Theodore Roosevelt and William Howard Taft were openly sympathetic to the installation of such a program, the Congress was not so inclined until 1912, when it authorized the Civil Service Commission to establish a Division (later Bureau) of Efficiency to develop a system of efficiency ratings on the premise that standard salaries should be adopted for similar kinds of work.

Despite the federal government's ambivalence toward position classification during this time period, there was considerable reform activity at the state and local level. In 1912 Chicago became the first jurisdiction to implement a position classification program. Later in the same year, Illinois was the first state to do so. Within the next two decades position classification plans were implemented by many of the largest state and local jurisdictions and certainly by all of the progressive ones.

In 1919 the Congress created the Congressional Joint Commission on Reclassification of Salaries. The Commission's report, issued in 1920, announced that "equal pay for equal work as a standard for employment does not prevail in the U.S. Civil Service." The Commission maintained that it was the lack of a comprehensive position classification plan that caused so many gross inequities in pay and concomitant problems of organizational structure, morale, excessive turnover, and inefficiency. Because the Commission was mandated to propose remedies for the problems it encountered, the Commission's staff developed a comprehensive classification system that evaluated positions according to duties, qualifications, and responsibilities.

The basic principles were codified in the Classification Act of 1923, which set up a method for job standardization, drew up grade levels and salary levels for each grade, created five services to group occupational categories, and established the Personnel Classification Board (later abolished in 1932 and transferred to the Civil Service Commission) as the central classifying authority. The 1923 Act was a major precedent or foundation for practically all position classification systems at the state, local, and national levels. The principles that were promulgated were very much reflective of the scientific management movement, which was very influential at that time, so it is hardly surprising that their implied view of the individual worker is that of a human interchangeable machine part.

The principles established in 1920 were as follows (*Report of Congressional Joint Commission on Reclassification of Salaries*, 1920):

1. That positions, not individuals, should be classified.
2. That the duties and responsibilities pertaining to a position constitute the outstanding characteristics that distinguishes it from, or marks its similarity to, other positions.
3. That qualifications in respect to education, experience, knowledge, and skill necessary for the performance of certain duties are determined by the nature of those duties. Therefore, the qualifications for a position are important factors in determining the classification of the position.
4. That the individual characteristics of an employee occupying a position should have no bearing on the classification of the position.
5. That persons holding positions in the same class should be considered equally qualified for any other position in that class.

In the two decades after the 1920 report, a period of extensive classification activity occurred. City, county, state, and federal government agencies conducted surveys of their positions and completed studies of how positions related individuals to organizations as part of the classification system. As the practice diversified, there was a perceived need to review position classification and appraise the state of the art.

B. Facts and Fallacies in Position Classification

In 1937, the Civil Service Assembly sponsored such an appraisal. It resulted in the formulation of a committee on position classification and pay plans in the public service, under the direction of Ismar Baruch. Baruch, who was chief of the U.S. Civil Service Commission's Division of Classification, was ideally placed as a director to see that the best expertise was available to produce the report and to ensure that the report would be used. The resulting 400+-page volume, published in 1942, was a unique document. It was (and is still considered by many) the authoritative source on position classification, and its use by practicing classifiers compared with the ministry's use of the Bible. The Baruch report, as it was called, remains the definitive statement of the theory and applied practice of position classification for the 1940s and 1950s. The report covered all the pertinent aspects of the practice, beginning with the role of personnel administration, and fundamental concepts and definitions to applications, methods, legal authority, development, installation, and maintenance. Although it is difficult to summarize the Baruch report in a few paragraphs, the basic concepts can be briefly identified. First, the meaning of position classification must be considered as the Baruch report stated it:

> Reduced to its simplest terms, classification of positions means the process of finding out, by obtaining the facts and analyzing them, what different kinds or "classes" of positions,

calling for different treatment in personnel processes, there are in the service; it further includes making a systematic record of the classes found and of the particular positions found to be of each class. The duties and responsibilities of the positions are the basis upon which classes are determined and the individual positions assigned or "allocated" to their appropriate classes. When every position has been allocated to its appropriate class, each class will consist of all positions, regardless of departmental location, that are sufficiently alike in duties and responsibilities to be called by the same descriptive title, to be accorded the same pay scale under like conditions, and to require substantially the same qualifications on the part of the incumbents (*Position Classification in the Public Service*, 1942, p. 3).

In an important footnote to the above, mention is made of the problem of excluding personal bias. The report adds: "This is an objective, impersonal basis. Allocations of positions to classes are based on the essential characteristics of the work performed in each position, and not on the education, experience, background, efficiency, or ability that the incumbent employees at the time may happen to possess or lack" (p. 36). With this purpose clearly stated, the report defines a position as

a group of current duties and responsibilities, assigned or delegated by competent authority, requiring the full-time or part-time employment of one person. Under this definition a position consists of assignments of duties and delegations of responsibilities. It comes into existence through the action of management or other controlling authority proceeding through supervisory operating officials who formally or informally specify work for individuals to do and delegate responsibilities for them to exercise (p. 43).

Each position was to be specified separately through completion of a position description or some form of joint statement by the employee and the supervisor of what the work duties and responsibilities are. This definition was further amplified by the recognition that position duties and responsibilities are changing and that position classification must stay tuned to these changes. But these changes had to be organizationally inspired and mandated as opposed to being based on employee interests. In one classic paragraph, the Baruch report reviews how to deal with the problem of matching the employee to the job, in this case referred to as a Phi Beta Kappa working as a janitor:

To be sure, in the cases we have just mentioned there may be an administrative error in matching employee to his job. Position-classification serves a very important function in bringing such administrative errors into focus. It displays the facts about the actual duties and responsibilities of the position to which the employee is assigned. If, in the interests of the employee or of the department, that assignment can be made more effective, it is a matter for correction, not through position-classification, but through placement procedures.

Another common reason for falling into an unconscious attempt to classify the employee rather than the position is failure to distinguish between the duties and responsibilities an employee performs or exercises and the relative degree of efficiency or effectiveness with which he carries them out (p. 45).

The Baruch report saw positions as individual units or microstructures within larger designations, which are referred to as classes, defined as follows:

A class of positions constitutes a group of positions which, irrespective of the particular operating units in which they are located, are, in respect to their duties and responsibilities, sufficiently alike for purposes of personnel administration. In a position-classification plan, the class is the fundamental unit (p. 392).

Basically, the class was the aggregate concept that provided the method for vertical and horizontal comparisons. Vertical comparisons were made inside each class and attempted to distinguish between higher and lower levels of work. Horizontal comparisons were made between job classes in order to relate each class to the others within the organization. Once these comparisons were made and documented, along with a set of procedures for updating the comparisons, the plan for position classification was completed and could be put into effect (Table 2).

All of the above concepts hinge on a final set of analytic factors that are the basis for comparisons of positions and classes of positions. These units of analysis obviously varied depending on the kinds of positions involved, but the Baruch report also discussed in depth how they may be used for measurement purposes. Four general areas were to be used:

1. Difficulty and complexity of duties
2. Nonsupervisory responsibilities
3. Supervisory and administrative responsibilities
4. Qualification standards

The Baruch report in essence summarized the basis of the traditional position classification system that emerged from the application of scientific management to personnel management. Baruch himself, writing in 1937 in a monograph entitled *Facts and Fallacies in Position Classification*, added an important caveat. He wrote that "a duties classification plan is not an end in itself but a tool or device for accomplishing the many and varied ends of personnel administration" (p. 3). It was a prophetic insight because traditional classification was very much the backbone of the traditional concept of public personnel management. In the aftermath of the Second World War, when public administration was confronting a different and more political environ-

Table 2   General Checklist of Questions Involved in Analyzing the Difficulty and Responsibility of a Position for Classification Purposes (Baruch report, 1942)

I.   Difficulty and compexity of duties
    a. Status of work when assigned
    b. Selection/segregation of assignments
    c. Procedure followed/employee initiations
    d. Control of work
    e. Variety and scope
II. Nonsupervisory responsibilities
    a. Reviewing work of others
    b. Independence of action or decision
    c. Responsibility for decisions
    d. Responsibility for safety
    e. Responsibility for security/money
    f. Responsibility for accuracy
    g. Responsibility for public contacts
III. Supervisory and administrative responsibilities
    a. Supervisory action required
    b. Degree of supervisory control needed
    c. Size of organization
    d. Importance, variety, and complexity
IV. a. Subject knowledge, education, previous experience, training, social skills, physical aptitude, others

---

Source: Adapted from Appendix E, Position Classification in the Public Service, Civil Service Assembly, Chicago, 1974, pp. 392–404.

ment, a different genre of public personnel management began to emerge. This new environment would focus considerable criticism on position classification.

C.   The Triumph of Technique Over Purpose

> At a time when the urgency, difficulty, and complexity of governmental performance are daily increasing, at a time when industrial personnel administration is moving toward a recognition of the values of experimental and thorough inquiry into human behavior, tempered in application by informality and flexibility in the human relations of organized effort, the public service becomes steadily more dependent upon a cold, impersonal, rigid quantification of human ability and worth in public employment.
>
>   Wallace S. Sayre, "The Triumph of Technique Over Purpose," 1948, p. 536

By the Second World War, there were substantial new pressures on the federal classification system. The sheer increase in numbers of positions and resulting deluge of classification actions work as governments grew made the idea of one central classifying authority impossible. Increasing numbers of while collar jobs were presenting problems in classifying for a system that was predominantly based on blue collar jobs. The result was a major revision of the system in the Classification Act of 1949.

The 1949 Act created the General Schedule (GS) pay plan with 18 grade categories to cover white collar workers. Blue collar workers were grouped into a craft, protective, and custodial (CPC) pay plan. Later amendments in 1954 would change the CPC pay schedule to a wage grade system in which blue collar workers were linked to local prevailing rates. Finally, the Classification Act of 1949 specified classification standards (i.e. detailed statements of job duties and qualifications for each grade level). The resulting framework was virtually permanent. Indeed, a 1989 report by the U.S. Merit Systems Protection Board noted that "these grade level criteria have come to be viewed as if they were 'cast in stone' since they have only had one minor modification in the last 40 years" (pp. 20–21).

The 1949 Act changes lessened some of the administrative difficulties but did not abate managerial pressures. The most constant complaint about classification procedures was that the system placed primary emphasis on the position rather than on the qualifications and abilities of an individual incumbent. This situation, critics maintained, generated dysfunctional activities in order to compensate for the inflexibility of the classification system. Administrators, recognizing the futility of maintaining such a principle, would compensate via administrative finesse, i.e., "fudging the system."

What the Baruch report provided was an irrefutable set of theory and principles for classifiers. Practice, however, was another matter. Classification practices were widely resisted by managers who ridiculed what they viewed as a rigid and static set of standards administered by unreasonable classifiers. In part, the problem was a lack of standards for classification actions and insufficient authority by classifiers to ensure conformity to rules and procedures. In the federal government, classifications, as Van Riper (1958) notes, "continued all through the war [World War II] to remain a major bone of administrative contention between the [Civil Service] Commission and nearly all government agencies" (pp. 388–389).

The problem in a nutshell was the felt need on the part of most government agencies to upgrade position levels in order to increase pay and prestige as a means of retaining employees in a highly competitive environment. Classification, on the other hand, was concerned about the lack of control and potential abuse that such agency demands represented. While agencies complained about nonresponsive, inflexible classification actions, classifiers rebutted with charges of unwarranted grade escalation or "grade creep."

The grade escalation controversy became the pivotal point in the deterioration of the traditional classification practice. Despite the passage of a new Classification Act in 1949, which remedied (at least legally) some of the older problems of insufficient standards, lack of authority, and inadequate audit procedures, criticism was unabated. Van Riper's history quotes an experienced practitioner:

> The Civil Service Commission is sacrificing quality for mass production, and is forcing standards on the agencies that are technically invalid for many reasons, and that in style and content are so ambiguous and incomplete as to leave the classifier in the same state of uncertainty that existed before they were issued" (1958, pp. 53–54).

Despite the unhappiness of agencies, the Civil Service Commission began to press its claims against grade escalation. In 1963, the Commission's Bureau of Programs and Standards released a research report, *The Nature and Meaning of Grade Escalation Under the Classification Act*. The report conceded that public sector grade escalation was "a sign of the times that would continue." Further, it should be expected because of the rapidly changing composition of the government work force, which was shifting significantly from low-level routine work to higher level professional/technical work. The report also indicated that this trend was prevalent in private industry, which was also experiencing escalation.

The report took a much harder line in its view of the causes, noting the following:

1. Some of the causes are basically good.
   a. Growth in research and development activities that contribute to our national security and that result in breakthroughs in the fight against disease.
   b. Better service or greater protection for the public, e.g., improvement in air traffic control.
2. Other causes are clearly bad.
   a. Reorganization specifically for the purpose of raising grades by spreading higher level duties thinly among a larger number of positions.
   b. Establishment of more organizational units than are really necessary to get more high-level supervisory jobs.
   c. Inflated position descriptions.
   d. Deliberate misclassification of jobs for purposes of adjusting to outside pay pressures.
3. Still other causes cannot be clearly labeled as good or bad.
   a. Decisions to establish a new organizational segment or to set up a new staff position, where the soundness of management judgment cannot be determined ahead of time.
   b. Management action to delegate decision-making authority on cases (e.g., claims or appeals to more positions in order to cut processing time; soundness of such management action often is not determinable in advance).

Causes of overstaffing and misclassification have not changed over the years. They are as follows:

1. Poor management practices resulting in excess personnel, improper distribution of assignments, poor utilization, and so forth.
2. Disregard of classification standards for recruiting advantages, for pirating purposes, or for empire building.

In 1964, Seymour S. Berlin of the U.S. Civil Service Commission wrote an article attempting to reconcile the manager's and the classifier's stands on grade escalation. Berlin argued that the ultimate responsibility for this unwarranted grade escalation belonged to the manager and that classification of jobs "is the result of management decisions which occur long before the position classifier takes his formal action. The classification of the job is all but final after the manager decides what duties are to be performed, how the position will relate to other jobs, etc" (p. 19). Berlin spared neither classifiers, who he felt regarded classification as an end in itself, nor managers, who in their attempts to beat the system were evading their responsibilities.

D. The Behavioral Critique

> The kind of workforce that classification plans were originally designed to accommodate no longer exists. . . . But now because of advances in the social sciences and radical changes in the nature of work and the workforce, conventional position classification systems are not only obsolete in terms of simply not being as efficient as other modes of organization but have also proved themselves to be counterproductive of the organizational mission.
>
> Jay M. Shafritz,
> *Position Classification: A Behavior Analysis for the Public Service*, 1973, p. 4.

Berlin's conclusion was basically that the classification system as it stood was sound; it simply was not being adhered to. Subsequent critics were prepared to take on the theory itself. Jay M. Shafritz probably provided the most comprehensive critique. Shafritz's work (1973) began with the problem of grade escalation, which he viewed as merely the "frontal attack on the entire classification process." He then noted the reluctance of classifiers to see the reality of the deterioration of the practice:

> Rather than officially accepting the fact that the classification process is being used to cure a pay problem, they will simply refuse to believe as classifiers what is obvious to them as individuals. Opinion surveys of government managers have consistently confirmed the fact that otherwise unwarranted adjustments to the classification plan are made in order to compensate for inadequacies in the pay plan. A U.S. Civil Service Commission questionnaire survey of the state classification programs specifically asked if the classification system has been used to solve any pay problems. Sixteen states admitted that their job evaluation systems were being "misused to solve pay problems" (p. 29).

Shafritz reviewed the many factors that he argued had made traditional classification practices obsolete. Not only had the work force changed, but the scientific management–oriented principles of traditional classification were counterproductive for more highly skilled, knowledge-oriented employees, and for highly flexible organizational structures with different relationships between managers and workers. The advent of public sector unions was another unforeseen development, he argued, that had changed the basis for classification. But Shafritz's major hypothesis was that classification ignored the behavioral implications of organization. This complex argument is based on his premise that "a long-recognized behavioral tenet holds that, 'when formal organizations come into operation, they create and require informal organizations.' Thus position classifications, being an integral part of the formal bureaucratic structure, unintentionally create informal organizational structures to compensate for the deficiencies of the formal structure" (p. 9).

Shafritz was laying groundwork for what he felt would be a new theory of classification in the postbureaucratic era that could deal with new forms of workers and organizations. The new theories of behavioral science would radically change the role of personnel. As Shafritz confidently concluded: "The present accounting and policing functions will gradually give way to an in-house consulting team specializing in the motivation and optimal utilization of its human resources" (p. 82).

The Shafritz behavioral critique was accompanied by others, most notably the work of Jay F. Atwood and Frank J. Thompson. Atwood (1971), a personnel practitioner with the state of California, argued a similar case for applying behavioral science principles to position classification. New dimensions to classification would be required to understand positions where "the sum of the total positions is greater than the sum of its individual tasks. Thus, we need to use 'position synthesis' rather than 'job analysis' to understand how the position and its particular incumbent relate in a multi-faceted organizational environment" (p. 77). Atwood's new breakthroughs in methods would, at a minimum, (1) use broader position/organizational data, (2) examine critical factors in individual–position relationships, and (3) apply behavior science/organizational dynamics to position classification.

Another part of the behavioral critique was provided by Frank J. Thompson (1976), who pursued the political approach. Thompson's article, as the title "Classification as Politics" implied, examined the political dimension. Thompson stated that the study of classification had focused too much on who wins and who loses and not enough on the dynamics of the process. To begin with, he indicated that there are four categories of classification systems, which are subdivided according to complexity (the relative number of classes existing) and precision (how specifically class labels describe work duties). His categories were as follows:

1. Focused—very precise labels, few classes
2. Differentiated—very precise labels, many classes
3. Elemental—imprecise labels, few classes
4. Blurred—imprecise labels, many classes

Thompson's categories, while speculative, were very provocative. He examined how these different categories (perhaps a better word is conditions) of classification practices might impact recruitment, pay, productivity, advancement, affirmative action, and other personnel practices. His conclusion added questions for our consideration:

> Classification is, then, replete with political implications. Regrettably, we know relatively little about such politics. What are the dynamics which lead some agencies to opt for one kind of classification over another? What characterizes bureaucratic politics when some seek to enlarge jobs in a government agency? What relationship in fact exists between classification and government productivity? Well documented answers to these and other questions are extremely scarce (p. 527).

The behavioral critique set off an alarm. Classification had to reform itself and incorporate into its reform new modes of responsiveness. Unfortunately, the forces of reform were already at work. They rushed to prescribe new cures for more effective practices, calculating that a pound of responsiveness might head off an ounce of true reform.

E. The System Response: Factor Evaluation in the 1970s

By 1967 the House Committee on Post Office and Civil Service had decided that "a comprehensive review should be made of all classification and ranking systems in the federal service." Thereupon a comprehensive survey of federal classification practices was undertaken by the subcommittee on position classification. The subcommittee's report was a detailed indictment of current practices. It found the following:

1. Although job evaluation and ranking should provide the basis for good personnel management, many believed it was not doing so.
2. Classification and ranking systems had not been adapted to, maintained, or administered to meet the rapidly changing needs of the federal government.

3.   Classification was not generally used as a management tool. Many officials commented that
     the only function of classification in their organization was a basis for fixing pay.

These findings were serious enough that they led to the passing of the Job Evaluation Policy Act
of 1970. This act asserted that it was the sense of the Congress that there be a coordinated classification system for all civilian positions and that the U.S. Civil Service Commission should exercise general supervision and control over it. The Civil Service Commission was authorized to
establish a planning unit that would submit its final report within 2 years and then cease to exist.
This unit became known as the Job Evaluation and Pay Review Task Force. The final report of
the task force, released in January 1972, is popularly known as the Oliver report after the task
force director, Philip M. Oliver. The Oliver report declared the federal government's classification and ranking systems obsolete.

The task force recommended a new job evaluation system. The new system was field-tested
and revised. Finally, in December 1975, the Civil Service Commission approved the implementation, over a 5-year period, of the factor evaluation system for nonsupervisory positions. The factor
evaluation, or factor comparison, system was designed to be accurate and flexible, yet simple and
relatively inexpensive. But even more important, it hoped to secure the active involvement of
operating management, thus helping to reduce the them-or-us mentality that was usually associated with traditional control-oriented classification methods (Table 3).

Actually, the federal government's use of a factor evaluation system was seen by some as a
return to the classification practices of the 1920s. And in truth, the first factor comparison system
was installed by Eugene J. Benge at the Philadelphia Transit Company in 1926. The factor comparison system was basically a hybrid of traditional position classification systems, but the differences are significant. In the case of traditional classifications, different combinations of factors were
used for different positions; the factor evaluation system uses the same factors for all positions.
In the case of traditional classifications grade levels were ascertained by the weight and eloquence
of narrative descriptions; the factor evaluation system determined grade levels by comparing positions directly to one another. In short, the factor evaluation system sought to take traditional classification concepts a step further into rationality.

Obviously, the main ingredient of a factor evaluation system is the factor—any of the various key elements individually examined in the evaluation process. Although there are an infinite
number of specific factors that pertain to differing jobs, the factors themselves are usually categorized within five groupings:

1.   *Job requirements*—The knowledge, skills, and abilities needed to perform the duties of a spe-
     cific job
2.   *Difficulty of work*—The complexity or intricacy of the work and the associated mental demands
     of the job
3.   *Responsibility*—The freedom of action required by a job and the impact of the work performed
     on the organizational mission
4.   *Personal relationships*—The importance of interpersonal relationships to the success of mis-
     sion accomplishment
5.   *Other factors*—Specific job-oriented elements that should be considered in the evaluation pro-
     cess, e.g., physical demands, working conditions, accountability, number of workers
     directed

Once the factors of a position have been identified, it can be ranked, i.e., the factors of one position can be compared to those of another. Such a factor comparison can have only three outcomes. Any given factor must be higher than, lower than, or equal to the factor of another posi-

Table 3 Comparison of Job Evaluation Systems (Nonsupervisory Positions)

Characteristics	Federal wage system	Position classification system (Traditional)[a] 1940s	Factor evaluation system 1970s
Occupation	Trades and labor	Clerical, technical, administrative, and professional	Clerical, technical, administrative and professional
Pay basis	Hourly rates of area WG and NAF schedules	Per-annum rates, national general schedule	Per-annum rates, national general schedule
Factors used in evaluating positions	1. Skill and knowledge 2. Responsibility (includes supervisory controls, guidelines, and scope and effect) 3. Physical effort 4. Working conditions	1. Qualifications required 2. Nature of supervision received 3. Guidelines 4. Originality required 5. Nature and variety of work 6. Recommendation, decisions, etc. 7. Purpose and nature of person-to-person work relationships (Physical demands and hazardous work environment, as important in particular occupations)	1. Knowledge required by the position 2. Supervisory controls 3. Guidelines 4. Complexity 5. Scope and effect 6. General contacts 7. Purpose of contacts 8. Physical demands 9. Work environment
Standards	Same factors used consistently in narrative descriptions of grade levels	Various combinations of factors—mostly narrative descriptions of grade levels; some quantitative and factor format standards	Same factors used consistently in benchmarks and factor level descriptions (each factor level carries a point value)
Application	Positions graded to highest level reflected in regular, recurring duties	Positions graded to highest level compared to standards	Positions graded by totaling points and converting to grade; all regular, recurring work considered

[a] The "traditional" position classification system typically covers supervisory positions as well as nonsupervisory positions. Because this chart compared systems for nonsupervisory positions, "Nature and Extent of Supervision Exercised over Work of Other Employees" is not included under "Factors Used."

tion. When positions are ranked by factors, all of the factors of each position are compared and an overall ranking is achieved.

The crucial focus of a factor comparison system is the benchmark—a specific job at a specific point within an array of evaluations. Each series of choices based on ranking one position as compared to another results in a composite or total of the choices. These, when assigned numerical values, yield a score that assigns position X and position Y to specific points within an array of evaluations. Each time such determinations are made, they add to the array, thereby increasing the number of benchmarks. Each addition to the number of benchmarks facilitates arriving at the ranking choices for other jobs not yet evaluated.

Finally, when all of the jobs within an organization have been evaluated, they all become benchmarks. Once this has been achieved, all the positions within an organization would have, in effect, been compared to each other; each would have found its place in the classification and pay plans because it was found to rank higher than, lower than, or equal to its neighboring positions.

In adapting general factor evaluation for the federal government, the system was based on the following nine factors:

1. *Knowledge required by the position*—This factor measures the nature and extent of information or facts that the worker must understand to do acceptable work (e.g., steps, procedures, practices, rules, policies, theory, principles, and concepts) and the nature and extent of skills/abilities necessary to apply this knowledge.

2. *Supervisory controls*—This factor covers the nature and extent of direct or indirect controls exercised by the supervisor, the employee's responsibility, and the review of completed work. Controls are exercised by the supervisor in the way assignments are made, instructions are given to the employee, priorities and deadlines are set, and objectives and boundaries are defined. Responsibility of the employee depends on the extent to which the employee is expected to develop the sequence and timing of various aspects of the work, to modify or recommend modification of instructions, and to participate in establishing priorities and defining objectives. The degree of review of completed work depends on the nature and extent of the review, e.g., close and detailed review of each phase of the assignment, detailed review of the finished assignment, spot-check of finished work for accuracy, or review only for adherence to policy.

3. *Guidelines*—This factor covers the nature of guidelines and the judgment needed to apply these guidelines. Jobs vary in the specificity, applicability, and availability of guidelines for performance of assignments. Consequently, the constraints and judgmental demands placed on employees also vary. For example, the existence of specific instructions, procedures, and policies may limit the opportunity of the employee to make or recommend decisions or actions; however, in the absence of procedures or under broadly stated objectives, the employee may use considerable judgment in researching literature and developing new methods.

4. *Complexity*—This factor covers the nature and variety of tasks, steps, processes, methods, or activities in the work performed, and the degree to which the employee must vary the work, discern interrelationships and deviations, or develop new techniques, criteria, or information. At the low end of the scale, the work involves few, clear-cut, and directly related tasks or functions.

5. *Scope and effect*—This factor covers the purpose of the assignment and the effect of work products both within and outside the organization. At the lower end of the scale, the purpose is to perform specific routine operations that have little impact beyond the immediate organizational unit. At the high end of the scale, the purpose is to plan, develop, and carry out vital administrative or scientific programs that are essential to the missions of the agency or affect large numbers of people on a long-term or continuing basis.

6. *Personal contacts*—This factor includes face-to-face contacts and telephone and radio dialogue with persons not in the supervisory chain. The nature of contacts ranges from those with

other employees in the immediate work unit to contacts with high-ranking officials outside the agency. In between are many variations.

7. *Purpose of contacts*—The contacts covered by this factor range from the factual exchanges of information to situations involving significant or controversial issues and differing viewpoints, goals, or objectives.

8. *Physical demands*—This factor covers the requirements and physical demands placed on the employee by work assignment. This includes physical characteristics and abilities (e.g., specific agility and dexterity requirements) and the physical exertion involved in the work (climbing, lifting, pushing, balancing, stooping, kneeling, crouching, crawling, or reaching). To some extent the frequency or intensity of physical exertion must also be considered. For example, a job requiring prolonged standing involves more physical exertion than a job requiring intermittent standing.

9. *Work environment*—This factor considers the risks, discomforts, or unpleasantness that may be imposed on employees by various physical surroundings or job situations.

It is important that factor ranking be viewed in a comparative perspective. Philip Oliver, the principal architect of the method, often emphasized that the system was essentially a recompilation of existing methods in the private and public sectors. In Table 4, which illustrates the four major

Table 4 Typology of Job Evaluation Plans

Category of method	Concept	Best applications
Ranking method	Rank order each position by value using some form of collective judgement. Positions evaluated as whole units.	Small organizations where all positions are common knowledge.
Classification method (traditional)	Sort positions into grades/classes using predetermined standards or descriptions to ascertain grade levels. Positions evaluated as whole units.	Stable, large organizations (traditional) where outside control is significant (especially if legislature is involved).
Point rating method	Uniform set of job factors are chosen as the basis for establishing the value of a job. Positions are then rated in terms of degrees on each factor with points assigned for each degree. Position evaluated as a cumulative score from its components.	Used extensively in private industry where flexibility is important and different perspectives are involved in determining value of positions/jobs.
Factor comparison method	Combines aspects of ranking and point rating. Predetermined selection of factors, weights for the factors, and key jobs (benchmark positions). Positions are then scored on each factor compared to benchmark positions. Position is then evaluated as cumulative score.	Recommended for large, dynamic public-sector organizations where extensive employee/ supervisory involvement is critical for acceptance.

Source: Adapted in part from R. F. Milkey, Job Evaluation After 50 Years, *Public Personnel Rev.*, January 1960.

categories of job evaluation plans (as adopted from Robert F. Milkey's 1960 work), factor comparison can be seen as a blend of the ranking and point rating methods. Of course, its application on a scale as large as the federal government or many state and municipal governments was a major development in and of itself.

To cement the significance of factor ranking and other, more sophisticated methods, an effort was made to replace the standard reference work, the Baruch report. Harold Suskin edited a comprehensive volume in 1977 that provided illustrations of the new methods of job evaluation, overviewed pay administration and legal issues, and surveyed applications and new developments portending change. Suskin himself wrote the descriptive review on factor ranking and explained the advantages as follows:

> All major job characteristics must be weighed under the factor ranking approach. Strengths and weaknesses of a job must be recognized and quantified. The classifier's judgment on each factor is placed squarely on the record for all to see. This eliminates much of the mysticism commonly associated with classification decisions.
>
> Job evaluation is a subjective decisionmaking process. The classification method involves a review of the job as a whole, as well as a single subjective judgment concerning the appropriate grade, skill level, or pay range. If that decision over-credits or under-credits the job as a whole, the job is placed in the wrong grade, skill level, or pay range. Factor ranking involves a series of subjective decisions (i.e., a decision concerning each factor). Errors tend to offset one another, and the end product is likely to be more valid. Numerous psychological studies have indicated that a series of subjective judgments usually produce more valid results than does a single subjective judgment (p. 98).

Although Suskin recognized that there would be disadvantages, these were generally categorized as being problems of implementation that would inevitably occur when any jurisdiction switched from a more subjective method to a much more objective, mechanically oriented process.

But one should understand what was really at variance. In Table 3, an abridged version of an old Civil Service Commission exhibit used in educating administrators about the differences among job evaluation systems is presented. As the table shows, the informational factors are not that different. What was more different was the method used by the classifiers in making the classification decisions.

Consequently few critics were surprised when the factor evaluation system proved not to be major surgery but only a Band-Aid for the wounds of the federal classification system and the pressing need for pay reform. It offered better and more efficient methods but it could not address the deterioration of the entire classification systems. By the early 1980s this was all too apparent, as the trend to reallocate positions upward (frequently referred to as "grade escalation" or "grade creep") continued unabated. In a 1983 federal survey, the Office of Personnel Management (OPM—the replacement for old U.S. Civil Service Commission) calculated that at least 14% of jobs are misclassified or overgraded.

In August of the same year, OPM issued a moratorium on the issuance of classification standards. This was a remarkable admission on the part of OPM as they in effect refused to put more resources into creating and updating standards when the system clearly needed total repair. The question was which path to take; should classification be "modernized" or should reform follow a totally new path, one which would incorporate a new vision for both classification as an organizational function and a personnel process?

F. Which Path to Reform: Modernization or Reengineering

The moratorium lasted until 1986 when OPM announced new initiatives to move toward more flexible and simplified standards. A major thrust of this movement was to experiment with "multioccupation classification guides" that were designed to be more general and compare similar work across different occupational categories to avoid being overly specialized or narrow. Finally new initiatives promised, again, more delegation of authority to agencies and more flexibility for managers.

But classification reform was to take a back seat to pay reform. In the 1980s, severe pay pressures were greatly distorting the classification system. As federal wages, especially for white collar occupations, fell behind private sector wages by 10–15% and then by 20% at the end of the decade, federal managers inflated the grades of jobs as their surest response to increase pay.

The result was a major change in the grade composition of the federal work force. Driven also by the impacts of increased automation, agencies "traded" lower grade positions at the GS 1–5 levels for significant expansion in the higher grades (GS 12–15). In 1982, the lower grades (GS 1–6) accounted for the largest slice of the general service grades (39%). By 1992, the largest slice was GS 11–13 at 37.7% compared to 30% for GS 1–6. (Fig. 2 and 3) (Hyde, 1993).

OPM's conscious effort to defer any significant change in classification reform led to growing unrest among agencies that wanted out of the centralized federal pay system anyway. By the early 1980s, the research and demonstration authority under Title VI of the Civil Service Reform Act had been invoked to sponsor several major experiments with broad banding. And OPM began lobbying for passage of a new Civil Service Simplification Act, which would have let agencies adopt grade banding as an option, as long as there were linkage points back to the central system.

The pressure to seriously consider grade or broad banding led to the commission of a major study by the National Academy of Public Administration, which released its report in July 1991, just after OPM was able to secure passage of pay reform. The deck now seemed clear to discuss major reform. Certainly the mood was right. As one federal personnel manager, Lyn Meridew Holley (chief of position classification at the customs service), noted in a 1990 article:

> The job classification system has been in a state of progressive deterioration for more than a decade, culminating in 1983 when OPM ceased altogether to develop or update job classification standards. The system for developing job classification standards (and training those who use them) has not been fundamentally improved since the 1950's, even while resources available to develop and update standards have shrunk, and the rate of change in occupations has increased. The job classification system should be redesigned, retooled, and recalibrated (p. 40).

G. The Path Not Taken: Broad Banding?

Change comes from experimentation and when the Civil Service Reform Act was put together in 1978, the reformers envisioned a series of special projects to develop such innovations. Title VI authorized demonstration projects in which existing civil service rules would be waived and new systems developed and evaluated. In 1980 one of the most ambitious demonstration projects ever undertaken was begun at the Naval Weapons Center in China Lake, California and the Naval Ocean Systems Center in San Diego. In the mid 1980s, a parallel effort was initiated at McClellan Air Force Base in a union environment. A third experiment involving classification reform was undertaken by the National Institute of Standards and Technology.

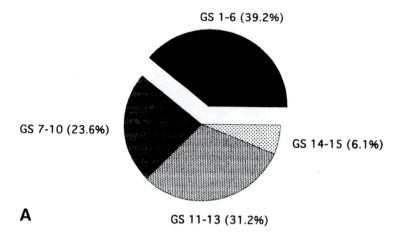

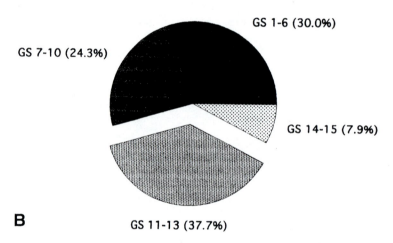

Figure 2 Grade distribution of GS employees; A, 1982 all agencies; B, 1992 all agencies.

What makes these particular demonstration projects so different is their reliance on a unique and more flexible classification system that aggregated separate grade levels into broader categories or pay bands. These demonstration projects thus used a totally different compensation scheme. In the case of China Lake, a performance appraisal system tied compensation to performance levels. At McClellan (called PacerShare), individual performance appraisals were to be replaced completely with a productivity gain-sharing system.

Why were these demonstrations so radical? The answer is they reengineered the federal job classification system. The traditional system was evolved into the General Schedule (GS) system, which defines nearly 450 different white collar occupations into 18 grades or compensation levels, and the federal wage system (FWS), which divides blue collar work into nearly 350 occupations with 15 grade levels. Organizational managers have to use the "system" to place people into their work roles—they write job descriptions for new hires which are reviewed and classified in terms of grade level before an authorization to fill the position can be given (Fig. 4).

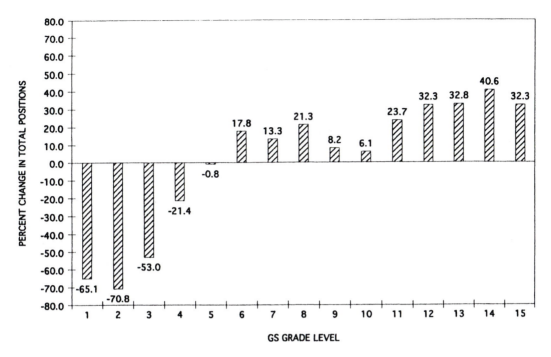

Figure 3   Change in GS grade levels, 1981–1982 to 1991–1992

The same system is confronted when work roles and duties change over time; the position must be reclassified if the supervisor wants to change the work roles, assignment, or compensation levels for individuals in the organization. Obviously, managers complain if there is extensive paper work (always), if there are delays (usually), and if they feel that classifiers are trying to tell them how to run or structure their organization (whether this is true or not, this impression is inevitable).

Perhaps in an era of centralization, stability, and prescribed work arrangements, the classification system was viable. In any organizational climate characterized by decentralization, rapid change, and discretionary work arrangements, managers may tend to view classification systems as excessively rigid, narrow, overspecialized, inefficient, and too time consuming.

The advantage of broad or pay banding comes from combining grade levels and simplifying occupational categories. In fact, broad banding is not an original idea developed just for the demonstration projects. In a 1968 report on job evaluation and ranking in the federal government, the idea of grade reduction was proposed as a solution to problems of rigidity and arbitrariness. It was felt that fewer overall grades with broader within-grade levels would provide more flexibility and authority for managers. Using the China Lake project as an example (see Fig. 4), the following steps were taken:

1. Five career paths were created covering separate major occupational groups, assuring that employees in comparable jobs would get comparable pay evaluations.
2. Each career path was divided into pay bands that combined at least two or more GS grades, giving each pay band a salary range of at least 50% (by comparison, the maximum range within a single GS grade is less than 30%).
3. Lastly, individuals are paid at least the minimum pay rate in their pay band with increases tied to either performance levels or some other type of incentive plan.

Career Group   **Pay Band**

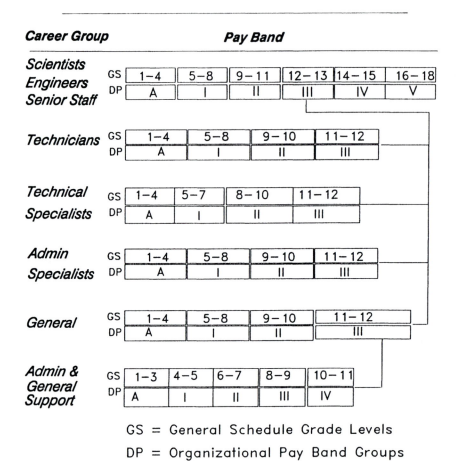

GS = General Schedule Grade Levels

DP = Organizational Pay Band Groups

Figure 4   Career paths and pay levels as related to current General Schedule.

Does broad banding work? Is this the next generation of classification? Every demonstration project authorized under Title VI requires a systematic evaluation. OPM itself has its own evaluation unit—the Office of Systems Innovation and Simplification (OSIS)—which has prepared major studies of both China Lake and McClellan. In the more recent case of McClellan, numerous difficulties including budget shortfalls and unexpected employee and union confrontations have delayed major assessments on this important project, but early results are very promising. But for all the promise, pay banding and a new generation of classification and compensation simplification is far from being a reality. In addition to determining the cost and budget impacts, there are other problems relating to pay comparability and performance appraisal. Critics are concerned that the drive to simplification will hinder comparisons between specific jobs making salary surveys more complex and blurring distinctions about job values within organizations. Others are worried about the increased pressure on performance appraisal practices. Broad banding shifts the classification focus from specific positions to more emphasis on an individual's performance within a broader pay band as determined by the manager.

Given the less than distinguished history of performance appraisal practices in government, some wonder as the U.S. MSPB (1989) questioned whether "Government's appraisal tools and processes are up to the demands of a system using broad pay bands?" Of course, the counterargument is that the above freedom, flexibility, and increased managerial discretion is precisely the goal of this potential innovation that links classification and compensation systems.

Of course, the organizational bottom line is cost. In the case of China Lake, the evaluations conclude that revised personnel practices that rely on broad banding for classification, appraisal, and pay are workable. However, both OPM and GAO advised caution in drawing general conclusions because of other mitigating factors and external events. Initially OPM noted that overall salary costs increased 6% more for the demonstration sites than the control sites. Not surprisingly, attitudinal surveys showed higher pay satisfaction among most employees at the demonstration sites and a greater sense of connectedness between pay and performance. A later OPM study showed that pay banding at China Lake does not have a dissimilar effect on salary costs as pay levels at the control sites have caught up to demonstration project levels.

This question about increased salary costs is important. The intent behind the demonstration projects was to prove that pay banding is budget-neutral, that it can work without increasing costs, or that the benefits produced would outweigh the costs. Probably most of the federal personnel community believes that pay banding will increase overall salary costs over time, as the MSPB noted in its 1989 review of OPM's Classification and Qualification Systems:

> Over a longer time span, the Board is still inclined to believe that pay banding will increase overall salary costs, all other things being equal. Of course, even if pay banding does increase costs, it may still be a valuable enhancement to the classification system (p. 32).

But this is an old problem—and one can only ask whether it really matters? On the last page of his now classic critique, Shafritz noted in 1973: "It has been found that savings are realized when the central budget agency removes personnel ceilings, while retaining budgetary ceilings." How difficult would it be to extend the same timeless rule back to classification and compensation levels within organizations. There must be some irony in the fact that to do so would be to essentially return to the personnel practice of over a century ago when lump sum appropriations for salaries were the rule and organizational heads had authorization to set salaries within budgetary ceilings. Or, one might conclude that that prospect is precisely what classification has fought against for over a century and understand its reluctance to follow it as a path for reform.

The report by NAPA on broad banding has moved the discussion to a full-scale debate between classification supporters who defend the framework of the system and want "modernization," and classification critics who want reform through "reengineering." Frank P. Cipolla of NAPA argued the case quite forcefully in a recent op-ed article:

> We need to fix the classification system *first*. It doesn't matter whether we adopt the NAPA broad banding model intact or whether we go to some other flexible system. The important thing is that we move away from the position-based approach to managing work and performance to one that focuses on the individual as a *contributor* to the work of the *team* or an organization. If we don't move in this direction we'll only be swimming up the TQM stream, treading water at best. In any case, we don't need pigeon-holing and unnecessary grade levels at a time when we are trying to flatten organizational structures and expand career broadening opportunities for employees.
>
> The current system pre-empts managers from fully exercising their responsibilities for managing work. Those who want to be accountable can't be because personnelists run the system. Those who don't want to be accountable can hide behind the barriers and restrictions of the current system and blame the personnelists. Too many personnelists aren't ready for a new system because they can't bring themselves to relinquish the control the current

system gives them. They rationalize by saying cynically that managers aren't ready, that it would take too much time to train them, and that going to a more flexible system run by managers necessarily would drive up costs. No matter which side of the fence you are on, as a minimum we ought to agree that line managers should be calling the shot on what shape a new classification system ought to take. . . .

As things stand now, it may well be two decades before the federal government decides to move in this direction. Why can't we be in the front wave for a change? Dragging a system which has its origins in the 19th century into the 21st century hardly seems in the public interest (p. 5).

H.   In Pursuit (or Retreat) of Modernization?

Cipolla's concerns were centered on the recent release of a report on the reform of the position classification system by a working group of the Interagency Advisory Group of Personnel Directors. This working group was established by OPM to develop final recommendations for system changes in classification, performance management, and pay-for-performance.

Its report, issued in June 1992 to the Director of OPM (entitled "Draft Framework of Policy and Program Initiatives for Performance Management and Position Classification"), argued that the basic structure of the classification system is adequate and that reform should concentrate on "simplification, automation, and redefinition of the roles of classifiers and managers." While the document does accept using alternative classification systems, such as grade banding, these would be approved on an "exception basis for occupations or organizational entities that can not accommodate to the general system".

A simple reading of the framework document will attest to the proposed path: modernization as opposed to reengineering. It begins: "For most of the work performed in the Federal civil service, the current classification framework of Title 5, USC, is adequate to achieve fundamental federal human resources goals such as equal pay for equal work and structuring work to accomplish missions. There are cases, however, where alternative structures may be needed to address unique circumstances." A vision statement follows that summarizes the direction of modernization as a destination point for the progress of classification over three-quarters of a century. To advocates, who have long extolled the need for redefining roles, simplifying standards, automating the system, and providing more training for managers, it will be seen as demonstrable proof of how far classification has come. To critics, who are committed to reengineering the system, "informating" the function, and devolving the process back into line management, it will validate how little real change has been made.

I.   Vision Statement for Position Classification

The federal government's General Schedule classification system is organized, managed, and supported in such a way that:

1.   Individuals available and qualified to perform the mission of an organization are the building blocks of the personnel system, the work and functions must first be organized in the most economically effective manner, with tasks and relationships sufficiently described to enable assignment of individuals.
2.   The classification system is viewed throughout the government as a useful, rational, and essential tool for supporting agency missions and for fostering equity and fairness to federal employees.

3. The classification system reflects and supports the principles of the federal government as a single employer.

4. Managers are responsible for organizing and structuring work in the most economically effective manner and to do so must understand the purposes, concepts, capabilities, and composition of the classification system with regard to their own specific situations.

5. Classifiers are proficient at accomplishing a primary role as consultants and advisors to managers on structuring organizations as well as individual jobs to attain agency goals and objectives with maximum effectiveness.

6. Employees understand the system and have full access to complete information about how their jobs are classified.

7. The classification system is simplified and automated in such a way that managers and personnel specialists everywhere have fast, user-friendly access to impartial, reliable, current, and technically sound classification determinations.

8. Alternatives to the government-wide classification system are available to solve agency-unique problems that cannot be put off under the general schedule.

A final decision has not been made on the future of federal classification. There is a new president, a new administration, a new director at OPM. And OPM is preparing its own evaluation of broad banding based on the demonstration project experience and the experience of other agencies that are exempted from Title V that have adopted pay banding. The PacerShare project is being reorganized out of existence and conversions made to bring federal employees there back into the GS system. There is a vigorous debate in classification circles about broad banding, pay and performance relationships, and emerging concerns about introducing quality teams as part of the quality management movement. In the 1990s, it may well be the latter—the quality management movement—that brings the most pressure to bear on classification and staffing.

IV. STAFFING AND PERFORMANCE: CONTOURS OF CHANGE

A. Work Redesign: The First Challenge?

A decade ago, this review predicted confidently that work redesign strategies would have tremendous impacts on the public sector. Partly because of technology and partly because of behavioral concerns, many were confident that the work environment would be so dynamic and fast changing that classification would have to change drastically to keep pace.

Indeed, the staffing literature on the 1970s and 1980s was filled with articles about work redesign, which was defined as "any activities that involve the alteration of specific jobs (or interdependent systems of jobs) with the intent of increasing both the quality of the employees' work experience and their on-the-job productivity." While primarily an experimental concept for private sector firms, it seemed destined to have large impacts on the public sector. And because so much of work redesign was aimed at increasing employee motivation and producing organizational change, classification would have to take work redesign very seriously. This reviewer predicted confidently that when work redesign hit the public sector in full force, classification would be in a real quandary.

The dilemma for classification was straightforward. Traditional classification was focused largely on job simplification. Classification, in response to work redesign experiments in the public sector, would have to be more decentralized; more sensitive to personal requirements, demands and capacities; and more self-administrable. There would be a certain irony, it was argued, as classification was increasingly relegated to mostly a training function for project managers and supervisors to assist them in evaluating new job arrangements and performance dimensions.

In defense of such predictions, the trend of work redesign was not clear. As a change strategy, it did seem to promise to alter, often radically, many of the basic premises of managing work assignments. As such, work redesign clearly built on the foundations established in the behavioral critique. Actually the opposite was the case. Most of the major tenets of work redesign were developed by the 1970s as an extension of the job enrichment movement. Shafritz (1978) in the first edition of his coauthored public sector personnel textbook included a chapter on work redesign. The chapter, itself rather unique in that it was part satire and part lecture on the future impact of work redesign, was entitled "Confessions of a Job Designer by 'X'."

In retrospect, the problem with work redesign was its premise usually summarized as changing work assignments in jobs to make them more rewarding, more satisfying, and therefore more motivating. A quarter of a century ago, changing the work itself to influence worker motivation seemed radical to large, centralized, heavily bureaucratized, command-and-control–oriented work environments.

At first, work redesign was epitomized by two types of approaches. The first approach, job enlargement, had roots going back to the 1950s in select progressive American and European factories. Job enlargement entailed increasing the variety of tasks performed at any level for the purpose of reducing boredom and repetitive actions. The second approach, usually attributed to Frederick Herzberg, a very influential management guru in the 1960s and 1970s, was to be more qualitative. Job enrichment allowed employees to plan, control, and take more responsibility in scheduling and even managing their own work.

The distinction made between the two approaches was that both were dimensions of work redesign. Enlargement was horizontal change wherein the range of actual work being done is changed. Enrichment was vertical change wherein employees participated in planning, organizing, leading, and controlling work functions. This was useful as long as job satisfaction was the primary premise.

Other leaders in the work redesign movement saw things in a wider context. Led by a number of British and European researchers and scholars, the idea of work redesign took on a new emphasis: mainly how to develop organizations and their systems of work organization that would provide for both individual and societal needs and change the scope of supervision and management from command and control to participation and democratization.

Thus, a more comprehensive assessment of work redesign (it was seen as a true work movement) saw a number of stages of concurrent emphasis but progressive evolution. Louis E. Davis and James C. Taylor (1972) at the forefront of the movement divided work redesign into four stages:

1. Task and job rationalization (or work simplification)
2. Changing of Job content
3. Changing of Role content
4. Self-maintaining of organizations

Task rationalization represented the ongoing past, involving engineering work assignments through the use of scientific management with time and motion study, work physiology, and the study of the worker–machine interface. These foci emphasized variables such as simplifying work assignments, reducing worker fatigue, and improving management and human engineering in work settings. Davis and Taylor included both job enlargement and enrichment in the job content stage, since both focused on intrinsic job satisfaction. The variables being changed were task variation and range, planning, regulation, and work control activities.

It was in the final two phases, role content and self-maintaining organizations, that Davis and Taylor saw a more sociological systems focus. Here work redesign was to be viewed in both an

Table 5 Evolution of Work Redesign: Periods, Emphasis, Concepts, and Techniques

Periods and emphasis (some significant theorists)	Concepts and techniques
1. Job simplification 1800s–1940s (Taylor, Scientific Management)	1. Rationalization of tasks and work; to replicate scientifically one most efficient way of producing output
2. Job enlargement 1955–1960s (Walker and Guest; Davis and Canter)	2. Horizontal task loading: changing positions by increasing number, control, and variety of tasks
3A. Job enrichment 1960s–1970s (Herzberg; Ford and Gillette)	3A. Vertical task loading: work redesign as the key to employees' psychological growth, emphasis on improving individual's responsibility, recognition, and achievement
3B. Integrated work/organizational redesign 1980s (Hackman and Oldham; Janson and Purdy; Lawler)	3B. Changing core job dimensions: skill variety, task identity and significance, autonomy; job redesign but as a motivational strategy and a design for employee development
4. Self-maintaining organizations 1980s–1990s (Emery and Trist; Davis)	4. Development of autonomous work teams: (emphasis on self-regulation through use of team building, new forms of organizations, new management roles)

organizational and a sociotechnical context, which could include worker democratization efforts. They concluded that changing jobs and job content was unlikely to produce real progress, stating flatly that "focusing on job revision, job enlargement, job enrichment, etc., will not fundamentally alter the organizational system, the roles of the organization's members and managers, the opportunity for self-regulation, or the flexibility or adaptability of the organization and its members" (Davis and Taylor, 1972) (Table 5).

This remarkably accurate prediction missed only the logical extension of its own argument, i.e., that enthusiasm for work redesign from most organizations, given their traditional concerns for command and control, was not likely to be strong, unless there would be a strong linkage to increased productivity and performance. Work redesign theory in the 1970s expanded its research scope to relationships between key work variables (variety, task identity, task significance, autonomy, and feedback) and expected outcomes (experienced meaningfulness of the work, experienced responsibility for work outcomes, and knowledge of actual results of work activity). The work of American behavior scientists (Lawler, 1972; Hackman and Suttle, 1977 and many others) focused on how core job dimensions impacted on personal motivation, productivity, and job satisfaction.

Interestingly, as Lawler reported in the early 1970s, their findings provided some interesting contradictions. In a summary article written in 1972, Lawler reported on work redesign research as it affected public sector organizations. He noted the following:

1. Work redesign affects work quality more strongly than it does productivity.
2. Work redesign strongly affects job satisfaction, involvement, and absenteeism (which are more personal than organizational values).
3. Interpersonal dimensions of work have little impact on worker satisfaction or performance.
4. Many managerial-professional jobs rate low on the core job dimensions (variety, task identity and significance, autonomy, and feedback).

5. Supervisors often misperceive the jobs of their subordinates (they rate the existence of the core job dimensions much higher than the employees themselves).
6. Supervisors are often major obstacles to job redesign efforts. (p. 13).

Lawler's findings, written a decade before the quality management movement, were quite prophetic. More than anything else, the inability of work redesign to demonstrate first how it would improve employee productivity made it questionable to most managers. In defense of this reviewer's prediction that work redesign would have a major impact on public organizations and public personnel management, the concluding line from the first edition read: "Work redesign will be a serious force when the productivity factors are matched, line for line, with individual quality of work life indicators such as stress reduction, increased self/group determination, and personal growth and development."

B. Round II: The Quality Circles Movement

If work redesign failed because of its inability to convince organizations of its potential impact on productivity, it set the stage for a different kind of renewal effort involving staffing and work, i.e., new templates for quality improvement. Work redesign had always championed the idea of participative management, using various forms of work teams to alter work systems and structures. But it was the advent of quality circles, due in part to the extensive use of them in Japanese management, that captured attention in the early 1980s.

Quality circles were very attractive to American organizations because they represented a form of *voluntary planned change*. Individuals assume self-determined roles on a voluntary basis to improve organizational outcomes and take responsibilities to plan, make, and maintain better quality. Since employees essentially volunteered their time to participate and continued to do their existing jobs, but used the circle meetings to concentrate their efforts on improving existing processes and outputs, organizations found them attractive.

Quality circles emerged in the early 1980s as a significant approach for dealing with barriers to organizational productivity and individual performance. Its origins were in the Japanese industrial experience where impressive productivity rates have been attributed to highly goal-oriented, solidified group activity within organizations. There was a certain irony, of course, in the fact that the Japanese attribute the original concept to American engineers who were working with developing Japanese firms in the 1950s. (Indeed, to this day Japan's industry-wide competition prize for quality is named the Deming Prize after the American quality guru W. Edwards Deming.)

The essential concept behind the quality circle was to enable a small number of key participants to do more than study or discuss problems, but to actually have the group plan for and implement actual solutions. In the early 1970s, the Lockheed Missile Division became one of the first American borrowers of the quality circles concept. By the early 1980s over a dozen federal agencies and numerous state and local government agencies had instituted quality circle programs.

The guiding premise was that the most significant expertise of the organization is in its employees. Quality circles became voluntary participant work groups, functioning autonomously in an attempt to focus worker expertise on work problems, especially quality problems. To establish quality circles within public sector organizations usually required consideration of three critical factors:

1. The commitment and cooperation of management, unions and employees, and the public
2. The establishment of a measurement concept that can serve as a basis for assessment of work environment and productivity changes
3. Identification and provision of some form of facilitative expertise to assist in organizing, focusing, and implementing quality circle deliberations.

Quality circles or quality improvement teams were generally defined as any group of workers from the same organizational area who meet for some period of time regularly to discuss quality problems, investigate causes, recommend solutions, and implement changes when approved by management. The guiding premise behind the quality circle was that problems in quality, productivity, and motivation are widespread; that management can't solve all the problems and (in many cases doesn't know many of the problems exist); that solutions are only possible when the organization relies on the innovative power within the work force. The goal then was to develop a participative management process in the organization that "empowered" workers to solve their own job quality-related problems.

The quality circle differed from teams or other task forces in that members selected problems to work on, analyzed problems and recommended solutions, had their own leadership, used trained facilitators, and generally had both leaders and members receive training in meeting skills, interpersonal communication, problem solving, etc. But most critical of all—the circle was to be totally voluntary. In some Japanese firms, where membership in quality circles was strongly encouraged, it was not uncommon for every member of the work force to belong to one or more quality circles.

There are also key differences in the types of problems that are addressed. Quality circles focused on logistical support problems and supply defects; administrative processes; division of functions, tasks, and work staffing; reports, records, and all supporting paper work; work flow; communications flow; safety; and technical training. They generally didn't get involved over wages and salaries, benefits, disciplinary and grievance policies, or employment and termination policies.

Most organizations using quality circles established some type of organizational steering committee. This committee oversaw and coordinated the establishment of quality circles, reviewed circle implementation plans, and helped select circle leaders and circle facilitators. If the organization decided to establish some type of reward or recognition program, the steering committee would oversee that effort as well as review the progress of circles to determine the overall worth or success of the effort.

So how, then, were quality circles unique? First, their objectives are focused primarily on quality, not productivity, not cost reduction, not anything else. Admittedly, quality improvement ultimately leads to productivity improvement, cost reduction, and enhanced performance—but these are long-range goals that are byproducts of the commitment to quality. The method of operation of the quality circle is also substantially different. All quality circle members supposedly function as equals. A consensus decision-making method is used to ensure that all views have been heard and accepted. Consensus means that all members have to agree or agree not to disagree. Even the discussion method at circle meetings favors brainstorming methods designed to get the maximum number of ideas without promoting high amounts of disagreement.

Quality circles had about a 5-year life span in most of the American organizations in which they were developed. Private sector organizations were the first to disband their circles and replace them with more informal team-building efforts. When circles failed, several internal factors were generally cited: (1) management ordering supervisors to volunteer as leaders or supervisors ordering employees to volunteer as members, (2) management assigning problems to circles rather than letting circles chose their own agenda, (3) within the circles, leadership trying to control circle activities or dominate the decision-making process.

But there were several major external factors. The advent of quality circles didn't change the levels of management or reduce hierarchy. In Japan, where the manager and administrator ratio is 1 to 27 workers and the typical number of layers in the organization is between 3–4, the quality circle was indispensable. In the United States, with 8:1 manager-to-employee ratios and 6–7 levels of hierarchy, quality circles were a luxury. Given that quality circles didn't reduce supervisory levels, eliminate hierarchy, and simply competed for management time and attention, it was not surprising when most researchers found little correlation between quality circles and productivity and performance. And when organizations first in the private sector in the mid-1980s and then the public sector in the late 1980s began downsizing and reducing the size of the work force, quality circle training, facilitators, and then quality circles themselves were rapidly jettisoned or replaced with more informal problem-solving teams or "chartered teams."

C. Work Teams and Quality Management: The Third Challenge

Unlike work redesign, which was seen primarily as a tool to fix job satisfaction, quality circles were viewed by many organizations as an important forerunner for involving the whole organization into the quality and competitiveness arena. By the mid-1980s, increasing numbers of private sector firms were developing total quality management efforts. The Defense Department and NASA, two organizations with extensive contractor ties, launched major efforts into TQM by the late 1980s and by 1990; TQM was at the forefront of American organizational management effort, in both the private and public sectors.

A detailed history and accounting of TQM goes well beyond the scope of this chapter, but one facet—indeed, what is often called its most important dimension—commands attention. This major dimension of TQM entailed new forms of collaboration or participation. Under the rubric of "work force empowerment," organizations use various forms of problem-solving work teams ranging from ad hoc corrective action or chartered work teams to more extensive organized process redesign and work reengineering teams. The purpose of all these participative efforts is similar—to engage work force members in the solution of quality problems.

What most distinguishes the level of effort in participative teams is the scope of the team's charter and its representation. Starting organizations concentrate their initial efforts by creating high-level teams of top managers and supervisors or quality improvement teams or councils within an organizational unit. Such efforts are often ad hoc with self-defined agendas that change with the subtraction or addition of new team members. More rigorous efforts involve "chartered" work teams (essentially a more structured problem-solving work group) or process teams. These groups investigate quality problems, chart work flows and linkage of production or service processes, and/or examine customer feedback or benchmarking data. Their recommendations for improvement are reviewed, changes are made, and progress is monitored.

But the real demarcation between less and more developed TQM organizations is the use of some form of cross-functional work team concept. Their working groups are called either work process redesign teams or work reengineering teams. Extensive use of process measurements is made, but there is greater emphasis on experimental design and innovation. The focus often goes beyond that: "Are the right things being done?" as opposed to "Are things being done right?" Work reengineering is the most ambitious step. Here the organization will restructure supplier relationships, production and service processes, organizational designs, and cross-individual work roles. Thus the focus is truly on strategic change.

Quality management places a premium on the work group cooperating and interacting as a team, as opposed to individual competition under direct organizational supervision. To overcome vertical specialization and organizational layering, TQM efforts are generally organized through some type of team effort representing different levels or functions of the traditional organization. Table 6 illustrates the key options in ascending order of significance. Most organizations embarking on TQM recognize the importance of employee empowerment. However, putting participation into practice is a different matter. What is at stake is more than asking employees to become more concerned about or committed to work quality. Organizations in the 1990s have learned that change through quality improvement must be enacted through some form of work group focused effort.

Table 6 A Typology of Quality Teams

Corrective Action or Quality Improvement Teams

Appointed or representative problem-solving work teams that meet regularly to diagnose quality problems within an organizational unit. They usually consist of supervisors and employees who prioritize problems and suggest solutions to the problems they have selected. Often a first step for getting started without having to plan or integrate efforts into an overall improvement process.

Chartered Teams

Problem-solving work groups that are formed after quality problems have been selected and improvement efforts are linked together. Chartered teams have specific problems to address; a charter detailing objectives, boundaries, and time frames; and, once solutions are proposed, are reformed or taken up into other efforts.

Work Process Teams

Work teams that are chosen to examine a specific work production or service process horizontally or from a customer's perspective. The team follows every aspect of input, throughput, and output to track quality, cost, and time factors; applying various SPC measurement tools. The group's mission is to focus on how a specific work process can be improved or made more reliable. *Engineering Redesign Teams or Cross-Functional Work Teams* Work teams that are chosen from different disciplines and units inside and outside the organization. The goal is to examine outputs and reinvent processes, technology applications, human work roles, and all other inputs to improve the product or service process. Engineering redesign questions every aspect of a process and considers experimental and other innovative methods to accomplish the process objectives.

This is difficult because it involves much more than simply beefing up the employee suggestion systems, conducting brainstorming sessions with small employee committees, or reenacting quality circles. TQM organizations have begun with chartered work teams, often led by external facilitators, that have focused on specific, high-priority quality problem targets. More developed TQM efforts are characterized by a willingness to experiment with major change and redefinition of entire work processes and service and production design structures. Since this constitutes radical change, there is often considerable resistance, both from managers within the organization who are being displaced and from workers who have developed considerable specialization and professional commitment to specific areas of expertise.

D. The Challenge to Staffing and Classification?

For a quality team concept to be successful, several variables must be considered. First, it is essential that teams be assigned whole tasks with identifiable, meaningful, and significant objectives that are linked to organizational priorities for performance improvement and change. Second, members of the team must have a number of different skills required for group completion of the tasks. Third, each team must be given autonomy to make decisions about methods through which work is accomplished. Finally, and most difficult of all from a personnel perspective, evaluation of the team is based on performance of the group as a whole rather than team contribution of the individual. Essentially, the classification, compensation, and performance appraisal concept must be group-based as opposed to individually based. There are other personnel implications that must be considered, such as the following:

Who selects the objectives for the team and ensures that the team's work plan and efforts are integrated into the organization's strategic objectives?

Who selects the team members, based on what criteria, and where do team members go when
the objective is accomplished? In the same vein, what guidelines does a team member use to
balance the host unit's needs with the quality team's needs?

Who owns the results, i.e., who is accountable for accomplishing the team's objectives and takes
over implementation of the results?

How will teams be trained, especially in facilitation, team work skills, and quality measurement
skills, in order to accomplish their work group objectives?

How will team members be evaluated and what are the implications for the organization's performance appraisal processes? Similarly, how will organizations provide recognition for the
efforts of work teams and reward team members for outstanding contributions?

How does the use of different types of quality teams and participative management alter the classification perspective and affect classification outcomes (if some form of broad banding system is not in place)?

V. A NOTE ON PLACEMENT AND STAFFING

It should not be too difficult to recognize that the preceding questions involve different categories
of problems. On the one hand, there is a set of organizational performance, coordination, and
strategic planning issues to which quality management has brought a new focus. On the other hand,
there is the age-old group of issues involving individual placement or how the organization puts
the right person in the right place.

A decade ago, this review (Hyde, 1982) noted that the placement problem was important but
largely ignored:

> The final dimensions of the staffing process focus on placing the individual into the organi-
> zation. Few functions should have as much importance as the critical tasks of matching in-
> dividuals to the positions that are best suited for their skills, attitudes, and abilities. In fact,
> this objective, so ideally stated, is very difficult to realize. Although many personnel admin-
> istrators talk about the challenge of matching the right person to the right position at the right
> time, this is all too often simply lip service. Placement, as important as it is, is virtually in-
> visible in public personnel management (p. 117).

Probably the largest reason that placement is seen as trivial is that most organizations treat "placement" through the recruitment, promotion, and career development processes. It would be better
to recruit top personnel (the higher level the better) and let them compete through promotion and
performance review for advanced assignments, or choose training and development program options that further lock them into their path of vertical specialization. Promotions in the public sector, especially on a competitive basis for single vacancies, are supposedly placement decisions.
In reality, considerations of promotion far outweigh the placement dimensions.

Granted there are exceptions. Many federal agencies like NASA, GAO, and others make
extensive use of co-op and internship programs. They bring new professionals into their organization, rotate them through different divisions, even assign them to details in different regions or
agencies, and provide them with extensive opportunities to work in different parts of the organization before "settling down" to a particular career path. And some of these organizations believe
that periodic transfer is important to keep people well versed in the complete range of organizational functions and missions.

But one need only look at the capstone of the federal civil service to see that the idea of "horizontal movement" has never truly taken hold. Less than 20% of all senior executive service take
lateral transfers and move from one challenging assignment to another. Whether or not a highly

mobile executive service was an objective of civil service reform has become irrelevant in the reality that it is not.

Rank-in-person systems, such as the uniformed services or the U.S. State Department's Foreign Service, which divorce placement from promotion, have made the most progress in the placement area. The volume of placements in these mobile career services can be quite high, especially when the typical assignment lasts only 1 or 2 years. In such environments, the costs to the organization of a poor placement are excessive; by the time the employee and/or his or her supervisor can make needed adjustments to get the full value from the employee's efforts, the tour of duty ends and the employee is reassigned. Furthermore, the worldwide scope of many rank-in-person services makes unattractive the option of curtailed assignments because of the expense and lost time frequently incurred in a long-distance curtailment and reassignment. Theoretically, both rank-in-person and rank-in-job systems must place a high value on correct placements, the former to avoid the dollar costs and loss of efficiency arising from curtailed or ineffective assignments, the latter to avert errors in promotion that a bad placement entails.

But most organizations have difficulty in seeing placement in its own right as a major function, instead of some smaller supporting process—or at least historically they have. How that will change in a quality team environment where there is real movement and reassignment to a variety of projects and process improvement efforts that cut across the organization and take people out of their "NWT" (a cute acronym for natural work team, which is actually a euphemism for the section you're assigned to for purposes of the organization's head count) is the real question.

Placement has traditionally been viewed as the final stage in bringing individuals into organizations. In an organizational world composed of numerous types of quality process and work teams using a broad-banding grade level approach, placement may finally become an ongoing process. It will be much more than reassignments, job rotations, or lateral transfers, it will have to address collective work team assignments, team member training, team member and unit assessments, even career planning.

The relationship between classification and placement in this new staffing environment will change dramatically. Marvin D. Dunnette (1966); a highly influential industrial psychologist in the decade of the 1960s who wrote perhaps the classic statement on the topic, summarized it thusly:

> The broad aim of personnel decision making is to estimate or measure as accurately as possible each person's individuality and to place him in an assignment for which his pattern of predicted job behavior is appropriate both to his own long-term goals and to the goals of his employer. Thus, personnel classification and job placement seek the optimal matching of men and jobs within the constraints dictated by available manpower and available jobs. When only a few jobs and many men are available, personnel classification and job placement give way to strategies of pure selection. When many jobs are available (as with most large industrial firms, government agencies, and the armed services), procedures directed toward optimal classification and placement may be realistically undertaken. The opportunity to use a classification strategy as opposed to pure selection is primarily a function of the size of the institution for which personnel decisions are being made and the diversity of jobs available for personnel assignment (pp. 183–184).

How much has changed in the span of a quarter century? Not only are half of those workers women, but the downsizing efforts and quality management processes designed to accomplish a true revolution in producing a new postbureaucratic paradigm in modern organizations are now the center stage. Dunnette's world view of institutions (and his criticism of the neglect of placement) was probably right then. But that seems long ago. Today at the crossroads leading to the 21st century, how work is to be defined is fundamental, even in the public sector, to the change that lies ahead. Michael Barzelay in his new work *Breaking Through Bureaucracy* summarized it thusly:

> [The bureaucratic strategy] . . . of defining work is failing to satisfy public servants. Younger members of the Workforce are less willing to accept close supervision. It is a reasonable inference that specifying organizational positions is an unsatisfactory way to characterize their identity and purpose at work. Another problem with the standard account is that citizens are skeptical about the value of work public servants do—and public servants know it. The bureaucratic paradigm offers late-twentieth-century public servants few tools for explaining to themselves and others why their work counts (p. 6).

VI. SUMMARY

What general conclusions can be reached about the state of the art in staffing and placement in the public sector, the art and science of placing individuals into organizations? Staffing is more than ever an area filled with contradiction and change. The larger process of staffing, constituted by classification and job evaluation on the one hand and placement and assignment on the other, is an integral bet controversial part of the personnel practice. The literature, while considerable, is often contradictory, with little attempt by advocates or critics to reconcile opposing positions. Classification specialists and managers and critics have disputed problems, causes, and remedies for decades, seemingly talking past each other. In fact, it may well be just that. In the early debates between the scientific management and human relations schools on organizational theory and behavior, reviewers would note that the premises, variables, and values that one school thought critical were ignored by the other and vice versa.

The current debate in classification over modernization and the new system of broad banding seems likely to emerge as a draw. Modernization will probably triumph in the system overall, and broad banding may become the exception of choice. The ultimate score in this match-up may well be how many and what kinds of organizations pursue broad banding and make the exception the rule.

Whether the remainder of this decade will resolve the major problems in staffing is open to question. A decade ago this review concluded on this cautionary note:

> A more probable outcome will be that new emphasis on work redesign, individual demands for quality of work life, and new forms of self-managing organizations will generate major new pressures that will make many of the old controversies obsolete. In the meantime, staffing will continue to emphasize formal organizational control and management objectives. As long as it does so, it will be beset by controversy and challenge.

It seems more likely that as governments (federal and state and local) go through their own variations of downsizing, technology displacement, and quality improvement efforts, that modernization and automation will not be enough. The entire public personnel function is now under a great pressure to change, to help lead the public sector's effort to be more competitive, and to provide greater value both in better services delivered and lower costs of performance. The above goals cannot be accomplished by simply working harder or getting harder working people to work in the public sector. It requires changing organizational structures, work processes and products, supervisory and worker relationships, and resource and information management. Staffing is absolutely critical in this change process; whether the change process is accomplished with or without the full participation of staffing and human resources management is the real question that remains.

REFERENCES

Atwood, J. F. (1971). Position synthesis: a behavioral approach to position classification, *Public Personnel Rev.*, April, 70–81.

Baruch, I. (1942, 1965). *Position Classification in the Public Service*, Public Personnel Association, Chicago.

Baruch, I. (1937). *Facts and Fallacies in Position Classification*, Civil Service Assembly, Chicago.

Barzelay, M. (1992). *Breaking Through Bureaucracy: A New Vision for Managing in Government*, University of California Press, Berkeley, California.

Berlin, S. S. (1964). The manager, the classifier, and unwarranted grade escalation, *Civil Service J.*, July–Sept, 1–8.

Boyett, J. H., and Conn, H. P. (1991). *Workplace 2000: The Revolution Reshaping American Business*, Penguin, New York.

Cipolla, Frank P. (1992). *Periscope, 13* (September).

Classifiers column (1988–1992), newsletter of the Classification and Compensation Society, 1730 K Street NW, Washington, DC. Civil Service Assembly (1942). *Committee on Position Classification and Pay Plans in the Public Service*, Chicago.

Cummings, T. G., and Srivatva, S. *Management of Work*, Kent State University Press, Kent, OH, 1977.

Davis, L. E., and Taylor, J. C., eds. (1972). *Design of Jobs*, Penguin Books, New York.

Dunnette, M. D. (1966). *Personnel Selection and Placement*, Brooks/Cole, Belmont, CA.

Epperson, L. L. (1975). The dynamics of factor comparison/point evaluation, *Public Personnel Manage.*, *4* (Jan.–Feb.).

Forrer, J. (1981). *A Federal Position Classification System for the 1980's*, U.S. Government Printing Office, Washington, DC.

Ganschinietz, B., and McConomy, S. (1983). Trends in job evaluation practices of state personnel systems, *Public Personnel Manage.*, *12*(1), 1–12.

Ghropade, J., and Atchison, T. J. (1980). The concept of job analysis: a review and some suggestions, *Public Personnel Manage.*, *9*(3), 134–139.

Gilbert, G. R., and Nelson, A. (1989). The pacer share demonstration project: implications for organizational management and performance evaluation, *Public Personnel Manage.*, *18*(2), 209–220.

Hackman, J. R., and Suttle, L. (1977). *Improving Life at Work*, Goodyear, Santa Monica, CA.

Holley, L. M. (1990). Pay reform and job classification, *The Bureaucrat, 19*(1), 40–44.

Hyde, A. C., and Shafritz, J. (1983). Position classification and staffing, *Public Personnel Administration: Problems and Prospects* (S. W. Hays and R. C. Kearney, eds.), Prentice-Hall, Englewood Cliffs, NJ.

Hyde, A. C. (1988). The new environment for compensation and performance evaluation in the public sector, *Public Personnel Manage.*, *17*(4), 351–358.

Hyde, A. C. (1992). The proverbs of TQM: recharting the course to quality improvement in the public sector, *Public Prod. Manage. Rev., fall*, pp. 22–38.

Hyde, A. C. (1993). An annotated glossary of TQM, Brookings Institution, Center for Public Policy Education, Washington, DC.

Jensen, O. A. (1978). An analysis of confusions and misconceptions surrounding job analysis, job evaluation, position classification, employee selection, and content validity, *Public Personnel Manage.*, *7*(4), 258–271.

Lawler, E. E. (1972). Worker satisfaction job design, and job performance, *Good Government, 89*(2).

Lawton, E. C., and Suskin, H. (1976). *Elements of Position Classification in Local Government*, IPMA, Chicago.

Maccoby, M. (1988). *Why Work*, Simon & Schuster, New York.

McCarthy, Eugene M. (1989). The Congress and the civil service: a history of federal compensation and classification, background paper for National Commission on the Public Service, Washington, DC.

McInnis, D. (1948). Does position classification work? *Personnel Admin., 10* (March).

Milkey, R. F. (1960). Job evaluation after 50 years, *Public Personnel Rev., Jan.*

National Academy of Public Administration (1986). *The Quiet Crises of the Civil Service: The Federal Personnel System at the Crossroad*, Washington, DC.

National Academy for Public Administration (1991). *Modernizing Federal Classification: An Opportunity for Excellence*, Academy Panel. NAPA, Washington, DC.

National Commission for the Public Service (1989). *Leadership for America*, Washington, DC.

Oliver, P. M. (1976). Modernizing a state job evaluation and pay plan, *Public Personnel Manage., 5*(3), 168–169.

Osborne, D. and Gaebler, T. (1992). *Reinventing Government*, Addison Wesley, Reading, Massachusetts.

Penner, M. (1983). How job-based classification systems promote organizational effectiveness, *Public Personnel Manage., 12*(3), 268–276.

Perlman, K. (1980). Job families: a review and discussion of their implications for personnel selection, *Psychol. Bull., 80*(1).

Remsay, A. S. (1976). The new factor evaluation system of position classification, *Civil Service J., 16*.

Report of the Congressional Joint Commission on Reclassification of Salaries (1920). House Document 686, 66th Congress, 2nd Session, Washington, DC.

Sayre, W. (1908). The triumph of techniques over purpose, *Public Admin. Rev., spring*, 134–136.

Shafritz, J. M. (1973). *Position Classification: A Behavioral Analysis for the Public Service*, Praeger, New York.

Shafritz, J. M., Balk, W., Hyde, A. C., and Rosenbloom, D. (1978). *Personnel Management in Government*, 5th Ed., Marcel Dekker, New York.

Siegel, G. B. (1989). Compensation, benefits and work schedules, *Public Personnel Manage., 18*(2), 198–208.

Smith, R. (1981). Job redesign in the public sector, *Rev. Public Personnel Admin., 2*(1), 63–84.

Special Task Force to the Secretary of Health, Education, and Welfare (1973). *Work in America*, MIT Press, Cambridge, MA.

Stahl, O. Glenn (1971). *The Personnel Job of Government Managers*, IPMA, Chicago.

Suskin, H., ed. (1977). *Job Evaluation and Pay Administration in the Public Sector*, International Personnel Management Association, Chicago.

Taylor, F. W. (1967). *The Principles of Scientific Management*, W.W. Norton, New York.

Thompson, F. J. (1976). Classification as politics, *People in Public Service*, (R.T. Golembiewski and M. Cohen, eds.), Peacock, Itsaca, IL, pp. 515–527.

Thompson, F. J., ed. (1991). *Classics of Public Personnel Policy*, Brooks Cole, Pacific Heights, CA.

U.S. Civil Service Commission, Bureau of Programs and Standards (1963). *The Nature and Meaning of Grade Escalation Under the Classification Act*, Washington, DC.

U.S. Civil Service Commission, U.S. Job Evaluation and Pay Review Task Force (1971), *Report on Survey of Job Evaluation and Pay for State Merit and Civil Service Systems*, Washington, DC.

U.S. Civil Service Commission (1978). *A Report on Study of Position Classification Accuracy in Executive Branch Occupations under the General Schedule*, Washington, DC.

U.S. Merit Systems Protection Board (1989). *OPM's Classification and Qualification Systems: A Renewed Emphasis, A Changing Perspective*, November.

U.S. Office of Personnel Management (1979). *Position Classification: A Guide for City and County Managers*, U.S. Government Printing Office, Washington, DC, November.

U.S. Office of Personnel Management (1991). *The Classifier's Handbook*, Washington, DC.

U.S. Office of Personnel Management, Classification and Performance Management Working Group (1992). Policy initiatives for position classification and performance management, June 10.

Van Riper, P. P. (1958). *History of the United State Civil Service*, Row Peterson, Evanston, IL.

Walker, J. H. (1980). *Human Resource Planning*, McGraw-Hill, New York.

White, R. D. (1984). Position analysis and characterization, *Rev. Public Personnel Admin., 4*(2), 57–67.

14

The Practice of Performance Appraisal

ARIE HALACHMI   Tennessee State University, Nashville, Tennessee

I. THE DIFFERENT USES OF PERFORMANCE APPRAISAL

A basic premise of performance appraisal is that a careful examination of the record can provide supervisors and organizations with important means for finding out what took place and what must be done to achieve an end. However, performance appraisal rarely meets the needs of the individual supervisor or employee. The general approach and the instruments in use during the process are intended to serve several personnel and management functions, such as:

1. *Providing a mechanism for getting subordinates to contribute to management development.* Here the review concentrates on the past. The emphasis is on the subordinate's perspective and perception of the supervisor's role in determining performance. Performance appraisal in this context is a vehicle for organizational development and for alerting and educating supervisors about how their own performance may influence what subordinates achieve. The focus of the review process is on the job situation rather than on the individual, the subordinate, or the supervisor. When a supervisor is not in a position to interact directly with service recipients on a daily basis, a trained subordinate can be a valuable source for important intelligence about the environment. Such an employee may be able to spot emerging trends and allow the supervisor, and the organization as a whole, to anticipate demands for a specific service and to prepare for it.

2. *Helping employees understand assigned responsibilities and their relationships to organizational goals.* The appraisal is a vehicle for improving productivity by motivating employees and generating concerns about results. Deriving individual objectives from the unit and the organizational objectives as well as the review of the progress toward achieving them provides supervisors with opportunities to educate employees. Teaching subordinates about the significance of their jobs, how they contribute to the overall mission of the organization, and how their performance influences the work of others is important and necessary for sound employee motivation.

3. *Informing employees about management expectations.* The preparations that take place before the beginning of the appraisal period allow supervisors to work on reducing uncertainty and helping employees channel their efforts in the desired direction. During meetings that occur before, during, and at the end of the appraisal period, supervisors inform employees about the relative emphasis management puts on each aspect of job performance and possible strategies for addressing management's expectations.

4. *Providing employees with periodic feedback regarding how well they are meeting performance standards.* The purpose of the appraisal is to provide employees with the necessary in-

put for updating, refining, or developing realistic compensation, career, and employment aspirations.

5. *Developing the necessary documentation for career and work-force planning.* The information collected as part of the appraisal is used by human resource management (HRM) departments and supervisors for making decisions about training (or retraining), compensation, promotion and transfer, or separation. The information may be used to make decisions about a single employee, a group of employees, or the whole organization. Personnel departments can use this information to improve the recruitment, selection, orientation, and placement of new employees.

6. *Generating data the organization may need for dealing with outside agencies and organizations, such as unions, courts, and labor/employment security agencies.* Some of the data may be collected to comply with legal or contractual requirements.

7. *Collecting data for purely internal purposes.* These might include assessing the need to redesign job classifications, job descriptions, organizational structure, work practices, standard operating procedures, and validity of selection processes, including test instruments.

8. *Complying with legal requirements or the conditions set for insurance, licensing, or accreditation.* Here performance appraisal is a means for achieving other goals that have to do with the general conditions within the organization and how the organization relates to the external environment.

9. *Asserting authority, establishing self-confidence, and meeting supervisors' needs for power, control, and status.* Here performance appraisal is a weapon empowering supervisors by communicating to subordinates that there are consequences when instructions are not followed.

II. GENERAL PROBLEMS WITH PERFORMANCE APPRAISAL

It is unlikely that any managerial problem has attracted more attention or so successfully resisted a solution than arriving at an acceptable, useful, and valid method of appraising performance (Henderson, 1980). Daley (1983), for example, notes that the problems with performance appraisal are twofold. First, the actual choice of an appraisal instrument often poses a trade-off between effectiveness (validity) and efficiency (reliability). The validity of appraisal techniques, according to Daley, roughly ascends as one goes from the essay approach to forced distribution, ranking, weighted checklists, force-choice checklists, graphic rating scales, critical incidents, and appraisal by objectives (Daley, 1983). At the same time, the complexity and cost of administering the appraisal goes up as well. Second, managers often attempt to gloss over these problems with a claim that despite these faults, such systems are better than nothing. By taking action administrators "did not contribute to building public employee confidence either in performance appraisal itself or in managerial abilities" (Daley, 1983). At the end, the use of questionable performance appraisal systems undermines the merit concept.

Several writers (Freidman, 1986; Marcoulides and Mills, 1988; Daley, 1991) trace the source of the problematic nature of performance appraisal to the appraisal instrument and the abilities of those using it. On the one hand, employees may be puzzled about what parts of their performance really count, or count more than others. Less educated, less skilled, and lower level employees tend to concentrate on a few aspects of the job they deem to be important for evaluation. Thus, they may emphasize activities and achievements that can be easily documented rather than those that may contribute to the overall better performance of the unit or the organization. Supervisors, too, may concentrate on the most measurable aspects of the performance and ignore other dimensions of the work for which comparative or objective standards are difficult to establish (Freidman, 1986).

Marcoulides and Mills (1988) suggest that the problem with the appraisal instruments is that they "are constructed in a manner that makes it difficult to measure actual job performance." The problems with the process used for administering them are due to various rater errors such as "halo error" (i.e., the tendency to give an employee high marks on all aspects because he or she is special in one respect), the central tendency error (i.e., the tendency to rate all employees as average), or the error of first impressions. Daley (1991) notes along the same lines that public employees have shown little confidence in specific performance appraisal systems (often graphic rating scales) or in the managerial abilities of those responsible for their implementation.

Another source of problems with performance appraisal is the illusive nature of the fit between the appraisal approach or the instrument in use, the abilities of the rater who uses it, and the purpose for which the appraisal is done. As pointed out earlier, performance appraisals are carried out for a variety of reasons. Consequently, the data from the appraisal review is in demand by many consumers within and outside the organization (Halachmi, 1992). As all the consumers attempt to influence the process and the rating instrument to make the results of the appraisal readily available for their divergent uses, the integrity of the process may be compromised. Yet, as Ammons and Condrey (1991) note, "Rarely do disgruntled employees, disillusioned taxpayers, or other critics of a given performance appraisal system bother to examine the conceptual viability of the approach taken in a particular instance, the consistency of the system design and implementation, or the presence or absence of the supporting conditions—including commitment and resources—necessary for successful performance appraisal." When the fit between the instrument or the approach, the rater, and the purpose for which the appraisal is done is poor, one of the problems likely to arise will concern merit pay.

The concepts of pay for performance and merit rating cannot be separated (Halachmi and Holzer, 1986). The pressure to introduce merit pay to the public sector is the synergistic result of several forces, e.g., the ever growing concerns of the public about the mounting cost of government; popular reaction to what seems to be capricious, arbitrary, and unresponsive bureaucracy; the simple and tangible nature of the concept; and the assumption that it is used successfully in the private sector. In reality, the concept of merit pay is anything but simple and straightforward, and it cannot be implemented successfully for appraising all job classifications because of inherent problems (Halachmi and Holzer, 1986; Perry, 1986; McNish, 1986; Pay for Performance Labor Management Committee, 1991). The U.S. General Accounting Office reported two findings that illustrate this point: first, "most employees supported the concept of pay for performance but were dissatisfied with its implementation," and, second, "they [employees] had few suggestions for improving the system" (*Pay for Performance*, 1990).

Karr (1992) notes that although 98% of the surveyed personnel managers of 270 large companies say employee pay should reflect performance, only 48% say their systems achieved that goal. One way the private sector deals with the discrepancy between compensation and performance is by replacing salary increases with rewards based on long-term financial or market performance. According to Karr, data from 2006 employers show 61% with a result-sharing program, up from 51% in 1991 (Karr, 1992). The relationship between pay and performance in the public sector may not be different from the one experienced in the private sector. However, dealing with a possible discrepancy between compensation and performance in the public sector is not as easy as in the private sector for at least three important reasons.

First, the two sectors use different mechanisms for determining compensation. In the private sector allocations for compensation can be made in advance or following the period for which the employee may get a bonus. Corporations commonly reward their highly valued employees following a good earnings report. In the public sector managers cannot look at the bottom line to determine how much of a profit might be shared with employees. Public funds allocated for salaries, or any other expenditure like a merit award, must be part of the approved budget. Even if the money for merit pay is budgeted, problems can still arise. A supervisor's decision not to use resources that were appropriated for compensation is likely to generate two sets of problems. One set of problems with the supervisor's own superiors, budget officer, auditors, and legislators may evolve when the unspent monies for compensation are returned or transferred for other uses. The supervisor may suffer the consequences of violating the norm requiring budgets to be spent as planned. Another set of problems may evolve as a result of the reactions of subordinates and their unions to the decision to forego salary raises or merit rewards. Employees develop all kinds of expectations when they know that there is a budget for performance awards. The frustration that may result from the lost opportunity may undermine the position and the supervisor's own career as a result of spoiled labor relations, loss of trust and leadership stature, or low morale and sagging productivity. Interestingly, the same seems to be true for the private sector as well. According to Bennet (1991), most [corporate] managers are unwilling to make distinctions among their employees and few companies force them to do so. Most pay scales in most organizations still move in lockstep: seniority and higher ranking jobs—not performance—confer higher pay.

Most supervisors are aware of these two sets of problems. Thus, they are not likely to withhold allocated resources even when employee performance does not justify the compensation, let alone a merit award (*Pay for Performance*, 1987). A syndicated column by Jack Anderson illustrates this point. According to Anderson (1983), "Five senior Energy Department officials have been identified by congressional investigators as responsible for serious lack of security at a government owned nuclear plant. Their fate: They have been given achievement medals and generous bonuses." This report is consistent with testimony before congress that performance has not been perceived as a major factor in determining who received performance awards and that awards have been viewed as inequitable (Ungar, 1989). In 1991 Constance Newman, the Director of the U.S. Office of Personnel Management, appointed a committee to review the Federal Performance Management and Recognition System (PMRS). Reporting back to the Director, "the Committee supported the concept of pay for performance for Federal managers [but] agreed that the current PMRS is neither fair nor effective" (*Advancing Managerial Excellence*, 1991).

Sometimes actions by the legislature or collective bargaining agreements may establish mandatory levels of compensation that leave supervisors with little authority over those levels. Under such circumstances the salary of subordinates may exceed that of their supervisors (McNish, 1986). At other times, budgetary allocations do not allow supervisors to match compensation with accomplishment (Allan and Rosenberg, 1986; McNish, 1986).

A second distinction between private and public merit systems is that public administrators, unlike their corporate counterparts, cannot reward or be rewarded by stock options whose value is tied to performance. Public employees are expected to do what is best for their clients and to enhance the public interest rather than the interest of the agency or its employees. For example, in the private sector employees can be rewarded for actions that prolong dependency and maintain a solid base of captive service recipients. In theory, public employees should be rewarded in many cases only for achieving the opposite result and elimination of the need for their services.

Third, in the private sector it is possible to think about a team effort with shared responsibilities. When the team does well, everybody can share the profit. When performance leaves a company behind its competitors, members of the team may lose their jobs or parts of their compensation. In the public sector, in many cases, competition is not an issue. It is hard to judge and compare the performance of government agencies. Bureaucrats are not supposed to benefit from the results of their own deeds even if those were successful. The rewards to employees in the public sector are often limited to changes in the level of appropriation (which may go up or down without regard to outstanding performance) or to career advancement (through promotion, transfer, or broadening of authority). The responsibility for mistakes belongs to individual office holders and is not shared by a group as a collective. Public administrators are accountable only for the decisions they make and the decisions made by their subordinates. Legally, they do not share the blame for decisions by peers or superiors, though they may suffer the consequences of mistakes in other parts of their agency.

III. PROBLEMS FACING MANAGERS ADMINISTERING PERFORMANCE APPRAISAL

Managers experience difficulty in the administration of performance appraisal for several reasons. First, a manager's role as evaluator is inconsistent with the role of supervisor. For example, the supervisor is expected to be nurturing and supportive rather than critical. However, the employee who is more impressed by criticism than by encouragement is less likely to trust and confide in the supervisor. According to Blau (1956), law enforcement agents were reluctant to reveal to their superiors their inability to solve a problem for fear that their ratings would be adversely affected. Thus, the evaluative part of the supervisory role interfered with the other parts necessary to good overall supervision.

A second administrative problem develops when supervisors find themselves evaluating subordinates who are colleagues, peers, or superiors in outside social, political, or professional organizations. If nothing else, supervisors may give such subordinates a better-than-deserved rating to avoid a confrontation or a decline in performance (Allan and Rosenberg, 1986).

Third, like other adults, managers may be reluctant to take a judgmental role. In the past, the use of social psychology was enough to explain such reluctance (Heisler et al., 1988). However, the proliferation of legal challenges of performance appraisals (Kleiman and Durham, 1981; Burchett and De Meuse, 1985) and the prospect of having to defend one's judgment in court provide an even more potent explanation. In order to prepare for the contingency of a lawsuit, supervisors must be trained to be sensitive to all that can go wrong during the evaluation. The paradox arises as supervisors become aware of all the possible problems and more apprehensive about passing judgment. Consequently, they may be reluctant to differentiate among employees (e.g., by giving all of them good or average ratings) and invite a challenge on the grounds that the appraisal does not differentiate among employees by level of performance. The reluctance of supervisors to articulate for subordinates the shortcomings of their performance (Foxman and Polsky, 1988) for social, psychological, or legal reasons creates an additional complication. According to Derven (1990), if a performance issue has continued for a substantial length of time, an implicit contract may have been formed, leading the employee to conclude that the behavior is acceptable. Thus, the rater's behavior may create a major behavioral and legal barrier to the improvement of performance.

IV. PERFORMANCE APPRAISAL APPROACHES

A. The Narrative Approach

The common denominator for the different appraisal techniques that comprise the narrative approach is the "story"—the detailed description that is used as the main input or the main output of the performance appraisal. In most cases the narrative is compiled by the supervisor and is considered to be a key component of that position. The narrative is expected to be detailed and may produce an appraisal that is as accurate as more formal methods of evaluation (Baird et al., 1985). Though narrative appraisals may be used as a stand-alone instrument for evaluating employees, they can be even more beneficial when used to supplement other instruments. The most common appraisal techniques to involve the narrative approach are critical incident, field review, and essay appraisal. The critical incident technique is discussed in the following section.

1. The Critical Incident

The critical incident method involves the recording of the highlights and the lowlights of employee performance. This approach acknowledges the fact that supervisors tend to base their assessment on an employee's most memorable achievement or mistake. Being aware of this reality, proponents of this technique strive to help the supervisor to be more systematic and even-handed. By keeping an ongoing log of special events, achievements, and mistakes, the supervisor can evaluate the employee on the basis of the whole record. The appraisal is therefore less likely to depend on the supervisor's recollections and ability to differentiate between events that took place before the last appraisal and those that took place since. Also, by reviewing a written record the evaluator is less likely to give more weight to recent events than earlier ones. Raters are expected to maintain a log on each employee. A record is created whenever the supervisor observes exceptional performances, such as carrying out responsibilities, getting along with other employees or clients, being prudent with the use of resources, and showing creativity, initiative, or organizational loyalty, etc. (Baker, 1988).

A supervisor may be trained and instructed to pay more attention to incidents of exceptional performance in some areas at certain times and in other areas at other times. For example, during one evaluation period an organization may decide to reduce the waste of office supplies in order to reduce expenses. During a second evaluation period the organization may decide to pay more attention to reducing clients' complaints. Requesting all supervisors to pay closer attention to incidents involving questionable use of supplies during the first period or to client satisfaction during the second period can have a dramatic effect on organizational performance across the board. Thus, this technique allows supervisors to be very responsive to changing circumstances and management priorities. Individual evaluations can be aligned with the overall performance targets of the organization by appraising subordinates' performance in those areas that management deems to be more critical to organizational success for a given period of time. Thus, the critical incident approach is less likely to produce an evaluation that seems irrelevant from management's point of view, e.g., when the individual employee scores high but the organization does poorly. It should be noted here that in order to generate maximum progress in a given area three conditions must be satisfied:

1. All subordinates and supervisors should be informed about management's priorities for a future evaluation period. At this time employees also should be informed about the relative importance and what to do about those issues that are going to become less significant, for evaluation purposes, even though those issues are still critical for organizational performance. By failing to address this last issue, an organization may forego the fruits of past efforts to improve productivity, when stress was placed on the very issues now deemed insignificant. For example, in the transition from an emphasis on conservation of supplies to an emphasis on client satisfaction, employees may give up any attempt to address the old priority in order to score well on their efforts to achieve the new priority. Consequently, an organization may lose some of the gains from the first period.
2. Proper training should be provided to all employees in advance. As a result of the training employees should know what constitutes desired and undesired performance, how each kind of performance may manifest itself, how it is to be observed, and how it is to be recorded.

3. All units should work out the specific implications of given evaluation priorities for their areas of responsibility before the beginning of the evaluation period. The aim is for all the subunits to start and pursue the same management priorities at the same time.

Figure 1 is an illustration of the kind of simple forms organizations may provide supervisors for recording incidents. A copy of each record should be shared and discussed with the employee either immediately or after accumulation of no more than three to five records. By discussing the report, the supervisor is supposed to encourage an employee's desired performance in the future. When supervisors have immediate access to computers, such forms may be completed and stored without much difficulty. However, many supervisors prefer to be more meticulous in creating written records of negative incidents than positive ones, not only to protect themselves should an employee decide to challenge a low evaluation but to avoid the need to deal orally with an employee about a negative evaluation.

In addition to management priorities for a given evaluation period, a supervisor may be asked to monitor closely certain kinds of behaviors in order to help make broader personnel decisions touching on promotion, transfer, training, or separation. Marking on the critical incident form key words such as *leadership, creativity*, and *punctuality*, and utilizing simple Likert scales that allow

```
EMPLOYEE NAME                           DATE_____

TIME AND PLACE OF OBSERVATION:

REPORTING SUPERVISOR:

WHAT DID YOU SEE?


WHAT WAS PARTICULARLY GREAT/BAD ABOUT IT?



HAVE YOU SEEN IT BEFORE?


WAS THE EMPLOYEE INFORMED ABOUT THE PREVIOUS OBSERVATION?

WHEN ARE YOU PLANNING TO SHARE THIS OBSERVATION WITH THE EMPLOYEE?

IF THERE IS A NEED FOR FOLLOWUP, INDICATE WHO ELSE WILL BE
INVOLVED?


ACTION(S) NEEDED:   ___AWARD, ___DISCIPLINE, ___TRAINING,

                    ___SECURITY, ___REVIEW, ___JOB DESCRIPTION,

                    ___PLACEMENT, ____OTHER:_____


NOTES:
```

Figure 1 Supervisor's report of an observation form.

the supervisor to rate the performance on a continuum from high to low, may facilitate easy tabulation at the end of the evaluation period. Recording incidents as part of an electronic database can also simplify the dissemination and retrieval of information about individual employees or about employees with specific attributes. Such a database can facilitate better human resources planning and utilization.

To secondary users of information about the performance of an individual employee, the access to records containing the details of what took place is very important. Common evaluation forms are short. They leave out the raw data used to compile them. Thus the user must depend on the integrity and ability of the supervisor to complete them truthfully. Being able to use the original records relieves secondary users from the need to rely on the recollection and the interpretations of events by the supervisor. As long as the details are accurate, secondary users of the data can form their own opinions about the performance of the individual.

When observing a certain behavior, the supervisor may form an opinion about the employee. Having an opportunity to reexamine an observation against the record of subsequent incidents, the supervisor may reach a different conclusion about the overall performance of a given employee. When the record is examined in perspective, along with other relevant entries, an overwhelming impression may be found to be related to an isolated incident that was an exception rather than the norm. Incidents that seem out of character may alert a supervisor (or any other user of the data) to possible flaws in the method of observation. They may suggest, for example, that a supervisor has indicated an outstanding (or poor) performance because of failures to observe the beginning or the end of a given episode and, thus, that the record is incomplete or unreliable. As a matter of fact, this possibility is one of the main weaknesses of the critical incident technique. It may be that for reasons that have to do with the personality, training, or abilities of the supervisor, or for reasons that have to do with the nature of the employee's job, a complete and accurate record cannot be compiled.

The quality of the record is dependent on the critical skills of the supervisor making the observations and his or her ability to create a detailed record. Critical skills of supervisors are important in all appraisal techniques. However, some employees seem to feel that the variability of a supervisor's critical skills make the critical incident technique more prone to subjective judgment and bias because it requires the supervisor to write a descriptive narrative in detail rather than to simply check a form. Accordingly, events that are less important but more suitable to simple description are more likely to be recorded. A related weakness of the technique is that it is time consuming. To save time supervisors are more likely to record mistakes than a good performance because the employee is expected to do a good job. Thus, from the employees' point of view, the deck is stacked against them because it contains a complete record of what they do wrong but an incomplete record of what they do right. Also, because creation of the record is time consuming, supervisors are likely to log more observations at the beginning and toward the end of the appraisal period. During these time spans, employees' behavior may not be typical because of their reaction to the appraisal they just got or by their anticipation of the one they expect or wish to get. The more typical behavior may be more likely to happen during the middle of the appraisal period, which will be less well documented than the behavior or events at either end of that period.

Another weakness of this approach is the incentive it gives employees to avoid responsibility and to hide mistakes (Henderson, 1984). At the same time, the critical incident approach encourages employees to engage in those activities that are likely to catch the eye of the supervisor and to earn them good points. The emphasis on such activities may come at the expense of doing more important things that cannot be observed by the supervisor for the record. In other words, the critical incident approach may encourage showmanship at the expense of substance.

B. Rating With Graphic Scales and Forms

Graphic scales and a variety of forms are designed by organizations to help supervisors and to facilitate a unified approach to performance appraisal for all employees in a given job classification. The various methods in this group share the premise that a meaningful evaluation of the employee can be achieved only in the context of what other employees, in the same job or in the same unit, are doing or are expected to do. Though the different approaches in this group may have a great potential, Daley (1991) has ample documentation to suggest that public employees have shown little confidence in performance appraisal systems (often graphic rating scales) or in the managerial abilities to implement them.

1. Behaviorally Anchored Rating Scales

Behaviorally anchored rating scales (BARS) provide the evaluator with a visual aid for relating specific descriptions of common behaviors to the various grades of performance as illustrated in Fig. 2. BARS are sometimes called *behavioral expectation scales* (BES) or *behavioral observation scales* (BOS) (Bernardin et al., 1976) to denote a slightly different approach for developing

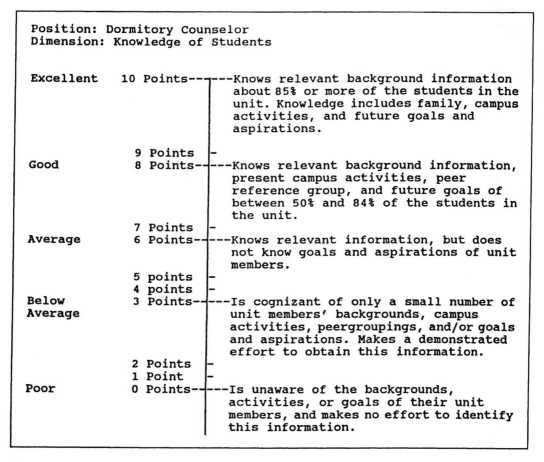

Figure 2 Behaviorally anchored ratings scales (BARS).

the scale. However, in all cases, the idea is to combine the descriptive benefits of the narrative approach to performance appraisal with a corresponding, predetermined, quantitative rating of anybody holding a given job. Typically, the scale is built around specific examples of desired/good or undesired/bad performance as illustrated in Fig. 2.

BARS were introduced in the early 1960s (Smith and Kindall, 1963) as a tool that is capable of a more equitable appraisal than previously available tools (Dessler, 1991). BARS are claimed to be superior to other approaches to the evaluation of employee performance because they change the role of the supervisor. Using BARS, the supervisor matches an observed behavior with a behavior statement on the scale rather than judging the merit of the behavior as desired or undesired. It was also argued that since effectiveness involves additional factors that are beyond the control of the individual, behaviorally based rating scales are more appropriate for assessing individual performance.

BARS are developed through a sequence of steps and require direct participation of both supervisors and subordinates who are thoroughly familiar with the job to be evaluated. First, one group of individuals familiar with the job is asked to describe typical behaviors employees exhibit while carrying out the job.

Second, these critical incidents are clustered together. Each cluster represents a significant dimension of the job. For example, all the descriptions of good, average, or poor performance concerning interactions with other employees are grouped together; those dealing with exercise of judgment form another category; and so on. Figure 2 illustrates the behavioral descriptions for the "planning and scheduling of projects" aspect of a given job. At the end of this step there are specific descriptions for each aspect of the job.

Third, several groups (e.g., subordinates, supervisors, former employees, clients, consultants) are asked to rate each of the behavioral descriptions on a seven- or a nine-point scale as effective (desired), average, or ineffective (undesired) performance.

Fourth, a subset of the behavioral description is selected to serve as an anchor. On the scale, each of these descriptions is a reference point. The supervisor has only to decide whether the individual's behavior matches the description, is slightly above it, or is slightly below it in order to generate a quantitative score as illustrated in Fig. 2.

Generating BARSs takes time. An organization may get hold of BARS that were developed elsewhere and speed up the process, but the need to involve supervisors and employees that are going to use the appraisal instrument cannot be avoided. The decision to introduce BARS is a commitment that requires the organization to move resources from other activities (Halachmi, 1992) and gamble that the possible future benefits may be larger than the immediate cost. Another important drawback is that, like many other methods of performance appraisal, BARS are likely to entice an employee to do what scores high on the evaluation instrument rather than what is right for the organization (Halachmi and Holzer, 1987). That is because the needs of the organization may change a long time before a revision of the assessment instrument takes place. The old BARS may allow employees to score high for behavior that has become dysfunctional due to changes in information technology, the law, or any other aspect of the environment. However, BARS have unique advantages that make them very attractive to many managers.

The process the organization must use for developing BARS increases the likelihood that the evaluation is meaningful. Since people who are familiar with different aspects of the job have an opportunity to contribute behavioral descriptors, an employee is not likely to be assessed on the basis of behavior that is inconsequential to the job. In other words, BARS may reduce the risk of a biased appraisal due to the halo effect by forcing the evaluator to refer to specific behaviors for each aspect of the job. Thus a behavior that renders a high score in one respect may not help the employee to earn a corresponding grade on a behavioral description that has to do with a different dimension of the job. Statistical results showed considerably less distortion, bias, and variance when BARS, are used for appraising an employee's performance (Shafritz et al., 1992). In addition, by involving subordinates, supervisors, and clients in determining whether a given behavior is exemplary, slightly less than exemplary, average, below average, poor, or undesired, the subjective nature of the assessment may be significantly reduced. Thus, BARS can help an organization achieve equity and fairness by assuring that the merit of a given performance is always assessed the same way and is not dependent on which of the supervisors is in charge. Finally, BARS can help the organization communicate to employees in advance what is considered to be an outstanding as opposed to an average performance. BARS may also facilitate the process of giving employees feedback and a better idea about what is expected of them. Such communication can be particularly potent when elements of the BARS, i.e., the desired behavior for each critical aspect of the job, are written into the job description (Shafritz et al., 1992). This in turn may help employees target their behavior to meet set standards instead of feeling that they are chasing an illusive goal.

Are BARS suitable for evaluating every employee in the organization? Schneier and Beatty (1979) claim that an organization stands to lose important information if only one type of performance appraisal approach is used to evaluate all employees. They recommend the use of BARS for assessing top management because "top executives may be better evaluated on behaviors which they, as individuals, control and demonstrate in the pursuit of measurable unit or group objectives" (Schneier and Beatty, 1979). In other words, effort to create the necessary conditions for attaining certain results can be a basis for appraising an individual employee. Such an allowance is important when it is not obvious that the individual worker deserves credit for desired results or when certain results are the outcome of a cumulative action by many individuals or of time.

2. Mixed Standard Scales

This approach is halfway between the BARS and the form-based rating approach. The mixed standard scale (MSS) was introduced in 1972 by Blanz and Ghiselli (Baird et al., 1985). It involves the use of three behavior statements for ascertaining how the individual performs with respect to different performance criteria. The statements are compiled following interviews with former job holders and experts as well as reviews of job descriptions. The three statements represent a scale from good to poor performance. The evaluator records on a form, as illustrated in Fig. 3, whether the employee performs above, at, or below the behavioral descriptor by marking (+), (0), or (-), respectively. The rating is calculated by adding the value of the rating for the group of three descriptors that represent each of the predetermined performance criteria.

On the rating form the statements are mixed and the supervisor cannot easily tell whether rating the employee above, below, or at the level indicated by the statement will lead to a higher or lower overall score. For example, a supervisor cannot tell without knowing the corresponding performance criterion whether "showing considerable initiative" is desired or not; it may be either one, depending on the criterion in use.

As an approach, MSS attempts to separate the task of determining the level of performance from the task of evaluating its merit. Proponents of this approach assert that by disguising the nature of the performance dimensions and the levels of performance it is possible to reduce rating errors due to the halo effect and leniency (Landy and Farr, 1983). Another advantage of the MSS approach is the ability to verify the observations of a given supervisor against the observations of fellow employees or even the employee's self-rating. Inconsistent marking for the three behavioral descriptors can alert management to a possible problem with the supervisor.

	Rating
1. Has normal self-confidence, with only occasional uncertainty. He usually is opened and assured. *(A)*	0
2. There is some lack of efficiency on his part. He may take too much time to complete his assignments and sometimes he does not really finish them. *(P)*	+
3. Both his written and oral reports are well-formulated, thorough and well thought out. They rarely need additional explanation. *(G)*	+
4. He is a little shy and uncertain. Occasionally avoids situations which require him to take a position. *(P)*	+
5. He is efficient enough, usually getting through his assignments and completes work in a reasonable time. *(A)*	+
6. Sometimes his reports are so incomplete and poorly organized that they are of little value, or must be done over. *(P)*	+
7. He is quick and efficient, able to keep his work on schedule. He really gets going on a new task. *(G)*	0
8. Behaves confidently. Reacts in all situations without hesitation and assurance. *(G)*	-
9. His reports are useful and meaningful, but they usually require some additional explanations. *(A)*	+

Figure 3 Mixed Standard rating scale. Items 2, 5, 7 represent the dimension of efficiency, items 1, 4, 8, self-confidence, and items 3, 6, 9 report making. "G," "A," and "P" stand for good, average, and poor performance.

The weakness of the approach has to do first of all with the negative reaction of supervisors. Not knowing whether they are rewarding or punishing an employee by marking a descriptor in one of the three ways, supervisors sense a loss of control over the final result. Also, because they do not know which of the behavioral descriptors corresponds to which dimension of performance, they experience a difficulty in providing employees with feedback to improve performance. Last but not least, as with the use of BARS, developing the rating scales, i.e., selection of valid behavioral statements, is time consuming and expensive. The need to assure relevancy of the rating instrument may require the organization to pay again and again for validating and reconstructing it periodically. To some managers, the relative difficulty of responding to possible legal challenges can make MSS less than attractive.

3. Graphic or a Form-Based Rating

As indicated by its name, this popular approach is based on a simple standard form. The form, as illustrated in Fig. 4, lists those job aspects on which employees are to be evaluated.

A supervisor uses the same basic form for each employee. For each item on the form the evaluator marks a five- to seven-point scale. Each point on the scale denotes a level of performance on a range from unacceptable to exceptional. A seven-point scale breaks this range into

SYSTEM 2B PATIENT/RESIDENT CARE EVALUATION FORM

Employee SSN ☐☐☐ – ☐☐ – ☐☐☐☐

Employee Name _____

Employee Pos. Number_____

Class _____ Work Center _____

Date Evaluation Due_____

Evaluation Type: System 2B

Purpose_____ ☐ Other (Do Not Use Label)

DEPARTMENT OF PERSONNEL
STATE OF TENNESSEE
JOB PERFORMANCE
PLANNING AND EVALUATION

TO THE SUPERVISOR: READ THE INSTRUCTIONS ON PAGE TWO
BEFORE USING THIS FORM.

SUPERVISOR'S SSN ☐☐☐ – ☐☐ – ☐☐☐☐

REVIEWER'S SSN ☐☐☐ – ☐☐ – ☐☐☐☐

System 2B ☐ Flex ☐ Probation ☐ Annual

JOB PERFORMANCE PLANNING DISCUSSION

Employee's Signature   Supervisor's Signature
                    MO   DAY   YR
          DATE ☐☐☐☐☐

FIRST INTERIM REVIEW	SECOND INTERIM REVIEW
Employee's Signature	Employee's Signature
Supervisor's Signature	Supervisor's Signature
MO DAY YR	MO DAY YR
DATE ☐☐☐☐☐	DATE ☐☐☐☐☐

TO THE EMPLOYEE BEING EVALUATED: Mark whether you Agree, Partially Agree, or Disagree with each rating.

TO THE SUPERVISOR: Carefully read the instructions on page two of this booklet before evaluating the employee's performance.

Exceptional
Superior
Good
Marginal
Not Acceptable
Not Applicable

AGREE / PARTIALLY AGREE / DISAGREE

JOB PERFORMANCE RESPONSIBILITIES

1. Following work instructions .... 1. ☐ 1 2 3 4 5 1 2 3
2. Adhering to work requirements and regulations .... 2. ☐ 1 2 3 4 5 1 2 3
3. Cooperating with co-workers .... 3. ☐ 1 2 3 4 5 1 2 3
4. Working without close supervision .... 4. ☐ 1 2 3 4 5 1 2 3
5. Using and maintaining tools, equipment, and supplies .... 5. ☐ 1 2 3 4 5 1 2 3
6. Providing therapeutic behavioral management/day-to-day interactions .... 6. ☐ 1 2 3 4 5 1 2 3
7. Providing health care/Assisting nurses ..... 7. ☐ 1 2 3 4 5 1 2 3
8. Providing direct care services .... 8. ☐ 1 2 3 4 5 1 2 3
9. Keeping records; charting and reporting .... 9. ☐ 1 2 3 4 5 1 2 3
10. Observing safety procedures and security measures .... 10. ☐ 1 2 3 4 5 1 2 3
11. Responding to difficult or emergency situations .... 11. ☐ 1 2 3 4 5 1 2 3
12. Cooperating in special assignments .... 12. ☐ 1 2 3 4 5 1 2 3
13. Providing training .... 13. ☐ 1 2 3 4 5 1 2 3
14. Checking on patients/residents .... 14. ☐ 1 2 3 4 5 1 2 3
15. Attending staffings and case conferences .... 15. ☐ 1 2 3 4 5 1 2 3
16. Maintaining cleanliness and neatness in work areas; doing laundry services .... 16. ☐ 1 2 3 4 5 1 2 3
17. Directing and assisting visitors .... 17. ☐ 1 2 3 4 5 1 2 3
18. .... 18. ☐ 1 2 3 4 5 1 2 3
19. .... 19. ☐ 1 2 3 4 5 1 2 3
20. .... 20. ☐ 1 2 3 4 5 1 2 3
21. .... 21. ☐ 1 2 3 4 5 1 2 3
22. .... 22. ☐ 1 2 3 4 5 1 2 3
23. .... 23. ☐ 1 2 3 4 5 1 2 3

OVERALL EVALUATION & RECOMMENDATION
(REVIEW THE APPROPRIATE DESCRIPTION
ON PAGE 12 OF THIS BOOKLET)

NOT ACCEPTABLE MARGINAL GOOD SUPERIOR EXCEPTIONAL
     ☐1   ☐2   ☐3   ☐4   ☐5

EMPLOYEE
1 AGREES
2 PARTIALLY AGREES
3 DISAGREES

DATE OF EVALUATION
MO DAY YR
☐☐☐☐☐☐

Employee's Signature   Date   Reviewer's Signature   Date

Supervisor's Signature   Date   Appointing Authority's Signature   Date

PR-0161
(Rev. 4-/)

1

Figure 4 Form-based evaluation.

smaller segments and allows the evaluator to better differentiate among employees. However, this accuracy may not come without a cost. First, the need to be more specific with respect to each aspect of the job, while serving the needs of the organization as a whole, may complicate the administration of the assessment instrument for the supervisor. After all, it is easier (e.g., less time consuming) to classify individuals into a few broad categories than into many specific ones. Second, differentiating among individuals with respect to specific aspects of their jobs increases the likelihood that an employee will question the fairness of the evaluation. According to the teachings of the equity approach to motivation (Adams and Rosenbaum, 1962), negative perceptions of the appraisal process may be a disincentive to individual productivity (Halachmi and Holzer, 1987).

One advantage of this approach, provided that supervisors use a simple evaluation form, is the ease with which the appraisal can be carried out. Using a simple form across the board allows for easy training of supervisors in the consistent use of the technique. A second advantage is that using the same simple form all over the organization may facilitate communication between management and employees and help employees get feedback from supervisors. A third advantage is that it provides staff units, and particularly those involved in human resource planning and training, with an easy way of periodically updating their database.

On the down side, the use of simple forms across the board may do injustice to employees in positions that are more demanding in certain aspects. For example, given the nature of the work in a public relations unit, rating an employee in public relations as average on creativity may make it difficult to recognize that the individual in question is more creative than another employee in accounting who is rated as exceptional on this item. Though creativity may mean the same in both cases, the expectations are different in each case, and thus different levels of effort and achievement may be required in order to score the same. Some organizations attempt to overcome this problem by assigning a relative weight to all items to indicate the importance of each item on the form for successful performance of different assignments. For example, the evaluation form for academic personnel in one university listed teaching, research, administration, and public service as the basic items for evaluating each faculty member. However, depending on specific assignments for each faculty member, the evaluator assigned different weights to the score for each of the four items. The weights reflected the relative amount of time or the relative importance of a given component for the overall evaluation. Thus, for those doing mainly research, for instance, the score on this item contributed more to the total score than any of the scores on the other items.

Another disadvantage of the form-based approach develops from the different ways the broad, nonspecific categories can be viewed by supervisors and employees. As illustrated by Fig. 4, the Tennessee Department of Personnel allows employees to record their level of agreement with the score assigned to each item by their supervisor. Other instruments request supervisors to cite specific examples in support of the rating on each element of the evaluation and allow subordinates to add to the evaluation instruments comments or documentation that challenge specific ratings. Consistent indication of a disagreement between a supervisor and a subordinate about the rating signifies a possible problem with the administration of the instrument.

4. Simple and Weighted Checklists

Simple checklists are very similar to rating scales. The supervisor is given a list of behavioral statements for each dimension of the job performance that is subject to the evaluation. Typically the rater reviews a list of about 50 items like those illustrated in Fig. 5. Each item describes a specific job behavior and performance characteristic that can be noted in the job analysis. The supervisor generates the evaluation by checking each item that seems to apply to the employee under review.

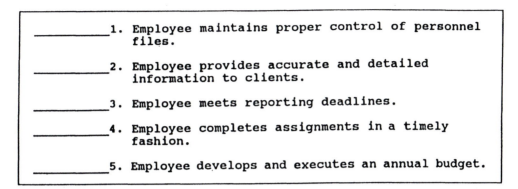

_____1. Employee maintains proper control of personnel files.

_____2. Employee provides accurate and detailed information to clients.

_____3. Employee meets reporting deadlines.

_____4. Employee completes assignments in a timely fashion.

_____5. Employee develops and executes an annual budget.

Figure 5 Five items from a simple checklist.

This method is very attractive because it is easily understood by raters and ratees. Both can see the connection between the rating process and the job description. Usually, use of this method does not involve any risk of misunderstanding. As a matter of fact, its simplicity may open clogged communication channels. By reviewing what supervisors check, subordinates get an opportunity to point out that a given aspect of their job performance was overlooked. This in turn may lead to a revision of the evaluation and to a more accurate and equitable documentation of employees' performance. The evaluation instrument allows comparisons and thus can be used as input for several personnel decisions such as compensation, incentives, training, promotion, transfer, or separation.

Simplicity is not only the strength of the weighted checklist; it is also the weakness. First of all it does not allow a fine differentiation among employees. A check mark can convey that the descriptor is applicable to a given employee. However, it does not say whether it is more or less applicable in comparison to another employee for which the same item was checked. In other words, the checked descriptor allows personnel departments to differentiate among the groups of employees for whom the descriptor is applicable but not among members of each group. Another disadvantage is that in order to keep it simple many aspects of the job and many responsibilities may be kept off the list. Consequently, employees may feel that the evaluation does not consider all that they actually do. Finally, the various items on the list carry the same weight, making the most menial of tasks equal in importance to the most portentous one (Henderson, 1984).

The weighted checklist attempts to remedy this last weakness by assigning a weight factor to each aspect of job performance. Thus, the various descriptors are not of the same importance. By assigning a value, a supervisor can also communicate to the employee what he or she deems to be of greater importance. Allowing supervisors and employees to influence and contribute to the development of the appraisal instrument is important (Baker, 1988), but it does not come without a cost.

The checklist methods become susceptible to the weaknesses that result from subjective judgment (e.g., halo effect, central tendency, or leniency–strictness bias) as the role of the supervisor evolves from recognizing performance to evaluating the relative importance of its various aspects. Thus, the attempt to cure one problem (i.e., assign a coefficient of importance to each descriptor) may lead to the creation of other problems and negate the usefulness of the appraisal. In order to retain the benefit of the weighted checklist without generating other rater-related problems, organizations must use outside experts to assign the various weights. From time to time such experts may be requested to review the relevancy of the evaluation instrument because changes in information technology or any other condition inside or outside the organization may require a corresponding modification of the assigned weights. In other words, the cost of developing the weighted checklist may be only the first installment. Subsequent reviews will lead to additional expenses and a dependency that would not be attractive to most administrators.

5. Force Choice Checklist

Efforts to combat leniency errors resulted in the development of the forced choice checklist during World War II. Here too the evaluation instrument involves the use of behavioral statements that are gathered into groups of two or five (Henderson, 1984). The checklist may include between 20 and 50 different groups. For each item, as illustrated in Fig. 6, the rater marks one of the boxes.

The design of the instrument is such that each descriptor appears to be equally desirable or undesirable. The items are selected based on their usefulness in differentiating between more and less successful performers. The rater determines which descriptor from a given group is the most and/or the least accurate portrayal of the job holder's behavior. However, the rater has no access to the background information that correlates desired and undesired behaviors with various levels of performance. If done correctly this background information establishes whether a given behavior is significant or insignificant for the ultimate performance on the job. The rater has no way of knowing with certainty how much a given descriptor contributes to the overall score and is not involved in calculating the total score. Thus, the rater cannot know whether the employee is getting a high or low rating. This process is expected to eliminate some problems that are common to other approaches to performance appraisal, such as central tendency or leniency errors.

Unfortunately, this method, too, is not tamper-proof. Experienced supervisors can develop a pretty good notion of which descriptors are likely to be considered significant or marginal for each job they supervise. After each round of appraisals, they are likely to sharpen their insights. Hence, with time they are likely to become more and more adept at selecting those descriptors

MOST DESCRIPTIVE	LEAST DESCRIPTIVE	ITEM
----	----	REVIEWS WORK OF SUBORDINATES AND PROVIDES ASSISTANCE AS NEEDED.
----	----	FOLLOWS UP ON ALL DELEGATED ASSIGNMENTS TO INSURE CONFORMANCE WITH OPERATING PROCEDURES.
----	----	REQUESTS EMPLOYEE OPINIONS AND USES THEM WHEN CONDITIONS PERMIT.
----	----	MEETS DEADLINES ON WORK ASSIGNMENTS.
----	----	PRAISES THOSE WHOSE WORK PLACE BEHAVIOR HAS EARNED RECOGNITION.

Figure 6 Forced choice checklist.

that would lend their subordinates the rating they wish them to have. Competent supervisors are likely to be challenged to unlock the secrets of the evaluation instrument to regain control over the end result. The less competent may be less challenged or less able to uncover the secrets. However, by the same token this second group may be less dependable in the use of the appraisal instrument as well.

A notable weakness of the forced choice approach is that the appraisal effort cannot be used as an opportunity or a means for providing feedback to subordinates. Assuming that such feedback can lead to better performance, this approach deprives the organization of some of the benefits of having an appraisal system. Use of this method can be costly. The total expenditure for using this method includes the cost of developing the initial instrument; the recurring cost of securing, updating, and maintaining the scoring manual; and the cost of having specialists transcribe each evaluation form to a rating score.

6. Ranking Systems

Ranking systems are based on one or both of the following assumptions: (1) The performance of a given employee can be appreciated only in relative, rather than objective, terms. (2) Because employees assess their own performance by comparison to the performance of other employees, the appraisal, if it is to be perceived as fair, must be based on the same approach. The first assumption reflects some problems with supervisors, e.g., the tendency to recognize those who are more like themselves rather than those who come closer to meeting some external, objective standard of excellence. The second assumption has to do with the way an employee's perception of the relationship between past efforts and present rewards will influence the motivation to exert additional effort in the future. Motivation theories like expectancy theory or equity theory (Wagner and Hollenbeck, 1992) use employee perceptions as a key element for explaining the connection between motivation and performance.

7. Simple Ranking

As suggested by its name, simple ranking requires the supervisor to rank employees from most productive to least productive. This method can be very efficient when the supervisor oversees a small group of employees who perform the same task. With small groups of five to eight persons, it takes little time to decide the rank order of employees at either end of the scale and a little longer to decide the right placement for those in the middle. The task gets complicated when some of the employees have responsibilities different from the rest, or when the group gets to be too large.

There is an advantage in allowing the supervisor to decide on the relevant criteria for rank-ordering employees. For example, supervisors can use considerations that are important to them, criteria they fully understand and can communicate to subordinates easily. However, the advantage turns out to be a disadvantage when one considers the possibility that the ranking can be capricious and arbitrary. Inconsistent ranking of the same group of employees by the same supervisor or by different supervisors can undermine the ability of central personnel departments to manage human resources effectively. The method is prone to legal challenges but very hard to defend because it is based on the subjective judgment of the supervisor.

8. Paired Comparison Method

This method requires the evaluator to establish the ranking for the employee in two steps. First, as illustrated in Fig. 7, for each evaluation item the supervisor compares the performance of an employee with the performance of every other employee. In each comparison the evaluator marks which employee performed better relative to the given item. Second, the number of times the employee scored better than any other employee is added up for each item.

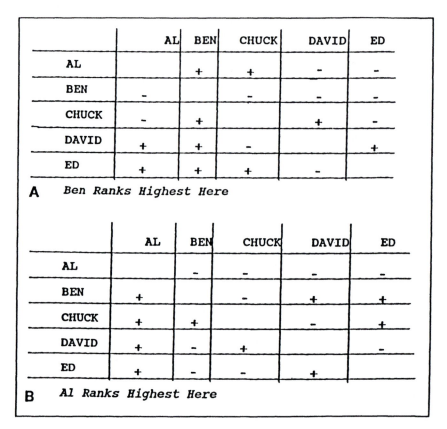

Figure 7   Ranking employees by the paired comparison method. A, for the trait "quality of work"; B, for the trait "creativity."

The paired comparison is an excellent way for collecting important data for human resources planning. When the appraisal is done by well-trained supervisors the organization can get a detailed picture about the contribution of each employee to the overall performance of a given unit. However, this method can be used without undue burden on supervisors only for small groups of employees. A supervisor can do the paired comparison for a 10-item appraisal instrument if he or she is responsible for five employees. A supervisor who oversees 20 employees would find this task to be a formidable and time-hogging proposition.

9.   Forced Distribution Method

This method requires the supervisor to classify employees by using a predetermined distribution pattern. A bell-shaped pattern, for example, represents a distribution where most employees are average performers but few are below or above the norm. As management decides how many (or what percentage of) employees may be classified as low or exceptional achievers, it decides what constitutes a poor, average, or above-average performance. Thus, for example, when management decides to use three categories of, say, good (20%), average (60%), poor (20%), the organization adopts a definition of quality different from when it places 5% of the employees in the exceptional category, 20% in the good category, 50% in the average category, 20% in bellow average, and 5% in the poor performer category. By varying the number and size of the categories, an organization can react to changes in the internal or the external environment. By redefining what constitutes each level of merit under the new conditions, it may differentiate among employees within its working units. Since the same pattern is usually applied across the board, the distribution becomes a tool for expressing or carrying out broader, or more basic, managerial policies. For example, in deciding how many employees can be classified as outstanding, management can determine in advance, and within the constraints of a given budget, how many employees are going to get a bonus and make sure that the amount is meaningful, or how many employees can become eligible for leadership training, educational grants, promotion, etc.

Forced distribution has several advantages. First, it allows employees to earn an excellent rating by forcing a supervisor to compare them to their immediate peers rather than using images or vague notions about what is happening in other parts of the organization. Second, it helps the organization to overcome the tendency of a supervisor to overrate the performance of employees who are hard to replace (Halachmi and Holzer, 1987). Thus, the appraisal is more likely to document performance than the ease of replacing certain employees, i.e., the reality of supply and demand for certain skills in a given labor market. Third, it may contribute to morale by placing equal value on good performance in all parts of the organization. Fourth, because forced distribution requires a supervisor to rank-order his or her subordinates, it can help the organization to minimize the prospect of a leniency or severity bias on the part of different supervisors. Fifth, the forced distribution is a strong antidote for dealing with the creeping merit syndrome, i.e., the tendency of supervisors to move further toward the higher end of the rating scale each time the employee is evaluated. It is not surprising that forced distribution was found to be attractive to managers in organizations where most employees have been ranking at four or better on a five-point scale. The inability to differentiate among different levels of achievement can undermine the motivation of the true achievers (Dessler, 1992). Sixth, the forced distribution method does not discriminate for or against employees in positions that have been held in the past mostly by men or mostly by women. Yet the forced distribution method is not without weaknesses. One problem with its use is that it treats all the different jobs as equally difficult or demanding. As such, it overlooks the fact that the average performance in one job classification is more demanding mentally and physically than the exceptional performance in another classification. Moving nurses from one hospital ward to another, for instance, may require them to do less than what they have done before but earn them a better rating than achieved in their previous assignment. Employees are quick to discover these kinds of inequities. Keeping in mind the teaching of the equity theory of motivation, it is not surprising that some employees will tend to react negatively to the use of this approach.

Another problem with the forced distribution approach is that it can be extremely unfair to employees in small units. Individual employees may be forced into the average or below-average classification in a small unit, even though the same performance would have earned them a better classification in a larger unit. Attempts to make smaller units a part of larger units for purposes of evaluation may open the door to a politicizing of the process. Thus, mail carriers may be classified differently for the same performance if they work out of different post offices. An attempt to treat all of them as employees of the same unit cannot eliminate the perception of favoritism, even when such a perception is not based on hard facts. Another reason that forced distribution can be unfair, or at least be perceived as unfair, is that management redefines the categories shortly before the end of the evaluation period. As can easily be understood, defining the categories before the appraisal takes place can distort the results of the appraisal for the purpose of implementing other policies such as the promotion, training, compensation, or retention of employees. From the viewpoint of employees and unions, these categories are being defined after the fact, leaving evaluated employees little discretion over their own level of performance. Employees tend to be hurt when they find out that what they consider to be extra effort on their part is not going to make a difference in their rating because only one employee can be classified as outstanding.

Other problems with forced classification are common to several other approaches. They include the risk of slanted appraisals due to the "similar-to-me bias," i.e., the tendency of supervisors to overrate those they think are like them, or the halo effect, i.e., the tendency to rate employees in all respects on the basis of how they rank relative to a single salient (but not necessarily the most important or relevant) respect. The forced distribution method tends to encourage such slanting by putting pressure on supervisors to classify employees artificially.

C. Management by Objectives

Although some of the early writing about management by objectives (MBO) goes back to the early 1950s, MBO did not reach prominence until the 1970s. In the public sector, performance by objectives gained notoriety in connection with the Civil Service Reform Act of 1978 (Daley, 1983). One possible reason for the interest in MBO is the concept of a contract between a supervisor and subordinate. This concept was akin to other contemporary thinking during the late 1960s and throughout the 1970s. For example, proponents of transactional analysis (TA) described building blocks of social and interpersonal relationships as contracts.

In MBO, the contract between the employee and the supervisor evolves from joint sessions in which both agree on what the employee is expected to achieve during a given period of time and the measures that are going to be used.

MBO is an attempt to value employee performance as a function of that individual's contribution to predetermined organizational goals. Merit is established not by comparing one employee's behavior or skills with those of other employees but on the basis of meeting the objectives as set forth in the contract. These objectives are derived from departmental goals, which in turn are derived from ultimate organizational goals. Thus as employees meet the objectives set in their individual work plans, they provide the means for achieving departmental goals and make it possible for the organization to progress toward a desired end. Theoretically, subordinates and supervisors at each level work together as necessary in order to meet the goals set for them by the next higher level in the hierarchy. By the same token, they are expected to meet periodically to review progress and revise the strategies they use to accomplish the job as necessary.

On its face the use of MBO reduces the supervisor's subjective influence on the performance appraisal. That, however, is not the reality. Employees may be manipulated and coerced into agreeing to work toward objectives that are not truly theirs. They may end up agreeing to pursue objectives they may not fully understand or ones they will never be able to achieve. Setting up MBOs can also become a tug of war between subordinates who want less responsibility, e.g., a smaller case load, and supervisors who try to push for higher quotas (Dessler, 1991). In the aftermath of such a match, supervisor and subordinate may be upset with each other—a condition that does not contribute to productivity. Another weakness of MBO has to do with the time factor. MBO is based on the premise that a measure of progress toward important objectives can be realized by the end of the appraisal period. Though in some cases this may be possible, in many others it is not. The results of a given effort may not manifest themselves within the given period, or they may appear all at once precluding a meaningful measurement. Also, it is somewhat naive to expect that a result that should be of significance for, let us say, several years can be accomplished within a quarter year, half a year, or even a year. As demonstrated in the private sector, products like the Hulahoop or companies like People Express can be very successful as they enter the market. However, that success measured as market share or revenues cannot be sustained over time. Immediate or short-term results may not be a good indicator of genuine quality performance—an argument that is used to explain why Japanese companies prosper where American companies fail.

Other problems with the use of MBO result from the use of unclear objectives. Problems may develop when the supervisor and the subordinate do not share the same understanding of what is meant by a given objective or when measuring progress toward the objective is not precise or can be done in more than one way. For example, at one public university state funding was a function of enrollment. In order to increase the appropriation to the university the vice-president for academic affairs requested that all academic departments increase the number of students recruited. The head of one department was very upset to receive a letter from the office of academic affairs requesting a more responsible behavior. It so happened that the net number of students in the department was increasing, but so was the rate of attrition. As a result of the new objective, the department attracted a large number of students who could not be expected to matriculate. In the long run, the tangible and intangible costs of admitting such marginal students were far greater than the short-term increase in state appropriation to the university. This incident corresponds to Daley's (1983) observation about the experience of using MBO by the state of Iowa: "There is ample willingness to comply with the requirements of the appraisal by objectives system even though there is a limited ability to do so correctly."

Like many other approaches to performance appraisal, MBO is time consuming. It involves completing and reviewing forms at the beginning of the appraisal period, at given intervals, and at the end of the appraisal period. The time employees and supervisors spend in connection with the use of MBO is time that is not available to them for carrying out their regular assignments.

D.   Self-Evaluation

Several approaches to performance appraisal require the employee to perform some kind of self-evaluation that a supervisor should use in developing his or her own evaluation of that employee. In the view of some, giving employees an opportunity to create a record of what they perceive to be an accomplishment is an indication of participative management (Daley, 1991). Thus, it is not uncommon to see on the rating instrument two lines for each entry as illustrated in Fig. 8. Workers

TEACHING EFFECTIVENESS (10=Exceptional)						
PROFESSOR	10	8	6	4	2	0 [Attach supporting documents]
DEPT. HEAD	10	8	6	4	2	0 [Attach explanation if different from employee's]
DEAN/DIRECTOR	10	8	6	4	2	0
GRAD. SCHOOL	10	8	6	4	2	0 [Mark only when applicable]
RESEARCH PRODUCTIVITY (5=Exceptional)						
PROFESSOR	5	4	3	2	1	0 [Attach supporting document]
DEPT. HEAD	5	4	3	2	1	0 [Attach explanation]
DEAN/DIRECTOR	5	4	3	2	1	0
GRAD. SCHOOL	5	4	3	2	1	0 [Mark only when applicable]

Figure 8   Two items from a self-appraisal instrument for university professors.

mark on the first line what they perceive to be their level of achievement relative to each objective. Supervisors use the same form to indicate their perceptions of the same performance. Some organizations prefer to use separate forms for the self-evaluation and the supervisor's evaluation. Proponents of the single-form instrument point out the saving on paperwork and the advantage of a visual picture that conveys how the two—supervisor and subordinate—perceive a given situation. Such a picture can help the supervisor or personnel department to detect problems and identify training needs or both. Proponents of the dual-form method advance two arguments in support of their position. One claim is that the self-evaluation is a working draft of the appraisal on which the subordinate provides input that helps the superior carry out his or her duty. From an organizational point of view, only the report of the supervisor establishes whether (or how much of) the objectives listed on the initial documents have been achieved. The other claim has to do with labor relations and legal concerns. The supposed advantage is that the use of two forms allows employees to forward copies of their own forms to their boss's supervisor or the personnel department in advance of the appraisal by the supervisor. Thus, if they disagree with the appraisal they can still sign it to indicate that it was discussed with them without being concerned that by doing so they are in agreement with it.

Advocates of MBO consider the opportunity for discussing self-evaluations with subordinates an important element of that approach. However, though self-evaluation can provide a basis for improving performance and giving the individual a sense of fair treatment, it can be the source of many problems. Harris and Schaubroeck (1988) note that several authors argued that self-rating can promote personal development, improve communication between supervisors and subordinates, and clarify differences of opinion. However, they conclude that "despite the alleged gains from self-ratings, empirical research shows frequent lack of agreement between self-ratings and those provided by other sources." One possible reason for this discrepancy may have to do with different expectations and role perceptions. Individuals have a view of what their job entails and what others expect of them that is significantly different from the understanding and expectations of others. Thus, an employee's notion of his or her job performance may differ from that held by other people (Thornton, 1980). A second possible reason for the discrepancy is that various raters may observe diverse dimensions of performance due to differences in organizational levels or the opportunities for observation. Consequently, they may arrive at different assessments of the same individual's performance. A third possible explanation may have to do with the personality of the individual employee and the role of defensive feelings.

The relationships between employee personality, performance, and self-perception are important but cannot be addressed as part of this chapter. The importance of this issue can be illustrated by the following two points. First, personality traits may influence how an employee carries out job assignments and how he or she perceives performance in different ways. High self-esteem may lead an employee to exert little effort due to misplaced self-confidence. High self-esteem may lead the same worker to inflate actual achievements. An employee with low self-esteem may do just the opposite, i.e., try harder and undervalue the results. Second, using attribution theory (De Vader et al., 1986) it is possible to see how individuals with internal or external loci of control may consider results a function of effort or of environmental circumstances, respectively.

Considering these two points, it is easy to see that self-evaluation can trigger psychological defenses that can influence subsequent performance and interpersonal relations. To be sure, employees may find it easier to deal with others' ratings of their performance after going through the motions of self-appraisal and articulating their own perception of worth. Performance targeting (Halachmi, 1992), as will be explained later in this chapter, offers a way of reducing the odds for triggering some mechanism of psychological self-defense by shifting the focus of the appraisal away from the individual. Self-appraisal, under performance targeting, is the employees' assessment of what worked, what did not work, and what needs to be done to improve future performance. This removes from the discussion their own responsibility, or the credit they can take, for any result.

On its face self-appraisal seems to be a promising approach. However, it cannot be used as the sole basis for HRM decisions. In connection with other appraisal instruments it can provide valuable information, but not without a cost and not without risking future performance.

E. Team Evaluations

Team appraisal is an ambiguous term. On the one hand, it denotes the subject of the evaluation, i.e., a collective rather than an individual employee. On the other hand, it suggests that the appraisal is performed by a group rather than by an individual supervisor.

Evaluation of team performance is useful because in most organizations successful operation results from timely contributions by many individuals. It may be dysfunctional to appraise the performance of one individual without considering the efforts of all those who made it possible for the employee to do a good job. Not only may that present an inaccurate assessment of the actual achievement, but it may discourage future cooperation by those whose contributions were essential but not salient enough to merit individual recognition.

Team evaluations and team awards escape some of the weaknesses of individual and whole organizational plans, such as gain sharing (Huret, 1991). Unlike schemes that evaluate and reward on an individual basis, the team approach considers the individual's contributions in the context of team results. Team incentive programs create inducements for cooperation and foster open discussions and problem solving among members of the group. To enjoy the benefits of a group incentive, individual members must be eager to suggest how the group can improve performance and what they intend to do to make it happen. Demonstrating concern about the group's performance and a willingness to do what the rest of the group deems necessary for success leads to high scores on the appraisal instrument.

Norman and Zawacki (1991) describe a team approach to team appraisal for self-managed groups. The evaluation in this case is produced by a committee of the individual's peers. Individuals work with the committee to document their contributions and achievements for the year on the basis of their own records and input from members of the committee. The committee develops an accurate and extensive document outlining job descriptions and responsibilities. These job requirements are used to identify the critical activities that demonstrate success, against which the employee is measured. The document establishes the group expectation for individual behavior. The involvement of the individual in developing this document resembles the MBO process and introduces an element of participation in goal setting. Each member of the team is expected to provide input for the evaluation of all other members of the group. This along with the individual's work with the committee to produce the evaluation may foster team work. The process provides team members who are serving on the committee with a sense of empowerment and, between evaluations, encourages the individual employee to share and to seek performance-related information from all members of the team. However, the committee approach to team evaluation can be time consuming. According to Norman and Zawacki (1991), the committee uses the help of outside management consultants. This, too, may add to delays and the overall cost of the appraisal. The committee approach suffers also from all the other pathologies of group thinking (Janis, 1982), and the process is not free from the risks of the halo effect. Also, coming from a committee of peers, the basis of the input from all members of the team may be perceived as more negative or more positive than it really is. This, in turn, may induce individuals to reach a wrong conclusion about their future as members of the group.

Evaluations by a team are sometimes promoted as a way of using experts or unbiased (but informed) third parties to make appraisals more objective by putting performance in perspective. The Performance Management and Recognition System Review Committee, for example, recommends that agencies that implement peer review consult with and include recognized professional or management associations as appropriate (*Advancing Managerial Excellence*, 1991). Team evaluation provides organizations with an important vehicle for collaborating with outside groups, such as organized labor. Since managers appoint the evaluating team and decide whether and how to use the appraisal it produces, there are no concerns about compromising authority or jurisdiction to outsiders. Such cooperation can reduce the odds for grievances.

Sometimes the use of team incentives necessitates the use of a team approach to performance evaluation. The typical team incentive plan consists of several elements, each with a different weight. The weight may reflect the organizational priorities or philosophy of management. When each element is arrived at by the use of a different instrument, there may be a need to adjust the raw score from each instrument so that scores can be expressed in the same numerical or qualitative terms. Thus, for example, the collective score may combine two kinds of data: first, the weighted (or adjusted) performance scores from a supervisor's evaluation of the individual's performance, self-evaluation, peer evaluations, or management's ranking of the team's performance; second, the adjusted performance indicators that reflect quantitative or qualitative changes in overall organizational productivity. Such indicators may link the individual's contribution and the group's achievements to organizational performance in areas such as reduction in cost per operation/service recipient, improvement (expansion) of service, reduction in errors (consumer complaints), facility/equipment utilization, etc. The indicators to be included in the formula and their relative weight may change as the organization changes priorities or its strategy for productivity improvement. As total quality management (TQM) makes its way into the public sector, we may witness a growing tendency to embrace a team approach to evaluation along with a team-based incentives program.

F. Subordinate Evaluation

It has been estimated that in over 95% of the performance appraisal programs the employee's supervisor compiles the rating (Mount, 1984). There are questions about the desirability of this practice since supervisory ratings are susceptible to intentional and unintentional bias. To overcome some of the problems with accuracy of appraisals by supervisors, it was suggested that organizations attempt to obtain ratings from alternative rating sources: peer ratings, self-ratings, and subordinate ratings (Mount, 1984). Peer and self-ratings are important sources of information about the individual's performance. However, as pointed out earlier, self-rating may not be consistent with ratings by others (supervisors or peers), because individuals and other raters may see the individual's performance differently.

An evaluation of a supervisor by subordinates costs more than an evaluation by the supervisor's own boss. The added cost results from the fact that instead of one person (i.e., the immediate superior) taking time away from regular activities to perform the evaluation, several people compile the ratings. According to Bernardin (1986), "Subordinate appraisal of managers is an assessment and development tool which has an excellent, albeit limited, track record and which deserves the same critical consideration which is given to highly publicized methods such as assessment centers, psychological testing, and management development programs." The Administrative Systems Center at Florida Atlantic University at Boca Raton, for example, requires that supervisors submit subordinates' appraisals prior to the manager's arrival at the center. These appraisals serve as a basis for training and development intervention. According to Bernadin and Beatty (1987), "Managers are extremely interested in these appraisals and consider them one of the most valid sources of feedback." In a study of managers at the U.S. Geological Survey, over 45% of the managers indicated that subordinate appraisal would be a "valid" or "highly valid" source of performance appraisal. Likewise, over 80% of the subordinates felt that their evaluations would be useful and legitimate (Bernardin, 1987).

Subordinate appraisal is a natural, and maybe necessary, element of an evaluation system that uses group incentives. Leadership qualities can determine whether the performance of a group amounts to more (or less) than the arithmetic sum of total contributions by members of the group. Indeed, Bernardin and Beatty (1987) cite research findings indicating a link between organizational effectiveness and subordinates' evaluation of their supervisors' leadership skills. The case for subordinate appraisal is even stronger where the evaluation by a supervisor is complemented by an assessment by one's peers. The rationales for the use of peer evaluation and group evaluation are as relevant to the case of appraisal by subordinates.

Bernardin (1986) lists three compelling reasons to support the formal use of subordinate appraisals of managers:

> First of all, subordinates are a valid source of information about their managers because they are in a better observational position to evaluate certain managerial dimensions than any other source of assessment. Second, because appraisals are often available from several subordinates, the multiple assessments have potential for greater validity than what is typically found in ratings by a single rater, most often the superior to the manager. Third, a formal system of subordinate appraisal of managers fits nicely into the employee commitment or involvement models which are gaining in popularity today.

Halachmi (1992) makes the claim for a systematic appraisal by subordinates as a source of input for decisions by the supervisor's superiors. The purpose of the appraisal by subordinates is not to rank the supervisor on leadership scales, a common practice in subordinate appraisals (Bernardin and Beatty, 1987). Rather, the purpose is to inform the supervisor's superior about the role of the supervisor in creating the necessary conditions for achieving a given objective. This in turn should provide the supervisor's superior with important feedback about the supervisor's own performance as well. Halachmi's concept of performance targeting is not an appraisal approach for facilitating better human resource management per se. Its primary concern is performance from a management point of view. It is concerned with the involved individuals from a personnel point of view (e.g., in terms of identifying training needs, opportunities for promotion, merit pay, demotion, accuracy of job descriptions) only to the extent that there is a need for action by line managers. This position is consistent with Mount's (1984) assertion that "the use of subordinate ratings as a source of feedback to the manager on performance strengths and weaknesses is quite different from using the ratings for administrative purposes such as salary."

The rationale for the appraisal of supervisors cannot guide an organization in modifying some instrument already in use for assessing subordinates so that it can be used for rating supervisors. Such modification would be more difficult than it at first appears. Some of the strengths but also some weaknesses of various instruments for assessing subordinates may hold true when they are used by subordinates to assess supervisors. For example, subordinates' ratings, like appraisals by supervisors, may be influenced by the halo effect, excess leniency or severity, or insufficient training, knowledge, or understanding of the job being rated (Mount, 1984; Bernardin, 1986). As a matter of fact, some of the problems are likely to be even more serious since, in comparison to supervisors, subordinates may be less experienced, mature, dependable, or trained to do the ratings. The risk of using an unreliable supervisor's appraisal is that instead of improving the quality of the information base the organization may end up muddling the picture. Because the supervisor represents a greater organizational investment than the subordinate, the danger is that the unreliable appraisal of a supervisor by a subordinate can do more harm to the organization than the slanted assessment of a subordinate by a supervisor.

Nevertheless, from an HRM perspective, there seems to be a case for the use of closely related (or even identical) instruments for assessing subordinates and supervisors. Collecting the same kind of data in a related fashion can help personnel departments in areas such as labor relations, organizational development, validity of selection/testing instruments, job description, compensation, and career planning. However, there is a need to compare the advantages of using the same (or modified but closely related) instruments with the possible disadvantages of using a single rating instrument for evaluating all employees. The right appraisal approach should allow the organization to compare the performance of a supervisor with that of other supervisors and not with the performance of subordinates.

As new organizational designs resemble less and less the traditional pyramid and as organizations move from mechanical to organic structures, subordinates' appraisals may become the only meaningful way to evaluate the performance of supervisors. Changes in demography, education, and information technology are going to reduce the risk of uninformed appraisals by inexperienced or immature subordinates. As more employees postpone retirement, the risk of inexperience and immaturity is greatly reduced. Because educational requirements for employment are going up, subordinates are more likely to be apt to comprehend the assessment instrument for appraising a supervisor. Information technology in general will allow subordinates to assess the performance of supervisors because they too will possess all the information the supervisor uses for making operational decisions.

If organizations are willing to invest in the training of employees, some of the weaknesses of subordinates' appraisals of supervisors can be eliminated. The value to the organization of getting employees to provide their superiors with feedback may be greater than the cost of such training.

V. PERFORMANCE TARGETING: A PROMISING ALTERNATIVE

Performance targeting shifts the focus from documenting and evaluating an employee's work to assessing the partnership between a subordinate and a supervisor. When this partnership works, the supervisor creates the necessary conditions for the subordinate to do his or her share to meet organizational objectives.

Performance targeting establishes not only the responsibilities of the subordinate but the supervisor's responsibilities as well. It replaces the MBO's passive "contract," to which employees are held accountable, with a functional relationship between supervisors and subordinates. This relationship requires an ongoing effort by the partners to accommodate and complement each other as a condition for a successful attainment of organizational goals.

Halachmi and Holzer (1987) argue that performance targeting should replace performance appraisal as the vehicle for improving performance. The MBO concept of management involves a joint effort by a supervisor and subordinate to decide what the subordinate should do to achieve organizational goals. The concept of performance targeting goes on to establish what the supervisor is expected to do to create the necessary conditions for the subordinate to do his or her share. Performance targeting is a joint effort by a supervisor and a subordinate to find out what must be done to meet organizational goals, what and how the employee can contribute toward that end, and what must be done by the supervisor to create the necessary conditions to help the subordinate contribute to those goals. MBO establishes an employment contract. Performance targeting creates a partnership.

In performance targeting, the supervisor's exchanges with a subordinate include information about the expectations of the supervisor's superiors. That does not assume, however, that the subordinate enters the discussion thoroughly ignorant of the expectations of the organization's hierarchy. In fact, the concept of performance targeting implies that the supervisor may get a better understanding of his own boss's expectations by reexploring them from a different perspective—that of the subordinate. The logic is simple. First, the subordinate may have informal information that may place official goals in a different, more objective, perspective—one closer to that of the supervisor's boss. Second, in the final analysis, the subordinate's perspective and understanding of what is involved, rather than the supervisor's, is going to influence what that employee does. To influence results, it follows that a supervisor must first understand the subordinate's perspective and personal interest. This approach implies that an employee cannot be taken for granted, that the employee is not passive or without an opinion about the job, and that the process of actuating involves interaction between the various management levels of the organization. Such an approach urges subordinates not to assume that the boss will magically know what help or information subordinates need and provide it to them (Gabarro and Kotter, 1980). It also urges them to understand that to achieve organizational goals they are dependent on their boss and their boss is dependent on them, even though they may wish it otherwise (Gabarro and Kotter, 1980). Performance targeting allows subordinate and superior to explore their mutual dependencies in terms of concrete issues and thus to find a way to accommodate each other's needs. It lets managers take advantage of the fact that the workers of the future will expect to have more and more say about what they do and how they do it, with less supervision (Brown, 1991). Performance targeting gives subordinates an opportunity to evolve into what Kelly (1988) calls "effective followers," i.e., those who think for themselves and carry out their duties with energy and assertiveness. Effective followers "see themselves—except in terms of line responsibility—as equals of the leaders they follow. . . . They can see that the people they follow are, in turn, following the lead of others, and try to appreciate the goals and needs of the team and the organization" (Kelly, 1988).

Performance targeting starts with the premise of McGregor's theory Y (1960) but goes on to change the pattern of communication as well as the employee's role in defining needs for accomplishing assigned tasks. Theory Y changes the boss's assumptions about and attitudes toward subordinates' behavior but retains a theory X-like pyramidal flow of communication and interactions. Theory Y is supervisor-oriented. The boss is expected to assume a non–theory-X posture but not to make allowance for the role that should be played by the subordinate. Performance targeting acknowledges the possibility of reversing the direction in which orders and reports flow, that power and information can run upward as well as downward (Yukl and Taber, 1981). Accordingly, performance targeting delineates the subordinate's role in defining his job, assigns responsibility, and requires accountability.

As a result of dealing with employees as active rather than passive participants, performance targeting can move the supervisor from a position where relationships with subordinates are contaminated by the prospects of rewards and punishment to a more comfortable position of guidance, support, and cooperation (Halachmi and Holzer, 1987). Performance targeting retains the functional aspects of performance appraisal because it preserves the notion of evaluation and accountability. However, it is relatively free from some of the older system's dysfunctions in terms of motivation. In particular, performance targeting concentrates less on doing what counts toward the evaluation (i.e., doing things right) and more on an ongoing search for what needs to be done (i.e., doing the right things).

In many work situations, persons who are both willing and able to accomplish a task successfully may be inhibited or prevented from doing so by situational characteristics beyond their control. According to Peters and Acinar (1980), "Inhibiting situational constraints are hypothesized to have their strongest effect on those persons with the greatest task-relevant abilities." As a process, performance targeting has the greatest promise for would-be high performers. Such employees are more likely to be in a position to accurately identify the kind of help they need to do their job and thus benefit greatly from involving their supervisor in the effort to solve problems in the workplace.

The joint efforts of supervisors and subordinates to identify constraints can help to clarify intentions. When a subordinate and a supervisor become aware of each other's intentions, they are more likely to find out what needs to be done, what each can or should do (achieve), and what their mutual responsibilities are. The role of intentions in work motivation and productivity is already clear in the research agenda (Tubbs and Ekeberg, 1991). However, from an organizational point of view, clarifying intentions to allow employees to be more effective followers (Wortman, 1982; Gabarro and Kotter, 1987; Kelly, 1988) may not be enough. To provide the organization with the necessary information for all the other functions of performance appraisal, performance targeting must go beyond superior–subordinate relations. The key, it seems, is the review of the documented performance not by the supervisor but by the superior.

A.   Performance Targeting and Performance Review

Evaluation of performance fulfills several needs of the organization. It provides important information an agency may use in connection with activities such as promotion, demotion, transfer, or separation of a particular employee; salary decisions for the individual employee and the management of compensation across the board; grievance handling, labor–management relations and negotiations; training and development; redesigning or rewriting job descriptions, as well as the reclassification of jobs; career planning, capacity building, and annual work plans; placement, orientation, and conflict resolution; decisions about restructuring or reorganization; and the introduction of planned change.

Because an employee's uses of time and resources are of the utmost importance to the organization, performance targeting requires the supervisor and subordinate to concentrate on those results. Any attempt to deal with the other organizational functions is likely to muddy the water by confusing the issue and diverting attention from the highest priority—evaluating results. Yet, the organization does need a system for gathering the information on those other functions and for determining the degree to which the interaction between the supervisor and the subordinate is target-oriented. This writer asserts that an important component of such a system is the requirement that the supervisor's report of the subordinate's performance be discussed first between the subordinate and the supervisor and then between the employee and the supervisor's boss. Such a review is necessary for proper evaluation of the supervisor's performance by his own boss (which, in turn, should be subject to review by that boss's superior). Another important attribute of such reviews is that they provide a measure of accountability and quality control, which results from knowing in advance that the appraisal is subject to review (Weekley and Gier, 1989).

As each boss reviews the performance appraisals produced by reporting supervisors in consultation with their subordinates, the organization gets a change to account for possible bias in the evaluative approach of various supervisors toward a person, a group, or a given performance dimension (Edwards, 1983). Consequently, at least for each level of the organization, the odds for consistency in appraisals increase. That consistency in turn may improve the quality of information supporting various organizational functions.

It is beyond the scope of this chapter to discuss all the functions possibly served by an employee's performance report that includes a review by the subordinate and the supervisor's boss. However, it would be hard to overemphasize its potential for improving the quality of the performance report. Specifically, the performance review can reduce the number of capricious and arbitrary ratings based on something other than the actual performance. It provides the employee with an opportunity to point out the role of the supervisor in creating the necessary conditions for the subordinate to achieve the desired targets. As such, it creates the necessary conditions for reminding the supervisor of his or her own responsibilities for a subordinate's performance. Consequently, the prospect of the performance review of a subordinate by one's own boss may induce a more responsible behavior toward the subordinate before, during, and after the evaluation period. This in turn may induce loyalty and organizational commitment that may result only as a function of an intrinsic sense of satisfaction due to improved performance.

Introducing a review of a subordinate's performance by the supervisor's boss deprives the supervisor of some authority. It can make the assessment of performance less capricious and arbitrary and introduce a notion of partnership. In short, it can flatten the organizational pyramid a little bit. Since the better educated work force of today has greater expectations for fairness and for having a say about what should be done, performance targeting and performance review may be the necessary steps in the right direction.

VI. CONCLUSIONS: WHAT ARE THE REQUIREMENTS FOR EFFECTIVE PERFORMANCE APPRAISAL?

Since performance appraisal drains important organizational resources, it behooves managers to take the necessary steps to facilitate its conduct. To justify the use of scarce resources, at least two perspectives must be accounted for in assessing any performance appraisal system: (1) the effectiveness of the system as judged by the appraiser and (2) the effectiveness of the system as judged by the subordinate, the appraisee. Ideally, performance appraisal should meet the needs of both (Lawler et al., 1984).

A demonstration of commitment and interest by the top echelons is a necessary but insufficient condition for a successful system. To satisfy the needs of appraisers and appraisees, top level managers must take specific steps to create the right atmosphere and proper conditions. Choosing an approach and developing appraisal instrument(s) commensurate with the demographic profile of supervisors and employees, organizational culture, and local mores are tall orders. However, there are some issues or considerations organizations must address, regardless of past experiences or the characteristics of their labor force. Without attention to issues, such as those listed hereafter, performance appraisal activities can be dysfunctional and have an adverse effect on organizational performance.

A. Requirement 1: Develop a Clear, Consistent, and Equitable Policy

There is no need to explain why a clear, consistent, and equitable policy can facilitate the administration of performance appraisal. However, it is not easy for organizations to meet those three conditions or attain them by declaring them in a single document.

A performance appraisal system that is not perceived to be equitable is dysfunctional because instead of getting more out of its financial and human resources it may get less. Questions about equity may force an agency to use resources for dealing with litigation and labor disputes. That can be a potent demotivator in simple cases and trigger deliberate attempts to undermine operations by disgruntled individuals or groups in extreme cases. Negative reactions to the appearance of a questionable equity on the part of outside groups can be costly. It can reduce the cooperation and good will of other organizations, clients, and others who identify with "wronged employee(s)." Such sympathizers are many times in a position to influence what resources are available to the agency and how it uses them. Under extreme conditions, an intervention by the court or a legislative body may strip management of exercising its discretion over decisions concerning hiring, firing, promotion, transfer, or level of compensation.

Assuring that the appraisal is equitable is not easy. Use of one approach or one instrument to evaluate all employees regardless of rank and job description leads to inequitable results. It may cause employees to be ranked higher or lower than they would have been if an approach more commensurate with their job content had been used. A uniform approach can subject some employees to a process that is less tolerable to them than to other employees. For example, with a policy that promotes team appraisal, subordinate appraisal of supervisors may not be congruous with organizational culture. A policy that applies to the evaluation of civilian employees of a National Guard unit may be inconsistent with the policies governing the evaluation of other individuals assigned to the unit, e.g., career officers from one of the armed forces or local members of the Guard.

Inconsistent application of the appraisal process or an indiscriminate use of an appraisal instrument may undermine the credibility of the process and the validity and usefulness of the results. Any one of these threats in turn may raise questions about equitability.

As pointed out earlier, each of the different approaches, processes, and instruments that can be used for performance appraisal has strengths and weaknesses. Some of these strengths and weaknesses may be true only for the general case, i.e., when used for appraising all employees regardless of job content or organizational level, while others apply only when the appraisal is used to evaluate a selected group of employees. A better understanding of the policy may bring an individual or a group of employees to question the possible consequences of using a particular approach to their case.

In order for employees to accept a given performance appraisal as fair, the policy governing its use and administration must be understood by most employees without much difficulty. However, an attempt to simplify the language may introduce ambiguity while the attempt to clarify may complicate the policy and will make it difficult to follow. In either case an attempt to clarify the policy, a necessary step for assuring a consistent and equitable appraisal system, may actually reduce them.

A clear, consistent, and equitable policy can facilitate the performance appraisal process. However, though organizations may be able to write policies that meet any two specifications, they may find it difficult to satisfy all three of them at the same time.

B.   Requirement 2: Provide Training of Raters

Because appraisals are both important and difficult, training of raters is invaluable (Sims et al., 1987). Training raters can help an organization overcome some of the inherited weaknesses of the system it uses. Training is a way for assuring that supervisors are aware of possible mistakes and know how to avoid them. It is also a vehicle for assuring that the instrument is applied uniformly across the board and that raters pay attention to and document those aspects of the performance that are important to the organization.

An effective training program can preempt some legal challenges to the way the organization conducts the appraisal of its employees. In the absence of formal training an agency will have to work harder to prove that its appraisal system is fair. At the same time, the training of raters increases the odds that the information the organization collects is dependable and that the cost of collecting unnecessary information is avoided. From an organizational perspective, undependable or unnecessary information not only generates an opportunity cost but may expose the organization to litigation by disgruntled employees.

C.   Requirement 3: Be Cost-Effective

In order for a performance appraisal system to be credible, it must be cost-effective. If the system is perceived to be less than cost-effective, employees and supervisors have little incentive to take it seriously. They will be right to conclude that the system is not going to be in place for long. In order for a system to be cost-effective, employees and supervisors must be convinced that investing the time and effort to do it right is the most promising way for all to achieve their desired ends. If one of the parties feels that the return on the investment in time or effort does not justify the trouble of participating in performance appraisal or that there is a more promising way for getting some desired ends, the system will fail.

To clarify this point we need to elaborate on what we mean by cost. To the organization, the cost of performance appraisal involves the expense of developing the system, training raters, and gaining the confidence of employees; producing the instruments for performing the rating; the opportunity cost of the time used for carrying out the various steps of the process, such as retrieval, analysis, dissemination, and storage of the data. Though most organizations do not keep a running tab on the actual expense, there is not reason to assume that it is negligible (Halachmi, 1992). To the supervisor the cost of performance appraisal consists of two elements. The first is in the price of failing to satisfy the expectations of a subordinate or one's own supervisor (Edwards, 1983). This price can be hefty and the supervisor may end up paying it for many years in terms of lost career opportunities, demotivation of subordinates, and the undermining of one's position within groups inside and outside the organization. The second cost is in the time and effort that were spent on the various steps of the appraisal instead of attending to other responsibilities. For the subordinate, one element of the cost is the expenditure of the efforts that could have been used in other ways to gain desired ends, e.g., promotion, transfer, or salary increase. The other element of the cost is the emotional setback that results from the frustration and the sense of being let down or taken advantage of by the organization and the supervisor.

D.   Requirement 4: Use Systematic Job Analysis for Updating Job Descriptions

Job analysis is a process undertaken to determine which characteristics are necessary for satisfactory job performance and to analyze the environmental conditions in which the job is performed (Singer, 1990). It is easy to see why there is a need to base the appraisal of performance on what the employee can reasonably be expected to achieve in order to have a plausible defense should the system be challenged in court. However, the administrative justification of the need is as, or even more, compelling.

Without a systematic job analysis, a manager is actually in the dark. The manager must have the information from job analysis for making rational rather than capricious decisions when placing employees or assigning jobs. The appraisal process generates important information about the validity of the job analysis and thus about its usefulness for improving productivity. Properly done, the appraisal may reveal, for example, that some employees spend more time than expected on a certain aspect of a job or that they are doing something they did not have to do. Thus, performance appraisal may indicate to the manager that the old job description is not relevant. Updating of job descriptions may be a key to improving productivity through better recruitment, training, and placement of employees. It can also be used for realignment of compensation to make it more commensurate with job demands. This in turn may influence productivity.

E. Requirement 5: Provide Opportunities and Means for Employees to Improve Performance

When performance appraisal is perceived as an exercise providing superiors with the justification for decisions about compensation and career, employees have little reason to be cooperative. We should not be surprised to find out that employees attempt to use the appraisal to outsmart the system, e.g., to exert the same effort but only on what seems to count, especially when the appraisal becomes a tool for maintaining discipline. For the very reasons that employees may be tempted to play games, they may be open and receptive to an appraisal system when they can see how it genuinely benefits them. Thus, employees are likely to be more forthcoming in sharing critical information when accepting the review of their accomplishments as an opportunity to find out how they are doing, where they can or need to do better, or where they can get help.

F. Requirement 6: Provide Employees with a Meaningful Say About the Definition of Desired Performance Objectives and the Standards or Means for Ascertaining the Degree of Progress Toward Them

Better educated employees have more and higher expectations about their jobs. Professional employees need to reconcile apparent conflict between professional and organizational loyalties (Halachmi, 1980). Allowing employees to participate in a meaningful way in setting objectives and in selecting the standards for measuring progress is recognizing that they too have something at stake. Such participation implies that the appraisal is not arbitrary and that what the employee deems to be important, and thus where efforts are directed, counts as much as other things important to the organization or the supervisor.

G. Requirement 7: Withstand Legal Scrutiny

As employees develop a higher stake in performance appraisal than in other components of the personnel system, employers would find it instructive to learn what factors employees feel contribute to a fair and accurate evaluation (Heiler et al., 1988). It is impossible to articulate complete guidelines for assuring the legality of a given approach to performance appraisal or the instruments that are being used to implement it. Thus, employers must follow up and monitor changes in legislation and decisions by state and federal courts as those matters constantly redefine the boundaries of what can and cannot be done. At the same time new legislation and court decisions reflect and influence employees' expectations. However, considering existing legislation, court decisions, and research findings about performance appraisal systems, organizations need to assure that their practices:

Have a proportional impact on protected classes
Are developed from a systematic job analysis
Emphasize work behavior rather than personal traits
Use clear standards of performance
Provide written instruction and training of raters
Set reasonable standards of performance for employees before the beginning of the process
Provide periodic feedback on how well standards are attained

Contribute to updates of job descriptions
Are used uniformly for all personnel and compensation decisions
Do not violate the rights of the supervisor or the employee as individuals
Are consistent with negotiated labor contracts

REFERENCES

Adams, J.S., and Rosenbaum, W.B. (1962). The relationship of worker productivity to cognitive dissonance about wage inequities, *J. Appl. Psychol., 46*: 161–164.

Advancing Managerial Excellence: A Report on Improving the Performance Management and Recognition System, Washington, DC, Performance Management and Recognition System Review Committee, November 5, 1991.

Allan, P., and Rosenberg, S. (1986). An assessment of merit pay administration under New York City's managerial performance evaluation system: three years of experience, *Public Personnel Manag., 15*: 279–309.

Ammons, D. N., and Condrey, S.E. (1991). Performance appraisal in local government: warranty conditions, *Public Product. Manage. Rev., 19*: 253–266.

Anderson, J. (1983). Officials' Wrongdoing Rewarded, *The Tennessean*, November 27.

Baird, L. S., Beatty, R.W., and Schneier, C. E. (1985). *The Performance Appraisal Source Book*, Human Resource Development Press, Amherst, MA.

Baker, J. (1988). *Causes of Failure in Performance Appraisal and Supervision*, Quorum Books, New York.

Barret, G., and Kernan, M. (1987). Performance appraisal and terminations: a review of court decisions since Brito v. Zia with implications towards personnel practices, *Personnel Psychol., 4*: 489–503.

Bennet, A. (1991). Paying workers to meet goals spreads, but gauging performance proves tough, *Wall Street Journal*, September 1, B1.

Bernardin, H.J. (1986). Subordinate appraisal: a valuable source of information about managers, *Human Resource Manage., 25*: 421–439.

Bernardin, H.J. (1987). A performance appraisal system, *Performance Assessment*, (R. Berk, ed.), Johns Hopkins University Press, Baltimore, 277–304.

Bernardin, H.J., and Beatty, R.W. (1987). Can subordinate appraisal enhance managerial productivity? *Sloan Manage. Rev., 28*: 63–73.

Bernardin, H.J., Alvares, K.M., and Cranny, C.J. (1976). A recomparison of behavioral expectations scales to summated scales, *J. Appl. Psychol., 61*: 564–570.

Blau, P. (1956). *Bureaucracy in Modern Society*, Random House, New York.

Brown, D.S. (1991). Free employee from close supervision, *Government Executive, 23*: 42.

Burchett, S.R., and De Meuse K. (1985). Performance appraisal and the law, *Personnel, 62*: 29–37.

Daley, D. (1983). Monitoring the use of appraisal-by-objectives in Iowa: research note, *Rev. Public Personnel Admin., 3*: 33–44.

Daley, D. (1991). Performance appraisal in North Carolina municipalities, *Rev. Public Personnel Admin., 11*: 32–50.

Derven, M. (1990). Assessment: the paradox of performance appraisal, *Personnel J., 69*: 107–111.

Dessler, G. (1991). *Personnel/Human Resource Management*, 5th Ed., Prentice Hall, Englewood Cliffs, NJ.

De Vader, C.L., Bateson, A.G., and R.G. Lord (1986). Attribution theory: a meta-analysis of attributional hypothesis, *Generalizing from the Laboratory to Field Settings* (E. Lock, ed.), Lexington Books, Lexington, MA, pp. 63–81.

Dumas, C. M., McIntyre, C., and Zelenock, K.L. (1990). Parate v. Isabor: resolving the conflict between the academic freedom of the university and the academic freedom of university professors, *J. Coll. Univ. Law, 16*: 713–730.

Edwards, M. R. (1983). Productivity improvement through innovations in performance appraisal, *Public Personnel Manage., 12*: 13–24.

Foxman, L., and Polsky, W. (1988). Career counselor: performance appraisal are not salary review, *Personnel J., 67*: 30–32.

Friedman, M. (1986). Ten steps to objective appraisal, *Personnel J., 67*: 30–32.

Gabarro, J. J., and Kotter, J. P. (1980). Managing your Boss, *Harvard Business Rev., 58*: 92–100.

Halachmi, A. (1980). Dealing with the conflict of loyalties: the continuing seminar and action research, *J. Health Human Res. Admin., 2*: 505–531.

Halachmi, A. (1992). Performance targeting and productivity, *Int. Rev. Admin. Sci., 58*: in press.

Halachmi, A., and Holzer, M. (1987). Merit pay, performance targeting and productivity, *Rev. Public Personnel Admin., 7*: 80–91.

Harris, M. M., and Schaubroeck, J. (1988). A meta-analysis of self-supervisor, self peer, and peer-supervisor ratings, *Personnel Psychol., 41*: 43–62.

Heisler, W. J., Jones, W.D., and Benham P.O. (1988). *Managing Human Resources Issues*, Jossey-Bass, San Francisco.

Henderson, R. L. (1980). *Performance Appraisal: Theory to Practice*, Reston, Reston, VA.

Henderson, R. L. (1984). *Practical Guide to Performance Appraisal*, Reston, Reston, VA.

Huret, J. (1991). Paying for team results, *HRM Magazine, 36*: 39–41.

Janis, I. L. (1982). *Groupthink*, 2nd Ed., Houghton Mifflin, Boston.

Karr, A. R. (1992). Pay for performance, *Wall Street Journal*, September 1, A1.

Kelly, R. E. (1988). In praise of followers, *Harvard Business Rev., 66*: 142–148.

Kleiman, L. S., and Durham, R. (1981). Performance appraisal, promotion and the courts: a critical review, *Personnel Psychol., 34*: 103–122.

Landy, F. J., and Farr J. L. (1983). *The Measurement of Work Performance*, Academic Press, New York.

Lawler, E. E., Mohrman, A. M., and Resnick, S. M. (1984). Performance appraisal revisited, *Organiz. Dyn., 13*: 20–35.

Marcoulides, G. E., and Mills, R. B. (1988). Employee performance appraisal: a new technique, *Rev. Public Personnel Admin., 8*: 105–112.

McGregor, D. (1960). *The Human Side of the Enterprise*, McGraw-Hill, New York.

McNish, L. C. (1986). A critical review of performance appraisal at the federal level: the experience of the PHS, *Rev. Public Personnel Admin., 7*: 42–56.

Mount, M. K. (1984). Psychometric properties of subordinate ratings of managerial performance, *Personnel Psychol., 37*: 687–702.

Norman, C. A., and Zawacki, R. A. (1991). Team appraisals—team approach, *Personnel J., 70*: 101–104.

Pay for Performance (1987). Washington, DC, GAO/GGD-87-28, January 21.

Pay for Performance (1990). Washington, DC, GAO/GGD/-91-1, October.

Pay-for-Performance Labor Management Committee (1991). *Strengthening the Link Between Pay and Performance*, Office of Personnel Management, Washington, DC.

Perry, J. L. (1986). Merit pay in the public sector: the case for the failure of theory, *Rev. Public Personnel Admin., 7*: 57–69.

Peters, L. H., and Acinar, E. J. (1980). Situational constraints and work outcomes, *Acad. Manage. Rev., 5*: 301–397.

Schneier, C. E., and Beatty, R. W. (1979). Combining BARS and MBO: using an appraisal system to diagnose performance problems, *Personnel Admin., 24*: 51–60.

Sims, R. R., Veres, J. G., and Heninger, S. (1987). Training appraisers: an orientation program for improving supervisory performance rating, *Public Personnel Manage., 16*: 32–46.

Smith, P. C., and Kindall, L. M. (1963). Retranslation of expectations: an approach to the construction of unambiguous anchors for rating scales, *J. Appl. Psychol., 47*: 149–155.

Thornton, G. C. (1980). Psychometric properties of self appraisals of job performance, *Personnel Psychol., 33*: 263–271.

Tubbs, M. E., and Ekeberg, S. E. (1991). The role of intention in work motivation, *Acad. Manage. Rev., 16*: 180–199.

Ungar, B. L. (1989). Comments on reauthorization of the performance management recognition system,

Testimony before the Subcommittee on Compensation and Employee Benefits Committee on Post Office and Civil Service, House of Representatives, July 18, GAO/T-CGD-89-36.

Weekley, J. A., and Gier, J. A. (1989). Ceilings in the reliability and validity of performance rating, *Acad. Manage. J., 32*: 213–222.

Wortman, M. S. (1982). Strategic management and changing leader–follower roles, *J. Appl. Behav. Sci., 18*: 371–383.

Yukl, G., and Taber, T. (1983). The effective use of managerial power, *Personnel, 60*: 37–44.

15

Compensation Administration and the Human Resource Management Function

ROBERT H. ELLIOTT and THOMAS VOCINO Auburn University at Montgomery, Montgomery, Alabama

I. INTRODUCTION

Employees provide their time, energy, expertise, and loyalty to organizations in exchange for assorted rewards. Traditionally, pay is the most widely recognized organizational reward, but compensation administration covers a much broader gamut of organizational incentives than the amount of money contained in each employee paycheck. While pay is still the most visible incentive, today's organizations in both the public and private sectors must put together a balanced package of inducements to be competitive in the contemporary changing work force. As Buford has indicated, "the task of management is to design a compensation system which attracts and retains a qualified workforce, motivates employees to put forth their best efforts, and achieves optimum returns for the dollars spent" (Buford, 1991).

This chapter will focus briefly on some of the major laws regulating the compensation function, concentrating in some detail on the Fair Labor Standards Act. Next, we will examine the relationship between compensation administration and other human resources management (HRM) processes used to attain internal equity such as job analysis, position classification, and job evaluation. External equity concepts using wage and salary surveys will also be discussed. Other worthwhile HRM tools used to attain individual equity in this area such as seniority and merit-based pay will also be highlighted. The final sections of this chapter will focus on three contemporary topics of interest to the field of compensation administration: alternative pay systems such as broad banding and gain sharing, the contemporary impact of unions and the collective bargaining process on compensation administration, and new developments in the area of fringe benefits.

II. LEGAL ASPECTS OF THE FIELD

Compensation administration is a highly regulated field with a multitude of federal laws setting the parameters that guide the establishment of HRM policies. Laws prohibiting exploitation of child labor, setting minimum wages, maximum hours, and specifying nondiscrimination based on numerous categories of legally protected groups are now commonplace decision-making criteria for HRMs trying to establish compensation policies. The major federal laws in this area are the Fair Labor Standards Act of 1938, the Equal Pay Act of 1963, the Civil Rights Act of 1964, and the

Age Discrimination Act of 1967. This chapter will focus specifically on the most wide ranging of the above laws, the Fair Labor Standards Act.

III. FAIR LABOR STANDARDS ACT

The landmark law governing compensation is the Fair Labor Standards Act (FLSA) passed by the Congress and signed by President Franklin D. Roosevelt in 1938. The FLSA established a minimum wage for covered groups of $0.25 per hour and limited the basic work week to no more than 44 hours. The New Deal official most responsible for this initiative was Frances Perkins, FDR's secretary of labor, who accepted that position with the understanding that she would be able to work for a national minimum wage and hours law (Berg, 1989).

Fair Labor Standards Amendments were enacted during the administration of President Harry Truman in 1949, raising the minimum wage 87% to $0.75 per hour on January 25, 1950. The Eisenhower administration enacted the Fair Labor Standards Amendments of 1955, which increased the minimum wage to $1.00 per hour on March 1, 1956. On February 2, 1961, President John F. Kennedy sent a special message to the Congress urging an increase of the minimum wage. The Fair Labor Standards Amendments of 1961 were enacted, raising the minimum wage on September 3, 1961 to $1.15 per hour and on September 3, 1963 to $1.25 per hour. The administration of President Lyndon B. Johnson enacted the Fair Labor Standards Amendments of 1966, raising the minimum wage to $1.40 per hour on February 1, 1967 and to $1.60 per hour on February 1, 1968 (U.S. House of Representatives, 1989, Education and Labor Committee, No. 101-160, pp. 10–11).

In the Supreme Court case of *Maryland v. Wirtz* in 1969, the Court ruled that the inclusion of state institutions under the FLSA by Congress did not exceed Congress's power under the Commerce Clause. In 1976, the Supreme Court overruled the *Wirtz* decision of 1969 and ruled that the Fair Labor Standards Amendments of 1966 and 1974, which had broadened the coverage of the Act to local and state governments, were unconstitutional to the extent that they interfered with the integral or traditional governmental functions of states and their political subdivisions. This decision, known as *National Leagues of Cities v. Usery*, only pertained to the minimum hourly wage rate and maximum hours provisions of the FLSA (U.S. House of Representatives, 1989, Education and Labor Committee, Report 101-11, pp. 8–9).

On November 1, 1977, President Jimmy Carter signed into law the Fair Labor Standards Amendments of 1977. "It has been a step in the right direction," President Carter stated. "The overall impact of this bill is good." This legislation produced four increases in the minimum wage. Beginning on January 1, 1978, the minimum wage would rise to $2.65 per hour. On January 1, 1979, it would rise to $2.90 per hour, on January 1, 1980 to $3.10 per hour, and on January 1, 1991 to $3.35 per hour (*Public Papers*, 1977, p. 147).

In 1985, the Supreme Court made state and local governments subject to the wage, hours, and record-keeping requirements of the FLSA. In *Garcia v. San Antonio Metropolitan Transit Authority*, a sharply divided Court ruled that the application of the provisions of the FLSA regarding minimum wage and overtime pay is not a violation of the U.S. Constitution and contrary to the established practices of the American federal system (Garcia, 1985). David O. Stewart, writing in the *ABA Journal*, suggested that additional Court appointments by Ronald Reagan might result in an overturning of *Garcia* (Stewart, 1985). This situation has not occurred and is not likely to occur for the foreseeable future with the White House being occupied by President Bill Clinton.

For the entire duration of his administration, President Reagan and the Republicans in the Senate successfully blocked legislation designed to increase the minimum wage. The Democrats, especially Senator Kennedy and Representatives Hawkins and Murphy, fought hard to keep the issue on the public agenda (Rovener and Cohodas, 1987).

With President George Bush supporting a minimum wage increase in his 1988 campaign for the nation's highest office, the Democrats once again pushed ahead with the legislation. Still, a traditional legislative debate arose, with the Democratic Party supporting labor and the Republican Party supporting business. Although he vetoed HR2, the President never reneged on his promise to give an increase to $4.25 per hour as long as it was included in legislation providing for a training wage. The president could have vetoed any minimum wage legislation and been sustained by the 35 Republican senators pledged to support any position he took on the issue. As President Bush did not belong to the ultraconservative wing of the Republican Party, he was able to compromise with Senator Kennedy and the AFL-CIO to give a minimum wage increase that both the President and Senator Kennedy could call a "victory for American workers" (Pytte, 1989; *Weekly Compilation*, 1989, p. 1765).

IV. THE RELATIONSHIP BETWEEN COMPENSATION AND OTHER PERSONNEL PROCESSES

A well-integrated strategy for compensation within an organization will necessarily consider numerous definitions of fairness and equity when making final compensation policies. Questions addressing the issues of internal equity, external equity, and individual equity are all relevant and must be answered when arriving at final decisions (Buford, 1991).

Internal equity, the consideration of what relevant skills are worth within the organization, may involve a detailed analysis of critical job tasks, and the knowledge, skills, and abilities (KSAs) needed to perform them. It normally requires arranging similar tasks and KSAs into classifications based on the premise that a structured classification system will bring about more order and fairness in the allocation of work. It may also involve an internal comparison of one job to another and the setting of organizational priorities on job worth. External equity, the consideration of what relevant skills are worth to the world outside one's own organizational boundaries, may involve an analysis of the forces of supply and demand, and may require survey research techniques needed to ascertain the value of those skills to other competing organizations. Finally, individual equity, the consideration of personalized contributions and their worth to the organization, may involve procedures such as pay-for-performance systems, worth based on seniority, and other reward-based factors.

A. Internal Equity

Organizations will differ somewhat in the extent to which they place a value on internal positions. A legal position within a law firm may be more paramount in the overall value structure than a legal position in an automotive corporation. A clerical supervisor's position may be more valuable to the organization than any of the numerous typist positions being supervised. Internal equity involves assigning compensation values to jobs based on attributes of the job deemed important to the organization.

Job analysis, position classification, and job evaluation are three management control tools useful in making final policy decisions concerning internal equity. Job analysis provides useful information on job tasks that must be performed and on the knowledge, skills, and abilities need to perform such tasks (Flanagan, 1954; Fine and Wiley, 1971; McCormick et al., 1972; Primoff, 1975; Levine et al., 1983; Roark and Burnett, 1984; Ghorpade, 1988; Siegel, 1992). Once job descriptions detailing the job work activities have been written, and once job specifications detailing the worker characteristics necessary in order to perform such activities have been established, then the nature of the job has been documented. Job analysis information is useful for many elements of the personnel system (see Fig. 1) but has always been especially important in making compensation-type decisions.

Since the Position Classification Act of 1923, the concept of equal pay for equal work has been an important guidepost for compensation decisions (Shafritz, 1973; Shafritz et al., 1991). Job analysis allows the organizations to better define the nature of the work involved; position classification allows managers to better organize all jobs within the organization, delineate authority, establish the chain of command, and provide equitable salary scales (Shafritz, p. 139). Thus, based on job analysis information, we find a number of jobs where proofreading, typing, filing, and other clerical responsibilities are being performed. A classification labeled "clerk-typist" may be created. Because some jobs require only the following of minutely detailed instructions and other jobs in this family require coordination, prioritizing, and leadership, a classification series may be established. The entry level of clerk-typist I may be followed by clerk-typist II, III, and IV as the amount of discretion in decision making, leadership, and responsibility increases. Pay rates are then tied to the position levels. Over the years, as government has become more complex and the nature of government work more varied, there has been a massive accumulation in the number of position classifications within most governmental bureaucracies. Currently, at the state and local level, classifications range from as high as 7300 in New York to as low as 551 in South Dakota (Winter, 1993). Recently, there have been calls for a complete revamping of the current systems of position classification used in the federal government. These advocates of reform favor a more flexible system of fewer broad-based classifications that would allow managers more discretion and authority (Cipolla, 1993). These efforts toward change will be discussed in a later section of this chapter.

Job evaluation is also an important management tool useful in making compensation decisions related to internal equity. Although there are numerous methodologies of job evaluation, they all involve using information on the nature of the job to determine the relative worth of different jobs to the organization (U.S. Civil Service Commission, 1965; Remsay, 1976; Treiman, 1979; Ganschinietz and McConomy, 1983; Siegel, 1992). Either implicitly or explicitly these systems consider jobs in relation to numerous factors considered important internally by the organization. Factors such as knowledge required, skill, effort, responsibility, external contacts, and supervision required are used to make internal job worth decisions. In some job evaluation systems, points are assigned for each of the various job factors deemed important, and point totals for each job can then be derived. Jobs can be compared to each other based on a point total standard.

Recently, the concept of comparable pay for work of comparable value to the organization or comparable worth has become an important issue within the field of compensation administration. Women have argued that for decades personnel systems built during earlier "male-dominated" times have resulted in the perpetuation of sex discrimination into current compensation decisions (*Gunther v. County of Washington*, 1981; Remick, 1981; *AFSCME v. The State of Washington*, 1985; Wittig and Turner, 1988). The issue of comparable worth has been fought in courts of law and across the table in collective bargaining sessions, and has served to place a more intense public spotlight on what were once arcane and mysterious personnel procedures.

B. External Equity

Organizations are constantly competing for skilled employees. Even in situations where the number of applications for a position may be numerous, the more relevant consideration may be the

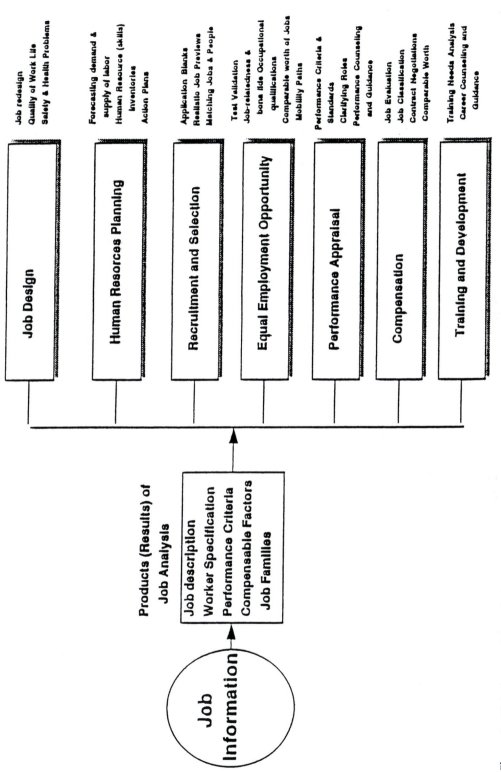

Figure 1 Links between job analysis and human resource management. (From Ghorpade, 1988, p. 6.)

quality of the applicant pool. In many public sector jurisdictions where 100 applicants may be received for one midlevel position, a crucial question that should be posed is, "Are these the best 100 applicants that could be received?" Many times, because the public sector does not take the time to investigate external equity considerations, the quality of service offered to the public may not be as high as is desirable.

In order to remain competitive for human resources in the external market, data on wage rates and benefits packages offered by competing organizations are a necessity. These data are normally obtained through wage and salary surveys. Important considerations in these surveys include determining the relevant labor market, the sample of organizational jobs to be included in the survey (benchmark jobs), and the outside organizations to be surveyed. General types of information needed from these organizations consist of items such as pay, benefits packages, size of the organization, and type of job evaluation systems used. More detailed information for each job in the sample may include, among other things, job titles, job descriptions, supervision given and received, and minimum qualifications used (Wallace and Fay, 1983; Siegel, 1992).

Once information such as that above has been collected, it is possible to begin to think in terms of developing an actual pay structure. In establishing the pay structure data from the external market survey, it is combined with the internal results of the job analysis and job evaluation studies. As can be seen in Fig. 2 and 3, a scatter diagram can be created graphically depicting the relationship between points from the job evaluation results (horizontal axis) and salary data from the external market survey (vertical axis). Benchmark jobs can then be located along the scatter diagram giving managers some idea as to their relative monetary value, based on internal and external equity considerations (Buford, 1991).

C. Individual Equity

Attention to the concept of individual equity can also be incorporated into this wage structure. Variations in compensation within an organization are necessary based on the individual characteristics of job holders. In systems where seniority is given a high priority, those employees who have been in a position for longer periods of time are given some financial credit for this factor. In systems where merit-based pay is an important decision-making criterion, employees who score higher on performance appraisals or produce more for the organization are usually entitled to differential pay increases. These programs have met with varying levels of success (Gabris and Mitchell, 1988; Perry and Petrakis, 1988; Lewis, 1991; Taylor and Vest; 1992; Siegel, 1992; Kellough and Lu, 1993).

These individual equity considerations are handled through the establishment of different pay grades and pay ranges within each of the pay grades. Individuals, through their own longevity or effort, can move through these pay grades and pay ranges at varying frequencies. For instance, a given pay range may contain 10 steps with each step representing a 1% pay increment. If an employee receives an outstanding performance appraisal, this may allow him or her to gain a three-step (3%) pay increase. Another employee who receives an average performance appraisal may only be entitled to a one-step (1%) pay increase.

Compensation determination is a complicated decision-making process in most organizations. Managers wish to be competitive externally and to have a solid internal rationale for final compensations policies. They also wish to create a compensation system that will allow for individual differences to be recognized and to reward those employees making the most valuable contributions to the organization. As the personnel field has become more legalistic over the past several decades, it is of paramount importance for managers to have a solid, defensible, nondiscriminatory rationale for their compensation decisions. Through the personnel management processes of

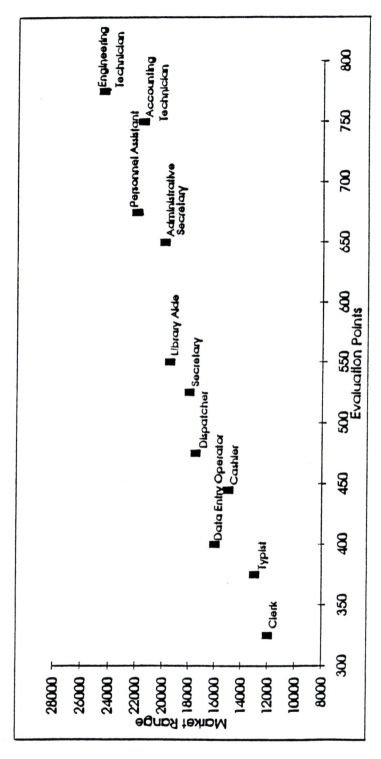

Figure 2   Scatter diagram for key clerical and technical jobs. (From Buford, 1991, p. 305.)

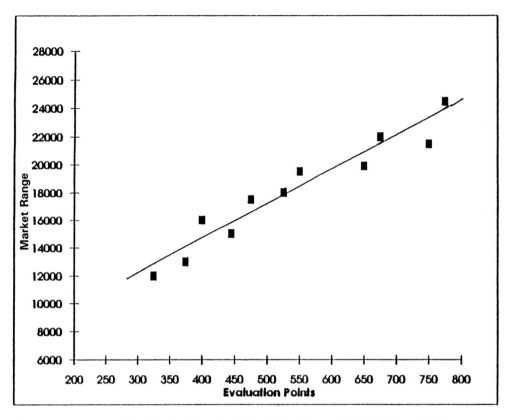

Figure 3   Wage trend line for clerical and technical jobs. (From Buford, 1991, p. 306.)

job analysis, job evaluation, market surveys, and performance appraisal systems, managers should be able to bring about a higher level of internal, external, and individual equity in arriving at their final compensation policies.

V.   PAY INNOVATIONS

Dissatisfaction with pay levels is not an uncommon occurrence within organizations; yet the magnitude of this dissatisfaction in the federal government has in recent years been growing to alarming levels. In poll results of over 4000 federal executive reported in 1988, 70% felt that their pay was unfair, and 74% felt that the merit pay and bonus systems being used in the federal government were unfair (Shafritz, 1991, p. 152).

Since the Pay Comparability Act of 1970, the federal government has been legally committed to the concept of pay comparability between federal pay rates and private sector pay rates for similar work, although it is not surprising that in tough economic times our political will has not matched our legal obligation. The salary gap between the federal wage rates and those in the private sector has been continuing to increase to the point where today common estimates place the gap at between 20% and 40% (Volcker Commission, 1989; U.S. GAO, April 1991) (see Fig. 4). A history of federal pay increases since 1978 can be seen in Table 1 (U.S. GAO, May 1990). This gap is particularly exaggerated in some urban areas. Average pay differences by 22 metropolitan

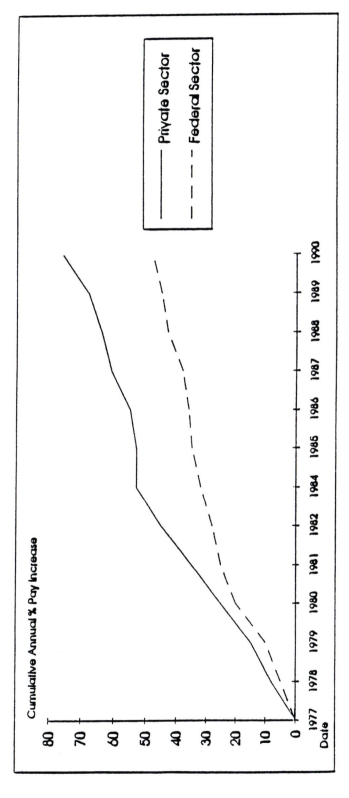

Figure 4 The federal/private sector pay gap has steadily widened since 1977. (From Recruitment and retention, General Accounting Office Report,

Table 1 History of General Schedule Pay Adjustments, % (1978–1990)

Month/year	Pay agent[a] determination	Increase provided	Pay gap
Oct 78	8.40	5.50	2.90
Oct 79	10.41	7.00	3.41
Oct 80	13.46	9.10	4.36
Oct 81	15.10	4.80	10.30
Oct 82	18.47	4.00	14.47
Jan 84	21.51	4.00	17.51
Jan 85	18.28	3.50	14.78
Jan 86	19.15	0.00	19.15
Jan 87	23.79	3.00	20.79
Jan 88	23.74	2.00	21.74
Jan 89	26.28	4.10	22.18
Jan 90	28.62	3.60	25.02

Source: Federal pay, General Accounting Office (GAO) Report, May 1990, p. 5.
[a] The president's pay agent (currently the secretary of labor and the directors of the Office of Management and Budget and the Office of Personnel Management) reports annually to the president on the pay adjustments necessary to keep federal pay with private sector pay.

statistical areas are displayed in Table 2 (GAO, April 1991). In its 1988 report entitled *Civil Service 2000*, the Office of Personnel Management (OPM) decried the fact that federal pay was noncompetitive (Johnston, 1988). In 1989, the Volcker Commission called for significant salary increases for the federal civil service.

These gaps have come about during times when federal, state, and local governments have been facing economic shortfalls requiring retrenchment and curtailments of basic services in order to balance budgets. In the federal government, the political climate had demanded "revenue-neutral" solutions to fiscal problems. Therefore, any cost increases for salary enhancements must be balanced by cuts in other administrative areas.

Recently, Secretary of Agriculture Mike Espy suspended employee award programs within his department. In doing this, he made it clear that he is not opposed to rewarding good employees, but that we must rethink every aspect of government. Under congressional budget reconciliation proposals, cash rewards and bonus programs that had become a staple of the federal employment system since they were established by Congress in 1954 were scheduled to be eliminated. Although studies indicate that savings to the government and to the American taxpayer far exceeded the monetary amounts of the awards themselves; in this climate, politically, they seem impossible to justify (Desky, 1993).

Recent policy initiatives indicate that this political climate is not likely to change. A report of the National Commission on the State and Local Public Service (Winter Commission) recently called for substantial changes in the civil service systems operated by state and local governments. Among the changes bearing directly on compensation, the report advocated simplifying the classification system; allowing "greater flexibility in rewarding good employees;" using "a small number of broad pay bands, usually three, to replace the complicated grade-and-step system currently in place" (Winter, 1993). Other areas of the report called for a reevaluation of the current pay-for-performance systems with an eye toward innovations such as "team-based pay-for-performance systems," and "gain sharing"—workers being allowed to split the saving from higher productivity efforts. Recently, the Clinton/Gore administration announced its game plan for "re-

Table 2   Average Private Sector Pay Advantage in 22 MSAs as of January 1, 1989

MSA	Average annual salary		Average private sector pay advantage	
	Federal	Private	$	%
Atlanta, GA	28,575	35,008	6,433	22.50
Baltimore, MD	31,350	37,183	5,833	18.60
Boston, MA	31,704	37,921	6,217	19.60
Chicago, IL	29,848	36,929	7,081	23.70
Dallas, TX	28,836	36,172	7,337	25.40
Dayton–Springfield, OH	34,491	37,540	3,049	8.80
Denver, CO	31,541	39,632	8,091	25.70
Detroit, MI	29,543	38,521	8,979	30.40
Harrisburg–Lebanon–Carlisle, PA	25,609	28,560	2,950	11.50
Houston, TX	39,468	52,884	13,416	34.00
Indianapolis, IN	29,189	34,406	5,216	17.90
Kansas City, MO–KS	26,447	30,909	4,462	16.90
Los Angeles–Long Beach, CA	27,734	36,716	8,982	32.40
New York, NY	27,805	36,115	8,310	29.90
Oakland, CA	27,303	35,545	8,242	30.20
Philadelphia, PA	28,153	35,008	6,856	24.40
St. Louis, MO	28,034	33,648	5,614	20.00
San Antonio, TX	21,740	23,049	1,309	6.00
San Diego, CA	26,643	33,942	7,299	27.40
San Francisco, CA	26,080	36,269	10,189	39.10
Seattle, WA	27,744	32,396	4,552	16.40
Washington, DC	33,903	40,668	6,765	20.00

Source: Federal pay, General Accounting Office (GAO) Report, April 1991, p. 5.

inventing government," which will call for further sacrifices among federal employees and additional downsizing of the federal work force (National Performance Review, 1993).

In this climate, new ideas about governmental systems are being demanded and civil service classification and compensation systems designed for an earlier day and time are being questioned. It is clear that given the current political climate, for public employees to enhance their financial standing, these improvements will have to be tied to increased productivity, performance, and results. It is with this thought in mind that the remainder of this section will explore some current pay innovations currently in process.

One noteworthy pilot research project commissioned by OPM under authority of the Civil Service Reform Act of 1978 is the Navy Personnel Management Demonstration Project ("China Lake") begun in 1980 in two California locations. Normal civil service regulations were waived for this project by Congress. The time frame for the project has also been extended by Congress and it is now scheduled to continue until 1995. The main thrust of this effort was to do away with the current cumbersome, rigid government classification structure and substitute a simpler classification system that consolidates a multitude of job series into five career paths, and combines several government service grades into broad pay bands—up to six (USMSPB, 1992). Here, the philosophy was that fewer overall grades with broader within-grade levels would allow managers more flexibility (Shafritz et al., 1991, p. 132). With this simpler design, compensation was then tied to performance using a performance appraisal system. Additional features of this project included higher than the minimum starting salaries for new hires and the use of recruitment bonuses (USMSPB, 1992).

A second project similar to the China Lake experiment is called the PACER SHARE (Gilbert and Nelson, 1989). This venture was implemented in February 1988 at McClellan Air Force Base, California, and is currently scheduled to expire in 1993. The effort is loosely based on the principles of total quality management (TQM) espoused by Dr. W. Edwards Deming (USMSPB, 1992) and, like China Lake, involves experimentation with a more simplified version of the classification system. The simpler structure consolidates 66 job series into six broad categories and combines white collar and blue collar pay grades into four broad bands. Additionally, a group performance rating is used instead of the individual performance rating, and the concept of gain sharing is employed. Within this system organizational productivity efforts are rewarded by distributing any cost savings equally between the agency and employees. Using this system, cost savings are only realized if the same work is performed for fewer labor dollars or more work is performed for the same labor costs (USMSPB, 1992). One additional feature of the PACER SHARE project that distinguishes it from the earlier China Lake project is that it takes place in a union environment (Shafritz et al., 1991).

The PACER SHARE project was only begun in 1988 and has not been as thoroughly evaluated as the China Lake experiment. PACER SHARE was immediately hit with budgetary shortfalls and unusual union configurations that have delayed thorough evaluation, but early results were labeled "very promising" (Shafritz et al., 1991, p. 133).

Initial evaluations of the China Lake project concluded that pay banding was a workable solution; however, most importantly in our revenue-neutral public sector economic environment, initial studies showed that overall salary costs at China Lake increased 6% over salary costs at the control sites. A later evaluation by OPM showed that pay levels at the control sites later caught up to those at the demonstration project levels (Shafritz et al., 1991). A more recent evaluation by OPM of these two projects plus a third similar project conducted by the National Institute of Standards and Technology (NIST) found that under broad banding it is easier to simplify classification than to contain salary costs. After more than 10 years of operation of the U.S. navy demonstration project, the additional cost of the system was around 2% of payroll (Schay, 1993). It was also found that this system may work more smoothly in organizations "looking to support a new culture, with effective communication channels and performance management systems in place. Organizations least likely to benefit from banding are those with a strong existing culture that values a traditional organizational hierarchy" (Schay, 1993). The OPM evaluation found that white collar, scientific, and professional organizations such as the navy and NIST programs accepted broad banding more than the mixed blue and white collar environments of the PACER SHARE experiment—a more traditional hierarchical organization (Schay, 1993).

It seems safe to conclude, at least at this point, that the jury is still out on both of these experiments; however, both offer some promise for simplifying and adapting an excessively rigid classification system that seems to cause more problems that it controls, and for developing new compensation options allowing more discretion for managers to reward both individual and group-based performance. This change may not arrive until the distant future, however, since OPM recently accepted a report of a working group of the Interagency Advisory Group of Personnel Directors that it not make government wide fundamental change or institute the broad banding model recommended in a 1992 study by the National Academy of Public Administration (NAPA). This negative decision comes at a time when more and more major corporations in the private sector are beginning to implement the broad banding concept in their organizations. In a recent report by Hewitt Associates, broad banding was described as "the most significant change in administering pay in the last two decades" (Cipolla, 1992).

VI. UNIONS AND PUBLIC SECTOR COMPENSATION

Since the passage of Proposition 13 in California in 1979, public sector unions have faced an increasingly hostile economic and political environment. Unions traditionally fare better in times of economic growth, and such times have only been distant memories for the vast majority of public sector officials. Instead of growth, most public sector jurisdictions have been faced with financial shortfalls necessitating the curtailment of public services, the imposition of user fees, and the reduction of the public sector work force. Politically, this time period included the well-publicized decertification of the PATCO union as Ronald Reagan drew the proverbial line in the sand, challenging the right of public employee unions to engage in illegal strikes. He also followed up by hiring replacement air traffic controllers to take the place of those PATCO members given notices of job termination.

At the local level, taxpayers have increasingly looked over the shoulders of elected officials as they have negotiated collective bargaining agreements. This taxpayer resistance combined with economic uncertainties has allowed other elected public officials to become more hardened and defiant in their bargaining postures, much to the detriment of the interests of public employee unions.

In the private sector, collective bargaining traditionally includes the right to bargain over pay. In the public sector, different laws and policies at each level of government in our federal system serve to regulate the collective bargaining process for public unions.

At the federal level, compensation is not a negotiable issue under the Civil Service Reform Act of 1978 (CSRA of 1978). For the vast majority of federal employees, their pay is set by a well-institutionalized process of moving through pay grades based on seniority and on performance indicators. Laws such as those discussed earlier in this chapter serve to regulate federal pay. In selected agencies of the federal government, because of past laws establishing alternative pay systems, pay is a bargainable issue. Two examples of this ability to bargain are the Tennessee Valley Authority (TVA) and the U.S. Postal Service (USPS).

At the state and local levels, in those two-thirds of the states that have institutionalized collective bargaining processes, it is more common to find pay to be a bargainable issue than at the federal level. Even here it is common to find legal limits set on many compensation issues such as pensions, health care, use of sick leave, and so on. (Coleman, 1990, p. 165).

Wherever collective bargaining takes place in the public sector, unions have been negatively impacted in some way by this changed political and economic climate. Whereas in the past unions might have bargained for pay increases, dental riders, and increased numbers of positions, the current collective bargaining climate for unions has forced them to change their bargaining strategies. Instead of negotiating an increased number of positions, they are now bargaining to maintain current staffing levels and avoid layoffs. Instead of negotiating pay increases, they are often bargaining to avoid pay reductions. A victory may indeed be maintaining a flat level of pay from the previous budget or bargaining a "golden parachute" for employees forced to retire because of cutbacks.

Even though unions have suffered in recent years, the public sector remains a segment of the work force that is heavily unionized. Within the federal government approximately two-thirds of the work force is represented by a union while approximately one-third of federal workers actually belongs to a union. At the state and local levels, approximately 45% of all workers belong to labor organizations (Kearney, 1992, pp. 21, 27). These percentages far exceed the percentages of private sector workers belonging to unions.

Public sector managers cannot afford to treat public employee unions lightly in the collective bargaining process. The unilateral relationships that existed with regard to pay policies in the past is fundamentally transformed when unions are present and have the right to bargain over compensation issues. No longer can the relationship be considered unilateral; it is now either bilateral or even multilateral in nature.

Particularly at the state and local levels where bargaining over pay is more common, employee unions can have a major impact on the city's budgetary process both through the substance of the negotiations and through delaying the highly politically charged time frame of the annual budget cycles. By effecting delays, local unions can drag out the bargaining process to the point where the budget is not submitted to the legislative body for its final approval in a timely manner. Under these conditions, management believes that it loses control. These feelings may arise because of a need for supplemental appropriations to continue operations when deadlines are not met, or because of intense pressures for settlement when budget deadlines are missed (Kearney, 1992, p. 166).

Based on the accumulated literature, the results of such negotiations have advantaged workers who are union members or who are covered under union contracts. Unions have had an impact on the pay process in public sector jurisdictions. The presence of unionization and collective bargaining tends to drive salaries and wages upward (Gallagher, 1978; Kearney, 1979; Zax, 1988; Louis and Stein, 1989; Valletta, 1989; Benecki, 1991). As Richard Kearney stated, "The mere presence of unions may influence compensation policies even in the absence of collective bargaining, through union lobbying and pressure activities" (1992, p. 179).

Although most of the evidence indicates that unions do have an upward pressure on employee salaries, the studies giving rise to these statements take place in a real-world setting; and, unlike a laboratory setting when every variable can be controlled, in the real world little external control is possible. The levels of organizational budgets and the percentages of those budgets devoted to employee pay and benefits are functions of a wide array of political and economic factors. For instance, bargaining laws regulating unions vary considerably from jurisdiction to jurisdiction below the federal level. Governmental structures such as mayor-council forms vs. city manager forms, nonpartisan elections, and at-large constituencies may impact the strength of unions and the shape of city budgets. Economic factors such as unemployment rates, city size, cost of living, and educational levels of the labor force may directly impact pay policies. Politically, factors such as hiring freezes, pay caps, and pay parity policies (e.g., between policemen and firemen within a given jurisdiction) may impact the role that unions can have.

Modern day unions may even provide a mechanism for savings to the taxpayer. This can come about because unions recognize that excessive gains for their employees may eventually provoke a taxpayer backlash. This backlash gives public officials enhanced power at the bargaining table and a redress of the imbalance in the union—management relationship will be achieved (Kearney, 1992, p. 192). Or this savings may be as a result of newly developed and innovative programs whereby the unions voluntarily cooperate with management in areas where they both stand to benefit. Examples of successful productivity bargaining programs reducing overtime pay (Mankin, 1977) or badly needed improvements in city sanitation efforts (Holzer, 1988) are only two among many. Joint labor–management committees (LMCs) have also made great strides in reducing the number and costs of accidents and illnesses on the job, and in implementing employee assistance programs (EAPs), which help to reduce employee dependency on alcohol and illegal drugs (Coleman, 1990, p. 114).

In summary, although the political and economic climate has been unfavorable to unions in recent years, modern unions are important public sector partners with management in compensation issues. Although compensation is generally not negotiable at the federal level, it is often thrown on the bargaining table at the state and local levels. Available evidence indicates that unions have had an upward impact on their members' compensation in the past and that unions can be formidable challengers to the timely closure of the annual budgetary process during negotiations. Unions have also worked voluntarily with management to achieve savings where the interests of their members were better served.

VII. FRINGE BENEFITS

In addition to salary and wages, governmental employees receive a number of "benefits." This compensation, which is most often called fringe benefits, is an important complement to employee cash compensation in that it helps government to provide a total compensation package that allows it to compete with the private sector in the recruitment and retention of employees. One of the key reasons for the growth of benefit packages is that fringe benefits are often of greater direct benefit to the employee than is the case with a salary or wage adjustment and these forms of compensation are not taxed (Hills, 1987, p. 90).

Some benefits such as health insurance, life insurance, and retirement plans are parts of traditional fringe benefit packages offered public employees, but the benefits picture is changing. No longer do we have the "typical" family situation where the father works outside the home with the mother not in the work force. The divorce rate, dual-career families, and the growth of single-family households have placed pressure on benefits systems that were designed for the single wage earner in the family with the mother not working outside the home (Chen, 1982, pp. 13–14).

With the changing demographics of the work force, the trend has been to investigate and implement new approaches to serving the needs of a changing work force that has more women and larger numbers of single parents for whom such services as child care are a critical need. But just as there is a call for a changing set of supplemental benefits to meet the needs of today's work force, there also exists tremendous pressure to control the costs of employee compensation.

Benefits to an employee are of critical importance. A Gallup survey sponsored by the Employee Benefit Research Institute indicates that by far the most important benefit to employees is that of health care coverage. Second in the hierarchy of benefit needs is that of retirement but a poor second relative to health insurance. It is apparent that with the downsizing of large corporations and the movement of many of these persons into new, small business, the total coverage is declining to the point where only 50% of all workers are projected to have health care coverage by the year 2000 (Salisbury, 1992, pp. 8–10).

The fringe benefits program offered by government represents a significant financial commitment. These programs, including health care, life insurance, retirement, and other benefits, approach 30–40% of government's employee compensation (Grossman, 1991; Kearney and Sears, 1985). From data collected in 1989 and 1990 from a comprehensive survey of private sector employers and state and local governments, the magnitude of the private/public sector commitment to benefit packages becomes much clearer. Overall, 80% of private sector employees are eligible for health care benefits whereas 93% of state and local government employees have these benefits. Another area of disparity is that of employer-provided life insurance. Here, nearly 9 of 10 state and local government employees have such a benefit available whereas only 4 of 5 private sector employees have a comparable benefit program—although life insurance programs are available in nearly every large corporation (Grossman, 1991).

In the matter of retirement benefits, virtually all state and local employees have a retirement program in which they may participate; in contrast, less than two-thirds of the private sector employees have defined pension programs in addition to federal social security. However, a much larger proportion (40%) of private sector employers than their state and local government (23%) have available a pension plan wholly financed by the employer (Grossman, 1991).

An area of great and growing interest to employees is that of the flexible benefits or cafeteria plan. Such plans from the employees' point of view have the appeal of the choice of utilizing only those benefits that are needed. Thus, if a spouse's benefits plan provides coverage such as health care, then the employee would be able to choose another benefit of direct utility such as financed educational leave or dependent care assistance (Meisenheimer and Wiatrowski, 1989).

The problem from an employer standpoint is that, as might be expected, employees are rational in their choice of specific benefits in that they select one that they will utilize. When a flexible benefits package is instituted rather than a standard benefits package for all employees, the result is a program that employees prefer, but it is also a program more expensive to administer (Kearney, 1985).

The pressures for changes from the standard package to the flexible package are due to changes in the composition of the American work force. Between 1968 and 1988, the percentage of women in the work force grew from 37% to 48% and the expectation is that this trend will continue. In addition, during this period the number of dual-income families has grown from 45% to 57% of the work force. Thus, persons in these situations are more interested in leave and child care programs that would not have been necessary in years past (Meisenheimer and Wiatrowski, 1989, p. 18).

While there is greater interest in flexible plans, they have been relatively slow to develop with only 13% of the work force covered by such programs in 1988. These plans are seldom an option for government employees and provide generally for cash compensation in lieu of foregoing health care and life insurance benefits. Increased vacation or sick leave does not seem to be an option in the relatively few public jurisdictions that provide flexible benefits (Meisenheimer and Wiatrowski, 1989, pp. 18–21).

With historically high federal budget deficits and revenue growth being relatively stagnant due to a less than robust economy at the state and local levels, governments have been under enormous pressure to control costs. In the 1980s, the focus of fringe benefit cost control was in the area of health care. Over a number of recent years the costs of health care have exceeded the rise in the rate of inflation. As major financiers of personal health care through Medicare, Medicaid, and other programs, federal and state governments have become increasingly concerned with the control of these costs. Thus, many states are implementing provisions for enhanced outpatient surgery, second options for elective surgery, and other programs, such as HMOs, which focus on prevention (Chollet and Friedland, 1987).

In sum, while the benefits area is likely to experience the greatest escalation of costs and a resultant battle over the level of benefits, the remainder of the 1990s will see substantial contention in the debate over the level of benefits in general. As well, if benefits programs are not managed carefully and spending escalates at a rapid rate, then it is less likely that employing organizations will be able to adjust and further expand their benefits programs to meet changing conditions (DeCengo, 1990).

VIII. CONCLUSION

The level of employee compensation is a critical variable in the politics and administration of government in the United States. As a variety of interests have sought increased compensation for work performed, this field has experienced a great deal of change, especially since the years of Franklin Roosevelt's New Deal. These changes accelerated in the 1960s because of a dramatically changing work force whose demographics carry with them a different set of needs than was the case with the married male who was the family breadwinner for the majority of the work force.

Now the growing number of once underrepresented minorities, single heads of families, and dual-career wage families has effected a changed set of salary and fringe benefit needs to which governments are continually attempting to respond. Advocacy for and experimentation with comparable worth, flexible classification systems, "cafeteria" benefits programs, and other innovations of compensation delivery have been and will be the reality of public sector compensation programs for the remainder of the 1990s.

Federal deficits and stagnant revenues at the state and local levels guarantee that government will be pressured to manage efficiently their employee compensation systems as seldom as has been the case in U.S. history. While the pressure of fiscal constraints tends to restrict the broadening of compensation levels, the changing demographics of the work force and the fact that a large majority of the public work force is represented by unions ensure that government will be forced to grapple with work force demands and that compensation will remain a paramount public personnel issue.

ACKNOWLEDGMENT

The authors acknowledge Mark A. Tyler's invaluable assistance in the preparation on this chapter.

REFERENCES

AVSCME v. The State of Washington, 770 F. 2d. 1401 (1985).

America in Transition: Benefits for the Future (1987). Employee Benefit Research Institute, Washington, DC.

Benecki, S. (1991). Municipal expenditure levels and expenditure levels and collective bargaining, *Ind. Rel., 17* (May): 216–230.

Berg, G. (1989). Frances Perkins and the flowering of economics and social policies, *Monthly Labor Rev., 112* (June): 28–32.

Bucci, M. (1991). Growth of employer-sponsored group life insurance, *Monthly Labor Rev. (October)*: 25–32.

Buford, J. A. (1991). *Personnel Management and Human Resources in Local Government*, Center for Governmental Services, Auburn, AL, pp. 263–330.

Chen, Y. (1982). Changing family role: their impact on benefit programs, *America in Transition: Implications for Employee Benefits* (Dallas L. Salisbury, ed.), Employee Benefit Research Institute, Washington, DC.

Chollet, D.J., and Friedland, R.B. (1987). Health care costs and public policy toward employee health plans, *Rev. Public Personnel Admin., 7* (Summer): 60–73.

Cipolla, F.P. (1992). Classification reform: more than a technical matter, *Periscope, 13* (Sept.): 5.

Coleman, C.J. (1990). *Managing Labor Relations in the Public Sector*, Jossey-Bass, San Francisco.

Crenshaw, P. (1990). Pay reform: is this the time? *The Bureaucrat, 19* (Summer): 11–17.

DeCenzo, D.A., and Holovich, S.J. (1990). *Employee Benefits*, Prentice-Hall, Englewood Cliffs, NJ.

Desky, J. (1993). Federal employee awards come under fire, *Public Admin. Times, 16* (August): 1.

Devens, R.M., Jr. (1992). The employee turnover and job opening survey, *Monthly Labor Rev. (March)*: 29–36.

Famulari, M., and Manser, M.E. (1989). Employer-provided benefits: employer cost versus employee value, *Monthly Labor Rev. (Dec.)*: 24–32.

Fay, C., Risher, J., and Hempel, P. (1991). Locality pay: balancing theory and practice, *Public Personnel Manage., 20* (Winter): 397–408.

Fine, S.A., and Wiley, W.W. (1971). *An Introduction to Functional Job Analysis*, Upjohn, Kalamazoo, MI.

Flanagan, J.C. (1954). The critical incidents technique, *Psychol. Bull., 15*: 327–358.

Ford, J. (1992). State-mandated employee benefits: conflict with federal law? *Monthly Labor Rev. (April)*: 38–42.

Gabris, G.T., and Mitchell, K. (1988). The impact of merit raise scores on employee attitudes: the Matthew effect of performance appraisal, *Public Personnel Manage., 17* (Winter): 369–385.

Gallagher, D.G. (1978). Teacher bargaining and school district expenditures, *Ind. Rel., 17*: 231–237.

Ganschinietz, B., and McConomy, S. (1983). Trends in job evaluation practices of state personnel systems, *Public Personnel Manage., 12* (Spring).

Garcia v. San Antonio Metropolitan Transit Authority, 469 U.S. 528 (1985).

Ghorpade, J.V. (1988). *Job Analysis: A Handbook for the Human Resource Director*, Prentice-Hall, Englewood Cliffs, NJ.

Gilbert, R.G., and Nelson, A. (1989). The Pacer Share demonstration project: implications for organizational management and performance evaluation, *Public Personnel Manage., 18* (Summer): 209–225.

Grossman, G.M. (1991). U.S. workers receive a wide range of employee benefits, *Monthly Labor Rev. (Sept.)*: 36–40.

Gunther v. County of Washington, 452 U.S. 161 (1981).

Hills, F.S. (1987). *Compensation Decision Making*, CBS, New York.

Holley, L.W. (1990). Pay reform and job classification, *The Bureaucrat, 19* (Summer): 40–42.

Holzer, M. (1988). Productivity in, garbage out: sanitation gains in New York, *Public Productivity Rev.* XI (Spring) 37–50.

Ingraham, P.W. (1993). Of pigs in pokes and policy diffusion: another look at pay-for-performance, *Public Admin. Rev., 53* (July/August): 348–356.

Johnston, W. (1988). *Civil Service 2000*, U.S. Government Printing Office, Hudson Institute, Washington, DC.

Kearney, R.C. (1979). The impact of police unionization on municipal budgetary outcomes, *Int. J. Public Admin., 1*(4): 361–379.

Kearney, R.C. (1992). *Labor Relations in the Public Sector*, 2nd. Ed., Marcel Dekker, New York. pp. 1–441.

Kearney, R.C., and Sears, C.J. (1985). Planning fringe benefits for the workforce of the future, *Public Admin. Q., 9* (Fall): 293–309.

Kellough, J.E., and Lu, H. (1993). The paradox of merit pay in the public sector, *Rev. Public Personnel Admin., 13* (Spring): 45–64.

Lawler, E.E. III (1990). *Strategic Pay: Aligning Organizational Strategies and Pay Systems*, Jossey-Bass, San Francisco.

Levine, E.L., Ash, R.A., and Bennett, N. (1980). Exploratory comparative study of four job analysis methods, *J. Appl. Psychol., 65*: 524–535.

Lewis, G.B. (1991). Pay and job satisfaction in the federal civil service, *Rev. Public Personnel Admin., 11* (Summer): 17–31.

Louis, G.B., and Stein, L. (1989). Unions and municipal decline, *Am. Pol. Q., 17* (April): 208–222.

Mankin, L.D. (1977). Public employee organizations: the quest for legitimacy, *Public Personnel Manage., 6* (Sept/Oct): 334–340.

McCaffery, R.M. (1988). *Employee Benefit Programs: A Total Compensation Perspective*, PWS-Kent, Boston.

McCormick, E.J., Jeanneret, P.R., and Mecham, R.C. (1972). "A study of job characteristics and job dimensions as based on the position analysis questionnaire (PAQ), *J. Appl. Psychol., 56*: 347–368.

Meisenheimer II, J.R. and Wiatrowski, W.J. (1989). Flexible benefits plans: employees who have a choice, *Monthly Labor Rev. (Dec)*: 17–23.

Milkovich, G.T., and Cogil, C.J. (1984). Measurement as an issue in analysis and evaluation of jobs, *Handbook of Wage and Salary Administration*, 2nd Ed. (M. L. Rock, ed.), McGraw-Hill, New York, 10/1–10/14.

National Performance Review (1993). *Creating a Government That Works Better and Costs Less*, U.S. Government Printing Office, Washington, DC.

Perry, J.L., and Petrakis, B.A. (1988). Can pay for performance succeed in government? *Public Personnel Manage., 17* (Winter): 359–367.

Primoff, E.S. (1975). *How to Prepare and Conduct Job-Element Examinations*, U.S. Government Printing Office, Washington, DC.

Public Papers of the Presidents, Jimmy Carter, 1977 (1977). U.S. Government Printing Office, Washington, DC.

Pytte, A. (1989). Ending minimum wage standoff took give and take from both sides, *Congr. Qu. Week. Rep., 47*: 2942–2943.

Remick, J. (1981). The comparable worth controversy, *Public Personnel Manage., 10* (Winter): 377–383.

Remsay, A.S. (1976). The new factor evaluation system of position classification, *Civil Service J., 16* (Jan–March).

Risher, H., and Fay, C. (1991). Federal pay reform: a response to an emerging crisis, *Public Personnel Manage., 20* (Fall): 385–395.

Roark, J.R., and Burnett, J.H. (1984). Objective methods of job analysis, *Handbook of Wage and Salary Administration*, 2nd. Ed. (M. L. Rock, ed.), McGraw-Hill, New York, 7/1–7/17.

Rovener, J., and Cohodas, N. (1987). Kennedy off and running with liberal agenda, *Congr. Q. Week. Rep., 45*: 117–119.

Salisbury, D.L. (1992). Introduction: the value of benefits, *Controlling the Costs of Employee Benefits* (Theresa Brothers, ed.), Conference Board, New York.

Schay, B.W. (1993). Broad banding: higher price tag or simplified system? *Periscope, 14* (Spring): 1, 6.

Shafritz, J.M. (1973). *Position Classification: A Behavioral Analysis for the Public Service*, Praeger, New York.

Shafritz, J.M., Riccucci, N.M., Rosenbloom, D.H., and Hyde, A.C. (1991). *Personnel Management in Government, Politics, and Process*, 4th Ed., Marcel Dekker, New York.

Siegel, G.B. (1992). *Public Employee Compensation and Its Role in Public Sector Strategic Management*, Quorum Books, New York.

Stanley, D.T. (1972). *Managing Local Government Under Union Pressure*, The Brookings Institution, Washington, DC.

Stewart, D.O. (1985). Court flip-flops on 10th amendment, *ABA J., 71*: 114–119.

Sturdivant, J.N. (1991). Challenges to the federal employer, *The Bureaucrat, 20* (Summer): 26–28.

Taylor, G.S., and Vest, M.J. (1992). Pay comparisons and pay satisfaction among public sector employees, *Public Personnel Manage., 21* (Winter): 445–454.

Treiman, D.J. (1979). *Job Evaluation: An Analytic Review*, National Academy of Science, Washington, DC.

U.S. Civil Service Commission (1965). *Basic Training Course in Position Classification*, U.S. Government Printing Office, Washington, DC.

U.S. General Accounting Office (GAO) (1990). *Federal Pay, Comparisons with the Private Sector by Job and Locality*, May, Washington, DC, pp. 1–70.

U.S. General Accounting Office (GAO) (1991). *Federal Pay, Private Sector Salary Differences by Locality*, April, Washington, DC, pp. 1–56.

U.S. House of Representatives (1989). Fair Labor Standards Amendments of 1989, Report 101-11, Committee on Education and Labor, Washington, DC.

U.S. House of Representatives (1989). Fair labor standards amendments of 1989, Report 101-260, Committee on Education and Labor, Washington, DC.

U.S. Merit Systems Protection Board (USMSPB) (1992). *Federal Personnel Research Programs and Demonstration Projects, Catalysts for Change*, Washington, DC, pp. 1–37.

Valetta, R.G. (1989). The impact of unionism on municipal expenditures and revenues, *Ind. Labor Rel. Rev., 42* (April): 430–442.

Volcker Commission (1989). *Report of the National Commission on the Public Service*, Washington, DC.

Wallace, Jr., M.J., and Fay, C.H. (1982). *Compensation Theory and Practice*, Kent, Boston, pp. 111–144.

Weekly Compilation of Presidential Documents (1989). Government Printing Office, Washington, DC, *25* (November 17): 1765.

Winter, W.F. (1993). Hard truths tough choices: excerpts from the first report of the national commission on the State and Local Public Service, *Governing, (August)*: 51.

Wittig, M.A., and Turner, G. (1988). Implementing comparable worth: some measurement and conceptual issues in job evaluation, *Comparable Worth, Pay Equity, and Public Policy* (R.M. Kelly and J. Bayes, eds.), Greenwood Press, New York, pp. 143–149.

Zax, J.S. (1988). Wages, non-wage compensation and municipal unions, *Ind. Rel., 27* (Fall): 301–317.

16

Pension Fund Management

N. JOSEPH CAYER   Arizona State University, Tempe, Arizona

I. INTRODUCTION

Most U.S. public jurisdictions offer retirement benefits in the form of pensions. Public pension funds have assets of more than $900 million and cover some 30 million employees and retirees (1993 Pensions Directory, 1993). Public employees have become nervous in recent years as they have observed many private pension systems reduce benefits or go broke entirely. While government pension funds seem to be in no danger of collapsing, they are stressed by many pressures (March, 1980; Hall and Smith, 1981; *Harvard Law Review*, 1977).

Public pension plans must address numerous issues among which are public policy regarding all aspects of pensions, type and level of benefit, who participates, type of governance or oversight of the plans, and funding and investment strategies of the plans. Internal management of the plans also requires attention to communicating with participants and managing day-to-day operations. This chapter attempts to address each of these major issues in terms of the problems associated with them and in terms of how the problems are addressed.

II. PENSION POLICY

Public pension plans exist at all levels of government. Of course, the national government has a retirement system that covers most of the federal service although there are specialized systems for some employees such as those in the foreign service. State and local government employees are covered by numerous systems as provided under state law (Klingner and Nutter, 1984; Retirement Research Committee Staff, 1992). While some states, such as Idaho and Mississippi, have one general system that covers all public employees, other states, such as Illinois and California, have statewide as well as local systems. Many states have a general plan as well as specialized systems for some employees, especially teachers, police, and fire personnel (Louisiana and Texas). Policies also differ as to whether participation is optional or mandatory for either employers or employees.

Retirement benefits tend to be relatively generous in the public sector, possibly because pay tends to lag behind the private sector. Retirement benefits often can be provided with the costs being passed on to future decision makers to deal with. As a result, it is politically easier for politicians to agree to improved pension provisions than to adopt higher pay structures that require immediate funding (Grosskopf, Hayes, and Sivan, 1983; Grosskopf, Hayes, and Kennedy, 1985).

National government policy also may affect pension plans although the U.S. Congress has been fairly systematic in excluding public systems from requirements imposed on private systems. For example, the Employment Retirement Income Security Act of 1974 (ERISA), which regulates private sector plans to protect participants, does not apply to the public sector. Similarly, fiduciary standards applied to private sector fund trustees do not apply to public pension systems (Klausner, 1986; Melbinger, 1992). The Tax Reform Act of 1986 does stipulate policy regarding taxability of pension benefits (Hennessy, 1987) and the Internal Revenue Code prohibits discrimination in benefit plans (Houk, 1989). Other general, nondiscrimination, and equal employment opportunity legislation may have impact on implementation of some retirement system pensions as well. State and local governments consistently oppose any efforts by Congress to impose ERISA regulations on them. Of course, individual states are at liberty to develop such standards for their own systems and Florida is touted by some as the model for reform along these lines (Klausner, 1986).

Systems are governed in varying ways as well. Typically, boards or commissions have responsibility for managing public pension funds. They make the policy and investment decisions although they normally have professional staff to run the day-to-day operations. Trustees sometimes find themselves in difficult positions, especially during times of fiscal austerity. Political leaders often see the retirement trust funds as attractive places from which to raid funds to help finance current services and general government activities. Trustees often find themselves in the middle between those political leaders and courts that hold them liable for the lack of funding (*Dadisman v. Moore*, 1988). Concerns of trustees who have a fiduciary responsibility to members of the plan and a report of a congressional task force are just two of the reasons that much attention has been focused on better management and control of public pension funds (U.S. Committee on Education and Labor, 1978).

III. TYPE AND LEVEL OF BENEFIT

Pension benefits usually are described as being either defined benefit or defined contribution plans depending on whether the benefit or contribution is fixed or variable (Lingo, 1984; Martin, 1989; Zorn, 1990). Most public sector systems are defined benefit plans while private sector retirement systems usually are defined contribution plans.

A. Defined Benefit Plans

Defined benefit plans are those in which the benefit is either a fixed amount or is determined by a formula. The formula usually factors in salary, age, and years of service. Thus, the benefit could be some flat percentage of salary (or average of salary over the last few years) at retirement, known as the flat benefit plan. Alternatively, a unit benefit formula would base the pension on a certain percentage (e.g., 2%) of salary multiplied by the number of years of service. There may be a minimum and a maximum benefit based on years of service. Defined benefit plans mean that the employees can count on a specific level of benefit at retirement based on the formula used by the system. Benefits do not result directly from the amount the employee contributes although the plans may, and usually do, require employee contributions.

Typically, defined benefit plans require a minimum of 5 or 10 years of service before an employee is guaranteed pension benefits or rights to take the money from the system upon leaving employment. This right to the benefit or the funds is known as vesting. Therefore, the employee is vested in the system after the prescribed period of time. Benefit formulae usually are applied to the highest 3 or 5 years of salary. The percentage applied to the salary also may vary over the years of service. Thus, annual salary may be multiplied by 1.5 for the first 10 years of service and 2.0 for the next 10 years and so on.

Minimum age requirements also tend to be part of the criteria for receiving benefits. Typically, 55, 60, and 62 years of age tend to be required of employees to qualify for retirement pensions. The Tax Reform Act of 1976 requires plans to start payout at 70-1/2 years regardless of whether the individual has retired.

Defined benefit plans have fixed benefits. Therefore, any change in level of benefits usually requires action by the pension system governing board or the jurisdiction's policymaking body. Many plans have provisions for some kind of cost-of-living adjustment (COLA). A formula usually exists for figuring the COLA; rarely is the pension adjusted to reflect 100% of cost-of-living increases. However, what is used to figure cost of living may bias the adjustment. The consumer price index (CPI) often is used as the basis for COLAs and many criticisms are raised regularly about some of the items included in figuring the CPI.

Defined benefit plans tend to favor the retiree's rights to benefits over the problems with adequately funding pension plans. As a result, policymakers are tempted to pass on costs to future policymakers and taxpayers. Costs are deferred to the future because it is easier for the policymakers to give the benefit if they do not have to find the funds to finance it (Moe, 1984). Any risks of the plan are the responsibility of the plan sponsor or the employer. From the employee's perspective, they are safe because they need not worry about loss of funding. In times of fiscal constraints, employers find it difficult to pay for the accumulated benefits of retirees (Mumy, 1978; Inman, 1982).

B. Defined Contribution Plans

Defined contribution plans require the participant to contribute some fixed amount, either a flat amount or a specified percentage of salary, to the plan over the course of employment. The amount contributed varies over time as earnings change. The amount of benefit varies depending on what the employee contributes over the course of employment and on the earnings on investment by the fund. The employee is not guaranteed any specified level of benefit upon retirement; rather, the benefit level depends on how much is put into the individual account of the employee. Typically, the employer and employee both contribute to the account. Earnings (ultimately paid as benefits) depend on how large the employee's account is, the employee's age at retirement, and how well the investments perform.

Defined contribution plans appear to be more fair to most people. The level of benefits corresponds to the level of contributions. The plans tend to be financially stable since benefits are paid only according to the ability of the plan to pay based on assets. Assets depend on contributions of participants as well as on how well the plan's funds perform on investments. The solvency of the plan tends to be favored over the level of benefit individuals receive. The participants in the plan bear the risks. Because defined contribution plans are fully funded, they do not exacerbate the fiscal woes of the jurisdiction. Because of these issues, public employers are looking increasingly at defined contribution plans, although defined benefit plans still dominate (Schaitberger, 1987; Vosti, 1993).

IV. WHO PARTICIPATES

Eligibility to participate in benefits programs, including pension plans, varies from jurisdiction to jurisdiction. Most public plans require all employees to participate, but increasingly, options are provided so that employees may have a choice of plans (Martin, 1989). Public universities are examples of systems where options exist. As a way of being competitive, public universities long have permitted faculty to participate in the state retirement system or to participate in an optional system such as the Teachers Insurance and Annuity Association and College Retirement Equities Fund. Now the options are even greater and employees other than faculty are given options. While the norm for other public employees still is mandatory participation in a particular retirement system, there are increasing numbers of cases where they can make their own choices (Haslanger, 1986). Thus, while participation in a retirement plan is required, employees are gaining choices among alternative plans.

Another aspect of who participates which has generated controversy is the inclusion of elected political officials in plans (Tilove, 1976; Zolkos and Phillip, 1992). Recent years have witnessed city councils and state legislatures placing themselves in such plans. While they typically have part-time salaries as elected officials, the pension plans often provide very generous benefits. The result is that taxpayers are forced to pay for these benefits, which often are out of proportion to what the full-time, permanent public service employee receives (Zolkos and Philip, 1992).

V. GOVERNANCE

Public pension systems are so numerous and varied that it is difficult to generalize about the ways in which they are governed (U.S. Bureau of the Census, 1987). Approximately half of the states have permanent commissions at the present time; the number keeps changing as commissions are established in reaction to some of the problems plans face (Salomone, 1989). Commissions have numerous functions including preparing the reports and recommendations on which policymakers develop policy for the systems. They also review proposed legislation and sponsor research into issues affecting their plans. Commissions typically have the responsibility for monitoring their state and local pension systems. Where commissions do not exist, pension plans may be administered by the human resources department or other agencies such as the budget and finance unit. In those cases, governance is viewed primarily as administrative in nature and the oversight function is provided by the policymaking body such as the state legislature or city council.

One of the major activities of the commission or administrator of the pension plan is serving as a trustee for the participants in the plan. The role of trustee involves making decisions on investment strategy for the plan. The investments and their implications are discussed in the following section. Here the role and responsibility of the trustee is examined.

Generally, trustees are governed by a fiduciary standard which binds trustees to "undivided loyalty to the fund or enterprise for which the trustee serves" (Langbein and Posner, 1980; *Meinhard v. Salmon*, 1928). As noted earlier, Congress has been systematic in exempting public pension systems from regulations applied to the private sector. Thus, the fiduciary standard spelled out above applies only if the states apply it through their statutes to their plans (Ingram and Copeland, 1982). Over the past few years, there have been numerous calls for national legislation to regulate public pension systems and apply the fiduciary standard to them because of concerns about the governance of public systems (Advisory Commission on Intergovernmental Relations, 1980). Participants in plans and elected political leaders have been alarmed by the lack of fiduciary standards, lack of reporting and disclosure of pertinent information about the system and the interests of the trustees, and conflict of interest. The Governmental Accounting Standards Board does now require public pension plans to publish financial reports and requires that certain information be included in them (Testin, 1991).

A recent controversy in Arizona in which the chairperson of the Arizona State Retirement System Board, another member, and the executive director all resigned over public disputes concerning pressure from one board member to direct investments to risky ventures is typical of problems that arise (Miller and Foster, 1993; Wiles, 1993). A similar situation led to controversy in Kansas (Chernoff and Philip, 1993; Vise, 1992). In most situations, the board or commission members tend to find themselves in the middle when political officials (governors or legislators) attempt to influence the investment policies and members of the system expect decisions based on investment performance and nothing else. As noted earlier, the State of Florida has passed reform legislation that addresses these concerns in that state.

The Internal Revenue Code also requires that plans treat all employees fairly. To do so, the managers of the plans must put all policies in writing and employees must be notified of available benefits. Standards require that the employee's spouse and dependents must also be covered. Another provision of the Code is that once established, the plan is expected to last indefinitely. These requirements usually are easily met by public sector plans although the quality of implementation varies.

Public pension systems often seem to be the last to adopt new technology in managing their plans. In recent years, however, efforts have been made by many state and local systems to improve management. In Oregon, for example, installation of a new retirement information management system has helped managers keep abreast of what is happening with their system and helped participants with better service (Amick, 1991). Other systems have utilized such technology as optical disks for managing records thus speeding service, reducing staffing needs, minimizing errors, saving space, and providing backup to stressed systems (Brown, 1991).

Another aspect of managing retirement systems is the integration or nonintegration with the social security system (Drucker, 1976; Haeworth, 1981 Universal Social Security Coverage Study Group, 1980;). Most private sector plans integrate social security benefits into their benefit formulas. Public sector plans, however, usually do not do so although there are exceptions. When plans are integrated, social security retirement benefits are taken into account in determining the appropriate level of benefits. With defined benefit plans, such integration would be particularly significant.

VI. FUNDING AND INVESTMENT STRATEGIES

A. Funding

Funding of public pension plans long has been problematic (Ehrenberg, 1980b; Metz, 1974; Munnell and Connolly, 1988; Zorn, 1987). As noted earlier, political leaders have from time to time attempted to curry political favor with public employees and system retirees by providing generous benefits to be paid in the future. They then move on to other offices or out of office and leave their successors with the responsibility of finding the money to pay for the benefits. Unfunded pension obligations have been very serious problems for state and especially local governments strapped for fiscal resources (Advisory Commission . . . , 1973; Mann, 1978; Ehrenberg, 1980a; Ferris, 1987). These funding problems are a feature of defined benefit programs as the benefits are guaranteed but the funding source is not always specified.

Funding may be on a pay-as-you-go basis or be provided for by reserve funding (Zorn, 1990; Testin, 1992). Pay-as-you-go is the system whereby obligations are funded as they arise. Thus, as employees retire and begin to receive benefits, the jurisdiction raises the revenue to cover the costs. In reserve funding, a retirement fund is established and both employees and employers typically contribute to it. The reserve fund also realizes income from return on investment. The fund is supposed to cover the cost of pension obligations although recent studies suggest that the majority of public pension plans are underfunded (Testin, 1992).

While most public funds now operate under reserve fund systems, there still are pay-as-you-go systems (U.S. Department of Commerce, 1980–1981). The state of Massachusetts is a good example of what often happens with pay-as-you-go systems. Prior to 1982, there were 105 different governmental retirement systems operating under state statute requiring pay-as-you-go financing (Whiston et al., 1985). Employees were deemed to have a contractual right to pension payments. At the same time, most of these systems did not use actuarial-based estimates for benefits. In 1983, state law was changed so that actuarial data had to be used and a Pension Reserves Investment Management Board (PRIM) was created to develop a statewide pooled investment fund, the Pension Reserves Investment Trust, which local governments could join. The separate systems may retain management of their own assets, or they may transfer assets to the PRIM board that will manage them, or they may purchase fund units from the Pension Reserves Investment Trust. As of 1985, governments in Massachusetts had $11 billion of unfunded pension obligations resulting from the old system of pay-as-you-go. The new program has gradually helped to finance those systems as state appropriations are available to those who join PRIM.

Underfunding or unfunded obligations are stated as a funding ratio. The funding ratio is figured by dividing plan assets by actuarial liability. The ratio should be 1; the lower it gets below 1, the less healthy a plan is. Some plans actually are overfunded meaning that they have ratios above 1, but they are the exceptions.

Reserve funding usually is recommended for a variety of reasons (Corriggio, 1987). Employers should be interested in reserve funding because the obligations can be planned for more carefully and bond ratings are not likely to be as affected by unexpected obligations. Reserve funding also makes negotiating with employee groups where that occurs more realistic as both sides can look at the projections for earnings of the funds and how they translate into available dollars for benefits. State and local governments are likely to face federal legislation requiring reserve funding if they do not do it on their own (Schwartz, Munley, and Aronson, 1983).

Employees have an obvious interest in reserve funding because the system protects their benefits. Reserve funding also provides better protection against retroactive reductions in benefits. Benefits also can be improved with good investments.

Reserve funding is in the best interest of the general public as well. Taxpayers benefit from the fact that reserve funding generally means that the ultimate cost to the public is lower because the reserve fund does earn interest to help with some of the costs. Also future fiscal problems are likely to be minimized with reserve funding.

Of course, defined contribution benefit systems do not pose as much of a funding problem. The funding decision is made up front in the level of contribution by the employer to the individual participant's account. Since benefits depend on how much is deposited in the specific account and on the return on investment of the retirement fund, the public jurisdiction does not have to be concerned about funding the benefit in the future.

In efforts to reduce current costs, many governments have developed incentives to get people to retire early (Jordan, 1992; LaRock, 1992). The rationale is that current expenditures from the general fund can be saved by getting people off the payroll. If the pension system already is funded, the costs are transferred there and current operating costs are reduced. Even if replacements are needed for some of the retirees, they usually can be hired at lower salaries. The rationale has been widely accepted, but the realities of practice do not seem to reflect the promise. Plans often are so attractive that many more people than expected accept the incentives (Jordan, 1992; Perlman, 1992). Often the early retirement programs fail because good plans are not in place to cover the work of those leaving. Often very good employees leave. Without careful planning and control, the agencies go right back and fill the positions of the retirees and the savings are not realized.

B. Investment Strategies

Investment strategies also have been the source of many problems for public pension systems (Hargadon and Shavers, 1989; Snell and Wolfe, 1990). Trustees of public pension funds have the responsibility to make investment decisions. It is expected that they have loyalty to the members of the system and may be covered by the fiduciary standard or other legal obligations requiring them to make their decisions based on the best interests of the members (Hutchinson and Cole, 1980). The prudent person principle usually applies to trustees of pension funds. That principle requires the trustee to

> act with the care, skill, prudence, and diligence under the circumstances that prevail that a prudent man acting in a like capacity and familiar with such matters would use in the conduct of an enterprise of a like character and with like aims (Employee Retirement Income Security Act, 1974).

In recent years, trustees have been under pressure from politically elected officials and others to make investment decisions on bases other than just the return on investment and security of the fund for members. Various plans for social investing and investing for economic development reasons are often pushed by elected officials and interest groups (Zorn, 1983). Social investing came about initially to foster certain social causes (Mares, 1979). For example, many pension plans, public and private, made decisions to divest themselves of stocks or other investments that had ties to the government and economy of South Africa as a way of bringing pressure on that government to abandon its policy of apartheid (Munnell, 1986). Other political or social causes may also be the source of investment decisions. Environmentalists may bring pressure to invest only in firms or activities that demonstrate a concern for protecting the environment.

Because assets of pension funds are large, public and private sector plans together have more than $3 trillion in assets, and are therefore very attractive targets for public officials looking for resources to fund government operations or to stimulate economic activity in the state or other jurisdiction (Litvak, 1981). Thus, pressure has mounted on public pension funds to target investment for such purposes (Munnell, 1983). For example, Alaska's public and teacher retirement systems targeted residential housing. During the oil boom those investments paid off, but now there are high delinquency rates on real estate loans and the plans are losing millions of dollars on their investments (Gregory, 1990). Kansas is another state in which public employee retirement systems lost large amounts of money in real estate investments (Chernoff and Philip, 1993).

Another interest of public policymakers is investment in home state activities so as to support local business and stimulate economic activity (Love, 1989). California, Connecticut, Kansas, and Los Angeles are examples of governmental jurisdictions that have engaged in these types of economically targeted investments, often with disastrous results for the pension funds (Vise, 1992). Even if the policy itself does not require such targeted investment, there often is a tendency for pressure to be placed on fund managers to favor local investment over others (Halpern and Halpern, 1990).

Even more alarming to many people is that state and local governments are viewing the assets of pension funds as sources of revenue to fund current programs and services (Deutschman, 1992; Zolkos, 1992; Chernoff, 1993). While the needs of state and local governments are great and taxpayers are reluctant to pay additional taxes, borrowing money from the pension assets proves to be a politically easy move in most cases. The problem in the long run is that those assets have to be restored so that benefits can be paid. At the same time, state borrowing from such funds usually does not carry interest or at least competitive interest with what can be earned by other investment. The result is that retirees are being asked to subsidize activities that should be the responsibility of the general citizenry and their governments.

Several factors normally determine investment decisions and their evaluation (McKenzie, 1989). Essentially return-oriented issues involve level of returns, returns relative to the plan's objectives, returns compared to other managers' performance, returns compared to indices such as stock indices or consumer price indices, volatility of returns, and allocation of assets. Other considerations include compliance with the plan's philosophy, guidelines, and processes for investment. The cost of investing, such as fees and the like, is also important. Ultimately, the satisfaction of the members with performance is the key issue. To insure that they react on the basis of accurate information, it is necessary to communicate effectively with them as well as all interested parties.

The performance of investments may be affected by the political decisions that direct investments in directions other than those related to return and health of the system. There is the potential for jeopardizing retirement security of retirees if the targeted investments do not work (Brauer, 1983).

Another ploy legislators use in balancing budgets is to manipulate the level of contribution they make to pension plans. They may just adjust the rate of contribution downward thereby saving money to apply to other parts of the budget. A more subtle method is to adjust the actuarial figures in such a way that estimates of the amount of money needed to fund the retirement system change (Melbinger, 1992). By changing actuarial figures to show a lower level of need, the amount that the state has to contribute can be reduced. Again, the long-term implications are not good for retirees or taxpayers. Eventually, the benefits have to be paid and taxpayers have to come up with the money or benefits have to be reduced. Neither is a positive outcome. Short-term benefits to the elected official tend to be the governing factor in these decisions. At the same time, these practices call attention to the plight of public pension funds and eventually may lead to congressional action to regulate public pension funds.

VII. CONCLUSIONS

Public sector pension plans are a major part of human resources systems (Siegel, 1992). They present challenges to public policymakers because they involve expectations of those who have given service to government and they cost money to operate. The interests of the members of the plans are very clear, but there are many others who have a stake in the systems and their interests are not always so clear. Among those with interests in public pension plans are the government officials, taxpayers, financial community, commission and board members, consultants, and society as a whole. These different interests may be affected politically, economically, and in terms of problems to be faced by society. The exact impact for each party varies from situation to situation.

Many of the problems that have arisen with public pension systems result from lack of agreement about exactly what pension plans should accomplish and how they should be funded and managed (Moe, 1984). The lack of agreement has resulted in policies that are inconsistent and lacking. For example, past tendencies to defer costs to the future for political reasons have left many jurisdictions under heavy financial burden. Funding inadequacies leave members anxious about the future and government officials concerned about where to find the needed money to operate them.

The changing demographics of the United States portends many effects for pension systems both public and private (Robertson and Kalman, 1986). The increasing number of people 65 years of age and over along with longer life expectancy means that the ratio of people employed to those retired is getting smaller. The smaller ratio has an impact on funding, especially with defined benefit plans. These trends are likely to lead to ever-increasing interest in changing to defined contribution plans in the public sector.

The increasing numbers of retirement age employees might lead to a higher retirement age, especially since it is no longer possible to require retirement at a certain age. The longer life span also has consequences for postretirement health care benefits and costs. With more need for health care, the health care system, which already is under extreme pressure, will experience even greater stress.

The diversity of the work force including dual-career couples and more women also will have effects. The likelihood is that there will be more experimenting with different types of plans. Flexibility to accommodate the needs of the individual employee also is certain to be a part of the future for pension plans.

Many of the cost implications of pension plans will probably lead to reforms that create multitiered plans. Because it is unfair to change systems and benefits after people have been retired, it is very likely that most jurisdictions will not institute policies that adversely affect retired members or current employees who have a contractual right to what was promised upon employment. On the other hand, generous provisions may be reduced for new employees thus creating a multitiered system. There is likely to be more interest in integrating social security benefits although national policy has put a freeze on it for the present. That policy always can be changed.

Among the most powerful lobby groups in the nation are retired persons. The American Association of Retired Persons (AARP) mobilizes people any time public policy affecting retiree interests is considered. AARP is very effective in getting its way with members of Congress and other public policymaking bodies.

Because public pension funds have so many assets and because there is increased interest in all public sector responsibility and accountability, there will be continued pressure for improvement in public pension systems management.

REFERENCES

Advisory Commission on Intergovernmental Relations (1973). *City Financial Emergencies*, ACIR, Washington, DC.

Advisory Commission on Intergovernmental Relations (1980). *State and Local Pension Systems: Federal Regulatory Issues*, ACIR, Washington, DC.

Amick, D. E. (1991). A new retirement information management system for Oregon: on time and on budget, *Gov. Fin. Rev., 7*(5) (Oct.): 11–14.

Bahl, R., and Jump, B. (1974). Budgeting implications of rising employee retirement system costs, *Nat. Tax J., 27* (Sept.): 479–490.

Brauer, M. A. (1983). Issues to consider in social investing, *Pension World, 19*(6) (June): 29–34.

Brown, S. (1991). Managing a retirement systems's records using optical disk technology, *Gov. Fin. Rev., 7*(1) (Feb.): 7–10.

Chernoff, J. (1993). Another pension benefit: funds could be used to fix infrastructure, *City and State (April)*: 5, 18.

Chernoff, J., and Philip, C. (1993). Using pension funds for investment, *City and State (March)*: 16, 21.

Copeland, R. M., and Ingram, R. W. (1983). Municipal bond market recognition of pension reporting practices, *J. Acc. Public Policy, 2*: 147–165.

Corriggio, H. J. (1987). Funding public employee pension plans, *Public Employee Benefit Plans-1987* (J. M. Lehman, ed.), International Foundation of Employee Benefit Plans, Brookfield, WI, pp. 65–71.

Dadisman v. Moore, 384 S.E.2nd 815 (W. Va. 1988).

Deutschman, A. (1992). The great pension robbery, *Forbes*, 125(1) (Jan.): 76–78.

The divestment dilemma (1986). *Gov. Fin. Rev., 2*(5) (Oct.): 7–11.

Drucker, P. F. (1976). *The Unseen Revolution: How Pension Fund Socialism Came to America*, Harper and Row, New York.

Ehrenberg, R. (1980a). Correlates of underfunding of public sector retirement systems, *Econ. Inquiry, 18* (July): 493–500.

Ehrenberg, R. G. (1980b). Retirement system characteristics and compensating wage differentials in the public sector, *Ind. Labor Rel. Rev., 33* (July): 470–483.

Emmert, M.L. (1989). Self-funding employee benefits, *Public Risk*: 4–6.

Employee Benefit Research Institute (1985). *Fundamentals of Employee Benefit Programs*, 2nd Ed., Washington, DC.

Employee Retirement Income Security Act, 1974 P.L. 93-406, 88 Stat. 829 (1974), Section 404.

Ferris, J. M. (1987). Local government pensions and their funding: policy issues and options, *Rev. Public Personnel Admin., 7*(3) (Summer): 29–44.

Gregory, D.L. (1990). Public employee pension funds: a cautionary essay, *Labor Law J., 42*(10) (Oct.): 700–705.

Grosskopf, S., Hayes, K., and Sivan, D. (1983). Municipal pensions, funding, and wage capitalization, *Nat. Tax J., 36* (March): 115–121.

Grosskopf, S., Hayes, K., and Kennedy, T. (1985). Supply and demand effects of underfunding of pensions on public employee wages, *Southern Econ. J., 51* (Jan.): 745–753.

Haeworth, R.A. (1981). *The Coming Revolution in Social Security*, Reston, Reston, VA.

Hall, A., and Smith, W. (1981). *Local Public Employee Pension Plans: Current Conditions and Prospects for the Future*, SRI International, Menlo Park, CA.

Halpern, P., and Halpern, K. D. (1990). What do we want from our public retirement systems? *Pension World, 26*(3) (March): 25–26.

Hargadon, C. A., and Shavers, P. S. (1989). Focus on retirement fund investing, *Public Manage., 71*(2) (Feb.): 10–11.

Harvard Law Review (1977). Public employee pensions in time of fiscal distress, *90* (March): 992–1017.

Haslanger, J. A. (1986). Do flexible plans undermine cost containment? *Pension World (May)*: 52–60.

Hennessy, E. A. (1987). Legal issues facing public plans, *Public Employee Benefit Plans—1987* (J. M. Lehman, ed.), International Foundation of Employee Benefit Plans, Brookfield, WI, pp. 1–17.

Houk, S. A. (1989). Section 89: employee benefit plan nondiscrimination, *Public Manage., 71*(2) (Feb.): 12–13.

Hutchinson, J. D., and Cole, C.G. (1980). Legal standards governing investment of pension assets for social and political goals, *Univ. Penn. Law Rev., 138*: 1340–1388.

Ingram, R. W., and Copeland, R.M. (1982). State mandated accounting, auditing and finance practices, *J. Acc. Public Policy (Spring)*: 19–29.

Inman, R. (1982). Public employee pensions and the local budget, *J. Public Econ., 19*: 49–71.

Jordan, A. (1992). The "gold watch" plan for cutting budgets, *Governing (July)*: 25–27.

Klausner, R. D. (1986). Fiduciary responsibilities: becoming the prudent man, *Public Employee Benefit Plans—1986* (M.E. Brennan, ed.), International Foundation of Employee Benefit Plans, Brookfield, WI, pp. 65–76.

Klingner, D., and Nutter, R. (1984). State and local government pension systems, *State and Local Government Administration* (J. Rabin and D. Dodd, eds.), Marcel Dekker, New York, pp. 371–384.

Langbein, J. H., and Posner, R. A. (1980). Social investing and the law of trusts, *Mich. Law Rev., 79* (Nov.): 72–112.

LaRock, S. (1992). Both private and public sector employers use early retirement sweeteners, *Employee Benefit Plan Rev., 47*(2) (August): 14–19.

Lingo, F. J. (1984). Capital accumulation plans for public employees, *Public Employee Benefit Plans—1984* (C.C. Hayne, ed.), International Foundation of Employee Benefit Plans, Brookfield, WI, pp. 117–123.

Litvak, L. (1981). *Pension Funds and Economic Renewal*, Council of State Planning Agencies, Washington, DC.

Love, J., et al. (1989). *Economically Targeted Investments*, Institute for Fiduciary Education, Sacramento.

Mann, D. (1978). Your pension system: financial difficulties? Three indicators to help you find out, *SPEER Newslett.*, National League of Cities, *1*(3) (Feb.): 1, 5–8.

March, Michael S. (1980). Pensions for public employees: present nationwide problems, *Public Admin. Rev., 40*(July/August): 382–389.

Mares, J. W. (1979). *The Use of Pension Fund Capital: Its Social and Economic Implications, Some Background Issues*, President's Commission on Pension Policy, Washington, DC.

Martin, L. A. (1989). Issues in local public pension plan management, *Public Manage., 71*(2) (Feb.): 2–4.

Martin, L. J., Ifflander, A.J., Cayer, N.J., and Gorrell, J.Z. (1986). Pension obligations and municipal bond ratings, *State Local Gov. Rev., 18* (Winter): 26–30.

McKenzie, C. (1989). Evaluating pension fund investment managers, *Public Manage., 71*(2) (Feb.): 8–9.

Meinhard v. Salmon, 164 N.E. 545 (N.Y. Ct. Appl. 1928).

Melbinger, M. S. (1992). The possibility of federal regulation of state and local government retirement plans, *Employee Benefits J., 17*(4): 23–27.

Metz, J. G. (1974). Public employee pensions: prospects for the future, *Tax Found. Tax Rev., 35* (July): 27–30.

Miller, E., and Foster, E. (1993). 2 pension officials felt jobs threatened, *Arizona Republic (July 3)*: 1, A2.

Moe, D. M. (1984). Pension plan design issues, *Public Employee Benefit Plans—1984* (C. C. Hayne, ed.), International Foundation of Employee Benefit Plans, Brookfield, WI, pp. 69–71.

Mumy, G. E. (1978). The economics of local government pensions and pension funding, *J. Polit. Econ., 86* (June): 517–527.

Munnell, A. H. (1983). The pitfalls of social investing: the case of public pensions and housing, *N. Eng. Econ. Rev., (Sept./Oct.)*: 20–41.

Munnell, A. (1986). Social investing: the case of South Africa, *Public Employee Benefit Plans-1985* (J. M. Lehman, ed.), International Foundation of Employee Benefit Plans, Brookfield, WI, pp. 13–20.

Munnell, A., and Connolly, A. (1988). Financing public pensions, *N. Engl. Econ. Rev., (Jan./Feb.)*: 30–42.

The 1993 pensions directory (1993). *Institutional Investor 27*(1) (Jan.): 117–137.

Perlman, E. (1992). It's a lose–lose situation, *City and State (Nov. 2)*: 3, 18.

Retirement Research Committee Staff (1992). 1990 comparative study of major public employee systems, *Public Employee Benefit Plans—1991* (M. J. Brzezinski, ed.), International Foundation of Employee Benefit Plans, Brookfield, WI, pp. 102–136.

Robertson, A. H., and Kalman, R. W. (1986). What is the future for public retirement systems? *Gov. Fin. Rev., 2*(5) (Oct.): 23–27.

Salomone, A. W. (1989). Public employee retirement commissions, *Public Manage., 71*(2) (Feb.): 5–7.

Schaitberger, H. A. (1987). Future trends in public retirement systems, *Public Employee Benefit Plans—1987* (J.M. Lehmen, ed.), International Foundation of Employee Benefit Plans, Brookfield, WI, pp. 53–63.

Schwartz, E., Munley, V., and Aronson, J.R. (1983). *Reforming Public Pension Plans to Avoid Unfunded Liability, 15*(5) May, Management Information Service, International City Management Association, Washington, DC.

Siegel, G. B. (1992). *Public Employee Compensation and Its Role in Public Sector Strategic Management*, Quorum Books, New York.

Snell, R. K., and Wolfe, S. (1990). *Public Pension Funds' Investment Practices*, National Conference of State Legislatures, Denver.

Testin, B. L. (1992). 1990 comparative study of major public employee retirement systems, *Public Employee Benefits Plans—1991*, (M. J. Brzezinski, ed.), International Foundation of Employee Benefit Plans, Brookfield, WI, pp. 102–136.

Tilove, R. (1976). *Public Employee Pension Funds*, Columbia University Press, New York.

U. S. Bureau of the Census (1987). *1987 Census of Governments, 4*(6), Employee retirement systems of state and local governments, Government Printing Office, Washington, DC.

U.S. Committee on Education and Labor, *Report of the Pension Task Force on Public Employee Retirement Systems* (1978). U.S. House of Representatives, March 15.

U.S. Department of Commerce, Bureau of the Census (1980–1981). *Finances of Employee Retirement Systems of State and Local Governments*, Government Printing Office, Washington, DC.

U.S. General Accounting Office (1979). *Funding of State and Local Government Pension Plans: A National Problem*, Washington, DC.

U.S. General Accounting Office (1980). *An Actuarial and Economic Analysis of State and Local Government Pension Plans*, Washington, D.C.

Universal Social Security Coverage Study Group (1980). *The Desirability and Feasibility of Social Security Coverage for Employees of Federal, State, and Local Governments and Private, Nonprofit Organizations*, U.S. Department of Health, Education and Welfare, Washington, DC.

Verbon, H. A. A. (1986). Altruism, political power and public pensions, *Kyklos, 39*(3): 343–358.

Vise, D. A. (1992). The pension fund that financed a sorority house, *Washington Post National Weekly Edition (December 14–20)*: 20.

Vosti, C. (1993). Defining quality benefit programs: governments try out private pension concept, *City and State, (Feb.)*: 15, 19.

Whiston, S. C., Martin, J., and Todisco, P. (1985). A pooled investment fund for local public retirement systems: the start-up experience in Massachusetts, *Gov. Fin. Rev., 1*(2) (June): 19–22.

Wiles, R. (1993). Major loss feared for state pension plan, *Arizona Republic (July 3)*: 1, A2.

Zolkos, R. (1992). Guvs eye pensions, city taxes, *City and State (June 1–14)*: 1, 21.

Zolkos, R., and Philip, C. (1992). Legislator's pensions soar, *City and State (August 10–23)*: 1–2.

Zorn, P. (1987). Public pension funding: preliminary results from a survey of current practices, *Gov. Fin. Rev.*, 3 (4) (August): 7–11.

Zorn, P. (1990). A survey of state retirement systems covering general employees and teachers, *Gov. Fin. Rev.*, 6 (5) (Oct.): 25–29.

Zorn, W. P. (1983). Public pension policy: a survey of targeting practices, *Govt. Fin., 12*(4): 47–53.

17

Budgeting Human Resource Requirements

W. BARTLEY HILDRETH   Wichita State University, Wichita, Kansas

I. INTRODUCTION

While the annual operating budget is the allocation device for public services, it also conveys the organization's approach to human resource management. The budget's strategic impact on the personnel system derives from the labor-intensive nature of public services. In recent years, the compensation of employees composed over 65% of all state and local government purchases and 40% in the federal government.[1]

Managers need to understand the relationship between budgeting and human resource (HR) management in order to effectively pursue the service delivery goals of the organization. The U.S. Office of Personnel Management (1990) specifies the goal of federal HR management as the creation of "a responsive system that enables each agency to attract, develop, and retain a quality and representative workforce needed to accomplish its unique mission." The statement, however, slights the responsibility of managers to meet tests of efficiency and effectiveness, especially in a time of fiscal constraint.

Fiscal stress is a recurring theme in the recent history of public administration. Since the mid-1970s, we have witnessed widespread use of austerity measures such as hiring freezes, layoffs, contracting out, privatization, and, most ubiquitous of all, "cutbacks" (Peterson, 1976; Levine, 1978; Rubin, 1982; Clark and Ferguson, 1983). Following a period of stability, if not growth, for most governments in the 1980s, the early 1990s represented another period of fiscal stress (Cromwell and Wirkus, 1990; Pagano, 1993). As budgets change, so too does the size, composition, and compensation of public employees (Johnson, 1982).

Service entities, such as governments, must continuously improve their provision and production of programs and activities to meet changing missions. The service delivery system is not static. The size and composition of the public work force reflects residents' service demands, measured by current (and past) service levels as well as future needs. Incremental theory suggests that the past predicts the future, with minor adjustments. Still, major shifts occur. As Lewis (1988)

---

[1] The federal government's lower percentage is due to its large amount of durable goods (e.g., weapons) purchased and transfer payments (U.S. Department of Commerce, 1992).

This is a revised and expanded version of Hildreth (1993b), published in the *International Journal of Public Administration*.

noted, fair share departmental employment increases (decreases) are not the norm in growing (declining) cities. In another example, as the Cold War threat subsided, budget debate turned on the amount to cut from the military, not whether to cut. These cuts affected the number of military and civilian employees of the Department of Defense and the reserve forces.

As the composition of the population changes, the demand and need for public services changes too. In a domestic, local example, an aging population has more need for emergency medical service specialists than for playground coordinators. Population shifts also affect the types of taxes and revenues that the governmental entity can levy on citizens. For example, individuals (such as retirees) on fixed incomes (e.g., pensions and/or social security) find increased charges for basic water and sewer services can materially affect their monthly budgets. This can lead to a reluctance to vote for tax increases or incumbent office holders who advocate increases in service fees and charges. In addition, the push for earmarked taxes of limited duration for popular services requires flexible personnel orientations; workers need only be employed for the 3-year duration of a special tax, for example. Thus, a budget responsive to changes in service demands is required, with efficiency and effectiveness as strong considerations.

The purpose of this chapter is to explore the interrelationships between financial policies and HR issues. The goal is to permit service delivery issues to guide budget decisions instead of having decisions premised merely on adding up the cost of existing staffing patterns. To achieve this goal, the first section scans factors influencing the budgeting of labor. The second section clarifies the basic elements of work force budgeting, as the focus of this discussion is termed. In closing, the role conflicts between the finance and HR functions are examined.

II.   INFLUENCES ON WORK FORCE BUDGETING

Work force budgeting is a comprehensive view of allocating resources recognizing that expenses flow from the use and remuneration of labor. It is incumbent on managers to acquire, deploy, and control human resources in the production of public goods and services. A number of factors influence the size, composition, and compensation of the work force. For our purposes, five areas are discussed: legal, political, financial, collective bargaining, and management. While there are many overlaps between these organizational influences, it helps to briefly introduce each one.

A.   Legal Conditions

Governmental units operate within changing legal conditions. Judicial and statutory pressures from the federal government, for example, impose work force constraints on state and local governments. The scope can be very precise or wide ranging. An example of a precise intervention is where a federal court orders a governmental unit to take remedial actions to correct constitutional deprivations. One illustration is the federal court's receivership over the Alabama Department of Mental Health and Mental Retardation for the State's failure to observe legally protected rights of adequate treatment (Yarbrough, 1981; Hildreth, 1985; Axelrod, 1989). The Court specified minimum staffing requirements to meet treatment standards.

A more wide-ranging intervention is the application of the Fair Labor Standards Act to state and local governments following the U.S. Supreme Court decision in *Garcia v. San Antonio Metropolitan Transit* (1985). This required subnational governments to revise their shift schedules, overtime provisions, and minimum wage levels. Before the case, state and local governments were not considered to be covered by the same minimal work standards required of business and industry.

State governments impose requirements on their local governments, termed mandates. Mandated staffing rations arise in areas such as minimum staffing of sewerage treatment facilities and landfills. In many states, statewide collective bargaining law structures and limits the workplace decisions of local executives with research suggesting that "strong bargaining laws stimulate union growth" (Zax and Ichniowski, 1990; but see Trejo, 1991). In some cases, state lawmakers also legislate the pay and benefits for local employees, including increases in employer pension contributions. It is relatively easy for one level of government to mandate that lower levels of government follow certain procedures, especially if no dollars accompany the mandate. Needless to say, this influences a subordinated government's work force size and compensation costs.

Public policy on compensation is expressed in federal and state legislation and in regulations imposed by executive branches of these governments. Table 1 illustrates the broad and frequently passed mandates affecting pay policies of public agencies (Hildreth and Miller, 1983). The legal constraints do, at times, conflict and appear illogical. Belcher (1974, p. 432) says, "Because these stated social goals express only a portion of our broader social and economic purposes, they are not always clear or consistent with one another." Perhaps the principle behind the panoply of laws governing pay is best stated by Belcher as:

> Public policy may be represented as stating that compensation must not be too low nor (at times) too high, but that within these limits compensation decisions should be left to the parties at interest. Also, in the interest of fairness, certain groups have been protected and all groups must be paid when such payment is due.

Legal constraints derive from political pressures, the next topic.

B. Political Context

Public organizations also operate in a political context. It should come as no surprise that personnel positions are considered political resources, a form of "political currency," as termed by Nalbandian and Klingner (1981). Positions are the currency of exchange in making policy (Thompson, 1975). New or changed programs are reflected in part by changes in personnel counts (Wanet, 1976).

Elected officials typically desire to impregnate the public entity with their own views, approaches, and people. The 1990 U.S. Supreme Court opinion of *Rutan v. Republican Party of Illinois* struck down the most blatant approach, applying political considerations in personnel decisions for nonpolicymaking positions. A new era of political behavior by federal and postal employees is likely due to a 1993 law relaxing Hatch Act restrictions on partisan political activity. The Hatch Act barred federal workers from participating in campaigns, holding public office, and soliciting campaign contributions. Within specified limits, workers can now take part in campaigns and solicit contributions to political action committees, such as those of unions.

Many newly elected chief executives, at least at the federal and state levels, impose an immediate hiring freeze, a severe form of HR planning (Newland, 1976; U.S. General Accounting Office, 1982; but see Ricciuti, 1982). Hiring freezes can serve to halt existing recruitment paths until the new administration develops substitute or additional hiring standards (Hamilton, 1993). This could be viewed as political patronage or, in a less pejorative manner, political accountability. A result of such practices is that across-the-board hiring freezes do not discriminate between effective and ineffective budget units. It impacts every budget unit, despite the fact that not every budget unit needs to be treated the same. Besides, since the turnover rate may be higher for some jobs (e.g., clerical) than for others (e.g., middle management), attrition can lead to situations where managers have to perform clerical functions, an inefficient allocation of resources (Hartman, 1982).

Several initiatives under former President Ronald Reagan displayed a new level of interest and concern in how to shape work force issues around political issues. In one strident example, efforts were taken to modify the federal employee health insurance program to avoid the funding

Table 1 Public Policy on Compensation

Policies	Description
1. Collective bargaining policies	Policies specify processes of bargaining for wages between employers and employees when used. Postal Reorganization Act of 1970 allows collective bargaining to determine postal workers' pay and fringe benefits.
2. Minimum wage laws	Policies setting a floor under wages and specifying pay for overtime work. Policies express social concern with earnings, standard of living, and adequate leisure. Opponents charge that laws create unemployment *and* inflation.
3. Prevailing wage laws	Policies set wage for workers on public projects at rates prevailing in the area on private projects. Federal Davis–Bacon Act, Walsh–Healey Act, and state/local laws. Policies mandate that public projects not compete unfairly with private projects for labor.
4. Minimum benefits laws	Policies place floor under benefits rather than wages that workers receive. Federal Social Security Act for participating employees at all levels, various retirement, health, and other laws at all levels. Policies express concern that a "social safety net" exist in areas of major insecurity such as health and old age.
5. Maximum pay policies	Policies avoid labor market conditions by placing ceiling on salaries. Salary adjustments for top career executives linked with elected officials' salaries.
6. Incomes policies	Policies that attempt to control the effects of rapid changes in economic conditions through controls on changes in wages paid. Federal laws prevail. Policies attempt to centralize control of economic cycles that wages influence.
7. Equal pay laws and anti-discrimination statutes	Policies prohibit compensation discrimination on the basis of various categories such as sex, race, religion, and national origin. Federal Equal Pay Act, Civil Rights Act, and state and local statutes.
8. Assurance of payment laws	Policies specify mode and interval of wage payment by employers to employees, regulate debt collection as part of compensation process, and prohibit political kickbacks as a condition of employment.
9. Pay comparability laws	Policies require salaries comparable to private sector be paid public employees. Federal Employees Pay Comparability Act of 1980 and many state and local policies. Policies prevent wage penalty for public service. May permit locality-specific salary adjustments to compensate for high private wage rates in excess of general federal pay rates.
10. Competitive pay policies	Policies to link pay to similar positions in both public and private sectors, and by locality. Federal Pay Comparability Act of 1990 established a phased process to make federal pay rates at least 95% of prevailing nonfederal rates in each locality where federal employees work by the year 2002.

Table 1   Continued

Policies	Description
11. Comparable worth policies	Policies requiring pay based on equal value of jobs. Equal Pay Act of 1963 and its relationship to Civil Rights Act of 1964. Concern discrimination based on sex. Requires judgment on value of respective jobs, not just those that are substantially equal.
12. Merit pay policies	Policies condition certain amounts of compensation of satisfactory or exemplary job performance. All merit systems—federal, state, and local—include such provisions. Federal Civil Service Reform Act creates structure for making performance–reward linkage tangible for high-ranking federal executives.
13. Cost-of-living adjustments (COLAs)	Policies allow compensation to adjust automatically to changes in cost of living. COLAs often result from collective bargaining. Policies permit pay decision to be made without direct annual legislative intervention or political responsibility.
14. Pay-for-performance policies	Policies to grant a one-time bonus or base pay expansion for efforts to increase productivity. Permitted by Civil Service Reform Act of 1978.
15. Gain-sharing policies	Policies permitting public employees to personally gain a share of the savings achieved through cooperative efforts to cut costs. Rewards organizational productivity.
16. Service benchmarking	Policies to measure accomplishment of services against competitive service delivery modes, thereby determining the need (if any), and allowable costs, for using public employees in service production. Includes contract-out policies.

Source: Adapted and revised from Hildreth and Miller (1983).

of abortions. Also, the administration sought to make the "Combined Federal Campaign"—a charity solicitation program whereby federal employees earmark withholdings—conform to its political preferences by adding right-to-work foundations while dropping family planning organizations as eligible organizations, thereby facilitating these organizations in gaining the receipt of federal employee charity contributions.

C.   Financial Constraints

Financial resources provide the means for accomplishing work force goals (Hildreth, 1989). Granted, wealthier communities can afford to pay higher levels of compensation than can a less well-endowed community. It is this disparity that fuels the interdistrict school finance litigation that is raging in various states. A deteriorating financial condition quickly forces attention to personnel costs due to the high percentage of total operating expenditures devoted to pay and employee benefit costs. As pointed out by Clark and Ferguson (1983), the basic work force issue in static, declining, or slow growth revenue cities is either (1) to hire more employees and pay them less, or (2) to hire less but pay existing employees more (but see Schneider, 1988). In many governments this means limiting future work force growth rather than forcing a reduction in the present work force size (Johnson, 1982).

Lewis (1988) studied the shifting composition of employment, by department, to reveal the effects of fiscal policy. In the process, he rejected incremental theory predictions of fair share change for explaining employment patterns in growing and declining cities. Policy preferences were at work. As Wanet (1976) found in his study of congressional budget behavior, personnel measures and dollars both should be studied to fully understand budgeting.

Tax and spending limits impose resource constraints on labor costs (Johnson, 1982). This has caused unions to lose benefits once negotiated, but not without some protest and fight. Property tax caps, as one form of limit, were found to exert downward pressure on wages but not aggregate payroll (Gyourko and Tracy, 1989). To make matters worse, HR managers find their roles greatly diminished in times of fiscal stress (Saltzstein and Bott, 1983).

D. Collective Bargaining

The degree to which the budget process incorporates work force costs is more difficult when the budget is not coordinated with the *collective bargaining process* (Hildreth, 1983b). If all labor contract changes were prospective in application, starting with the next budget year, then coordination problems would be minimized. Budget planning is complicated, however, when officials approve a labor contract changing pay or benefits immediately or retroactively to the start of the fiscal year. A governmental unit may respond to this uncertainty by "padding" the budget with sufficient money to cover any expected labor contract costs. This padding may be overt or covert, typically the latter (Toulmin, 1988; Riordan, 1991). Union leaders either assume there are reserves (or "pads") set aside or simply do not care. In the latter case unions assert that it is management's job to balance the budget after taking into account the various costs of services; merely crying that the treasury is "empty" draws little sympathy. This view may change once unions are fully apprised of the financial condition and have an opportunity to consider the implications.

Government budgets respond to union-sponsored changes in pay and fringe benefits in two basic ways (Benecki, 1978). First, collective bargaining pressures can lead to a change in the budget. Even when the total budget remains unchanged after collective bargaining, it can mask changes within the budget. That is, particular departments or functions may obtain disproportionate gains, such as fire (Benecki, 1978) or police (Woska, 1988) gaining in budget share compared to other departments.

Second, collective bargaining can influence the distribution of budget shares within a government department. Higher wage settlements, without corresponding new dollars flowing into an office, require a proportional decrease in nonpayroll expenses. Some units may gain at the expense of other spending units. An example is the street maintenance unit of a street and highway department's budget growing to cover wage settlements, meaning that some other unit has to bear a disproportionate cut. Fundamentally, internal resource reallocations are required to accommodate wage settlements in a fixed budget scenario (Benecki, 1978; Zax and Ichniowski, 1988), unless extreme measures are taken (Advisory Commission on Intergovernmental Relations, 1985).

Government structure is a variable that appears in the research on collective bargaining outcomes. For example, a reformed city, known by its city manager form of government, may be less effective in minimizing labor costs than a strong mayor form (O'Brien, 1992), but more effective in offsetting the negative effect of unionization on black employment (Mladenka, 1991).

E. Management Capacity

The management capacity of the jurisdiction also influences work force issues. Gargan (1981) defines capacity as the ability to do what is required and expected. Since most very small local governments are dependent on part-time or even relatively low-skilled individuals to serve as the sole "administrator" and/or "staff," there is little capacity to move beyond simple payroll and other payment concerns. Even in larger organizations, the division of labor between HR and finance functions often hinders a comprehensive approach to the budget requirements of work force issues (Cornia et al., 1985).

Governors are not immune from problems in controlling government work forces. A study of state government personnel levels under changes in administrations found that conservative governors increased the staffing levels to achieve political control over highly tenured (civil service) state bureaucracies. In the study, Jarrett (1981) concluded that "state elections for governors, while important in many respects, do not provide a true opportunity for altering state government (personnel) growth, even when clear-cut choices between candidates are provided" (p. 91).

The capacity to adopt productivity initiatives is hindered by shortsighted HR orientations. Osborne and Gaebler (1992) paint a disturbing picture of the costs associated with contemporary personnel rules, at least in terms of the negative implications for delivery of services that add value to clients and citizens. Furthermore, the movement toward greater utilization of user charges and service fees to fund government services can conflict with artificial limits on personnel, for example. Basically, if a budget unit has to operate under personnel staffing ceilings, it cannot add people to administer new user fee programs. An agency has little incentive to identify self-supporting user fee opportunities if it cannot staff at levels to generate the fees. Even new ventures are stillborn if labor is unavailable. Efforts to enhance productivity or to adopt other management improvement programs depend on a close examination of the way HR requirements are budgeted.

III. ELEMENTS OF WORK FORCE BUDGETING

Work force budgeting is a function of how services are designed to utilize labor inputs and the payment for that labor. This section examines work force design, pay policies, and the employee benefits portfolio. It closes on the need for comprehensive work force compensation policies.

A. Work Force Design

Work force design is the traditional way to control the number and type of workers. The basic approach is to restrict the number of authorized positions. According to this logic, if the number of positions is controlled, then the basic budget issue is only how much to pay for each position. Naturally, this begs the point of what the employees should be doing with their work time. While the use of a personnel ceiling, as this is called, has come under attack as an ineffective management device (U.S. General Accounting Office, 1977), elected officials find it a very effective political statement.

This section explores the budgeting aspects of the following work force design issues:

1. Organizational structure
2. Status as employee
3. Work hours and tenure status
4. Minimum staffing
5. Work process
6. Sizing the work force

1. *Organizational Structure*

Organizational structures and jobs are influenced by two size indicators—resources and the work force (Rabin et al., 1981). The growth of either promotes structural complexity and fragmentation. More funds and/or more people typically yield more coordination structures and division of labor. Organizational decline may reverse this trend, resulting in long-term relaxation of command and control structures (Sutton and D'Aunno, 1989). The demise of the Soviet Union is a striking illustration of this point. On the negative side, threats of resource reductions lead to individual anxiety and organizational rigidity, such as centralization of decision making, more rules governing behavior, and the conservation of resources. Decreases in work force size also lead to individual anxiety but only short-term organizational rigidity; over the long term, it is posited that rigidity is reduced (Sutton and D'Aunno, 1989; but see McKinley, 1992).

Centralization of decision making is a problem in government (National Performance Review, 1993). Public employees whose jobs require dealing directly with the public—such as teachers, police officers, social workers, and nurses—have "line" responsibilities while "staff" employees grow in number, salary, and prerequisites of position. Much of the antigovernment sentiment appears based on the bureaucratic or "red tape" layers of administrative approval that line workers must follow to deliver public services. Public education is one area where the "bloat" in central office administration is emerging as a potent argument for more decentralized control of school-based decisions. One prevailing characteristic of the early 1990s was the widespread reduction in middle management positions in public, private, and nonprofit sectors of the economy as all types of organizations attempted to flatten their organizational structure. By removing layers of management overhead, the goal was to make the organization more responsive to customers.

2. Status as Employee

The common gauge of the HR complement in any organization is a direct measure of the number of positions authorized and filled. Unfortunately, this measure masks HR costs reflected in other budget categories or line items, hidden to some degree from a cursory look at the records. A review of some of the most utilized screens would have to include function shifting and mandates, contracting out, professional service contracts, and volunteer labor.

(*a*) *Function Shifting and Mandates.* When a government faces a barrier in providing a particular function or service, one overused option is to shift the responsibility to another entity, with or without financial help. The federal government has entered into many functions that were more legally and politically feasible if carried out by states and localities. In some (but not all) cases, the federal government has paid for the programs and services (or at least a share of the costs). In one large case, the federal budget shows an outflow to state governments to conduct Medicaid programs but does not show the large number of personnel slots required to administer this joint federal–state program. Thus, the size of the federal work force appears much smaller than if the program was strictly an in-house function. Without the federal government providing the funding stream, these programs and services might not receive state or local funding at all, or receive funding at the same level as that forthcoming from federal coffers.

State and local governments utilize similar practices to shift their functions "off-budget." They create special authorities to perform particular programs. As a byproduct, the staffing of such an enterprise is not shown on the general government's personnel roster. In another strategy, the government pays a contract fee, with the budget showing an outlay to the named agency instead of a direct personnel slot.

A mandate is the requirement placed on one party to do something on the authority of someone superior. This requirement to perform a service typically translates into payroll expenditures. State and local governments deal with many requirements to provide certain staffing levels in order to qualify for federal funds or to meet federal standards. Assessing the costs of mandates and halting their growth is a major issue of continuing interest to subordinate governments (U.S. Conference of Mayors, 1993; National Association of Counties Research, 1983).

(*b*) *Contracting Out.* When the federal government contracts for a service or good (such as a major weapons system), the contractor's payroll represents the labor requirements for accomplishing the task. The funding for the position, however, comes from the federal government. There is a similar result when state and local governments contract for garbage services and road construction. In fact, the contractors are engaged to acquire specialized talent that is either not on the government's direct payroll or, if present, has other obligations.

Governments contract out services or programs in an announced attempt to achieve economies and efficiencies, but with a variety of impacts (Chandler and Feuille, 1991). However, an analysis of the financial rationale given for such efforts should withstand scrutiny (Hildreth, 1983a). Substitution of costs may result, with real impact. Governments have instituted service contracts with a provision requiring the contractor to hire the displaced public employees, but this change of employers means employees lose retirement and other benefits. While this helps the public treasury conserve funds, it sends ripples through the remaining work force.

(*c*) *Professional Service Contracts.* Many governmental units enter into professional service contracts without following the normal practice for government purchases of soliciting competitive bids. Public officials use professional services to acquire specialized talent (e.g., legal expertise) or to achieve an independent appraisal of certain government practices (e.g., external auditors). When organizations downsize, letting employees go (through early retirement or reductions in force, for example) some of the same workers are hired back as consultants to fill the specialized needs they once provided as full-time employees (Cascio, 1993). Consultants can work at home due to personal computers and related technological advances, blurring the boundaries between professional services and contracted-out services. By only looking at the personal services category of a budget, the scope and expense of professional services is neglected. Reframing the question as to the need for a service, regardless of where to locate the worker (in-house or externally), may help.

(*d*) *Volunteer Labor.* All types of agencies rely on volunteers for substantial service delivery functions. Fire departments in many smaller communities are staffed solely by volunteers. Social service agencies rely on donated labor for internal functions as well as direct care of employees. By law, hospice service agencies, for instance, must utilize a large contingent of volunteer help in order to satisfy Medicare reimbursement terms. Many government units have well-organized volunteer staffing programs. It is important, however, to evaluate the economic costs and benefits of these alternative staffing programs (Brudney and Duncombe, 1992).

3. Work Hours and Tenure Status

Except for political appointees, public sector employees normally enjoy a longstanding, permanent (tenured) position. Instead of owing their job continuity to political factors, public employees faced selection and retention decisions based on more or less objective measures of job qualifications. This merit principle gained currency at the turn of the 20th century and has continued to date, although not universally followed by all governments.

A significant movement in work force design is the use of part-time workers instead of full-time, permanent employees. Smaller municipalities, for example, have more part-time employees per capita than larger cities, but this is offset by the larger cities having more full-time employees (Pagano, 1993). The part-time labor trend is less designed to meet workers' preferences than to cut labor costs (Tilly, 1991).

The difference between full-time and part-time employees represents a work force decision with implications for the budget. A full-time employee, or one with a certain number of weekly work hours, qualifies for most employee benefits such as holiday and sick leave, health insurance, and retirement benefits, to name some of the highest cost items. In contrast, part-time employees are generally excluded from receiving employee benefits.

Changes in fiscal condition and service delivery missions have led public agencies to rely on seasonal or temporary personnel. Summer recreation activities, winter sports (in snow-prone areas), summer grounds maintenance, and intensive construction efforts all represent reasons for using temporary personnel. Temporary personnel can work either full time (e.g., 40 hr/week) or part time (less than 40 hr/week).

While temporary workers offer a valid approach for handling peak service periods, the tendency is to extend their use for meeting normal service demands. Someone hired as an "emergency" for 30, 60, or 90 days may find himself or herself in a more permanent position, but without the full compensation accorded to a full-time, permanent employee. Plus, the "temporary" *need* may subside without termination of the "temporary" *individual*.

Private business has responded to the need by providing temporary staffing firms. In the health care setting, nurse pools have evolved into a viable source of temporary staffing (Hildreth, 1983). These "rent-a-person" options are especially useful when service demands or funding sources are uncertain; as service demands stabilize or funding sources firm up, more permanent staffing can be implemented.

One advantage for the rent-a-person option is the need to pay only the agreed-on, fixed rate. Pay and employee benefits are covered by the temporary hiring serive from the fixed price paid by the public jurisdiction. Adjacent jurisdictions may differ in their practice, with one using a temporary hiring service and the other directly hiring nontenure-earning workers.

Four organizational settings illustrate the sweeping utilization of part-time employees. Universities and colleges, for example, hire nontenure-track faculty to meet special needs and/or high-demand teaching areas. In fact, one study found that temporary employees conduct a third of all faculty work (Bowen and Schuster, 1985). In a second example, the federal government has become increasingly dependent on part-time workers, accounting for about one-fifth of the overall increase in federal employment. The growth of the work force with nonpermanent appointments reflects, in part, intensive efforts to encourage agencies (other than the postal service) to depend more on temporary workers. The growth also is taking place at higher grades, and in professional, administrative, and technical occupations (U.S. General Accounting Office, 1986; U.S. Congressional Budget Office, 1987). While most temporary appointments remain in the clerical occupational group, it is a declining percentage (General Accounting Office, 1989).

Nonprofit service delivery agencies are creative, by necessity, in designing low-cost service productions, as the third example illustrates. A counseling service can use contract social workers and pay them for the time actually spent with a client at the agency's offices. By controlling the scheduling of the client session, the agency makes the contract worker be on call for a multihour time slot, deal with long time gaps between client sessions, and incur last minute client cancellation, all assigned nonpay status.

The fourth work force design illustration involves the structure of the U.S. military in the wake of the cold war. Current policy relies on reserve forces to augment the active military; thus the size and composition of one affects the other. For the active military to place more reliance on the reserves for critical skills or for quick response in times of crises introduces uncertainty into the projection of military goals. Reserves, however, provide an alternative to a large, active force (RAND, 1992).

Part-time employment has differential impacts in society, a concern for the public sector policymaker, if not by the public employer. While "voluntary" part-time work meets workers' needs, "involuntary" part-time work is a more direct effect of labor markets. Workers are forced to accept temporary work status if that is the only job available. More women than men work part time involuntarily (*Working Women*, 1993). The conflicting roles of public policymakers—as employers *and* policy role models—makes dealing with this effect difficult.

Social changes have led to an increase in the use of job sharing. Job sharing is where two people occupy one position resulting in part-time, permanent work for each. Sidestepping the debate over job sharing, there is one budgetary impact to consider. There is the potential for higher compensation costs, especially if the same employee benefits are given to part timers as full timers (Nollen, 1982).

4. *Minimum Staffing*

Staffing levels are set in some cases by legal preconditions, contract requirements, or shift necessities. Constitutional challenges to the care given by state jails and mental health hospitals have led to consent decrees specifying minimum staffing by qualified persons (Hildreth, 1985). Labor unions, especially those in public safety, often seek to specify the minimum number of employees required on each shift. When this level of staffing is not met, "off-duty employees are called to duty at overtime rates" (Woska, 1988, p. 553). In 1984, Cleveland public safety unions sought, but failed in their bid for, voter support on an amendment to the city charter mandating minimum police and fire staffing. The unions dismissed claims that this would unduly hamper the mayor or lead to similar moves by other worker groups.

Practical reasons also dictate minimum staffing levels. A two-person patrol car has a clear staffing impact. A shift for one emergency medical unit, fire truck, or patrol area requires a certain number of employees to respond to a call for service. Even garbage collection efforts require a certain minimum staffing component, depending on the technology in use (rear loader, side loader, etc.).

As such, minimum staffing designs carry a cost. Shifting from a one-person police patrol unit to a two-person patrol mode has a financial impact. The trend to community policing requires more police to "walk the beats." It is incumbent on policymakers, therefore, to consider the work force staffing requirements of service proposals, even to the point of reexamining existing work processes.

5. *Work Process*

Organizations do not employ individuals out of social benevolence; there is a job to perform. As Chester Barnard (1938) said, an organization is a consciously coordinated mechanism for two or more individuals to achieve a stated purpose. The *purpose* is paramount, not employment per se.

Production lines conjure up images of various individuals working on a product moving down the assembly belt. While service delivery of most governments may not appear on the surface to be so assembly line–oriented, in fact many core business functions involve a variety of skilled persons performing different functions at various stages of a process. It is this work specialization and staging of events that helps determine the organization's need to hire and retain people (as opposed to acquiring and maintaining machines).

Too frequently in government (and nonprofit agencies), leaders and workers forget that the production of goods and services are the purpose of the entity. The value added by each step in a production deserves to be continuously evaluated. Recently, this has become known as "reengineering" or "reinventing" government (Osborne and Gaebler, 1992). It draws much from the total quality management philosophy, with its own implications for human resource management (Blackburn and Rosen, 1993).

It is critical to recognize that work flows across departmental boundaries. In fact, departments make staffing decisions to meet the demands imposed by other internal units. As noted by Ostrenga et al. (1992, p. 23), if work is viewed strictly on a departmental basis, "efforts to streamline the work may result merely in a shifting of problems downstream, or in creating additional problems, complexity, or rework" elsewhere in the organization. Costs are incurred in work processes. A consequence of streamlining a work process is its impact on labor costs and the need to resize the work force to meet newly defined tasks.

6. *Sizing the Work Force*

Work force planning provides an organization with a coherent method for estimating the size, composition, and skill requirements of its people to meet organizational objectives. Work force planning involves an analysis of the current staffing profile—or "stock"—and the "flow" of employees into and out of the various positions required to do the work. A work force planning effort also incorporates expectations of future organizational activities and service. Data on the stock, flow, and expected work changes provide an organization with the essentials for modeling future work needs. Decision makers can use such information to make more informed staffing decisions regarding the use and composition of employees. Alternative staffing options—part time vs. full time, temporary vs. permanent, direct employee vs. contracted employee, etc.—receive due consideration in such planning.

Planning offers a methodology for dealing with service demands. Governmental entities provide services to meet real or perceived constituent demands. Public workers influence services levels by identifying and exploiting unmet needs or opportunities (Jones et al., 1980). Service demands pinpoint the skills needed to provide the services. This is usually translated into the type of needed positions (and related expenses). The budgeting process may hinder work force planning. According to Hyde and Whitman (1977, p. 67), "Increases in demand may not be accurately forecast for fear of driving the budget too high; conversely, decreases in demand may not surface if the forecasting of them would lead to budget reduction."

Work force planning can provide advance notice of impending staffing excesses relative to demand shrinkages. Without such efforts, reductions in force (RIFs) can be more disruptive than necessary. It costs money to let an employee go. In the federal government, forced RIFs require expenditures for lump sum annual leave payments, severance pay, unemployment compensation, and early retirement. Announced savings can dissipate quickly as previously separated employees are replaced and agencies award contracts or employ overtime to perform separated employees' functions.

Despite its utility, little work force planning is conducted by public organizations (Feldt and Andersen, 1982; Johnson, 1982; Ledvinka, 1994). Work force planning offers an opportunity to better deal with a number of issues, such as equal employment opportunity (Ledvinka and Hildreth, 1984). Efforts to use work force planning to help make RIF decisions are rare (Andersen et al., 1978; Andersen and Feldt, 1978). Instead, "changes in work force size are the result of a political (i.e., negotiating) process and not a function of human resource planning, even where planning exists" (Johnson, 1982, p. 47). A look beyond the current budgetary year is rare, with negative implications for work force planning (Andersen et al., 1978; Lane and Wolf, 1990).

A flexible work force enhances managerial discretion, but with costs shifted in employees, often unwillingly. Unionization gains momentum when existing work groups face job uncertainties. A balance of sorts is possible. At the federal level, the Senior Executive Service (SES) provides a cadre of experienced civil service employees willing to move between a wide range of executive positions (within certain guidelines) to meet changing presidential preferences (Perry and Miller, 1991). A few states have explored similar approaches (Sherwood and Breyer, 1987).

Structuring the time and effort of labor to meet the service delivery mission is only one piece of the work force puzzle. Pay and benefit policies also demand attention, as are outlined in the next two sections.

B. Pay Policies

A primary focus of budget debate is pay policy. The degree to which the budget allocates resources for pay increases is one of the most common departure points in any debate over a public budget. What determines the pay level for employees? Should employees receive a raise and, if so, of what amount? Should the raise be added to the salary base, thereby increasing the base for future raises, or should the raise constitute a one-time payment that has no lasting impact on the base? These and other questions rage throughout the budgeting process. This section surveys the basics of pay, overtime, employee negotiations over pay, automatic pay adjustments, salary compression, and pay-for performance systems.

1. *Pay Plans*

An employee's pay reflects internal and external labor markets. Internal structures are the meat of personnel management practices. Civil service systems have long included pay plans to help structure compensation decisions. A pay plan builds a systematic schedule of job positions arranged according to approximately similar duties and responsibilities (called a classification system). It rewards rank and time in grade, a form of maturity internal to the organization. Typical classification systems have many levels—starting at GS-1 and rising to GS-15, for example—with a set number of steps or gradations for each level. The intent of most efforts is to have the classification and pay schedule cover the entire jurisdiction's work force (with the possible exception of appointed and elected officials). Each level conveys a separate pay amount or, as shown in Table 2, a minimum and maximum. This specificity helps neutralize the system against contamination by partisan or organizational politics, but it hinders managerial flexibility.

Subjectivity enters into pay decisions, however. Managers may bargain and cajole to have their workers placed in particular positions in the "uniform plan." Unions seek influence over pay policy too. Unions have gone to the voters to gain approval for favorable wage formulas to be

Table 2 Pay Plan Design

Job title (department)		Annual Salary Range ($)		
	Grade	Minimum	Midpoint	Maximum
Corporal (Uniform patrol)	16	22,938	27,525	32,112
Electrician (Wells/lifts)				
Meter Maintenance Supervisor (Finance)				
Personnel Technician (Personnel)				
Utility Billing Supervisor (Finance)				
Legal Assistant (Legal)	17	24,031	28,836	33,643
Planning Coordinator				
(Planning and Development)				
Utility inspector (Public Works Admin.)				
Athletic director (Recreation)	18	25,122	30,147	35,170
Center/waterfront director (Recreation)				
Detective (Detective)				
Lead mechanic (Fleet management)				
Master building inspector				
(Planning and development)				

Source: City of North Myrtle Beach, South Carolina, Budget, Fiscal Year 1993–1994.

incorporated into city charters, for instance (Katz, 1979). More frequently, police and firefighter employee groups band together to separate their pay levels from all other employee groups while at the same time disagreeing on which of the two deserve to get paid the highest scale. Needless to say, a single, unified pay system is under constant pressure.

Challenges to the traditional pay plan include merit pay and "broad-banding" positions. Merit pay (a topic discussed later in the chapter) has pay set according to individual performance, not the easiest way to establish pay levels in government. One innovation is to draw broad bands of positions. By collapsing numerous job classifications into just a few broad bands, managerial discretion is enhanced. This permits a more fluid assignment of workers to meet changing managerial perceptions of what is needed to provide acceptable levels of goods and services, and to compete with the private sector. However, driven by equity concerns, unions are not very supportive of such innovations.

External labor market conditions are powerful forces in worker compensation (Groshen, 1990). Employers compete for labor. Historically, government pay levels were considered lower than private sector pay, but job security features helped offset that deficiency. Comparisons of equal work confirm the underpayment (U.S. General Acounting Office, 1991; Lewis, 1992). After adding in employee benefits to the compensation package (but not placing an economic value on added job security), the pay disparity is reduced to the point of parity or even overpayment relative to the external market (Miller, 1993). Based on similar education and experience, public workers earn more than private sector workers (Lewis, 1992). Public compensation premiums relative to the services industry, arguably the more appropriate labor market competition, add pressure for prudence (Miller, 1993). With federal employee quit rates (numbers of employees leaving as a percentage of total employment) remarkably stable and low over time, most federal employees must perceive their jobs to be worth more to them than a job elsewhere (Lewis, 1991). Calls to modify the incentives of federal employees are viewed as ways to invigorate the public service (National Commission on the Public Service, 1989; National Performance Review, 1993).

2. Overtime Pay

When staffing levels and workloads are at capacity, one way to avoid hiring additional labor is to encourage existing workers to do the needed work. This is normally accomplished by the use of overtime pay or compensation levels that are in addition to the standard pay amount. Overtime rates vary, from standard 1-1/2 times the regular rate to more than double the hourly rate, depending on the hour of the day (after normal work hours), day of the week (Sunday work), or nature of the work performed (hazardous duty). The application of the Fair Labor Standards Act (FLSA) to state and local government in 1985 introduced some consistency into overtime practices. Additional guidance is offered through statutes and collective bargaining contracts. In terms of collective bargaining, the FLSA does not bar state and local governments from refusing to negotiate overtime.

Controlling overtime use is not easy. Cities facing severe financial pressures find that they cannot commit to hiring needed firefighters and police officers, for instance. This situation can lead to an overuse of overtime, with employees likely to enjoy the extra pay for awhile, but if continued too long the situation often degenerates to a point of employee bitterness, and perhaps even litigation.

Overtime can result from employees pacing their work to gain overtime pay, thus lowering efficiency and increasing costs. In one instance, public safety personnel were accused by a city manager of abusing overtime by taking sick leave on days when they were supposed to work so that other employees could work on days they were supposed to have off, thereby earning overtime. When absent, the work is shifted to those on the job, leading to overtime pay under some labor contracts. In the early 1980s, the Cleveland (Ohio) Board of Education sought to change a custodian labor contract requiring time-and a-half pay to each building custodian when there was no assistant custodian present in the building in the noon lunch hour. Another example of overtime misuse results from the practice of basing future pension benefits on the employee's final year's earnings, including all overtime payments. Attempts to change such practices often meet stiff employee opposition, including court suits contesting managerial authority.

A predictable level of overtime utilization is just another item to figure into budget estimates and presents no particular problem. At a calculable point, overtime costs justify adding a new employee. This contrasts with the unplanned, unpredictable situation facing most jurisdictions. Crime waves, large fires, visits by dignitaries (such as a presidential visit), utility system failures, natural disasters, etc., can result in enormous overtime liabilities. The work is performed to meet the immediate need; the bills come in after the fact.

A common tendency is to underestimate the need for overtime expenditures at the time of budget preparation but reality sets in once service demands build during the year. An arbitrary overtime budget amount can help balance a budget during budget adoption but lead to budget deficits later. The City of Kent, Ohio provides a case in point. In the early 1980s, the city budgeted the same amount for overtime each of 4 years even though (1) actual overtime incurred always exceeded the amount, (2) service demands increased each year, and (3) base payroll increased. In the Kent example, overtime to provide minimum staffing represented almost one-half of all overtime in the fire department with overtime created to pay for coverage on holidays representing another 30%. The remaining overtime met the more conventional definition of service demands in excess of staffing.

As such, overtime policies (or the lack of any) can have serious budgetary implications. Work force design contributes to the use (and abuse) of overtime. The linkage of overtime costs to artificial personnel ceilings was noted by Standard and Poor's Corporation (1991, p. 25), a bond rating firm: "Often, overtime is used as a head-count management tool to restrain the growth of the personnel roster. As a result, shortages of key personnel, such as fire fighters, at critical times will often yield unanticipated overtime expenditures." The firm proceeded to quantify the extent of overtime in major states, cities, and counties, serving notice to potential governmental issuers of debt that the use of overtime is an issue during credit review, thereby requiring tighter management policies.

3. *Employee Negotiation Over Pay*

The influence of unionization on state and local government pay policy is a theme that has generated a large body of literature. The basic question—does public sector unionization lead to higher wage and salary levels—has been examined along two lines (Lewin et al., 1979; Zax, 1988; Zax and Ichniowski, 1988). The first line of research attempts to find out which occupational group within a single government unit gets the most out of unionization. Illustrative of this work is research that indicates that firefighters are the most effective wage gainers under collective bargaining, achieving roughly a 5% wage increase as a result of unionization (Lewin et al., 1979). Firefighters may be effective because they can translate into political support the potent weapon of citizens' sympathy with the plight of firefighters having to deal with a dangerous job. More concretely, direct union political activity translates into higher compensation and employment (O'Brien, 1992; Gely and Chandler, 1993). Zax (1988) found a spillover effect with bargaining units helping increase the compensation of their own members as well as other municipal employees.

A second line of research examines pay differentials across juridictions. It is generally assumed that pay levels are primarily local decisions with labor market competition varying from city to city and from region to region. Applicable law, however, may remove pay from being a formal subject of bargaining in one government but not another. Research has uncovered other factors affecting pay differentials, such as the degree of unionization. Zax (1988:315) points out that public sector labor relations has no clear meaning of "unionization," with the strength of unions increasing "as employees move through organization [of the union] into recognition, and as cities move from nonbargaining to bargaining." Compensation levels were found to be higher for employees in cities with more powerful degrees of unionization. In sum, the two lines of research indicate that unionization's impact on pay depends on variables such as the type of employee group and characteristics of the labor–management relationship.

Collective bargaining over pay (and benefits) in the federal government is denied by the Civil Service Reform Act of 1978. As might be expected, labor officials feel that bargaining for pay could be viable; but, interestingly, less valuable than bargaining for benefits (Naff, 1993).

4. Salary Compression

Limits on legislative pay may effectively cap the pay of others in the employ of a government. This means that politics, not the market, dictates pay limits. Elected officials are prone to link their pay level to civil service pay policies. Since many politicians are hesitant to face the electors after voting themselves a pay increase, civil service salary and wage levels are effectively capped in such situations until politicians gain the wherewithal to press for their own pay increase. As such, politically imposed and maintained pay lids negate labor market pricing. This can thwart the recruitment of professionals and top business executives into government. As a survey of federal workers revealed, the highest ranked item cited as a reason for leaving the federal service was pay compared to what could be earned outside the federal government but, interestingly, an equal number said this was a reason to stay (U.S. General Accounting Office, 1992a).

Congress is ingenious in designing a pay system to tilt in its favor. One method is to have the pay for members of Congress established by an independent commission whose recommendations become law unless disproved by Congress. This effectively removes some of the bitter pay decision from the direct hands of Congress. Congress has found it hard to withstand appearances of citizen disfavor with congressional pay raises and has avoided taking all scheduled pay increases. This also affects executive branch pay levels. High-level civil servants find their pay held captive to congressional pay limits, with many SES executives at the maximum salary level despite different levels of responsibility.

Pay compression is not only an issue in the political linkage of congressional pay and federal executives. Salary structures internal to an organization may disregard time and grade. Higher ranking organizational members may receive less pay than received by lower ranking employees, even those new to the organization. Public agencies at state and federal levels also must contend with arbitrary limits. Universities, both public and private, face pay compression since they must pay market rates for new faculty. If there is strong demand for a particular field or discipline, then market salary levels are likely to exceed the amounts paid to existing faculty members who for various reasons are unable or unwilling to place their services to the market test. Pay compression is especially a problem for senior faculty members confronted with newly minted PhDs joining the faculty at higher salaries. In such situations, market conditions and merit win over internal maturity. To rectify pay compression requires the allocation of more funds to compensate for the inequity. In a survey of academic leaders by Snyder et al. (1992), actions to "combat salary compression . . . were to increase awards to promotions in rank, set salary floors, . . . promote more rapidly, and increase travel funds as an alternative form of compression" (p. 21).

5. Automatic Pay Adjustments

During periods of high inflation, employees demand, and frequently receive, multiyear labor contracts with assurances that wages and salaries will increase in each future year by a certain factor, such as in proportion to cost-of-living changes. As inflation subsides and/or fiscal stringency occurs, these cost-of-living adjustments, or COLAs, become subjects of union "give-backs" to employers in exchange for job security. The COLAs gained by New York City unions over many years were modified in return for the U.S. govenment's loan guarantee to the city during its mid-1970s fiscal crisis. At a minimum, a COLA ensures workers that their buying power remains constant despite inflation. Escalators, however, can result in increased payroll costs in the height of the inflationary period, harming the governmental entity in its fiscal struggle over inflation. Klay (1981) advocates a delayed lump sum adjustment to offset the loss of income brought on by inflation, but structured in a manner to delay its fiscal impact on the employer. This type of payment can be linked to an economic incentive to improve productivity.

6. *Pay-for-Performance*

A concern with the productivity effort (or lack of it) by public employees has fostered the call for pay-for-performance systems. The public sector trails the private sector in linking pay to individual performance or true merit. These arrangements lead to one-time bonuses and/or expansions in base pay for worker efforts to increase productivity on the work site. Gain sharing is one type of pay policy that permits employees to personally gain a share of the savings achieved through individual initiative to improve productivity. These programs require a change in fiscal thinking (especially for gain sharing) and a yearly budget for a pool of resources from which to pay the performance incentives. Civil Service reform in the late 1970s led to several experiments but no systemic change in the way federal employees earn their pay (Siegel, 1992). A persistent problem in implementing merit pay in the federal government, and in states that have adopted pay-for-performance systems, is the lack of consistent funding. When such programs are subject to the whim of the budgetary process, their value in promoting productivity suffers. Despite the advantages that pay-for-performance systems offer to manager–employee relationships, resource scarcity looms as the major implementation hurdle (Ingraham, 1993; Kellough and Lu, 1993).

Limits on salary levels lead employers and employees to other forms of compensation. A myopic focus on salary levels omits the often "hidden" side of compensation policy: employee benefits.

C. Employee Benefits

The basic concept behind an employee benefit is to provide the employee with a form of compensation other than a wage or salary. Just as with direct pay, employee benefits have developed to meet variously defined needs of workers, or employer perceptions of those needs (Quattrociocchi, 1981; Hildreth and Miller, 1983). Fiscal pressures combined with changing demographics of the work force presage even more attention to the benefit package (Guy, 1993).

Public employees enjoy a wide range of employer benefits. As recently as 1990, 96% of full-time workers in state and local government were covered by retirement plans. Insurance and paid leave programs were widespread: 93% of full-time employees were covered by medical insurance, 62% by dental insurance, 88% by life insurance, and 95% by paid sick leave. However, part-time employees were much less likely to have the same benefit package (Hedger, 1992). To complicate matters for some workers, public sector unions have agreed to cuts in benefit programs for yet-to-be-hired employees but not for current ones, setting up a two-tier system (Walters, 1993). Although there are numerous forms of employee benefits in use, this section considers key monetary benefits only, excluding nonmonetary programs as illustrated by suggestion boxes and sports leagues.

Public sector benefit programs have a major impact on employment decisions. While the pay level may be less than a private sector position, benefits are often more rewarding (Moore, 1991;

U.S. General Accounting Office, 1992a). Once employed, employee benefit programs help retain workers. A random sample of federal employees revealed that of 37 factors listed, 10 were rated by more than half of all respondents as being key reasons for staying with their public employer. As shown below, work force design and benefit programs represented most of the important reasons to stay in the federal service, shown with the percentage of respondents listing the item:

Annual leave program	79%
Sick leave program	75%
Job security	71%
Opportunity to work freely on your own	65%
Retirement system	63%
Opportunity to apply abilities	62%
Opportunity to work on challenging assignments	58%
Current duties/responsibilities	57%
Progress you have made in the federal government	55%
Work schedule used	53%

Source: U.S. General Accounting Office, 1992.

Some of the most ingenious machinations in management and finance occur in the design of employee benefit programs. Due to favorable tax laws, individuals perceive a gain by getting "paid" in the form of a benefit instead of straight pay. The organization can benefit also. For example, the organization can provide employees a larger compensation package by agreeing to pay generous pension benefits and health care coverage. Policymakers can avoid current tax increases by pushing the costs of such benefits into another budget year—typically decades away. To the extent that governments have to pay and report on an actuarial basis, this form of shifting the liability into the future is reduced if not eliminated. Tight budgets in the last few years have led states to reduce (or forego) their annual contributions to public employee pension systems. This is hard to resist when the pension system is in healthy financial shape (as some are), but it occurs even when pension systems have unfunded actuarial liabilities.

1. Benefit Politics

Employee benefit programs can advance political agendas. According to some theories of government growth, political incumbents have an incentive to grant government employees new or expanded benefits (or pay) in order to gain their support at the ballot box. This is bolstered by the evidence that the size of the public employee work force influences the growth of that state's public spending (Garand, 1988).

The Reagan administration demonstrated a keen mastery for using the employee benefits arena to meet financial and ideological (political) strategies. This was pointed out earlier as efforts to deny federal employee health care coverage of abortions and the attempts to influence which organizations would be eligible to participate in the Combined Federal Campaign. Another episode, instigated by the Reagan appointee director of the Office of Personnel Management, equated civil service retirement benefits with welfare, that all-too-frequent subject of political ridicule. Needless to say, this proposition did not go without equally strong objection (Rosen, 1986).

State government political preferences are evident when the design of benefit programs for public employees is placed alongside social welfare programs. In attempting to limit entitlement programs, such as Medicaid, states have a tendency to require recipients to clear more stringent hurdles before gaining coverage (such as obtaining second opinions) than states require of their own employees (Noah, 1991). This policy inconsistency makes little sense to nonemployee tax-payers, much less the recipients of the harsher rules.

2. Benefit Stability

Employee benefit programs, and their features, are set by longstanding labor contracts, person-nel systems, or other legal structures. Changes or enhancements may result from budget crises, new labor contracts, laws, competitive practice, or market pricing. A change during the budget year compounds the problem of coping with higher costs. Economic conditions may influence program utilization, causing costs to escalate (e.g., more vacation use by one person causes other workers to pick up the slack, on overtime). All of these impact the baseline budget, confounding budget planning (Forsythe, 1993).

An all-to-frequent area of budget instability is health insurance. Governments enter into group insurance contracts to reimburse employees or directly pay for employee medical and hospital care costs. When insurance contracts come up for renewal (or are unilaterally reopened by the insur-ance company) after the budget has already been prepared and adopted, the contract renewal price may exceed the amount budgeted. The jurisdiction therefore faces a reallocation decision with funds conserved in other accounts reprogrammed into the deficit health account, unless revenues are exceeding forecasts.

Governmental entities have learned that managing health care costs is prudent. This usually involves the shifting of any benefit increase to the employees. That is, the jurisdiction places a ceiling on the amount of benefit dollars it will contribute per employee. Any amounts required to maintain or obtain a given benefit above the funded ceiling becomes the employee's responsibil-ity. Shifting costs to employees is seen as a way to introduce more cost discipline into benefit use. According to this view, as the employee becomes more financially responsible for costs, more cost-conscious buying occurs. This preserves the baseline budget. Public agencies also have to be vig-ilant against private employers restricting health coverage for spouses of public employees, effec-tively shifting family benefit costs to the often generous government employee health benefit program.

3. Union Influences

As in the pay area, unions can influence employee benefit choices, with two impacts most notice-able (Ichniowski, 1980; Zax, 1988). First, unions can increase the probability that a jurisdiction will offer a particular benefit. Emergency medical specialists may demand special AIDS protec-tion gear beyond that required by safety laws, and school custodians may require double pay for after-hours work, for example.

Second, employee benefit programs can evolve in ways unanticipated at first. Mitchell and Smith (1991) found that "unionized employers are less likely to fund future pension obligations fully" (p. 1). Extra pay or overtime is an example where unions seek coverage expansion. Con-tinuing the case of the school custodians, once the union secured a provision for double pay, it later requested minimum periods of time (2 hr) for any call-back, even if the call-back lasted only 30 min.

4. Form of Benefits

Employee benefits are provided as cash payments and as economic value in kind. A typical cash payment is overtime for work performed. However, two forms of cash payment are for time not worked (Woska, 1988). One cash form is earned time off, found as vacation and sick leave, holiday pay, and compensatory time off. As revealed earlier, federal employees view cash benefit programs as strong motivators. The other form of cash payment for time not worked includes paid time away from primary duties, including coffee breaks, military leave, jury duty, sabbaticals, etc. It is wise for organizations to track and calculate the full costs of these payment forms (Woska, 1988).

In addition to cash payment forms, employee benefits also are provided as a subsidy or in-kind amount. Housing for military personnel, for example, is provided as either a housing allowance (a cash payment) or the provision of family housing on a military base (an in-kind economic value). Combined, these housing benefits account for about 24% of the regular military compensation of a member of the armed service (U.S. Congressional Budget Office, 1993). Most budgets fail to fully disclose the costs of employee benefits programs that provide an economic value (cash and in-kind) to workers.

5. Benefit Portfolios

Individuals have different preference structures. Changing demographics of the workplace call for more employee flexibility over employee benefits (U.S. General Accounting Office, 1992c; Guy, 1993). One approach for dealing with the question of choice is to employ the cafeteria approach to employee benefits. After providing a minimum package (including any legally required benefits), employees get a set number of benefit "dollar values" to "buy" selected benefit options, including high or low levels of health benefits. Under this system, an employee desiring only a bare, minimum level of health coverage could direct the remaining benefit dollar value into a more highly valued benefit, such as more paid vacation days.

Regardless of the amount of employee discretion, benefit programs must be measured against their costs. The benefits portfolio is not without its costs. As Woska (1988) pointed out, a number of benefit programs provide pay for time not worked, with significant budget costs. A change in any single employee benefit program could make an employee assume more financial risk but lessen the employer's financial liability. This is the tough choice facing public leaders each budget cycle.

D. Total Work Force Budgeting

The preceding sections have shown that work force design, pay issues, and the benefit portfolio combine to greatly structure an organization's budget. A large share of most governmental units' operating budgets, especially in local government, is allocated for employee pay and benefit costs. To look at any of the three issues separate from their budgetary impact is folly. A more integrated budgetary approach is needed.

The government compensation debate traditionally focuses on pay issues with much less attention given to employee benefits (especially misused or costly ones). Recent attempts to redefine the issue into one of "total compensation" have failed. A proposal before Congress that was not enacted defined total compensation as

> including payments and entitlements which are provided by an employer for an employee in exchange for the performance of work and which costs the employer money, either directly or indirectly, now or in the future; are of value to an employee in one or more ways, such as by adding cash to an employee's current income, by creating a present value to the employee based on the prospect of future receipt, or by providing an employee with compensated time off; . . . and are measurable (Federal Employee Compensation Reform Act, proposed, 1979).

The purpose of the proposed statute was to turn compensation decisions from an unfocused concern over pay, pension, overtime, sick leave, and so forth into a very integrated one of the total costs of salary and benefits. The purpose was to gain control over the proliferation of employee benefits. However, there has been little interest in Congress to implement total compensation, partly due to costs (Siegel, 1992), measurement problems (U.S. General Accounting Office, 1980), and politics (Hartman, 1982).

To arrive at the total compensation of a government worker (or work force) is one goal. Another goal is to make comparisons to similar calculations in the private sector. Public sector pay policies have traditionally recognized, but not followed, the need for compensation comparability with the private sector. The idea is to match comparable jobs in business and government, and to see what variation exists (U.S. General Accounting Office, 1991). Policymakers then have to confront the impact, if any, of labor market compensation on service delivery. Usually comparability only focuses on pay, excluding employee benefits such as retirement programs. Total compensation comparability has the distinction of expanding the comparability concept to include employee benefits.

Recognizing that labor costs must include the economic value of pay and employee benefits, the concept of total compensation comparability still has merit (Moore, 1991). To implement it, however, requires computing the dollar value of all employee benefits and revealing that value combined with the pay level. This conveys the need to comprehensively examine the budgeting of personnel requirements and to reexamine the budget format to see what might foster more disclosure of total work force compensation.

IV. WORK FORCE DISCLOSURE STRATEGIES

Human resource management is a creative and dynamic arena despite its image to many public executives (Sampson, 1993). Managers use the HR management system to encourage and deploy people in accomplishing service delivery goals. Strategic interests are advanced by tactics to expand or reduce the work force, suggesting a need to briefly review some of the more common ones.

A. Budget Expansion Tactics

Budgets can conceal labor costs, even as they both grow. Once a new line or staff function is started, the almost natural tendency is to expand the scope of responsibilities, requiring additional personnel. Theories of bureaucracy predict this behavior (Downs, 1966), partly building on division of labor and specialization (Gerth and Mills, 1946). As Kaufman (1976) concludes, growth in agencies is inherent. Several forces may accelerate growth, namely demographic, economic, or technological developments (Rabin et al., 1981). Executives and (more in frequently) legislators may erect (short-term) barriers that slow, but do not stop, growth. Incremental decision making fuels budget growth (Lindbloom, 1959). Executives gain prestige and other rewards for managing larger asset bases, making growth a goal by itself (Borcherding, 1977).

This chapter has already hinted at many expansion tactics that also mask the full labor costs of programs. For example, one is the "transfer of slots" from one level of government to another, expecially as used by the federal government to fund positions in state and local governments to perform a nationally determined program (e.g., Medicaid). Hiring temporary employees also helps by avoid staffing limits. Two other tactics deserve expanded treatment.

1. *Temporary Assignments*

The executive office of the president has become infamous for its use of the "temporary assignment." Why is it practiced in the White House? Presidents face almost inscrutable press attention. When the president is on a cost cutting (or budget containing) rampage, it is not politically advantageous for the president's staff to increase, but past presidents have found it useful to cast aspersions on all the other agencies and bureaucrats. As a result, presidents are prone to announce that they will not let their office staff grow like the rest of government.

Presidents find that contemporary events and issues require quick attention and exhaustive analysis, some more political in nature than others. The result is a heavy workload for the assigned staff. To get around the self-imposed constraints on the size of the staff to meet service demands, the staff expands. To be too open about the expansion invites political damage, especially if the president is striving to maintain an image as one against the growth of government. Rather than take a direct route, other executives agencies, including the Defense Department, detail (or assign) their staff over to the White House for "temporary" duty. So while the position appears under the lending agency's budget, the person actually receives his or her job duties from another organizational unit, in this case an office of the president.

Efforts to delimit the use of temporary assignments have not been altogether successful. For instance, if the temporary assignment extends beyond 180 days, offices of the White House are supposed to reimburse the lending agency. During this 6-month period there are rules also. Under the principles of appropriations laws, the lending agency must be reimbursed for these employee costs unless the duty will aid the lending agency in accomplishing a purpose for which it receives appropriations. Furthermore, lending agencies are not suppose to hire individuals exclusively for details to the White House; but they do. This has emerged as a controversial practice, especially with Schedule C workers, or those employees exempted from the competitive service because they are to be either policy determining or involve a close and confidential working relationship with a key official. While the U.S. General Accounting Office (1992b), an arm of Congress, has advocated the need for tighter controls, the executive branch's Office of Personnel Management has maintained the need for flexibility.

2. Employees as Consultants

Governmental units and agencies facing hiring ceilings find it convenient to enter into consulting contracts for the performance of particular duties and responsibilities. With sufficient personal service funding, an internal staff would perform the requisite responsibilities. However, when the stability of funding is in question, consulting contracts fit the bill for hiring the talent as long as funds last.

The financial control system may inadvertently foster the use of consultants instead of full-time workers. A contributing element is the budget format. Typically, the budget provides different categories for personal services (direct employee salaries, wages, and benefits) and professional services (engineering, legal, accounting/auditing, management services, etc.). Still another budget category reveals service delivery expenses, providing a convenient avenue for some consulting contracts. Regardless of the way recorded, the effect is the same; the jurisdiction receives services that otherwise would be performed by an employee, if one was hired. Thus, adequate funds might be available in a professional services budget (or operating services) category but not in the personal services category. In one example of circumventing personnel ceilings, a governor's office contracted with a public university department to hire selected people who in turn were tasked to work in the governor's office.

Consultants offer certain advantages over the direct hiring of new staff. Permanent employees impose long-term costs that are difficult to reduce without layoffs. The jurisdiction may save on employee benefit costs by hiring a consultant instead of directly hiring a new staff member. Also, service demand fluctuations may dictate the use of consultants. Still, the tactical employment of consultants hides their true nature and value.

B. Budget Reduction Tactics

Since pay and employee benefits consume a predominant percentage of the ongoing costs of providing public service most budget reduction strategies target personnel costs. This section provides a short description of many (but by no means all) of the methods employed to reduce personnel costs. The items are not listed in any priority or preference ordering.

1. *Freeze hiring*. An unfilled position saves money. Thus, a common approach is to delay filling vacant positions. In fact, a freeze in hiring is often announced by incoming mayors, governors, and presidents. Selective hiring during the freeze requires care, else the signals to spenders and to the public are muddled. Appendix A provides an elaborate set of criteria used in Volusia County, Florida to fill selective positions during a hiring freeze. A freeze should generate personnel savings, but it may impose a cost in terms of ineffective work force planning and staffing. This is especially the case when the freeze applies to all vacant positions, even those that might significantly retard revenue collection or essential services. If a personnel ceiling is imposed but the personnel services funds remain, then the manager may attempt to contract out the work to external firms (Hartman, 1982).

2. *Freeze promotions*. Promotions usually mean higher levels of compensation. Thus, delays in promotions generate savings but at a cost of morale, incentives, and fair play. This is due to the impact of such freezes on some while those who received promotions in the recent past are seldom subjected to a retroactive application of the same treatment.

3. *Train to avoid lost employee time*. Employees who do not work but still draw a wage or salary cost the organization money. While this applies to underworked employees, it is clearly directed at avoidable, on-the-job injuries and lost work due to avoidable sick leave. The organization might also gain higher productivity results by a training program to inform employees on how to do their work more safely and with greater efficiency.

4. *Cut overtime*. To get employees to work past a normal work schedule, the organization often offers premium pay (typically, one-and-a-half times the standard pay level). Employees can get addicted to the extra pay and structure their labor contracts or work patterns to ensure that the premium pay will be forthcoming each pay period. The organization may have to plan on a certain amount of overtime to cover peak service periods (e.g., water line breaks at night, special events, police work, snow removal, or other "on-call" activities). The real problem emerges when overtime becomes uncontrollable. At a calculable point, the organization would save money by hiring a new employee instead of continuing to pay overtime to one or more employees.

5. *Use temporary employees*. A permanent, full-time employee receives a full package of benefits and pay. From strictly a cash budget viewpoint, it may be cheaper to hire a qualified temporary to cover peak demand periods or specialized tasks. An advantage to using temporaries is that they are subject to quick termination. Employers can become addicted to temporaries, keeping them on the payrolls long after the "temporary" situation has expired. Furthermore, when temporaries work alongside more permanent employees but receive less pay for the same work, morale can sink.

6. *Use volunteers*. Similar to temporaries, volunteers can supplement the work force. Also, they are usually providing their time for little, if any pay. This feature greatly restricts who might serve as a volunteer and for how long. Volunteers often come from groups such as retirees, spouses of wage earners, civic-minded individuals, and students. Careful supervision and placement of volunteers is required.

7. *Freeze, reduce, or cut budgeted raises*. The expectation of a raise is a motivator for many employees. To freeze, reduce, or cut an expected raise has the opposite effect. Since internal pay plans often use grade and step structures, with yearly movement into a new step (up to a maxi-

mum), employees come to expect the yearly salary enhancement. Anything that disrupts this pattern is sure to cause severe displeasure. An employee (or union) lawsuit could subsequently go against the employer especially if the budgeted raise is called for in a labor contract. Courts have on occasion required employers to pay the affected employees the delayed raises and lost interest earnings, thwarting any anticipated budget savings.

8. *Extend review periods between wage/salary changes.* To reward longevity, personnel systems usually specify certain future points when a pay increase will be considered. Often this is on the anniversary date of hiring, say yearly. Extending the period from every 12 months to every 18 months cuts costs. While the idea is repugnant to employees, it does delay pay increases. If not done for the entire work force, the time extensions may be viewed as a form of reverse favoritism.

9. *Reduce or change benefits.* Employees are prone to forget that their employer pays for a range of benefits that the employee may use only sparingly or just takes for granted (such as disability insurance, life insurance, etc.). Employers can reduce the range of benefits or the extent of coverage of an individual benefit program. Instead of paying the full costs of the employee's premium for disability insurance, the employees might obtain group rates but require the employee to pay the premium if that benefit is chosen.

10. *Impose benefit cost sharing.* The employer may want to shift more of a benefit cost to the employees, especially if the premiums are rising in costs. For example, instead of paying for all health care costs of employees, the employer might require employees to pay all costs up to a deductible amount and a percentage of all additional costs (a copayment). Thus, if an employee wants to retain the past level of health insurance, that employee has to pay the full price increment.

11. *Reduce work week.* If a pay level is assumed to compensate for a certain work week (40 hr/week), then a forced reduction in the work week requires a corresponding pay reduction. This generates large personnel cost savings but affects the service delivery function and the employees' morale and economic livelihood. The State of Louisiana used this approach on several occasions to balance its budget.

12. *Furlough or forced leave without pay.* Similar in effect to a reduced work week, employees are required to take off one or more days (e.g., Fridays) as an unpaid day of leave. The State of Idaho used this in 1982, the City of New Orleans employed it in late 1986, and Moore, Oklahoma used it in 1992. New Hampshire's governor tried, but failed (on legal grounds), to institute a half-day-per-month furlough in 1991.

13. *Salary deferral.* To avoid layoffs or work week reductions, employees are required (or asked to voluntarily agree) to accept a deferral of a portion of wages or salary, perhaps 8 hr of the 40-hr week. In one state example, pay checks were calculated on 32 hr; the amount due for the deferred 8 hr was listed in a special account to be taken as additional leave time or paid off at the time of separation. Not so long ago, thousands of employees for the State of Michigan voluntarily agreed to this layoff alternative when the state faced a serious budget crisis. The government obtains current cash flow savings without a reduction of current services in exchange for an obligation to pay in the future (Jarrett, 1986).

14. *Encourage early retirement.* Usually the highest paid employees are the ones with the longest organizational tenure. If motivated, these employees might consider retiring earlier than planned. A common practice is to offer a financially attractive early retirement package to such employees so that they are likely to accept the offer. The retirement package can be very costly since it has to take into account large accrued annual and sick leave payouts as well as the lump sum "incentive" amount, up to a full year's pay. The organization accepts this large, one-time cost in order to reduce its future recurring budgets. This can disrupt service delivery if not well planned.

Part of the loss is experienced talent and the organization's memory of key practices. To achieve the cost savings of an early retirement program, the position must be eliminated and not refilled. Due to the sudden nature of many early retirement programs, succession planning does not take place. However, this appears to be less of a problem in government than in private business.

15. *Downgrade position.* To downgrade a position is to place an employee in a lower grade. This usually imposes a loss of income, either immediately or, for federal employees, after years. Even if done through a systematic reclassification of jobs, the stigma is longlasting.

16. *Contract out functions.* The private sector has demonstrated an increasing willingness to assume public service responsibilities for a fee. Certain functions (e.g., garbage collection, janitorial, accounting, debt collection, etc.) are frequent candidates. Public managers have learned that contracting out can save money under certain assumptions about the level and quality of expected services.

17. *Pay absorption.* Pay absorption results when all or part of a pay raise has to be financed out of existing budget authority instead of new funds. As used by the federal government (U.S. Congressional Budget Office, 1983), this practice effectively reduced other administrative expenses since the affected agency was required to save funds from unfilled positions or reduce other expenses, and use the funds instead to meet the salary account. The Office of Management and Budget used pay absorption rates to guide agencies in how much to request from Congress in supplemental funds for pay adjustments. Congressional appropriations committees then determined what percentage of the full cost of planned raises the agency had to absorb; the remainder of the planned raise was how much additional funding Congress appropriated. While at first Congress treated pay absorption as a temporary absorption with full funding forthcoming in the next budget cycle, it lead to permanent absorptions. States have used pay absorption to deal with pay increases. One year in Ohio's budget cycle, state universities were required to absorb the costs of pay increases out of the existing budget levels for a period of time. In this case the state used pay absorption to preserve its cash flow. The state remitted 10% less than the full amount of funds necessary to pay the first half of the year's salary budget even though the university had to pay all the first-half amount. The state remitted 60% of the yearly salary total in the second half of the year, thus covering the entire year's budgeted salary level, albeit not in two equal allocations. This forced the universities to absorb the extra 10% of all payroll from other administrative accounts during the first half of the year.

18. *Adopt an attrition policy.* Attrition is a reduction in the number of employees as a result of voluntary resignations, retirements, transfers, or death. For the organization, attrition offers a strategic opportunity to eliminate a position. Agencies have different attrition rates, even in the same jurisdiction. A full attrition policy is ineffective because some vacanies must be filled while other positions may not carry equal value. One tactic is to replace less than the number leaving, e.g., hiring one replacement for every three empty slots. An attrition policy shifts more work to the remaining employees. This impact on productivity has potentially positive (if there is undercapacity to start with) and negative (straining already overworked employees) implications. Attrition is often carried out in conjunction with a hiring freeze to prevent the replacement of an open position. Attrition is one of the most common budget reduction techniques and is a centerpiece of President Bill Clinton's announced deficit reduction efforts, as it was of previous presidents.

19. *Reduction in force (RIF).* To achieve a work force reduction, an employee may be subject to an involuntary separation (Dennis, 1983; Rich, 1986). This is analogous to a layoff in the private sector. An RIF may be unavoidable when an entire service activity or program is abolished. Needless to say, the involuntary loss of a job is highly stressful to the individual even if the employer maintains a listing to recall laid-off workers as job openings occur. The relationship be-

tween attrition savings and RIF savings is often overlooked. A study by the U.S. General Accounting Office (1985) notes: "An agency that cuts staffing levels by means of attrition must bear the cost of salaries of the employees who exceed the staffing goal until they, or their equivalent, leave. The salary cost of reducing staff by attrition is equal to the gross salary savings from a RIF. As shown in [Table 3 and Fig. 1], once staffing is reduced to the targeted level, the savings in salary are the same from that point on, regardless of how the reduction was accomplished." The cost effectiveness of alternative reduction strategies requires close examination (Greenhalgh and McKersie, 1980).

   20. *Limit bumping and retreat rights.* Civil service systems often permit employees facing RIFs or layoffs to bump newer employees. Seniority, not merit, controls in such settings. This leads to "overqualified" (i.e., more senior) workers taking lower level jobs merely to continue their employment. Limiting such bumping to one career path (e.g., lawyers not bumping into secretarial jobs), only one or two steps in any career sequence, and basing it on performance, not seniority, overcomes the worst aspects of this situation. A related provision is "retreat rights," meaning that an employee can retreat in the face of a work force reduction to a job previously held, therefore bumping a lower employee. Again, limits on such retreat rules guard against the negative implications.

   21. *Manipulate pension payments.* Most public entities contribute to an employee retirement program as a form of fringe benefit. Pension plans are built on the accumulation of employer as well as employee contributions (plus investment earnings on these cash assets). The financial strength of a pension system is the degree to which current assets are estimated to cover the long-term value of benefits. Actuarial estimates of the required contribution levels are based on many assumptions, including (but not limited to) potential investment returns, projected rate of inflation, demographic composition of the covered work force, mortality and disability rates and expected

Table 3 Relationship Between RIF Savings and Attrition Savings: A Hypothetical Example

Assumptions		
Total no. of employees at start of year	=	2000
Target no.	=	1900
No. positions to eliminate	=	100
Attrition rate per year	=	10%
Attrition rate per month	=	0.008%
Average salary per year	=	$24,000
Average salary per month	=	$2000

End of month	Employees remaining of 100 exceeding end-of-month target	Av. no. employees during the month	Mean monthly salary ($)	Salary savings (or cost of employees exceeding target) ($)
0	100	92	2,000	184,000
1	84	76	2,000	152,000
2	68	60	2,000	120,000
3	52	44	2,000	88,000
4	36	28	2,000	56,000
5	20	12	2,000	24,000
6	4	0	2,000	0
				624,000

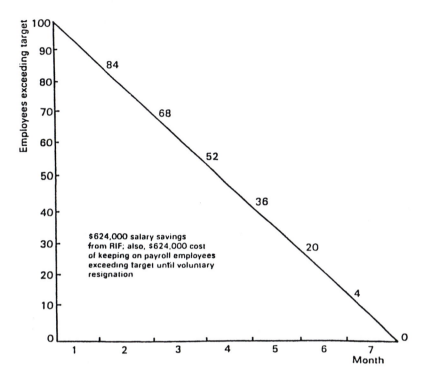

Figure 1. Hypothetical example of the relationship between RIF savings and attrition savings. (The actual relationship of the reduction of employees over time is slightly curvilinear, as the base number of remaining employees [to which the attrition rate is applied] is reduced each month. The relationship has been shown here for simplification as a straight line. The actual calculation of salary savings uses the more accurately curvilinear approach.)

employee career paths. States have been known to grab a pension surplus (when pension assets exceed career paths. States have been known to grab a pension surplus (when pension assets exceed liabilities). But can pension contributions be cut during austerity efforts? In many instances, pension funding is a mandatory appropriation. As a contractual obligation embodied in some state constitutions, arbitrary cutbacks in pension benefits are not possible. Still, reductions in the employer's contribution have proven successful (but they are contentious) in some cases. For example, the City of Philadelphia recently slid one year's pension contribution liability into the next fiscal year, thereby freeing up budget resources. Another manipulation is to change the assumptions on which future estimates of a pension plan are built. By raising the assumed rate of earnings on the fund's assets (interest earnings), lower pension costs result—almost miraculously. For example, a 1% increase in the assumed investment return rate, holding other assumptions constant, can result in a 20–25% reduction in the required annual contribution. This is due to the fact that higher investment earnings mean that the employer has to contribute less to maintain the same employee benefit structure.

22. *Change work rules.* The rules by which employees conduct their work impact costs, not just benefits. Labor contracts often are filled with restrictions on managerial assignment of duties. Of course, employees and their unions object strenuously to any change.

23. *Simplify the work process.* Streamlining the process by which a service is delivered helps eliminate bottlenecks and inefficiencies. This leads to changes in factors of production (e.g., less

labor, or the substitution of equipment for labor). A focus on the needs of customers and recipients often leads to reengineering the work process.

C. Disclosure Strategies

A listing of various budget expansion and budget reduction tactics does not adequately convey the costs of such action. Managerial choices can negatively affect individual productivity. Short-term financial costs can outweigh savings, with the full benefit of the savings not showing until later. Budget practice is part of the problem and the solution. In the budgeting of HR requirements, there are three work force disclosure strategies; control, modified, and service. There are parallels in this scheme to the three-prong management control concept advanced by Anthony (1965), as refined by Schick (1966). The labeling of the strategies is intended to convey a hierarchy of strategies with each level imposing more financial disclosure about the linkages between the work force and the service delivery goals of the organization.

1. Control Strategy

Under the control strategy, the focus is on the amount of dollars devoted to pay and employee benefits, and the number of employees. This is accomplished, however, in ways that make it nearly impossible to isolate choices for achieving organizational goals.

Table 4 Control Budget Format ($)

Code	Object classification	FY 92 actual	FY 93 budgeted	FY 93 estimated	FY 94 budgeted
011	Salary, regular	70,289	53,219	53,190	74,639
014	Overtime	636	500	450	500
021	FICA	4,968	4,029	4,023	5,636
022	Employee retirement	6,547	5,211	5,203	7,288
023	Employee insurance	5,763	4,275	4,250	5,900
030	Training	564	270	270	505
040	Workers compensation	1,880	1,477	1,475	2,066
050	Awards	255	255	255	255
	Subtotal	90,902	69,236	69,116	96,789
110	Clothing/uniforms	420	846	600	784
111	Materials/supplies	1,256	1,608	1,600	1,997
112	Office supplies	71	155	155	155
113	Printing/binding	0	375	300	375
120	Communications	478	375	375	425
130	Contractual services	28,388	24,750	22,500	31,000
131	Repair/maintenance	2,074	900	700	3,400
132	Professional services	0	100	0	100
140	Subscriptions/dues	60	90	90	90
150	Vehicle operations	554	750	500	1,000
151	Fuel	1,699	1,600	1,500	2,200
	Subtotal	35,000	31,549	28,320	41,526
	Total	125,902	100,785	97,436	138,315

Source: Animal and Nuisance Control Department, City of North Myrtle Beach, South Carolina, Budget, Fiscal Year 1993–1994.

In this basic form of disclosure of work force expenditures, each budgeted department or subunit has separate line items for wages and salaries, overtime, social security (FICA), retirement, group health insurance premiums, among other items. Table 4 provides a sample control budget format, with its myriad items by which to dictate spending. In a variation of the same strategy, line items are totaled into the category called personal services. Wage and salary costs are almost always reflected in this manner; benefit costs deviate from this practice. For example, employee benefits may be presented as a lump sum amount under a general administrative (e.g., finance) unit, or one that is only a pass-through account without any service activity or employees—termed a nondepartmental account in many jurisdictions. Thus, instead of showing the planned benefit expenditures for each particular department (e.g., police), all benefits are shown in one lump sum for the entire jurisdiction. This separates the service delivery unit from a major aspect of the service cost, requiring a cost allocation plan to link the nondepartmental account to the appropriate organizational unit (cost center).

An enhancement to the basic form of disclosure is an enumeration of authorized positions vs. the number of positions actually filled (MacManus, 1984). This faciliates the control of positions. Taken together, the information provided by the control strategy is rich in detail but weak in substance. The primary focus is on the number of employees, not the dollars allocated. As with line item budgeting, this form of work force strategy is the foundation for control, not management.

2. Modified Strategy

For personnel staffing levels to reflect flexible work schedules and to be compared over time and across jurisdictions, a modified disclosure strategy is needed. A technique that facilitates the disclosure of work force choices is the use of full-time equivalents (FTE); a method of converting a position into one year of work. A full-time position (one FTE) equals 2080 hr of work (a 40-hr work week × 52 weeks). By adopting the FTE method, a combination of part-time slots equals a full-time position. The FTE method for budgeting personnel slots is consistent with, and advances, the utilization of part-time employees, such as in job sharing (where the schedules of two part-time employees are arranged to cover the duties of a single full-time position). Personnel ceilings, even when defined by FTEs, are oppressive restrictions on managers (National Performance Review, 1993). In fact, yearly FTE ceilings were instituted as a replacement for limits measured by those on the payroll on a specific day of the year (U.S. General Accounting Office, 1981 and 1977).

A multiyear staffing profile, by department, allows budget reviewers to see the ebbs and flows of departmental staffing levels. This is important since one change in staffing can have an impact on the unit's current and future budget needs. By itself, the mere presentation of the number of authorized slots for each of several years masks the work performed (or not performed), as well as the quality of the work. Obviously, the same number of people can do more or less, depending on many factors, including individual motivation, leadership, and adequate support in terms of supervision, equipment, and supplies.

It helps to show changes in the number of positions that are contained in the budget as it moves from a departmental request, to the chief executive's recommendation, and in the approved budget to the legislative body. The City of Phoenix uses this style of presentation. Just as budget levels are likely to change as the typical budget travels through its decision-making gauntlet, so too should personnel numbers (Wanet, 1976). In fact, due to the labor-intensive nature of public service, spending levels are likely to be driven by decisions regarding changes in personnel.

A comparative staffing analysis helps judge the appropriate work force size against a standard of comparison. Ratios of staffing to another variable, such as population or per capita income, are possible, both for the aggregate work force (city employees per 1000 population) and for each department (police officers per capita). Before using such comparative figures, caution is required because governmental units differ in many respects (social, economic, and political to name just three major categories). To reduce budget analysis to one ratio (e.g., police officers per capita) may be specious.

Why should governments make comparisons against standards given the limitations of such analyses? For instance, if governments are going to reduce the staffing and if there is a local inability to determine performance by more quantitative standards, one alternative is to use a ratio as a baseline to detect any deviations. Comparative staffing analyses draw attention to variations from a standard, whether the standard is the average for similar jurisdictions or some other comparison group (Berne and Schramm, 1986). This signals the need for additional analysis on the appropriateness of the variance. A trend analysis of several ratios, over time, serves to improve the utility of this information.

In summary, the operating premise of the modified disclosure strategy is that single-year staffing information is less useful than comparative figures, for the same unit over several years and in comparison with similar jurisdictions. Using FTEs as the unit of analysis facilitates flexible work design, a requirement of contemporary management.

3. Service Strategy

Governments can move from a focus on the number of personnel being budgeted to the service goals that employees are hired to achieve. Table 5 shows a program budget where the focus is on the service, with position counts as collateral information. This fosters managerial discretion, but further improvements are possible with a focus on the service delivery process and service costs. Relating the efficiency and effectiveness of service delivery to the actual production process is important. Flow charts of client processing systems help identify the points where labor is required

Table 5 Program Budget

Service	FY93 adjusted ($)	FY94 budget ($)	Increase/ (decrease) ($)	Permanent full-time FY94 positions
Stabilize and transport medical patients by responding to 90% of EMS calls within 4.5 min with minimum of one unit and two emergency personnel.	4,833,461	4,836,334	2,873	142.5
Reduce the average damage and loss per structure fire by responding to 90% of structural fires, automobile accidents, or equivalent emergency incidents within 4.5 min with a minimum of three fire and rescue units including 10 or more personnel in order to control the incident and provide life services to citizens affected.	1,234,946	1,235,842	896	33.5

Source: Extract from Fire Department, City of Hampton, Virginia.

to satisfy service goals. The emphasis is on service results, not personnel numbers. It requires organizing around processes of tasks that yield a needed customer service. Budgets that enhance this form of organization are rare, but the heightened emphasis on total quality management should stimulate more work.

For managers to meet service goals requires management of total costs rather than personnel positions. Since budgeting does not operate in a static economic environment, adoption of the service strategy might help deal with stressful budget periods. The service approach to work force budgeting compliments productivity improvements and follows many of the newer precepts of reengineering the organization along with timeless concepts of cost accounting and performance budgeting. It also is consistent with the precepts and suggestions contained in the National Performance Review (1993), a Clinton administration program to improve government.

A step in this direction is the adoption of responsibility centers, or cost/profit centers as they are called in business. A responsibility center is the lowest organizational unit for which management has an interest in knowing the full costs of conducting an activity. Responsibility centers in a police department of a medium-sized municipality might include foot patrol, vehicle patrol, court assignments, detention, community relations, records management, communications, juvenile relations, investigation, research, court liaison, and leadership (Rhode Island Department of Community Affairs, 1983). In each cost center, the costs of personnel assigned, if only for certain portions of the workday or period, must be recorded against the particular responsibility center. A police officer may actually spend one-third of the time on foot patrol, one-third on vehicle patrol, and one-third on court appearances. If so, the police officer's compensation costs would be allocated to each of the three responsibility centers. This permits development of indicators such as personnel hours per crime cleared and total costs per crime cleared. A problem with such fine distinctions in time allocations is that they make discontinuation of one responsibility center less clear-cut, if part of an employee's time is devoted to a function that will end, but the only part assigned to a function that continues to be funded. Advantages of a cost system are numerous (Coe and O'Sullivan, 1993). This action encourages managers to focus on cost per unit of service (Forsythe, 1993). An example of this type of information is shown in Appendix B.

A recent initiative by the Governmental Accounting Standards Board (GASB) examines the possiblity of incorporating service effort and accomplishment measures in state and local government financial reports. It builds on the comparative indicators identified with the previous disclosure strategy. The GASB initiative is part of a large effort to "seek ways to provide information useful in assessing not only how much and on what an entity is spending its resources, but also what its citizens are getting from the use of public funds and how efficiently and effectively those funds are being used" (Hatry et al., 1990). This effort supports the call by Kwiecinski and Williamson (1984): "Work force budgeting is a process to develop workload standards as a tool which can be used in determining appropriate departmental staffing levels." At the federal level, the Chief Financial Officers Act of 1990 and the 1993 Government Performance and Results Act should provide vehicles for change (Hildreth, 1993a). This agenda presages more attention to service outcomes than dollars budgeted for salaries and benefits, strictly focusing on the number of funded positions.

V. FISCALIZING HR ACTIONS

Work force issues are typically handled by line agencies with general policy guidance established by the HR office, but the finance officer is involved too. The roles of the parties involved are instructive for understanding work force budgeting. A significant difference exists in how chief executives view budgeting (finance) executives in contrast to personnel (HR) heads. Central to the success of most public chief executive officers (city manager, mayor, governor, or president) is the exercise of financial strategy. HR management does not seem to rise to the same level of concern. This carries over in who is considered part of policymaking, and it is not the personnel manager (Sampson, 1993). While the HR office has primary responsibility for recruitment, selection, and development of employees, the finance (and budget) office has the responsibility to monitor the financial implications of all work force decisions (Thompson, 1975). Without such monitoring, the fear is that negative budget variances (overspending an account, for instance) may result. This increases the demand for more direct fiscal oversight over many HR actions. As demonstrated by Rich (1982) in his study of New York City personnel practices during a time of severe fiscal pressure, agency heads faced hard choices choosing a course of action between fiscal monitors, employee/union members, and constituent groups, a gauntlet sure to make agency heads earn their pay. In spite of such difficult operating environments, current management initiatives favor giving line managers more responsibility for all it takes to achieve mission-driven results (Barzelay and Armajani, 1990).

Internal controls over work force costs rest on the working relationship between the finance and HR functions. Most are before-the-fact, ex ante controls. Including a finance staff member on a labor contract negotiation team is a common way to gain assurance that budget considerations are given adequate review during intense negotiation sessions (Barbour, 1976; Friedman, 1983). Another common requirement is for all personnel staffing requests to go through central offices, such as the finance (or budget) office (Herzik, 1991; Cornia et al., 1985; see also Hamilton, 1993). Under such a system, the finance office ensures that (1) the new or changed position is authorized for funding in the budget and (2) funds are currently available. Even if the position is authorized through the budget, funds must be available. A cash flow problem or some other financial disruption might have changed the jurisdiction's financial position since the budget's adoption several months earlier. Merely having an authorized position does not necessarily mean that funds are available to pay the new or changed compensation. To handle such situations, the routine paperwork flow is often from the hiring work unit through both the personnel and finance offices. Work units resist the notion that budget problems outside their control should deny them their authorized work force staffing complement. The fact remains that most governments do not immunize one department from the problems caused by others.

Even when a staffing request overcomes the above hurdles, the finance office still has several ongoing responsibilities. The processing of payroll checks is the most visible function, but one with many subtleties. The finance office may want to change the payroll process for purely financial reasons. To do so may help the jurisdiction overcome a liquidity problem. When the State of California faced a liquidity problem in 1992, it issued "warrants" insteady of checks to workers, vendors, and state tax refund recipients. This promise-to-pay certificate was accepted by banks from their customers. The banks charged the state interest for holding the certificates until the state made up the amount. The effect was to achieve a cash flow advantage by delaying the actual payment of cash.

Finance functions gain cash flow advantages without having to resort to such external machinations. This arises from the fact that wages and taxes are paid after the work is performed. The organization therefore gains any interest earned on the retained funds until wages and taxes are paid. Since financial officers have a never-ending quest to earn interest on idle cash (and to avoid paying big bills), it may be advantageous to change payroll dates to achieve longer accrued payables. This can occur by pushing one pay period into another fiscal year to save one pay period's cash outlays in a tight end-of-year budget. In the fourth quarter of fiscal year 1988, the State of Louisiana delayed payroll checks by an additional 2 days per pay period, effectively pushing an entire 2-week payroll into the next fiscal year. In a repeat of a 1987 manipulation, but done in the early 1990s to meet deficit control limits, part of the U.S. Defense Department's payroll was delayed in order to push the payment into the subsequent fiscal year. While these activities may further budget success in the short run, they indicate more serious structural budget problems, with the service delivery system not sustainable by the likely level of resources.

Some budgets are based on the assumed cost savings of expected personnel vacancies. The total amount of funds budgeted for personnel, calculating all positions times their respective salaries, is usually the maximum amount that will be expended by a jurisdiction, making forecasting of expenditures easier than that of revenues (Frank, 1992). When a position becomes vacant, it typically takes several weeks to refill, and as a result, the amount of unpaid salary accumulates. The vacancy reserve, as it is called, also increases when a new employee's salary is lower than that of the person leaving. Significant amounts are accumulated by delaying the hiring process, especially where employee turnover is greatest. From this perspective, turnover is a lucrative asset (Falton and Todor, 1982).

To utilize this vacancy lag, budgeteers reduce the personnel budget by calculating the anticipated savings from delayed hiring and subtracting it from the maximum budget. A simple example shows how it works. If an agency's personal services budget category is estimated at $400,000, a reserve for unused salaries of $20,000 reduces the $400,000 budget figure to $380,000. The $20,000 is an estimate of the vacancy reserve. Understandably, this amount should be a conservative estimate determined from historical, or known, turnover rates, the average time necessary to fill a vacancy, and the difference between old and new salaries. Reserves for unused salaries range from 1% to 5% of the total personnel budget, but vary by organization.

Jurisdictions differ in the strategy for using the vacancy reserve. The overall personal services budget category may be reduced by the expected amount, or the saved funds may be reallocated later in the year. The funds may represent departmental spending flexibility through a transfer between personnel and other spending categories (if allowed). For example, universities often permit major academic units (e.g., college of business) to retain salary savings from its subunits for reallocation as one-time expenses, such as travel and research grants. Another approach is not to budget for vacancies, or at least not all expected savings, and to allow the resulting vacancy savings to become part of the end-of-year fund balance. By necessity, however, if the assumed vacancy savings do not materialize as expected, strict budget controls (e.g., delaying or not replacing positions to achieve savings) and budget cuts result. Furthermore, a myopic focus on vacancy savings disregards any concern over where the cuts occur within the organization and the impact (if any) on service delivery.

As demonstrated, HR managers face a steady encroachment in their functional responsibilities by "fiscal managers" (Rich, 1982). As defined by Rich (p. 99), the new actor in the personnel scene is the "political budgeteer, " the one who decides "who got what and how much." Applying strict budgetary control to HR requirements has its costs. Micromanagement of personnel actions by budget offices thwart managerial discretion (Wilburn and Worman, 1980). In an age of customer-driven agency missions, a focus on head counts (i.e., personnel numbers) is as short-sighted as arbitrary limits on the replacement of open positions. The core issue is the cost of the deliverable service. Since labor makes up a large share of most public services (despite the technological advances to date), a focus on costs requires evaluation of the proper mix of HR requirements (e.g., volunteer, parttime, fulltime, benefit types and levels, etc.) that will best factor into a cost-effective service. Managers closest to the service recipient or client have to have flexibility to make critical HR choices and be held accountable for such decisions. To make the point clearer, former state budget director Dall Forsythe (1993, p. 421) reminds the budget control advocate that "financial management is not the final goal" of the organization.

VI. SUMMARY

In summary, the budgeting of HR requirements is the very essence of a service organization, especially a governmental jurisdiction. Individuals build their lives around the expectation of continuity of work even though a few sometimes forget that they are expected to do a satisfactory level of work in return. The annual operating budget is supposed to take into consideration the expendables such as wages, salaries, and employee benefit costs. When labor costs exceed the availability of resources or the desired service levels, the budget process can impose a change. There remains a concern, however, that short-run budget considerations impose a significant burden on the functioning of an HR system (U.S. General Accounting Office, 1985). This chapter supports the proposition that service delivery goals should guide budget decisions instead of simply having decisions premised on adding up the cost of existing staffing patterns.

Human resources are costs that require funding from taxpayers, rate payers, or service users. Managers must acquire, deploy, and control human resources to produce public goods and services. At the same time, governmental units tend to centralize financial control. As a result, it has been asserted that central budget offices, "should exhibit greater sensitivity to human resource issues" (Lane and Wolf, 1990). A humane and ethical bureaucracy, however, has to meet tests of efficiency and effectiveness. It is therefore important for the finance and personnel functions to take careful, deliberate, and coordinated action in financing work force activities lest one adversely influence the other to the detriment of effective management of public services.

APPENDIX A*

Filling Positions During a Hiring Freeze

Hiring freezes are common strategy for reducing expenditures over the short term. The Department of Management and Budget of Volusia County, Florida designed a scoring system to evaluate requests to fill positions during a hiring freeze. The following table lists the evaluation criteria, weighing, and points that make up that system.

An agency requesting approval to fill a position must rate the position on its relative importance within the agency and its impact on operations if it remains vacant. The criteria for scoring the request are grouped accordingly under "position impact" and "vacancy impact." Each criterion, in turn, is weighted (e.g., funding availability for the position is given a weight of 6% of the total 100%).

There are two or more possible responses for each criterion. Each response is assigned a point value (e.g., 5 points for external support). Responses under some criteria are assigned a point range. The score for each criterion is determined by multiplying the points for the chosen response by the percentage weight for that criterion (e.g., 5 points × 7.5%). The scores for all of the criteria are then tallied to calculate the total score. In theory, the higher the tally, the greater justification there is for filling the position.

Managers must make some tough choices as they fill positions during a hiring freeze. This scoring system does not make those decisions any easier but does help to measure the results.

*Reprinted with permission of Government Finance Officers Association, 180 N. Michigan Ave., Suite 800, Chicago, IL 60601.

Criteria for Evaluating Position Requests

% Weight	Criteria	Points
	Position Impact (30% of total score)	
7.5	Position Support	
	•External (public)	5
	•Internal support	2
4.5	Type of Position by Category	
	•Administrative support/clerical	2
	•Professional/technical	2
	•Manual/skilled worker	4
	•Public health/safety	5
4.5	Position Revenue Link/Funding Source	
	•Property tax-supported/internal service	1
	•Partially tax-supported	2
	•Enterprise	4
	•Fully grant-funded	5
	•Partially grant-funded	3
	•Direct revenue link	1-5
4.5	Positions—Division	
	•Number of similar positions by category	
	(0–1) 5 pts. (2–4) 3 pts. (5+) 1pt.	
	•Percent of similar positions by category	
	(75–100) 5 pts. (50–74) 3 pts. (25–49) 2pt. (<25) 1Pt.	
3.0	Positions - Department	
	•Number of similar positions by category	
	(0–1) 5 pts. (2–4) 3 pts. (5+) 1pt.	
	•Percent of similar positions by category	
	(75–100) 5 pts. (50–74) 3 pts. (25–49) 2pt. (<25) 1Pt.	
6.0	Funding Availability	
	•Available	5
	•Marginal	2
	•None	0
	Vacancy Impact (70% of total score)	
28.0	Service Delivery—Vacancy will result in:	
	•Elimination of the service	5
	•Significant delay in providing service	3-4
	•Slight delay in providing service	1
	•None	0
21.0	Financial	
	•Overtime	
	- Cost exceeds position	5
	- Cost between 75% and 100%	4
	- Cost between 25% and 74%	3
	- Costs less than 15%	1
	•Additional cost of filling position (subtract):	
	>$10,000	3
	>$5000	1
	$0	0
21.0	Reason for Vacancy	
	•Management decision	5
	•Attrition	1
	•Transfer	2
	•New positions authorized in current fiscal year	5

APPENDIX B*

Performance Indicator: Road Striping Work Orders

The Sunnyvale City Council has budgeted $2752 for 90 employee work hours to prepare 64 striping work orders, with 90% completed within 45 days after determining the need to apply stripe to roadway.

Program	Traffic engineering
Objective	Determine street painting and signs needed to restripe roadway, with 90% completed within 45 days.
Task	Prepare striping work order
Production Unit	Work order

	Planned
Number of units	64 work orders
Unit cost	$43
Work hours	90
Cost	$2752

REFERENCES

Advisory Commission on Intergovernmental Relations (1985). *Bankruptcies, Defaults, and Other Local Government Financial Emergencies,* Advisory Commission on Intergovernmental Relations, Washington, DC.

Andersen, D.F., and Feldt, J.A. (1978). *Cost Estimates for Alternative Reduction in Force Strategies: A Markov Simulation,* New York State Continuity of Employment Committe, Albany, NY.

Andersen, D.F., Balk, W., Feidt, J., and Zimmerman, V. (1978). *Comprehensive Workforce Planning in New York State: A Policy and Organizational Analysis,* New York State Continuity of Employment Committee, Albany, NY.

Anthony, R. N. (1965). *Planning and Control Systems: A Framework for Analysis,* Graduate School of Business Administration, Harvard University, Boston.

Axelrod, D. (1989). *A Budget Quartet,* St. Martin's Press, New York, chap. 2.

Barbour, G. J., Jr. (1976). How to price a negotiated labor settlement, *State and Local Gvmt Rev. 8*(3) (Sept.): 78–79.

Barnard, C. I. (1938). *The Functions of the Executive,* Harvard University Press, Cambridge, MA.

Barzelay, M., and Armajani, B. J. (1990). Managing state government operations: changing visions of staff agencies, *J. Policy Anal. Manage., 9* (Summer): 307–338.

Belcher, D. W. (1974). *Compensation Administration,* Prentice-Hall, Englewood Cliffs, NJ.

Benecki, S., (1978). The impact of unionization of the budget shares of common municipal functions, Working Paper Series 78-77, The Ohio State University, Columbus, Ohio.

Berne, R., and Schramm, R. (1986). *The Financial Analysis of Governments,* Prentice-Hall, Englewood Cliffs, NJ.

Blackburn, R., and Rosen, B. (1993). Total quality and human resources management: lessons learned from Baldridge award-winning companies, *Acad. Manage. Exec., 7*(3): 49–66.

Borcherding, T.E. (ed.) (1977). *Budgets and Bureaucrats,* Duke University Press, Durham, NC.

Bowen, H. R., and Schuster, J. H. (1985). Outlook for the academic profession, *TIAA/CREF Res. Dialogues, 6* (Dec.).

Brudney, J. L., and Duncombe, W. D. (1992). An economic evaluation of paid, volunteer, and mixed staffing options for public services, *Public Admin. Rev.* (Sept./Oct.) *52*(5): 474–481.

---

*Source: Sunnyvale, California, Performance Audit and Budget System.

Cascio, W. F. (1993). Downsizing: what do we know? What have we learned? *The Executive, 7*(1) (Feb.): 95–104.

Chandler, T., and Feuille, P. (1991). Municipal unions and privatization, *Public Admin. Rev., 51*(1) (Jan./ Feb.): 15–22.

Clark, T. N., and Ferguson, L. C. (1983). *City Money: Political Processes, Fiscal Stress and Retrenchment,* Columbia University Press, New York.

Coe, C. K., and O'Sullivan, E. (1993). Accounting for the hidden costs: a national study of internal service funds and other indirect costing methods in municipal governments, *Public Admin. Rev. 53*(1) (Jan./ Feb.): 59–63.

Cornia, G. C., Timmons, W. M., and Varley, D. A. (1985). Cooperation betweeen personnel and budget offices during position requests and reclassifications, *State and Local Gvmt. Rev., 17* (Winter): 180–187.

Cromwell, B.A., and Wirkus, I. A. (1990). State and local red-ink: crisis or opportunity, *Federal Reserve Bank of Cleveland Economic Commentary* (July 15).

Dalton, D.R., and Todor, W.D. (1982). Turnover: A lucrative hard dollar phenomenon, *Acad. Manage. Rev., 7*(2): 212–218.

Dennis, H.C., Jr. (1983). Reductions in force: The federal experience, *Public Personnel Manage. 12*(1) (Spring): 52–62.

Downs, A. (1966). *Inside Bureaucracy,* Little, Brown, Boston.

Feldt, J. A. and Anderson, D.F. (1982). Attrition versus layoffs: how to estimate the costs of holding employees on payroll when savings are needed, *Public Admin. Rev.,* (May/June): 278–282.

Forsythe, D. W. (1993). Financial management and the reinvention of government, *Public Prod. Manage. Rev., 14*(4): (Summer): 415–423.

Frank, H.A. (1972). Expenditure forecasting, *Handbook of Public Budgeting,* (J. Rabin, ed.), Marcel Dekker, New York, pp. 167–209.

Friedman, M. (1983). Calculating compensation costs, *Budget Management: A Reader in Local Government Financial Management* (J. Rabin, W. B. Hildreth, and G. J. Miller, eds.), Institute of Government, University of Georgia, Athens, pp. 116–127.

Garand, J. C. (1988). Explaining government growth in the U.S. states, *Am. Polit. Sci. Rev., 82* (Sept.): 837–849.

Garcia v. San Antonio Metropolitan Transit (1985), 105 S. Ct. 1005.

Gargan, J.J. (1981). Consideration of local government capacity, *Public Admin. Rev. 41*(6) (Nov./Dec.): 649–658.

Gely, R., and Chandler, T.D. (1993). Public sector union political activities and departmental/expenditures, Working Paper, Department of Management, Louisiana State University, Baton Rouge.

Gerth, H. H., and Mills, C.W. (1946). *From Max Weber: Essays in Sociology,* Oxford University Press, New York.

Greenhalgh, L., and McKersie, R.B. (1980). Cost-effectiveness of alternative strategies for cutback management, *Public Admin. Rev. 40*(6) Nov./Dec.; 575–584.

Groshen, E. L. (1990). How are wages determined? *Federal Reserve Bank of Cleveland Economic Commentary,* Federal Reserve Bank of Cleveland (Feb. 15).

Guy, M. (1993). Workplace productivity and gender issues, *Public Admin. Rev.* (May/June): 279–282.

Gyourko, J., and Tracy, J. (1989). Public sector bargaining and the local budgetary process, Working Paper, National Bureau of Economic Research.

Hamilton, K. (1993). The staffing function in Illinois State government after *Rutan, Public Admin. Rev. 53*(4) (July/August): 381–386.

Hartman, R. W. (1982). Federal employee compensation and the budget, *The Federal Budget: Economics and Politics,* (J. M. Boskin and A. Wildavsky, eds.), Institute for Contemporary Studies, San Francisco, pp. 263–280.

Hatry, H. P., Fountain, J. R., Sullivan, J. M., and Kremer, L. (eds.) (1990). *Service Efforts and Accomplishments Reporting: Its Time Has Come,* Governmental Accounting Standards Board, Norwalk, CT.

Hedger, D. (1992) Benefit in state and local governments address family concerns, *Monthly Labor Rev., 115* (March): 32–37.

Herzik, E. B. (1991). Improving budgetary management and fostering innovation: expenditure control budgeting, *Public Prod. Manage. Rev., 14* (Spring): 237–248.

Hildreth, R. P. (1983). Registered nurses in supplemental nurse staffing agencies: the short-term effect on changes in labor-force participation, unpublished Ph.D. dissertation, University of Alabama in Birmingham.

Hildreth, R. P. (1985). Monitor's Report to the Court, Vol. 2, U.S. District Court Middle District, Montgomery, Alabama.

Hildreth, W. B. (1983a). Applying professional disclosure standards to productivity financial analyses, *Public Prod. Rev., 17*(3): 269–287.

Hildreth, W. B. (1983b). Collective bargaining impacts on local government management, *Readings in Public Administration: Institutions, Processes, Behavior, Policy,* 4th ed., (R. T. Golembiewski and F. K. Gibson, eds.), Houghton Mifflin, Boston, pp. 271–281.

Hildreth, W. B. (1989). Financing strategy, (eds.) *Handbook of Strategic Management* (J. Rabin, G.J. Miller, W.B. Hildreth, eds.), Marcel Dekker, New York, pp. 279–300.

Hildreth, W. B. (1993a). Federal financial management control systems: an integrative framework, *Public Budget Fin. 13*(1): 77–86.

Hildreth, W. B. (1993b). Budgeting the workforce: influences, elements, disclosure strategies, and roles, *Int. J. Public Admin., 16*(7): 985–1014.

Hildreth, W. B., and Miller, G. J. (1983). Compensation and reward systems: public-sector pay and employee benefits, *Handbook on Public Personnel Administration and Labor Relations,* (J. Rabin, T. Vocino, W. B. Hildreth, and G. J. Miller, eds.), Marcel Dekker, New York, pp. 159–191.

Hyde, A. C. and G. Whitman, Workforce planning: the state of the art, *The Public Personnel World,* (J. Shafritz, ed.), International Personnel Management Association, Chicago, 1977, pp. 65–73.

Ichniowski, C., (1980). Economic effects of the firefighters' union, *Ind. Labor Rel. Rev. 33:* 198–211.

Ingraham, P. (1993). Pay for performance in the states, *Am. Rev. Public Admin. 23*(3) (Sept.): 189–200.

Jarrett, J. E. (1981). Gubernatorial control of state government work forces, *State Gvmt, 54:* 87–92.

Jarrett, J.E. (1986). Strategies and innovations in productivity improvement, *LBJ School of Public Affairs, Public Affairs Comment, 33*(1) (Fall).

Johnson, A. T. (1982). Cutback strategies and public personnel management, *Rev. Public Personnel Admin. 3*(1) (Fall): 41–55.

Jones, B.D., Greenberg, S., and Drew, J. (1980). *Service Delivery in the City: Citizen Demand and Bureaucratic Rules,* Longman, New York.

Katz, H.C., (1979). Municipal pay determination: the case of San Francisco, *Ind. Rel., 18:* 44–58.

Kaufman, H. (1976). *Are Government Organizations Immortal?* Brookings Institution, Washington, DC.

Kellough, J. E., and Lu, H. (1993). The paradox of merit pay in the public sector: persistence of a problematic procedure, *Rev. Public Personnel Admin.* 13(2) (Spring): 45–46.

Klay, W. E. (1981). Combating inflation through wage negotiations: a strategy for public administration, *Public Admin. Rev. 41* (5) (Nov./Dec.): 520–526.

Kwiecinski, A. M., and Williamson, R. P. (1984) Controlling the workplace by planning for people: Metro-Dade County, *Public Admin. Rev. 44* (March/April): 163–168.

Lane, L. M., and Wolf, J. F. (1990). *The Human Resource Crisis in the Public Sector: Rebuilding the Capacity to Govern,* Quorum Books, Westport, CT.

Ledvinka, J. (1994). "Human Resource Planning," Chapter 8 in this volume.

Ledvinka, J., and Hildreth, W. B. (1984). Integrating planned change intervention and computer simulation technology: the case of affirmative action, *J. Appl. Behav. Sci. 20:* 125–140.

Levine, C. (1978). Organizational decline and cutback management, *Pub. Admin. Rev., 38* (July/August): 316–325.

Lewin, D., Hurton, R. D., and Kuhn, J. W. (1979). *Collective Bargaining and Manpower Utilitization in Big City Governments,* Allanheld, Osmun, Montclair, NJ.

Lewis, G. B. (1988). The consequences of fiscal stress: cutback management and municipal employment, *State and Local Gvmt Rev. 20*(2) (Spring): 64–71.

Lewis, G. B. (1991). Turnover and the quiet crisis in the federal service, *Public Admin. Rev. 51*(2) (March/April): 145–155.

Lindblom, C. (1959). The science of "muddling through," *Public Admin. Rev., 19* (April): 79–88.

MacManus, S. A. (1984). Coping with retrenchment: why local governments need to restructure their budget document formats, *Public Budget. Fin. 4*(3) (Autumn): 58–66.

McKinley, W. (1992). Decreasing organizational size: to untangle or not to untangle. *Acad. Manage. Rev. 17*(1): 112–123.

Massey, J., and Straussman, J.D. (1981). Budget control is alive and well: case study of a county government, *Public Budget. Fin., 1*(4) (Winter): 3–11.

Miller, Glenn H., Jr. (1993). Profligacy or providence? Changes in employment and compensation of state and local government workers, *Public Budget. Fin. 13*(1) (Spring): 95–106.

Mitchell, D. S., and Smith, R.S. (1991). Pension funding in the public sector, Working Paper No. 3898, National Bureau of Economic Research (Nov.).

Mladenka, K. R. (1991). Public employee unions, reformism, and black employment in 1,200 American cities, *Urban Affairs Q. 26*(4) (June): 532–548.

Moore, P. (1991). Comparison of state and local employee/benefits and private employee benefits, *Public Personnel Manage., 20*(4) (Winter): 429–439.

Naff, K. C. (1993). Toward the year 2000: issues and strageties for labor-management relations, *Int. J. Public Admin. 16*(6): 813–839.

Nalbandian, J., and Klingner, D. (1981). The politics of public personnel administration: towards theoretical understanding, *Public Admin. Rev. 41*(5), (Sept./Oct.): 541–549.

National Association of Counties Research, Inc. (1983). Living with mandates: a guide for elected officials, *Budget Management: A Reader in Local Government Financial Management* (J. Rabin, W. B. Hildreth, and G. J. Miller, eds.), Institute of Government, University of Georgia, Athens, pp. 39–52.

National Commission on the Public Service (1989). *Leadership for America: Rebuilding the Public Service,* Lexington Books, Lexington, MA.

National Performance Review (1993). *From Red Tape to Results: Creating a Government That Works Better and Costs Less,* Government Printing Office, Washington, DC.

Newland, C. (1976). Public personnel administration: legalistic reforms vs. effectiveness, efficiency, and economy, *Public Admin. Rev. 36* (Sept./Oct.): 529–537.

Noah, T. (1991). Instead of tax rises, Michigan tries to cure deficit with cutbacks, *Wall Street Journal,* October 30, pp. A1, A6.

Nollen, S.D. (1982). *New Work Schedules in Practice,* Van Nostrand Reinhold, New York.

O'Brien, K.M. (1992a). Compensation, employment, and the political activity of public employee unions, *J. Labor Res. 13*(2) (Spring): 265–273.

O'Brien, K.M. (1992b). Form of government and collective bargaining outcomes, *Public Fin. Q. 20*(1), (Jan.): 64–76.

Osborne, D. and Gaebler, T. (1992). *Reinventing Government,* Addison-Wesley, Reading, MA.

Ostrenga, M. R., Azan, T. R., McIlhattan, R. D., and Harwood, M. D. (1992). *The Ernst and Young Guide to Total Cost Management,* John Wiley and Sons, New York.

Pagano, M. A. (1993). Balancing cities' books in 1992: an assessment of city financial conditions, *Public Budget. Fin., 13*(1) (Spring): 19–39.

Perry, J.L., and Miller, T.K. (1991). The Senior Executive Service: Is it improving managerial performance. *Public Admin. Rev. 51*(6) (Nov./Dec.): 554–563.

Peterson, G. E. (1976). Finance, *The Urban Predicament* (W. Gorham and N. Galzer, eds.), Urban Institute, Washington, DC, pp. 35–118.

Quattrociocchi, S.M. (1981). Fringe benefits as private social policy, *New Strategic Perspectives on Social Policy* (J. D. Tropman, M. J. Dluhy, and R.M. Lind, eds.), Pergamon Press, New York, pp.422–433.

Rabin, J., Miller, G. J., Hildreth, W. B., and Lynch, T. D. (1981). Public Bureaucracy, *Contemporary Public Administration* (T. Vocino and J. Rabin, eds.) Harcourt Brace Jovanovich, New York, pp. 40–63.

RAND (1992). Personnel cuts call for careful knife, panel cautions, *RAND Res. Rev. 15* (Winter): 3–6.

Rhode Island Department of Community Affairs (1983). Monitoring Performance, *Budget Management: A Reader in Local Government Financial Management* (J. Rabin, W.B. Hildreth, and G.J. Miller, eds.), Institute of Government, University of Georgia, Athens, pp. 106–115.

Ricciuti, J. R. (1982). Federal personnel cuts: a blessing still disguised, *J. Policy Anal. Manage., 2*(3): 457–461.

Rich, W. C. (1982). *The Politics of Urban Personnel Policy; Reformers, Politicians and Bureaucrats*, Kennikat Press, Port Washington, NY.

Rich, W. C. (ed.) (1986). Symposium: reduction-in-force policy: issues and perspectives, *Public Admin. Q. 10*(1) (Spring), 3–6.

Riordan, T. H. (1991). *Building the Budget, Mun. Fin. J. 12*(2) Summer: 79–89.

Rosen, B. (1986). Crises in the U.S. civil service, *Public Admin. Rev. (May/June):* 207–211.

Rubin, I. S. (1982). *Running in the Red*, State University of New York Press, Albany, NY.

Rutan v. Republican Party of Illinois (1990). 110 S. Ct. 2729.

Staltzstein, A.; and Bott, V. (1983). Personnel policy making in times of crisis: California public personnel directors face the aftermath of proposition 13, *Am. Rev. Public Admin. 16*(2/3): 195–207.

Sampson, C.L. (1993). Professional roles and perceptions of the public personnel function, *Public Admin. Rev. 53*(2) (March/April): 154–160.

Schick, A. (1966). The road to PPB: The states of budget reform, *Public Admin. Rev. 26* (Dec.): 243–258.

Schneider, M. (1988). The demand for the suburban public work force: residents, workers, and politicians, *J. Politics, 50* (Feb.): 89-107.

Sherwood, F.B., and Breyer, L.J. (1987). Executive personnel systems in the States, *Public Admin. Rev. 47*(5) (Sept./Oct.): 410-416.

Siegel, G. B. (1992). *Public Employee Compensation and Its Role in Public Sector Strategic Management*, Quorum Books, New York.

Snyder, J. K., McLaughlin, G.W., and Montgomery, J.R. (1992). Diagnosing and dealing with salary compression, *Res. High. Educ., 33*(1); 113-124.

Standard and Poor's Corp. (1991). Overtime pay needs attention, *Standard & Poor's Credit Week* (May 27): 23-25.

Sutton, R. I., and D'Aunno, T., (1989). Decreasing organizational size: untangling the effects of money and people, *Acad. Manage. Rev., 14* (April): 194-212.

Thompson, F. J. (1975). *Personnel Policy in the City: The Politics of Jobs in Oakland*, University of California Press, Berkeley.

Tilly, C. (1991). Reasons for the continuing growth of part-time employment, *Monthly Labor Rev. 114* (March): 10-17.

Toulmin, L.M. (1988). The treasure hunt: budget search behavior by public employee unions. *Public Admin. Rev. 49*(1) (March/April): 620-630.

Trejo, S. J. (1991). Public sector unions and municipal employment, *Ind. Labor Rel. Rev. 45*(1) (Oct.): 166-180.

U.S. Conference of Mayors (1993). *Impact of Unfunded Mandates on U.S. Cities*, Washington, DC.

U.S. Congressional Budget Office (1983). *The Budgetary Treatment of Federal Civilian Agency Pay Raises: A Technical Analysis*, Washington, DC.

U.S. Congressional Budget Office (1987). *Federal Civilian Employment*, Washington, DC.

U.S. Congressional Budget Office (1993). *Military Family Housing in the United States*, Washington, DC.

U.S. Department of Commerce (1992). *Survey of Current Business 72* (Jan.): Table 3.8B, p. 45.

U.S. General Accounting Office (1977). *Personnel Ceilings: A Barrier to Effective Manpower Management*, Washington, DC (June 2).

U.S. General Accounting Office (1980). *Problems in Developing and Implementing a Total Compensation Plan for Federal Employees*, Washington, DC.

U.S. General Accounting Office (1981). *Improving the Credibility and Management of the Federal Work Force Through Better Planning and Budgetary Controls*, Washington, DC (July 17).

U.S. General Accounting Office (1982). *Recent Government-wide Hiring Freezes Prove Ineffective in Managing Federal Employment*, Washington, DC (March 10).

U.S. General Accounting Office (1985). *Reduction in Force Can Sometimes Be More Costly to Agencies Than Attrition and Furlough,* Washington, DC.

U.S. General Accounting Office (1986). *Federal Workforce: New Authority to Make and Extend Temporary Appointments,* Washington, DC.

U.S. General Accounting Office (1989). *Federal Workforce: Temporary Appointments and Extensions in Selected Federal Agencies,* Washington, DC.

U.S. General Accounting Office (1991). *Federal Pay: Private Sector Salary Differences by Locality,* Washington, DC.

U.S. General Accounting Office (1992a). *Federal Employment: How Federal Employees View the Government as a Place to Work,* Washington, DC.

U.S. General Accounting Office (1992b). *Personal Practice: Details of Schedule C Employees to the White House,* Washington, DC.

U.S. General Accounting Office (1992c). *The Changing Workforce: Demographic Issues Facing the Federal Government,* Washington, DC.

U.S. Office of Personnel Management (1979). *Integrated Salary and Benefits Programs for State and Local Governments,* Superintendent of Documents, Washington, DC.

U.S. Office of Personnel Management (1989). *Manage to Budget Programs: Guidelines for Success.* Office of Systems Innovation and Simplification, Washington, DC.

U.S. Office of Personnel Management (1990). *Strategic Plan for Federal Human Resources Management,* U.S. Government Printing Office, Washington, DC.

Walters, J. (1993). The chastening of the public employees, *Governing* (Jan.): 26–30.

Wanet, J. (1976). Personnel measures of budgetary interaction, *Wes. Polit. Q., 29*: 295–297.

Wilburn, R.C., and Worman, M.A. (1980). Overcoming the limits to personnel cutback: lessons learned in Pennsylvania, *Public Admin. Rev.* (Nov./Dec.): 609–612.

Working Women (1993). March 20.

Woska, W. J. (1988). Pay for time not worked: a public-sector dilemma, *Public Admin. Rev. 48*(1) (Jan/Feb.): 551–556.

Yarbrough, T. E. (1981). *Judge Frank Johnson and Human Rights in Alabama,* University of Alabama Press, Tuscaloosa.

Zax, J. S. (1988). Wages, nonwage compensation, and municipal unions, *Ind. Rel., 27* (Fall): 301–317.

Zax, J., and Ichniowski, C. (1988). The effects of public sector unionism on pay, employment, department budgets, and municipal expenditures, *When Public Sector Workers Unionize* (R. B. Freeman and C. Ichniowski, eds.), University of Chicago Press, Chicago, pp. 323–361.

Zax, J. S., and Ichniowski, C. (1990). Bargaining laws and unionization in the local public sector, *Ind. Labor Rel. Rev. 43* (April): 447–462.

18

Comparable Worth and Pay Equity: From Legal Principle to Negotiating Point

LARRY S. LUTON and MARSHA L. REILLY   Eastern Washington University, Cheney, Washington

I.   INTRODUCTION

Historically women have not received monetary compensation for the work they do at a rate that compares favorably to the compensation men have received for the work they do. The difference between the pay men receive and that which women receive is often referred to as the pay gap. In the United States the gap can be documented as far back as 1815 (Wilborn, 1986, p. 8), and current trends do not portend its demise in the foreseeable future. In 1939, the median earnings of women in full-time jobs was approximately 64% of the male rate of pay (Klingner, 1988, p. 46). In 1990 the Bureau of the Census reported the figure for women as 71% of the median earnings of men in full-time jobs.

Although there is considerable disagreement over the causes of (and potential cures for) this pay gap, it is clear that they are interwoven with the rest of the American society's values and practices in complex ways. Some people believe that the gap results from a bias against women, and studies have shown that "people tend to favor men over women in otherwise identically defined situations" (Aaron and Lougy, 1986). A somewhat more specific explanation that is often given for the gap is occupational segregation: women and men have tended to obtain employment in different occupations, each finding employment in jobs that society deemed "appropriate" for them. For example, men have been more likely to find employment as truckdrivers, firefighters, or construction workers, whereas women have been more likely to find employment as secretaries, flight attendants, or nurses. There are those who say that these occupational patterns are simply the result of choices men and women have made, but the dynamics behind the development of such job segregation patterns are too complex to be explained simply as the cumulative result of multiple instances of individuals making rational, economic choices. The societal messages regarding which occupations are appropriate for men and which are appropriate for women affect the decisions of both the job seeker and the employer.

Whatever the reason behind occupational segregation, "women's jobs" tend to receive lower compensation than "men's jobs." One reason sometimes given for this pattern of disparity is the differential in unionization (Nelson et al., 1980), but there is no inherent reason why men would unionize more than women. Women have also been employed more often than men in part-time positions, which are compensated at lower rates than full-time jobs. Again, the factors that create these patterns involve more than the historical results of the economic market.

It is also true that women have moved in and out of the work force more frequently than men. Married men have the highest labor force participation rate. Married women have the lowest labor force participation rate (Polachek, 1984, p. 42). But again, the roles that society has encouraged men and women to take in its noneconomic institutions have had considerable impact on the development of that pattern: "single-never-married males and females have roughly similar lifetime work behavior patterns" (Polachek, 1984, p. 42).

The concept of comparable worth (providing comparable pay for work of comparable value) arose as the women's work issue of the 1980s because it appeared to be a policy direction that could counter the effects of social traditions and economic practices that supported the continued existence of the pay gap. In none of the advanced industrialized nations has the pay gap been significantly reduced without some kind of government-authorized deliberate intervention. Even then, reduction of the gap has usually proceeded rather slowly.

Some would counsel dependence on the market system to discover the appropriate wage rate for jobs, whether those jobs are filled by men or women. It is argued by advocates of the market system that it best reflects the values actually held in the society. As the status and power of women changes the market system will reflect those changes.

Others note that the compensation rates for many jobs are already set through the use of job classification systems. These systems are designed to evaluate the knowledge, skills, and abilities required to do a job; to place their exercise within a work context; and to evaluate the value of the job to the employer. Although most of these systems operate within parameters that reflect the market, the basic purpose of the systems is to attempt to establish equitable pay for a variety of jobs in a variety of specific settings. All but the smallest of the government jurisdictions in the United States utilize some kind of classification system.

The principles underlying comparable worth are similar to those found in most job classification systems that are based on professional job evaluation procedures, but with regard to comparable worth the motivation for appealing to those principles derives from the hope that they provide a foundation for attacking the pay gap. This hope is based on the belief that at least a significant portion of the pay gap is due to a societal bias against females that is reflected in the rates of compensation paid to "female jobs." Through the conscious policymaking involved in designing a classification system, deliberate action can be taken to change the traditions that have undervalued women's jobs.

Although the term *comparable worth* originated in a 1974 study of the compensation system for Washington State employees (U.S. General Accounting Office, 1985), when Congress was considering the Equal Pay Act of 1963, it discussed the concept of comparable worth but rejected it in favor of a more narrow concept of equal pay for equal work (Doherty and Harriman, 1981). Equal pay for equal work is now a well-established American legal principle aimed at pay equality among all those performing the same or similar work. But when it comes to establishing fair compensation rates for dissimilar work, no operable and generally acceptable principle has yet been established. Comparable worth and pay equity (providing equitable pay for any and all work) are much more controversial concepts than equal pay for equal work. As abstract concepts both comparable worth and pay equity seem to be supported by compelling logic—how can one justify not paying equitably or not compensating comparably for work of comparable value? But the difficulty has come in establishing an agreed on basis for deciding what jobs are comparable in value and what pay is equitable in comparison to other rates of pay for other jobs.

In the 1970s public employees at both the state and local levels began to push for the adoption of the concept of comparable worth in their classification and compensation systems. Sometimes the employees held a strike to try to pressure their employers to address the gap. Sometimes they went to court to press their case. Other times they lobbied for legislative redress. They also found that union negotiations regarding compensation were potential avenues for addressing the gap. In some places (e.g., the City of San Jose, the State of Washington, and the State of Minnesota), studies were conducted to examine the extent of the pay gap between male and female employees. Once the gap was documented by official studies, employees began to push for action to narrow the gap.

Having witnessed this process at the lower levels of government, the federal government has thus far resisted the suggestion that it conduct a study to determine the male—female wage gap among its employees. One head of the Equal Employment Opportunity Commission during the 1980s was so hostile to the concept of comparable worth that he called it "looney" (*Boston Herald*, 1984). Taking note of the Reagan and Bush administrations' hostility to the concept of comparable worth, proponents of deliberate action to reduce the pay gap now prefer the term *pay equity*.

As the terminology used by proponents has moved from comparable worth to pay equity, the institutional mechanism for addressing the pay gap has changed from legal challenges to legislative lobbying and collective bargaining negotiations. In the United States, comparable worth as a legal principle has failed, but pay equity may continue to make progress through policymaking or negotiated agreements.

This chapter will review the key ideas and historical developments related to the comparable worth/pay equity issue as it has evolved in the United States. It will begin with a review of the key terms and theoretical issues, proceeding through the relevant federal legislation, legal cases, and state and local case studies. It will then review some of the developments in other nations. Finally, it will speculate about the future of comparable worth/pay equity.

II. IMPORTANT TERMS AND ISSUES

In order to understand the implications of laws, legal cases, and policies relating to comparable worth/pay equity, it is necessary first to understand some of the key terms and theoretical issues underlying them. This section discusses many of the terms and theoretical issues fundamental to comparable worth/pay equity.

A. Comparable Worth and Pay Equity

Because of the history of the comparable worth debate, many people think of "comparable worth" and "pay equity" as two phrases pointing to the same idea (e.g., Neuse, 1991, p. 766). For them the basic idea that something needs to be done to address the pay gap can be referred to by either term. Others are quite specific in their distinction between the two terms. Cook (1991, p. 101) sees pay equity as the goal of closing the gap and comparable worth as the means of measuring the size of the gap. Similarly, Shafritz et al. (1992, p. 252) describe comparable worth as a compensation-deriving method aimed at achieving pay equity. The authors of this chapter see the terms as pointing to the same goal of reducing or eliminating the pay gap, but note that comparable worth was the term used more frequently when that goal was sought through arguments based on legal principles. Pay equity is a more general term that appears more suitable for inclusion in legislative and collective bargaining discussions aimed at reducing or eliminating the pay gap in particular jurisdictions.

B. Pay Gap

The pay gap is the difference between women's wages and men's. Because the statistic used to indicate "women's pay" and "men's pay" varies from report to report, figures are not always exactly the same.

Whichever statistic is used, however, women's jobs traditionally have been undervalued and, as a result, compensated less than men's jobs, even when educational requirements and the level of responsibility are higher, such as in the case of nurses receiving less pay than tree trimmers in Denver (Heen, 1984, p. 217; Hutner, 1986, p. 136).

Advocates of comparable worth maintain that the pay gap is due to sex discrimination perpetuated by traditional social values and stereotypic portrayal of women as homemakers and men as breadwinners. These values were dominant in American culture until World War II, when the demand for factory workers to support the war effort put women to work in record numbers. Since then, women have steadily entered the labor force in increasing numbers; between 1960 and 1980 their participation rate increased from approximately 38% to 53% (Tienda et al., 1987). By 1991 that figure had increased to nearly 58% (U.S. Dept. Labor, 1992, p. 78). The median earnings of women have fluctuated between 57% and 70% of male median earnings since 1960 (see Table 1).

C. "Crowding" and Occupational Segregation

The influx of women into the labor force has been attributed to the supply and demand of the labor market, a shift from an industrial to a service economy, and, most important, social acceptance of female employment (Tienda et al., 1987). However, this approval was conditional on appropriate and acceptable positions for women.

The reluctance of employers to hire women for positions other than what was socially acceptable, and the reluctance of women to enter positions contrary to their sexual identity led to "crowding," or occupational segregation of women into positions deemed appropriate for women—primarily service, nurturing, and human relationship positions (i.e., teachers, secretaries, nurses, social workers). Occupational segregation is a contributing factor in the pay gap because "women's jobs" have historically been compensated at a lower rate than "men's jobs." In 1980 the five occupations with the highest compensation rates (physicians, dentists, lawyers, podiatrists, and medical science teachers) had average mean earnings of $43,805. The percentage of females in those occupations averaged 10%. In that same year the five lowest paid occupations (child care workers in private households, house servants, housekeepers and butlers, and child care workers outside of private households) had average mean earnings of $5863. The percentage of females in those occupations averaged 91% (Wilborn, 1986, p. 18). The National Academy of Sciences (Trieman and Hartmann, 1981) reported that the more women there are in a profession, the lower the wage.

D. "Male Jobs" and "Female Jobs"

Since establishing comparable worth is dependent on identifying the differences in rates of pay between male jobs and female jobs that have the same value to their employer, the task of defining male jobs and female jobs is very important. As different jurisdictions have struggled with this task, the most common definition has been as follows: a job in which 70% of its incumbents are female is a female job; and, likewise, a job in which 70% of its incumbents are male is a male job.

Advocates of pay equity claim that labor market discrimination and occupational segregation are to blame for the development of male and female jobs. Those forces have concentrated women into a relatively small number of jobs that offer low pay with little opportunity for advancement. Women also face barriers when entering traditional male occupations. Those women who are able to advance or enter traditional men's occupations often face a hostile environment and in many instances are harassed by male coworkers.

Table 1   Median Earnings of Men and Women, 1960–1990

Year	Men's median earnings	Women's median earnings	% of women's to men's earnings
1960	5434	3296	0.606
1961	5663	3341	0.600
1962	5826	3457	0.593
1963	6070	3556	0.586
1964	6284	3710	0.590
1965	6598	3816	0.578
1966	6955	4026	0.579
1967	7289	4198	0.576
1968	7814	4568	0.585
1969	8668	5077	0.586
1970	9184	5440	0.592
1971	9631	5701	0.592
1972	10538	6053	0.574
1973	11468	6488	0.566
1974	12162	7174	0.600
1975	12934	7719	0.635
1976	13859	8312	0.600
1977	15070	8814	0.585
1978	16062	9641	0.600
1979	17514	10550	0.602
1980	19173	11591	0.604
1981	20692	12457	0.602
1982	21655	13663	0.631
1983	22506	14488	0.644
1984	24004	15422	0.642
1985	24999	16252	0.650
1986	25894	16843	0.650
1987	26722	17504	0.655
1988	27342	18545	0.678
1989	28605	19643	0.687
1990	29172	20586	0.706

Source: U.S. Department of Commerce, Bureau of the Census, Current Population Reports, Consumer Income Series P-60, Money Income of Families and Persons in the U.S. (Median Income of Persons by Selected Characteristics 15 Years Old and Over), various issues.

Becker (1986) discusses several barriers facing women in entering and advancing in the labor market. Ideology of gender is taught to boys and girls at a very young age and reinforced in public schools where, for example, boys are encouraged to take shop and girls home economics. The ideology becomes part of their sexual identity and, as a result, women have not entered into traditional male jobs, and employers have been reluctant to hire women for these jobs because it conflicts with traditional values. Gender ideology and the fact that men's work has traditionally been regarded as more important, and therefore valued more than women's work, has resulted in an unconscious bias in valuing the work of women. Stereotypes of men as better supervisors, more assertive and more reliable than women, have also proved detrimental to women, affording them fewer opportunities for advancement. Institutionalized rules, such as seniority systems and age limits for apprenticeship programs, have kept women from advancement and entrance into male-dominated jobs because these systems do not address women's employment patterns (i.e., maternity leave). Additionally, information regarding male jobs is often passed through male networks and thus is not as readily available to women. As a result, women are continually steered into women's jobs.

E. The Market Defense

While no one would argue with the fact that women's work is paid less than men's work or that women are concentrated within a narrow margin of low-paying occupations, the primary focus of the comparable worth debate is whether or not the pay gap is fairly attributed to sex discrimination. Proponents of comparable worth argue that the effects of past discrimination are deeply rooted in the wage structure of the market system. Opponents argue that there have been no reliable studies that prove that the pay gap results from discrimination in the market (Finn, 1984, p. 102).

Neoclassical economic theory contends that the pay gap is due to the competitive forces of supply and demand and rejects the concept that work has "value" or "worth" to the employer other than that determined in the market. Some opponents insist that when occupational segregation results from discrimination, remedies are available under Title VII of the Civil Rights Act of 1964; therefore, "imposing comparable worth in the form of a minimum wage in female-dominated occupations is both inefficient and inequitable" (Fischel and Lazear, 1986b, p. 950). Fischel and Lazear (1986a) also argue that women freely choose their occupations and that the resulting segregation is therefore not a function of discrimination.

To the degree that the institutional barriers mentioned above interfere with the dynamics of a free market system, the free market arguments against discrimination as the explanation for the pay gap are threatened.

F. Human Capital

A portion of the pay gap has also been attributed to women's lower investment in human capital. A person's human capital is determined by how much that person has invested in himself or herself in ways that contribute to increased productivity—factors such as education, training, experience, and work history. Various explanations have been given for women's human capital investment. Some of them are as follows: they work primarily to supplement their husbands' income and are not interested in climbing the career ladder; they prefer part-time work or flexible schedules; they are more vulnerable to relocation due to husbands' career choices; and they do not invest in schooling or training compatible with the labor market (Levin, 1984, p. 127; Bayes, 1988, p. 17).

Work history, or labor force attachment, is a predominant factor in women's lower human capital investment. This lower investment is attributed primarily to women leaving the work force to give birth and raise children. Employers may be reluctant to hire or train women because of their lower attachment to the labor force.

Studies have been done to examine the disparity between males and females in human capital investment in order to determine what percentage of the pay gap is due to discrimination. Treiman and Hartmann (1981, p. 22) report that one-fourth to one-half of the pay gap is due to investment in human capital. The remaining difference most often has been attributed to discrimination (Hartmann, 1984, p. 13).

However, the fact that women have less human capital investment than men also may be due to discrimination. "Human capital studies underestimate the effect of sex discrimination on wages because the factors the studies use to explain wage disparities are themselves infected with discrimination" (Wilborn, 1986, p. 16). Some refer to this as "noninvidious" or efficient discrimination. As they see it, if male sex is an accurate statistical representation for greater productivity, attachment, and/or commitment to wage labor, employers can reasonably pay women less (Fischel and Lazear as cited in Becker, 1986, p. 936).

G. Job Evaluation

Comparable worth advocates see formalized job evaluation as the primary means to achieve pay equity. Job evaluation is a system used to rank order position categories according to their comparative value within an organization and thereby determine pay scales. The concept of job evaluation is not new; it was first recommended to Congress by the Civil Service Commission in 1902 as a way to establish uniform compensation for equal work. In 1919 Congress appointed a commission to study salary inequities of public employees. The Classification Act of 1923 resulted from the commission's study and a federal position classification system was established (Moore, 1985). By 1940, many large employers adopted job evaluation in order to more effectively mediate pay level disputes during union negotiations. Instead of negotiating salaries for individual positions, employers were allowed to negotiate salaries for entire job classes; when job content changed, evaluation was used to determine a new rank order and pay scale (England, 1992, p. 189). During World War II, the National War Labor Board concluded that the best way to ascertain the "worth" of a job was through a job evaluation process that determined compensation on the basis of skill, effort, and job content (Wesman, 1988).

Job evaluation has evolved since World War II, and today there are four major methods in use: position ranking, position classification, factor comparison, and point factor. Position classification and factor comparison methods of job evaluation are the ones most often used by public jurisdictions (Moore, 1985, p. 64). The point factor method is preferred by comparable worth advocates because it orders jobs by their value to the employer. Most pay equity studies conducted by states and local governments to date have used a point factor evaluation system (Moore, 1985, p. 64; England, 1992, p. 193).

Comparable worth opponents argue that job evaluation systems preclude employers from being responsive to changes in market wages and that job evaluation "must not interfere with the competitive capability of the enterprise" (Clarke, 1984, p. 200). But when surveys are conducted to determine prevailing wage rates, some employers survey higher paying firms for men's jobs, while surveys for female-dominant jobs are taken from lower paying firms (Grune, 1984, p. 5). Even when surveys are done correctly, the market may reflect a gender bias of the society. For example, Grune reports that wage increases are more responsive to shortages of engineers or plumbers, but this has not been true in shortages for nurses. Job evaluation systems allow for a policy decision to avoid such a bias.

Opponents also argue that job evaluation factors are subjective rather than objective (Cumming, 1984, p. 200). Biases are evident in the job evaluation systems currently used throughout industry. Typically, compensable factors such as physical exertion are prevalent in male-dominated jobs, while factors such as fine motor skills are absent or deemphasized in female-dominated jobs (Beatty and Beatty, 1984, pp. 73–74). Also, personal assessment of job factors, such as physical difficulty, dirty or dangerous work, and the like, vary among respondents. Tree trimmers see their jobs as being physically difficult and dangerous because of the heights and machinery involved with their work. On the other hand, nurses, who typically deal with life-threatening situations and are exposed to blood, feces, urine, and disease, see their work as clean because of their attempts to keep the environment in which they work sterile (Remick, 1984, p. 114). By being deliberate about avoiding such gender biases, job evaluation systems can help avoid their unconscious institution-alization.

Job evaluation has been used for many years to rationalize the wage and salary structure of industry and organizations. According to Scholl and Cooper (1991, p. 17), it has only been since the suggestion was made that it be used as a method of eliminating gender-based pay differentials that the reliability and validity of job evaluation has been questioned.

H.   Economic Consequences

Finally, it has been said that imposing comparable worth will hurt and not help women because a wage increase will force employers to cut staff in those female-dominated positions, thereby putting more women out of work. It has also been said that the economic consequences of com-parable worth would have dire effects on the economy, thereby restricting the ability of the Unit-ed States to compete in world markets (Bergen, 1984, pp. 215–217). But adopting significant comparable worth policies in Minnesota and Australia has not resulted in the predicted negative consequences (Aaron and Lougy, 1986, p. 41; Rothchild and Watkins, 1987). In Washington State, it was argued that implementation of comparable worth would cost billions of dollars (Hutner, 1986, pp. 179–180). However, the actual figure totaled approximately $571 million over an 8-year period, or 2.59% of the total expenditures for all state salaries and benefits (U.S. General Accounting Office, 1992, p. 26). It would seem that economic projections cannot accurately ascertain the costs of implementation of comparable worth any better than they can determine the costs of discrim-ination.

III.   LEGISLATIVE AND POLICY HISTORY

Receiving equal pay for equal work has been a legal issue since before the women's rights and suffrage movements of the 19th century. However, it wasn't until World War II, when record numbers of women entered the work force and did jobs that had previously been done by men, that the issue received serious consideration. Unions were the primary supporters of equal pay, not necessarily because they supported women in the work force, but because they recognized that postwar wages for these previously male jobs might be reduced. Therefore, they repeat-edly brought claims before the National War Labor Board (NWLB), which was established by President Roosevelt to aid in labor relations and to mediate wage disputes during the war. In 1942, the NWLB set a precedent for pay equity through General Order No. 16, which ordered the inclusion of an equal pay clause in a contract between the General Motors Corporation and the United Auto Workers. This order stated that "slight or inconsequential changes in a job as a reason for setting up a wage differential against women employees" was unacceptable (Steinberg, 1984, p. 7).

During its tenure, the NWLB was successful in establishing an equal pay policy and, toward the end of the war, broadened the concept to comparable worth, although this extension was never enforced (Steinberg, 1984, p. 7; Blum, 1991, p. 38). At the conclusion of World War II, it was assumed that women would leave the work force but for various reasons this did not occur. However, the fight for pay equity continued.

From 1945 to 1962, women's groups continuously lobbied Congress to pass legislation re-quiring equal pay for comparable work. Every year the bills were defeated, opposed by groups such as the U.S. Chamber of Commerce and the National Association of Manufacturers on the grounds that the term "comparable work" was too vague and passage of such a bill could destroy the wage structure that took years to perfect (Hutner, 1986, p. 28; Wesman, 1988, p. 15).

As a compromise, the term "equal work" was substituted for "comparable work," and the Equal Pay Act of 1963 finally passed. This Act requires employers to pay the same wage to men and women workers doing equal work—equal work being defined as "jobs the performance of which requires equal skill, effort and responsibility, and which are performed under similar working conditions." The courts have interpreted this to mean that jobs must be substantially identical, even though titles may differ (i.e., janitor vs. maid). The Equal Pay Act, then, did not resolve wage discrimination in sex-segregated jobs where women were paid lower wages than men for jobs that required more skill (e.g., nurses vs. custodians).

In 1964, Title VII of the Civil Rights Act was passed. Title VII makes it unlawful for an employer "to discriminate against any individual with respect to compensation, terms, conditions, or privileges of employment, because of such individual's race, color, religion, sex, or national origin." It also prohibits discrimination with regard to hiring, classification, assignment, promotion, and discharge. Although the original intent was to stop discrimination against blacks, the inclusion of sex discrimination was added in the U.S. House of Representatives at the last minute by civil rights opponents who hoped that the inclusion would cause the bill to fail (Patten, 1988, p. 40). Much to their dismay, the bill passed in the House and moved to the Senate. At this point, concern was raised over the inclusion of sex as a class protected against discrimination and the bill's perceived conflicts with the Equal Pay Act. As a result, the Bennett Amendment was added to Title VII:

> It shall not be an unlawful employment practice under this title for any employer to differentiate upon the basis of sex in determining the amount of the wages or compensation paid to employees of such employer if such differentiation is authorized by the provisions of Section 6(d) of the Fair Labor Standards Act of 1938 as amended (29 USC 206(d)) [i.e., the Equal Pay Act].

While the intent of the Bennett Amendment was to clarify the relationship of Title VII to the Equal Pay Act, the word "authorized" caused considerable confusion. Are sex discrimination claims filed under Title VII limited to "equal pay for equal work," as provided under the Equal Pay Act? Or does the term refer to the four affirmative defenses (merit, seniority, quantity and quality of work, or any other factor other than sex) for paying unequal wages under Title VII? The ambiguity of the Bennett Amendment was not resolved until 1981 when the Supreme Court ruled in *County of Washington v. Gunther* that the term "authorized" did in fact refer to the four affirmative defenses. The Court ruled that sex discrimination compensation claims were not limited to equal work situations. Although the Court refused to address directly the comparable worth issue, it left the door open (Hutner, 1986; Patten, 1988).

Other federal mandates impacting gender discrimination include Executive Order 11246, signed by President Johnson in 1965. This Order forbade discrimination against minorities in employment decisions. It was broadened in 1968 through Executive Order 11375 to include sex-based discrimination. Together these executive orders imposed affirmative action obligations on federal agencies and federal contractors and their subcontractors, and required written affirmative action plans. The Department of Labor's Office of Federal Contract Compliance Programs (OFCCP) was charged with enforcement responsibilities for federal contractors, and the Equal Employment Opportunity Commission (EEOC) was established to investigate and reconcile employment discrimination complaints and grant the right of complainants to seek a remedy in court (Blum, 1990, p. 22).

Comparable worth continued to be an issue of heated debate throughout the 1970s, although attempts to pass legislation continued to fail. The Carter administration drafted proposals mandating comparable worth for federal contractors, but the Reagan administration quickly rejected these proposals and limited OFCCP affirmative action activities (Hutner, 1986, p. 2).

Although specific comparable worth legislation has not been adopted at the federal level, other legislative actions have greatly reduced gender discrimination and indicate that sentiment is moving toward more equitable treatment of women in the workplace. First, the Pregnancy Disability Act of 1978 required employers to treat disabilities arising from pregnancy and birth the same as any other disability. Prior to this act, insurance benefits offered by employers did not cover pregnancy. Sick leave was not granted for pregnancy because it was strictly a female disability. However, these same benefits had been granted to men who required prostate surgery, a disability affecting only men (Kelly, 1991, pp. 182–183). Second was the Retirement Equity Act of 1983, which provided that men and women who make equitable contributions to a retirement plan shall receive equal pension benefits. Before it was enacted, retired women received smaller pensions than men based on the fact that women were expected to live longer and therefore draw benefits for a longer period of time.

The most recent legislation having an effect on comparable worth is the Civil Rights Act of 1991 (CRA 1991). This was enacted primarily because Congress wished to reverse the effect of Supreme Court rulings that limited the rights of individuals claiming employment discrimination. Specifically, CRA 1991 allows for recovery of compensatory and punitive damages in cases of intentional discrimination. The purpose of that provision was to further deter employers from discrimination, particularly regarding sexual harassment. Most important, the meaning of "business necessity" has been restored to the interpretation before the *Wards Cove* decision, and the burden of proof in disparate impact cases has been shifted from plaintiffs to respondents.

In 1971, *Griggs v. Duke Power Co.* (401 U.S. 424) provided the legal basis of burden of proof in disparate impact cases. In that decision, the Supreme Court held that employment practices adopted without a discriminatory intent, but with a discriminatory effect on minorities and women, were illegal. In *Griggs,* the employer required intelligence testing not related to actual requirements of the job. The Supreme Court ruled the employer was required to prove that the disparate impact resulted from a practice that was a business necessity. In order to show that the practice is a business necessity, an employer must show that it has a significant relationship to successful job performance or that a practice is a significant business objective of the employer other than monetary, social, moral, political, or religious. In *Wards Cove*, the Supreme Court overruled this requirement holding that although the employer must produce evidence justifying an employment practice, the plaintiff has the burden of persuasion.

Other benefits of CRA 1991 include the establishment of a Glass Ceiling Commission to study artificial barriers preventing women and minorities from entering high-level business positions, and the right to challenge discriminatory seniority systems.

So, despite the recent progress with regard to gender equity on other fronts, it has been almost 30 years since the last federal legislation that directly dealt with pay equity.

IV. LEGAL CASES

Much of the legal activity around the comparable worth issue in the 1970s and 1980s was in the judicial arena, but as we begin to move through the 1990s it looks as if the activity in that arena is essentially finished—and without the U.S. Supreme Court ever hearing a test case (Hyde and Graham, 1991; England, 1992). The closest that the Supreme Court ever came to a ruling on comparable worth was in the *County of Washington v. Gunther* (1981), when it said that gender-based compensation claims under Title VII are not to be judged only by the equal work standard of the Equal Pay Act. At that point, many people thought they saw an opening for gender-based discrimination suits that went into claims of inequitable pay for similar jobs. Surely the court meant to establish some broader standard. But the Williams assessment in 1984 appears in retrospect to have been correct: "The courts simply have not accepted the proposition that the intrinsic worth of different jobs can be established to a legally acceptable standard of certainty" (Williams, 1984, p. 154).

So, is there a broader standard than equal pay for equal work? If there is, what implications does it have for the broader goal toward which comparable worth has aimed—reducing or eliminating the pay gap?

As one reviews the key legal cases relating to comparable worth, it becomes evident that disparate impact claims made simply as comparable worth claims were not upheld but that disparate impact claims based on comparable worth studies as well as other kinds of evidence, and intentional discrimination (or disparate treatment) claims, were more likely to obtain a favorable court ruling. As early as 1977, the Eighth Circuit indicated its unwillingness to allow a comparable worth study to determine the wage structure for the State of Iowa (*Christensen v. State of Iowa*, 1977). In 1980 a Michigan district court said that it would not accept claims based solely on comparable worth theory (*Gerlach v. Michigan Bell Telephone Company*, 1980). The Court allowed, however, that evidence of undervaluation of female jobs based on a comparable worth study might be relevant in a claim based on some other theory of wage discrimination. Another Michigan district court refused to engage itself in comparing the relative worth of various dissimilar jobs, noting that comparable worth was not a legally recognized theory but that intentional discrimination was (*Power v. Barry Bounty, Michigan*, 1982). Still, intentional discrimination is often not the problem, and even when it is, it is often almost impossible to prove. In *California State Employees Association v. California* (1989), a district court judge rejected the claim of intentional discrimination because it was not shown "that the state selected particular pay policies *because of* any alleged discriminatory effects upon women state employees" [emphasis added].

Even *Gunther*, which seemed to create a broader standard than equal pay for equal work and was seen as having potentially opened the door to comparable worth claims under Title VII, was no endorsement of the comparable worth theory. The Court in that case specifically noted that the "respondents' claim is not based on the controversial concept of 'comparable worth'" (p. 166). But what was that broader standard, if it was not comparable pay for comparable work? Following that ruling by the Supreme Court, lower courts continued to find claims based on the comparable worth theory insufficient (*Spaulding v. University of Washington*, 1984), but claims of intentional discrimination were found to be actionable (*Connecticut State Employees Association v. State of Connecticut*, 1983).

One broadening of the standard might involve insisting that those who conducted comparable worth studies base their compensation policies on those studies. Perhaps conducting a comparable worth study and then failing to act on the implications of its results would be actionable as intentional discrimination. Some courts found that such a refusal would be actionable (*Connecticut State Employees Association v. State of Connecticut*, 1983; *Plemer v. Parsons-Gilbane*, 1983). But the last case to deal with that issue at the circuit court level, (*AFSCME v. State of Washington*, 1985) said that conducting a comparable worth study and then not implementing its findings is not evidence of intent to discriminate. Furthermore, the opinion in that case was written by Anthony Kennedy, who is now a Supreme Court justice, and he suggested in that opinion that to treat such actions as evidence of intentional discrimination would discourage employers from conducting comparable worth studies because it would punish employers who undertook the effort.

If the definition of intentional discrimination has not been broadened, then perhaps the kinds of defenses that are acceptable in disparate impact cases (which do not require a finding that the discrimination is intentional) have been reduced. Prior to *Gunther* courts had found that a bona fide classification system qualified as a "factor other than sex" and was therefore under the protection of the Bennett Amendment's four affirmative defenses, i.e., as acceptable reasons for practices that unintentionally have a disparate impact upon members of a protected class (*Cayce v. Adams*, 1977). But to qualify as an acceptable defense, classification systems must be applied in a gender-blind manner. For example, even when the classification system is facially nondiscriminatory, if officials knowingly overgrade a male employee and then refuse either to give that same upgrade to a female employee who is doing substantially equivalent work or to downgrade the male employee, then that is not acceptable.

Prior to *Gunther*, courts had also found that defenses based on the implications or impact of the marketplace on the setting of wages would be found acceptable as a "factor other than sex" (*Christensen v. State of Iowa*, 1977; *Lemon v. City and County of Denver*, 1980). Furthermore, *Christensen* found that even after a job evaluation study had judged two jobs to be of comparable worth, different wage rates could be justified based on market conditions. *Gunther*'s finding that the Bennett Amendment incorporated the four affirmative defenses of the Equal Pay Act had virtually no impact on this aspect of the lower courts' findings. Courts after *Gunther* continued to find the market defense acceptable (*Kouba v. Allstate Insurance Company*, 1982; *Briggs v. City of Michigan*, 1982; *AFSCME v. State of Washington*, 1985; *California State Employees Association v. State of California*, 1989).

Courts did, however, begin to find defenses that claimed to be among the four affirmative defenses which were not acceptable. Pay differentials cannot be justified by referring to traditional industry practice as a factor other than sex when the traditional industry practice has been to sex-segregate jobs and then pay female jobs lower rates than substantially similar male jobs (*Thompson v. Sawyer*, 1982). Different geographic locations cannot justify different pay if males and females are doing the same work under the same classification system, unless good cause is shown for a geographic exception (*Grumbine v. U.S.*, 1984). The willingness of a female to accept lower pay for the same work is also an insufficient defense (*Grayboff v. Pendleton*, 1984).

But the future of disparate impact claims in general is clouded at this time. In *AFSCME v. State of Washington*, Justice Kennedy said that disparate impact may only be applied to "a specific, clearly delineated employment practice at a single point in the jobs election process" (1985, p. 1407). It cannot be applied to the overall impact of a complex compensation system. Further, in a race discrimination case (*Wards Cove Packing Co. v. Antonio*, 1989), the Supreme Court reduced the usefulness of disparate impact analysis in job discrimination cases. They found that statistical disparity within a company is not sufficient evidence of discrimination; they said the appropriate statistical test is one that compares the composition of the at-issue jobs with the composition of the relevant labor market. They further specified that the statistical disparities must be traceable to specific employment practices. They also said that the burden of persuasion remained with the complainant even after disparate impact was shown. All the employer is required to do is to produce evidence that the disparity might have resulted from a legitimate business practice. But that portion of *Antonio* which kept the burden on the complainant has in effect been overruled by passage of the Civil Rights Act of 1991, which puts the burden of proof on the employer once disparate impact has been shown.

When one combines the patterns found in these cases with the clear opposition of the Reagan and Bush administrations to the concept of comparable worth and the impact of the judicial appointments made by those administrations during the 12 years from 1981 through 1992, it is difficult to avoid the conclusion that if any progress is to be made in the near future on reducing the pay gap, it is not likely to come through action in federal courts. As Paula England concluded, "It is clear that, absent new legislation, the federal courts will not be effective vehicles for ending the wage discrimination of the sort at issue in comparable worth" (1992, p. 250).

V. STATE AND LOCAL EXPERIENCES

Since comparable worth has not been accepted in the United States as a basic legal principle and has not been favorably viewed by recent federal administrations, one might expect that there would be a push to get it instituted at the state and local levels. According to the U.S. General Accounting Office (1986), an overwhelming majority of the states have engaged in some kind of relevant legislation. In 1989 the National Committee on Pay Equity listed only five states that had taken no action on pay equity. But although over 20 states have appropriated funds designated for improving pay equity, only Minnesota has passed a statewide pay equity statute (Graham and Hyde, 1991, p. 810). In addition, by 1990 at least 1500 local governments had adopted some type of comparable worth adjustment (Shafritz et al., 1992, p. 264).

The experiences at the state and local levels are widely varied, ranging from states like New York and Connecticut, both of which instituted tens of millions of dollars in adjustments, to North Carolina, which stopped its comparable worth study prior to its completion. Still, a fair taste of the wide range of experiences can be obtained by briefly examining the experiences in three states: California, Washington, and Minnesota.

At the state level, California has had difficulty moving on comparable worth because of a strong partisan division—the Republican governor has been opposed, and the Democratic legislature has been in favor. This has resulted in vetoes of any comparable worth legislation. Efforts to obtain comparable worth through the courts have also failed (*California State Employees Association v. State of California*, 1989). At the local level, however, comparable worth agreements have been reached. San Jose was one of the first cities in the nation to have its name associated with comparable worth. In that city a 1981 strike action eventuated in a union-negotiated agreement. Also in Los Angeles pay equity was negotiated through collective bargaining. In San Francisco a union-negotiated agreement was put to the voters and rejected in 1985. The agreement was then modified and obtained voter approval in 1986. Since then, fiscal woes have placed pay equity adjustments behind regular salary increases in the local union's priorities.

Washington State was one of the leaders in promoting comparable worth. In the early 1970s complaints of wage discrimination against female state employees led the governor to order an investigation. A preliminary study found the possibility of wage discrimination, so Norman D. Willis and Associates was hired to do a more complete study. It initially found a wage gap of approximately 20% and that study was updated over the years without any substantial changes being made. Implementation of authorized steps to close the gap faltered for two reasons: a new governor who was opposed to comparable worth and, later, insufficient funding. In 1982 the union filed suit under Title VII (*AFSCME v. State of Washington*, 1985). The union won a widely reported but short-lived victory at the district court level, but lost in a unanimous appellate court reversal. Before the Supreme Court could take up the case, the union and the state reached a settlement that provided $482 million to attempt to close the gap by 1993. The settlement was a good example of the difference between a legal victory and a negotiated agreement. Despite the number of years that the issue had been alive in Washington State, the settlement did not provide for back pay. It also used the lower paid female jobs in its calculation of the average wage of a job with x number of Willis points and that lowered the target comparable worth line (Luton and Thompson, 1989).

The Minnesota experience is rather unique (Rothchild and Watkins, 1987). In that state there existed bipartisan support for comparable worth that spanned different governors' terms. A number of independent studies in the mid-1970s showed a pay gap between male and female state employees. In 1979 Hay Associates was hired by the Department of Employee Relations to establish a job evaluation system. In 1981 a legislative task force was established to study state pay practices. In 1982 the legislature passed the State Employees Pay Equity Act, which required (1) comparable worth implementation in all state agencies and (2) annual reports to the state legislature to ensure implementation was accomplished. In 1983 the cost of implementation was estimated at $26 million and the legislature appoved a 2-year plan that would appropriate a little more than half of what was needed. In 1985 the other half was appropriated for adjustments in the next 2 years. Not satisfied with success at the state level, the legislature in 1984 passed the Local Government Pay Equity Act requiring that all local governments (cities, counties, and school districts) implement comparable worth. The legislature gave those local governments flexibility in the kind of study that they would do but insisted that any pay gaps be addressed. A review of implementation at the local level due in 1992 expected to find 70% in compliance (Watkins, 1992).

An examination of the impact of the Minnesota comparable worth legislation concluded that the dire predictions of comparable worth opponents did not materialize: "No employees had wages reduced or frozen, and no employees were laid off as a result of the pay equity program. There have been no strikes or lawsuits. There has been no creation of a new bureaucracy to manage the process, no change in the state's ability to attract and retain qualified workers or to meet its fiscal responsibilities" (Rothchild and Watkins, 1987, p. 26). Similarly, predictions that women would lose jobs and that they would not move into nontraditional jobs have proven inaccurate. The number of women working for the State of Minnesota has increased by 6% and the number of women state employees working in nontraditional jobs has increased by 19% (Rothchild and Watkins, 1987, p. 26). Finally, predictions of lower morale resulting from comparable worth implementation have not been supported. Eighty percent of both men and women Minnesota State employees say that they support the pay equity program (Rothchild and Watkins, 1987, p. 27).

In California, Washington, and Minnesota, much of the success in adopting and implementing comparable worth has been due to union activity, but Hawaii and Oregon have experienced the down side of depending on union negotiating to achieve comparable worth. In both of these states the unions were willing to sacrifice comparable worth as they negotiated on behalf of all their members (Cook, 1991, p. 108). As comparable worth becomes one of the items on the negotiation table, it is subject to being negotiated away in favor of other considerations.

VI. EXPERIENCES OF OTHER NATIONS

Although most of this chapter has focused on comparable worth and pay equity in the United States, it is important to note that other nation-states have dealt with this issue. In industrialized nations around the world, comparable worth has been discussed and/or adopted—with varied results. This section will review the experiences of Australia, New Zealand, the European Economic Community (EEC), Britain, Canada, and Sweden.

Comparable worth has come a long way in Australia. Its history of wage-setting practices is one of government-sanctioned compulsory arbitration. In a key 1912 case, a judge justified different wages for women because, unlike men, they did not generally support a family. In a later case, that same judge began the practice of fixing the female pay rate as a percentage of the basic male wage, and that rate was officially established at 54% until 1949 when it was increased to 75% (Willborn, 1986, p. 89). The principle of equal pay for work of equal value was adopted in 1972 (Aaron and Lougy, 1986, pp. 40–41; Gregory et al., 1989). Because the government establishes, through its tribunals, the pay of nearly 90% of all employees (Willborn, 1986, p. 87), the result of the adoption of that principle and the establishment of a serious implementation schedule and system was that by the end of the decade base pay for women had risen from 74% to 94% of that of men (Aaron and Lougy, 1986, p. 40). The impact of such a dramatic change remains in dispute. Some researchers claim that it had a smaller-than-expected but nonetheless real deleterious effect on female employment. Others claim that no such impact resulted.

Although New Zealand has a history and traditions similar to those of Australia, in the early 1970s it began to chart a significantly different course with respect to comparable worth (Willborn, 1986, p. 90). Different wage rates for men and women were officially sanctioned as early as 1903 and the legislature put its authority behind different rates in 1934 and 1945. The Minimum Wage Act of 1945 set the female minimum rate at about 60% of the male minimum. "Although the legislature enacted statutes requiring equal pay for government employees in the 1960s, it was not until the 1970s that equal pay became a legal requirement in the private sector" (Willborn, 1986, p. 91). The Equal Pay Act of 1972 required that women be paid the same as men for the same work and, if only females were engaged in that kind of work, women should be paid the same rate as a hypothetical man performing the same work. This approach resulted in the hourly earnings of females rising from 71.3% of male earnings in 1973 to 78.5% in 1977 (Willborn, 1986, p. 92), not nearly the dramatic results found in Australia.

Article 119 of the 1961 Treaty of Rome, which set up the EEC, provided that "each Member State shall ensure and . . . maintain the application of the principle that men and women should receive equal pay for equal work" (Hutner, 1986, p. 35). Defining "equal work" proved so difficult that it was not until 1975 that the EEC adopted a directive implementing Article 119. That directive, which went into effect in 1978, defined equal work as "the same work or work to which equal value is attributed" (Hutner, 1986, p. 35). It also prohibited job classification systems from engaging in gender discrimination. A 1979 report on compliance with the directive was not good, so the European Commission began to pressure members toward compliance, and this pressure has had an effect (Willborn, 1986, p. 80; Hutner, 1989, p. 37).

Before 1975 Britain, a member of the EEC, explicitly countenanced pay discrimination on the basis of gender. Wage agreements contained provisions authorizing different rates of pay for men and women who performed the same work (Gregory et al., 1989). The Equal Pay Act of 1970, which took effect in 1975, included three provisions designed to change this situation. The first was an equal-pay-for-equal-work clause. The second provided that if a job evaluation found a female job of equal value to a male job, there should be a change of pay for the female job. It did not, however, require that job evaluations be done. Third, "if a female pay rate with no male equivalent was included in a wage agreement, the act provided that the female pay rate must be at least equal to the lowest level of the male pay provision in the agreement" (Gregory et al., 1989, p. 232). By 1977 the female/male ratio had improved by 21.6%.

When the Canadian Parliament adopted its Human Rights Act in 1977, it included a provision for equal pay for work of equal value. Although implementation of that provision was not always smooth, it was eventually incorporated into the national framework (Cadieux, 1984). Since then, five provinces and the Yukon territories have passed pay equity legislation of some sort but there are significant differences in the legislations' specific provisions (Ames, 1991). For example, Manitoba defined a male-dominated job and a female-dominated job as one for which at least 70% of the incumbents are male or female, respectively. Ontario defined a female-dominated job as one for which at least 60% of the incumbents are female and a male-dominated job as one for which at least 70% of the incumbents are male. Both provinces, however, also included a proviso that any job class might be designated as gender-dominated if the employer and the bargaining agent agreed on that designation. While Manitoba required that agreements be reached with all the bargaining units representing employees of a given employer, Ontario allowed employers to deal with each bargaining unit separately, which meant that "even if equity [were] established within bargaining units, great inequities [might] still exist across units" (Ames, 1991, p. 880). Further, Manitoba required that female-dominated jobs be paid comparably to the average of comparable male-dominated jobs, but Ontario allowed female-dominated jobs to be paid comparably to the lowest paid comparable male-dominated job.

Finally, the Swedish experience demonstrates the connection between the pay gap and general social values that was mentioned at the beginning of this chapter (Martin and Thorsin-Hamm, 1991). In the Swedish welfare state much more governmental authority has been placed behind attempts to bring those who have been disadvantaged by traditional practices to a more equitable station in life. The pay gap is considerably smaller than that found in the United States: "The aggregate wage of white collar Swedish women working in the private sector is 70% of that of men. The aggregate wage of female Swedish industrial workers is about 91% of that of men. Comparable figures in the public sector are 91% in the national government . . . , 87% in local/municipal government . . . and 75% in regional/county government" (Martin and Thorsin-Hamm, 1991, pp. 898–899). Still disparities between male and female pay and other indicators of social status continue to exist. According to recent studies, "only 16% of the exceedingly powerful official government policy-making board and commission memberships" were female, and only 15% of the union leadership were women (p. 899). The Swedish example thus demonstrates that comparable worth, even when generally accepted, is no panacea for treating status disparities between men and women.

VII. THE FUTURE OF COMPARABLE WORTH

Public sector managers have utilized Equal Employment Opportunity (EEO) policy as a means for women and minorities to gain equal access to "white male jobs" along with equal pay for equal work (England, 1992, p. 304). Because equal pay for equal work is a firmly established legal principal, diminishing job segregation will certainly strengthen pay equity. However, it fails to address a key concern addressed by comparable worth and pay equity—traditional women's work is undervalued. Women should not have to change occupations to receive fair compensation for their work.

Taking into account the many achievements and failures of comparable worth and pay equity in the past, what is the outlook in the 1990s for achieving a national policy on comparable worth? A careful look at the politics of this controversial issue may offer some insight.

In 1976, President Carter campaigned on a platform of comparable worth and under his administration this policy made significant progress through enforcement agencies. Budgets and staff were increased in EEOC and OFCCP, and civil rights advocates were assigned to key positions (Blum, 1991, p. 24). While the OFCCP doubled the number of contractors barred from receiving federal contracts due to noncompliance with affirmative action laws (p. 24), the EEOC delineated a policy of comparable worth. Under the direction of Eleanor Holmes Norton, the tactic employed by the EEOC was to advance comparable worth on an incremental basis. Two important victories were achieved: the *Gunther* decision, which ruled that wage discrimination charges are not limited to the equal work standard and the commissioning of a comparable worth study by the National Academy of Sciences (Blum, 1991, p. 50). The study assessed factors contributing to the pay gap and concluded that up to 50% of the gap was due to discrimination (Hartmann, 1984, p. 13). The report also recommended that job evaluation be used to establish comparable worth policies (pp. 16–21).

These victories were short-lived. The Reagan administration actively opposed comparable worth. OFCCP and EEOC enforcement activities were limited; the U.S. Civil Rights Commission urged Congress and federal agencies to reject comparable worth; and the dozen comparable worth-related bills initiated in Congress between 1984 and 1985 were rejected (Chi, 1988, p. 112).

Comparable worth fared no better under the Bush administration. The 1988 Republican platform repudiated the concept, and Bush's speeches addressing employment discrimination were limited to equal pay for equal work (Killingsworth, 1990, p. 6).

Although President Clinton's promise to select a cabinet that "looks like America" sounded like an encouraging note for advocates of comparable worth, at the time this chapter was finalized it remained to be seen whether his campaign promises would find their way into his administration. Even though his cabinet appointments included more women than previous administrations, he could still be faulted for not living up to the promise. In addition, the fate of some of his key female nominees for appointments in the Justice Department (Zoe Baird, Kimba Wood, and Lani Guinier) was not encouraging for equity advocates.

It might also be noted that President Clinton's approval ratings as of this writing did not bode well for a second term. It seems unlikely that a national comparable worth policy would be instituted under Ross Perot, a Republican president, or a more conservative Democratic president. It is also unlikely under any of the three non-Clinton scenarios that enforcement activities would be maintained at a level similar to those under the Carter administration. For these reasons, comparable worth will most likely fare better at the state and local levels.

Successes at state and local levels indicate that comparable worth may well continue to be a major issue into the 1990s. As of 1989, 45 states and 1500 local governments had initiated some type of comparable worth action, and funding for pay equity studies has been provided by more than 20 states. The success of comparable worth has been attributed to three factors: region, party dominance, and unionization. Comparable worth bills have been introduced in eastern and midwestern legislatures. State successes have been achieved mainly in Democrat-dominated legislatures, by states that have also ratified the Equal Rights Amendment, and in states that have collective bargaining laws (Chi, 1988, pp. 100–111).

It would appear that the most promising avenue to achieving pay equity is through unions. To date, public sector unions have made the most progress toward this goal, both in court cases and in labor negotiation agreements. While court litigation offers high visibility, the cost is high and progress slow. Money spent on lawyers and expert witnesses, it is argued, could be used more effectively in resolving pay disparities (Wilborn, 1986, p. 57). Also, past litigation has shown that courts have taken a conservative view of equal pay for comparable work; unless specific federal legislation is passed, it does not appear that this position will be redefined.

Advancement of comparable worth through union efforts will most likely occur as a result of contract negotiations. Unions have been very successful in bargaining with states and local governments to conduct comparable worth studies and implement pay equity policy. Moreover, studies show that unionized women paid on an hourly basis receive 30% higher wages than nonunionized women; however, only 14% of the total women in the work force are union members (Wesman, 1988, p. 23). Unions also offer other avenues for achieving pay equity—the grievance process and possible arbitration, petitioning enforcement agencies, and strikes, all of which have had success.

The future of comparable worth may depend significantly on personnel managers and their management style. According to Grider and Shurden (1987, pp. 81–86), the precedent set by *Gunther* indicates that personnel managers should take a proactive role in accommodating comparable worth. They suggest that managers conduct a review of job analysis/job evaluation programs for indication of bias; review compensation programs; conduct a human resource inventory; and review corporate strategic plans and establish premises for future human resource programs (p. 86).

In the United States, a final factor in the success comparable worth might expect in the 1990s can be seen in the results of the 1992 elections. Record numbers of women ran for office and women made noteworthy gains in representation at state and national levels. Future elections may well see a continuation of that trend. Furthermore, the Clinton/Gore ticket did promise to "protect women's rights in the workplace" and to "ensure fair wages for all workers." Despite the early difficulties of the Clinton administration, it should be expected that pay equity advocates will press the administration to deliver on those promises. Therefore, pay equity will most likely continue to be a significant issue.

REFERENCES

Aaron, Henry J., and Lougy, Cameran M. (1986). *The Comparable Worth Controversy*, The Brookings Institution, Washington, DC.

AFSCME v. State of Washington (1985). 770 F.2d 1401 (9th Cir.).

Ames, L. J. (1991). Legislating equity: a comparison of provincial legislation in Manitoba and Ontario requiring pay equity, *Int. J. Public Admin., 14* (special issue): 871–892.

Bayes, Jane (1988). Occupational sex segration and comparable worth, *Comparable Worth, Pay Equity, and Public Policy* (Rita Mae Kelly and Jane Bayes, eds.), Greenwood Press, New York, pp. 15–47.

Beatty, Richard W., and Beatty, James R. (1984). Some problems with contemporary job evaluation systems, *Comparable Worth and Wage Discrimination* (Helen Remick, ed.), Temple University Press, Philadelphia, pp. 59–78.

Becker, Mary E. (1986). Barriers facing women in the wage—labor market and the need for additional remedies: a reply to Fischel and Lazear, *Univ. Chicago Law Rev. 53* (Summer): 934–952.

Bergen, Orville V. (1984). A business viewpoint on comparable worth, *Equal Pay for Unequal Work* (Phyllis Schlafly, ed.), Eagle Forum Education and Legal Defense Fund, Washington, DC, pp. 209–217.

Blum, Linda M. (1991). *Between Feminism and Labor: The Significance of the Comparable Worth Movement*, University of California Press, Berkeley and Los Angeles.

Boston Herald (1984). Comparable pay "looney": Civil Rights Chief, November 17, p. 2.

Briggs v. City of Michigan (1982). 536 F.Supp. 435 (W.D. Wisc.).

Bureau of the Census, U.S. Department of Commerce (various issues). *Current Population Reports*, Consumer Income Series P-60, Money Income of Families and Persons in the U.S.

Cadieux, Rita (1984). Canada's equal pay for work of equal value law, *Comparable Worth and Wage Discrimination: Technical Possibilities and Political Realities* (Helen Remick, ed.), Temple University Press, Philadelphia, pp. 173–196.

California State Employees Association v. State of California (1989). 724 F.Supp. 717 (N.D. Cal.)

Cayce v. Adams (1977). F. Supp. 606 (D.D.C.).

Chi, Keon S. (1988). *Comparable Worth in State Government: Comparable Worth, Pay Equity, and Public Policy* (Rita Mae Kelly and Jan Bayes, eds.), Contributions in Labor Studies, Vol. 22, Greenwood Press, New York.

Christensen v. State of Iowa (1977). 563 F.2d 353 (8th Cir.).

Clark, Edwin R. (1984). The relationship of wages to profits, *Equal Pay for Unequal Work* (Phyllis Schlafly, ed.), Eagle Forum Education and Legal Defense Fund, Washington, DC, pp. 199–201.

Connecticut State Employees Association v. State of Connecticut (1983). 31 FEP Cases 191 (D. Conn.).

Cook, A. H. (1991). Pay equity: theory and implementation, *Public Personnel Management: Current Concerns—Future Challenges* (Carolyn Ban and Norma M. Riccucci, eds.), Longman, New York, pp. 100–113.

County of Washington v. Gunther (1981). 452 US 161.

Cumming, Charles M. (1984). Practical considerations in job evaluation, *Equal Pay for Unequal Work* (Phyllis Schlafly, ed.), Eagle Forum Education and Legal Defense Fund, Washington, DC, pp. 193–197.

Doherty, M. H. and Harriman, A. (1981). Comparable worth: the equal employment issue of the 1980s, *Rev. Public Personnel Admin., 1* (Summer), pp. 11–31.

England, Paula (1992). *Comparable Worth: Theories and Evidence*, Walter de Gruyter, New York.

Finn, Michael (1984). The earnings gap and economic choices, *Equal Pay for Unequal Work* (Phyllis Schlafly, ed.), Eagle Forum Education and Legal Defense Fund, Washington, DC, pp. 101–123.

Fischel, Daniel R., and Lazear, Edward P. (1986a). Comparable worth and discrimination in labor markets, *Chicago Law Rev.*, *53*: 891–918.

Fischel, Daniel R., and Lazear, Edward P. (1986b). Comparable worth: a rejoinder, *Chicago Law Rev.*, *53*: 950–952.

Gerlach v. Michigan Bell Telephone Company (1980). 501 F. Supp. 1300 (E.D. Mich).

Grayboff v. Pendelton (1984). 36 FEP Cases 350 (N.D. Ga.).

Gregory, R. G. Anstie, R., Daly, A., and Ho, V. (1989). Women's pay in Australia, Great Britain, and the United States: the role of laws, regulations, and human capital, *Pay Equity: Empirical Inquiries* (Robert T. Michael et al., eds.), National Academy Press, Washington, DC, pp. 222–242.

Grider, Doug, and Shurden, Mike (1987). The gathering storm of comparable worth, *Business Horizons*, *30* (July/Aug.): 81–86.

Griggs v. Duke Power Co. (1971). 401 U.S. 424.

Grumbine v. U.S. (1984). 586 F.Supp. 1144 (D.D.C.).

Grune, Joy Ann (1984). Equal pay through comparable worth, *Equal Pay for Unequal Work* (Phyllis Schlafly, ed.), Eagle Forum Education and Legal Defense Fund, Washington, DC, pp. 3–10.

Hartmann, Heidi I. (1984). The case for comparable worth, *Equal Pay for Unequal Work* (Phyllis Schlafly, ed.), Eagle Forum Education and Legal Defense Fund, Washington, DC, pp. 11–24.

Heen, Mary (1984). A review of federal court decisions under Title VII of the Civil Rights Act of 1964, *Comparable Worth and Wage Discrimination* (Helen Remick, ed.), Temple University Press, Philadelphia.

Hutner, Frances C. (1986). *Equal Pay for Comparable Worth: The Working Woman's Issue of the Eighties*, Praeger, New York.

Hyde, Albert C., and Graham, Michael (1991). Comparable worth in the United States: legal and administrative developments in the 1980s, *Int. J. Public Admin.*, *14* (special issue): 799–821.

IUE v. Westinghouse Electric Corp. (1980). 631 F.2d 1094 (3d Cir.).

Kelly, Rita Mae (1991). *The Gendered Economy*, Sage, New York.

Killingsworth, Mark R. (1987). Heterogeneous preferences, compensating wage differentials, and comparable worth, *Quarterly Journal of Economics*, *102* (November): 727–742.

Klingner, D. E. (1988). Comparable worth and public personnel values, *Rev. Public Personnel Admin.*, *9* (Fall): 45–60.

Kouba v. Allstate Insurance Co. (1982). 691 F.2d 873 (9th Cir.).

Lemons v. City and County of Denver (1980). 620F. 2d 228 (10th Cir.), cert denied, 449 US 888.

Levin, Michael (1984). The earnings gap and family choices, *Equal Pay for Unequal Work* (Phyllis Schlafly, ed.), Eagle Forum Education and Legal Defense Fund, Washington, DC, pp. 125–139.

Luton, Larry S., and Thompson, Suzanne (1989). Progress in comparable worth: moving toward non-judicial determination—problems and prospects, *Rev. Public Personnel Admin.*, *9* (Spring): 79–85.

Martin, J. A., and G. Thorsin-Hamm (1991). Swedish and American approaches to improving working women's status: context and comparable worth, *Int. Public Admin.*, *14* (special issue): 893–922.

National Committee on Pay Equity (1989). *Pay Equity Activity in the Public Sector 1979-1989: Executive Summary*, National Committee on Pay Equity, Washington, DC.

Nelson, B. A., and Opton, E. M., Jr., and Wilson, T. E. (1980). Wage discrimination and the "comparable worth" theory in perspective, *Univ. Michigan J. Law Ref.*, *13* (Winter): 233–301.

Neuse, S. M. (1991). From comparable worth to pay equity: into the 1990s—an introduction to the symposium, *Int. J. Public Admin.*, *14* (special issue): 763–772.

Patten, Thomas H., Jr. (1988). *Fair Pay*, Jossey-Bass, San Francisco.

Plemer v. Parsons-Gilbane (1983). 713 F.2d 1127 (5th Cir.).

Polachek, S. W. (1984). Women in the economy: perspectives on gender inequality, *Comparable Worth: Issue for the 80's: A Consultation of the U.S. Commission on Civil Rights*, *1*: 34–53.

Power v. Barry Bounty, Michigan (1982). 539 F.Supp. 721 (W.D. Mich.).

Remick, Helen (ed.) (1984). *Comparable Worth and Wage Discrimination*, Temple University Press, Philadelphia.

Rothchild, Nina, and Watkins, Bonnie (1987). Pay equity in Minnesota: the facts are in, *Rev. Public Personnel Admin., 7* (Summer): 16–28.

Scholl, Richard W. and Cooper, Elizabeth (1991). The use of job evaluations to eliminate gender based pay differentials, *Public Personnel Management, 20* (Spring): 1–18.

Shafritz, J. M., Riccucci, N. M., Rosenbloom, D. H., and Hyde, A. C. (1992). *Personnel Management in Government: Politics and Process*, 4th ed., Marcel Dekker, New York.

Spaulding v. University of Washington (1984). Case no. C74-91M (W.D. Wash. Dec. 17, 1981).

Steinberg, Ronnie J. (1984). A want of harmony: perspectives on wage discrimination and comparable worth, *Comparable Worth and Wage Discrimination* (Helen Remick, ed.), Temple University Press, Philadelphia.

Thompson v. Sawyer (1982). 678 F.2d 257 (D.C. Cir.).

Tienda, D. J., Smith, Shelley A., and Ortiz, Vilma (1987). Industrial restructuring, gender segregation, and sex differences in earnings, *Am. Sociol. Rev., 52*(2): 195–210.

Treiman, D. J., and Hartmann, Heidi I. (1981). *Women, Work and Wages: Equal Pay for Jobs of Equal Value*. National Academy Press, Washington, DC.

U.S. Department of Labor (1992). *Employment and Earnings*. Bureau of Labor Statistics, Superintendent of Documents, U.S. Government Printing Office, Washington, DC.

U.S. General Accounting Office (1985). *Options for Conducting a Pay Equity Study of Federal Pay and Classification Systems*, GAO/GGD-85-37 (March 1).

U.S. General Accounting Office (1986) *Pay Equity: Status of State Activities*, GAO/GGD-86-141BR (Sept.).

U.S. General Accounting Office (1992). *Washington State Efforts to Address Comparable Worth*, GA1.13:GGD-91-87BR (July 1).

Wards Cove Packing Co. v. Antonio (1989). 109 S.Ct. 2115.

Watkins, Bonnie (1992). Reassessing comparable worth: the Minnesota experience, *P.A. Times, 15* (April 1): 8.

Wesman, Elizabeth C. (1988). Unions and comparable worth; progress in the public sector, *J. Collect. Negot. Public Sect., 17* (1): 13–26.

Willborn, Steven L. (1986). *A Comparable Worth Primer*, D.C. Heath, Lexington, MA.

Williams, Robert E. (1984). Comparable worth: legal perspectives and precedents, *Comparable Worth: Issue for the 80s*.

19

Race Norming, Validity Generalization, and Employment Testing

MITCHELL F. RICE and BRAD BAPTISTE Louisiana State University, Baton Rouge, Louisiana

I. INTRODUCTION

Employment tests have been a valuable tool for employers seeking qualified, efficient, and productive employees for over a century. While tests are seen as an effective method available for predicting job performance, they often have a disparate impact on minority groups that as a whole score lower than nonminorities (US DOL, 1983a). As a result contemporary employers must find ways to choose a productive work force while at the same time attempting to develop a diversified and balanced work force (Brown, 1991). To accomplish this task many employers rely on employment agencies such as the United States Employment Services (USES)—a branch of the U.S. Department of Labor (DOL)—to tap into the local labor pools. Over 19 million persons apply annually for jobs through the 1800 local USES offices, and 3.5 million persons permanently or temporarily become employed (Wigdor and Hartigan, 1990). It is advantageous for individual employers to use employment services because these agencies implement affirmative action techniques, which shield the employer against liability in employment-related race discrimination lawsuits (Wigdor and Hartigan, 1990).

Test scores can be used in primarily three ways to make employment decisions: (1) top-down hiring—hiring individuals in declining order of their test scores; (2) within-group scoring—hiring individuals in declining order of their test scores after classifying them into demographic groups (e.g., race or ethnic groups); and (3) minimum competency hiring—hiring individuals randomly who have exceeded some minimum cut-off score (Wigdor and Hartigan, 1988; Hunter and Hunter, 1984). One of the most widely used affirmative action techniques utilized by the USES has been the implementation of "within-group score conversion" or "score adjustment strategy," commonly referred to as "race norming," in the scoring of employment tests (Interstate Conference of Employment Security Agencies, 1992). The USES implemented race norming with little publicity and no public debate in 1981. The policy took effect shortly after Ronald Reagan became president. By the mid-1980s race norming had developed into a highly controversial issue sparking heated debate between supporters and opponents.

This chapter discusses race norming in employment testing, illustrates how widespread the use of race norming had become nationally, and discusses judicial cases and decisions concerning race norming and validity generalization (VG). The chapter also briefly discusses the findings of the National Academy of Sciences (NAS) study of the General Aptitude Test Battery (GATB),

VG, and race norming. The GATB is a most popular employment test being administered annually to some 10 million potential civil servants (Bronner, 1991) and some 600,000 job applicants in various states (La Franiere, 1991). Further, some 18 million individuals a year take various tests of USES (Hacker, 1991).

II. WHAT IS RACE NORMING?

Race norming is an affirmative action technique combining a compensatory scoring system that is used to adjust applicant test scores so the number of individuals chosen for referral, and ultimately for selection, will reflect racial proportions in the actual population (Blits and Gottsfredson, 1990). The technique was developed by psychologists, test researchers, and statisticians seeking to eliminate racial imbalance and sampling error from tests. The scientific term used by most supporters of the policy is "within-group scoring" (National Review, 1991). The practice resulted from negotations between USES and the DOL legal staff, the Equal Employment Opportunity Commission (EEOC), and the Department of Justice in 1972 (Wigdor and Hartigan, 1988). To race-norm a test, each individual's raw score is given a percentile ranking within the individual's own ethnic group. In other words, every individual's score is compared and ranked against others of the same race. These scores, however, are not ranked in reference to the entire test-taking population (Wigdor and Hartigan, 1988). The individual's converted percentile score is then reranked with all converted percentile test scores and the highest percentile scores become referrals for employment opportunities (Blits and Gottfredson, 1990a). The effect of within-group percentile referral is to increase the proportion of minorities referred in comparison with a raw score, top-down referral system.

Research indicates various ethnic groups perform at different levels on standardized employment tests. Historically, Asians and whites have obtained higher raw scores than other races (US DOL, 1983a). Minorities typically score in the following descending order: Hispanics, African-Americans, and Native American Indians (US DOL, 1983a). These minority groups as a whole score significantly lower than whites and Asians (US DOL, 1983a). Because of this disparity, a testing agency only referring individuals with the highest overall test scores would refer a disproportionate number of whites and Asians as compared to other minority individuals. This would ultimately cause a work force not reflecting the population, which is considered a disparate impact on minorities. Therefore, race norming is seen as an approach to prevent those who score better on employment tests, mainly whites and Asians, from disproportionately getting most jobs (Holland, 1991). Specifically, race norming or within-group scoring is a race-conscious practice used to enrich the employment opportunities of black and Hispanic job seekers who take the GATB. According to Kelman (1991: 1192), "race-norming simply reflects a substantive commitment to interpreting raw scores in a fashion that facilitates the hiring of workers that do poorly on tests." Race-norming also attempts to correct for predictive bias, "the systematic under- or over-prediction of criterion performance for people belonging to groups differentiated by characteristics not relevant to criterion performance" (American Educational Research Association, 1985: 93). Simply stated, predictive bias exists in a test if members of a racial group typically or characteristically score lower than members of another racial group and the differences are not reflected in job performance (Shapiro et al, 1989).

The following example is illustrative of race norming. Five individuals, an American Indian, a black, an Hispanic, an Asian, and a white, apply for a blue collar job advertised at their local job service. The GATB is administered to all of the individuals and they all receive the same raw score (i.e., each person answered 300 questions correctly). These scores are then given a percentile ranking within each individual's ethnic group. These percentile scores, not the raw scores, are then reported to the employer. The Asian and white individuals both received a percentile score of 44, the Hispanic received a 67, the black received an 83, and the American Indian a percentile ranking of 89 (Brown, 1991). The rankings are different because each person is compared with members of his or her own race, not with the entire population of individuals who took the test at that time. These scores were being reported to employers with no indication of the individual's race, no raw score, and no statement explaining that the scores had been race-normed (Tenopyr, 1991). Table 1 illustrates the percentile conversion table used in race-norming test scores. Race norming was to become a popular practice used by the states in their employment referral systems. By the mid 1980s thirty-five states were using race norming to some degree in their employment referral systems (Barrett, 1991). This number had increased to thirty-eight states by mid-1990 (New York Times, 1991).

III. ALTERNATIVE METHODS TO RACE NORMING

There are other forms of test score manipulation available to testing and referral agencies, but none of these methods had approached the use and popularity of race norming. One such method is referred to as *banding*. Banding is a system in which the entire set of test scores is divided into several bands. Once this is accomplished, the band whose racial composition most closely resembles that of the population is selected above all the others and indiviuals are randomly chosen from within this group. This procedure may result in the elimination of the very highest and the very lowest scoring bands because these are normally overrepresented by majority and minority individuals, respectively. The band most often chosen falls in the middle to lower-middle region of the overall testing population (Holland, 1991).

Another alternative used in the E. F. Wonderlic Personnel Test is called "minimum–maximum qualification range." In this case all high and low scores are eliminated until the remaining group has roughly equal proportions of minority and majority individuals. A referral group is then randomly selected from this pool (Holland, 1991).

The *low-cutoff method* is also popular among referral agencies, and it is endorsed by the EEOC. In this method the lowest 20% of applicants tested are eliminated from the referral pool. The remaining 80% of the individuals scoring above this low cutoff value are subjected to a random selection process prior to referral. The problem with this method is that it results in an 85% average loss of production and has been shown to result in lower minority hiring rates than other available methods. Not all methods result in a loss of productivity. Most similar methods average only a 15% loss in productivity (Holland, 1991).

Table 1 Percentile Conversion[a]

	I	II	III	IV	V
Black	79	59	87	83	73
Hispanic	62	41	74	67	55
Other	39	42	47	45	42

[a] Jobs are grouped into five broad families: family I includes such jobs as machinists, cabinet makers, and tool makers; family II includes helpers in many types of agriculture, manufacturing, and etc.; family III includes professional jobs such as accountants, chemical engineers, nurses, editors; family IV includes bus drivers, bookkeepers, carpet layers; family V includes exterminators, butchers, file clerks. A raw score of 100 would convert to the percentile rankings shown in the table.
Source: Virginia Employment Commission, U.S. Dept. of Labor, Employment and Training Administration, *Validity Generalization Manual* (Section A, Job Family Scoring).

IV.   VALIDITY GENERALIZATION VS. RACE NORMING

Although the terms *validity generalization* (VG) and *race norming* have been used interchange-ably, it is important to note that the two terms are not synonymous. VG was developed in 1983 as a statistical technique allowing agencies to validate tests for groups of similar occupations, called job families (US DOL, 1983b). This method eliminates the need to perform time-consuming, com-plicated, expensive, and often statistically impossible validation studies for every job title (US DOL, 1983b). Validity is a measure of how well an employment test actually predicts future job perfor-mance (Society for Industrial and Organizational Psychology, 1987). VG analysis supports the idea that if the validity of a test is known for a reasonable sample of jobs, then its validity for other similar jobs will fall within a relatively small range. Stated another way, VG analysis provides the predictive validity of a test for similar jobs not studied. Figure 1 illustrates a sample regres-sion line for a valid test estimating future job performance. The graph has a positive slope, meaning low test scores are correlated with poor job performances and high scores with good job perfor-mances. The more accurate test will have higher validity, and employment tests must be validat-ed to be both useful to the employer and legal. Prior to VG, a validity study was required for each combination of test and job title to which the test was applied. If a study was not conducted, then the testing agency could not prove that the test was a valid predictor of performance in the given occupation (US DOL, 1983b).

VG allowed USES to administer the GATB to applicants in all job classifications. The GATB has been used for employment testing since 1947, but it had only been validated for about 500 of the over 12,000 occupational titles listed in the *Dictionary of Occupational Titles* (DOT) (Holland,

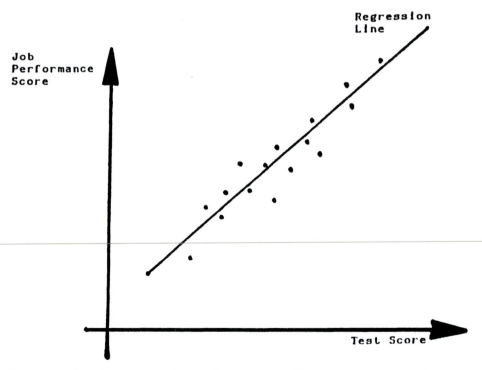

Figure 1   A hypothetical scatterplot showing the relationship between test scores and job performance scores for some validity study.

1990). The DOT, first devised by USES in 1939, classifies jobs according to a scheme of broadly defined performance requirements and is considered a basic tool for matching workers and employers (Wigdor and Hartigan, 1988).

In 1983 a new and improved version of the GATB extended the applicability of the test by generalizing (VG) from the 500 jobs originally covered to all 12000 jobs in the U.S. economy (see Hunter, 1982). This new version was termed the VG-GATB referral system by USES. By the end of 1986, some 38 states had used the new referral system on a trial or experimental basis (Hartigan and Wigdor, 1989).

The GATB is divided into nine aptitudes tested by various written and manual tests. Table 2 lists these aptitudes and the tests used to evaluate each item. For instance, an applicant's verbal aptitude is evaluated by a written vocabulary test, while manual dexterity is measured with a pegboard test titled "Place and Turn."

The ability to validate entire job families using VG dramatically increases USES value to employers. The procedure is designed to increase test vitality, which means an increase in the economic benefits enjoyed by employers. It is estimated that poor selection procedures cost the American economy $80–100 billion in lost productivity annually (Hartigan and Wigdor, 1980; US DOL, 1983b). On this point Olian and Guthrie (1987: 201) make the following observation:

> The ability to identify potentially successful employees correctly translates into dollar savings for an employer. These savings occur both directly (lower socialization and initial training costs and higher quality and quantity of performance among incumbents) and indirectly (more promotable workers, fewer separations due to poor performance, and associated reductions in severance and replacement costs).

Hunter and Hunter (1984) calculated that if the GATB were used as a basis for allocation decisions annual savings of between $2.5 billion and $15.6 billion could be realized by the federal government as an employer.

VG is different from race norming. Race norming is an affirmative action test score manipulation technique. Race norming is designed to eliminate disparate impact on minorities who take the tests. VG analysis determines the extent to which a test predicts job performance for similar jobs. However, both VG and race norming are involved with the GATB and it is this involve-

Table 2   The Nine Aptitudes Measured by the GATB and the Tests Used for Each

Symbol	Name	Test(s)
G	General intelligence	Vocabulary + arithmetic Reasoning + three-dimensional space
V	Verbal aptitude	Vocabulary
N	Numerical aptitude	Computation + arithmetic reasoning
S	Spatial aptitude	Three-dimensional space
P	Form perception	Tool matching + form matching
Q	Clerical perception	Name comparison
K	Motor coordination	Mark making
F	Finger dexterity	Assemble + disassemble
M	Manual dexterity	Place + turn

Source: USES Test Research Report No. 44, 1983, p. 17.

ment that generated additional controversy. If the purpose of the VG-GATB is to measure abilities related to job performance and to refer suitable workers to employers, the issue is whether norming or within-group scoring enhances or weakens this process. For job seekers (blacks and Hispanics) with very low scores on the GATB, VG-GATB referral will lead to predictable, negative outcomes—no job referrals. Race norming adjusts these lower scores to higher scores and indicates that these individuals have done better than they actually have (the raw scores were lower). For example, a black applicant with Job Family IV within-group score of 70%, will have the same referral status of a white applicant with a within-group of 70%, although their raw scores on the VG-GATB were 283 and 327, respectively. The percentile within-group scores are reported to employers with no reference to the applicant's identity. Since only the within-group scores are reported, at least two types of misinterpretation can occur on the part of employers:

1. The employer could easily assume that all individuals with the same reported score achieved the same raw score on the GATB.
2. The employer might also be led to assume that all candidates with the same percentile score on the test would have the same expected performance of the job (Hartigan and Wigdor, 1989).

Understanding the difference between VG and race norming may eliminate confusion when the two terms are substituted for one another in the literature.

V.   NATIONWIDE USE OF VG AND RACE NORMING

USES has almost 50 years of experience and research regarding the use of the GATB to predict job performance, which makes it the most widely used and validated employment test presently available to employers (US DOL, 1983b). USES monitors the extent to which the GATB is used and has performed similar surveys on the use of VG and race norming.

When race norming began to be publicly scrutinized, USES contacted the Interstate Conference of Employment Security Agencies Inc. (ICESA) to conduct a survey to assess the nationwide use of the GATB, VG, and race norming. The survey was completed in January 1992 and results were reported to the individual state employment service administrators in a March 11, 1992 memorandum from the ICESA Equal Opportunity Committee Chair (ICESA, 1992). According to the survey, 50 of the 53 state employment service agencies were using the GATB to evaluate job candidates (ICESA, 1992). However, the use of VG and race norming was perhaps the most interesting aspect of the survey.

ICESA reported the use of VG and race norming during two time periods. The first period was prior to September 1990 and the second period was between September 1990 and January 1992. It was during 1991 the opposition to race norming intensified to the point of declaring its use illegal for testing agencies (National Review, 1991). Table 3 shows that 34 states were utilizing VG-GATB with race norming to some extent as of September 1990. However, following the controversy of 1991, utilization of VG-GATB declined to only eight participating states by January 1992. Of these remaining states, Iowa was preparing to eliminate the use of VG-GATB, and Montana and North Dakota had discontinued race norming. In all, 26 of the original 34 participating states discontinued the use of VG-GATB and 28 were no longer using race-norming techniques. However, 10 of these states reported that they planned to reinstate an improved VG-GATB program by 1993 (ICESA, 1992).

Employers were reported to be "generally frustrated" and considered the loss of race norming as a "loss of a valuable hiring tool"; for this reason USES requested individual state participation in federal, state, and local research projects designed to improve the validity of VG-GATB and lessen its disparate impact. Twenty-seven states expressed a desire to participate in federally funded

Table 3 VG-GATB Users

State	As of Sept. 1990	As of Jan. 1992
Alaska	ODO	SW
Arkansas	SS	Not used
Colorado	SS	Not used
Delaware	SW	Not used
Florida	SS	Not used
Georgia	SW, ODO	Not used
Illinois	SW	Not used
Indiana	ODO	Not used
Iowa	SW	Phasing out
Kansas	SS	Not used
Kentucky	SW, ODO	Not used
Maine	SS	SS
Minnesota	SS	Not used
Missouri	SS	Not Used
Montana	SS	SS, fewer race norms
Nebraska	SW	Not used
New Jersey	SS	Not used
New Mexico	SW	Not used
New York	SW	Not used
North Carolina	SW	Not used
North Dakota	SW	SW, no race norms
Ohio	ODO	INA
Oklahoma	SW	Not used
Oregon	SS, ODO	Not used
Pennsylvania	SW	Not used
South Carolina	SS	Not used
South Dakota	SS	SS
Tennessee	SS	Not used
Texas	SW	Not used
Utah	SW, ODO	Not used
Vermont	SW, OCA	SW, OCA
West Virginia	SW	Not used
Wisconsin	SS	SS, ODO

SW, statewide; SS, selected sites; ODO, on demand only; OCA, only for counseling and assessment.
Source: ICESA January 1992 GATB Survey of SESAs.

validity improvement research studies, but only 6 states were willing to develop or participate in state or local projects requiring the use of their own funds. In regard to research on race norming, only 4 states wanted to participate on a state and local level, while 26 were willing to participate in federal research programs (ICESA, 1992). Basically, there appeared to be a general interest in the research projects as long as they did not involve the use of state and local funds.

VI. THE DEMISE OF RACE NORMING

As noted earlier, race norming of the GATB was developed under the Carter administration and was put into policy practice by the DOL under the Reagan administration. Race norming was never debated or approved by the Congress and the Reagan administration had no input in the implementation of this policy. However, in 1986 the U.S. Department of Justice (DOJ), under the direction of Assistant Attorney General for Civil Rights, William Bradford Reynolds, challenged VG-GATB on the basis it represented reverse discrimination that was in violation of Title VII of the 1964 Civil Rights Act. However, the DOJ agreed to drop its pursuit of this matter if DOL would agree not to expand the system beyond 1986 boundaries before conducting research to justify the system's results (Wigdor and Hartigan, 1988). DOL agreed not to extend the system until a panel of the NAS completed "a thorough, scientific evaluation" of the GATB referral system including within-group scoring.

Further, congressional concern developed during the following years. Most notably an amendment to the 1991 Civil Rights Bill was proposed by Democratic Congressman Henry Hyde of Illinois. In addition, Republican Senate Minority Whip Alan Simpson of Wyoming introduced a similar bill to outlaw the practice (Brown, 1991). However, the amendment to the 1991 Civil Rights Bill was deleted by the Republicans because the election was quickly approaching and they did not want the Democrats to be able to charge them with "racial politics" (Brown, 1991). The White House hoped that Congress would take it upon itself to abolish the practice so President Bush would be shielded from any negative fallout.

Further, polls showed whites, 85% of the electorate, were extremely opposed to any preferential treatment of minorities. In fact, a March 20–23, 1991 poll found that 77% of the voters did not approve of race norming while only 16% agreed with the policy (Brown, 1991). Democrats were upset with Hyde for openly challenging the policy and drawing attention to it (Brown, 1991). Hyde's proposal was defeated in the House Judiciary Committee by a 21-13 vote, strictly party line (Brown, 1991; Civil Rights Act of 1991). However, when President Bush signed the bill into law in November, 1991, a provision was included in the final bill that outlawed race norming (LaFraniere, 1991).

VII. THE COURTS, VALIDITY GENERALIZATION, AND RACE NORMING

A. Validity Generalization Cases

The landmark *Griggs v. Duke Power Co.* (1971) case led the way for litigation involving more specific areas of employment discrimination such as questions regarding the use of VG in employment tests. According to Sharf (1989), by 1987 five case precedents involving VG had been argued in federal district courts. Of these, the court had ruled in favor of VG four times.

B. *Friend v. Leidinger*

Friend v. Leidinger was argued on October 3, 1977 in the U.S. District Court of Virginia. This was a class action suit filed by black firemen against the city of Richmond, Virginia. These plaintiffs claimed the city violated 22 provisions of the Civil Rights Act of 1964 because Fire Bureau Employment policies were discriminatory against them as a class. Further, the plaintiffs alleged that there was the excessive punishment and garnishment of wages for accidents involving black employees compared to those involving whites; they were promoted at a lower rate than whites; they were intentionally given lower job-performance ratings than whites; and they were subjected to racial insults from their coworkers. The plaintiffs also challenged the validity of the city's testing procedures for employment and promotions.

Judge Warriner ruled in the city's favor for various reasons. First, no discriminatory impact was demonstrated by the plaintiff's evidence. Most importantly, a prima facie case of race discrimination can be rebutted by a state or municipality by evidence of lack of discriminatory purpose, and evidence showed that fire officials had demonstrated no discriminatory intent. In fact, fire officials had, in the court's opinion, made sincere efforts to eliminate discrimination.

Some interesting arguments were presented concerning employment testing. The firemen claimed the test had not been validated for the position of fireman in the City of Richmond and therefore they claimed the test was not job related. However, the city claimed the test would be statistically impossible to validate in Richmond due to small sample size. The city argued the test was valid because it had been validated in 55 jurisdictions in the State of California. The city's justification was that the job of fireman in both places (in Richmond and California) was essentially the same, therefore VG allowed the test to be used. The court ruled that this use of VG was appropriate according to EEOC guidelines. In addition, the defendants provided evidence that the number of blacks hired was proportional to the black population in Richmond. The court also felt blacks were sufficiently represented in high-ranking city government positions to rule out any intentional race discrimination by city officials. The court decided that there was not enough evidence to rule on the subject of tests for promotional purposes. For these, and many other reasons, the court ruled completely in favor of the defendants.

C. *Pegues v. Mississippi State Employment Services, Etc.*

The *Pegues* case is a very important one because of the unusual nature in which it was filed. A class action suit was brought about by female and black applicants who claimed the Mississippi State Employment Service had racially and sexually discriminated against them through its referral methods. The plaintiffs challenged the validity of the GATB and SATB (a smaller state-developed test designed for specific jobs). The plaintiffs were poorly educated individuals who were not qualified for the positions they were seeking and were unwilling to relocate. Some of the plaintiffs, including Mrs. Pegues, had been placed in developmental programs to eliminate these employment barriers, but many showed no interest in the programs and eventually dropped out. This case is most important because it placed the burden on the plaintiffs to show that they or their class had suffered or were likely to suffer race or sex discrimination. In this case the plaintiffs were unable to do so.

D. *Van Aken v. Young*

The courts have not always ruled in favor of VG. In *Van Aken v. Young* (1982), the concept of VG was completely disregarded. This case involved a class action suit by white firefighter applicants in Detroit who claimed that they had been overlooked in favor of less qualified minorities and females. They claimed that the city's affirmative action policy constituted reverse discrimination and further claimed that the written tests used to choose firefighters were valid measures of job performance. The Court did not agree and ruled that the city had admitted to a long history of race and sex discrimination within the fire department. Evidence presented overwhelmingly substantiated this point. In some years over 300 firefighters would be hired, none were female or black. The city developed an affirmative action plan to choose the highest qualified minority and female individuals even if more qualified white or male applicants were to be passed over. This procedure was put in place until the racial and gender proportions of hire applicants reflected city populations. The court examined the practice and found it to be an appropriate means of reversing past discriminatory practices.

One of the plaintiff's arguments is germane to VG. The plaintiff claimed that the written exam should have been used to strictly rank-order all applicants and relied on the expert testimony of noted validity expert Dr. John Hunter, Professor of Psychology, Michigan State University. However, his testimony was not convincing. Hunter relied on VG to claim that the fireman's written test was valid because good academy performance correlated well with job performance. Hunter was rebuked so powerfully that Judge Gilmore wrote in his memorandum of decision that:

> Hunter was completely destroyed on cross-examination. He admitted he knew nothing specific about the Detroit Fire Department Academy and its curriculum, and stated that the ability to be a fire fighter depended just as much upon fast reading ability as agility and ability to climb ladders and do other physical tasks that fire fighters perform. He was unable to explain how a person in a wheelchair, who could get the highest grade on a written exam, could be an active fire fighter. He further testified that there was a high correlation between cognitive ability and the ability to be a good lemon picker. Most of Hunter's testimony lacked credibility, and the Court is completely disregarding it.

In Hunter's defense, it must be noted that the fireman's test did not have the same statistical power of the GATB or even the E. F. Wonderlic Test. However, this decision was a major defeat of the VG technique. The decision clearly illustrated the weakness of relying on VG in all cases. The VG method seems to have the greatest utility when the tests are the same and the jobs being tested are very similar. The decision in the case seems to say that when these requirements are not met the courts will not be kind to the use of VG.

E.   *EEOC v. Atlas Paper Box Company*

EEOC v. Atlas Paper Box Company was heard on January 30, 1987 in the U.S. District Court of Tennessee. At issue was the use of the E. F. Wonderlic Personnel Test as a predictor of applicant performance in the clerical department of the company. The EEOC claimed the company had used the test as a way to keep blacks from obtaining salaried, clerical office positions.

The court held that EEOC must meet three requirements if the plaintiffs were to prove their case:

1. EEOC must prove the existence of a pattern and practice of race discrimination by Atlas.
2. To prove disparate impact EEOC must show that applicants were selected in a significantly different pattern than the application pool.
3. EEOC must prove that the use of these procedures was motivated by race discrimination.

EEOC was unable to meet these requirements. One reason was the expert testimony provided again by Dr. John E. Hunter, of Michigan State University, who testified that the Wonderlic Test was a good measure of cognitive skills. He also testified that the test was fair and better predicted job performance than any other criteria such as interviews or previous work history. Although Atlas had conducted no validation study of its own, statistically impossible with the given sample size, Hunter testified that studies conducted by other agencies had shown the test to be valid for clerks.

The Court examined extensive hiring records and found no evidence of race discrimination. The court did not find that blacks had been rejected in favor of less qualified white applicants. In addition, very few blacks had ever applied for positions compared to whites. For instance, in 1975 only 6% of the applicants applying for clerical positions were black, and none had scored higher than the lowest scoring white hiree. Many other examples such as this can be found in hiring records dating all the way back to 1969. However, testimony from the EEOC indicated that during the period 1969–1979, Atlas's hiring practices exhibited statistically significant adverse impact on blacks. Yet, expert testimony from Dr. Thomas E. Geraghty from the University of Tennessee, Chattanooga presented testimony that found no statistically significant adverse impact from 1978 to 1984. Interestingly, EEOC agreed with this testimony.

In its decision, the Court found that the plaintiff had failed to show disparate treatment or disparate impact and the defendant had successfully shown that the Wonderlic Test was not used simply as a means to discriminate. The policy of VG was upheld without question and Atlas Box Company received a favorable ruling because it had consistently applied a policy of hiring the most qualified applicant regardless of race.

F. The Railroad Cases

One example of VG at work is illustrated in cases involving the Consolidated Rail Corporation (1986). The suits alleged tests given to applicants in the engineer training program (ETP) were not valid predictors of their future job performance since the tests had not been individually validated. Conrail admitted that no validity study had been performed on the two written exams used to evaluate applicants in the ETP. However, Conrail claimed that the tests accurately evaluated specific knowledge required in the job, and that the tests and the job duties were similar ("almost identical") to those of a close competitor, Burlington Northern.

Burlington Northern locomotive engineers had been subjected to tests for many years and sufficient data was available to validate the tests for the job of engineer. The plaintiffs argued that the equipment used was different and could not allow the same test to be applied across companies. The court ruled that the equipment was sufficiently similar to allow a capable operator of one locomotive to operate a different type of locomotive both safely and efficiently. Because Conrail's tests were similar to those of Burlington Northern, which had been validated, the Court ruled in favor of the defendant Conrail. The position and its duties were the same and the test was seen as a valid predictor under the concept of VG.

VIII. RACE-NORMING COURT CASES

Following the *Griggs* decision many employers began to abandon testing altogether fearing charges of discrimination. Some employers recognized the need for affirmative action, yet desired the utility of tests. Procedures were developed to satisfy both requirements. A technique called the "bottom line" defense was developed. This technique normally involved tests utilizing the low cutoff method as a prescreening device followed by preferential selection of minorities from the remaining group. Minorities were to be selected until the racial proportions were appropriate. Employers hoped that the minority employees being chosen to satisfy the bottom line would shield them from adverse impact claims. They further reasoned that if the bottom line were satisfied tests would not have to be validated. This reasoning was not accepted in the 1982 Supreme Court case of *Connecticut v. Teal*. The *Teal* case is a landmark race-norming case, and resulted in the virtual abandonment of tests by many employers (Blits and Gottfredson, 1990).

The *Teal* case focused on a group of black Connecticut State employees who were eliminated from consideration for permanent supervisory positions because they failed a written exam. The state relied on the bottom line defense in this case citing the fact that blacks in supervisory positions were proportional to blacks in the population. The test being administered had not been validated and the black employee passing rate was only 68% of the white passing rate. The courts have established that a test is fair if minority passing rates are within at least 80% of majority passing rates. This was referred to as the four-fifths rule. Therefore, this test had an adverse impact on minorities and because this test had not been validated—the Court ruled in favor of the plaintiff.

A. *Guardians v. New York*

The case of the *Guardians Association of the New York City Police Department v. Civil Service Commission of the City of New York* was decided in the Second Circuit U.S. Court of Appeals on

July 31, 1980. The plaintiffs were minority candidates for the position of entry level police officer. They claimed that a rank-ordered entrance exam was not valid and resulted in disparate impact on minority hiring. The city had four other requirements including a physical examination, agility test, psychological profile, and background check. However, these requirements were graded on a pass–fail basis and their legality was not questioned by the plaintiffs. Only the rank-ordered test was under scrutiny. The Court under Judge Sifton affirmed and remanded the case in parts. The court found the test to have disparate racial impact because whites passed the test at a rate of 45.9%, while blacks and Hispanics had 17% and 20.5% passing rates, respectively.

The Court further ruled that the test had content validity, and the state had conducted appropriate studies to assure that this test met EEOC guidelines. The problem was that the test did not differentiate well enough among all individuals. There existed a cluster of individuals surrounding the cutoff level. Thus, the test did not sufficiently differentiate between individuals to justify rank ordering. Because this procedure resulted in disparate impact Title VII of the Civil Rights Act of 1964 had been violated.

The Court ordered the City to discontinue using the exam unless adjustments eliminating adverse impact were made. The judge ordered the development of a new procedure and required that it be approved by the Court prior to its use. The judge also ruled that strict adherence to the EEOC guidelines was not necessary as long as the results did not violate Title VII. The state offered to institute an interim quota system, but the Court rejected it as unnecessary. Based on the court's requirements, it would seem that if the City had race normed the results and hired accordingly it probably would have been acceptable.

B. *Bushey v. New York State Civil Service*

The *Bushey* case involved the failure of minority passing rates to meet the four-fifths rule (see *Teal* case) in comparison to nonminority success rates on a promotional examination in the New York Department of Corrections. Originally minorities only passed the test at a rate of 25% compared to 49% for whites. The state then instituted a score adjustment procedure whereby minority candidates' raw scores were adjusted with bonus points. Whites challenged this procedure as reverse discrimination since qualified whites were not being selected in preference to apparently less qualified minorities. A district court agreed that the procedure was illegal, but on appeal the Court ruled it was justified. The Court noted that the system did not eliminate any eligible nonminority candidates from the referral pool, nor did it absolutely bar nonminorities from advancement. The Court held the procedure valid because of its ability to limit the adverse impact of the test and because it was only temporary in nature. This was a major victory for supporters of race norming and similar affirmative action procedures.

C. *Hannon v. Barry*

In the *Hannon* case (1987), the District of Columbia had developed an affirmative action plan requiring hiring quotas of minority candidates at levels above race proportions in the actual population. The District held that this action was required to reverse past discriminatory practices. The United States, plaintiff in this case, argued that statistics showed that the work force of Washington, D.C. already had proportional minority representation and any affirmative action plan would tend to discriminate against nonminorities. The Court agreed and judged that in the absence of any current discrimination an unnecessary affirmative action plan violated Title VII of the Civil Rights Act. Further, the Court added that the District had failed to consider non–race-based alternatives, and their goal of achieving racial parity was constitutionally invalid. Accordingly, the

Court ruled in favor of the plaintiff and declared the affirmative action plan in violation of Title VII.

The above cases are only a sample of the myriad of VG and race norming cases brought before courts. The decisions tended to favor affirmative action procedures except in cases where little or no effort appears to have been made to validate the procedures or monitor their results. The employer seems to carry most of the burden of proof in these cases.

IX. THE NATIONAL ACADEMY OF SCIENCES STUDY

Due to a 1986 agreement with the DOJ, a study of the VG-GATB and race norming was required to be conducted by a neutral organization before VG-GATB could be extended beyond its 1986 boundaries (Wigdor and Hartigan, 1990). The National Academy of Sciences (NAS) was contracted to conduct the study, which took more than 2 years to complete, and many important topics and rumors were addressed using scientific methods and advanced statistical procedures. The results of these studies are published in over 50 detailed reports issued by USES. Much of the work conducted by NAS involved repeating advanced statistical experiments originally conducted by J. E. Hunter in the 1970s and early 1980s (Hartigan and Wigdor, 1989).

The Committee's report offered a number of policy recommendations for the fair and reasonable use of the GATB (Tenopyr, 1990; Hartigan and Wigdor, 1989). The NAS found the GATB to be of reasonable quality, having a moderately meaningful relationship to job performance. The Committee supported the use of VG, but added that GATB scores alone are not enough to refer and finally choose employees. The Committee recommended that GATB score adjustments be maintained to equalize the chance of referral for whites, blacks, Hispanics, and other minority individuals who would all do well on the job. Further, the Committee recommended full disclosure of both the race-normed and raw scores to the applicant and the employer. The NAS also recommended that score adjustment be used with other multiple criteria such as educational history and past work experience to choose employees (Hartigan and Wigdor, 1989). Finally, the Committee realized and admitted that the use of race norming will result in some economic loss. It estimated this loss of efficiency to be between 10% and 20%. This loss in production is the cost of providing minority workers the same chance of referral as able majority workers (Hartigan and Wigdor, 1989).

X. CONCLUSION

On the subject of race norming there appears to be experts on both sides of the issue. It is an emotional subject touching the lives of millions of individuals. Race norming generates controversy because it revolves around our human concept of and need for fairness, and it is unlikely that any policy developed will ever be fair to everyone. Blacks and other minority groups want employment tests that allow them to compete and provide them an equal opportunity for employment. Whites, on the other hand, feel cheated as individuals if they are overlooked for a position in favor of an apparently less qualified minority member.

Supporters of race norming typically present logical, unemotional, and scientific evidence to support their positions. Yet critics of VG and race norming are normally highly emotional and almost pleading. Blits and Gottfredson (1990b) consider VG and race norming to be Marxist, and argue that America will once again be thrown into a feudalistic society where lineage and birth would predict a person's rights and standing in their community (Blits and Gottfredson, 1990b). However, race norming appears to be an effective and useful technique allowing employers to reap most of the economic benefits of testing, while accomplishing equal employment opportunity and diversity goals.

ACKNOWLEDGMENTS

Research support was provided by a Summer 1993 Research Grant, College of Business Administration, Louisiana State University.

REFERENCES

American Educational Research Association, American Psychological Association, and National Council on Measurement in Education (1985). Standards for Educational and Psychological Testing, American Psychological Association, Washington, DC.

Barrett, Laurence I. (1991). Cheating on the Tests, *Time (June 3)*:57.

Blits, Jan H. and Gottfredson, Lindson S. (1990a). Employment Testing and Job Performance, *The Public Interest (Winter)*:18–25.

Blits, Jan H. and Gottfredson, Linda S. (1990b). Equality or Lasting Opportunity, *Society (March/April)*:4.

Bronner, Ethan (1991). Scoring of Job Test Under Fire. Chicago Tribune (May 25):2.

Brown, Peter A. (1991). Normin Stormin, *New Republic (April)*:13.

Connecticut et al v. Winnie Teal et al., 102 S. Ct. 2525 (1982).

EEOC v. Atlas Paper Box Co., U.S. District Court, E. D. Tennessee, Southern District, No. CIV-1-83-251, January 30, 1987, 680 F. Suppl. 1184 (1980).

Equality Through Double Standards (1991). *National Review (June 10)*:14.

Frazier et al., and Cox et al. v. Consolidated Rail Corporation, et al., U.S. District Court, D. C., Nos. 85-845 and 83-0514, July 31, 1986.

Griggs v. Duke Power Co., 401 U.S. 424 (1917).

Guardians Association of the New York City Police Department Inc. v. Civil Service Commission of the City of New York, U.S. Court of Appeals, 2nd Circuit, No. 849, Docket 80-7027, July 31, 1980, 630 F 2.d 79 (1980), cert. denied 452 U.S. 940 (1981).

Hacker, Holly K. (1991). Adjusted Federal Employment Tests Stirs Controversy. *New York Times (June 6)*:A5.

Hartigan, John A. and Wigdor, Alexandra K. (eds.) (1989). *Fairness in Employment Testing* National Academy Press: Washington, DC.

Holland, Robert G. (1990). Big Brother's Test Scores, *National Review (September 3)*:35–37.

Holland, Robert G. (1991). Race norming by any other name, *National Review (July 29)*:36.

Hunter, John E. (1982). *Test Validation for 12,000 Jobs: An Application of Job Classification and Validity Generalization Analysis to the General Aptitude Test Battery (GATB),* Report to the U.S. Employment Service.

Hunter, John E. and Hunter, R. F. (1984). The validity and utility of alternative predictors of job performance, *Psychological Bulletin 96*:72–95.

Interstate Conference of Employment Security Agencies, Inc. (1992). ICESA GATB/VG Survey, *(March)*, Unpublished, ICESA, Washington, DC.

James Bushey et al v. New York State Civil Service Commission, U.S. Court of Appeals, 2nd Circuit, No. 779, Docket No. 83-7893, April 16, 1984, 733 F. 2d. 220 (1984), cert. denied 469 U.S. 1117 (1985).

Kelman, Mark (1991). Concepts of discrimination in "general ability" job testing, *Harvard Law Review 104*:1157–1247.

LaFraniere, Sharon (1991). Labor Department to revamp aptitude test, *The Washington Post (December 14)*:A13.

Marvin K. Hammon et al, United States of America v. Marion S. Barry Jr. Mayor, D.C., et al., U.S. Court of Appeals, D.C. Circuit, Nos. 85-5669, 85-5670, and 85-5671, February 27, 1987, 813 F. 2d 412 (D.C. Cir. 1987).

Neal VanAken et al v. Coleman A. Young et al, U.S. District Court, E.D. Michigan, Southern District, Cir. A. No. 77-62443, June 8 1982, 541 F. Suppl. 448 (1982), affirmed 750 F.2d 43 (1983).

Olian, Judy D. and Guthrie, James P. (1987). Cognitive ability tests in employment: ethical persepctives of employers, *Research in Corporate Social Performance and Policy* (9):185–212.

Pegues v. Mississippi State Employment Service Inc, U.S. District Court, N.D. Mississippi, Delta Division, No. 72-4-5, March 7, 1980, 488 F. Suppl. 239 (1980), affirmed in part and reversed in part, 699 F. 2d 760 (5th Circuit), cert. denied, 464, U.S. 991 (1983).

Race norming test become a fiery issue (1991). *New York Times (May 19)*:Section 4.

Shapiro, Martin M., Slutsky, Michael H., and Watt, Richard F. (1989). Minimizing unneccessary racial differences in occupational testing, *Valparasio University Law Review 23 (Winter)*:213–265.

Sharf, James C. (1987) Litigating personnel measurement policy, keynote address, Conference on Fairness in Employment Testing, October 1. Newport Beach, CA.

Society for Industrial and Organizational Psychology (1987). *Principals for the validation and use of personal selection procedures*, 3rd ed., Society for Industrial and Organizational Psychology, College Park, MD.

U.S. Department of Labor (1983a). Fairness of the General Aptitude Test Battery: Ability Difference and Their Impact on Minority Hiring Rates. (USES Test Research Report No. 43, U.S. Department of Labor, Washington, D.C.

U.S. Department of Labor (1983b). Overview of Validity Generalization for the U.S. Employment Service. *USES Test Research Report No. 43*, U.S. Department of Labor, Washington, D.C.

Wigdor, Alexandra K. and Hartigan, John A. (1990). The Case of Fairness, *Society (March/April)*:13.

Wigdor, Alexandra K. and Hartigan, John A., eds., (1988). *Interim Report: Within Group Scoring of the General Aptitude Test Battery*, National Research Council, Washington, DC.

20
Personnel Training and Development

G. DAVID GARSON and DENNIS M. DALEY   North Carolina State University, Raleigh,
North Carolina

Training has mushroomed as a profession in public administration. The diverse work force and often rapidly changing environment that the 21st century promises only adds to the need for professional training (Hudson Institute, 1988). Larger municipal, state, and federal jurisdictions routinely rely on in-house professional training staff to meet a large proportion of their employee training and staff development needs. The trend is for this in-house capability to become larger and more inclusive over time. Yet traditional providers of learning such as universities and consulting firms will continue in the role of providers of that training which is characterized as complex or requires special features. For the foreseeable future the training market will continue to be characterized by a burgeoning multiplicity of providers, learning designs, and subject competency areas.

In this chapter we examine the goals of the training process and of management development. In addition to discussing assumptions about goals and objectives, the relation of training to career management is outlined. We look at the problem of assessing training needs, training trainers, establishing learning designs in relation to adult learning theories, and evaluating training and development programs from a human resource investment viewpoint. This discussion of the training process is followed by a brief survey of some specific modes and formats of learning designs. A concluding section outlines possible directions for further research in this much practiced but little studied area.

I. THE NATURE OF THE TRAINING AND DEVELOPMENT PROCESS

The public service training function in the United States has undergone a long evolution. A considerable road has been traveled between the 1917 Smith–Hughes Act funding vocational training and the 1978 Civil Service Reform Act, vesting the new U.S. Office of Personnel Management (OPM) with a broad mandate for coordinating governmental training at the federal level. Today virtually all major branches of the federal government, along with many state and local jurisdictions, have instituted formal training programs. Since the 1958 Government Employees Training Act, we have witnessed a rapidly proliferating spread aided in part by funding under the now-defunct 1970 Intergovernmental Personnel Act (IPA).

A.   Objectives of Training and Management Development

Prior to the introduction of any training program an organization must first determine if training is indeed the appropriate response to its perceived problem. Donald Klingner and John Nalbandian (1985, p. 234) note that training is only one of five possible responses to performance problems. Training is inappropriate wherever problems are deemed bothersome but insignificant, are due to inadequate selection criteria, arise because employees are unaware of what is expected of them, or arise because employees lack incentives for performance. These problems are dealt with by ignoring them, by the application of job analysis, by orientation and performance appraisal feedback, or by the implementation of an explicit performance reward system. Only when performance problems are attributable to inadequate employee skills does training become the appropriate response.

OPM identifies goal clarity as an essential prerequisite for successful training. Clear goals must be communicated throughout the organization (OPM 1979a, p. 2). Without the setting of clear training goals, later evaluation is rendered impossible. More important, such a failure sets the stage for serious problems in the development program.

The call for clarity of objectives is not just a platitude. A few common scenarios can be used to illustrate how easily deficiency in this area can lead to organizational failure of training programs. For example, training can arouse expectations of career development and mobility that management is unprepared or unable to satisfy—or even address! In such a situation the posttraining environment may be one of hostility and resentment with low morale undercutting whatever productivity gains the substantive training may have provided.

As another illustration, trainers may design programs that emphasize interpersonal skills because subordinates enjoy such training and because the trainers are experienced in it. Yet if management thinks that training is changing skill levels in a technical sense, misunderstanding results. Training may become viewed as "too soft" or "just an escape from the job." The common result of such a mismatch between trainers' and managers' goals for training is underbudgeting of investment in human resources and relegation of the training function to the backwaters of the organization. Often this is a result of training programs in which participant selection is through self-nominations rather than involving or requiring managerial merit selection.

The interface between training and organizational goals is critical. With regard to equal employment opportunity, affirmative action, and multicultural diversity, for instance, training programs may either diminish or perpetuate ethnic, racial, and sexual inequalities in the agency's work force. Poor training may also create "tunnel vision" whereby the organization focuses on existing operating procedures at the expense of consideration of alternatives. Training is related to goal setting in an agency planning processes as well as in the making of career assignments, the appraisal on performance, and other aspects of job management. Without the setting of clear organizational goals for the training function, the common result is management failure to utilize training effectively and consistently in relation to other administrative systems.

Establishing goals for training assumes a certain relationship between the employees and management. Two extreme views contrast the differences here. Anchoring one extreme are uncritical advocates of "improving interpersonal relations" and of "team approaches to management." Here one may find the belief that most organizational problems are basically "people problems." It is thought that if these are treated properly through training such problems will disappear. At the opposite pole are radical critics who believe that most organizational problems are due to inherent oppositions of real interests, including class, ethnic, and gender interests. Such critics do not believe that better communication or improved training can substantially change existing modes of production and service delivery.

As usual, the truth may lie in the middle. Training is not a panacea. It should not be forced to serve in place of other forms of employee development and interest articulation. On the other hand, training can smooth organizational processes by increasing understanding of the rules of the game. Training may address needs perceived as affecting the entire organization or as applying to an individual employee. It can focus on adding to an organization's overall level of knowledge or on the treatment of specific deficiencies.

There are many specific organizational objectives to which training may be directed. These include such areas as labor relations (cf. Zack, 1978), race relations (O'Brien and Gubbay, 1979; Kohls, 1985), and productivity management (Lovell, 1979). Service educational activities such as preretirement counseling (Bradford, 1979) may also be included. Common training topical areas include management skills/development, supervisory skills, technical skills/knowledge, communication skills, basic computer skills, new methods/procedures, customer relations/services, clerical/secretarial skills, personal growth, executive development, employee labor relations, wellness, sales skills, customer education, and even remedial basic education (Geber, 1989, p. 50). Almost any topic may be the object of training.

Given the multiplicity of possible training objectives, the question is not so much what as how. That is, there is no list of training objectives that could be given here as "correct" and universally applicable. Rather, the setting of training objectives is particularized to the specific organization. How training objectives are set is the distinguishing criterion, not which objectives are selected.

In an organization with a mature training function, training objectives are set in two ways. First, objectives must be integrated with the organization's overall approach to career management and reward structure. An organization that emphasizes training in managerial skills, for example, will not ordinarily base its career system on sole reliance on outside recruitment of formally credentialed applicants. Such a system would thwart the career incentives motivating effective participation in the training process. Likewise, an organization whose reward structure is geared to daily output penalizes participation in training in broader or longer range management competencies.

Second, training objectives must be set on the basis of assessed training needs (Steadham and Clay, 1985; Rummler, 1987). Not only does the needs assessment process afford an opportunity for employee participation (and hence self-investment in the training concept); it also assures a linkage between organizational objectives, task structures, supervisory perceptions, and employee desires. Although complete harmony of these four elements is an almost unachievable ideal, each must be considered. The setting of training objectives cannot be done well by a manager sitting in the solitude of his or her office, nor can it be left as an ambiguous "something everyone understands." The relation of training objectives to career management and to needs assessment is the subject of the two sections that follow.

B. Training's Relation to Career Management and Reward Systems

In planning for the federal system of executive resources boards, OPM (1979b) identified 10 prerequisites for an effective executive development system:

1. Top management support for executive development
2. Formation of a high-level executive resources board
3. Clearly articulated and communicated goals
4. Design of an executive development planning system (e.g., treating training, job rotation, retirements)

5. Merit selection of participants in development programs
6. Management candidate development programming (e.g., self-assessments, management training, exposure to future colleagues, varied job assignments, coaching and counseling)
7. Management member development programming (e.g., professional updating, sabbaticals, and other growth opportunities
8. Use of development program graduates in task forces, interagency assignments, and job assignments
9. Staff and budgetary support for the development function
10. Implementation of an evaluation–feedback system for the development program

Although OPM was considering management development for higher level administrators, many of the same considerations apply to training at lower levels. The list of 10 prerequisites of effective executive development raises many issues relating training to career management issues of selection, implementation, and evaluation.

For example, is merit selection of development program participants really necessary? Clearly, in one sense it is not. Most training in the public sector is in the form of on-the-job orientation to existing organizational practices and technical procedures. Although the individual may be hired on merit considerations, this on-the-job training is usually an automatic and universal accompaniment to simply being hired. On most jobs there is adequate incentive to perform satisfactorily and, therefore, to "learn the ropes." For training and development that is more basic (e.g., communications skills) or more specialized (e.g., policy analysis) than the job technically calls for, there may not be clear incentive. Merit selection typically involves the supervisor or superior in the recruitment of candidates for training and development. This serves to increase the likelihood of follow-through on the job after training is over and also enhances the status of the training experience.

Of course, the reason merit selection is often an effective motivator of participation in training and development is that it suggests other things. Merit selection, particularly by superiors, suggests that superiors are interested in the career development of subordinates. To be credible this interest must be manifested in other ways as well. Point 8 in the prerequisites of effective executive development is critical here. Training is most successful in the long run if management's policy is to use it. This seeming truism is often violated in practice. Organizations may find it difficult to adjust traditional job assignment patterns to give priority to utilization of individuals who have received relevant training. Agency leaders may be unaccustomed to the concept of varied job assignments as a method of career development, preferring instead the seeming security of long-term narrow specialization and tracking.

OPM's prerequisites of effective executive development also raise many issues of implementation. Training is logically complemented by a system of coaching and counseling (point 6), for example, but this requires either retraining of managers or expansion of staff specialists. Top management support (point 1) and continued high-level attention (point 2) are costly in terms of executive time and energy, yet nearly all studies of training cite the importance of these elements, at least for executive and management development. Job assignments (point 6) and released time (point 7) are equally disruptive of "normal" management scheduling, yet implementation of training programs integrated with career management requires a great deal of management on this score.

Evaluation (point 10) is perhaps the most critical area relating training to career management. Though evaluation is discussed in Section I.F, it may be noted here that greatest interest attaches to attempts to evaluate training through assessment of its impact on job performance and, more broadly, on career performance. The employees themselves will often so assess training efforts. If no relation is seen to back-home job performance and recognition for job performance through the reward structure, cynicism toward the training program will develop.

In summary, it may be said that career management provides a supportive environment for a successful training and development effort. It is true that most training proceeds without any systematic approach to career management. It is also the case that most training, particularly in the public sector, is little connected to the organization's reward structure, if at all. Nonetheless, these are matters that come at a cost as well as a savings to the organizations that forego them. The cost generally appears in a complacent employee attitude toward training, if not outright deprecation of its value. Likewise, just as the employee often fails to see the relation of training to career development and rewards, so the manager often fails to see the connection of training to the needs of administrators.

C. Assessing Training Needs

Comprehensive training or executive development efforts normally include a needs asesssment at the outset (Steadman and Clay, 1985; Rummler, 1987). Needs assessments may draw information from analysis of individual employees, management plans and concerns, or environmental factors affecting the organization. Regardless of the type of assessment approach adopted, the general objective is to determine training and development needs specifically and concretely in order to translate needs into learning tasks. An ancillary objective is to involve potential trainees and their superiors in all phases of the needs assessment process (Braun, 1979; Boyer and Pond, 1987; Schneier et al., 1988).

McGehee and Thayer (1961) outline three levels to the analysis of training needs: organizational, operational/job, and individual/personal. Organizational analysis focuses on the general treatment needs necessary for implementing or carrying out the human resource planning process. It concentrates on those functions that help to maintain the existing organizational structure, enhance its efficiency or updating operations, and nurture the organizational culture. Job analysis is devoted to delineating the specific skills and competencies involved in the tasks that compose an individual job. Training is directed at ensuring that the individual possesses these skills and competencies. Personal analysis needs assessment focuses on the organization–person fit. The advantages of individual, technical competence can be dissipated if the individual fails to successfully integrate into the organization's social structure.

An organizational approach to needs assessment focuses on environmental factors. An example is the study of client preferences for employees' role behavior as a criterion for setting behavioral training objectives (Folley, 1969). Assessment may also be based on the discrepancy between organizational competencies and those prescribed by professional standards nationally, Likewise, simple awareness of trends in current affairs (e.g., affirmative action and diversity, collective bargaining, productivity, automation and MIS) may clearly dictate externally imposed training needs on the organization.

Many of these concerns are brought together in the efforts for fostering Total Quality Management (TQM). Mostly associated with W. Edwards Deming (1986) and recognized in the United States through the Malcom Baldridge awards, these are efforts at crafting the effective organization through the empowerment and training of its members (Cocheu, 1989).

In a planning context, organizational needs assessment could be associated with career management and work force planning. Training is greatly enhanced in an organization if career ladders have been established. Career ladders are job systems in which any rung (position) is obtainable by specified training and experience in a previous rung. Work force planning based on service load projections can provide general estimates of growth and turnover. From this may be derived a projection of the needed flow through job pathways in the career management system. These projections, finally, are parameters for determining the scope and substance of the organization's training function over time.

Another organizational assessment approach is the organizational climate survey (Zemke, 1979). Though often used in early phases of organizational development efforts, such surveys are useful in identifying training and management development needs as well. Surveys can be an efficient means of gathering data on commonly perceived organizational problems often not noticed in policy-centered management planning. Training in conflict management, communications, team building, job design, and similar "humanistic" content areas may well seem more salient to the organization's "bottom line" if surveys reveal a climate marked by discontent, low morale, or confusion about organizational goals. Though not ordinarily used in this manner, surveys could also serve as a means of identifying employee-perceived priorities regarding potential training topics.

Job analysis needs assessments that focus on how a specific job operates may be either manager-centered or individual-centered. Management-centered approaches to needs assessments for training and development are often discounted as "topdown" and "theory X" in assumptions. However, as Malcolm Knowles (1978, p. 173) said, "When there is evidence that training does not (1) respond to what managers report they want and need, and (2) lead to organizational change, then something is amiss." If the management-centered needs analyst is sometimes accused of being autocratic, the stereotyped countercharge is that the individual-centered approach degenerates into making training an enjoyable diversion from work or a steppingstone up and out of the organization.

Such dangers are inherent in training. The stereotyped debate above misses the point, however. Management cannot efficiently maximize return on human resource investment if it is not carefully and individually targeted. Individuals cannot be motivated by training unless there is a clear expectancy that it is the path to a goal. This requires training to be a subordinate element in overall management planning.

Advocates of management-centered approaches to needs assessment cite certain advantages. First, of course, such approaches help mesh the training program with organizational objectives as determined by management. These objectives may take into account a variety of needs about which the individual employee may be totally unaware. Second, by involving management more closely in the training planning process, legitimation of the training effort is gained that is instrumental to success. Third, management-centered approaches avoid confusing training assessment with judgmentally directed performance appraisal (Daley, 1993).

From the employee viewpoint, individual-centered needs assessment may seem like a demand to "confess weaknesses" that may lower the employee's standing in the eyes of those who rate his/her performance, creating defensiveness (Meyer et al., 1965; Meyer, 1991). Where such systems are employed it becomes imperative that the employee provided information not be used or appear to be used in any judgmental decisions (i.e., retention, dismissal, promotion, or pay). Hence, both Meyer (1991) and Daley (1993) advocate the use of developmental appraisal processes in such circumstances.

Analysis of individual employees is the commonsense approach to training needs assessment. The simplified model is to assess employees' strengths and weaknesses, and to provide remedial training for the latter. Remedial training is not the only type, however. Other types include training for advancement, training in response to displacement, and training for growth. In these forms training may serve to advance career management, aid in implementing technological and other organizational changes, or enrich the organization through the diffuse benefits of continuing education.

This information may be obtained from performance appraisal systems (Daley, 1993) or from employee surveys (Brinkerhoff, 1986). In either case training needs are basically assessed by asking the employees (Graham and Mihal; 1986). Individual-centered approaches usually include measures designed to ascertain the organization–person fit. Besides including training programs primarily designed to aid in an individual's growth and development, they include assessments as to whether that specific individual matches the present or projected human resource needs of the organization.

These personal analyses could also be used to ascertain whether the individual employees in question actually possessed the ability to learn (Fleishman and Mumford, 1989; Geber, 1989). In addition to ability itself, the motivation to seek or participate in training (Hicks and Klimoski, 1987) as well as other personal attributes and attitudes play a role in determining trainability (Noe, 1986; Noe and Schmitt, 1986). Often overlooked in our concern for equity and fairness is the fact that real people are indeed different. They not only bring with them different personalities but different and meaningful job potentials. An individual's ability to learn specific tasks and skills is an important consideration in the overall assessment of training needs (Robertson and Downs, 1989).

In individual-centered needs assessments, remedial training commonly utilizes skills testing and performance testing. Such tests may be administered by written or oral examination, simulation, peer evaluation, superior's evaluation, or self-rating. The simplest, least scientific, but perhaps most common method is to translate the job description into a list of task elements and corresponding skills. The potential trainee is then asked to rate himself or herself in terms of perceived proficiency in each of the skill areas. Training for advancement or for displacement is often assessed similarly, except that the new position to which the employee will be moving is used as the base. In training for growth, the individual-centered approach to needs assessment may utilize the interest inventory as well (Maslow, 1976, p. 10-4).

Organizational, job, and personal needs assessment approaches are not mutually exclusive. In fact, each serves to inform the training designer in a different way. Ideally, a multimethod approach to needs assessment would be the rule in learning design. However, even this would not solve all problems. Ultimately, well-designed training depends on social science. Unless the cause–effect relationships of administrative behavior are well understood, training techniques (media usage, experiential learning) are apt to be in advance of the state of the art of training substance. The complete trainer is also an action researcher, concerned with the study of the causes of desirable job performance (Gagne, 1962). When training breaks its bond to these broader educational concerns, it erodes the basis for its long-term credibility.

A wide array of specific techniques are available for assessing training needs. Besides the obvious sources derived from management and employee requests for training (for themselves or others), information on training needs can be gathered through attitudinal surveys, focus groups, and advisory committees. Employee skill inventories and assessment centers can serve to point out areas in need of attention. Performance measures such as those provided by performance appraisals, work samplings, critical incidents, output or result reports, as well as information from program evaluations and management audits can be used (Newstrom and Lilyquit, 1979, p. 56).

D. Competencies of Trainers

The range of concerns suggested by this brief review of needs assessment only begins to suggest the knowledge base that would be possessed by a first-rate trainer. Training is not something "anyone can do." Moreover, training is not a single, homogeneous role. The Training Leadership Division of the then–U.S. Civil Service Commission (now Office of Personnel Management, or OPM), for example, has developed separate competency guidelines for five major training roles: career counselor, consultant, learning specialist, program manager, and training administrator (U.S. Civil Service Commission, 1976). Although all require certain core competencies (e.g., abilities in communication, data gathering, analysis, planning; knowledge of adult learning theory, training resources and techniques, group process skills), each has distinct competency prerequisites.

The training consultant, for example, is an individual who is able to negotiate with organizational clients regarding the scope of training. This includes the ability to develop detailed plans for job study, project planning and scheduling, and cost–benefit analysis. Also included in this role is ability in arranging meetings, conducting interviews, and gathering information on organizational goals, objectives, and work processes. This ordinarily requires the ability to plan and conduct reliability/validity studies of training programs. The consultant must be able to select, plan, and implement performance analyses, conduct evaluation studies, and facilitate long-range organizational planning to meet future training needs.

A learning specialist holds a role most often associated with the term "trainer." Such an individual must be competent in analyzing learning populations, conducting task analyses, writing learning objectives, researching relevant literature, and developing evaluation techniques. The specialist also prepares lesson plans, of course, organizing content based on a sequence of learning objectives. Specialists must be familiar with a wide variety of learning strategies and tools and have a general familiarity with adult learning theory. Among these competencies will be the ability to utilize audiovisual production equipment, graphics and printing, and interactive computer-assisted instructions as appropriate. This role also requires public information skills and abilities to relate to various client groups in the selection, design, and evaluation of a learning program.

Training program managers are individuals with general policy-planning skills combined with substantial expertise in their specific application to the training function. Program managers must be able to carry out all aspects of budgeting, contracting, and personnel administration for the training program. This includes development of specifications for requests for proposals (RFPs), cost estimation of projects, and procurement management. The manager also interfaces the training program with legislative and governmental requirements that affect it, including management of all reporting processes. As the external representative of the program, the manager also articulates program objectives, provides ongoing technical assistance to the staff, and oversees the evaluation process.

Training administrators must have the ability to maintain and coordinate support services. This includes scheduling of training and role orientations. Many of these are practical in nature. Suessmuth (1978, pp. 6–11) cites many of these orientations: strong motivation, good social relations skills, showmanship, analytic intelligence, emotional self-awareness and willingness to change, experience in what is to be taught, and empathy with others. Even more practical criteria are willingness to travel, to work erratic hours, and to work for a rate of pay that has typically been submanagerial in level.

When one combines these various competencies, role elements, and other requirements, it is easy to see that hiring a first-rate trainer is no small challenge. Many of these skills are precisely the ones that would enable an individual to attain a much higher position in the organization than the training division ordinarily allows. When the manager does find a first-rate individual who possesses all of the needed characteristics, it is apt to be someone who has foregone other opportunities because he or she likes the teaching role and is personally interested in adult learning (Fetteroll, 1985; Brinkerhoff, 1987).

The various learning styles that adults bring to the process need be considered in providing education and training (Sims and Sims, 1991). In addition to students possessing different learning styles, teachers and trainers may also have preferences with regard to teaching methods.

Education is an interactive process. This is especially true in the case of adult workers. They are much more likely to question the value and style of the education and training they are receiving or subject to. Unlike younger students, adults possess a degree of knowledge as to what needs to be done. With regard to professional educational courses or training sessions, they are to some extent themselves already experts on the topics under discussion. Matching teacher and student teaching/learning style preferences is an important part of the process (Sims and Sims, 1991).

E. Adult Learning Theory

The psychological aspects of human development indicate that adults pass through a series of life stages. These life stages influence their perceptions and relationships with themselves, the world at large, and their work lives. Career development, motivation, commitment, and job satisfaction are all affected by an individual's life stage (Schott, 1986).

More specifically, life stages affect adult learning. Methods designed to serve children and adolescents or even young college students are not necessarily appropriate for the education and training of mature, adult workers and professional colleagues. While adults already come to us with an innate propensity for learning, schools and organizations can influence how well they learn (Knowles, 1987).

The professional trainer is very apt to have been educated in and be a firm advocate of a rather definite theory of adult learning—andragogy. Though hardly the only viewpoint, this dominant perspective is perhaps most associated with Malcolm S. Knowles, who has contrasted the teaching of adults as a separate science from traditional teaching (which is primarily focused on children and adolescents) requiring different principles. This perspective is heavily rooted in what may be termed the humanistic theory of motivation.

Knowles's theory of adult learning reflects humanistic psychology's assumptions that motivation is best based on self-direction. Knowles (1978, pp. 55–59) cites four premises differentiating andragogy from pedagogy:

1. Normal maturation moves individuals from total dependency toward increasing self-directedness as a self-concept; lack of self-direction creates cognitive dissonance in mature individuals.
2. Mature individuals have acquired rich resources useful in learning through experiential approaches (e.g., discussion, laboratory exercises, simulations, field experience, team projects); pedagogic approaches (lectures, canned audiovisual presentations, assigned reading) become decreasingly useful with maturation.
3. With maturation, readiness to learn becomes increasingly a function of perceived developmental need (e.g., in the learner's roles as worker, spouse, parent, leisure consumer, etc.); readiness to learn is decreasingly a function of academic pressure, though it may be stimulated through exposure to role models, through self-diagnosis, and other means.
4. With maturation, orientation to learning becomes decreasingly subject-centered and increasingly problem-centered.

In summary, the andragogic approach is an attempt to place the adult learner at the center of the training and development effort. Walter Broadnax (1979, pp. 520–522), formerly with the Federal Executive Institute, the OPM's leading executive unit, likewise summarizes andragogy as a learner-centered approach marked by self-examination by the student, followed by student setting of change expectations, student formulation of cause–effect change hypotheses, and, finally, student testing of these hypotheses in action-based learning.

What does the adult student approach mean in practice for training? Training will be based ordinarily on student self-assessment of learning needs and self-determination of learning goals, often calling for an individualized approach. Learning will be related to life problems and will be based on a problem-solving orientation. Physical conditions of learning will treat adults as adults (e.g., provision for comfort and other amenities), usually in a coequal, seminar setting (e.g., no individuals sitting behind one another). Attention will be given by the trainer to trust-building activities and to the downplaying of competitive pressures. The teacher will expose his or her own assumptions, values, and needs as a colearner and will involve students as information providers, discussion leaders, and resources.

Students will participate in setting learning objectives. They will ordinarily learn through self-organized project groups at least part of the time, as well as through individualized study, learning–teaching teams, and other self-selected modes. The teacher often will function as a resource, assisting in arranging role plays, discussion of cases, and application of learning to life problems. Criteria for measuring progress are developed on a mutually acceptable basis with students and final assessment is by self-evaluation (Knowles, 1978, pp. 77–79).

Knowles's humanistic approach to adult education is not necessarily in contradiction to a second major theory used in adult learning, i.e., stimulus–response theory. This theory, associated with B. F. Skinner and behaviorism, holds that learning is primarily a function of reinforcement (this is also the foundation on which the various motivational reward theories such as that offered by expectancy theory are based). What is learned results not from simulation toward learning but from reward for learning (Skinner, 1971).

Stimulus–response (S-R) theory could be used to support the view that any method of instruction can be effective so long as the content is geared to the desired behavior, enables the individual to engage in the desired behavior, and then rewards the individual for it.

Trainers have usually seen behaviorism as an adjunct to adult learning, not a contradiction of it (Knowles, 1978, p. 61). S-R theory is cited to support the need for clear leaning objectives, action-based learning, and back-on-the job recognition of and reward for learning (cf. Murphy, 1972). Behaviorism is generally compatible, for example, with (1) the views of basic learning texts such as that of Bass and Vaughn (1966), (2) feedback about learned improvement followed by corresponding reinforcement, as well as (3) action-based learning and explicit integration with and transfer back to the learner's job.

Behaviorism is also associated with the advocacy of behavioral learning objectives and competency-based testing in training and development. Behavioral objectives are stated learning goals that are concrete and specific with regard to (1) the desired, observable behavior to be learned, (2) how the behavior is to be demonstrated, and (3) the standards for evaluating the behavior (Verduin et al., 1977). Behavioral objectives are said to improve teacher–student communication, establish clear goals, set the basis for evaluation, allow individualization of learning, improve accountability for learnings and increase efficiency.

A competency-based curriculum (Verduin et al., 1977, chap. 11) is one based on many such behavioral objectives. These curricula are developed as a nested set of general goals, intermediate objectives, and situation-specific task mastery elements. Although the competency-based approach has very wide appeal in training circles, largely because of its capacity to place training on a more accountable, results-oriented basis, it is not without pitfalls and shortcomings. These include the danger of reducing curricula to rote memory approaches, overemphasizing specific skills at the expense of more important underlying attitudes and thought processes, trivialization of the subject matter, inappropriate forcing of content into behaviorist formats, and the practical drawback of the time necessary to write behavioral objectives and track them for each student.

Though supported by psychometricians and the prestigious Educational Testing Service, competency-based exams often assume a "catechism" aura. An example was the test for Georgia's Certified Public Manager (CPM) Program (Henning and Wilson, 1979), locking instructors into a rather rigid, mass duplication version of training to conform to tightly set behavioral objectives. International City Management Association and correspondence courses generally also have the same tendency. Thus, although the andragogic approach is consistent with action-based teaching, the behavioral measurement of action-based learning—a seemingly logical corollary—may be in tension with the creative, flexible, and self-evaluative aspects of andragogy.

The question of behavioral rewards, like that of behavioral objectives, is also a matter of controversy in learning theory. Some, in fact, oppose direct rewards (e.g., though salary increments) for learning. The above-mentioned Georgia CPM Program, for instance, is explicitly not tied into the state's reward structure because of the desire not to flood the courses with participants motivated mainly by money. It is thought, perhaps correctly, that such participants would be a dead weight on the program and that learning could proceed better if conducted primarily for those with a motivation toward learning itself.

At least for culturally deprived trainees, there is evidence that a closer tie of behavior to reward may be necessary (Porter, 1973). There is also evidence that learned behaviors wear off after several months if not rewarded (Fleischman, 1953). Skinner (1948), of course, advocates behaviorist reward systems across the board from infancy through adult learning. Although trainers still strongly disagree on the topic of relating training to reward, the combined tendencies in public administration toward (1) increased use of performance-based personnel appraisal systems, personnel appraisal management by objectives, and the like, and (2) the emphasis on productivity, performance basing for merit pay, and incentive systems suggest that the future holds a strong attraction for linking training to performance objectives, and performance to reward systems.

General applications in the learning process help us in the design of specific training methods (see Section II below). To be effective, the development of training programs focused on imparting skills or competencies must include (1) goal setting, (2) behavioral modeling, (3) practice, and (4) feedback (Wexley and Latham, 1991).

Training must be focused on specific goals. The general lessons learned with regard to the inherent value in goal setting are equally applicable in the training arena. Employees must know what it is they are expected to learn and why it is important for their future job performance.

Approaches that provide the employee with a model of what is actually desired are better able to achieve this. Behavioral models demonstrate the skills or competencies that are to be learned (Robinson, 1985). Computer tutorials and audiovisual presentations of correct procedures and methods are ideal examples; more so are the techniques that employ simulations and role playing in which the employee actually experiences or goes through what is to be learned. (Cascio, 1992, pp. 244–245).

Continuing in this vein, learning requires practice if the material is to be retained. The frequent repetition of tasks provides for familiarity and confidence (Cascio, 1992, pp. 245–246). Repeated practice sessions enable the trainer to avoid fatigue and better manage and focus on what is to be learned. Repeated sessions also reinforce and strengthen the learning process. This is an approach that characterizes the performance appraisal training for supervisors under the North Carolina Performance Management System.

Finally, employees need feedback on what their skill levels are and what they need to do in order to correct or improve their performance. Feedback must be both immediate and specific. It must be provided as soon as possible to the event while memories are fresh and vivid. Otherwise, good practices may be overlooked and bad practices repeated. Feedback must also be specific. When correcting mistakes it must not only clearly identify what is wrong but also include guidance or instruction on what is desired.

F. Evaluating Training and Development

The issue of relating training to performance and to reward immediately plunges human resources management into the question of training program evaluation. Here the debate ranges from those who believe that training carries diffuse but crucial benefits that cannot easily be measured to those who believe that cost–benefit techniques can yield specific and meaningful dollar value bottom lines for training programs. In this debate, there is a very slow trend toward more explicit, quantitative, and sophisticated evaluations, though assessments of the loosest sort still predominate. The trend exists, however, because, as Hickerson and Litchfield (1978, p. 54) have pointed out: "The key to management acceptance (of training) is demonstrating that training is an accountable service." In trying to provide such an accounting, four types of basic evaluation modes have been attempted. These are based respectively on satisfaction, learning, behavior, and effectiveness.

Professional education and training should be subject to rigorous cost-benefit analyses. It is perhaps the failure to subject personnel practices, in general, and education and training programs, in particular, to evaluations that has allowed them to languish (Ammons and Nietzielski-Eichner, 1985; Slack, 1990). The application of thorough evaluations to these and other personnel practices would help to assess their contributions and, thereby, to establish their value to the organization.

Before discussing the alternative evaluation levels, certain considerations that apply to all types should be listed. First, we may note that evaluation is best viewed as a component of designing an overall information system for the training effort. Such a record-keeping system includes information gathered in the needs assessment phase, characteristics of the trainees, and individual performance data when available (Marsh, 1976). Legal requirements such as affirmative action, union agreements, or terms of grants often impose additional reporting on the information system and training program (Walsh and Waites, 1976).

One factor that is paramount in early consideration of information system needs is baseline data. Although evaluation of a sort can be and is done after the fact, the most desirable forms of assessment provide for baseline data on before-training performance levels as well as posttraining levels. Performance auditing is one approach to documenting these levels, suitable when performance is amenable to work-engineering measurement techniques (Rummler, 1987). Ideally, not only baseline but also longitudinal data would be gathered, though few have done so in evaluating training programs (Beaumont, 1979, p. 498). Even more ideally and more rarely, such measurements could be undertaken in an experimental design utilizing treatment (training) and control (randomized or matched pair) groups (Parker, 1978).

The impact of education and training is evaluated on the extent to which it produces satisfactory reactions, learning, behaviors, or effective results (McGehee and Thayer, 1961; Kirkpatrick, 1975, 1987; Ammons and Nietzielski-Eichner, 1985). While progressively more demanding, each of these four categories contributes useful information on the overall effectiveness of training.

The most common type of evaluation is the satisfaction or reaction survey. The trainee is simply asked to rate the course, the instructor, and various learning elements (exercises, readings, cases, speakers, films) on a Likert scale ranging from strong satisfaction to strong dissatisfaction. Usually, open-ended questions are also included to elicit more concrete criticisms and suggestions useful in redesigning curricula. The satisfaction survey approach is direct and useful, involves learners in course feedback, and is easy and inexpensive to administer. It rests on the commonsense premise that if learners feel that the training was poor, that they didn't learn much, that the instructor was boring, and that the readings were unrelated to the real world, then training probably was poor.

Even simple reactions to the education courses and training sessions—the hot coffee and fresh donuts school—can be important sources of information. Comments on the content, teacher/trainer styles and methods, and perceived utility can be quite helpful (Ammons and Nietzielski-Eichner 1985). The social environment and opportunity to interact with others afforded by educational opportunities and training programs is an important, added ingredient in creating a highly motivated work group. In many circumstances the informal dialogue between participants contributes more to the education and training than the formal sessions (Sims and Sims, 1991).

There are any number of problems with the satisfaction survey approach when used as the sole evaluative method. First, it is biased by the "gratitude" effect. Learners tend to say kind things about the training because it seems more polite and because most people like to think of themselves as kind and nice. Second, the satisfaction survey is biased by the "Hawthorne effect." By this is meant that the extra management attention of the training and evaluation rather than the training itself may cause satisfied responses. Third, this approach is biased by the effects of psychological self-investment. Participants have invested their time, energy, and perhaps money in training, and this investment, like all forms of participation, fosters favorability and acceptance. Failure to hold attitudes of acceptance creates cognitive dissonance with the fact of self-investment. Fourth, the satisfaction survey is biased by subjectivity. Learners often are not in a position to rate their own learning, or may be distracted by other values (enjoyment, for example), which may infuse all their responses. This is the problem of individuals who note several years later that their most hated high school teachers were the ones who taught them the most. It is also the problem of contamination of subjective surveys by environmental factors (e.g., comfortable surroundings, prestigious sponsorship, high-status colearners), favorable reaction to which confounds evaluation of the actual training delivered.

The satisfaction survey can be adapted slightly in the direction of the second form of evaluation, i.e., the assessment of learning. This form seeks to measure not learner satisfaction, feelings, and reactions but rather objective amount learned. A hybrid form is to ask learners to evaluate their own amount of learning. Hickerson and Litchfield (1978), for example, advocate an evaluation form on which learners set program objectives and rank their importance before training and then evaluate the job appropriateness of the learning experience and their ability to accomplish their objectives after the training.

Although this shifts the focus from reaction to the instructor and materials to emphasis on learning objectives, it is still quite subjective. Because individuals are notoriously disinclined to admit skill weaknesses and because the gratitude effect and other biases of satisfaction surveys are still present, this method also tends to make training "look good" unduly. An improvement would be to measure skill accomplishment self-assessment both pre- and posttraining. This would partially control for the hiding of weaknesses but not for the gratitude and other effects. Another improvement of the hybrid forms is to interview learners months after the learning experience. At this time, they may be asked not only whether they perceive the training to have increased accomplish capacity but also to identify specific instances of accomplishment they perceive to have resulted from training. Though still subjective, the greater concrete accountability of this approach encourages realistic response and diminishes gratuitous generalities (Garson, 1979). Other refinements include asking respondents about the amount learned in comparison with other training programs or if they would like to take an additional course of the same type or recommend the given course to fellow employees. Though still subjective, such items also help puncture glittering generalities and bring responses down to a more concrete level.

Learning the material presented in an educational or training program is an initial, necessary condition in an effective endeavor. Information not presented or not received and not correctly understood by the individual is information that is not going to be used. Learning measurements assess the potential inherent in an educational process. Learning techniques can assess how well the basic fundamentals are understood (Ammons and Nietzielski-Eichner, 1985).

The objective learning approach to evaluation is, of course, the academic standard. This conventionally takes the form of written examinations. Other forms are "hands-on" demonstration of skills, successful completion of individual or team projects, simulations (e.g., in assessment centers), and interactive computer exercises. When this approach to evaluation is combined with pre- and posttest training measurement and with a curriculum with clear learning objectives in the first place, it results in stable, reliable estimates of knowledge, skill, and attitude transfer in the training process. Panel studies may be necessary, however, if learning attrition and decay is of concern, as when knowledge, though organizationally important, will not be reinforced through continuous practice on the job. Reliability can be further improved through multimethod testing and through averaging ratings of multiple assessors, though these refinements are probably not necessary for most applications. Highest reliability requires panel testing of the training and a matched control group.

The learning approach to evaluation, in spite of its advantages, is not without its drawbacks. In comparison with the satisfaction approach, it fails to tap the effect of training on morale and organizational climate. A training program could, for example, pound great deal of knowledge into employees' skulls (satisfying the learning-oriented type of evaluation) in a way that created deep resentments entirely undermining the organizational changes toward which training was ostensibly directed. The most serious objection to the learning approach (and the satisfaction approach as well) is that it does not measure directly whether knowledge and attitude acquisition actually translates into behavior on the job and desired effect on the organization.

This last objection is important for two reasons. First, we are all aware that "head knowledge" does not necessarily mean that a person can accomplish tasks well. If this were true, academic credentials would be the only form of evaluation necessary. What is less understood but equally important to recognize is that just as knowledge does not necessarily translate into effective action, the same is true of attitudes. As Ehrlich (1969) noted some time ago, studies of the relation of attitudes to behavior are a poor predictor of behavior. For example, because certain human relations attitudes and knowledge have been acquired through training does not necessarily mean the individual's behavior will change no matter how sincerely the acquired attitudes are held or how deeply the new knowledge is understood (see Tarter, 1969. 1970).

While adult learnings will themselves endeavor to apply what they have learned, modern educational and training programs should focus on assisting them in this. Work behaviors and, ultimately, organizational results become measures of a successful training program. Learning needs to be applied in the workplace and in turn those behavioral applications should lead to the desired organizational outcomes. While they are perhaps more general in their focus, professional educational programs need to be held to the same standards. Like training, eduction imparts substantive knowledge.

Subsequent assessments can measure the long-term continuance of learned behaviors. Monitoring should detect improvements in the quality. Employee attitudes should also be more favorable (Ammons and Nietzielski-Eichner, 1985).

The behavioral approach to training evaluation is widely acknowledged to be preferable to the satisfaction and learning approaches. At the simplest level, the behavioral approach is performance testing, substituting obervation and rating of student demonstration of skills for pencil-and-paper tests (Verduin et al., 1977, pp. 165–171). As Malcolm Knowles notes, there is a wide variety of types of behavioral evidence of learning. Skills may be evaluated through on-the-job demonstration, performance exercises, or videotape performances rated by observers. Understanding can be evaluated in problem-solving action exercises, research projects leading to policy recommendations, or development of personal management plans. Attitudes may be evaluated through role playing and simulations of critical incidents with peer and staff feedback and rating (Knowles, 1978, p. 201) (Fig. 1).

Kirkpatrick (1975) presented several case examples of behavioral approaches to evaluation. One study used the before-and-after measures of on-the-job performance for the training and for

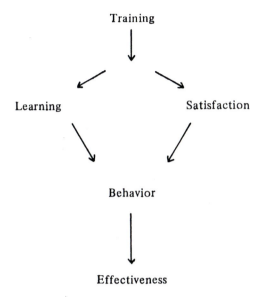

Figure 1 Training–effectiveness linkages.

the control group. In another study with a different research design, before-and-after content analysis (in this case, of interview records for suprvisors trained in democratic leadership) was used to assess performance changes. Other designs include before-and-after studies, preferably with control groups, based on performance ratings by superiors, based on peer evaluations, and based on subordinates' impressions. Finally, many organizations collect other forms of behavioral data that may be pertinent to evaluation of training: absenteeism rates, turnover rates, downtime, piece rates, quality control measures, and behaviorally anchored rating scales used in performance appraisal (see Beatty and Schneier, 1977, pp. 88–107, 219).

Finally, organizational productivity should show signs of improvement. While many factors—many of which are beyond our control or influence—contribute to these outcomes, this is nevertheless the *sine qua non* for any organizational activity.

The fourth and final approach to evaluation centers on the measurement of organizational effectiveness. Just as it is possible for learned knowledge and attitudes to fail to affect individual behavior, so it is possible that behavior will fail to affect the effectiveness of the organization in attaining its goals. To take an obvious and extreme case, training is wasted and no amount of learned behavior change is helpful to an organization seeking to achieve impossible goals. Though it is often true that the sum of improvements individual behaviors will contribute to, if not equal, the magnitude of overall improvement in organizational effectiveness, this is an empirical question that will vary by circumstance. As Figure 1 suggests, each step in the training process must be evaluated in its own right.

This fourth approach calls on the training evaluator to assess the proportion of variance organizational goal achievement attributable to factors that can be improved through training. If effectiveness is 90% determined by budgetary, political, and environmental factors that training cannot affect, then this must be taken into account. There may be two programs that improve individual behavior equally, but if one is in a 90% constrained system and the other is at the opposite end of the spectrum, the two programs must be evaluated very differently. This raises questions of organizational equity. In essence, the effectiveness approach holds the training function hostage to factors that may be beyond its control. "If our directors asked us to prove that training increases productivity," one trainer writes, "we'd find ourselves taking responsibility for variables that are both beyond our control and not accounted for in the evaluation system" (Leifer, 1979, p. 13). On the other hand, a human resource accounting philosophy is properly founded only on an accountability-for-effects basis. Accountability for what one may not control is a problem of all management-by-effects systems, not just those in training evaluations.

In complex organizations, effectiveness-based evaluations may assume a state-of-the-art of management science that does not exist. A complete approach would assume that a multivariate input–output model of the firm can be constructed that simulates organizational performance over time; that the input measures can include training investments; and that the output measures reflect organizational effectiveness (as opposed simply to client, paper, or materials turnover). In the public sector, effectiveness measurement has become considerably more sophisticated (cf. Urban Institute, 1974; HUD, 1976; Hatry et al., 1977). Human resource accounting, however, is best in its infancy (Cascio, 1982). Overall, the input side of the information base needed to construct the simulation model for effectiveness measurement is largely missing, and even the output side is still in great controversy and development.

Because of the still-developing state of the art, and partly because of the lack of sophistication of trainers in causal modeling, the effectiveness approach to training evaluation takes a simpler approach in practice. What is done is to skip causal analysis entirely and directly correlate training investment in time period 1 with improvement in effectiveness measures in time period 2. Effectiveness measures may include such items as unit productivity or cost–benefit ratios (Caldwell, 1964). In evaluation of training program effectiveness in training agencies themselves, effectiveness measures may include placement rates, longevity on the job, or posttraining compensation rates (cf. Employment Training Division, 1978). Because (1) many other factors besides training affect effectiveness and (2) the simpler effectiveness approach in practice today bypasses statistical controls through causal analysis of input–output data, the effectiveness approach can be validly undertaken only in a research design employing before–after measurements and a control group.

From problems such as these, Leifer (1979) concludes that trainers must convince managers that ultimate bottom line cost effectiveness measurement is the wrong approach to training evaluation, which must be viewed, like education, as having valuable but more general and less measurable benefits. On the other hand, many training environments are far less complex and lend themselves to effectiveness measurement. Such, for example, is the case of language training for Asian employees reported by O'Brien and Gubbay (1979), where the authors relied for validity on supervisor performance evaluations. Assuming that this individual behavior change did affect organizational effectiveness (as it would in the production-based setting the authors utilized), this seems a fully satisfactory approach. Though books have been written about training evaluation (cf. Kirkpatrick, 1975), it is still true that a general lack of empirical support or refutation for training programs characterizes the field, hampering its growth and opening the door for continual questioning of its professional credibility (Campbell, 1971; Ammons and Nietzielski-Eichner, 1985; Slack, 1990).

Even if these measures can be taken for assuring effective training programs, they can still fail to infuse the organization with an added degree of productivity. The Conference Board (1985) notes a number of reasons for the failure of training programs:

No on-the-job rewards for behavior and skills learned in training (58%)
Insufficient time to execute training programs (55%)
Work environment not supporting new behaviors learned in training (53%)

Lack of motivation among employees (47%)
Inaccurate training requiring analyses (40%)
Training needs changing after program had been implemented (35%)
Management not supporting training program (30%)
Insufficient funding of training program (21%)

Most of these reasons address general organizational rather than specific issues related to the individual training programs. They also indicate the extent to which the application of training and development still suffers from a lack of being taken as a serious management tool.

II. METHODS OF TRAINING AND DEVELOPMENT

In contrast to the relative neglect of training evaluation, the training profession has evolved training methods to a sophisticated level. By combining adult learning theory with advances in communications technology, the modern training office in a large organization is apt to be a telecommunications, multimedia production, and curriculum development center employing staff with a variety of skills drawn from education, public and business administration, communications, graphics, engineering, and the arts. Behind the attention-getting glitter of such methods as videotape and interactive feedback are a very wide range of approaches to education and development, many of them quite traditional. Campbell, et al. (1970) divide these into three major divisions: on-the-job training methods, information presentation methods, and simulation methods. The sections that follow discuss these in turn.

A. On-the-Job Training Methods

On-the-job training (OJT) methods are the oldest forms of training. Apprenticeship is the classic example, traceable to ancient times. Other methods include off-line training, on-line training and coaching, job rotation, committee rotation, and internships. Though the methods of training are subject to intense faddism (Campbell, 1971, p. 565), there is great stability as well.

1. Internships and Apprenticeships

Apprenticeship is the oldest training model in America and encompasses over a quarter million apprentices, mostly in the building trades (Saltzman et al., 1976, pp. 25–27; Rorabaugh, 1986). There is a Bureau of Apprenticeship and Training in the U.S. Department of Labor, and many states have apprenticeship councils. Apprenticeship programs are supported by national legislation, such as the National Apprenticeship Act of 1937, the Veteran's Readjustment Assistance Act of 1952, and the Comprehensive Employment and Training Act of 1973. In the United States, apprenticeship programs have usually not occurred in semiprofessional, professional, or managerial career tracks. Unlike Europe, American apprenticeship has been rare even in office skill areas. In the public sector it is almost unknown.

Nonetheless, there are training counterparts to apprenticeship in the public sector (Riccucci 1991). Less than 10% of all apprenticeships take place in the public sector and nearly a third of these apprenticeships occur among the military and civilian employees of the Defense Department. Yet apprenticeships are employed in numerous state and local governments.

Booth and Rohe (1988) note that apprentice programs for firefighters, police, and corrections are widespread means used for recruiting women and minority candidates. The Police Department in Blacksburg, Virginia, for example, operates an in-service "internship" program for all patrol officers. Officers serve for one month under an experienced investigator, assisting in criminal investigation and arrests (Connors, 1978, p. 162). Charlotte, North Carolina places newly hired engineering employees of the Department of Public Works in a new entry level job classification, civil engineer I. These new employees are then placed under the formal sponsorship of a civil engineer II, who oversees the employees' rotation for 6-month work programs in each division of the agency (Hopson, 1978, p. 16). Other analogies to apprenticeship exist in cooperative education programs in which students alternate between work experience and academic training.

Specialized apprentice programs are also found in other areas such as the Wisconsin Department of Transportation's Electrical Highway Technicians and various positions in the Alaska Marine Highway Department (Riccucci, 1981, p. 187).

Internship programs are well developed in public administration. They are, for example, a criterion in the standards applied by the National Association of Schools of Public Affairs and Administration in their peer review accreditation of master's programs in public management. This has helped foster the development of numerous state and local internship programs. The State of Mississippi previously funded an internship program that linked the state's four graduate public administration programs to state-funded positions in various state agencies (Gabris and Mitchell, 1989). At the University of Utah the Hinckley Institute of Politics coordinates local, state, and national intern placements. In addition to the myriad local and state public internship programs (e.g., Dade County, Florida; Kansas City, Kansas; Long Beach, California; and Phoenix, Arizona), the U.S. Office of Personnel Management oversees the Federal Graduate Internship program, established in 1978 to complement the longstanding internship program for undergraduates. Supplementing these are several internship programs run by Housing and Urban Development (HUD) and other federal departments.

The Presidential Management Internship Program, providing excellent management experiences at a high level, is rather more in the nature of a managerial apprenticeship than of an internship. It is a 2-year program leading to a career appointment in the federal civil service. It has become the chief means for the recruitment of outside midlevel managers by the federal government. Both New York and New Jersey have established similar state level programs.

Though not under the label of apprenticeship, this type of training is likely to increase in the future. There is a great interest in the mentoring concept inherent in apprenticeship and internship, for example. Roche found that two-thirds of top executives listed in the "Who's News" column of the *Wall Street Journal* had had mentors able and willing to share knowledge and information, and studies of this sort have aroused great appreciation (Roche, 1979; OPM, 1980a, p. 7; Wilson and Elma, 1990). Second, partly for affirmative action reasons, the personnel profession has become far more attuned to the concept of entry level semiprofessional or assistant job classifications, which are, in effect, apprenticeship-type positions. Such transitional classifications are also likely to spread as career management becomes more prevalent in the public sector. Though seemingly a 19th century concept, apprenticeship is a surprisingly vital idea that may, on close inspection, seem to be a highly motivating, participative, and cost-efficient training method.

2. Off- and On-line Training and Coaching

On-the-job training programs (OJT) are another ancient training model. Off-line versions, sometimes called "vestibule training" (Strauss and Sayles, 1980. p. 411), are relatively rare in the public sector because most government agencies are willing to undertake the risks to service delivery that on-line OJT carries. However, there are striking exceptions. Strauss and Sales, for instance, note that NASA "could not provide on-the-job training for astronauts and instead use a simulated moon environment." On-line OJT remains far more prevalent in the public sector.

OJT is attractive because it provides direct, realistic training in the specific methods actually required by the position. OJT also provides immediate performance feedback in most situations and the motivation of active involvement of peers and superiors in the training process. It has the added advantage of being a form of learning that can be utilized by many individuals for whom the intellectual skills required in classroom training would constitute a barrier to performance and employment/promotions, a barrier not always truly germane to the actual requirements of the job. Finally, OJT may allow an agency to provide compensation to the learner that it could not provide for traditional classroom learning. This compensation may be an additional motivator in the learning process and may remove a financial barrier having a discriminatory effect in the organization's intake process.

An example of OJT is provided by the Hollywood, Florida Police Department. This department utilizes a specialized squad of field training officers who train new officers while doing actual police work using methods consistent with uniform department standards and policy. This in-service training, moreover, is provided for veteran as well as new police officers (Darlins, 1978, p. 160).

Other uses of OJT are training in new technology or management procedures, as in the introduction of productivity systems (Lovell, 1979; Andrews, 1979). Problem-oriented coaching in supervision, as through the performance appraisal process, is yet another form of OJT (Calhoon and Jerdee, 1976; Wolf and Sherwood, 1981).

3. *Job Rotation and Committee Assignment*

Job rotation, unlike apprenticeship and OJT, assumes that the organization derives a generalized benefit from training the employee in related jobs as well as his or her own job. In the private sector, this has sometimes been carried quite far. The Pet Foods Plant of General Foods in Topeka, Kansas, for example, was designed around the job rotation concept (Brower, 1975, pp. 71–71). At this plant, the production force was divided into teams that rotated tasks among group members. Training was assumed by the team and remuneration was based not on longevity or hierarchical advancement but on the number of skills learned. Rotation and the team concept also enabled the company to dispense with a variety of other hitherto separate roles such as maintenance, certain personnel work, safety, and quality control. Under this form of organization, the plant was operated by 72 rather than the normal complement of 110 employees. Similarly, the Aluminum Company of Canada has reported increased levels of cooperation and coordination following job rotation (Archer, 1975, p. 263). On the other hand, it is clear that rotation does not always yield productivity results (King, 1974).

The Greyhound Financial Corporation is another example of the use of job rotation albeit with a small company on the rebound following a substantial downsizing experience. Faced with the negative effects of career plateauing and the lack of traditional promotional opportunities, management personnel are provided with new, developmental challenges through an extensive program of job rotation (Northcraft, et al., 1992).

Job rotation reflects a number of aspects considered desirable from an andragogic point of view. It is based on experiential learning. It is peer-assisted. It provides direct feedback and generally involves the employee's superiors in the training process. Rotating committee assignments are analogous in purpose and function. Through learning by doing, the employee gains competence in new areas, confidence in self increases, and useful networks of cooperating individuals are built up through formal and informal association.

4. *Summary*

OJT methods, though ancient, are surprisingly in line with contemporary learning theory. More widely used than any other approach, these methods may be attractive to managers and supervisors precisely because they can be integrated into the line organization of the agency. Their use may lessen or even eliminate the need for a specialized training staff function.

Nevertheless, as Sackman (1975) noted, OJT methods have several serious drawbacks. They typically require a 1:1 training ratio, expensive to any organization not willing just to "overlook" the ratio because a separate training line doesn't appear in the budget. Such methods are also high risk. Shouldn't the danger of poorly servicing governmental clients be taken as seriously as industry takes the risk of OJT to production? Moreover, OJT methods tend to train employees in an unsystematic, noncomprehensive manner, usually without any attempt at accountability or evaluation. In this training, learners rarely benefit from the application of even the most elementary learning principles provided by professional trainer (e.g., OJT follows work flow rather than organizing learning from easiest to most difficult).

B. Information Presentation Methods

If on-the-job methods are the classic industrial mode, information presentation is the traditional educational mode of instruction. Though the lecture format comes quickest to mind and is perhaps still the most popular information presentation method, this mode also includes use of small group discussions, case methods, audiovisual techniques, and computer-assisted instruction (CAI). Also, information presentation can be undertaken in a variety of formats: university credit courses, institutes, short courses and conferences, and correspondence courses.

1. Classroom Instruction

Though associated with the university, classroom instruction has strong advocates in many quarters (Donaldson and Scannell, 1986; Broadwell, 1987). For instance, Designers of the Opportunities Industrialization Centers (OIC) training programs, oriented to disadvantaged clients, concluded: "We are convinced that classroom training, when successfully completed, tends to produce more permanently trained individuals than do other kinds of training" (Employment Training Division, 1978, p. 5). Compared to individuals trained by on-the-job methods, the OIC evaluators found that classroom-trained learners (1) were more likely to stay on the job after placement, (2) were less likely to need later retraining, (3) had more choice of occupations, and (4) were more likely to be promoted. Moreover, classroom training did not displace needed jobs, allowed more counseling and assessment, and gave program stability in the face of fluctuating employer interest. Finally, because most employers expected those hired to come to the job already trained, classroom training avoided much of the "remedial" stereotyping associated with special on-the-job training efforts.

In spite of such testimonials, classroom instruction has something less than a first-rate reputation in the training profession. Alan Campbell, former director of the OPM, stated: "Let me say a word about purchasing executive development from universities-based on my experience I urge you not to buy what it is that many of them will attempt to sell you" (OPM, 1979b, p. 7). Such statements are not incompatible with the OIC view cited earlier. Rather, Campbell's position reflects a widespread feeling that learning designs must be tailored to specific organizational situations on the basis of objective assessments of needs. The "classroom" may be all right, but it shouldn't be located in an "ivory tower."

Classroom instruction is offered today by nearly everyone. Not only universities and community colleges offer courses for public managers, but also government institutes and research bureaus, extension services, professional associations, consulting firms, personnel departments, training divisions, and many line agencies provide this training. The instruction explosion makes generalization difficult, but probably the most common format is the short course (Reith, 1987). Offered for 1–5 days, the short course provides training in a specialized area (e.g., communications skills, information management, environmental impact analysis, performance appraisal, sexual harassment, Americans with Disabilities Act, Employee Assistance Programs) in a "bite size" that can be taken out of the in-service learner's schedule with a minimum of disruption. Typically, the classroom lecture format is combined with small group discussion and brainstorming, audiovisual presentations, and the simulation of real-life situations.

Short-course formats are sometimes criticized for their in-and-out nature, which lacks follow-through. In contrast to academic courses, such instruction rarely leaves adequate time for the important gestation period needed by many learners. Short courses, generally not offered for credit, may also be prone to dispense with evaluation of the participants, because the sales of short courses to agencies discourages anything that lowers participant satisfaction (e.g., grades, difficult readings, time-consuming projects). For this reason, academics and others frequently raise questions about short-course quality. These questions exist, of course, because training evaluation is inadequate or absent.

2. Printed and Programmed Instruction

Programmed or printed instruction is the most common companion of classroom instruction and is the mainstay of most self-instructional approaches. Correspondence instruction, for instance, is based mostly on printed materials (Salinger, 1976; Baker, 1985). Correspondence instruction is also linked to video presentations. Many public broadcasting stations air video courses as part of their Saturday morning line-up. These broadcasts are offered often in conjunction with means for the viewer to obtain college credit. Case study, the core of the Harvard Business School approach and that used in some public administration programs, is also based on printed materials (Pigors, 1987); so is nearly all programmed instruction designed for self-study. Well-designed printed instruction is highly efficient and can result in impressive cost savings in reducing training time. It also allows home study and later refresher sessions at the convenience of the learner.

Printed and programmed instruction has other advantages as well. It allows the learner to pause, back up, or skip ahead in the learning sequence on an individualized basis. Far more branching options (specialized explanations or topics) are possible in this method than in other learning technologies. Also, self-diagnostic checks and self-scoring quizzes can be incorporated into printed instruction to provide immediate feedback on learning in a nonevaluative, low-pressure context.

The disadvantages of print are equally many. It is the wrong method for trainees deficient in verbal or reading skills. It may further de facto discrimination in the intake process, which could be avoided by using other training methods. It is difficult to anticipate all learner needs and usually requires a more personal backup system to field additional questions. Also, it is difficult to find talented writers who are capable of presenting material in an interesting and clear manner. Perhaps most important, many skills, particularly those dealing with human relations, are difficult to learn without the experience of group interaction. Group discussion will also ordinarily enrich the learner's insights into the subject by bringing out points not considered, by creating a sense of "ownership" of the material through participation, and by allowing brainstorming and other creative learning techniques based on group methods.

More and more, programmed instruction is included as part of a computer-based learning package (King, 1986; Hart, 1987; Madlin, 1987). CAI possesses all the advantages found in programmed instruction and, in addition, often allows for an interactive environment in which the trainee can practice the skill being taught. The "what if" aspect of many computer packages allows the trainee to explore the limitations and possibilities inherent in a new method.

3. Audiovisual Methods

Though classroom and print-based instruction have many advantages, the sad experience of so many students in suffering through boring lectures and even more boring required readings creates a strong attraction to audiovisual (A-V) techniques as an alternative. There is a natural tendency for the organization just beginning a training function to seek to compete with television. The high technology and the powerful impact of well-done audiovisual productions seems to many the ideal answer to training problems (Wallington, 1987).

Audiovisual methods include much more than motion pictures and videotape, of course. Also included are slide and slide–tape presentations, transparencies, opaque projection, audio tapes, flip charts and easel graphics, interactive computer video disks, and the simple chalkboard. The high-technology end of audiovisual production is not necessarily the best medium for every occasion.

Good A-V production requires tremendous effort. Some of the costs are obvious: the need to develop a story board, to write a script, to employ actors or train staff, to pay music copyright fees, not to mention the costs of lighting, sound mixing, directing, editing, duplicating, and special effects and graphics. Unfortunately, many of the cost factors that inflate Hollywood costs are present in the humble organization A-V production as well. Worse, viewers may expect the organization to meet commercial standards of production. There are indirect costs too. Production takes a great deal of time, which may be disruptive to the organization. Once completed, it is difficult to change and may soon become outdated. In the classroom, it may isolate the instructor from communication with students or seem a "canned presentation" and poor substitute for "live" teaching. It is also nonparticipatory, allowing no individualization and providing no feedback.

These problems have been somewhat overcome with the introduction of interactive videos in recent years. While sophisticated and hence costly, the interactive videos are keyed to the trainee's responses as to what information is presented and the expected results therefrom (Parker, 1988). Interactive videos have been especially useful in training police officers for crisis situations.

Often the simplest productions may be best, such as the 6-minute film used in Newport News, Virginia, in which the city manager explains the pay and classification plan for new employees (Reynolds, 1978, p. 41). In fact, visual presentations are best utilized when the information to be presented is kept to simple levels, avoiding complexity and overcrowding of visual imagery. Better uses of the medium include multiuse, open-ended problem visuals in which a situation is presented on video. Analysis and discussion, however, are left to the classroom leader. Videotaping students themselves can also be a valuable form of instant feedback, allowing either self-evaluation or greater class insight into group process.

4. *Summary*

Information presentation methods of training are still the heart of the training profession. A well-designed combination of classroom techniques (lectures, questions, and small group discussion), printed material (cases, self-instructional materials, review quizzes, and readings), and A-V presentations (transparencies, videotapes of student performances) is difficult to beat. Such a combination can transfer a great deal of information that allows a maximum of feedback, individualization, and efficient reproducibility for a variety of training targets. If there is a major failing, it is that information presentation techniques, in spite of case materials and audiovisuals, may fail to provide a sufficient immersion in "doing" because many believe that learning by doing is ultimately the only way to consolidate learning (Rogers, 1969). For such individuals (perhaps the majority of those trained in adult learning theory), action-based learning techniques have been developed as the professional trainer's counterpart to the advantage of on-the-job approaches.

C. Action-Based Methods

Lesson plans designed by professional trainers are very likely to include not only content-oriented presentation of information but also an opportunity to gain deeper insight into content through some action-based learning experience (Suessmuth, 1978; chap. 2; Verduin et al., 1977, chap. 7). Three broad categories of methods are roleplays and simulations; laboratory and behavioral methods; and organization development activities. Although these are not necessarily mutually exclusive, they do represent different emphases within the training profession.

1. Role Plays and Simulations

Role playing and simulation exercises are among the most common forms of training today. They basically encompass the important concept of behavioral modeling. An example is the training provided by a consortium of 12 law enforcement agencies in Marin County, California (Hill and Brindley, 1978, p. 161). This training centers on four to six simulated exercises conducted over a 6-week period. Trainees go through field experiences that are role-played by actors. Trainee performance in these simulations is rated by training officers, who evaluate the extent of use of recommended procedures, safety, public relations, and other criteria. Exercises revolve around such incidents as emergency first aid at auto crash scenes, arrest and search situations, and suspicious vehicle stops. Through such "live" experiences, training seeks to assure that knowledge and attitude-oriented learning is translated into action and behavior.

Role plays ordinarily involve breaking a larger class into smaller groups. Group research suggests that small groups (three to five members) are most satisfying to participants and reach consensus sooner, but medium-sized groups (six to eleven), though slower to organize, often make higher quality decisions (Cooke, 1987). The problem with larger groups is their tendency to decompose into smaller, informal subgroups. Also, large size may inhibit expression for some participants. Various other concerns raised by Janis (1972), such as aspects of groupthink, can also affect such processes.

The instructor in a role play often circulates from one small group to another, not to participate but to answer process questions and to gather impressions useful in leading end-of-role-play class discussions. The instructor may also function as a rulekeeper, intervening to establish or reestablish basic role play facts. This may be needed when an occasional participant goes to extremes in improvisation, changing the nature of the simulation learning objectives. The instructor usually is also firm in discouraging "stepping out of role" in the middle of a role play, as when students stop to explain how they would feel in real life. These comments can be saved for later discussion. The instructor may also act as a process controller. For example, the instructor may intervene to discourage aggression and personalization of conflict. Role reversal, where participants exchange roles, is an empathy-creating technique used in this regard. Videotaping also improves role play feedback and empathetic insight in many situations.

Simulations need not be involved and complex. They are readily available from commercial suppliers, (e.g., Creative Universal's performulations kit for role-playing superior–subordinate relationships); from professional associations (e.g., some of the setups available from the American Political Science Association); from adaptation of examples distributed through the training press (e.g., Pfeiffer and Jones, 1974,, 1980; Morris and Cinnamon, 1974); and from examples designed for academic use (Henry, 1982; Huddleston, 1992). Instructions for the preparation of original role plays also exist (Sackman, 1974).

Role play and simulation have drawbacks as well as advantages. The advantages of providing ego-involving behavioral practice and reinforcement for learning objectives are so great that trainers sometimes rely on this approach almost exclusively. There are two major disadvantages, however. First, some people learn best in traditional ways. In this author's experience, training evaluations tend to show that whereas most participants value role playing, there is almost always a significant minority who prefer information presentation techniques. Second, role playing is very time consuming. To hurry the role-playing experience is unwise and creates learner dissatisfaction with the training experience. For instance, one role play can easily fill up an entire 3-hour training session; informational content might be decreased as the role play component of training is increased. This makes role playing most valuable when the content is interpersonal relations and least valuable when the content is technical information.

2. Laboratory and Behavioral Methods

Laboratory and behavioral methods of training are other action-based approaches that are commonly used (Shore, 1985). Popularized in the 1960s by the National Training Laboratories (NTL), the laboratory approach came to be associated with sensitivity training. In sensitivity training groups (T groups), organization members—often middle management—seek to improve interpersonal skills through open communications, direct personal feedback, and confrontation. Though it may utilize role playing, the emphasis is not on simulation of actual situations but rather on providing a vehicle for expression of emotions and beliefs. The NTL approach emphasizes personal development (Dupre, 1976, p. 37-5), and the psychological techniques employed provide just that: powerful personal experiences from which many individuals claim benefit. Others charge that the encouragement of openness merely fosters conflict and even inflicts serious psychological damage on vulnerable group members.

Because of charges of this sort and because of the lack of clear linkage of sensitivity training to organizational goals, the T-group approach to training fell from favor in the 1970s, though it is still common. Instead, laboratory methods tended to evolve in the direction of organization development, discussed below, or were combined with more goal-oriented and problem-solving approaches. Gaming is an objectives-oriented laboratory adaptation of role playing that started to become popular in this period, for example. Various approaches to instrumented team learning are another example of a behavioral approach that evolved at least in part from the laboratory tradition (Mouton and Blake, 1975).

These approaches are often more familiarly known under the rubric of assessment centers. The assessment center is a managerial tool noted for its usefulness in the selection process where it serves as a battery of tests measuring a candidate's abilities to perform job-related tasks. However, virtually the same assessment center can serve to introduce an individual to the nature and demands of a new job (Byhan, 1971; Sackett, 1982; Yeager, 1986; Moses, 1987; Ross, 1985). The assessment center, such as that used in the North Carolina State University Master of Public Administration program, can also be used to identified individual weaknesses and strengths; this information is then used to coordinate remedial training and strengthening programs for the individual.

3. Organization Development Methods

Out of those enthusiasts for laboratory approaches in the 1950s and 1960s, organization development (OD) has since become a field unto itself, with ramifications far outside the scope of this chapter (see French and Bell, 1978; Garson and Williams, 1981: chap. 6; Varney, 1987). Included in OD are such techniques as team building (Dyer, 1977; Shaw, 1985; Christen, 1987), survey feedback (Nadler, 1977), and leadership development (Blake and Mouton, 1969; Reiner and Morris, 1987). Other techniques include role analysis, process consulting, conflict management, and various aspects of management development.

After dramatic, even revolutionary claims made for OD, and after over a decade of practice, it is difficult to discern any great changes. However, meaningful if not great changes are indeed evident (Golembiewski, 1985). This is partly because most OD efforts are not intended to be experiments in creating participatory organizational structures even though, as training methods,, participation is encouraged. Moreover, the focus of OD as training is on process (leadership styles, organizational climate, interpersonal communication and role clarification, goal setting) and not on structural change (power relationships, benefit flows, accountability). Indeed, the "team" ideology of OD-type training suggests that harmony can be achieved through teamwork (process) apart from structure. Also, there in much evidence that OD techniques improve employee satisfaction.

4. Summary

The action-based approaches to training are here to stay. They serve to provide a behavioral basis for the learning process and are especially desirable for those situations and individuals where learning by doing works best but on-the-job training is too risky, too expensive, or otherwise inappropriate. Role playing provides a flexible and vivid medium by which the instructor can allow students to experience content through interaction with others. Simulation, along with sensitivity training, gaming, and other forms of laboratory learning such as organization development team-building groups, provides not only experiential learning but also an ego-involving basis for group participation and peer feedback, prompting group discussion more effectively than most information presentation techniques.

The action-based approaches often involve drawbacks too. They are time consuming, generally require reduction in information transfer, and not all learners learn best through activity. Great care must be taken to structure interpersonal interaction, and action-based techniques may thrust the trainer into the undesirable role of amateur group psychologist. It is not always true that bringing out into the open latent conflicts, emotions, and discontents is wisest for the organization or the individual, though the action-based approaches generally assume that it is. These approaches also carry a participative ideology that is used to legitimate them as teaching methods (in opposition to hierarchical and autocratic information presentation techniques). Thus, OD advocates, and even laboratory trainers, may implicitly, or even explicitly, carry into training content not desired or warranted by the organization's needs and options.

III. DIRECTIONS FOR FUTURE TRAINING RESEARCH

In a symposium on public sector training, Chester Newland, its editor, observed that "training needs to be disciplined against established theory and hard research" (1979, p. 407). Scientific research is generally thought to be characterized by multivariate research on causal propositions carried on by investigators free of interest conflict with regard to the subject. Research presented in the Newland symposium reflected, through no fault of the editor, the fact that the state-of-the-art in training research rarely meets either criterion of scientific inquiry. Research is generally not cast in terms of well-defined propositions and hypotheses. On those rare occasions when it is, research is zero-order correlative rather than multivariate and causal. Perhaps of even greater concern the great bulk of training research is conducted and published by trainers with a vested interest in the outcome of the research, or by professional evaluators commissioned by agencies with training projects where the evaluator has a vested interest in continued contractual relations with the given or similar agencies. A review a decade later by Thomas Roback (1989) reached the same conclusions as regards the nature of research in this area.

The changing work force environment has focused greater attention on the importance of training and development. Organizations have recognized this and endeavored to meet the increasing demands placed on them. Unfortunately, most of this effort has been directed at the applied aspects of training (Roback, 1989, p. 143). The more difficult assessment and evaluative arenas as well as those more involved with basic research have received less attention (Saari et al., 1988; Roback, 1989).

While a primitive state of training research still characterizes many fields of public management, the Civil Service Reform Act introduced significant changes. A review of public management research by the Public Services laboratory of Georgetown University, commissioned by the U.S. Office of Personnel Management (then U.S. Civil Service Commission), concluded: "At present there is no established machinery to define a research agenda on public management, formulate priorities, and gain recurrent review and updating in terms of new needs identified and research completed" (Mushkin et al., 1978, p. 83). The same study, it should be noted, did not find training research to be among the 10 top research priorities identified by their panel sample of public managers and experts (pp. xviii–xix). Similar benign neglect of training research as a priority was also evident in the conference on the setting of public management research agendas sponsored by OPM, GAO, GSA, and OMB (OPM, 1980b). In response to such reports the Civil Service Reform Act directed OPM to take a more active role in personnel research. Since then OPM has held research conferences and has instituted a series of publications entitled *Personnel Research Highlights* that disseminates abstracts of pertinent research findings. A research agenda has been established in which training and development composes one of the seven major categories.

If a governmental agency were to put public sector training research on a new basis, what would the research agenda be? The agenda advocated by G. David Garson over a decade ago in the first edition of this book is—somewhat unfortunately—still quite relevant and, hence, bears repeating. Three major priorities can be discerned dealing, respectively, with the linkages shown in Fig. 1.

The first of these linkages is that between training and learning. Questions that arise here are those dealing with the relative effectiveness of various modes and techniques of instruction on the amount of learning achieved. Investigation must deal with several classes of variables: type of instruction, nature of the instructor, characteristics of the learners, substance of the instruction, and various situational variables (e.g., organizational climate, relation of training to the incentive system, relation of training to unionism and other forms of employee participation, and time frame). Over the past decade progress has been greatest in this area of research (Sims and Sims, 1991).

The second generation of this line of research would recognize the emerging de facto consensus among trainers that some combination of types of instruction is best. Assessing the synergistic effects of such hybrids would be a more complex process, requiring either larger samples (to enable more elaborate statistical controls) or experimental design (control groups). This type of research, however, is needed to definitively identify current trends in training practice, which while becoming more eclectic and complex remain based on anecdotal justifications for the most part.

The second key linkage for research is that of the transference between learning and behavior. A great deal of money is wasted each year on the false assumption that learning equals behavior. For example, most race relations and diversity training is of this type. Similarly, interpersonal skills training can often fall into this category because it is not matched to specific organizational problems. Even technical training may "fail" because the underlying problem is in fact not technical in its nature.

This line of research has been frustrated because of the slow development of performance data in line agencies. With line managers preoccupied with "putting out fires" and trainers feeling that it is "not their role" to impose performance measurement, this key element in the data collection base for study of the learning–behavior linkage is lost.

What little that has been done still selects out learning situations in which the performance measures are already collected by agencies (e.g., absenteeism records), utilizes performance appraisals (often of a subjective and unreliable type), or simulates behavior in the laboratory (often with young, student subjects) where it is difficult to recreate actual job pressures and incentives. In spite of these difficulties, research of this type is crucial to the training profession. Because it is not generally available at present, it is rare for a public manager to know if training investment (in spite of evidence of learning) has actually improved employee performance. At best trainers now rely on second-order gratitude effects in the form of posttraining supervisory ratings.

The third linkage meriting priority in a research agenda on public sector training is that between learned behavior and organizational performance. If training cannot be tied to ultimate objectives, such as effectiveness, responsiveness, or equity, it will never achieve the status in government it deserves.

What future awaits the training function in the public sector? The politics of scarcity teaches the lesson that training may be among the first items cut as governments face the difficult decades ahead. Indeed, the training function started to grow at a time when funds may be unavailable to make the leap that would carry the state-of-the-art of training research to the level where convincing data could be generated, enabling training to be evaluated in terms of cost effectiveness as compared to other management investments. In an informational society training and development are now the quintessential forms of investment. It would be unfortunate if notions formed derived from a decaying manufacturing environment were to mire us in the past and cost us our future.

REFERENCES

Ammons, D. N., and Nietzielski-Eichner, P. A. (1988). Evaluating supervisory training in local government: moving beyond concept to a practical framework, *Public Personnel Manag. 14*(3): 211–230.

Andrews, M. A. (1979). *Management Information Service Guide to Management Improvement Projects*, Vol. 3, MIS, Phoenix, p. 62.

Archer, J. T. (1975). Achieving joint organizational, technical, and personal needs. *The Quality of Working Life*, Vol. 2 (L. E. Davis and A. B. Cherns, eds.), Free Press, New York, pp. 253–268.

Argyris, C. (1964). *Integrating the Individual and the Organization*, Wiley, New York.

Baker, J. F. (1985). Correspondence and home study, *Human Resources Management and Development Handbook*, (W. R. Tracey, ed.), American Management Association, New York, pp. 1273–1283.

Bass, B. M., and Vaughn, J. A. (1966). Training in industry, *The Management of Learning*, Wadsworth, Belmont, CA.

Beatty, R. W., and Schneier, C. E. (1977). *Implementors' Manual for Personnel Administration*, Addison-Wesley, Reading, MA.

Beaumont, E. (1979). Training evaluation: opportunities and constraints. *South. Rev. Public Admin., 2*: 498–510.

Berne, E. (1964). *Games People Play*, Grove Press, New York.

Blake, R. R., and Mouton, J. S. (1964). *The Managerial Grid*, Gulf, Houston.

Blake, R. R., and Mouton, J. S. (1969). *Building a Dynamic Corporation Through Grid Organization Development*, Addison-Wesley, Reading, MA.

Booth, W. S., and Rohe, C. A. (1988). Recruiting for women and minorities in the fire service: solutions for today's challenges. *Public Personnel Manage., 17* (Spring): 53–61.

Boyer, C. E., and P. Pond (1987). Employee participation and involvement, *Training and Development Handbook, 3rd ed.* (R. L. Craig, ed.), McGraw-Hill, New York, pp. 771–784.

Bradford, L P. (1979). It's time you considered pre-retirement training, *Training* (June): 52–54.

Braun, A. (1979). Assessing supervisory training needs and evaluating effectiveness, *Train. Dev. J., 33*: 3–10.

Brinkerhoff, R. O. (1986). Expanding needs analysis, *Train. Dev. J., 40,*(2): 64–65.

Brinkerhoff, D. W. (1987). Recruiting and selecting the human resource development staff, *Training and Development Handbook, 3rd ed.* (R. L. Craig, ed.), McGraw-Hill, New York, pp. 65–74.

Broadnax, W. D. (1979). Values clarification and executive development, *South. Rev. Public Admin., 2*: 511–525.

Broadwell, M. M. (1987). Classroom instruction, *Training and Development Handbook, 3rd ed.* (R. L. Craig, ed.), McGraw-Hill, New York, pp. 383–397.

Brower, M. (1975). Experience with participation and self-management in U.S. industry, *Admin. Soc., 7*: 65–84.

Byhan, W. (1971). The assessment center as an aid in management development, *Train. Dev. J.*, 10–21.

Caldwell, L. K. (1964). Measuring and evaluating personnel testing, *The Public Personnel World* (J. M. Shafritz, ed.), International Personnel Management Association, Chicago, 1977, pp. 251–265.

Calhoon, R. P., and Jerdee, T. H. (1976). *Coaching in Supervision*, University of North Carolina Institute of Government, Chapel Hill.

Campbell, J. P., Dunnette, M. D., Lawler, E. E., and Weick, K. E. (1970). *Managerial Behavior, Performance, and Effectiveness*, McGraw-Hill, New York.

Campbell, J. P. (1971). Personnel training and development, *Annu. Rev. Psychol. 22*: 565–602.

Cascio, W. F. (1978). *Applied Psychology in Personnel Management*, Reston, Reston, VA.

Cascio, W. F. (1982). *Costing Human Resources: The Financial Impact of Behavior in Organizations*, Van Nostrand Reinhold, New York.

Christen, J. C. (1987). Team building, *Training and Development Handbook, 3rd ed.* (R. L. Craig, ed.), McGraw-Hill, New York, pp. 442–455.

Cocheu, T. (1989). Training for quality improvement. *Train. Dev. J. (Jan.)*: 56–62.

Conference Board (1985). *Trends in Corporate Education and Training*, The Conference Board, New York.

Connors, J. E., Jr. (1978). *Management Information Service Guide to Management Improvement Projects*, Vol. 2, MIS, Blacksburg, VA, p. 162.

Cooke, P. (1987). Role playing, *Training and Development Handbook, 3rd ed.* (R. L. Craig, ed.), McGraw-Hill, New York, pp. 430–441.

Daley, D. M. (1993). *Performance Appraisal in the Public Sector: Techniques and Applications*, Quorum Books, New York.

Darling, E. W. (1978). *Management Information Service Guide to Management Improvement Projects*, Vol. 2, MIS, Hollywood, FL, p. 160.

Demings, W. E. (1986). *Out of Chaos*, MIT Center for Advanced Engineering Studies, Cambridge, MA.

Donaldson, L., and Scannell, E. E. (eds.) (1986). *Human Resource Development: The New Trainer's Guide*, Addison-Wesley, Reading, MA.

Dupre, V. A. (1976). Human relations laboratory training, *Training and Development Handbook*, 2nd ed. (R. L. Craig, ed.), McGraw-Hill, New York, pp. 37-1–37-15.

Dyer, W. G. (1977). *Team Building*, Addison-Wesley, Reading, MA.

Ehrlich, H. (1969). Attitudes, behavior, and the intervening variables, *Am. Sociologist, 4*: 29–34.

Employment Training Division (1978). *Classroom Training: The OIC Approach: CETA Program Models*, U.S. Department of Labor, Washington, DC.

Fetteroll, E. C., Jr. (1985). Selecting and training the trainer, *Human Resources Management and Development Handbook* (W. R. Tracey, ed.), American Management Association, New York, pp. 1387–1394.

Fleischman, E. A. (1953). Leadership climate, human relations training, and supervisory behavior, *Personnel Psychol., 6*: 205–222.

Fleischman, E. A., and Mumford, M. A. (1989). Causes of individual differences, *Human Perf.*, 2(3): 201–223.

Fleischman, E. A., Harris, E. F., and Burtt, H. E. (1955). *Leadership and Supervision in Industry*, Ohio State University Bureau of Educational Research, Columbus.

Folley, J. D., Jr. (1969). Determining the training needs of department store sales personnel, *Train. Dev. J. 23*: 11–17.

French, W. L., and Bell, C. H., Jr. (1978). *Organization Development*, 2nd ed., Prentice-Hall, Englewood Cliffs, NJ.

Gabris, G. T., and Mitchell, K. (1989). Exploring the relationship between intern job performance, quality of education experience, and career placement, *Public Admin. Q., 12*(4) (Winter): 484–504.

Gagne, R. M. (1962). Military training and principles of learning, *Am. Psychologist, 18*: 83–91. Cited in E. H. Schein (1964). How to break in the college graduate, *Harvard Business Rev., 42*: 68–76.

Garson, G. D. (1979). The institute model for public sector management development, *Public Personnel*

Manage., *8*: 241–255.

Garson, G. D., and Williams, J. O. (1981). *Public Administration*, Allyn and Bacon, Boston.

Geber, B. (1989). The limits of HRD, *Training* (*May*): 25–33.

Geber, B. (1989). Industry report: who, how what, *Training* (*Oct.*): 49–63.

Golembiewski, R. T. (1985). *Humanizing Public Organizations*, Lomond, Mt. Airy, MD.

Graham, J. L., and Mikal, W. L. (1986). Can your management development needs surveys be trusted?" *Train. Dev. J.* 40(3): 38–42.

Hart, F. A. (1987). Computer-based training. *Training and Development Handbook, 3rd ed.* (R. L. Craig, ed.), McGraw-Hill, New York, pp. 470–487.

Hatry, H. P., Blair, L. H., Fisk, D. M., Greiner, J. M., Hall, J. R., and Schaenman, P. S. (1977). *How Effective Are Your Community Services?* Urban Institute, Washington, DC.

Henning, K. K., and Wilson, L. D. (1979). The Georgia Certified Public Manager Program, *South. Rev. Public Admin.*, *2*: 424–435.

Henry, N. (1982). *Doing Public Administration*, Allyn and Bacon, Boston.

Herzberg, F. (1966). *Work and the Nature of Man*, World, Cleveland, OH.

Herzberg, F. (1976). *The Managerial Choice: To Be Efficient and To Be Human*, Dow Jones–Irwin, Homewood, IL.

Hickerson, K. A., and Litchfield, H. L., III (1978). Professionalism versus salesmanship: focusing on evaluation procedure at John Deere, *Train. Dev. J.*, *32*: 53–59.

Hicks, W. D., and Klimoski, R. J. (1987). Entry into training programs and its effects on training outcomes: a field experiment, *Acad. Manage. J.*, *30*: 542–551.

Hill, R., and Brindley, P. (1978). *Management Information Service Guide to Management Improvement Projects*, Vol. 2, MIS, Marin County, CA, p. 161.

Hopkins, C. O., Ritter, K. L., and Stevenson, W. W. (1972). *Delphi: A Planning Tool*, Oklahoma State Department of Vocational and Technical Education, Stillwater.

Hopson, R. S. (1978). *Charlotte, N. C. Management Information Service Guide to Management Improvement Projects*, Vol. 2, MIS, Charlotte, NC, p. 16.

HUD (1976) *A Guide for Local Evaluation*, HUD, Washington, DC.

Huddleston, M. W. (1992). *The Public Administration Workbook*, Longmans, New York.

Hudson Institute (1988). *Service 2000*, Washington, DC.

Jain, H. C. (1975). Managerial education: the weak link. *The Labour Gazette*, *11*: 800–803.

Janis, I. (1972). *Victims of Group Think*. Houghton Mifflin, Boston.

King, A. S. (1974). Expectation effects in organizational change, *Admin. Sci. Q.*, *19*: 221–230.

King, J. (1986). Computer based instruction, *Human Resource Development: The New Trainer's Guide* (L. Donaldson and E. E. Scannell, eds.), Addison-Wesley, Reading, MA, pp. 79–85.

Klingner, D. E., and Nalbandian, J. (1985). *Public Personnel Management: Contexts and Strategies*, Prentice-Hall, Englewood Cliffs, NJ.

Kirkpatrick, D. L. (1975). *Evaluating Training Programs*, American Society for Training and Development, Madison, WI.

Kirkpatrick, D. L. (1987). Evaluation, *Training and Development Handbook, 3rd ed.* (R. L. Craig, ed.), McGraw-Hill, New York, pp. 301–319.

Knowles, M. S. (1978). *The Adult Learner: A Neglected Species*, 2nd ed., Gulf, Houston.

Knowles, M. S., (1987). Adult learning, *Training and Development Handbook, 3rd ed.* (R. L. Craig, ed.), McGraw-Hill, New York, pp. 168–179.

Kohls, L. R. (1985). Intercultural training, *Human Resources Management and Development Handbook* (W. R. Tracey, ed.), American Management Association, New York, pp. 1125–1134.

Leifer, M. (1979). Remember evaluation data usually doesn't prove anything, *Training* (*June*): 6ff.

Lewin, K., Lippitt, R., and White, R. K. (1939). Patterns of aggressive behavior in experimentally created social climates, *J. Social Psychol.*, *10*: 271–299.

Likert, R. (1961). *New Patterns of Management*, McGraw-Hill, New York.

Likert, R. (1967). *The Human Organization*, McGraw-Hill, New York.

Lippitt, G. L., and Nadler, L. (1967). Emerging roles of the training director, *Train. Dev. J.*, *21*. Cited in

P. H. Chaddock (1976). Selection and development of the training staff, *Training and Development Handbook, 2nd ed.* (R. L. Craig, ed.), McGraw-Hill, New York, pp. 3-1-3-17.

Lovell, C. (1979). Training for productivity improvement: Long Beach, CA, *South. Rev. Public Admin.*, 2: 458–474.

Luthans, F., and Kreitner, R. (1975). *Organizational Behavior Modification*, Scott, Foresman, Glenview, IL.

Marini, F., ed. (1971). *Toward a New Public Administration*, Chandler, Scranton, PA.

Madlin N. (1987). Computer based training comes of age, *Personnel*, 64(11): 64–65.

Marsh, N. D. (1976). Training records and information systems, *Training and Development Handbook, 2nd ed.* (R. L. Craig, ed.), McGraw-Hill, New York, pp. 5-1-5-36.

Maslow, A. H. (1954). *Motivation and Personality*. Harper and Row, New York.

Maslow, A. P. (1976). The role of testing in training and development, *Training and Development Handbook, 2nd ed.* (R. L. Craig, ed.), McGraw-Hill, New York, pp. 10-1-10-13.

McClelland, D. C. (1953). *The Achievement Motive*, Appleton-Century-Crofts, New York.

McGehee, W., and Thayer, P. W. (1961). *Training in Business and Industry*, Wiley, New York.

McGregor, D. (1960). *The Human Side of Enterprise*, McGraw-Hill, New York.

Meyer, H. H., Kay, E., and French, J. R. P. (1965). Split roles in performance appraisal, *Harvard Business Rev.*, 43: 123–129.

Meyer, H. H. (1991). A solution to the performance appraisal feedback enigma, *Acad. Manage. Exec.*, 5(1) (Feb.): 68–76.

Milkovich, G. T., and Boudreau, J. W. (1991). *Human Resource Management*, Irwin, Homewood, IL.

Morris, K. T., and Cinnamon, K. M. (1974). *A Handbook of Verbal Group Exercises*, Applied Skills Press, Kansas City, MO.

Moses, J. L. (1987). Assessment centers, *Training and Development Handbook, 3rd ed.* (R. L. Craig, ed.), McGraw-Hill, New York, pp. 248–262.

Mouton, J. S., and Blake, R. R. (1975). *Instrumented team learning: behavioral approach to student centered learning*. Florida State University, Tallahassee, FL.

Murphy, I. R. (1972). Is it Skinner or nothing? *Train. Dev. J.*, 26: 2–8.

Mushkin, S. I., Sandifer, F. H., and Familton, S. (1978). *Current Status of Public Management Research Conducted by or Supported by Federal Agencies*, Public Service Laboratory, Georgetown University, Washington, DC.

Nadler, D. A. (1977). *Feedback and OD*, Addison-Wesley, Reading, MA.

Newland, C. A. (1979). Public sector training: diversity, dispersion, discipline, *South. Rev. Public Admin.*, 2: 402–408.

Newstrom, J., and Lilyquit, J. (1979). Selecting needs analysis methods, *Train. Dev. J. (Oct.)*: 56.

Noe, R. A. (1986). Trainee's attributes and attitudes: neglected influences on training effectiveness, *Acad. Manage. Rev.*, 11: 736–749.

Noe, R. A., and Schmitt, N. (1984). The influence of trainee attitudes on training effectiveness: test of a model, *Personnel Psychol.*, 39: 497–523.

Northcraft, G. B., Griffith, T. L., and Shalley, C. E. (1992). Building top management muscle in a slow growth environment: how different is better at Greyhound Financial Corporation, *Acad. Manage. Exec.*, 6(1) (Feb.): 32–41.

O'Brien, J., and Gubbay, D. (1979) Training to integrate the multiracial workforce, *Personnel Manage.*, 11: 21–23.

Office of Personnel Management (1979a). *Executive Development: An Overview for Agency Officials*, Document XD-1, OPM, Washington, DC.

Office of Personnel Management (1979b). *Executive Development and the Senior Executive Service*, Document XD-2, OPM, Washington, DC.

Office of Personnel Management (1980a). Mentoring process studied in various federal agencies, *Public Manage. Res.*, 1: 7.

Office of Personnel Management (1980b). *Setting Public Management Research Agendas*, OPM, Washington, DC.

Parker, A. (1988). America's new learning technology, *Personnel Administrator* 33(9): 62–132.

Parker, T. C. (1976). Statistical methods for measuring training results, *Training and Development Handbook, 2nd ed.* (R. L. Craig, ed.), McGraw-Hill, New York, pp. 19-1–19-23.

Pfeiffer, J. W. (1980). *The 1980 Annual Handbook for Group Facilitators*, University Associates, San Diego, CA.

Pfeiffer, J. W., and Jones, J. E. (1974). *A Handbook of Structured Experiences for Human Relations Training* (7 vols), University Associates, San Diego, CA.

Pigors, P. (1987). Case method, *Training and Development Handbook, 3rd ed.* (R. L. Craig, ed.), McGraw-Hill, New York, pp. 414–429.

Porter, L. W. (1973). Turning work into nonwork: the rewarding environment, *Work and Nonwork in the Year 2000* (M. D. Dunnette, ed.), Brooks Cole, Monterey, CA.

Reiner, C. A., and Morris, H. (1987). Leadership development, *Training and Development Handbook, 3rd ed.* (R. L. Craig, ed.), McGraw-Hill, New York, pp. 519–536.

Reith, J. L. (1987). Meetings, conferences, workshops, and seminars, *Training and Development Handbook, 3rd ed.* (R. L. Craig, ed.), McGraw-Hill, New York, pp. 398–413.

Reynolds, T. (1978). *Management Information Service Guide to Management Improvement Projects*, Vol. 2, MIS, Newport News, VA.

Riccucci, N. M. (1991). Apprenticeship training in the public sector: its use and operation for meeting skilled craft needs, *Public Personnel Manage.*, *20*(2) (Summer): 181–193.

Roback, T. H. (1989). Personnel research perspectives on human resource management and development, *Public Personnel Manage.*, *18*(2) (Summer): 138–161.

Robertson, I. T., and Downs, S. (1989). Work-sample tests of trainability: a meta-analysis, *J. Appl. Psychol.*, *74*: 402–410.

Robinson, J. C. (1985). Behavior modeling training, *Human Resources Management and Development Handbook* (W. R. Tracey, ed.), American Management Association, New York, pp. 1158–1174.

Roche, G. R. (1979). Much ado about mentors, *Harvard Business Rev. (Jan.–Feb.)*: 14–16.

Roethlisberger, F. J. (1941). *Management and Morale*, Harvard University Press, Cambridge, MA.

Rogers, C. R. (1969) *Freedom to Learn*, Merrill, Columbus, OH.

Rorabaugh, W. J. (1986). *The Craft Apprentice*, Oxford University Press, New York.

Ross, J. D. (1985). Update on assessment center: implications for public sector selection, *Rev. Public Personnel Admin.*, *5*(3) (Summer): 1–8.

Rummler, G. A. (1987). Determining needs, *Training and Development Handbook, 3rd ed.* (R. L. Craig, ed.), McGraw-Hill, New York, pp. 217–247.

Saari, L., Johnson, T., Mclaughlin, S., and Zimmerle, D. (1988). A survey of management training and education practices in U.S. companies, *Personnel Psychol.*, *41*: 731–743.

Sackett, P. (1982). A critical look at some common beliefs about assessment centers, *Public Personnel Manage.*, *11*(2) (Summer): 140–147.

Sackman, M. (1975). Make your own simulations to train public managers in collective bargaining, *The Public Personnel World* (J. M. Shafritz, ed.), International Personnel Management Association, Chicago, pp. 257–263.

Salinger, R. D., (1976). Correspondence study, *Training and Development Handbook, 2nd ed.* (R. L. Craig, ed.), McGraw-Hill, New York, pp. 38-1–38-14.

Saltzman, A. W., Maly, R. J., and Hartshorn, G. R. (1976). Vocational and technical education, *Training and Development Handbook* (R. L. Craig, ed.), McGraw-Hill, New York, pp. 25-1–25-14.

Schott, R. (1986). The psychological development of adults: implications for public administration, *Public Admin. Rev. 46*(6): 657–667.

Scneier, C. E., Guthrie, J. P., and Olian, J. D. (1988). A practical approach to conducting and using the training needs assessment. *Public Personnel Manage.*, *17*: 191–205.

Shaw, M. E. (1985). Work team development training, *Human Resources Management and Development Handbook* (W. R. Tracey, ed.), American Management Association, New York, pp. 1113–1124.

Shaw, M. E., Corsini, R. J., Blake, R. R., and Mouton, J. S. (1980). Role playing, *A Practical Manual for Group Facilitators*, University Associates, San Diego, CA.

Shore, M. (1985). The Action system in learning, *Human Resources Management and Development Handbook* (W. R. Tracey, ed.), American Management Association, New York, pp. 1425–1433.

Sims, R. R., and Sims, S. J. (1991). Improving training in the public sector, *Public Personnel Manage.* *20*(1) (Spring): 71–82.

Skinner, B. F. (1948). *Walden II*, Macmillan, New York.

Skinner, B. F. (1971). *Beyond Freedom and Dignity*, Knopf, New York.

Slack, J. D. (1990). Information, training, and assistance needs in municipal governments, *Public Admin. Rev. 50*(4): 450–457.

Steadman, S. V., and Clay, M. A. C. (1985). Needs assessment, *Human Resources Management and Development Handbook* (W. R. Tracey, ed.), American Management Association, New York, pp. 1338–1352.

Strauss, G., and Sayles, L. R. (1980). *Personnel: The Human Problems*, 4th ed./, Prentice-Hall, Englewood Cliffs, NJ.

Suessmuth, P. (1978). *Ideas for Training Managers and Supervisors*, University Associates, San Diego, CA.

Tarter, D. (1969). Toward prediction of attitude–action discrepancy, *Social Forces*, *47*: 398–404.

Tarter, D. (1970). Attitude: the mental myth, *Am. Sociologist*, *5*: 276–278.

Thayer, F. C. (1973). *An End To Hierarchy! An End to Competition!* New Viewpoints, New York.

Urban Institute (1974). *Measuring the Effectiveness of Basic Municipal Services*, International City Management Association, Washington, DC.

U.S. Civil Service Commission (1976). *The Employee Development Specialist Curriculum Plan*, Bureau of Training, Training Leadership Division U.S. Civil Service Commission, Washington, DC.

Varney, G. H. (1987). Organization development, *Training and Development Handbook, 3rd ed.* (R. L. Craig, ed.), McGraw-Hill, New York, pp. 537–563.

Verduin, J. R., Miller, H. G., and Greer, C. E. (1977). *Adults Teaching Adults*, Learning Concepts, Austin, TX.

Wallington, C. (1987). Audiovisual methods, *Training and Development Handbook, 3rd ed.* (R. L. Craig, ed.), McGraw-Hill, New York, pp. 500-516.

Walsh, J., and Waites, J. A. (1976). Legal and legislative aspects of training, *Training and Development Handbook, 2nd ed.* (R. L. Craig, ed.), McGraw-Hill, New York, pp. 6-1-6-11.

Wexley, K. N., and Latham, G. P. (1991), *Developing and Training Human Resources in Organizations*, 2nd ed., Scott, Foresman, Glenview, IL.

Wilson, J. A., and Elma, N. S. (1990). Organizational benefits of mentoring, *Acad. Manage. Exec. 4*(6) (Nov): 88–94.

Wolf, J. F., and Sherwood, F. (1981). Coaching: supporting public sector executives on the job, *Public Admin. Rev., 41*(1) (Jan./Feb.): 73–76.

Yeager, S. J. (1986). Use of assessment center by metropolitan fire department, *Public Personnel Manage., 15*(1) (Spring): 51–64.

Zack, A. M. (1978). The retraining of arbitrators, *Arbitration J., 33*: 31–33.

Zemke, R. (1979). Employee attitude and opinion surveys, *Training* (June): 21–33.

21
Promotion of Personnel—Career Advancement

STEVEN W. HAYS University of South Carolina, Columbia, South Carolina

RICHARD C. KEARNEY University of Connecticut, Storrs, Connecticut

I. INTRODUCTION

The promotion process includes those activities that contribute to the identification and screening of candidates for advancement to increasingly responsible positions. As such, it is closely related to the recruitment and selection functions, from which many of its techniques are borrowed. In addition, because progressive organizations place a high value on advancing the professional and technical accomplishments of their workers, it is also influenced by training and development activities.

Depending on certain particulars of the situation, a single promotion might involve a job analysis, the writing and advertising of a position announcement, the application of various interview and testing strategies, and the assumption of decision responsibility by one or more agency personnel. While typical textbook discussions often leave the impression that employee screening halts once the new workers are successfully hired, the reality is that almost all workers are "selected" many times during their careers. Each step up the career ladder involves a selection of some type, although the level of formality that guides the process varies widely from agency to agency and jurisdiction to jurisdiction.

Because it is the virtual Siamese twin of selection, the promotion process shares many of that function's frailties and failures. Deciding between and among candidates—even if the decision is guided by "objective criteria"—is a process fraught with pitfalls. As is discussed elsewhere in this volume, the difficulties inherent in the validation of tests, or even of minimum job requirements, are legendary. This problem is compounded when there is an unabashed reliance on subjective criteria, as is often the case when promotions are based on "hunch," personality (in the case of internal candidates), and even "performance" (as assessed by notoriously flawed performance appraisals). Partly as a result of these factors, Peter Drucker estimated that the promotion "batting average" for American managers is about 0.333, meaning that the wrong decision is made two-thirds of the time (1985, p. 95).

If Drucker's observation is not unduly pessimistic, then both government and industry are paying a huge price for poor promotional decision making. The most obvious byproduct would be the lower levels of performance attributable to the presence of many overemployed workers in most organizational settings. More subtle consequences would rain down from the impact that such decisions would have on the rest of the labor force. Promotions are probably *the* most significant incentive that any organization can offer. For many workers, at least, the opportunity to be considered for advancement is a critical enticement that has been positively linked to motivation (Weiner and Vardi, 1980), organizational commitment (Sheldon, 1971; Stumpf and Hartman, 1984), loyalty (Solomon, 1992), and a variety of other workplace behaviors that covary with these constructs (e.g., low rates of turnover, absenteeism, and tardiness; improved quantity of work) (Steers, 1977; Mowday et al., 1979). In addition to destroying employee morale, poor promotional decisions tear at the foundation of the organization's authority structure. The steady progression of workers who prove to be incompetent or who are widely regarded as undeserving is one of the quickest ways to diminish management's credibility and to call all other decisions into question. The "Peter principle"—the tendency to promote individuals to their level of incompetence—may pervade, and ultimately cripple, any organization.

An organization's promotion philosophy also has a number of indirect effects on employee behavior. If career paths are designed around narrow specialties, intraorganizational mobility is a likely casualty. Workers will be reluctant to transfer between departments for fear that they will lose their "place" in the promotion queue. A preference for external candidates (lateral entry) encourages turnover, while the uninterrupted practice of promoting internally often contributes to dysfunctional behaviors among competing candidates searching for an advantage over their peers. Similarly, promotion paths that become very predictable—as when elevation to high-level jobs always come through the same department—produce logical responses on the part of employees. Competition becomes very intense for transfers into the fast-track department, while assignment to departments that appear to be promotional deadends are interpreted as punishment. In short, promotion patterns quickly become decision premises that guide the career choices of all employees.

Given the extreme importance of promotion policies to the internal health of an organization, one might expect that the topic has been thoroughly explored by researchers and practitioners. In reality, however, it is clearly one of the *least* studied functions of personnel management. Many personnel textbooks, especially those focusing on *public* personnel administration, do not even have a relevant listing in their indexes (much less in their tables of contents!). Likewise, the subject makes only an occasional appearance in research journals. Although tremendous research energy has been focused on personnel functions that are directly relevant to employee advancement, such as performance evaluation and test validity, issue-specific research on promotion practices and policies is a rarity.

Even in the face of this surprising inattention, the importance of promotion to the public personnel system has never been greater. Unfortunately, much of this increasing significance stems from contemporary challenges that are altering the career options of civil servants throughout the nation. This chapter begins with an overview of the changing context of public promotional policies, with emphasis on the seemingly ever-decreasing career mobility of civil servants. Later sections describe the design characteristics of different types of public career systems and address various techniques by which promotion decisions are made in most government agencies. The chapter concludes with an examination of the affirmative action and equal opportunity dilemmas that influence managerial decisions concerning employee promotions.

II. PROMOTIONS IN A CHANGING GOVERNMENTAL CONTEXT

For much of the post–World War II era, the career advancement opportunities offered by government generally surpassed those available in many areas of the private economy. Public service jobs were being created at a remarkable pace, as evidenced by the fact that government employment increased at triple the rate of the private sector between 1954 and 1974 (Rosow, 1976).

Spurred on by advancing professionalization and the enhanced occupational status of the civil service, large segments of two postwar generations invested their high career aspirations in government employment. Job growth logically translated into promotional opportunities. Each successive wave of employees climbed the bureaucratic hierarchy as fresh faces were being recruited to fill the jobs left behind.

When the rate of government growth started to level off during the 1970s, civil servants began to feel the initial effects of a phenomenon that becomes more pronounced each year. Job mobility and career advancement opportunities have become progressively more scarce, thereby producing a "career plateau" throughout most of the public service (see, e.g., Wolf, 1983; Pergl, 1990). Simply stated, this means that government career ladders are congested with too many employees competing for too few promotional opportunities. This problem is exacerbated by the fact that most of the employees whose careers are plateaued belong to the baby boom generation; they are well educated, ambitious, and upwardly mobile.

The effects of the career plateau dilemma are dramatically illustrated in a number of recent studies and reports. These reveal that many of the government's "best and brightest" are "locked into positions and pay scales well beyond their expected time of advancement" (Wolf, 1983 p. 160). In 1990, for example, there were 13 workers in competition for each high-level executive grade position in the federal government (Pergl, 1990 p. 40). Because most of these these workers are reaching the plateau at an earlier age—the average age is now 42, down from 47 since 1980—most have little hope of ever making substantial progress up the career ladder. Competition for each promotion is extraordinarily fierce and is complicated by the increasing presence of women and minorities in the labor pool. Another dysfunction that is thought to spring from limited career mobility is that a form of professional myopia sets in. Without clear career options, workers are not challenged sufficiently, thereby reducing their levels of innovation and creativity (Rich, 1984).

Similar situations prevail in just about all other governmental jurisdictions, with the possible exception of those in especially prosperous or high-growth locations. Studies focusing on the Illinois and Wisconsin personnel systems, for instance, indicate longstanding problems with career plateaus. The Illinois project reported that a lack of upward mobility is one of the most serious employee complaints and noted that more than 40% of the work force has "topped out" at the maximum pay grade with little chance of promotion beyond that point (Illinois Commission on the Future, 1991). Employees in Wisconsin face a similar fate. Wisconsin public servants were found to experience reasonable amounts of upward mobility very early in their careers, only to reach a plateau after 5 years. Not surprisingly, more than three-quarters of the respondents in that study expressed strong dissatisfaction with the lack of advancement opportunities (Wisconsin Employment Relations Study Commission, 1977).

A predictable offshoot of this situation can be found in the attrition and attraction problems that currently prevail in some civil service systems. Workers separating from the public service, as well as prospective workers who turn down job offers, frequently cite inadequate advancement potential as a primary consideration in their decisions. Almost 46% of the federal "quits and refusals" mention this factor, which is surpassed only by pay and job availability as a reason for leaving (U.S. General Accounting Office, 1990). Among different employee groups, professional and public safety workers are especially sensitive to the shortage of promotional opportunities; almost 70% of them list it as a determining factor. The U.S. Merit Systems Protection Board (1987) found a comparable response pattern among workers who had not yet expressed an intention to quit their federal jobs. Its survey of federal workers revealed that inadequate promotional opportunities are *the* most commonly mentioned strong reason for leaving government service" (cited by 45% of the respondents). Only 26% of the workers mentioned career advancement as a reason for *staying* in government (U.S. Merit Systems Protection Board, 1987 p. 3). Further evidence that these opinions have permeated the pool of potential recruits to government posts can be found in the Volcker Commission report (1990). It mentions compressed career ladders as a major impediment to the recruitment of college graduates to the public service. Only 3% of the graduates who were surveyed expressed optimism that they could successfully ascend to the high-level posts in federal agencies.

Although career plateaus are certainly the most current (and probably the most notorious) problem with public career ladders, civil service systems have other traits that complicate the promotion process in ways that may seem peculiar to private sector managers. The ultimate effect of these factors is, for the most part, to further limit the career mobility of civil servants. The three most prominent characteristics are the classification-based nature of public personnel systems, career ladder compression, and (ironically) government's supposedly "open" approach to staffing.

A. Promotion and Position Classification

Perhaps the defining characteristic of public career systems is their long-term attachment to formal position classifications. Most civil service systems are decidedly *rank-in-job* (position-oriented) rather than *rank-in-person* (person-oriented). Thus, the classification and compensation scheme essentially dictates the height and width of the career ladder. Classifications that are narrowly drawn, and those that include many explicit qualification standards, effectively inhibit movement between classes. An employee classified as an accounting technician I may be justified in aspiring to the level of accounting technician II or III, but cannot reasonably expect to move beyond that particular career ladder. The next level—such as senior accountant—will probably require educational and/or experiential qualifications (such as an MBA or CPA) that are beyond the technician's reach. Movement to an altogether different career ladder, such as personnel technician, is even more unlikely because it involves a completely new specialty with differing qualification requirements. As a consequence, most employees are unable to rotate among jobs in the organization or to expand their opportunities for career mobility.

The confining nature of employee classifications generates an additional problem that is almost pandemic in government: due to low promotional ceilings, the only way to reward loyal and competent workers is to engineer classification upgrades. Once a worker reaches the final step in his or her pay grade, no additional raises or promotions are possible, except for any cost-of-living adjustments that may be provided. To circumvent this obstacle, positions are routinely classified upward in order to justify greater pay (and perhaps status) for valued employees. This "grade creep," as it is often called, quickly distorts the entire classification system. Likewise, it gives the promotion "system" a completely haphazard character that defies planning and human resource development goals.

Another common trait of rank-in-job career systems is their tendency to be relatively ad hoc in terms of recruitment. Instead of planning systematically for future personnel needs, they "tend to search for people to fill specific positions when the positions are open" (Golembiewski and Cohen, 1970 p. 56). Promotions are made to fill specific vacancies, which places extreme emphasis on the specialized qualifications delineated by the hiring agency. This favors internal candidates, but also exposes employees to highly random and unpredictable career progressions. An extraordinarily talented worker may languish for years in a position because there is no turnover among the superiors in her career ladder; less competent workers may get promoted merely because high levels of turnover open up advancement opportunities in their job series (Leich, 1960).

For some time now, the job classification system has been recognized as "arcane, antiquated, and unwieldy" (Shoop, 1992 p. 16). Calls for reform have resulted in a few celebrated innovations, such as the creation of the federal Senior Executive Service (SES) and "broad banding," but have not diffused very far across bureaucracies or levels of government. Except for a few pocket of rank-in-person career systems, most of the public service remains rank-in-job.

From the perspective of the promotion process, the person-oriented approach to career management appears more rational, planned, and effective in utilizing human capital. Because it is the established approach to personnel management in Japan, it almost automatically achieves a measure of credibility among many American managers (Bowman, 1986). If the system is objectively administered (this may be a big if, as evidenced by criticisms of the SES), members of the labor pool are continually rated in comparison to their peers. Foreign service officers, for example, compete annually against their contemporaries for promotions that are based on annual evaluations by their supervisors. When a vacancy occurs, candidates are assigned on the basis of their talents and abilities rather than according to arbitrarily determined qualifications. An employee's career may thus involve any number of job assignments in different functional or technical areas.

Although generally regarded as being superior to the rank-in-job format, person-oriented career systems are not without their critics. The chief complaint is that they are too closed and elitist for American society. They usually operate in a start-at-the-bottom, work-your-way-up fashion that strictly precludes lateral entry or open competition for jobs. This raises fears that an insulated and unresponsive "governing class" will result (Golembiewski and Cohen, 1970 p. 56).

Some rank-in-person systems also take a personal toll on their members, since employees who fail to gain promotions on a regular basis are typically forced to resign from the service. While this tactic obviously culls ineffective workers from the ranks, it may also contribute to the promotion of marginal employees or those who merely rise to their level of incompetency (the Peter principle).

A closely related problem arises when personal friendships, sympathy, or civil service restrictions on demotion and dismissal lead to the "up-and-out-of-the-way" promotion. Instead of cutting ineffective workers loose from their organizational umbilical cord, there are strong informal pressures to "keep them in the family," even if this involves make-work assignments and bogus promotions. Within rank-in-job career settings, where civil service rules make it very difficult to terminate workers for cause, "turkey farms" are sometimes established. These are organizational dumping grounds for workers who could not perform in their original assignments. They are a convenient (albeit wasteful) way to clear dead wood out of the career ladder expeditiously and legally. Because civil service rules generally prohibit grievances arising from promotions, workers who are "promoted" into a turkey farm have no legal recourse.

B. Career Ladder Compression

Another typical characteristic of many government career ladders is the simple fact that they are short. Unless one is employed in a very large agency or one that uses a person-oriented career system, the number of potential promotions for most workers is severely restricted.

This problem is attributable to a number of causes, including job classification, unreasonable qualification standards, and (contrary to popular opinion) relatively flat organizational structures. In recent years, the seemingly endless barrage of public sector budget cuts has further compressed career ladders since personnel replacements and promotions are early casualties of austere economies. Because a single promotion tends to create several additional opportunities within the same career ladder, the elimination of any position exerts a negative multiplier effect on all potential career opportunities (Wolf, 1983 p. 162).

An additional downward tug on the promotional ladder arises from the fact that the highest level jobs are simply unavailable to career civil servants. The public sector career path does not lead to the top of the organization because policy level jobs are ordinarily reserved for political appointees. As the Volcker Commission pointed out, this can "discourage talented men and women from remaining in the career service, or entering in the first place"(1990 p.18). Not only must ambitious individuals abandon any hope of ever truly being in charge of the agency, they must also contend with political appointees whose commitment and competence are often subject to question (see Stahl, 1990). These factors, combined with uncompetitive salaries at the upper levels of management (Rosow, 1976; Cox and Brunelli, 1992), produce a low promotion ceiling that is virtually impermeable.

C.   Open Staffing Practices

Compared to the practices that prevail in much of business and industry, career systems in government are putatively much more open. Modern civil service systems were founded on the ideal of open and objective competition for government jobs. Theoretically, at least, every civil service vacancy is subject to being filled through an open competition. Thus, applicants for these jobs need not be currently employed within the agency, or even within government generally. Except in a few person-oriented professions—such as in the military, the U.S. Foreign Service, the Forest Service, and the public safety specialties—lateral entry at any level is possible.

Obviously, the degree of openness within any public agency depends on many factors, both formal and informal. Where there is no tradition of progressive personnel management, or where the merit system is weak and/or ignored, managerial discretion usually prevails. In such settings, competition for desirable vacancies is usually restricted to employees already in the agency. Conversely, jurisdictions that operate highly articulated merit systems often mandate that *every* qualified applicant be given an equal chance to compete for vacancies. In these settings, public postings of job opportunities and formalized screening strategies (perhaps through written exams) are normal fixtures. Whether or not external candidates actually have a fair chance at the job is, however, frequently debatable. The conventional wisdom holds that even in the absence of explicitly preferential treatment (such as the use of seniority as a selection criterion), internal candidates often have the upper hand. They are the first to know about choice vacancies and also have a much better understanding of the "lay of the land." As will be discussed more thoroughly below, the debate over open vs. closed (external recruitment vs. internal promotion) career systems has many dimensions.

Based on these characteristics, it is possible to offer two very rough generalizations concerning promotional opportunities and career mobility in the public sector. The first, as has been reiterated above, is that career ladders in government are unusually low and unattractive relative to those in the private sector. Government agencies may be able to compete for personnel on the basis of fringe benefits, job security, or intrinsic satisfactions (the public service ethic), but they cannot generally rely on advancement opportunities for a competitive edge (U. S. General Accounting Office, 1990).

The second generalization is an outgrowth of the first: the rate of job mobility among public servants is not as high or as rapid as that which occurs at comparable levels of business and industry. Although there is a paucity of data to demonstrate this point, the few studies that have been performed appear to support the contention firmly. A 1988 *Harvard Business Review* comprehensive analysis of executive mobility concluded that the career pattern of high-level American managers in the *private* sector is "three years per job, five years per company" (*Harvard Business Review*, 1988, p. 119). The average public manager, in contrast, stays in one or two organizations for the majority of his or her career. Of the public executives who have been surveyed, only about one-third to one-half have worked in more than one governmental jurisdiction, and less than

25% have work experience in more than two different organizations (Frankel and Pigeion, 1975; Allan, 1977; Wright, Wagner, and McAnaw, 1977; Hays and Kearney, 1992). Only one study concluded that public sector executives have significantly higher rates of job mobility than those reported above (Peason, 1984). Thus, lateral entry appears to be more common in the private sector, while the public sector favors promotion from within (Haas and Wright, 1987). While there are unquestionably pockets of public workers with much higher rates of job mobility (such as school principals), they are the exception rather than the rule.

A complete explanation of the low level of public sector job mobility is not feasible at this time, given the weak body of empirical evidence relating to civil servant career paths. It *is* possible, however, to identify a few factors that clearly contribute to the phenomenon.

Some authors have suggested that the public sector's liberal pension plans coupled with impediments that limit their transportability between jurisdictions make movement increasingly unlikely as an employee accrues seniority (Bacon, 1980; Dickson et al., 1980; March, 1983). The heightened professionalization of public management also has certainly played a role. The civil service is regarded as a career by most contemporary public administrators, many of whom have acquired specialized training that is applicable only to the governmental setting. Once employed in a public agency, these influences are continually reinforced. Although the public recruitment process is legally open to all applicants, government employment sometimes has the feel of a closed and insular community. Most of a person's contacts, as well as timely information concerning career opportunities, are tied to the public agency in which one is employed. The folklore of public management has long maintained that the trick to getting ahead professionally is to get "into the system" (i.e., finding a job in a particular agency or jurisdiction), then to look for advancement opportunities arising within the organization. To the extent that this philosophy is shared by civil servants, the typical public sector career path is quite narrow.

III. POLICY OPTIONS IN PROMOTION SYSTEM DESIGN

Before the ultimate decision to promote one candidate over another can be made, a variety of preliminary questions must be resolved. Who will be allowed to compete for the promotion, and on what criteria will the choice be based? Who will exercise decision authority, and how much latitude will that person (or persons) enjoy? The answers are in part dictated by the character of a jurisdiction's personnel system, which in turn is influenced by historical and technological factors. This section identifies some of the variables and policy options that must be taken into consideration when one analyzes a jurisdiction's approach to promotion and employee advancement.

A. Custom and Technology

In many organizational settings, worker expectations concerning the operation of the career system are firmly fixed by custom and tradition. Career paths adhere to time-honored practice and are tenaciously defended by their members. Where rank-in-person career systems predominate, and in almost all paramilitary organizations, promotional opportunities are jealously parceled out only to workers who have been in the organization for a number of years. Police and fire departments expect employees to start at the bottom and serve lengthy apprenticeships before competing for advancement.

A rigid caste system operates in other venues. Due either to technical requirements or tradition (and sometimes to both), strictly enforced barriers segregate workers performing roughly equivalent jobs. University faculties, for instance, are notorious for the vigor with which they enforce a caste system over graduate students and research personnel who lack formal faculty appointments. Similarly, the technical and professional norms of the health field preclude nurses' aides from becoming nurses, and nurses from becoming physicians (at least not without acquiring the requisite professional credentials).

Another set of promotion groundrules is established by the technology of the work being performed. Industries that use highly complex technologies, where the efforts of numerous professional and technical specialists are coordinated and integrated (Mintzberg, 1979), often maintain separate career ladders for engineers, accountants, production, and other types of workers. These career ladders converge only at the top of the organizations, at which point vice presidents and chief executive officers may be selected from any of the various professional groups (Grant and Holmes, 1991).

Because most government work is service-based, it utilizes a relatively simple technology. Work is generally divided into administrative and clerical/technical categories, thereby resulting in two distinct career ladders. New employees are hired expressly into one track or the other, and rarely does a worker succeed in crossing over. The isolation of each ladder is perpetuated not only by custom but by widely differing port-of-entry requirements. Workers hired into an administrative track theoretically have the potential to be promoted all the way up to agency director. Therefore, entry requirements are set at a correspondingly high level. One problem that may result from the enforcement of demanding entry requirements is that new workers are overqualified for the work that they perform early in their careers. Boredom and turnover are a likely consequence (Hall, 1976).

A different type of dual career ladder has emerged in response to the proliferation of professional workers in government (see Mosher, 1984). Professionals oftentimes do not welcome promotions with the same degree of eagerness exhibited by clerical and administrative workers. Within traditional career ladders, a promotion usually means that the professional will no longer be plying his or her trade but will be shifted into a purely managerial role. For individuals with deep professional values, this is frequently too high a price to pay. It requires them to sacrifice their professional attachments and to assume duties for which they are often poorly prepared (both technically and temperamentally). Many of the most troublesome instances of workers who were "Peter-principled" involve those who, on the basis of professional or technical accomplishments, received promotions into administrative tracks.

Dual career ladders offer organizations a convenient way to reconcile these employees' desire for advancement with their professional orientations. Parallel, nonadministrative career ladders are established to reward valued professional employees with high status and salaries while keeping them in an occupational track that does not substantially alter the nature of work they perform. Civil engineers in a state highway department, for example, might be placed in a career ladder containing such designations as associate engineer, senior engineer, senior engineering consultant, and master engineer. In addition to an impressive title and salary increase, those individuals who rise to the top rung may be rewarded with such perks as private offices, greater freedom in project selection, and sabbatical leaves (Goddard, 1990).

Parallel career tracks are especially common in settings employing numerous research and high-tech personnel, and are also recommended for attorneys and health professionals. At the present time, one of the federal government's major retention problems involves turnover among attorneys. This dilemma is largely attributable to the fact that, due to a compressed career ladder, few attorneys are ever able to climb beyond grade GS-12 (U. S. General Accounting Office, 1990). A separate career ladder is the obvious solution, but the idea has not yet been widely adopted in the federal service outside NASA and similar agencies. Although professionally driven dual career ladders can be found in many state and local jurisdictions, their popularity is not as high in government as it is in business and industry.

B.   Centralization vs. Decentralization

The extent to which a personnel system is centrally regulated and controlled is another significant factor affecting who and how promotion decisions are made. In the few remaining jurisdictions that contain powerful civil service commissions, policies governing all phases of the recruitment, selection, and promotion functions are subject to commission authorship and/or review (International Personnel Managers Association, 1973). Likewise, executive personnel systems that are closely monitored by the jurisdiction's chief executive (be it mayor, manager, or governor) will probably function in a hierarchical manner.

Generally speaking, the greater the level of centralized control, the more open a personnel system will be. That is, personnel policies will require that vacancies be filled through open searches following closely prescribed procedures. Public posting of the vacancy, strictly enforced notification requirements, and explicitly delineated review and selection guidelines are predictable fixtures in such settings. Because highly centralized civil service systems make heavy use of single-point-of-entry recruitment, the infrastructure already exists within the personnel office to advertise, recruit, and test applicants for job vacancies. Written examinations are frequently used for such purposes when selecting or promoting many categories of state and local workers, especially those in clerical and technical fields; they are not used as frequently in the federal sector.

Once these preliminary steps are completed, a list of *certified* candidates is compiled. A given number of applicants from this *eligibility list* (or *promotion register*) will then be referred to the manager charged with appointing authority. For many years the notorious "rule of three" restricted the decision to the top three candidates on the eligibility list; managerial discretion has since been expanded in most jurisdictions by the adoption of rules of 5, 10, and even 20. As you will remember from the discussions in Chapters 9 and 11, the promotion process described here is essentially identical to the procedures that prevail during recruitment and selection.

Although many state and local personnel systems remain highly centralized, there is a discernable trend toward decentralization. This movement is intended to give line managers greater latitude and flexibility in dealing with human resource demands. Centralized bureaucratic arrangements usually mean that front line managers confront long delays and rolls of red tape in accomplishing any task. These problems are especially acute in the personnel management arena, where for much of this century far more emphasis was placed on policing the system than on making it function efficiently (Van Riper, 1957 pp. 101-102). Foot dragging in the processing of appointments and promotions has reportedly cost public agencies many quality applicants, since truly talented individuals usually have many career options and are thus unwilling to wait around while the wheels of government slowly turn. Moreover, there is a growing sense that the managers who are closest to service delivery are better able to assess their human resource needs than staff technicians in a central personnel office.

An example of a decentralized approach to promotion is the one that currently exists in the federal government. Instead of screening candidates and making referrals to the agencies, the Office of Personnel Management's (OPM) role is to provide guidance and ground rules on how the process should advance. OPM requires that promotions be based on merit, that agencies recruit broadly enough to assure high-quality candidates, that supervisory evaluations be valid and job-related, and that agencies maintain records and respond to inquiries from the public regarding the promotion decisions that are made (OPM, 1979). Beyond these requirements, OPM also provides written guidance on evaluating employees for promotion, and on how to assemble and manage the promotion panels (which usually consist of three to seven managers) that many federal agencies use to screen candidates.

By placing more discretion in the hands of line managers, decentralization probably contributes to the tendency to promote internal candidates over applicants from outside the organization.

Generally speaking, the higher the level of formality in the search process, the more likely that external candidates will be successful. Because centralized systems are usually the most formal, they are most likely to ensure that a wide net is cast in the recruitment process. In contrast, decentralization runs the risk of yielding to parochialism. For reasons that will be discussed in the next section, the granting of preference to internal candidate is a very tempting option for most managers.

Another potential effect of decentralization is that it may accentuate the influence of departmental barriers on the internal movement of workers. If communication between departments is poor, or if tensions exist, the ability of workers to rotate throughout the organization may be constrained in a decentralized personnel setting. "Inside" candidates will probably still receive preference, but the definition of who is an outsider will be unusually narrow. This problem is ameliorated to some extent under a more centralized arrangement, where the personnel office can act more effectively as a clearinghouse in aiding internal mobility. Ultimately, however, if the personnel rules permit operating managers to exercise wide discretion over promotion decisions, then a preference for internal candidates—defined quite narrowly—may be a probable result.

C. Internal vs. External Candidates

An implicit theme of much of the preceding discussion is the critical significance of the "inside—outside" option in promotions. According to O. Glenn Stahl, "Achieving the proper balance between inside and outside recruitment lies at the heart of good personnel administration" (1983 p. 163). This quote is based on the reasonable premise that the exclusive use of either promotion from within or external recruitment will be dysfunctional to the organization. The two strategies for filling vacancies obviously need to be used in tandem, but determining the appropriate mix is an eternal conundrum for managers.

The case for promoting internal candidates is based largely on common sense (much of which can be quite compelling). Within career paths that have already been described as narrow and compressed, civil servants need at least to be offered the promise that they can compete for the few advancement opportunities that arise. Nothing is more demoralizing to employee morale than a belief that promotional opportunities are limited or that stated career ladders are management fiction (Hays and Reeves, 1984 pp. 203–204). In addition to feeling cheated, workers who are passed over for promotion in preference to external applicants will probably experience a marked decline in job satisfaction and incentive to perform (Kerr and Slocum, 1987; Mowday et al., 1982). The elevation of internal candidates maintains the perception that career paths are open, thereby reducing attrition and promoting job performance. In short, promoting workers from within keeps the labor force docile (if not happy), while outside recruitment is likely to stir discontent.

Although the perceived impact on employee morale is the most frequently cited justification for promotion from within, a number of practical advantages bolster the argument. Long service in an organization represents a type of apprenticeship that matures and seasons employees. Because they come to the new job with a reservoir of knowledge about the organization and its idiosyncrasies, there is little need for on-the-job training and a lengthy startup period. Moreover, as long-time employees accumulate experience, their coworkers have an opportunity to observe how candidates for promotion respond to different types of stimuli. This process of getting to know a person can be of critical importance in the appointment of managerial personnel. The case study literature is replete with horror stories describing how new (external) hires undergo Dr. Jekyl/Mr. Hyde transformations as soon the ink is dry on their employment contracts. Likewise, the performance traits of internal candidates are more readily judged against organizational selection criteria, since they have been observed in action over an extended period of time (Heneman et al. 1989, p. 374).

Finally, promotion from within avoids the inevitable attraction problems that plague the recruitment process. Candidates from outside the organization usually demand higher salaries than current employees. One rule of thumb is that external recruits can rarely be lured from their old jobs without at least a 25% increase in salary. The turnover of externally hired personnel is also much higher than that of internally promoted workers, owing in part to the difficulties inherent in moving families and to the unavoidable "surprises" that almost always surface in a new position (Byrne, 1971). On the way out the door, the oft-heard refrain is "The job wasn't as advertised!"

Perhaps the best way to summarize the case for internal promotion is to suggest that, at least from the viewpoint of those in the bureaucratic trenches, it is more comfortable and reliable than external recruitment. The comfort is derived from the preservation of the employees' hope for advancement as well as from the relief at not having to explain the hiring of an outsider to loyal coworkers who lusted after the vacancy. An additional increment of comfort is derived from the fact that the promoted person will fit in. The importance of this latter factor is attested to in the notable body of research evidence establishing a correlation between internal promotion and work force homogeneity (Jackson et al., 1991). The reliability springs from the fact that the promoted candidate is a known quantity whose talents and limitations are obvious, and who probably represents no appreciable threat to the status quo. This is truly a seductive combination.

How, then, is the recruitment of external candidates justified? Although there are fewer arguments supporting this approach to staffing, they are no less substantive or valid. The chief reason why organizations need to recruit some outside talent is to avoid excessive inbreeding. Without the infusion of different ideas and perspectives, organizations can become less creative and responsive to external demands. If all promotions are routinely made from within, employees are prone to rely on conformity rather than imagination and risk taking in order to maximize their chances for promotion. An army of "yes-men" (and women) results, and stagnation soon follows. Occasional new blood is needed to keep any organization vital.

An additional argument for the acquisition of external talent is that organizations frequently need to go outside in order to attract needed skills that are not possessed by any position incumbents. Where promotions from within are the norm, organizations easily fall prey to the recruitment stereotyping syndrome. There is a tendency to make the job fit an internal candidate (the process is often called "cloning"). This is a very unfortunate impulse, since each vacancy represents a wonderful opportunity for management to engage in a serious planning and job analysis exercise. Without a position incumbent to guard turf, there is no better time to conduct an objective analysis.

Relatedly, if the current work force is weak (or even average), or if the organization has not done an effective job of developing its personnel, promotion from within will merely perpetuate mediocrity. It is naive to assume that the best possible candidate already exists in the organization when the potential labor pool is so enormous. Although it takes time, effort, and money to recruit external candidates, the organizational payoff can be great.

Given compelling arguments both pro and con, is it possible to reconcile the two? Is there a golden mean between promotion from within and external recruitment? In typical ivory tower fashion, the standard textbook response goes something like this: With effective human resources planning, an organization should continually search for the perfect mix of strategies for filling vacancies. Through techniques such as skills inventories and replacement charting (which links, position by position, the skills inventory with projected attrition), management ought to be able to identify positions that will be externally filled well in advance of their becoming vacant. If the skills of current employees can't be upgraded sufficiently to help them qualify for the promotion, then all affected workers should be made aware of management's intention to go outside for a replacement. And, more to the point, there is widespread consensus that most searches ought to be conducted with at least one eye on the outside labor market. Preference can certainly be granted to internal candidates during the evaluation process, but truly superior external candidates who emerge during the search should be given a fair chance at the job.

D. Evaluation Criteria: Seniority vs. Merit

Whichever policy an organization implements in regard to the internal–external puzzle, the choice of screening criteria will play an important role. An evaluation formula that grants credit for seniority will undoubtedly favor internal candidates, while requirements for high educational achievement will probably strengthen the chances of external applicants.

Except for seniority, the criteria used in making promotion decisions are essentially the same as those applied to initial selection. The major difference is that, generally speaking, promotion criteria are more loosely defined and more generously interpreted. Informality frequently prevails, which tends to preserve the discretion of appointing officials. This general rule holds in all but two important areas: where written examinations are used and where collective bargaining agreements give unions a say in promotion decisions.

The situation surrounding the use of written examinations is thoroughly discussed in Chapter 11. Suffice it to say here that they are not popular among line managers for the purpose of making promotional decisions. While support exists for the use of written and/or performance exams for some classes of technical and clerical workers, their use declines markedly as one ascends the hierarchy. The more abstract or "managerial" the job, the less likely that a formal test will be used in making promotion decisions. Instead, work history and various appraisals of past and future (predicted) performance are viewed as being better indicators of probable success. As will be discussed later, different types of screening mechanism have been developed to assess the various skills required for management.

The union position is that all bargaining unit jobs (other than entry level) should be filled through promotion from within and that seniority should be the major criterion in promotion decisions (Kearney, 1992 pp. 236–237). In jurisdictions that permit unions to bargain over promotion policy, most contracts (about 80%) require that at least some consideration be given to seniority (Bureau of National Affairs, 1983). If the union lacks the formal right or the bargaining power to set promotion policy, it may then try to influence the process by having union representatives appointed to promotion panels (this is common in the federal government).

Organized labor's fondness for seniority is predicated on that factor's perceived objectivity. Once an agreement is reached concerning how seniority will be calculated (i.e., must service be continuous and unbroken to count? is service in a different agency or jurisdiction included?), management cannot "play games." With other forms of evaluation, there is always the risk that management will use the inherent subjectivity to stifle dissent, punish troublemakers, and reward toadies. Thus, seniority is viewed as being both democratic and protective of workers' rights (Abraham and Medoff, 1984).

Seniority is also defended on performance-based grounds. Union officials argue (sometimes without even blushing) that seniority correlates with ability, since workers learn from job experience (critics contend that one year of experience may be experienced five times). Likewise, rewarding employees in this way is viewed as an important incentive to the organization to invest in human resources development. If workers are destined to be promoted on the basis of long-term job experience, then management would be foolish to ignore their training needs. Another argument that is sometimes offered is that promotion on the basis of seniority rewards employee loyalty and is pleasing to the organization's sense of justice and fairness. This logic is equally present in the contention that promotions based on seniority will occasion less resentment among the workers. Because everyone (presumably) can add (or at least count years of experience), the calculation of "why" someone was promoted leaves no room to suspect that favoritism influenced the decision.

Research findings do not generally support the performance-based arguments marshaled in defense of seniority. Extensive job experience does not correlate closely with productivity or performance (Maranto and Rogers, 1984; Mills, 1985). Given this conclusion, it should not be surprising to discover that the use of seniority as a prime screening criterion has been found to result in the promotion of poor performers over effective ones (Abraham and Medoff, 1985; Mills, 1985). Yet, despite such findings, promotions tend to go to the most experienced employees in over 95% of the unionized settings in which the collective bargaining contract contains a strong promotion clause (Abraham and Medoff, 1985). Even in nonunion organizations, promotion from within tends to prevail, with seniority the deciding factor (Kearney, 1992 pp. 236–237). But unfortunately, as expressed by one researcher, promotion on the basis of seniority "can weaken the opportunity to assign a worker to the job that produces the most profitable match"(Schnell, 1987 p. 1976). And, as discussed below, seniority sometimes obstructs affirmative action plans in limiting the promotional opportunities of recently hired members of protected classes.

Given the shortcomings of seniority as a measure of promotion potential, managers have little else to rely on other than performance. This is certainly a more viscerally pleasing criterion, since managers don't have to contemplate the specter of a work force in which aged incompetents occupy the high-level positions. Although some unspecified amount of credit for seniority is often factored into promotional decisions, the bulk of the evaluation rests on various assessments of job performance. Past performance is never a guarantee of future performance—especially considering that promotions involve changing responsibilities—but it is probably the most reliable indicator available.

Most of the arguments in favor of performance-based promotions are so obvious as to seem tautological. Promotions constitute an important form of reward, and our culture generally believes that rewards ought to be earned. Allocating promotions on the basis of effort and performance helps to maintain the authority structure by perpetuating the belief (myth?) that the most capable among us are in charge. Similarly, to spur the rest of the work force to greater levels of performance, merit needs to be a prominent criterion in the evaluation and reward system. If other factors creep in, such as sucking up to the boss or defaming one's competition, then that behavior will likely spread until the decision cues are once again changed.

While few will disagree that merit is an (if not *the*) appropriate criterion, getting the management community to agree on an adequate definition or measure of performance is an entirely different matter. Current textbooks frequently draw a distinction between performance and ability, with the latter concept now being used to refer to *potential* performance in a new job. The development of evaluation strategies that provide some predictive validity to estimates of future management potential has become a preoccupation of personnel professionals.

Meanwhile, controversy continues to rage over the best ways to evaluate present performance. The fundamental weakness of all such evaluation is its subjectivity. Try as we might, appraisals of worker performance are inevitably influenced by personalistic considerations and chance. Survey after survey reveals that civil servants do not trust the performance evaluation process. Workers consider their evaluations to be unreliable and prone to favoritism that is both personally and politically motivated (see, e.g., U. S. Merit System Protection Board, 1989; U. S. General Accounting Office, 1992). Significant numbers of federal executives, for instance, consistently report that evaluation results are manipulated by political appointees to promote partisan objectives. Similarly, nearly one-half of the respondents to an MSPB survey (1989) noted that they have personally witnessed promotions being allocated on the basis of friendship rather than merit (U.

S. General Accounting Office, 1984, 1987). This problem appears to be especially acute in the federal service, perhaps simply because the U.S. government attracts much closer scrutiny than other public jurisdictions. If state and local personnel systems were to be examined closely, there is little question that similar findings would be common.

Because these sentiments are so widespread, promotions made on the basis of performance evaluation run the risk of being viewed as illegitimate. Workers who are passed over for promotion attribute their lack of success—either rightly or wrongly—to office politics, favoritism, and other ego-pleasing explanations.

Efforts to objectify performance measurement have produced an amazing array of assessment technologies, none of which appears to be truly satisfactory. In addition to rating scales, management-by-objectives, critical incidents, and untold other approaches (see Chapter 13), managers have resorted to a number of proxies. The candidates' education levels is one favorite, since they are easily assessed and appear objective. If applicants for a promotion seem roughly equal on the basis of other measures, it is a simple matter to pare the list by excluding those who do not, for example, have an advanced degree. This contributes to "credentialism," which (much to the delight of many universities) has filled classrooms with MPA students. Another proxy for performance is the variety of experiences that an applicant can claim. Those who engaged in a formal or informal program of job rotation are theoretically advantaged by this criterion, unless the evaluator is suspicious that such candidates "couldn't keep a job." It is also true that even more subjective proxies, such as the supervisor's assessment of worker cooperation or loyalty, frequently enter into the decision calculus. Thus, while performance is the accepted means of allocating promotions, the level of decision sophistication is often embarrassingly low.

IV. EVALUATION STRATEGIES

Widespread dissatisfaction with traditional forms of performance evaluation has stimulated an energetic search for alternatives. Although supervisory assessment of employee performance remains the bedrock component of promotion screening, just as it does in other merit determinations, civil service systems are exhibiting an ever-increasing willingness to innovate and experiment. Some completely new assessment approaches have been devised, while other more traditional methodologies are merely being applied in different ways.

If these emergent techniques have any common theme, it is that of *multiple indicators*. Because reliance on a single evaluation indicator—the supervisor's rating of employee performance—has proven to be such a disappointment, additional sources of information are being exploited. One approach is to expand the number of individuals feeding information into the evaluation process; the other is to increase the variety of performance indicators available for each promotion candidate.

A. Nonsupervisory Evaluation Formats

Although it represents an assault on bureaucratic notions of hierarchy and authority, some support exists for soliciting the opinions of peers and subordinates concerning a worker's performance and/or promotion potential. Seldom used as the exclusive source of information, the input of coworkers and followers supplements more traditional indicators.

Of the two techniques, *peer appraisal* is probably the most common. It has been used for generations in some rank-in-person settings, such as universities and the military. The specific tactics that are used to collect attitudes concerning one's peers are diverse, but usually tend toward the simple and direct (Burke, 1972; Kane and Lawler, 1978). Rather than filling out exhaustive questionnaires, workers are asked to provide a summary judgment of some type. This may involve responding to an up-or-down question, such as, "Should John be promoted, and why?" The military is fond of asking all members of a unit to rank-order one another. The form might read: "You are isolated behind enemy lines. Who in this platoon would you like to be in command under this situation? Rank, in descending order of preference, everyone in the platoon."

The advantages and disadvantages of peer ratings are fairly obvious. Few people are as familiar with an employee's strengths and weaknesses as his or her coworkers. They are in a good position to provide insights concerning personality and performance traits. Since they perform comparable tasks, their understanding of a job's nuances and complexity is unparalleled, thus providing insights that are difficult to replicate in any other context. For these same reasons, ironically, their judgments may also be unreliable. Opinions may be colored by personal animosities or friendships, agreement or disagreement over specific style and policy issues, and competition among one another for recognition and advancement.

Peer evaluations are rarely used outside of the settings mentioned above, *except* when included as part of an assessment center (a topic that is discussed later). But they receive surprisingly positive support from the sparse research record that focuses on them specifically. Applications in the military reflect reasonable levels of reliability and worker satisfaction with the fairness of the process (Weitz, 1958). The record is not quite as good in some other applications, such as in the evaluation of police personnel (Eisenberg, 1980; Love, 1981), but is sufficient to ensure that the use of peer evaluation will probably expand as experience is gained.

Subordinate rating of candidate for promotion is another promising technique that is just beginning to be investigated by researchers (Bernardin and Beatty, 1987). The means by which subordinate perceptions are integrated into managerial evaluations span the gamut from simplistic to elegant. One easy approach is to have an employee's subordinates complete the same evaluation instrument that is normally used by the candidate's superiors. Results are then contrasted and compared; if major discrepancies exist, the subordinate may be interviewed. Much more sophisticated experiments have been conducted in some corporations, where workers receive training on the specific behaviors and job dimensions they should evaluate among their superiors.

Here, too, the pros and cons are readily apparent. The biggest advantage is that subordinate evaluation erodes the isolation and insulation of the management group (Bernardin and Beatty, 1987 p. 72). By telling it like it is, subordinates can help to unveil the truth about their manager's style, performance, and demeanor. Care must obviously be taken to guard against the defamation of a manager by employees with an axe to grind. By the same token, managers who know that their subordinates will have input into a critical promotion decision may become preoccupied with campaigning; they'll spend too much time "being nice" and not pay enough attention to their real responsibilities. For these reasons, anonymity of respondents (who participates in the evaluation) and response (what they say) are essential to maintaining the integrity of the process. Some authors also worry about the inability of many subordinate to provide valid feedback on managerial performance (Hegarty, 1974). Their perspectives are often so different and their understanding of contextual factors so constrained that they are inappropriate sources of evaluative information (see Mount, 1984).

In contrast to these criticisms, most analyses indicate that subordinate evaluations are extraordinarily reliable. One classic study from the 1950s revealed that, even though two-thirds of the supervisors were surprised by their subordinates' comments and criticisms, only 7% thought that the comments were unfair or invalid (Maloney and Hinrichs, 1959). More recent research shows that subordinates are especially helpful in evaluating such performance dimensions as leadership, information dissemination, crisis handling, and resource allocation. They are less effective in appraising the superior's external performance, including spokesperson, negotiator, and resource acquisition (Bernardin and Beatty, 1987 p. 69). Another project concluded that, in the promotion of officers within a state highway patrol, subordinate ratings were "better predictors of subsequent supervisory performance than assessment centers at approximately one-twentieth the cost" (as quoted in Bernardin and Beatty, 1987 p. 68). A follow-up study reinforced this conclusion, asserting that subordinate ratings "outperform" assessment centers in predicting supervisory performance (McEvoy and Beatty, 1989 p. 37). Since assessment centers are widely reputed to be the most reliable predictor of promotional potential, findings such as these will certainly generate additional interest in the subordinate rating technique.

One other potential source of evaluation input comes from the promotion candidates themselves. *Self-appraisal* is occasionally offered up as a useful complement to supervisory and subordinate evaluation (Mabe and West, 1982). This technique is generally thought to be most appropriate to management development, whereby employees engage in self-analysis in order to identify strengths and weaknesses (Markus and Wurf, 1987). In such a low-risk setting, self-appraisal can be an effective aid to learning (Mani, 1992).

As a means of making promotion decisions, however, self-appraisal appears to have a fatal flaw. Making judgments about oneself is never a dispassionate act, and it is especially problematic when the stakes are very high (George and Smith, 1990 p. 175). The empirical evidence is fairly overwhelming that managerial employees are not very adept at making objective assessments of their performance. Likewise, the predictive validity of self-appraisals is consistently shown to trail that of both supervisory and subordinate ratings (Harris and Schaubroek, 1988). These facts do not appear to be influenced by a manager's level of experience or independent measures of competence. In short, while self-assessments may be a useful training and development strategy, they are not sufficiently reliable to be applied to promotion decisions.

B. Multiple Indicators: Assessment Centers

With the notable exception of legally imposed validation requirements, the most revolutionary development in employee screening in the past 30 years has been the assessment center. Originally developed and refined as a means of selecting intelligence agents (spies), assessment centers have quickly become one of the most popular techniques for selecting managers and for diagnosing and predicting management potential. They are often associated with initial selection, but their most celebrated applications are in evaluation of candidates for promotion.

Assessment centers differ from conventional selection procedures in a number of important ways. The three most striking characteristics are the choice of predictors, the range of skills and abilities evaluated, and the manner in which participants are rated.

All assessment centers utilize multiple predictors, although wide variations exist in the specific ones chosen for any particular evaluation process. Most involve various work sample exercises, including in-baskets, leaderless group discussions, and simulations. Aptitude tests, extemporaneous presentations, management games, essay writing, and a large number of other possible indicators might also be used. If the center has been properly planned, each predictor is designed only after a careful job analysis.

A distinguishing trait of the assessment center is its total concentration on the measurement of ability and potential, not present or past job performance. Although participants ordinarily complete long questionnaires and work histories prior to the center experience, the exercises themselves are intended to probe skills and talents that are thought to translate into management potential. Among the commonly assessed dimensions are leadership, organizing and planning, initiative, analytical ability, management style, subordinate development skills, stress tolerance, ability to delegate, behavior flexibility, human relations competence, oral and written communication skills, and originality (Howard, 1974; Klimoski and Brickner, 1987).

Because most of these concepts are highly abstract, the actual assessment of participant performance takes place under close scrutiny in a controlled setting. Centers are usually conducted off-site in order to ensure standardized conditions. Some are completed in about a day, but most full-blown centers torment their participants for 2 days or more. Participants are usually evaluated in groups ranging in size from 2 to 12.

One of the most important innovations is the use of multiple raters who have (hopefully) been carefully trained. From three to six raters judge all of the participants in every exercise. The center designers go to extreme efforts to ensure interrater reliability, including the use of preevaluation briefings, standardized evaluation formats and criteria, and postmortem discussions. Raters are commonly drawn from the administrative level immediately above that for which the participants are competing, but may also be representatives of peer groups or even subordinates of the subject position.

Public jurisdictions frequently trade raters back and forth, such as when police lieutenants from surrounding cities serve as raters for another city's promotional evaluations. Public school principals, similarly, are often used by school boards and state education departments to help screen candidates for promotion to vice principal and principal.

The premise used in selecting raters is the same that guides the test designers who use Job Knowledge Experts to identify and validate a position's KSAs (knowledge, skills, and abilities): individuals who have performed the job, or who are otherwise very familiar with it, are best able to assess candidate performance. It is important to note, however, that some experts believe that psychologists who specialize in assessment methodologies are the most effective raters. This contention has been confirmed in meta-analyses of assessment center validities (Gaugler et al., 1987). However, since the cost of conducting an assessment center is already very high, it is unlikely that many public agencies can afford to go to the additional expense of hiring consultant psychologists to serve as raters. Solace can found in the fact that the predictive validity of centers using managers and peers as raters is still quite impressive (Klimoski and Brickner, 1987).

The popularity of assessment centers within public personnel systems has exploded during the past 20 years. Surveys reveal that more than 40% of the responding jurisdictions use them for one or more screening purposes (Lowry, 1992). This is a startling figure, since only a handful of public agencies had experimented with assessment centers as late as in the mid-1970s (DiLauro, 1979). Their use appears to be most widespread in evaluating candidates for selection and promotion in the police and fire services, but they are also widely applied in more general management settings.

Thanks to their amazing popularity, assessment centers have attracted an almost unprecedented level of research interest. For the most part, the research record tends to confirm the advantages that this evaluation technique offers. Specifically, assessment centers appear to measure what they purport to measure. Interrater reliability is generally high, and validity coefficients in the range of 0.50–0.60 have been reported (Heneman et al., 1989, p. 380). This high validity insulates them from legal challenge to some extent, since no assessment center recommendation has yet been negated by court order (Frank and Preston, 1982; Frank et al., 1988). Their reputation is that of an unbiased screening device which is not affected by such participant traits as race, gender, age, educational level, or prior assessment center experience (Klimoski and Brickner, 1987, p. 244). Moreover, their utility extends not just to the promotion function (Cascio and Silbey, 1979), but to training and career planning (Lorenzo, 1984). Their greatest validity appears to be in assessing advancement potential (Gaugler et al., 1987; Klimoski and Strickland, 1977).

Despite this rosy scenario, a few words of caution are in order. Although well-designed assessment centers have been shown to have high predictive validity, their reliability fluctuates with situational variables. Some centers have *not* been accurate predictors, a fact that can be variously attributed to poorly designed exercises, inadequately trained raters, incomplete specification of target competencies, inept selection of participants, and an infinite number of other design flaws (Dulewicz, 1991). Relatedly, there are serious differences of opinion in the professional community over many highly technical facets of assessment center design. One of the hottest debates is over the decision rules that should govern the raters' ultimate recommendations: whether consensus should be the rule and, if so, how it should be achieved (pooling of scores? arithmetic computation?) (Lowry, 1988, 1991). Different approaches yield inconsistent results.

Assessment centers thus are a good idea, but a jurisdiction can't just slap one together in a slip-shod manner and expect it to perform adequately. There is still much that is not understood about their design and operation. This point was eloquently argued in a 1987 article that asks, "Why do assessment centers work?" (Klimoski and Brickner, 1987). The authors conclude that there is no clear answer. They suggest that the best explanation may be that "assessment centers predict managerial success because the ratings obtained reflect the level of intellectual functioning of candidates" (Klimoski and Brickner, 1987, p. 251). Since intelligence has long been associated with managerial performance, this conclusion is not surprising. One must ask the obvious question, however: whether the high costs of conducting an assessment center (figures for each participant are often estimated to be in the thousands of dollars) are justified if all we are measuring is a trait that can be evaluated with an aptitude test. While no one is seriously questioning the utility of assessment centers at this time, additional research is clearly needed to enrich our understanding of why and how they work.

C. Promotability Ratings

To be of any use to decision makers, the information gleaned from the various evaluation formats must be systematically aggregated and analyzed. The results of this analysis are often expressed in terms of an employee's *promotability rating*, which is nothing more than a verbal or numerical representation of where that person stands in the promotion queue. In the military, for instance, officers at one time were placed in any of three ratings categories: "promote ahead of contemporaries," "promote with contemporaries," or "promote behind contemporaries." A rating in the last category, incidentally, was a one-way ticket to civilian status.

Recently, the promotability rating concept has taken on a slightly different meaning. It is now used to describe a specific information collection strategy that is distinct from other forms of evaluation. Like many assessment centers, the intent is to gather information that is expressly targeted at promotion potential. Unlike assessment centers, the information is gathered from the promotion candidates' coworkers, not from the candidates themselves. Peers, subordinates, and superiors—in one combination or another—are asked to judge how an individual is likely to perform at the next organizational level. The evaluation is not concerned with the candidate's current level of job performance except to the extent that it reflects positively or negatively on promotion potential. Workers taking part in the evaluation are usually asked to rate the candidate on specific dimensions using a closed-ended questioning methodology, such as a Likert scale.

An example of how this process looked in one public agency is offered by Cederblom (1991). He describes the approach used to promote officers in the Washington State Patrol. The 60 candidates for promotion were provided with an orientation, at which time the process was described and explained. They were all asked to rate each other's promotability on the basis of four job dimensions: judgment, administrative skill, personal impact (leadership, interpersonal ability), and work involvement (initiative, adaptability). These dimensions had been identified and refined by high-level department personnel in earlier meetings. Participants were instructed to rate only those individuals with whom they had worked frequently. Ratings were assigned on a five-point Likert scale ranging from "an outstanding prospect for promotion" to "an individual who is not promotable at this time." The results of this exercise were then averaged for each dimension, and an overall average was calculated separately from peers and higher ranking officers. According to the author, the process was reliable and valid, and reflected high interrater agreement and participant satisfaction.

Because there has been so little experience with this approach to promotion, it is premature to become too excited about its potential. Based on the promising evidence to date, however, the outlook for promotability rating methodology may be bright. Its reliance on peer ratings seems reasonably sound, given a growing body of support for their predictive validity (Schmitt et al., 1984). Expense is another factor that may ensure that experimentation continues. Compared to assessment centers, a promotability rating program is an extraordinarily cheap investment. Within the current financial picture in state and local government, any human resource technique that offers a good return for a modest expenditure can probably count on growing popularity.

D. So Who Gets Promoted, and How?

Although sketchy, the research record contains a few intriguing clues concerning factors that aid and impede progress up the career ladder. Among the institutional contributors to career mobility are a number of obvious independent variables. One's promotional opportunities are influenced in manifest directions by organizational size and complexity, the age and turnover rates of the work force, and the individual's skill level (Anderson et al., 1981). Likewise, certain staffing practices exert predictable effects. The number of temporary workers that an organization employs, for instance, has been found to be a hidden escalator that boosts full-time employees up the hierarchy (Barnett and Miner, 1992). If you are ambitious, then, the lesson here is to become highly skilled and then to find employment in a large and complex organization with an aged and/or temporary work force.

Other personal variables that correlate, either positively or negatively, with one's promotion potential include age, seniority, educational level, and job performance. Education, job tenure, and current job performance are the most salient criteria in promotion decisions (Cox and Nkomo, 1985; 1992, p. 200). When age is separated from the contaminating effect of work experience (job tenure), it tends to inhibit promotions for both younger and older workers (Cox and Nkomo, 1992). The effects of education and job tenure tend to diminish with time, serving as major determinants on initial job acquisition and early promotions, but becoming increasingly irrelevant as one's career progresses. Workers' performance ratings, in contrast, remain critical to promotion decisions throughout a career (Cox and Nkomo, 1992). Interestingly, the timing of one's first promotion has been established as an important predictor. Promotion in early career is "significantly related to later successes, including mobility ceiling and floor and probability of future promotions" (Anderson et al., 1981, p. 535).

The effects of gender and race are also matters of great importance. Frankly, the research findings concerning the career progress of women as opposed to men are confusing. Although the "glass ceiling" is real, as evidenced by aggregate data on the paucity of women in the upper reaches of bureaucracy, individually focused data indicate that the playing field is level or nearly level. After controlling for education and experience, Stewart and Gudykunst (1982) found that females are receiving a higher number of promotions than men. Gregory Lewis's analysis of federal personnel records produced an equally surprising conclusion. He found "strikingly similar promotion probabilities for white men and women, once a variety of individual characteristics are accounted for" (1986, p. 406). Most earlier research, however, consistently showed that males experience greater mobility than females (see, e.g., Kanter, 1977). It is tempting to conclude that times have changed and that the glass ceiling is permeable, but it remains difficult to do so because of the overwhelming evidence that women continue to experience career impediments (Guy, 1993). There is far less ambiguity about the impact of race, which continues to affect minorities adversely in the promotion battles. Seemingly irrelevant factors that correlate positively with career mobility include religious beliefs and club memberships (Pellegrin and Coates, 1957).

A final approach to research in this area attempts to establish linkages between organizational characteristics and the types of promotion policies that are used. Halaby's classic study (1978) of promotion practices in a sample of public agencies reveals several interesting patterns. The newer an agency, the more likely it is to emphasize subjective evaluations (performance appraisal) in promotional decisions. Older agencies, meanwhile, are more prone to use "fixed criteria," such as seniority and test scores. The professionalization of an agency's work force leads to an emphasis on examinations for promotional purposes, at the expense of seniority and performance evaluation. Geographic region also appears to be related; Halaby found that "bureaus outside the South promote more on the basis of examinations and seniority and less on the basis of evaluations" than those in Southern states (1978, p. 480). While the effect of civil service regulations is relevant to some of these findings, they remain significant even when that variable is controlled. As you can see, this finding—as well as many of the others noted above—raise more questions about the who's and why's of promotion than they answer.

V. APPROACHES TO CAREER DEVELOPMENT

Unlike many private companies, public agencies do not ordinarily provide much tender loving care to employees seeking assistance with their career planning needs. Whereas most large corporations spend a considerable amount of energy preparing their managers to progress up the career ladder (Saari et al., 1988), specially focused efforts of this nature are unusual in government employment. Most of the broad-based surveys that have been conducted on career development practices yield tiny response rates from government jurisdictions (see, e.g., Walker and Gutteridge, 1979).

This apparent inattention is easily understood in the context of several interrelated factors. First, civil service systems are not generally known to follow a human *resources* approach to personnel management. Attractive fringe benefit packages are typical, but employees are not always treated as valuable assets to be nurtured and developed. Compared to much of business and industry, public agencies invest far fewer resources in attracting qualified workers, in orienting them once hired, and in upgrading their skills. Embarrassingly low training budgets most especially attest to the low premium that public employers usually place on employee development. The government spends "about three quarters of one percent of its payroll dollars on civilian training, compared with three to five percent in the most effective private firms" (Volcker Commission, 1990, p. 43).

This problem is exacerbated meanwhile by the crushing budget crisis in contemporary public management. Employee services that might otherwise be provided in prosperous times are viewed as unjustifiable frills when reductions in force lurk as a constant threat. Pronounced limitations on civil service career ladders act as another disincentive to the provision of career development programs. In the midst of declining advancement opportunities, why raise unrealistic expectations among the work force? Moreover, there is undoubtedly a tendency in many jurisdictions to avoid such programs on the grounds that they would merely encourage their employees to pursue occupational opportunities elsewhere. By pointing out career options or by enhancing worker's professional skills, the "brain drain" from government to the private sector might be accelerated.

Despite this grim outlook, career development activities are not completely ignored in government. There have been some success stories, such as the public sector's effectiveness, relatively speaking, in advancing the careers of minorities and women (Roback, 1989).

If current expressions of concern about the state of the public labor force carry any weight whatsoever, then intensified efforts to prepare civil servants for promotions may be in the offing. A common theme in all of the recent calls for civil service reform is that more energy must be spent preparing public managers for career advancement (see, e.g., Hudson Institute, 1988; Volcker Commission, 1990; Illinois Commission on the Future of Public Service, 1991). Addressing training inadequacies and providing civil servants with focused career planning assistance are regarded as relatively inexpensive means of both retaining workers and improving their ability to deal with the pressing demands of modern day public service (Wexley and Latham, 1981). In so doing, government can "enhance the relationship between the individual and the organization" so that both benefit (Crites, 1982, p. 20).

Virtually any form of training is potentially relevant to an employee's promotional potential and thus can legitimately be referred to as career development. Merely being invited to participate in high-level training exercises is often an early indication that a worker is on the promotion fast track (Ford and Noe, 1987). However, our focus here is not on career development activities generally, but on those few proactive efforts that are specifically intended to ease workers up the career ladder. The two that are discussed most frequently in the public management literature are career planning workshops and employee mentoring.

A. Career Planning Workshops

To some extent, all organizations provide their employees with assistance and guidance in the complexities of the promotion process. If used effectively, the performance evaluation process is a forum in which systematic feedback can be given to the worker concerning promotion potential and opportunities. Informal counseling by peers and/or personnel department staff is an even more frequent reality in most settings (Walker and Gutteridge, 1979, p. 11). As an organization's commitment to career development increases, so does the level of formality that is present within assessment and counseling sessions.

A formal counseling strategy that is universally applicable to most employee development objectives is the *career planning workshop*. This is a generic name for a wide array of career planning approaches that share certain common goals (Marsh, 1980). Most strive to enhance the employees' self-awareness, to improve their understanding of organizational processes as they relate to career management, and to identify self-improvement measures that might increase their promotion potential.

Although it isn't appropriate to describe a "model" workshop, since they appear in such extreme diversity, some follow a predictable pattern. The workshops are ordinarily held at the work site, and participation is voluntary. The initial activity usually consists of some type of career/life planning exercise that is intended to get the participants involved in self-assessment. Often using tools borrowed from the organizational development literature, facilitators will have the employees write their own obituaries, develop chronological personal lifelines (which, in terms of their careers, specify where they have been in the past, where they are now, and where they would like to go in the future), or complete questionnaires that otherwise probe self-perceptions and goals (see, e.g., French and Bell, 1984). The next phase generally involves some form of skills assessment. The techniques used in this regard range from the very simple (questionnaires and discussion) to the highly sophisticated (full-blown assessment centers).

Once these diagnostic exercises have been completed, counselors meet individually with participants to discuss career development options. If, for example, an employee's aspirations don't mesh with his or her current skill level, additional training programs may be recommended. In a highly developed personnel management setting, the information gleaned from these workshops may even be used to orchestrate transfers and job rotations that contribute to the workers' career development objectives (see, e.g., Hanson, 1982; Cross, 1983; Gutteridge and Otte, 1983; Nightingale, 1988).

The Internal Revenue Service's program to facilitate employee advancement to managerial positions offers an interesting example of a career development workshop in the public service (Mani, 1992). The workshop, which focuses heavily on self-assessment, is conducted in three sessions held 2 weeks apart. The first 6-hr session is devoted to completing a battery of "canned" appraisal instruments, including the Personal Value Statement (Oliver, 1987), the Strong Interest Inventory, the Myers–Briggs Indicator (Myers and McCaulley, 1988), and various scales intended to measure leadership and personal "style" (Dore, 1973). In subsequent sessions, the employees receive feedback on how to interpret the results of the instruments. When meeting individually with counselors, they have the option to invite their supervisors to join in the discussion. The assumption is that the employee's superior can help "to validate the self-assessment instruments" and to formulate individual development plans (Mani, 1992, pp. 8–9). A final group session is used to discuss the participants' perceptions of how their self-assessments compare to the organization's expectations of good managers. This input is used to decide whether or not to revise their career goals and individual development plans.

Managerial perceptions of the effectiveness of career planning workshops are generally very positive (Hanson, 1982; Gutteridge and Otte, 1983). In addition to the obvious payoffs in worker satisfaction and motivation, the workshops offer managers a chance to bring their employees' activities into conformity with organizational expectations. In other words, career development workshops provide a nonthreatening context in which managers can make recommendations to workers concerning needed alterations in work habits, training requirements, and job mobility.

Given these advantages, some organizations have sought less expensive alternatives to the multiday workshop format. One increasingly popular option is the production of career development *workbooks*. Often used in tandem with an abbreviated workshop program, these books "equip individuals with the questions necessary to guide introspective thinking about job and career objectives, personal strengths and limitations, and development needs" (Walker and Gutteridge, 1979, p. 14). Workbooks typically include self-analysis exercises, readings about the agency and alternative job opportunities, and guidance on how to establish personal development plans. Completion of the books is self-paced and requires individual initiative on the part of the employee (Ford and Lippett, 1977). Upon completion of the books, employees are encouraged to solicit guidance and advice from their supervisors or personnel department staff. Although not as effective as a complete workshop (Gutteridge and Otte, 1983, p. 25), workbooks can be used to stimulate career development activities simultaneously throughout an organization. They save time and coordination costs, but can be fairly expensive to develop since they need to be tailored to the needs of each agency.

B. Mentoring

Mentoring represents a less structured approach to career advancement. A mentor is defined as "someone with whom you had a relationship at any stage of your career in which he or she took a personal interest in your career and helped to promote you and who guided or sponsored you" (Roche, 1979, p. 14). One survey found that over 70% of all public managers benefitted from two or more mentors during their careers (Henderson, 1985).

Much of the literature on mentorship focuses on how mentors assist their proteges' careers. The benefits include sponsorship, exposure, visibility, coaching, protection, counseling, friendship, and challenging assignments (Kram, 1983). Individuals who receive personal attention from mentors report significantly higher levels of career success and satisfaction than employees who are not mentored (Riley and Wrench, 1985; Fagenson, 1989). Extensive mentorship experience also correlates with the absolute number of promotions and with salary growth (Dreher and Ash, 1991). These striking advantages of mentorship are thought to be related to the assistance mentors give their proteges in the area of organizational socialization. They "guide and protect" the subordinate, and "convey the necessary knowledge and information concerning organizational history, goals, language, politics, people and performance" (Chao et al., 1992, p. 622). Clearly, workers who have access to this type of information concerning their organization's "realpolitik" have a marked advantage over those who do not.

Mentor relationships are most common (and probably most helpful) early in one's career, but even older managers report high levels of mentor involvement. Public executives are more likely than their private sector counterparts to acquire external mentors (such as college professors) and to have mentors who are high-level (agency director) managers (Henderson, 1985). Women executives typically have more mentors than their male counterparts, and most of their mentors tend to be female (Henderson, 1985). Given the relative paucity of women in high-level management positions, this connection between mentoring and advancement might logically be interpreted as an obstacle to the promotional opportunities of women (Hale, 1993). Yet, since women report the higher number of mentor relationships, the problem does not appear to be a serious impediment.

Mentorships have no doubt existed since formal organizations first emerged. Mentor–protege relationships tend to spring up spontaneously whenever managers and subordinates "hit it off." Once the many advantages of mentorship become generally recognized, organizations began to try "to formalize these relationships as part of the planned career development of junior managers and professionals" (Chao et al., 1992, p. 620). Whereas informal mentorships are not managed, structured, or technically "recognized" by the organization, formal mentor programs are intentionally designed to fulfill specific career management objectives. For example, some agencies assign mentors to minority managers, or to all junior management personnel, as part of their orientation and socialization efforts. Similarly, junior faculty members are assigned senior professors as mentors under a recent demonstration funded by the Lilly Foundation (Swanson, 1992).

Although having any mentor is better than not having one at all, mentorship relationships engineered through a formal program are far less fruitful than those that arise naturally from personal interaction (Chao et al., 1992). The satisfaction level of workers in informal arrangements is higher, and they report more promotions and salary increases than those in formally sanctioned programs. These differing results are probably attributable to the bad matches that will inevitably result when mentors are assigned and to resentment that probably is generated on both sides of the relationship. The mentor may resent the time and energy demands of the assignment, while the protege may feel uncomfortable (or even demeaned) with the arrangement. Another potential dilemma is that mentoring may result in a mutual dependency relationship under which the employee loses self-sufficiency and the mentor refuses to "let go" (Vertz, 1985).

Despite the superiority of informal mentorship relationships, there is plenty of evidence to suggest that structured programs will be worthwhile in certain situations. One logical application is to the transitional employee who has just been promoted to a managerial position from a technical or professional specialty. These employees typically encounter serious difficulties in switching organizational gears and can likely benefit immensely from the advice of a seasoned veteran. Guidance of any type, either from a "coaching" program (Wolf and Sherwood, 1981) or a formal mentorship assignment, could be invaluable to these neophytes. The major conditions that need to guide the assignments are that participation be strictly voluntary and that the mentorship program be part of a broader career-planning effort (Phillips-Jones, 1983).

VI. THE AFFIRMATIVE ACTION/EEO DILEMMA

Employer discrimination on the grounds of race, color, gender, religion, and national origin is forbidden by Title VII of the 1964 Civil Rights Act and Equal Employment Opportunity Act of 1972 for virtually all personnel decisions, promotion included. Handicapped persons are similarly protected by the Vocational Rehabilitation Act of 1973 and the Americans with Disabilities Act of 1990. The Age Discrimination in Employment Act of 1967, as amended in 1978, prohibits discrimination in employment decisions based on a person's age (for individuals aged 40–70). Through regulatory actions of the U.S. Equal Employment Opportunity Commission and its state affiliates, various executive orders, and a raft of federal and state court decisions, the classes protected in the above statutes may benefit from affirmative actions to select and advance their members in public and private organizations. In addition, veterans of the U.S. Armed Forces receive certain affirmative action–type preferences under the Veterans Preference Act of 1944 and the Vietnam Era Veterans Readjustment Assistance Act of 1974, and related state statutes. Within the broad environment of these statutory, regulatory, and judicial actions all employees are entitled to due process and equal protection of the laws, and designated classes of employees and job applicants are extended special considerations.

With regard to promotions the dilemma for employers is twofold: how to implement techniques for carrying out these laws and edicts, and how to balance longstanding seniority-based promotion systems against equal employment opportunity (EEO) and affirmative action (AA) policies. A wide assortment of techniques has been applied to improve the promotional opportunities of individuals in protected classes. In-service training can be expanded for subject matter knowledge, special skills, and basic skills (e.g., reading and mathematics). Increasingly, public and private employers are picking up workers where the schools have left them off in order to bring them up to the knowledge and skill levels needed. Minority groups, deprived in the educational process for various reasons, typically benefit disproportionately from these types of training and educational opportunities (Stahl, 1983, p. 141). Existing training programs can also be adapted to the special needs of minorities and other protected class individuals. For example, immigrants or Latinos with weak English language capabilities may receive intensive language training. Handicapped persons may be given special accommodations to help them adjust to job requirements (e.g., a reader for the sight-impaired).

Another technique for advancing EEO/AA policies is job redesign. For instance, bridge positions may be erected to provide a path out of occupational ghettos such as basic clerical work and low-status laborer jobs. (A specific example would be technical software training for a clerk-typist.) More broadly, restrictive examination and certification rules can be loosened to expand managers' ability to promote AA candidates. Generally, so long as there is the will and the determination to give protected class candidates every reasonable opportunity to compete for open positions through job-related procedures, a way can be found. And as long as promotion criteria are demonstrably related to the requirements of the position as required by *Griggs v. Duke Power Company* (1971), promotion decisions are likely to be defensible in the courts.

Veterans preference rules have been in place and enforced since World War II in most public jurisdictions. Whether the rationale is a continuing reward for service to one's country or readjustment assistance to veterans moving into the civilian work force (Stahl, 1983, pp. 134–135), the practice is widespread across federal, state, and local employment. Typically, eligible veterans (i.e., those who served during war time or periods of national emergency) are granted an extra 5 points on government selection and promotion exams (with 10 points or absolute preference for disabled veterans). In many jurisdictions wives of disabled veterans and widows of veterans receive similar preference. In some states (e.g., Michigan) preference points must be used within a specified period of time after release from active duty. In others (e.g., Massachusetts) veterans receive preference for life (Hays and Reeves, 1984, p. 209).

Veterans preference has resulted in a very high percentage of former members of the armed forces in government employment, especially at the federal level (44% in 1981; see Stahl, 1983, p. 135). The vast majority of veterans, of course, are white males, so the practice of veterans preference has been controversial and inimical to affirmative action (Elliott, 1986; Tummala, 1987). Nonetheless, veterans preference has been consistently upheld by the U.S. Supreme Court. In *Massachusetts v. Feeney* (1978), the Court ruled that even though the Bay State's preferential scheme had exercised a "severe" impact on employment opportunities for women, it is constitutional because its discriminatory effects are not deliberate. As of the early 1990s, the racial and gender composition of the U.S. Armed Forces had changed dramatically from 15 years before, and the percentage of African-Americans, Latinos, and women has continued to climb in all branches and ranks of the service. In many cases, representation of protected classes exceeded those groups' proportions in the national population. The U.S. military branches are generally believed to be color-blind in their promotional decisions today, and much progress has been made in opening up new opportunities for women. As members of protected classes muster out of the service, they too will benefit from veterans preference. The practice will continue to be controversial, no doubt (e.g., women are still underrepresented and discrimination against homosexuals remained the rule in early 1993), but what was once an occupational disadvantage for blacks and Latinos has now become an advantage.

A more delicate dilemma is how to retain widely accepted seniority-based promotion systems while at the same time advancing qualified women, minorities, and other protected classes who have been subjects of employment-related discrimination in the past. Although one might presume that some day, as members of protected classes increasingly enter and progress in all occupations within public and private organizations, this problem will be self-limiting, it is at least equally likely that there will always be new immigrant groups and other identified classes in the U.S. society that require special employment and promotion considerations.

As noted, unions strenuously seek seniority-based promotion systems and react with vigor to any perceived challenge to them, whether from management (wanting to hire laterally) or from protected classes striving for access to positions historically denied to them. Generally, bona fide seniority systems are protected by Title VII of the Civil Rights Act of 1964. For instance, seniority may be used as a decision rule for layoffs if there is not a history of employment discrimination and if the seniority criterion is applied in a neutral, nondiscriminatory fashion (*Waters v. Wisconsin Steelworkers*, 1974; *Watkins v. Steelworkers Local 2369*, 1975).

Several recent Supreme Court decisions have addressed the nexus between seniority systems and affirmative action plans directly. In *Weber v. Kaiser Aluminum and Steel Corporation and United Steelworkers* (1979), the Court held that race may be considered as a factor in hiring and promotion decisions, even when less senior members of an organization benefit. in *Memphis Firefighters Local No. 1784 v. Stotts* (1984), the Supreme Court dealt with a direct clash between a city's court-ordered affirmative action plan for hiring and promotion of blacks and a union-negotiated seniority system, ruling that the Memphis fire department could legally use seniority as the basis for layoffs even though the dismissals disproportionately affected black firefighters. Thus, bona fide seniority systems take precedence over AA plans when layoffs are required. The *Stotts* decision was later affirmed in *Wygant v. Jackson* (1986).

In other recent cases, the Court has upheld AA plans for promotion. *U.S. v. Paradise* (1987) addressed a court-ordered affirmative action program to remedy the systematic exclusion of blacks from the ranks of Alabama state troopers. The program was not complied with by Alabama authorities despite continuous federal court oversight, leading the Supreme Court to uphold a lower court's order that one qualified black officer had to be promoted for each white officer until appropriate black representation was attained. Finally, *Johnson v. Transportation Agency* (1987) was concerned with a voluntarily adopted AA promotion plan. In this case, a woman who scored slightly lower on a promotion exam, and who was not recommended by the promotion review board, was promoted over a higher rated male into a job category that had never previously contained a female. The Court found that the preferential promotion plan was enforceable since it was aimed at remedying underrepresentation and nonpromotion of women. The Court did not stipulate any specific goals but did require that goals be established. It thus appears that the federal courts will look with favor on preferential promotional policies that are *voluntary* and that are intended to redress *conspicuous imbalances* in the affected job categories. The situation is less clear in regard to nonvoluntary (e.g., judicially imposed) programs and to those implemented in settings where past problems with discrimination are not so painfully evident.

VI. CONCLUSION

As in the case of any personnel action that affects employees' status, compensation, and well-being, promotion decisions provoke conflict and controversy. It has always been so. However, the hard-pressed personnel manager may not have to devote as much attention to the promotions dilemma in the future, albeit for an unfortunate reason. As the growth of government at all levels has tapered off and even been reversed through layoffs, attrition, and downsizing, and as public services are increasingly contracted out to private and nonprofit providers, the opportunities for promotion in governmental organizations have diminished. Compounding the problem is the anticipated progression of baby boomers up the organizational hierarchy even as promotional opportunities diminish. The glut created by this population bulge will also make it difficult for younger workers, who also happen to be more female and minority than their predecessors, to climb organizational ladders. Career plateaus may be reached more quickly and with greater frustration than in the recent past.

The challenge to the personnelist during this period of limited or no growth in government is to find nonpromotional incentives and inducements to keep workers reasonably satisfied and to prevent costly turnover among the most mobile employees. Flexible pay, hours, and benefits can help, as can job redesign and the addition of new career tracks. Meanwhile, training and development opportunities can raise the knowledge, skills, and abilities of incumbent employees and prepare them for promotion openings when they do appear.

For researchers, the challenge is essentially the same as that confronting personnel practitioners. Both groups need to emphasize innovation and experimentation. The primary focus of future research, however, must be on the practical consequences of varying approaches to promotion and career development. Despite the volumes that have been written on such topics as the inside promotion/external recruitment debate, for example, the research record contains a stunning lack of focus on the true implications and consequences of one promotion format over the other. Similar gaps exist throughout the literature on promotion (with the exception of empirical analyses of various evaluation methodologies). Topics that will almost certainly need to be explored more fully include the human costs of limited career mobility, the productivity advantages (if any) of rank-in-person career systems, and the impact of personnel system decentralization on who gets promoted. Hopefully, as these blanks are filled in through empirical research, personnelists will have a much better understanding of the probable effects of various career system design options. Until that time, most of the innovation in this area of personnel management will continue to be driven by intuition and guesswork.

REFERENCES

Abraham, K., and Medoff, J. (1985). Length of service and promotions in union and nonunion work groups, *Ind. Labor Rel. Rev., 39* (April): 408–420.

Allan, P. (1977). Career patterns of top executives in New York City government, *Public Personnel Rev., 33*: 114–117.

Anderson, J., Milkovich, G., and Tsui, A. (1981). A model of intra-organizational mobility, *Acad. Manage. Rev., 6* (4): 529–538.

Bacon, A. (1980). A note on selecting the appropriate pension funding method for localities, *Public Admin. Rev., 40* (May-June): 265–269.

Barnett, W., and Miner, A. (1992). Standing on the shoulders of others: career interdependence in job mobility, *Admin. Sci. Q., 37* (June): 262–281.

Bernardin, H., and Beatty, R. (1987). Can subordinate appraisals enhance managerial productivity? *Sloan Manage. Rev., 28* (Summer): 63–73.

Bowman, J. (1986). Japanese management: personnel policies in the public sector, *Public Personnel Manage., 15* (spring): 197–217.

Bureau of National Affairs (1983). Basic patterns in seniority provisions, *Daily Labor Rep. (March 25)*: E1–E2.

Burke, R. (1972). Why performance appraisals fail, *Personnel Admin.* (May–June): 32–40.

Byrne, D. (1971). *The Attraction Paradigm*, Academic Press, New York.

Cascio, W., and Silbey, V. (1979). Utility of assessment center as a selection device, *J. App. Psychol., 64*: 107–118.

Cederblom, D. (1991). Promotability ratings: an underused promotion method for public safety organizations, *Public Personnel Manage., 20* (Spring): 27–34.

Chao, G., Walz, P., and Gardner, P. (1992). Formal and informal mentorships: a comparison of mentoring functions and contrast with nonmentored counterparts, *Personnel Psychol., 45* (Autumn): 619–636.

Cox, T., and Nkomo, S. (1986). Differential performance appraisal criteria: a field study of black and white managers, *Group Organiz. Stud., 11*: 101–119.

Cox, T., and S. Nkomo (1992). Candidate age as a factor in promotability ratings, *Public Personnel Manage., 21* (Summer): 197–210.

Cox, W., and Brunelli, S. (1992). America's protected class, *The State Factor, 18* (Feb.): 1–31.

Crites, J. (1982). Testing for career adjustment and development, *Train. Dev. J.,* (Feb.): 20–28.

Cross, L. (1983). Career management development: a system that gets results, *Train. Dev. J.* (Feb.): 54–63.

Dickson, E., Hovey, H., and Peterson, G. (1980). *Public Employee Compensation: A Twelve City Comparison*, Urban Institute, Washington, DC.

DiLauro, T. (1979). Training needs assessment: current practices and new dimensions, *Public Personnel Manage.* (Nov.-Dec.): 350–359.

Dore, R. (1973). LEAD (Leadership: employee-orientation and differentiation questionnaire), *The 1973 Annual Handbook for Group Facilitators* (J. Jones and J. Pfeiffer, eds.), University Associates, San Diego, Ca.

Dreher, F., and Ash, R. (1990). A comparative study of mentoring among men and women in managerial, professional, and technical positions, *J. App. Psychol., 75*: 539–546.

Drucker, Peter F. (1985). How to make people decisions, *Management* (Nov.): 95–99.

Dulewicz, V. (1991). Improving assessment centres, *Personnel Manage.* (June): 50–55.

Eisenberg, T. (1980). An examination of assessment center results and peer ratings, *The Police Chief:* 46–47.

Elliott, R. (1986). The fairness of veterans preferences in a state merit system: the employee's view, *Public Personnel Manage., 15* (Fall): 311–323.

Fagenson, E. (1989). The mentor advantage: perceived career/job experiences of proteges versus nonproteges, *J. Organiz. Behav., 10*: 309–320.

Ford, F., and Lippett, G. (1977). *A Life Planning Workbook*, University Associates, La Jolla, Ca.

Ford, J., and Noe, R. (1987). Self-assessed training needs: the effects of attitudes toward training, managerial level, and function, *Personnel Psychol., 40*: 39–53.

Frank, F., Bracken, D., and Struth, M. (1988). Beyond assessment centers, *Train. Dev. J. (March)*: 65–67.

Frank, F., and Preston, J. (1982). The validity of assessment center approach and related issues, *Personnel Admin., 27* (June): 87–95.

Frankel, L., and Pigeion, C. (1975). Municipal managers and chief administrative officers: a statistical profile, *Urban Data Service Rep., 7* (Feb.): 1–17.

French, W., and Bell, R. (1984). *Organizational Development*, Prentice Hall, Englewood Cliffs, NJ.

Gaugler, B., Rosenthal, D., Thornton, G., and Bentson, C. (1987). Meta-analysis of assessment center validity, *J. Appl. Psychol., 72* (3): 493–511.

George, D., and Smith, M. (1990). An empirical comparison of self-assessment and organizational assessment in personnel selection, *Public Personnel Manage., 19* (Summer): 175–190.

Goddard, R. (1990). Lateral moves enhance careers, *Human Resource Mag., 35* (Dec.): 69–74.

Golembiewski, R., and Cohen, M. (1970). *People in Public Service*, Peacock, Itasca, Il.

Grant, P., and Holmes, J. (1991). Putting professionals and managers on equal footing, *Personnel, 68* (July): 17–18.

Griggs v. Duke Power Company (1971). 401 U.S. 424.

Gutteridge, T., and Otte, F. (1983). Organizational career development: what's going on out there? *Train. Dev. J. (Feb.)*: 22–26.

Guy, M. (1993). *Women and Men of the States*, M.E. Sharpe, Armonk, N.Y.

Haas, P., and Wright, D. (1987). The changing profile of state administrators, *J. State Gvmt, 60* (Nov.–Dec.): 270–278.

Halaby, C. (1978). Bureaucratic promotion criteria, *Admin. Sci. Q., 23* (Sept.): 466–484.

Hale, M. (1993). Mentoring, *Women and Men of the States* (M. Guy, ed.), M.E. Sharpe, Armonk, New York, pp. 89–108.

Hall, D. (1976). *Careers in Organizations*, Goodyear, Santa Monica, Ca.

Hanson, M. (1982). Career/life planning workshops as career services in organizations: are they working? *Train. Dev. J. (Feb.)*: 58–63.

Harris, M., and Schaubroeck, J. (1988). A meta-analysis of self-supervisor, self-peer, and peer-supervisory ratings, *Personnel Psychol. 41*: 43–62.

Harvard Business Review (1988). Worldwide executive mobility, *Harvard Business Rev., 66* (July–August): 105–123.

Hays, S., and Kearney R. (1992). State personnel directors and the dilemmas of workforce 2000: a survey, *Public Admin. Rev., 52* (July-August): 380–388.

Hays, S., and Reeves, T. Z. (1984). *Personnel Management in the Public Sector*, Allyn and Bacon, Boston.

Hegarty, W. (1974). Using subordinate ratings to elicit behavioral changes in supervisors, *J. Appl. Psychol., 59*: 764–766.

Henderson, D. (1985). Enlightened mentoring: a characteristic of public management professionalism, *Public Admin. Rev., 45* (Nov.–Dec.): 857–863.

Heneman, H., Schwab, D., Fossum, J., and Dyer, L. (1989). *Personnel/Human Resource Management*, Irwin, Homewood, Il.

Howard, A. (1974). An assessment of assessment centers, *Acad. Manage. J. (March)*: 115–134.

Hudson Institute (1988). *Civil Service 2000*, U.S. Office of Personnel Management Career Entry Group, Washington, DC.

Illinois Commission on the Future of Public Service (1991). *Excellence in Public Service: Illinois' Challenge for the 90s*, Chicago Community Trust, Government Assistance Project.

International Personnel Managers Association (1973). *Guidelines for Drafting a Public Personnel Administration Law*, Chicago.

Jackson, S., Brett, J., Sessa, V., Cooper, D., Julin, J., and Peyronnin, K. (1991). Some differences make a difference: individual dissimilarity and group heterogeneity as correlates of recruitment, promotions and turnover, *J. Appl. Psychol., 76*: 675–689.

Johnson v. Transportation Agency, Santa Clara, California (1987). 55 U.S.L.W. 4379.

Kane, J., and Lawler, E. (1978). Methods of peer assessment, *Psychol. Bull. 85*: 555–586.

Kanter, R. (1977). *Men and Women of the Corporation*, Basic Books, New York.

Kearney, R. (1992). *Labor Relations in the Public Sector*, Marcel Dekker, New York.

Kerr, J. and Slocum, J. (1987). Managing corporate culture through reward systems, *Acad. Manage. Exec., 1*: 99–108.

Klimoski, R., Brickner, M. (1987). Why do assessment centers work: the puzzle of assessment center validity, *Personnel Psychol. 40*: 243–260.

Klimoski, R., and Strickland, W. (1977). Assessment center: valid or merely prescient, *Personnel Psychol. 30*: 353–361.

Kram, K. (1983). Phases of the mentor relationship, *Acad. Manage. J., 26*: 608–625.

Leich, H. (1960). Rank in man or job? Both! *Public Admin. Rev., 20* (Spring): 92–99.

Lewis, G. (1986). Gender and promotions, *J. Human Resources, 21*: 406–419.

Lorenzo, R. (1984). Effects of assessorship on managers' proficiency in acquiring, evaluating, and communicating information about people, *Personnel Psychol., 37*: 617–634.

Love, K. (1981). Accurate evaluation of police officer performance through the judgment of fellow officers: fact or fiction? *J. Police Sci. Admin., 9*: 143–148.

Lowry, P. (1988). The assessment center: pooling scores or arithmetic decision rule? *Public Personnel Manage. 17* (Spring): 63–71.

Lowry, P. (1991). The assessment center: reducing interassessor influence, *Public Personnel Manage., 29* (Spring): 19–26.

Lowry, P. (1992). The assessment center: effects of varying consensus procedures, *Public Personnel Manage., 21* (Summer): 171–183.

McEvoy, G., and Beatty, R. (1989). Assessment centers and subordinate appraisals of managers: a seven-year examination of predictive validity, *Personnel Psychol., 42*: 37–52.

Mabe, P., and West, S. (1982). Validity of self-evaluation of ability: a review and meta-analysis, *J. Appl. Psychol. 67*: 280–296.

Mani, B. (1992). Developing quality leadership: preparing to meet and to match organizations' and employees' needs for effective leadership skills, paper presented at the Southern Political Science Association Annual Meeting, Atlanta, Nov. 6, 1992.

Maloney, P., and Hinrich, J. (1959). A new tool for supervisory self-development, *Personnel, 36* (July): 46–53.

Maranto, C., Rogers, R. (1984). Does work experience increase productivity? A test of the on-the-job training hypothesis, *J. Human Resources, 19*: 341–357.

March, M. (1983). Retirement benefits for public employees, *Public Personnel Administration: Problems and Prospects*, (S. Hays and R. Kearney, eds.), Prentice-Hall, Englewood Cliffs, NJ, pp. 153–172.

Markus, H., and Wurf, E. (1987). The dynamic self-concept, *Annu. Rev. Psychol. 38*: 299–337.

Marsh, P. (1980). The career development workshop, *Public Personnel Managment*, (M. Levine, ed.), Brighton, Salt Lake City, pp. 250–262.

Massachusetts v. Feeny (1978). 422 U.S. 256.

Memphis Firefighters Local Union No., 1784 v. Stotts (1984). 467 U.S. 561.

Mills, D. Q. (1985). Seniority versus ability in promotion decisions, *Ind. Labor Rel. Rev., 38* (April): 421–426.

Mintzberg, H. (1979). *The Structuring of Organizations*, Prentice-Hall, Englewood Cliffs, NJ.

Mosher, F. (1984). *Democracy and the Public Service*, Oxford University Press, New York.

Mowday, R., Porter, L., and Steers, R. (1982). *Employee–Orientation Linkages: The Psychology of Commitment, Absenteeism, and Turnover*, Academic Press, New York.

Mowday, R., Steers, R., and Porter, L. (1979). The measurement of organizational commitment, *J. Voc. Behav., 14*: 224–247.

Mount, M. (1984). Psychometric properties of subordinate ratings of managerial performance, *Personnel Psychol. 37* (Winter): 687–701.

Myers, I., and McCaulley, M. (1988). *Manual: A Guide to the Development and Use of the Myers-Briggs Type Indicator*, Consulting Psychologists Press, Palo Alto, CA.

Nightingale, H. (1988). Battle bureaucracy with temporary transfers, *Harvard Business Rev., 66* (July–August): 124–126.

Oliver, J. (1987). *The Personal Value Statement: An Experiential Learning Instrument*, University Associates, San Diego.

Peason, W. (1984). Organizational mobility among state executives, *Rev. Public Personnel Admin., 5* (Fall): 57–67.

Pergl, G. Plateau prevention, *Gvmt Exec. (Jan.)*: 40–43.

Phillips-Jones, L. (1983). Establishing a formalized mentoring program, *Train. Dev. J. (Feb.)*: 38–42.

Rich, W. (1984). Career paths for public managers: upward but narrow, *Personnel, 61* (July-August): 24–32.

Riley, S., and Wrench, D. (1985). Mentoring among women lawyers, *J. App. Social Psychol., 15*: 374–386.

Roback, T. (1989). Personnel research perspectives on human resource management and development, *Public Personnel Manage., 18* (Summer): 138–161.

Roche, G. (1979). Much ado about mentors, *Harvard Business Rev., 57* (Jan.–Feb.): 14–28.

Rosow, J. (1976). Public sector pay and benefits, *Public Admin. Rev., 36* (Sept.–Oct.): 538–543.

Saari, L., Johnson, T., McLaughlin, S., and Zimmerle, D. (1988). A survey of management training and education practices in U.S. companies, *Personnel Psychol., 41* (Winter): 731–743.

Schmitt, N., Gooding, R., Noe, R., and Kirsch, M. (1984). Meta-analysis of validity studies published between 1964 and 1982, *Personnel Psychol., 37*: 307–422.

Schnell, J. (1987). An ordered choice model of promotion rules, *J. Labor Research., 8* (Spring): 159–178.

Sheldon, M. (1971). Investments and involvements as mechanisms producing commitment to the organization, *Admin. Sci. Q., 16*: 143–150.

Shoop, T. (1992). Class action, *Gvmt Exec., 24* (Feb.): 16–18.

Solomon, C. (1992). The loyalty factor, *Personnel J., 71* (Sept.): 62–68.

Stahl, O. G. (1983). *Public Personnel Administration*, Harper and Row, New York.

Stahl, O. G. (1990). A retrospective and prospective. The moral dimension, *Public Personnel Administration: Problems and Prospects*, (S. Hays and R. Kearney, eds.), Prentice-Hall, Englewood Cliffs, NJ, pp. 308–321.

Steers, R. (1977). *Organizational Effectiveness: A Behavioral View*, Goodyear, Santa Monica, CA.

Stewart, L., and Gudykunst, W. (1982). Differential factors influencing the hierarchial level and number of promotions of males and females within an organization, *Acad. Manage. J., 25* (3): 586–597.

Stumpf, S., and Hartman, K. (1984). Individual exploration to organizational commitment or withdrawal, *Acad. Manage. J., 27*: 308–329.

Swanson, M. (1992). Junior, senior faculty paired in mentoring program, *USC Times*, September 25.

Tummala, K. (1987). Veteran's preference in the state of Montana: equal employment or affirmative action? *Public Personnel Manage., 16* (Summer): 159–171.

U.S. General Accounting Office (1984). *An Assessment of SES Performance Appraisal Systems*, Washington, DC, (May).

U.S. General Accounting Office (1987). *Blue Collar Workers: Appraisal Systems Are in Place, But Basic Refinements Are Needed*, Washington, DC (June).

U.S. General Accounting Office (1990). *Recruitment and Retention*, Washington, DC (Sept.).

U.S. General Accounting Office (1992). *Senior Executive Service: Opinions About the Federal Work Environment*, Washington, DC (May).

U.S. Merit Systems Protection Board (1987). *Federal Personnel Policies and Practices: Perspectives From the Workplace*, Washington, DC (Dec.).

U.S. Merit Systems Protection Board (1989). *The Senior Executive Service: Views of Former Federal Executives*, Washington, DC (Oct.).

U.S. Office of Personnel Management (1979). *Manager's Handbook*, Washington, DC (Nov.).

United States v. Phillip Paradise (1987). 107 S.Ct. 1053.

Van Riper, P. (1958). *History of the United States Civil Service*, Peterson, Evanston, IL.

Vertz, L. (1985). Women, occupational advancement, and mentoring: an analysis of one public organization, *Public Admin. Rev., 45* (May–June): 415–422.

Volcker Commission (1990). *Leadership for America: Rebuilding the Public Service*, D.C. Heath, Lexington, MA.

Walker, J., and Gutteridge, T. (1979). *Career Planning Practices*, American Management Association, New York.

Waters v. Wisconsin Steelworks (1974). 502 F.2d. 1309 CA-7.

Watkins v. Steelworkers Local 2369 (1975). 516 F.2d. 41 CA-5.

Weber v. Kaiser Aluminum and Steel Corporation and United Steelworkers Union (1979). 443 U.S. 193.

Weiner, Y., and Vardi, Y. (1980). Relationship between organization, career commitments, and outcomes: an integrative approach, *Organiz. Behav. Human Perf., 26*: 81–96.

Weitz, J. (1958). Selecting supervisors with peer ratings, *Personnel Psychology, 11* (Winter): 25–35.

Wexley, K., and Latham, G. (1981). *Developing and Training Human Resources in Organizations*, Scott Foresman, Glenview, IL.

Wisconsin Employment Relations Study Commission (1977). *Wisconsin Civil Service*, Department of Administration, Madison.

Wolf, J. (1983). Career plateauing in the public service: baby boom and employment bust, *Public Admin. Rev., 43* (March–April): 160–165.

Wolf, J., and Sherwood, F. (1981). Coaching: supporting public executives on the job, *Public Admin. Rev., 41* (Jan.–Feb.): 73–76.

Wright, D., Wagner, M., and McAnaw, R. (1977). State administrators: their changing characteristics, *State Gvmt., 50*: 152–159.

Wygant v. Jackson Board of Education (1986). 476 U.S. 267.

22

Turnover of Personnel

PETER W. HOM   Arizona State University, Tempe, Arizona

RODGER W. GRIFFETH   Georgia State University, Atlanta, Georgia

PAULA PHILLIPS CARSON   University of Southwestern Louisiana, Lafayette, Louisiana

This chapter examines the phenomenon of employee turnover, namely, the *voluntary cessation of organizational membership by an individual who receives monetary compensation for participation* (Mobley, 1982). Given this definition, our examination thus excludes job transfers and involuntary terminations, such as dismissals, retirements, layoffs, and death. While significant in their own right, these forms of organizational withdrawal fall outside the traditional purview of turnover research. Notwithstanding this narrow definition, turnover has attracted well over 1000 studies this century (Steers and Mowday, 1981). Employers worry about resignations because of their financial and nonfinancial costs (Cascio, 1991), while organizational scientists view turnover as a significant behavioral manifestation of job alienation or dissatisfaction (Hulin, 1991). To structure this literature review, we divide this chapter into four primary sections: (1) review of empirical studies of turnover causes; (2) examination of turnover consequences; (3) synthesis of theoretical models of turnover; and (4) descriptions of methods to control turnover.

I. TURNOVER CAUSES AND CORRELATES

Many reviews of turnover antecedents and correlates have appeared over the years (Mobley, 1982; Mobley et al., 1979; Muchinsky and Tuttle, 1979; Porter and Steers, 1973; Price, 1977; Steers and Mowday, 1981). This chapter updates those early reviews and refines them using a technique known as meta-analysis. Meta-analysis is superior to traditional reviews, wherein a reviewer draws conclusions from subjective analysis of empirical findings (Hunter and Schmidt, 1990). For example, a narrative reviewer may conclude that job satisfaction is unrelated to turnover because their correlations fluctuate across different samples. Some studies find positive correlations, others negative, and still others nonsignificant ones. This interpretation may be erroneous because conflicting findings may be artifactual. Statistical artifacts, such as sampling error and uneven instrument reliabilities across studies, may underlie apparently disparate correlations. Moreover, narrative reviews overlook the paltry sample sizes of many empirical findings. Small samples weaken statistical power, undermining the statistical significance of variable relationships (Hunter and Schmidt, 1990).

Instead of informal inspection, meta-analysis statistically summarizes measures of variable association from different studies. Unlike qualitative reviews, this procedure more precisely estimates the "true" relationship between two variables (and their generality) by correcting for methodological artifacts. Typically, meta-analysis averages correlations from different studies (weighing by their sample sizes) to correct for sampling error and then adjusts that mean correlation for random measurement errors (cf. Hunter and Schmidt, 1990). Importantly, this "population" correlation discloses *strength* of variable relationship, whereas narrative reviews seek to establish whether or not that relationship exists. Finally, meta-analysis estimates generality of the relationship, determining whether between-study variability in correlations is real or illusory. If genuine, other situational or population variables (i.e., moderators) condition this relationship. In other words, the association between two variables is not constant but changes across different settings or populations.

Recognizing these advantages, scholars have increasingly applied meta-analyses to accumulate turnover findings (Carsten and Spector, 1987; Cotton and Tuttle, 1986; Hom et al., 1992a; Mathieu and Zajac, 1990; McEvoy and Cascio, 1985, 1987; Premack and Wanous, 1985; Steel and Griffeth, 1989; Steel et al., 1990a; Steel and Ovalle, 1984; Tett and Meyer, 1992; Wanous et al., 1992; Williams and Livingstone, 1989). Nevertheless, these meta-analyses investigated a few select turnover determinants and correlates, such as perceived alternatives (Steel and Griffeth, 1989) or organizational commitment (Mathieu and Zajac, 1990). Only Cotton and Tuttle (1986) comprehensively reviewed a broad array of turnover causes, although they only assessed significance of their relationships to turnover. In this chapter, we update Cotton and Tuttle's review by including studies undertaken since their meta-analysis and extend their analysis by measuring magnitude of predictor–quit associations.

A. Meta-analytical Procedure

First, we reviewed the research literature, using computerized sources and a manual search of leading journals in organizational behavior, to uncover correlations between turnover and its antecedents (and sample sizes and reliability estimates). [If other association indices were available, we transformed those statistics into correlations using Schwarzer's (1989) meta-analysis program.] Moreover, we relied on previous turnover meta-analyses and narrative reviews to identify relevant studies. Our review excluded studies on aggregate quit rates because our focus was to explain individual turnover. Turnover rates constitute a different construct than individual turnover, even though quit rates are computed by aggregating individual quits within organizations or departments (Hulin et al., 1985). That is, the meaning of the turnover construct changes across different levels of aggregation (Rousseau, 1985; Terborg and Lee, 1984). Attesting to shifting meaning, job vacancy rates correlate differently with aggregate and individual quits (Hulin et al., 1985; Steel and Griffeth, 1989). Finally, we classified turnover antecedents using Mathieu and Zajac's (1990) taxonomy.

Following Hunter et al.'s (1982) procedure, we corrected correlations (and their variances) for sampling and measurement errors, the foremost sources of spurious between-study variation (Premack and Hunter, 1987). To correct sampling error, we first averaged correlations between turnover and a given predictor, weighing by sample size. Next, we adjusted this correlation for unreliability by inserting the predictor's reliability coefficient (averaged across different samples) into the classic attenuation correction formula (Schmidt and Hunter, 1990, p. 119). [We did not correct turnover for dichotomy or base rate given the ongoing controversy surrounding such corrections (Bass and Ager, 1991; Steel et al., 1990b; Williams, 1990).]

Three procedures tested the "true" generality of each predictor–quit correlation. Specifically, these tests estimated *nonartifactual* variation of this correlation, detecting whether or not (unknown) moderators condition this correlation. One moderator test assessed the degree to which statistical artifacts explain variance in observed correlations (Hunter and Schmidt, 1990). Because our meta-analysis only corrected for sampling error and unreliability, we defined 60% (or more) artifactual contribution as signifying no moderators (cf. Hom et al., 1992; Mathieu and Zajac, 1990). Second, a χ^2 test revealed whether between-study variance in observed correlations was solely attributable to sampling error (cf. Wanous et al., 1992). Third, we computed 95% credibility intervals (using variances fully corrected for experimental artifacts) around "true" population correlations (Whitener, 1990). Credibility intervals including zero signal moderators and suggest correlations can assume signs opposite to that of the population correlation. If these tests reject an invariant relationship, then the population estimate constitutes an average of different correlations from distinct subpopulations (Hunter and Schmidt, 1990). To specify these subpopulations, a meta-analytical researcher would pursue additional moderator analyses (cf. Hom et al., 1992). Such analyses, however, are beyond the scope of this chapter, whose primary objective is a basic overview of turnover research.

Tables 1 and 2 show correlations between causal antecedents and voluntary quits, reporting the number of samples and overall sample size on which they were based and moderator tests of their between-sample stability. The population correlation (r_{pop}) represents the best measure of the relationship between turnover and a determinant because this index was derived from double corrections for measurement and sampling errors. At the same time, the three moderator tests indicate whether or not this population correlation generalizes across different settings, populations, or circumstances. On the whole, moderator findings tempered all generalizations, showing that most correlations change across settings or populations. Specifically, most indices of the contribution of artifactual variance to observed variance fell below the 60% threshold value, suggesting that statistical artifacts did not fully account for between-study variation in correlations. Moreover, most credibility intervals included zero and most χ^2 tests were significant (signifying that sampling error did not entirely underlie between-study variance). Given these caveats, we nevertheless proceeded with some tentative conclusions (see Table 1).

Table 1 Meta-analysis of Turnover Predictors: Individual Determinants

Predictor	k	N	r_{obs}	r_{cor}	V_{pop}	%	95% Credibility interval	χ^2
Cognitive ability	2	1879	−0.09	−0.09	0.0035	30.19	−0.19 to 0.01	6.62*
Education	29	8915	0.07	0.07	0.0030	52.21	−0.04 to 0.17	55.54*
Training	4	3394	−0.07	−0.08	0.0074	15.69	−0.24 to 0.09	25.49*
Job performance	28	6556	−0.17	−0.17	0.0235	14.58	−0.47 to 0.13	192.09*
Sex	15	6451	−0.08	−0.08	0.0126	15.39	−0.30 to 0.14	97.46*
Marital status	23	7599	0.01	0.01	0.0076	28.48	−0.16 to 0.18	80.76*
Kinship responsibilities	9	5354	−0.10	−0.10	0.0053	26.90	−0.25 to 0.04	33.46*
Relatives	2	440	0.22	0.22	0.0000	100	0.22 to 0.22	1.75
Children	4	727	−0.14	−0.14	0.0000	100	−0.14 to −0.14	0.63
Tenure	38	12954	−0.13	−0.14	0.0281	10.60	−0.47 to 0.19	358.59*
Weighted application blanks	6	1329	0.31	0.33	0.0704	5.84	−0.19 to .85	102.73*

*$p < .05$.

Note: k = the number of samples; N = total number of individuals in the k samples; r_{obs} = mean observed correlation; r_{cor} = weighted correlation corrected for attenuation; V_{pop} = population variance; and % = percentage of variance due to statistical artifacts. Marital status was coded as married = low score; single = high score. Sex was coded as male = low score; female = high score.

1. Personal Characteristics

Most personal attributes modestly predicted resignations, albeit their predictive strength varied. In particular, intelligent, trained, and effective employees remained employed compared with their less competent or trained counterparts. Indeed, the inverse correlation between performance and exits contradicts conventional views that more capable personnel more readily resign—presumably because they have more employment options (cf. Jackofsky, 1984). While disputing this view, moderator tests nonetheless suggest positive performance–quit correlations may emerge under some conditions (McEvoy and Cascio, 1987). For example, Allison [1974; cited in Price (1977)] and Schwab (1991) discovered that productive scholars more often left research universities. Unlike other occupations, scholarly accomplishments of academicians (i.e., publications) are objectively measured and externally visible to other employers. Given credible, objective performance records, accomplished scholars can more easily resign for other employment, yielding a positive performance–quit relationship.

Contrary to popular stereotypes, women did not quit their jobs more readily than men; rather, they were more loyal employees ($r = -0.08$). Still, kinship responsibility [a complex measure of family obligations based on number of children, their age, and marital status (Blegen et al., 1988)] and number of children improved retention, while number of relatives in the community accelerated organizational exits. Not surprisingly, employees with long company tenure quit less often than short-tenure employees [possibly reflecting senior personnel's greater long-term job investments (Rusbult and Farrell, 1983)]. Finally, the weighted application blank correctly identified unstable personnel. Like an employment test, this procedure scores a job applicant's responses to questions on an application blank based on a scoring key that empirically differentiates between short- and long-term employees (Cascio, 1976). (We will return to this methodology later.)

2. Position Attributes

Positional qualities (i.e., job characteristics, leadership, coworker relations, compensation, promotions, and role states) also predicted dissolution of organizational membership (see Table 2). Generally speaking, poor positional attributes motivated turnover, albeit moderator tests indicate that unfavorable conditions do not invariably induce exits. Job scope (overall complexity and challenge of work duties), leader–member exchange (close rapport between superior and subordinate), and role clarity most reduced resignations. Surprisingly, pay and pay satisfaction modestly decreased terminations, although routine omission of other compensation forms—notably, fringe benefits and incentive pay (Heneman, 1985; Price and Mueller, 1981, 1986)—surely understated compensation's impact.

3. Company Climate

Organizational characteristics minimally affected quits, possibly reflecting their remote causal status (cf. Mobley et al., 1979; Price and Mueller, 1981, 1986). Predictably, centralization escalated turnover. Even so, company attributes may sizably influence turnover rates while scarcely affecting individual quits (cf. Alexander, 1988; Price, 1977; Terborg and Lee, 1984). As noted earlier, causal determinants may differentially affect aggregate and individual quits because the turnover construct may shift meaning across different levels of aggregation (Rousseau, 1985).

4. Job Satisfaction

Consistent with most theoretical perspectives, job dissatisfaction foreshadowed resignations (Mobley, 1977; Porter and Steers, 1973; Price and Mueller, 1986; Steers and Mowday, 1981). Dissatisfied employees [presumably reacting to impoverished work conditions (cf. Mobley et al., 1979; Price and Mueller, 1986)] more readily abandoned present employment. Moreover, met expectations—a leading source of job satisfaction, according to prevailing thinking (Porter and

Table 2 Meta-analysis of Turnover Predictors: Situational Determinants

Predictor	k	N	r_{obs}	r_{cor}	V_{pop}	%	95% Credibility interval	χ^2
Job characteristics								
Job scope	3	583	−0.30	−0.33	0.0000	100	−0.33 to −0.33	2.17
Routine	6	3707	0.08	0.09	0.0011	64.69	0.03 to .016	9.35
Work satisfaction	6	2299	−0.13	−0.14	0.0347	7.72	−0.50 to 0.23	77.72*
Leadership								
Participation	5	1584	−0.08	−0.08	0.0031	53.50	−0.19 to 0.03	9.35
Leader–member exchange	3	161	−0.21	−0.23	0.0167	55.65	−0.48 to 0.03	5.39
Supervisory satisfaction	14	3002	−0.10	−0.10	0.0018	74.53	−0.19 to −0.02	18.82
Leader communication	8	5185	−0.11	−0.11	0.0020	45.71	−0.20 to −0.03	17.54*
Coworker relations								
Cohesion	3	412	−0.12	−0.14	0.0000	100	−0.14 to −0.14	1.90
Integration	4	3394	−0.08	−0.10	0.0042	29.29	−0.22 to 0.03	13.95*
Coworker satisfaction	11	1313	−0.10	−0.10	0.0033	74.19	−0.22 to 0.01	14.84
Compensation								
Salary	7	3763	−0.06	−0.06	0.0025	42.59	−0.16 to 0.04	16.44*
Pay satisfaction	16	4094	−0.03	−0.04	0.0071	41.69	−0.20 to 0.13	38.43*
Distributive justice	7	3836	−0.06	−0.07	0.0010	68.99	−0.13 to −0.01	10.17
Reward equity	2	274	−0.02	−0.02	0.0154	40.03	−0.26 to 0.22	5.00*
Promotional Opportunity	8	4942	−0.08	−0.09	0.0406	4.36	−0.48 to 0.31	185.09
Role States								
Role Clarity	2	259	−0.20	−0.24	0.0000	100	−0.24 to −0.24	0.03
Role Overload	3	2627	0.10	0.11	0.0000	100	0.11 to 0.11	0.27
Company Climate								
Centralization	4	2506	0.08	0.09	0.0022	46.08	0.00 to 0.18	8.69*
Supportiveness	2	256	0.02	0.02	0.0052	62.47	−0.12 to 0.16	3.20
Job Satisfaction								
Job Satisfaction	66	23421	−0.18	−0.19	0.0133	19.04	−0.42 to 0.03	352.07*
Met Expectations	8	1435	−0.12	−0.13	0.0086	41.94	−0.31 to 0.05	19.13*
Alternative Employment								
Attraction & Availability	27	10447	0.10	0.11	0.0084	28.48	−0.07 to 0.29	96.01*
Comparison with Job	7	1635	0.24	0.26	0.0092	33.44	0.08 to 0.45	21.47*

*$p < .05$.

Note: k = the number of samples; N = total number of individuals in the k samples; r_{obs} = mean observed correlation; r_{cor} = weighted correlation corrected for attenuation; V_{pop} = population variance; and % = percentage of variance due to statistical artifacts.

Steers, 1973; Wanous, 1980; Wanous et al., 1992)—also predicted turnover. Put differently, employees quit jobs if their work experiences disconfirm preentry expectations about their jobs, while they remained employed if those experiences confirmed initial expectations.

5. Alternative Employment

Organizational scientists and labor economists universally proclaim that employment elsewhere stimulates job changes (Forrest et al., 1977; Gerhart, 1990; Mobley, 1977; Mobley et al., 1979; Price and Mueller, 1986). Despite its theoretical centrality, our meta-analysis [and other reviews (Hulin et al., 1985; Steel and Griffeth, 1979)] found that perceived attraction and availability of other jobs modestly promoted individual quits. These findings also conflict with labor economic studies, which find strong relations between unemployment rates and quit rates (Mobley, 1982; Hulin et al., 1985). Here again, these discrepancies underscore that individual quits and quit rates constitute different constructs and that extrapolating labor–economic findings to explain *individual* turnover risks the ecological fallacy (Hulin et al., 1985; Rousseau, 1985).

6. Withdrawal Cognitions

A fundamental tenet of modern turnover theories is that decisions to withdraw from the workplace best portend subsequent withdrawal (Mobley, 1977; Price and Mueller, 1986; Rusbult and Farrell, 1983; Steers and Mowday, 1981). The present meta-analysis corroborated this supposition, revealing that intentions to seek alternatives or to quit best predicted job exits (cf. Steel and Ovalle, 1984) (see Table 3). Similarly, organizational commitment, which encompasses propensity to withdraw from the job (cf. Mathieu and Zajac, 1990; Mowday et al., 1982), foreshadowed employment changes. Thus, employees lacking company identification severed employment ties more readily than did committed employees.

While verifying predictive superiority of withdrawal cognitions, our meta-analysis surely underestimated their predictive efficacy by including those studies assessing cognitions and quits over lengthy time lags or having few leavers (Hom et al., 1992a). Turnover researchers have long shown that long time spans between measurements of withdrawal decisions and actions weaken their association, as do extreme quit base rates (attenuating turnover variance) (Carsten and Spector, 1987; Steel and Ovalle, 1984; Steel and Griffeth, 1979; Hom et al., 1992a). Meta-analytical inclusion of such studies doubtlessly understated predictive accuracy of withdrawal cognitions under more auspicious conditions of short time lags and near-50% quit rates. Indeed, large nonartifactual between-study variation—uncovered by moderator tests—and broad credibility intervals suggest closer withdrawal cognitions–quit agreements under certain circumstances.

7. Expected Utilities of Withdrawal Acts

Consistent with various social-psychological models (Ajzen, 1991; Bagozzi and Warshaw, 1990; Fishbein and Ajzen, 1985; Triandis, 1979), our meta-analysis showed that termination decisions emerge from conscious calculations of perceived costs and benefits of withdrawal actions. Rather than impulsively quit over poor work conditions, many employees formulate withdrawal decisions after considering withdrawal's anticipated outcomes. Therefore, they would desert their workplace if they believe that job seeking or quitting will bring about valued consequences (e.g., obtain a better job elsewhere), while avoiding or minimizing negative repercussions (e.g., loss of sizable job investments).

8. Motivation

Various employee motivations also shaped turnover. Specifically, job involvement (psychological identification with the job) and internal motivation (self-esteem based on job accomplishments) decreased job withdrawal (Kanungo, 1982). Moreover, sociologists widely contend that workplace norms of efficiency and bureaucratic control clash with professional standards and ethical codes, imposing job stress and conflict on professional employees (Abbott, 1988; Kramer, 1974; Raelin, 1986). Despite their persuasive arguments and observations, this meta-analysis found that professionalism (adherence to professional values and standards) did not influence professional employees' withdrawal. Finally, job stress provoked more job terminations, while managerial orientation (strong drive to manage people) slowed managerial exodus (cf. Butler et al., 1983).

9. Other Withdrawal Actions

Our meta-analysis showed that other acts of withdrawal from aversive work conditions, such as absenteeism and lateness, foretold later turnover. Such positive covariation between milder forms of work avoidance and quitting—the most extreme and irrevocable avoidance form—supports a progression-of-withdrawal model (Hulin, 1991; Rosse and Miller, 1984), wherein dissatisfied employees progressively enact more extreme manifestations of job withdrawal over time (cf. Rosse, 1988).

In summary, these meta-analytical findings carry significant theoretical and practical implications. They suggest which managerial interventions effectively forecast and control voluntary quits, a subject addressed in a later section. They also identify causal antecedents that any viable model of turnover must incorporate. All the same, we caution that our meta-analyses uncovered limits to our generalizations about turnover causes. Many moderator tests suggest that the effects of these turnover determinants (including directions of those effects) vary across situations and populations. Such persistent evidence of inconsistency suggests turnover that theorists overstate the generality of their formulations, overlooking boundary conditions. Finally, our meta-analysis omitted other influential antecedents too rarely examined to include in a meta-analysis.

II. TURNOVER CONSEQUENCES

Having reviewed the determinants of turnover, this section reviews conceptual and empirical literature on its consequences (Mobley, 1982; Mowday et al., 1982; Price, 1977, 1989; Staw, 1980). Following Mobley's (1982) classification scheme, Table 4 summarizes potential benefits and disadvantages for leavers and employers. At the outset, we note that the consequences of turnover may be curvilinear or vary with different conditions (Price, 1989; Staw, 1980).

A. Negative Organizational Consequences

Undoubtedly, the turnover consequence attracting most attention is financial costs (Blakeslee et al., 1985; Cascio, 1991). According to human resource accounting, separation, replacement, and training costs embody exit expenses (Cascio, 1991; Flamholtz, 1985). Separation costs are costs created by quitting itself (e.g., exit interviews), whereas replacement costs include expenses incurred to replace leavers. Training costs represent a third cost factor, comprising company expenditures to orient and train replacements and costs due to their substandard productivity.

To illustrate these cost categories, Table 5 depicts their components from Hom's (1992) study on the cost of quits among mental health professionals. Following previous work (Cascio, 1991; Whiting, 1989) and preliminary interviews, Hom (1992) designed a survey to assess turnover costs in mental health agencies. Completing this survey, 24 agency directors answered questions about each major cost factor for key clinical positions. This study further identified special attrition costs for these professions, namely, case transfer (supervisory time to communicate the histories of leaver's clients to other clinicians assuming these clients) and client revenue losses (because fewer clients are served during the time a clinical position is vacant and during orientation of new

Table 3 Meta-analysis of Turnover Predictors: Immediate Precursors and Other Attitudes

Predictor	k	N	r_{obs}	r_{cor}	V_{pop}	%	95% Credibility interval	χ^2
Withdrawal cognitions								
Search intentions	16	3649	0.27	0.30	0.0064	42.03	0.14 to 0.45	40.14*
Quit intentions	70	78078	0.31	0.35	0.0266	4.81	0.03 to 0.67	2173.19*
Withdrawal cognitions	4	486	0.28	0.30	0.0022	78.26	0.21 to 0.39	5.12
Organizational commitment	36	10867	−0.18	−0.19	0.0127	21.92	−0.42 to 0.03	164.58*
Withdrawal expected utility								
Expected utility of search	6	1175	0.21	0.22	0.0072	42.65	0.05 to 0.38	14.19*
Expected utility of quit	7	1349	0.23	0.25	0.0000	100	0.25 to 0.25	5.62
Motivation								
Job stress	5	779	0.17	0.19	0.0000	100	0.19 to 0.19	1.18
Internal motivation	2	1681	−0.12	−0.13	0.0000	100	−0.13 to −0.13	0.24
Job involvement	8	2816	−0.13	−0.17	0.0147	24.04	−0.40 to 0.07	33.27*
Professionalism	4	3390	−0.01	−0.02	0.0000	100	−0.02 to −0.02	2.77
Managerial motivation	2	753	−0.14	−0.15	0.0001	95.72	−0.17 to −0.12	2.10
Withdrawal actions								
Lateness	2	413	0.14	0.15	0.0000	100	0.15 to 0.15	0.00
Absenteeism	8	1410	0.23	0.23	0.0000	98.34	0.21 to 0.24	8.14

*$p < .05$.
Note: k = the number of samples; N = total number of individuals in the k samples; r_{obs} = mean observed correlation; r_{cor} = weighted correlation corrected for attenuation; V_{pop} = population variance; and % = percentage of variance due to statistical artifacts.

replacements). The latter cost parallels productivity losses theorized by human resources accounting scholars, who contend that leavers lose productivity before exiting and new replacements are inefficient during their probation period (Mobley, 1982). Although typically omitted due to measurement problems (Cascio, 1991), productivity losses are more amenable to quantification in service personnel attrition as "foregone client revenues" (cf. Darmon, 1990; Whiting, 1989).

Following Cascio's (1991) formulas, the first author computed the cost of one turnover incidence from each clinical job and overall exit cost for individual agencies (i.e., an agency's summary costs due to all resignations for all jobs). These formulas typically factored in fully loaded compensation, namely, base pay and fringe benefits. Figure 1 shows median cost of one turnover occurrence for each job, while Figure 2 exhibits overall turnover costs for individual agencies. Not surprisingly, turnover costs varied across different occupations (cf. Cascio, 1991; Wanous, 1980). Different job markets and complexity may underlie disparate recruiting and training costs across jobs (Staw, 1980). As Table 5 attests, voluntary terminations can impose sizable financial burden on organizations. In 1991, the median agency cost was $57,902, while combined costs for all 24 agencies was $3,071,484.

Table 4 Turnover Consequences

Favorability of consequence	Organizational consequences	Leaver consequences
Negative consequences	• Financial costs for separation, replacement, and training • Productivity or service losses • Increased administrative burden • Business opportunity costs • Increased work load for stayers • Disrupted work routine of stayers • Reduced morale and retention among stayers	• Lost seniority and perks • Lost pension and other benefits • Sever friendships • Job transition stress • Financial costs of moving • Terminate social network of family members • Loss of valued community services • Disrupt spousal career
Positive consequences	• Displace poor performers • Loss of abrasive co-workers • Enhanced promotional opportunities for stayers • Empowerment of stayers • Infusion of new knowledge and technology by replacements • Reduced labor costs through downsizing	• Obtain better job elsewhere • Avoid stressful former job • Renewed work commitment • Pursue extraorganizational endeavors • Live in more desirable community • Improve spousal career

Table 5   Costs of Turnover Among Mental Health Professionals

- Separation Costs
  —Exit interviews: interviewer and interviewee time
  —Administrative costs: remove name from records, etc.
  —Unused vacation time: disburse unused vacation time
  —Lost client revenues: service fewer clients during vacancy period
  —Overtime pay: pay employees to assume leaver's work
  —Temporary employment: hire temps to assume leaver's work
  —Case consultation: transfer leaver's clients to others

- Replacement costs
  —Advertisements: communicate job vacancies
  —Personal recruitment: college recruitment, job fairs, etc.
  —Application processing: process and review applications
  —Entrance interviews: interviewer time
  —Application selection: interviewer time
  —Miscellaneous costs: tests, travel/relocation reimbursements, etc.

- Training costs
  —Formal orientation: instructor and trainee time
  —Formal job training: instructor and trainee time
  —Offsite training: course costs and trainee time
  —On-the-job training: Trainee time to develop proficiency and informal instruction by superior
  —Client revenue loss: fewer clients serviced by replacements

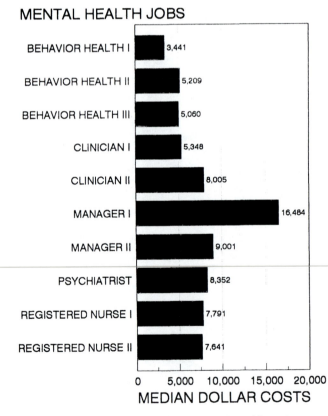

MENTAL HEALTH JOBS

Job	Median Dollar Costs
BEHAVIOR HEALTH I	3,441
BEHAVIOR HEALTH II	5,209
BEHAVIOR HEALTH III	5,060
CLINICIAN I	5,348
CLINICIAN II	8,005
MANAGER I	16,484
MANAGER II	9,001
PSYCHIATRIST	8,352
REGISTERED NURSE I	7,791
REGISTERED NURSE II	7,641

MEDIAN DOLLAR COSTS

Figure 1   Turnover costs for mental health positions (per one turnover incidence).

AGENCY

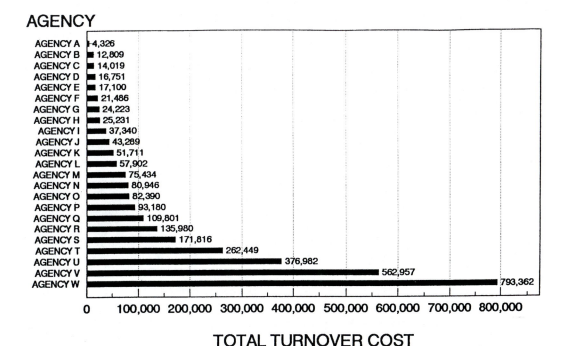

AGENCY	
AGENCY A	4,326
AGENCY B	12,809
AGENCY C	14,019
AGENCY D	16,751
AGENCY E	17,100
AGENCY F	21,486
AGENCY G	24,223
AGENCY H	25,231
AGENCY I	37,340
AGENCY J	43,289
AGENCY K	51,711
AGENCY L	57,902
AGENCY M	75,434
AGENCY N	80,946
AGENCY O	82,390
AGENCY P	93,180
AGENCY Q	109,801
AGENCY R	135,980
AGENCY S	171,816
AGENCY T	262,449
AGENCY U	376,982
AGENCY V	562,957
AGENCY W	793,362

0   100,000   200,000   300,000   400,000   500,000   600,000   700,000   800,000

TOTAL TURNOVER COST

Figure 2   Total turnover costs per agency.

In contrast to well-documented financial costs, other negative exit ramifications for firms secured less empirical attention. For one, research on the ubiquitous view that voluntary quits lower organizational productivity, i.e., ratio of company goods and services to inputs, is remarkably scarce (Price, 1977, 1989). Indeed, Price (1977) argued that cost data do not directly show that turnover impairs productivity. Nonetheless, there are good reasons and indirect evidence to suggest productivity losses. Specifically, leavers exhibit more absenteeism and lateness prior to quitting (Rosse, 1988); a missing employee obviously cannot produce (Rhodes and Steers, 1990). Along these lines, Mobley (1977, 1982) theorized that leavers' efficiency deteriorates before quitting (while productivity suffers during the time a leaver's job remains vacant; cf. Whiting, 1989). Moreover, new replacements may produce fewer goods or services than experienced incumbents who left, which research on age–productivity relationships affirms (Price, 1977; Waldman and Avolio, 1986). Finally, termination disrupts the work of remaining employees, whose work may be interdependent with that of the leaver or who may assume the leaver's duties (Mobley, 1982; Staw, 1980). Employees must also adjust to replacements' work style and habits and interrupt work to train them (Louis et al., 1983; Mowday et al., 1982).

Notwithstanding such productivity reversals, turnover may enhance productivity in some cases. That is, poor performers may quit and be replaced with superior personnel. The present and other meta-analyses (McEvoy and Cascio, 1987; Williams and Livingstone, 1989) documented this productivity gain. Generally speaking, marginal performers exit more than effective performers because most merit pay schemes distribute fewer rewards to marginal performers, who become dissatisfied and quit (Staw, 1980; Williams and Livingstone, 1989; Zenger, 1992). Given potential contradictory effects, turnover's *net* impact on productivity is thus uncertain (Price, 1989). Recently, Ulrich et al. (1991) estimated this net effect, finding lower quit rates in financially successful Ryder Truck Rental districts. While a noteworthy finding, they did not statistically control other firm-performance determinants, and their finding may not generalize beyond service firms.

Several studies further revealed that turnover decreases another dimension of organizational effectiveness—namely, delivery of client service (Price, 1977). Presumably, turnover worsens customer service because short-staffed offices or stores delay or withhold service (Darmon, 1990). Given exits by experienced incumbents, new employees may serve clients less competently, while leavers' departure may dissolve customers' loyalties to the firm if they became friends (Darmon, 1990). Indeed, internal research at Automatic Data Processing finds a strong association between retaining employees and clients (Shellenbarger, 1992). Finally, quit rates and poor service may arise from poor employee morale or commitment, a byproduct of ineffective human resource management (Schneider and Bowen, 1985; Ulrich et al., 1991). Consistent with this reasoning, Ulrich et al. (1991) documented that lower quit rates characterized Sears stores noted for service quality.

Furthermore, a few studies established that terminations by health or mental health providers diminish patient care (Price, 1977). In a pioneering study, Kahle (1968) first identified an indirect causal link between personnel turnover and suicides among patients in a mental health hospital. Although finding no correlations between quit rates and patient suicides, he nonetheless argued that excessive turnover overtaxes staff, who may overlook patients' suicide signals. In a follow-up study, Coser (1976) showed that departure of a psychiatrist or senior resident who supervises and trains residents in a mental hospital preceded each wave of patient suicides. She theorized that superiors' exits weakened psychiatric trainees' preparation and social support and thus their capacity to recognize suicidal clues. Finally, Spector and Takada (1991) measured various resident and facility attributes of 80 nursing homes (including staff quits) to predict quality of nursing care. Their logistic regression disclosed that low RN turnover enhances functional improvements (i.e., residents can independently bathe and eat) above and beyond other predictors of patient care.

Apart from current company productivity, anecdotal evidence abounds about lost business opportunities due to key personnel turnover (Mobley, 1982). For example, Gomez-Mejia et al. (1990) related numerous incidents of top level scientists and engineers quitting corporate research laboratories to start competing companies. In addition, turnover may expand administrative staffing to handle the extra recruiting and training created by attrition (Price, 1977). Various reviews upheld this staffing impact (Price, 1977, 1989).

Finally, some scholars propose that turnover lowers attitudes and stability among remaining employees (Mowday et al., 1982). This supposition is based on the rationale that valued colleagues' abandonment weakens group cohesion (Price, 1977) and that imputed motives for job exits represent negative social cues about the job (Mowday et al., 1982). Moreover, knowledge of leavers' alternative employment may decrease job satisfaction (i.e., the present position seems inferior in light of superior alternatives; Hulin et al., 1985) and stimulate consideration of other job opportunities (Mobley, 1982). Suggesting these effects, many reviewers have concluded that quits reduce integration and thus satisfaction (Mobley, 1982; Mowday et al., 1982; Price, 1977, 1979). All the same, such demoralization is not universal. Rather, Krackhardt and Porter (1985) discovered that strength of friendship ties between remaining employees and leavers (in a social network structure) ironically *promoted* employee satisfaction and commitment. Apparently, employees may form more positive job attitudes to rationalize why they remained while their friends quit. While provocative, Krackhardt and Porter's findings require replication. Their sample comprised adolescents who worked for extra spending money rather than economic survival in fast-food restaurants where turnover ran 200% annually.

B. Positive Organizational Consequences

Meta-analytical findings that poor performers quit more than high performers suggest that turnover is not necessarily bad (McEvoy and Cascio, 1987; Williams and Livingstone, 1989). Indeed, Dalton et al. (1981) have long argued that turnover researchers overstate exit costs because they ignore who quits employment. To correct this perspective, Dalton et al. advanced the notion of functional turnover—the resignation of marginal performers. Their turnover actually benefits employers, who may replace them with superior performers [presuming productivity gains offset replacement and training expenses (Darmon, 1990)]. To illustrate how gross quit rates are misleading, Dalton et al. (1981) classified whether employees quitting a bank were marginal or effective performers. Although the 32% quit rate seemed alarming, only 58% of quits comprised high performers—or dysfunctional turnovers.

Beyond functional turnover, turnover may benefit firms through the replacement's infusion of new knowledge and technology (Price, 1977), while top management exits may lay the groundwork for shifts in established organizational policy (Staw, 1980). Several literature reviews confirmed the former innovation impact (Mobley, 1982; Mowday et al., 1982; Price, 1977, 1989; Staw, 1980). In particular, R&D team studies indicate that excessive group longevity (i.e., low turnover) decreases R&D performance (Katz, 1980, 1982; Price, 1977). Given criticality of external technical knowledge and new ideas, long-term R&D teams become ineffective because they increasingly rely on customary work patterns and insulate themselves from outside information that threatens comfortable, predictable work habits. From Katz's (1982) study of 50 R&D teams, Figure 3 shows that lengthy group membership reduces team performance. As for managerial quits, Finkelstein and Hambrick (1990) found that long-tenured executive teams followed more persistent company strategies that mirrored industry norms, whereas short-tenured teams adopted more novel strategies deviating from industry patterns.

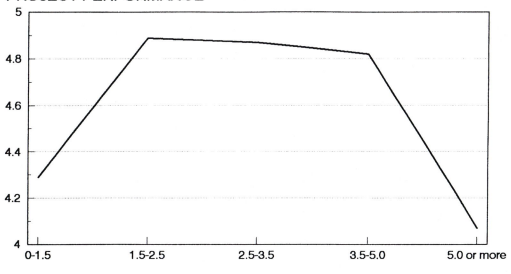

Figure 3 Project performance as a function of group longevity for R&D teams.

Moreover, voluntary attrition—without replacements—may lower labor costs, a primary thrust of large corporations downsizing to meet global competition (Balkin, 1992; Henkoff, 1900; Jacob, 1992; Nussbaum, 1991). For instance, annual American Management Association surveys found that a third of American companies have cut payrolls in the past 3 years (Henkoff, 1990), while 3.5 million lost jobs since 1987 (Lesly and Light, 1992). Voluntary quits represent a less costly means to downsize than layoffs, early retirement inducements, or job buyouts (Balkin, 1992; Faltermayer, 1992). Although popular, layoffs incur financial losses (e.g., severance pay and outplacement services), demoralize survivors, and damage public relations (hurting future recruitment) (Ashford et al., 1989; Davy et al., 1991; Faltermayer, 1992).

Finally, turnover writers identified various potential turnover benefits for remaining employees, although empirical findings are scant (Price, 1977, 1989; Staw, 1980). Turnover may expand promotional opportunities for continuing members through new job openings vacated by leavers and through diminished competitions for promotions (Mobley, 1982; Staw, 1980). In a similar vein, managerial turnover may empower subordinates (Price, 1977). Conceivably, incoming managers who replace leavers are uncertain about their authority because they lack familiarity with their position. Given uncertainty, they may initially rely on their subordinates for background information and advice. In line with this logic, Price (1977) interpreted several empirical studies as showing that managerial exits (and succession) decentralize power. Finally, Staw (1980) claimed that the departure of colleagues involved in interpersonal disputes may lower coworker conflicts.

C. Negative Leaver Consequences

Empirical research and anecdotal evidence identify sundry negative consequences for people who quit—notably, relinquishing various rewards of organizational membership (Mobley, 1982; Staw, 1980). Turnover theories have long envisioned that quitters may lose job seniority (and its associated perks) and nonvested pension and other benefits (Mobley, 1977; Rusbult and Farrell, 1983). Their forfeiture inhibits turnover (cf. Hom and Griffeth, 1991). Quite likely, lost health care benefit poses the most pressing leaver cost in present times. To illustrate, an Associated Press telephone poll of 1005 adults nationwide (December 1990) reported that 15% said they or a family member changed jobs or *remained* in a job due to health benefits (Lewin, 1991). Explaining "job-lock," the *New York Times* recounted stories about employees whose cancer or heart disease, or whose dependents' long-term treatment, prevented them from resigning because the new employer's insurer rejected coverage for preexisting conditions (Lewin, 1991). Similarly, labor economic research affirmed that pension coverage retards job turnover (Ippolito, 1991). Apart from lost benefits, leavers may surrender friendships at work (Rusbult and Farrell, 1983).

What is more, socialization and turnover researchers have suggested that quitters may face transition stress during entry into a new company (Mobley, 1982; Feldman and Brett, 1983). Leavers typically secure another job elsewhere (Hom and Griffeth, 1991; Mobley et al., 1979; Turban et al., 1992). While superior to the present job in many ways, new employment may still disappoint leavers, failing to confirm their preentry expectations and inspiring dissatisfaction and turnover (Wanous, 1980; Wanous et al., 1992). Contributing to reality shock, new employees must master crucial socialization tasks, such as developing job proficiency and achieving group acceptance (Feldman, 1975, 1988). We caution, however, that reality shock has mostly been shown for new entrants to the labor force. New employees having extensive work histories may face lesser, if not different, socialization problems (Feldman and Brett, 1983).

Additionally, leavers may confront additional losses if they relocate to new geographic regions (Mobley, 1982; Mowday et al., 1982; Rusbult and Farrell, 1983). Obviously, leavers bear the financial costs of moving, especially if they do not receive full reimbursements from their new employer or they move to a locale whose the cost of living is higher (Mowday et al., 1982). For an indirect cost estimate, Turban et al. (1992) reported that companies spent $4 billion to relocate employees. Apart from moving expenses, relocating leavers may sever the social support network for themselves and their families (Mowday et al., 1982; Zedeck and Mosier, 1990). Similarly, noncustodial divorced parents who move may separate from their children, whereas custodial parents may face lawsuits from former spouses (trying to preserve visitation rights) if they relocate (Lublin, 1992). Turnover theorists have overlooked social costs to leavers' families, who must adapt to a new community without support from friends or extended family. Yet research on expatriate managers attests to such family dislocation, finding that families must adjust to a new cultural milieu. Otherwise, family failure to culturally adapt results in premature termination of overseas assignments (Dowling and Schuler, 1990).

Beyond these relocation costs, leavers and their families may lose valued community services, such as family physicians and good schools (Rusbult and Farrell, 1983). Suggesting these losses, Turban et al. (1992) showed that long-term *community* tenure discouraged relocations to new jobs elsewhere. Finally, leavers' geographic mobility may disrupt the careers of working spouses (Mobley, 1982; Zedeck and Mosier, 1990). Here too, Turban et al. (1992) found that married employees refused offers by employers to relocate more than single employees, whereas Milliken et al. (1990) reported that 25–30% of employees declined promotions requiring relocations, mainly to avoid disrupting spousal careers.

D. Positive Leaver Consequences

Finally, leavers may reap certain benefits from turnover (Mobley, 1982; Staw, 1980). For one, leavers may assume a better position—one that better matches their talents and interests—or escape a stressful job (Mowday et al., 1982). Indeed, a new position may rejuvenate leavers, instilling greater work commitment (Mobley, 1982). Moreover, leavers—assuming new (or no) employment—may have more time to participate in extraorganizational endeavors, such as family or avocational pursuits (Hom and Griffeth, 1991; Hom et al., 1992a; Hulin et al., 1985). For example, surveys consistently find that young nurses often resign to bear or raise children (Cavanagh, 1989). Furthermore, relocation may provide leavers and their families with better schools, safer communities, or more attractive climates (Mowday et al., 1982; Turban et al., 1992). Finally, leavers' relocation may allow their spouse to accept a better career assignment elsewhere. Nursing surveys indicate that many nurses quit because their spouse transferred elsewhere (Donovan, 1980).

In summary, voluntary turnover introduces various consequences for leavers and employers. This section underscored that turnover effects can be contradictory. Some are advantageous for organizations or individuals, while others are disadvantageous. Importantly, many theorized turnover repercussions have not been empirically substantiated. Given such contradictory and difficult-to-quantify outcomes, practitioners and scholars may find it impossible to gauge turnover's net impact (Staw, 1980). Needless to say, consideration of potential exit outcomes would improve managerial evaluations of cost/benefits of turnover interventions, suggesting their potential side effects. While reducing quits, some programs may produce counterproductive effects, such as retaining marginal employees.

III. EXPLANATIONS OF TURNOVER

Theoretical models of employee turnover have proliferated since March and Simon's (1958) seminal explanation of organizational participation (Hulin et al., 1985; Lee and Mitchell, 1991; Mobley, 1977; Mobley et al., 1979; Price and Mueller, 1981, 1986; Rusbult and Farrell, 1983; Sheridan and Abelson, 1983; Steers and Mowday, 1981). Rather than introducing another model, this section suggests an integrative theoretical framework that builds on contemporary formulations, incorporating constructs and construct linkages that comply with empirical findings. In particular, we review empirical tests of prevailing theoretical accounts and meta-analyses of turnover correlates. Figure 4 shows this integrative conceptualization.

A. Job Attitudes → Withdrawal Cognitions

A hallmark of all turnover conceptualizations, including the present model, is that poor attitudes mobilize the termination process. Traditional thinking (e.g., Mobley, 1977; March and Simon, 1958; Porter and Steers, 1973; Price, 1977) contends that job dissatisfaction induces turnover cognitions, presuming that dissatisfying work conditions motivate escape (Hulin, 1991). In recent years, turnover theories (Price and Mueller, 1986; Steers and Mowday, 1981) have incorporated organizational commitment, positing that commitment to company values and goals undermines withdrawal thoughts (Mowday et al., 1982). Supporting this expanded set of attitudinal causes, meta-analyses found both attitudes predict withdrawal thoughts (Hom et al., 1992a; Mathieu and Zajac, 1990), while confirmatory factor analyses affirmed their conceptual independence (Brooke et al., 1988; Mathieu and Farr, 1991). Indeed, commitment scholars contend that commitment predicts quits more accurately than does satisfaction (Porter et al., 1974) because resignation implies rejecting the company, not necessarily the job (which can be assumed elsewhere) (Hom and Hulin, 1981). Given these theoretical rationale and facts, our model includes commitment and satisfaction as affective states initiating withdrawal cognitions.

Contemporary models embracing commitment and satisfaction nonetheless conflict over their place in a structural network of withdrawal precursors. Early theoretical statements proposed that commitment mediates satisfaction's influence on terminations (Price and Mueller, 1986). Although consistent with cross-sectional recursive models (Price and Mueller, 1986; Williams and Hazer, 1986), this preliminary perspective has been disputed by more rigorous tests. In particular, panel research (Farkas and Tetrick, 1989) and nonrecursive models (Mathieu, 1991) uncovered reciprocal causality between attitudes, albeit showing satisfaction affects commitment more than the reverse causation (Mathieu, 1991). Other research further doubted strict mediation through commitment, revealing that both attitudes independently shaped quit decisions (Farkas and Tetrick, 1989; Vandenberg and Scarpello, 1990). On these grounds, our model specifies reciprocal influence between satisfaction and commitment and their direct effects on withdrawal cognitions (Hom and Griffeth, 1991).

B. Withdrawal Cognitions → Turnover

Conventional thought differentiates various turnover cognitions, such as thoughts of quitting and search intentions (cf. Dalessio et al., 1986; Hom et al., 1992a). Despite allusions to different acts (quitting vs. seeking), withdrawal cognitions have not been empirically differentiated by recent confirmatory factor analyses (Hom and Griffeth, 1991; Hom et al., 1989; Sager et al., 1992). Rather, recent findings sustained a more parsimonious conception, holding that molecular withdrawal cognitions represent different facets of a molar construct (Miller et al., 1979; Steers and Mowday, 1981). Based on these findings, our conceptual framework submits a general withdrawal cognition that subsumes specific withdrawal intentions (cf. James and James, 1989).

Following Steers and Mowday (1981) and Hom and Griffeth (1991), we also envision that withdrawal cognitions can directly activate turnover. Unlike customary viewpoints (e.g., Mobley, 1977; Mobley et al., 1979), this direct pathway takes into account impulsive quitting (Mobley,

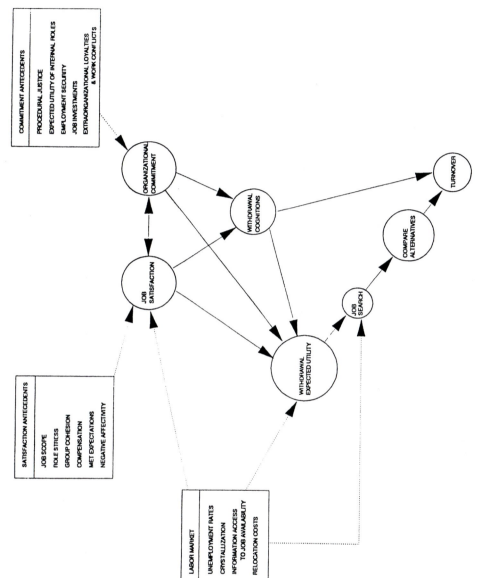

Figure 4 Integrative conceptualization of prevailing theoretical accounts and meta-analysis of turnover correlates.

1977), labor market exits by peripheral employees (Hulin et al., 1985), search unemployment (Baysinger and Mobley, 1983), relocation to distant communities (Hom and Griffeth, 1991), and decisions to pursue extrawork activities (e.g., childrearing or childbearing responsibilities; Hom et al., 1984; Hom and Griffeth, 1991). In short, this withdrawal cognitions-to-quit pathway acknowledges that many employees may quit without first assuming alternative jobs.

C. Withdrawal Cognitions → Job Search

Like Steers and Mowday (1981), the withdrawal-cognitions-to-job-search path implies that some employees deciding to quit seek other employment before leaving. This withdrawal route deviates from the conventional tenet that employees develop turnover cognitions after seeking and comparing alternatives (cf. March and Simon, 1958; Mobley, 1977; Price and Mueller, 1981; Rusbult and Farrell, 1983). Indeed, growing empirical evidence refutes this search-to-withdrawal-cognitions sequence. For example, Gerhart (1990), Carsten and Spector (1987), and Hom et al. (1992a) found that unemployment rates moderate the impact of quit decisions on turnover. Yet if employees enter the labor market and form impressions of alternatives before making quit decisions, then unemployment rates (a proxy for perceived alternatives) should *not* condition the quit intentions–quit relationship. Rather, these moderating effects suggest that employees develop quit intentions before seeking a new job. Thus, poor job markets undermine initial plans to quit work (attenuating the quit intention–quit relation), whereas expanding job markets allow premeditated withdrawal cognitions to translate into quitting. Furthermore, path analytical tests made tenable this withdrawal cognitions → search → quit chain (cf. Griffeth and Hom, 1990; Hom et al., 1984, 1992a; Hom and Griffeth, 1991).

D. Withdrawal Expected Utilities → Job Search

Adopting Mobley's (1977) and Fishbein-Azjen's (1975) rationale, our model posits that prospective quitters first evaluate perceived costs and benefits of quitting and job seeking before pursuing alternatives. In the same vein, theories of alternative responses to job dissatisfaction specify that expected utility (perceived consequences) of responses dictate their choice (Hulin, 1991; Rosse and Miller, 1984). In line with these views, empirical research consistently finds that expected utility of quitting affects terminations (Hom and Hulin, 1981; Prestholdt et al., 1987) or that anticipated exit costs inhibit a broad pattern of exit responses, including job seeking and quitting (Rusbult et al., 1988; Withey and Cooper, 1989).

Unlike popular conceptions of separate expected utilities for job search and quitting (cf. Hom et al., 1984; Laker, 1991; Lee, 1988; Sager et al., 1988; Steel et al., 1981), we argue that these utilities reflect different aspects of a broader construct of withdrawal expected utility. We reason that these expected utilities are inextricably codetermined (cf. Mobley, 1977) because quit and search decisions are often made together (Hom and Griffeth, 1991). This view accords with emerging formulations that classify diverse actions to avoid the job—namely, transfer, job seeking, and turnover—into a general response family (exit) (cf. Farrell, 1983; Rosse and Hulin, 1985; Rusbult et al., 1988; Withey and Cooper, 1989). Upholding our global conception, Hom and Griffeth (1991) found that search and quit expected utilities represented the same latent factor in a confirmatory factor analysis.

Consistent with Mobley (1977) and Steers and Mowday (1981), we specify that positive withdrawal expected utility stimulates job pursuits. After uncovering alternatives, job seekers would then compare them against their present position. Should this comparison favor an alternative, the employee would choose this job and quit. In line with this argument, empirical data substantiated a sequence wherein job search precedes job comparisons (Hom et al., 1984; Hom and Griffeth, 1991; Lee and Mowday, 1987; Steel et al., 1981).

E.   Other Empirical Support for Structural Network

Thus far, we discussed empirical support for segments of the proposed nomological network. More direct evidence is forthcoming from Hom and Griffeth (1991) and Griffeth and Hom (1992), who more completely validated structural linkages relating attitudes to quits with structural equation modeling (SEM) procedures. Moreover, turnover meta-analyses lend further support to the general causal sequence embedded within our framework: job attitudes → withdrawal cognitions → quit. While varying in sample compositions and corrections for statistical artifacts, separate meta-analyses still identically ordered these determinants in predictive strength. Specifically, withdrawal cognitions [$r = 0.30$ (present meta-analysis); $r = 0.45$ (Tett and Meyer, 1992)]—or, more specifically, quit decisions [$r = 0.35$ (present meta-analysis); $r = 0.36$ (Hom et al., 1992a); $r = 0.50$ (Steel and Ovalle, 1984)]—predicted quitting more accurately than did satisfaction [$r = -0.19$ (present meta-analysis); $r = -0.18$ (Hom et al., 1992a); $r = -0.28$ (Steel and Ovalle, 1984); $r = -0.24$ (Tett and Meyer, 1992$]$ and commitment [$r = -0.19$ (present meta-analysis); $r = -0.38$ (Steel and Ovalle, 1984); $r = -0.35$ (Tett and Meyer, 1992)].

F.   Satisfaction Determinants

Following a traditional framework set by Mobley et al. (1979) and Price and Mueller (1981, 1986), we also identify exogenous determinants whose effects on terminations are mediated by job attitudes. Based on theory and research, we classify separate antecedents for satisfaction and commitment. Given their different foci, we expect specific aspects of the job to shape satisfaction, while organizational characteristics should affect commitment. In line with this taxonomic premise, Brooke et al. (1988) and Mathieu and Farr (1991) showed antecedents differently correlated with commitment and satisfaction. They also found antecedents correlated with both attitudes, but their analyses did not control interdependency between attitudes (Mathieu, 1991). Given correlated attitudes, a determinant of one attitude may spuriously correlate with the other attitude (Mathieu and Zajac, 1990). While we concede possible multiple effects on both attitudes, our taxonomic description of attitudinal causes nevertheless delineates which antecedents most shape a given attitude for heuristic purposes.

1.   Job Complexity

This formulation specifies emotional reactions to job duties as emanating from facets of job complexity. This proposition draws from theories of job characteristics, proposing that job dimensions, such as task identity and autonomy, mold job affect by instilling meaning, personal responsibility for outcomes, and knowledge of accomplishments into work (Hackman and Oldham, 1980). Empirical research has established that job complexity enhances job satisfaction (Fried, 1991; Loher et al., 1985) and retention (Griffeth, 1985; Katerberg et al., 1979; McEvoy and Cascio, 1985). Still, our proposal that satisfaction primarily translates job scope's effects on commitment or withdrawal cognitions remains untested.

2.   Role Stress

Moreover, role stress—namely, role ambiguity and conflict—should decrease job satisfaction. That supposition derives from theories of role stress, which submits that ambiguous or conflicting role demands evoke role strain (Kahn et al., 1964; Netemeyer et al., 1990). Many studies affirmed that role stress promotes dissatisfaction and resignations (Fisher and Gitelson, 1983; Jackson and Schuler, 1985; Lyons, 1971; present meta-analysis). Affirming satisfaction mediation, recent SEM analyses showed that role stress boosts withdrawal cognitions via job satisfaction (Klenke-Hamel and Mathieu, 1990; Netemeyer et al., 1990).

3. *Group Cohesion*

Apart from work attributes, group cohesion provides satisfaction and thereby stabilizes employment. Organizational demography theory offers an explanation for our claim (Pfeffer, 1983). Supposedly, demographically dissimilar members of a work group hold different values and outlooks, which lessen mutual attraction and intragroup communication. The result is weakened group cohesion and greater strife, stimulating exits. Predictably, Jackson et al. (1991) and McCain et al. (1983) found greater quit rates in work groups marked by demographic diversity, whereas O'Reilly et al. (1989) pinpointed dissension within heterogeneous groups accelerates member exits. Other research adds credence to our proposition, showing that coworker satisfaction (or integration) sustains job incumbency (Cotton and Tuttle, 1986; Price and Mueller, 1981; present meta-analysis).

4. *Compensation*

Our theory shares the ubiquitous view that compensation (and compensation satisfaction) builds job longevity through job satisfaction (Hulin et al., 1985; Price and Mueller, 1981, 1986). Borrowing from social exchange and equity models, many turnover authors proclaim that insufficient financial inducements for employee contributions to the firm spawn feelings of inequity and thus induces job exits (Hulin et al., 1985; Rusbult and Farrell, 1983). Management and labor economic studies uphold this contention, finding that low pay or pay dissatisfaction underlies job dissatisfaction (Ironson et al., 1989; Lawler, 1971, 1981) and turnover (present meta-analysis; Blakemore, et al., 1987; Cotton and Tuttle, 1986; Mobley, 1982; Wilson and Peel, 1991). More revealing, Motowidlo (1983), Price and Mueller (1981, 1986), and Rusbult and Farrell (1983) directly verified our mediational sequence: pay → satisfaction → quitting.

5. *Leader–Member Exchange*

We further submit that dissatisfaction (and hence turnover) may derive from poor leader–member exchange (LMX), (Graen and Scandura, 1986). Graen and his associates (Dansereau et al., 1975; Graen and Scandura, 1986) found that superiors develop more effective working relationships with select subordinates (high LMX). Leaders exchange various inducements beyond the formal employment contract with these employees, such as job latitude and decision-making influence. In return, high-LMX subordinates reciprocate with higher contributions toward unit functioning. This mutual interpersonal exchange, in turn, fosters subordinate morale and loyalty, which empirical data have borne out (Ferris, 1985; Graen and Ginsburgh, 1977; Graen et al., 1982). Although scant, empirical findings on the satisfaction mechanism are equivocal. Ferris (1985) and Graen et al. (1982) found that partialing out overall job satisfaction did not nullify LMX–turnover correlations, suggesting that satisfaction does not fully mediate the influence of LMX. Yet Williams and Hazer (1986) upheld a causal network wherein leader consideration (an aspect of LMX) bolsters satisfaction and thus retention decisions.

6. *Met Expectations*

We comply with Porter and Steers' (1983) theory of met expectations, which declares that new employees become dissatisfied (and hence withdraw) if the job disconfirms their initial job expectations. Supporting our supposition, Wanous et al.'s (1992) meta-analysis found that met expectations reinforce satisfaction and retention, affecting satisfaction more than retention. Additionally, recent SEM tests more directly confirmed that job affect translates the effects of met expectations onto exits (Bacharach and Bamberger, 1992; Farkas and Tetrick, 1989; Hom et al., 1992b).

7. Negative Affectivity

Finally, negative affectivity—a personality trait reflecting a chronic predisposition to evaluate oneself, others, and situations (e.g., work settings) unfavorably—may shape feelings toward the job and job changes (Staw et al., 1986). Empirical work affirmed that negative affectivity arouses dissatisfaction (Staw et al., 1986) and quit decisions (George, 1989). Still, empirical data on its quit effect are still absent. Logically, we would expect that negatively affective employees would more readily change jobs given their inclination toward disparaging their jobs.

G. Commitment Determinants

1. Procedural Justice

Our conceptualization further states that procedural justice, i.e., fair procedures to allocate organizational rewards, should underpin company commitment and thereby bolster organizational participation (Folger and Greenberg, 1985; Folger and Konovsky, 1989). This hypothesis rests on Folger and Konovsky's (1985) rationale that procedural equity instills employee confidence that employers will fairly distribute many rewards in the long run. Lacking faith in the reward system, employees would not commit to the firm and discontinue their careers there. In line with this perspective, Folger and Konovksy (1989) documented that equitable distribution of pay raises strengthens bonds of loyalty between employees and company, whereas Miceli et al. (1991), using SEM analysis, validated a causal pathway in which pay system fairness improves satisfaction, in turn reducing quit intentions.

2. Expected Utility of Internal Roles

Furthermore, prospects for attaining desirable work roles inside a company may engender commitment and stability (Mobley, 1982). Mobley (1982; Mobley et al., 1979) posited that expectations of assuming desirable positions inside the firm, i.e., "expected utility of internal roles" (e.g., promotion), may account for why some dissatisfied employees do not quit. In the same vein, Hulin et al. (1985) suggested that "efforts to change the work situation"—through transfers, promotions, or demotions—represent alternative means to desert an unpleasant job. Hulin et al.'s formulation thus implies that successful job changes inhibit termination decisions and behavior (cf. Jackofsky and Peters, 1983).

Various research streams corroborate commitment-binding effects of attractive roles within the firm. Many empirical works reveal that promotional opportunities underlie quit decisions (Cotton and Tuttle, 1986; present meta-analysis) and company commitment (Mathieu and Zajac, 1990). Although specifying other mediators, recent SEM tests also support a basic promotions → commitment → turnover pathway (Griffeth and Hom, 1990; Price and Mueller, 1986). Hom et al.'s 1989) confirmatory factor analysis, however, did not differentiate between expected utility of other internal roles and job satisfaction. Given its prominence in modern thought (e.g., Hulin, 1991; Mobley et al., 1979), expected utility of internal roles nonetheless merits additional research to verify its explanatory power.

3. Employment Security

Furthermore, employment security may be a prime commitment underpinning. We base this contention on Ashford et al.'s (1989) reasoning that employees perceiving their companies to be undependable in carrying out their commitments to them would in turn lose trust and commitment to their companies. Sharing this view, Kerr and Slocum (1987) described employee's commitment to the firm as an exchange for the firm's long-term commitment to the individual (i.e., job security). Likewise, Japanese observers widely claim that the exalted loyalty and productivity of Japanese workers stem from lifetime employment in corporations (Lincoln, 1989; Lincoln and Kalleberg, 1985; Marsh and Minnari, 1977). Affirming the present supposition, Ashford et al. (1989) found that employees fearing layoffs felt less committed to the employer and planned to quit, whereas Davy et al. (1991) documented with SEM analysis that job insecurity feelings → commitment → quit decisions among survivors of corporate layoffs.

4. *Job Investments*

Our framework also recognizes that job investments (e.g., nonportable pension benefits, job-specific training, seniority perks) are an essential basis for organizational commitment and retention. Leading turnover theorists specify that potential forfeiture of job investments deters turnover (Mobley, 1977; Rusbult and Farrell, 1983) and underlies the well-supported association between job tenure and turnover (Cotton and Tuttle, 1986; Mobley, 1982; present meta-analysis). Derived from Becker's (1960) side-bet model, commitment writers similarly conceive compliance or calculative commitment as identification based on extrinsic inducements (Mathieu and Zajac, 1990; Meyer et al., 1989, 1990; O'Reilly and Chatman, 1976). In this commitment form, employees become bound to a firm because they have sunk costs invested in the firm and fear losing those investments (Mathieu and Zajac, 1990). Supporting this commitment factor, turnover studies affirmed that perceived costs of quitting inhibit resignations (Hom et al., 1984; Lee, 1988; Rusbult and Farrell, 1983; Steel et al., 1981), while Mathieu and Zajac's (1990) meta-analysis found that calculative commitment reduces withdrawal intentions and actions.

5. *Extraorganizational Loyalties*

Finally, extraorganizational loyalties represent another commitment antecedent. In growing numbers, turnover theorists promulgate that competing commitments jeopardize company loyalty (Mobley, 1982; Mobley et al., 1979; Price and Mueller, 1981, 1986; Steers and Mowday, 1981). Psychological attachment to extraorganizational pursuits, such as professionalism and family responsibilities, represents the core idea behind various conceptions of extrawork influences (Lee and Mowday, 1987; Price and Mueller, 1981, 1986). Still, empirical findings failed to sustain their presumed detrimental effects on job incumbency (Blegen et al., 1988; Lee and Mowday, 1987; Price and Mueller, 1981, 1986). For example, sociologists have long observed that professionals' loyalty to their occupation interferes with company loyalties due to their conflicting values and norms (Dean et al., 1988; Kramer, 1974; Raelin, 1986; Von Glinow, 1988). For example, nursing graduates are often dismayed by hospitals' norms of efficiency and bureaucratic control, which hamper their ability to serve patients according to school-bred professional standards (Kramer, 1974). Contrary to such observations, empirical inquiries regularly find that professional and organizational commitments positively covary and that professionalism inhibits turnover (Aranya et al., 1981; Curry et al., 1985; Ferris and Aranya, 1983; Mathieu and Zajac, 1990; Price and Mueller, 1981; Morrow and Wirth, 1989).

Similarly, demographic proxies of family responsibility (e.g., marital status, family size) have not shown clear-cut effects on turnover (Mobley, 1982; Mobley et al., 1979; Muchinsky and Tuttle, 1979; Porter and Steers, 1973). Rather, demographic effects vary with gender and family composition. For example, family size and marital status may bolster quits among women—who traditionally carry primary family obligations—but inhibit quits among men who are traditionally family breadwinners (cf. Mobley, 1982; Porter and Steers, 1973). Likewise, family composition displayed conflicting effects. That is, the size of the nuclear family (especially number and presence of young children) accelerates female turnover, whereas size of the extended family (comprising relatives) in the community prolongs company tenure among women (and men) (Blegen et al., 1988; Donovan, 1980; Gerson, 1985; Huey and Hartley, 1988; Price and Mueller, 1981). In summary, simple demographic proxies often misleadingly index family obligation. Their widespread usage betrays an oversimplification of their meaning because marital status and family size may historically symbolize family obligations for women but not for men. To more firmly establish family effects, future research must develop more direct measures of family obligations or develop more valid demographic indices, showing that they reflect family burdens (cf. Blegen et al., 1988). For example, Kossek (1990) suggests assessing the configuration of children's ages rather than counting number of children (toddlers have different needs than school age children) and household *employment* configuration rather than marital status (single parents have more family responsibilities than dual-career or traditional nuclear families).

6. *Time and Behavioral Conflicts*

Based on this limited review, we contend that turnover studies overlooked interrole conflict—or work interference with extraorganizational commitments (Hom and Griffeth, 1991; Mobley, 1982; Ralston and Flanagan, 1985). Conflict between job and off-job domains may arise from time conflicts or incompatible behavioral demands (O'Driscoll et al., 1992; Zedeck and Mosier, 1990). Thus, competing loyalties will accelerate organizational exits (and perhaps, discontinue work force participation) only if work schedules interfere with participation in extrawork endeavors (Gerson, 1985; Hom and Griffeth, 1991) or if behaviors at work conflict with extrawork (or extraorganizational) values (e.g., bureaucratic-professional conflict; Aranya and Ferris, 1983). These two sources of job conflict parallel traditional role stress dimensions: role overload (insufficient time to do the job) and person–role conflict (perceived incongruency between role requirements and personal values) (Miles, 1976). Although scarce, growing evidence shows that job conflicts with extraorganizational endeavors [including professional standards (Aranya and Ferris, 1983)] promote withdrawal cognitions and weaken organizational commitment (Bacharach and Bamberger, 1992; Hom et al., 1989). More revealing, a recent path analytical test confirmed that excessive work hours increase job interference with off-job activities, which thereby diminishes commitment (Driscoll et al., 1992).

Moreover, interrole conflict may clarify contradictory findings about effects of extraorganizational attachments on withdrawal. That is, employees dedicated to extrawork endeavors, such as childrearing, leisure, or community service, are motivated to quit only if their present work hours (excessive or inconvenient hours) hamper or preclude involvement in those undertakings (Mobley, 1982). By a different logic, employees committed to their occupation more readily change jobs if they cannot follow professional standards to carry out job duties (cf. Hom et al., 1992b; Huey and Hartley, 1988). All told, neglected time-based or behavioral conflicts may moderate how extraorganizational interests affect turnover. To fully understand extraorganizational influences, future investigations should not only consider work–family conflicts but also other extrawork pursuits, such as leisure and community service (O'Driscoll et al., 1992; Hom et al., 1989).

H. Labor Market Determinants

Finally, we specify that job market determinants—embodying various factors (suggested by different theorists)—exert multiple, complex effects on the termination process (Hom et al., 1992a; Steel and Griffeth, 1989). Like Hulin et al. (1985), we posit labor market influences on job satisfaction, contending that attractive perceived alternatives diminish evaluations of the present job ("greener grass syndrome"); (cf. Schneider, 1976). Moreover, we follow Mobley's (1977) reasoning that unemployment rates [especially in one's local community or occupation (Hulin et al., 1985)] affect expected utility of job seeking. Additionally, job market factors (notably, relocation costs) enter into mental calculations of the costs and benefits of quitting (Hom and Griffeth, 1981; Steel and Griffeth, 1979) (as do job investments via commitment). Finally, labor market antecedents may shape the course of the job search (Hom et al., 1992a; Mobley et al., 1979; Steers and Mowday, 1981). Specifically, limited information about available positions or poor vacancy rates may undermine job search, preventing job seekers from finding suitable alternative employment.

All the same, research studies find that current proxies of perceived alternatives are weak or inconsistent quit predictors or moderators of quit determinants (Hom et al., 1992a; Hulin et al., 1985; Steel and Griffeth, 1989). Explaining disappointing findings, Griffeth and Hom (1988a) and Steel and Griffeth (1989) maintained that common operationalizations poorly proxy the complex, multifaceted employment market. By comparison, objective joblessness indices have moderated the impact of attitudes and quit decisions and directly impacted quits (Carsten and Spector, 1987; Gerhart, 1990; Hom et al., 1992a). While encouraging, we still recommend developing measures to directly assess varied labor market perceptions (instead of indirect proxies using unemployment rates) to verify more firmly theoretical propositions (Steel and Griffeth, 1989).

IV. METHODS TO REDUCE TURNOVER

Prescriptions for reducing turnover abound (Bellus, 1984; Half, 1982; Moore and Simendinger, 1989; Roseman, 1981; Watts and White, 1988). However popular, these recommendations rest on frail empirical foundations. At best, practical remedies derive from case studies or anecdotal evidence. Thus, conclusions that certain practices stem job exits are often unwarranted and perhaps fallacious. The following discussion thus suggests promising interventions that have garnered stronger empirical support. Specifically, we review experimental tests of turnover reduction methods and studies documenting reliable turnover determinants (McEvoy and Cascio, 1987). At the very least, correlational studies establish that a variable reliably predicts turnover more than case studies—and, by extension, its manipulation may change turnover (Campbell and Stanley, 1963). Table 6 provides an overview of the various methods for turnover control.

Table 6 Turnover Reduction

- Newcomer socialization
  - —Realistic job previews
  - —Socialization programs
- Job characteristics
  - —Job enrichment
  - —Social cues
  - —Work space attributes
- Leadership
  - —Leader–member exchange
- Compensation
  - —Procedural fairness
  - —Variable pay
  - —Retention incentives and fringe benefits
- Employee selection
- Extraorganizational conflicts
  - —Alternative work schedules
  - —Family leave
  - —Child and dependent care
  - —Telecommuting

A. Socialization Assistance

1. *Realistic Job Previews*

Turnover is largely concentrated among new employees (Mobley, 1982; Wanous, 1980). Elevated newcomer exodus implicates inadequate or incomplete socialization to the organization as a root cause (Feldman, 1988; Fisher, 1986). Socialization theorists uniformly contend that reality shock impedes adaptation to a new work role (Feldman, 1988; Wanous, 1980). Acknowledging the ubiquity and impact of reality shock (Dean et al., 1988), organizational scientists have developed realistic job previews (RJPs), which communicate information about a job to newcomers during recruitment or orientation to forestall disillusionment (Wanous, 1980).

By now, extensive research has corroborated RJPs' efficacy for reducing early attrition in many occupations (McEvoy and Cascio, 1985; Premack and Wanous, 1985; Reilly et al., 1981; Wanous and Collela, 1989). To illustrate, Hom et al. (1992b) developed RJPs for certified public accountants and registered nurses. Using an experimental design, they delivered this RJP to some new employees, while withholding this preview from others (control group). A year later, fewer RJP recipients quit than did unforewarned newcomers; 8.5% of RJP nurses quit vs. 17.8% of control nurses [χ^2 (1, N = 155) = 2.95, p < 0.10] while 6.4% of RJP accountants quit vs. 23% of control accountants [χ^2(1, N = 98) = 3.70, p < 0.05]. On the whole, RJPs modestly reduce quits; current estimates find a 0.12 correlation between RJPs and job survival (Wanous and Collela, 1989).

Despite their effectiveness, controversies over why RJPs work and practical RJP design persist (Premack and Wanous, 1985; Wanous, 1989). Over the years, many explanations for how RJPs operate have emerged (Dugoni and Ilgen, 1981; Ilgen and Seely, 1974; Meglino et al., 1988; Porter and Steers, 1973; Wanous, 1980). By and large, empirical tests inconsistently or sparingly support these mechanisms (Hom et al., 1992b; Premack and Wanous, 1985; Wanous and Collela, 1989). The theory of met expectations is an exception to this generalization (Porter and Steers, 1973). This theory contends that new employees typically hold naive and inflated expectations about their job (Wanous, 1980). Because of naivete, they eventually learn that their initial expectations do not conform to workplace realities (Dean et al., 1988). Disconfirmed expectations, in turn, induce dissatisfaction and exits. Upholding this interpretation, Premack and Wanous' (1985) meta-analysis revealed that RJPs deflate initial expectations, whereas Wanous et al.'s (1992) meta-analysis found that met expectations (whether manipulated or measured) enhance satisfaction and job survival. Moreover, Hom et al. (1992b) validated a mediational pathway, wherein RJPs → met expectations → job satisfaction → turnover, using SEM analysis.

RJP researchers have also examined means to enhance RJP efficacy. For example, RJPs may best foster retention if delivered to job candidates during recruitment—before they decided to accept the job—rather than during orientation (Wanous and Collela, 1989). As a result, prehire RJPs can reduce reality shock as well as let job candidates self-select themselves out of the job if they perceive a poor fit between themselves and the job (Wanous, 1980). These reasons notwithstanding, posthire RJPs reduce quit as effectively as prehire RJPs, although no test has directly compared them (Dugoni and Ilgen, 1981; Hom et al., 1992b; Horner et al., 1979; Meglino et al., 1988).

RJP studies have also considered various modes of communication, including booklets, audiovisual media, work samples, and interviews to convey realistic job data (Wanous and Collela, 1989). By far, booklet previews represent the most popular medium due to ease of development and administrative convenience. Fortunately, these practical advantages do not limit booklet effectiveness. In their meta-analysis, Premack and Wanous (1985) found that booklet and audiovisual RJPs similarly decreased turnover, albeit audiovisual media also improved performance. Furthermore, Colarelli (1984) directly compared RJP booklets with realistic communications by job incumbents. He conjectured that incumbent descriptions enhance attention and comprehension (due to face-to-face interactions), provide more relevant information addressing applicant's unique concerns, and represent more candid (booklets might omit facts the firm does not wish to formally acknowledge) and credible (incumbents are job experts) sources than booklet RJPs. In line with this reasoning, Colarelli found that incumbent RJPs reduced turnover among new bank tellers (3-month quit rate: 14.6%) more than did RJP booklets (44.9% quit rate).

To improve efficacy, RJP investigators increasingly construct job previews to accurately and fully reflect job content (Reilly et al., 1979). In particular, they follow test content validation to develop RJP booklets (Ghiselli et al., 1981). To this end, they first elicit statements about the job from preliminary interviews with incumbents and superiors. Their statements are then compiled into a survey, in which another incumbent sample independently verifies statement truthfulness (cf. Dean and Wanous, 1984). Majority opinion (e.g., 70% consensus) then dictates which statements are included in the final RJP booklet. Unfortunately, optimal development for other RJP media awaits further examination.

2. Reality Shock Orientation

Kramer and Schmalenberg (1977) designed a "bicultural training" orientation to help nursing graduates adjust to hospital life. More intensive than RJPs, this program has nursing graduates attend 90-min weekly "rap sessions" for their first 6 weeks of employment. During the fourth week, new nurses read Kramer and Schmalenberg's workbook about common sources of reality shock, such as sporadic feedback and personal feelings of incompetency. Four to five months after hospital entry, nurses attend conflict resolution workshops—first together with peers, and then later with head nurses—where they role play behaviors to deal with routine workplace conflicts.

Several quasi-experimental studies have shown that bicultural training decreases nursing turnover (Holloran et al., 1980; Kramer, 1977). For example, Kramer (1977) exposed half of 260 new nurses to bicultural training, while the other half received traditional orientation. After a year's employment, 90.2% of bicultural nurses remained employed, but 60% of control nurses had quit. Since its inception, "reality shock" components (e.g., lectures, rap sessions) have been introduced into present day hospital orientations, which also develop nurses' clinical skills (Borovies and Newman, 1981). Weiss's (1984) evaluation of these more eclectic programs showed that 7% of trained nurses resigned compared with 31% quit rates for untrained nurses.

3. Socialization Programs

In sharp contrast to bountiful theoretical writings, descriptions about successful socialization practices are modest (Louis et al., 1983). Adding to this knowledge void, Louis et al. (1983) surveyed new business graduates, having them report availability and helpfulness of various socialization practices. Their results in Figure 5 show that peers, supervisor, and senior coworkers most assisted newcomers, corroborating the prominence accorded by socialization models to these socialization agents (Feldman, 1988). By comparison, newcomers regarded formal programs, such as orientation sessions and offsite residential training, as less helpful. Notwithstanding popular writings, mentors or sponsors were neither available nor helpful to new employees (Kantor, 1977). Louis et al. (1983) also measured newcomer attitudes, correlating them with socialization experiences. Figure 6 shows which socialization practices most improved satisfaction and tenure intentions, namely, favorable offsite residential training and business trips.

B. Job Enrichment

According to prevailing theories, employees find work motivating and attractive to the extent they learn (knowledge of results) that they personally (experienced responsibility) performed well on a job that they care about (experienced meaningfulness) (Hackman and Oldham, 1980). These

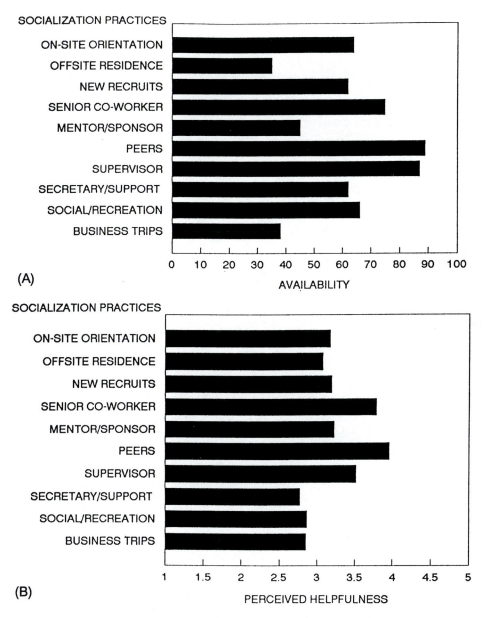

Figure 5 Availability and helpfulness of socialization practices; (A), availability; (B), helpfulness.

"critical psychological states" derive from the presence of the following job characteristics: skill variety (using various skills and talents); task identity (doing whole, identifiable pieces of work); task significance (doing work that substantially impacts others' work or lives); autonomy (freedom to schedule work and work methods); and job feedback (obtaining direct, clear information about performance) (Hackman and Oldham, 1980). Given this rationale, job enrichment—through introduction of job characteristics—should enhance employment longevity.

SOCIALIZATION PRACTICES

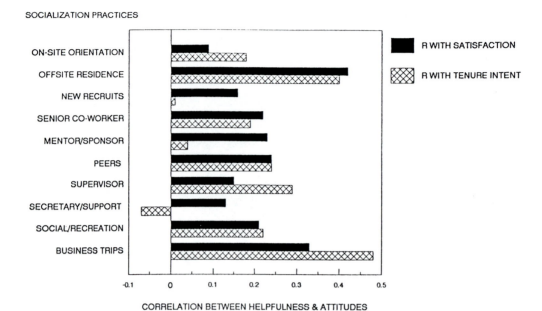

Figure 6   Correlations between helpfulness of practice and job satisfaction and tenure intentions.

1. Job Enrichment Effects

Diverse research streams support job enrichment as a means for turnover abatement. Meta-analyses find that job characteristics reliably predict exit determinants—notably, job satisfaction and organizational commitment (Loher et al., 1985; Mathieu and Zajac, 1990). Additionally, turnover studies find that job characteristics moderately forecast terminations (Katerberg et al., 1979; Price and Mueller, 1981, 1986). More definitely, field experiments establish that enriching work reduces job withdrawal (Griffeth, 1985; McEvoy and Cascio, 1985). Indeed, a meta-analysis concluded that job enrichment lowered quits more than did RJPs; the enrichment effect size was 0.17 compared with 0.09 for RJPs (McEvoy and Cascio, 1985).

2. Social Cues

Besides objective task attributes, socially constructed realities underlie job attitudes (Salancik and Pfeffer, 1978; Zalesny and Ford, 1990). Social information-processing theory contends that the social environment, i.e., others' communications about the workplace, can shape employee perceptions and attitudes toward the job (Salancik and Pfeffer, 1978). Specifically, social cues from coworkers or superiors (e.g., written job descriptions, verbal remarks) may focus attention on particular task dimensions about a job. Attending to salient job aspects, employees may develop attitudes conforming to those task "definitions." Alternatively, others' commentaries about the job may connote a socially acceptable evaluation of a job, implying an appropriate attitude for the employee to espouse (Zalesny and Ford, 1990).

Laboratory experiments and correlational studies have shown that social cues can mold job perceptions and attitudes, although these effects are neither strong nor consistent (Griffin, 1987; Zalesny and Ford, 1990). Extending this research, Griffin (1983) compared objective job enrichment with social cues in a field experiment. Specifically, he trained superiors to make remarks about various job characteristics to subordinates whenever appropriate. For example, whenever an employee did an autonomous task, the superior would call attention to this job quality. Over a 4-month period, supervisors made five task comments per day. In other departments, Griffin (1983) however enriched work content. This experiment revealed that supervisory remarks about qualities of enriched work enhanced task perceptions and attitudes as much as did job enrichment. By extension, Griffin's findings suggest that social cues that increase awareness of positive job attributes—that exist but go unnoticed—might enhance employee retention.

3. *Workspace Characteristics*

Physical environmental characteristics might also shape job perceptions and attitudes (Oldham, 1988). Drawing from overstimulation theory, Oldham and his colleagues argued that physical workplace features can excessively stimulate employees (Oldham and Fried, 1987; Oldham and Rotchford, 1983). That is, social density (number of people within a work area) and room darkness (offices having dim lighting and drab wall colors that seem spatially restricted) increase distractions, feelings of invaded privacy, and perceived crowding, while enclosures (number of walls or partitions surrounding work areas) and interpersonal distance (distance between colleagues) reduce these environmental impressions. Stimulus overload, in turn, increases work dissatisfaction and avoidance. Moreover, work space features can shape job attitudes through task perceptions. In open offices, employees may perceive less autonomy due to hindrance with freedom to work from unwanted intrusions and less task identity because their contribution seems like a small piece of the work of the entire office (Oldham and Rotchford, 1983).

Testing this theory, Oldham and his colleagues found that workplace attributes moderately explained work satisfaction (31% of its variance) and turnover (24% of its variance) (Oldham and Fried, 1987; Oldham and Rotchford, 1983). Office properties also displayed interactive effects, such that simultaneous presence of dark rooms, few enclosures, closely spaced work areas, and densely filled offices, most engendered demoralization and exits. Using a quasi-experiment, Oldham (1988) also evaluated office changes on claims adjusters initially working in open-plan (three) offices (no interior walls or partitions) of an insurance firm. During his study, two offices converted into more private office configurations, while a third office remained unchanged (control group). Compared to the control office, employees moving to a low-density open plan or partitioned office reported more privacy, less crowding, and higher work satisfaction. In conclusion, work space shelter from overstimulation represents a promising means to curb work avoidance and awaits further validation.

C. Leader–Member Exchange

Graen and his associate (cf. Dansereau et al., 1975; Graen and Scandura, 1986) emphasized the leader's role for assimilating newcomers and maintaining loyalty among established incumbents. Their research identified two types of exchanges between superior and subordinate. One kind is high LMX, wherein a superior offers various inducements beyond the formal employment contract, such as job latitude, decision-making influence, information, and social support, to some subordinates. In return, these subordinates reciprocate with greater departmental allegiance and obligations and expanded time and energy. Instead of interpersonal exchange, superiors use formal authority with other subordinates (low LMX), who strictly do their job descriptions in return for pay and benefits. Comparing these two exchanges, Graen and his colleagues found that high-LMX members express higher satisfaction and quit less than low-LMX members (Dansereau et al., 1975; Ferris, 1985; Graen and Cashman, 1975; Graen and Ginsburgh, 1977; Graen et al., 1982).

Since that preliminary research, Graen and his associates (Graen et al., 1982; Graen et al., 1986; Scandura and Graen, 1982) designed and evaluated a training program for leaders to develop effective exchanges with subordinates. Lasting 6 weeks, this program uses lectures and role playing to instruct managers about the LMX model, active listening skills, techniques for sharing mutual expectations and resources, and practicing one-to-one sessions. After training, managers meet with each subordinate and follow a prepared script to communicate each other's concerns and expectations about each other's job and their working relationship. Compared with untrained managers, Graen and his colleagues showed that LMX training improves productivity and morale. By virtue of enhanced job attitudes, LMX training might similarly sustain job incumbency, although future research must verify such turnover reduction.

D. Compensation Practices

Employers universally believe that poor wages contribute to resignations (Liebtag, 1987). To illustrate, partners in public accounting firms cite pay dissatisfaction as a major reason for staff quitting (Hom et al., 1988). Indeed, a fundamental principle of compensation administration is assuring that current wages are competitive with community rates to forestall turnover (Milkovich and Newman, 1990). Likewise, former employees attribute their departure to inadequate salaries or fringe benefits in exit surveys or interviews (Donovan, 1980; Huey and Hartley, 1988; Sigardson, 1982; Silvers and Valencia, 1990). Along these lines, an Associated Press telephone call of 1005 adults nationwide (December 1990) reported that 15% declared that they or a family member changed jobs or *remained* in a job due to health benefits (Lewin, 1991). Employees (or their dependents) having a long-term disease may endure "job-lock" because a new employer's insurer may reject coverage for preexisting conditions.

Contrary to testimonials about pay's centrality for job stability, turnover research generally uncovers weak and inconsistent relationships between pay (and pay satisfaction) and individual exits (Mobley et al., 1979; Mobley, 1982; Motowidlo, 1983; Weiner, 1980). Yet various methodological artifacts possibly subverted these associations. For one, turnover studies typically examined wages in one job or firm, restricting pay variance and hence pay–quit correlations (cf. Steel and Griffeth, 1989). In contrast, labor economic studies, which sample multiple firms (e.g., national samples), reveal stronger wage effects on individual quits (Blakemore et al., 1987; Mitchell, 1983; Shaw, 1987). Importantly, routine measurement of base pay (Price and Mueller, 1981, 1986) overlooked other major compensation forms (Heneman, 1985), namely, fringe benefits and incentive pay, which represent growing proportions of pay packages (Gomez-Mejia and Balkin, 1992). Compounding this oversight, turnover research typically neglected pay system characteristics, which compensation scholars have recently found to underpin pay satisfaction and quit decisions (Folger and Konovsky, 1989; Miceli et al., 1991). Given these weaknesses, extant turnover work surely understated the impact of pay practices on quitting. With this caveat in mind, the next section extrapolates from compensation research to identify promising pay interventions for decreasing terminations.

1. Setting Base Pay

Theories of pay satisfaction contend that pay satisfaction derives from perceived fairness of the pay amount (distributive justice) and pay practices (procedural justice) (Folger and Greenberg, 1985; Heneman, 1985; Miceli and Lane, 1991; Lawler, 1981). To meet employee perceptions of fair pay amounts, firms must base pay on personal job inputs (e.g., job performance, education) and job characteristics (e.g., working conditions, job complexity) that employees deem *relevant* contributions to the firm (Lawler, 1971, 1981). Furthermore, employees compare their pay to earnings of others doing similar work (in or outside the firm). Thus, firms must also ensure that pay is relatively consistent across jobs of similar worth (or difficulty) and match community wages for those jobs (Miceli et al., 1991).

Nonetheless, prevailing compensation practices may not necessarily satisfy employees' standards for equitable base pay. Employers often use job evaluation—a procedure rating jobs on various dimensions of personnel requirements and job complexity (known as compensable factors)—and salary surveys to establish base pay for jobs (Henderson, 1989; Milkovich and Newman, 1990). These practices seek internal and external equity by paying wages to jobs that are commensurate to their complexity and demands and to their wages in the external marketplace. These compensation decisions rarely involve employee input (Milkovich and Newman, 1990). For example, job evaluation techniques may judge a job's worth differently or use different compensable factors (or weight them differently) than job incumbents. Similarly, wage surveys may sample pay referents different than those employees consider in pay comparisons. Despite their oft-times care and rigor, these pay practices may not achieve "fair" salaries and thus promote loyalty (through pay satisfaction).

Apart from distributive equity, traditional pay programs miss many elements embodying procedural equity (Milkovich and Newman, 1990). Drawing from Leventhal (1980) and Folger and Greenberg (1985), Table 7 describes those rules for procedural justice and their extension for compensation administration. Recent compensation work affirmed that both procedural and distributive fairness underpin pay satisfaction (Folger and Konovsky, 1989; Miceli et al., 1991). Indeed, Folger and Konovsky (1989) found that perceived fairness of merit pay decisions—based on regular performance feedback, appraisal reviews that develop ratees and solicit their views, and extensive supervisory observations—enhanced organizational commitment more than did perceived equity of the pay raise.

In a rare study, Gomez-Mejia et al. (1982) built many features of procedural fairness into a new pay structure for Control Data Corporation managers. For instance, Gomez-Mejia et al. (1982) elicited compensable factors from 26 personnel executives and had 50 managers revise a preexisting job evaluation scale to improve its validity for evaluating their work. Rather than a job evaluation committee, 449 managers then used this new scale to evaluate their jobs. (Their ratings were computer-scored to derive an overall index of a job's worth and then checked against norms for that job for accuracy.) Gomez-Mejia et al. then used incumbents' job evaluations to assign jobs into pay grades (and hence pay rates), forming a new pay structure (cf. Milkovich and Newman, 1990). Afterwards, Gomez-Mejia et al. solicited feedback from compensation managers, who endorsed this pay plan as correctly assigning wages based on job worth and predicted that employees would welcome this plan. In summary, these findings suggest that improvements in procedural fairness in pay administration will yield dividends in higher morale and retention (Greenberg and McCarthy, 1990). Additional work remains to replicate and extend Gomez-Mejia et al.'s intriguing results.

2. Skill-Based Pay

Skill- or knowledge-based pay plans constitute an emerging alternative to the traditional job-based pay plan and promise higher procedural and distributive fairness of base pay (Ledford, 1990; Milkovich and Newman, 1990). Rather than paying for job content, these approaches base pay on depth of incumbent knowledge in one professional or technical job or mastery of multiple production jobs (LeBlanc, 1990; Ledford and Bergel, 1990; Ledford et al., 1990). Preliminary evaluations suggest that skill-based pay plans quicken salary progression because employees earn raises as quick as they can master new skills (Ledford, 1990). Apart from higher pay, skill-based plans involve more consistency, accuracy, and representativeness in pay decisions, fostering procedural justice. For example, employees only receive a pay hike if they meet clear standard criteria (master a defined skill block) according to a certification panel comprising superiors and peers (Ledford, 1990). Not surprisingly, case studies find that skill-based pay promotes job satisfaction (Ledford and Bergel, 1990) and retention (LeBlanc, 1990).

Table 7 Illustration of Justice Rules for Compensation

Justice rules	Setting base pay	Pay increases
Consistency		
Allocation procedures are consistent across persons/time	Apply same job evaluation to all jobs	Apply same performance standards to all subordinates
Bias suppression		
Minimize personal self-interest in allocation procedure	Safeguards against depressed job evaluation of jobs dominated by women	Performance ratings are free from personal prejudices
Accuracy		
Base allocation on accurate information	Base job evaluation on accurate, up-to-date job descriptions	Document performance ratings with behavioral examples
Correctability		
Opportunities to modify or reverse allocation decisions	Employee opportunity for job audits if jobs are placed in wrong pay grades	Employee opportunity to disagree with performance rating
Representativeness		
Allocation process represents concerns of all recipients	Job evaluation committee includes representatives from all functional areas	Multiple-rater appraisal comprises ratings from knowledgeable raters
Ethicality		
Allocations do not violate prevailing moral standards	Company complies with stated objective of equitable pay differentials	Maintain confidentiality of individual employees' performance ratings

3. *Variable Pay*

Tying financial rewards to job or firm performance (or variable pay) can potentially curb dysfunctional turnover. Several studies corroborate that contingent-pay schemes slow exits by effective performers—who benefit from performance incentives—but accelerate exits by marginal performers (functional quits) (Bishop, 1990; Williams and Livingstone, 1989; Zenger, 1992). Quoting Fama (1980), "When the firm's reward system is not responsive to performance . . . the best are the first to leave" (p. 292). Moreover, some research finds that variable pay reduces overall quit rates, possibly due to higher remuneration to most employees (Blakemore et al., 1987; Leonard, 1987; Wilson and Peel, 1991).

Unfortunately, merit pay programs—the prevailing scheme for distributing variable pay—often fail to motivate higher performance (Heneman, 1990). Their inefficacy can be primarily traced to their reliance on superiors to evaluate employee performance (Gomez-Mejia and Balkin, 1992; Lawler, 1990). Yet many employees regard supervisory judgments as inherently biased and thereby doubt whether their accomplishments would truly earn just compensation (Gomez-Mejia and Balkin, 1992). These suspicions are not groundless for appraisal studies have long documented pervasive rating errors in performance evaluations (cf. Bernardin and Beatty, 1984; Murphy and Cleveland, 1991).

While beyond the scope of this chapter, we briefly review research on ways to enhance validity and fairness of performance ratings, and thereby efficacy of merit pay schemes. Specifically, Table 8 summarizes findings from examinations of employee reactions to performance reviews (Cederblom, 1982; Murphy and Cleveland, 1991), showing how to increase appraisal fairness (Dipboye and dePontbriand, 1981; Folger and Konovsky, 1989; Greenberg, 1986; Landy et al., 1978). For example, Greenberg (1986) found that employees regarded performance appraisals as fair if they could challenge superior ratings, provide input before final ratings, and their superior consistently applied standards and knew their work.

Table 8 Credible and Fair Appraisal Reviews (Improving Appraisal Attitudes)

- Performance measurement
  - Consistent performance standards
  - Relevant performance dimensions
  - Behavioral performance dimensions
  - Solicitation of subordinate views
  - Frequent supervisory observations
  - Supervisory knowledge of job requirements
  - Accounted for performance obstacles
- Performance feedback
  - Frequent feedback
  - Specific feedback for behavioral change
  - Rationale for performance rating
- Performance planning
  - Set specific and clear goals
  - Discussion of plans for performance improvements
  - Resolution of difficulties about job duties
  - Periodic review of goal progress
- Recourse
  - Allowing expressions about performance rating
  - Allowing opportunity to appeal performance rating

Besides appraisal validity, certain ways of reward distribution boost effectiveness of merit pay schemes (Gomez-Mejia and Balkin, 1992; Lawler, 1990). Reviewing merit pay studies, Heneman (1990) identified several allocation practices promoting "line of sight," i.e., employees' belief that performance translates into monetary rewards (Lawler, 1981). Such confidence in the reward system inspires work motivation as well as loyalty of high performers, who would leave if they did not believe that incentives are dispensed for achievement (Zenger, 1992). For one, objective links between pay and performance reinforce line-of-sight perceptions, as do meaningful pay increases (that outstrip inflation) and sufficient variability of pay hikes. More than this, paying bonuses rather than merit pay increases that are permanently rolled into base salaries enhances contingency beliefs (Lawler, 1990). Instead of annuities, such merit bonuses carry greater motivational impact since employees must re-earn bonuses in successive years (Heneman, 1990). In addition, distributing merit raises in one pay check (lump sum distribution) sustains motivation more than common distribution of raises across multiple pay checks, "burying" reward amount (Lawler, 1981). In summary, implementing fair and credible appraisals and line-of-sight reward allocation may enhance the capacity of merit pay schemes to retain superior personnel.

4. Group Incentives

Increasingly, employers grant bonuses based on company profits or operational efficiency (Gomez-Mejia and Balkin, 1992; Milkovich and Newman, 1990). Although reviews attest to their productivity gains (Bullock and Lawler, 1984; Welbourne and Gomez-Mejia, 1988), turnover impact of group incentives has rarely been examined. Nevertheless, several theories persuasively argue that profit sharing or gain sharing programs may affect terminations, while a recent British study discovered that profit sharing reduced overall voluntary quits (Wilson and Peel, 1991).

Given their motivational impact (cf. Gerhart and Milkovich, 1990), group incentives might stem the migration of effective performers, especially if bonuses are proportional to individual accomplishments (cf. Balwin, 1982). Beyond this, lucrative incentive systems may boost pay satisfaction and overall retention, such as Lincoln Electric's sizeable bonuses (Balwin, 1982). Additionally, efficiency-based plans usually involve employee participation (soliciting suggestions), thereby increasing perceived fairness of pay administration (Blinder, 1989). For example, the Scanlon plan sets up a plant-wide committee comprising labor and top management to administer the bonus plan (Frost, 1978). As noted earlier, procedural justice raises pay satisfaction and loyalty (Folger and Greenberg, 1985; Folger and Konovsky, 1989). Furthermore, employees may accumulate large pension benefits from profit-sharing plans (Gomez-Mejia and Balkin, 1992), making it costly for them to quit (Hulin et al., 1985; Rusbult and Farrell, 1983). Finally, group incentive plans possibly enhance job security (Irrgang, 1972; Gomez-Mejia and Balkin, 1992), which in turn breeds company loyalty (Davy et al., 1991; Greenhalgh and Rosenblatt, 1984). By lowering fixed labor costs (e.g., base pay), firms can promise more secure employment by withholding bonuses during economic downturns instead of laying off staff (Irrgang, 1972; Lawler, 1990).

5. Stock ownership

For various reasons, stock ownership—through stock grants [e.g., employee stock ownership plans (ESOP)] or stock purchase plans—may foster organizational loyalty (Klein, 1987; Labich, 1992). First, stock grants may enhance satisfaction and retention because they constitute a benefit of company membership (Hulin et al., 1985; Rusbult and Farrell, 1983). Second, ESOP shares (which vest over time) and stock options (or restricted stock) may prolong tenure because employees must stay employed for a certain duration to obtain fully vested ESOP shares or to exercise options (Klein, 1987; Lawler, 1990). Premature terminations would forfeit these stock benefits (Mobley, 1977;

Rusbult and Farrell, 1983). Third, stock ownership may diminish unfriendly takeovers by outsiders (since employees can vote for who runs the firm) and thus reinforce job security and retention (avoiding the downsizing or dismantling that follows takeovers) (Faltermayer, 1992). Supporting our line of reasoning, Klein (1987) found that employees owning substantial ESOPs expressed more firm commitment, while Wilson and Peel (1991) showed that firms having share ownership schemes experienced lower quit rates.

6. Retention Incentives

High-tech and military organizations have long experimented with financial incentives to retain staff. For example, reenlistment bonuses have bolstered military reenlistments (Lakhani, 1988). In a similar manner, high-tech companies award special inducements to retain technical employees ("key contributors") whose special skills or proprietary knowledge profoundly contribute to firm success (Gomez-Mejia et al., 1990). Most often, high-tech firms distribute large cash awards for outstanding scientific achievements. Besides cash, many companies grant stocks (or phantom stocks) to key contributors. Additionally, some companies offer special budgets for equipment or conference travel to talented scientists, while other firms even fund their new ventures. Such intrapreneurship satisfies key contributors' intellectual and entrepreneurial pursuits, besides discouraging their departure to form new competing businesses (Gomez-Mejia et al., 1990).

7. Fringe Benefits

Although roughly consuming 39% of payroll (Barber et al., 1992), employee benefits have rarely been demonstrated to enhance retention and morale, underlying reasons for their existence (Dreher et al., 1988; Milkovich and Newman, 1990). All the same, anecdotal reports widely disclose that potential forfeiture of accumulated pension benefits postpones retirement (Cahan, 1986; Stricharchuk, 1987) or threatened loss of health benefits discourages quits (Lewin, 1991). As well, employee surveys and public opinion polls attest to the broad significance of benefits, especially health care (Dwyer and Garland, 1991).

All the same, a few empirical studies suggest that certain benefits or benefit practices may prolong job tenure (Barber et al., 1992; Ippolito, 1992; Williams and Dreher, 1992). For one, extensive benefit coverage may reduce turnover. Suggesting this impact, Dreher et al. (1988) showed that ample benefits elevated benefit satisfaction [which may enhance job stability (Hulin et al., 1985)], while Williams and Dreher (1992) found that broad coverage lures more job applicants (and by extension, enhances job attraction for current incumbents). More directly, labor economic research established that pension coverage and pension accumulations deter quitting (Ippolito, 1991; Mitchell, 1983).

Moreover, organizations often tie benefit levels (e.g., pension, vacation time) to years of service (Milkovich and Newman, 1990). Although routinely done, the impact on job longevity of seniority-based benefits has only recently been examined (Ippolito, 1991). While pension loss upon premature quits before full vesting is well known, Ippolito (1991) established that exits *after* full vesting also yield sizable losses, which accumulate with tenure [in common defined benefits plans (Milkovich and Newman, 1990)]. Based on years of seniority and final salary, most benefit formulas distribute smaller pensions to vested leavers (at retirement) because they index benefits to leavers' last wage, not later (and higher) retirement age salary. Analyzing data from 109 pension plans, Ippolito (1991) calculated pension capital losses for 6416 employees and found that large anticipated pension forfeiture lengthens employment. This striking demonstration may account for one of the most durable facts about turnover; quit rates decline with rising job tenure (Mobley, 1982).

Moreover, certain fringe benefits may promote satisfaction and retention more than others (Miceli and Lane, 1991). Medical benefits and stock are most desired, but benefit preferences also vary with personal values (risk aversion, leisure demands), family responsibilities, and age (Miceli and Lane, 1991; Milkovich and Newman, 1990). For example, Williams and Dreher (1992) found that banks offering more paid time off more quickly filled vacant teller positions, indicating that young women—who constituted most tellers—most prized this benefit given their parental obligations. To provide valued benefits, organizations must first identify their work force's benefit preferences. Employee surveys more accurately diagnose benefit desires than do demographic profiles (Barber et al., 1992; Milkovich and Newman, 1990).

However generous, benefit coverage fosters morale and retention only if employees understand and appreciate their benefits (Dreher et al., 1988; Miceli and Lane, 1991). Yet most employees are unaware of or underestimate their fringe benefits (Wilson et al., 1985), and such ignorance or misunderstanding can undermine benefits' payoffs in higher satisfaction and loyalty (Dreher et al., 1988). Therefore, communication programs—notably, small-group meetings and personalized benefit statements—are vital for promoting benefit effectiveness through improved knowledge of benefits and their costs to employers (Barber et al., 1992; Miceli and Lane, 1991; Milkovich and Newman, 1990; Wilson et al., 1985).

Furthermore, organizations must limit benefit expenses imposed on employees, who increasingly share the cost of benefit coverage (Dreher et al., 1988). To illustrate, Dreher et al. (1988) showed that employee costs (e.g., higher medical premiums and deductibles) worsen benefit satisfaction. On the other hand, employee contributions to benefit coverage increase understanding of benefit value and perceived benefit coverage (Wilson et al., 1985). Finally, flexible benefit plans—wherein employees can choose benefits—improve benefit knowledge and attainment of desired benefits (Miceli and Lane, 1991). Upholding this latter reason, Barber et al. (1992) found that introduction of a flexible benefits plan bolsters benefit satisfaction and knowledge, while Williams and Dreher (1992) showed that benefit flexibility shortens vacancy periods for job openings. By extension, these findings imply that flexible benefits may stabilize employment among job incumbents.

E. Employee Selection

1. Weighted Application Blanks

Employers often screen out job applicants based on perceived job instability—or the "hobo" syndrome (Hulin, 1991)—to ensure a more stable work force (Kinicki et al., 1990). To date, weighted application blanks (WABs) best identify unstable personnel (Cascio, 1976; Cotton and Tuttle, 1986; Schmitt et al., 1984). WABs are application forms that have been converted to selection tests. This conversion requires an initial comparison between long- and short-term employees' responses to application blank items (completed during hiring), identifying items evoking different responses from these groups (Gatewood and Feild, 1987). Using these items, the test developer computes a scoring key, assigning different scores to groups' dissimilar answers to each item. Next, new job applicants complete the application blank and their item responses are scored using the new answer key. The sum of item scores becomes a test score assessing propensity for stable employment, and applicants whose WAB scores suggest this predisposition would be rejected.

Despite their effectiveness, few organizations use weighted application blanks, fearing discrimination charges (Gatewood and Feild, 1987). That is, inquiries about certain demographic characteristics violate state fair employment statutes and screening out applicants with certain background attributes (e.g., residence) may disproportionately exclude minorities or women (Gatewood and Feild, 1987). Apart from adverse effects, the apparent irrelevancy of many biodata items (e.g., age, home ownership) may prompt discrimination lawsuits (Breaugh and Dossett, 1989). Thus, companies may incur litigation costs to defend such "unfair" questions and suffer damaged public relations. Besides, statistical evidence that questionable biodata items are job-related may not convince a judge that WABs should be used or alternative tests having less adverse impact are missing (Breaugh and Dossett, 1989).

Breaugh and Dossett (1989) described a more rational basis for choosing biographical predictors of turnover. Traditional empirical keying provides little understanding into why biodata items predict a criterion and requires huge samples to design a scoring key. Rather, they recommended that WABs include only biodata items that are verifiable (promoting applicant honesty) and logically correspond to turnover according to well-known psychological theories. Such criteria would improve WABs' face validity and thus discourage lawsuits from rejected job candidates (Breaugh and Dossett, 1989).

Following these criteria, Breaugh and Dossett developed a WAB to predict bank teller turnover. In particular, they chose tenure on the previous job, following the well-accepted maxim that "past behavior is the best predictor of future behavior." Because reality shock induces turnover, they also selected employee referrals (a recruitment source) and relevancy of prior work experience to index realism of expectations (Wanous, 1980). Finally, their WAB comprised educational attainment because turnover research finds that overeducated personnel are more likely to quit due to their ample job opportunities (Cotton and Tuttle, 1986). In combination, these biodata items moderately predicted turnover ($r = 0.44$). In conclusion, the Breaugh–Dossett WAB procedure is a practical (bypasses large-sample scoring-key development) and defensible (using job-related items) way to choose biographical predictors of turnover.

2. Personality Measures

In contrast to WAB efficacy, personality measures have poorly predicted terminations. Reviews (Barrick and Mount, 1991; Griffeth and Hom, 1988b; Muchinsky and Tuttle, 1979; Schmitt et al., 1984) consistently estimated modest correlations (typically, 0.18 or less) between personality (and vocational interests) and turnover. Several reasons underlie such disappointing findings (Mobley, 1982). Personality and interest inventories are prone to faking by respondents, who present themselves favorably when seeking employment (Bernardin, 1987) and when participating in research studies (Aronson et al., 1990). Importantly, personality measures are often arbitrarily chosen without thought as to their theoretical correspondence to turnover (Barrick and Mount, 1991; Weiss and Adler, 1984).

Notwithstanding these findings, recent theory-based personality measures more accurately predict job stability. One research stream pinpoints a "negative affectivity" trait (NA) (Staw et al., 1986) as a dispositional source of job satisfaction. The NA personality unfavorably evaluates self, others, and situations, and consequently experiences negative emotional states (Brief et al., 1988; George, 1990). Given this tendency, NA individuals process work cues negatively and thus feel more job dissatisfaction (Staw et al., 1986). Impressively, Staw et al. (1986) demonstrated that NA measures takened during adolescence reliably forecasted adult job attitudes—predicting satisfaction as long as 50 years later. Thus, adolescents viewing life negatively eventually judged their adult work unfavorably. Other research extended Staw et al.'s provocative findings, showing that NA promotes absenteeism and termination intentions, while discouraging prosocial actions (George, 1989, 1990).

A second research stream suggests that person–environment fit also forecasts turnover (Chatman, 1991). Following interactional psychology (Schneider, 1987), O'Reilly et al. (1991) reasoned that shared and deeply held values of organizational members embody organizational culture and that congruency between employee values and those cultural values underlies organizational commitment (O'Reilly and Chatman, 1986). To assess person–organization fit, O'Reilly et al. (1991) designed the Organizational Culture Profile (OCP). The OCP compares employees and organizations on values (enduring preferences for a specific mode of conduct or end state of existence [Rokeach, 1973]), which are relevant and commensurate descriptors of both entities.

Specifically, the OCP identifies value profiles for the firm and individual and uses template matching to assess profile similarity (Caldwell and O'Reilly, 1990; O'Reilly et al., 1991). Following a Q-sort procedure, respondents sort 54 value statements (drawn from writings on company culture) into nine categories that range from most to least characteristic of the existing or ideal company, distributing a certain number of statements into each category (item pattern: 2–4–6–9–12–9–6–4–2). To develop the culture profile, firm experts (e.g., managers) sort value statements according to which they describe the company; their responses are then averaged. For individual profiles, employees sort statements according to personal preference for each value in their ideal company. Correlation between employee and firm profiles yields a person–company fit score. In a preliminary test, O'Reilly et al. (1991) and Chatman (1991) showed that new accountants' OCP scores foreshadowed later job attitudes and retention, albeit the latter prediction was a modest 0.16 correlation.

Approaching person–job fit differently, Bernardin (1987) developed a forced choice personality inventory for customer service representatives working for a newspaper. Unlike most personality tests, this inventory controls faking by having respondents choose a descriptor from a pair of descriptors matched for social desirability; however, only one descriptor represents a valid choice. Specifically, Bernardin interviewed job incumbents and superiors to identify discomforting work events, writing statements about these events. Then he generated statements about vexing situations irrelevant to the job and recruited college students to rate the discomfort level of relevant and irrelevant statements. The resulting inventory included multiple pairs of statements; each pair comprised one relevant and one irrelevant statement that were equally annoying. From each pair, respondents would select the most irritating description. In a concurrent validation design, current incumbents completed this personality test and those who chose valid statements more likely resigned ($r = 0.31$). Thus, employees who felt more distressed by common job stressors, i.e., poor fit, more readily terminated. However, replications with predictive validation designs are warranted because research participants may lack motivation to distort their personality responses.

In summary, contemporary research suggests higher utility of personality tests for turnover management. First, organizations might screen out NA or mismatched job applicants to obtain a more stable, satisfied work force (Chatman, 1991; Staw et al., 1986), although evidence on NA predictions of turnover is missing. All the same, existing NA measures appear easily fakable and may be impractical for applicant selection. Instead, employers might use NA scores to place NA newcomers in work groups with positive affective tones (i.e., shared norms of positive affectivity) to curb their morose affect (George, 1990). Elevated moods may in turn lower withdrawal. By comparison, the OCP is more immune to intentional distortions because OCP items are expressed in socially neutral or slightly positive terms (cf. Bernardin, 1987). [O'Reilly et al. (1991) also found that social desirability did not bias OCP firm profiles.] Besides hiring, OCP company profiles may serve as realistic organizational previews for prospective employees, enabling them to better self-select themselves for their ideal organizational cultures (Schneider, 1987; Wanous, 1980). Furthermore, wider usage of forced choice methodology would reduce fakability of personality tests (Bernardin, 1987). Finally, morale-boosting interventions (e.g., job enrichment) may have limited success given affective dispositional roots of job attitudes (Staw et al., 1986). All the same, such interventions may still raise mean satisfaction levels, even without changing the rank ordering of individuals' attitudes (Arvey et al., 1989).

F.   Managing Interrole Conflicts

The popular press and academic writings increasingly emphasize changing work force demographics. During the past 20 years, women have rapidly joined the labor force and will account for 63% of new entrants to the work force between now and the turn of this century (Kossek and Grace, 1990; Milliken et al., 1990). Remarkably, mothers of preschoolers, 60% of whom work (Shellenbarger, 1992), are and will remain the fastest growing segment of the work population (Milliken et al., 1990). By the same token, single-parent and dual-earner families increasingly dominate the working population, outnumbering the traditional nuclear household comprising a male breadwinner and mother raising two children (Bernstein et al., 1991; Farrell, 1992; Zedeck and Mosier, 1990). In another development, 25% of the working age population care for aging relatives—a doubling in growth since 1980 (O'Reilly, 1992; Shellenbarger, 1992). These demographic changes bode growing conflict between work and family duties for employees, especially women who historically assumed primary domestic obligations (Kossek, 1990; Raltson and Flanagan, 1985; Zedeck and Mosier, 1990). For example, a Department of Labor study found that one of three women who stopped working in 1986 did so to devote more time to home or children compared with one in 100 men who did so (Mattis, 1990), while a Yankelovich Clancy Shulman survey revealed that 28% of working mothers in 1990 wanted to quit to become full-time mothers and homemakers (Spiers, 1992).

Such rising interrole conflict may become a prime stimulant of turnover (Driscoll et al., 1992; Hom et al., 1989; Kossek, 1990). To illustrate, career studies of nurses find that 40% drop out of the job market primarily to fulfill family responsibilities (Donovan, 1980), and a survey in a public utility found that female employees more often considered quitting for childrearing (Kossek, 1990). To address this prospective cause, various interventions have been proposed and implemented to help employees balance work and family responsibilities (Bernstein et al., 1991; Schwartz, 1992). For example, a nationwide study of 2600 pregnant women by the National Council of Jewish Women discovered that women whose firms accommodated their pregnancy remained on the job 1-1/2 months longer than those working for less accommodating firms, while a U.S. Census Bureau study found that 71% of women receiving maternity benefits returned to their jobs within 6 months of childbirth compared with 43% of those without these benefits (Trenk, 1990). The following section discusses the most promising approaches catalogued by Zedeck and Mosier (1990): (1) maternity and parental leaves; (2) child and dependent care services; (3) alternative work schedules; and (4) telecommuting. Indeed, the Families and Work Institute developed an index to measure whether or not a company is family-friendly, shown in Table 9 (Bernstein et al., 1991).

1.   Family Leave

Exit interviews and surveys find that many women drop out of the labor force—temporarily or permanently—to meet childbearing or childrearing responsibilities (Gerson, 1985; Huey and Hartley, 1980). Given such extrawork roles, many writers recommend available maternity or parental leave to reduce job exits (Cook, 1989; Johnson, 1990). Nonetheless, American leave policy is typically restricted in work force coverage, remuneration, job guarantees, duration, and health benefit extensions compared with European plans. For example, only 40% of working women have any partially or fully paid maternity leave, which they largely receive through disability or sickness benefits (Zedeck and Mosier, 1990). Moreover, leave policies generally do not guarantee that the women can return to their jobs if they remain off work more than 6–8 weeks, the standard "disability" period following childbirth (Zedeck and Mosier, 1990). In addition, only 67% of firms

Table 9   Company Family Friendliness

Policy	Maximum score
Flexible schedule	105
Family leave	40
Financial assistance	80
Corporate giving and community service	60
Dependent care services	155
Management change	90
Work–family stress management	80
Total possible score:	610

Source: From Families and Work Institute.

with health insurance plans continue to pay for coverage during maternity leave (Bernstein, 1991a). Furthermore, fewer companies offer any paid paternity leave, although only 37% of large firms offer job-guaranteed, unpaid leaves (ranging from 1 to 6 months) to fathers (who mostly decline leaves) (Zedeck and Mosier, 1990). Despite these official statistics, a Families and Work Institute in-depth survey of four northern states uncovered far more pervasive maternity (83%) and paternity (60%) leaves if informal practices are combined with written leave policies (Bernstein, 1991a).

Notwithstanding their growing legislation (Nobile, 1990), family leave policies have received little empirical support that they truly curb job exits, a prime motive for their usage (Bernstein et al., 1991). Studies noted above do suggest that firms accommodating pregnancies had fewer female quits (Trenk, 1990), albeit these firms implement other family-responsive measures in addition to parental leave. In the wake of alarming statistics that 23% of women returning to work after childbirth later quit, Aetna Life and Casualty introduced family leave (Trenk, 1990). This family leave, wherein new mothers can take up to 6 months off without pay, combined with part-time work schedules halved turnover (12%).

2.   Child and Dependent Care Services

Increasingly, businesses provide daycare services, usually information and referral programs, or flexible spending accounts (Goff et al., 1990; O'Reilly, 1992; Zedeck and Mosier, 1990). On- or near-site child care is most preferred by employees with children but is also the costliest daycare service (Kossek, 1990; Zedeck and Mosier, 1990, Yalow, 1990). Although Goff et al. (1990) found that onsite child care did not reduce work–family conflicts, Campbell Soup Company claimed that onsite child care at its headquarters lowered quits (Yalow, 1990). More revealing, Milkovich and Gomez (1976) found that mothers with young children enrolled in a company-sponsored day care quit less than mothers who did not enroll their children in this program, while Youngblood and Chambers-Cook (1984) found that available daycare service decreased quit intentions.

3.   Alternative Work Schedules

Organizations have also experimented with alternative work schedules to help employees balance home and work duties. For one, experimental tests find that flexitime reduces absenteeism but not turnover (Dalton and Mesch, 1990; Ralston and Flanagan, 1985). In contrast to flexitime, compressed work schedules—which entails longer but fewer work days—allow employees more time to deal with interrole conflict (Pierce and Dunham, 1992). In fact, compressed workweeks with more recuperative days off can ameliorate the disruptive family and physiological effects of shift rotation, a leading cause of turnover (Choi et al., 1986; Newby, 1980; Zedeck et al., 1983). In line with this reasoning, Pierce and Dunham (1992) supported compressed workweeks, showing that police officers enrolled in this work schedule developed higher job satisfaction and felt less interference with extrawork demands.

Moreover, case studies and other empirical work indicate that part-time work and job sharing, wherein two employees share responsibility for a full-time position, can reduce turnover (Shellenbarger, 1992; Zedeck and Mosier, 1990). Hospitals have long experimented with part-time and temporary work to retain nurses and lure inactive nurses back to nursing (Bogdanich, 1991; Huey and Hartley, 1988; Laird, 1983; Newby, 1980; Wandel et al., 1981). In other occupations, working mothers also credit part-time schedules for work reentry (Johnson, 1990)—as many as one-third of part-time or job-sharing women in a Catalyst survey (Mattis, 1990)—while 39% of women in a 1990 national survey believed that women should work only part-time if they have young children (Bernstein, 1991b). Furthermore, part-time schedules, as well as slower tracks to partnerships in professional firms, are becoming more prevalent among professional and managerial women (Ehrlich, 1989), although such "mommy" tracks may derail their careers and eventually speed their exodus from corporate America (Schwartz, 1989). More indicative, 68% of employers surveyed by Catalyst believed that part-time work and job sharing improved female retention, while NationsBank Corp retained valued employees by offering them job sharing (Shellenbarger, 1992).

4. Telecommuting

Telecommuting—or doing work at home and then electronically transferring results to the office—may improve working parents' capacity to care for children due to higher availability during the day and avoidance of commuting time (Zedeck and Mosier, 1990). In an early study, interviews with female office employees disclosed that telecommuting allowed them to better care for their children (and reinforced their organizational commitment) (Olson and Phillips, 1984). Nonetheless, these office personnel earned lower pay and benefits and experienced *more* conflict over simultaneous demands of work and family roles. By comparison, male professionals reported less work stress (due to fewer interruptions and office politics) and commuting stress, while having more opportunities for leisure (e.g., pursuing recreation during weekdays to avoid weekend crowds).

In closing, many businesses are experimenting with various approaches to help employees balance work and family obligations. Despite their expansion, most family-responsive measures are based on weak or nonexistent empirical support. By and large, testimonials or employer perceptions justify family assistance programs (Goff et al., 1990; Kossek and Grace, 1990). What is more, the few empirical evaluations of efficacy are plagued by various methodological shortcomings, including lack of control groups and extraneous confounds (Miller, 1984). For example, companies often simultaneously introduce multiple family benefits, preventing isolation of the impact of a particular intervention (cf. Trenk, 1990). In light of the rising work force clamor for family benefits, more scholarly research is merited to validate which approaches effectively promote job occupancy (Kossek and Grace, 1990).

REFERENCES

Abbott, A.D. (1988). *The System of Professions*, University of Chicago Press, Chicago, IL.
Ajzen, I. (1991). The theory of planned behavior, *Organiz. Behav. Human Decision Process.*, *50*: 179–211.

Alexander, J.A. (1988). The effects of patient care unit organization on nursing turnover, *Health Care Manage. Rev., 13*: 61–72.

Aranya, N., and Ferris, K.R. (1984). A reexamination of accountants' organizational–professional conflict, *Account. Rev., 1–15.*

Aranya, N., Pollock, J., and Amernic, J. (1981). An examination of professional commitment in public accounting, *Account, Organiz. Soc., 6*: 271–280.

Aronson, E., Ellsworth, P.E., Carlsmith, J.M., and Gonzales, M.H. (1990). *Methods of Research in Social Psychology*, McGraw-Hill, New York.

Arvey, R.D., Bouchard, T.J., Segal, N.L., and Abraham, L.M. (1989). Job satisfaction: environmental and genetic components, *J. Appl. Psychol., 74*: 187–192.

Ashford, S.J., Lee, C., and Bobko, P. (1989). Contention, causes, and consequences of job insecurity: a theory-based measure and substantive test, *Acad. Manage. J., 32*: 803–829.

Bacharach, S., and Bamberger, P. (1992). Causal models of role stressor antecedents and consequences: the importance of occupational differences, *J. Voc. Behav., 41*: 13–34.

Bagozzi, R.P., and Warshaw, P.R. (1990). Trying to consume, *J. Consumer Res., 17*: 127–140.

Balkin, D.B. (1992). Managing employee separations with the reward system, *The Executive, 6*: 64–71.

Balwin, W. (1982). This is the answer, *Forbes*, July 5.

Barber, A.E., Dunham, R.B., and Formisano, R.A. (1992). The impact of flexible benefits on employee satisfaction: a field study, *Personnel Psychol., 45*: 55–75.

Barrick, M.R., and Mount, M.K. (1991). The big five personality dimensions and job performance: a meta-analysis, *Personnel Psychol., 44*: 1–26.

Bass, A.B., and Ager, J. (1991). Correcting point-biserial turnover correlations of comparative analysis, *J. Appl. Psychol., 76*: 595–598.

Baysinger, B., and Mobley, W. (1983). Employee turnover: individual and organizational analysis, *Research in Personnel and Human Resources Management, Vol. 1.*, (K. Rowland and G. Ferris, eds.s), JAI Press, Greenwich, CT, pp. 269–319.

Becker, H.S. (1960). Notes on the concept of commitment, *Am. J. Sociol., 66*: 32–42.

Bellus, D. (1984). Turnover prevention: third-year staff accountants, *J. Account., 158*: 118–122.

Bernardin, H.J. (1987). Development and validation of a forced choice scale to measure job-related discomfort among customer service representatives, *Acad. Manage. J., 30*: 162–173.

Bernardin, H.J., and Beatty, R.W. (1984). *Performance Appraisal: Assessing Human Behavior at Work*, Kent, Boston.

Bernstein, A. (1991,a). Family leave may not be that big a hardship for business, *Business Week*, june 3, p. 28.

Bernstein, A. (1991,b). Do more babies mean fewer working women? *Business Week*, August 5, pp. 49–50.

Bernstein, A., Weber, J., and Driscoll, L. (1991). Corporate america is still no place for kids, *Business Week*, Nov. 25, pp. 234–237.

Bishop, J.H. (1990). Job performance, turnover, and wage growth, *J. Labor Econ., 8*: 363–396.

Blakemore, A., Low, S., and Ormiston, M. (1987). Employment bonuses and labor turnover, *J. Labor Econ., 5*: 124–135.

Blakeslee, G.S., Suntrup, E.L., and Kernaghan, J.A. (1985). How much is turnover costing you? *Personnel J.*, (Nov.): 98–103.

Blegen, M.A., Mueller, C.W., and Price, J.L. (1988). Measurement of kinship responsibility for organizational research, *J. Appl. Psychol., 73*: 402–409.

Blinder, A.S. (1989). Want to boost productivity? Try giving workers a say, *Business Week*, April 12, p. 10.

Bogdanich, W. (1991). Danger in white: the shadowy world of "temp" nurses, *Wall Street Journal*, Nov. 1, pp. B1, B6.

Borovies, D.L., and Newman, N.A. (1981). Graduate nurse transition program, *Am. J. Nurs.*, (Oct.): pp. 1832–1835.

Breaugh, J.A., and Dossett, D.L. (1989). Rethinking the use of personal history information: the value of theory-based biodata for predicting turnover, *J. Business Psychol., 3*: 371–385.

Brief, A.P., Burke, M.J., George, J.M., Robinson, B.S., and Webster, J. (1988). Should negative affectivity remain an unmeasured variable in the study of job stress, *J. Appl. Psychol., 73*: 193–198.

Brooke, P., Russell, D.W., and Price, J.L. (1988). Discriminant validation of measures of job satisfaction, job involvement, and organizational commitment, *J. Appl. Psychol., 73*: 139–145.

Bullock, R.J., and Lawler, E.E. (1984). Gainsharing: a few questions, and fewer answers, *Human Res. Manage., 23*: 23–40.

Butler, R.P., Lardent, C.L., and Miner, J.B. (1983). A motivational basis for turnover in military officer education and training, *J. Appl. Psychol., 68*: 496–506.

Cahan, V. (1986). The shrinking nest egg: retirement may never be the same, *Business Week*, Dec. 8, pp. 114–116.

Caldwell, D.F., and O'Reilly, C.A. (1990). Measuring person-job fit with a profile-comparison process, *J. Appl. Psychol., 75*: 648–657.

Campbell, D.T., and Stanley, J.C. (1963). *Experimental and Quasi-Experimental Designs for Research*, Rand McNally, Chicago.

Carsten, J.M., and Spector, P.E. (1987). Unemployment, job satisfaction, and employee turnover: a meta-analytic test of the Muchinsky model, *J. Appl. Psychol., 72*: 374–381.

Cascio, W.F. (1976). Turnover, biographical data, and fair employment practices, *J. Appl. Psychol., 61*: 576–580.

Cascio, W.F. (1991). *Costing Human Resources: The Financial Impact of Behavior in Organizations*, 3rd ed., Kent, Boston.

Cavanagh, S.J. (1989). Nursing turnover: literature review and methodological critique, *J. Adv. Nurs., 14*: 587–596.

Cederblom, D. (1982). The performance appraisal interview: a review, implications, and suggestions, *Acad. Manage. Rev., 7*: 219–227.

Chatman, J.A. (1991). Matching people and organizations: selection and socialization in public accounting firms, *Admin. Sci. Q. 36*: 459–484.

Choi, T., Jameson, H., Brekke, M.L., Podratz, R.O., and Mundahl, H. (1986). Effects on nurse retention: an experiment with scheduling, *Medical Care, 24*: 1029–1043.

Colarelli, S.M. (1984). Methods of communication and mediating processes in realistic job previews, *J. Appl. Psychol., 69*: 633–642.

Cook, A.H. (1989). Public policies to help dual-earner families meet the demands of the work world, *Ind. Labor Rel. Rev., 42*: 201–215.

Coser, R.L. (1976). Suicide and the relational system: a case study in a mental hospital, *J. Health Social Behav., 17*: 318–327.

Cotton, J.L., and Tuttle, J.M. (1986). Employee turnover: a meta-analysis and review with implications for research, *Acad. Manage. Rev., 11*: 55–70.

Curry, J.P., Wakefield, D.S., Price, J.L., Mueller, C.W., and McCloskey, J.C. (1985). Determinants of turnover among nursing department employees, *Res. Nurs. Health, 8*: 397–411.

Dalessio, A., Silverman, W.H., and Schuck, J.R. (1986). Paths to turnover: a re-analysis and review of existing data on the Mobley, Horner, and Hollingsworth turnover model, *Human Rel., 39*: 245–264.

Dalton, D.R., and Mesch, D.J. (1990). The impact of flexible scheduling on employee attendance and turnover, *Admin. Sci. Q., 35*: 370–387.

Dalton, D.R., Krackhardt, D.M., and Porter, L.W. (1981). Functional turnover: an empirical assessment, *J. Appl. Psychol., 66*: 716–721.

Dansereau, F., Graen, G., and Haga, W.J. (1975). A vertical dyad linkage approach to leadership within formal organizations, *Organiz. Behav. Human Perf., 13*: 46–78.

Darmon, R.Y. (1990). Identifying sources of turnover costs: a segmental approach, *J. Market., 54*: 46–56.

Davy, J.A., Kinicki, A.J., and Scheck, C.L. (1991). Developing and testing a model of survivor responses to layoffs, *J. Voc. Behav., 38*: 302–317.

Dean, R.A., and Wanous, J.P. (1984). Effects of realistic job previews on hiring bank tellers, *J. Appl. Psychol., 69*: 61–68.

Dean, R.A., Ferris, K.R., and Konstans, C. (1988). Occupational reality shock and organizational commitment: evidence from the accounting profession, *Acc. Organiz. Soc., 13*: 235–250.

Dipboye, R.L., and dePonbriand, R. (1981). Correlates of employee reactions to performance appraisals and appraisal systems, *J. Appl. Psychol., 66*: 248–251.

Donovan, L. (1980). What nurses want, *RN, 43*: 22–30.

Dowling, P.J., and Schuler, R.S. (1990). *International Dimensions of Human Resource Management*, PWS-Kent, Boston, MA.

Dreher, G.F., Ash, R.A., and Bretz, R.D. (1988). Benefit coverage and employee cost: critical factors in explaining compensation satisfaction, *Personnel Psychol., 41*: 237–254.

Dugoni, B.L., and Ilgen, D.R. (1981). Realistic job previews and the adjustment of new employees, *Acad. Manage. J., 24*: 579–591.

Dwyer, P., and Garland, S.B. (1991). A roar of discontent, *Business Week*, November 25, pp. 28–30.

Ehrlich, E. (1989). The mommy track, *Business Week*, March 20, pp. 126–134.

Faltermayer, E. (1992). Is this layoff necessary? *Fortune*, June, pp. 71–86.

Fama, E.F. (1980). Agency problems and the theory of the firm, *J. Polit. Econ., 88*: 288–307.

Farkas, A.J., and Tetrick, L.E. (1989). A three-wave longitudinal analysis of the casual ordering of satisfaction and commitment on turnover decisions, *J. Appl. Psychol. 74*: 855–868.

Farrell, C. (1992). Where have all the families gone? *Business Week*, June 29, pp. 90–91.

Farrell, D. (1983). Exit, voice, loyalty, and neglect as responses to job dissatisfaction: A multidimensional scaling study, *Acad. Manage. J., 26*: 596–607.

Feldman, D.C. (1976). A contingency theory of socialization, *Admin. Sci. Q., 21*: 433–452.

Feldman, D.C. (1988). *Managing Careers in Organizations*, Scott, Foresman, Glenview, IL.

Feldman, D.C., and Brett, J.M. (1983). Coping with new jobs: a comparative study of new hires and job changers, *Acad. Manage. J., 26*: 258–272.

Ferris, G.R. (1985). Role of leadership in the employee withdrawal process: a constructive replication, *J. Appl. Psychol., 70*: 777–781.

Finkelstein, S., and Hambrick, D.C. (1990). Top-management-team tenure and organizational outcomes: the moderating role of managerial discretion, *Admin. Sci. Q., 35*: 484–503.

Fishbein, M., and Ajzen, I. (1975). *Belief, Attitude, Intention and Behavior: An Introduction to Theory and Research*, Addison-Wesley, Reading, MA.

Fisher, C.D. (1986). Organizational socialization: an integrative review, *Research in Personnel and Human Resources Management* (K. Rowland and G. Ferris, eds.), JAI Press, Greenwich, CT.

Fisher, C.D., and Gitelson, R. (1983). A meta-analysis of the correlates of role conflict and ambiguity, *J. Appl. Psychol., 68*: 320–333.

Flamholtz, E. G. (1985). *Human Resource Accounting*, Jossey-Bass, San Francisco.

Folger, R., and Greenberg, J. (1985). Procedural justice: An interpretive analysis of personnel systems, *Research in Personnel and Human Resources Management, Vol. 3* (K. Rowland and G. Ferris, eds.), JAI Press, Greenwich, CT, pp. 141–183.

Folger, R., and Konovsky, M.A. (1989). Effects of procedural and distributive justice on reactions to pay raise decisions, *Acad. Manage. J., 32*: 115–130.

Forrest, C.R., Cummings, L.L., and Johnson, A.C. (1977). Organizational participation: A critique and model, *Acad. Manage. Rev., 2*: 586–601.

Fried, Y. (1991). Meta-analytic comparison of the job diagnostic survey and job characteristics inventory as correlates of work satisfaction and performance, *J. Appl. Psychol., 76*: 690–697.

Frost, C.F. (1978). The Scanlon plan: anyone for free enterprise? *MSU Business Topics (Winter)*: pp. 25–33.

Gatewood, R.D., and Feild, H.S. (1987). *Human Resource Selection*, Dryden Press, Hinsdale, IL.

George, J.M. (1989). Mood and absence, *J. Appl. Psychol., 74*: 317–324.

George, J.M. (1990). Personality, affect, and behavior in groups, *J. Appl. Psychol., 75*: 107–116.

Gerhart, B. (1990). Voluntary turnover and alternative job opportunities, *J. Appl. Psychol., 75*: 467–476.

Gerson, K. (1985). *Hard Choices*, University of California Press, Berkeley.

Ghiselli, E.E., Campbell, J.P., and Zedeck, S. (1981). *Measurement Theory for the Behavioral Sciences*, W.H. Freeman, San Francisco.

Gomez-Mejia, L.R., and Balkin, D.B. (1992). *Compensation, Organizational Strategy, and Firm Performance*, South-Western, Cincinnati, OH.

Gomez-Mejia, L.R., Balkin, D.B., and Milkovich, G.T. (1990). Rethinking your rewards for technical employees, *Organiz. Dyn., 18*: 62–75.

Gomez-Mejia, L.R., Page, R.C., and Tornow, W. (1982). A comparison of the practical utility of traditional, statistical, and hybrid job evaluation approaches, *Acad. Manage. J., 25*: 790–809.

Goff, S.J., Mount, M.K., and Jamison, R.L. (1990). Employer supported child care, work/family conflict, and absenteeism: a field study, *Personnel Psychol., 43*: 793–809.

Graen, G.B., and Cashman, J. (1975). A role-making model of leadership in formal organizations: a developmental approach, *Leadership Frontiers* (J.C. Hunt and L.L. Larsons, eds.), Kent State University Press, Kent, OH.

Graen, G.B., and Ginsburgh, S. (1977). Job resignation as a function of role orientation and leader acceptance: a longitudinal investigation of organizational assimilation, *Organiz. Behav. Human Perf. 19*: 1–17.

Graen, G.B., and Scandura, T.A. (1986). A theory of dyadic career reality, *Research in Personnel and Human Resources Management* (K. Rowland and G. Ferris, eds.), JAI Press, Greenwich, CT.

Graen, G.B., Liden, R., and Hoel, W. (1982). Role of leadership in the employee withdrawal process, *J. Appl. Psychol., 67*: 868–872.

Graen, G.B., Scandura, T.A., and Graen, M.R. (1986). A field experimental tests of the moderating effects of growth need strength on productivity, *J. Appl. Psychol., 71*: 484–491.

Greenberg, J. (1986). Determinants of perceived fairness of performance evaluations, *J. Appl. Psychol., 71*: 340–342.

Greenberg, J., and McCarty, C.L. (1990). Comparable worth: a matter of justice, *Research in Personnel and Human Resources Management, Vol. 8* (G.R. Ferris and K. Rowland, eds.), JAI Press, Greenwich, CT, pp. 265–301.

Greenhalgh, L., and Rosenblatt, Z. (1984). Job insecurity: toward conceptual clarity, *Acad. Manage. Rev., 9*: 438–448.

Griffeth, R.W. (1985). Moderation of the effects of job enrichment by participation: a longitudinal field experiment, *Organiz. Behav. Human Decision Process., 35*: 73–93.

Griffeth, R.W., and Hom, P.W. (1988a). A comparison of different conceptualizations of perceived alternatives in turnover research, *J. Organiz. Behav., 9*: 103–111.

Griffeth, R.W., and Hom, P.W. (1988b). Locus of control and delay of gratification as moderators of employee turnover, *J. Appl. Social Psychol., 18*: 1318–1333.

Griffeth, R., and Hom, P. (1990). *Competitive Examination of Two Turnover Theories: A Two-Sample Test*, Paper presented at the 50th Annual Convention of the Academy of Management, San Francisco, August.

Griffin, R.W. (1983). Objective and social sources of information in task redesign: a field experiment, *Admin. Sci. Q., 28*: 184–200.

Griffin, R.W. (1987). Toward an integrated theory of task design, *Research in Organizational Behavior* (L.L. Cummings and B.M. Staw, eds.), JAI Press, Greenwich, CT.

Hackman, J.R., and Oldham, G.R. (1980). *Work Redesign*: Addison-Wesley, Reading, MA.

Half, R. (1982). Keeping the best—employee retention in public accounting, *CPA J., 52*: 34–38.

Heneman, H.G. (1985). Pay satisfaction, *Research in Personnel and Human Resources Management, Vol. 3* (K.M. Rowland and G.R. Ferris, eds.), JAI Press, Greenwich, CT.

Heneman, R.L. (1990). Merit pay research, *Research in Personnel and Human Resources Management, Vol. 8* (G.R. Ferris and K. Rowland, eds.), JAI Press, Greenwich, CT, pp. 203–263.

Henkoff, R. (1990). Cost cutting: how to do it right, *Fortune (April)*: pp. 40–49.

Henderson, R. (1989). *Compensation Management*, Prentice-Hall, Englewood Cliffs, NJ.

Holloran, S.D., Mishkin, B.H., and Hanson, B.L. (1980). Bicultural training for new graduates, *J. Nurs. Admin.*, pp. 17–24.

Hom, P.W. (1992). *Turnover Costs among Mental Health Professionals*, unpublished manuscript, Department of Management, College of Business, Arizona State University, Tempe.

Hom, P.W., and Griffeth, R. (1991). Structural equations modeling test of a turnover theory: cross-sectional and longitudinal analyses, *J. Appl. Psychol., 76*: 350–366.

Hom, P.W., Griffeth, R.W., and Sellaro, C.L. (1984). The validity of Mobley's (1977) model of employee turnover, *Organiz. Behav. Human Perf., 34*: 141–174.

Hom, P.W., Bracker, J.S., and Julian, G. (1988). In pursuit of greener pastures, *New Accountant*, *4* (Oct.): 24–27.

Hom, P.W., Kinicki, A., and Domm, D. (1989). Confirmatory validation of a theory of employee turnover, *Proceedings of the 49th Annual Conference of the Academy of Management*, (F. Hoy, ed.), Academy of Management, Ada, Ohio, pp. 219–223.

Hom, P.W., Caranikas-Walker, F., Prussia, G.E., and Griffeth, R.W. (1992a). A meta-analytical structural equations analysis of a model of employee turnover, *J. Appl. Psychol., 77*: 890–909.

Hom, P.W., Griffeth, R.W., Palich, L.E., and Bracker, J.S. (1992b). Realistic job previews for new professionals: a two-occupation test of mediating processes, unpublished manuscript, Department of Management, Arizona State University, Tempe.

Horner, S.O., Mobley, W.H., and Meglino, B.M. (1979). *An Experimental Evaluation of the Effects of a Realistic Job Preview on Marine Recruit Affect, Intentions, and Behavior*, Technical Report 9, Center for Management and Organizational Research, Columbia, SC.

Huey, F.L., and Hartley, S. (1988). What keeps nurses in nursing, *Am. J. Nurs., 88*: 181–188.

Hulin, C.L. (1991). Adaptation, persistence, and commitment in organizations, *Handbook of Industrial and Organizational Psychology*, 2nd ed., *Vol. 2* (M.D. Dunnette and L.M. Hough, eds.), Consulting Psychologists Press, Palo Alto, CA.

Hulin, C.L., Roznowski, M., and Hachiya, D. (1985). Alternative opportunities and withdrawal decisions: empirical and theoretical discrepancies and an integration, *Psychol. Bull., 97*: 233–250.

Hunter, J.E., and Schmidt, F.L. (1990). *Methods of meta-analysis*, Sage, Newbury Park, CA.

Hunter, J.E., Schmidt, F.L., and Jackson, G.B. (1982). *Meta-analysis: Cumulating Research Findings Across Studies*, Sage, Beverly Hills, CA.

Ilgen, D.R., and Seely, W. (1974). Realistic expectations as an aid in reducing voluntary resignations, *J. Appl. Psychol., 59*: 452–455.

Ippolito, R.A. (1991). Encouraging long-term tenure: wage tilt or pensions? *Ind. Labor Rel., Rev., 44*: 520–535.

Ironson, G.H., Smith, P.C., Brannick, M.T., Gibson, W.M., and Paul, K.B. (1989). Construction of a job in general scale: a comparison of global, composite, and specific measures, *J. Appl. Psychol., 74*: 193–200.

Irrgang, W. 1972). *The Lincoln Incentive Management Program*, Lincoln Lecture Series, College of Business, Arizona State University, Tempe.

Jackofsky, E.F. (1984). Turnover and job performance: an integrated process model, *Acad. Manage. Rev., 9*: 74–83.

Jackofsky, E.F., and Peters, L.H. (1983). Job turnover versus company turnover: reassessment of the March and Simon participation hypothesis. *J. Appl. Psychol., 68*: 490–495.

Jackson, S.E., Brett, J.F., Sessa, V.I., Cooper, D.M., Julin, J.A., and Peyronnin, K. (1991). Some differences make a difference: individual dissimilarity and group heterogeneity as correlates of recruitment, promotions, and turnover. *J. Appl. Psychol., 76*: 675–689.

Jackson, S.E., and Schuler, R. (1985). A meta-analysis and conceptual critique of research on role ambiguity and role conflict in work settings, *Organiz. Behav. Human Decision Process., 36*: 16–78.

Jacob, R. (1992). The search for the organization of tomorrow, *Fortune* (May): pp. 92–98.

James, L.A., and James, L.R. (1989). Integrating work environment perceptions: Explorations into the measurement of meaning, *J. Appl. Psychol., 74*: 739–751.

Johnson, A.A. (1990). Parental leave: is it the business of business? *Human Resource Plann., 13*: 119–131.

Kahn, R.L., Wolfe, D.N., Quinn, R.P., Snoek, J.D., and Rosenthal, D.A. (1964). *Organizational Stress: Studies in Role Conflict and Ambiguity*, Wiley, New York.

Kahne, M.J. (1968). Suicides in mental hospitals: a study of the effects of personnel and patient turnover, *J. Health Social Behav., 9*: 255–266.

Kantor, R.M. (1977). *Men and Women of the Corporation*, Basic Books, New York.

Katerberg, R., Hom, P.W., and Hulin, C.L. (1979). Effects of job complexity on the reactions of part-time workers, *Organiz. Behav. Human Perf., 24*: 317–332.

Katz, R. (1980). Time and work: toward an integrative perspective, *Research in Organizational Behavior*, *Vol. 2*, (B. Staw and L.L. Cummings, eds.), JAI Press, CT, pp. 81–127.

Katz, R. (1982). The effects of group longevity on project communication and performance, *Admin. Sci. Q., 27*: 81–104.

Kanungo, R.N. (1982). Measurement of job and work involvement, *J. Appl. Psychol., 67*: 341–349.

Kerr, J., and Slocum, J.W. (1987). Managing corporate culture through reward systems, *The Academy of Management Executive, 1*: 99.

Kinicki, A.J., Lockwood, C.A., Hom, P.W., and Griffeth, R.W. (1990). Interviewer predictions of applicant qualifications and interviewer validity: aggregate and individual analyses, *J. Appl. Psychol., 75*: 477–486.

Klein, K.J. (1987). Employee stock ownership and employee attitudes: a test of three models, *J. Appl. Psychol., 72*: 319–332.

Klenke-Hamel, K.E., and Mathieu, J.E. (1990). Role strains, tension, and job satisfaction influences on employees' propensity to leave: A multisample replication and extension, *Human Relations, 43*: 791–808.

Kossek, E.E. (1990). Diversity in child care assistance needs: employee problems, preferences, and work-related outcomes, *Personnel Psychol., 43*: 769–791.

Kossek, E.E., and Grace, P. (1990). Taking a strategic view of employee child care assistance: a cost-benefit model, *Human Resource Plann., 13*: 189–202.

Krackhardt, D., and Porter, L. (1985). When friends leave: a structural analysis of the relationship between turnover and stayers' attitudes. *Admin. Sci. Q., 30*: 242–261.

Kramer, M. (1974). *Reality Shock: Why Nurses Leave Nursing*, Mosby, St. Louis, MO.

Kramer, M. (1977). Reality shock can be handled on the job, *RN, 63*: 11.

Kramer, M., and Schmalenberg, C. (1977). *Paths to Biculturalism*, Contemporary Publishing, Wakefield, MA.

Labich, K. (1992). The new pay game, *Fortune, (OCT.)*: pp. 116–119.

Laird, D.D. (1983). Supplemental nursing agencies—a tool for combatting the nursing shortage, *Health Care Manage. Rev., 8*: 61–67.

Laker, D. (1991). Job search, perceptions of alternative employment and the turnover decision, *J. Appl. Business Res., 7*: 6–16.

Lakhani, H. (1988). The effects of pay and retention bonuses on quit rates in the U.S. Army, *Ind. Labor Rel. Rev., 41*: 430–438.

Landy, F.J., Barnes, J., and Murphy, K. (1978). Correlates of perceived fairness and accuracy of performance appraisal, *J. Appl. Psychol., 63*: 751–754.

Lawler, E.E. (1971). *Pay and Organizational Effectiveness: A Psychological View*, McGraw-Hill, New York.

Lawler, E.E. (1981). *Pay and Organizational Development*, Addison-Wesley, Reading, MA.

Lawler, E.E. (1990). *Strategic Pay*, Jossey-Bass, San Francisco.

LeBlanc, p.V. (1990). Skill-based pay case number 2: Northern Telecom. *Compens. Benefits Rev.*, pp. 39–56.

Ledford, G.E. (1990). Three case studies on skill-based pay: an overview, *Compens. Benefits Rev.*, pp. 11–23.

Ledford, G.E., and Bergel, G. (1990). Skill-based pay case number 1: General Mills. *Compens. Benefits Rev.*, pp. 24–38.

Ledford, G.E., Tyler, W.R., and Dixey, W.B. (1990). Skill-based pay case number 3: Honeywell ammunition assembly plant. *Compens. Benefits Rev.*, pp. 57–77.

Lee, T. (1988). How job satisfaction leads to employee turnover, *J. Business Psychol., 2*: 263–271.

Lee, T.W., and Mitchell, T.R. (1991). The unfolding effects of organizational commitment and anticipated job satisfaction on voluntary employee turnover, *Motiv. Emotion, 15*: 99–121.

Lee, T.W., and Mowday, R.T. (1987). Voluntarily leaving an organization: an empirical investigation of Steers and Mowday's model of turnover. *Acad. Manage. J., 30*: 721–743.

Leonard, J.S. (1987). Carrots and sticks: pay, supervision, and turnover, *J. Labor Econ., 5*: 136–152.

Lesly, E., and Light, L. (1992). When layoffs alone don't turn the tide, *Business Week*, Dec. 7, pp. 100–101.

Leventhal, G.S. (1980). What should be done with equity theory? *Social Exchange* (K. Gergen, M.S., Greenberg, and R.H. Willis, eds.), Plenum Press, New York.

Lewin, T. (1991). High medical costs hurt growing numbers in U.S., *New York Times*, April 28, pp. 1, 14–15.

Liebtag, B. (1987, October). Compensation curves. *Journal of Accountancy*, pp. 75-79.

Lincoln, J.R. (1989). Employee work attitudes and management practices in the U.S. and Japan: evidence from a large corporation survey, *Cal. Manage. Rev., 31*: 89–106.

Lincoln, J.R., and Kalleberg, A.L. (1985). Work organization and workplace commitment: a study of plants and employees in the U.S. and Japan, *Am. Sociol. Rev., 50*: 738–760.

Loher, B.T., Noe, R.A., Moeller, N.L. and Fitzgerald, M.P. (1985). A meta-analysis of the relation of job characteristics to job satisfaction, *J. Appl. Psychol. 70*: 280–289.

Louis, M.R., Posner, B.Z., and Powell, G.N. (1983). The availability and helpfulness of socialization practices, *Personnel Psychol. 36*: 857–866.

Lublin, J.S., (1992). After couples divorce, long-distance moves are often wrenching, *Wall Street Journal*, Nov. 20, pp. 1, 8.

Lyons, T.F. (1971). Role clarity, need for clarity, satisfaction, tension, and withdrawal, *Organiz. Behav. Human Perf., 6*: 99–110.

March, J.G., and Simon, H.A. (1958). *Organizations*, Wiley, New York.

Marsh, R.M., and Mannari, H. (1977). Organizational commitment and turnover: a prediction study, *Admin. Sci. Q., 22*: 57–75.

Mathieu, J.E. (1991). A cross-level nonrecursive model of the antecedents of organizational commitment and satisfaction, *J. Appl. Psychol., 76*: 607–618.

Mathieu, J.E., and Farr, J.L. (1991). Further evidence for the discriminant validity of measures of organizational commitment, job involvement, and job satisfaction. *J. Appl. Psychol., 76*: 127–133.

Mathieu, J.E., and Zajac, D. (1990). A review and meta-analysis of the antecedents, correlates, and consequences of organizational commitment, *Psychol. Bull., 108*: 171–194.

Mattis, M.C. (1990). New forms of flexible work arrangements for managers and professionals: myths and realities, *Human Resource Plann., 13*: 133–146.

McCain, B.E., O'Reilly, C., and Pfeffer, J. (1983). The effects of departmental demography on turnover: the case of a university, *Acad. Manage. J., 26*: 626–641.

McEvoy, G.M., and Cascio, W.F. (1985). Strategies for reducing employee turnover: a meta-analysis, *J. Appl. Psychol., 70*: 342–353.

McEvoy, G.M., and Cascio, W.F. (1987). Do good or poor performers leave? A meta-analysis of the relationship between performance and turnover, *Acad. Manage. J., 30*: 744–762.

Meglino, B.M., DeNisi, A.S., Youngblood, S.A., and Williams, K.J. (1988). Effects of realistic job previews: a comparison using an enhancement and a reduction preview, *J. Appl. Psychol., 73*: 259–266.

Meyer, J.P., Paunonen, S.V., Gellatly, I.R., Goffin, R.D., and Jackson, D.N. (1989). Organizational commitment and job performance: it's the nature of commitment that counts, *J. Appl. Psychol., 74*: 152–156.

Meyer, J.P., Allen, N.J., and Gellatly, I.R. (1990). Affective and continuance commitment to the organization: evaluation of measures and analysis of concurrent and time-lagged relations, *J. Appl. Psychol., 75*: 710–720.

Miceli, M., and Lane, M.C. (1991). Antecedents of pay satisfaction: a review and extension, *Research in Personnel and Human Resources Management, Vol. 9* (G.R. Ferris and K.M. Rowland, eds.), JAI Press, Greenwich, CT.

Miceli, M.P., Jung, I., Near, J.P., and Greenberger, D.B. (1991). Predictors and outcomes of reactions to pay-for-performance plans, *J. Appl. Psychol., 76*: 508–521.

Miles, R.H. (1976). Role requirements as sources of organizational stress, *J. Appl. Psychol., 61*: 172–179.

Milkovich, G.T., and Gomez, L. (1976). Day care and selected employee work behavior, *Acad. Manage. J., 19*: 111–115.

Milkovich, G.T., and Newman, J.M. (1990). *Compensation*, BPI/Irwin, Homewood, IL.

Miller, H., Katerberg, R., and Hulin, C. (1979). Evaluation of the Mobley, Horner, and Hollingsworth model of employee turnover, *J. Appl. Psychol., 64*: 509–517.

Miller, T.I. (1984). The effects of employer-sponsored child care on employee absenteeism, turnover, productivity, recruitment or job satisfaction: what is claimed and what is known, *Personnel Psychol., 37*: 277–289.

Milliken, F., Dutton, J.E., and Beyer, J.M. (1990). Understanding organizational adaptation to change: the case of work-family issues, *Human Resource Plann., 13*: 91–107.

Mitchell, O.S. (1983). Fringe benefits and the cost of changing jobs, *Ind. Labor Rel. Rev., 37*: 70–78.

Mobley, W.H. (1977). Intermediate linkages in the relationship between job satisfaction and employee turnover, *J. Appl. Psychol., 62*: 237–240.

Mobley, W.H. (1982). *Employee Turnover: Causes, Consequences, and Control*, Addison-Wesley, Reading, MA.

Mobley, W.H., Griffeth, R.W., Hand, H.H., and Meglino, B.M. (1979). Review and conceptual analysis of the employee turnover process, *Psychol. Bull., 86*: 493–522.

Moore, T.F., and Simendinger, E.A. (1989). *Managing the Nursing Shortages*, Aspen, Rockville, MD.

Morrow, P.C., and Wirth, R.E. (1989). Work commitment among salaried professionals, *J. Voc. Behav., 34*: 40–56.

Motowidlo, S.J. (1983). Predicting sales turnover from pay satisfaction and expectation, *J. Appl. Psychol., 68*: 484–489.

Mowday, R.T., Porter, L.W., and Steers, R.M. (1982). *Employee-Organization Linkages*, Academic Press, New York.

Muchinsky, P.M., and Tuttle, M.L. (1980). Employee turnover: an empirical and methodological assessment, *J. Voc. Behav., 14*: 43–77.

Murphy, K.R., and Cleveland, J.N. (1991). *Performance Appraisal*, Allyn and Bacon, Boston.

Netemeyer, R.G., Johnston, M.W., and Burton, S. (1990). An analysis of role conflict and role ambiguity in a structural equations framework, *J. Appl. Psychol., 75*: 148–157.

Newby, J.M. (1980). Study supports hiring more part-time RNs. *Hospital*, Sept. 1, pp. 71–73.

Nobile, R.J. (1990). Leaving no doubt about employee leaves, *Personnel, 67*: 54–60.

Nussbaum, B. (1991). I'm worried about my job! *Business Week*, Oct. 7, pp. 94–104.

O'Driscoll, M.P., Ilgen, D.R., and Hildreth, K. (1992). Time devoted to job and off-job activities, interrole conflict, and affective experiences, *J. Appl. Psychol., 77*: 272–279.

Oldham, G.R., (1988). Effects of changes in workspace partitions and spatial density on employee reactions: a quasi-experiment, *J. Appl. Psychol., 73*: 253–258.

Oldham, G.R., and Fried, Y. (1987). Employee reactions to workspace characteristics, *J. Appl. Psychol., 72*: 75–80.

Oldham, G.R., and Rotchford, N.L. (1983). Relationships between office characteristics and employee reactions: a study of the physical environment, *Admin. Sci. Q., 28*: 542–556.

Olson, M.H., and Primps, S.B. (1984). Working at home with computers: Work and nonwork issues, *J. Social Issues, 40*: 97–112.

O'Reilly, B, (1992, May 18). How to take care of aging parents, *Fortune*, pp. 108–112.

O'Reilly, C.A., and Chatman, J. (1986). Organizational commitment and psychological attachment: the effects of compliance, identification, and internalization, *J. Appl. Psychol., 71*: 492–499.

O'Reilly, C.A., Caldwell, D.F., and Barnett, W.P. (1989). Work group demography, social integration, and turnover, *Admin. Sci. Q., 34*: 21–37.

O'Reilly, C.A., Chatman, J., and Caldwell, D.F. (1991). People and organizational culture: a profile comparison approach to assessing person-organization fit, *Acad. Manage. J., 34*: 487–516.

Pfeffer, J. (1983). Organizational demography, *Research in Organizational Behavior, Vol. 5* (L.L. Cummings and B.M. Staw, eds.), JAI Press, Greenwich, CT.

Pierce, J.L., and Dunham, R.B. (1992). The 12-hour work day: a 48-hour, eight-day week, *Acad. Manage. J., 35*: 1086–1098.

Porter, L.W., and Steers, R.M. (1973). Organizational, work, and personal factors in employee turnover and absenteeism, *Psychol. Bull., 80:* 151–176.

Porter, L.W., Steers, R.M., Mowday, R.T., and Boulian, P.V. (1974). Organizational commitment, job satisfaction, and turnover among psychiatric technicians, *J. Appl. Psychol., 59*: 603–609.

Premack, S.L., and Wanous, J.P. (1985). A meta-analysis of realistic job preview experiments, *J. Appl. Psychol., 70*: 706–719.

Prestholdt, P.H., Lane, I.M., and Mathews, R.C. (1987). Nurse turnover as reasoned action: development of a process model, *J. Appl. Psychol., 72*: 221–227.

Price, J.L. (1977). *The Study of Turnover*, Iowa State University Press, Ames.

Price, J.L. (1989). The impact of turnover on the organization, *Work and Occupations*, *16*: 461–473.

Price, J.L., and Mueller, C.W. (1981). A casual model of turnover for nurses, *Acad. Manage. J.*, *24*: 543–565.

Price, J.L., and Mueller, C.W. (1986). *Absenteeism and Turnover of Hospital Employees*, JAI Press, Greenwich, CT.

Raelin, J.A. (1986). *The Clash of Cultures*, Harvard Business School Press, Boston.

Ralston, D.A., and Flanagan, M.F. (1985). The effect of flexitime on absenteeism and turnover for male and female employees, *J. Voc. Behav.*, *26*: 206–217.

Reilly, R.R., Sperling, S.M., and Tenopyr, M.L. (1979). Effects of job previews on job acceptance and survival of telephone operator candidates, *J. Appl. Psychol.*, *64*: 218–220.

Reilly, R.R., Brown, B., Blood, M.R., and Malatesta, C.Z. (1981). The effects of realistic previews: a study and discussion of the literature, *Personnel Psychol.*, *34*: 823–834.

Rhodes, S.R., and Steers, R.M. (1990). *Managing Employee Absenteeism*, Addison-Wesley, Reading, MA.

Rokeach, M. (1973). *The Nature of Human Values*, Free Press, New York.

Roseman, E. (1981). *Managing Employee Turnover*, AMACON, New York.

Rosse, J.G. (1988). Relations among lateness, absence, and turnover: is there a progression of withdrawal? *Human Rel*: *41*: 517–531.

Rosse, J.G., and Miller, H.E. (1984). Relationship between absenteeism and other employee behaviors, *Absenteeism: New Approaches to Understanding, Measuring, and Managing Employee Absence* (P.S. Goodman and R.S. Atkin, eds.), Jossey-Bass, San Francisco.

Rousseau, D. (1985). Issues in level in organizational research: multilevel and cross-level perspectives, *Research in Organizational Behavior*, *Vol. 7* (L.L. Cummings and B.M. Staw, eds.), JAI Press, Greenwich, CT.

Rusbult, C.E., and Farrell, D. (1983). A longitudinal test of the investment model: the impact of job satisfaction, job commitment, and turnover of variations in rewards, costs, alternatives, and investments, *J. Appl. Psychol.*, *68*: 429–438.

Rusbult, C.E., Farrell, D., Rogers, G., and Mainous, A.G. (1988). Impact of exchange variables on exit, voice, loyalty, and neglect: an integrative model of responses to declining job satisfaction, *Acad. Manage. J.*, *31*: 599–627.

Sager, J., Varadarajan, P., and Futrell, C. (1988). Understanding salesperson turnover: a partial evaluation of Mobley's turnover process model, *J. Personal Sell. Sales Manage.*, *8*: 20–35.

Sager, J., Griffeth, R.W., and Hom, P.W. (1992). A structural model assessing the validity of turnover cognitions. Unpublished manuscript, Department of Marketing, University of North Texas, Denton.

Salancik, G.R., and Pfeffer, J. (1978). A social information processing approach to job attitudes and task design, *Admin. Sci. Q.*, *23*: 224–253.

Scandura, T.A., and Graen, G.B. Moderating effects of initial leader-member exchange status on the effects of a leadership intervention, *J. Appl. Psychol.*, *69*: 428–436.

Schmitt, N., Gooding, R.Z., Noe, R.D., and Kirsch, M. (1984). Meta-analyses of validity studies published between 1964 and 1982 and the investigation of study characteristics, *Personnel Psychol.*, *37*: 407–422.

Schneider, B. (1987). The people make the place, *Personnel Psychol.*, *40*: 437–453.

Schneider, B., and Bowen, D.E. (1985). Employee and customer perceptions of service in banks: Replication and extension, *J. Appl. Psychol.*, *70*: 423–433.

Schneider, J. (1976). The "greener grass" phenomenon: differential effects of a work context alternative on organizational participation and withdrawal intentions, *Organiz. Behav. Human Perf.*, *16*: 308–333.

Schwab, D.P. (1991). Contextual variables in employee performance–turnover relationship, *Acad. Manage. J.*, *34*: 966–975.

Schwartz, F.N. (1989). Management women and the new facts of life, *Harvard Business Review*, Jan.–Feb., pp. 65–76.

Schwarzer, R. (1989). *Meta*, National Collegiate Software, Durham. NC.

Shaw, K. (1987). The quit propensity of married men, *J. Labor Econ.*, *5*: 533–560.

Shellenbarger, S. (1992). Managers navigate uncharted waters trying to resolve work-family conflicts, *Wall Street Journal*, pp. B1, B10.

Sheridan, J.E., and Abelson, M.A. (1983). Cusp catastrophe model of employee turnover, *Acad. Manage. J.*, *26*: 418–436.

Sigardson, K.M. (1982). Why nurses leave nursing: a survey of former nurses, *Nurs. Admin. Q.*, *7*(Fall): 20–24.

Silvers, A., and Valencia, F. (1990). Labor absorption and turnover in the maquila industry, *Arizona Rev. (Spring)*: pp. 17–23.

Spector, W.D., and Takada, H.A. (1991). Characteristics of nursing homes that affect resident outcomes, *J. Ag. Health*, *3*: 427–454.

Spiers, J. (1992). The baby boom is for real. *Fortune*, Feb. 10, pp. 101–104.

Staw, B.M. (1980). The consequences of turnover, *J. Occup. Behav.*, *1*: 253–273.

Staw, B.M., Bell, N., and Clausen, J.A. (1986). The dispositional approach to job attitudes: A life time longitudinal test, *Admin. Sci. Q.*, *31*: 56–77.

Steel, R.P., and Griffeth, R.W. (1989). The elusive relationship between perceived employment opportunity and turnover behavior: a methodological or conceptual artifact? *J. Appl. Psychol.*, *74*: 846–854.

Steel, R.P., and Ovalle, N.K. (1984). A review and meta-analysis of research on the relationship between behavioral intentions and employee turnover, *J. Appl. Psychol.*, *69*: 673–686.

Steel, R., Lounsbury, J., and Horst, W. (1981). A test of the internal and external validity of Mobley's model of employee turnover, *Proceedings of the 24th Annual Conference of the Midwest Academy of Management* (T. Martin & R. Osborn, eds.). Southern Illinois University, College of Business Administration, Carbondale, IL, pp. 333–345.

Steel, R.P., Hendrix, W.H., and Balogh, S.P. (1990a). Confounding effects of the turnover base rate on relations between time lag and turnover study outcomes: An extension of meta-analysis findings and conclusions, *J. Organiz. Behav.*, *11*: 237–242.

Steel, R.P., Shane, G.S., and Griffeth, R.W. (1990b). Correcting turnover statistics for comparative analysis, *Acad. Manage. J.*, *33*: 179–187.

Steers, R.M., and Mowday, R.T. (1981). Employee turnover and postdecision accommodation processes, *Research in Organizational Behavior*, Vol. 3 (L. Cummings and B. Staw, eds.), JAI Press, Greenwich, Ct, pp. 235–281.

Stricharchuk, G. (1987). Retirement prospects grow bleaker for many as job scene changes, *Wall Street Journal*, Aug. 26., pp. 1, 15.

Terborg, J.R., and Lee, T.W. (1984). A predictive study of organizational turnover rates, *Acad. Manage. J.*, *27*: 793–810.

Tett, R.P., and Meyer, J.P. (1992). Job satisfaction, organizational commitment, turnover intention, and turnover: path analyses based on meta-analytic findings. Unpublished manuscript, Department of Psychology, University of Western Ontario, London, Ontario, Canada.

Trenk, B.S. (1990). Future moms, serious workers, *Manage. Rev.*, *(Sept.)*: pp. 33–37.

Triandis, H.C. (1979). Values, attitudes, and interpersonal behavior, *Nebraska Symposium on Motivation* (H.E. Howe, Jr., ed.), University of Nebraska Press, Lincoln, pp. 159–259.

Turban, D.B., Campion, J.E., and Eyring, A.R. (1992). Factors relating to relocation decisions of research and development employees, *J. Voc. Behav.*, *41*: 183–199.

Ulrich, D., Halbrook, R., Meder, D., Stuchlik, M., and Thorpe, S. (1991). Employee and customer attachment: Synergies for competitive advantage, *Human Resource Plann.*, *14*: 89–103.

Vandenberg, R.J., and Scarpello, V. (1990). The matching model: An examination of the processes underlying realistic job previews, *J. Appl. Psychol.*, *75*: 60–67.

Von Glinow, M.A. (1988). *The New Professionals*, Ballinger, Cambridge, MA.

Waldman, D.A., and Avolio, B.J. (1986). A meta-analysis of age differences in job performance, *J. Appl. Psychol.*, *71*: 33–38.

Wandelt, M.A., Pierce, P.M., and Widdowson, R.R. (1981, January). Why nurses leave nursing and what can be done about it, *Am. J. Nurs.*, *81*: 72–77.

Wanous, J.P. (1980). *Organizational Entry: Recruitment, Selection and Socialization of Newcomers*, Addison-Wesley, Reading, MA.

Wanous, J.P. (1989). Installing a realistic job preview: ten tough choices, *Personnel Psychol.*, *42*: 117–134.

Wanous, J.P., and Colella, A. (1989). Organizational entry research: current status and future directions.

Research in Personnel and Human Resources Management (G. Ferris & K. Rowland, eds.), JAI Press, Greenwich, CT, pp. 59–120.

Wanous, J.P., Poland, T.D., Premack, S.L., and Davis, K.S. (1992). The effects of met expectations on newcomer attitudes and behaviors: a review and meta-analysis, *J. Appl. Psychol.*, *77*: 288–297.

Watts, L.R., and White, E.C. (1988). Assessing employee turnover, *Personnel Admin.*, *33*: 80–85.

Weiner, N. (1980). Determinants and behavioral consequences of pay satisfaction: a comparison of two models, *Personnel Psychol.*, *33*: 741–757.

Weiss, H.M., and Adler, S. (1984). Personality and organizational behavior. *Research in Organizational Behavior, Vol. 6* (B.M. Staw and L.L. Cummings, eds.), JAI Press, Greenwich, CT, pp. 1–50.

Weiss, S.J. (1984). The effect of transition modules on new graduate adaptation, *Res. Nurs. Health*, *7*: 51–59.

Welbourne, T.M., and Gomez-Mejia, L.R. (1988). Gainsharing revisited, *Compens. Benefits Rev.*, *20*: 19–28.

Whitener, E.M. (1990). Confusion of confidence intervals and credibility intervals in meta-analysis, *J. Appl. Psychol.*, *75*: 315–321.

Whiting, L. (1989). *Turnover Costs: A Case Example*. Unpublished manuscript, Ohio Department of Mental Health, Columbus.

Williams, C.R. (1990). Deciding when, how and if to correct turnover correlations, *J. Appl. Psychol.*, *75*: 732–737.

Williams, C.R., and Livingstone, L.P. (1989). A second look at the relationship between performance and voluntary turnover. Unpublished manuscript, Department of Management, Texas Christian University, Fort Worth.

Williams, L.J., and Hazer, J.T. (1986). Antecedents and consequences of satisfaction and commitment in turnover models: a reanalysis using latent variable structural equation methods, *J. Appl. Psychol.*, *71*: 219–231.

Williams, M.L., and Dreher, G.F. (1992). Compensation system attributes and applicant pool characteristics, *Acad. Manage. J.*, *35*: 571–595.

Wilson, N., and Peel, M.J. (1991). The impact on absenteeism and quits of profit-sharing and other forms of employee participation, *Ind. Labor Rel. Rev. 44*: 454–468.

Wilson, M., Northcraft, G.B., and Neale, M.A. (1985). The perceived value of fringe benefits, *Personnel Psychol.*, *38*: 309–320.

Withey, M.J., and Cooper, W.H. (1989). Predicting exit, voice, loyalty, and neglect, *Admin. Sci. Q.*, *34*: 521–539.

Yalow, E. (1990). Corporate child care helps recruit and retain workers, *Personnel J.* pp. 48–55.

Youngblood, S.A., and Chambers-Cook, K. (1984). Child care assistance can improve employee attitudes and behavior, *Personnel Admin.*, *29*: 45–46, 93–95.

Zalesny, M.D., and Ford, K.J. (1990). Extending the social information processing perspective: New links to attitudes, behaviors, and perceptions, *Organiz. Behav. Human Dec. Process.*, *47*: 205–246.

Zedeck, S., and Mosier, K.L. (1990). Work in the family and employing organization, *Am. Psychologist*, *45*: 240–251.

Zedeck, S., Jackson, S.E., and Summers, E. (1983). Shift work schedules and their relationship to health, adaptation, satisfaction, and turnover intentions, *Acad. Manage. J.*, *26*: 297–310.

Zenger, T.R. (1992). Why do employers only reward extreme performance? Examining the relationships among performance, pay, and turnover, *Admin. Sci. Q.*, *37*: 198–219.

23

Motivation of Personnel: A Synthesis of Current Research

NATALIA TROGEN and BARTON WECHSLER   Florida State University, Tallahassee, Florida

I. INTRODUCTION

Motivation has long been a central concern for organizational scholars as well as managers; its centrality in both domains derives from its key role in explaining individual and organizational performance. In studying work motivation, scholars seek to understand the factors or processes which activate individual effort, while managers hope to gain mechanisms for influencing the effort of employees directed to organizational goals.

In the organizational behavior literature, work motivation is typically described as the set of psychological processes that cause the initiation, direction, intensity, and persistence of behavior (Pinder, 1984). Current approaches to motivation embrace a variety of theories; some have received strong empirical support, while others deal with unresolved ambiguities or inadequacies (Klein, 1989). In this chapter we review and evaluate the current status of motivation theory, emphasizing some of the most recent theoretical developments. Our review is organized in terms of several streams of research considered integral to the study of motivation, including (1) content theories, (2) cognitive choice theories, and (3) self-regulation theories (Kanfer, 1990). Although this framework is somewhat different from the traditional organization of the literature, it is consistent with the most important emerging developments.

II. CONTENT THEORY

Content theories emphasize the role of personality, values, and motives as a basis for motivated behavior. Some scholars (Kanfer, 1990) identify this research as the need–motive–value approach, which allows for the inclusion in this category of a number of diverse theoretical perspectives, including job characteristics theory as well as approaches dealing with the role of external and internal rewards.

Research on content theories has an extensive history; early developments can be roughly categorized into three types: laundry lists of needs [e.g., Murray's (1938) account of more than 20 needs]; shorter, more synthetic and theoretic lists [e.g., Maslow's (1954) hierarchy of needs or Alderfer's (1969) ERG theory]; or single-item approaches [e.g., McClelland's (1961) need for achievement (Snyder and Williams 1982)]. Despite their continuing prominence in the popular literature, few of the traditional need theories have received much empirical support and they are generally out of scholarly favor. In addition to empirical shortcomings, scholars have identified a variety of theoretical ambiguities and methodological problems in these approaches (Kanfer, 1990).

A. Job Characteristics Theory

In contrast to the large number of motives identified in traditional need achievement theories, the theories mentioned in the remainder of this section concentrate on the operation of a single or small set of psychological motives (Kanfer, 1990). One of the most popular and relevant streams of contemporary research is concerned with the effect of characteristics of the task or the work itself on motivation (Graen et al., 1986; Champoux, 1980). Theories of this type regard growth need strength as an important moderator of psychological and behavioral response to the task environment (Champoux, 1980). Researchers have sought to determine the fundamental structure of job characteristics and the normative effects of job structure on affective responses (Kanfer, 1990). Graen and his colleagues argue that only employees having strong growth needs are predicted to develop strong internal motivation when working on complex, challenging jobs (Graen et al., 1986). Other organizational members, without strong needs for growth, will be less likely to take advantage of opportunities provided by a job high in motivational potential. Results from their work suggest that employee growth need strength moderates the relationship between growth and productivity, "work itself" attitudes, and internal work motivation of employees (Graen et al., 1986).

B. Self Theory

Snyder and Williams (1982) describe a "molar and integrated" formulation of need satisfaction theory: *self theory* is based on the premise that human beings have a fundamental need to maintain or enhance the phenomenal self. Self theorists contend that all behavior is primarily a function of what goes on inside the person, of how all objective situations are perceived as opportunities for or threats to the fundamental maintenance and enhancement of the individual. Self theorists do not regard lower performing employees, for example, as lacking motivation or as unresponsive to organizational stimuli. Instead, they contend that individuals are always motivated to maintain or enhance their self concept.

The difference between a high-performing individual and one who is a low performer, therefore, cannot be understood in terms of different levels of motivation. Both individuals are motivated, according to this approach, but the high performer perceives performance as a means of maintaining or enhancing self while the low performer does not. Increased performance involves the creation of an organizational context in which all the employees perceive high performance as a viable and desirable strategy for maintaining and enhancing specific attributes of the self relevant to the particular performance involved.

Interestingly, it has been found that cultural differences influence the response to work motivation factors. For instance, there are significant differences among different nationalities with respect to the perceived importance of various outcomes and the level of satisfaction experienced on the job as a result of achieving them (Kanungo and Wright, 1983). For example, British managers appear to place much greater importance on individual achievement and autonomy goals than do their French counterparts, while the relative emphasis placed on extrinsic job factors is practically reversed. French managers place greater emphasis on organizationally controlled, interpersonally mediated job factors than do the British. In general, the British appear to have higher needs for self-actualization, while the French have stronger needs for security and comfortable working conditions (Kanungo and Wright, 1983).

C. Intrinsic and Extrinsic Rewards

Many theories of individual performance are concerned with the processes by which rewards energize, sustain, and direct behavior. Work-related behavior can be motivated by many different kinds of rewards, including pay, praise, promotion, alleviation of boredom, and a sense of accomplishment. All of these rewards can be characterized as one of two types: intrinsic or extrinsic. There is now some controversy in the literature about the assignment of a reward to one or the other of the categories, largely having to do with the ambiguity of the distinction commonly made between them (Guzzo, 1979). It has generally been understood that *intrinsic rewards* are obtained when the individual does not receive any apparent rewards from performing a task except those that derive from the task itself. *Extrinsic rewards*, on the other hand, are described as those which do not have inherent connections between the task itself and the reward earned for performing the task. However, this distinction is increasingly regarded as problematic. According to Guzzo (1979), the problem is that all activities have consequences or outcomes, making it inappropriate to say that some activity can be engaged in for its own sake. Consequences can be private, internal to the actor, not visible to the observer. While this may lead an observer of the activity to regard it as being performed independent of any extrinsic consequences or rewards, clearly this may not be the case.

Some scholars have approached the problem differently, using Maslow's hierarchy of needs as a means of distinguishing the two types of rewards. Lawler (1969), for instance, identifies extrinsic rewards as satisfying lower order needs of the individual, such as the need for safety or security. Intrinsic rewards are considered as those satisfying higher order needs, such as self-esteem and self-actualization. This definition is also not without problems. For example, if we consider money, the most commonly employed reward in work organizations, to be only an extrinsic reward since it is used to satisfy lower order needs, then we cannot easily explain how the acquisition of money can enhance the individual's feelings of self-esteem or achievement. Since individuals in everyday life often gain higher order outcomes from monetary and other extrinsic rewards, such a formulation appears to be of limited utility.

Still another way of distinguishing between intrinsic and extrinsic rewards was suggested by attribution theorists (De Charms, 1968; Deci, 1975a, 1975b; Deci et al., 1981). From the attribution theory perspective, intrinsic rewards are those associated with cognition of personal causality for behavior and extrinsic rewards are those associated with cognition of external causality of behavior (DeCharms, 1968). This approach has been criticized because many activities can be shown to have both an external and internal cause simultaneously. A different way of thinking about rewards, which takes us beyond a simple dichotomy, is suggested by Guzzo (1979) who regards reward as entities which vary simultaneously on several attributes. Thus, rewards can be social or nonsocial in origin, immediate or delayed, symbolic or tangible, self-generated or not, long or short duration, etc.

Finally, Deci (1975a) has long argued that intrinsic and extrinsic rewards are incompatible as motivating forces. In laboratory experiments, he has shown that the provision of extrinsic rewards diminishes the effect of intrinsic rewards associated with performance of the task itself. The generalizability of these findings, however, is not well established. In most work organizations, the utility of both intrinsic and extrinsic rewards are nearly universally accepted.

III. COGNITIVE CHOICE THEORIES

Cognitive choice theories are concerned with the psychological processes by which individuals determine, in the context of organizational life, the level of effort they will expend on work activities. These theories have enjoyed considerable attention in the scholarly literature, as well as varying levels of criticism (Kanfer, 1990). An important trend, which underlies our treatment of these theories, is the effort to find a basis for unifying the disparate theoretical perspectives.

A. Expectancy Theory

Expectancy theory is easily the most widely known of the cognitive choice models and, in our view, provides the most useful framework for thinking about a unified process perspective on motivation. Vroom (1964) did much of the early work establishing the conceptual foundations for an expectancy-based approach to motivation theory. According to Vroom (1964, p. 17), "An expectancy is defined as a momentary belief concerning the likelihood that a particular act will be followed by a particular outcome." In other words, the expectancy theory holds that an individual's choice to act in a certain way is based on expectations that accomplishing the task will lead to the attainment of valued outcomes.

While expectancy theory has been regarded as theoretically powerful and useful in a variety of contexts, many scholars regard its primary value to be in its diagnostic capacity. Expectancy theory leads to an examination of such things as (1) the value members of the organization give to organizational and social rewards, (2) the quantity and variety of intrinsic rewards provided by the organization, (3) the extent to which high performance is seen as leading to specific rewards, and (4) the extent to which individuals believe they can reach specified performance levels (Vroom, 1964).

A second benefit of expectancy theory is that it is consistent with a number of motivational techniques familiar to and frequently employed by management. Procedures such as contingent or incentive rewards systems, job enrichment, and goal setting (including management-by-objectives) have direct basis in expectancy theory. Goal setting, for example, may be conceived as the process by which the instrumental relationship between specific levels of performance and rewards such as recognition, supervisor approval, and feelings of accomplishment are made explicit (Ilgen et al., 1981).

Expectancy models predict that, all things being equal, performance will increase as effort–performance expectancy increases. In other words, the higher the expectancy for success the higher the performance. Managers should find that performance is maximized in situations where the setting of challenging goals is linked with attempts to establish significant performance-related expectancies (Garland, 1984). These attempts would involve building up what Bandura (1982) has called "self-efficacy," which is confidence in one's ability to accomplish the specific action required in the situation.

Since Vroom's original work, a number of researchers (Ilgen et al., 1981; Locke et al., 1986) have developed elaborated models of expectancy theory. Some formulations identify three variables as playing the crucial role in the intensity of the force toward a certain course of actions: (1) effort performance expectancy—the belief that a certain level of effort will lead to a certain performance level; (2) instrumentality—the belief that a certain performance level will lead to other valued outcomes; and (3) valence—the anticipated satisfaction to be derived from these other valued outcomes (Ilgen et al., 1981; Locke et al., 1986). According to these researchers, there can be multiple outcomes and therefore multiple instrumentalities and valences attached to a given performance level. For example, high performance may result in more recognition, more money, and a promotion. The individual's choice to perform at a specific level is based on the expectancy that effort will lead to that level of performance, the belief that performance will be instrumental to the achievement of rewards, and the value the individual places on the rewards provided (Locke et al., 1986).

Effort–performance expectancy and instrumentality found in expectancy theory are similar to the concepts of self-efficacy expectancy and outcome expectancy in self-efficacy theory (Bandura, 1982). Effort–performance expectancy and self-efficacy expectancy both represent the beliefs of individuals about their capacity to perform at certain levels. Instrumentality and outcome expectancy are both concerned with the utility of performance for achieving outcomes (Locke et al., 1986).

In contrast, Eden (1988) argued that expectancy is a perception of the situation rather than a belief about the capacity of the individual; changes in expectancy, and therefore in performance, can be best achieved by targeting the situation rather than the individual. Eden (1988) also differentiates "trait expectancy" from "state expectancy." Trait expectancy is a cognition about self-competence, which varies relatively little across situations. State expectancy is a cognition about performance which varies across situations.

Figure 1 depicts performance as determined by trait and state expectancy as well as goal difficulty. In practical terms, however, state expectancy should be treated as the key element in managerial interventions designed to increase motivation. Research on the Pygmalion effect (see below) and goal setting theory provide examples of how state expectancy can be increased. These results suggest that the combination of high expectations and hard goals is generally promising. Trait expectancy is much harder to increase than state expectancy because personality traits are more resistant to change than are characteristics of jobs.

In still another elaboration of expectancy theory, Garland (1985) explains the linkages between individual goals and performance in terms of two mediating constructs: performance expectancy and performance valence. This theory (see Fig. 2) proposes that individuals form expectancies associated with different levels of performance, not just that level represented by some specific task goal. Performance expectancy is defined as a probability composed of the sum of an individual's subjective probabilities for reaching each of a number of different performance lev-

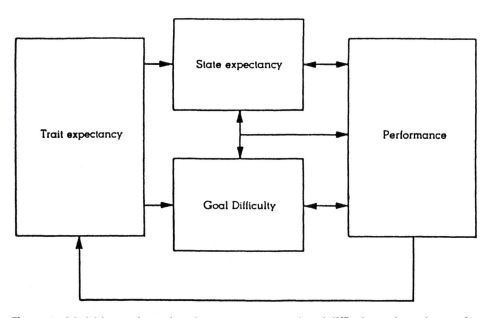

Figure 1 Model integrating trait and state expectancy and goal difficulty as determinants of performance.

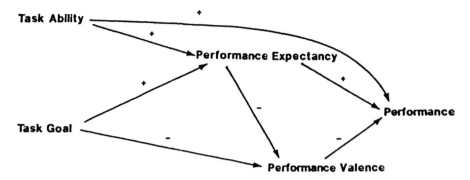

Figure 2   Theoretical model of the linkages between task goals and performance.

els. The second construct, performance valence, is defined as the sum of those satisfactions an
individual anticipates will be associates with each of a number of different performance levels. A
task goal, according to Garland, is an image of a future level of performance that the individual
wishes to achieve. Task ability is defined as an individual's skills in executing those mental and
physical acts that contribute positively to task performance. Although performance is determined
by task abilities and goals (aspiration levels), this relationship is mediated by calculations of the
probability of achieving a specific level of performance and the valence associated with its achievement.

As the figure suggest, higher task goals result in higher performance expectancy and lower
performance valence. Performance valence exerts a direct (negative) influence on performance;
lower valence leads to higher levels of performance. Performance expectancy exerts both direct
and indirect (positive) effects on performance. Task ability influences performance both directly
and indirectly through its influence on performance expectancy.

A related phenomenon, described by Rosenthal and Jacobson (1968), is the Pygmalion effect in which educational performance is associated with the performance expectations of teachers. Their research seemed to find that teachers unwittingly communicate performance expectations to their students and thereby increase the likelihood that their expectations will be fulfilled.
This effect has been extensively studied, with experimental replication having been achieved in
an organizational setting other than a school. Studies by Eden and Ravid (1982) not only replicated the Pygmalion effect but also showed that high expectations communicated by authority figure
led subordinates to expect more of themselves and to perform at higher levels.

A very similar concept is discussed in the literature under the label of the "self-fulfilling
prophesy" (Jussim, 1986). In general this refers to situations in which expectations about the
behavior or performance of someone lead that person to behave in ways to confirm the first person's expectations (Jussim, 1986). There has been a substantial amount of empirical research
(Brophy and Good, 1974; Brockner, 1979; Allington, 1980) and several theoretical reviews (Braun,
1976) have been devoted to this concept. As shown in Fig. 3, expectations (positive or negative)
about the individual can produce differential treatment which, in turn, has self-fulfilling effects on
performance levels, thus confirming the initial expectations (Jussim, 1986).

B.   Integration with Other Approaches

Although goal setting theory will be presented more completely and explicitly later in the chapter, the current discussion, related to the integration of expectancy and goal setting theory, requires

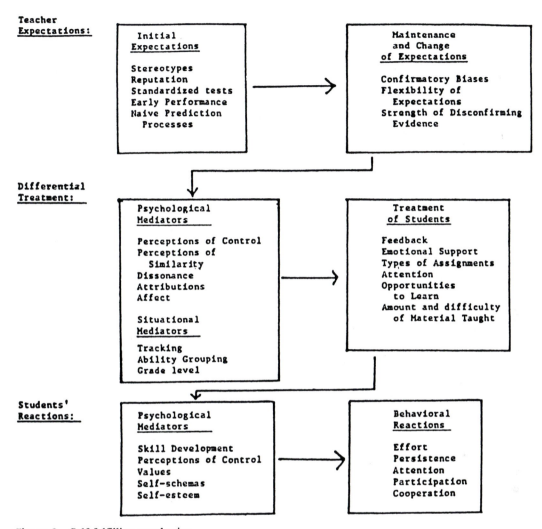

Figure 3 Self-fulfilling prophecies.

some examination of the conflict between the two theories. Basically, this takes the form of opposite predictions about the relationship of expectancy to performance. From an expectancy theory perspective, if instrumentality and valence are held constant, then expectancy will be positively related to performance. Easy goals are associated with both higher expectancy and higher levels of performance. Goal setting theory, on the other hand, postulates that performance is heightened by challenging goals; goal setting theory suggests that higher performance is associated with lower expectancy.

Locke et al. (1986) identify the fundamental reason for the conflict as differences between levels of analysis in different studies (within-group vs. between-group). They also stress the importance of appropriate construct measurement. According to these authors an integration of goal setting theory, expectancy theory, and self-efficacy theory is clearly possible. Their proposed integration is shown in Fig. 4.

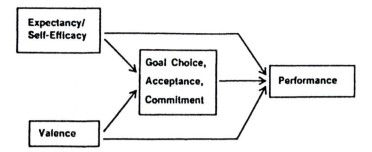

Figure 4 Outline of a model integrating goal setting, expectancy, and self-efficacy theories.

In this model, expectancy/self-efficacy, as well as valence, affects goal choice, acceptance, and commitment. Performance is directly influenced by expectancy/self-efficacy, goals, and valence. Although the model omits some variables relevant to motivation, it does provide a structure for integration, which might be the foundation for a more elaborate, more fully integrated approach.

IV. SELF-REGULATION THEORIES

A. Self-Management Theory

Some of the most interesting recent developments in the motivation literature have focused on the influence of individual organization members on themselves. These developments can be traced to the social learning literature (Bandura, 1977a; Davis and Luthans, 1980; Wexley and Latham, 1981; Latham and Napier, 1984) and related work in self-control (Mahoney and Arnkoff, 1978; Carver and Scheier, 1981; Mills, 1983). Also related to this emerging stream of research are more traditional goal-oriented approaches (Locke, 1968).

Self-management strategies have been found to be a useful tool for reducing resistance to change, for setting goals, and for maintaining a high level of activity toward achieving the goal. Several specific self-management strategies have been identified in the literature, including self-observation, self-goal setting, cueing strategies, self-reinforcement, self-punishment, and rehearsal (Mahoney and Arnkoff, 1979). To date, the value of self-management techniques have been mostly demonstrated in clinical rather than organizational settings.

The self-management model is anchored in two contingencies—goal setting–goal accomplishment and goal accomplishment–goal outcomes—and the control individuals have over these two contingencies. The process involves four steps: setting goals, monitoring, evaluating, and reinforcing behavior (Erez and Kanfer, 1983). The concept of self-management is also implemented, at least in part, through other motivational techniques such as job enrichment, quality control, time management, and the use of extrinsic and intrinsic rewards (Luthans and Davis, 1979; Mahoney and Arnkoff, 1979; Andrasik and Heimbergs, 1982).

However, Mills (1983) notes that self-management is not exempt from organizational influence or control. He argues that it is more meaningful to conceptualize self-management as an organizational strategy which shifts important aspects of the control process from management and the formal organizational structure to organizational members. Factors such as professional orientation and normative system of members can provide leadership not supplied by the formal supervisor and can, as a result, provide for greater predictability in behavior.

In a similar vein, Manz (1986) proposes self-leadership as a comprehensive self-influence perspective by which individuals lead themselves toward performance of organizational tasks. He identifies three contributions of the self-leadership approach: (1) it allows for addressing a wider range (higher level) of standards for self-influence; (2) it more fully incorporates the role of intrinsic work motivation; and (3) it suggests some additional strategies for employee self-control.

Conceptually, self-management can be viewed as a set of strategies that assists employees in structuring their work environment and in establishing self-motivation and that facilitates appropriate behaviors for limiting deviations from behavioral standards. Self-leadership, on the other hand, encompasses self-management behavior but is also concerned with leading the self-influence system at superordinate levels. Manz (1986) stresses that the concept of self-leadership is proposed to stimulate a broader view of self-influence that takes into account the important role of the intrinsically appealing aspects of work ("natural" rewards). Figure 5 illustrates the difference between self-management and self-leadership.

The self-efficacy concept developed by Bandura (1982) is also related to self-regulation theories. Self-efficacy is concerned with how people judge their capabilities and how perceptions of their own efficacy affect their motivation and behavior (Bandura, 1982). According to self-efficacy theory, for example, individuals avoid activities believed to exceed their coping capabilities but willingly take on those activities perceived as manageable. Perceptions of self-efficacy also determine how much effort individuals will make and the duration of their persistence in the face of obstacles. When faced with difficulties in performing a specific task, individuals with a strong

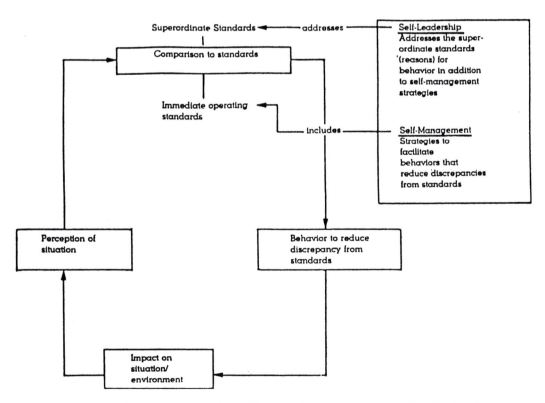

Figure 5   A cybernetic control system view of the role of self-management and self-leadership.

sense of efficacy undertake greater efforts; in effect, they have a greater capacity to cope with challenges. Judgments that individuals make about their capabilities influence the way in which they deal with environmental changes. Individuals with low self-efficacy perceptions tend to experience a sense of defeat and imagine potential difficulties as harder than they really are. These attitudes not only create stress but actually impair performance; individuals lacking confidence in their efficacy divert attention from how to best perform the task at hand and become paralyzed by concerns over failings and potential mishaps. In contrast, persons who have a strong sense of efficacy devote their attention and effort to the demands of the situation and are spurred to greater effort by challenging situations (Bandura, 1982).

Since behavior is influenced more by perceptions about the achieved performance than by actual performance, perceived self-efficacy is an efficient predictor of subsequent behavior (Bandura, 1982). As Bandura stresses, individuals register significant gains in self-efficacy when their actual experiences disconfirm inaccurate judgments about their capacity and when they gain new skills to manage threatening activities. As individuals gain an increasing sense of their ability to cope with aspects of their environment, they also gain self-assurance that serves them well in mastering subsequent challenges. Bandura also emphasizes the role of selected information in judging personal capabilities; the cognitive processing of efficacy information is strongly influenced by the types of cues people have learned to use as indicators of their capacity and the decision rules they employ for integrating efficacy information from different sources.

Self-efficacy has three dimensions. *Magnitude* applies to the level of task difficulty that a person believes he or she can attain; *strength* refers to whether the conviction regarding magnitude is strong or weak; and *generality* indicates the degree to which the expectations are generalized across situations (Bandura, 1977b). Recent research (Atkinson, 1964; Bandura, 1982; Bandura and Cervone, 1983) identifies three self-influences: *self-evaluation, perceived self-efficacy*, and *self-set goals*. Each of these influences has been shown to affect the individual's level of motivation. Bandura and Cervone (1983) found that each of the constituent self-influences contribute differentially to motivation, depending on the direction and magnitude of the difference between individual standards and attainments. The study showed, for instance, that perceived self-efficacy operated as a moderator, regardless of whether achievements were significantly below goals or whether achievement levels exceeded goals. From these results, one could conclude that motivation is best maintained by individuals who have a strong sense of self-efficacy, allowing them to withstand failure.

B. Theory of Deontic Work Motivation

Deontic motivation, although not a new concept in the field, until recently received little attention in the motivation literature. Schwartz (1983) apparently resurrected the concept, introducing the term "deontic," which is derived from the Greek word for duties. As it has been developed, the concept of deontic motivation refers to motivation determined by the feeling of obligation. The motive force for deontic motivation is based on self-perception: individuals attempt to achieve what they perceive to be their "ideal self," rejecting the "actual self." Individuals feel pride or self-esteem for having lived up to the standards of their ideal self. In this framework, self-esteem derives not so much from a capacity to act (self-efficacy) as from a feeling of worthy or moral conduct.

Deontic motivation is based on the generation and discharge of obligation. For instance, acceptance of inducements is perceived as generating obligation, while work discharges the obligation (Schwartz, 1983). According to Schwartz, there is some tendency, at least in the extreme, for deontic motivation to incline individuals toward activities that are socially useful and altruistic.

C. Goal Theory

Comprehensive theories of motivation, based on such concepts as instinct, drive, and conditioning, have not generally succeeded in explaining human action and have been gradually replaced by more bounded theories (Locke et al., 1981). These modern approaches do not attempt to explain all phenomena that might be related to motivation; instead, their domains are more limited. Goal setting theory is one example of the more restricted, middle-range approaches.

Goal setting has come to play a very important role in managerial strategies for enhancing employee motivation. In addition, many organizational scholars regard goal setting theory as the most empirically supported contemporary theory of work motivation (Locke et al., 1981). According to the theory, goals represent an end state toward which individuals strive and serve as immediate and proximate regulators of action (Erez and Kanfer, 1983).

Goals are generally regarded as closer to the point of individual action than needs, values, and generalized attitudes. Many laboratory and field studies have examined the effects of goal setting on task performance (Bryan and Locke, 1967; Chidester and Grigsby, 1984; Mento et al., 1987). This extensive stream of research deals mostly with the effects of setting various types of goals or objectives for task performance and with other factors affecting the effectiveness of goal setting.

According to Locke and his colleagues, a goal is "what an individual is trying to accomplish; the object or aim of an action" (Locke et al., 1981, p. 126). Other scholars (Erez and Kanfer, 1983) use different concepts in place of goal, including performance standard, work norm, objective, or even deadline, but all carry the essential meaning of goal.

There are four mechanisms by which goals are said to affect task performance: (1) directing attention and action; (2) mobilizing energy expenditure or effort; (3) prolonging effort over time; and (4) motivating the individual to develop relevant strategies for goal attainment (Locke et al., 1981). The nature of the goal itself or its dimensions influence its effects on performance. Among the dimensions studied are goal specificity or clarity and difficulty. Goal specificity or clarity is concerned with the degree of precision with which a goal is defined. Goal difficulty has to do with the extent to which the required level of task performance is challenging to the individual.

The concepts of "task" and "goal" are interrelated—in fact, some studies identify task accomplishment as a goal. For instance, Garland (1985) writes that when some explicit standard of quality or quantity is included in the task, it should be considered an assigned goal. In most studies, however, the term "goal" refers "to attaining a specific standard of proficiency on the task, usually within a specified time limit" (Locke et al., 1981, p. 126). Most research has found a positive relationship between goal difficulty and task performance: harder goals lead to higher performance than easier goals (Locke et al., 1981; Matsui, 1981; Garland, 1982). Positive relationships have also been found between specificity of goals and level of performance: specific difficult goals lead to better performance than vague goals such as "do your best" (Wofford, 1979; Locke et al., 1981). These effects assume certain contingencies, including that (1) the individual has sufficient knowledge and ability to attain the goal, (2) the individual accepts and remains committed to the goal, and (3) the individual has feedback showing progress in relation to the goal (Locke et al., 1986).

1. Role of Feedback

Feedback represents that subset of information available to organizational members describing how well they are meeting various goals. This information about goal performance includes that which is provided by the task itself, by the individual member, and by organizational peers and coworkers as well as by direct supervisors and other superordinates (Ashford and Cummings, 1983). Much of the theoretical work in this area has centered on formulating a rationale for the positive effects of feedback on performance and in describing the conditions which delimit its effects.

In early goal setting studies, attempts were made to separate the effect of feedback from the effects of goal setting itself, in the hopes of determining whether feedback directly influences performance or whether its effects were necessarily mediated by goal setting activity. The conclusion was that both feedback and goal setting were necessary for achieving a higher level of performance (Locke, 1967; Locke et al., 1968). Recent research has suggested that feedback stated in terms of performance improvement, rather than failure to reach the goal, is more effective since it increases confidence in the abilities of the individual to ultimately reach the goal (Garland, 1984).

Bandura and Cervone (1983) found that neither goals alone nor performance feedback alone affects motivational level. When first adopted, goals alone produced a performance gain, but they did not generate any further increases in motivation without knowledge of performance (feedback). Analysis of performance effort (motivation) derived from self-set standards under conditions of feedback alone supports the view that both performance knowledge and a standard of comparison are needed to produce motivational effects (Bandura and Cervone, 1983).

Ashford and Cummings (1983) stress the importance of feedback as an individual resource. The value of feedback as a personal resource for attaining organizational goals depends on its potential for fulfilling the following functions: (1) providing usable information under conditions of uncertainty, (2) reflecting the relative importance of various goals within a particular setting, and (3) helping to achieve a sense of competence. Some degree of uncertainty is necessary for feedback to be valuable to an individual. If an individual operates in complete certainty about what constitutes an appropriate response and how that response will be evaluated by others, feedback is not informative and does not provide increased knowledge. Evaluations of the response direct individuals to pursue goals that are regarded as important to the organization and provide them with information about their capacity to achieve organizational goals and, relatedly, their worth to the organization. According to Ashford and Cummings (1983), where feedback fulfills these functions it will come to be seen as a valuable resource and individuals should be motivated to seek it.

Feedback given to employees, whether inherent in the situation or derived from behavior, signals the expected payoffs associated with specific behaviors or with the achievement of a range of goals (Ashford and Cummings, 1983). Individuals can use such feedback cues to maximize their total satisfaction, which they accomplish by allocating their energies across an array of organizational goals. Based on feedback, an individual may decide to devote more effort toward those goals having the greatest probable payoff or toward that goal that seems obtainable only with extra effort. Information from the task itself and from others is sufficient to allow the making of judgments about competence. Feedback, therefore, is a central and necessary resource for understanding the work environment, making self-evaluations, and developing and sustaining feelings of competence (Ilgen et al., 1979).

2. Task Characteristics as Moderators of Goal Effects

Twenty years of empirical research has established that specific, challenging goals lead to higher performance than easy or vague goals (Locke et al., 1981; Kanfer, 1990). In the late 1980s, as research turned to the theoretical limits of goal setting (Garland, 1985; Wood et al, 1987), scholars attempted to identify those variables that moderate the positive performance effects of goals. Among the most potent variables in this respect were task complexity, goal commitment, monetary incentives, participation, and individual differences (Locke et al., 1981; Naylor and Ilgen, 1984; Austin and Bobko, 1984).

Wood et al. (1987) used meta-analytical procedures to assess the moderator effects of task complexity for goal setting studies conducted from 1966 to 1985. Three sets of analyses were conducted: (1) goal difficulty results, (2) goal specificity–difficulty results, and (3) all studies collapsed across goal difficulty and goal specificity–difficulty. Generally, goal setting effects were strongest for easy tasks (e.g., reaction time and brainstorming) and weakest for more complex tasks (e.g., business stimulations, scientific and engineering work, and research productivity).

Goal importance has been found to have a significant impact on performance. Hollenbeck and Williams (1987) studied the presence of multiple goals under conditions that specified priorities among these goals. Goal importance, they argued, has implications for goal setting applications; specifically, it implies that the positive effect of goals on task performance would be increased by the importance attributed to those goals relative to other work- or even non–work-related outcomes. This effect is even more pronounced for individuals who closely monitor their behavior in terms of performance goals (Hollenbeck and Williams, 1987). For them, feedback indicating even a minor difference between goals and performance may be motivating. For others, even major gaps between goals and performance may not bring forth corrective effort.

3. Goal Acceptance

Goal acceptance plays a significant role in moderating the effects of goal setting. Given potential discrepancies between goals set externally and the willingness of individuals to engage in serious efforts to attain them, goal acceptance must necessarily be considered an important moderator variable. Situations in which individuals manifest low acceptance of organizational goals are so common in life situations that nearly all of the work on leadership and management is oriented to motivating subordinates to accept organizational goals (Erez and Kanfer, 1983).

Goal acceptance depends on the perceived outcomes associated with goal implementation (Erez and Kanfer, 1983). Acceptance is more likely if the individual perceives the goal as leading to personally valuable outcomes. Also influencing goal acceptance is the locus of goal setting; goals which are set externally tend to have lower acceptance levels than goals set by the affected individual. Studies (Mandler and Watson, 1966; Thompson, 1981) have demonstrated that people prefer choice and self-control over no choice and external control. That is why in goal setting the degree of worker participation affects goal acceptance.

One strategy suggested as a means of achieving higher levels of goal acceptance is to coordinate external control with personal motivation (Meyer and Gellatly, 1988). Assigned goals are presumed to influence task performance through their effect on personal goals; assigned goals provide implicit information about the level of performance that is acceptable or attainable. This information, in turn, sets a standard for estimating performance capabilities, determining the desirability of any given level of performance, and shaping personal goals. Assuming that individuals have normal aspirations for at least the appearance of competency, they will strive to meet or exceed this implicit standard. Those who are assigned a relatively easy goal can achieve their implicit standard with little difficulty and therefore have little incentive to work harder. On the other hand, employees who are assigned a relatively more difficult goal are motivated to exert considerably more effort (Meyer and Gellatly, 1988).

Assigned goals not only influence performance indirectly through their influence on personal goals, but also directly since most individuals assigned very difficult goals set personal performance goals at or above their ability ceiling (Garland, 1983). Garland (1983), for example, demonstrated that higher levels of motivation produced by a challenging goal are not diminished even when the goal is unlikely to be attained by most individuals to whom it is assigned. Also, the presence of normative information about goal difficulty did not significantly affect performance.

In another study, Erez and Zidon (1984) tested the hypothesis that goal acceptance moderates the relationship of goal difficulty to task performance. They found positively linear relationships between performance and difficulty where goals are accepted and negatively linear ones where they are rejected.

4. Goal Commitment

The literature distinguishes goal commitment from the acceptance of difficult goals, which refers specifically to a goal assigned by another person as a referent (Locke et al., 1981). Goal acceptance does not necessarily require that the individual be bound to the external standard. Commitment is the more inclusive concept, referring to an individual's determination to achieve a goal regardless of its origins. Commitment can apply to any goal, whether it is set by the individual or assigned by someone else. Acceptance, therefore, may be regarded as one type of commitment, referring specifically to an externally assigned goal (Locke et al., 1981).

Goal commitment plays a more crucial role in predicting performance than goal acceptance (Hollenbeck and Klein, 1987). For example, one can initially accept a goal and yet not demonstrate subsequent commitment to that goal over time (Hollenbeck and Klein, 1987). Goal commitment, which implies determination to achieve the original goal, was one of the first potential moderating variables recognized by Locke (1968). The idea that goal commitment was a necessary condition for the goal difficulty effect received empirical support and was central to early theorizing in goal setting (Hollenbeck and Klein, 1987).

More recently, however, Hollenbeck and Klein (1987) reexamined the contribution of goal commitment to goal setting research. Building on the existing literature, they developed a revised model of the goal commitment process, using it to reinterpret past goal setting research. Their model (see Fig. 6) identifies the antecedent factors that may enhance commitment to difficult goals. The antecedents of commitment are divided between those that affect goal valence or attractiveness and those that affect goal expectancy; these are further delineated by whether they are of a personal or a situational nature. Additionally, this suggests that the primary function of goal commitment is to moderate the relation between goal difficulty and task performance.

5. Role of Monetary Incentives in Goal Setting Theory

Research indicates that monetary incentives can affect task performance independently of goal level (Riedel et al., 1988). In the context of goal setting, monetary incentives also play an important role, affecting the degree of goal commitment. In other words, an individual appears more inclined toward higher levels of performance if a monetary reward is offered than if it is not (Locke, 1968). Riedel et al. (1988), for instance, conducted a study to determine the mechanism by which monetary incentives influence goal choice, goal commitment, and task performance. They found that financial incentives influence the process of goal choice; it is through their effect on the choice of goals that monetary incentives influence both goal commitment and task performance.

These effects are complex and occur across several stages. In the first stage, the availability of financial incentives influence pay instrumentality. More specifically, the presence of incentives affects individual perceptions about the amount of pay associated with alternative levels of performance. Next, an individual chooses from alternative performance goal levels perceived to be most attractive. This perception of attractiveness is based on various beliefs and feelings a person has regarding the likelihood that performing at certain levels will lead to particular outcomes, suggesting that the process of goal choice may be linked to expectancy theory concepts and processes. Also, incentives appear to induce choice of more difficult goals and improve performance outcomes. However, both goal difficulty and goal commitment seem to depend significantly on the amount of the financial incentive offered. Finally, goals mediated the effects of monetary rewards on performance.

6. *Participation in Goal Setting*

Participation is generally regarded as an effective means of achieving higher levels of employee goal commitment and performance (Locke et al., 1981). Previous research shows that participation in goal setting may contribute to performance in two ways. First, it can lead to setting higher goals than without participation; and second, it can lead to greater goal acceptance or commitment.

B. Control Theories

One of the most important recent developments in self-regulatory theories of organizational behavior and human performance is control theory (Bandura, 1982; Kanfer, 1990). Control theory places more emphasis on behavior maintenance than on behavior change and, therefore, less emphasis on the need for self-imposed or external reinforcement to activate and maintain the self-regulatory process.

Organizations, of course, impose multiple controls of varying types as part of the management process, always with the aim of ensuring sufficient levels of compliance to achieve organizational goals. One view suggests that the control process involves applying rational control mechanisms (work standards, appraisal and reward systems) to influence employees through external means to assure that the organization achieves its goals (Lawler and Rhode, 1976). An alternative approach views each person as possessing an internal control system (Manz, 1986). Although organizations present employees with certain values and beliefs packaged as organizational cultures or corporate visions, members of the organization hold their own systems of values, beliefs, and visions for the future. Therefore, while organizations provide organizational control systems that influence people, these systems do not control individual actions directly. Rather, the impact of organizational control mechanisms is determined by the way they influence, in intended as well as unintended ways, the self-control systems within organization members (Manz, 1986).

There is a strong linkage between control theories and general theories of self-regulation: both study the impact of external (organizational) and internal (self) loci of control on motivation and performance. From an organizational perspective, recognizing and facilitating employee self-regulating systems poses a viable and more realistic view of control than views centered entirely on external influence (Manz, 1986).

Carver and Scheier (1981), for example, highlight the role of individual differences in self-focus. From their perspective, individuals may direct their attention in one of two directions: inward toward the self or outward toward the environment. Self-control processes included four stages: (1) input perceptions of existing conditions, (2) comparison of this perception to the standard, 3) output behaviors reducing discrepancies between the performance and the standard, and (4) a consequent impact on the environment.

C. An Integrated Control Theory Model of Motivation

A growing number of scholars (e.g., Campion and Lord, 1982; Lord and Hanges, 1987; Klein, 1989) have attempted to employ the control theory framework to develop an integrated approach to motivation. Progress in this effort has led some to call for the combination of all theoretical approaches to work motivation into a single metatheory (Klein, 1989). According to Klein, the use of control theory as an integrating framework makes sense for the following reasons: (1) its dynamic structure easily allows the integration of other theories; (2) it is parsimonious, and even as the other theories are incorporated, it can remain a simple heuristic; (3) its focus is directed to cognitive processes, whose absence has been a source of criticism of current approaches (Klein, 1989).

In control theory, the feedback loop is the fundamental building block of behavior. In its simplest form it consists of five elements: (1) a *referent standard or goal* that the system attempts to maintain or achieve; (2) a *sensor* or input function that measures or gathers information important to the system; (3) a *comparator* which compares the sensed information to the standard; (4) a *decision mechanism* by which the system decides what action to take in order to reduce any discrepancy between the sensed information and the standard; and (5) an *effector* or output function that enables the system to interact with this environment (Lord and Hanges, 1987). Figure 6 provides an illustration of these feedback mechanisms.

Although human systems are often too complex to map in this simple way, they tend to operate similarly—utilizing feedback to ensure the attainment of goals. In human control systems, however, feedback involves much more than the mechanical sensing of the environment. Also, goals are not predetermined and there are several alternatives for reducing discrepancies. Nonetheless, complex behaviors can be explained by hierarchies of feedback loops (Klein, 1989).

An integrated control theory model of motivation can be developed using the feedback loop as the essential component. The model incorporates feedback, goal setting, expectancy, and attribution theories and, according to Klein (1989), it could be extended to include several other theories (e.g., social learning theory, need theories, etc.). Figure 7 illustrates Klein's approach.

From Klein's perspective, this integrated model of work motivation is advantageous for several reasons: (1) it focuses attention on the cognitive processes underlying motivation; (2) it focuses attention on the self-regulation of behavior; (3) it allows scholars to derive numerous propositions regarding the nature of goals and feedback; cognitive, behavioral, and affective reactions over time to goals, performance, and feedback; and role of attributions, expectancies, and goal hierarchies in determining those reactions (Klein, 1989, pp. 168–169).

V. CONCLUSIONS

Over the past two decades, motivation theory has been in turmoil (Kanfer, 1990); many of the most prominent and popular approaches have been challenged (e.g., need theory) and no single

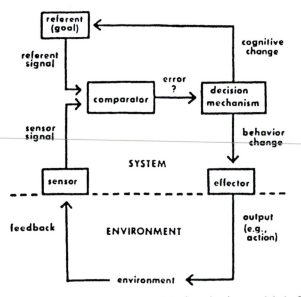

Figure 6 Control systems model of motivation modeled after Powers (1973).

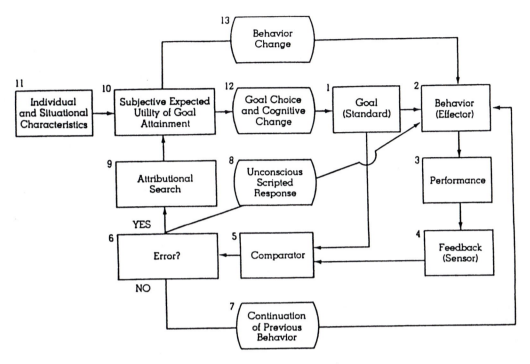

Figure 7   An integrated control theory model of work motivation.

theory has received universal support. At various times in this period, scholars have expressed a lack of confidence in the direction and potential of motivation research. Nonetheless, as our review suggests, there has been a great volume of research in recent years and some real theoretical progress. Similarly, learnings from these ongoing streams of research provide managers with new insights and tools.

Among the most promising theoretical developments are the emergence of models which integrate previously contending candidates for paradigm dominance. The work of Hollenbeck and Klein (1987), for example, draws on expectancy theory to explain important aspects of goal theory and brings together what has often been regarded as competing perspectives (Locke, 1980). Other theorists have brought together control theory and goal setting theory, information processing and control theory, and a variety of other interesting amalgamations (Kanfer, 1990). These remain promising efforts.

Organizations and their managers, especially those in the public sector, have not taken full advantage of more established motivation theories, let alone some of the newer developments. After nearly 20 years of cutback management, however, the old questions of motivating employees have become even more important. Insights about the relationship between individual differences and the motivating potential of tasks, the importance of performance contingent rewards, and the need to provide both intrinsic and extrinsic outcomes need to be better incorporated into management understanding and practice. Similarly, as organizations become flatter and the ratio of supervisors to workers declines, self-management and self-motivation strategies also merit attention.

Effort is rightly regarded as a key to individual and organizational performance. Despite the obvious limitations remaining in our knowledge of motivation, current research directions promise further contributions and greater understanding in the future.

REFERENCES

Allington, R. (1980). Teacher interruption behaviors during primary grade oral reading, *J. Educ. Psychol., 72*: 371–377.

Andrasik, F., and Heimbergs, S. (1982). Self-management procedures, *Handbook of Organizational Behavioral Management* (L.W. Frederickson, ed.), Wiley, New York, pp. 219–247.

Ashford, S.J., and Cummings, L.L. (1983). Feedback as an individual resource: personal strategies of creating information, *Organiz. Behav. Human Perf., 32*: 370–398.

Atkinson, J. (1974). *An Introduction to Motivation*, Van Nostrand, New York.

Austin, J., and Bobko, P. (1984). The application of goal setting: Some boundary conditions and future research, *Proceedings of the 44th Annual Meeting of the Academy of Management*, (J. Pearce II and R. Robinson, Jr., eds.), pp. 197–201.

Bandura, A. (1977a). *Social Learning Theory*, Prentice-Hall, Englewood Cliffs, NJ.

Bandura, A. (1977b). Self-efficacy: toward a unifying theory of behavioral change, *Psychol. Rev., 84*: 191–215.

Bandura, A. (1982). Self-efficacy mechanism in human agency, *Am. Psychologist, 37*(2): 122–147.

Bandura, A. (1983). Self-evaluative and self-efficacy mechanisms governing the motivational effects of goal systems, *J. Personality Social Psychol., 45*(5): 1017–1028.

Bandura, A., and Cervone, D. (1983). Differential engagement of self-reactive influences in cognitive motivation, *Organiz. Behav. Human Dec. Process., 38*: 92–113.

Braun, C. (1976). Teacher expectations: sociopsychological dynamics, *Rev. Educ. Res., 46*: 185–213.

Brockner, J. (1979). The effects of self-estem, success-failure, and self-consciousness on task performance, *J. Personality Social Psychol., 37*: 1732–1741.

Brophy, J., and Good, T. (1974). *Teacher–Student Relationships: Causes and Consequences*, Holt, Rinehart and Winston, New York.

Bryan, J., and Locke, E.A. (1967). Goal setting as a means of increasing motivation, *J. Appl. Psychol., 51*: 274–277.

Campion, M.A., and Lord, R.G. (1982). A control system conceptualization of goal setting and changing process, *Organiz. Behav. Human Perf., 30*: 265–287.

Carver, C.S., and Scheier, M.F. (1981). *Attention and Self-Regulation: A Control Theory Approach to Human Behavior*, Springer-Verlag, New York.

Carver, C.S., and Scheier, M.F. (1982). Control theory: a useful conceptual framework for personality-social, clinical, and health psychology, *Psychol. Bull., 92*(1): 111–135.

Champoux, J.E. (1980). A three sample test of some extensions to the job characteristics model of work motivation, *Acad. Manage. J., 23*(3): 466–478.

Chidester, T., and Grigsbym N. (1984). A meta-analysis of the goal setting performance literature, *Proceedings of the 44th Annual Meeting of the Academy of Management*, (J. Pearce II and R. Robinson, Jr., eds.), pp. 202–206.

Davis, T., and Luthans, F. (1980). A social learning approach to organization behavior, *Acad. Manage. Rev., 5*: 281–290.

De Charms, R. (1968). *Personal Causation*, Academic Press, New York.

Deci, E.L. (1975a). *Intrinsic Motivation*, Plenum Press, New York.

Deci, E.L. (1975b). Notes on the theory and metatheory of intrinsic motivation, *Organiz. Behav. Human Perf., 15*: 130–145.

Deci, E.L., Nezlak, J., and Sheiman, S. (1981). Characteristics of the rewarder and intrinsic motivation of the rewardee, *J. Personality Social Psychol, 40*: 1–10.

Eden, D. (1988). Pygmalion, goal setting, and expectancy: compatible ways to boost productivity, *Acad. Manage. Rev., 13*(4): 639–652.

Eden, D., and Ravid, G. (1982). Pygmalion effect versus self-expectancy: effects of instructor- and self-expectancy on trainee performance, *Organiz. Behav. Human Perf., 30*: 351–364.

Erez, M., and Kanfer, F. (1983). The role of goal acceptance in goal setting and task performance, *Acad. Manage. Rev., 8*(3): 454–463.

Erez, M., and Zidon, I. (1984). Effect of goal acceptance on the relationship of goal difficulty to performance, *J. Appl. Psychol., 69*(1): 69–78.

Garland, H. (1982). Goal levels and task performance: a compelling replication of some compelling results, *J. Appl. Psychol., 67*(2): 245–248.

Garland, H. (1983). Influence of ability, assigned goals, and normative information on personal goals and performance: a challenge to the goal attainability assumption, *J. Appl. Psychol., 68*(1): 20–30.

Garland, H. (1984). Relation of effort-performance expectancy to performance in goal-setting experiments, *J. Appl. Psychol., 69*(1): 79–84.

Garland, H. (1985). A cognitive mediation theory of task goals and human performance, *Mot. Emot., 9*(4): 345–367.

Graen, G., Scandura, T., and Graen, M. (1986). A field experimental test of the moderating effects of growth need strength on productivity, *J. Appl. Psychol., 71*(3): 484–491.

Guzzo, R.A. (1979). Types of rewards, cognition, and work motivation, *Acad. Manage. Rev., 4*(1): 75–86.

Hollenbeck, J.R., and Klein, H.J. (1987). Goal commitment and the goal-setting process: problems, prospects, and proposals of future research, *J. Appl. Psychol., 72*(2): 212–220.

Hollenbeck, J.R., and Williams, C.R. (1987). Goal importance, self-focus and the goal-setting process, *J. Appl. Psychol., 72*(2): 204–211.

Ilgen, D.R., Fisher, C., and Taylor, M (1979). Consequences of individual feedback on behavior in organizations, *J. Appl. Psychol., 64*: 359–371.

Ilgen, D.R., Nebeker, D.M., and Pritchard, R.D. (1981). Expectancy theory measures: an empirical comparison in an experimental simulation, *Organiz. Behav. Human Perf., 28*: 189–223.

Jussim, L. (1986). Self-fulfilling prophecies: a theoretical and integrative review, *Psychol. Rev., 93*(4): 429–445.

Kanfer, R. (1990). Motivation theory and industrial and organizational psychology, *Handbook of Industrial and Organizational Psychology*, 2nd ed., Vol. 1, (M.D. Dunnette and L.M. Hough, eds.), Consulting Psychologists Press, Palo Alto, CA, pp. 75–170.

Kanungo, R.N., and Wright, R.W. (1983). A cross-cultural comparative study of managerial job attitudes, *J. Int. Business Stud. (Fall)*: 115–129.

Klein, H.J. (1989). An integrated control theory model of work motivation, *Acad. Manage. Rev., 15*: 150–172.

Latham, G., and Napier, N. (1984). Practical ways to increase employee attendance, *Absenteeism*, (P. Goodman and R. Atkins, eds.), Jossey-Bass, San Francisco, pp. 322–359.

Lawler, E.E. (1969). Job design and employee motivation, *Personnel Psychol., 22*: 426–435.

Lawler, E.E. and Rhode, J. (1976). *Information and Control in Organizations*. Goodyear, Pacific Palisades, CA.

Locke, E.A. (1967). Motivational effects of knowledge of results: knowledge or goal setting? *J. Appl. Psychol., 51*; 324–329.

Locke, E.A. (1968). Toward a theory of task motivation and incentives, *Organiz. Behav. Human Perf., 5*: 157–189.

Locke, E.A. (1980). Latham versus Komaki: a tale of two paradigms, *J. Appl. Psychol., 65*: 16–23.

Locke, E.A., Bryan, J.F., and Kendall, L.M. (1968). Goals and intentions as mediator of the effects of monetary incentives on behavior, *J. Appl. Psychol., 52*: 104–121.

Locke, E.A., Latham, G.P., and Erez, M. (1988). The determinants of goal commitment, *Acad. Manage. Rev., 13*(1): 23–39.

Locke, E.A., Motowidlo, S.J., and Bobko, P. (1986). Using self-efficacy theory to resolve the conflict between goal-setting theory and expectancy theory in organizational behavior and industrial/organizational psychology, *J. Social Clin. Psychol., 4*(3): 328–338.

Locke, E.A., Shaw, K.N., Saari, L.M., and Latham, G.P. (1981). Goal setting and task performance: 1969–1980, *Psychol. Bull., 90*(1): 125–152.

Lord, R.G., and Hanges, P.J. (1987). A control system model of organizational motivation: theoretical development and applied implications, *Behav. Sci., 32*: 161–177.

Luthans, F., and Davis, T. (1979). Behavioral self-management (BSM): the missing link in managerial effectiveness, *Organiz. Dyn., 8*: 42–60.

Mahoney, M.J., and Arncoff, D.B. (1978). Cognitive and self-control therapies, *Handbook of Psychotherapy and Therapy Change*, (S. Garfield and A. Borgin, eds.), Williams and Williams, Baltimore, pp. 689–722.

Mahoney, M.J., and Arncoff, D.B. (1979). Self-management: theory, research and application, *Behavioral Medicine: Theory and Practice*, (J.P. Brady and D. Pomerleau, eds.), Williams and Williams, Baltimore, pp. 75–96.

Mandler, G., and Watson, D. (1966). Anxiety and the interruption of behavior, *Anxiety and Behavior*, (C.D. Spielberger, ed.), Academic Press, New York, pp. 262–288.

Manz, C.C. (1986). Self-leadership: toward an expanded theory of self-influence processes in organizations, *Acad. Manage. Rev., 11*(3): 585–600.

Maslow, A.H. (1954). *Motivation and Personality*, Harper and Row, New York.

Matsui, T., Okada, A., and Mizuguchi, R. (1981). Expectancy theory prediction of the goal theory postulate, "The harder the goals, the higher the performance," *J. Appl. Psychol., 66*(1): 54–58.

McClelland, D.C. (1961). *The Achieving Society*, Van Nostrand Reinhold, Princeton, NJ.

Mento, A., Steel, R., and Karren, R. (1987). A meta-analytic study of the effects of goal setting on task performance, *Organiz. Behav. Human Dec. Process., 39*: 52–83.

Meyer, J.P., and Gellatly, I.R. (1988). Perceived performance norm as a mediator in the effect of assigned goal on personal goal and task performance, *J. Appl. Psychol., 73*(3): 410–420.

Mills, P.K. (1983). Self-management: its control and relationship to other organizational properties, *Acad. Manage. Rev., 8*(3): 445–453.

Mitchell, T.R., Rothman, M., and Liden, R.C. (1985). Effects of normative information on task performance, *J. Appl. Psychol., 70*(1): 48–55.

Murray, H.A. (1938). *Explorations in Personality*, Oxford University Press, New York.

Naylor, J., and Ilgen, D. (1984). Goal-setting: a theoretical analysis of a motivational technology, *Research in Organizational Behavior*, (B. Staw and L. Cummings, eds.), JAI Press, Greenwich, CT, pp. 95–140.

Pinder, D. (1984). *Work Motivation*, Scott, Foresman, Glenview, IL.

Riedel, J.A., Nebeker, D.M., and Cooper, B.L. (1988). The influence of monetary incentives on goal choice, goal commitment, and task performance, *Organiz. Behav. Human Dec. Process., 42*: 155–180.

Rosenthal, R.A., and Jacobson, L. (1968). *Pygmalion in the Classroom: Teacher Expectations and Pupils' Intellectual Development*, Holt, Reinhart and Winston, New York.

Schwartz, H.S. (1983). A theory of deontic work motivation, *J. Appl. Behav. Sci., 19*(2): 204–214.

Snyder, R.A., and Williams, R.R. (1982). Self theory: an integrative theory of work motivation, *J. Occup. Psychol., 55*: 257–267.

Thompson, S. (1981). Will it hurt less if I can control it? A complete answer to a simple question, *Psychol. Bull., 90*: 89–101.

Vroom, V.H. (1964). *Work and Motivation*, Wiley, New York.

Wexley, K., and Latham, G. (1981). *Developing and Training Human Resources in Organizations*, Scott, Foresman, Glenview, IL.

Wofford, J.C. (1979). A goal-energy-effort requirement model of work motivation, *Acad. Manage. Rev., 4*(2): 193–201.

Wood, R.E., Mento, A.J., and Locke, E.A. (1987). Task complexity as a moderator of goal effects: a meta-analysis, *J. Appl. Psychol., 72*(3): 416–425.

24

The Practice of Employee Discipline

ARTHUR L. FINKLE   Rider University, Lawrenceville, New Jersey

The organization's work rules are the critical mass which drives the operation of the different and sometimes complex activities of doing work through other people. It is critical to the organization to abide by these work rules. Failure to abide by these rules results in the breakdown of the organization's operation. Accordingly, the organization has to create the means by which to enforce its control over its organization. Employee discipline is a form of training that enforces the organization's rules (Mathis and Jackson, 1982).

This chapter will explore employee discipline in generic terms, although differences do exist in different economic sectors. We will refer to the organization (as opposed to the company, agency or government) and to the employee (as opposed to the union).

We shall define progressive discipline, explain its gradations, and display a sample disciplinary price list. Next, we will present checklists for preparing a disciplinary case for management and for the employee. Finally, we shall list some steps in presenting the case.

Historically, in the preindustrial era and in the early industrial era, discipline was oftentimes used as a negative sanction to socialize and motivate people to accept the factory system whereby a monetary payment was exchanged for work produced. The concept of work rules—when to begin work, when to end work, how to establish goals, and how to coordinate different work units—were completely foreign to the rural populace. Initially, this socialization was enforced by corporal punishment, fines, dismissal at will, and on-the-job moral education (Wren, 1981).

In the industrial era (early 1900s), scientific management theorists treated the employee as an investment to be carefully trained, supervised, and sustained. Indeed, as Henri Fayol stated, "general opinion is deeply convinced that discipline [abiding by work rules] is absolutely essential for the smooth running of business and that without discipline no enterprise could prosper" (Fayol, 1981, p. 104).

Later on, a humanistic treatment of the employee shaped current disciplinary attitudes and procedures. The Wagner Act (1935) guaranteed employees the right to join in associations and to formulate grievance procedures. The National Labor Relations Board (NLRB) which was a creation of the Wagner Act, enforced this statutory right (Holly and Jennings, 1988).

These current attitudes and procedures have had a profound effect on management. Management had always possessed unilateral decision-making powers of all of its organization's functions. Nobody questioned its authority to make unfettered managerial decisions on staffpower, capital, production, materials, and methods. However, the rise of unions and their legitimacy guaranteed by the National Labor Relations Act provided for the *bilateral sharing* of staffpower decision-making.

Management feels uncomfortable in this new role and consciously or unconsciously resents this diminution of authority. This uncomfortable managerial role is clearly seen when investigating employee discipline. (It should be noted that Holly and Jennings counsel that if a nonunion company does not provide a "fair" employee discipline system, that company is vulnerable to unionization.)

For example, an employee disciplinary system must have specific standards. There must be a clear definition of the work rules, just cause to impose sanctions and specific procedures, including that the rules must be clear and specifically communicated, clear and consistent, specific steps to resolve the issues, a standard of evidence, and a presumption of innocence (Sloane, 1991).

The incidence of discipline depends on the type of organization. For example, paramilitary organizations (police or correction agencies), hospital employees, and assembly line operators require strict adherence to the work rules and thus receive a large amount of disciplinary actions. In a 1987 study of workers in the state government hospital systems, 25% of all employees were disciplined in 4 states, 10--24% were disciplined in 10 states, and 0-9.9% were disciplined in 21 states. In addition, in Florida where the state contracted out hospital services to a private operator, there was virtually no difference in the percentage of employees who were disciplined in the public and private sectors (Finkle, 1987). In another study of correctional facilities by the Rider Institute of Policy Research, there was a bimodal distribution of disciplinary actions of 5-20% and another of 35-43% of all employees (Finkle and Doherty, 1987).

I. LEGAL RAMIFICATIONS

Union employees have more employee disciplinary procedural rights than nonunion employees. For example, the Supreme Court required the opportunity for union representation when discipline is an issue (*Weingarten v. U.S.*, 449 U.S. 1034, 1980). The NLRB recently ruled that nonunion employees are not entitled to this right.

Union employees in the public sector enjoy an additional right to be apprised of the reason for termination and have an opportunity to explain their side of the issue (*Cleveland Board of Ed. v. Loudermill*, 470 U.S. 532, 1985).

Nevertheless, during the past 30 years, the federal and state governments have provided legislation which protects all employees against certain arbitrary actions. For example, major antidiscrimination acts (Equal Pay Act of 1963, Title 7 of the Civil Rights Act of 1964, Age Discrimination Act of 1967, and Americans with Disabilities Act of 1990) provide protections for employees in protected groups from discriminatory and invalid personnel actions which are not demonstrably related to the job. There are also major employee protections to insure a safe work place (Occupational Safety and Health Act of 1970), including the right to demand on-the-job safety and health on the job without fear of reprisal.

In addition, the state courts are beginning to award wrongful discharge suits by tearing down the wall of the "employment-at-will" concept. This concept holds that an employment contract can be terminated at will by either an employer or an employee. Thus, an employee may resign for any reason and an employer can "fire" an employee for any reason and not have to give the employee an explanation. However, employees are taking their dismissals to court and the courts are generally finding that employers do not have a blanket right to "fire" the employee.

The courts have categorized three types of employee rights in protection of their employment: public policy exceptions, implied contracts, and additional considerations. The case law in 20 states holds that an employee cannot be fired for performing his or her legal duties. Thus, it is against public policy to fire an employee who refuses to lie in court to protect the employer or who refuses to sell a product known to be dangerous. Thirteen states have held that company employee manuals, handbooks, or interviews may constitute an "implied contract" to which an employer is legally bound. In New Jersey, for example, the court in *Peirce v. Ortho Pharmaceutical Corp.*, 84 N.J. 58, held that an employee handbook was an enforceable employment agreement with respect to termination proceedings. Seven states provide for additional consideration to employees when something in addition to their employment is contracted. In Florida, the Court in *Chatelier v. Robinson* found for an employee who sold his business in exchange for a lifetime employment contract, but was subsequently fired (Dessler, 1991).

II. PROGRESSIVE DISCIPLINE

While the best employee discipline is self-discipline, the concept of progressive discipline is assessed for employee wrongdoing in order to make a positive effort to correct unacceptable behavior and to give the transgressor increased (progressive) amounts of disciplinary actions for each subsequent infraction. Thus, the progressive discipline concept uses the psychological idea of extinction of unacceptable behavior by negative reinforcement. Progressive discipline also implies that there is an effort at rehabilitating the employee's performance (Nigro and Nigro, 1976). Dr. Paul Hersey captures this idea:

> In constructive [progressive] discipline, you attempt to correct performance in a timely manner without making the person angry or defensive. The goal is turning performance around, and providing people an opportunity for positive growth. . . not slam dunking someone (Hersey, 1985).

To be most effective, corrective intervention should be immediate, expected, consistent, and impersonal. To delay corrective action, while comfortable for procrastinators, delays improvement. Inaction by itself bespeaks decision-making by paralysis—clearly not the type of organizational impression one wants to convey. The corrective action should be expected. If a work rule is not enforced, it becomes all the more difficult to impose a penalty. Corrective action should be consistent. Sloppy enforcement of one rule encourages disregard for other rules. Corrective action should also be impersonal. Indeed, the problem should be separated from the person. The intention is to correct incorrect or unacceptable behavior of a person rather than correcting an incorrect or unacceptable person. The interview should focus on the undesired behavior, the seriousness of conforming to work rules, and a plan of action (Strauss and Sayles, 1980).

There are generally three gradations of discipline. Corrective actions (oral warning, written warning, counseling) are actions which intend to improve employee performance to adhere to the work rules. Such actions are not held against the employee unless the employee commits a subsequent infraction. For example, when a person is late for work for the first time, the supervisor may counsel the employee that he or she is crucial to the work unit and that all employees are expected to report to work on time. However, the importance of being to work on time depends on the nature of the work. For example, in the production, health care, and paramilitary (law enforcement) sectors, lateness cannot be tolerated. An assembly line cannot be partially staffed. A hospital ward cannot be left unattended due to the potential life-and-death decisions. A prison cannot be left unattended.

Minor disciplinary actions (approximately 5 or fewer days suspension/fine or official reprimand) indicate an increased severity of infraction and actually include a monetary penalty of up to one week's pay. Some firms even go so far as to fine employees, but this practice is seldom used because the employee not only has to pay the fine but has to work in lieu of suspension. Fines are generally used only in restitution situations when equipment is damaged through negligence. Official reprimands often serve the purpose of corrective discipline without any financial penalty. For instance, in using our lateness example, if an employee is late a third time, he or she would be assessed an official reprimand which is a written document that is placed in an employee's official personnel file. A subsequent offense would result in a 1- to 5-day suspension.

Major disciplinary action (more than 5 days suspension, demotion, removal) necessarily involves a serious violation of the work rules and a consequent major penalty. While the loss of 2 weeks pay usually communicates the severity of the offense to employees, some companies will issue up to 6-month suspensions. In suspensions incurred beyond a pay period, management will often allow the employee to take intermittent days off so that the employee will be able to remain on the payroll for at least a day to receive health benefits coverage. The ultimate penalty, of course, is removal. For example, if our late employee continues to be late beyond the 5-day suspension, he or she could be assessed a major suspension, from a 6-day suspension to termination.

However, studies have confirmed that the frequency of firings is miniscule due to several factors. For managers, the act of separation is unpleasant, particularly when the manager knows that there will be a stigma attached to the worker when he or she applies for another job (or for unemployment insurance when there is a penalty waiting period). For organizations, personnel turnover costs will necessarily be incurred when someone replaces the fired employee. Organizations will also have to pay increased unemployment rates if its separation rates are high. Discharged employees are increasingly filing lawsuits for wrongful discharge, discrimination or union bias, thus tying up organizational resources and time. Finally, organizations want to have a "wholesome" public image and do not want to be viewed as "ruthless" (Sloane, 1983).

Moreover, removal in a union–management context is a form of "economic capital punishment" and arbitrators are reluctant to uphold termination proceedings (Holly and Jennings, 1988).

In addition, there are other actions which are not technically employee discipline, but which represent de facto "dehiring" practices, such as resignations not in good standing and forced resignations ("either you resign or you will be fired").

Progressive discipline usually uses a "disciplinary price list" which shows the type of rule infraction and the penalty for each occurrence of that infraction. Types of infractions could include employee attendance (excessive absenteeism, unreasonable excuse for lateness, absence from work without permission), performance (sleeping on duty, serious mistake due to carelessness, failure or excessive delay in carrying out an order), personal conduct (reporting to work unfit for duty, verbal abuse of a patient, fighting on the work premises), safety (negligence in performing duties, loss or careless control of keys, contributing to the escape of an inmate, violation of traffic laws while operating a company vehicle), and miscellaneous offenses (intentional abuse of authority, violation of a rule, regulation, policy, procedure, order, or administrative decision).

Two examples will illustrate the progressivity of penalty. First, reporting to work unfit for duty may carry a penalty ranging from counseling to a written warning; the second infraction will carry a range of a written warning to an official reprimand; the third infraction will carry an official reprimand to removal; and the fourth infraction will result in removal from the job. Second, physical or mental abuse of a patient, resident, or employee will result in removal for the first infraction (New Jersey Department of Human Services, 1981). A sample disciplinary price list is shown in Table 1. Lest we think that the disciplinary price list is used mechanically, this list serves merely as a guide to communicate the standards of behavior, performance, and safety required of employees.

In all cases, there will be mitigating and aggravating factors which will influence a decision made on discipline. The courts have determined that mitigating and aggravating factors are, including but not limited to:

Table 1 Sample Disciplinary Price List

Type of offense	1st Min–Max	2nd Min–Max	3rd Min–Max	4th Min–Max
Attendance				
Excessive absence	C-WW	WW-OR	OR-R	R
Unreasonable excuse for lateness less than 15 min	C-OW	OW-WW	WW-OR	OR-R
Abuse of sick leave	WW-OR	OR-10D	10D-R	R
Leaving assigned work without permission	5D-R	R		
Performance				
Neglect of duty which could result in danger to person or property	C-WW	WW-OR	OR-R	R
Sleeping while on duty	5D-R	R		
Unsatisfactory performance rating	C-R/d	R/d		
Physical/mental inability to perform duties	R/D			
Personal Conduct				
Reporting to work unfit for duty	C-WW	WW-OR	OR-R	R
Physical or mental abuse of a patient, client, resident, or employee	R			
Fighting or creating a disturbance on company property	OR-R	R		
Insubordination	C-R	5D-R	R	
Falsification	C-R	R		
Safety and Security				
Negligence in performing duty resulting in injury to persons or property	5D-R	R		
Failure to report loss of tools	1D-10D	10D-R	R	
Loss or careless control of keys	OR-5D	5D-10D	10D-R	R
Violation of traffic laws while operating company vehicle	C-1D	1D-5D	10D-R	R
Failure to use safety devices	OR-2D	2D-R	R	
General				
Violation of a rule, regulation, policy, procedure, order or administrative decision	C-R	5D-R	R	
Intentional abuse or misuse of authority of position	C-R	5D-R	R	

C, counseling; OW, oral warning; WW, written warning; R, removal; OR, official reprimand; D, suspension; d, demotion.

1. Employee's length of service
2. Employee's employment history
3. Employee's awards, commendations
4. Employee's prior disciplinary history including corrective actions
5. Employee's amount of prior training
6. Employee's amount of supervision
7. Undue amount of time in processing disciplinary charges
8. Bad faith on the part of the supervisor (poor interpersonal relations, retaliation for a prior incident, etc.)
9. Extenuating circumstances (illness in the family, family tragedy, medical/psychological problem beyond the employee's control)

To use the mitigating/aggravating elements, we can turn to our earlier employee example. If the employee had a seriously ill child and had to make arrangements for child care or medical care, then perhaps the employee would receive the benefit of the doubt. Perhaps he or she would change shifts or secure other arrangements to care for his or her child. On the other hand, if this employee were a short-time employee, working in a probationary period, then he or she might be dismissed because lateness in a window period intending to impress management bodes poorly for future occurrences of lateness.

III. DISCIPLINE WITHOUT PUNISHMENT

An alternative to progressive discipline is discipline without punishment. This alternative assumes that the employee desires to adhere to the work rules of the organization and any work rule violations are the result merely of oversights or the employee's not being informed of the correct behavior. Because suspensions are punitive in nature and they result both in loss of income (to the employee) and in lack of productivity (to the organization), the corrective action is: oral reminder, written reminder, paid one-day leave, and, finally, a decision to stay with the organization or not. In this system, there is no loss of income to the employee and there is no downtime to the organization (Dessler, 1991).

IV. WHAT HAPPENS AFTER A WORK RULE IS ALLEGEDLY VIOLATED?

When a work rule is allegedly violated, a process is generally triggered which requires both management and the employee to prepare a case against the action and to defend the action. What follows are checklists for both management and the employee in preparation of the case. Thereafter, we will discuss the actual presentation of the case before an arbitrator.

V. MANAGEMENT'S CHECKLIST OF PREPARING A DISCIPLINARY CASE

Since management has the burden of proof, it has a higher standard than the union to prepare a case. Accordingly, we will focus on the important features to sustain a disciplinary action, with particular emphasis on major disciplinary cases in a departmental hearing. It is intended to assist management personnel as they prepare a case at the departmental (first) level.

There are basically seven steps which management should follow in preparing for such cases.

A. Employee Identification

While this step seems elementary, many cases have been lost because of management's inability to ascertain the correct employees involved in alleged wrongdoing. In fact, there might have been numerous employees assigned to a particular location and identification is crucial. Once the particular employee is denoted, his or her employment status is then recorded as a permanent employee, a temporary employee, or an at-will employee. These designations are crucial because usually only permanent employees have hearing rights. Otherwise, there is a common law right of presenting an administrative action in the courts by a prerogative writ, when there is no administrative remedy. Occasionally, determining the employee status can be confusing. For example, an employee serving in a working test period is treated as a temporary employee with no hearing rights. On the other hand, a temporary employee with permanent status in another title may have the rights of a permanent employee for a hearing.

Next, management has to identify the bargaining group of the employee. Such groups vary greatly from state to state. For example, New York State has 787 local government bargaining units and Hawaii has only 4. But obviously it is important to ascertain the employee's unit so that the appropriate union may be notified and the appropriate procedure may be used. Oftentimes, different unions collectively bargain using different hearing procedures (Kearney, 66).

B. Time

The date and time of occurrence is recorded as well as the day of the week and the shift. Oftentimes, an incorrectly recorded time of day cuts the ground out from prospective witnesses who worked shifts different from the alleged offender. Thus, when management alleges that the action at issue occurred on the second shift, but is recorded on the third shift, the third shift employees' testimony becomes not credible and the alleged action becomes overwhelmingly suspect.

C. The Interview and Statement

Every effort should be made to interview the accused individual as soon as possible after the alleged occurrence. The individual should be asked:

What happened?
When did it happen?
Where did it happen?
How did it happen?
Why did it happen?
Who did what?

An oral statement from the employee should then be reduced to writing. In this way, the facts and circumstances will be memorialized when memories are fresh. Later on, memories may dim or vanish altogether. After securing any statement (including those of witnesses), the competency and credibility of the individual should be considered. Some criteria to use for competency are the capacities to recall, to relate, and to perceive what was happening. A statement from an attending physician, psychologist, or social worker may also be required, particularly if the mental capacity of an institutionalized witness is sought. In addition, the credibility of the alleged offender or a witness should be determined. The interviewer should ask:

Is the statement believable and accurate?
Is the statement contradicted by another witness?
Is the statement suspicious?
Does the individual have something to hide or a motivation to protect another person?
Does the interviewee seem vague or uncertain?
Does the interviewee's statement change as you talk to him or her?

Does the statement seem unusual, e.g., too precise a memory of an event that occurred a long
   time ago?

Does the interviewee's general demeanor reveal a falsehood, i.e., failure to look at the interviewer or extremely nervous or edgy?

D.   Interview All Possible Witnesses

It is management's duty to interview all possible witnesses to ascertain the truth. Oftentimes those
whom you do not interview may appear at the hearing to contradict your case and to render it
indefensible. Therefore, it is imperative that all eyewitnesses and hearsay witnesses be interviewed
for the probative (truthful) value of their statements. Witnesses in administrative hearings are not
generally granted immunity as in criminal proceedings. Therefore, management's opportunity to
seek the truth is greatly enhanced because failure to cooperate could result in a charge of insub-
ordination.

E.   Evidence

Evidence includes all means by which a fact is established or disproved. Evidence must be competent (trustworthy), relevant (on point), and material (has a bearing on the matter at issue).
Generally, cases in administrative law are decided on the basis of a preponderance of sufficient
credible evidence [see *Spagnuolo v. Bonnett*, 16 N.J. 546 (1954)]. Therefore, management is
obligated to prove beyond 50% of the doubt that the accused wrongdoer actually committed the
specified act subject to disciplinary action. Some procedures for what to collect as evidence are
as follows:

Physical evidence, such as broom handles, bricks, dice, pieces of glass, ripped clothing, etc.
Photographs of the individual who was harmed and/or the location at issue. Such photographs must
   be taken as soon as possible and the taker must sign and date the back of the photo.
Diagrams or maps, to the scale of the location at issue, may be drawn with name of drawer and
   date indicated at bottom.
Relevant memoranda, letters, schedules, log books, sign-in sheets, etc.
Record of prior disciplinary actions.
Record of accused employee's training and performance evaluations.
Accused employees' job specifications.
Relevant administrative orders, policies, and procedures.

F.   Look for Aggravating and Mitigating Factors

There can be no arbitrary punishment for a wrongful act. Each act has to be interpreted within
the context of the occurrence, the intention of the purported wrongdoer, and the gravity of actual
danger or harm. These factors may aggravate or mitigate penalties. Such factors include:

Employee's performance ratings
Prior disciplinary record and dates of such occurrences
Employee's awards and good service record
Instances of misconduct informally adjudicated (warnings, reprimands)
Training
Supervision given the employee
Length of service
Delay in processing charges (more than 3 months, 6 months, 1 year, more)
Bad faith on the part of the supervisor (personal animosity, bias, political motivation, or prior abor-
   tive attempts to discipline the employee)

As an example, the penalty to a 20-year employee who is convicted of neglect of duty is different from that of a 2-year employee. In this case, significant mitigating factors are the employee's length of service, performance record, and prior disciplinary record.

G. Charge and Specification

Finally, management may issue a charge against the employee. The charge may be cited from those on the Sample Disciplinary Price List on page 607.

In addition, management must issue a specification which recites the act or acts for which the disciplinary act is alleged. Special care must be taken to prepare the specification (the recitation of the facts of the case—the time, the place, the alleged wrongful act). The courts have generally ruled that a charge may be modified but a specification cannot be so modified because the alleged wrongful act could not have been changed.

H. Summary

With this checklist, management and unions should be better prepared to seek the truth and to achieve equity in personnel disciplinary situations. In this way, the disciplinary process can help to guarantee a democratic workplace where a sense of fairness will prevail in the work force, thus assuring more a productive work force.

V. THE EMPLOYEE'S CHECKLIST OF PREPARING A DISCIPLINARY CASE

The basic principle underlying most discipline is "just cause." This standard is generally written or implied in union contracts, personnel manuals, or other binding employment documents.

The employee should ask certain questions to determine whether just cause is satisfied for disciplining an employee:

1. Was the employee adequately warned of the consequences of his or her conduct? The warning may be communicated by word, by action, or by writing? Of course, outrageous behavior, such as fighting on the job or incoherence due to substance abuse is so serious that the employee should have known that such behavior was punishable.
2. Was the employer's rule reasonably related to the efficient and safe operation of the job?
3. Did management make a fair and objective investigation prior to giving a disciplinary penalty? Did management investigate and verify the charge before taking action or did it "shoot from the hip?" Did management selectively overemphasize certain facts and points, ignoring factors which would support the grievant's case? Was management at fault by not explaining the rules to the alleged wrongdoer? Was a management employee at fault, but not disciplined, for the same offense?
4. Were the rules, orders, and penalties consistently applied? Was the penalty punitive or vindictive rather than corrective and remedial? Was the discipline timely? Was the alleged wrongdoer informed as to the level of performance expected of him or her? Did the violation break the contract, the administrative directive, or past practice?
5. Was the penalty reasonably related to the seriousness of the offense and the past record? Were mitigating and aggravating factors considered in the decision?

VI. PRESENTATION OF THE CASE

In most cases, nonlawyers present a disciplinary case. There may be as few as one or as many as nine steps before the case ripens to go to arbitration or to another quasi-formal dispute resolution process (administrative law, mediation, fact finding, etc.). Ninety-nine percent of all union contracts provide for a resolution mechanism for disciplinary actions (Holly and Jennings, 1988).

The most common resolution method involves four steps. Usually, at the first step the employee (with or without the shop steward) presents the case to the first-line supervisor. If the case is not resolved, a union grievance committee member presents the case to the organization's employee (labor) relations representative. If the case is still not resolved, the entire union grievance committee presents the case to the labor relations manager and the general operations management official. If the third step is unsuccessful, the case goes to arbitration where an impartial arbitrator makes a decision.

A.   Arbitration

Arbitration is the most definitive type of third-party intervention in which the arbitrator usually has the power to determine and dictate the settlement terms (Dessler, 1991).

The arbitrator conducts the hearing in an informal manner. But no matter how informal the hearings are, they must proceed in an orderly and reasonably efficient manner, making it inevitable to compare arbitration proceedings with legal trials. Accordingly, we shall present a guide to union officials and management officials who may be asked to present a disciplinary case before an arbitrator.

B.   Rules of Evidence

The legal rules of evidence in the American (English) system of law have evolved over hundreds of years. The rules of evidence exist to assure the triers of facts (jurors presumably not schooled in the law) in lawsuits that relevant proof will be admitted. After the relevant proof is submitted, it has to withstand cross-examination from which the juror can then ascertain the truth. However, since labor arbitration involves an arbitrator (who is generally experienced in weighing the facts and in deciding such cases), the arbitrator is not likely to be led astray the way that inexperienced jurors may.

C.   The Case Presentation

In a lawsuit, the moving party presents the case first. However, in a disciplinary proceeding, the power to establish the disciplinary standards and the power to make the personnel action resides in management. Therefore, most labor contracts provide for the initial presentation to be performed by management. Management usually also has the burden of proof (the establishing of proof against rebutting evidence of the other side that the allegations are correct). The party which has the burden of proof has to convince the arbitrator to believe its case based on some standard of evidence. A "preponderance of the credible evidence" is that amount of evidence which would lead a reasonably cautious mind to a given conclusion. On a scale of zero to 100, where zero is no proof at all and 100 is an absolute certainty, a "preponderance of the credible evidence" would be something more than 50. "Clear and convincing" evidence would total approximately 67. [Most disciplinary cases are decided by the clear and convincing standard of evidence, (Holly and Jennings, 1988)].

D.   The Opening Statement

In the opening statement, the parties present the issues and their version of the facts which will be demonstrated by proof. Experienced participants usually prepare their opening statements by writing their notes, thus giving them the advantage of methodically thinking through their case and giving the arbitrator an orderly picture of the presentation or arguments.

E. Witnesses

Although some witnesses are sworn in, the practice is not to swear in witnesses. The questioner (both management and labor) should ask the witness the questions he or she will ask prior to the hearing so that all the facts are known beforehand. Among lawyers, a cardinal principle is to ask only those questions in which the answer is known. The witness is the most important link to the case because the demeanor and credibility of the witness will probably determine which version of the facts will be adopted by the arbitrator.

F. Direct Examination and Objections

Direct examination of the witness is conducted by asking the witness to recite his or her version of the facts. If the witness is verbal and able, the presenter may ask the witness to recite the facts without asking too many questions. If the witness is not too verbal or is limited in any way, the presenter may ask a series of questions which adduce the facts. However, leading questions (in which the questioner suggests the answer by the form of the question, "You saw that he really was asleep?") may not be asked during direct examination.

Although the hearing is informal, the opposing side may object to certain lines of questions or to leading questions. The general rule is to raise the objection before the question is answered because after the question is answered the damage is done.

The arbitrator may also ask questions to help him or her better understand the case.

G. The Facts

Certain facts may be stipulated, in which both sides agree on certain facts. In this way, the facts in dispute become narrower so that the hearing will become more efficient. In addition, either side may introduce documents which have a bearing on the case, such as the contract, the job performance form, the time sheets, diary accounts, etc. These documents are presented to the arbitrator who will mark them in evidence. A copy should also be provided to the other side.

H. Firsthand Knowledge of the Facts

Our legal system generally requires that the most reliable sources of information be used as the source of information. Thus, a witness who observed the facts is crucial to the case. In some cases, hearsay evidence (testimony of a statement by someone other than the witness) is admissible in arbitration. Even our formal legal system permits exceptions to the introduction of hearsay evidence:

1. Testimony taken at a former hearing or in another suit
2. The admissions of the opposing party
3. Declarations made by a person against his interest
4. Declarations made by a party shortly before death
5. Other kinds of spontaneous declarations concerning a mental state or some excited utterance made along with, or as part of, the happening of some event
6. Records of past recollection
7. Business records
8. Official written statements (Siegel, 1978)

I. Opinion Testimony

In a court of law, only an expert may render an opinion on a conclusion of fact. However, in an arbitration hearing, a witness can draw on memory recall, inferences, and reflection when in actuality giving an opinion. For example, a witness is able to say, "He was drunk," based on observation and memory and inference.

J. Cross-examination

In American law, the truth is borne out when the witness is subject to cross-examination. In this way, the credibility of the witness and the factual scenario are evaluated.

A questioner should emphasize a witness's lack of credibility or unfamiliarity with the facts. The questioner should never go on a "fishing expedition." It will only result in a restatement of the witness's own position. The questioner should keep meticulous notes to question exactly the facts at issue.

K. Redirect and Recross-Examination

An act of fundamental fairness, the questioner may redirect questions to the witness after being cross-examined, usually on the specificity of the facts at issue. Then the cross-examiner may re-cross-examine the witness. In this way, if the facts hold up, the arbitrator will be persuaded.

L. Final Arguments and Briefs

The final arguments summarize the events of the hearing. They should reflect the original opening statement and should reflect on the conduct of the hearing to show that the facts have been sustained by the evidence. Arguments will be presented to show that the opposing party's facts are not credible or logically consistent. Sometimes, the arbitrator will request a posthearing brief in which the parties will present a summary of all legal issues, legal and work rule citations, and proofs.

As the reader can see, presenting a case before an arbitrator cannot be properly accomplished without adequate preparation. It is imperative that the presenter be prepared. We recommend ample use of the checklist to prepare a case. We also recommend that the presenter be schooled by the national union, a local attorney, a veteran arbitrator, or local university faculty. With some experience comes resultant confidence and competence.

REFERENCES

Dessler, Gary (1991). *Personnel/Human Resource Management*, 5th ed. Prentice Hall, Englewood Cliffs, NJ.

Fayol, Henri. (1986), General principals of management, *Organization Theory* (D.S. Pugh, eds.), Penguin Books, New York, pp. 101–123.

Holly, William H., and Jennings, Kenneth M. (1988). *The Labor Relations Process*, 3rd ed., Dryden Press, Chicago, IL.

Finkle, Arthur L. (1987). Public employee discipline in state government, *Int. J. Public Admin.*, 9(5): 554.

Finkle, Arthur L., and Doherty, Donald R. (1987). Custody disciplinary study. Unpublished study of the Rider Institute of Policy Research.

New Jersey Department of Human Services, (1981). Administrative Order 4:08—Disciplinary Action Program.

Nigro, Felix, and Nigro, Lloyd. (1976). *The New Public Personnel Administration*, F. E. Peacock, Itaska, IL.

Siegel, Boaz (1961). *Proving Your Arbitration Case*, Bureau of National Affairs, Washington, DC.

Sloane, Arthur A., and Witney, Fred (1991). *Labor Relations*. 7th ed., Prentice-Hall, Englewood Cliffs, NJ.

Sloane, Arthur A. (1983). *Personnel: Managing Human Resources*, Prentice-Hall, Englewood Cliffs, NJ.

Strauss, George and Sayles, Leonard R. (1980). *Personnel: The Human Problems of Management*, 5th ed., Prentice-Hall, Englewood Cliffs, NJ.

Wren, David A. (1979). *The Evolution of Management Thought*, 2nd ed., Wiley, New York.

25
Productivity and Quality Management

MARC HOLZER   Rutgers University at Newark, Newark, New Jersey

I. PRODUCING PUBLIC SERVICES

Productive management, public and private, has evolved from simple "common sense" in the late 19th century to complex systems in the late 20th century (Holzer, 1992). Today, to produce public services, the best public organizations have developed multiple, reinforcing capacities, as summarized in Fig. 1 (Holzer and Callahan, 1993). Government agencies which have been formally recognized as high achievers, as the state-of-the-art:

Integrate advanced management techniques
Apply quality management principles
Use measurement as a decision-making tool
Work hard to motivate employees
Adapt new technologies, and
Develop public–private partnerships

This chapter will concentrate on one contemporary approach to productivity improvement, total quality management (TQM), and its implications for the processes of human resource management. The opportunities and problems which we can identify through this lens are not necessarily confined to TQM-type projects, but suggest the subtleties of systemic problem solving in any ambitious management capacity-building project. It is important to recognize that TQM is not a new invention. Rather, it is an innovative repackaging of several decades of public sector productivity improvement, as is evidenced by the *Public Productivity and Management Review* (17 volumes and more than 500 articles from 1975 to 1994), the *Productivity Improvement Handbook for State and Local Government* (Washnis, 1980, 1492 pages), and the *Public Productivity Handbook* (Holzer, 1992, 705 pages). The TQM movement in government also draws heavily on decades of industrial quality improvement work in the private sector, such as that of Deming (1986) and Juran (1988). Although neither TQM nor quality improvement was a term generally found in the public sector literature as late as 1988, the past several years have witnessed an accelerated improvement and publication movement under this terminology. In many cases, what were formerly "productivity" projects are now redescribed as "quality" efforts.

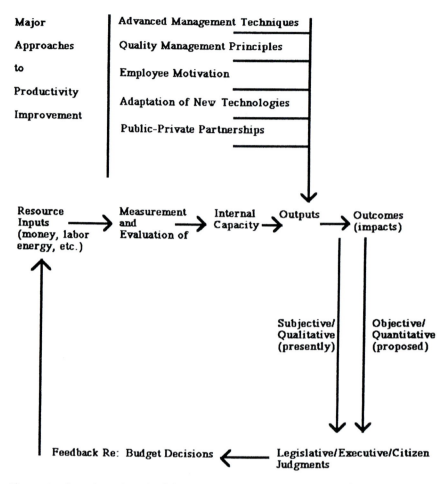

Figure 1   Overview of productivity and performance.

II.   MANAGEMENT FOR QUALITY

Total quality management, directed at public or private sector productivity improvement, is one of the most recent reformulations of management theory. It is a theory-based improvement strategy which allows public managers to increase the capacity for agency-wide cooperation, responsiveness to customer needs, and process improvement. Although TQM and similar efforts are popularly associated with the private sector (Crosby, 1979; Imai, 1986; Juran, 1988; Ciampa, 1992), elected and appointed officials have come to recognize that traditional, management-oriented productivity efforts alone may not lead to sufficient improvements in service quality as perceived by the public. Standard management methods—such as strong executive leadership, top-down control, intensive quality inspections, and tight audits—have proven insufficient in motivating employees toward higher productivity. According to Milakovich (1992), "Despite the best intentions, the application of these methods has not eliminated complaints of inefficient or ineffective services, wasted resources, or lack of responsiveness by public employees." Osborne and Gaebler, in *Reinventing Government* (1992) are essentially in pursuit of improved productivity, and they weave in quality as an important aspect of productivity improvement.

There are many definitions of TQM, and each is reminiscent of previous definitions of productivity improvement. Cohen and Brand (1993, pp. xi–xii) define TQM as follows:

Total implies applying the search for quality to every aspect of work, from identifying customer needs to aggressively evaluating whether the customer is satisfied.
Quality means meeting and exceeding customer expectations.
Management means developing and maintaining the organizational capacity to constantly improve quality.

According to the authors, "The same principles of total quality management used in private industry are creating a quiet revolution in the public sector . . . . To improve quality of service, increase productivity, and reduce waste, more and more government managers—from Little Rock to Washington—are turning to TQM."

According to Hyde (1992; U.S. Department of Defense, 1990, p. 11), the Defense Department's extensive experience through the 1980s has produced what is perhaps the most appropriate definition:

TQM is both a philosophy and a set of guiding principles that represent the foundation of a continuously improving organization. TQM is the application of quantitative methods and human resources to improve materials and services supplied to an organization, all the processes within an organization, and the degree to which the needs of the customer are met, now and in the future. TQM integrates fundamental management techniques, existing improvement efforts, and technical tools under a disciplined approach focused on continuous improvement.

The Federal Quality Institute (Mizaur, 1992), the federal government's overall commitment to TQM, offers an even more succinct explanation:

Quality management is a strategic integrated management system for achieving customer satisfaction through the involvement of all employees and continuous improvement of all the organization's processes and use of resources.

Figure 2 summarizes the FQI's approach as an inverted pyramid, in contrast to the traditional top-down management hierarchy. FQI recognizes that "all three stakehold agendas—that of customer, employee, funder—must be served equally" (Mizaur, 1992). The FQI conceptualization emphasizes seven key factors for successful implementation (Hyde, 1992; U.S. FQI Handbook, 1991):

1. Top management support
2. Customer focus
3. Long-term strategic planning
4. Employee training and recognition
5. Employee empowerment and teamwork
6. Measurement and analysis of products and processes
7. Quality assurance

Hyde (1992) is of the opinion that this seven-part route is a conceptual middle course between the strategic planning–quality education–training analyses promulgated by such TQM gurus as Juran (1988) and Crosby (1979) on the one hand, and the statistical analysis–participative management approach advocated by Deming (1986) and some Japanese experts.

TQM is sufficiently diverse in its conceptualization to have spawned many different formulas under the same rubric. When comparing just three prescriptions, as in Table 1, the extent of overlap is surprisingly limited. This underscores the complexity of truly *total* quality management

Traditional Management Focus

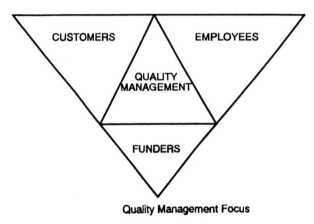

Quality Management Focus

Figure 2   Federal Quality Institute approach to TQM.

as well as the lack of a unified conceptual framework. It also points to the need to build an orga-
nization-specific plan by deriving appropriate steps from the experiences of employees, through
their participation, and of other organizations, through published cases and other analyses.

EXAMPLES OF SUCCESS

Although the FQI type of approach is also characteristic of private sector quality efforts, the director of the institute feels that governments' tasks are more complex: "Private sector customer
agendas are often straightforward. . . . Even with multiple customers . . . there is usually substantial
congruence on the primary agenda. However, in many Government agencies customer agendas
may be varied, complex, or competing" (Mizaur, 1992). Despite that difficulty, quality improvement has been achieved at the federal, state, and local levels as evidenced by many cases.

The federal government is often accorded leadership in government quality efforts. It follows,
according to Hyde (1992), that "quality management seems both logical and inevitable" at the state

Table 1 TQM Prescriptions Compared

Federal Quality Institute
1. Top mangement leadership and support
2. Customer focus
3. *Long-term strategic quality planning*
4. *Employee training and recognition*
5. Employee empowerment and teamwork
6. Measurement and analysis of products and processes
7. Quality assurance

Swiss (1992) has an alternate seven-point formulation:
1. The customer is the arbiter of quality
2. Quality should be built into the product or service rather than weeding out failures through inspection
3. *Quality calls for consistency*
4. Group or team performance is emphasized rather than individual performance
5. TQM is a continuous process
6. Success is dependent on the participation of the workers
7. TQM requires the total commitment of the organization

The U.S. General Accounting Office (GAO) (1991) surveyed high-scoring Baldridge Award applicants (the Baldridge Award is a national competition, administered by the Departmnet of Commerce, primarily for the private sector) and concluded that six features were important:
1. Corporate attention is focused on meeting customer quality requirements
2. Management leads the way in disseminating TQM values throughout the organization
3. Employees are asked and empowered to continuously improve all key business processes
4. *Management nurtures a flexible and responsive corporate culture*
5. *Management systems support fact-based decision making*
6. *Partnerships with suppliers improve product or service delivery*

Note: Steps that differ substantially from other prescriptive plans above are highlighted in italic.

and local level. Actually, quality improvement in government, particularly state and local government, is not unusual, and in some cases clearly predates the FQI, and sometimes even the government-wide TQM movement. The Local Government Information Network (LOGIN, 1992) database, for example, contains more than 550 examples of programs with a quality component dating back through the 1980s. West et al. (1993) estimate "that twenty-five percent of all cities over 25,000 population use TQM in at least one functional area . . . most often police work, parks and recreation services, personnel management, and budgetary reporting." They attribute adoption of TQM to the interests of chief administrative officers, to public complaints, and to budget pressures. Cohen and Brand (1993) cite dozens of examples at all levels of government. Many of these, such as dramatic improvements in vehicle maintenance at the New York City Department of Sanitation, have been described as productivity improvements prior to the TQM movement (Contino and Giuliano, 1991). Two award-winning quality-oriented cases from the Exemplary State and Local Awards Program are described in Appendix A.

At the federal level there are now many cases, although the most prominent are primarily military. The Department of Defense's dates to the early 1980s and predates the establishment of the FQI by at least 5 years. For example, the seven finalists for the 1993 Federal Quality Improvement Prototype (QIP) Award included: United States Air Force Medical Center, Wright-Patterson AFB, OH; Arnold Engineering Development Center, Arnold AFB, TN; Defense Logistics Services Center, Battle Creek, MI; Naval Supply Center, Oakland, CA; Naval Aviation Depot, Cherry

Point, NC; Royalty Management Program, Minerals Management Service, Department of the Interior, Lakewood, CO; and the Naval Air Warfare Center, Aircraft Division, Lakehurst, NJ. In 1992 award winners included the Defense Contract Management District Northeast, Boston, MA; the Department of Veterans Affairs, Philadelphia; the Public Services and Administration Patent and Trademark Office of the Department of Commerce, and the Department of Labor's Wage and Hour Division, San Francisco Region (Federal Quality Institute, 1992a–d).

The most successful civilian case at the federal level may be the Ogden Service Center of the Internal Revenue Service, which received the 1992 Presidential Award for Quality. According to Keehley and Medlin (1991), prior to the award Ogden had made great strides in instilling quality as a core value and establishing quality measures as key operational indicators, illustrating how "quality" organizational change could be accomplished. The following is taken from the Executive Summary of the 1992 Presidential Award for Quality:

> In 1985, Ogden Service Center was caught in a crisis, along with the entire Internal Revenue Service. We initiated Total Quality Management principles throughout our organization. Because we soon realized it takes both managers and employees working together to achieve quality, the Internal Revenue Service changed the definition from Total Quality Management to Total Quality Organization.
>
> Incorporating quality into an organization the size of our Service Center is a complex task. During the 1991 filing season, 6,300 federal employees processed over 26 million tax returns, collected over $100 billion, and processed refunds for taxpayers totaling $9 billion. Many other important functions are performed in the Center, including the correction of errors, answering taxpayer correspondence, and ensuring compliance to tax regulations.
>
> In order to begin transforming our immense organization into a Total Quality Organization, we have implemented a series of interlocking driving principles designed to generate continuous improvement. These principles are: structure, commitment, education, customer focus, involvement and recognition.
>
> Our structure includes councils, a value system, quality improvement teams, task teams, and ways to measure quality progress. To date, quality improvement teams have saved $3,730,959 and our quality initiatives have saved $7,571,789. This gives us a total cost benefit of over $11 million. Our partnership with the National Treasury Employees Union strengthens the overall structure of our quality improvement process.
>
> Our structure is the mainspring of our driving principles. By adding other interlocking principles, we are building a Total Quality Organization. Commitment from all levels—top management, the Union, and employees—accelerates the progress of the quality movement and sets the principle of education in motion. We discovered that when we put quality up front, in our training, we effectively communicate the quality vision to our employees.
>
> We amplify the power of these principles by focusing on our customers. At Ogden Service Center, we re-examined the word "customer." To improve customer service, we literally started from the inside out by identifying our internal and external customers and their needs.
>
> Involvement expands our quality improvement process. We find that involving our employees in the process gives them the buy-in necessary to generate teamwork and pride of ownership. Every employee is part of the team that evolves into a Total Quality Organization.
>
> Recognition is an important principle used to generate enthusiasm in our workforce. We have many ways to recognize our employees as they make quality happen through their day-to-day accomplishments. The celebration of success is limited only by the imagination and creative abilities of our employees.

The force we generate through our driving principles enables us to face the challenges of change. We realize the quality process is not an easy one, but has many rewards. As long as we remain focused on our quest for excellence, we will provide quality service to our customers.

IV. RED FLAGS FOR TQM SYSTEM BUILDING

Despite an impressive compendium of successful cases, public sector quality improvement programs in the 1990s may suffer from the same problems and mistakes encountered by private sector firms in the 1980s. According to Hyde (1992), these may include dysfunctional internal competition, weak employee participation below a meaningful threshold, distrust by managers and nonparticipating employees, uneven implementation, insufficient training, and inconsistent implementation of quality efforts.

These problems of quality management, which are suggested by private sector experiences, are generic and overlap substantially with the public sector context. But TQM implementers within government may face particular human resource problems, most of which are as characteristic of previous attempts to build comprehensive public sector productivity management systems as they are of contemporary quality management efforts: employee participation and trust, training, and personnel management (Holzer, 1992).

A. Employee Empowerment and Trust

Decisions made at the top often remain at the top. In the case of TQM, this adage cautions that everyone must "buy in" or else the effort will be no more than a semantic exercise. Resistance to top-down decisions will render them of little consequence at the operating level. For example, measurement, which provides the necessary feedback for quality management, cannot ignore feedback from employees as to the validity, reliability, and sufficiency of hard data. Unions, which are much more prevalent in the public sector, should be considered partners in quality. That partnership cannot, however, be manipulative or given only lip service. Real partners have meaningful input into decisions regarding the design and implementation of quality systems.

The concept of teamwork—beyond just the notion of participatory decision making—is a key to TQM. The Presidential Award for Quality gives it a weight of 20 points (of 100) in the award criteria. In their study of TQM in the Florida Department of Transportation (DOT), Bowman and French (1992) found that 73% of respondents agreed that the "team concept is excellent," 66% credited management with ongoing involvement, more than 60% identified strong team leadership, and more than 70% noted "explicit guidelines for team tasks." But these positives can be negatives in TQM cases which are neither well planned nor well managed. Management may fail to be involved. Team leadership may be weak. Guidelines may be vague. And even in a successful case, Bowman and French also found that only a minority (some 48%) of respondents "felt that teams have the power to make necessary changes," a conclusion which suggests inadequate empowerment. As the authors conclude:

> Thus, although managers are involved with quality, provide resources, and assume leadership roles, some of them support the team concept less often than others. Perhaps a minority is offering pseudo commitment, and its members are not willing to provide real ownership to employees. The lack of trust in DOT is, of course, one of the most troubling findings. A trusting environment is integral to success, and DOT must deal with its vulnerability to this key feature of TQM. Creating such an atmosphere is, like TQM, a long-term, day-by-day process; one important way to do this is to continue work on team problem solving.

Without trust and a firm management commitment, quality initiatives—and any other agency intitiatives—are likely to deteriorate.

One danger in employee involvement, especially within the TQM envelope, is the extent to which it will parallel or bypass the union. In those cases the gains to be made through participation may run up against the losses resulting from political alienation of the union hierarchy. The most effective systems might involve both union and workplace committees. In both sectors the most effective organizations are those which treat unions as real partners, not imagined enemies. Excellent union relationships are especially important in the more heavily unionized public sector.

Employee participation may also be hindered by the very impetus for TQM—scarce resources and the need to cut back. Cutback management usually increases work force paranoia, and with good reason: its history has been saturated with layoffs, reductions in real wages, and overtly political (rather than productive) decisions (Levine, 1980). How can employees be expected to accept a new approach, TQM, to shrinking government? One answer, perhaps, is to convince them that TQM will result in more rational cuts and reallocations than the traditional political and off-the-cuff decisions. TQM also offers the possibility of maximizing the efficacy of service delivery to needy clients and the public, a public service argument which may be especially salient to public servants.

B. Training

TQM is complicated, and in any complex undertaking managers and employees must be carefully trained. Deming (1986), for example, emphasizes the critical role of training and education. On the "hard" side, that training must extend to the nuts and bolts of measurement and work process analysis. On the "soft" side, it must equip employees and managers to work harmoniously as teams, but in a manner which emphasizes constructive critique. Just the notion of self-directed work teams is enough to define major training needs: teamwork, problem solving, creativity, supervision, management, customer relations, group management, work process improvement, etc. These needs will require cash expenditures for outside trainers or time away from work for in-house trainers and employee trainees.

TQM's team-based orientation defines a particular need for multiskilled employees. Whether incorporating job enlargement (i.e., a horizontal expansion of tasks) or job enrichment (i.e., a vertical broadening of responsibilities), training must keep ahead of, or at least apace of, employees' needs to improve their proficiency and skills. To the extent that training is underfunded or defined as "on the job," its insufficiency becomes at least a bottleneck to improved quality, at most a fatal constriction.

Supervisory training is equally important. As TQM begins, it is unlikely that may supervisors will understand its fundamentals, resource requirements, behavioral constraints, and subtleties. They must be trained first, and must be trained well. And their training must be more than cognitive; their subjective, internal biases toward traditional patterns of authority must be reversed as a prerequisite to working with, rather than directing, the work force.

The Presidential Award for Quality, administered by the Federal Quality Institute, accords training 10 points and asks that a nominee describe a comprehensive training strategy based on a systematic needs analysis, provide evidence that quality-oriented training has reached all levels of management and the work force, provide data for a sufficient fiscal investment in quality training, and describe the organization's indicators of training effectiveness.

The International City Management Association, for example, has developed a comprehensive approach to TQM training in response to pressures to deliver quality services with constrained resources (i.e., productivity). Its training package, "Total Quality Management: Strategies for Local Government" (1993), focuses on customers, teamwork, process improvement, data-based decision making, and continuous improvement activities. At the course's conclusion, participants should have a better understanding of:

The importance of meeting and/or exceeding customer expectations
How improvement of work processes and systems leads to continuous improvement
The organization's role in managing change while fostering staff support and commitment
The roles and responsibilities of managers in creating and promoting quality improvement initiatives, and
How to use quality tools and effective problem-solving techniques

There is also a great deal of TQM-type training offered as seminars, primarily for the private sector. Typically, these programs focus on the Japanese experience, the criteria for the Baldridge Award, successful implementation in various firms, and the future of quality management. One such seminar, offered nationally, is built around a particular book, *Total Quality Management: The Road of Continuous Improvement* (Capezio and Morehouse, 1992). Another, "Eight Principles of a Quality Work Environment," is a video workshop with an accompanying text (Lebow, 1992).

C. Personnel Management

Although TQM is so comprehensive an effort as to affect all subsystems of public organizations, it may have especially important impacts on the personnel system with respect to performance appraisal and compensation. As Hyde (1992, p. 33) suggests,

> Performance appraisal is the lead target because (in theory) it is so central to how people are managed and how organizations communicate formally with the work force. In a nutshell, the main problems are focus and context. TQM assumes that the major problems faced by most organizations are the lack of a quality focus caused by the work system and production process. Quality is achieved when workers (the emphasis being plural) cooperate with each other, not compete, and when they rely on customer feedback as the best measurement of whether the system is working effectively. Individual performance appraisal negates every point just listed. Individuals are held accountable and evaluated against performance standards for a work system that is assumed to be optimal. And appraisals are focused on individual, not group, actions, which in turn breeds individual competition, not group cooperation. Essentially, TQM advocates prefer getting rid of individual performance appraisal completely.

Daly (1992) adds that "in TQM, performance appraisal is viewed at best as a minor tool. At worst, it becomes one of Deming's (1986) seven deadly sins. For Deming, far more is gained by dealing with problems from a systemic perspective than by attempting to personalize them." That is, systemic TQM is not compatible with judgments of individual performance; individual appraisal is not compatible with systemic problem solving processes. Daly allows, however, that "an appraisal system can prove useful, especially when employed in a developmental approach . . . focus[ing] on the positive, helping aspects of the personnel process."

Furthermore, because TQM incorporates a substantial "dose" of measurement, it may stimulate fears associated with scientific management. As with turn-of-the-century failures, measurement of work is often perceived as harassment of workers. The typical stereotype is of a scientific management specialist holding a stopwatch over an employee, with punitive motives.

Compensation also becomes a problem of performance. Are financial rewards to be distributed based on individual performance, which is the dominant mode in traditional public and private organizations, or on the basis of group performance? Within TQM, individual bonuses or merit raises run up against a logical, systemic problem: if performance is based on group problem solving, mutual support and quality measured at the service—not employee—level, then compensation should follow suit. And, as Hyde suggests above, individual competition may sour the very environment which successful TQM must build.

As a demonstration personnel project, the Department of Defense undertook an unusually comprehensive personnel reform effort. According to Gilbert (1992), Project Pacer Share in the Department of Defense undertook four major prerequisites to quality management:

1. Pay banding and job series consolidation, by reducing as many as 15 pay grades to 4. The intended results included providing added flexibility in work, enlarging job responsibilities, increasing motivation, reducing costs, and producing more timely products.
2. Elimination of performance appraisal, by replacing annual appraisal with overall team-focused performance on a day-to-day basis. The intended results included building greater trust within the team and organization, reducing costs, improving labor relations, and fostering teamwork.
3. Creation of a temporary corps that could be hired or released as resources warranted. The intended results were to protect career employees and eliminate problems associated with RIF (reduction in force) procedures.
4. Productivity gain sharing, with half of gains being distributed to the work force and half to the Air Force parent organization. Intended results included rewarding organizational performance, increasing employee accountability and ownership, and encouraging production.

V. IMPLEMENTING TQM INTELLIGENTLY: CONSULTING PUBLISHED RESOURCES

Fortunately, TQM has spawned dozens of books and newsletters, and hundreds of articles. Unfortunately, the sheer amount of information available maybe overwhelming. As the discussion above indicates, there is obviously no singular right way. It would be a mistake to attempt to transplant any specific guidelines, especially private sector guidelines, into a particular public sector organization. Each innovating organization or individual must develop a synthesis, and then adjust or modify that plan with the full participation of middle management and employees. Those individuals should also have access to the same publications.

One way to facilitate that dialogue, especially with individuals who are easily overwhelmed by technical or academic explanations, is to focus the discussion through concise lists and diagrams. Several lists—alternative approaches to TQM—appear above, as do the FQI graphics. Others abound in the literature, and one of the most useful is the Quality and Productivity Management Association's "Basics of TQM." (Fig. 3), a seven-step implementation process: assess, organize, plan, raise awareness and educate, involve, improve, and review (*Commitment Plus*, 1991).

In addition to the many trade books on the subject of TQM from private sector perspectives, such as Deming (1986), Juran (1988), Fiegenbaum (1954), and Crosby (1979), public sector TQM efforts should, at the minimum, consult quality management publications oriented to government. One of the most current and comprehensive publications is *Federal Quality News*, the newsletter of the Federal Quality Institute, which is published monthly. FQI also publishes a multivolume series *Total Quality Management in the Federal Government: Introduction: How to Get Started: Appendix to Book #1: Education and Training.* The very comprehensive *Federal TQM Documents Catalog and Database User Guide* contains several hundred entries. Other periodical publications include the *Newsletter of the International Society for Quality Government*, and the "Quality Developments" section of the *Public Productivity and Management Review. QPM, (Quality and Productivity Management)* is a useful magazine which bridges public and private concerns. A few TQM books are especially helpful as they are oriented to government rather than the private sector. These include such titles as *Excellence in Government: Total Quality Management in the 1990s* (Coopers and Lybrand), which is a guide to implementation in the public sector and includes hundreds of real world examples from federal, state and local governments. The *Public Productivity Handbook* (Holzer, 1992) has an extensive chapter called "Total Quality Management for Public Service Productivity Improvement," by Michael Milakovich.

TQM has also generated a literature specific to certain functional areas, such as health care and higher education, functions which tend to cross the public–private boundaries. In health care, for example, Gaucher and Coffey (1993) have written a comprehensive guide "providing healthcare leaders and practitioners with field-proven, practical guidance for implementing TQM." Although their prescriptions are similar to the generic lists above—continuous improvement, team-based problem solving, and attention to customer needs—they build an applied bridge which provides an advantage to professionals in health care. "TQM in Higher Education," a symposium published by Virginia Tech (Virginia Productivity Center, 1993), offers a reasoned discussion of change and several successful cases, but with the caveat that institutions of higher education may not be as accepting of quality changes as more pressured organizations such as those in health care.

VI. CONCLUSION

The real test of TQM is its staying power. Does government have the capacity—the resources—to implement it properly? Or will it fail for the same reasons that plagued other formulas? In the last quarter century formula-based failures have ranged over ZBB (zero base budgeting), MBO (management-by-objectives), PPBS (planning–programming–budgeting system), TPM (total program management), OD (organizational development), and probably a dozen others. Those failures (or "insufficiencies," to use a euphemism) have been a function of overwhelming complexity, insufficient investment, unnecessarily high expectations, and equally unnecessary employee resistance. TQM probably has a better opportunity to succeed, but only if it is implemented carefully, cooperatively, and with long-term goals in mind. But as Jonathan Walters (1992) reminds us, "At this point it is not clear that very many people in government really understand TQM, or have an appreciation for just how much work is involved in applying it." Unfortunately, many public sector productivity programs have been aborted for lack of political patience (Hayes, 1978). The reelection horizons of elected officials are much shorter than the period in which TQM (or other productivity) investments are likely to "pay off." And the payoff might primarily be improved quality, i.e., services as program outcomes, rather than cost savings. This suggests that the prerequisite to effective TQM is effective education of politicians and good government groups, with the objective of agreeing on modest short-term goals toward the likelihood of major long-term accomplishments.

APPENDIX: EXEMPLARY STATE AND LOCAL AWARD WINNERS WITH A QUALITY FOCUS

A quality improvement approach (EXSL Award 1989) has helped San Diego improve services despite cuts following voter approval of Proposition 13 in 1978. At that time the attitude of many employees at the City of San Diego continued to reflect the resentment of having to increase their productivity without the personnel, training, equipment, and office space they perceived as necessary to do their work. The city manager wanted to change the attitude of employees at all levels of the organization, training them to act as "if our customers had a choice, they'd choose us." In February 1988, his office requested proposals from all department directors for programs de-

TQM Implementation Process

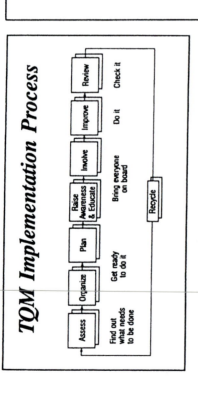

Assess → Organize → Plan → Raise Awareness & Educate → Involve → Improve → Review

- Assess — Find out what needs to be done
- Organize — Get ready to do it
- Plan — Get ready to do it
- Raise Awareness & Educate / Involve — Bring everyone on board
- Improve — Do it
- Review — Check it

Recycle

Step 4: Raise Awareness and Educate

WHAT

- The Need for Quality Improvement
- What Quality/TQM Is
- Mission, Vision, Guiding Principles
- Tools and Techniques
- Implementation Plan
- Everyone Involved
- What's In It for Me

HOW

- Meeting, Articles, Speeches, Videos
- Teamwork Training
- Tools and Techniques Training
- Skills Training
- Success Stories
- Recognition/Celebrations
- Walking the Talk
- Networking

Step 1: Assess
Find Out What Needs To Be Done

TECHNIQUES

- Interviews
- Surveys
- Focus Groups
- Benchmarking
- National Quality Award Criteria
- ISO Criteria
- Performance Data

WHO

- External Customers
- Internal Customers
- Suppliers
- Employees
- Competition
- Best-In-Class
- TQM Leaders

Step 5: Involve
Bring Everyone On Board

TECHNIQUES

- Problem-Solving Groups
- Process Improvement Teams
- Cross Functional Teams
- Self-Directed Teams
- Whole Job
- Suggestions

TRADITIONAL MANAGER

MGRS
Employees
Operations

"My job is to make sure you get the work out, on schedule and at the lowest possible cost. Do it this way."

CONSULTATIVE MANAGER

Customers
Employees
MGRS

"My job is to help you produce the best possible product or service, within our means. What do you need?"

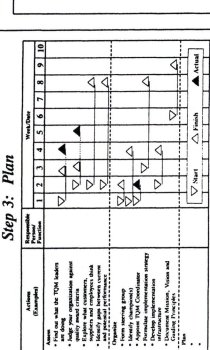

Step 2: Organize
Get Ready to Do It

WHO
- Executive Steering Group
- TQM Coordinator
- Implementation Infrastructure

WHAT
- Mission, Vision, Guiding Principles
- Choose Strategy
- Tools and Techniques
- Resources
- Tie to Business Plan

Step 6: Improve
Do It

KEYS
- Customer Focus
- Vision & Guiding Principles
- Continuous Improvement Mindset
- Management Involvement
- Employee Commitment
- Training & Communication
- Measures
- Aligning Policies & Practices

PITFALLS
- Ignoring the Keys
- Program or Quick-Fix Approach
- Not Enough Time Spent Up Front
- Use of Fad Tools or Techniques
- Lack of Patience
- Not Walking the Talk

Step 7: Review
Check It

- Progress Against the Plan
- Resurvey Customers, Employees
- Cycle/Delivery Times
- Quality/Service Indicators
- Benchmarks
- Cost of Quality
- Financial Indicators
- Recognize/Celebrate/Reward

Step 3: Plan

Figure 3   Basics of TQM. (From *Commitment Plus*, Quality and Productivity Management Association.)

signed to enhance citywide services to customers, citizens and employees. Three departments—Building Inspection, Parks and Recreation, and Fire—were selected to participate in the first phase of such a program. The experiment has been successful, and key components which have developed from the program include:

1. Development of performance measures to assist each department in monitoring the effectiveness of their service
2. Development and administration of pre- and post-citizen surveys
3. Development of a quarterly service-oriented employee newsletter
4. Citywide training in customer service philosophy and techniques
5. Inclusion of a customer service function and standards in each employee's performance evaluation
6. Revision of citywide policies and procedures to streamline them for service to the customer
7. Development of a telecommunications system to improve communication to city customers

In 1988 Pinellas County, Florida established a comprehensive quality improvement program (EXSL Award 1990). It seeks greater employee involvement as the means to more efficient, higher quality services to county residents. The concepts of employee empowerment and participation have driven this program, as evidenced by increased team building and the flow of innovative ideas emanating from county employees. Achievements are rewarded with monetary incentives as well as paid leave and public recognition. Achievement categories include prevention, damage control, community commitment, and leadership. Employees of the county are honored at various banquets, savings, and other events which foster a greater sense of involvement and participation. Financial savings have topped $1 million to date, while total costs have been only approximately $20,000 per year for printing, incentives, awards, and the like. Savings have been realized through the more efficient use of resources, time management, and employee-generated innovations. The program has stressed specific quality objectives, including preserving the environment and water resources, recycling, and improved public safety. A seven-member Quality Planning Council has established a set of standards and goals for the efficient operation of the county government. Sound, productive management also occurs outside the total quality umbrella, and may include a range of techniques such as restructuring, organizational development, strategic planning, facility planning, and performance standards.

REFERENCES

Bowman, James S., and French, Barbara J. (1992). Quality improvement in a state agency revisited, *Public Prod. Manage. Rev.*, *16*(1): 53–64.

Capezio, Peter, and Morehouse, Debra (1992). *Total Quality Management: The Road of Continuous Improvement*, National Seminars Group, Rockhurst College Continuing Education Center, Shawnee Mission, KS.

Ciampa, D. (1992). *Total Quality*, Addison-Wesley, New York.

Cohen, Steven, and Brand, Ronald (1993). *Total Quality Management in Government: A Practical Guide for the Real World*, Jossey-Bass, San Francisco.

Commitment Plus (1991). Newsletter of the Quality and Productivity Management Association, 300 N. Martingale Rd., Suite 230, Schaumburg, IL 60173.

Contino, R. A., and Giuliano, J. (1991). Productivity gains through employee participation at the New York City Department of Sanitation, *Public Prod. Manage. Ref.*, 15(2): 185–190.

Crosby, P. B. (1989). *Quality is Free: The Art of Making Quality Certain*, McGraw-Hill, New York.

Daley, Dennis M. (1992). Pay for performance, performance appraisal, and total quality management, *Public Prod. Manage. Ref.*, *16*(1): 39–52.

Deming, W. E. (1986). *Out of the Crisis*, MIT Center for Advanced Engineering Study, Cambridge, MA.

Excellence in Government: Total Quality Management in the 1990s (1991). Coopers and Lybrand, Arlington, VA.

EXSL (Exemplary State and Local Award Program) (1992). National Center for Public Productivity, Rutgers University, Newark, NJ.

Federal Quality Institute (1992). Quality Improvement Prototype Award—1992. Department of Veterans Affairs, Philadelphia, PA. U.S. Government Printing Office, Washington, DC.

Federal Quality Institute (1992). "Quality Improvement Prototype Award—1992. Public Services and Administration Patent and Trademark Office, Department of Commerce, Arlington, VA." U.S. Government Printing Office, Washington, DC.

Federal Quality Institute (1992). Quality Improvement Prototype Award—1992. U.S. Department of Labor, Wage and Hour Division, San Francisco Region. U.S. Government Printing Office, Washington, DC.

Federal Quality Institute (1990-94). *Total Quality Management in the Federal Government: (1) Introduction: (2)How to Get Started: (3) Appendix to Book #1: (4)Education and Training.* Federal Quality Institute, U.S. Office of Personnel Management, Washington, DC. These volumes, as well as the very comprehensive *Federal TQM Documents Catalog and Database User Guide* (with several hundred entries), are available through the Federal Quality Institute, Information Center, 401 F St. NW, Rm. 331, Washington, DC 20001.

Federal Quality News. Newsletter of the Federal Quality Institute, U.S. Office of Personnel Management, Information Center, 401 F St. NW, Rm. 331, Washington, DC 20001.

Federal TQM Documents Catalog and Database User Guide, Federal Quality Institute, U.S. Office of Personnel Management, Washington, DC.

Fiegenbaum, A. V. (1954). *Total Quality Control*, McGraw-Hill, New York.

Gaucher, Ellen J., and Coffey, Richard J. (1993). *Total Quality in Healthcare: From Theory to Practice*, Jossey-Bass, San Francisco.

Gilbert, G. Ronald (1992). Quality improvement in a federal defense organization, *Public Prod. Manage. Rev., 16*(1): 65–76.

Hayes, Frederick O'Rourke (1978). *Productivity Improvement in State and Local Government*, Lexington Books, Lexington, MA.

Holzer, Marc (ed.) (1992). *Public Productivity Handbook*, Marcel Dekker, New York.

Holzer, Marc, and Callahan, Kathe (eds.) (1993). Fiscal pressures and productive solutions: proceedings of the Fifth National Public Sector Productivity Conference, *Public Prod. Manage. Rev., 16*(4): 331–348.

Hyde, Albert C. ed. (1992). Implications of total quality management for the public sector, *Public Prod. Manage. Rev., 16*(1): 23-76.

Hyde, Albert C. (1992b), The proverbs of total quality management: recharting the path to quality improvement in the public sector, *Public Prod. Manage. Rev.*, 16(1): 25–38.

Imai, M. (1986). *Kaizen: The Key to Japan's Competitive Success*, McGraw-Hill, New York.

International City Management Association (1993). Total Quality Management: Strategies for Local Government, Washington, DC. Training package consists of Module 1: The Meaning of Total Quality Management; Module 2: The Road to Quality; Module 3: Making the Transformation; Module 4: Prerequisites to Implementation; Module 5: Procedures and Tools; Selected Reading: Total Quality Initiatives in Specific Local Governments.

International Society for Quality Government Newsletter (1993). St. Paul, MN.

Juran, J. M. (1988). *Juran on Leadership for Quality*, McGraw-Hill, New York.

Keehley, Patricia, and Medlin, Steve (1991). Productivity enhancements through quality innovations, *Public Prod. Manage. Rev., 15*(2): 217–228.

Lebow, Rob (1992). *A Journey Into the Heroic Environment*, Lebow Company, Bellevue, WA.

Levine, Charles H. (ed.) (1980). *Managing Fiscal Stress: The Crisis in the Public Sector*, Chatham House, Chatham, NJ.

Milakovich, Michael (1992). Total quality management for public service productivity improvement, *Public Productivity Handbook*, (Marc Holzer, ed.), Marcel Dekker, New York.

Mizaur, Donald (1993). Quality government is government of the people, by the people, for the people, *Public Prod. Manage. Rev.*, *16*(4).

Osborne, D., and Gaebler, T. (1992). *Reinventing Government: How the Entrepreneurial Spirit Is Transforming the Public Sector*, Addison-Wesley, Reading, MA.

Presidential Award for Quality: Ogden Internal Revenue Service Center (1992). Federal Quality Institute, Washington, DC.

Presidential Award for Quality Program (ongoing). Federal Quality Institute, Washington, DC.

QPM (Quality and Productivity Management). Virginia Productivity Center, College of Engineering, Virginia Tech, Blacksburg, VA.

Swiss, J. (1992) Adapting total quality management (TQM) to government, *Public Admin. Rev.*

Virginia Productivity Center (1993). TQM in higher education, *QPM: Quality and Productivity Management*, Virginia Tech. *10*(2): Blacksburg, VA.

Walters, Jonathan (1992). The cult of TQM, *Governing*, *5*(8): 38–44.

Washnis, George (1980). *Productivity Improvement Handbook for State and Local Government*, Wiley, New York.

West, Jonathan P., Berman, Evan M., and Milakovich, Michael E. (1993). Implementing TQM in local government: the leadership challenge, *Public Prod. Manage. Rev.*, *17*(2).

26
Strategic Human Resource Management

DONALD E. KLINGNER   Florida International University, North Miami, Florida

I. INTRODUCTION

Strategic human resource management is the purposeful resolution of human resource administration and policy issues so as to enhance a public agency's ability to accomplish its mission. It requires an *understanding* of how organizational human resource management functions relate to one another and to their environmental context, a *vision* of the strategic importance of human resources, and a *commitment* on the part of elected officials, personnel managers, supervisors, and employees to work for change.

The analysis will first (1) define public personnel management as functions, processes, values, and systems; (2) describe the history of public personnel management as the dynamic of conflict and compromise among competing values and systems; and (3) discuss the shared roles of political leaders, personnel managers, supervisors, and employees.

Second, it will discuss the changing realities that continue to shape public personnel administration: (1) demands for "reinventing government"; (2) uncontrolled benefit cost increases; (3) increasing legal liability risks; (4) a more diverse work force; (5) dual labor markets; (6) divergent views of public employees as capital assets or production costs; and (7) alternative instrumentalities for providing public services.

Third, it will show how the impact of these influences on public personnel management have led to the emergence of strategic human resource management as a concept and as a reality. The components of this concept are (1) recognition that human resource management is a critical corporate function; (2) shift in managerial focus from position management to work management and employee management; (3) clear differentiation between "asset" and "Kleenex" jobs based on divergent concern for asset accountability and personnel cost control; (4) for asset jobs, a clear focus on employee training and development; (5) for asset jobs, a clear focus on employee involvement and participation; (6) for asset jobs, a shift in focus from equal employment opportunity/affirmative action compliance to work force diversity; (7) for asset jobs, an emphasis on family-centered leave and benefit policies; (8) enhanced human resource management information systems; and (9) increased entrepreneurial behavior.

Fourth, it will present some examples of how public and private employers have successfully implemented the components of strategic human resource management as the emergent model of personnel administration.

II. PUBLIC PERSONNEL MANAGEMENT

A. Functions, Process, Values, and Systems

Public personnel management can be viewed as functions, process, values, and systems (Klingner and Nalbandian, 1993). First, it is the *functions* (planning, acquisition, development, and sanction) needed to manage human resources in public agencies. Planning includes the budgeting, human resource planning, dividing tasks among employees, deciding how much jobs are worth, and position management. Acquisition includes recruitment and selection of employees. Development includes orienting, training, motivating, and evaluating employees to increase their knowledge, skills, and abilities. Sanction is the establishment and maintenance of expectations and obligations that employees and the employer have toward one another.

Second, personnel management is the *process* by which a scarce resource (public jobs) is allocated. Public jobs are scarce resources because they are limited by tax revenues and they have enormous significance for the course of public policymaking generally. Because public jobs are scarce and important, there is intense competition for them among individuals and more broadly among advocates of competing public personnel values and systems.

Third, public personnel management may be seen as the continuous interaction among four fundamental societal *values* that often conflict. The goal of much policymaking is to develop compromises among two or more of the values. The goal of those who must actually carry out the policies is to develop and implement rules, regulations, procedures, and practices that will effectively fulfill the four functions within a spirit of compromise.

1. Responsiveness is the belief that government answers to the will of the people expressed through elected officials. Political and personal loyalty to elected officials are best ensured through an appointment process that considers political loyalty, along with education and experience, as an indicator of merit. Often, in order to promote responsive government, the filling of a number of public jobs is made the prerogative of authorized elected officials. The decision to contract out for goods or services is often made on two levels—an explicit level based on the objective of obtaining goods or services more efficiently, and an implicit level based on the desire to reward the prospective contractor for support of a candidate or elected official.

2. Efficiency is the desire to maximize the ratio of outputs to inputs in any management process. Efficiency means that decisions about who to hire, reassign, or promote should be based on the knowledge, skills, and abilities (KSAs) of applicants and employees. Merit is defined traditionally in terms of KSAs and performance rather than political loyalty. Efficient service is often best achieved through privatization and contracting out, rather than through public agencies and employees, because of the belief that the private sector's profit motive and emphasis on reduction of unnecessary personnel costs enables it to provide services more cheaply.

3. Individual rights emphasizes that individual citizens will be protected (by the Bill of Rights as well as the Fourteenth Amendment to the Constitution) from unfair actions of government officials. In addition to these legal protections, public employees' rights are maintained through job security and due process (civil service), and through merit system rules and regulations that protect public employees from inappropriate partisan political pressure, and provide job security and due process. In a parallel fashion, public employees who are union members will have recourse to work rules, contained in collective bargaining agreements, that protect them from arbitrary management decisions.

4. Social equity is the belief that individuals should be accorded preference in selection and promotion in public positions based on previous sacrifices (veterans) or discrimination (minorities and women) that prevent them from competing fairly for jobs. Like individual rights, social equity is concerned with fairness. But unlike individual rights, it is the social aspect of equity that provides its group orientation. Social equity emphasizes fairness to such groups as women, racial minorities, the disabled, and veterans, who would otherwise be disadvantaged by a market economy that accepts the legitimacy of discrimination in hiring and in pay.

Fourth, public personnel management is personnel *systems*—the laws, rules, and regulations used to express these abstract values in fulfilling personnel functions (PADS). There are several basic public personnel systems: political systems, civil service, collective bargaining, and affirmative action (AA). Civil service is the predominant, and the only complete, system (because it includes all four functions and can incorporate all four competing values).

1. Political systems are those whereby personnel functions and decisions are carried out with political motives and objectives uppermost. They are characterized by legislative or executive approval of individual hiring decisions, particularly for policymaking positions. Political appointees serve at the discretion of those who appoint them; they may be fired any time, particularly if successful job performance depends on political philosophy or loyalty.

Contracting out for public services may fall into the political system because the decision to contract out, and the choice of contractor, both are at least partly motivated by politics as well as concerns for efficiency. And even if the contract bid and selection process is run fairly (with sealed bids and an objective analysis of contractors' qualifications), contracting out is still political because private sector personnel policies and practices differ in many respects from those of civil service systems based on merit. The contracting out system is supported by legislators, elected officials, and many private sector interest groups who compete to decide what services shall be contracted out, how many jobs will be involved, and who will receive the contracts—political supporters or those who have not made any contributions.

2. Civil service systems are designed with two objectives: the enhancement of administrative efficiency and the maintenance of employee rights. Proponents of civil service systems think that staffing public agencies rationally (based on jobs needed to carry out specific programs and the KSAs needed to accomplish these goals) and treating employees fairly are the best ways to maintain an efficient and professional public service. This means providing good pensions and health benefits; giving equal pay for work of comparable worth; hiring and promoting on the basis of KSAs; treating employees impartially on the job; and protecting employees from partisan political influences.

Overall policy objectives of civil service systems are controlled by elected officials, who often appoint agency heads responsible for managing the bureaucracy. The legislature (Congress, a state legislature, or a local governing body) maintains control over resources by limiting the total number of employees an agency can hire, staffing levels in particular agencies or programs, and the personnel budget (money allocated for wages, salaries, and benefits).

Civil service systems are supported by citizens and groups who want to keep "politics" out of public personnel decisions and run government like a business, by employees holding civil service jobs, by job applicants seeking fair consideration for public jobs, and by federal court decisions upholding the job security rights of civil service employees. Together, these outcomes are considered desirable by those who support the notion of a professional public service as the best way to achieve the values of efficiency and individual rights and a bureaucracy responsive to political direction.

3. Collective bargaining is a specialized personnel system that exists within civil service systems. Under collective bargaining, employees negotiate with management over such items as wages, benefits, and conditions of employment. In all cases, contracts negotiated between an agency's managers and leaders of the union representing its employees are subject to the approval of the appropriate legislative body (Congress, a state legislature, a county or city commission, or a school board) because these political bodies are the only ones that can legally make a policy decision. Contracts may also provide for additional protections for individual employees against disciplinary action or discharge, an obvious indication of the intermingling of civil service and collective bargaining systems. Because some overlap exists in the grievance procedures available under civil service and collective bargaining systems, employees are usually required to select one procedure, but not both.

Collective bargaining systems are supported by employee organizations (unions or professional associations). They reflect the values of individual rights (of union members). Even though collective bargaining is commonly associated with negotiation over wages, the primary motive is to ensure equitable treatment by management.

4. Affirmative action (AA) is a specialized personnel system that usually exists within civil service systems. For the AA system to operate, the governmental jurisdiction must have acknowledged an imbalance in the percentage of minorities in its work force and those qualified minorities in a relevant labor force. Alternatively, members of a group protected against discrimination may have sued the public employer, resulting in a judicial ruling requiring the agency to give special consideration to members of the "protected class" in various personnel decisions, especially hiring and promotion.

Affirmative action is supported by female, minority, and handicapped job applicants and employees, and by the interest groups supporting them. It is also supported by social equity advocates who contend that the efficacy of representative democracy depends on the existence of a representative bureaucracy.

B.   Conflict and Compromise

The history of public personnel management in the United States can be understood conceptually as conflict and compromise over job allocation among competing personnel systems and values. Although several alternative systems—or all four—can be present in an agency simultaneously, in reality one or two systems are dominant within society—and the culture of the organization—at any one time. Over time, personnel systems will reflect the dominant values in a particular jurisdiction. The more stable the values, the more permanent the personnel system and practices will become. When the governing body consists primarily of advocates of one personnel system and the values it enhances, personnel systems tend to have a clear and recognizable influence on the entire range of personnel functions. When the governing body consists of advocates of each of these alternative personnel systems and values, the actual practice of personnel management in government agencies may be weak, unstable, or poorly articulated, i.e., different systems may have a differential impact on different personnel functions. Disagreements over individual selection and promotion decisions reflect more basic disagreements over the criteria (decision rules) by which scarce public jobs should be allocated. Or personnel policies and practices may be operated at two levels—an ideal level of desirable law, rules, and practice; and actual practices that may not be supported by law and regulations but are widely used by personnel specialists and line managers to get the job done.

Civil service systems are the predominant public personnel system because they have articulated rules and procedures for performing the whole range of personnel functions. Other systems, though incomplete, are nonetheless legitimate and effective influences over one or more personnel functions. While personnel functions remain the same across different systems, their organizational location and method of performance differ depending on the system.

Conflict among values and public personnel systems is limited and regulated by the dynamic realities of the competition itself. Each value, carried to its extreme, creates distortions that limit the effectiveness of human resource management because other values are artificially suppressed.

this means that attempts by each system or value to dominate lead inevitably to stabilizing reactions and value compromises. For example, responsiveness carried to extremes results in the hiring of employees solely on the basis of patronage, without regard for other qualifications; or in the awarding of contracts based solely on political considerations (graft and corruption). Efficiency, carried to extremes, results in overrationalized personnel procedures, e.g., going to decimal points on test scores to make selection or promotion decisions, or making the selection process rigid in the belief that systematic procedures will produce the "best" candidate. Individual rights, carried to extremes, results in overemphasis on seniority or overemphasis on due process and rigid disciplinary procedures (as opposed to the rights of the public, managers, and other employees to have employees who are competent, diligent, and not liability risks). And social equity, carried to extremes, results in personnel decisions being made solely on the basis of group membership, disregarding individual merit or the need for efficient and responsive government.

C. Shared Roles

Responsibility for the design and implementation of personnel systems is shared among three general groups: political leaders, personnel directors and specialists, and line managers and supervisors. Political leaders (legislators, executives, and their political appointees) are responsible for establishing the objectives and constraints for personnel systems. Agencies must be created, program priorities established, and funds allocated to meet program objectives before jobs can be designed or positions filled. This is true regardless of which system (political appointment, civil service, collective bargaining, or affirmative action) dominates the way personnel functions are performed.

Personnel directors and specialists are responsible for designing and implementing personnel systems, or for supervising those who do so. In civil service systems, they usually work within a personnel department that functions as a staff support service for line managers and supervisors. Personnel directors and specialists both help line managers use human resources effectively, and constrain their personnel actions within the limits imposed by political leaders, laws, and regulations.

Most public personnel management functions are performed by managers and supervisors who operate personnel systems rather than by the personnel departments that design them. Supervisors are responsible for the routine activities that influence the effectiveness with which employees are acquired and utilized, and that determine the nature of the relationship between employees and the organization, which is the most important factor in personnel management.

When public personnel directors perform the same functions regardless of the system in which they operate, the system has profound effects on the relative importance of these functions, their organizational location, and their method of implementation. The authority of personnel managers varies widely. Those working in predominantly political systems have little authority beyond that given to them by political leaders and are concerned mainly with acquisition. Those working in civil service systems are more constrained by laws and have responsibilities for a wider range of functions. Those working with collective bargaining systems are responsible for negotiating and administering collective bargaining agreements with unionized employees, who are also members of civil service systems. Those working in AA systems are usually AA officers, with predominant responsibilities for acquisition.

It is overly simplistic to say that public personnel directors work within one system or another. It is much more likely that an individual director will be in charge of the personnel function in an agency that includes several personnel systems. Thus, while someone might be in charge of labor relations, that person might report to the personnel director; the same would be true for the AA officer in many public agencies. The role of the personnel director involves significant elements of role conflict because the director is responsible not only for supervising all the personnel functions but for resolving conflicts in how they are performed based on alternative values and decision rules.

Public personnel management may be viewed as a technical specialty or as a profession. Traditional personnel managers (those who operate within a consensus on one system and its underlying values) tend to define themselves, and to be defined by others, as technical specialists working within a staff agency. Contemporary personnel managers (those who operate as interpreters or mediators among competing systems and values) tend to define themselves, and to be defined by others, as professionals whose role involves a blend of technical skills and ethical decision making (Daniel and Rose, 1991).

III. PRESSURES FOR CHANGE

Public personnel management, like all systems, is fundamentally responsive to external pressure for change. Consequently, changes in societal conditions (political, social, economic, and technological) impact the outcome of the conflict among public personnel systems and values, and in turn the way in which personnel functions (planning, acquisition, development, and sanction) are performed. There are seven changing realities that continue to shape public personnel management: (1) demands for "reinventing government," (2) uncontrolled benefit cost increases, (3) increasing legal liability risks, (4) a more diverse work force, (5) the continued development of dual labor markets, (6) divergent views of public employees as capital assets or production costs, and (7) alternative instrumentalities for providing public services.

A. Demands for "Reinventing Government"

"Reinventing government" is both the title of a popular book and a slogan epitomizing the need to enhance work measurement, productivity, and accountability in government agencies (Osborne and Gaebler, 1992). First, irrespective of the level of inputs or the types of activities engaged in by public agencies, what are their outputs? This is the pressure for identification of agency objectives and measurement of work products. Second, they have had to defend the productivity of public agencies by comparing outputs to inputs. These comparisons are against the agency's previous performance, or the performance of competing public agencies or private companies providing the same service. The objective here is increased productivity—doing more with less. Third, whether or not they are productive, public agencies are under constant pressure to respond to policy objectives established by elected officials. This is true regardless of the clarity of mission, competing objectives, or level of resources.

As it applies to personnel management, this means that traditional civil service systems or collective bargaining relationships have often not met these objectives. Therefore, personnel managers must experiment with alternative systems (instrumentalities) that will enable agencies to *manage to budget* and *manage to mission* (National Academy of Public Administration, 1991; U.S. Office of Personnel Management, 1990).

B. Uncontrolled Benefit Cost Increases

Benefits (primarily employer-financed health benefits, pensions, sick leave, and paid holidays and vacation) constitute a large and increasing share of personnel costs (Blostin et al., 1988). With respect to health benefits, there is widespread agreement today that there are serious problems with the health care delivery system in the United States. Growing at twice the rate of inflation, medical costs have climbed from $248 billion in 1980 to $600 billion in 1990 (this is 12% of our gross national product) (Luthans and David, 1990). And despite this high cost, there are tremendous inequities in the distribution of health care benefits. Many Americans are denied health care because they cannot afford it. In 1984, 34.7 million Americans (17.4%) had neither private nor public health insurance coverage (Chollet and Friedland, 1987).

The increased cost of medical technology and increased longevity are primarily responsible for the increase in health costs. Our present system is geared toward the development of high-technology advances that provide a longer life span for the elderly at a high price; it is driven by a third-party reimbursement system that discourages cost control or cost–benefit analysis. As a result, retirees are creating a staggering liability for employers. Today, it is estimated that total employer liabilities for health care coverage for current employees are $85 billion for those Americans who are covered by employer-financed plans (Allan, 1988).

C. Increasing Legal Liability Risks

Beginning in the 1970s, the legal liability of public agencies and employees began to change as a consequence of changes in the Supreme Court's interpretation of immunity from civil suit for violations of constitutional rights accorded applicants, employees, and clients (Klingner, 1988). Briefly, the transition from *sovereign immunity* to *limited immunity* involved the restriction of immunity to those acts which were officially sanctioned by law or regulations. At the same time, Court's concern for equal protection of employment rights for protected classes increased concern for discrimination against veterans, racial and ethnic minorities, women, and the disabled. The result was increased liability risk for public personnel administrators with respect to workplace safety, affirmative action, sexual harassment, employee privacy, and due process violations. In addition, the consequences of this increased liability have been enhanced by an increase in litigation and court awards of compensatory and punitive damages against all employers, including public agencies.

D. A More Diverse Work Force

The Hudson Institute's report on the changing work force predicts that the next decade will bring about a change in its composition (Johnston and Packer, 1987). Chief among these demographic changes are an older work force, one comprised more of women and minorities, and one requiring technical and professional skills increasingly in short supply because of growing deficiencies in our educational system (Thomas, 1990). This change means that personnel managers, no matter what mix of personnel systems they utilize, will be forced not only to move toward accepting diversity, but embracing it in order to accomplish agency mission.

The challenge of channeling diversity into productivity is complicated by the breadth of expectations members of diverse cultures bring to their work, both as individuals and as members of those cultures. Differences are not assets without an organizational commitment to respect, tolerance, and dignity. Without these virtues, differences consume organizational resources without positive results. The broader the differences, the more pressure we can expect on organizational processes designed to negotiate and resolve differences in expectations and obligations. The concept of justice and fair play may become as important within organizations marked by diversity as they are in our society generally. And the protection of these rights will increasingly be an administrative rather than a judicial responsibility.

E. Continued Development of Dual Labor Markets

In recent years, concern has grown over the "glass ceiling"—the perceived lack of promotional opportunities for women and minorities in organizations where managerial and professional positions are filled primarily by white males. In one respect, it is only natural that the evolution of affirmative action means a shift in focus from entry level jobs to promotional opportunities. However, concern for the glass ceiling has obscured a larger macroeconomic issue—gradual but persistent displacement of career jobs for *all* employees, not just women and minorities, and their replacement by lower paying and less stable service jobs. An understanding of this phenomenon requires some understanding of labor market theory.

There are three conflicting approaches to understanding the character of labor markets and the responses of individuals to them. Conventional explanations include human capital theories and job search theories. Human capital theories view unemployment as one aspect of the wage-setting process. People are unemployed because their marginal value product (i.e., their abilities, skills, and productive capacities) is less than the prevailing market wage and therefore insufficient to make it worthwhile for employers to hire them. Job search theories treat unemployment as the outgrowth of a job search process where workers have limited information, uncertainty, or faulty expectations about the labor market. While in theory this type of "frictional" unemployment is temporary and always resolved, in reality the imperfect operation of market forces means that some minimal level of unemployment is inevitable.

The concept of a dual labor market was introduced 20 years ago by Doeringer and Piore (1971) in an effort to move beyond what they considered the inadequacy of conventional explanations for persistent unemployment and underemployment among minorities and women in the United States. The dual labor market approach postulates a labor market which is divided into primary and secondary sectors. High-paying, steady jobs (professional, technical, and managerial) are filled primarily by white males through the primary labor market (Doeringer and Piore, 1975). Low-paying, unstable, and dead-end jobs in the secondary sector are commonly filled by women and minorities. The labor market is segmented in that the markets remain separate, relatively high qualifications for jobs filled through the primary market, and a relative lack of developmental or promotional opportunities in jobs filled through the secondary market, tend to perpetuate a glass ceiling for women and minorities concentrated in jobs filled through the secondary labor market.

There are many examples of the growth of segmented labor markets in the United States. These include the movement of major corporations to two-tier wage structures beginning in 1985 (Foegen, 1986; Jennings and Traynham, 1988), an increase in the total number of leased employees from 150,000 in 1986 to 450,000 in 1990 (Odds and ends, 1990), and increased hiring of part-time and temporary employees by employers who wish to circumvent personnel ceilings, collective bargaining agreements, or civil service rules (Wessel, 1985). Indeed, the fastest growing public personnel systems (contracting and privatization) have become more prevalent precisely because they utilize the lower pay and benefits (personnel costs) which make it attractive to fill jobs through the secondary labor market.

Economic projections indicated that the service sector will be responsible for generating the most jobs during the next decade (McGahey, 1987). And while employers will increasingly be required to utilize minorities and women because of changing work force demographics, job development will be most likely to occur not in the primary labor market but in those dead-end service and industrial jobs which have traditionally been filled through the secondary labor market (Hudson Institute, 1988). And these are jobs in which minorities and women are already overrepresented (U.S. Bureau of Labor Statistics, 1989).

F. Divergent Views of Public Employees as Assets or Costs

Pay and benefits are the ways in which the employer rewards employee performance and the way in which human resources are developed and maintained. And depending on the personnel system, pay and benefits are regarded as an increasingly important motivator of employee retention and performance, or an increasingly uncontrolled employee cost. This divergence is tied to two opposing organizational view of employees—the "career" model and the "Kleenex" model—which reflect basic conflict among personnel systems throughout the range of personnel functions.

1. The Career Model

The career model is based on the assumption that employees are societal and organizational assets who bring human capital (knowledge, skills, and abilities) to the labor market (Schiller, 1984). The concept of human capital emerged in the 1960s to explain rates of investment and return in human resources for both societies and organizations. This concept underlies civil service systems and collective bargaining systems in the public sector, human resource asset accounting models in private industry, and national manpower (human resource) development programs.

Within organizations, the concept of human capital led to the development of *human resource asset accounting*—the application of capital budgeting principles common in facilities management (buildings and equipment) to proposed personnel programs as well (Pyle, 1970; Flamholtz, 1974). Programs such as training, retention of key staff, or enhanced benefit packages might have high initial operating budget costs; and they would also result in a long-term increase in the value of human resource assets. Other programs such as early retirement or layoffs might considerably reduce operating expenses in the short run yet result in an eventual greater decrease in the value of the company's human resource assets.

On a societal scale, Schultz (1961) used human investment theory to explain past economic growth rates. Chiswick and Mincer (1972) cite human investment theory as a determinant of income distribution. The optimalities of resource allocation within education and between education and other sectors were explored by Dougherty and Psacharopoulos (1977). This concept has also been used to explain a great part of the residual increase that has puzzled scholars examining economic growth in the 1950s (Psacharopoulos, 1985).

The human resource asset concept can be seen as an organizational or societal application of the economic concept of segmented (dual) labor market theory. That is, managerial, professional, and skilled technical employees hired by major public and private sector employers through primary labor market mechanisms into career positions are considered human resource assets. The relatively high job status, security, pay, and benefits that go with these positions are considered essential for long-term human resource asset maintenance and development.

2. The Kleenex Model

The Kleenex model is based on the assumption that employees should be viewed primarily as personnel costs rather than human resource assets. Because pay and benefits are the largest operating expense for most organizations, and because personnel costs can be cut by reducing or eliminating benefits, an increasingly larger percentage of employees is hired into semiskilled or service positions through secondary labor market mechanisms. This explains the rapid increase in temporary, seasonal, and part-time employment—public and private. The implication that Kleenex employees are a disposable commodity rather than a human resource is apt: Kleenex employees typically have less status, lower pay, less job security, and fewer benefits (O'Rand, 1986). Because these employees may usually be discharged "at will," employers can reduce benefit costs and legal liability risks.

To be sure, the societal implications of segmented labor market theory are profoundly troubling to many dual labor market theorists, who have suggested several mechanisms to increase the stability and equity of employment in the secondary sector (Doeringer and Piore, 1975). However, these mechanisms have not had much success (Piore and Sabel, 1984; Doeringer, 1990).

The breakup of traditional mass production industries has meant that business development now requires smaller firms, more entrepreneurial activity, and more flexible work practices. And these characteristics are not designed to produce labor market equity and stability.

The organizational tensions generated when professional and high-skilled career employees work side by side with service and semiskilled Kleenex employees has troubled many employees, supervisors, and personnel managers. Nor is it always easy to determine whether use of the primary or secondary labor market results in long-term cost savings. While the secondary market offers the advantage of lower short-term pay and benefit costs, there are also many examples from the public and private sectors in support of the conclusion that management of employees as human resources results in long-term benefits, not just for employees but for employers as well (Morgan and Tucker, 1991).

G. Alternative Instrumentalities for Providing Public Services

A traditional objective of civil services systems is to achieve both individual rights and government efficiency. Efficiency is the maximization of the ratio of outputs to inputs in any management process. In the personnel world, efficiency means that decisions about who to hire, reassign, or promote should be based on the knowledge, skills, and abilities (KSAs) of applicants and employees (rather than favoritism or political loyalty).

But more recently, critics have argued that efficient service is often best achieved through privatization and contracting out rather than through public agencies and employees. Critics contend that the private sector's profit motive and emphasis on the bottom line (reduction of unnecessary personnel costs) enables it to provide services more cheaply. And desires for both political payoffs and political accountability make provision of public services through contracts and privatization more attractive.

As a consequence, much of the growth in public agency employment has been through contract services and a secondary labor market of part-time temporary, and seasonal employees. Employers (public and private sector) consider this market a valuable strategy for reducing benefit costs and legal liability. And the threat of privatization or contracting out is a powerful strategy for breaking unions or gaining give-backs during contract renegotiation. thus, pressures for work measurement, productivity, and political accountability have highlighted the advantages of the Kleenex model for doing more with less, at least in the short run. And the increased use of a secondary labor market composed primarily of Kleenex jobs coincides with increased use of alternative instrumentalities (personnel systems) as a means of enhancing work measurement, productivity, and accountability.

Primary alternative instrumentalities are (1) mandated services, (2) contracting, (3) privatization, and (4) market mechanisms.

1. Mandated Services

Governments frequently seek to relieve themselves of responsibility for providing services by enacting legal mandates which make private contractors or other levels of government responsible for provision of "public" services. For example, municipal planning and zoning officials can require that developers pay (and pass on to new homeowners) the increased cost of providing infrastructures (schools, fire service, streets and curbs) in new subdivisions. And governments often attempt to pass costs to one another. For example, local and state officials in South Florida have often sought increased state and federal money to provide for the increased level of public services required by the influx of Caribbean refugees—an issue they say is more appropriately addressed by the national government rather than by local authorities.

2. Contracting

The decision to contract out for goods or services is often made on two levels—an explicit level based on the objective of obtaining goods or services more efficiently, and an implicit level based on the desire to reward the prospective contractor for support of a candidate or elected official. Examples of contracts awarded on the basis of both explicit and implicit criteria include procurement of weapons by the military from private defense contractor, or from state highway construction and maintenance.

3. Privatization

While contracting places responsibility for providing a specified good or service in an outside contractor, privatization turns the entire range of services performed by a government agency to an outside organization. The outside organization may be a quasi-public corporation (such as airport authorities or port authorities which are chartered by governments but have independent financial authority) or a private corporation financially independent of government but subject to government regulation (such as a municipal golf course, solid waste contractor, or transportation department).

Privatization is attractive to those who wish not only to enhance efficiency but to reduce the size of government by exchanging public employees for private sector counterparts.

4. Market Mechanisms

For those governments that cannot provide services themselves, cannot pass them to another level of government, cannot contract out, and cannot privatize, there is a remaining response: stop providing the service and let those who wish to purchase it, and who can afford to do so, make arrangements with private providers. Examples are many: private recreation facilities (Disney World), private security and burglar alarm companies, and so forth.

IV. STRATEGIC HUMAN RESOURCE MANAGEMENT CAPABILITY

Strategic human resource management has emerged as a concept and an organizational capability because of the impact of the above realities on public personnel management. Conceptually, it consists of the following elements: (1) recognition that human resource management is a critical corporate function, (2) a shift in managerial focus from position management to work management and employee management, (3) a clear differentiation between "asset" and "Kleenex" jobs based on divergent concerns for asset accountability and personnel cost control, (4) for asset jobs, a clear focus on employee training and development, (5) for asset jobs, a clear focus on employee involvement and participation, (6) for asset jobs, a shift in focus from EEO/AA compliance to work force diversity, (7) for asset jobs, an emphasis on family-centered leave and benefit policies, (8) enhanced human resource management information systems, and (9) increased entrepreneurial behavior among public personnel managers.

A. Recognition That Human Resource Management Is a Critical Corporate Function

Public personnel management refers to the techniques and policy choices related to agency human resource management. Taken together, these techniques and choices send messages to employees, managers, and external stakeholders about the value the agency places on human resources. In an organization with an effective human resource management capability, these messages are clear and positive. For managers and employees within the agency, this is the message: "We need you to achieve our mission." For elected officials outside the agency, the message is: "Employees are a cost and an asset. Personnel management is the function by which productive agencies reduce costs and maintain assets." And for the personnel director, the message is: "You are the lead member of the management team in developing, implementing and evaluating human resource policies and programs."

B. Shift in Managerial Focus From Position Management to Work Management and Employee Management

Traditionally, legislators and chief executives have sough to maintain bureaucratic compliance, efficiency, and accountability through budgetary controls and *position management* (limiting the number and type of personnel an agency can employ). Frequently, position and budgetary controls are combined through the imposition of average grade level restrictions.

Within agencies, public personnel directors have sought to achieve efficient allocation of work and equitable allocation of rewards through *work management*—the development of maintenance of classification and pay systems. This also decreases the opportunity for political favoritism by providing that pay be based on a realistic assessment of duties and qualifications, rather than as a reward for political responsiveness.

Employees have a third perspective—*employee management*. They want their individual skills and abilities to be fully utilized in ways that contribute to a productive agency and to their own personal career development. They want to be managed as individuals, through a continual process of supervision, feedback, and reward. Most supervisors share this perception. They want to be able to match employees with work needs, flexibly and creatively, so that they can get their jobs done. They want to be able to use and reward employees based on their contributions to a work unit. At heart, they see job descriptions and job classification systems as "administrivia," needed to justify budget requests and to keep the folks in personnel happy, but not related to agency mission nor day-to-day supervision.

Due to a variety of political and economic pressures, the focus of public personnel management changed from management of positions, as was the case under traditional civil service systems to accomplishment of agency mission through work management and employee management (Chief Financial Officers Act of 1990; and U.S. Office of Personnel Management, 1989). For public personnel managers accustomed to working primarily within civil service systems, this has meant recognizing the need for increased flexibility and experimentation in many areas such as rank-in-person personnel systems, broad pay banding, and group performance evaluation and reward systems (Shoop, 1991). Outside civil service systems, it includes contracts, leased employees, and other secondary labor market mechanisms.

C. Clear Differentiation Between "Asset" and "Kleenex" Jobs Based on Divergent Concerns for Asset Accountability and Cost Control

In the absence of coherent national strategies for public pension system reform, health care, cost control, or human capital investment, public personnel directors have had to adopt reasonable organizational level policies for asset accountability and cost control. These workplace policies are as follows: (1) filling "career" jobs (professional, managerial, scientific, and technical positions) through a primary labor market offering relative high benefits and operating under civil service, AAs, and collective bargaining system rules' (2) using Kleenex employees hired through secondary labor market mechanisms to meet fluctuating employment needs, and (3) excluding high-risk applicants from "career" employment (Masi, 1987b; Reichenberg, 1988; Turk, 1989; Emery, 1989; Heacock and Orvis, 1990; World Health Organization, 1990; Klingner and O'Neill, 1991).

First, employers continue to hire managerial, professional, scientific, and technical employees through civil service systems into "career" positions. The relatively high job status, security, pay and benefits that go with these positions are considered essential for long-term employee retention and productivity. This includes preventive education through employee wellness programs and treatment through employee health plans. However, health insurance carriers (and self-insured employers) have also responded to the cost of medical care by increasing premium costs, reducing benefits, lengthening the period within which health care benefit claims may be excluded as preexisting conditions, or adopting subbenefit limitations on coverage for health problems that may be considered preventable because they are "lifestyle choices" (e.g., smoking, alcoholism, drug abuse, or AIDS) (Faden and Kass, 1988). Benefit managers for self-insured agencies are even responding, on a case-by-case basis, to advance questions from health care providers about whether reimbursement for specific treatments will be authorized.

Second, employers have tried to "cap" benefit costs and liability risks by greater use of secondary labor market mechanisms (such as contract or temporary employment) to meet fluctuating work loads.

Third, whenever possible given the limits of available technology and the applicability of handicap laws protecting applicant rights (Jenks, 1987), employers have sought to reduce benefit costs by excluding high-risk applicants from career employment through civil service systems (Masi, 1987a; Klingner, et al., 1990). The ability to predict long-term health risks by evaluating employee health profiles was originally developed as a component of employee wellness programs to prevent serious health problems among current employees. But because career employees incur high benefit costs (Holton, 1988; Solovy, 1989), and because these costs correlate with health indicators, medical health indicators are also being used as selection criteria (Rowe, et al., 1987).

In selecting applicants for positions filled through civil service systems, employers are moving from narrowly focused screening methods (such as the use of back x-rays to determine whether laborers are physically able to lift or carry) to more generalized health indicators that may indicate the applicant is a long-term health risk because his or her general indicators are outside normal limits (Uzych, 1986). Examples include abnormal weight to height, abnormal electrocardiogram, abnormal blood chemistry (such as cholesterol levels), history of heavy drinking (as determined by liver enzyme activity), history of substance abuse (as determined by urinalysis), or likelihood of developing AIDS (determined by AIDS antibody tests) (Slater, 1990).

D. For Asset Jobs, a Clear Focus on Employee Training and Development

The *Workforce 2000* study concludes, "The income generating assets of a nation are the knowledge and skills of its workers" (Johnston and Packer, 1987, p. 116). Judged by this standard, the United States currently is suffering from the absence of concerted public policy which ties together educational development, national human resource development, industrial policy, and economic growth. Public and private employers uniformly express alarm at the ineffectiveness of our educational system in producing the skilled workers needed by high-technology industries. Lack of high-tech job training or retraining capacity is a major obstacle to retention of manufacturing jobs, which have fallen to their lowest level in 20 years.

Consequently, two contradictory trends follow from the "shakeout" occurring in the economy between career jobs and Kleenex jobs. First, employers reduce the requisite KSAs of most Kleenex jobs by job redesign or work simplification techniques. For example, cash registers at many fast-food restaurants show pictures of food items on the keys rather than numbers, so that cashiers without arithmetic skills can still perform adequately. Ironically, by increasing the monotony and diminishing the learning opportunities in Kleenex jobs, these personnel practices contribute to the perpetuation of segmented labor markets and the glass ceiling.

Second, employers accept the human resource asset assumptions underlying career jobs filled through primary labor market mechanisms. That is, employees are human capital whose retention and utilization depend on appropriate placement and continued development (Argyris, 1980). A close relationship between the employee development and corporate human resource policy helps the organization in three respects: (1) it focuses planning and budget analysis on human resources; (2) it facilitates cost–benefit analysis of current training and development activities; and (3) it facilitates communication and commitment of organizational goals through employee participation and involvement (Rosow and Zager, 1988; Bernhard and Ingols, 1988).

Organizational productivity improvements focus both on individual performance and work group effectiveness. Therefore, training and development include not only individual job skills but improvement in employees' work relationships. Examples are team building and organizational development (French and Bell, 1990), total quality management (Deming, 1988), and training for diversity (Solomon, 1989).

E. For Asset Jobs, a Clear Focus on Involvement and Participation

Performance management is the management of resources to agency mission. This includes not only financial resources but human resources as well. It is here that human resource managers have an advantage over their financial counterparts. Financial resources are finite and fixed. In an era where policy and program initiatives are predicated on "budget neutrality," managers and supervisors have come to conclude that financial managers respond to problems by telling the organization to do the same with less, or more with the same amount of money. Human resource managers recognize that employees are a resource, and a variable one. That is, even in the absence of significant financial rewards, employee performance will continue to improve if the characteristics of work and the climate of the organization are appropriate.

The assumption underlying all new ways of designing work is that high internal work motivation, "growth" satisfaction, general job satisfaction, and work effectiveness result when people experience their work as meaningful, when they feel responsible for the quality and quantity of work produced, and when they have first-hand knowledge of the actual results of their labor. These psychological states are likely to result from work designed to incorporate the following characteristics: variety; work with a beginning and identifiable end; work of significance; and work characterized by autonomy and feedback. Jobs that are high in these qualities are said to be "enriched" and to have a high motivating potential. Whether high internal motivation, satisfaction, and productivity actually do result in holders of these kinds of jobs depends on differences in the workers' knowledge and skill, their growth need strength (such as the need for self-esteem or the esteem of others), and by context satisfaction (including such aspects of work as pay, supervision, and working conditions). Obviously, these psychological states and work characteristics are most likely to accompany career positions filled by asset employees.

Results of research into this model have been generally supportive. For example, federal agency work force quality objectives emphasize the connection between the quality of the work environment and the quality of individual, team, and organizational performance (Advisory Committee on Federal Workforce Quality Assessment, 1992, p. 20). At an operating level, they have resulted in the adoption of personnel policy innovations first as experiments, and then as options the supervisor and personnel director use to match employees with work, and to generate good individual and team performance. These include delegation, flexible work locations and schedules, job sharing, management by objectives (MBO), and total quality management (TQM).

All these examples of managing for performance have a common thread—working with employees as unique human resources rather than as uniform inputs to a production process. For example, delegation and MBO are fundamentally not management techniques, but assumptions and values related to the human resource development and employee involvement in accomplishing the mission of the agency (Sashkin, 1984). Flexible work scheduling and locations are not just troublesome exceptions to normal working hours and duty stations; they are innovative ways of using people's talents which are made possible by new work technologies (Mellado, et al., 1989).

Moreover, they are necessary because of changing role expectations and cultural norms. Those who promote work force diversity as a new approach to productivity (rather than just a new name for affirmative action) believe that different races, ethnicities, and sexes bring diversity to the workplace, and that this diversity introduces variations on white male management styles which can make organizations dramatically more effective. For example, some researchers conclude that women have a more interactive and nurturing management style which makes organizations more flexible and effective utilizers of human resources (Rosener, 1990).

Human resource managers and supervisors have a unique and irreplaceable role in the agency. Within the parameters set by legislators and chief executives, they must develop and implement corporate human resource systems for maintaining and improving the performance of individual employees and work groups. This requires an understanding of what employees need to perform well (adequate skills, clear instructions, feedback, and rewards), as well as insight into the impact of equity theory and expectancy theory on employee effort and performance. Most important, it requires understanding of the critical role played by human resource specialists in managing a variable, strategic resource (employees) so as to achieve agency objectives.

Public personnel managers share responsibility with managers and political leaders for developing and implementing personnel systems—the rules and procedures by which personnel functions occur. These choices involve the implicit or explicit selection of alternative personnel systems, each reflecting different dominant values. And it is not surprising that the selection of alternative systems sends a different message to employees.

For example, placement of a job within civil service systems or within a collective bargaining unit implies that the dominant value will be protection of employee rights, along with a message to employees: "You are a human resource asset: we need your knowledge, skills and ability to attain productive and responsive agency performance." On the other hand, placement of a job within another instrumentality (outside contract or a temporary payment for services agreement) implies that the dominant value will be short-term productivity and send the following message to employees: "Your perform a needed service, but you are not a permanent asset employee. Rather, you are a replaceable or expendable production unit whose service can be controlled by contract compliance procedures or the sanction process, and who can be hired and fired to match fluctuations in work load."

Because these messages are quite different, and because personnel activities are interrelated, public personnel managers have had to be much more explicit with employees about which messages are sent to which groups of employees. And they have had to be aware that employee productivity is affected by these messages, and by the dissonance between them—not only for Kleenex employees, but for asset ones as well. And concern for social equity values has meant that public personnel managers are responsible for making sure that access to career employment is equitably distributed among protected classes. Otherwise, public employment loses the representativeness that is required for maintenance of both democratic values and effective public service.

And the lengthy and cumbersome selection process characteristic of career positions actually serves many purposes for managers, political leaders, personnel directors, and applicants.

Managers accept the costly and tedious screening of large numbers of applicants as necessary to compensate for the generally uneven quality of job applicants. Political leaders under pressure to fill vacancies with friends or campaign contributors can refer people to the personnel department and then blame the personnel director or the selection process if a particular applicant is not hired. Personnel directors dislike being criticized by political leaders, managers, and applicants for the cumbersome selection process, but they also find that a ritualized selection process, which includes procedures and criteria favored by adherents of alternative personnel systems, also tends to regulate the conflict among systems over each selection. And applicants, like players in any lottery, may get symbolic satisfaction from the opportunity to apply for high-status jobs, regardless of the slight chance that they will actually be accepted. The equality of opportunity to apply for career positions fosters the belief among most applicants that the number of career positions is large and that it is relatively easy to advance from Kleenex positions filled through the secondary labor market to career positions filled through the primary labor market.

F.   For Asset Jobs, a Shift in Focus from EEO/AA Compliance to Work Force Diversity

Work force diversity is not just a variant on civil rights or AA (Rodarmor, 1991). While the two concepts are related, they differ in three important respects. Work force diversity is broader and more individualized; it focuses on accomplishment of agency missions rather than compliance with sanctions; and, as a result, its locus of control is internal rather than external.

The objective of AA is the full representation of protected classes of employees within the agency work force, proportionate to their share of the appropriate labor market. Personnel directors who focus on AA compliance therefore tend to regard employees as members of classes and use these categories to drive or influence personnel decisions. The focus of AA is therefore on inputs (number and percentage of positions filled by members of particular groups). And the locus of control is external, in that it is based on review of personnel practices by AA compliance agencies.

The concept of work force diversity implies a broader and more individualized perspective on diversity—not just AA categories, but a range of knowledge, skills, and abilities which managers must recognize and factor into personnel decisions. The importance of this change is accentuated by agency managers' changing focus on work management rather than position management. Once agency managers and personnel directors have changed their focus from position management to work management, they are forced to alter their focus on employees from *categorical* to *individual*. Good managers have always done this, of course. They have recognized that the secret of assigning the right employee to the right job means (1) determining the important tasks of the position, (2) specifying the combination of KSAs needed to accomplish these tasks, and (3) picking the employee who has the best combination of requisite KSAs (Loden and Rosener, 1991).

Second, work force diversity differs from AA in that it focuses on *outputs*—what combination or balance of KSAs is needed to get the work done—rather than *inputs*—what is the racial and ethnic composition of the work force? Work force diversity is therefore linked to a number of other recent trends such as performance management, MBO, delegation, and results-oriented job descriptions (RODS). All of these focus on work and on mission accomplishment rather than on position management or process conformity.

Third, work force diversity differs from AA in that its locus of control is internal rather than external. Agency managers must ask, "Is the agency allocating resources appropriately so as to accomplish its mission?" rather than "Is our work force sufficiently representative to avoid externally imposed sanctions by affirmative action compliance agencies?" or "Are our personnel policies and procedures adequate to avoid externally imposed sanctions by affirmative action compliance agencies?" Thus, acceptance of work force diversity goes hand in hand with increased accountability of agency managers for mission accomplishment and increased focus on employees as resources rather than as positions to be controlled (Solomon, 1989; Haight, 1990).

G. For Asset Jobs, Emphasis on Family-Centered Leave and Benefit Programs

Family-centered leave and benefit programs are integrally related to employee involvement and participation as well as work force diversity. First, the productivity of asset employees is directly related to their involvement and participation, which in turn is related to the extent to which the employer provides services and benefits which help employees meet family obligations. Second, because women are the traditional caregivers in our society, the effectiveness of an employer in attracting a diverse work force depends on the provision of these same services and benefits. Major components of a family-centered corporate human resource policy for asset employees are (1) flexible benefits, (2) family leave, (3) child care and elder care support programs, (4) alternative work locations and schedules, and (5) employee-centered supervision.

1. Flexible Benefits

The high cost of benefit programs means that employers will seek to maximize their attractiveness to employees by offering benefit flexibility. Flexible benefit programs are sometimes called cafeteria plans because they offer employees a menu of benefits. They are developed by costing the employer's contribution to each of a variety of employer-sponsored benefit programs and allowing employees to select alternative mixes of benefit packages depending on their needs. For the employees this has the major advantage of full utilization of benefits without duplication or gaps. This makes the employer's benefit package of greater value to the employee and is a tool for recruitment and retention (Cafeteria Plans, 1990).

There are administrative and financial barriers to flexible benefit programs. First, given the wildly fluctuating cost of alternative benefits, it may be difficult for the employer to constantly calculate (and recalculate) the comparative costs of all options. Second, reconfiguring alternative benefit packages on a constant cost basis may be difficult for employees, who are unable to project benefit usage or the relative utility of alternative benefits accurately. Third, full employee utilization of benefits may increase benefit costs for the employer (who may have been able to reduce costs by relying on such overlaps as duplicate health insurance for two employees in a family). Fourth, increased benefit costs tend to compel health and life insurance providers toward uniform defined benefit programs to reduce "shopping" from one program to another. In this environment, the advantages of flexible benefit programs may tend to diminish.

2. Family Leave

Changing family roles have resulted in numerous single-parent households. Under these conditions, sick leave policies must reflect parental responsibilities to care not only for themselves but for children and parents as well. And because medical emergencies and day care crises are seldom predictable, policies and supervisory practices must be flexible in this regard.

Parental leave means the legal entitlement of parents to job retention rights if they need to be absent from the workplace to care for a relative. These retention rights apply after a person has exhausted paid sick leave or annual leave; they remain in place for a considerable period (6 months to a year); and they apply in cases of elder care, childbirth, or adoption. Either parent would be eligible. There are several arguments in favor of parental leave. First, the high cost of health care could be reduced if home care provided by a family member were an alternative to hospitalization or care in an extended care facility. Second, because nonworking parents are present in only 11% of American households, no home care will be provided unless employees are guaranteed job retention rights. Third, the United States is alone among major industrialized countries in not offering these benefits. Other countries have recognized that, for employees facing childbirth, adoption, or terminal care for a parent, the long-term negative consequences of a forced choice between remaining on the job or giving up their employment rights is not socially justifiable.

A recent study indicated that parental leave could be implemented easily and inexpensively. The 3-year study was conducted in four states that passed parental leave laws during the 1980s. The survey found that 91% of respondent personnel directors reported no difficulty with implementation of the laws; 67% said they relied on other employees to do the work (rather than hiring replacement employees); and the percentage of working women who took leave and the length of leave was virtually unchanged by the legislation (Taylor, 1991). While opponents of nationally mandated parental leave legislation use this research to demonstrate that most employers are already offering these benefits voluntarily, proponents argue that the same data justify the mandatory extension of these benefits to all employees.

3.   Child Care and Elder Care Support Programs

The increased number of single-parent families (and two-parent families in which both parents work) has led to increses in employer-operated child care facilities. At first, this was seen primarily as an employee benefit. But as agencies began to face shortages of qualified employees, child care has been demonstrated to be necessay to recruit or retain qualified female employees (such as in hospitals or on military bases). In an era of increased work force diversity, it is simply essential to recognize that employees' ability to find satisfactory child care arrangements will reduce job stress, turnover, sick leave abuse, and other causes of low productivity (Child Care, 1987).

There are some issues with employer-subsidized child care. These include cost, fee setting, and liability risks. But these are technical concerns rather than major impediments to the adoption of child care policies and programs. And the fundamental value orientation of child care remains unassailable. If employees are a human resource and an asset, then children are the seed corn from which future assets are developed for use by the employer and the society.

One innovative proposal allows closer cooperation between employers, parents, and the local school board by allowing parents to place their children in schools close to the job rather than close to home. This reduces the length of time school-aged children go without supervison and makes it easier for parents to leave work for child care emergencies without so much use of leave or disruption of employer productivity.

4.   Alternative Work Locations and Schedules

In the past, all employees were expected to have identical working hours anad a fixed job location, but this is no longer true. First, changes in technology (primarily communications and computers) have meant that employees can work productively at decentralized workstations or even at home. Second, the need for more flexible service delivery and the complex child care and elder care arrangements necessitated by two-career families have resulted in the development of part-time and flexible work schedules. Last, the focus on employees as resources has led to the development of variable models of resource use that have proved effective at achieving performance.

Under flex time, all employees are expected to work during core hours (such as 9:00–3:00). Depending on agency needs and personal preferences, each employee is free to negotiate a fixed work schedule with different start or end times. Research on flex time experiments in both the public and private sectors generally reveals positive results in employee attitudes and in the reduction of absenteeism, tardiness, and in some cases even increases in productivity.

Job sharing is the splitting of one job between two part-time employees on a regular basis. There are obvious advantages for employees (flexible part-time work rather than a choice between full-time work or no work at all) and the agency (mentoring, light-duty work). But the employees must coordinate their activities with each other, with their supervisor, and with clients/customers inside and outside the agency. and the agency must develop policies for contributions and division of pensions, health care, and other benefits.

Employees may work away from the office, provided suitable outside workstation is available. This works best for professionals who can work independently and yet remain in contact with the agency through phone systems, a computer, and a modem. The advantage to the agency is that it may be able to get work done just as well and to attract individuals who value independence and flexibility. The downside, of course, is predictable things like communication and control, and unpredictable ones like workplace health and safety, and workers' compensation claims.

5. Sensitive Supervision

As with all aspects of public personnel management, the quality of the relationship between the supervisor and the employee is of much more importance in determining the climate of the organization than the mere existence of family-centered leave policies, childcare and eldercare support programs, and alternative work settings and schedules. Organizations which wish to attract and keep asset employees by supporting "family values" need to select and train supervisors who are sensitive to these issues.

H. Enhanced Human Resource Management Information Systems

The collection and use of information for program planning, control, and evaluation purposes is essential to work measurement, productivity, or responsiveness by public management. And while these data have always been collected and used on at least an ad hoc and piecemeal basis, there are many reasons why more systematic data collection and reporting are now necessary: heightened concern for productivity and accountability, establishment of public personnel management as a corporate function, and increased awareness of the interrelationship of personal functions (Whitman and Hyde, 1978).

The relationship between the HRMIS and *planning* occurs during the budget preparation and approval process. Revenue estimates are matched against program proposals. The cost of proposed programs depends on such factors as the number and type of employees, their pay and benefits, and the training they will need. All these data are collected and stored as part of the budget and payroll system. Affirmative action is the personnel activity that dominates *acquisition* of human resources. The extent to which social equity considerations will influence selection is determined by the extent to which particular groups are underutilized and the validity of the selection criteria. Both utilization analysis and empirical validation techniques are dependent on computerized applicant data such as race, sex, age, test scores, and performance evaluations. Employee *development* involves the comparison of performance and productivity data against organizational objectives. Performance appraisal systems and organizational productivity data are routinely computerized. Training needs assessment can be based on a comparison of computerized skill inventories against jobs' required KSAs. The *sanction* process concerns the involvement of outside organizations such as unions or contract compliance officers in personnel policymaking.

To sum up, an HRMIS is used to collect and store data, to produce reports used to control and evaluate current programs, and to develop simulations to support policy decisions. Therefore, a good HRMIS is one that provides the kind of information needed to the people who need it when they need it. The personnel director must decide what the system needs to do before computer specialists decide how to do it; the HRMIS must be designed to be compatible with the larger organizational management information system (MIS); and computerization should be recognized as a change in work technology that also involves such issues as employee acceptance, job redesign, and training. Because the costs of some applications are high, HRMIS systems designers need to balance them against user expectations and capabilities.

An HRMIS can also provide essential assistance to political leaders and stakeholders who wish an agency's programs to remain responsive to policy pressures originating outside the agency. In these cases, data supportive or critical of an agency's performance are compiled into reports that "drive" the agency's planning, control, and evaluation activities. Elected officials, agency managers, or interest groups use these reports to induce changes in organizational policies or procedures (or to compel those changes, if legal sanctions were involved).

I. Public Personnel Managers as Entrepreneurs

Public personnel management may be viewed as static or dynamic. Traditional personnel mangers view the field as narrow and static. They picture it as a collection of administrative techniques applied within a structure of rules, policies, and laws that clearly define the limits of acceptable professional behavior. They see themselves as continually acting within a consensus on one system and its underlying values. They tend to define themselves, and to be defined by others, as technical specialists working within a staff agency.

More contemporary public personnel managers view the field as emergent and dynamic. They tend to define themselves, and to be defined by others, as interpreters or mediators among competing systems, stakeholders, and values. They see themselves as professionals whose role involves a blend of technical skills and ethical decision making, and as key players in developing corporate human resource management strategy. The essence of this emergent professional public personnel management role is *synergy*, the exploitation of pressure points whereby conflicting systems compete and converge, and the reconciliation of conflicting values, changing conditions, competing stakeholders, and a diverse work force into a coherent and dynamic whole.

Over the past 10 years much research has been conducted concerning organizational innovation. Most of the research, however, has been about technical innovation, not administrative innovation. Yet the strategic design of human resource management systems and structures for the purpose of making agencies more effective is an administrative innovation. This leads to the issue of what causes or enhance administrative innovation in public agencies.

After controlling for external and organizational variables, research studies conclude that the professional role, and the self-perception of that role, is the major factor that leads key agency players to undertake and successfully complete administrative innovations. Those who see themselves as professionals, who recognize the dynamism and conflict inherent in their roles, are more likely to innovate. Both the extent to which they represent a departure from traditional organization policy and practice and the scope of their application (the number of employees they affect) are likely to be greater (Sabet and Klingner, 1993).

Innovation carries the risk of failure, for it represents experimentation with the unknown. Therefore, those organizations interested (for their own survival's sake) in encouraging innovation must select human resource managers (and other managers) who are experienced and positive risktakers. Fortunately, the same systems, structures, and rewards the organization uses to exploit dynamism and conflict also create the situations to which public personnel directors must respond. By creating these situations, and by encouraging managers to respond creatively and take some risks, the agency can use dynamism not only to force change and augment human resources, but to develop personnel managers who have leadership ability as well as technical skills.

V. STRATEGIC HUMAN RESOURCE MANAGEMENT IN ACTION

The above analysis has shown that strategic human resource management is best seen as a set of characteristics, an "ideal type" that is more useful as an analytical model of where public personnel management is headed than as an actual description of personnel policies and practices in any one organization. These are the characteristics: (1) recognition that human resource management is a critical corporate function; (2) a shift in managerial focus from position management to work management and employee management; (3) a clear differentiation between "asset" and "Kleenex" jobs based on divergent concerns for asset accountability and personnel cost control; (4) for asset jobs, a clear focus on employee training and development; (5) for asset jobs, a clear focus on employee involvement and participation; (6) for asset jobs, a shift in focus from EEO/AA compliance to work force diversity; (7) for asset jobs, an emphasis on family-centered leave and benefit programs; (8) enhanced human resource management information systems; (9) increased entrepreneurial behavior among public personnel managers.

The following examples show strategic human resource management in action a variety of organizational settings. Like all examples of emergent trends, they are often fragmentary and hesitant. But taken together, they show how far-sighted personnel managers have continued to respond to environmental change.

A. Recognizing Human Resource Management as a Critical Corporate Function

The U.S. Office of Personnel Management has developed a *Strategic Plan for Federal Human Resource Management* (1990) which is based on the vision of effective human resource management throughout the federal government, which enables agencies to recruit, develop, and retain a quality and representative work force.

The office of the assistant secretary for personnel (ASPER) of the U.S. Department of Health and Human Services has in recent years undergone a series of reorganizations aimed at creating a model for a human resource management capability in federal agencies (Boyle, 1991; U.S. Department of Health and Human Services, 1991; Klingner, 1991).

B. Shift in Focus from Position Management to Work Management and Employee Management

The federal government sponsored a 17-agency review of the position classification system originally created in 1949 under Title V. The review, conducted by the National Academy of Public Administration (1991), concluded that agencies could make significant changes (such as broad banding) within existing law. The feasibility of these changes has been demonstrated by a decade of experimentation through the demonstration projects operated by a number of federal agencies and authorized by the Office of Systems Innovation and Simplification, U.S. Office of Personnel Management.

The U.S. Public Health Service has implemented an alternative personnel system to enhance effectiveness in the recruitment and utilization of medical personnel (U.S. Merit Systems Protection Board, 1991).

In its most dramatic restructuring in the past 25 years, the U.S. Postal Service announced plans to eliminate 25% of its 120,000 managerial jobs and overhaul its military-style hierarchy (Where things stand, 1992).

C. Clear Differentiation Between "Asset" and "Kleenex" Jobs Based on Divergent Concerns for Asset Accountability and Personnel Cost Control

The Advisory Commission on Federal Workforce Quality recently (August 1992) concluded that "despite widespread . . . anecdotal evidence, the quality of employees [in the engineering, scientific, and computer fields] is not generally deficient and has remained fairly constant over time" (Advisory Committee on Federal Workforce Quality, 1992, p. x).

The University of California developed an early retirement program for faculty which reduced short-term pay and benefit costs by offering selected faculty (those who almost meet minimum age and seniority criteria for retirement) a limited "window of opportunity" during which they can retire at close to full benefits. The University maintained productivity by using adjunct or nontenured faculty to teach classes. The asset loss represented by professors who retired early was considered a less significant factor, based on a conscious comparison of short-term operating costs with long-term human resource asset values.

D. For Asset Jobs, a Clear Focus on Employee Training and Development

At Aetna Life and Casualty (Hartford, CT), over 1000 workers have been hired through a cooperative eduction effort with local organizations that focuses on reading and written communication skills (Bennett, 1989).

IBM has adopted a high-skill employee empowerment approach as part of its full-employment, no-layoffs policy. When managers at its Austin (Texas) plant estimated they could save $60 million by buying circuit boards elsewhere rather than manufacturing them, IBM management had other ideas. They cut costs by upgrading worker skills, organized workers into teams, and gave teams responsibility for quality control, repairs, and materials ordering. Skill requirements for manufacturing jobs were increased, and education and training costs increased to 5% of payroll. The bottom line result was that productivity increased 200%, quality was up 500%, and inventory was cut 40%. The plant employs more people than ever before (Karr, 1990).

E. For Asset Jobs, a Clear Focus on Involvement and Participation

Madison, Wisconsin is home to model TQM programs in both state and local governments. For example, the motor equipment division of the city's department of public works used managerial tools and participative decision making to better understand their customer's needs and to identify basic underlying causes for excessive vehicle downtime. The time invested in these efforts led to improved customer satisfaction and procedures throughout all departments to reduce repair downtime. At a time when staff was reduced by 17%, vehicles service increased by 25% (Klingner and Nalbandian, 1992).

Florida Power and Light (FPL) won the coveted Deming Award in 1991 for successful efforts by work teams to increase customer satisfaction and reduce costs. These efforts equipped the public utility to perform successfully when Hurricane Andrew devastated Miami's southern suburbs a year later.

F. For Asset Jobs, a Shift in Focus from EEO/AA Compliance to Work Force Diversity

Corning Glass Works evaluates managers on their ability to "create a congenial environment" for diverse employees (Schmidt, 1988).

Mobil corporation created a special committee of executives to identify high-potential female and minority executive job candidates, and to place them in line management positions viewed as critical for advancement through the glass ceiling (How companies help, 1987).

Dr. Charles McCabe, President of Miami-Dade Community College, recently won a MacArthur Foundation Award for educational leadership, including a 10-year emphasis on work force diversity as a key to community involvement and mission achievement (Ruff, 1992).

G. For Asset Jobs, an Emphasis on Family-Centered Leave and Benefit Programs

A number of commentators and researchers have reported on employers' increased family-centered benefit programs (Morgan and Tucker, 1991, pp. 11–14). These include:

IBM: year-long maternity leave with supervisory job retention rights

Stride-Rite (Cambridge, MA): onsite child care and daytime eldercare

Merck & Co. (Rahway, NJ): parent-run child care centers

Joy Cone (Hermitage, PA): split shifts and flexible shift assignments at its factories

Arthur Anderson & Co.: part-time benefited professional positions, child care

United States Hosiery Corporation (Lincolnton, NC): child care, sick room for mildly ill children

Lotus Development Corp. (Cambridge, MA): month-long paid parenting leave to mothers, fathers, and adoptive parents

Johnson and Johnson corporate philosophy includes the following statement: "We must be mindful of ways to help our employees fulfill their family obligations"

Working Mother magazine identified 10 companies as extremely progressive for family career issues and career opportunities for women: Aetna Life & Casualty (CT), Beth Israel Hospital (MA), Corning (NY), Fel-Pro (IL), IBM (NY), Johnson and Johnson, (NJ), Merck & Co. (NJ), Morris and Foerster (CA), St. Paul Cos. (MN), SAS Institute (NC).

H   Enhanced Human Resource Management Information Systems

The U.S. Public Health Service has developed a KSA-based management information that aids in placing professional, technical, and scientific personnel through a person-based personnel system (Sherwood, 1991).

A consortium of federal agencies, led by the U.S. General Accounting Office, recently noted:

As one looks to the future, it becomes clear that human resource management skills will become simultaneously more essential and more difficult to apply . . . . Supervisors will increasingly face the challenge of relating to staff from diverse backgrounds. People from differing backgrounds often communicate, behave and respond differently. As managers and supervisors, we must be able to accept differences in style, focusing instead on the results achieved (Goldstein, 1989).

The Federal Quality Institute notes that managers' and directors' personal development requires that they train themselves to thrive in a contingent environment where objectives are diverse and means–end relationships are uncertain—and that they train and reward subordinates for taking similar risks and for learning from them.

VI. SUMMARY

Strategic human resource management is a concept and an organizational capability in many public and private organizations. Its characteristics are (1) the recognition that human resource management is a critical corporate function, (2) a shift in managerial focus from position management to work management and employee management, (3) a clear differentiation between asset and Kleenex jobs based on divergent concerns for asset accountability and personnel cost control, (4) for asset jobs, a clear focus on employee training and development, (5) for asset jobs, a clear focus on employee involvement and participation, (6) for asset jobs, a shift in focus from EEO/AA compliance to work force diversity, (7) for asset jobs, an emphasis on family-centered leave and benefit programs, (8) enhanced human resource management information systems, and (9) increased entrepreneurial behavior among public personnel managers.

Strategic human resource management will continue to develop because of underlying changes which continue to shape public personnel management as an emergent profession: (1) demands for reinventing government in ways which enhance work measurement, productivity, and accountability, (2) uncontrolled benefit cost increases, (3) increasing legal liability risks, (4) a more diverse work force, (5) the continued development of dual labor markets, (6) divergent views of public employees as capital assets or production costs, and (7) alternative instrumentalities for providing public services.

Strategic human resource management is the purposeful resolution of human resource administration and policy issues so as to enhance a public agency's ability to accomplish its mission. It requires an *understanding* of how organizational human resource management functions relate to one another and to their environmental context, a *vision* of the strategic importance of human resources, and a *commitment* on the part of elected officials, personnel managers, supervisors and employees to work for change.

REFERENCES

Advisory Committee on Federal Workforce Quality (1992). *Federal Workforce Quality Measurement and Improvement,* Advisory Committee on Workforce Quality, Washington, DC.

Allan, I. (1988). Financing and managing public employee benefit plans in the 1990's, August. *Gvmt. Fin. Rev.*, 4: 32.

Argyris, C. (1980). Making the undiscussable and its undiscussibility discussable, *Public Admin. Rev.*, 40(May–June): 205-213.

Bennett, A. (1989). As pool of skilled help tightens, firms move to broaden their role, *The Wall Street Journal*, May 8, 1.

Bernhard, H., and Ingols, C. (1988). Six lessons for the corporate classroom, *Harvard Business Rev.*, 88(Sept.-Oct.): 40-48.

Blostin, A., Burke, T., and Lovejoy, L. (1988). Disability and insurance plans in the public and private sector, *Monthly Labor Rev.*, (Dec.): 9-17.

Boyle, P. (1991). *New Directions for the 90's: Building a "Corporate" Human Resource Capability*, Department of Health and Human Services, Washington, DC, May.

Cafeteria Plans, Wellness Programs Gaining in Popularity, *Employee Benefit Plan Rev.*, (July 1990): 90-92.

Chief Financial Officers Act of 1990 (Public Law 101-576), November 15, 1990.

Child care and recruitment boost flexible plans (March 1987). *Employee Benefit Plan Rev.*, 32-33.

Chiswick, B. R., and Mincer, J. (May–June 1972). Time series changes in personal income inequality in the United States from 1939, with projections to 1985, *J. Polit. Econ.*, 80: 34-71.

Chollet, D., and Friedland, R. (1987). Health care costs and public policy toward employee health plans, *Rev. Public Personnel Admin.*, 7: 68.

Daniel, C., and Rose, B. (1991). Blending professionalism and political acuity: empirical support for an emerging ideal, *Public Admin. Rev.*, 51: 438-441.

Deming, W. (1988). *Out of the Crisis*, MIT Center for Advanced Engineering Study, Cambridge, MA.

Doeringer, P. (ed.) (1990). *Turbulence in the American Workplace*, Oxford University Press, New York.

Doeringer, P., and Piore, M. (1971). *The Internal Labor Market*, D.C. Health, Lexington, MA.

Doeringer, P., and Piore, M. (1975). Unemployment and the "dual labor market," *The Public Interest*, *38*: 67–79.

Dougherty, C., and Psacharopoulos, G. (1977). Measuring the cost of misallocation of investment in education, *J. Human Resources*, 12: 446–459.

Emery, A. (1989) AIDS strategies that work, *Business and Health (June)*: 43–46.

Faden, R., and Kass, N. (1988). Health insurance and AIDS: the issue of state regulatory Activity," *Am. J. Public Health*, *78*: 437–438.

Flamholtz, E. (1974). *Human Resource Accounting*, Dickenson, Encino, CA.

Foegen, J. (1986). Split-level wages: reluctantly approved by labor unions and reinforced by keen foreign competition, *Business Econ. Rev.*, *32*: 34–35.

French, W., and Bell C., (1990). *Organizational Development*, 4th ed., Prentice-Hall, Englewood Cliffs, NJ.

Goldstein, I. (1989). Managing for performance in the public sector, *GAO J.*, *7*: 51.

Haight, G. (1990). Managing diversity, *Across the Board*, *27* (March): 22–30.

Heacock, M., and Orvis, G. (1990). AIDS in the workplace: public and corporate policy, *Harvard J. Law Public Policy*, *13*: 689–713.

Holton, R. (1988). AIDS in the workplace: underwriting update, *Best's Review, Property–Casualty Edition*, pp. 96–98.

Hudson Institute (1988). *Opportunity 2000: creating affirmative action strategies for a changing workforce*, Hudson Institute, Indianapolis, IN.

Jenks, J. (1987). Protecting privacy rights, *Personnel J.*, *66*: 123–126.

Jennings, K., and Traynham, E. (1988). The wages of two-tier pay plans, *Personnel J.*, *67*: 56–63.

Johnston, W., and Packer, A. (1987). Workforce 2000: Work and Workers for the Twenty-first Century, Hudson Institute, Indianapolis, IN.

Karr, A., (1990). Workplace panel is urging changes in schools, on job, *Wall Street Journal*, June 19, C-15.

Klingner, D. (1988). The personal liability of state and local personnel directors: legal, organizational and ethical implications, *Public Personnel Manage.*, *17*: 125–134.

Klingner, D. (1991). *ASPER and Corporate Human Resource Capability in DHHS: Analysis and Evaluation*, U.S. Department of Health and Human Services, Office of the Assistant Secretary for Personnel, Washington, DC, June 12.

Klingner, D., with O'Neill, N. (1991). *Workplace Drug Abuse and AIDS: A Guide to Human Resource Management Policy and Practice*, Greenwood/Quorum, Westport, CT, ch. 9 and app. B.

Klingner, D., and Nalbandian, J. (1993). *Public Personnel Management: Contexts and Strategies*, 3rd ed., Prentice-Hall, Englewood Cliffs, NJ.

Klingner, D., O'Neill, N., and Sabet, M. (1990). Drug testing in public agencies: are personnel directors doing things right?, *Public Personnel Manage.*, *19*: 391–397.

Loden, M., and Rosener, J. (1991). *Workforce America! Managing Employee Diversity as a Vital Resource*, Business One Irwin, Homewood, IL.

Luthans, F., and David, E. (1990). The healthcare cost crisis: causes and containment, Personnel, *67*: 24.

Marshall, S. (1992). *Personal Interview*, U.S. Office of Personnel Management, Office of Systems Innovation and Simplification, Washington, DC, Oct. 10.

Masi, D. (1987a). Company response to drug abuse from the AMA's national survey, *Personnel*, 63: 40–46.

Masi, D. (1987b). AIDS in the workplace: what can be done?, *Personnel*, 64: 57–60.

McGahey, R. (1987). Minorities and the labor market: twenty years of misguided policy, *Social Policy*, *17*: 5–11.

Mellado, C., Mellado, R., and Armendariz, F. (1989). Apples's new approaches to affirmative action, *Hispanic Engineer* (Spring): 32–36.

Morgan, H., and Tucker, K., (1991). *Companies That Care*, Fireside, New York.

National Academy of Public Administration (1991). *Modernizing Federal Classification: An Opportunity for Excellence*, NAPA, Washington, DC.

Odds and ends (1990). *Wall Street Journal*, March 6, C-1.

O'Rand, A. (1986). The hidden payroll: employee benefits and the structure of workplace inequality, *Sociol. Forum*, *1*: 657–683.

Osborne, D., and Gaebler, T. (1992). *Reinventing Government*, Addison-Wesley, Reading, MA.

Piore, M., and Sabel, C. (1984). *The Second Industrial Divide: Possibilities for Prosperity*, Basic Books, New York.

Psacharopoulos, G. (1985). Returns to education: a further international update and implications, *J. Human Res.*, *20*: 583–597.

Pyle, W. (1970). Monitoring human resources—"on line," *Mich. Business Rev.*, *22*(July): 19–32.

Rodarmor, W. (1991). The diversity project's Troy Duster, *Cal. Month.*, *102*(Sept.): 40–45.

Rosener, J. (19990). Ways women lead, *Harvard Business Rev.*, *68* Nov.–Dec.): 119–125.

Rosow, J., and Zager, R. (1988). *Training—the Corporate Edge*, Jossey-Bass, San Francisco.

Rowe, M., Russell-Einhorn, M., and Weinstein, J. (1987). New issues in testing the work force: genetic diseases, *Labor Law J.*, *38*: 518–523.

Ruff, J. (1992). Unpublished dissertation proposal, Florida International University, Department of Public Administration.

Sabet, M., and Klingner, D. (1993). Professionalism and administrative innovation, *J. Public Admin. Res. Theory.*, *3*, 2(April): 252–266.

Sashkin, M. (1984). Participative management is an ethical imperative, *Organ. Dyn.*, *12*(Spring): 5–22.

Schiller, B. R. (1984). *The Economics of Poverty and Discrimination*, (4th ed.), Prentice-Hall, Englewood Cliffs, NJ, p. 39.

Schmidt, P. (1988). Women and minorities: is industry ready?, *New York Times*, Oct. 16, p. 25.

Schultz, T. W. (1961). *Education and Economic Growth: Social forces Influencing American Education*, National Society for the Study of Education, Chicago.

Sherwood, R. (1991). *Personal interview*, U.S. Department of Health and Human Services, U.S. Public Health Service, Washington, DC, May 12.

Shoop, T. (1991). Paying for performance, *Government Executive*, pp. 16-18.

Slater, K. (1990). Likely Methuselahs get more life-insurance breaks, *Wall Street Journal*, June 7, pp. C1, C8.

Solomon, C. (1989). Firms address workers' cultural variety: the differences are celebrated, not suppressed, *Wall Street Journal*, Feb. 10, p. B-1.

Solovy, A. (1989) Insurers, HMOs and BC-BS plans talk about AIDS, *Hospitals*, *63*(Jan. 20): 24.

Taylor, P. (1991). Study of firms finds parental leave impact light, *Washington Post*, May 23, p. A9.

Thomas, R. (1990). From affirmative action to affirming diversity. *Harvard Business Review*, *68*: 107-117.

Turk, H. (1989). AIDS: the first decade, *Employee Rel. Law J.*, *14*: 531–547.

U.S. Bureau of Labor Statistics (1989). *Monthly Labor Rev.*, (Nov.).

U.S. Department of Health and Human Services, Office of the Secretary (1991). *General Reorganization: Statement of Organization, Functions and Delegation of Authority*, USDHHS, Office of the Secretary, Assistant Secretary for Personnel Administration, Washington, DC.

U.S. Merit Systems Protection Board (1991). *The Title 38 Personnel Systems in the Department of Veterans Affairs: An Alternative Approach*, USMSPB, Washington, DC.

U.S. Office of Personnel Management (1989). *Manage to Budget Programs*, Office of Systems Innovation and Simplification, Personnel Systems and Oversight Group, PSOG-203, Washington, DC.

U.S. Office of Personnel Management (1990). *Strategic Plan for Federal Human Resource Management*, Office of Systems Innovation and Simplification, Washington, DC, Nov.

U.S. Office of Personnel Management (1991). *Federal Total Quality Management Handbook*, Federal Quality Institute, Washington, DC, May.

Uzych, L. (1986). Genetic testing and exclusionary practices in the workplace. *J. Public Health Policy* (*Spring*): 37–57.

Wessel, D. (1985). Split personality: two-tier pay spreads, but pioneer firms encounter problems, *The Wall Street Journal*, Oct. 14, p. 1+.

Where things stand (1992). Postal service restructures, *PA Times*, *15*(9)(Sept. 1): 3.

Whitman, T., and Hyde, A. (1978). HRIS, matching the right person to the right position, *Defense Manage. J. (March)*: 28–35.

World Health Organization (1990). *Guidelines on AIDS and First Aid in the Workplace*, WHO AIDS Series 7, Geneva.

27

Volunteers in the Delivery of Public Services: Magnitude, Scope, and Management

JEFFREY L. BRUDNEY   University of Georgia, Athens, Georgia

> "Ask not what your country can do for you—ask what you can do for your country."
> President John F. Kennedy, 1961.

> "The old ideas are new again because they're not old, they are timeless: duty, sacrifice, commitment and a patriotism that finds its expression in taking part and pitching in."
> President George H. Bush, 1989.

> "I challenge a new generation of young Americans to a season of service . . . and others who are still young in spirit to give of themselves in service, too."
> President William J. Clinton, 1993.

More than three decades spanned the inaugurations of Presidents Kennedy, Bush, and Clinton, yet on that most visible of occasions all three expressed remarkable continuity in encouraging Americans to engage in voluntary service. The particular concepts or vehicles for public sector volunteerism have changed over time: Kennedy is best remembered for the Peace Corps, Bush for the "points of light," and Clinton for incipient plans for national and community service, still in the formulation stages in the early 1990s. Other recent presidents have also promoted volunteerism. The "Volunteers in Service to America" program, or VISTA, began under President Johnson. In his 8 years in office, President Reagan took seemingly every opportunity to extol volunteering, proclaiming in a 1982 speech typical of his administration, "The volunteer spirit is still alive and well in America." In addition to the prominence his volunteer work has brought to the Habitat for Humanity organization, President Carter is the founder of the Atlanta Project, a broad-scale initiative to reinvigorate the civic culture as well as infrastructure of that city through massive voluntary and philanthropic effort.

As these actions illustrate, expansion of the number and types of people who do volunteer work, as well as the range of their activities, has been public policy for at least the past 30 years (Chambré, 1989). This endorsement of volunteerism forms part of a venerable tradition in America, dating back to the seminal observations of Alexis de Tocqueville in the 1830s, who characterized Americans as a nation of inveterate "joiners" in self-help and mutual assistance associations. Susan J. Ellis and Katherine H. Noyes document an even longer *History of Americans as Volunteers* (1990), encompassing the colonial and precolonial eras.

Volunteerism is not the exclusive province of one political party or philosophy. Nor despite contemporary interest in the cost-saving aspects of the approach should it be considered only a stop-gap measure to combat harsh economic realities or a cynical ploy for governments to offload significant responsibilities. Volunteers have been active in providing public services in periods of munificence as well as scarcity, usually preceding the formal introduction of government. Indeed, many consider volunteerism to be woven into the very fabric of American democracy and culture (see Kramer, 1981; Park, 1983).

This chapter focuses on a crucial area in which this tradition manifests itself: the involvement of volunteers in the delivery of public services. The chapter consists of five sections. It begins with a definition of volunteers to government agencies. Next, it considers the magnitude of citizen participation in services, followed by a discussion of the scope or breadth of volunteer involvement. The chapter then turns to the costs and benefits of the approach. The final section provides a comprehensive treatment of the design and management of government-based volunteer programs.

I.   VOLUNTEERS TO GOVERNMENT AGENCIES: A DEFINITION

Like many other signal concepts in public administration, "volunteerism" and "volunteer" elude facile definition. The present analysis treats *service-oriented* or "operations" volunteering occurring under the auspices of a *government agency*. Here, the approach concentrates on volunteers who donate time to an institution in the public sector rather than to a private (e.g., a charitable or nonprofit) organization.

As implied by this definition, for the purposes of this chapter, volunteer activity occurs in an *organizational context*. Participants engage in "formal" volunteering, in which they contribute their energy and talents in programs sponsored by government agencies. Thus, management of volunteers arises as a central concern for the public administrator. "Informal" volunteering, by contrast, consists of spontaneous acts of helping not mediated by an organization, usually undertaken to aid an acquaintance, friend, or relative (e.g., babysitting or housewatching).

In a seminal article, David Horton Smith (1972) defines service volunteers as individuals who donate their time to help other people directly, in the realms of health, welfare, housing, education, recreation, rehabilitation, and so forth. Their activities are "widely perceived as the heart of volunteerism . . . the countless individual acts of commitment encompassing an endless variety of volunteer tasks" (Park, 1983, p. 118). This conception highlights the involvement of volunteers in delivering direct or final services to the public, but it also embraces their assistance in organizational support functions, such as internal maintenance (e.g., clerical duties) and fundraising and advocacy on behalf of government agencies.

The hallmark of the volunteer concept is that individuals do not receive monetary compensation for their labor. In fact, the most authoritative mass sample surveys probing this behavior—a series of biennial surveys commissioned by the Independent Sector Organization and conducted by Gallup, Inc.—as well as many other surveys, operationalize volunteering as "working in some way to help others for no monetary pay" (see Hodgkinson et al., 1992).

Some controversy attends the meaning of compensation, however. Smith (1972) and other scholars allow that volunteers are entitled to reimbursement for out-of-pocket expenses incurred in this activity, such as mileage, meals, and parking. More problematic is the fact that many individuals normally classified as volunteers do receive remuneration, albeit at a partial or subsistence level. The Peace Corps, VISTA, and some fire departments, emergency medical service (EMS) organizations, and state parks provide volunteers with a nominal stipend well below prevailing wage rates (see Smith, 1972; Pattakos, 1982; Farr, 1983; Marando, 1986). These examples suggest that the relationship between volunteering and compensation may be a matter of degree.

Jacqueline deLaat (1987, p. 104) tried to formalize this relationship by proposing that volunteering may be considered job-related work that is "undercompensated," as when a certified public accountant charges reduced rates to charitable organizations. While provocative, this formulation raises serious impediments to operationalization and has not been accepted in the literature. However, receipt of a modest stipend or subsistence payment is widely regarded to fall within the volunteer concept.

Despited the absence (or relative absence) of monetary compensation, volunteering should not be confused with self-sacrifice. As will be illustrated below, findings from survey research indicate that participants have a variety of motivations, both self-interested and altruistic, for engaging in volunteer activity. They also reap substantial benefits, including sociability, career exploration and development, various forms of personal enhancement, and even better health (e.g., Clary, Snyder, and Ridge, 1992; Clotfelter, 1985).

Just as volunteering is not aimed at material gain, it cannot be mandated or coerced; compulsion significantly alters the character of the endeavor (Van Til, 1988, pp. 5-9). Recently, this provision, too, has aroused controversy. Individuals sanctioned to undertake public service activities by the courts, such as prisoners and defendants ordered into restitution or community programs, are not usually considered volunteers. But what about students "sanctioned" (required) by school systems to participate in community service or volunteer work as a condition for graduation? In 1992, Maryland became the first state to require its students to perform community service to graduate from high school; many cities, including Washington, DC, and Atlanta, Georgia, have such a provision (Haberek, 1992). Opponents argued that although they endorsed the concept of youth service, "it seemed incongruous to mandate volunteerism" (Haberek, 1992, p. 5). As national and community service commands greater attention from states and localities, stemming in no small part from President Clinton's interest in these initiatives, the traditional definition of *volunteer* may expand.

In sum, for the purposes of this chapter, volunteers are people who donate time to a public program or agency; their activity occurs in an organizational context. Normally, this behavior is not mandated or coerced, but undertaken willingly. Although the activity is not conducted for monetary profit, a volunteer may receive payment for out-of-pocket costs or modest living expenses.

II. MAGNITUDE OF VOLUNTEER INVOLVEMENT IN THE DELIVERY OF PUBLIC SERVICES

Although the great majority of volunteers donate their time to the nonprofit sector, a significant amount of volunteering is directed to public organizations. According to a Gallup survey of the U.S. populace conducted in 1990, 28% of all volunteer assignments reported by a national sample were for government organizations. Converted to a full-time equivalent basis, about one-quarter (26%) of the time contributed by volunteers went to government (Hodgkinson et al., 1992, p. 7). These estimates of the extent of volunteer involvement in the delivery of public services substantiate less precise judgments reached in earlier research. For example, an expert panel convened in 1980 speculated that government agencies operate as many as 20–30% of all organized volunteer programs in the United States, and that probably another 20–30% of these programs are linked to the public sector through funding or other arrangements (Rydberg and Peterson, 1980, pp. 19–20).

Strong evidence exists that the level of volunteer involvement in government service provision is increasing. In 1985, a Gallup survey established that just over one in five volunteers contributed time to government (Gallup, 1986, p. 5)—compared to about one in four volunteers in the 1990 survey (see above). Economist Burton A. Weisbrod (1988, p. 202) estimates that the number of full-time equivalent volunteers to government (calculated on the basis of 1700 hours per year) grew by 50% from 1977 to 1985, from 0.8 million to 1.2 million.

The trend in growth is most evident among local governments. Based on a survey conducted in 1982, the International City-County Management Association (ICMA) estimated that 56.5% of cities over 4500 population employed volunteers in at least one service domain (Shulman, 1982). By 1985, according to a survey by Sidney Duncombe (1985), the figure had swelled to more than 70% (72.6%). Similarly, among counties, from preliminary results of a 1990 survey of chief elected officials, the National Association of Counties (1990, p. 6) determined that "within the last five years there has been a 13 to 50 percent increase in the number of county-sponsored volunteer programs and a similar 33 to 50 percent expansion of existing programs. The use of volunteer assistance by counties is growing significantly."

The ICMA replicated its survey of local governments in 1988. James M. Ferris (1992) analyzed changes in local service delivery patterns, based on those cities that completed both surveys. He, too, concludes that during the 1980s cities increased volunteer involvement significantly. On the average, city use of volunteers grew from 3.4% of all services delivered in 1982 to 4.2% in 1988, and from 4.6% of direct services to 6.1% (changes statistically significant at $p < 0.01$). Contrary to expectation, the incidence of contracting for services by cities appears to have declined over this period (again, changes statistically significant at $p < 0.01$).

In light of the heightened rhetoric advocating privatization of services, this pattern of increases in volunteerism combined with a decrease in contracting may seem anomalous. Yet, it is fully consistent with the interpretation of volunteer involvement as an alternative service delivery approach—and one that can make the work life of public employees far more rewarding and less threatening than contracting (Brudney, 1987, 1990b).

III. SCOPE OF VOLUNTEER INVOLVEMENT IN PUBLIC SERVICE DELIVERY

The best data available on the service domains in which volunteers donate their time emanate from surveys of local governments. The 1988 ICMA survey documents the importance of volunteer participation in government services to meeting societal needs (Morley, 1989). At least one-fourth of the national sample of cities over 4500 population reported using volunteers in the areas of culture and the arts (41%), food programs (37%), museum operations (34%), recreation (26%), and programs for the elderly (25%). A minimum of 10% of cities used volunteers in fire prevention and suppression (19%), emergency medical service (18%), ambulance service (17%), crime prevention/patrol (16%), libraries (13%), child welfare (11%), and drug/alcohol treatment (10%). In his 1985 survey, Duncombe (1985) found that volunteers assisted cities in more than 60 types of work.

A survey conducted by the National Association of Counties (1990) offers parallel results. Based on returns from 1322 of the universe of 3107 counties, the survey showed that at least one county used volunteers in 133 of the 135 service areas polled. The study grouped these data into 15 service domains: Volunteer involvement was highest in public safety (54.5%), social services (29.2%), parks and recreation (20.2%), public health (16.6%), and community development (8.2%).

The extent of volunteer participation in the delivery of local government services may well be greater than intimated by these findings, especially in certain functional areas. Consider fire prevention and suppression and emergency medical services, for example. The 1988 ICMA survey placed the incidence of volunteer involvement in these domains at about 20% of cities (see above). By contrast, according to knowledgeable estimates, over 25,000 volunteer fire departments with a membership of more than 1 million individuals (80% of the total firefighting force) protect three-fourths of the geographic area of the United States (see Perkins, 1987, 1990). Similarly, 65% of the EMS labor force is thought to be volunteer, and over 5000 volunteer organizations with some 180,000 members likely provide this service to about 30% of the population. Other research documents very high levels of volunteer involvement in these service domains (see Norris et al., 1993). Relatively low survey response rates may provide at least a partial explanation. The response rate for cities to the 1988 ICMA survey was just 40.2% (Ferris, 1992), and the National Association of Counties (1990) survey generated a similar cooperation rate of 42.5%.

Unfortunately, data on volunteer involvement comparable in representativeness and scope to those collected for local government do not exist for other levels of government. Nevertheless, available evidence suggests that the participation of service volunteers in federal agencies and among the states is also substantial.

With respect to the states, since 1974, ACTION, officially designated as the "Federal Domestic Volunteer Agency," has sponsored a grant program to assist in the establishment of state offices of volunteerism (SOVs). Over the course of the program, ACTION has awarded grants totaling approximately $3 million; nearly all states have participated. The SOVs promote and coordinate existing volunteer programs within state government and aid in the design and development of additional offices and programs. They also facilitate and support federal volunteer efforts as well as the activities of private voluntary organizations (Schwartz, 1989). Throughout the late 1980s and early 1990s, the National Assembly of State Offices of Volunteerism numbered about 30 state offices; another 7–10 states had a formal representative or contact person to coordinate and sustain volunteer efforts.

The SOVs represent a complex federal–state interaction. Volunteers are also active in state-operated functions, such as human services, corrections, parks and recreation, public health, education, and tourism (Allen et al., 1989). For example, 60% of state park systems employ volunteers to provide visitor services (Myers and Reid, 1986).

At the federal level, ACTION and the Peace Corps have an established mission and reputation for enlisting volunteers. ACTION resulted from President Nixon's Reorganization Plan Number 1 of 1971, which attempted to consolidate federal volunteer programs into a single organization responsible for promoting citizen volunteerism. With a volunteer complement that numbers in the hundreds of thousands, ACTION houses most of these programs, including Volunteers in Service to America, citizen participation and volunteer demonstration projects, and older American volunteer programs (retired senior volunteer, foster grandparents, and senior companion programs). Once a part of ACTION but autonomous since 1981, the Peace Corps places over 5000 Americans in voluntary service in over 60 countries worldwide.

President Clinton has pledged to stimulate volunteerism, particularly among young people, through federal initiative. While his nascent plans for national and community service have not yet crystallized, they appear to be modeled mainly after ACTION and the Peace Corps: in general, volunteer service is to be full-time, and participants are to receive a stipend. However, unlike the Peace Corps, which enrolled only about 16,000 volunteers at its zenith, Clinton hopes to enlist hundreds of thousands of volunteers in national and community service and to tie their participation to forgiveness of college loans.

By no means are volunteer programs in the federal government limited to those agencies with a formal mission in this arena. The national government also sponsors 4-H Clubs and extension programs of the Cooperative Extension Service of the Department of Agriculture; the Volunteers in the Parks of the National Park Service of the Department of the Interior; the Income Tax Counseling for the Elderly (TCE) and Volunteer Income Tax Assistance (VITA) programs of the Internal Revenue Service of the Department of the Treasury; and the Service Corps of Retired Executives (SCORE) volunteers of the Small Business Administration. Additional federal agencies which support volunteer programs include the Department of Housing and Urban Development, the Department of Health and Human Services, the Department of Justice, the Department of Transportation, the Environmental Protection Agency, and the Forest Service.

Aside from studies of city and county governments, systematic data are limited on the participation of service volunteers in the public sector. These sources suggest that volunteers assist large numbers of government offices at all levels and that this practice is increasing.

IV.   VOLUNTEER INVOLVEMENT IN THE PUBLIC SECTOR: COSTS AND BENEFITS

In one sense, the increased use of volunteers in the delivery of public services presents an anomaly. Scholars and practitioners alike acknowledge the special burdens this mode of service provision may impose on government organizations. These disadvantages can be organized into three categories.

A.   Potential Disadvantages of Volunteer Involvement

The first set of possible disadvantages centers on funding the volunteer program. Although the labor donated by citizens to public agencies is not compensated monetarily, the support structure essential to harnessing this labor and operating the program effectively does necessitate expenditures. Political jurisdictions and individual agencies may not be prepared (fiscally or psychologically) to underwrite necessary program obligations, such as reimbursement of volunteers' work-related expenses, provision of liability insurance protection, orientation and training of citizens, and so forth—especially for ostensibly "free" services. In addition, paid staff time, a cost to the organization and nearly always at a premium, must normally be devoted to program administration and supervision of volunteers.

A second set of difficulties concerns the putative shortcomings of volunteers as workers. Familiar criticisms accuse volunteers of poor work, high levels of absenteeism and turnover, and unreliability in meeting work commitments. Just as problematic, the recourse to volunteers presumes a sufficient supply of citizens to government agencies to meet their demands for productive labor. But with the growing dependence of the public and nonprofit sectors on volunteers, recruitment may well constitute the most serious obstacle to effective implementation of this approach to service delivery (Duncombe, 1985; Brudney, 1990a).

Third, volunteer programs may precipitate political and labor tensions that undermine the potential benefits of the approach. For example, weak support for the program from top elected or appointed officials, or from department heads and supervisors who must often oversee the volunteers, sends the wrong message to paid staff and citizen participants alike about the legitimate role and value of volunteers. Lack of organizational support or direction can exacerbate natural apprehensions between paid and unpaid staff, jeopardize working relationships crucial to program success, and draw objections from public employee unions. Moreover, by filling in during periods of budgetary cutback and retrenchment, volunteers may inadvertently fuel popular misconceptions regarding the number of paid staff actually needed by an agency to meet work obligations, let alone to perform with full effectiveness.

Nevertheless, the introduction of volunteers may offer substantial compensating benefits to public organizations in four primary areas.

B.   Potential Advantages of Volunteer Involvement

The advantages that have excited greatest attention center on potential economic and productivity gains. First, since a well-designed and operated volunteer program requires expenditures of its own (see above), popular claims that volunteers are the "answer" to deficits in public budgets appear highly exaggerated. In fact, unless cuts are exacted elsewhere in the agency budget, volunteer involvement can add marginally to outlays. Yet, because volunteers promise dramatic saving in labor and fringe benefit costs, their use can help an organization to limit costs in achieving a given level of service, or to boost service quality or amount for a fixed level of expenditure (Karn, 1983; 1982–83). Although this characteristic is often referred to as the "cost savings" potential of volunteer involvement, a more apt term is *cost effectiveness*.

Second, volunteers may assist governments in augmenting capability. The additional labor, skills, and energy brought by citizens can enable organizations to provide services that would otherwise not be possible; increase the level or the kinds of services or programs offered; and buttress operations in emergency and peak load periods. Volunteers contribute to the resource base necessary for innovation in government. In addition, they can bolster agency ability to do more with available resources. As the coproduction literature has long observed, not only can citizens supplement the work of public employees, but also they can relieve service agents of routine functions, thus freeing them to pursue the tasks for which their professional training and expertise qualify them (e.g., Parks et al., 1981). As a result, their work may have greater effectiveness.

A volunteer contingent offers public organizations further economic benefits. Although experts caution that volunteering should not be treated as a credentialing process for paid employment with an agency, trained volunteers are an attractive and convenient source of proven recruits. President Clinton has repeatedly cited this advantage of his proposed plan for national and community service—to create a huge new corps of police officer and teacher trainees who will eventually occupy paid positions.

Third, volunteers may raise the quality of government services. For example, they may bring to the public workplace specialized skills (e.g., legal, computer, technical) not possessed by employees that yield improvements in services or programs. Many volunteers find rewarding personal contact with service recipients; in national surveys, the motivation expressed most frequently for volunteering is to do something useful to help other people (e.g., Hodgkinson et al., 1992). By devoting detailed attention to agency clients—time which agency personnel frequently lack—volunteers may personalize and enhance the delivery of public services. Clary (1987) shows that more readily than employees, volunteers are able to build relationships with clients characterized by acceptance, approval, empathy, care, regard, respect, understanding, and trust. Through interaction with service recipients, volunteers can help to "humanize" the delivery of governmental services, lending them a more personalized and informal quality (e.g., Wineburg and Wineburg, 1987; Naylor, 1985). Not only does the emotional support provided by volunteers help to raise clients' self-esteem and self-confidence; it also increases the willingness to accept and profit from the tangible forms of assistance offered by government organizations.

Finally, volunteer involvement can yield substantial benefits to an agency and its leadership in the community. A sound volunteer program can build the job skills and experience of participants; improve relations with the citizenry; and promote greater public awareness of the pressures and constraints on government. For example, a study of literacy programs in California reveals that library administrators enlisted volunteers as a strategy to expand their base of activities, develop and consolidate political support among elected officials and the larger community, and enhance the credibility and attractiveness of library programs (Walter, 1993). Volunteer participation offers other practical advantages through generating advice and guidance on government programs and activities, and by increasing public support for these endeavors.

Volunteers can also engage in critical support functions with external constituencies normally precluded to government employees, such as fundraising and lobbying. Despite possible apprehension surrounding their use, volunteers have proven effective advocates of agency interests who help to further organizational missions, achieve increased appropriations, and thereby preserve government budgets and paid positions (e.g., Marando, 1986). Lobbying campaigns by volunteers helped to shield the California public library system from the depredations of Proposition 13 (Walter, 1987) and the U.S. Small Business Administration from repeated attacks by President Reagan and his appointees (Brudney, 1990b). The exposure of citizens to the public sector through volunteering appears to breed respect and approbation rather than contempt or ridicule. No evidence exists that volunteers are motivated by a desire to cut government budgets (or staff); on the contrary, they are much more likely to press for increases in the policy domains where they have chosen to give their time and talents.

Through volunteering, citizens identify policy arenas that they believe require greater attention; offer feedback to public administrators on community conditions; and expand agency capability to provide services and assistance in response to these needs. One citizen participant writes that "frontline volunteers . . . know what's going on and are more willing to tell you what is as distinguished from what you might prefer to hear" (Williams, 1993b, p. 11). Most volunteers live in the communities where they donate their time and possess some familiarity with local resources and formal and informal helping networks. Using this knowledge, public organizations can engage more effectively in outreach and case finding in the community, as well as tailoring assistance to individual circumstances. In sum, volunteers assist in making governmental institutions more accessible to the citizenry.

C. Realization of Costs and Benefits from Volunteer Involvement

Although the above listing of costs and benefits is often attributed to volunteer involvement, surprisingly little research has examined how prevalently these disadvantages and advantages are actually realized by governments that use the approach. Despite the mounting interest of elected officials, public administrators, and academic researchers in volunteers, few studies have systematically evaluated these effects in large representative samples of public organizations or jurisdictions. In fact, just two surveys of local governments that enlist volunteers have addressed the issue: a national survey of 534 cities completed by Sydney Duncombe (1985) and a more recent survey of 250 Georgia localities by Jeffrey L. Brudney (1993). While Duncombe questioned cities on only four potential benefits of the approach and six reputed problems, Brudney probed a much more extensive inventory of 14 advantages and a like number of disadvantages.

The surveys reveal very comparable results regarding the costs and benefits to governments of involving volunteers in the delivery of services. By a substantial margin, the most common drawback to volunteer participation reported by local officials is recruitment ("getting enough people to volunteer"), cited by 39% of Georgia's local governments and 56.2% of Duncombe's (1985) national sample.

The next most frequently mentioned set of problems stem from funding the volunteer program. Approximately one in five of the Georgia local governments listed as disadvantages providing liability insurance for volunteers (22%, vs. 21% in the national survey), a general lack of funding for the program (20%), and inadequate funds for reimbursement of the work-related expenses of volunteers (19%). Nearly as many pointed to insufficient time for paid staff to train and supervise volunteers properly (16%).

Local governments apparently encounter the putative shortcomings attributed to volunteers as workers somewhat less often. Just 5% of the Georgia sample mentioned as a disadvantage poor work by volunteers (6% in the national survey); 12% cited high turnover and 14% unreliability in meeting work commitments. Problems with volunteer absenteeism seem a bit more common, cited by 17% of the Georgia sample (16% in the national survey).

Among the Georgia local governments, the political and labor difficulties sometimes associated with volunteer involvement occur with very low frequency. A scant 8% of the sample reported that use of volunteers had led to misconceptions by the citizenry regarding the number of paid staff needed by government. Slightly less acknowledged problems arising from lack of support for the program from department heads or supervisors (7% vs. 16% in the national survey) or from top elected or appointed officials (5%). Remarkably, just 3% mentioned poor working relationships or mistrust between paid and unpaid staff members; none of the Georgia localities cited union objections to the use of volunteer workers.

With respect to the perceived advantages of volunteer involvement in the delivery of public services, the most common benefit perceived is cost savings, reported by 82% of localities in both the Georgia and national samples. High percentages also cite advantages in the categories of expanding government capability, improving community relations, and enhancing service quality.

In the first of these areas, 64% of the Georgia local governments reported that volunteers had enabled them to provide services that would otherwise not be possible. Almost half (48%) indicated that volunteers had allowed them to do more with available resources. Approximately one in four noted that use of volunteers had led to an increase in the level of services or programs offered (28%), expansion of staff in emergencies and peak load periods (27%), and expansion in the kinds of services or programs provided (22%).

The participation of volunteers in government services also appears to have a salient effect on relations with the community. About half of the Georgia localities stated that volunteer involvement had led to improvements in community relations in general (48%) and to greater public support for government programs (46%, vs. 25% nationally). Less frequently mentioned as benefits, volunteers raised public awareness of the pressures and constraints on government (28%) and provided useful advice and guidance on programs (24%). Approximately one-third of these governments indicated that volunteers had gained valuable job skills and experience from their involvement (31%).

Finally, volunteers contributed to perceived enhancements in the quality of public services. According to the findings from the Georgia study, benefits in this category arise principally from the specialized skills possessed by volunteers applied in service to government (34%, vs. 40% in the national survey) and general improvements in the quality of public services and programs (32%). While few of the Georgia localities seemingly recognize the benefits that volunteers might generate through devoting more detailed attention to clients (8%), a much larger percentage in the national survey did so (45%).

The findings from these surveys support two primary conclusions regarding the costs and benefits local governments likely derive from the participation of volunteers in the delivery of services. First, they help to explain why volunteer involvement has increased over the past decade and to resolve the anomaly with which this section began: The volunteer approach certainly has its limitations, but these drawbacks apparently occur with much lower frequency than the anticipated benefits of the method. While a possible element of rationalization should be acknowledged in the responses (government officials may want to assure themselves that the benefits outweigh the costs), the great similarity in results from two distinct surveys (with very different samples, items, and time points) defies a simple interpretation as mere artifact.

Second and notwithstanding, the potential benefits of volunteer involvement are not realized universally by local governments. Variation across these institutions in the adoption and implementation of appropriate techniques for administration and management of the volunteer program may be responsible (see Brudney and Brown, 1993). These elements are discussed below.

V. DESIGN AND MANAGEMENT OF THE VOLUNTEER PROGRAM

A volunteer program is a vehicle for facilitating and coordinating the work of volunteers and paid staff toward the attainment of agency goals. The core program functions consist of:

Establishing the rationale for volunteer involvement
Involving paid staff in volunteer program design
Integrating the volunteer program into the organization
Creating leadership positions for the volunteer program
Preparing job descriptions for volunteer positions
Recruiting volunteers
Meeting the needs of volunteers
Managing volunteers
Evaluating and recognizing the volunteer effort

A.   Establishing the Rationale for Volunteer Involvement

No matter how overburdened an organization, constrained its human and financial resources, eager for fresh input and innovation, and enthusiastic about the potential contribution of citizens, its volunteer program should not begin with recruitment. An agency must resist the temptation to enlist volunteers until the groundwork for their sustained involvement has been put in place. Unfortunately, well-intentioned but premature calls for help can breed apprehension among paid staff and frustration among volunteers, and, worse still, exacerbate the very problems volunteerism was intended to solve. Such a result would reinforce negative stereotypes about volunteers and undermine their credibility as a vital service resource; it must be circumvented.

The initial step in planning the volunteer program should be to determine the purposes for introducing the new participants into the organization. The foundation for an effective program rests on a serious consideration by the agency of the rationale for citizen involvement and the development of a philosophy or policy to guide this effort.

As demonstrated above, volunteers can offer a variety of advantages to public agencies. While officials may center on cost savings as the catalyst for seeking volunteers, additional or different purposes may drive a volunteer program. Organizational leadership may pursue volunteers to interject a more vibrant dimension of commitment and caring into its relationships with clients. Or, the goal may be to learn more about the community, nurture closer ties to citizens, and strengthen public awareness and support. Volunteers may be needed to reach clients inaccessible through normal organizational channels, i.e., to engage in "outreach" activities (e.g., May et al., 1991; Dorwaldt et al., 1988; Young et al., 1986). They may be called on to provide professional skills, such as computer programming, legal counsel, or accounting expertise, not readily available to an agency. The purpose may be to staff an experimental or pilot program otherwise doomed to fiscal austerity. Enhancing responsiveness to client groups offers yet another rationale.

Agencies have also recognized the merit of volunteers in the area of fund or resource raising. Because the public tends to perceive them as neutral participants who will not directly benefit from monetary donations to an agency, organizations very frequently engage citizens for this task. In a 1989 national survey, nearly half (48%) of volunteers reported assignments in fundraising (Hodgkinson et al., 1992, p. 46).

At this initial stage, public officials need to review carefully statute law and or organizational policy that may impact prospective volunteer involvement. One particularly noteworthy example is a federal regulation that proscribes national agencies from using volunteers, except in emergency situations affecting the safety of human life or the protection of property, unless a law has been passed specifically exempting the agency (Title 31, Section 1342 of the United States Code). Congress has overridden the provision in a number of instances. Case studies attest that organizational policy can exert comparable effects on volunteer involvement, either to retard a program (Utterback and Heyman, 1984) or to strengthen and promote it (Holme and Maizels, 1978).

The large number of possible purposes that can be met by a volunteer program attests to the vitality of the approach. Before seeking volunteers, agency leaders should settle on the ends for their organization. An explicit statement of goals advances several important facets of program design and functioning. First, it begins to define the types of volunteer positions that will be needed and the number of individuals required to fill these roles. Second, it aids in delineating concrete objectives against which the program might be evaluated once in operation.

Finally, a formal statement of the philosophy underlying volunteer involvement and the specific ends sought can help to alleviate possible apprehensions of paid staff concerning, for example, professional prerogatives and job security. Clarifying the goals for volunteer participation can help to check negative speculation and begin to build a sense of program ownership on the part of employees—especially if they are included in planning for the volunteer program.

B. Involving Paid Staff in Volunteer Program Design

A precept in the field of organizational development is to include groups to be affected by a new policy or program in its design and implementation. Involvement builds the knowledge base for developing policy and inculcates a sense of ownership and commitment very useful in gaining acceptance for innovation.

Because the introduction of volunteers into an agency can impose dramatic changes in work life, the participation of paid staff is especially important (Graff, 1984, p. 17). The sharing of needs, perspectives, and information among agency leadership, employees, and prospective volunteers that ensues plays a pivotal role in determining how the volunteer program might be most effectively designed, organized, and managed to further attainment of agency goals. At the same time, the process helps to alleviate any concerns paid staff may harbor regarding volunteer involvement and its implications for the workplace.

Participants in planning sessions should work to develop policies and procedures governing volunteer involvement. Agency guidelines should address all aspects of volunteer participation, including attendance and absenteeism, performance review, grievance procedures, record keeping, reimbursement, confidentiality requirements, suspension and termination, and so forth (McCurley and Lynch, 1989, p. 22). In all areas, policies should be as comparable as possible to pertinent guidelines for employees.

The establishment of explicit policies for volunteers is associated with positive results for citizen participants, the agency, and clients. Such policies demonstrate that the agency takes volunteer involvement seriously and values its contribution to goal attainment. By setting standards as high for volunteers as for paid staff, an agency builds trust and credibility, increased respect and requests for volunteers from employees, a healthy work environment, and, perhaps most important, high-quality services (e.g., Wilson, 1984; Deitch and Thompson, 1985; Goetter, 1987; McCurley and Lynch, 1989). As one long-time volunteer states, "Administration should desire and continually express the need for high standards. Everyone prefers being involved in an organization he or she can be proud of and brag about" (Williams, 1993a, p. 8).

Formal guidelines and expectations for the volunteer program greatly facilitate the tasks of managing for consistent results, handling problem situations, protecting volunteer rights, and motivating performance. Explicit policies for the program help to solidify the "psychological contract" linking volunteers to the agency and thus may reduce turnover. In one study, Jone L. Pearce (1978, pp. 276–277) found that those organizations most successful in clarifying the volunteer–agency relationship enjoyed the lowest rates of turnover. While these agencies distributed notebooks with all written policies, formal job descriptions, and training manuals to citizen participants, the organization with the highest turnover in Pearce's sample did not have this information available.

Although volunteers may not yet be known to the agency and thus involved in initial discussions concerning program planning and design, once this effort is launched and in operation, they should definitely have input into major decisions affecting the program. Just as for paid employees, citizens are more likely to invest in and commit to organizational policies and provide useful information for this purpose if they enjoy ready access to the decision-making process.

Participation in decision making is a key element of the "empowerment" movement in volunteer administration. The term has not been defined with precision, but it connotes a genuine sharing of control over the volunteer program with citizen participants; more attentive listening to volunteer ideas and preferences; and greater recognition of the time, skills, and value provided to organizations through this approach. Empowerment is thought to result in increased ownership of the volunteer program by participants and, hence, greater commitment and effectiveness (for a full discussion, see Scheier, 1988–89, 1988a, 1988b; Naylor, 1985).

C. Integrating the Volunteer Program into the Organization

As these comments suggest, the volunteer program must be organized to respond to the motivations and requirements of both volunteers and employees. With respect to volunteers, the program should have mechanisms for determining the types of work opportunities sought and meeting those preferences, and for engendering an organizational climate in which volunteers can pursue their goals with the acceptance (if not always the avid endorsement) of paid personnel. From the perspective of staff, the program must have structures and procedures in place to assume the task of volunteer administration and to generate a pool of capable citizens matched to the tasks of participating offices and departments.

To accomplish these goals, the volunteer program must be linked to the structure of the organization. While a small agency may accommodate volunteers with minimal structural adaptations, larger organizations need to consider alternative structural configurations for integrating volunteers into their operations (Valente and Manchester, 1984, pp. 56–57). In order of increasing comprehensiveness, these arrangements are: ad hoc volunteer efforts; volunteer recruitment by an outside organization with the agency otherwise responsible for management; decentralization of the program to operating departments; and a centralized approach.

Volunteer efforts may arise spontaneously in an ad hoc fashion to meet exigencies confronting an organization, especially on a short-term basis. Often, citizens motivated to share their background, training, and skills with organizations that need them are the catalyst. Fiscal stress, leaving an agency few options, may quicken the helping impulse. The Service Corps of Retired Executives (SCORE), an association of primarily retired businesspersons who donate their time and skills to assist the U.S. Small Business Administration (SBA) began in this manner in the early 1960s, when a group of retirees approached the SBA to offer assistance in treating its huge constituency (Brudney, 1987). The responsiveness and alacrity with which an ad hoc effort can be launched and operating are inspiring. Within 6 months of its inception, SCORE supplied 2000 volunteers to the SBA; in even less time, in response to a federal court order, the State of Alabama had deployed biracial teams of volunteer trainers to teach new federal requirements to election poll workers (Montjoy and Brudney, 1991). Crisis and emergency situations can provoke an even more spectacular response from volunteers.

Spontaneous help from citizens can infuse vitality (and labor) into an agency and educate officials to the possibilities of volunteerism. Offsetting these advantages, however, is the fact that only selected parts or members of the organization may be aware of an ad hoc citizen effort and, thus, involve volunteers. Moreover, because levels of energy and zeal ebb as emergencies are tamed or fade from the limelight of publicity or attention, the ad hoc model of volunteer involvement is very vulnerable to the passage of time. A volunteer program requires not only a different type of ongoing, rather than sporadic, commitment from citizens, but also an organizational structure to sustain their contributions and make them accessible to all departments and employees. Unless the agency takes steps to institutionalize participation, it risks squandering the long-term benefits of the approach.

A second option for an agency is to rely on the expertise and reputation of an established organization, such as the United Way and its affiliates, or a voluntary action center or a volunteer clearing house, to recruit volunteers, but to retain all other managerial responsibilities internally. Since recruitment is the most fundamental program function and, arguably, the most problematic, regular professional assistance in this area can be highly desirable. This arrangement can be particularly useful to an agency just starting a volunteer program. Some organizations have extended this model to contract with local volunteer centers for a much greater range of program functions (Haran et al., 1993).

As in the delegation of any organizational function, however, quality control presents a necessary caution. Recruiters must be familiar with the needs of government for voluntary assistance to ensure that referrals approximate the desired profile of backgrounds, interests, and skills. A recruiter may also deal with several client organizations, so that the priority attached to the requests of any one of them is unclear. More importantly, trusting recruitment to another organization is a deterrent to developing the necessary capacity internally—which is an essential aspect of a successful volunteer program. While public organizations should nurture positive relationships with community agencies to attract volunteers and for many other purposes, they should endeavor to build and implement their own mechanisms for recruitment as well.

A volunteer program can be decentralized to individual departments within an organization. The primary advantage of this approach is the flexibility to tailor programs to the needs of specific organizational units and to introduce volunteers where support for them is greatest. Yet, duplication of effort across several departments, difficulties in locating sufficient expertise in volunteer management to staff multiple programs, and problems in coordination—particularly restrictions on the ability to shift volunteers to more suitable positions or to offer them opportunities for job enrichment across the organization—are significant liabilities. The selective approach can also unwittingly generate disincentives for managers to introduce volunteers (Brudney, 1989, p. 117). Top agency officials may mistakenly equate nonpaid work with "unimportant" activities to the detriment of a particular department or manager, or they may seize on the willingness to enlist volunteers as a pretext to deny a unit essential increases in budget and paid personnel.

Despite these limitations, the decentralized approach may serve an agency quite well in starting a volunteer program. The results of this effort might guide the organization in moving toward more extensive implementation. Alternatively, a lack of tasks appropriate for volunteers across the agency, or, perhaps, strong opposition from various quarters, may confine voluntary assistance to selected departments.

The final structural arrangement is a centralized volunteer program serving the entire agency. In this model, a single office or department is responsible for management and coordination of the program, with volunteers deployed and supervised in line departments. The office provides guidelines, technical assistance, screening, training, and all other administration for volunteer activity throughout the agency. The advantages of centralization for averting duplication of effort, assigning volunteers to meet their own needs as well as those of the organization, and producing efficient and effective voluntary services are considerable. Yet, the success of this design rests on attaining broad support for volunteer involvement across the organization, especially from top management. If such backing is not forthcoming, the other structural arrangements may serve the agency admirably.

D. Creating Leadership Positions for the Volunteer Program

Regardless of the structural arrangement utilized to integrate the volunteer program into an agency, this component requires a visible, recognized leader. All program functions benefit from the establishment and staffing of a position bearing overall responsibility for management and representation of the volunteers. The position goes by a variety of names, but here it is called *director of volunteer services* (DVS) to signify the importance of the role.

The manner by which the office is staffed sends a forceful message to employees regarding the significance of the volunteer program to the agency and its leadership. While organizations have experimented with a variety of staffing options (e.g., paid personnel who have other primary duties), none so manifestly demonstrates a sense of organizational commitment and purpose as does a paid DVS position. Establishing the office as close to the apex of the formal hierarchy as feasible reinforces the sense of resolve. Unfortunately, available evidence suggests that agencies do not routinely attend to necessary supports for the position (for a review, see Brudney, 1992, pp. 272–273).

The DVS should enjoy prerogatives and responsibilities commensurate with positions at the same level of the organizational hierarchy, including participation in relevant decision and policymaking, and access to superiors. In this manner, the incumbent can represent the volunteers before the relevant department(s) or the organization as a whole, promote their interests, and gain greater use and recognition of volunteers. A part-time or full-time (as necessary) paid position lodges accountability for the program squarely with the DVS; presents a focal point for contact with the volunteer operation for those inside as well as outside the organization; implements a core structure for program administration; and rewards the officeholder in relation to the success of the volunteers.

Other important duties further substantiate the need for a dedicated DVS position (Ellis, 1986, pp. 45–49). The DVS is responsible for volunteer recruitment and publicity, a critical function requiring active outreach in the community. The incumbent must communicate with departmental and organizational officials to ascertain workloads and requirements for voluntary assistance. Assessing agency needs for volunteers, enlarging areas for their involvement, and educating staff to the approach are not a one-time exercise, but an ongoing responsibility of the DVS. The DVS interviews and screens all applicants for volunteer positions, maintains appropriate records, places volunteers in job assignments, provides liaison supervision, and monitors performance. The office must coordinate the bewildering array of schedules, backgrounds, and interests brought by volunteers to an agency. The DVS bears overall responsibility for orientation and training, and evaluation and recognition, of volunteers. Since employees are typically unfamiliar with volunteer administration, training may need to extend to them as well; the DVS is the in-house source of expertise on all facets of volunteer involvement and management. As the chief advocate of the program, the DVS endeavors not only to express the volunteer perspective but also to allay any apprehensions of paid staff and to facilitate productive working relationships.

Given the number and importance of the duties assigned to the DVS, as the volunteer effort increases in size, additional positions of program leadership will likely need to be created. Paid employees might staff these positions, but they also offer strong empowerment and growth prospects for especially dedicated volunteers (see above).

E. Preparing Job Descriptions for Volunteer Positions

The fundamental building block of a thriving volunteer program is the job description. Pardoxically, no intrinsic basis exists to create or classify a position as paid or volunteer. Even among agencies that have the same purpose or mission, or that work in the same substantive or policy domain, a given position can be classified differently (e.g., computer programmer, day care provider, receptionist). Within an agency, moreover, job definitions are dynamic, so that volunteers can give way to paid service professionals in some areas (e.g., Becker, 1964; Schwartz, 1977; Park, 1983; Ellis and Noyes, 1990) and gain responsibility from them in others (e.g., Brudney, 1987).

Absent an intrinsic basis to designate a task or position as volunteer or paid, the *process* by which work responsibilities are allocated assumes paramount importance. As elaborated above, the most enduring method is for top agency officials and employees (and if possible, volunteers) to work out in advance of program implementation explicit understandings regarding the rationale for the involvement of volunteers, the nature of the jobs they are to perform, and the boundaries of their work (Wilson, 1976; Brown, 1981; Graff, 1984; Ellis, 1986). This agreement should designate (or provide the foundation for distinguishing) the jobs assigned to volunteers and those held by paid staff.

A second desirable step in the job design process consists of a survey of employees, or personal interviews, to acquaint them with the potential contributions of volunteers, and to ascertain key factors about their jobs, such as tasks they most enjoy performing, those they dislike, and those for which they lack sufficient time or expertise. Since employees may not have background information regarding the assistance that volunteers might lend to them and to the agency, the survey or interview, or in-service training, should provide resource material regarding volunteers, such as a listing of the jobs that unpaid staff are already performing in their agency or in similar organizations (compare McCurley and Lynch, 1989, pp. 27–28).

Contrary to popular stereotypes, not all volunteer positions are in supportive roles to employee jobs. In some Maryland counties, paid staff support the activities of volunteers in delivering recreation services rather than the reverse (Marando, 1986), and at the SBA, paid staff facilitate the work of volunteers who counsel agency clients on sound business practices (Brudney, 1987, 1990). Many organizations rely on donated labor for highly technical, professional tasks, such as accounting, economic development, and computer applications. The crucial factor in the delegation of tasks is that the parties take into account the unique capabilities that staff and volunteers might each bring to meeting organizational needs and goals.

To allocate work responsibilities efficiently among employees and volunteers, Ellis (1986, pp. 89–90) recommends that an agency reassess the job descriptions of paid staff. Prime candidates for delegation to volunteers are tasks with the following characteristics:

Those performed periodically, such as once a week, rather than on a daily or inflexible basis
Those that do not require the specialized training or expertise of paid personnel
Those that might be done more effectively by someone with specialized training in that skill
Those for which the position occupant feels uncomfortable or unprepared
Those for which the agency lacks in-house expertise
Those that can be performed in concentrated time blocks conducive to a part-time schedule

The intent of these guidelines is to achieve the most effective deployment of both paid and nonpaid personnel. The respective tasks should be codified in formal job descriptions not only for paid but also nonpaid workers. Accompanying the two sets of job descriptions should be an explicit proviso that neither group will occupy the positions reserved for the other.

Studies undertaken by the International City–County Management Association on volunteer programs in local governments indicate that "volunteer job descriptions are really no different than job descriptions for paid personnel. A volunteer will need the same information a paid employee would need to determine whether the position is of interest" (Manchester and Bogart, 1988, p. 59). Specifications for volunteer positions should include job title and purpose; benefits to occupant; qualifications for position; time requirement (e.g., hours per week); proposed starting date (and ending date, if applicable); job responsibilities and activities; authority invested in the position; and reporting relationships and supervision.

The job description provides the foundation for other key elements of the volunteer program. Based on the description, applicants for volunteer positions should be *screened* for relevant competencies and interests, as well as pertinent background and qualifications. They should be *interviewed* by officials from the volunteer program and/or the agency to ensure a suitable fit of citizen and organizational needs. These new members will require an *orientation* to the agency and its volunteer component. Among the topics that orientation activities should address are the overall mission and specific objectives of the organization, its traditions and philosophy, its operating rules and procedures, the distinctive environment of the public sector (e.g., norms of accountability, accessibility, equity, and due process), the rationale and policies of the volunteer program, and the roles and interface of paid and nonpaid staff members. Finally, as needed, *training* should be provided to citizens to assume the tasks outlined in volunteer job descriptions.

F. Recruiting Volunteers

As discussed above, recruitment of citizens is likely the largest obstacle to a viable volunteer program. Yet, in a series of national surveys conducted by the Gallup Organization over the past decade, approximately half of the U.S. populace report volunteering in the past year. Close examination of the series reveals, however, that with respect to the aims of building or sustaining volunteer programs in government, the estimated rate is markedly inflated (Brudney, 1990a). It includes all acts of volunteering, both formal (to an organization) and informal (outside of organizational auspices), regular (on a continuous basis) or sporadic (one time only or episodic), and to all types of institutions (secular or religious). After correcting for these factors, Brudney (1990a) estimates that the effective pool of volunteers for public agencies is probably only about one-third the size suggested by the national surveys. Moreover, this group is highly prized not only by government but by nonprofit organizations and an increasing number of private businesses.

A long-term strategy for recruiting volunteers is the development of an organizational culture that welcomes and recognizes them as full partners in attending to agency missions, goals, and clients. This process should begin with an explicit statement of the philosophy and goals underlying the volunteer program, codified in agency policy (see above). More immediate steps than the often painfully slow one of creating a receptive organizational culture are open to public managers as well.

The most persuasive recruitment mechanism is the availability of nonpaid positions that appeal to the needs of potential volunteers, especially for challenge, interesting or meaningful work, personal growth, career exploration, and/or social interaction. Such an admonition can easily be misinterpreted to mean that every volunteer job must present close contact with clients, ample opportunity for self-expression, ready means for acquisition of job skills, and so on—but that implication is erroneous. Because volunteers are richly diverse in the ends sought through this activity, public (and other) organizations will enjoy success in recruiting them to the degree that they can offer a range of jobs to appeal to a diversity of motivations. An organization should no more allocate exclusively routine, repetitive tasks to volunteers than it should place volunteers solely in highly ambitious work assignments.

Public managers can turn to other practical methods to stimulate recruitment. Facilitation strategies include extending the opportunity to volunteer beyond traditional working hours (evenings and weekends); reimbursement of all out-of-pocket expenses incurred by volunteers, including meals and child care; providing nonpaid jobs that can be performed outside the agency (e.g., in the home or automobile); placing a fixed term on a job assignment, subject to renewal by the volunteer and the agency; and encouraging volunteer activity on a group basis (e.g., by the family, church/synagogue, club/association, and work or other organization). Group-based volunteering allows participants to transport a known, supportive environment to the activity. Recruiters of volunteers should not hesitate to look in their own backyard. As Table 1 shows, many volunteers either received service previously from the organization or program, or have a friend or relative involved in the program or who benefits from it.

No matter how worthwhile their volunteer programs (or how desperate or obvious the need for citizen assistance), public managers should not assume that citizens will take the initiative to learn about them and to commit their time. According to the national Gallup surveys, only about one in five volunteers seek out the activity on their own. By contrast, most are asked to become involved by someone participating in the program or benefiting from it. Thus, public managers must practice outreach. Agency officials should make every effort to publicize the volunteer program and its opportunities for service at the workplace, school, church, synagogue, neighborhood group, civic and other associations, and so forth. In addition, because they can relate experience first-hand, satisfied volunteers make excellent recruiters.

G. Meeting the Needs of Volunteers

An effective volunteer program marries organizational demands for productive labor with the disparate motivations that volunteers bring to an agency for donating their time. Voluminous research has been concerned, directly or indirectly, with the motivations that activate volunteers. A major conclusion emanating from this research is that these motivations are complex and

Table 1 Motivations for Involvement in Volunteer Work by Year, 1965–1991 (In Percentages)

Motivation	1965	1974	1981	1985	1987	1989	1991
Help people	37	53	45	52	—	—	70
Do something useful	—	—	—	—	56	62	61
Enjoy doing volunteer work	31	36	29	32	35	34	39
Interest in activity or work	—	—	35	36	—	—	—
Sense of duty	33	32	—	—	—	—	—
Religious concerns	—	—	21	27	22	26	31
Could not refuse request	7	15	—	—	—	—	—
Friend or relative received service[a]	—	22	23	26	27	29	29
Volunteer received service	—	—	—	—	10	9	17
Learning experience[b]	—	3	11	10	9	8	16
Nothing else to do, free time	—	4	6	10	9	10	8
Thought work would keep taxes down	—	—	5	3	—	—	—

[a] In 1974, this category referred exclusively to respondents' children: in 1989, this category stated that a family member or friend would benefit.
[b] In the 1974 study, this category referred to the idea that volunteer work can lead to a paid job.
Note: The percentages do not add up to 100 because respondents were permitted multiple responses. In the 1965 and 1974 surveys, volunteers were asked about the reason for doing their first "nonreligious" volunteer work. In the 1981, 1985, 1987, 1989, and 1991 surveys, the motivations also pertain to "informal" volunteer work, i.e., work that does not involve a private sector association or formal organization.
Source: Much of these data appear in Chambré (1989). The data are adapted from U.S. Department of Labor (1969); ACTION (1974); Gallup Organization (1981); and Hodgkinson and Weitzman (1986, 1988, 1990, 1992).

mutifaceted, and that they may serve a variety of functions for the individual volunteer, including values, understanding, career, social, esteem, and protective dimensions (Clary et al., 1992).

Although the reasons for volunteering are rich and diverse, several large, national surveys extending back a quarter of a century reveal a markedly consistent and interpretable pattern of professed motivations. Table 1 displays the reasons for involvement in volunteer work expressed most often by representative samples of Americans in seven different surveys, the earliest taken in 1965 and the most recent in 1992.

According to these data, the most common stimulus for volunteering is to "do something useful to help others" or to "help people", stated by nearly a majority of respondents and usually more in each survey. Approximately one in four mention "religious concerns" as a reason for their volunteer activity. About 10% of volunteers, rising to 17% in 1991, state as a motivation that they had previously benefited from the activity; perhaps their volunteer work is motivated by a desire to "give something back" for the services they had earlier received.

While such altruistic motivations appear to drive a great amount of volunteering, more instrumental motivations, such as "enjoy doing volunteer work" and "had an interest in the activity or work," are prominent as well. In the survey findings summarized in Table 1, between 29% and 39% of respondents professed these motivations. Similarly, in the surveys conducted in the 1980s and in 1992, another 8–11% identified volunteering as a learning experience. The educational or training benefits of this opportunity are especially important to individuals who seek entry or reentry into the job market. In addition, a substantial number of volunteers (22–29%) state that they have a friend or relative either involved in the activity in which they volunteer or who would benefit from it.

The data in Table 1 suggest that many people seem to hold simultaneously both other-directed and self-interested motivations for volunteering. In order to capture some of the richness of these motivations, the surveys allowed multiple responses, and in each survey the cumulative percentages surpass 100.0%. Volunteering thus appears to spring from a mixture of altruistic and instrumental motivations. Volunteers can—and most likely do—pursue both types of rewards at the same time. One can certainly help others, derive strong interest and satisfaction in the work, learn and grow from the experience, and enjoy the company of friends and coworkers in the process. Jon Van Til (1988, pp. 1–9) observes that volunteering is helping behavior deemed beneficial by participants, even though this action "may contribute to individual goals of career exploration and development, sociability, and other forms of personal enhancement."

The data in Table 1 seem to dash another stereotype regarding volunteer involvement. Although public officials frequently turn to volunteers to achieve cost savings, this motivation is not widely shared by citizens. Very few of them apparently engage in this activity with the motivation to spare organizational funds or the conviction that their "work would keep taxes down" (only 3–5% of volunteers).

Research suggests that as volunteers join organizations and contribute time, their motivations evolve. While strong altruistic or service motivations may lead individuals to seek productive outlets for donating labor, as might be expected, once they have begun to assist an organization, the immediate rewards of the work experience—such as the social aspects of volunteering, the characteristics of the job, the potential for self-development, and so forth—tend to rise in salience.

In one study, Pearce (1983) discovered that volunteers from diverse work settings stated that they joined an organization for predominantly service reasons, but that friendships and social interaction became more influential in their decision to remain with it. While the motivations to help others, support organizational goals, and make a contribution decreased in importance (albeit the scores remained at high levels), the rewards of meeting people and enjoying the company of friends and coworkers increased. Similarly, in a study of volunteers to local government, the importance attached by participants to doing something useful to help others or benefiting a family member or friend diminished over time, but interest in or enjoyment of the work grew as a motivation (Sundeen, 1989).

Pearce concludes (1983, p. 148), "The rewards individuals expected from volunteering are often not the rewards most salient to them once they have become volunteers." If not anticipated and addressed, this shift in the expected rewards from the experience can result in rapid and ruinous turnover of volunteers. The volunteer program must be designed to counteract this possibility. Toward this end, agencies should offer entry level counseling and careful placement to assist volunteers in reaching their personal goals and attempt to foster a work environment conducive to their efforts. Training programs and orientation sessions should also present an accurate depiction of the rewards of volunteering with the agency, so that citizens—and the organizations they serve—do not fall prey to unrealistic expectations.

Agencies need to respond to likely changes in the motivations of volunteers. While an organization may have a standard set of activities for recruiting volunteers, retaining them is a dynamic process of reviewing performance, growth, and aspirations with citizen participants, and modifying work assignments accordingly. Depending on the circumstances and preferences of individual volunteers, organizations may offer a variety of inducements to motivate their continued involvement. These include greater contact with clients or service recipients, increased influence in policy development, participation in problem solving and decision making, a series of steps toward greater work responsibilities, opportunities for training, supportive feedback and evaluation, and letters of recommendation and other aids for securing paid employment.

H. Managing Volunteers

In the field of volunteerism, at least one truism bears repeating: managing volunteers is different than managing employees. The basic reason for divergence is that volunteers are much less dependent on the organization than are paid staff members, who must take their livelihood from it. Almost always, volunteers can leave the agency and find comparable opportunities for their labor with far less effort, inconvenience, and uncertainty and apprehension than can employees. As a result, mangers and supervisors do not have as much control over volunteers.

This difference in control helps to explain some oft-noted characteristics of volunteer workers. Volunteers can afford to be more selective in accepting job assignments. Because social interaction seems to heighten the volunteer experience, participants may place high value on this feature of the job and workplace. Volunteers may insist on substantial flexibility in work hours. They may not be as faithful in observance of agency rules and regulations, particularly those they deem burdensome or "red tape." Many volunteers apparently regard these formal aspects of the job and agency as inimical to the spirit and practice of help freely given, and may show little patience with them. Exacerbating this situation is that nearly all who volunteer do so on a part-time basis and, thus, have less access than full-time staff to information about organizational policy, procedures, and changes to them.

Given the relative autonomy of volunteers, a heavy-handed approach to supervision can be expected to elicit antagonism and turnover rather than compliance and productivity. The standard organizational inducements for employees—the three "p's" of pay, promotion, and perquisites—are not operative for volunteers. Similarly, conventional organizational sanctions are likely to prove abortive. For example, referring a problem to hierarchical superiors for resolution or disciplinary action (or threatening to do so) is far less apt to sway volunteers than employees.

While these differences may leave the impression that volunteers cannot be "managed," that inference is erroneous. In fact, the conclusion is decidedly more positive: the foundation for effective management of volunteers rests on applying different techniques and incentives than commonly used for paid employees to motivate and direct work behaviors toward agency goals. Managerial investment in building trust, cooperation, teamwork, challenge, growth, achievement, values, excitement, purpose, and commitment are much more effectual strategies for this purpose than are the conventional methods. Moreover, as Thomas J. Peters and Richard H. Waterman (1982) discuss in their highly influential study *In Search of Excellence*, America's best-run companies use the same approach for paid employees—with enviable results.

Based on a careful examination of a volunteer program servicing a large, urban public library system, Virginia A. Walter (1987, p. 31) found that administrators who embraced this style of "management by partnership" enjoyed greater success in dealing with volunteers and meeting objectives than did officials intent on control. In a major investigation of the volunteer SCORE program sponsored by the Small Business Administration, Brudney (1990, pp. 112–114) reached a similar conclusion. The volunteer business counsellors who assisted the SBA sometimes fit the stereotypes attributed to volunteer workers: they displayed low tolerance for necessary government paperwork and "bureaucracy," uneven knowledge of SBA rules and procedures, and keen interest in deciding what cases they would accept or reject for counseling. Nevertheless, SBA staff rated the performance of the volunteers as comparable to their own on signal dimensions, including quality and timeliness of service to clients, and dependability in meeting work commitments. Like Walter (1987), Brudney (1990) attributes these beneficial results to the partnership approach to managing the volunteer program adopted by the SBA and SCORE. While the agency provides general oversight and support to the program, it entrusts substantial autonomy and discretion to the volunteers.

Underlying the partnership model must be a framework to facilitate the task of volunteer supervision. In particular, government agencies must elucidate the behaviors expected from nonpaid staff to channel volunteer talents and energies productively. Toward this end, SCORE utilizes such devices as screening, orientation, training, and instructional materials (handbooks, videos, and so forth); it also stipulates a probationary period for new members and standards of volunteer activity and conduct necessary to maintain full-membership status. The procedures discussed earlier in this chapter complement these techniques for building mutual understanding of the volunteer–agency relationship. Developing a coherent philosophy for volunteer involvement, preparing guidelines for the volunteer program, creating formal positions for volunteers, preparing the relevant job descriptions, and interviewing applicants and placing them in mutually satisfactory work assignments are potent means to define what volunteer service means to the agency and to citizens, and to coordinate the needs and motives of both parties. Probably no factor aids more in supervising volunteers (or paid staff) than placing them in positions where they can put their strongest motivations and best skills to work.

In short, effective management of volunteers calls for more than changes in managerial style, although these adjustments are certainly important. The volunteer program must also provide a structure to impart a shared conception of volunteer service. Absent such a framework, managerial adaptations in themselves are likely to prove unavailing.

I. Evaluating and Recognizing the Volunteer Effort

According to researchers, the evaluation function is carried out less often and less well than other central elements of the volunteer program (e.g., Utterback and Heyman, 1984; Allen, 1987). A national survey of 534 cities over 4500 population that involve volunteers in service delivery found that only a handful (11.6%) had made or sponsored an evaluation study (Duncombe, 1985, p. 363). A survey of Georgia local governments (Brudney and Brown, 1993) confirmed that evaluation of the volunteer program is not a common practice (undertaken by 4.8% of these units). Understandably, organizations that rely on the assistance of volunteers may be reluctant to appear to question through evaluation the worth or impact of well-intentioned helping efforts. In addition, officials may be apprehensive about the effects of an evaluation policy on volunteer recruitment and retention, and on public relations. Nevertheless, for individual volunteers and the paid staff who work with them, as well as for the overall volunteer program, evaluation and recognition are essential activities.

The fears of organizational leadership notwithstanding, volunteers have cogent reasons to view appraisal of their work favorably. A powerful motivation for volunteering is to achieve worthwhile and credible results; evaluation can guide volunteers toward improvement on this dimension. No citizen contributes his or her time to have the labor wasted in misdirected activity, or to repeat easily remedied mistakes and misjudgments. That an organization might take one's work so lightly as to countenance such wasteful behavior is an insult to the volunteer and an affront to standards of professionalism underlying effectiveness on the job. If allowed to persist, this behavior can erode the foundations of expected conduct essential to management of the volunteer program (see above).

Evaluation of performance, moreover, is actually a form of compliment to the volunteer (Ellis, 1986, pp. 81–82). A sincere effort at appraisal indicates that the work merits review, and that the individual has the capability and will to do a better job. For many who contribute their time, volunteering offers an opportunity to acquire or hone desirable job skills and/or to build an attractive resumé for purposes of paid employment. To deny constructive feedback to those who give their time for organizational purposes, and who could benefit from this knowledge and hope to do so, is a disservice to the volunteer.

Government agencies can utilize several approaches for evaluating volunteer performance. Perhaps most often the volunteer's supervisor will prepare the appraisal. Alternatively, the responsibility may rest with the director of volunteer services or with the personnel department in larger organizations. A combination of these officials might also handle the task. To broaden this agency-based perspective, volunteers might evaluate their own accomplishment and experience in the agency. The assessment should tap volunteer satisfaction with important facets of the work assignment, including job duties, schedule, support, training, opportunities for personal growth, and so on. The self-assessment is also a valuable tool to obtain feedback on the management and supervision of volunteers; employees should learn from the process as well. Regardless of the type of evaluation, the goal ought to be to ascertain the degree to which the needs and expectations of the volunteer and the agency are met, so that job assignments can be continued, amended, or redefined as necessary.

Agency officials might recognize and show their appreciation to volunteers through a great variety of activities: award or social events (luncheons, banquets, ceremonies), media attention (newsletters, newspapers), certificates (for tenure or exceptional achievement), expansion of opportunities (for learning, training, management), and, especially, personal expressions of gratitude from employees or clients. A heart-felt "thank you" may be all the acknowledgement many volunteers want or need. Others desire more formal recognition. The director of volunteer services should make letters of recommendation available to all volunteers who request them. Recognition is a highly variable activity that optimally should be tailored to the wants and needs of individual volunteers. It should be ongoing rather than reserved for special occasions.

Some agencies choose to recognize volunteers who both demonstrate very strong aptitude for a paid position and seek employment by considering them for job vacancies (e.g., police auxiliaries). One of the advantages of a solid volunteer program is that it will often help participants build or augment job skills (see above). One volunteer administrator refers to this process as a "try-before-you-buy" opportunity for the organization (Thornburg, 1992, p. 20). The advantages afforded by this policy notwithstanding, volunteering should not be seen as a necessary credential or requirement for paid employment with an organization.

In general, volunteer-based services require the participation not only of citizens but also paid staff. If organizational officials are committed to having volunteers and employees work as partners, program functions of evaluation and recognition should apply to both members of the team. Though frequently overlooked in job analysis, employees expected to work with volunteers should have pertinent responsibilities written into their formal job descriptions. Equally important, performance appraisal for the designated positions must assess requisite skills in volunteer management. Just as demonstrated talent in this domain should be encouraged and rewarded, an employee's resistance to volunteers, or poor work record with them, should not go overlooked and, implicitly, condoned in the review. As necessary, the organization should support training activities for paid staff to develop competencies in volunteer administration.

Similarly, recognition activities for volunteer programs normally focus on citizen participants rather than on both members of the team. Employees value recognition as well, especially when awards ceremonies, social events, media coverage, agency publications, and the like bring their efforts and accomplishments to the attention of organizational leadership. Agency personnel files should also document employee achievement as noted by individual volunteers and the director of volunteer services. By taking seriously the evaluation and recognition of paid staff with regard to their collaboration with volunteers, agency officials provide incentives for an effective partnership.

In most agencies, the overriding goal of the volunteer program is to exert a positive effect on the external environment and/or to improve the circumstances of clients. Periodically, the program should undergo an evaluation of the impact or progress it has registered toward such objectives. Too often, what passes for evaluation in this case is a compilation of such factors as the number of volunteers, hours donated, and clients contacted or visited. Some studies supplement these figures with the estimated "dollar value" of the services contributed by volunteers, based on the market price the organization would otherwise have to pay to employed personnel to accomplish the same tasks (for a complete discussion of the methodology, see Karn, 1983, 1982–83).

Impressive and significant though these data may be—normally documenting tremendous levels of contributed effort and monetary value across public and nonprofit institutions—they tap the inputs or resources to a volunteer program rather than its results or accomplishments. Some researchers complain, too, that this approach slights the monetary costs associated with the volunteer program, e.g., for paid staff supervision, reimbursement for expenses, and use of organizational resources and facilities (Utterback and Heyman, 1984, p. 229). Others lament that volunteers remain an "overlooked and undervalued asset" (Darling and Stavole, 1992).

Hence, public organizations should undertake additional forms of evaluation. Much as they might be expected to do for other departments or units, at regular intervals agency officials should assess the outcomes of the volunteer program against its stated mission or goals. Volunteer activity is other-directed; it should do more than gratify citizen participants and accommodate employees. Officials need to review the aggregate performance of the volunteers in assisting clients, addressing community problems, expediting agency operations, and meeting further objectives. Not only does the assessment yield information that can improve functioning of the program, but also it reinforces for all concerned—citizens, employees, and clients—the importance attached by the organization to the volunteer effort.

A second recommended type of assessment is a process evaluation of the volunteer program. The purpose is to determine that procedures to meet essential program functions, such as those discussed in this chapter, are in place and operating effectively. Additionally, the evaluation should attempt to gauge the satisfaction of volunteers and paid staff members with the program, as well as their perceptions concerning its impact on clients and the external environment. Continuing struggles in recruiting suitable volunteers, arresting high rates of volunteer burnout and turnover, relieving staff antagonisms, reaching mutually agreeable job assignments, and so forth point to flaws in program design that must be addressed. By diagnosing such difficulties and suggesting solutions, a process evaluation can enhance progress toward achievement of program objectives.

VI. CONCLUSION

This chapter has presented an extensive discussion of the role, magnitude, and importance of volunteer involvement in the provision of government services. It has elaborated a definition of volunteers to public agencies; the level and scope of volunteer participation in service delivery; the benefits and drawbacks of this approach; and crucial issues for the design and management of volunteer programs. All available evidence and research point to the increased involvement of volunteers in the public sector. This chapter can assist public officials and administrators in enhancing the application and advantages of the approach for their agencies and clients—and for the volunteers who ultimately make these programs feasible and effective.

REFERENCES

ACTION (1974). *American Volunteer, 1974*, Washington, DC.

Allen, N. J. (1987). the role of social and organizational factors in the evaluation of volunteer programs, *Eval. Prog. Plann.*, *10*(3): 257–262.

Allen, J. W., et al., (eds.) (1989). *The Private Sector in State Service Delivery: Examples of Innovative Practices*, Urban Institute, Washington, DC.

Becker, D. G. (1964). Exit lady bountiful: the volunteer and the professional social worker, *Social Serv. Rev.*, *38*(1): 57–72.

Brown, K. (1981). What goes wrong and what can we do about it? *Vol. Act. Lead.*, (Spring): 22–23.

Brudney, J. L. (1987). Coproduction and privatization: exploring the relationship and its implications, *J. Vol. Act. Res.*, *16* (July–Sept.): 11–21.

Brudney, J. L. (1990a). The availability of volunteers: implications for local governments, *Admin. Soc.*, *21 (Feb.)*: 413–424.

Brudney, J. L. (1990b). *Fostering Volunteer Programs in the public Sector: Planning, Initiating, and Managing Voluntary Activities*, Jossey-Bass, San Francisco.

Brudney, J. L. (1993). Volunteer involvement in the delivery of public services: advantages and disadvantages, *Public Prod. Manage. Rev.*, *16*(3): 283–297.

Brudney, J. L., and Brown, M. M. (1993). Government-based volunteer programs: toward a more caring society. Presented at the Independent Sector Spring Research Forum, San Antonio, TX, March 18–19.

Brudney, J. L., and Duncombe, W. D. (1992). An economic evaluation of paid, volunteer, and mixed staffing options for public services, *Public Admin. Rev.*, *52* (Sept./Oct.): 474–481.

Chambré, S. M. (1989). Kindling points of light: volunteering as public policy, *Nonprofit Vol. Sect. Q.*, *18*(3): 249–268.

Clary, E. G. (1987). Social support as a unifying concept in voluntary action. *J. Vol. Act. Res.*, *16*(4): 58–68.

Clary, E. G., Snyder, M., and Ridge, R. (1992). Volunteers' motivations: a functional strategy for the recruitment, placement, and retention of volunteers, *Nonprofit Manage. Lead.*, *2*(4): 333–350.

Clotfelter, C. T. (1985). *Federal Tax Policy and Charitable Giving*, University of Chicago, Chicago, IL.

Darling, L. L., and Stavole, R. D. (1992). Volunteers: the overlooked and undervalued asset, *J. Vol. Admin.*, *11*(1): 27–40.

Deitch, L. I., and Thompson, L. N. (1985). The reserve police officer: one alternative to the need for manpower, *Police Chief*, *52*(5): 59–61.

DeLaat, J. (1987). Volunteering as linkage in the three sectors, *J. Vol. Act. Res., 16*(1 and 2): 97–111.

Dorwaldt, A. L., Solomon, L. J., and Worden, J. K. (1988). Why volunteers helped to promote a community breast self-exam program, *J. Vol. Admin., 6*(4): 23–30.

Duncombe, S. (1985). Volunteers in city government: advantages, disadvantages and uses, Nat. Civic Rev., *74*(9): 356–364.

Ellis, S. J. (1986). *From the Top Down: The Executive Role in Volunteer Program Success*, Energize, Philadelphia, PA.

Ellis, S. J., and Noyes, K. H. (1990). *By the People: A History of Americans as Volunteers, Revised Ed.* Jossey-Bass, San Francisco.

Farr, C. A. (1983). *Volunteers: Managing Volunteer Personnel in Local Government*, International City Management Association, Washington, DC.

Ferris, James M. (1992). Initiatives in local government service delivery: a view from the United States, University of Southern California, School of Public Administration.

Gallup, Inc. (1981). *Americans Volunteer, 1981*, Gallup Organization, Princeton, NJ.

Gallup, Inc. (1986). *Americans Volunteer, 1985*, Gallup Organization, Princeton, NJ.

Goetter, W. G. J. (1987). When you create ideal conditions, your fledgling volunteer program will fly, *Am. School Board J., 194*(6): 34–37.

Graff, L. L. (1984). Considering the many facets of volunteer/union relations, *Vol. Act. Lead., (Summer)*: 16–20.

Haberek, J. (1992). Maryland—first state to mandate community service for students, *Vol. Act. Leadership (Summer)*: 5.

Haran, L., Kenney, S., and Vermilion, M. (1993). Contract volunteer services: a model for successful partnership, *Leadership (Jan.-March)*: 28–30.

Hodgkinson, V. A., and Weitzman, M. S. (1986). *The Charitable Behavior of Americans: A National Survey*, Independent Sector, Washington, DC.

Hodgkinson, V. A., and Weitzman, M. S. (1988). *Giving and Volunteering in the United States: Findings from a National Survey*, Independent Sector, Washington, DC.

Hodgkinson, V. A., and Weitzman, M. S. (1990). *Giving and Volunteering in the United States: Findings from a National Survey*, Independent Sector, Washington, DC.

Hodgkinson, V. A., and Weitzman, M. S. (1992). *Giving and Volunteering in the United States: Findings from a National Survey*, Independent Sector, Washington, DC.

Hodgkinson, V. A., and Weitzman, M. S., Toppe, C. M., and Noga, S. M. (1992) *Nonprofit Almanac, 1992-1993: Dimensions of the Independent Sector*, Jossey-Bass, San Francisco.

Holme, A., and Maizels, J. (1978). *Social Workers and Volunteers*, Allen and Unwin, London.

Karn, G. N. (1983-83). Money talks: a guide to establishing the true dollar value of volunteer time. I. *J. Vol. Admin., 1* (Winter): 1–17.

Karn, G. N. (1983). Money talks: a guide to establishing the true dollar value of volunteer time. II. *J. Vol. Admin., 1* (Spring): 1–19.

Kramer, R. M. (1981). *Voluntary Agencies in the Welfare State*, University of California Press, Berkeley.

Manchester, L. D., and Bogart, G. S. (1988). *Contracting and Volunteerism in Local Government: A Self-Help Guide*, International City Management Association, Washington, DC.

Marando, V. L. (1986). Local service delivery: volunteers and recreation councils, *J. Vol. Admin., 4*(4): 16–24.

May, K. M., McLaughlin, R., and Penner, M. (1991). Preventing low birth weight: marketing and volunteer outreach, *Public Health Nurs., 8*(2): 97–104.

McCurley, S., and Lynch, R. (1989). *Essential Volunteer Management*, VMSystems and Heritage Arts Publishing, Downers Grove, IL.

Montjoy, R. S., and Brudney, J. L. (1991). Volunteers in the delivery of public services: hidden costs . . . and benefits, *Am. Rev. Public Admin., 21*(4): 327–344.

Morley, E. (1989). Patterns in the use of alternative service delivery approaches, *Municipal Year Book, 1989*, International City Management Association, Washington, DC.

Myers, P., and Reid, A. C. (1986). *State Parks in a New Era: A Survey of Issues and Innovations*, Conservation Foundation, Washington, DC.

National Association of Counties (1990). *The Volunteer Toolbox: Visions for Improving the Service of America's Counties*, National Association of Counties, Washington, DC.

Naylor, H. H. (1985). Beyond managing volunteers, *J. Vol. Act. Res.*, *14*(2 and 3): 25–30.

Norris, D. F., Mandell, M. B., and Hathaway, W. E. (1993). Volunteers in emergency medical service: a case study from rural America, *Public Prod. Manage. Rev.*, *16*(3): 257–269.

Park, J. M. (1983). *Meaning Well Is Not Enough: Perspectives on Volunteering*, Groupwork Today, South Plainfield, NJ.

Parks, R. B., et al. (1981). Consumers as coproducers of public services: some economic and institutional considerations, *Policy Stud. Rev.*, *9*(7): 1001–1011.

Pattakos, A. N. (1982). *Volunteers and the Provision of Local Government Services: A Preliminary Issue Paper*, International City Management Association, Washington, DC.

Pearce, J. L. (1978). *Something for Nothing: An Empirical Examination of the Structures and Norms of Volunteer Organizations*, Doctoral dissertation, Yale University.

Pearce, J. L. (1983). Participation in voluntary associations: how membership in a formal organization changes the rewards of participation, *International Perspectives on Voluntary Action Research* (D. H. Smith and J. Van Til, eds.), University Press of America, Washington, DC.

Perkins, K. B. (1987). *Volunteer Firefighters in the United States: A Sociological Profile of America's Bravest*, Report to the National Volunteer Fire Council, Farmville, VA.

Perkins, K. B. (1990). Volunteer fire and rescue corporations: structure, process, and survival, *Nonprofit and Voluntary Sector the Structures and Norms of Volunteer Organizations*. Quarterly, 19(4): 359–370.

Peters, T. J., and Waterman, R. H., Jr. (1982). *In Search of Excellence: Lessons from America's Best-Run Companies*, Warner Books, New York.

Rydberg, W. D., and Peterson, L. J. (eds.) (1980). *A Look at the Eighties: Crucial Environmental Factors Affecting Volunteerism*, Aid Association of Lutherans, Appleton, WI.

Scheier, I. H. (1988a). Empowering a profession: what's in our name? *J. Vol. Admin.*, *6*(4): 31–36.

Scheier, I. H. (1988–89). Empowering a profession: leverage points and process, *J. Vol. Admin.*, *7*(2): 50–57.

Schwartz, F. S. (1977). The professional staff and the direct service volunteer: issues and problems, *J. Jewish Communal Serv.*, *54*(2): 147–154.

Schwartz, M. I. (1989). *The State Office of Volunteerism Manual*, ACTION, Washington, DC.

Shulman, M. A. (1982). *Alternative Approaches for Delivering Public Services*, International City Management Association, Urban Data Service Reports, no. 14, Washington, DC.

Smith, D. H. (1972). Types of volunteers and voluntarism, *Vol. Admin.*, *6*(3): 3–10.

Sundeen, R. A. (1989). Citizens serving government: volunteer participation in local public agencies, *Working Papers for the Spring Research Forum, Independent Sector*, Washington, DC.

Thornburg, L. (1992). What makes an effective volunteer administrator? Viewpoints from several practitioners, *Vol. Act. Lead.*, *(Summer)*: 18–21.

U. S. Department of Labor (1969). *Americans Volunteer*, Department of Labor, Manpower administration, Washington, DC.

Utterback, J., and Heyman, S. R. (1984). An examination of methods in the evaluation of volunteer programs, *Eval. Program Plann.*, *7*(3): 229–235.

Valente, C. F., and Manchester, L. D. (1984). *Rethinking Local Services: Examining Alternative Delivery Approaches*, International City Management Association, Washington, DC.

Van Til, J. (1988). *Mapping the Third Sector: Voluntarism in a Changing Social Economy*, Foundation Center, New York.

Walter, V. A. (1987). Volunteers and bureaucrats: clarifying roles and creating meaning, *J. Vol. Act. Res.*, *16*(3): 22–32.

Weisbrod, B. A. (1988). *The Nonprofit Economy*, Harvard University Press, Cambridge, MA.

Williams, R. M. (1993a). Advice to administrators: ask why, *Leadership (April–June)*: 8.

Williams, R. M. (1993b). Advice to administrators: get out of your office, *Leadership* (*Jan.-March*): 11.

Wilson, M. (1976). *The Effective Management of Volunteer Programs*, Johnson, Boulder, CO.

Wilson, M. (1984). The new frontier: volunteer management training, *Train. Dev. J.*, *38*(7): 50-52.

Wineburg, C. R., and Wineburg, R. J. (1987). Local human service development: institutional utilization of volunteers to solve community problems, *J. Vol. Admin.*, *5*(4): 9-14.

Young, C. L., Goughler, D. H., and Larson, P. J. (1986). Organizational volunteers for the rural frail elderly: outreach, casefinding, and service delivery, *Gerontologist*, *26*(4): 342-344.

28
Professionalism and the Public Sector

JOHN J. GARGAN   Kent State University, Kent, Ohio

I   INTRODUCTION

This chapter is concerned with the relationship between government and the professions, a relationship that is close and of long standing. The relationship is iterative. Professions form when occupations become increasingly specialized and knowledge intensive. Governmental officials seek out professionals for advice when confronted with unfamiliar problems. As the number and influence of professions grow, public authorities are called on to protect both the public and the professions by regulating admission to professional practice and by overseeing those in practice. Throughout the political system, governments are major employers of professionals of all types.

"Professionalization," notes Brown (1992, p. 6), "depends on the creation and maintenance of at least three things: knowledge, practitioners, and clientele." In modern societies professional status is not ascribed but achieved. To be considered a professional the practitioner must be able to demonstrate to a clientele competence based on mastery of a body of knowledge and allied skills. Though the relevant skills are derived from the knowledge they are applicable to concrete problems.

The body of knowledge is gained, after extended study, typically in a university graduate program accredited by the profession at large and/or licensed by the state. Within universities the neophyte receives the accumulated wisdom and the state-of-the-art of the profession, is socialized to professional norms, and develops some sense of professional identity. Training and experience inculcate an orientation to the world, a vocabulary, and "common ways of perceiving and structuring problems and of attacking and of solving them" (Mosher, 1978, p. 147).

Professionals interact with clients. The interaction delineates a power relationship. A critical determinant of the professional's power is the client's dependence on the professional for assistance (Larson, 1977). Simultaneously, a profession must create a want; a profession without a clientele is an oxymoron. It is difficult to envision the role of teachers without students, medical doctors without patients, soldiers without enemies, and priests without sinners.

Desired outcomes of the interaction result when the professional addresses a client's needs and transforms a client's condition from a less positive to a more positive state. Achievement of desired outcomes in such public services as education, health care, welfare, and police and fire protection demands coproduction, i.e., the active involvement and participation of both professional and client (Whitaker, 1980; Brudney and England, 1983). Ultimately, the success of the individual professional and his or her profession is a function of the quality of practitioner–clientele interactions and judgments by the clientele of the value of the interactions.

Two dynamics bound the quality of the interactions: (1) the pace of change in core knowledge of a profession and (2) the stability of the context within which practitioners operate. The legitimacy of a profession is determined by its core knowledge. The context of professional practice must be supportive of the values which the profession seeks to maximize.

When a profession's extant core knowledge and associated substantive, methodological, and theoretical issues are undergoing attack or rapid change, the profession as a whole must be concerned with the emergent knowledge and the mechanisms available for transmitting the new knowledge to practitioners in the field. A crisis can develop. Notes Ostrom (1974, pp. 11–12):

> If the methods of studying, teaching and practicing the subject matter . . . have become problematical, then the profession can*not* have much confidence in what it professes. The practice of a profession rests upon the validity of the knowledge which it professes. When the confidence of a profession in the essential validity of its knowledge has been shattered, that profession should be extraordinarily modest about the professional advice it renders while keeping up its appearance.

The provision of professional knowledge to clients in a neutrally competent manner is an ethical axiom of all professions. That knowledge is provided with neutral competency does not mean that the knowledge is neutral. In practice, some body of theory, empirical findings, and exemplary practices are brought to problem situations. Where alternative theories, empirical findings, and exemplary practices are available, the choice of guiding theory decides the parameters of likely professional solutions.

Professions can be practiced successfully only in appropriate contexts. Most generally, if professions are to be accepted the context must be supportive of the notion of utilizing abstract knowledge and deferring to the technical competence and skill of sanctioned individuals. Context is shaped by societal conditions: cultural, social, economic, and political.

When conditions change, so does the context. As the maturation of the "baby-boom generation" demonstrated, the specialized knowledge of thousands of pediatricians became less relevant as millions of children grew from infancy to puberty. The need for the well-honed skills of military strategists has shrunk as the threat of major war has diminished. Should a clientele question the existence of a deity, let alone the ability of individual humans to interact with it, the specialized knowledge, extensive training, and technical skills of the religious professional may become suspect.

II. GOVERNMENT AND PROFESSIONS

The current hegemony of professional power has led to extensive study of the professions. Students and practitioners of personnel policy have done much thinking, research, and writing on the government–professional relationship, particularly at the national level. A segment of this work has related to the roles and functions of professionals *in* government, those using their advanced knowledge and skills in public rather than private or nonprofit sector jobs. Another segment of the work has related to professionals *of* government, those engaged in the supervision, management, and administration of public business.[1]

---

[1] Of great assistance in conceptualizing profesionalism in the public sector were Eulau's 1972 Presidential Address to the Annual Meeting of the American Political Science Association (1973) and Frederick Mosher's *Democracy and the Public Service* (1982).

Students and practitioners need to be attentive to both types of professionals. Elected officials are pushed to professionals *in* government for recommendations when new issues emerge on public agendas. The conduct of government and the public's judgments of its adequacy are molded by the performance of professionals *of* government. Considerable debate regarding epistemological and praxis issues has been evident for both types of professionals.

Since 1960 the public administration community has taken on some of the trappings of a profession even if it lacks a compact on primary purpose, goals, and focus. Over the same period, the conduct of politics and government has been altered, becoming much more fragmented and factionalized. The major institutions which dominated in the 1960s have been replaced by more fluid, open, and activist-shaped policy subgovernments in the 1990s (Heclo, 1989; Berry, 1989).

A. Assessing Professionals *in* Government

It is as societies develop that knowledge derived from empirical evidence and technology-related skills become bases of power.[2] For professions to enjoy a privileged position the need for such advance knowledge and skills to deal with matters of security and social and economic life must obviously be recognized. There must also be sufficient resources to support a professional class. The number and range of professions present in a society are indicators of modernity.

As with professionalism generally in the larger society, concern for professionalism in government arises only at some density of activity. When public responsibilities are very limited, as in 18th century and early 19th century American cities, public work is done when it is obvious to everyone that it needs to be done, and then often by standing volunteer committees or by ad hoc arrangements. With urbanization and the growth of an industrial and manufacturing economy, the context of public action and problems targeted becomes more intricate and requires the attention of those who claim to hold special knowledge and skills.

It is significant that while the adoption of new approaches to problem solving and governmental organization in the United States was inevitable, the specific form of the approaches and organization was not. Through the late 19th century and into the 20th century extended maneuvering occurred over the details of changes in the form and focus of governmental and political power. In this maneuvering, professionals from many fields were sources of proposals for enhancing the efficient operation of an expanding administrative state *and* participants seeking benefits from the political process (Skowronek, 1982; Wiebe, 1967).

Increased public sector professionalism was advantageous for the nation's political leadership. Lowi (1993, p. 262) states that meritorious administrators

> could be entrusted with the great powers and responsibilities of government not merely because they were trained in their craft and would spend a lifetime in the agency dealing with the problems of that agency, but because they added to their professionalism and training a willingness to subordinate their abilities to the wishes of the elected officials. "The neutral civil servant" was the key to legitimacy, not the professionalism by itself.

1. *Public Sector Growth*

A public sector of sufficient size to require the attention of professionals *in* and *of* government is of recent origin in the United States. For most of the nation's history, military and civilian employment were limited. Through the 19th century, the number of military personnel varied with the intensity of operations, peaking at the height of military conflicts and then returning to preconflict

---

[2] Control of information and knowledge is central to the postindustrial society and to power of professionals. On this significant point see, among many others, Toffler (1990), Ohmae (1990), and Bell (1973).

levels. In 1860, for example, there were 27,958 in uniform, by 1865 1,062,848, and by 1871 42,238. Civilian employment was dominated by mail delivery, the function most essential to a nationwide communication system. At midcentury the post office, with 21,391 employees, employed 81% of civilians in the federal government.[3]

By 1901 postal employees still made up 57% of all federal nonmilitary employees. When federal civilian employees in defense work are added to the postal workers better than three-quarters (75.5%) of all federal civilian employees at the turn of the century are accounted for.

Expansion of governmental activity in the more recent past can be traced through two variables—the amount of money spent by government and the number of individuals working for government (Peters, 1985). Table 1 shows change in the two variables during the past 60 years. The years selected for data reporting bracket periods of major policy change in American government and politics.

The general trend in public sector spending is clear, increasing from 10% of GNP in 1929 to 36% in 1990. The overall increase involved striking changes in the spending patterns by levels of government. Before the Great Depression, the American political system, measured in fiscal terms, was a grandly decentralized one. Most of the 10% of GNP spent in 1929 was spent by the state–local segment; 53.8% of total public spending was by local governments. Of the 36% of GNP spent in 1990, nearly two-thirds (64.4%) was accounted for at the national level.

Less dramatic than the changes in spending have been those in employment. The number of civilians employed by government has increased as a percentage of total employment, from 6.5% in the pre-Roosevelt years to 15.1% toward the end of the Reagan–Bush years. Employment growth has occurred throughout the system but most has been in the state–local sector, and particularly at the local level which constitutes three-fourths of the state–local total. Federal civilian employment, to which considerable political rhetoric and attention have been directed, after increasing during the New Deal and World War II years, has actually decreased as a percentage of civilian employment since 1950.

Spending and employment are related but are not equivalents. When the range of governmental activities and responsibilities is limited and labor-intensive, the relationship is positive and strong. The relationship weakens as the range of activities and responsibilities is broadened and alternative means of providing and delivering the associated services are adopted. Decisions at the national level to make greater use of transfer payments and to rely on private and third-party providers to deliver services have led to increases in federal spending with no concomitant increase in federal employment (Walker, 1991; Kettl, 1993).

2. What Professionals in Government (and Other Public Employees) Do

Table 1 reveals an overall pattern of growth in spending and employment. Since there is no reason to assume that all functions of government should grow at the same rate, the table's composite figures may mask differences in functional growth patterns.

At the national level, the scope of public activity has changed in response to unprecedented international responsibilities, new notions of social service entitlement, and political pressures on Congress for programs to meet constituency needs (Wilson, 1975). With World War II and the Cold War, national defense was a major claimant of public spending. In 1945, nearly nine-tenths

---

[3] The historic data on civilian and military employment discussed in this section are drawn primarily from Chapter Y, Government Employment and Finances, of the United States Bureau of the Census (1976) volume, *The Statistical History of the United States*. For additional trend data, Fabricant's study (1952) is still useful to the analyst of public sector change.

Table 1 Public Sector Activity: Government Spending as a Percentage of GNP and Civilian Government Employment as a Percentage of Total Employment, by Year, 1929–1990, and Level of Government

Measure	1929	1950	1960	1970	1980	1990
Percent GNP						
Federal spending	2.5	14.3	18.2	20.5	22.5	23.2
State–local spending	7.5	7.8	9.7	13.2	13.3	12.8
Total spending	10.0	22.1	27.9	33.7	35.8	36.0
Percent Total Employment						
Federal employment	1.2	3.6	3.7	3.7	2.9	2.6
State–local employment	5.3	7.3	9.7	12.9	13.1	12.5
Total public employment	6.5	10.9	13.4	16.6	16.0	15.1

Source: Data from Advisory Commission on Intergovernmental Relations (1992): United States Bureau of the Census (1976); Peters (1993, p. 32).

(89.5%) of federal spending was for national defense. For each year from 1951 to 1961 over half of the federal budget was for national defense purposes. Defense spending as a percentage of federal outlays decreased in a more or less consistent fashion from 1962 to 1982. From 1983 to the present, spending on national defense has been over 25% of federal outlays and between approximately 5% and 6.5% of GNP (Historical Tables, Budget of the United States Government, Fiscal Year 1990).

The second major superfunction and area of growth in federal spending has been that of human resources. The human resources category encompasses several policy areas including training, employment, social services, health, and veterans benefits. The most important of the policies in the human resources are Social Security, Medicare, and income security. From the late 1940s to the late 1960s, with short-term decreases during the Korean War years, human resources spending ranged from roughly one-quarter to one-third of federal spending. During the 1970s and 1980s, spending on human resources increased so as to consistently exceed 50% of federal spending.

As increased spending on national defense reflects the emergence of the United States as a world power, increased spending on human resources reflects the maturation of the welfare state or the growth of the social service state. Basic to this maturation or growth has been an expanding and increasingly expansive definition of entitlement in both philosophical and technical senses.

As the scope of the national government's responsibilities has changed, so too has its work force. Within the public work force, professionals *in* government, according to Frederick Mosher, have generally been of two classes. The first is a class of "general professionals," those who are employable in both the public and private sectors (lawyers, doctors, engineers, accountants). The second class is one of "public service professionals" (military officers, foresters, meteorologists, diplomats, intelligence agents) who are concentrated in government (Mosher, 1982, p. 116; Levine, 1986, p. 202). For many public service professionals career opportunities have been primarily, if not exclusively, in government.

Because of the level of knowledge and skill needed to satisfy statutory obligations and political expectations, particular agencies may employ several types of professionals—both types of professionals *in* government (general and public service professionals) as well as professionals *of* government. The professional culture of the agency will be defined by an elite whose professional background best fits its functional responsibilities (lawyers in the Justice Department or state attorney general's office, public health doctors in health offices, engineers in highway departments, accountants in budgeting and financial management offices). The work of the corps of elite professionals is usually supported by other line professionals, as well as staff and administrative professionals.

The expanding focus of the public sector has so increased the range of professional types needed that to study governmental employment is to examine professionalism in all its varieties. At the same time, the greater part of public sector employment is concentrated in a limited number of functions at each level of government. The work of the professionals (and other employees) involved in these primary functions affects measures of overall governmental capacity and public and media perceptions of performance.

3. Professionals in Government: The National Government

Conforming to the rationales of public goods and functional assignment in a federal system, national defense and delivery of the mail continue to be primary purposes of employment in the national government, just as in the 19th century. Active duty military personnel and postal service employees were 53% of total federal employment in 1992. Through the 1960s, military personnel alone, among the most highly professionalized of professionals in government, comprised just over half of the total. From the early 1970s on, the share of total national government employment accounted for by uniformed military personnel declined toward 40%.

The relative importance of functional professionalism in the national government is indicated in Table 2 which reports, by executive department for 1992, the number of civilian employees and departmental employment as a percentage of total executive branch employment (Budget of the United States Fiscal Year 1994, 1993, p. 38). Care needs to be taken in interpreting the data. While developments in executive departments are clearly related, the executive branch is not of a single piece. Reference to a civilian work force in the federal government can be misleading. A Hudson Institute report (1988, pp. 31–32) declares:

> In terms of mission, organization, and skills, there is no such thing as "the Federal government." There is only an aggregation of different agencies, each of which has different goals, different structures, and different employee needs.

Though the six departments listed in Table 2 deal with only selected national government responsibilities, they employ more than three-quarters of executive branch civilian workers. Over half of executive branch civilian employment is related to preparing for future wars (Department of Defense) or coping with the human costs of past wars (Department of Veterans Affairs). Lesser numbers of professionals and support employees are involved in the four other departments which

Table 2 Executive Branch Civilian Employment: Number of Employees, Percentage of Total, and Cumulative Percentage, by Department, 1992

Department	Number (000)	Percent Total	Cumulative percentage
Defense	972.9	44.8	44.8
Veterans Affairs	229.0	10.6	55.4
Treasury	162.8	7.5	62.9
Health and Human Services	128.8	5.9	68.8
Justice	91.7	4.2	73.0
Interior	75.3	3.5	76.5

Source: Data from Budget of the United States Fiscal Year 1994.

Table 3 State–Local Public Employment: by Function, 50-State Mean Percentage of Total, 1991, and 50-State Mean Percentage Change, 1971–1991

Function	Mean percent 1991	Percent change 1971–91
Elementary/secondary education	38.0	50.9
Higher education	12.7	79.0
Hospitals	7.2	26.7
Highways	4.8	6.6
Police protection	4.9	68.8
Welfare	3.4	117.9
Corrections	3.3	270.1
Health	2.5	193.1

Source: Data from United States Bureau of the Census (1972, 1992).

collect taxes, direct social welfare programs, oversee the administration of justice, or manage extensive natural resources and a park system.

Involved in the work of the departments listed in Table 2 is the full range of Mosher's general and public service professionals, from nuclear scientists, to accountants, to contract negotiators, to foresters. The civilian employees of the federal government, like their military counterparts, represent well the concept of professionals in government. And the levels of professionalism are increasing. The Congressional Budget Office reported in the late 1980s that the federal work force was becoming increasingly better educated and more professional. The growing upper echelon white collar component of that work force—18% professional, 24% administrative, 17% technical—was greater than in the total economy (Congressional Budget Office, 1987, p. 5).

4. Professionals in Government—The State–Local Sector

Despite scholarly attention to professionals in the national government, any reference to professionalism in the civilian public sector is, in the main, a reference to the state–local sector. This is because state–local employment surpasses federal employment by multiples of 4–5:1. Within the state–local sector the local sector is two to three times greater than the state.

In Table 3 are reported the 50-state mean percentage of total state–local employment accounted for by several major functions.[4] Also reported is the 50-state mean percent change, 1971 to 1991, in each functions's percentage of total employment.

Most state–local public employment is concentrated in few functions, as at the national level. Over half the total is in education—elementary, secondary, and higher. By training, experience, traditions, and codes of ethics, those employed in education represent a major segment of the professionals in government. Educators utilize substantial portions of state–local budgets and their performance is immediately apparent to families in all locales. As a result, the spending and performance of education professionals have been closely monitored in recent years.

Considerable numbers of professionals are engaged in state-local functions, aside from education. Many of them, along with technical and semiskilled workers, are involved in custodial work,

---

[4] Because of differences among the states as to the assignment of functional responsibilities to state and/or local governments, it is necessary to combine state and local employment for comparative purposes. Table 3 lists the major, but not all, state-local functions.

caring for those who are ill or need help in coping in contemporary society (hospitals) or controlling persons who have broken the law (corrections). Maintaining basic transportation systems (highways) accounts for another major group of workers. Police protection, on average, accounts for 5% of state–local employment. Welfare and health functions involve smaller but significant percentages.

The most dramatic percentage increases in state–local employment from 1971 to 1991 were in the functions which have accounted for lesser percentages of total employment: corrections, health, welfare. These are also state–local functions (along with education) whose professionals and technicians, professionals *in* government, encounter political pressure for new approaches to problems. In many instances, the professionals find the state-of-the-art in the core knowledge and technical skills of their fields challenged by nonprofessionals—elected officials, clientele, and citizen taxpayers.

Another perspective on the penetration of state–local employment by the professions can be gained from data gathered by the Equal Employment Opportunities Commission (EEOC) (1992). For each state, EEOC reports employment in several occupation categories, *exclusive of education*, by the state and its local governments.

The EEOC category labels are descriptive. Criteria used to designate jobs holders as professionals are familiar to those who have worked with the scholarly literature. Professionals possess "specialized and theoretical knowledge which is usually acquired through college training or through work experience and other training which provides comparable knowledge" (United States Equal Employment Opportunity Commission, 1992, p. xxxv). The occupations included in the category cover the gamut of professions. Among them are social workers, doctors, registered nurses, economists, dieticians, lawyers, system analysts, engineers, vocational rehabilitation counselors, librarians, management analysts, airplane pilots, and navigators.

Even with education excluded, professionals in government dominate state–local employment. The professional category is the largest in Table 4 and accounts, on average, for 23.2% of the state–local total. There is interstate variation in the employment of professionals (over 30% of the total in Utah and Vermont vs. 16% in Kansas and New Hampshire) but the variation is generally less than in the other categories. The coefficient of variation for professionals is the next to the smallest in the table.

Table 4 State–Local Noneducation Public Employment: State Mean Percentage of Total and Coefficient of Variation, by Major Job Category, 1991

Job category	Mean ($N = 49$)	CV
Officials and administrators	6.2	21.9
Professionals	23.2	14.2
Technicians	9.2	22.7
Protective service workers	15.5	18.1
Paraprofessionals	7.7	30.6
Administrative support	17.6	12.7
Skilled craft workers	8.6	22.2
Service-maintenance	12.0	22.0

Source: Data from United States Equal Employment Opportunity Commission, 1992.

B. Assessing Professionals *of* Government

In their appraisal of federal personnel Lane and Wolf (1990, p. 63) cite three types of competencies which are relevant to any discussion of public sector professionalism:

> First, there are the technical competencies—the basic occupational skills necessary to execute the varied tasks of governance. Next are the program and agency competencies—those capabilities required to activate administrative processes which create and deliver programs and execute public policies. Third, there is governance competency—that composite of special abilities which federal workers must possess in order to work effectively in and among political institutions at all levels of governmental activity.

The first competencies, involving technical skills, are the domain of professionals *in* government. The second and third competencies, involving agency administration, policy implementation, and interorganizational communication and negotiation have been perennial concerns of professionals *of* government.

Professionals of government have come to occupy pivotal posts in American government and politics. Contemporary life is shaped, in the most fundamental ways, by decisions made within, and actions taken on behalf of, large-scale bureaucracies. The quality of the decisions and actions is shaped by the talents of those in managerial and administrative leadership positions. Understanding the behavior of these leaders and the efficacy of the bureaucracies within which they operate has been a primary challenge to public administration scholars, including those interested in public sector professionalism (Ostrom, 1974,1980; Buchanan, 1985).

Professionals of government are the supervisors, managers, and executives from the career service who answer for the success or failure of government undertakings and enterprises. The short-term conduct of the public bureaucracy and the long-term performance of the modern administrative state are fundamentally determined by the talents of these individuals. The responsibilities of professionals of government include components of program management (effective supervision of the implementation of public programs and the on-line employees involved), resource management (oversight of well-developed budgeting, accounting, information, and personnel systems), and policy management (guidance of strategic planning, priority setting, and system design).[5]

Each of the management components includes technical and political elements though in differing combinations. Over the course of a career the individual professional of government typically moves through a series of positions in which the skill and knowledge requirements shift from the more specialized and technical to the more conceptual and political. The movement may be by two routes. The *professional administrator* begins as a professional *in* government and takes on management responsibilities. The *administrative professional* begins as a professional *of* government and moves through the administrative ranks (Kearney and Sinha, 1988, p. 572).

Professionals of government are important because of their positions in governmental organizations rather than their numbers. As a proportion of the public sector work force, the professionals of government component is limited. The Congressional Budget Office estimates that in the mid-1980s 2% of the federal government's white collar employees were managers and 11% were in supervisory jobs (Congressional Budget Office 1987, p. 4). For state–local employment,

---

[5] The primary management categories—program management, resource management, and policy management—are drawn from Burgess (1975). Though Burgess was concerned primarily with management in local governments, his categories are obviously applicable to other levels.

Table 4 shows the category "officials and administrators" with the smallest average percentage (6.2%).

Despite their limited numbers, professionals of government have received sustained attention, particularly at the senior levels. The attention is warranted. Those who achieve the upper grades of the civil service accept major responsibilities for policy management. Often they are expected (or assumed) to carry institutional memory, to be able to invoke intricate bureaucratic expertise, and to exhibit well-honed political dexterity. To be successful these higher civil servants need to become "specialists in generalization" (Smith, 1984, p. 16).

This is easier said than done. Constitutional provisions for the separation and sharing of powers among the branches of government blur lines of authority and responsibility for civil servants. Personnel systems in the United States have generally been designed to favor specialists over generalists. Changes in the properties of generalization complicate matters. For example, as federal policy has relied less on the direct delivery of services and more on contracts with third-party providers, senior managers have had to adapt operating styles and learn new technical skills (Lane and Wolf, 1990).

Reformers have encouraged for some time national and state career services capped by a cadre of nonpartisan public administration generalists. Frequently mentioned as models have been the British and French higher civil servants. Recommendations for an American version of such systems have been made and in some instances adopted.

The most successful case of the career public administration generalist has been the city manager plan. Formulated in the first two decades of the 20th century, the plan set formalized boundaries between politics and administration as called for by major scholars of public administration (Stillman, 1974, p. 11). In government, the policy process was understandably conflictual but the neutrally competent manager was charged with implementing policies as effectively, efficiently, and economically as possible. Though the manager's term was controlled by city council, tenure in office was contingent on meritorious performance. Embodied in the plan was the faith that, independent of political factors, effective management could enhance communities. This faith remained intact long after many in the public administration field had changed perspectives on the separation of politics and administration.

At the national level, serious efforts have been put forth on behalf of public administration professionals. The second Hoover Commission recommended a senior civil service in the 1950s, and the recommendation continued to be put forth, in differing forms, by other groups during the 1960s and 1970s, by President Nixon in 1971, and by Hugh Heclo in 1977 (1977, pp. 249–253).

The 1978 Civil Service Reform Act established the Senior Executive Service (SES), a new and separate category of federal executives. Those selected for the SES were to be given senior rank in person, freed from specific positions, and made available for a variety of assignments. They were to be, in practice, "a corps of executive smoke-jumpers, ready to drop in and quell administrative brushfires wherever they might break out" (Huddleston, 1991, p. 179).

The SES was to comprise primarily of the most talented applicants from the "supergrades" of the career service but was also was to include a limited number of noncareer political appointees. These senior executives were to be positioned at the interface of political appointees and the permanent bureaucracy and were to facilitate action on legitimate immediate objectives of the former and protect the long-term interests of the latter. For superior performance, they were to be given bonuses, as in the private sector; repeated inferior performance would result in a loss of rank and a return to the career service or retirement. As envisioned by its supporters, the new service properly used had "the potential of creating, over a period of time, the professional managerial corps the United States government needs so urgently" (Sundquist, 1979, p. 9).

Whatever the promise in 1978, the SES was viewed from the mid-1990s as *not* having "evolved into the mobile corps of generalist managers envisioned by some of its planners" (Cipolla,

1993, p. 24). The reasons are several. SES morale declined when bonuses for performance proved to be less available than pledged. Federal executive salaries lagged those in private business during the 1980s. The number of noncareer political appointees to the SES has limited opportunities open to careerists and, equally important, has brought to major jobs individuals with "little public service experience, and worse, with little commitment to public service" (Huddleston, 1992, p. 112). Training opportunities have been inadequate and the goal of mobility within and between agencies has proven elusive (Huddleston, 1991, pp. 178–180). While much was made initially of a policy management executive corps, in practice, according to close observers, SES positions have required sophisticated technical skills along with administrative experience (Huddleston, 1988–1989, p. 413).

The increasing emphasis on professionals of government has not been limited to Washington. Integral to the revitalization of state government during the past three decades have been changes in state personnel systems. Expanded civil service coverage, better recruitment programs, and new training opportunities have been undertaken in most states.

Among other changes, adaptations have been made in state personnel systems to permit greater flexibility in the assignment of career employees. In a number of states, full-scale SESs have been developed (Sherwood and Breyer, 1987) and in others increasing use has been made of exempt managers "who serve at the will of and pleasure of their political superiors because of their role in policymaking and execution" (Roberts, 1988, p. 21).

How successful state SESs and exempted mangers will be remains to be seen. Much depends on the political cultures of individual states and how governors reconcile the competing demands on them for political patronage and for policy and administrative expertise (Roberts, 1991). Even with improvements in state government organization, many governors continue to share executive power and to face extraordinarily difficult management problems. Hence the importance of politically astute professionals of government. Contemporary governors, like presidents, need help of a special kind. Each

> can face performance expectations that outstrip his or her institutional resources and capacity to perform. Thus, both come to prize "responsive competence" over "neutral or organizational competence" (Roberts, 1988, p. 34).

The extensive adoption of the city manager plan, creation of an SES in the national government, and experimentation with state level SESs and exempted managers have been important developments. Each constitutes a partial test of public administration theory. Valid theory and the core knowledge, technical skills, and exemplary practices derived from it are requisites for an encompassing public administration profession of which professionals of government would be the applied practitioners.

While the underlying theory of their work is being tested in applied settings, public administrators have taken steps to legitimate their profession. In 1977, the National Association of Schools of Public Affairs and Administration (NASPAA) adopted standards for master's degree programs whereby programs meeting the requisite standards are rostered and accredited by NASPAA (Daniels and Johansen, 1985). The National Council of the American Society for Public Administration approved a code of ethics in 1984. Certified Public Manager programs in several states have fostered arrangements to meet the training and development needs of supervisors, managers, and executives in state governments (Van Wart, 1992) and an American Academy of Certified Public Managers has been instituted. In combination, the steps resemble those taken by other occupations moving towards recognition as professions.

III. THE FUTURE OF PROFESSIONALS *IN* AND *OF* GOVERNMENT

The capacity of the public sector to implement policies and to respond to social problems is a function of the ability to marshall expert knowledge and skill. In a complex and interdependent world governmental effectiveness is a societal imperative. How well that imperative is met will be determined at least in part by the quality of professionals in and of government.

During any political era, the quality of public professionals depends on the interplay of developments relating to three overlapping realms:

The structural arrangements—legal, organizational, and sectoral—through which government is conducted, including the recruitment and promotion of career employees.

The policy and political preference orderings, as filtered through the attitudinal and ideological orientations, of the governing coalition, political activists, and general public.

The prevailing theoretical frameworks which guide thinking, research, and action in public administration. The frameworks may be comprehensive or partial.

A. Structural Arrangements

Because they promote certain values and condition the exercise of public power, structural arrangements are rarely neutral. For most of U.S. history, the structure of federalism, the separation of powers, and the organizational arrangements within the executive and legislative branches at each level of government have conditioned attacks on problems. Alterations in the way in which governmental work is done—transfer of responsibility for social services from the political party to a central public bureaucracy or to a private voluntary organization—and the ways in which personnel are recruited and promoted—abolition of political appointees and the use of examinations and neutral competence criteria—work to the advantage of some values and interests and to the disadvantage of others.

The relevance of structural arrangements is periodically demonstrated. The realities of federalism have complicated the government–professional linkage. During the last half of the 19th century, for example, attention was given by military theorists and career officers to conditions of professionalism in the U.S. Army. The theorists and officers looked to Prussia and elsewhere for models of highly centralized and hierarchical organization, general staff, and in-service education. The emergence of any national professional army was delayed by the fact of a state-based militia which was called into national service as needed. In that structure, state governors exercised de jure and de facto military authority, including the granting of officer commissions in the militia. That governors could use the commissions as a form of political patronage complicated the argument that rank and promotion should be based on proficiency (Ambrose, 1964, chap. 6; Weigley, 1984, chaps. 8 and 9).

Structural constraints are real but not immutable. During the 1930s, when localism and states' rights were still potent political forces, administrative agencies in state governments were reorganized and modernized. Some of the changes were in response to local political demands for greater efficiency to avoid fiscal disaster. Others were imposed by national legislation and New Deal administrators. Implementation of programs under the jurisdiction of agencies like the Social Security Board, the U.S. Employment Service, and the Office of Education carried merit system or staffing requirements as conditions for receiving funds (Benson, 1941, chap. 6; Patterson, 1969, chap. 8). During the 1970s, a new generation of federal officials, like their predecessors in the 1930s, faced an intergovernmental dilemma. Recognizing that the success of federal grant programs was contingent on the administrative capacity of state and local governments and the knowledge and technical skills of subnational professionals in government, federal officials sponsored initiatives to build state and local management capacity and professional competence (Macaluso, 1975).

Other modifications in structural arrangements have upgraded the status of professionalism in government. A defining characteristic of U.S. government from the 1930s to the 1960s was the administrative agency wherein career professionals were given considerable discretionary power to deal with very specialized areas such as communications, pharmaceutical drugs, and interstate commerce. In many instances, the discretionary powers given these agencies combined "investigative, prosecutorial, and adjudicative functions" (Freedman, 1978, p. 139) so as to marshall technical expertise and experience in dealing with very intricate problems. Thus was the career professional able to serve the public interest by overriding the intrinsic limitations of the separation of powers doctrine.

The negative impacts of specific structural arrangements on governmental professionalism frequently have been judged to be obvious and substantial. A study of the federal government's problems in recruiting, retaining, and utilizing scientists and engineers, archetypical professionals *in* government, was reported in 1990 by the National Research Council's Office of Scientific and Engineering Personnel (Campbell and Dix, 1990). One conclusion of that study was that

> perceptions about factors affecting the federal government's ability to recruit and retain scientists and engineers have remained basically the same for the past 30 years, in spite of specific efforts by OPM and individual agencies to enhance such recruitment and retention (p. 2).

Among the factors identified in the report were inadequate pay, delays in job offers, paperwork, and a ceiling on opportunities. These considerations are not unique to scientific and engineering professionals. Indeed, these factors (or other in the same vein) have received considerable attention in recent years. The National Commission on the Public Service, chaired by the exemplary public servant Paul Volcker, studied conditions influencing the future of the federal work force (National Commission on the Public Service, 1989). The same has been done for state and local governments by the National Commission on the State and Local Public Service (National Commission on the State and Local Public Service, 1993; Thompson, 1993).

In speeches and writing Volcker has referred to an emerging "quiet crisis" based on the difficulties faced by the federal, state, and local governments in attracting highly qualified individuals to public sector careers. Failure to attract some of the best and brightest of each generation to government service means that there is an inevitable dilution of governing capacity. On this, the final report of the National Commission on the Public Service (1989, p. 4) reaches a pessimistic conclusion applicable to all levels of government:

> If these trends continue, America will soon be left with a government of the mediocre, locked into careers of last resort or waiting for a chance to move on to other jobs.

Dealing with the quiet crisis at the national, state, and local levels requires action on several fronts, including structural arrangements. According to the Volcker Commission report (1989, p. 5) major action must follow the three themes of leadership, talent, and performance. Leadership refers to building political support for the career service. Talent refers to the recruitment and retention of the most capable and representative of college graduates. Performance refers to the development of a culture of excellence and an incentive system which rewards by pay and by training/promotion opportunities.

Structural arrangements are determinants of the level and quality of public sector professionalism. On occasion, the courts have intervened to eliminate political criteria in hiring and promotion which work to the disadvantage of professionals. As the reformers recognize, civil service rules and labor union provisions designed to assure members of the career service that their legitimate interests are protected can become outdated regulations that protect incompetent employees.

Arrangements are not unbiased; different arrangements advance different interests. To change arrangements is to change the interests favored. The future of professionalism will be shaped, in part, by the extent of agreement on the governmental objectives to be achieved thorough professionalism and structural arrangements. Lacking agreement, changing structure will make little difference since, as Wildavsky (1988, p. 755) counsels, "Quality or merit or talent matters . . . only when people are close enough on objectives. So long as political dissensus prevails, bureaucrats will remain the flakcatchers of American society."

B.   Governing Coalitions

The stature of governmental professionalism is determined by prevailing political regimes and the associated attitudes and ideologies of those holding power. Political regimes are based on ideas, institutions, and policies which, in combination, constitute approaches to governing (Harris and Milkis, 1989). Where the ideas, institutions, and policies do not support the assumptions of professionalism, as in the latter half of the 19th century (Skowronek, 1982), calls for reform which disrupt the priorities of regime leaders will likely go unheeded. Professionalism triumphs only when it is welcome.

Exemplary professional practices are rarely ends in themselves but are means of attaining political ends. Within a regime, the relationship between professional and political variables is causal and the causal order is from political to professional. The causal structure is dynamic. Evidence of the detrimental consequences of a lack of professional knowledge and skills may force political leaders to recruit new professionals and adopt new practices. As the worth of the new professionals is demonstrated, their practices become part of the routines of governing.

Alternatively, political considerations can override professional advice and the best intentioned policies. To reward election supporters, presidents, mayors, and governors may appoint unqualified amateurs to agency positions which governmental careerists think are properly theirs. To counter charges in legislative bodies and the mass media of being "soft on crime" or "lax on welfare reform," the same executives may adopt tactics which are opposed by their agency advisors, professionals in government.

Involved here are classic issues associated with public administration's politics–administration dichotomy. However difficult it is to demark the dichotomy's points of separation, most professionals *in* and *of* government, except those at the highest levels, perform on the administrative side. Also at play are different interpretations of the meaning of governing. William Schneider (1992, p. 32) writes that

> professionalism and politics don't mix. In fact, Americans see them as antithetical. The very notion of a professional politician strikes voters as an oxymoron. Professionalism is the art of problem-solving, of coming up with the right answer. Politics is the art of the possible, of balancing interests. The politician finds workable answers by balancing public opinion, organized interests, and the interests of his or her own career.

The different interpretations lead to a conundrum for those analyzing public sector performance. For career service professionals (along with semiprofessional and nonprofessional personnel) to be successful in their work, the political context within which they operate must be supportive. The context of the past quarter century has worked to the disadvantage of the service. Beverly Cigler (1990) argues that a "paradox of professionalization" prevails. At the very time the public service has become more professional and competent, public support for government and political institutions has declined.

The data are unambiguous. Since the mid-1960s, with some pauses, opinion polls and attitude surveys have revealed growing public distrust of government and a declining faith in the ability of government to deal effectively with problems. A 1992 poll found that 70% of respondents were "dissatisfied with the overall performance of the national government" and a 1993 poll indicated that 69% felt that the "Federal government creates more problems than it solves" (American Enterprise, 1993, p. 89). Reading the context accurately, politicians at all levels have sought to exploit the public's disenchantment by campaigning for office as governmental "outsiders." Denunciations are leveled against a specific agency for squandering public funds, the bureaucracy for being unresponsive to citizen demands, and the government at large, because it is ungovernable.

The campaign rhetoric addresses a public discontent based, at least in part, on the apparent inability of government to deal with problems. In an ironic sense the "paradox of professionalization" may well reflect the success of public sector professionals. Much of what government does entails routine services basic to a well-ordered society and civilization—utilities, social security, licensing and record keeping, public health, transportation, police and fire protection. Routine does not mean faultless; but most of the basic services are delivered at an adequate level most of the time. Nor does routine imply simplicity; routine activities like those cited are based on very sophisticated professional knowledge and technical skills.

To avoid system overload the critical basics must be performed adequately before demands can be made for action on new concerns. Frequently, action is sought of government experts not because of market failures but because of a lack of knowledge as to what should or can be done, as with AIDS as a public health issue. Or bureaucratic professionals in government are expected to handle impossible jobs (Hargrove and Glidewell, 1990) and to ameliorate political tensions resulting from policies based on mutually exclusive values, as with proposals for the treatment of mental illness and teenage pregnancy.

The intractability of many contemporary problems results not from a lack of technical knowledge, though that clearly is a factor in many instances, so much as from the difficulties involved in resolving conflicting values. Professionals in an administrative agency may be charged to resolve a problem in such a way as to best protect the public interest or to maximize economy and efficiency. When the governing coalition lacks attitudinal or ideological hegemony (as during the latter years of the Reagan–Bush era), elected officials may assign responsibilities to professionals or to technical experts in order to avoid choice making among competing or mutually exclusive values. Some time ago Herbert Simon (1957, pp. 56–57) commented on the need to distinguish between value and expert judgments:

> Democratic institutions find their principal justification as a procedure for the validation of value judgments. There is no "scientific" or "expert" way of making such judgments, hence expertise of whatever kind is no qualification for the performance of this function. If the factual elements in decision could be strictly separated, in practice, from the ethical, the proper roles of representative and expert in a democratic decision-making process would be simple.

The political attitudes and ideologies of power holders have very practical consequences for professionals in and of government. A governing coalition and its political entrepreneurs maintain and expand their support constituencies by advocating new programs and, in recent years, new modes of producing and implementing those programs (Mollenkopf, 1983; Walker, 1991).

Public policy is a form of patronage which can be designed to favor particular locales and groups (region A. vs. region B, central city vs. suburb, elderly vs. young) and be made the responsibility of, and administered on behalf of, particular interests (national government vs. state governments, public agency vs. private nonprofit organization vs. for-profit firm). From the perspective of the public sector professional, changes in policy form alter the character of program responsibilities, patterns of communications, and leadership of issue networks. Change in policy form may also lead to changes in the kinds of professional knowledge and skill deemed most relevant to governing.

The relevance of changing political attitudes on governing coalitions and the longer term implications for governmental professionals can be seen in recent national developments in regulatory policy. Since the New Deal, the administrative agency with regulatory responsibilities has epitomized "structural specialization" (Redford, 1969, p. 39) in government and has been the domain of professionals and their technical expertise (Freedman, 1978, pp. 51–52). But modifications have been made. In their study of changes in regulatory policy, Richard Harris and Sidney Milkis (1989) view the 1970s as years of revolutionary policy change with political roots in the 1960s. The 1980s, they claim, were years of counterrevolutionary attempts to undo the change, with political roots in dissatisfaction with the policies and an invigorated conservative movement.

According to Harris and Milkis, a new regulatory regime emerged in the 1970s. Involved was a new focus on social regulation—environmental quality, public health, occupational safety, consumer protection, equal opportunity. Also characterizing the new regime were new participants and approaches to regulation. The role of the courts in regulatory decision making was expanded, detailed criteria for the decision making were to be generated by congressional subcommittees, and public lobbyists were to be included in the regulatory processes as representatives of the general public and its interests. Though the Reagan administration challenged the premises of the new approach, such as the economics of the social regulations, and brought conservative leadership to regulatory agencies, the general structure of the social regulatory regime survived.

Changes in approaches to regulation are symptomatic of major governance developments which have eroded the autonomy and power of professionals in government. The bases of professionalism—specialized knowledge, technical skill, and current information—are increasingly dispersed. No longer are knowledge, skill, and information used solely by neutrally competent professionals to promote a universal public interest. Instead, they are also employed by action intellectuals who seek to gain ideological ends and to promote alternate public interests.

In recent years, as a case in point, many elected officials have looked to "think tanks" for advice. Frequently the advice has reflected unabashedly the liberal or conservative orientations of the organizations' policy analysts and their explicit propositions and preferred methodologies. The advice of these analysts is of quality equal to that from those in government. No longer is expertise and expert knowledge monopolized by those in official positions (Wildavsky, 1988, p. 753).

The growing clout of nongovernmental bodies as independent sources of professional expertise and policy suggestions raises the possibility of strategic programmatic change from one administration or political regime to the next. This means, in turn, that the number, type, and responsibilities of professionals in and of government may fluctuate with transformations in the attitudes and ideologies of those holding power in governing coalitions.

Professionals who remain in government service through successive regimes may find themselves coping with problems in dramatically altered circumstances as administrations change. Knowledge and skills appropriate to a set of problems in one administration could prove inappropriate or irrelevant to the same set of problems in another. Professionals in government can become discontented if new approaches are at variance with their concepts of good practices. Organizational arrangements which increase productivity but limit employee and citizen autonomy and participation, for example, may violate professional codes of ethics (Fischer and Zinke, 1989, p. 852). In such cases the professional faces very difficult personal choices.

C. Theoretical Frameworks

Contributing to the mystique of the professions and to the power of professionals relative to their clientele is control of a body of theory and abstract and esoteric knowledge and related technical skills drawn from the theory. It is mastery of knowledge and skills that empowers the professional. In this empowerment the university plays a pivotal role. Within the university, professional knowledge is formulated and transmitted and individuals are credentialed as learned in the appropriate knowledge and eligible for licensing (Larson, 1984, p. 53).

While theory, knowledge, and universities are essential to professional life, they have not been the sources of most professions. Professions have typically originated in a set of practices and activities directed to the need of some clientele and carried out by amateurs, artisans, or members of an established profession (Kirschner, 1986). As experience is gained, clientele is satisfied, and the number of practitioners grows, the practices and activities are defined as sufficiently specialized to become a profession. When the profession is fully developed, its subject matter becomes effectively depoliticized and recognized by society and the state as the near-exclusive province of professional experts. In time, attention is directed to rationales of purpose and the theoretical bases of knowledge and exemplary practices.

For the past century, the public administration community has engaged in a search for an overarching theory of public administration (Gargan, 1989). Such a theory would provide a framework for addressing critical questions and guide developments, including those related to professional practice.

The number of topics, breadth of coverage, and scope of activities that would need to be covered by such a theory of public administration impedes its formulation. Leading figures have suggested proceeding *as if* public administration was a profession even though its theoretical base was not fully developed. A quarter century ago Waldo (1968, p. 10) proposed that *"we try to act as a profession without actually being one, and perhaps even without the hope or intention of becoming one in any strict sense."* More recently, after an extensive review of major public administration theory publications, Denhardt (1990) concluded that a prevailing viewpoint among theorists would be

> that public administration is best viewed as a profession drawing from many different theoretical perspectives. Since no single discipline can currently provide the range of knowledge needed by administrators in the public sector, it seems reasonable to bring coherence to programs through their professional orientation (p. 63).

Theory generation in public administration is arduous. Complicating the efforts of public administration theory generators and those concerned with public sector professionalism is that they are called on to provide frameworks of understanding and explanations of phenomena in the midst of ongoing activities of governing. It is necessary to track simultaneously basic theoretical research and applied decisions and actions. Theories or partial theories are frequently tested as they are articulated.

Even lacking a general theory, there are matters of ongoing concern for professionals of government. As noted in Tables 1 and 3, the bulk of public employment is at the state and local levels and concentrated in a limited number of functions. While managing large complex organizations, like the Department of Defense, is a paramount concern of contemporary public sector professionals, most of the governing and administration that takes place in the United States is within fairly small state bureaus and commissions, public universities, municipalities, counties, as well as school and special districts. The measure of professionalism and the overall quality of public sector performance in these latter units would be upgraded by greater attention to raising basic management practices to meet minimal criteria of adequacy. Among these basics would be budgeting and accounting, record keeping and storage, personnel testing and training, and facilities planning.

That professionals of government must be able to perform these basic management tasks, *regardless of theories, forms, or purposes of the public sector*, is self-evident. Movement beyond the basics is problematic. Those wishing to go further may turn to practices produced in other fields. Episodically the practices will be proclaimed as salient for public management—zero base budgeting, strategic planning, total quality management. One mark of a true professional of government is the ability to recognize which of the practices are nostrums and which can truly improve the quality of government.

If the public administration community lacks consensus on a guiding theory, the analyst of professionalism must look elsewhere for answers to elementary questions:

What constitutes the body of core knowledge that defines the profession?

From what sources—theoretical, philosophical, intellectual schools, disciplines—is this body of core knowledge derived?

Where does one go—academic institutions, training facilities, midcareer programs—and what sources does one use—professional journals, applied periodicals, in-house discussion groups, seminars—to learn and to keep abreast of the body of core knowledge and developments in the body of core knowledge?

These questions are fundamental and not easily answered. Involved are issues of epistemology and subissues of methodology, propositions, data, evidence, and proof. For public administration these are macrolevel concerns about which there are competing frameworks and schools of thought.

Competing frameworks and schools of thought guide approaches to public problems and structure institutional arrangements and professional practices for dealing with social and public issues. By way of illustration, Rohr (1986) gave significant attention to the constitutional legitimacy of the Public Administration, and therefore professionals *in* and *of* government, as a "balance wheel" among the three branches of government. Similarly, Ingraham and Rosenbloom (1990, p. 212) established that three intellectual perspectives have competed for control in American public administration and have shaped the nation's political culture. A management perspective relates to the executive, a political perspective to the legislature, and a legal perspective to the courts. Each perspective advocates

> different values and procedural and structural arrangements for the operation of public administration, each views the individual citizen in a remarkably different way, and each adopts a different perspective on how to develop knowledge (Rosenbloom, 1989, p. 14).

Approaches to public employment and public service have diverged as one or another of these perspectives has prevailed. The divergence of recommendations has been even more pronounced as a result of competition among theories on such rudimentary points as the nature and ends of government. Thus, LaPorte (1971, p. 32) explains that *"the purpose of public organization is the reduction of economic, social, and psychic suffering and the enhancement of life opportunities for those inside and outside the organization."* Alternatively, Tullock (1988, p. 6) also explains that "the Public Choice point of view is that we only turn to the government if there is reason to believe that the government will be less imperfect than the market."

The positions of LaPorte and Tullock are not inherently mutually exclusive. However, for the teacher, student, or practitioner seeking advice on what public sector professionals actually do and should do, finding common ground is difficult. It makes a good deal of difference whether government is viewed as an instrument for the solution of longstanding individual and societal ills or as a natural monopoly. If government is a potential instrument of positive social change, observers should not be surprised when continuing social pathologies are attributed to the insensitivity of economic elites or a lack of opportunities for participation in the policy process by ordinary citizens. If government is a monopoly, observers should not be surprised when operations are inefficient and those in power allocate program cost and benefits in such a way as to produce social waste.

That theoretical positions are, for all practical purposes, incompatible does not mean that they cancel each other out in the political realm. Competing paradigms and schools of thought involve more than contention among academic factions. When used as the bases for policy initiatives, theoretical positions can fundamentally reorder the conduct of government and the roles and responsibilities of professionals in and of government. The orientation of the New Public Administration is reflected in pressures on the professionals to demonstrate greater concern for issues of equity, social justice, and environmental quality. That orientation is also apparent in the increased openness of the political system, including formal requirements regarding the conduct of public business and mandates that public sector professionals include citizens and clientele in their policy deliberations.

Perhaps even more dramatic have been the policy and professionalism implications of the Public Choice approach to government. Based in schools of economic and political science thought, public choice has furnished the intellectual infrastructure for a redefinition of modes by which government is carried out and the responsibilities of professionals within the government.

An essential component of the redefinition is the privatization of a portion of the public sector (Starr, 1989) and the expanded use of contracts, regulations, grants, loans, and tax provisions. Some federal agencies such as the Environmental Protection Agency during the 1980s came to rely on contractors to handle much of their program and even administrative responsibilities. Kettl (1988, p. 4) refers to the increased use of these strategies at all levels as "government by proxy" and points out that they

> have grown into the predominant form of government activity. Each strategy relies on proxies—intermediaries responsible for actually producing the goods or services—in place of direct administration of programs by the government.

In this new order, the effectiveness of public programs is contingent on the activities of large numbers of individuals working on aspects of the program in and out of governments. To be successful, professionals *in* government must integrate their work with that of counterparts employed on contracts or grants in third-party settings.

With the diversity of organizational arrangements now used to provide, produce, and deliver services (Savas, 1987) professionals *of* government continue to run individual agencies but must learn new techniques of negotiation and coordination among multiple organizational units and governmental levels ("transorganizational management") (Wise, 1990, p. 145). Precisely which techniques are most salient to these new professional responsibilities is not readily apparent. Nor is it readily apparent as to what the most effective ways of teaching the techniques to present and future supervisors, managers, and administrators are (Kettl, 1991).

This cursory examination of fragments of New Public Administration and Public Choice thought is intended to be suggestive rather than conclusive.[6] What public sector professionals do and how they do it is conditioned by prevailing theories. The 1980s and 1990s have proven to be

---

[6]LaPorte and Tullock are juxtaposed simply to make the point of theoretical diversity within the public administration community. To understand policy choices of the quarter century it is essential that the analyst be familiar with the theoretical orientations of decision makers and their advisors, including the professionals in and of government.

years of seminal thinking in theories related to public administration and public policy. Creative attempts have been made to reconceptualize public administration as a field of inquiry (White and McSwain, 1990; Behn, 1992). The relationship between public administration and the governance process has been reviewed through new lenses (Wamsley et al., 1990). Longstanding ideas on constraints on rationality in the policy process have been reassessed and presented in new ways (Lindblom, 1990).

The creative thought has not yet led to a consensus on a core body of knowledge that is to guide public sector professionalism. Continued differences between competing schools of thought lead to contrasting interpretations of the same reality. Where the differences are so fundamental as to be irreconcilable, some mechanism must be used to decide which shall prevail. In matters related to the public realm, public policy, and professionals in and of government, the distribution of political power and the consequences of recommendations by the competing schools for that distribution of power will be determining.

If untoward damage to the next generation of public sector professionals is to be avoided, that political power must be exercised wisely. This will require political elites, academicians, and practitioners to give careful thought to a theory of governing capacity. If successful, that theory will indicate the roles and responsibilities of professionals in and of government in meeting the governing requirements of the political system and in satisfying the expectations of elected officials and citizens.

REFERENCES

Advisory Commission on Intergovernmental Relations (1992). *Significant Features of Fiscal Federalism, Volume 2*, Washington, DC.

Ambrose, S. E. (1964). *Upton and the Army*, Louisiana State University Press, Baton Rouge.

American Enterprise (1993). Public opinion and demographic report, *The American Enterprise*, 4(2): pp. 89–90.

Behn, R. D. (1992). Management and the neutrino: the search for meaningful metaphors, *Public Admin. Rev.*, 52: 409–419.

Bell, D. (1973). *The Coming of Post-Industrial Society*, Basic Books, New York.

Benson, G. C. S. (1941). *The New Centralization*, Farrar and Rinehart, New York.

Berry, J. M. (1989). Subgovernments, issue networks, and political conflict, *Remaking American Politics* (R. A. Harris and S. M. Milkis, eds.), Westview Press, Boulder, CO, pp. 239–260.

Brown, J. (1992). *The Definition of a Profession*, Princeton University Press, Princeton, NJ.

Brudney, J. L., and England, R. E. (1983). Toward a definition of the coproduction concept, *Public Admin. Rev.*, 43: 59–65.

Buchanan, J. M. (1985). *Liberty, Market, and State*, New York University Press, New York.

Budget of the United States Fiscal Year 1994 (1993). U.S. Government Printing Office, Washington, DC.

Burgess, P. M. (1975). Capacity building and the elements of public management, *Public Admin. Rev.*, 35: 705–716.

Campbell, A. K., and Dix, L. S. (1990). Executive summary, *Recruitment, Retention, and Utilization of Federal Scientists and Engineers* (A. K. Campbell and L. S. Dix, eds.), National Academy Press, Washington, DC, pp. 1–36.

Cigler, B. A. (1990). Public administration and the paradox of professionalization, *Public Admin. Rev.*, 50: 637–653.

Cipolla, F. P. (1993). Federal executive turnover: crisis or opportunity? *The Public Manager*, 22: 23–25.

Congressional Budget Office (1987). *Federal Civilian Employment*, U.S. Government Printing Office, Washington, DC.

Daniels, M. R., and Johansen, E. (1985). Role of accreditation in the development of public administration as a profession: a theoretical and empirical assessment, *Public Admin. Q.*, 8: 419–441.

Denhardt, R. B. (1990). Public administration theory: the state of the discipline, *Public Administration* (N. B. Lynn and A. Wildavsky, eds.), Chatham House, Chatham, NJ, pp. 43–72.

Eulau, H. (1973). Skill revolution and the consultative commonwealth, *Am. Polit. Sci. Rev.*, *67*: 169–191.

Fabricant, S. (1952). *The Trend of Government Activity in the United States Since 1900*, National Bureau of Economic Research, New York.

Fischer, F., and Zinke, R. C. (1989). Public administration and the code of ethics: administrative reform or professional ideology? *Int. J. Public Admin.*, *12*: 841–854.

Freedman, J. O. (1978). *Crisis and Legitimacy: The Administrative Process and American Government*, Cambridge University Press, Cambridge, UK.

Gargan, J. J. (1989). The public administration community and the search for professionalism, *Handbook Of Public Administration* (J. Rabin, W. B. Hildreth, and G. J. Miller, eds.), Marcel Dekker, New York, pp. 965–1026.

Hargrove, E. C, and Glidewell, J. C. (eds.). (1990). *Impossible Jobs in Public Management*, University Press of Kansas, Lawrence.

Harris, R. A., and Milkis, S. M. (1989). *The Politics of Regulatory Change*, Oxford University Press, New York.

Heclo, H. (1977). *A Government of Strangers: Executive Politics in Washington*, Brookings Institution, Washington, DC.

Heclo, H. (1989). The emerging regime, *Remaking American Politics* (R. A. Harris and S. M. Milkis, eds.), Westview Press, Boulder, CO, pp. 289–320.

Historical Tables, Budget of the United States Government, Fiscal Year 1990. (1989). U.S. Government Printing Office, Washington, DC.

Huddleston, M. W. (1988–89). Is the SES a higher civil service? *Policy Stud. J.*, *17*: 406–419.

Huddleston, M. W. (1991). The Senior Executive Service: problems and prospects for reform, *Public Personnel Management* (C. Ban and N. M. Riccucci, eds.), Longman, New York, pp. 175–189.

Huddleston, M. W. (1992). To the threshold of reform: the Senior Executive Service and America's search for a higher civil service, *The Promise and Paradox of Civil Service Reform* (P. W. Ingraham and D. H. Rosenbloom, eds.), University of Pittsburgh Press, pp. 99–115.

Hudson Institute (1988). *Civil Service 2000*, U. S. Office of Personnel Management, Washington, DC.

Ingraham, P. W., and Rosenbloom, D. H. (1990). Political foundations of the American federal service: rebuilding a crumbling base, *Public Admin. Rev.*, *50*: 210–219.

Kearney, R. C., and Sinha, C. (1988). Professionalism and bureaucratic responsiveness: conflict or compatability? *Public Admin. Rev.*, *48*: 571–579.

Kettl, D. F. (1988). *Government by Proxy*, CQ Press, Washington, DC.

Kettl, D. F. (1991). Privatization: implications for the public work force, *Public Personnel Management* (C. Ban and N. M. Riccucci, eds.), Longman, New York, pp. 254–264.

Kettl, D. F. (1993). *Sharing Power: Public Governance and Private Markets*, Brookings Institution, Washington, DC.

Kirschner, D. S. (1986). *The Paradox Of Professionalism*, Greenwood Press, New York.

Lane, L. M., and Wolf, J. F. (1990). *The Human Resource Crisis in the Public Sector*, Quorum Books, New York.

LaPorte, T. R. (1971). The recovery of relevance in the study of public organizations, *Toward a New Public Administration* (F. Marini, ed.), Chandler, Scranton, PA, pp. 17–48.

Larson, M. S. (1977). *The Rise of Professionalism: A Sociological Analysis*, University of California Press, Berkeley.

Larson, M. S. (1984). The production of expertise and the constitution of expert power, *The Authority Of Experts* (T. L. Haskell, ed.), Indiana University Press, Bloomington, pp. 28–80.

Levine, C. H. (1986). The federal government in the year 2000: administrative legacies of the Reagan years, *Public Admin. Rev.*, *46*: 195–206.

Lindblom, C. E. (1990). *Inquiry and Change*, Yale University Press, New Haven.

Lowi, T. J. (1993). Legitimizing public administration: a disturbed dissent, *Public Admin. Rev.*, *53*: 261–264.

Macaluso, A. C. (1975). Background and history of the Study Committee on Policy Management Assistance, *Public Admin. Rev.*, *35*: 695–700.

Mollenkopf, J. H. (1983). *The Contested City*, Princeton University Press, Princeton, NJ.

Mosher, F. C. (1978). Professions in public service, *Public Admin. Rev.*, *38*: 144–150.

Mosher, F. C. (1982). *Democracy and the Public Service, 2nd ed.*, Oxford University Press, New York.

National Commission on the Public Service (1989). *Leadership for America: Rebuilding the Public Service*, Lexington Books, Lexington, MA.

National Commission on the State and Local Public Service (1993). *Hard Truths/Tough Choices*, Nelson A. Rockefeller Institute of Government, Albany, NY.

Ohmae, K. (1990). *The Borderless World: Power and Strategy in the Interlinked Economy*, Harper Business, New York.

Ostrom, V. (1974). *The Intellectual Crisis in American Public Administration*, University of Alabama Press, Birmingham, AL.

Ostrom, V. (1980). Artisanship and artifact, *Public Admin. Rev.*, *40*: 309–317.

Patterson, J. T. (1969). *The New Deal and the States: Federalism in Transition*, Princeton University Press, Princeton, NJ.

Peters, B. G. (1985). The United States: absolute change and relative stability, *Public Employment in Western Nations* (Richard Rose et al., eds.), Cambridge University Press, Cambridge, UK, pp. 228–261.

Peters, B. G. (1993). *American Public Policy*, Chatham House, Chatham, NJ.

Redford, E. S. (1969). *Democracy in the Administrative State*, Oxford University Press, New York.

Roberts, D. D. (1988). A new breed of public executive: top level exempt managers in state government, *Rev. Public Personnel Admin.*, *8*: 20–36.

Roberts, D. D. (1991). A personnel chameleon blending the political appointee and careerist traditions: exempt managers in state government, *Public Personnel Management* (C. Ban and N. M. Riccucci, eds.), Longman, New York, pp. 190–204.

Rohr, J. A. (1986). *To Run a Constitution*, University Press of Kansas, Lawrence.

Rosenbloom, D. H. (1989). *Public Administration, 2nd ed.*, Random House, New York.

Savas, E. S. (1987). *Privatization: The Key to Better Government*, Chatham House, Chatham, NJ.

Schneider, W. (1992). Off with their heads, *The American Enterprise*, *3*(4): 28–37.

Sherwood, F. P., and Breyer, L. J. (1987). Executive personnel systems in the states, *Public Admin. Rev.*, *47*: 410–416.

Simon, H. A. (1957). *Administrative Behavior*, 2nd ed., Free Press, New York.

Skowronek, S. (1982). *Building a New American State: The Expansion of National Administrative Capacities, 1877–1920*, Cambridge University Press, Cambridge, UK.

Smith, B. L. R. (1984). The U. S. higher civil service in comparative perspective, *The Higher Civil Service in Europe and Canada* (B. L. R. Smith, ed.), Brookings Institution, Washington, DC, pp. 1–19.

Starr, P. (1989). The meaning of privatization, *Privatization and the Welfare State* (S. B. Kamerman and A. J. Kahn, eds.), Princeton University Press, Princeton, NJ, pp. 16–48.

Stillman, R. H. II (1974). *The Rise of the City Manager: A Public Professional in Local Government*, University of New Mexico Press, Albuquerque.

Sundquist, J. L. (1979). Jimmy Carter as public administrator: an appraisal at mid-term, *Public Admin. Rev.*, *39*: 3–11.

Thompson, F. J. (1993). Revitalizing state and local public service, *The Public Manager*, *22*: 32–34.

Toffler, A. (1990). *Powershift*, Bantam Books, New York.

Tullock, G. (1988). *Wealth, Poverty, and Politics*, Basil Blackwell, New York.

United States Bureau of the Census (1972). *Public Employment in 1971*, U. S. Bureau of the Census, Washington, DC.

United States Bureau of the Census (1976). *The Statistical History of the United States*, Basic Book, New York.

United States Bureau of the Census (1992). *Public Employment: 1991*, U. S. Bureau of the Census, Washington, DC.

United States Equal Employment Opportunity Commission (1992). *Job Patterns for Minorities and Women in State and Local Government 1991*, Washington, DC.

Van Wart, M. (1992). Connecting management and executive development in the states, *Public Prod. & Manage. Rev.*, *15*: 477–486.

Waldo, D. (1968). Scope of the theory of public administration, *Theory and Practice of Public Administration: Scope, Objectives, and Methods* (J. C. Charlesworth, ed.), American Academy of Political and Social Science, Philadelphia, pp. 1–26.

Walker, D. B. (1991). American federalism from Johnson to Bush, *Publius*, 21: 105–119.

Wamsley, G. L. et al. (1990). *Refounding Public Administration*, Sage, Newbury Park, CA.

Weigley, R. F. (1984). *History of the United States Army*, Indiana University Press, Bloomington.

Whitaker, G. P. (1980). Coproduction: citizen participation in service delivery, *Public Admin. Rev.*, *40*: 240–246.

White, O. F., Jr., and McSwain, C. J. (1990). The Phoenix Project: raising a new image of public administration from the ashes of the past, *Images and Identities in Public Administration* (H. D. Kass and B. L. Catron, eds.), Sage, Newbury Park, CA, pp. 23–59.

Wiebe, R. H. (1967). *The Search for Order: 1877–1920*, Hill and Wang, New York.

Wildavsky, A. (1988). Ubiquitous anomie: public service in an era of ideological dissensus, *Public Admin. Rev.*, *48*: 753–755.

Wilson, J. Q. (1975). The rise of the bureaucratic state, *Public Interest*, *41*: 77–103.

Wise, C. R. (1990). Public service configurations and public organizations: public organization design in the post-privatization era, *Public Admin. Rev.*, *50*: 141–155.

Index